THE OXFORD HANDBOOK OF

EUROPEAN UNION LAW

THE OXFORD HANDBOOK OF

EUROPEAN UNION LAW

Edited by

ANTHONY ARNULL

and

DAMIAN CHALMERS

OXFORD
UNIVERSITY PRESS

OXFORD
UNIVERSITY PRESS

Great Clarendon Street, Oxford, OX2 6DP,
United Kingdom

Oxford University Press is a department of the University of Oxford.
It furthers the University's objective of excellence in research, scholarship,
and education by publishing worldwide. Oxford is a registered trade mark of
Oxford University Press in the UK and in certain other countries

First Edition published in 2015

Impression: 1

Published in the United States of America by Oxford University Press
198 Madison Avenue, New York, NY 10016, United States of America

British Library Cataloguing in Publication Data
Data available

Library of Congress Control Number: 2015934489

ISBN 978-0-19-967264-6

Printed and bound by
CPI Group (UK) Ltd, Croydon, CR0 4YY

Jacket illustration: Castle and Sun, 1928 (no 201), by Paul Klee.
Private ollection/Giraudon/Bridgeman Images

PREFACE

······················

IT is a truism that the European Union has grown out of (nearly) all recognition since its birth as the European Coal and Steel Community in the early 1950s. The number of Member States has grown from six to 28 (there always seem to be more waiting in the wings) and the substantive scope of the Treaties on which it is founded might now surprise even Jean Monnet and Robert Schuman. At the same time, scholarship on European Union law has become more diverse in style and critical in attitude. The doctrinal works aimed mainly at students and practitioners that once dominated the academic literature have now been joined by theoretical, contextual, and interdisciplinary material. This 'new wave' literature is frequently hostile to particular developments or sceptical of the direction in which 'the project' is travelling.

All this makes European Union law an ideal subject for an Oxford Handbook. Once of concern principally to specialists, it is now an established part of the curriculum in law schools across the Continent and beyond, and a focus for the scholarly activity of many of those who work in them. The complexity and depth of Union law now approximates that of a developed national system. Indeed, Union law is associated with the evolution of many sectors of modern law in the Member States. Whilst there were national rules on, for example, trade marks, the environment, or asylum prior to the Union, the modern development and systematization of the law in fields such as these has largely been realized or prompted by Union law. Moreover, the variety of Union legal forms and the contingency of Union legal authority have made Union law an important interface between many legal and non-legal academic traditions. The result is that an understanding of the subject is essential, not just for legal practitioners and policy makers, but also for those who study the Union from other disciplinary perspectives.

The striking range of approaches now evident in the literature on Union law reflects the unique theoretical problems it poses. With some of the characteristics of an international legal regime and some of the characteristics of a federation, what is the right level of analysis? Are its concepts to be measured against national legal standards or some other yardstick? What does it mean for certain concepts, such as the separation of powers or sovereignty, to be developed outside a domestic legal paradigm? Are some of its norms, such as those relating to fundamental rights, to be compared with those of international treaties or national legislation or some other source? Questions like these may lead to a rethinking of familiar concepts as the very novelty of the Union legal context challenges traditional assumptions about their meaning and operation. Issues about how law manages conflicts are raised by the very contestedness of Union law, which may give rise to conflicts not just around the content of a given norm but also over whether the Union has authority to enact it and who is responsible for its implementation and enforcement.

The Oxford Handbook of European Union Law comprises 38 chapters divided into eight sections examining how we are to conceptualize Union law; the architecture of Union law; making and administering Union law; the economic constitution and the citizen; regulation of the market place; economic, monetary, and fiscal union; the Area of Freedom, Security, and Justice; and what lies beyond the regulatory state. Each chapter summarizes, analyses and reflects on the state of play in a given area, and suggests how it is likely to develop in the foreseeable future. The authors, who come from a range of different backgrounds and adopt a range of academic perspectives, were asked to assume some basic knowledge of the legal framework within which the Union operates and what it seeks to achieve, but not detailed familiarity with the particular area of Union law under discussion. Our hope was that the resulting collection would offer a unique and authoritative guide to the richness of the debates that Union law generates, one that would be widely used both inside and outside academia by those who are interested in the law underpinning the Union and its policies, including advanced students of law and other disciplines, policy makers, and legal practitioners. It is for others to judge how successfully that hope has been realized.

We would like to thank Alex Flach at OUP for first suggesting an Oxford Handbook on European Union Law and his colleague Natasha Flemming for shepherding the collection through to publication. We would also like to thank Jenny Papettas of Birmingham Law School for helping to sub-edit some of the chapters. Our greatest debt, however, is to our authors for agreeing to take part in this venture and tolerating with such magnanimity our occasional reminders and all too frequent requests for items of information we should have asked for before. Chapters were completed between December 2013 and September 2014, though some small changes were incorporated subsequently.

AA

DC

January 2015

Table of Contents

PART III MAKING AND ADMINISTERING EU LAW

PART IV THE ECONOMIC CONSTITUTION AND THE CITIZEN

PART V REGULATION OF THE MARKET PLACE

PART VI ECONOMIC, MONETARY, AND FISCAL UNION

PART VII AREA OF FREEDOM, SECURITY, AND JUSTICE

PART VIII BEYOND THE REGULATORY STATE?

Notes on the Contributors

Zoe Adams is an LLM candidate at the European University Institute, Florence, Italy and a former Researcher at the Centre for Business Research, University of Cambridge, United Kingdom.

Fabian Amtenbrink is Professor of European Union Law at Erasmus University, Rotterdam, the Netherlands.

Kenneth Armstrong is Fellow in Law at Sidney Sussex College, Cambridge.

Anthony Arnull is Barber Professor of Jurisprudence, University of Birmingham.

Loïc Azoulai is Professor of European Union Law at the European University Institute, Florence.

Andrea Biondi is Professor of European Union Law and the Director of the Centre for European Law at the Dickson Poon School of Law, King's College London.

Michal Bobek is Professor of European Law at the College of Europe, Bruges, and Research Fellow at the Institute of European and Comparative Law, University of Oxford.

Damian Chalmers is Professor of EU Law, London School of Economics and Political Science.

Monica Claes is Professor of European and Comparative Constitutional Law at the Faculty of Law, Maastricht University, the Netherlands.

Paul Craig is Professorial Fellow in English Law at St John's College, Oxford.

Deirdre Curtin is Professor of European Law at the University of Amsterdam and part-time Chair in European and International Governance at the Utrecht School of Governance, University of Utrecht, the Netherlands.

Gareth Davies is Professor of European Law at the Department of International Law, Vrije Universiteit Amsterdam, the Netherlands.

Mark Dawson is Professor of European Law and Governance at the Hertie School of Governance, Berlin.

Simon Deakin is Professor of Law in the Faculty of Law and Director of the Centre for Business Research at the University of Cambridge.

Nadine El-Enany is Lecturer in Law at Birkbeck School of Law, University of London.

Paul Farmer is a barrister and partner in Joseph Hage Aaronson LLP, London.

Richard Fentiman is Professor of Private International Law at the University of Cambridge.

Christopher Harding is Professor of Law in the Department of Law and Criminology, Aberystwyth University.

Christophe Hillion is Professor of European Law at the Law School, Europa Institute, University of Leiden, the Netherlands.

Thomas Horsley is Lecturer in European Law at Liverpool Law School, University of Liverpool.

Alison Jones is Professor of Law at the Dickson Poon School of Law, King's College London.

Jan Klabbers is Professor of International Law at the University of Helsinki, Finland.

Jan Komárek is Lecturer in EU Law at the London School of Economics.

Panos Koutrakos is Professor of European Union Law at City University, London.

Dorota Leczykiewicz is Marie Curie Fellow at the European University Institute in Florence and a Research Fellow of the Oxford Institute of European and Comparative Law.

Maria Lee is Professor of Law at University College London.

Tatevik Manucharyan is a researcher at the Faculty of Law, University of Amsterdam, the Netherlands.

Niamh Moloney is Professor of Law at the London School of Economics.

Elise Muir is Associate Professor of EU Law at the Faculty of Law, Maastricht University, the Netherlands.

Niamh Nic Shuibhne is Professor of European Union Law at the University of Edinburgh.

Okeoghene Odudu is Herchel Smith Senior Lecturer in Law at Emmanuel College, Cambridge.

Elisabetta Righini is a Member of the Cabinet of Vice-President Joaquín Almunia, European Commission, and a Visiting Professor at Kings College London.

Robert Schütze is Professor of European Law at Durham University and Director of the Durham European Law Institute.

Catherine Seville is Director of Studies in Law and Vice Principal at Newnham College, Cambridge.

Melanie Smith is Reader in Law at Cardiff Law School, Cardiff University.

Eleanor Spaventa is Professor of European Union Law at Durham Law School, Durham University.

Phil Syrpis is Reader in Law at University of Bristol Law School.

Takis Tridimas is Professor of European Law at the Dickson Poon School of Law, King's College London.

Alexander Türk is Professor of Law at the Dickson Poon School of Law, King's College London.

Neil Walker is Regius Professor of Public Law and the Law of Nature and Nations at the School of Law, University of Edinburgh.

Andrew Williams is Professor of Law at the University of Warwick.

Bruno de Witte is Professor of European Law at the University of Maastricht, the Netherlands.

PART I

CONCEPTUALIZING EU LAW

CHAPTER 1

THE PHILOSOPHY OF EUROPEAN UNION LAW

NEIL WALKER

I. Introduction: A New Horizon

WHAT do we mean by the philosophy of European Union (EU) law, and how do we go about studying it? A simple parsing exercise suggests that the philosophy of EU law builds upon two prior and broader areas of philosophical inquiry. The first is the philosophy of law in general, while the second is the philosophy of the European Union in general. By bringing these two sets of inquiries within a single horizon, the philosophy of European Union law can enrich our understanding of both.

The philosophy of law in general has typically been concerned with basic questions about the nature of law.[1] It asks what, if any, are the essential, distinctive or typical characteristics of law. The search breaks down into a number of more focused, though interrelated areas of inquiry. We may identify four. First, whence does law in general, including the law in general of any particular jurisdiction, derive its justification—its basic claim to authority? Secondly, what is the ideal content of law, and what are the standards or other interpretive criteria by which we can determine the proper meaning of the law? Thirdly, what are the conditions of

---

[1] See eg John Gardner, 'Law in General' in *Law as a Leap of Faith: Essays on Law in General* (2012) Ch 5.

the validity of law, understood in the sense of 'social normativity'? How, regardless of objective justification, do laws come to be 'socially upheld as binding standards'[2] and what, more generally, are the operative conditions of law as an effective mode of intervention in the world? How, in other words, does law work *as* law? Fourthly, what are the 'systemic' properties of a legal system, or the coherent qualities of 'the law' considered in holistic terms?

For its part, the philosophy of the EU in general is most appropriately understood as a branch of social or political philosophy.[3] Is the EU properly conceived of as a polity, and if so, what type of polity? In what respects is it like a state, or like an international organization, or like neither? What, if any, is its deep social purpose? What does it offer and how does it justify itself to its constituents, whether Member States, individual citizens, consumers or special interest holders? What type of moral or political claim, if any, does it make on these constituents?

The philosophy of EU law, in turn, should be considered as a two-way street, circulating back and forward between our two prior domains of inquiry. It should provide insight into the special case of the EU and its law from the perspective of our philosophical reflections on law in general. And, conversely, albeit as a secondary consideration, it should augment our understanding of law in general in light of the distinctive character of the EU and the special case of EU law. In a nutshell, how does our appreciation of the essential, distinctive or typical characteristics of law refine or extend our understanding of EU law, and how does our understanding of the EU and of EU law refine or extend our sense of the general characteristics of law?

How, then, to proceed? Our two-way inquiry will track the four core legal philosophical themes introduced above, considering each in light of the peculiarities of the EU case. It begins with the fundamental question of the overall justification of the authority of the European Union legal order. It is here that legal philosophy and social and political philosophy stand in closest connection, for this question requires us to look at the justifications of the EU as a socio-political project more generally, as these have influenced and been influenced by its special conditions of origin and its particular transformative dynamic. The protracted attention given to this part of our inquiry reflects its key standing in any consideration of the EU as a philosophically significant entity. Our inquiry continues with reflections on the deep normative orientation and interpretive grain of EU law. It then asks how EU law operates as an effective framework of practical reasoning. And finally, questions of the integrity or coherence of EU law, in particular its relationship, both continuous and discontinuous, with other legal systems, are examined.

---

[2] Joseph Raz, *The Authority of Law: Essays on Law and Morality* (1st ed, 1979) 134.

[3] See eg Heidrun Friese and Peter Wagner, 'Survey Article: The Nascent Political Philosophy of the European Polity' (2002) 10 *Journal of Political Philosophy* 342.

These questions are closely connected. Authoritative foundations are linked to the justification of the normative core and associated matters of interpretation. The efficacy of EU law is linked to its coherence and integrity. And efficacy, as we shall see, is also intimately connected to authority. Equally, the strengths and fragilities associated with the integrity of EU law are also tied to unresolved questions about the authority and appropriate purpose and meaning of EU law. Nevertheless, it is best to engage with these four themes separately and in sequence, precisely so as to best appreciate the character of their relationship.

Before we examine each theme, a methodological note is in order. Much of what we are calling the philosophy of the EU, from underlying justification and basic principles and values to bespoke conceptions of the role of law and the nature of legal order, is implicit rather than explicit.[4] This itself is connected to the distinctive novelty of the EU and its law. As a still evolving system, and one that does not easily conform to any developed genus, reflection on the ideal character and distinctive ontology of the EU and its law tends to be of two contrasting types. Either it assumes a highly speculative and aspirational form, reflecting the remote prospect of its fullest realization; or it is instead tentative, recondite, and incremental. In that latter vein, it is marked by an emphasis upon 'doing' before 'hearkening',[5] of practice before theory, and, indeed, of a meta-theoretical temper which embraces a theoretical type that is itself strongly practice-dependent. One consequence of this is that some of the philosophically interesting positions on the EU lack refined articulation. Just as they are in some measure embedded in practice, so too they have to be inferred from that practice, which means that this commentator—indeed, any commentator—on the internal philosophy of the EU and its law must perforce be prepared to go beyond reportage and engage in a constructive interpretation and elaboration of that internal philosophy.

II. Authoritative Foundations

1. Remote Origins

The idea of Europe long predates the late twentieth century debates and struggles over its institutional form. The usage of the term in any approximation of its modern continental territorial designation dates back to the fifteenth century,[6] but

---

[4] See further, Neil Walker, 'Legal Theory and the European Union: A 25th Anniversary Essay' 25 *Oxford Journal of Legal Studies* (2005) 281.

[5] Joseph Weiler, *The Constitution of Europe* (1999) Ch 1.

[6] Douglas Hay, *Europe: The Emergence of an Idea.* (2nd ed, 1968).

only with the secular Enlightenment did it begin to replace Christendom as *the* key signifier of a unitary civilization. This emergent sense of Europe as a distinctive and common place had social and political dimensions, and these supply the deep and intertwined philosophical roots of the modern conception of the European Union. On the one hand, early modern Europeans, or at least their elites, came to recognize themselves as sharing certain social forms and beliefs. On the other hand, early modern Europe also began to be viewed as the object of a common political design or plan.

Reflecting the close connection between these two dimensions, eighteenth-century thinkers as diverse as Kant, Montesquieu, Voltaire, Vattel, Constant, Robertson, and Burke developed an understanding of Europe as a site of both social similarity and political balance.[7] This harmonious Enlightenment image did not survive the French Revolution and the subsequent continental wars. Yet the notion of Europe as an overlapping cultural space in which many political units and ethnic types must be accommodated persisted, feeding a sense of continental interdependence—and of nascent identity—unknown in other global regions.[8] The content of that overlapping cultural space—the raw material for any social philosophy in the new Europe—included matters such as shared religion, parallel imperial experiences and ambitions, and notably, both common systems of law and close trading and commercial bonds. And the many political projects of continental union, going back as far as the French Duc de Sully's Grand Design of 1620, fed off this shared heritage and common practice.

Yet, as one writer puts it, the pan-European political project has always been 'formally at odds with itself',[9] fundamentally challenged by the very conditions that invite it. Westphalian Europe was where the idea of the modern sovereign state attained an early maturity, and so the political recognition of Europe as a discrete object could only be of an entity whose basic structure and distinctive configuration was one of prior and embedded political plurality. On the one hand, this underlying structure made for a fragile, often broken, inter-state accommodation; hence the basic attraction of projects of union. On the other hand, some such projects of union, in their overweening ambition, threatened to destroy the very diversity that was Europe's distinctive political inheritance.

The approach to Europe's political reconstruction has always taken different forms, reflecting both horns of this dilemma. Some projects have been premised on consensus, but—recalling an earlier point—have remained largely 'theoretical' in the speculative sense. They are 'pure' philosophical resources to be retrieved from the archives, if at all, only as political circumstance permits. The more 'applied'

---

[7] Perry Anderson, *The New Old World.* (2009) Ch 1.

[8] Anthony Pagden (ed), 'Europe: Conceptualizing a Continent,' in Pagden, A. (ed), *The Idea of Europe: From Antiquity to the European Union* (2002) 34.

[9] Anderson (n 7) 477.

projects in this longer historical perspective have tended to operate through territorial conquest or imperial design. This suggests not only a contrast, but also a relationship born of contrast, and one whose pattern continues to mark the institutional dynamics of twentieth century Europe. In 1929, for example, the French Prime Minister Aristide Briand, operating between two projects of conquest—in the shadow of the First World War and in anticipation of the Third Reich—floated through the League of Nations the idea of a consensual federation of European states. The immediate origins of the contemporary continental polity, when theoretical speculation finally achieved settled institutional form, can also be seen largely as a response to the unilateral vision of regional domination which provoked the Second World War.[10]

2. Competing Philosophies of Post-War Settlement

Yet, even though joined by a shared reaction against the forced union of conquest and by a commitment to peaceful collaboration, there were from the beginning competing visions of the nascent post-War Europolity. That competition reflects the tensions of a political experiment that simultaneously depends upon and challenges the state-sovereignty template of the modern age, as well as the complexities of the relationship between that basic question of political design and the broader sense of a common social bond and philosophy. Translated into the puzzle of foundational legal authority, we may express this distinction between political design and social philosophy through a basic discrimination between two sorts of applied philosophical question. In the first place, there is the *structural* question of the appropriate legal form and shape of the new post-state entity. Secondly, there is the *substantive* question of the key social purposes influencing that political form, and of the general jurisdictional focus and range appropriately conveyed by that political form.

As regards the *structural* question, the available models of the legal polity are typically understood as three in number.[11] They are, in turn, a neo-federalist position, treating Europe's destiny as involving some approximation of a continental state. At the other extreme, is a statist position, which comprehends the European good as ultimately reducible, rather like the typical international regime, to the inter-governmentally negotiated aggregate interests of the Member States. Located between these two, is a supranational, or in some conceptions, transnational

---

[10] Weiler (n 5); Peter Lindseth, *Power and Legitimacy: Reconciling Europe and the Nation-State* (2010), Chs 2–3; Jan-Werner Muller *Contesting Democracy: Political Ideas in Twentieth-Century Europe* (2011) Ch 4; Anderson (n 7) Ch 9.

[11] See eg Justine Lacroix and Kalypso Nicolaïdis, 'European Stories: An Introduction' in *European Stories: Intellectual Debates on Europe in National Context* (2010).

position,[12] which envisages the new Europe not as a trade-off between different levels of state or state-like authority but as transcending the logic of statehood in a new model of political design. These positions should be treated with some circumspection. There are variations in specification as well as in labelling. More significantly, once we move beyond the stylizations of their authors, or of their supporters or critics, the triptych is probably better viewed as a spectrum, and one in which there is a significant pull to the new model at the centre and so towards the discontinuity rather than the continuity of the European project with the state tradition.

In the founding phase, the structural competition was framed by a division between an ambitious and overtly neo-federalist conception of the new Europe, one, premised on the equality of the citizens of all Member States, and a narrower conception of continental integration. The former envisaged a grand political project for a post-bellum continent dedicated to learning and perpetually applying the geopolitical lesson of uncoerced co-existence under a jurisdictionally open framework of policy sharing or co-ordination. Ambitious to mark a new continental beginning, this approach, as, for example, anticipated in Altiero Spinelli's pan-European Ventotene Manifesto of 1940,[13] was one that strongly favoured a 'big bang' foundational solution. From the outset, and in many of its later iterations—notably as one important vision supporting the failed Future of Europe Convention of 2003–5—the language and methods of documentary constitutionalism have been to the fore in this neo-federalist approach.

The second, narrower but more influential, founding conception was based upon a platform of common or pooled economic affluence and other manifest common goods. This apparently more modest approach spanned a range of candidate perspectives. One such perspective was developed by prominent founders such as Jean Monnet and Robert Schuman[14] whose long-term aspiration was also a neo-federalist one, but premised instead upon a process of gradual accretion from a narrow basis through a series of limited innovations. This incremental approach was famously summed up in the 1950 Schuman Declaration's pronouncement that 'Europe should not be made all at once, or in accordance with a single plan'—a commitment supplying the platform for the ECSC Treaty of the following year.

The so-called 'Monnet method' was the touchstone for much of the subsequently influential neo-functionalist theorizing of EU integration.[15] Neo-functionalism holds that in order to maximize the effectiveness of core areas of market-making

---

[12] See Lacroix and Nicolaidis (n 11). They use the term 'transnational', but include within that the position of Weiler (n 5), which is self-styled as 'supranational'. See further, text at n 18.

[13] See eg Michael Burgess, *Federalism and the European Union: The Building of Europe, 1950-2000*; Derek Urwin 'The European Community from 1945-85' in M. Cini, (ed.), *European Union Politics*. (2nd ed, 2007) 13–29.

[14] Schuman was the French Foreign Minister from 1948 to 1953. Monnet, a career diplomat, was widely regarded as the visionary mind behind the Schuman Plan.

[15] See eg Ernst Hass, *The Uniting of Europe* (1958).

economic integration, appropriately supportive regulatory conditions should 'spill over' into adjacent sectors of economic and social policy: whether, say, the equalization of product safety standards or the removal of gender discrimination to provide a level playing-field in the labour market. Such spill-over would gain momentum from the gradual transfer of loyalties from state to regional level in line with the social logic of a sectorally differentiated institutional formation, and from the progressive self-assertion of higher tiers of governance benefiting from their accumulation of regulatory capacity to embrace the greater technical complexity of multi-sectoral accommodation. Along these channels, furthermore, it was predicted that economic and social integration would eventually and inevitably give rise to political integration.

Others envisaged a more strictly bounded approach to European integration. For those, such as the followers of German ordoliberalism, for whom the optimal operation of the market required its ring-fencing from the exercise of social policy,[16] or for those who supported Hans Ipsen's idea of the EU as a special purpose association for economic integration,[17] as for many other pragmatic statists identifying discrete arenas of overlapping interest, the making of a common economic area was an end in itself. Europe should be no more than a delegated market-making framework, enhancing the common pool of resources and economic welfare of all Member States, but in so doing excluded from state-based market-correcting social and welfare policy. The key legal register of this approach, rather than the familiar public-law model of documentary constitutionalism, was instead the constitution of an economic order through shared basic institutions of private law.

Patently, then, in the early diversity of political models, we observe a corresponding diversity of *substantive* social philosophies. The neo-federal vision from the outset involved a jurisdictional outlook in which Europe would have a scope and precedence of authority akin to that of the higher level of a (federal) state, while the neo-functional, ordoliberal and intergovernmental views restricted themselves, at least in the shorter term, to the core economic freedoms and other measures necessary to make a common market. Yet we should not overstate the distinction between these different angles of approach. Economic policies typically figure large within wider political projects and ambitions at the national or supranational level; conversely, as the neo-functionalists, amongst others, stress, visions of the polity framed by economic considerations are bound to concern themselves with the wider societal and political infrastructure supporting the economic vision.

---

[16] Ernst Mestmacker, 'On the Legitimacy of European Law' (1994) *RabelsZ* 615; for analysis, see eg Damian Chalmers, 'The Single Market: From Prima Donna to Journeyman' in J. Shaw and G. More (eds), *New Legal Dynamics of European Union* (1995) 55–72; Christian Joerges, '"Good Governance" in the European Internal Market: An Essay in Honour of Claus-Dieter Ehlermann' (2001) *EUI Working Papers*, RSC No. 2001/29; Alan Milward *The European Rescue of the Nation-State* (2nd ed 2000).

[17] Hans-Pieter Ipsen, 'europaische Verfassung—Nationale Verfassung' (1987) EuR 195.

Through these connections we find a gradual drift and refinement of structural models from either starting point—moving away from wide neo-federal ambition and narrow state-centred economistic arguments alike towards a new 'third way' centre of debate.

From the one side, one of the best-known and influential public philosophies of the EU, and one of the fullest attempts to specify supranationalism as a structural vision of the legal and political order, elevates economic prosperity to a polity-defining ideal within a broader understanding of the EU's mission. According to Joseph Weiler, the common market should not be justified just on wealth-maximizing grounds. As important has been the wider political prize of lasting peace—another defining ideal for a continent ravaged by two World Wars and a longer history of conflict—that the settled practice of economic co-operation and a common dignity born of the collective overcoming of poverty could help secure.[18] In turn, he argues, these complementary ideals of peace and distributed prosperity are best consolidated in an arrangement that treats Europe's transnational domain neither as a neutral inter-national arena for the pursuit of state interests nor as a form of continental proto-nationalism or incipient statehood. Instead, Europe should be cultivated in a legal-institutional space properly called '*supra*national' because situated above the Member States and standing in a transformative relationship to them. Rather than emulate or replace the state, supranationalism undertakes to honour the goods of belonging and originality associated with nation statehood. At the same time, it seeks to overcome the insularities and tame the excesses of national sentiment under a new voluntary discipline of 'constitutional tolerance',[19] exercised by the still formally sovereign members *inter se* in accordance with their new edifice of common regulation.

From the other side, many narratives of European Union which began from the economic core have branched out in reflection or anticipation of the expanding scope of the polity, though often retaining the ontological commitment to 'individualism'[20] and a 'market'[21] conception of citizenship prioritizing economic freedom. For example, Giandomenico Majone's work on a European 'regulatory state'[22] shares with ordoliberalism the idea that supranationalism should transcend partisan politics. Here, however, the invisible hand of the market is supplemented by the expert hand of the technocrat. In Majone's conception—one that enjoyed extended success in capturing the sensibility of a significant part of the Brussels elite—these additional regulatory measures are not concerned with macro-politically sensitive

[18] Weiler (n 5) Ch 7

[19] Joseph Weiler, 'A Constitution for Europe: Some Hard Choices' (2003) 40 *Journal of Common Market Studies* 563

[20] Alexander Somek, *Individualism* (2008)

[21] Michelle Everson, 'The Legacy of the Market Citizen' in Shaw and More (eds) (n 16) 73.

[22] See eg Majone, 'From the Positive to the Regulatory State: Causes and Consequences of Changes in the Mode of Governance' (1997) 17 *Journal of Public Policy* 139.

questions of distribution. Rather, they attend to risk-regulation in matters such as product and environmental standards where expert knowledge is paramount, and where accountability, it is argued, is best served by administrative law measures aimed at transparency and enhanced participation in decision-making by interested and knowledgeable parties rather than the volatile preferences of broad representative institutions.

What we see in Majone, and various other gradualist conceptions, is a movement from a narrowly economic delegation model to a somewhat broader 'demarcation'[23] model. Legitimation still flows primarily through the authorization of Member States, but that authorization increasingly tends to be indirect rather than direct. What is stressed is some combination of the modesty, relative non-contentiousness, specialist requirements and containable character of the supranational remit. The EU is treated variously, and often cumulatively, as the recipient and 'trustee' of a clearly delimited mandate,[24] as the disinterestedly efficient or expert 'technocratic'[25] instrument for the realization of common commitments, as a transnationally pooled extension of the modern administrative state,[26] or as the indispensable and relatively uncontroversial transnational means to pursue a range of the shared interests of national states and citizens towards a positive net 'output'.[27]

3. The Philosophical Reflections of Maturity

Yet the adequacy of these justificatory models—both those, like Weiler's, that stress the legitimating force of an original mission embracing economic convergence as just one part of a wider polity vision; and those, like Majone's, that stress the containable and largely consequential and derivative nature of the growing non-economic agenda—is challenged by the relentlessly expansionary dynamic of the Union.[28] They have become less plausible claims in a supranational polity with a broader and deeper policy agenda, with a bureaucracy and agency structure increasingly distant from national control, with a membership that has risen from an original six to twenty eight, with multiple veto points that work against any rolling back of community legislative reach still less constitutional competence, and

---

[23] Neil Walker, 'Surface and Depth: The EU's Resilient Sovereignty Question' in J. Neyer and A. Wiener (eds), *Political Theory of the European Union* (2011) Ch 10, 101.

[24] See eg Majone, 'Delegation of Powers and the Fiduciary Principle' in his *Dilemmas of European Integration* (2005).

[25] Christopher Lord and Paul Magnette, 'E Pluribus Unum? Creative Disagreement about Legitimacy in the EU' (2004) 42 *Journal of Common Market Studies* 183.

[26] Lindseth (n 10).

[27] As in Fritz Scharpf's 'output legitimacy' *Governing in Europe: Effective and Democratic?* (1999).

[28] A point Weiler himself recognized in due course; see eg Joseph Weiler, 'Integration Through Fear' (2012) 23 EJIL 1–5.

which is, consequently, faced with the erosion of a comfortable 'permissive consensus'[29] amongst key national elites across Europe. In short, the very conditions that demand a higher threshold of legitimation of common action have tended to leave the Union less favourably placed to reach that threshold. For as the EU increasingly sought market-making or market-correcting interventions involving politically salient choices, it simultaneously reduced the capacity of states to act independently in these policy areas. The robust legal protection of the single market, which acted as a guarantor of wider and narrower visions of the economic polity, was suited to a formative context where market-making measures impinged only lightly on other social policy objectives; or, at least, where states retained the procedural means to prevent politically controversial collective commitments in pursuit of these other objectives, and so were slow to make such commitments in situations with obvious winners and losers. But the expansion of negative integration beyond the narrow market-making sphere, and the concomitant growth of positive integration to fill the policy gap, altered the dynamic of collective action. In particular, the Single European Act and the Treaty reforms of the 1990s cumulatively advanced the twin strategy of expanding the scope of supranational competence into traditional statist strongholds of monetary, social and security policy and providing new qualified majoritarian means to facilitate the exercise of that expanded jurisdiction. And compounding the potential of this development to jeopardize specific national interests, the post-Cold War Enlargement programme reduced the specific weight of particular national voices—especially smaller and medium size states—in the formation of coalitions that could confidently endorse the direction of the new policy lines.

These legitimacy-challenging considerations, which also supply the rudiments of the recent euro crisis, have provoked two further categories of response in terms of the general justification of EU authority. Again, the distinction between structural and substantive considerations is pertinent, as is the distinction between more or less federalist responses to the structural question.

(a) The New Structural Agenda—Integration or Disaggregation?

In the first place, at the structural level, there is a renewed stress on viewing the overall legitimacy of the EU in original rather than derivative terms—as a self-justifying rather than a state-dependent entity. This new emphasis, in turn, divides into *integrated* and *disaggregated*[30] approaches. The *integrated* approach, with its revival of a neo-federal agenda, has been more prominent, both in the academy and as a matter of public philosophy. Here the independent authority of

---

[29]   See eg Liesbet Hooghe and Gary Marks, 'A Postfunctionalist Theory of European Integration: From Permissive Consensus to Constraining Dissensus', (2008) 39 *British Journal of Political Science* 1–23.
[30]   Walker (n 23) 103.

the EU is understood in terms of a notion of constituent power[31] that may revert more or less explicitly to a statist template of understanding.[32] The EU may not have been born free, but at a certain point of its development of an increasingly capacious and contentious agenda for the allocation of rights, risks and resources, the key to its legitimacy, has come to lie with the collective self-determination of all whom this agenda affects.

The justification of the EU, therefore, has begun to be understood as depending upon a process of democratic reflexivity—a collective self-homologation, related to but going beyond the self-norming that supplies the generative code of the legal order. This democratization process has often been linked to a 'deliberate political act to re-establish Europe', as Joschka Fischer put it in his famous Humboldt speech in 2000—widely acclaimed as a key catalyst for the subsequent Constitution-making project. And in addition to, and often seen as flowing from this kind of meta-democratic constitutional commitment,[33] a legitimating form of democratic reflexivity also requires robust representative institutions at the quotidian level of political decision making.

But a full-blown democratic approach to the justification of supranational authority is vulnerable to various objections. One questions its basic plausibility, insisting upon the resilience of the so-called democratic deficit. This challenge to the democratic credentials of the Union stresses the record of voter apathy and weak transnational political party organization, notwithstanding progressive empowerment of the European Parliament over 30 years, indicates the continuing marginalization of national Parliaments despite recent subsidiarity-inspired reforms, emphasizes the limited transparency and poor accountability of Council and Commission, and, at the meta-democratic level, cites the failure of quasi-populist initiatives such as the (Constitutional) Convention on the Future of Europe to nurture a fertile democratic subsoil. On this view, the lack of a European *demos*, culturally self-understood as such, means that the motivation for a committed, contestatory democracy remains significantly deficient.[34]

A second objection recalls the theme of the EU as a dependent polity, questioning the normative appropriateness of a solution that foregrounds democracy. A key danger of supranational democratic overreach is that euro-democracy stands in a negative-sum relationship with—and so risks curtailing and chilling—democracy

---

[31] See eg Hans Lindahl, 'The Paradox of Constituent Power: The Ambiguous Self-Constitution of the European Union' (2007) 20 *Ratio Juris* 485.

[32] See eg Federico Mancini, 'Europe: The Case for Statehood' (1998) 4 ELJ 29–42; E. Eriksen, *The Unfinished Democratisation of Europe* (2009).

[33] But by no means necessarily so. See eg Simon Hix, *What's Wrong with the European Union and How to Fix it* (2008).

[34] See eg Andrew Moravcsik, 'What Can we Learn from the Collapse of the European Constitutional Project?' (2006) 47 *Politische Vierteljahresschrift* 2.

in its culturally more appropriate forum of the nation state(s).[35] Take the recent debate over the single currency, sovereign debt, and the relationship between monetary and fiscal integration, in which the social legitimacy of the EU has been more profoundly challenged than ever before. This deep controversy turns on the legitimate boundaries of supranational policy intervention into traditional areas of national democratic competence through regulatory mechanisms that themselves lack the courage of collective democratic conviction. Instead, they rely upon intrusive forms of 'executive federalism'[36] and a culture of 'integration through fear',[37] which, in a vicious circle, further undermines the capacity of the European level to attract democratic support.

A third and related objection revisits the demarcation argument. It holds that in its appeal to the trumping authority of the collective will, the case for democracy fails to capture the more limited and specialist mandate of the EU. Given its location in the overall architecture of national, continental and global political authority, the argument for a thoroughgoing democratic ethos suited to an entity whose *raison d'être* is one of collective self-determination should not apply, even if some aspects of the EU's authority do require democratic legitimation.[38]

The *disaggregated* model takes a very different approach to democratic reflexivity. Democracy becomes an adjective rather than noun—a mobile virtue of policy communities of discrete practical engagement where people have the knowledge and motivation to put things in common, rather than a holistic virtue of the large community of the 'demos'. What we need, on this view, is not mass ballot-box democracy, but a multiplicity of finely grained engagements of knowledgeable and mutually responsive constituencies aimed at providing context-specific optimizations of the common good. And if we look closely, it is argued, we can find such contexts in the EU across many different policy areas and mediated through such deliberative mechanisms as Comitology[39] and the Open Method of Co-ordination.[40]

But there is a level of analysis problem here. Democracy can certainly be disaggregated, often doing its best work in local micro-contexts. However, unless we hold that there are no mutual 'externalities' between discrete policy areas which require trans-contextual evaluation; that there should be no broader conception of the public interest (distributive fairness, equal rights protection etc) guiding individual sectoral choices; and that, underpinning these other concerns, there is no

---

[35] See eg Dieter Grimm, 'Integration by Constitution' (2005) 3 *International Journal of Constitutional Law* 193.

[36] Jurgen Habermas, *The Crisis of the European Union: A Response* (2012).

[37] Weiler (n 28).   [38] See eg Moravcsik (n 34).

[39] See eg Christian Joerges, 'Deliberative Political Processes Revisited: What we have Learnt about the Legitimacy of Supranational Decision-Making' (2006) 44 *Journal of Common Market Studies* 779.

[40] See eg Charles Sabel and Jonathan Zeitlin, 'Learning from Difference: The New Architecture of Experimental Governance in the European Union' (2008) 14 *European Law Journal* 271.

need for, or no threat to, the constitutive public goods of trust, respect, solidarity and mutual tolerance in the disaggregated approach, then there is something lacking. In particular, the disaggregated approach disregards the twofold quality of the 'demos'; that it represents a shorthand for those constitutive goods—respect, trust, solidarity and tolerance—which by their input not only make the broader democratic framework possible in terms of providing its motivational wherewithal, but are also among its greatest accompanying virtues and outputs. So, the fact that we find alternative routes to democratic practice at disaggregated sites despite the absence of these constitutive goods as motivational impulses at the input stage, only addresses one half of the problem. It can do nothing to cure or compensate for the absence of these constitutive goods as independently virtuous companions and dividends of the democratic process.

The structural debate about the appropriate democratic philosophy of the European Union remains very much alive. The integrated and disaggregated approaches each arguably needs the other to help address its own shortcomings. There remains a deep-rooted sociological problem about the conditions for democratic motivation, and a susceptibility to resort to a circular or boot-strapping approach, in which the capacity to achieve the institutional conditions of democratic maturity seems to depend upon a common political commitment that is elusive in the absence of just such a prior institutional achievement. There also remains a deeper normative question, trailed in the third critique of the integrated approach, concerning the appropriate centrality of the democratic ideal supranationally.

In this complex terrain, the idea of a 'right to justification'[41] has recently been mooted to allow a more context-sensitive justificatory methodology for different sectors and levels of supranational decision. On this view, voice may be more or less appropriate than say, output efficiency or expertise, as a way of justifying common action at different levels and different sectors. So, provided we respect that logic of appropriateness, we need not make rigid choices for or against the priority of democracy in general or in particular institutional contexts. Such an approach, however, for all its promise, still cannot easily overcome the sociological deficit of supranational democracy, however qualified, or resolve the meta-question of who gets to decide what pattern and degree of democracy is appropriate and sufficient in fulfillment of the right to justification.[42]

---

[41] See Rainer Forst, *The Right to Justification: Elements of a Constructivist Theory of Justice* (2007); and as specifically applied, with some variation, to the EU, see Jurgen Neyer, *The Justification of Europe: A Political Theory of Supranational Integration* (2012).

[42] See eg Neyer, 'Justice, not Democracy; Legitimacy in the European Union' (2010) 48 JCMS 903–921; and (from a critically democratic perspective), see Danny Nicol's reply, and the riposte by J. Neyer (2012) 50 *JCMS* 508–522, 523–529. See also Forst 'Transnational Justice and Democracy' *Normative Orders Working Paper* 4/11.

(b) The New Substantive Agenda: The Return to Ideals

Turning, more briefly, to new substantive approaches, we encounter arguments that address the problem of authority in the post-foundational phase neither by dismissing the very idea of mission legitimacy as an anachronism for a mature polity nor by viewing democratic process as a sufficient alternative. Rather, they adjust the mission to the demands of the twenty-first century. On one view, indeed, the historical problem of the EU lies neither in the rigidity of its mission nor in its having become stale or exhausted, but in an abiding failure to treat seriously enough the development of a deep and distinctive purpose and set of guiding values.[43] Candidates for a renewed substantive mission include a globalized peace agenda, emphasis upon human rights and the rule of law, and a more expansive notion of freedom based upon material capacity rather than non-interference.[44] All of them seek to track, reinforce or reshape current trends in EU law and policy. Within the last sub-category, one approach that has achieved particular prominence since the onset of the financial crisis sets out to correct a historically 'unbalanced' preference for economic rights over social solidarity and collective provision.[45]

Additionally, the increasingly outward-looking perspective of the EU—witnessed in its Enlargement programme, its Neighbourhood Policy, its foreign and defence policy and its closer engagement with the processes and consequences of globalization generally, has meant that much of the intense engagement with a value-based *raison d'être* has been in this area.[46] The idea of 'normative power Europe',[47] for example, champions an approach to the spreading of influence that leads by continental example and via conditional agreements rather than through military or other more coercive forms of authority. The structural model of supranationalism itself may be presented as a template of co-operative transnational government for emulation in other regions.[48] And by taking a prominent role in matters such as climate change, global health, development aid and anti-terrorism, the EU promotes its contribution to these substantive global goods as a defining feature of its mandate.[49]

[43] See eg Andrew Williams, *The Ethos of Europe* (2010) esp. Ch 7; Philp Allott, *The Crisis of European Constitutionalism: Reflections on the Revolution in Europe* (1996) 34 *Common Market Law Review* 339.

[44] See eg Williams (n 43) Chs 2–6.

[45] Mark Dawson and Floris De Witte, 'Constitutional Balance in the EU after the Euro-Crisis' (2013) 76 *Modern Law Review* 817; see also Andrea Sangiovanni, 'Solidarity in the European Union: Problems and Prospects' in J. Dickson and P. Eleftheriadis (eds) *Philosophical Foundations of European Union Law* (2012) 384.

[46] Gráinne de Búrca, 'Europe's Raison D'Etre' in Dimitry Kochenov and Fabian Amtenbrink (eds) *The European Union's Shaping of the International Legal Order* (2013).

[47] Ian Manners, 'Normative Power Europe: A Contradiction in Terms?' (2002) 40 *Journal of Common Market Studies* 235.

[48] See eg Rachel Kleinfeld and Kalypso Nicolaidis, 'Can a Post-Colonial Power Export the Rule of Law? Elements of a General Framework' in G. Palombella and N. Walker (eds), *Relocating the Rule of Law* (2009) 139.

[49] See eg de Búrca, (n 46).

III. The Interpretation of EU Law

Issues of underlying mission and purpose lead naturally to the question of how EU law should be approached as an object of interpretation. A major area of recent development in legal philosophy concerns the role of the judge or other privileged interpreter in deciding disputes under the law. Positivist and non-positivist theories offer differing answers. Positivists treat the law as a matter of rules derived from the socially acknowledged authoritative sources of the legal order in question, and so understand legal interpretation as the proper application of these rules. Non-positivists understand law, and its interpretation, as extending beyond the 'posited' materials of a legal system to include background principles or other independent moral or ethical considerations.[50] In EU law, this basic philosophical distinction is not insignificant, yet has been less crucial than in many settings in producing distinctive understandings of the limits of legal interpretation. This is partly a reflection of the comparatively recent emergence of this kind of inquiry in the EU context. This is due, in turn, not only to the relative novelty of EU law itself and its attendant legal-philosophical scholarship, but also to the formalist emphasis of the civilian tradition—the prevalent legal tradition throughout the EU—on the importance of a closed system of authority in which all legal questions are resoluble by means of resources and styles of reasoning internally prescribed by law. Yet the limited resonance of the positivist/non-positivist divide in accounting for the role of the EU judge also has to do with the creative way in which the language of sources has been used to allow broader consideration of the basic goods of the legal order to be entertained within legal interpretation.

Of central significance here is the emphasis on general principles of EU law. This is the register in which both external discussion and insider (in particular judicial) contemplation of the key interpretive guides to EU law takes place. In the academic literature, general principles are categorized in different ways,[51] but again we may usefully draw on the distinction between structure and substance. Structural principles are those such as primacy, attribution of competences, institutional balance, subsidiarity and sincere co-operation. Each is structural in the sense that it reflects and addresses the peculiar architecture of the EU as an entity that is horizontally and vertically dispersed—both multi-institutional and allocated across state and

[50] For a useful analysis of these background theoretical orientations in the EU context, see George Letsas, 'Harmonic Law: The Case against Pluralism' in J. Dickson and P. Eleftheriadis, (eds) (n 45) 77; see also Julie Dickson and Pavlos Eleftheriadis, 'Introduction: The Puzzles of European Law' 1, also in Dickson and Elepftheriadis (n 45).

[51] For a full overview of these categorizations, see Takis Tridimas, *The General Principles of EU Law* (2nd ed, 2006) Ch1; see also Armin von Bogdandy, 'Founding Principles' in A. von Bogdandy and J. Bast (eds) *Principles of European Constitutional Law* (2010).

inter-state levels. What we are concerned with here is the internal articulation of those normative premises that, in combination, give detailed shape to the EU as a 'supranational' ideal in the broader structural sense conveyed in the previous section. In the second place, substantive principles refer to supposedly 'compelling'[52] or 'axiomatic'[53] legal principles somehow inherent in the idea of legal order. These include the rule of law itself, but also fundamental rights protection, equality, proportionality, legitimate expectations and rights of legal defence.

While there is some agreement over the broad content of these principles, various tensions in their treatment reflect underlying philosophical disagreement. To begin with, and bearing upon the distinction between positivist and non-positivist understandings, the increasing prominence of general principles in the interpretation of EU law is a consequence both of a more candid acceptance of the compelling force of certain self-standing moral and ethical ideas in the interpretation of EU law, and of the expansion, since the Treaty of Maastricht, of the already strong strain of formalism towards an explicitly textual approach to the recognition of general principles. Understood as causal forces, these two phenomena are mutually supportive, yet this leaves unresolved the matter of which provides the authoritative basis for general principles. Whether we are discussing, say, the relationship between the Charter of Fundamental Rights and the general recognition of rights as fundamental to the EU legal order, or the relationship between general ideals of solidarity or equality and their various articulations in the preambles and texts of European Treaties and laws, the question of whether the enactment is the source of the principle in question or merely a medium for recognizing its prior existence remains.

Secondly, there is a tension between 'bottom-up' and 'top-down' understandings of general principles. Whereas the structural principles are viewed as *sui generis*, the substantive principles are understood as of broader origins and significance. On the one hand, there has long been a strong emphasis upon the 'common constitutional traditions' of the Member States as a source of inspiration and comparative learning both within the jurisprudence and in the academic commentary.[54] On the other hand, stress is often placed upon the universal significance of the rule of law and associated values, in some case associated with a natural law conception of their foundations.[55] Again, these approaches can be understood as mutually supportive in practice, but there remains an underlying difference—at least of emphasis. On one side, the accent is on the common legal-ethical horizon of a small group of Western European states gradually extended to Central Europe. On the other

---

[52] H. G. Schermers and D. Waelbroeck, *Judicial Protection in the European Union* (6th ed, 2001) 28.
[53] G. Issac, *Droit Communautaire General* (3rd ed, 1992) 145.
[54] See eg Tridimas (n 51) 5–11.
[55] See eg Schermers and Walebroeck (n 52) 28–30.

side, the emphasis is upon moral principles that transcend and should engage any conceivable legal order.

Thirdly, and finally, there is tension over the extent to which the general principles of the legal order—whether 'posited' or not and whether 'bottom-up' or 'top-down'—should be understood as permanent or long-term ideals set apart from the vicissitudes of the EU as a political order, or as sensitive to the changing role and purpose of the EU political order. On one view, the confident maturity of the legal order is indicated in its relative autonomy from these circumstances. On another view, the restricted purview of the discussion of general principles is instead a reflection and indictment of what—to recall discussion in the previous section—is seen as the broader failure of the EU to develop a forthright and morally defensible mission for the twenty-first century.[56] From that perspective, the relative autonomy of the legal order from deeper ethico-political concerns is understood as a symptom of, and apology for, that broader moral shortcoming, rather than accepted in general terms as the self-standing virtue of any legal order seeking to protect itself from undue political influence.

IV. The Efficacy of EU Law

Leaving behind the question of ideal interpretation, which bites most deeply in the 'hard case', let us turn to the general efficacy of EU law. Given what we know about the foundation of the EU and its claim to authority, on what basis, and with what consequences for the overall supranational project, does EU law operate as binding law? And in what sense, if at all, are these operative conditions distinctive to EU law? Here we find a number of different theoretical positions, corresponding to familiar philosophical strains of how law operates as a form of practical reason. These strains are in turn, instrumental, formal, congruent and constitutive. They need not be incompatible, but different approaches to the general efficacy of EU law will emphasis one or more strains over others, and perhaps at the expense of others.

In the first place, we must recognize the force of the instrumental argument for law as the basic motor of supranationalism—the key means to the end of European integration. Writing in the early 1980s, before the gradual development of Qualified Majority Voting (QMV) and the Treaty-based expansion of legislative jurisdiction beyond the market-making core, Weiler drew attention to the 'dual character of

---

[56] Williams (n 43) Ch 7.

supranationalism[57] as a key evolutionary dynamic. At that stage, developed legal supranationalism in the internal market, particularly the Court of Justice's assertion of the formal properties of the EU as an autonomous legal system, stood in stark contrast to a modestly conceived political supranationalism. Yet the two were strategically related. The early prominence of legal supranationalism did not occur in spite of political underdevelopment, but was encouraged or acquiesced in precisely *because* political supranationalism remained so modest, with the Member States retaining a veto power in most areas of European policy making. The persistence of the national veto in supranational forms of legislative integration also provided reassurance to those who might otherwise have been concerned that legal constitutionalism offers too much encouragement to a federalist vision. The most basic key to the attractiveness of law as the agent of supranationalism, therefore, lay in the fine balance that is struck. It depended on its regulatory capacity to steer, to consolidate and, typically through judicial recognition of the claims of private litigants, to guarantee positive-sum intergovernmental bargains across wide-ranging aspects of economic integration and other more limited aspects of market-correcting regulation, *yet* to do so without threatening key national political prerogatives. More specifically, the law's instrumental value was twofold. It provided a legible and stable method of charting and co-ordinating the supranational settlement. Additionally, in a context of market making where the temptation for each national member of the continental trade-liberalizing cartel to engage in protectionism while exploiting the general opening of the markets of the other national members posed a significant collective action problem, it performed a vital disciplining function. The consistent application and enforcement of the rules of the game by independent legal institutions was crucial in forestalling free-riding and rendering common commitments more credible.[58]

Structural factors reinforced the instrumental attractiveness of legal constitutionalism. The empowerment of the Court of Justice responded to a conception of the supranational settlement understood, in the language of organizational economics, as an incomplete contract. Framework texts, even the relatively detailed codes of successive EU treaties, allow a degree of open texture. In so doing, they lower the bar of prerequisite consensus and allow judicial adaptation of the text to changing conditions without new resort to the drawing board. The resulting margin of judicial manoeuvre is key to reconciling stability and flexibility in any constitutive context; all the more so in the EU, where the political conditions for regular textual reform were for long unfavourable. The Court of Justice, then, became a vital mechanism to avoid conflict or gridlock arising from the divergence

---

[57] Weiler, 'The Community System: The Dual Character of Supranationalism', (1981) *Yearbook of European Law* 267.

[58] Martin Shapiro, 'The European Court of Justice', in P. Craig and G. de Búrca, *The Evolution of EU Law* (1st ed, 1999) 321.

of national political interests. As a 'trustee court'[59] delegated significant power to bind its national principals and to expand its zone of discretion, it could 'complete' the supranational contract in incremental fashion. It would do so both by advancing the material agenda of integration case by case and by adjusting the balance, so sensitive in the mixed polity context, in boundary conflicts over the powers of the diversely-sourced institutions.[60]

The fiduciary role of a trustee court in the making of a legal constitution, however, is not legitimated solely through considerations of system functionality. Performative factors also matter, and here the tradition of legal formalism, underpinned by the predominately civilian roots of the Member States, is significant. A position of judicial neutrality, assiduously cultivated in the context of a Court composed of senior jurists from all Member States and delivering judgment in a typically laconic and scrupulously non-partisan 'legalese', has lent cumulative authority to the Court's decision making.[61] The fact that so much of the jurisdiction of the EU and its judicial organs could be articulated in terms of (primarily economic) rights has reinforced this formalist mindset and self-presentation. It has meant that the Court of Justice, for all that it inevitably retained a considerable margin of discretion in the polity-building phase, could nevertheless lay the constitutional foundation stones in a manner closely associated with its own ostensibly apolitical authority as an adjudicatory organ—in the language of individual rights and remedies so familiar from the historical lexicon of modern European domestic adjudication.[62]

The prominent success of EU law as part of the European project also depends upon a basic congruence between many of the earlier and predominantly economic understandings of the logic of integration and the basic modality of law. As already noted, for the ordoliberals, the Treaty of Rome supplied Europe with its own economic constitution, a supranational market–enhancing system of rights whose legitimacy *required* the absence of democratically responsive will formation and consequential pressure towards market-interfering socio-economic legislation at the supranational level, a matter best left instead to the Member States. Ordoliberal theory, then, provides a classic model of how an autonomous legal order, through generating and ring-fencing a framework of economic exchange centred on the four freedoms, provides a platform for the efficient operation of a capitalist economic logic. And Ipsen's theory, to which Majone's contemporary regulatory approach is a notable successor, also continues to operate within a logic of demarcation. In drawing a sharp distinction between the value-judgments of

---

[59] Alec Stone Sweet, 'The European Court of Justice' in P. Craig and G. de Búrca (eds.) *The Evolution of EU Law* (2nd ed, 2011) 121.

[60] See eg Shapiro (n 58) 321–322; Fritz Scharpf ,'Legitimacy in the Multilevel European Polity' in P. Dobner and M. Loughlin (eds), *The Twilight of Constitutionalism?* (2010) 89.

[61] See eg Weiler, (n 5) Ch.5.   [62] See eg Stone Sweet (n 59); Scharpf (n 60).

distributive politics and narrower expert or stakeholder dominated areas of risk regulation and cost-benefit analyses, these approaches were bound to favour a specifically *legal* decision-making method—a technique well versed and widely validated both in the jurisdictional matter of drawing and protecting the boundaries of the non-political and in the development of process rights and responsibilities within that non-political sphere.

As we have already seen, however, the conditions that placed law—understood in instrumental, formal or congruent terms—at a premium in an earlier phase of European integration, are challenged in a polity more broadly and transparently concerned with the negative-sum allocation of risks and resources. Legal instrumentalism becomes less attractive when the ends become more controversial. Legal formalism, too, becomes less adequate the more the law is implicated in controversial policies of positive integration. The idea of congruence between the demarcation-dependent methodologies of European integration and law's boundary-maintenance attributes fades as the supranational agenda becomes more open ended. As these strands have weakened, however, another way of conceiving of law in the EU has obtained a new prominence. Increasingly, what has been sponsored in recent years is the idea of law as somehow constitutive of the political conditions necessary to overcome the crisis of legitimacy of a polity unable to bear the social consequences of its distributive logic.

For some time, this brand of thinking was closely tied up with the idea of a new constitutional founding. Yet, as we have seen, the notion of a written constitution as a kind of meta-democratic catalyst, working through the symbolic force, the participatory breadth and epistemic depth of its settlement terms, foundered in *fact* on the practical failure of the 2005 Constitutional Treaty and *in theory* on the tendency to assume as a constitutional *precondition* the common social commitment that could not emerge other than as a constitutional dividend.[63] Today, in consequence, the constitutional language is more muted, but there remains a strain of constitutive theory, closely associated with Habermas, that continues to invest in the solidarity-generating potential of law.[64]

This argument depends upon drawings clear distinction between the condition of *Sittlichkeit*, understood as an embedded form of common ethical life, and *solidarity,* understood as an active ethical bond entered into 'on the expectation of reciprocal conduct—and on confidence in this reciprocity over time'.[65] Whereas the former relies on a pre-political community of attachment, the latter does not. What matters, instead, is the fair appeal to mutual interests inscribed in the substantive

---

[63] See eg Neil Walker, 'Europe's constitutional momentum and the search for polity legitimacy' (2005) 3 *International Journal of Constitutional Law* 211–238; Moravcsik (n 34).

[64] See eg Habermas (n 36); see also his 'Democracy, Solidarity and the European Crisis' *Social Europe Journal* 07/05/2013 http://www.academia.edu/4259473/Democracy_Solidarity_And_The_European_Crisis_By_J%C3%BCrgen_Habermas.

[65] Habermas, 'Democracy, Solidarity and the European Crisis' (n 64).

terms of the bond and the belief of each party in the long-term credibility of the commitment of all others. Even if a widely negotiated written constitutional settlement were a feasible option, therefore, to the extent that it declares as a symbolic dividend the prior affinity of 'We the People', it may be unnecessary, and arguably inappropriate as a solidarity platform. What would be both appropriate and necessary, however, and what has been conspicuous by its absence in the euro crisis, with its accelerating grant of discretionary powers to executive bodies intended to shore up a historically compromised model of monetary stability,[66] is an inclusive and transparent form of law making producing general norms that speak explicitly, and with settled commitment, to a renewed reciprocity of interests among all Member States. In this broader sense, law's constitutive function depends much more on the substance of what is agreed than on the legal style in which it is agreed.

V. The Systemic Character of EU Law

Legal philosophers have long been interested in the idea of legal system, and for obvious reasons. We all recognize that one of the distinguishing features of the law, indeed what makes the law 'the law' and not just a bundle or jumble of 'laws', concerns how it hangs together as a whole. Legal system, or legal order, or even legal jurisdiction, then, are all at root metaphors we use to explore that holistic sense of law. Granted, the systemic quality will be more important for some than for others. Legal positivists, with their stress on the authoritative sources of law, are likely to see the relevant tests of the law's validity and bindingness for most if not all intents and purposes as being 'jurisdiction-relative'.[67] Yet even natural lawyers, on the one hand, who may take a less bounded view of law's moral writ,[68] or legal realists or pragmatists on the other, who may, by contrast, take a more context-specific approach to legal justification, are bound to acknowledge something significant for our understanding of law in law's systematic capacity for self-organization in terms of rule hierarchies and interlocking institutions of law creation, law application and law adjudication.

If legal system is so important, however, then the EU poses an obvious puzzle. The EU, with its partial jurisdiction, its Treaty-dependent foundations and its reliance on state institutions for much of the enforcement and some of the basic

---

[66] See eg Dawson and De Witte (n 45); Damian Chalmers, 'The European Redistributive State and a European Law of Struggle' (2012) 18 *European Law Journal* 667.

[67] Neil MacCormick, *Questioning Sovereignty* (1999) 14.

[68] See eg John Finnis, 'The Truth in Legal Positivism' in J. Finnis, *The Philosophy of Law* (2011) 174.

legislative elaboration of its normative order, lacks the comprehensiveness of reach, original and unchallenged supremacy, and wide capacity to absorb other legal materials on its own terms that the typical state-centred legal system has.[69] Even in its own internal framework, it may lack the institutional and normative integrity of a fully coherent legal system, an argument particularly pronounced in the immediate post-Maastricht era with the introduction of an institutional division between mainstream internal market law, Justice and Home Affairs and common foreign and defence policy in the so-called Three Pillar system.[70] And the EU's credentials as a coherent legal whole are all the more challenged externally, where we contemplate considerable intersection and complex interdependence with the laws of the Member States.

Does this mean that the EU has no legal system, or at least no independent legal system of its own, but is merely a satellite or extension of the 28 Member State legal systems? Or is the EU part and parcel of one large, conglomerate legal system also embracing the legal systems—or rather sub-systems—of all the Member States? Or is the EU best viewed as possessing its own legal system, distinct from those of the Member States even though densely interconnected with them?[71]

Those who pursue the first option, stress the sovereignty in the last instance of the states as 'Masters of the Treaties', often invoking in justification of this reading their primary democratic credentials.[72] Those who pursue the second option tend, conversely, towards a monistic understanding of the supranational order, accepting the self-understanding of the EU legal order, with its pivotal doctrines of supremacy and direct effect and its claim to an overarching standard of legal certainty, as the best overall conception of the relationship between European law and national law.[73] Those who pursue the third option, often called constitutional pluralists, stress the co-existence of national and supranational systems with overlapping and interlocking jurisdictions, note the absence of any general hierarchical rule or other method for resolving the relationship between these orders, and urge some other method of reconciling the different legal systems.[74] On normative grounds,

---

[69]   See eg Joseph Raz *The Authority of Law* (2nd ed, 2009) 116–120.

[70]   See eg Deirdre Curtin, 'The Constitutional Structure of the Union: A Europe of Bits and Pieces' (1993) 30 *Common Market Law Review* 1.

[71]   Julie Dickson, 'Towards a Theory of European Union Legal Systems' in J. Dickson and P. Eleftheriadis (eds) (n 45) 25, 47.

[72]   See eg Grimm (n 35).

[73]   See eg Julio Baqero Cruz, 'The Legacy of the Maastricht-Urteil and the Pluralist Movement' (2008) 14 *European Law Journal* 389.

[74]   See eg Neil MacCormick, 'Beyond the Sovereign State' (1993) 56 *Modern Law Review* 1; Neil Walker, 'The Idea of Constitutional Pluralism' (2002) 65 *Modern Law Review* 317; Miguel Maduro, 'Contrapunctual Law: Europe's Constitutional Pluralism in Action' in N. Walker (ed) *Sovereignty in Transition* (2003) 532; Mattias Kumm, 'The Jurisprudence of Constitutional Conflict: Constitutional Supremacy in Europe before and after the Constitutional Treaty' (2005) 11 *European Law Journal* 262. See also, M. Avbelj and J. Komarek (eds) *Constitutional Pluralism in the European Union and Beyond* (2012).

they might query the trumping significance of the state's claim to democratic priority on the one hand, or the necessity of the EU's unqualified claim to an umbrella legal certainty on the other. In addition, on descriptive grounds, often pointing to well-known cases of tension between national constitutional courts and the Court of Justice over the extended jurisdictional ambition of the EU post-Maastricht, they claim the structural inevitability of an unresolved relationship of authority between national and supranational levels. In other words, regardless of the desirability of a pluralist starting point, in the special circumstances of the EU it may simply be unavoidable.

The pluralist hypothesis provokes two key sets of questions. First, if we accept its diagnosis as persuasive, how do we treat the heterarchical space between legal systems? Here the options include: so-called 'radical pluralism',[75] in which the solutions are strategic rather than legal, or at least follow no context-independent legal formulae beyond the particular bridging mechanism agreed between the discrete legal systems in question; 'contrapunctual law',[76] where the law between systems develops, through inter-court and other inter-institutional dialogue, as a kind of melodious blend from different starting points; and an abstract-normative approach, where brokering ideas such as legality, due process, subsidiarity and respect for fundamental rights are elevated to the status of trans-systemic, 'cosmopolitan' principles.[77]

This last approach, with its emphasis upon a generally applicable normative solution, already stretches our sense of systemic pluralism. This leads to a second and more fundamentally challenging question voiced by those who are sceptical of pluralism's basic premises. On this sceptical view, pluralism offers an unhelpful or at least an inadequate conceptual framework. In one variant of scepticism, pluralism is inadequate because, by concentrating so much on the authoritative foundations and co-ordinates of discrete systems, it fails to appreciate that the character of EU law is best grasped precisely in the interaction between systems—in 'relations, of mutual reference, between EU institutions and Member State institutions which share and exchange norms and normative powers to create, apply and enforce norms'.[78] On this account, the coherence of EU law is captured by focusing not on the institutional dimension of the relevant legal systems in play, which in a multi-system environment is apt instead to reveal disorder and incoherence, but on

[75] See in particular, Neil MacCormick, 'The Maastricht-Urteil: Sovereignty Now' (1995) 1 *European Law Journal* 259. He later modified this position: see in particular, MacCormick, *Questioning Sovereignty* (1999) Ch 7.

[76] Maduro (n 74).

[77] Mattias Kumm, 'The Moral Point of Constitutional Pluralism: Defining the Domain of Legitimate Institutional Civil Disobedience and Conscientious Objection' in J. Dickson and P. Eleftheriadis (eds) (n 45) 216.

[78] Keith Culver and Michael Giudice 'Not a System but an Order: An Inter-Institutional View of European Union Law' in J. Dickson and J. Eleftheriadis (eds) (n 45) 54, 68.

the emergent coherence of the inter-institutional dynamics themselves, in this way characterizing the EU as a 'distinct non-systemic legal order'.[79]

A second critique of pluralism is still more radical, and goes directly to its positivist foundations. On this view, once we overcome the positivist preoccupation with the sources and pedigree of different systems of rules, then it no longer makes sense to treat the relationship between national and European courts over the jurisdictional limits and proper meaning of EU law as one where different authoritative sites compete and require to be reconciled. Instead, if we see law as providing a form of practical reason in which the right answers depend upon an appropriate consideration of the normative materials regardless of *who* decides, rather than upon the authority of the decision-maker, then there is nothing to prevent us from looking at the European case as a form of 'harmonic law',[80] with all parties engaged in a common and cumulative interpretive exercise.

Disagreement persists over the value of the pluralist perspective and is unlikely to be resolved. This is so because pluralist and non-pluralist perspectives alike rest their case not only on the explanatory adequacy of their positions, but also on their ability to provide a normatively attractive picture of a legal configuration that is still in the process of becoming. The argument, then, is not just about the best account of how the world is, but also about how through that construction we can also influence and aid the *reconstruction* of a distinctive, in some respects even unprecedented, and certainly unsettled model of legal authority.

The debate over the systemic character of EU law is an appropriate place to conclude our discussion. It illustrates well both the interconnectedness of our various philosophical questions and the fertile relationship between the philosophy of EU law and the philosophy of law more generally. As regards the first point, the pluralist debate is clearly bound up with controversies over how we resolve the basic structural question of the kind of authority-claiming entity or polity the EU is. Additionally, by casting doubt upon the idea of EU law as a single interpretive community, the pluralist understanding suggest possible objections or limits to the idea of European law as a distinct and integrated forum of principle. And by indicating that European law is not necessarily to be understood in singular terms, the pluralist perspective may also help us to refine our understanding of the success or otherwise of some of the ways—whether instrumental, formal, congruent or constitutive—that law is modelled as a form of practical reasoning in the European case. As regards the second point, more clearly than the other themes we have examined, the debate over legal pluralism and legal system in the supranational context not only highlights how EU law offers a new site for the hosting of older and wider debates within legal philosophy, but may also prompt us to consider afresh the terms of these older debates and the answers provided by them.

---

[79] Culver and Giudice (n 78) 76.
[80] Letsas (n 50), and in the same volume, Pavlos Eleftheriadis, 'Citizenship and Obligation' 159.

BIBLIOGRAPHY

Perry Anderson, *The New Old World* (2009)

Matej Avbelj and Jan Komarek (eds), *Constitutional Pluralism in the European Union and Beyond* (2012)

Julio Baqero Cruz, 'The Legacy of the Maastricht-Urteil and the Pluralist Movement' (2008) *14 European Law Journal* 389

Armin von Bogdandy, and Jurgen Bast (eds), *Principles of European Constitutional Law* (2010)

Paul Craig and Gráinne De Búrca (eds), *The Evolution of EU Law* (2nd ed., 2011)

Julie Dickson and Pavlos Eleftheriadis (eds), *Philosophical Foundations of European Union Law* (2012)

Dieter Grimm, 'Integration by Constitution' (2005) 3 *International Journal of Constitutional Law* 193

Jurgen Habermas, *The Crisis of the European Union: A Response* (2012)

Christian Joerges, 'Deliberative Political Processes Revisited: What We have Learnt about the Legitimacy of Supranational Decision-Making' (2006) *44 Journal of Common Market Studies* 779

Hans Lindahl, 'The Paradox of Constituent Power: The Ambiguous Self-Constitution of the European Union' (2007) *20 Ratio Juris* 485

Neil MacCormick, *Questioning Sovereignty* (1999)

Jurgen Neyer, *The Justification of Europe: A Political Theory of Supranational Integration* (2012)

Charles Sabel and Jonathan Zeitlin, 'Learning from Difference: The New Architecture of Experimental Governance in the European Union' (2008) *14 European Law Journal* 271

Alexander Somek, *Individualism* (2008)

Neil Walker (ed), *Sovereignty in Transition* (2003)

Joseph Weiler, *The Constitution of Europe* (2003)

Andrew Williams, *The Ethos of Europe* (2010)

CHAPTER 2

···

LEGAL REASONING IN EU LAW

···

JAN KOMÁREK

I. The Variety of Legal Reasoning in EU Law

···

1. Legal Reasoning and Reason Giving in EU Law

Legal reasoning in general 'refers to reasoning about the requirements and application of law'.[1] Thus defined, it is not confined to legal officials or courts alone, although most of the scholarship on legal reasoning focuses on precisely this.[2] Legal reasoning is part of a wider social practice of giving reasons, which involves reasoning in very different contexts, public or private. *Legal* reasoning is relatively prominent, however, due to law's central role in contemporary liberal

---

[1] Larry Alexander and Emily Sherwin, *Demystifying Legal Reasoning* (2008) 1.

[2] For works devoted to the ECJ see Gerard Conway, *The Limits of Legal Reasoning and the European Court of Justice* (2012); Gunnar Beck, *The Legal Reasoning of the Court of Justice of the EU* (2012); Suvi Sankari, *European Court of Justice Legal Reasoning in Context* (2013); Elina Paunio, *Legal Certainty in Multilingual EU Law: Language, Discourse and Reasoning at the European Court of Justice* (2013). Before 2012 the only book-length treatments of legal reasoning in EU law were Joxerramon Bengoetxea, *The Legal Reasoning of the European Court of Justice: Towards a European Jurisprudence* (1993) and Anna Bredimas, *Methods of Interpretation and Community Law* (1978). In 1976 the ECJ organized a conference devoted to the interpretation of EU law, and papers were subsequently published by the Court.

democracy as both enabling and constraining political power. It also provides a medium of communication between politics, other social systems, and society at large.[3]

Several values and aims promoted by reason giving can be identified.[4] They can be roughly divided into two groups. The first concerns primarily the addressees of legal decisions. Legal reasoning thus aims at

- showing the decision makers' *respect* for the addressees of their decisions;
- inducing addressees' *compliance* with the decision;
- facilitating addressees' *agreement* with the decision, although this last aspect is contestable;[5]
- increasing addressees' *autonomy* in the sense that they can better understand the consequences of the decision and the possible courses of action they may take in response to it;
- facilitating addressees' *criticism* of the decision.

The second set of values and aims relates to decision makers. Reason giving therefore can:

- *constrain* decision makers' *discretion*;
- *limit the arbitrariness* of decision makers' decisions;
- make the decision makers *accountable* to citizens.

To what extent these values and aims are fulfilled in practice depends on how institutions actually reason in their decisions. One way or another, they concern the legitimacy of the reason giving institution.

In the context of the EU, all institutions issuing legal acts have the duty to give reasons. Article 296 TFEU provides: 'Legal acts shall state the reasons on which they are based and shall refer to any proposals, initiatives, recommendations, requests or opinions required by the Treaties.'[6] Article 41 CFR formulates the duty to give reasons as part of the right to good administration, which includes 'the obligation of the administration to give reasons for its decisions', which is further affirmed by Article 47 CFR on the right to defence.[7]

---

[3] See Jürgen Habermas, *Between Facts and Norms*, trans William Rehg (1996).

[4] The following is based on Mathilde Cohen, 'Reasons for Reasons' in D. Gabbay, P. Canivez, S. Rahman, and A. Thiercelin (eds), *Approaches to Legal Rationality* (2010) 119.

[5] As admitted by Cohen (n 4) 135–137. The reservation concerning this argument concerns the desirability of 'incompletely theorized agreements' in pluralist societies, whereby people can agree on specific outcomes for different reasons that are left unarticulated. See particularly Cass R. Sunstein, *Legal Reasoning and Political Conflict* (1996) Ch 2.

[6] On the duty to give reasons in EU law see Vlad Perju, 'Reason and Authority in the European Court of Justice' (2009) 49 *Virginia Journal of International Law* 307, 315–327.

[7] Joined Cases C-584/10 P, C-593/10 P, and C-595/10 P *Commission v Kadi*, judgment of 18 July 2013, para 100.

The standards of reasoning differ in relation to each institution. They are partly determined by other provisions of EU law[8] and partly by the ECJ's case law. According to the Court, the reasons provided must enable the person affected by the legal act in question to decide whether to seek its judicial review and the Court to exercise such review.[9] This rationale for reason giving can become problematic, since the context of judicial review may be conducive to standards and practices that do not necessarily reflect the rationales of public justification mentioned above.[10]

It is important to bear in mind that the duty to give reasons broadly conceived does not entail just strictly *legal* reasons (understood here as reasons about the requirements and application of EU law).[11] For example, the Commission's legislative proposals contain reasons of a pragmatic nature, referring to economic rationales for the proposed action. The concrete shape of *legal* reasoning within different contexts will differ primarily in the level of its institutionalization. The standards of reasoning are relatively stable, corresponding to the aim pursued by the entity providing reasons. In what follows I attempt to distinguish various contexts in which the standards of legal reasoning differ.

2. Contexts of Legal Reasoning

(a) Adjudication

In the context of adjudication, by both courts and other public authorities, it is helpful to distinguish legal reasoning in *argument* and in *justification*.[12] The former aims at persuading before the decision is taken, whereas the latter seeks legitimation and acceptance of the already adopted decision or legal act.[13] Most

---

[8] For EU administrative authorities see point 3 of the Code of Good Administrative Behaviour for Staff of the European Commission in their Relations with the Public, which covers all EU staff. The Code is annexed to the Rules of Procedure of the Commission [2000] OJ L 308/26. For the ECJ see Art 36 of the Protocol (No 3) on the Statute of the Court of Justice of the European Union, as amended [2012] OJ L 112/21. The general duty to give reasons can be also further specified by rules concerning particular fields of activity of EU institutions. See eg Art 9(4) of Reg No 1049/2001 regarding public access to European Parliament, Council and Commission documents [2001] OJ L 145/43.

[9] See Case 24/62 *Germany v Commission* [1963] ECR 63, 69.

[10] See n 4. See Mathilde Cohen, 'Reason-Giving in Court Practice: Decision-makers at the Cross-Roads' (2008) 14 *Columbia Journal of European Law* 257.

[11] See n 1.

[12] See Bengoetxea (n 2) 143–145 for a helpful discussion. This distinction is different from that between discovery and justification made below, in that here, even when arguing for a certain outcome, the reasoner engages in the context of justification.

[13] One can of course contend that justification also aims at persuading the relevant audiences. This persuasion cannot, however, change the content of the ultimate decision (since it has already been taken) and is addressed to the external context of the decision making institution.

typically, parties argue a case before the court or judges seek to persuade their colleagues within the chamber that decides it. The distinction is important since the standards of legal reasoning in argument do often differ from those in justification.[14]

Before the ECJ, government lawyers can, for example, point to the case law of courts in their jurisdiction in order to shape the interpretation of a provision of EU law, whereas the ECJ never refers to judgments of national courts in its decisions for *this* purpose.[15] It is a well-known fact, however, that such arguments figure in the internal judicial discourse within the ECJ, either in so-called *notes de recherche* prepared by the Research and Documentation Directorate, or contained in particular judges' *notes en délibéré* addressed to their colleagues within the chamber.

Mitchel Lasser observed the 'bifurcation' of ECJ judicial discourse into two communicative channels. The first is contained in the Court's judgments and the second in the opinions of Advocates General.[16] In fact, the variety of judicial discourses is much richer since, as just mentioned, there are various texts prepared in the course of the ECJ's decision making which all contain different forms of reasoning.

(b) Legislative Law Making

In the legislative context, argumentative legal reasoning appears in documents that seek to establish that the proposal conforms to the relevant provisions of EU law or that its adoption is even required. Such reasoning does not differ substantially from that contained in documents submitted by EU institutions to the ECJ in the course of judicial process. Still, we know rather little about the power of legal argument outside adjudication—for example, whether it is capable of changing outcomes of negotiation in the legislative process or serves only as a cover for pragmatic political goals.

On the other hand, eventually adopted texts often contain simple references to Treaty provisions (concerning the legal basis for the adopted text or concerning subsidiarity and proportionality). Increasingly, however, even legislative texts will include precise references to the case law of the ECJ, especially in the fields

---

[14] See in general John Bell, 'The Acceptability of Legal Arguments' in Neil MacCormick and Peter B.H. Birks (eds), *The Legal Mind: Essays for Tony Honoré* (1986) 45.

[15] It of course uses national case law when it uses a provision of national law in its decision (eg when it assesses its compatibility with EU). For a very clear exposition of various uses of foreign law see Michal Bobek, *Comparative Reasoning in European Supreme Courts* (2013) Ch 12.

[16] Mitchel Lasser, *Judicial Deliberations: A Comparative Study of Judicial Transparency and Legitimacy* (2004) Ch 7.

strongly influenced by the Court,[17] instead of vague invocations of the 'established practice of the ECJ'.

Apart from the legal reasoning that forms part of the legislative process and its outcomes, there are various interpretive guidelines adopted by EU institutions in order to secure the uniform application of legislative rules. They are not formally binding,[18] but in practice they can be more important than the vague provisions of the legislation or even the rulings of the ECJ.

(c) Legal Doctrine and Public Discourse

Legal reasoning also appears within less institutionalized contexts, in doctrinal works or in contributions to public discourse.[19] In some legal cultures, commentaries on important pieces of legislation have considerable status—and so do their authors.[20] Mitchel Lasser showed the importance of doctrinal notes of selected judgments of the French *Cour de cassation*, written by the French professoriate (*la doctrine*), which allow the *Cour*'s audience to grasp fully the significance and meaning of rulings that contain very brief (and sometimes rather obscure) legal reasoning.[21]

One can also claim that not only is the Official Journal (or European Court Reports) an important communication medium for legal rules, but domestic media that report on EU legislation and the ECJ decisions are as well. There is no reason, therefore, to exclude from examination legal reasoning contained in the general media, especially once we are interested in the wider functions of legal reasoning. This is arguably best captured by the discourse theory of law and democracy, which understands legal reasoning as a communicative action connecting different social systems and mediating their claims.[22]

---

[17] See particularly Dir 2004/38/EC on the right of citizens of the Union and their family members to move and reside freely within the territory of the Member States amending Reg (EEC) No 1612/68 and repealing Dirs 64/221/EEC, 68/360/EEC, 72/194/EEC, 73/148/EEC, 75/34/EEC, 75/35/EEC, 90/364/EEC, 90/365/EEC, and 93/96/EEC, [2004] OJ L158/77; Dir 2006/123/EC on services in the internal market [2006] OJ L376/36 or Dir 2011/24/EU on the application of patients' rights in cross-border healthcare [2011] OJ L88/45.

[18] In the sense that they do not bind the ECJ when interpreting the legal act in question; they are also published in section C of the Official Journal.

[19] For a prominent example of the latter see Roman Herzog and Lüder Gerken, 'Stop the European Court of Justice' *Frankfurter Allgemeine Zeitung*, 8 September 2008; the English translation available here: http://www.cep.eu/fileadmin/user_upload/Pressemappe/CEP_in_den_Medien/Herzog-EuGH-Webseite_eng.pdf.

[20] On legal commentaries in Germany see eg David J. Gerber, 'Authority, Community and the Civil Law Commentary: An Example from German Competition Law' (1994) 42 *American Journal of Comparative Law* 531.

[21] See Lasser (n 16) 39–46.   [22] Habermas (n 3).

II. Legal Reasoning in the Context of the Decision Making of the ECJ

1. Discovery and Justification

As already mentioned, legal reasoning contained in judicial decisions is most often taken as a paradigm of legal reasoning. Joxerramon Bengoetxea explains this by the fact that 'legal reasoning manifests itself most clearly in the decisions and judgments of the courts, which have to prove that their decisions conform with the law'.[23] More precisely, analyses of legal reasoning concentrate on the *text* of judicial decisions, and exclude other documents produced in the process of judicial decision making, which entails legal reasoning at various stages and in various forms. They also exclude the processes of reasoning that occur inside the judicial mind.

This focus on judicial decisions is most probably due to pragmatic reasons: judicial decisions are widely accessible. In the case of the ECJ, they are all available on the Court's website, whereas other documents produced throughout the judicial process are not (and some of them are even kept secret).[24] Getting inside the heads of the members of the ECJ is even more complicated. Some judges have reflected publicly on how they approach their work, and occasionally articles based on interviews with them appear in law journals.[25] These, like judges' writings, have only a limited value as it is of course impossible to control for judges' unconscious self-stylization or even manipulation.

Studies of legal reasoning, therefore, often distinguish between the contexts of discovery and justification.[26] The former refers to the process of forming an opinion and adopting a decision, whereas justification comprises legal reasoning contained in judicial decisions or other official documents, including submissions by parties, which present their argument to the Court.

Various *factors of discovery*[27] intervene at the stage of adopting the decision:

- the *personality of the judge* (his political views, psychological predispositions, social background, the jurisdiction he comes from, previous experience in law, etc);

---

[23] Bengoetxea (n 2) 160.

[24] See Alberto Alemanno and Oana Stefan, 'Openness at the Court of Justice of the European Union: Toppling a Taboo' (2014) 51 *Common Market Law Review* 97.

[25] See eg Sonia Morano-Foadi and Stelios Andreadakis, 'Reflections on the Architecture of the EU after the Treaty of Lisbon: The European Judicial Approach to Fundamental Rights' (2011) 17 *European Law Journal* 595.

[26] Among various studies of the ECJ's legal reasoning, Joxerramon Bengoetxea, Neil MacCormick, and Leonor Moral Soriano, 'Integration and Integrity in the Legal Reasoning of the European Court of Justice' in Gráinne de Búrca and Joseph H.H. Weiler (eds), *The European Court of Justice* (2001) 43, especially at 48–60, go arguably farthest in applying the distinction to various stages of the judicial process before the ECJ.

[27] For a brief discussion of these factors see Bengoetxea (n 2) 115.

- the *organization of the judicial process*: whether there is an oral hearing where judges have direct contact with the parties, whether it is judges or their secretaries who write the judgment, the composition of the court and its organization (division into various chambers and the role of their presidents);
- the *court's outside context*: the views of other political institutions and public opinion;
- *legitimate legal reasons*: these ought to, or at least can, be used in legal argument—in other words, law is important for judicial decision making, despite some overstated accounts of judges completely free of any legal constraint.

Some legitimate legal reasons that inform the context of discovery can later become part of the context of justification, which appears in official documents. Both processes, discovery and justification, can be either 'highly ordered and formalized' or 'quite unsystematic and haphazard'.[28] As mentioned, it would be a mistake to think that legal rules play no part in the process of discovery—they are of course among the factors determining the decision. Similarly, writing the decision can be part of the process of discovery, since even then the judge can revise the conclusion that she arrived at before she sat and started to write the judgment.[29] These two processes are thus not sharply distinguished and the judge can go back and forth until the decision is publicly announced.

For some time legal theorists were reluctant to study the context of discovery, but more recently studies using insights from psychology, cognitive science, or behavioural economics have started to abound.[30] Such studies are arguably more difficult to conduct, since they often require access to judges and internal documents from the Court, but many observations about the context of discovery can be made by using appropriate social science methods.[31]

American legal realists were probably the first to study the context of discovery.[32] Their concerns explain why we should study both contexts. They were interested in the causes of judicial decisions and how best to make an argument before a court: the knowledge one cannot get from a mere reading of judicial decisions. They also wanted to formulate rules that would better reflect the actual causes of judicial decisions in order to make law more accessible and

---

[28] Richard Wasserstrom, *The Judicial Decision: Toward a Theory of Legal Justification* (1961) 27.

[29] See Chad M. Oldfather, 'Writing, Cognition, and the Nature of the Judicial Function' (2008) 96 *Georgetown Law Journal* 1283.

[30] See Steven L. Winter, *A Clearing in the Forrest: Law, Life, and Mind* (2001).

[31] For a programmatic statement in this respect see Arthur Dyèvre, 'Unifying the Field of Comparative Judicial Politics: Towards a General Theory of Judicial Behaviour' (2010) 2 *European Political Science Review* 297–327.

[32] See particularly Jerome Frank, *Law and the Modern Mind* (1930) and Karl N. Llewellyn, *The Common Law Tradition: Deciding Appeals* (1960).

socially responsive.[33] These are all concerns no less relevant now than they were almost a hundred years ago.

2. Legal Reasoning in the Context of Discovery

A significant part of the context of discovery has little to do with reasoning understood as an intellectual process of searching for a decision and the reasons that support it, possibly complemented by their express articulation.[34] Many *factors of discovery*, the central category in this context,[35] simply influence the Court and are important for understanding the outcomes of its decision making process, but do not entail reasoning in the more precise sense suggested here. In what follows, I will therefore focus on factors of discovery that entail reasoning.

For example, the use of analogy presupposes that a 'mental leap' is made from one case to another. There are now numerous studies of what induces the creation of analogy in the human mind and how this is relevant for legal argument.[36] Deduction means inference from a more general rule to a more specific one, but is far more complex than the traditional studies of legal reasoning assume.[37] These are all mental processes that involve some sort of reasoning, often unarticulated, but very important for the outcome. In this chapter I do not have the ambition to present the emerging scholarship on legal reasoning in the context of discovery in its entirety. Instead I point to some insights that can inform our understanding of the reasoning practices of the ECJ and its members, especially those that still await proper attention from scholars.

The process of discovery can be broken down into several distinct steps:

(a) defining the case;
(b) finding a tentative solution; and
(c) articulating reasons.

(a) Defining the Case

The context of discovery comprises several stages which all lead to the eventual decision that needs to be justified by legal reasoning, which is made publicly

---

[33] What American legal realists actually wanted remains controversial; see Frederick Schauer, Foreword to William Twining, *Karl Llewellyn and the Realist Movement* (2nd ed, 2013) ix–xxiv.

[34] See Christopher Kirwan, 'Reasoning' in Ted Honderich (ed), *The Oxford Companion to Philosophy* (2nd ed, 2005), 791.

[35] See n 27.

[36] See particularly Dan Hunter, 'Reason Is too Large: Analogy and Precedent in Law' (2001) 50 *Emory Law Journal* 1197.

[37] See Winter (n 30) 309–331.

available as part of the final decision.[38] The first step in the process of discovery concerns the definition of the case: 'what it is all about.' This means determining the factual background of the case (the 'real-life situation') together with its initial legal classification and the identification of the key issue(s). These processes are mutually interconnected, since among the numerous characterizations of events and fact patterns only those which are *relevant* are selected for the delimitation of a case. At the same time, how the judge perceives the facts determines the selection of legal provisions potentially relevant for adjudication on them.

An example from EU law can help to illustrate this point: in domestic cases concerning contracts of sale it may be irrelevant what the origin of the object of the contested transaction is and it does not even need to be mentioned in judgments. In the context of EU law, this fact can be of paramount importance, since it may trigger the application of EU provisions on the free movement of goods, which require some cross-border element in the transaction. Some of its characteristics (such as requirements on labelling) will not be relevant in domestic law, but can become decisive when the ECJ assesses whether they can constitute a barrier to trade.

Practically, the case is defined in the first instance by the parties (in direct actions to the ECJ) or the referring court (in preliminary references) and can have a great influence on the final outcome. This occurs not only in the context argument before the Court, but also as part of a more mundane administrative handling of the case inside it. For example, each case is given certain keywords, which accompany it throughout the process and appear as 'headings' in the text of the judgment (and Advocate General's Opinion).

This initial formal categorization is important in many respects. It signals to potential participants whether they should intervene. Bengoetxea, MacCormick and Moral Soriano note that *Martínez Sala*[39] went unnoticed by most governments since it was categorized as a social security case, in spite of the fact that it raised fundamental questions of EU citizenship. Only later did it become recognized as a transformative case that had a deep impact on subsequent case law of the Court.[40]

Categorization also determines how the case is approached. The ECJ is often criticized for viewing fundamental rights through the perspective of the internal market. *Schmidberger* is taken as a paradigm case of this type of criticism.[41] As is well known, it concerned a conflict between the freedom of expression and the free movement of goods. The former belonged to protesters who blocked the Brenner motorway in order to exert pressure on the competent authorities to regulate traffic

---

[38] Or Opinion in case of an Advocate General. In fact this concerns all legal documents, which provide reasons, since the 'right' reasons firstly need to be 'discovered' and then articulated in the given document.

[39] Case C-85/96 *Martínez Sala v Freistaat Bayern* [1998] ECR I-2691.

[40] Bengoetxea, MacCormick, and Moral Soriano (n 26) 52.

[41] Case C-112/00 *Schmidberger* [2003] ECR I-5659. See particularly the case comment by Christopher Brown, (2003) 40 *Common Market Law Review* 1499.

on the road and control the environmental deterioration of the region surrounding it. The right to the free movement of goods was invoked by a transport undertaking affected by the protest. The Court adjudicated the case as a potential violation of market freedom, which was nevertheless justified in this case by the protesters' exercise of the freedom of expression. This was seen as a perverse reversal of priority between constitutionally protected rights and market-based freedoms. The burden of justification was on the side of the right holders rather than companies who invoked their freedom to engage in business activity. The ECJ is not, however, a 'human rights court' and its jurisdiction is triggered by the application of EU law norms that mostly have instrumental objectives related to the establishment of the internal market. The case therefore must be framed as a case about free movement in order to get before the ECJ, which then structures the analysis in a way that may seem offensive to human rights advocates. The problem lies with EU law, however, and not the Court.

Complex cognitive processes are involved at the stage of categorization of the case and can influence, if not determine, the final decision of the court. Karl Llewellyn gave an account of this process, which he called getting a 'situation-sense' of the case. Its core was 'the sizing up of the "case" into some pattern',[42] which was for Llewellyn 'of the essence of getting to the case at all'.[43] He knew all too well that 'the shape it starts to take calls up familiar, more general patters to fit it into or to piece it out or to set it against for comparison'.[44] In other words, it was changing from a concrete problem situation to an ideal type situation, comprising some typical fact patterns and applicable legal and policy principles.

(b) Finding a Tentative Solution: Easy or Hard?

The foregoing discussion deals with the question whether the case at hand is to be treated as an easy or a hard one.[45] The easiest, but far from unproblematic, definition of an easy case is that it is a case where the judge is convinced that there is only one right decision, which can be legally justified. The classification of the case therefore follows from the judge's internal perspective.

Objectively or, as Elina Paunio puts it, 'from a hermeneutical viewpoint', it is a far more difficult process, and in her opinion 'no way of clearly distinguishing between hard cases and easy cases exists'.[46] This is because this classification already requires interpretation—which does not need to be shared by all participants in the judicial process, especially the opposing parties who brought the case to court. In a way it is therefore always subjective. In some sense, it is therefore true that all cases are at least *potentially* 'hard', although *in practice* many instances of

---

[42] Llewellyn (n 32) 268.   [43] Llewellyn (n 32) 268.   [44] Llewellyn (n 32) 268.
[45] For a discussion of the distinction see particularly Bengoetxea (n 2) 183–207.
[46] Paunio (n 2) 232.

the application of law are 'easy'—and as such they will never get before the court. In what follows I will focus on the subjective classification of a case, made by the judge in the context of discovery.

At the stage of discovery the judge forms an opinion, ideally in deliberation with her colleagues (and possibly also legal secretaries in her chambers) and at the same time listening to the parties (and the Advocate General at the ECJ). She can have a feeling what the right decision is, but until it is formally decided (in collegiate courts sometimes by taking a vote), it can always be reformulated and changed. The sources of doubt, which can turn an easy case into a hard one, are manifold and relate to the factors of discovery mentioned above:[47]

1. The political and societal context of the case
2. The moral or ethical convictions of the judge
3. Legal indeterminacy.

(1) The *political and societal context* of the case can make it hard. In spite of that it can be absolutely clear what the legally justified, right decision in the case at hand is. For outsiders to identify such a case can be difficult, however, since the availability of the legally justified decision allows the Court to hide the controversy ensuing from the wider context. The only available indication can in the end be the fact that the case was assigned to the Grand Chamber or that the Court held an additional hearing to discuss a particularly difficult issue raised by the case.[48]

Consider for example *Banca popolare di Cremona*,[49] concerning the compatibility of Italian tax legislation with the Sixth Directive.[50] Advocate General Jacobs found the legislation contrary to the Directive in his first Opinion delivered in March 2005. At the same time, he recognized the concern of the Italian government that the duty to repay the tax collected contrary to the Directive could amount to more than €120 billion. The ECJ's case law allows in such instances, under strict conditions, the postponement of the temporal effects of its ruling to allow the state to remove the incompatibility and avoid an avalanche of claims that can potentially follow the ruling. Those who have already initiated proceedings for recovery are, however, excluded from the limitation.[51]

The problem in *Banca popolare di Cremona* was that the number of claims already made was too high; the temporal limitation would therefore not protect

---

[47] See n 27. Many factors of discovery however steer the court to a single solution, rather than inducing uncertainty as regards the result.

[48] Bengoetxea (n 2) 195–207 discusses several indications of at least an implicit recognition of the distinction between easy and hard cases by the ECJ.

[49] C-475/03 *Banca popolare di Cremona* [2006] ECR I-9373.

[50] Sixth Council Dir 77/388/EEC of 17 May 1977 on the harmonization of the laws of the Member States relating to turnover taxes—Common system of value added tax: uniform basis of assessment [1977] OJ L145/1.

[51] See Juha Raitio, 'Legal Certainty, Non-retro-activity and Periods of Limitation in EU Law' (2008) 2 *Legisprudence* 1.

Italy's treasury in the way intended. Jacobs consequently proposed to limit the effects of the ECJ's judgment absolutely and rule only for the future, giving Italy some time to comply with the requirements of the Court's judgment. Jacob's proposal then became the subject of another hearing, which happens only exceptionally, when the Court intends to focus on a question raised by an Advocate General which was nevertheless not properly discussed at the first hearing. Fifteen governments took part in this second round, focusing on the question of temporal limitation—the incompatibility of the Italian legislation was no longer questioned.

The judgment does not mention any of this: it comes to the opposite conclusion from both Advocates General (the second Opinion was delivered by Stix-Hackl, since Francis Jacobs had left the Court in the meanwhile) and finds that there is no violation of the Directive. One can of course only guess how divisive the issue of temporal limitation was at the Court; the outcome, however, both avoids the ruling on the issue of temporal limitation and protects the Italian government from excessive repayments of the contested tax.

(2) Reasons for doubt can relate to *morality and ethics*. Here again there may be a perfectly legally justified, *single* right answer;[52] that answer can nevertheless appear to the judge to be unacceptable because of her personal moral and ethical convictions.[53] We still know very little about the personal characteristics of individual judges in this respect.[54] The appointment process is very overt and it officially focuses on the legal qualifications of candidates—as if their personalities did not matter.[55] I have already mentioned examples of cases where the Court dealt with deeply divisive issues—without acknowledging it in the text of the judgment.[56]

(3) More often, however, doubts arise when the law seems to give no clear answer at all (European Continental theory in particular calls such situations 'gaps in law'),[57] or, conversely, when there are too many available answers that can be legally

---

[52] Whether this can be the case (and a conflict between law and morality can materialize before a judge) depends on the conception of law adopted: for exclusive legal positivists (paradigmatically H.L.A. Hart or Joseph Raz), morality remains outside law (and such conflicts are therefore possible), whereas for inclusive legal positivists (Wil Waluchov) or interpretivists (Ronald Dworkin), morality is part of law and there is one right answer in both (this last claim is not universally held, however, and sets Dworkin apart from many other interpretivists).

[53] See Jeffrey Brand-Ballard, *Limits of Legality: The Ethics of Lawless Judging* (2010).

[54] For a pioneering work, see particularly Antonine Cohen, ' "Ten Majestic Figures in Long Amaranth Robes": The Formation of the Court of Justice of the European Communities' in Antoine Vauchez and Bruno De Witte (eds), *Lawyering Europe: European Law as a Transnational Legal Field* (2013) 21.

[55] For a still rather rare account of the appointment process see Lord Mance, 'The Composition of the European Court of Justice', the text of a talk given to the UK Association for European Law, 19 October 2011, King's College London.

[56] See Floris de Witte, 'Sex, Drugs & EU Law: The Recognition of Moral and Ethical Diversity in EU Law' (2013) 50 *Common Market Law Review* 1545, for a critique of such approach by the ECJ.

[57] For a discussion in the context of EU law see Julio Baquero Cruz, 'Constitutional Gaps in European Community Law' in *Melanges en hommage à Jean-Victor Louis*, Vol 1 (2003) 29.

justified and appear equally correct—in short, when the law is indeterminate.[58] This is what legal theory considers proper hard cases, ensuing from within the law.

There are many ways to contend that there are no gaps in law. Hans Kelsen provided a legal-positivist one: in the absence of a general norm the judge 'does not fill a gap of actually valid law, but…adds to the actually valid law an individual norm to which no general norm corresponds'.[59] Ronald Dworkin and 'interpretivists', on the other hand, claim that a judge is 'guided by law as integrity, which does not limit law to what convention finds in past decisions [essentially, positive law] but directs him also to regard as law what morality would suggest to be the best justification of these past decisions'.[60] What these two answers share is that they both invest courts and judges with immense power, which is difficult to square with traditional notions of political legitimacy based on the idea of democratic self-government.[61]

In the context of EU law, Dworkinian *integrity* is often reinterpreted as *integration*.[62] The overall normative orientation of the EU is thus understood as the creation of 'an ever closer union among the peoples of Europe' and results in 'the in-built *communautaire* tendency' of the Court's interpretation.[63] The ECJ, which is called upon to 'ensure that in the interpretation and application of the Treaties the law is observed',[64] is the faithful agent of the EU legal system understood in this pro-integrationist way and has made decisions that go far beyond the text of the Treaties.

The problem is of course that there is no consensus as regards the ultimate goals of European integration (its *finalité*), and that what can seem self-evident to scholars writing from the perspective of the ECJ, who do not seem to have a problem with conflating integrity and integration, can be controversial outside that circle. Legal historians and legal sociologists have recently started to discover that the pro-integration orientation of most of EU law scholarship was the product of a deliberate effort by a 'transnational legal elite'.[65] The *Van Gend en Loos* ruling

---

[58] See Brian Leiter, 'Legal Indeterminacy' (1995) 1 *Legal Theory* 481–492.

[59] Hans Kelsen, *General Theory of Law and State* (1946) 147.

[60] Ronald Dworkin, *Law's Empire* (1986) 119–120.

[61] This is in fact true mainly for positivist accounts, since Dworkin's theory can be taken as an attempt to make adjudication in hard cases compatible with the idea of liberal democratic government, since it in fact denies that judges have discretion in such cases, being limited by the requirement of integrity. The democratic critique of Dworkin must therefore be a different one, concerning the competence of judges to discover the normative theory, which underlies the legal system and their power to impose their discoveries upon the discoveries made by elected bodies.

[62] See particularly Bengoetxea, MacCormick, and Moral Soriano (n 26) 82–85. See also Samantha Besson, 'From European Integration to European Integrity: Should European Law Speak with Just One Voice?'(2004) 10 *European Law Journal* 257.

[63] Beck (n 2) Ch 10.   [64] Art 19(1) TEU. See also Baquero Cruz (n 57) 39.

[65] See n 54 and Bill Davies and Morten Rasmussen (eds), 'Special Issue: Towards a New History of European Law' (2012) 21 *Contemporary European History* 305.

was not an incontestable result of the uniquely right reading of the Treaties, but a hard-won victory of four over three judges in a divided Court.[66]

At a more philosophical level, one can also argue that Dworkin expressly limited the validity of his theory to a given political community (the USA), which does not exist in the EU,[67] or, if we accept that the EU is equally a union of states and their peoples, precisely this equivocal character of the EU distinguishes it from truly united political communities, where integrity can play a gap-filling role.

In more practical terms, this means that the scope for argument is much greater in EU law, since every legal system participating in European integration can lay a claim to its own integrity, which must not be displaced by the requirements of EU law unless we understand integrity as the absolute primacy of the EU (rule of) law. In positive terms, this idea finds expression in Article 4(2) TEU on the protection of Member States' national identities.

Once we reject the idea of the EU legal system as complete and underpinned by a uniform normative theory that can be discovered, it is difficult to deny that the ECJ is constrained much less strongly than its national counterparts—and that many cases are in fact 'hard'. This is true also as a matter of practical politics and its theoretical reflection by social theory: the mechanisms of embedding the Court in the EU political system are much weaker than the ones existing in the Member States.

Those seeking refuge in theories of interpretation that seek to constrain courts, developed in other legal systems, will in my view search in vain. The first of these theories, 'textualism', which prescribes strict adherence to the text of an interpreted rule, ignores many problems of linguistic indeterminacy.[68] In order to solve them, it needs to overcome the text and becomes self-defeating. Some characteristics of EU law exacerbate the problem of linguistic indeterminacy even more. The existence of (at the moment) 24 different and yet formally equal linguistic versions of the same rule is the most important among them.

The second approach, 'originalism', is even more futile in the context of the EU for reasons already discussed above: in spite of occasional invocations of the 'founding fathers' of the EU or the 'original intent of the Treaties' by some authors, the moment of founding does not play such a strong symbolic role, that would translate into authority, as it does in the context of the USA.[69]

The indeterminacy of EU law ensues not only from the openness of legal norms in the EU legal system, but also from the absence of a strong agreement on how

---

[66] See Morten Rasmussen, 'From *Costa v ENEL* to the Treaties of Rome: A Brief History of a Legal Revolution' in Miguel Poiares Maduro and Loïc Azoulai (eds), *The Past and Future of EU Law: The Classics of EU Law Revisited on the 50th Anniversary of the Rome Treaty* (2010) 69, 79–81.

[67] See Theodor Schilling, 'The Jurisprudence of Constitutional Conflict: Some Supplementations to Mattias Kumm' (2006) 12 *European Law Journal* 173, 180.

[68] This is of course overly simplistic and the adherents of textualism will feel mistreated. Given the scope of this chapter I would only refer to Antonin Scalia, *A Matter of Interpretation* (1997).

[69] Conway (n 2) represents best this US-inspired approach.

to interpret them—what particularly Continental lawyers call the 'legal method'. I take up this issue in Section II.3.2, which deals with justification, since it is in that context that legal method is formulated.

(c) Articulating Reasons

Writing the decision is usually considered a part of the context of justification, which is, however, misleading: as already mentioned, the justification is complete only when the decision, including justification, is handed down and publicly announced. That the writing of the decision is part of the context of discovery is nicely confirmed by an expression sometimes used by those who draft judicial decisions: 'it won't write.'[70] It is the stage when they realize that the desired solution cannot be supported by legitimate legal reasons and they have to reconsider it.

It is well known that at the ECJ, legal secretaries *(référendaires)*, who are heavily constrained by the Court's linguistic rules and conventions, furthermore transposed into numerous institutional arrangements,[71] produce the majority of its written output. At the same time, there is a wealth of written material produced (at least partially) by judges, especially the already mentioned *notes en délibéré* that they exchange with their colleagues. The need to write down an argument (or to defend in deliberation with other judges an argument prepared by the judge's legal secretaries) disciplines the judge and narrows down the range of available solutions.[72] This of course does not exclude the possibility that the ECJ will occasionally deliver decisions that fail to provide a credible or even plausible justification—where, in other words, the impossibility of writing down a desired decision did not stop the Court from delivering it.

3. Legal Reasoning in the Context of Justification

One reason why students of legal reasoning focus on justification is pragmatic—as already mentioned, all decisions of the ECJ can be found on the Court's website, and most of them are available in all official languages of the EU. But some theorists present a normative claim too. They claim that the published opinions 'give us, and are meant to give us, something quite other than an account of coming to a view individually or collectively. Instead, they give an account of what makes a decision

---

[70] See Patricia M. Wald, 'The Rhetoric of Results and the Results of Rhetoric: Judicial Writings' (1995) 62 *University of Chicago Law Review* 1371, 1375.

[71] See particularly Karen McAuliffe, 'Hybrid Texts and Uniform Law? The Multilingual Case Law of the Court of Justice of the European Union' (2011) 24 *International Journal for the Semiotics of Law* 97.

[72] 'Cold realists' will probably laugh at this point, believing that 'anything goes'. For a response, see Lawrence B. Solum, 'On the Indeterminacy Crisis: Critiquing Critical Dogma' (1987) 54 *University of Chicago Law Review* 462.

the right legal decision upon the legal case or answer'.[73] This approach therefore does not expect the written decision to provide *actual* reasons that led to the decision.[74] It assumes a particular theory of the Court's legitimacy and accountability, based on legal argument, *as written* in the public decision rather than that *used* in reaching the decision.[75]

When it comes to articulating what the criteria of the right legal decision actually are, scholars tend to turn to the ECJ itself. This lay at the heart of Bengoetxea's pioneering study: 'to reconstruct the Court's doctrine of interpretation as explicitly developed by the Court in its judgments and as implicitly followed in some of its other judgments.'[76] Bengoetxea thus combined a theoretical account of justification in judicial process in general with an analysis of selected decisions of the ECJ. This approach was followed by his more recent successors—although with different background theories of law and interpretation in mind and with varying levels of sophistication.[77]

In general, a 'doctrine of justification' should provide criteria that make the application of law objective, and thus consistent with the liberal conception of the rule of law which dominates post-war legal (and political) thinking in Europe and in the USA.[78] The doctrine is formed by the 'class of legal reasons'.[79] The class comprises:

(a) *sources* of law;
(b) methods of *interpreting* the sources of law;
(c) rules on the legal construction of relevant facts;
(d) *meta-rules* concerning the relationship between the above.

In what follows I take each in order.

(a) The Sources of Law in the Context of Justification

The notion of the 'sources of law' has been quite loaded in the history of legal thinking, especially on the European Continent, which underwent a significant

---

[73] Bengoetxea, MacCormick, and Moral Soriano (n 26) 44.

[74] On sincerity in legal justification see Bengoetxea (n 2) 161–164. More generally, see Mathilde Cohen, 'Sincerity and Reason Giving: When May Legal Decision-Makers Lie?' (2010) 59 *DePaul Law Review* 1091.

[75] For a conceptualization of this and competing models see Lasser (n 16) Chs 10 and 11.

[76] Bengoetxea (n 2) 6.

[77] Bengoetxea's background theories were institutional legal positivism and a theory of legal justification as a special case of rational discourse as formulated by Neil MacCormick and Robert Alexy.

[78] At an abstract level, I follow here Jules L. Coleman and Brian Leiter, *Determinacy, Objectivity and Authority in Law and Interpretation* (1995) 203. For the historical argument about post-war Europe see Jan Werner Müller, *Contesting Democracy: Political Ideas in Twentieth-Century Europe* (2011) Ch 4.

[79] This is a constitutive category of the doctrine of justification similarly as 'factors of discovery' within the context of discovery.

transformation in the course of the nineteenth century towards the dominance of legislation. Many debates on the sources of law had to do with ideological changes that reflected the democratization of the political systems of European states and the industrialization of their political economies.[80] The focal point of such debates was usually the question of the formal status of judge-made law—*la jurisprudence*—which was for some time (although for a much shorter period than is usually believed) denied classification as a proper source of law. Behind such debates was either a scepticism regarding courts and judges until the first half of the twentieth century, or optimism, expressed most forcefully through the establishment of constitutional-judicial review of legislation in post-war Europe.

EU law doctrine has largely avoided such debates. This is best captured by the characterization of the ECJ's case law. In the view of one leading monograph on the judicial system of the EU, the case law of the Court, 'though in theory not formally binding—is often the most important source of law'.[81] In line with this pragmatic approach, we can list the sources that the ECJ can legitimately use in the justification of its decisions in the following way:[82]

1. EU primary law: the TEU, TFEU and protocols attached to them, the ECFR and the explanations referred to in the ECHR;
2. EU secondary law listed in Article 288 TFEU, which is explicitly given binding effect: Regulations, Directives, and Decisions;
3. The case law of the CJEU;
4. The general principles of EU law, which include interpretive canons;
5. International law, which comes in many different forms, including the case law of international courts and international customary law;
6. Common constitutional traditions of the EU Member States;
7. EU soft law;
8. Preparatory works (*travaux préparatoires*).

It is important to stress that this is not a list of the sources of EU law as such, but a list of legitimate sources that can be used in the justification of the ECJ's decisions. The catalogue would thus be different for other institutions. For example, the Commission's discretion is limited by various Guidelines concerning its enforcement policies, which do not however constrain the Court in a similar way.[83] It would also be different in the

---

[80] For an insightful and brief overview see Philippe Jestaz, 'Les sources du droit: le déplacement d'un pole à un autre' (1996) 27 *Revue générale de droit* 5. See also Shirley Robin Letwin, *On the History of the Idea of Law*, ed Noel B. Reynolds (2005) 91–199.

[81] Henry G. Schermers and Denis F. Waelbroeck, *Judicial Protection in the European Union* (6th ed, 2001) 133.

[82] For a similar list see Bengoetxea (n 2) 225–227 and also Bengoetxea, Ch 2.

[83] Such as Guidelines on the method of setting fines imposed pursuant to Article 15(2) of Regulation No 17 and Article 65(5) of the ECSC Treaty [1998] OJ C9/3. These were at stake in Case C-397/03 P *Archer Daniels Midland* [2006] ECR I-4429, where the ECJ held in para 91 that 'whilst rules of conduct designed to produce external effects, as is the case of the Guidelines, which are

context of discovery (where the range of legitimate sources can be wider) and in the submission of the parties, as already mentioned above.

(b) Methods of Interpretation

The methods of interpreting the sources of law refer to the type of argument one can make with these sources. An impressive comparative study once identified 'a "common core" of *at least* 11 basic types of argument',[84] which were then subsumed under four standard categories:

1. Linguistic arguments;
2. Systemic arguments;
3. Teleological arguments;
4. Arguments from intention.[85]

The ECJ uses arguments from all four categories, although their concrete shape often differs from that found in national or international law, in relation to the specific character of EU law. As most analysts observe, it is sometimes difficult clearly to separate different methods, and the categorization used here is by no means the only possible or even universal one.[86]

(1) *Linguistic arguments*, sometimes referred to as grammatical, semiotic, textual, or literal arguments, seek to derive the meaning of a norm from its literal expression in the legal text. They meet particular difficulties in the multilingual context of the EU. The Court emphasizes that the 'provisions of European Union law must be interpreted and applied uniformly in the light of the versions existing in all the languages of the European Union'.[87] This at once imposes two rather conflicting rules: the *equivalence* of all versions of the linguistic expression of a legal norm and at the same time the *uniformity* of the norm's meaning. In cases of conflict between various language versions, systemic and teleological arguments will prevail.[88] In addition, 'even where the different language versions are entirely in accord with one another', the Court insists that EU law 'uses terminology which is peculiar to it'.[89] In the Court's words, 'it must be emphasized that legal concepts

---

aimed at traders, may not be regarded as rules of law which the administration is always bound to observe, they nevertheless form rules of practice from which the administration may not depart in an individual case without giving reasons that are compatible with the principle of equal treatment'.

[84] See Robert R. Summers and Michele Taruffo, 'Interpretation and Comparative Analysis' in Neil MacCormick and Robert S. Summers (eds), *Interpreting Statutes: A Comparative Study* (1991) 461, 464, emphasis in the original.

[85] See Neil MacCormick and Robert S. Summers, 'Interpretation and Justification' in MacCormick and Summers (n 84) 512–516.

[86] Various authors use different classifications; see Bengoetxea (n 2) 233–262; Paunio (n 2) 20–49; Beck (n 2) 187–224; Bredimas (n 2).

[87] Case C-476/11 *HK Danmark*, 26 September 2013, para 42.

[88] *HK Danmark* (n 87), para 42.

[89] Case 283/81 *CILFIT v Ministero della Sanità* [1982] ECR 3415, para 19.

do not necessarily have the same meaning in [Union] law and in the law of the various Member States'.[90]

(2) *Systemic arguments* put the interpreted provision into a wider context and seek to establish an interpretation which would cohere with the rest of the legal system. The Court thus looks at recitals to legislation, other provisions of the same legal text, relevant other secondary legislation, general terms and concepts used by EU law, and also the general principles of EU law.[91] As mentioned above, these general principles include 'interpretive canons', general guides of interpretation, such as the *a fortiori* argument, *a contrario, lex specialis* or *lex superior* or *per analogiam*.[92] These establish systemic relationships between different possible interpretations of a legal norm and give priority to one of them.

(3) *Teleological arguments* refer to the purpose of the legal norm, its function in the overall legal scheme and the consequences of the selected interpretation.[93] What distinguishes the ECJ's approach is its frequent recourse to 'meta-teleological' arguments, invoking the *thelos* of the whole legal order, and the function and consequences of a particular interpretation adopted. In particular, the Court would thus refer to the effectiveness, uniformity, legal certainty, and the protection of individual rights as such meta-purposes of the EU legal order.[94] It will sometimes use the expression 'the spirit of the Treaties' to refer to such meta-considerations, concerning the legal order as a whole.

(4) *Arguments from intentions* relate closely to both systemic and teleological arguments as they inquire into the intentions of the authors of the legal provisions under interpretation.[95] In the EU law context, however, the ECJ's most consequential decision, *Van Gen en Loos*, rejected the argument from the intentions of the authors of the Treaties, which was expressly invoked by AG Roemer in support of the rejection of the direct effect of the Treaties.[96] That is perhaps why it does not get as much attention as other methods of interpretation, with few exceptions.[97]

---

[90] *CILFIT* (n 89) para 19.   [91] Beck (n 2) 191–207.

[92] On the notion of interpretive canons see eg James J. Brudney and Corey Ditslear, 'Canons of Construction and the Elusive Quest for Neutral Reasoning' (2005) 58 *Vanderbilt Law Review* 1.

[93] Some authors thus distinguish purposive, functional, and consequentialist arguments.

[94] See Lasser (n 16) 211–236.

[95] See Richard Plender, 'The Interpretation of Community Acts by Reference to the Intentions of the Authors' (1982) 2 *Yearbook of European Law* 57.

[96] Compare Opinion of AG Roemer in Case 26/62 *Van Gend en Loos* [1963] ECR 1, 19 with the judgment (12 and 13).

[97] See Plender (n 95); Conway (n 2); and Søren Schønberg and Karin Frick 'Finishing, Refining, Polishing: On the Use of Travaux Préparatoires as an Aid to the Interpretation of Community Legislation' (2003) 28 *European Law Review* 149.

(c) Legal Construction of Relevant Facts

Judicial decisions are usually delivered on particular facts: these facts make up a case, which is construed in the process of discovery.[98] As Kim Lane Scheppele reminds us, '[l]egal texts are generally interpreted to determine their implications for a specific empirical instance'.[99] In other words, '[t]he question that judges routinely ask is not, What does this (legal) text *mean*? but rather, What does this (legal) text mean *for this case*?'.[100] Surprisingly, however, legal theory pays rather little attention to the process of legal construction of relevant facts in the process of adjudication, especially in the process of justification.[101]

One may object here that 'facts are brusquely treated' in most decisions of the ECJ,[102] and that such theory would be of no interest here. That is not true, however—one can find numerous instances where the ECJ carefully examines the facts of one case to determine whether its previous decision is relevant to the present one.[103] Moreover, one should distinguish between (at least) two different kinds of fact that play a role in the ECJ's adjudication: decisional and foundational facts.[104]

Decisional facts are relevant to the application of law in a particular case. As already mentioned, they need to be construed by the court as much as the applicable law. The choice of relevant facts determines the choice of applicable law and vice versa: the fact that a product moved across borders can be irrelevant in many contexts. It is the requirement of Article 34 TFEU that makes it important in adjudication concerning the free movement of goods.[105]

The Court seems to have ignored this *inevitable* 'mutual construction of facts and rules' when it interpreted the notion of the same acts in the context of the *ne bis in idem* principle.[106] In *Van Esbroeck* it held that 'the relevant criterion for the purposes of the application of that [principle] is identity of the material acts, understood as the existence of a set of facts which are inextricably linked together, *irrespective of the legal classification given to them or the legal interest protected.*'[107]

---

[98] See Section II.2.a. The nature of such facts will differ, but even in the so-called abstract review of legislation one can speak of 'facts'—meaning the legislation under review.

[99] Kim Lane Scheppele, *Legal Secrets: Equality and Efficiency in the Common Law* (1988) 87.

[100] Scheppele (n 99).

[101] See only relatively recently David L. Faigman, *Constitutional Fictions: A Unified Theory of Constitutional Facts* (2008), which is focused on the US constitutional doctrine and constitutional adjudication before federal courts.

[102] See Lasser (n 16) 105.

[103] See Jan Komárek, 'Reasoning with Previous Decisions: Beyond the Doctrine of Precedent' (2013) 61 *American Journal of Comparative Law* 149, 152–153.

[104] Suzanna Sherry, 'Foundational Facts and Doctrinal Facts' (2011) *University of Illinois Law Review* 145.

[105] See the discussion following n 38.

[106] Art 54 of the Convention implementing the Schengen Agreement of 14 June 1985 between the Governments of the States of the Benelux Economic Union, the Federal Republic of Germany and the French Republic on the gradual abolition of checks at their common borders [2000] OJ L 239/1.

[107] Case C-436/04 *Van Esbroeck* [2006] ECR I-2333, para 42, emphasis added.

The Court added that facts must be 'inextricably linked… together in time, in space and *by their subject-matter*'.[108] But the subject-matter is provided by law and its classifications. Only then do we know, for example, that it was important that Mr Van Esbroeck was smuggling drugs between Belgium and Norway, while we can ignore the means by which he did so. If, however, it was later revealed that the smuggling was part of an organized activity, the Court could find that this constituted a separate set of facts—although 'materially' (what Mr Van Esbroeck was actually doing), the conduct would be the same.[109]

Foundational facts substantiate a particular interpretation of law; they are used to justify a particular legal doctrine. The ECJ thus, for example, established a particular notion of an average consumer 'who is reasonably well informed and reasonably observant and circumspect'.[110] The notion of a 'reasonable consumer' makes an empirical assumption about actual consumers, who in fact can behave quite differently, which can lead to quite different regulatory strategies. The ECJ's conception of a reasonable consumer justifies a strategy that gives preference to individual consumers' choice over collective policies that aim at protecting vulnerable consumers in a more paternalistic manner.[111] The change in the Court's assessment of doctrinal facts on which a particular doctrine was built can lead to the doctrinal shift.

In addition, this kind of fact brings challenges for the justification of the ECJ's decision, especially for the 'standards of proof': what kind of evidence can be raised to challenge factual assumptions concerning a particular legal doctrine? Should not the Court state doctrinal facts more openly and give a more explicit account of why those facts were considered determinative?

(d) In Search of a Meta-theory of Interpretation

Different interpretative methods can lead to conflicting results. A complete doctrine of justification must therefore include meta-rules of interpretation,[112] which put the other three elements of the doctrine discussed above, especially the methods of interpretation, in order. Some legal systems have specific legislated rules. In the European context, Article 1 of the Swiss Civil Code is perhaps the most famous, since it acknowledges that judges can act as legislators in specific circumstances. The Vienna Convention on the Law of Treaties also contains rules on interpretation in Articles 31 to 33.[113]

---

[108] *Van Esbroeck* (n 107) para 38.
[109] Later cases revealed the difficulties brought about by this approach to *ne bis in idem*. See particularly C-288/05 *Kretzinger* [2007] ECR I-6441 and Case C-367/05 *Kraaijenbrink* [2007] ECR I-6619.
[110] Case C-465/98 *Darbo* [2000] ECR I-2297, para 20.
[111] The latter inform consumer protection policies in some EU Member States, such as Italy. See Marco Dani, 'Assembling the Fractured European Consumer' (2011) 36 *European Law Review* 362.
[112] Sometimes called second-order criteria of interpretation.
[113] See Richard K. Gardiner, *Treaty Interpretation* (2008).

No such rules exist in EU law. The ECJ's ruling in *CILFIT* comes perhaps closest to the explicit statement of the doctrine of justification in EU law. *CILFIT* specified circumstances in which a court of final appeal is relieved of its duty to submit a preliminary reference, because 'the correct application of Community law may be so obvious as to leave no scope for any reasonable doubt as to the manner in which the question raised is to be resolved'.[114]

After the ECJ spends a number of paragraphs on the linguistic method,[115] it concludes: 'Finally, every provision of Community law must be placed in its context and interpreted in the light of the provisions of Community law as a whole, regard being had to the objectives thereof and to its state of evolution at the date on which the provision in question is to be applied.'[116] This would suggest the priority of the linguistic method, further controlled by the application of systemic and teleological interpretation—what Gunnar Beck calls a three-stage model of justification, identified by the already mentioned comparative study.[117] As Beck, however, points out, whereas linguistic arguments provide a starting point, they have comparatively weaker status in EU law. Second, there is no clear hierarchy between different arguments. Instead, the ECJ uses what Beck calls a 'cumulative approach', mingling all sorts of argument, which moreover exhibits an 'in-built *communautaire* tendency'.[118] This, however, is not very satisfactory if the doctrine of justification seeks to guarantee the objectivity of the application of law as a central element of liberal democratic regimes.[119]

4. The ECJ's Judicial Style

It is a commonplace in the EU legal scholarship to criticize the ECJ for 'the cryptic, Cartesian style' of its decisions 'with its pretence of logical legal reasoning and inevitability of results', which 'is not conducive for a good conversation with national courts'.[120] Indeed, the Court's decisions are highly formalized and structured, they use a formulaic language speaking impersonally in the name of the institution as a whole, and they present the solution to the case at hand as the only possible one. The Court is very inconsistent in addressing arguments raised by the parties (sometimes these are not even mentioned, sometimes the Court engages in them at quite some length) and no dissent is published. The only alternative voice

---

[114] *CILFIT* (n 89) para 16. See Bengoetxea (n 2) 232.   [115] See n 87.

[116] *CILFIT* (n 89) para 20.

[117] Beck (n 2) 147–155 referring to MacCormick and Summers (n 85).

[118] Beck (n 2) Chs 9 and 10.   [119] See n 78.

[120] All quotes from Joseph H.H. Weiler, 'Epilogue: The Judicial Après Nice' in de Búrca and Weiler (n 26) 215, 225. See also Joseph H.H. Weiler, 'Epilogue: Judging the Judges—Apology and Critique' in Maurice Adams, Henri de Waele, Johan Meeusen, and Gert Straetmans (eds), *Judging Europe's Judges: The Legitimacy of the Case Law of the European Court of Justice* (2013) 235.

one can hear from Luxembourg is that of its Advocates General, whose position has however been undermined by procedural reform adopted in the wake of the Treaty of Nice. Overall, the ECJ is rather secretive: a lot of information concerning both individual cases and the functioning of the Court is never revealed.[121]

Many of the features just mentioned are due to the institutional design of the Court and the very features of the EU legal order. The formulaic language, for example, is imposed on the Court by the requirement to publish most of its decisions in all official languages of the EU. Those who draft the Court's decisions (mostly the legal secretaries of individual judges—the *référendaires*) are forced to write in 'Court French', which sounds foreign even to French native speakers.[122] It saves translation costs. The collegiate style of writing and the absence of dissenting opinions is (said to be) due to the rather short, but renewable mandate of the judges, which limits their independence and the willingness to speak in their own voice.

Still, as mentioned, the case for a more argumentative style is repeatedly made in the literature. Whether it is sound depends to a large extent on the relationship between legal reasoning and authority and legitimacy—an issue which needs to be left to another enquiry.

BIBLIOGRAPHY

Maurice Adams, Henri de Waele, Johan Meeusen, and Gert Straetmans (eds), *Judging Europe's Judges: The Legitimacy of the Case Law of the European Court of Justice* (2013)

Joxerramon Bengoetxea, *The Legal Reasoning of the European Court of Justice: Towards a European Jurisprudence* (1993)

Joxerramon Bengoetxea, Neil MacCormick, and Leonor Moral Soriano, 'Integration and Integrity in the Legal Reasoning of the European Court of Justice' in Gráinne de Búrca and Joseph HH Weiler (eds), *The European Court of Justice* (2001)

Gunnar Beck, *The Legal Reasoning of the Court of Justice of the EU* (2012)

Gerard Conway, *The Limits of Legal Reasoning and the European Court of Justice* (2012)

Ole Due, 'Understanding the Reasoning of the Court of Justice' in Gil Carlos Rodríguez Iglesias (ed), *Mélanges en homage à Fernand Schockweiler* (1999) 73

Mark A. Jacob, *Precedents and Case-based Reasoning in the European Court of Justice: Unfinished Business* (2014)

Jan Komárek, 'Judicial Lawmaking and Precedent in Supreme Courts: The European Court of Justice Compared to the US Supreme Court and the French Cour de cassation' (2008–2009) 11 *Cambridge Yearbook of European Legal Studies* 399

Thijmen Koopmans, 'The Theory of Interpretation and the Court of Justice' in David O'Keeffe and Antonio Bavasso (eds), *Judicial Review in European Union Law*, Vol 1 (2000) 45

---

[121] See Alemanno and Stefan (n 24).   [122] For an insightful account see McAuliffe (n 71).

Mitchel Lasser, *Judicial Deliberations: A Comparative Study of Judicial Transparency and Legitimacy* (2004)

Elina Paunio, *Legal Certainty in Multilingual EU Law: Language, Discourse and Reasoning at the European Court of Justice* (2013)

Vlad Perju, 'Reason and Authority in the European Court of Justice' (2009) *49 Virginia Journal of International Law* 307

Suvi Sankari, *European Court of Justice Legal Reasoning in Context* (2013)

CHAPTER 3

STRADDLING THE FENCE

THE EU AND INTERNATIONAL LAW

JAN KLABBERS

I. INTRODUCTION

IN a zoo full of strange creatures, the European Union manages to stand out as one of the strangest. Set up as an international organization, endowed with certain tasks by Member States on the basis of a set of treaties, the EU is no longer generally regarded as a normal international organization (if it ever was, and whatever the word 'normal' might signify[1]); to think of the EU as performing tasks set up by its Member States seems hopelessly inadequate; and the set of Treaties has, colloquially at any rate, evolved into a constitution. In short, the EU is a strange animal, a unicorn amidst a coterie of strange creatures, and this is so whether one studies it from the perspective of an international lawyer or whether the adopted angle is that of a domestic lawyer. Indeed, it might well be one of the brilliant aspects of the EU legal order that it is capable of being analysed from a variety of perspectives—none of them fully convincing perhaps, but many of them plausible.[2]

---

[1] On this, see Jan Klabbers, 'Unity, Diversity, Accountability: The Ambivalent Concept of International Organisation' (2013) 14 *Melbourne Journal of International Law* 149.

[2] One private law authority has held the EU to be a 'Jack-in-the-box', popping up whenever least expected. See Thomas Wilhelmsson, 'Jack-in-the-Box Theory of European Community Law' reproduced in Lars D. Eriksson and Samuli Hurri (eds), *Dialectic of Law and Reality: Readings in Finnish Legal Theory* (1999) 437.

The relationship of the EU with international law—public international law, that is—has always been highly ambivalent. The EU is, in many ways, a creature of international law, yet has done its best to distance itself from international law.[3] This is not a recent phenomenon; it is already visible in the early case law of the Court of Justice of the European Union (CJEU) when the European Coal and Steel Community was the only European Community in existence. This ambivalence will function as the red thread running through this chapter, the contention being that the EU feels very comfortable when sitting on the fence: it does not want to be seen as firmly embedded in international law, as this would entail having to live up to what the International Court of Justice has referred to as the 'general rules of law'[4] which may not always be to the EU's benefit. Neither does the EU aspire to full-fledged statehood, as such a position would, again, come with a legal status and obligations that it might not be all that keen on.

This chapter aims to discuss the relationship between the EU and (public) international law, and will do so by looking closely at three discrete topics. First, I plan to discuss the status of the EU in the international legal order. This will involve in particular questions of international legal personality and the utilization within the EU of the venerable implied powers doctrine. Second, I plan to discuss the status of international law in the EU legal order: what is the effect of international law in EU law? And third, how does the EU—in particular its courts—handle conflicts between EU law and international law? The last two topics are fairly familiar tropes on which an impressive amount of literature is available,[5] and thus will not be discussed in great detail. The first, however, is less familiar, and therefore warrants a bit more time and attention.

Institutionalization, reception, and collision are not the only ways in which the two legal orders intersect. It should be acknowledged, for instance, that the EU has concluded a large number of treaties and so contributes generously to the solidification and development of the law of treaties, although it is probably inappropriate to suggest a separate law of treaties to serve the EU's interests.[6] Likewise, the EU, by adopting

---

[3] For a subtle argument that the EU is still best seen as a creature of international law, see Bruno de Witte, 'The European Union as an International Legal Experiment' in Gráinne de Búrca and J.H.H. Weiler (eds), *The Worlds of European Constitutionalism* (2012) 19.

[4] See *Interpretation of the Agreement of 25 March 1951 between the WHO and Egypt*, advisory opinion [1980] ICJ Reports 73, para 37: the ICJ held that international organizations are bound to respect treaties they have concluded, their internal rules, and the 'general rules of international law'.

[5] On the reception of international law in the EU legal order, see, amongst others, the excellent study by Mario Mendez, *The Legal Effects of EU Agreements: Maximalist Treaty Enforcement and Judicial Avoidance Techniques* (2013), and Enzo Cannizzaro, Paolo Palchetti, and Ramses A. Wessel (eds), *International Law as Law of the European Union* (2012). On collision, see generally Jan Klabbers, *Treaty Conflict and the European Union* (2008), while the *Kadi* jurisprudence has spawned a cottage industry of theorizing on the relationship between the EU and international legal order. See eg De Búrca and Weiler (n 3).

[6] The suggestion is made in Delano Verwey, *The European Community, the European Union and the International Law of Treaties* (2004).

positions both internally and externally, contributes quite a bit to the development of international law on a number of substantive topics, for better or for worse,[7] with topics including such things as international terrorism,[8] the recognition of states,[9] or the responsibility of international organizations under international law;[10] and it plays an important role within the United Nations and other international organizations.[11]

It is also important to note that the intersection of the two legal orders engages what may, for want of a better term, be described as purely internal considerations. Thus, the precise division of competences between the EU and its Member States is of great importance, as are the various techniques developed for managing this relationship. In a nutshell, the EU is exclusively competent in a few policy areas (most prominently external commercial relations, broadly defined since the entry into force of the Lisbon Treaty[12]), and shares treaty-making competences with its Member States in various other policy areas, or supplements those Member State powers. The main technique for making this work is the institution of mixity, under which both the EU and its Member States separately become parties to international treaties.[13] This, in turn, may have ramifications, both internal (eg relating to the CJEU's jurisdiction) and external, when it comes to the international responsibility of the Union. In addition, the EU has developed the technique of the so-called disconnection clause: some international agreements contain a clause allowing the EU's Member States to apply EU law in their relations inter se, while applying the terms of the international agreement to the other Treaty partners.[14] I will largely leave these issues aside though, as they tend to have a greater bearing on EU law than on relations between the EU and international legal orders.

---

[7] See generally Frank Hoffmeister, 'The Contribution of EU Practice to International Law' in Marise Cremona (ed), *Developments in EU External Relations Law* (2008) 37.

[8] See eg Jan Klabbers, 'Europe's Counter-terrorism Law(s): Outlines of a Critical Approach' in Malcolm Evans and Panos Koutrakos (eds), *Beyond the Established Legal Orders: Policy Interconnections between the EU and the Rest of the World* (2011) 205.

[9] The EU adopted a set of guidelines on recognition in late 1991; these are reproduced in (1992) 31 *International Legal Materials* 1486.

[10] See generally Malcolm Evans and Panos Koutrakos (eds), *The International Responsibility of the European Union* (2013).

[11] See generally Jan Wouters, Frank Hoffmeister, and Tom Ruys (eds), *The United Nations and the European Union: An Ever Stronger Partnership* (2006).

[12] Art 207 TFEU now includes most notably trade in services and foreign direct investment in the concept of common commercial policy.

[13] The seminal study is Joni Heliskoski, *Mixed Agreements as a Technique for Organizing the International Relations of the European Community and its Member States* (2001); see also Christophe Hillion and Panos Koutrakos (eds), *Mixed Agreements Revisited: The EU and its Member States in the World* (2010).

[14] The seminal piece is Constantin P. Economidès and Alexandros G. Kolliopoulos, 'La clause de deconnexion en faveur du droit communautaire: une pratique critiquable' (2006) 110 *Revue Générale de Droit International Public* 273.

The status of the EU in international law and the status of international law in the EU legal order represent two sides of the same coin, but with a twist: the coin is skewed in the sense that international law is generally considered the overarching, 'higher', legal order.[15] In particular the recent *Kadi* saga before the CJEU, however, suggests that this image needs to be nuanced: as I will explain below, EU law may be *lex specialis* when viewed against the background of the *lex generalis* of international law, but it does not follow therefore that international law is hierarchically superior. Nor, for that matter, does it follow that EU law is by definition superior to international law—the relationship between the two is characterized by a high degree of complexity and ambivalence.

This is made possible, in part, by the circumstance that the EU Treaties remain virtually silent on the role and impact of international law, with the exception of what is now Article 351 TFEU which, on the face of it, lends priority to treaties concluded by EU Member States before they joined the EU. Beyond this, the EU Treaties contain very little on the relationship with international law.[16] It lacks a provision on the effect of international law in the EU legal order, for instance. As a result, much of the relevant law had to be developed by the CJEU without much formal political guidance, and in doing so the Court has enthusiastically both carved out a special position for the EU and done its utmost to protect that special position. As the following will suggest, the EU has always been highly ambivalent towards international law, and has carved out an ethos to justify this: what matters—and has always mattered—is the protection of the integrity of the EU legal order and the autonomy of EU law. Threats from the Member States must be averted, as must threats stemming from international law.

II. The EU as an International Institution

In the aftermath of the Second World War, representatives of six European States met in Paris in 1951 and concluded the Treaty establishing the European Coal and Steel

---

[15] As suggested by Ramses A. Wessel, 'Reconsidering the Relationship between International and EU Law: Towards a Content-based Approach?' in Cannizzaro, Palchetti and Wessel (n 5) 7, 11.

[16] There is on a more detailed point a provision allowing the Member States to conclude treaties inter se with a view to complementing EU law. This has been used sparingly, however, and is generally construed so as not to raise issues relating to public international law (see also, briefly, Section IV). For a discussion, see Bruno de Witte, 'Using International Law for the European Union's Domestic Affairs', in Cannizzaro, Palchetti, and Wessel (n 5) 133.

Community. This proved to be an inspired move, as it entailed an answer to an awkward and serious political conundrum: how to build up a strong Germany (if only to fend off communism) without allowing Germany to reassert itself as a military power.[17] The result was the ECSC, set up as an international organization but with a unified command in the form of a High Authority with far-reaching decision making and (quasi-)legislative powers. The ECSC was a curious creature: an international organization unlike other organizations, in the sense that decision making was not ultimately carried out by the Member States acting jointly in a plenary body, but that much depended on the High Authority, while the Court of Justice too was given serious powers.

Not surprisingly, this structure gave rise to various legal questions that would soon present themselves in litigation. What was surprising, however, was the Court's reluctance to look to international law in finding answers to those questions: in those cases where international law could have been invoked, the Court turned a blind eye, as if desiring already at this early stage to extricate the ECSC from its moorings in international law. This stands in some contrast to quite a few federal systems, where resort to international law in disputes between the various federal units may not be unheard of.[18]

Thus, in *Fédéchar*, the CJEU held that the High Authority was endowed with certain implied powers, a doctrine by then well established in (international) institutional law and, indeed, to some extent referred to by the Court: 'it is possible to apply a rule of interpretation generally accepted in both international and national law, according to which the rules laid down by an international treaty or a law presuppose the rules without which that treaty or law would have no meaning or could not be reasonably and usefully applied.'[19] Interestingly, the Court here, a few years after the landmark opinion of the International Court of Justice (ICJ) in *Reparation for Injuries*, opted to apply a far more modest version of the implied powers doctrine than the ICJ's in *Reparation*.[20] Also intriguing, and perhaps already signalling an awareness of the hybrid nature of the ECSC (neither pure international law nor domestic law), is that the Court justified itself by pointing to both international law and domestic law, instead of merely relying on international law.

---

[17] A very useful overview of the early phase of the European integration process is offered by Max Jansen and J.K. de Vree, *The Ordeal of Unity* (2d ed, 1985).

[18] See eg *Virginia v Tennessee*, 148 U.S. 503 (1893), although debate is possible on whether the law at issue in that case is to be considered a manifestation of international law. Notably though, the US Supreme Court invoked international legal authority in the form of writings by Vattel and Wheaton.

[19] See case 8/55 *Fédération Charbonnière de Belgique v High Authority* ECR English Special Edition 292, 299.

[20] In *Reparation*, the ICJ held that an implied power could not only be derived from an express power, but even from the functions of an organization at large. See *Reparation for Injuries Suffered in the Service of the United Nations* [1949] ICJ Reports 174. For discussion, see Jan Klabbers, *An Introduction to International Institutional Law* (2d ed, 2009) 59–64.

Another relevant question related to delegation of powers from the institutions of the ECSC to other entities. This arose in *Meroni*, with the Court eventually holding that the objectives of the ECSC were binding not only on the ECSC itself, but also on its institutions 'within the limits of their respective powers'. This created an institutional balance—a system of checks and balances—from which it followed that a delegation of discretionary powers by any of the institutions would not be acceptable. After all, a delegation of a discretionary power would upset the institutional balance.[21] Contrary to *Fédéchar*, here the Court's decision is roughly in line with established international precedent, in particular the *Effect of Awards* opinion of the ICJ concerning the delegation of a judicial task by the UN General Assembly to a United Nations Administrative Tribunal. Yet, at no point does the Court refer to *Effect of Awards*—if anything, its decision is grounded on an amalgam of administrative law. While the Court remains silent on whence its inspiration springs, AG Roemer devoted some attention to delegation of powers in administrative law and in Community law[22] but not, notably, in international law.

Likewise, in *Algera*, decided in July 1957, concerning administrative decisions regarding employment of officials, recourse was had to principles of administrative law, without paying any attention to the fairly rich experience of other international civil service tribunals.[23] The League of Nations Administrative Tribunal had already decided 37 cases after its creation in 1927,[24] and its successor, the International Labour Organization (ILO) Administrative Tribunal, would make its 30th decision the day after *Algera* was decided, but none of this was reflected in *Algera*.

Following the relative success of the ECSC, two new Communities were created in 1958: the European Economic Community (EEC) and the European Community for Atomic Energy, having a structure roughly similar to that of the ECSC, albeit with less far-reaching powers for the Commission (analogous to the High Authority) and a greater role for the inter-governmental Council of Ministers. This basic structure has remained largely intact since the late 1950s, although several modifications have been made. The powers of the Assembly (now the European Parliament) have markedly expanded; a Court of Auditors has been added to the

---

[21] See Case 9/56 *Meroni & Co v ECSC* ECR English Special edition 133, 152. Meroni's continued relevance is discussed in Deirdre Curtin, *Executive Power of the European Union: Law, Practices, and the Living Constitution* (2009), and was recently upheld by the CJEU in Case C-270/12 *United Kingdom v European Parliament and Council* (ESMA), judgment of 22 January 2014.

[22] See *Meroni* (n 21) 190, per AG Roemer.

[23] See Joined Cases 7/56, 3/57 to 7/57 *Algera and others v Common Assembly* ECR English Special Edition 39. The same applies to the Court's first civil service case, Case 1/55 *Kergall v Common Assembly* ECR English Special Edition 151.

[24] See C.F. Amerasinghe, *The Law of the International Civil Service as Applied by International Administrative Tribunals*, vol. 1 (2nd ed, 1994) 52. The International Institute for Agriculture also set up an Administrative Tribunal, in 1931, but this never decided any cases (53).

formal institutions of the EU; a new court has been created to assist the CJEU, first under the name Court of First Instance, now known as the General Court,[25] and, most importantly perhaps, the early informal summit meetings have become institutionalized under the heading of European Council.

Other changes too have taken place: the Union has expanded from the original six Member States to the current number of 28, since the accession of Croatia in the summer of 2013. Over the years, the Union has also expanded its field of activities, first within the existing Communities, later also adding such activities as migration policy, foreign policy and defence, and criminal law to the fold.

Nonetheless, the early ambivalence concerning the position of the EU in international law has remained: the early ECSC cases had set the tone. Gradually, the CJEU had paved the way for its famous *Van Gend and Loos* doctrine. The EU was not a creature of international law pure and simple, but 'constitutes a new legal order of international law for the benefit of which the states have limited their sovereign rights, albeit within limited fields, and the subjects of which comprise not only Member States but also their nationals'.[26] The formulation still marked a large degree of ambivalence or, if you will, a studied straddling of the fence: the EU was still 'of international law', but represented a 'new legal order'; the Member States had 'limited their sovereign rights', but only 'within limited fields'. The EU was neither international nor national, neither fish nor fowl. And the Court could happily decide that while, normally speaking, the effects of international law in domestic law depend on what domestic law has to say, the EU case was different: the effects of EU law in the domestic law of its Member States had to depend on EU law in order to do justice to the grand project of European integration.[27]

This line of thinking, as is well known, continued throughout the quasi-constitutional cases following *Van Gend and Loos*. In *Costa v ENEL*, for instance, the Court explicitly contrasted EU law with 'ordinary international treaties';[28] the (then) EEC Treaty created its own legal system which 'became an integral part of the legal systems of the Member States',[29] a formula that once again implies a comfortable sitting on the fence.

When it came time to systematize the international legal relations of the Union (its 'external relations', in the generally accepted Eurocentric phrase), the first relevant case would again display considerable ambivalence, and did so in two ways. In *ERTA*, at issue was whether transport agreements with third parties could be concluded by the Union, or would still have to be concluded by the individual

---

[25] Additionally, more recently a specialized Civil Service Court has been created.

[26] See Case 26/62 *Van Gend & Loos v Netherlands Internal Revenue Administration* ECR English Special edition 1 at 12.

[27] For further discussion, see Jan Klabbers, *International Law* (2013) 297–299.

[28] See Case 6/64 *Costa v ENEL* ECR English Special Edition 585, 593.

[29] Case 6/64 *Costa* (n 28).

Member States: did the Union have the power to conclude such agreements, or had the power remained with the Member States?[30]

Without providing any explanation, the Court started its analysis by bluntly stating that the EU was to be considered an international legal person.[31] It provided no authority or justification for this statement, other than the pithy terms of what was, at the time, Article 280 EEC, which provided merely that 'The Community shall have legal personality'. The point is not that the Court's conclusion was unjustifiable, for clearly an argument could be made to bolster its conclusion. Thus, Article 281 EEC at the time specified the EEC's capacity under domestic law, so an *a contrario* type of argument could have been made: if Article 281 related to domestic personality, then Article 280 could be seen to relate to international personality.[32] Or it could have been argued, along the lines of the ICJ's opinion in *Reparation*, that the international legal personality of the EU could be derived, in part, from the circumstance that its Member States had expected the EU to engage in international relations.[33]

In fact, reliance on the external activities would arguably have been more plausible than the Court's analysis. When the EEC Treaty was concluded, it was decidedly uncommon for any international organization to contain any clause relating to its possible personality under international law. The UN Charter, as is well known, did (and does) not have such a provision, and neither do the constitutions of many of the international organizations created at roughly the same time as the EU. Indeed, examples of international organizations set up between, roughly, the 1940s and 1960s with a clear provision on international personality seem to be non-existent, at least among major organizations, and much the same applies to the European entities established around the time the EU was created.[34] The Western European Union and North Atlantic Treaty Organization did not have anything on personality; the Council of Europe merely provides for privileges and immunities (Article 40), and while the Organization for European Economic Cooperation (OEEC) had a

---

[30] *ERTA* is often discussed as laying the foundation for the EU's external action, but rarely from an international legal perspective.

[31] Note that AG Dutheillet de Lamothe did not address the matter.

[32] This is not airtight though: one could just as plausibly argue that Art 281 elaborated the general proposition of Art 280, in which case a finding of international legal personality based on Art 280 would be inappropriate. This is the approach taken by Jacobs, holding that Art 280 was concerned not with international personality, but 'with more mundane matters of domestic law'. See Francis Jacobs, 'Direct Effect and Interpretation of International Agreements in the Recent Case Law of the European Court of Justice' in Alan Dashwood and Marc Maresceau (eds), *Law and Practice of EU External Relations: Salient Features of a Changing Landscape* (2008) 13.

[33] See *Reparation*, where the ICJ held that the external activities of the UN could only be explained on the basis of its having international legal personality.

[34] I have made use of the texts of the constituent instruments as assembled in Louis B. Sohn (ed), *International Organisation and Integration: Annotated Basic Documents of International Organizations and Arrangements: Student Edition* (1986). The one exception is the WEU, which is not covered in that volume, while the OEEC/OECD's Supplementary Protocols are also not reproduced (but the OECD Treaty itself is).

special protocol on legal capacity and privileges and immunities, this addressed the OEEC's 'juridical personality' in domestic law.[35]

Among universal organizations, references to domestic personality were common, but references to international personality remained absent: the constitutions of UNESCO, the World Health Organization, the International Civil Aviation Organization, the International Maritime Organization (created as the Intergovernmental Maritime Consultative Organization), the International Atomic Energy Agency, the International Bank for Reconstruction and Development, the International Monetary Fund, and the Food and Agriculture Organization[36] said nothing whatsoever about international legal personality,[37] and on other continents too clauses were absent, with neither the constitutions of the Organization of American States nor the Organization of African Unity (as it was first created; it has been superseded by the African Union) specifying the status of the organization in international law. Ironically, the only well-known exception was the ECSC Treaty, whose Article on personality (Article 6) elaborated what personality would mean in international relations as well as under the domestic laws of the Member States.

The standard approach with most of these organizations was to provide for domestic legal personality, often in terms of legal capacity, and often in conjunction with privileges and immunities in respect of the domestic laws of the Member States. In addition, many constituent instruments would include clauses on the possibility of entering into relations with states or other entities (including other international organizations) or concluding all kinds of arrangements. These would, it was generally thought, either presuppose international legal personality, or be constitutive of such personality—either way, a specific grant of international legal personality was deemed unnecessary. Ironically perhaps, it was probably the discussion on the international legal personality (*vel non*) of the EU following its creation at Maastricht[38] that inspired treaty makers to start thinking of including a clause on the international legal personality of their entities—some of the constituent documents of the newer organizations now explicitly refer to personality under international law.[39]

---

[35] This is clear from the preamble, and also follows from the 2nd Supplementary Protocol to the OECD Convention, as this outlines that in Canada and the USA, specific domestic legal instruments govern the OECD's legal status.

[36] The latter three may be considered somewhat ambivalent in that their constitutions refer to legal personality (without adjective) and then continue by specifying capacity under domestic law. Still, contextually, they would seem to be geared towards establishing personality under domestic, not international law. For discussion as to the uses of a specific clause granting domestic personality, see Klabbers (n 20) 44–46.

[37] Much the same applies to the older International Labour Organization.

[38] I have addressed this at some length in Jan Klabbers, 'Presumptive Personality: The European Union in International Law' in Martti Koskenniemi (ed), *International Law Aspects of the European Union* (1998) 231.

[39] This applies eg to the European Forest Institute set up in 2003.

The second reason why *ERTA* marks the continued ambivalence of the EU towards international law resides in its use of the implied powers doctrine—or what is sometimes held as its use of the implied powers doctrine.[40] The Court eventually seemed to derive the EU's Treaty making power in the field of transport from the general Treaty, thus following (seemingly) *Reparation*. But on closer scrutiny, the Court did no such thing, and it is telling that neither the Court nor its Advocate General even once referred to *Reparation*. Instead, the external transport power was justified predominantly under reference to what was at the time Article 5 EEC, the Community fidelity clause (*Gemeinschaftstreue*[41]), laying down an obligation on the Member States to abstain from measures which might jeopardize attainment of the Union's objectives. Hence, the conclusion by individual Member States of agreements with third parties could possibly encroach upon the exercise by the Union of its proper competences, and therefore the agreement should be concluded by the Union, not the individual Member States. This looks a little like an application of the implied powers doctrine à la *Reparation*, but differs in the source of implication: it is not geared towards enabling the organization to utilize a power in order to exercise its functions effectively, but arguably goes a step further: it is no longer about the Union having a power, but about whether the Member States are pre-empted.[42]

Indeed, this is exactly the construction AG Dutheillet de Lamothe envisaged, and while he appreciated its benefits from a policy perspective, he was unwilling to suggest it as a matter of law: 'the argument of implied and automatic transfer of authority outside the cases laid down by the Treaty meets with very serious objections.'[43] For him, the EEC Treaty was based, in particular with respect to external relations, on a strict notion of conferred powers, and to derive an implied power from a general doctrine of pre-emption was too much to swallow. If there would indeed be a need for an external transport power, then the general grant of what was at the time Article 235 EEC (now Article 352 TFEU) could be used: the Council could legislate so as to provide the Community with the necessary power.[44] Either way, it is striking that neither the Court nor its Advocate General wanted to rely on

[40] Denys is somewhat ambivalent, providing *ERTA* as an example of implied powers (at 122) that goes further than the doctrine usually goes in US federal relations, where implied powers need to be attached to explicitly conferred powers rather than to the objectives of functioning of an entity (at 131). Surprisingly perhaps, she does not discuss the *Reparation* version of implied powers. See Christine Denys, *Impliciete bevoegdheden in de Europese Economische Gemeenschap: Een onderzoek naar de betekenis van 'implied powers'* (1990). Engström suggests that *ERTA* and the doctrine of parallelism it launched are best seen as manifestations of the implied powers doctrine. See Viljam Engström, *Constructing the Powers of International Institutions* (2012) 50–52.

[41] Now Art 4, para 3 TEU.   [42] For further discussion, see Klabbers (n 20) 62–64.

[43] See *ERTA*, per AG Dutheillet de Lamothe, 291.

[44] The Advocate General was even reluctant to apply the narrow version of implied powers, as known from US federal law, according to which an implied power can be derived if necessary to give effect to an explicit power. *ERTA* (n 43) 293.

the international law doctrine of implied powers—outside inspiration was looked for, to some extent, in US federal law, but not in international law.

Thus, some of the pivotal cases[45] in the EU's judicial history demonstrate a marked ambivalence towards international law: the European edifice is built on international legal foundations (the Treaties), but the superstructure refuses to think of itself in terms of international law. The CJEU has done its best, in *Fédéchar, Meroni, Van Gend and Loos, Costa v ENEL*, and *ERTA*, to create something of special distinction: a unique creature, owing at least as much to federal inspirations or curious amalgams of administrative law as it does to international law—and perhaps more.

Recent developments suggest, moreover, that the Court's ambivalence to international law is unlikely to undergo any radical changes. Despite the avowed willingness of the Member States to accede to the European Convention on Human Rights, the Court displays a marked reluctance to apply said Convention; and with regard to a putative European Patent Court subsuming, in part, the Court's jurisdiction, it once again held that such a new court would be incompatible with the EU treaties.[46]

III. The Reception
of International Law

If the Court has been reluctant to build the EU on models familiar from international law when it comes to such basic concepts as legal personality and implied powers, on a more practical level too its reluctance to embrace international law can only be considered marked.[47] Remarkably, and despite the existence of a strong narrative heralding the EU as friendly disposed towards international law in combination with the circumstance that EU law itself is generally directly effective in the domestic legal orders of the Member States, the general position with respect to international law in the EU legal order is that international law shall not be directly applied or relied upon.[48] This holds true with respect to treaties to which

---

[45] Most of these cases are central to the early constitutionalization narrative relating to the EU: see Eric Stein, 'Lawyers, Judges, and the Making of a Transnational Constitution' (1981) 75 *American Journal of International Law* 1.

[46] See Opinion 1/09 of 8 March 2011.

[47] See in much more detail Jan Klabbers, 'In Defense of the Realm: Receiving the International' in Robert Schütze and Takis Tridimas (eds), *The Oxford Principles of EU Law* (2015). The leading monograph is Mendez (n 5).

[48] Note that analytically and theoretically, providing international law with direct effect is not the only way of demonstrating *Völkerrechtsfreundlichkeit*; in practice though, it is its most prominent

the Union is a party, and it holds true with respect to other manifestations of international law, such as customary international law, or even the more diffuse category of international legal concepts that are indispensable but difficult to classify in terms of their source—enforcement jurisdiction is an example. There is only one exception, and that is the group of treaties made up by association, free trade, and partnership agreements in their various guises. This is not surprising, as it is here that international law serves as a useful tool for the exportation of EU law. Where, on the other hand, international law aims to be imported, the Court has invariably put a stop to things.

This, of course, is not to say that the Court does not consider the EU to be bound by international law. The case law contains many suggestions that treaties concluded by the EU are binding on the EU (as well as its institutions and Member States), following what used to be Article 300 TEC (now Article 216, paragraph 2, TFEU). Equally, there are sufficient admonitions that the Court considers the EU bound by customary international law, be it the law of treaties[49] or the law of the sea.[50] But it is to suggest that when it comes to admitting international law into the EU's legal order, the CJEU and General Court are less sanguine than is often proposed—their approach can hardly be qualified as *völkerrechtsfreundlich*.[51]

Analytically, the effect of international law in the Community legal order can arise in various types of situations.[52] First, there is the situation in which a plaintiff argues that behaviour by the Union violates his or her legal right under international law. This could happen, hypothetically, when the Commission fines a company for antitrust behaviour or imposes countervailing duties on a company; when the Union authorities assume jurisdiction over ships captured on the high seas; or similar situations—these are the hard cases of direct effect, so to speak. Second, there is the review of legality: a plaintiff may argue that a Union rule, applied to him or her, may be in violation of international law—this is less a matter of direct effect (in that the individual is not relying directly before the EU courts on the international rule in question) but rather, at the risk of convoluting terminology, of indirect effect: the argument is that the EU rule violates international law, and is not directed at the action itself.

Third, it may happen when a domestic measure (be it legislation or otherwise) is thought to be in violation of international law as mediated by EU law: the EU may be

---

and likely manifestation. See also Jan Klabbers, 'International Law in Community Law: The Law and Politics of Direct Effect', (2002) 21 *Yearbook of European Law* 263.

[49] See eg Case C-162/96 *Racke v Hauptzollamt Mainz* [1998] ECR I-6133.

[50] See eg Case C-286/90 *Anklagemyndigheden v Poulsen and Diva Navigation* [1992] ECR I-6019.

[51] See eg Jan Klabbers, *The European Union in International Law* (2012). Note also that the EU's position has been characterized as 'exceptionalist', although ostensibly without pejorative connotations. See Magdalena Lickova, 'European Exceptionalism in International Law' (2008) 19 *European Journal of International Law* 463.

[52] The list is not exhaustive, but probably covers the most common situations.

a party to a Treaty which is not, or questionably, implemented. Fourth, action taken by one of the EU institutions may be considered in tension with the EU's obligations under international law. And finally, there is the infringement action: the Commission may start proceedings against a Member State for failing to live up to one of the EU's international commitments.

As far as the pure incidence of direct effect is concerned, the Court has been very reluctant to allow individuals to rely directly on rights granted in external agreements, with one broad category of exceptions: the association agreements, including free trade agreements and the so-called 'Europe' agreements which preceded full membership of the various eastern European Member States. This category of treaties was the first large group to reach the courts, and it is not impossible that the relative warmth with which the courts embraced these agreements has influenced perceptions.

The Court has, generally speaking, held in these cases that agreements concluded by the EU 'form an integral part of Community law'.[53] While their objectives may differ from those of the EU, and while such treaties need not be based on reciprocity, their provisions may nonetheless have direct effect, depending on the nature of the treaty concerned and on whether the provision concerned is sufficiently precise and unconditional.[54] Indeed, as Koutrakos has observed, with this class of treaties direct effect is effectively assumed and follows naturally from their purpose: 'To rule out the possibility of producing direct effect would be tantamount to ignoring its *raison d'être* as the foundation for gradual integration between the Contracting Parties.'[55] The possibility of direct effect even extends to decisions taken by bodies set up under such treaties (eg decisions taken by Association Councils[56]), and on some occasions such provisions have been capable of having horizontal direct effect, ie in relations between private parties.[57]

This generous approach could well have instigated some political unrest: it might entail, for example, the free inflow of migrants from associated countries into the EU. In such circumstances, the Court nevertheless was able to impose some limits, for example by means of limiting the scope of the provisions to be held directly effective,[58] or by insisting that within the field of operation of a directly effective norm, nonetheless the domestic rules on entry, work permits, and the like could continue to apply.[59] At any rate, these treaties are not all that disruptive of the legal

---

[53] See Case 181/73 *Haegeman v Belgium* [1974] ECR 449.

[54] See Case 87/75 *Bresciani v Amministrazione Italiana delle Finanze* [1976] ECR 129; Case 270/80 *Polydor v Harlequin* [1982] ECR 329; and Case 104/81 *Hauptzollamt Mainz v Kupferberg* [1982] ECR 3641.

[55] See Panos Koutrakos, *EU International Relations Law* (2006) 238.

[56] See Case 192/89 *Sevince v Staatssecretaris van Justitie* [1990] ECR 3641.

[57] See Case C-438/00 *Deutscher Handballbund eV v Maros Kolpak* [2003] ECR I-4135; Case C-265/03 *Igor Simutenkov v Ministerio de Educacíon y Cultura and Real Federacíon Espanola de Futbol* [2005] ECR I-2579.

[58] See Case C-416/96 *El-Yassini v Secretary of State for the Home Department* [1999] ECR I-1209.

[59] See Case C-268/99 *Jany and others v Staatssecretaris van Justitie* [2001] ECR I-8615.

orders of the Member States, having less far-reaching consequences than the EU treaties themselves; hence, their warm reception could easily be justified.

This stands in sharp contrast to the second biggest group of cases coming before the Court: those involving the General Agreement on Tariffs and Trade/World Trade Organization (GATT/WTO) law, in which, as is well known, international law is kept firmly at arm's length: the Court has steadfastly refused to provide GATT/WTO law with direct effect in the EU legal order. The decision in *International Fruit Company* set the tone: since the EU was not a party to the GATT, the Court first had to analyse whether the EU would be bound to begin with, and subsequently whether GATT law could be directly effective.[60] It established the bonds of legal obligation between the EU and the GATT by means of a succession theory:[61] by handing over exclusive competences to the EU, the Member States had intended to transfer their GATT obligations to the EU. Moreover, this was accepted by the EU's partners in the GATT, as testified by their behaviour. At the same time, the Court held that GATT law could not, based on the nature of the GATT itself, be directly effective: it left too much to negotiations and discretion. This then provided a brilliant result: the EU could shield itself against the foreign trade ambitions of its Member States, while simultaneously shielding itself against intrusion by GATT law into the EU legal order. And while some expected that the change from GATT to WTO would inspire a change in the Court's attitude,[62] this never materialized. The Court has remained insistent that WTO law leaves too much to negotiations to be considered directly effective,[63] even once the WTO has given its final decision on the compatibility of action with WTO law and the period of grace granted to members to rectify the situation has come to an end.[64] The policy rationale is clear: granting direct effect to WTO law would limit the discretion enjoyed by the EU's authorities in trying to negotiate a settlement within the WTO.[65] In addition, the Court has declined claims that cross-retaliation caused by the EU's violations of WTO law would engage the EU's non-contractual liability.[66]

---

[60] See Cases 21-24/72 *International Fruit Company NV and others v Produktschap voor Groenten en Fruit* [1972] ECR 1219.

[61] Also successfully applied in Case 38/75 *Nederlandse Spoorwegen* [1975] ECR 1439 (with again exclusive competence at stake), but rejected in later cases involving non-exclusive competences, such as *Intertanko*. For discussion, see Robert Schütze, 'The "Succession Doctrine" and the European Union', in Anthony Arnull, Catherine Barnard, Michael Dougan, and Eleanor Spaventa (eds), *A Constitutional Order of States? Essays in EU Law in Honour of Alan Dashwood* (2011) 459.

[62] See eg Joanne Scott, 'GATT and Community Law: Rethinking the "Regulatory Gap"' in Jo Shaw and Gillian More (eds), *New Legal Dynamics of European Union* (1995) 147.

[63] See Case C-149/96 *Portugal v Council* [1999] ECR I-8395.

[64] See Case C-377/02 *Leon van Parys v Belgisch Interventie- en Restitutiebureau* [2005] ECR I-1465.

[65] Moreover, none of the major trading blocs (USA, Japan) allows WTO law to be directly effective. Hence, the EU would place itself in a disadvantageous position vis-à-vis its competitors if it were the first to succumb.

[66] See Joined Cases C-120 and 121/06 P *FIAMM and others v Council and Commission* [2008] ECR I-6513. For discussion, see Anne Thies, *International Trade Disputes and EU Liability* (2013).

Still, over the years, the Court has developed three exceptions (if that is the word to use). Under the *Fediol* exception,[67] where EU law provides a remedy for violations by third parties of WTO law, this WTO law can be applied by the Court. Under *Nakajima*, the Court can also test the legality of EU law in the light of WTO law in situations where the EU law concerned is meant explicitly to implement WTO law in the EU legal order.[68] While these are useful exceptions, they have had fairly little practical impact: according to Mendez, only one subsequent claim has been upheld on either of these two bases.[69]

Of greater relevance then is the third exception: even where WTO law is not directly effective, existing EU law must be interpreted 'as far as possible' in harmony with WTO law. In other words, the Court has created a duty to interpret in conformity with WTO law (in *International Dairy Arrangement*), but as the caveat 'as far as possible' indicates, it is a duty of limited scope, leaving quite a bit of leeway.[70]

The remaining treaties to which the EU is a party form a relatively small group that has not yet given rise to much litigation. It comprises environmental treaties, maritime and other transport agreements and even the odd human rights treaty.[71] Here, the Court's attitude seems mainly inspired by the substance of the international norm concerned, and while not unwilling to accept international law, the international law at issue must improve on EU law or else be interpreted in such a way as to shield the EU from international responsibility. The Court has accepted the direct effect of a convention on air carrier liability, but in doing so refashioned the contents of the provision concerned in such a way that it remained compatible with the much stricter requirements EU law set on air carriers.[72]

In *Étang de Berre*,[73] the Court held directly effective a provision that called for a licensing system for the discharge of substances into waters that could affect the pollution of the Mediterranean Sea, in the expectation that since neither the French nor the EU authorities has established such a system (and no declaration concerning division of competences had been filed), the EU could possibly incur international responsibility. Here, then, direct effect gave domestic courts the tools to help enforce the underlying international agreement, and might therewith prevent responsibility from being incurred.[74]

---

[67] See Case 70/87 *Fediol v Commission* [1989] ECR 1781.

[68] See Case C-69/89 *Nakajima All Precision Co. v Council* [1991] ECR I-2069.

[69] See Mendez (n 5) 248.

[70] See Case C-61/94 *Commission v Germany* [1996] ECR I-3989, para 52

[71] The EU is a party to the Convention on the Rights of Persons with Disabilities, and is expected to accede to the European Convention on Human Rights. On the latter, see Jan Klabbers, 'On Myths and Miracles: The EU and its Possible Accession to the ECHR' (2013) 1 *Hungarian Yearbook of International and European Law* 45.

[72] See Case C-344/04 *IATA and ELFAA v Department of Transport* [2006] ECR I-403.

[73] See Case C-213/03 *Pêcheurs de l'Étang de Berre v EDF* [2004] ECR I-7357.

[74] The suggestion is made by Frank Hoffmeister, 'Curse or Blessing? Mixed Agreements in the Recent Practice of the European Union and its Member States', in Hillion and Koutrakos (n 13) 249, 265.

Most well known (though not a matter of direct effect) is how the Court held Ireland in violation of its EU law obligations when it brought cases involving the MOX plant to international tribunals other than the CJEU. While the UN Convention on the Law of the Sea, to which the EU is a party, facilitates this, the Court held that doing so would risk undermining the unity of EU law: since the UN Convention has become part of EU law, any dispute involving two Member States is a dispute under EU law, over which the CJEU has exclusive jurisdiction.[75] The case is arguably best seen as an example of the CJEU strengthening the position of EU law (however mediated) vis-à-vis its Member States, and something similar applies to the duty of consistent interpretation it posited with respect to the Aarhus Convention in *LZ VLK*.[76]

While the Court has long acknowledged that the EU is bound by customary international law, it is less adept at applying it in ways that international lawyers would recognize. In *Opel Austria*, the General Court felt the need to 'feign application'[77] of customary international law by channelling it through the EU law concept of the protection of legitimate expectations;[78] in *Abuja*, the same General Court made a curious category mistake, treating Greece's reluctance to uphold an agreement that explicitly provided for provisional application as a violation of the obligation not to defeat the object and purpose of a Treaty pending entry into force rather than as simply a breach of agreement;[79] and in *Racke* it saw nothing wrong with applying the controversial *rebus sic stantibus* doctrine to a situation where the Council had (partly) suspended the operation of a free trade agreement with Yugoslavia after the outbreak of hostilities in the latter.

Finally, sometimes the Court is asked to assess the effects of treaties to which the EU itself is not a party, but which binds all (or a large majority of) its Member States. Here too, the CJEU has been happy to sit on the fence, as exemplified by its consistent attitude towards the European Convention on Human Rights. Having initially found that EU law and human rights law had no connection whatsoever,[80] the Court later changed its approach and has found that the EU is bound to respect

---

[75] See Case 459/2003 *Commission v Ireland (Mox Plant)* [2006] ECR I-4635, paras 123–128.

[76] See Case C-240/09 *Lesoochranárske zoskupenie VLK v Ministerstvo zivotného prostredia Slovenskej republiky* [2011] ECR I-1255.

[77] The lovely phrase is Kuijper's: see Pieter Jan Kuijper, 'The European Courts and the Law of Treaties: The Continuing Story', in Enzo Cannizzaro (ed), *The Law of Treaties Beyond the Vienna Convention* (2011) 256, 271.

[78] See Case T-115/94 *Opel Austria GmbH v Council* [1997] ECR II-39. For extended discussion, see Jan Klabbers, 'How to Defeat a Treaty's Object and Purpose Pending Entry into Force: Toward Manifest Intent' (2001) 34 *Vanderbilt Journal of Transnational Law* 283.

[79] See Case T-231/04 *Greece v Commission* [2007] ECR II-63. On appeal, the ECJ seemed to decide on the basis of provisional application, using good faith (the idea underlying the obligation not a defeat a treaty pending entry into force) as an 'additional basis'. See Case C-203/07 P *Greece v Commission* [2008] ECR I-8161, para 64.

[80] See Case 1/58 *Stork v High Authority* ECR Special English Edition 17.

human rights and in doing so is inspired by the common constitutional traditions of its Member States as well as international agreements through which the Member States cooperate,[81] but it has declined the chance to give its approval to accession to the Convention.[82] Moreover, while occasionally willing to apply human rights law, it will do so explicitly by way of exception to the EU's own fundamental freedoms.[83]

Sometimes EU law explicitly aims to implement international law commitments of all the Member States. In such cases, while the CJEU considers itself justified in looking at the underlying Convention for inspiration and guidance,[84] it will stop short of applying the international norm or norms concerned if these are difficult to reconcile with EU law. This became abundantly clear in *Kadi*, where the Court (as is by now very well known) decided partly to invalidate a Council Regulation for being incompatible with the EU's system of fundamental rights protection, despite the Regulation being intended to implement a Security Council resolution. While substantively this has been heralded as a great step for human rights, there is nonetheless widespread recognition that in deciding the way it did, the Court fenced off EU law against intrusion by international law.

IV. Collision between EU Law and International Law

A different category[85] (but not entirely) is formed by agreements concluded between one or more Member States on the one hand, and one or more third parties on the other hand.[86] This is a different category mostly for numerical and internal EU reasons: Article 351 TFEU protects agreements concluded by Member States before the EU was created or before they joined the EU, but with large multilateral treaties this is a difficult rule to apply. By way of example, most Member States were parties to the ECHR before they joined the EU, but not all; Germany is a well-known exception. Hence, this would have the awkward result that the Convention would be

---

[81] See eg Case 4/73 *Nold v Commission* [1974] ECR 491.

[82] See Opinion 2/94 (*European Convention on Human Rights*) [1996] ECR I-1759; in Opinion 2/13, the Court held that the negotiated accession agreement was incompatible with EU law.

[83] See Case C-112/00 *Schmidberger v Austria* [2003] ECR 5659.

[84] See eg with respect to the 1951 Refugee Convention and 1967 Protocol, Case C-31/09 *Bolbol v BAH* [2010] ECR I-5539, and Case C-364/11 *El Kott and others v BAH* 19 December 2012.

[85] For a general overview of the different kinds of agreements that may be involved, see Allan Rosas, 'The Status in EU Law of International Agreements Concluded by EU Member States' (2011) 34 *Fordham International Law Journal* 1304.

[86] See generally Klabbers (n 5).

protected as far as most Member States would be concerned, but not with respect to Germany. This would mean differential treatment, and therewith be unpalatable. Consequently, in practice, Article 351 is mostly thought of as applying to bilateral treaties, although it is also applied to multilateral treaties establishing (or thought to establish) 'bilateralizable' legal relationships.

This approach is facilitated by the very first decision on Article 351 TFEU, in *Commission v Italy*.[87] Italy had invoked GATT rules in order to escape from EU law, but the Court wanted none of that, and firmly held that Article 351 TFEU existed to protect rights of third parties under international agreements, but did not exist to protect Member State rights. In doing so, it had to construe GATT as involving sets of bilateral rights and obligations, and this construction has stuck ever since, despite occasional feeble explorations of other conceptions.[88]

Consequently, Article 351 TFEU is not thought to apply to treaties concluded between Member States inter se, not even those concluded before the EU itself came into being: the provision serves solely to protect the legal interest of non-Member States.[89] Hence, the validity or legality of treaties between Member States inter se is usually considered solely from the perspective of EU law, regardless of their validity or legality under public international law. A good example is the *Pringle* case involving the 2011 European Stability Mechanism Treaty: at no point does international law feature in the arguments of the parties or in the Court's analysis.[90]

That said, the CJEU has been decidedly stingy in allowing 'anterior' treaties to continue to be applied. In many cases, any conflict between an international agreement and EU law has been 'defined away', with the Court in one case even going so far as to ascribe binding force to a later treaty that was still under negotiation.[91] In other cases it gratefully used the circumstance that an agreement had been amended at some point in time to disqualify it as anterior for purposes of the application of Article 351 TFEU,[92] and in yet other cases it left ultimate findings to the domestic courts that submitted the preliminary reference involving Article 351.

Moreover, the Court has been very strict in applying the second paragraph of Article 351 TFEU, which holds that Member States shall terminate all incompatibilities between the agreement in question and EU law. This involves at the very least a duty to

---

[87] See Case 10/61 *Commission v Italy* [1961] ECR 1.

[88] See in particular the conclusions of AG Warner in Case 34/79 *R v Henn and Darby* [1979] ECR 3795.

[89] See Case 235/87 *Annunziata Matteucciv Communauté Francaise of Belgium and others* [1988] ECR 5589.

[90] See Case C-370/12 *Thomas Pringle v Government of Ireland, Ireland, and Attorney General*, judgment of 27 November 2012. Much the same already applied to the Court's analysis in Joined Cases C-181/91 and C-248/91 *European Parliament v Council and Commission (Bangla Desh aid)* [1993] ECR I-3685.

[91] See Case 812/79 *Attorney General v Burgoa* [1980] ECR 2787. The later treaty between the EU and Spain would have abrogated the earlier one on which Mr Burgoa relied.

[92] It did so in most of the *Open Skies* cases, eg Case C-466/98 *Commission v United Kingdom* [2002] ECR I-9427.

seek renegotiation, and the practical feasibility of doing so is not considered much of an argument; in cases involving Portugal, the fact that treaty partners included states in serious disarray (Yugoslavia, Angola) did not soften the Court's stance.[93]

In the end, very few treaties (and thus treaty partners of Member States) have benefited from the protection seemingly so gracefully offered by Article 351 TFEU. In 2005, the Court held that an ILO agreement to which Austria was a party was protected, in that, like ILO agreements generally, it could only be terminated once every ten years.[94] More recently, in 2011, it held that an Investment Protection Agreement concluded by Slovakia with Switzerland was protected under Article 351 TFEU.[95] The matter was complicated as at issue was not just a bilateral treaty, but also a private law contract protected by that same bilateral treaty. Had Slovakia cancelled the contract (for running against an EU Directive), it could have amounted to unlawful expropriation, with the consequence that Slovakia could have faced a huge compensation claim. In those circumstances, it was perhaps better not to rock the boat and consider the Slovak–Swiss agreement protected under Article 351 TFEU. The Court's reasoning on this point is sparse, however; it is largely confined to noting that the agreement does not contain a denunciation clause.[96]

V. CONCLUSION

The position of the EU vis-à-vis international law has given rise, amongst academic commentators, to a variety of interpretations. Many have suggested that, traditionally, the EU has been open and receptive towards international law, and to the extent that the EU requires special protection, this stems from the circumstance that it is to be seen, in vivid terms, as the offspring of international law: it cannot (yet?) stand on its own.[97] Others suggest that the EU has traditionally been open and receptive, but that it has hardened its stance in recent years, as illustrated by decisions such as *Kadi*

---

[93] See Case C-62/98 *Commission v Portugal* [2000] ECR I-5171; Case C-84/98 *Commission v Portugal* [2000] ECR I-5215.

[94] See Case C-203/03 *Commission v Austria* [2005] ECR I-935.

[95] See Case 264/09 *Commission v Slovakia* [2011] ECR I-8065.

[96] Case 264/09 *Commission v Slovakia* (n 95) para 46. One cannot but wonder whether the circumstance that the EU is now itself empowered to act in the field of foreign investment helps explain the judgment: forcing Slovakia to depart from an investment contract for reasons internal to EU law might not inspire much confidence in the EU's investment practices. From a different angle, the two cases are seen as heralding a more internationalist approach on the part of the Court; see eg Magdalena Lickova, *La dynamique de la complexité en matière de relations extérieures des états membres de l'Union européenne* (2013) 305.

[97] See Christiaan Timmermans, 'The EU and Public International Law' (1999) 4 *European Foreign Affairs Review* 181.

and *Intertanko*.[98] The main proposition underlying the present chapter is, by contrast, that the EU has always employed an ambivalent attitude towards international law.

There may be good reasons for doing so. Not all manifestations of international law are morally commendable, as the *Kadi* saga has underlined,[99] and international law has the awkward side-effect of empowering national bureaucracies at the expense of democratic organs.[100] It is at least arguable that the CJEU has protected the autonomy of the EU legal order and the integrity of EU law at least in part for reasons of substance,[101] with EU law offering a higher level of protection to individuals or other concerns than the corresponding international norm.[102]

In those circumstances, slavishly following international law need not always be the preferred course of action, although for an entity that has always based itself on the rule of law, disregard of the law (no matter its source) may come at a price.[103] But whether or not international law is slavishly followed and adapted within the EU, it might be useful to offer an empirically solid perspective on the position of the EU vis-à-vis international law, and accept the EU's attitude as ambivalent rather than welcoming.

BIBLIOGRAPHY

Gráinne de Búrca and J.H.H. Weiler (eds), *The Worlds of European Constitutionalism* (2012)

Enzo Cannizzaro, Paolo Palchetti, and Ramses A. Wessel (eds), *International Law as Law of the European Union* (2012)

Viljam Engström, *Constructing the Powers of International Institutions* (2012)

Jan Klabbers, 'International Law in Community Law: The Law and Politics of Direct Effect' (2002) 21 *Yearbook of European Law* 263

Jan Klabbers, *Treaty Conflict and the European Union* (2008)

Jan Klabbers, *The European Union in International Law* (2012)

Panos Koutrakos, *EU International Relations Law* (2006)

Pieter Jan Kuijper, 'The European Courts and the Law of Treaties: The Continuing Story' in Enzo Cannizzaro (ed), *The Law of Treaties Beyond the Vienna Convention* (2011) 256

Mario Mendez, *The Legal Effects of EU Agreements: Maximalist Treaty Enforcement and Judicial Avoidance Techniques* (2013)

Allan Rosas, 'The Status in EU Law of International Agreements Concluded by EU Member States' (2011) 34 *Fordham International Law Journal* 1304

---

[98] See eg Gráinne de Búrca, 'The ECJ and the International Legal Order: A Re-evaluation', in de Búrca and Weiler (n 3) 105.

[99] Its most sophisticated international law justification to date is Antonios Tzanakopoulos, *Disobeying the Security Council: Countermeasures against Wrongful Sanctions* (2011).

[100] See eg J.H.H. Weiler, 'Dialogical Epilogue', in de Búrca and Weiler (n 3) 262, 263.

[101] See eg Wessel (n 15); also Jan Klabbers, 'The Validity of EU Norms Conflicting with International Obligations', in Cannizzaro, Palchetti, and Wessel (n 5) 111.

[102] This can be said to apply eg to *Kadi* (human rights) and *Intertanko* (environmental protection), and perhaps *IATA and ELFAA* (consumer protection) as well.

[103] See Klabbers (n 48).

PART II

THE ARCHITECTURE OF EU LAW

CHAPTER 4

....

EU COMPETENCES

EXISTENCE AND EXERCISE

....

ROBERT SCHÜTZE[*]

I. INTRODUCTION

....

WHAT constitutional principles govern the existence and exercise of Union competences? Article 5 TEU specifies three such principles:

The *limits* of Union competences are governed by the principle of *conferral*. The *use* of Union competences is governed by the principles of *subsidiarity* and *proportionality*.[1]

The first principle is the principle of conferral. It limits the existence of Union competences in two ways. Quantitatively, EU competences must have a limited material scope. Qualitatively, on the other hand, a particular competence type determines the legal ability of the Union to act within such a material field. These two constitutional limits to Union competences will be—respectively—discussed in Sections I and II.

Article 5 TEU however mentions two additional principles, namely, the principle of subsidiarity and the principle of proportionality—both of which limit the 'use' of Union competences. According to the principle of subsidiarity, the Union

* Thanks go to the editors, and the European Research Council. The research leading to this chapter received funding under the European Union's Seventh Framework Programme (FP/2007-2013) / ERC Grant Agreement n. 312304.
    [1] Art 5(1) TEU (emphasis added).

must act 'only if and in so far as the objectives of the proposed action cannot be sufficiently achieved by the Member States, either at central level or at regional and local level, but can rather, by reason of the scale or effects of the proposed action, be better achieved at Union level'.[2] The principle safeguards—like the principle of conferral—federal values. It determines which governmental level should exercise its competences, where both are equally competent. This contrasts with the third—and broader—principle of proportionality. The latter generally insists in Article 5(4) TEU that 'the content and form of Union action shall not exceed what is necessary to achieve the objectives of the Treaties'. The proportionality principle's traditional function within the Union legal order has been to safeguard liberal values, but it has also received a federal dimension. The two constitutional principles of subsidiarity and proportionality will be—respectively—analysed in Sections III and IV.

II. Conferral I:
Limiting Union Competences

Traditional international law considers states to be sovereign; and within a unitary state the government—in the broad sense of the term—is considered to be 'omni-competent'. When the British parliament legislates, it is thus regarded to enjoy a competence to do all things.[3] The European Union is however not a 'sovereign state'. It does not enjoy inherent—sovereign—powers. Its powers are *conferred* and limited powers. The constitutional principle that embodies this position is called the 'principle of conferral'. It can be found in Article 5(2) TEU, which states:

Under the principle of conferral, the Union shall act only within the limits of the competences conferred upon it by the Member States in the Treaties to attain the objectives set out therein. Competences not conferred upon the Union in the Treaties remain with the Member States.[4]

The formulation in Article 5(2) TEU suggests a picture in which the Union enjoys only those—limited—competences expressly conferred by the Treaties, whereas the

---

[2] Art 5(3) TEU.

[3] In the words of A. Dicey, *Introduction to the Study of the Law of the Constitution* (1982) 37–38: 'The principle of Parliamentary sovereignty means neither more nor less than this, namely that Parliament thus defined has, under the English constitution, the right to make or unmake any law whatever: and, further, that no person or body is recognised by the law of England as having a right to override or set aside the legislation of Parliament.'

[4] Art 5(2) TEU.

Member States retain those competences *not* conferred upon the Union. This picture is however seriously misleading, and that in two ways. First, the Union has historically been able to significantly 'expand' its competences into policy areas that were not expressly mentioned in the Treaties. In particular, the rise of teleological interpretation and the extensive use of 'general competences' have meant that the Union has come to enjoy a (bounded) competence to expand its own competences (Section 1). Secondly, it is incorrect to assume that the Member States only retain those competences not conferred in the Treaties. For with the exception of one very limited category of Union competence, the Union and the Member States 'share' their competences in such a way that they may both act in a field in which the Union is competent to act (Section 2).

1. Interpreting Union Competences

(a) Teleological Interpretation in General

If the Union must act 'within the limits of the competences *conferred upon it by the Member States*',[5] should this not mean that the Member States are able to determine the scope of the Union' s competences?

A strict reading of the principle of conferral would indeed deny the Union the power autonomously to interpret its own competences. Yet this solution encounters serious practical problems. For how is the Union ever to work if every legislative bill were to need the consent of every Member State? (Classic international organizations solve this dilemma in the following way: they allow international organizations a degree of interpretative autonomy but insist that the interpretation of international treaties must be in line with the clear—historical—intentions of the Member States.[6] Legal competences must thus be interpreted restrictively.) By contrast, a soft principle of conferral allows the holder of a competence to interpret its own competences widely. Instead of looking at the historical will of the founders, the Union is here allowed to use teleological interpretation. The latter looks behind a legal text in search of a legal solution to a social problem that may not have been anticipated when the text was drafted. Teleological interpretation may thus sometimes constitute a 'small' amendment of the original provision.

Has the Union adopted the strict or the soft principle of conferral? After a brief period of following the international law logic,[7] the Union wholeheartedly embraced the constitutional method of teleological interpretation. This technique can—for example—been seen at work in the famous controversy surrounding the

---

[5] Art 5(2) TEU (emphasis added).

[6] In international law, this principle is called the 'in dubio mitius' principle. In case of a doubt, the 'milder' interpretation should be preferred.

[7] See eg Case 8/55, *Fédération Charbonnière de Belgique v High Authority of the European Coal and Steel Community*, [1955] ECR 245.

adoption of the (first) Working Time Directive.[8] The Directive had been based on a legal competence within Title X on 'Social Policy'. That specific competence in Article 153 TFEU here allowed the Union to 'encourage improvements, especially in the working environment, as regards the health and safety of workers'.[9] But did it entitle the Union to adopt legislation on the general organization of working time?[10] Protesting that such a reading would undermine the principle of conferral, the United Kingdom strongly contested this teleological reading. Insisting that there was no thematic link to health and safety, it claimed that the Union legislator had acted *ultra vires*. The Court, however, did not think so and fully backed the Union legislator. The Court's endorsement of the use of teleological reasoning by the Union legislator was as follows:

There is nothing in the wording of Article [153 TFEU] to indicate that the concepts of 'working environment', 'safety' and 'health' as used in that provision should, in the absence of other indications, be interpreted restrictively, and not as embracing all factors, physical or otherwise, capable of affecting the health and safety of the worker in his working environment, including in particular certain aspects of the organisation of working time.[11]

This gave judicial permission to broad teleological interpretations of Union competences. In the past, the European Court has indeed accepted—almost[12]—every autonomous interpretation by the Union legislator.

(b) General Competences in Particular

The teleological 'elasticity' of Union competences is particularly high for the 'general' competences of the Union. These are competences that do not deal with a 'specific' policy area but rather grant the Union the power to act in the pursuit of a general Union aim.

---

[8] Case C-84/94, *United Kingdom of Great Britain and Northern Ireland v Council*, [1996] ECR I-5755.

[9] Ex-Article 118a (1) EEC. This competence is today Art 153(1)(a) TFEU, which allows the Union to support and implement the activities of the Member States as regards the 'improvement in particular of the working environment to protect workers' health and safety'.

[10] Section II of Directive 93/104 regulated the minimum rest periods. Member States were obliged to introduce national laws to ensure that every worker is entitled to a minimum daily rest period of eleven consecutive hours per twenty-four hour period (Art 3), and to a rest break where the working day is longer than six hours (Art 4). Art 5 granted a minimum uninterrupted rest period of twenty-four hours in each seven-day period, and determined that this period should in principle include Sunday. Art 6 established a maximum weekly working time of forty-eight hours. Finally, the Directive established a four weeks' paid annual leave (Art 7).

[11] Case C-84/94 (supra n 8), para 15. The Court, however, annulled the second sentence of Art 5 of the Directive that had tried to protect, in principle, Sunday as a weekly rest period. In the opinion of the Court, the Council had 'failed to explain why Sunday, as a weekly rest day, is more closely connected with the health and safety of workers than any other day of the week' (para 37).

[12] For an exception to the rule, see: Case C-376/98, *Germany v Parliament and Council (Tobacco Advertising)*, [2000] ECR I-8419. For a discussion of this case, see R. Schütze, *European Constitutional Law*, (2012), 158 et seq.

The two most general competences of the Union here are Article 114 and Article 352 TFEU. According to the former, the Union enjoys a horizontal competence to harmonize national laws so as to create the internal market. The latter allows the Union to act where it is 'necessary, within the framework of the policies defined in the Treaties, to attain one of the objectives set out in the Treaties, and the Treaties have not provided the necessary powers'.[13] Article 352 TFEU can thereby be used in two ways. It can be employed to supplement a policy title in which the Union is already given a specific competence, but where the latter is deemed—despite teleological interpretation—insufficient to achieve the desired objective. However, and more importantly, the horizontal competence can also be used to legislate in a policy area that has no specific title within the Treaties. From the point of view of the principle of conferral, this second use of the competence is of course the more dangerous one. For it allows the Union to enter into policy areas that theoretically are outside the Treaties.

How should we characterize Article 352 TFEU? The competence is a borderline provision;[14] and many a label has been given to it.[15] But does Article 352 give the Union a 'competence-competence'? The concept of competence-competence refers to the—sovereign—power to grant itself 'new' competences.[16] Does Article 352 come close to this idea? The traditional answer offered by European constitutional theory is a resolute 'No': since the European Union is not a (sovereign) federal state, it cannot have the power to grant itself new competences. However, once we abandon the (sovereignist) pre-conceptions of classic constitutional thought, a more nuanced evaluation might be in order. For is it not 'the very purpose of [Article 352] to bridge the divide between the [Union] objectives and powers through an *expansion* of the competences of the [Union]'?[17] Does a competence to act where the Treaties have 'not provided the necessary powers' not exhibit *some* characteristics of a competence-competence?

Some authors have—mistakenly—tried to solve this disparity between constitutional theory and practice by distinguishing between a legislative and a

---

[13] Art 352 TFEU (emphasis added).

[14] The wording of the provision is already paradoxical as it speaks of giving the Union a power where 'the Treaties have not provided the necessary powers'—suggesting that the Article would somehow be 'outside' the Treaty framework, (cf D.W. Dorn, *Art. 235 EWGV—Prinzipien der Auslegung—Die Generalermächtigung zur Rechtsetzung im Verfassungssystem der Gemeinschaften* (1986), 40–41.

[15] The provision has been—*inter alia*—described as a 'provision to expand competences' (cf BVerfGE 89, 155—*Maastricht*, 196: 'Kompetenzerweiterungsvorschrift'); '[an] instrument for extending [Union] powers', cf Tizzano, *The Powers of the Community,* in Commission of the European Communities (ed), *Thirty Years of Community Law* (1981) 43, 50); as well as an 'ad hoc procedure for granting new powers to the Community', cf A. Giardina, 'The Rule of Law and Implied Powers in the European Communities' (1975) *Italian Yearbook of International Law* 99 at 102).

[16] On the emergence of the concept in German federal doctrine, see R. Schütze, *European Constitutional Law,* (supra n 12) 55–56.

[17] L.-J. Constantinesco, *Das Recht der Europäischen Gemeinschaften* (1977) 278 (translation—RS).

judicial competence-competence of the Union.[18] But is the European Court not an institution of the *Union*; and has the Union judiciary not allowed the Union legislator—almost—complete freedom to interpret its own competences? Importantly, however, the Union legal order does accept some limits to the scope of its competence sphere.[19] The best label for Article 352 may therefore be *bounded* or partial competence-competence. This strange character of being a competence that is partly within and partly without the Treaty has been recognized by the German Constitutional Court;[20] and the 2011 British European Union Act equally insists that Article 352 should not be interpreted by the Council of Ministers—a Union institution—on its own and now requires prior ministerial authorization from the British Parliament.[21] From a national perspective, these procedural safeguards of federalism

[18] J. Weiler, 'The Autonomy of the Community Legal Order: Through the Looking Glass' in J. Weiler, *The Constitution of Europe* (1999). Weiler's analysis is inconsistent in a number of ways. First, it is already hard to accept that 'the ECJ, in adopting its position on judicial *Kompetenz-Kompetenz*, was not following any constitutional foundation but rather an *orthodox* international law rationale' (290–1, emphasis added). But how can we square this statement with the following assertion—only a few pages later—that within an 'orthodox' international organization 'should there be a disagreement over the interpretation of a clause within a treaty, an agreement of all parties will normally be the final word as either an authentic interpretation or a de facto amendment' (293–4)? If *that* is the orthodox international law doctrine, then the Court's judgment in Case 43/75 *Defrenne v Sabena* [1976] ECR 455 followed a constitutional rationale in that it opted against the 'ordinary' international law doctrine that permitted States to interpret 'their' Treaty. Be that as it may, a serious inconsistency arises with Weiler's second claim (312): 'The assumption that a [Union] without a legislative *Kompetenz-Kompetenz* cannot contain a court without judicial *Kompetenz-Kompetenz* . . . is false.' How can that be? How can one grant judicial *Kompetenz-Kompetenz* as 'the competence to declare or to determine the limits of the competences of the [Union]' (288) and yet, deny that if there is no other legal authority to set limits to the scope of its legislative powers, the Union can determine the limits of its legislative competences?

[19] Cf Opinion 2/94 (Accession by the European Community to the European Convention of Human Rights), [1996] ECR I-1759, esp. paras 29–30.

[20] In its Lisbon Decision, the German Constitutional Court referred to the 'indefinite' scope of Art 352 TFEU, whose use—coming close to a Treaty amendment—required the consent of the German parliament, see BVerfGE 123, 267 (Lisbon), para 328: 'Because of the indefinite nature of future application of the flexibility clause, its use constitutionally requires ratification by the German *Bundestag* and the *Bundesrat* on the basis of Art 23.1 second and third sentence of the Basic Law. The German representative in the Council may not express formal approval on behalf of the Federal Republic of Germany of a corresponding lawmaking proposal of the Commission as long as these constitutionally required preconditions are not met.'

[21] Cf European Union Act (2011), Part 1—Section 8 ('Decisions under Art 352 of TFEU'): '(1) A Minister of the Crown may not vote in favour of or otherwise support an Art 352 decision unless one of subsections (3) to (5) is complied with in relation to the draft decision. (2) An Art 352 decision is a decision under the provision of Art 352 of TFEU that permits the adoption of measures to attain one of the objectives set out in the EU Treaties (but for which those Treaties have not provided the necessary powers). (3) This subsection is complied with if a draft decision is approved by Act of Parliament. (4) This subsection is complied with if—(a) in each House of Parliament a Minister of the Crown moves a motion that the House approves Her Majesty's Government's intention to support a specified draft decision and is of the opinion that the measure to which it relates

recognize that a Union measure adopted under Article 352 TFEU comes close to a small and informal Treaty amendment.

2. Constitutional Saving Clauses

All policy areas outside the scope of the Treaties remain within the exclusive competence of the Member States. Yet, as we saw above, the scope of the EU Treaties has been dramatically extended over the years. Can we nonetheless find matters that fall *within* the scope of the EU Treaties but are constitutionally guaranteed to remain within the exclusive competences of the Member States?

From the very beginning, certain provisions within the Treaties could—theoretically—be read as constitutional guarantees for national exclusive powers. One of the potential candidates is Article 36 TFEU. The provision allows Member States to justify a violation of the free movement of goods on grounds of public morality, public policy and public security. But had these policy fields remained within the exclusive powers of the states; or, was the Union here also entitled to legislate? The European Court clearly rejected the exclusive competence reading in *Simmenthal*.[22] Holding that Article 36 TFEU was 'not designed to reserve certain matters to the exclusive jurisdiction of Member States',[23] it found that the States could not insist on their stricter national standards where Union measures provided for the necessary protection of the interests mentioned in Article 36 TFEU.

Reacting to this early defeat, the Member States increasingly tried to use subsequent Treaty amendments to insert provisions within Union competences that

---

is required as a matter of urgency, and; (b) each House agrees to the motion without amendment. (5) This subsection is complied with if a Minister of the Crown has laid before Parliament a statement specifying a draft decision and stating that in the opinion of the Minister the decision relates only to one or more exempt purposes. (6) The exempt purposes are—(a) to make provision equivalent to that made by a measure previously adopted under Art 352 of TFEU, other than an excepted measure; (b) to prolong or renew a measure previously adopted under that Article, other than an excepted measure; (c) to extend a measure previously adopted under that Article to another member State or other country; (d) to repeal existing measures adopted under that Article; (e) to consolidate existing measures adopted under that Article without any change of substance . . .'

[22] Case 35/76, *Simmenthal v Italian Minister of Finance* [1977] ECR 1871; as well as Case 5/77, *Tedeschi v Denkavit* [1977] ECR 1555.

[23] *Simmenthal* para 14. However, for a judicial 'slip of the tongue', see Case 265/95, *Commission v France* [1997] ECR 6959, paras 32–33: 'Article [34 TFEU] therefore requires the Member States not merely themselves to abstain from adopting measures or engaging in conduct liable to constitute an obstacle to trade but also, when read with Art [4(3) TEU], to take all necessary and appropriate measures to ensure that that fundamental freedom is respected on their territory. In the latter context, the Member States, which retain exclusive competence as regards the maintenance of public order and the safeguarding of internal security, unquestionably enjoy a margin of discretion in determining what measures are most appropriate to eliminate barriers to the importation of products in a given situation.'

aim to 'reserve' national powers within the Treaties. The insertion of such 'constitutional saving clauses' is well illustrated within the area of social policy, where Article 153(4) and (5) TFEU now state:

4. The provisions adopted pursuant to this Article:
   – shall not affect the right of Member States to define the fundamental principles of their social security systems and must not significantly affect the financial equilibrium thereof,
   – shall not prevent any Member State from maintaining or introducing more stringent protective measures compatible with the Treaties.
5. The provisions of this Article shall not apply to pay, the right of association, the right to strike or the right to impose lock-outs.

We find another illustration of general validity in Article 168 TFEU,[24] which commits the Union to 'respect the responsibilities of the Member States for the definition of their health policy and for the organisation and delivery of health services and medical care', and in particular excludes any Union measures affecting 'national provisions on the donation or medical use of organs and blood'.[25] This thematic exclusion is joined by a second constitutional exclusion. For the Union's public health competence only allows the Union legislator to adopt incentive measures 'excluding any harmonisation of the laws and regulations of the Member States'.[26]

What is the constitutional nature of these 'shall-not-affect' and 'excluding any harmonisation' clauses? Do they guarantee an exclusive competence to the Member States? The answer to this question depends on whether these 'savings clauses' only apply to the special competence within which they are placed; or whether they constitute a general constitutional limit to all the Union competences.

The Court seems to have expressed a strong inclination *against* the second—wider—view in *Germany v Parliament and Council (Tobacco Advertising)*.[27] The case involved a challenge to the adoption of the Tobacco Advertising Directive. Despite its public health aim,[28] the Directive had not been based on Article 168 but on Article 114 TFEU—the general harmonization competence

---

[24] The EU Treaties also acknowledge specific constitutional guarantees; see Protocol (No 35) 'On Art 40.3.3. of the Constitution of Ireland', which states: 'Nothing in the Treaties, or in the Treaty establishing the European Atomic Energy Community, or in the Treaties or Acts modifying or supplementing those Treaties, shall affect the application in Ireland of Art 40.3.3 of the Constitution of Ireland.' For an analysis of the 'Irish abortion' Protocol, see D. Curtin, 'The Constitutional Structure of the Union: A Europe of Bits and Pieces' [1993] 30 *CML Rev* 17, 47–49.

[25] Art 168(7) TFEU.   [26] Art 168(5) TFEU.

[27] Case C-376/98, *Germany v Council (Tobacco Advertising)* [2000] ECR I-8419.

[28] The Court freely admitted, '[t]he national measures *affected* [were] to a large extent inspired by public health policy objectives' (*Germany v Council (Tobacco Advertising)* (n 27) para 76 (emphasis added)).

of the Union. Germany objected to that competence and insisted—among other things—that the 'excluding any harmonisation' clause in Article 168(5) TFEU extended to Article 114. Could Article 168(5) TFEU negatively limit Article 114 TFEU? The Court disagreed. Article 168(5) TFEU did 'not mean that harmonising measures adopted on the basis of other provisions of the Treaty cannot have any impact on the protection of human health'.[29] '[T]he [Union] legislature cannot be prevented from relying on that legal basis on the ground that public health protection is a decisive factor in the choices to be made.'[30] The constitutional saving clause in Article 168 could thus *not* operate to limit Article 114; and if that conclusion were to be generalized, it would mean that the Union's 'saving clauses' cannot go beyond the scope of the legal base of which they form part.

In conclusion: the Union legal order has traditionally not committed itself to safeguard a 'nucleus of sovereignty that the Member States can invoke, as such, against the [Union]'.[31] There is no express constitutional recognition of a list of exclusive Member State competences. (Even if Article 4(2) TEU, reserves *national* security questions to the 'sole responsibility of each Member State', there is of course a *Common* Foreign and *Security* Policy of the Union within which national security concerns may need to be evaluated.) However, with the Lisbon Treaty another attempt at safeguarding national powers has been made in the form of Article 4(2) TEU. The provision aims at protecting the 'constitutional identities' of the Member States and reads as follows:

The Union shall respect the equality of Member States before the Treaties as well as their national identities, inherent in their fundamental structures, political and constitutional, inclusive of regional and local self-government. It shall respect their essential State functions, including ensuring the territorial integrity of the State, maintaining law and order and safeguarding national security.

The meaning of the clause is still highly controversial, and—despite some early pronouncements from the Court—it remains to be seen whether it will develop into a general external limit to all Union competences.[32]

---

[29] *Germany v Council (Tobacco Advertising)* (n 27) para 78.

[30] *Germany v Council (Tobacco Advertising)* (n 27) para 88.

[31] K Lenarts, 'Constitutionalism and the Many Faces of Federalism' [1990] *American Journal of Comparative Law* 205, 220.

[32] For an excellent overview of the potential functions of the provision and the early case law see B. Guastaferro, 'Beyond the *Exceptionalism* of Constitutional Conflicts: The *Ordinary* Functions of the Identity Clause' (2012) 31 *Yearbook of European Law* 263. For a case referring to Art 4(2) TEU, see *Sayn-Wittgenstein v Landeshauptmann von Wien*, Case C-208/09, (2010) ECR I-13693.

III. Conferral II: Classifying Union Competences

Why does the Union have different competence categories? The idea behind a typology of competences is to qualitatively limit a competence. Different types of competences constitutionally determine the 'degree' of power enjoyed within a particular policy field. An exclusive competence thus 'excludes' anyone else from acting within the same policy area. By contrast, a non-exclusive competence permits the co-existence of two legislators; yet it may limit one legislator to adopt supporting measures only.

What types of competences exist within the Union legal order? The original Treaties betrayed no sign of a distinction between different competence categories. Different categories of Union competence were only 'discovered' in the course of the 1970s.[33] The Treaties today distinguish between various categories of Union competences in Article 2 TFEU:

1. When the Treaties confer on the Union exclusive competence in a specific area, only the Union may legislate and adopt legally binding acts, the Member States being able to do so themselves only if so empowered by the Union or for the implementation of Union acts.
2. When the Treaties confer on the Union a competence shared with the Member States in a specific area, the Union and the Member States may legislate and adopt legally binding acts in that area. The Member States shall exercise their competence to the extent that the Union has not exercised its competence. The Member States shall again exercise their competence to the extent that the Union has decided to cease exercising its competence.
3. The Member States shall coordinate their economic and employment policies within arrangements as determined by this Treaty, which the Union shall have competence to provide.
4. The Union shall have competence, in accordance with the provisions of the Treaty on European Union, to define and implement a common foreign and security policy, including the progressive framing of a common defence policy.
5. In certain areas and under the conditions laid down in the Treaties, the Union shall have competence to carry out actions to support, coordinate or supplement the actions of the Member States, without thereby superseding their competence in these areas. Legally binding acts of the Union adopted on the basis of the provisions of the Treaties relating to these areas shall not entail harmonisation of Member States' laws or regulations.

---

[33] On this development, see R. Schütze, 'The European Community's Federal Order of Competences: A Retrospective Analysis' in M. Dougan and S. Currie (eds), *50 Years of the European Treaties: Looking Back and Thinking Forward* (2009), 63.

The Treaties here expressly recognize four general competence categories: exclusive competences; shared competences; coordinating competences; and complementary competences. Articles 3–6 TFEU correlate the various Union policies to a particular competence type (Section 1). These four general competence categories are joined by a separate competence category for the Common Foreign and Security Policy under Article 2(4) TFEU. The latter is but one expression of the special competence rules applicable in the external relations field (Section 2).

1. Internal Competences: General Rules

(a) Exclusive Competences: Article 3 TFEU

Exclusive competences constitutionally guarantee that only one public authority is entitled to act autonomously. For the European legal order, exclusive competences are thus defined as areas, in which 'only the Union may legislate and adopt legally binding acts'. The Member States will here only be able to act 'if so empowered by the Union or for the implementation of Union acts'.[34]

What are the policy areas of constitutional exclusivity? In the past, the Court has judicially qualified very few competences as exclusive competences. The first exclusive competence was discovered in the context of the Common Commercial Policy (CCP).[35] A second area of exclusive competence was discovered in relation to the conservation of biological resources of the sea in *Commission v United Kingdom*.[36] Article 3 (1) TFEU now expressly mentions five policy areas: (a) the customs union; (b) the establishment of the competition rules necessary for the functioning of the internal market; (c) monetary policy for the Member States whose currency is the euro; (d) the conservation of marine biological resources under the common fisheries policy; and (e) the common commercial policy.

In the past, the Court has interpreted these exclusive competences rather restrictively.[37]

(b) Shared Competences: Article 4 TFEU

Shared competences are the 'ordinary' competences of the European Union. Unless the Treaties expressly provide otherwise, a Union competence will be shared with

---

[34] Art 2 (1) TFEU.

[35] Opinion 1/75 (Draft understanding on a local cost standard) [1975] ECR 1355.

[36] Case 804/79, *Commission v United Kingdom*, [1981] ECR 1045.

[37] With regard to the CCP, this has even led to some 'deformations', cf R. Schütze, *From Dual to Cooperative Federalism: The Changing Structure of European Law*, (2009), 167ff. For a recent and restrictive definition of 'monetary policy', see *Pringle v Government of Ireland, Ireland and The Attorney General*, Case C-370/12, EU:C: 2012: 756, esp. paras 50 et seq.

the Member States.[38] Within a shared competence, 'the Union and the Member States may legislate';[39] yet, according to the formulation in Article 2(2) TFEU, both appear to be prohibited from acting at the same time: '[t]he Member States shall exercise their competence to the extent that the Union has not exercised its competence.' This formulation invokes the geometrical image of a divided field: the Member States may only legislate in that part which the European Union has not (yet) entered. Within one field, either the European Union or the Member States can exercise their shared competence.[40]

When viewed against the constitutional status quo, this is a misleading definition of shared competences. For in the past fifty years, shared competences have allowed the Union and the Member States to act *in the same field at the same time*. Indeed, depending on the political discretion of the Union legislator, the latter may decide to exercise its shared competences in three—typified—ways. Under rule preemption, the Union act will only outlaw those national norms that literally violate European law. Under obstacle preemption this is extended to national norms that violate the aim behind the Union act.[41] In both situations, Union and national law will however apply simultaneously in a given situation. By contrast, under field pre-emption the Union act excludes all national law within its field of application; and the formulation in Article 2 (2) TFEU appears to be exclusively based on that third pre-emption type. It seems to demand 'automatic [field] preemption of Member State action where the Union has exercised its power'.[42] However, this reading of Article 2(2) TFEU not only contradicts past constitutional practice,[43] it equally seems doubtful today, since the Treaties expressly mention the idea of minimum harmonization under shared competences.[44]

---

[38] Art 4 TFEU states that EU competences will be shared 'where the Treaties confer on it a competence which does not relate to the areas referred to in Art 3 and 6', that is, areas of exclusive or complementary EU competence.

[39] Art 2(2) TFEU.

[40] The Union may, however, decide to 'cease exercising its competence'. This reopening of legislative space arises 'when the relevant EU institutions decide to repeal a legislative act, in particular better to ensure constant respect for the principles of subsidiarity and proportionality'. See Declaration (No. 18) 'In relation to the delimitation of competences'.

[41] R. Schütze, *European Constitutional Law*, (n 12), 363 et seq.

[42] P. Craig, 'Competence: Clarity, Conferral, Containment and Consideration' [2004] 29 *EL Rev* 323, 334. The Treaties however clarify that such field preemption would 'only' be in relation to the legislative act (see Protocol (No. 25) 'on the Exercise of Shared Competence': 'With reference to Art 2 of the Treaty on the Functioning of the European Union on shared competence, when the Union has taken action in a certain area, the scope of this exercise of competence only covers those elements governed by the Union act in question and therefore does not cover the whole [competence] area').

[43] Cf R. Schütze, *From Dual to Cooperative Federalism* (n 37) Ch 4.

[44] See Art 4 (2) (e) TFEU on the shared 'environment' competence.

(c) Coordinating Competences: Article 5 TFEU

Coordinating competences are defined in the third paragraph of Article 2 TFEU; and Article 5 TFEU places 'economic policy', 'employment policy' and 'social policy' within this category. (The inspiration for this third category appears to have been the absence of a political consensus among the Treaty-makers. Whereas one group wished to place economic and employment coordination within the category of shared competences, an opposing view advocated their classification as complementary competence.[45]) The constitutional character of coordinating competences remains largely undefined. Articles 2 and 5 TFEU only tell us that the Union has a competence to provide 'arrangements' for the Member States so as to allow them to exercise their competences in a coordinated manner. The Union's coordination effort will thus typically involve the adoption of 'guidelines' and 'initiatives to ensure coordination'.

(d) Complementary Competences: Article 6 TFEU

The term 'complementary competence' is not used in Article 2 (5) TFEU. However, it appears to be the best way generally to refer to 'actions to support, coordinate or supplement the actions of the Member States'.[46] Article 6 TFEU lists seven areas: the protection and improvement of human health; industry; culture; tourism; education, vocational training, youth and sport; civil protection; and administrative cooperation. This should be an exhaustive list in light of the residual character of shared competences. The contours of this competence type are—again—largely unexplored but it appears to be a defining characteristic of complementary competences that they do 'not entail harmonization of Member States' laws or regulations'.[47]

2. External Competences: Special Rules

The Treaties do not generally distinguish between internal and external competences. (Within the areas of Union competences listed in Articles 3–6 TFEU, we do indeed find a number of external competences.[48]) There are however two

---

[45] Cf Convention Presidium CONV 724/03 (Annex 2), p. 68.   [46] Art 2(5) TFEU.

[47] Art 2(5) TFEU—second indent.

[48] eg the common commercial policy is listed under the Union's exclusive competences (see Art 3(1)(e) TFEU), environmental policy is listed as a shared competence (see Art 191(4) TFEU: 'Within their respective spheres of competence, the Union and the Member States shall cooperate with third countries and with the competent international organisations. The arrangements for Union cooperation may be the subject of agreements between the Union and the third parties concerned'); and public health is listed as a complementary competence (see Art 6(a) TFEU, and Art 168(3) TFEU: 'The Union and the Member States shall foster cooperation with third countries and the competent international organisations in the sphere of public health').

exceptions to this rule. First, Article 2(4) TFEU specifically isolates the Common Foreign and Security Policy (CFSP) competence from the ordinary competence categories; and secondly, Article 3(2) TFEU provides a source of exclusivity for the conclusion of international agreements that goes beyond the competence areas listed in Article 3(1) TFEU.

Let us look at both special constitutional arrangements in turn.

(a) The Sui Generis Nature of the CFSP Competence

What is the nature of the Union's CFSP competence? This has been a question ever since its introduction by the 1992 Maastricht Treaty. According to one view, the CFSP competence was a 'classic' international law competence that would not allow the Union to adopt supranational European law.[49] A second view, by contrast, argued that the CFSP competence forms part of one and the same European legal order.[50] The Lisbon Treaty has adopted this second view. While recognizing that the CFSP 'is subject to specific rules and procedures',[51] CFSP law will 'have the same legal value' as ordinary EU law.[52]

The Treaties nonetheless treat the CFSP competence as a distinct competence category.[53] In what way does it differ from the 'ordinary' competences of the Union? We may find a first answer to this question in Article 24 TEU. The provision declares that '[t]he adoption of legislative acts shall be excluded' within the CFSP area. What will this mean? If the reference to 'legislative acts' here simply formally refers to acts adopted under a legislative procedure, then Article 24 TEU would state the obvious. (Neither the ordinary nor any of the special legislative procedures apply within the CFSP.) If the formulation were however given a material meaning, then Article 24 TEU would signal that the competence could not be used for the adoption of generally applicable norms.

A second key to the nature of CFSP competences might be found in Declaration 14 to the European Treaties. The latter states that the CFSP competence 'will not affect the existing legal basis, responsibilities, and powers of each Member State in relation to the formulation and conduct of its foreign policy, its national diplomatic service, relations with third countries and participation in international

---

[49] M. Pechstein and C. Koenig, *Die Europäische Union* (2000), 5ff. The thesis that Union law differed from Community law had gained support from ex-Art 47 (old) EU, and Case C-402/05P, *Kadi and Al Barakaat International Foundation v Council and Commission*, [2008] ECR I-6351, para 202: 'integrated but separate legal orders.'

[50] K. Lenaerts and T. Corthaut, 'Of Birds and Hedges: the Role of Primacy in Invoking Norms of EU law' (2006) 31 *EL Rev* 287 at 288.

[51] Art 24 (1) TEU.   [52] Art 1 TEU and Art 1 TFEU.

[53] Art 40 TEU makes a clear distinction between the CFSP competence and 'the Union competences referred to in Arts 3–6 of the Treaty on the Functioning of the European Union'.

organisations'.[54] This formulation confirms the 'special' or 'sui generis' nature of the CFSP competence.[55]

(b) Article 3(2) TFEU: Subsequently Exclusive Treaty Powers

There exists a second exception to the 'ordinary' competence categories of the Union in the external relations field. It can be found in Article 3(2) TFEU, which concerns the Union's competence to conclude international agreements. It states:

The Union shall also have exclusive competence for the conclusion of an international agreement when its conclusion is provided for in a legislative act of the Union or is necessary to enable the Union to exercise its internal competence, or in so far as its conclusion may affect common rules or alter their scope.

The provision breaks the logic of constitutionally fixed areas of exclusive competence in Article 3(1) TFEU. It acknowledges the dynamic growth of exclusive competences in the external sphere.[56] According to Article 3(2) TFEU, the Union may thus 'obtain' exclusive treaty-making power in one of three situations. These three situations aim to codify three famous judicial doctrines.

According to the first situation, the Union obtains an exclusive treaty-making power when the conclusion of an international agreement 'is provided for in a legislative act'. This formulation has been called the 'WTO Doctrine'. For in Opinion 1/94 on the compatibility of the WTO Agreement with the Treaties,[57] the Court held that '[w]henever the [Union] has concluded in its internal legislative acts provisions relating to the treatment of nationals of non-member countries or expressly conferred on the institutions powers to negotiate with non-member countries, *it acquires exclusive external competence in the spheres covered by those acts*'.[58] The second situation mentioned in Article 3(2) TFEU grants the Union an exclusive treaty power, where this 'is necessary to enable the Union to exercise its internal competence'. This appears to codify the 'Opinion 1/76 Doctrine',[59] albeit in a much less restrictive form. Finally, the third situation in Article 3(2) appears to refer to the Court's famous 'ERTA doctrine'.[60] According to the latter, each time the Union 'adopts provisions laying down common rules', 'the Member States no longer have the right, acting individually or even collectively, to undertake obligations with third countries which affect those rules'.[61]

---

[54] Declaration (No. 14) concerning the Common Foreign and Security Policy.

[55] M. Cremona, 'The Draft Constitutional Treaty: External Relations and External Action' [2003] 40 *CML Rev* 1347 at 1354.

[56] For a criticism of this dynamic view, see R. Schütze, *European Constitutional Law,* (supra n 12), 203 et seq.

[57] Opinion 1/94 (WTO Agreement), [1994] ECR I-5267.

[58] WTO Agreement (n 57) para 95 (emphasis added).

[59] Opinion 1/76 (Laying-Up Fund), [1977] ECR 741.

[60] Case 22/70, *Commission v Council (ERTA)*, [1971] ECR 263

[61] *Commission v Council (ERTA)* (n 60) para 18—emphasis added.

IV. Subsidiarity: Safeguarding
Federal Values

In political philosophy, the principle of subsidiarity has come to represent the idea 'that a central authority should have a subsidiary function, performing only those tasks which cannot be performed effectively at a more immediate or local level'.[62] The principle therefore has a positive and a negative aspect.[63] It positively encourages 'large associations' to assist smaller ones, where they need help; and it negatively discourages the assignment 'to a greater and higher association what lesser and subordinate organisations can do' (Quadragesimo Anno, §79). The Union legal order recognizes the subsidiarity principle as a general constitutional principle governing the exercise of Union competences.[64] It can be found in Article 5(3) TEU, which states:

Under the principle of subsidiarity, in areas which do not fall within its exclusive competence, the Union shall act only if and in so far as the objectives of the proposed action cannot be sufficiently achieved by the Member States, either at central level or at regional and local level, but can rather, by reason of the scale or effects of the proposed action, be better achieved at Union level.

This definition states that the subsidiarity principle will only apply to the Union's non-exclusive powers. Unlike the principle of conferral, it is thus not a principle governing all types of federalism but it will only apply within a legal order based on a philosophy of *cooperative* federalism.[65] (Within such a system, two legislators can act within the same sphere, whereas dual federalism is premised on the idea that the Union and the Member States can only act within mutually exclusive spheres.)

The wording of Article 5(3) TEU is undoubtedly a textual failure. The Treaty definition in Article 5(3) TEU indeed recognizes two subsidiarity tests. The first can be called the *national insufficiency test*. The Union is here allowed to act, where the objectives of the proposed action cannot—in absolute terms—be sufficiently achieved by the Member States. The second test is a *comparative efficiency test*, according to which the Union should not act unless it can—in relative

---

[62] Oxford English Dictionary: 'subsidiary' and 'subsidiarity'.

[63] C. Calliess, *Subsidiaritäts- und Solidaritätsprinzip in der Europäischen Union*, (1999), 26.

[64] From the—abundant—literature, see only: G. Berman, 'Taking Subsidiarity Seriously: Federalism in the European Community and the United States' [1994] 94 *Columbia Law Review* 331; D. Z. Cass, 'The Word that Saves Maastricht? The Principle of Subsidiarity and the Division of Powers within the European Community' [1992] 29 *CML Rev* 1107; G. Davies, 'Subsidiarity: The Wrong Idea, in the Wrong Place, at the Wrong Time' [2006] 43 *CML Rev* 63; K. Lenaerts and P. van Ypersele, 'Le Principe de Subsidiarité et son Contexte: Étude de l'Article 3B du Traité CE' [1994] 30 *Cahier de Droit Européen* 3.

[65] On the meaning of that concept, see R. Schütze, *From Dual to Cooperative Federalism* (n 37), Introduction.

terms—better achieve the objectives of the proposed action. (The unresolved question arising from a combination of these two tests thereby is this: is the Union entitled to act where it is—in relative terms—better able to tackle a social problem, but where the Member States could—in absolute terms—nonetheless achieve the desired result?) And to make matters worse, the formulation 'if and in so far' in Article 5(3) TEU potentially offers two versions of the subsidiarity principle. The first version concentrates on the 'if' question by asking *whether* the Union should act at all (subsidiarity in a *strict sense*). The second version, by contrast, concentrates on the 'in-so-far' question by asking *to what extent* the Union should act (subsidiarity in a *wide sense*).[66]

In light of these textual ambivalences, two approaches have evolved to give concrete meaning to the subsidiarity principle. The first approach focuses on subsidiarity as a judicial standard, while the second concentrates on subsidiarity as a political safeguard of federalism.

1. Subsidiarity: A Judicial Safeguard of Federalism

(a) In General: (Legislative) Subsidiarity

What is the judicial content of the subsidiarity principle in the Union legal order? The principle of subsidiarity has remained a subsidiary principle of European constitutionalism. The reason for this shadowy existence lies in the absence of clear conceptual contours. The European Court has here primarily been responsible, since the Court has made a few—bad—conceptual choices, which have driven the principle of subsidiarity into a constitutional corner.

The Court seems to have taken the wrong turn in *United Kingdom v Council (Working Time)*.[67] The United Kingdom had applied for the annulment of the Working Time Directive. Its argument was twofold. First, it claimed 'that the [Union] legislature neither fully considered nor adequately demonstrated whether there were transnational aspects which could not be satisfactorily regulated by national measures, whether such measures would conflict with the requirements of the [Treaties] or significantly damage the interests of Member States or, finally, whether action at [European] level would provide clear benefits compared with action at national level'. Secondly and substantively, Britain argued that the principle of subsidiarity should 'not allow the adoption of a directive in such wide and prescriptive terms as the contested directive, given that the extent and the nature of legislative regulation of working time vary very widely between Member States'.[68]

---

[66] K. Lenaerts, 'The Principle of Subsidiarity and the Environment in the European Union: Keeping the Balance of Federalism' [1994] 17 *Fordham International Law Journal* 846 at 875.

[67] Case C-84/94 (n 8).   [68] Case C-84/94 (n 8) para 46.

How did the Court respond to both subsidiarity challenges? The Court offered an interpretation of subsidiarity that has structured the judicial vision of the principle ever since. It held:

> Once the Council has found that it is necessary to improve the existing level of protection as regards the health and safety of workers and to harmonise the conditions in this area while maintaining the improvements made, achievement of that objective through the imposition of minimum requirements necessarily presupposes [Union]-wide action, which otherwise, as in this case, leaves the enactment of the detailed implementing provisions required largely to the Member States. The argument that the Council could not properly adopt measures as general and mandatory as those forming the subject-matter of the directive will be examined below in the context of the plea alleging infringement of the principle of proportionality.[69]

This judicial definition contained two—fundamental—conceptual choices. First, the Court assumed that wherever the Union wished to 'harmonise' national laws, that objective could never be achieved by national action and thus necessarily required Union legislation. This view answers the national insufficiency test with a mistaken tautology: as only the Union can harmonize laws—*quaere*: what about international agreements harmonizing national laws?—the Union would pass the first subsidiarity test! However, had the Court now continued to adopt the broad subsidiarity version not much would have been lost. Yet this is where the Court took a second—bad—turn. For it decided against the idea of subsidiarity in a wider sense and relegated the review of the intensity of European legislation to the principle of proportionality under Article 5(4) TEU.[70] (And as we shall see below, it is there that the Court made a third important choice. In analysing the proportionality of the European law, it ruled that 'the Council must be allowed a wide discretion in an area which, as here, involves the legislature in making social policy choices and requires it to carry out complex assessments'. The Court would thus apply a low standard of judicial scrutiny that will be further discussed in Section IV.)

(b) In Particular: Executive Subsidiarity

The wording of the subsidiarity principle in Article 5(3) TEU refers to any action by the Union. This does include *executive* action.[71] The principle of subsidiarity,

---

[69] Case C-84/94 (n 8) para 47.

[70] Admittedly, case law has remained somewhat ambivalent on this point. While in some cases it has incorporated the intensity question into its subsidiarity analysis (cf Case C-491/01 *The Queen v Secretary of State for Health, ex p British American Tobacco (Investments) Ltd and Tobacco et al.* [2002] ECR I-11453, as well as Case C-55/06, *Arcor v Germany,* [2008] ECR I-2931), other jurisprudence has kept the subsidiarity and the proportionality principles at arm's length (cf Case C-84/94, *United Kingdom v Council (Working Time Directive)* (supra n 8); as well as Case C-103/01 *Commission v Germany,* [2003] ECR I-5369).

[71] C.D. Ehlermann, 'Quelques réflexions sur la communication de la Commission relative au principe de subsidiarité' (1992) *Revue du marché unique européen,* 215.

when applied to the executive branch, asks whether the Member States or the European Union will better achieve the administration of European law. Executive subsidiarity thereby operates *independently* from the principle's application in the legislative sphere. Thus, even when *centralized legislative* action by the Union is justified under the subsidiarity principle, the latter may nonetheless mandate the *decentralized execution* of European legislation by the Member States.

What criteria have the European Courts developed to clarify the contours of executive subsidiarity? Are they, perhaps, clearer than in the legislative sphere? The issue arose in *France Télécom v Commission*.[72] The French undertaking had been subject to a Commission investigation under Regulation 1/2003 and challenged its legality on the ground that the French competition authority would have been better able to deal with the case. The Commission, on the other hand, insisted that Regulation 1/2003 'preserve[d] the Commission's power to act at any time against any infringement of Articles [101 and 102]'. Moreover, 'where the Commission has competence to apply the [FEU] Treaty directly in individual cases, the principle of subsidiarity cannot be interpreted in a manner that deprives it of such competence'.[73] In its judgment, the Court—rightly—distinguished the Commission (preliminary) power to undertake inspections from the formal initiation of proceedings for the purposes of Article 11(6) of the Regulation.[74] Yet, it—wrongly—held that the subsidiarity principle could never limit the Commission's power to enforce the competition rules.[75]

The General Court's judgment represented a serious blow to the idea of an independent judicial analysis of executive subsidiarity. (The Court appears to leave executive subsidiarity completely in the hands of the European institutions. This reliance on the political safeguards of federalism is misplaced, especially in the context of the executive function.) For while Article 291(3) TFEU envisages 'mechanisms for control by Member States' as a general rule, these may not apply in specific executive regimes—like competition law. Indeed, the idea of an independent subsidiarity analysis for the executive function has been reinforced under the Lisbon Treaty. According to Article 291 TFEU, the Commission should only possess implementing powers '[w]here uniform

---

[72] *France Télécom SA v Commission*, Case T-339/04, [2007] ECR II-521. The case is extensively discussed by F. Rizzuto, 'Parallel Competence and the Power of the EC Commission under Regulation 1/2003 According to the Court of First Instance' [2008] *European Competition Law Review* 286.

[73] *France Télécom SA v Commission* (n 72) paras 72–3.

[74] A. Bardong, 'Article 11 of Regulation 1/2003' in G. Hirsch et al. (eds), *Competition Law: European Community Practice and Procedure* (2008), at 1645: 'As was the case under Art 9(3), Regulation 17/62, Art 11(6) is not triggered when the Commission merely initiates work on a case, or when it takes investigatory measures. It is clear that the Commission can exercise its powers of investigation before it formally opens proceedings.'

[75] *France Télécom SA v Commission* (n 72) para 89.

conditions for implementing legally binding acts are needed'. While this provision concerns the *competence* of the Commission to adopt executive acts, it betrays the clear intention to subject the executive function to a subsidiarity rationale. This idea would be undermined if the European legislator could transfer wide implementing powers to the Commission, the exercise of which would not be subjected to an independent subsidiarity review.

2. Subsidiarity: A Political Safeguard of Federalism

Due to the lack of judicial enforcement of the subsidiarity principle, a second approach gradually gained prominence. It is the constitutional attempt to develop subsidiarity into a political safeguard of federalism. This second enforcement method is embodied in Protocol (No. 2) 'On the Application of the Principles of Subsidiarity and Proportionality'. Importantly, the Protocol only applies to 'draft *legislative* acts',[76] that is, acts to be adopted under the ordinary or a special legislative procedure. Unlike the judicial enforcement of subsidiarity that theoretically covers legislative, executive and external competences of the Union, this second approach is thus confined to the Union's *legislative* competences. For these legislative competences, the Protocol establishes 'a system of monitoring'. Each Union institution is called upon to ensure respect for the principle;[77] and this means in particular that they must forward draft legislative acts to national Parliaments.[78]

How have national parliaments been involved in the subsidiarity review? According to the Subsidiarity Protocol, each national parliament may, within eight weeks, produce a reasoned opinion stating why it considers that a European legislative draft does not comply with the principle of subsidiarity.[79] Each parliament will thereby have two votes.[80] Where these negative votes amount to one-third of all the votes allocated to the national parliaments, the European Union draft 'must be reviewed'.[81]

---

[76] Protocol (No. 2) 'On the Application of the Principles of Subsidiarity and Proportionality' Art 3 (emphasis added).

[77] Protocol (No. 2) 'On the Application of the Principles of Subsidiarity and Proportionality' (n 76) Art 1.

[78] Protocol (No. 2) 'On the Application of the Principles of Subsidiarity and Proportionality' (n 76) Art 4.

[79] Protocol (No. 2) 'On the Application of the Principles of Subsidiarity and Proportionality' (n 76) Art 6.

[80] Protocol (No. 2) 'On the Application of the Principles of Subsidiarity and Proportionality' (n 76) Art 7 (1).

[81] For an analysis of the first activation of the yellow card mechanisms, see F. Fabbrini and K. Granat, '"Yellow Card, but no Foul": The Role of the National Parliaments under the Subsidiary Protocol and the Commission Proposal for an EU Regulation on he Right to Strike' (2013) 50 *CML Rev* 115.

This is called the 'yellow card' mechanism. For unlike a red card, the Union legislator 'may decide to maintain, amend or withdraw the draft'.[82] The yellow card mechanism is slightly strengthened in relation to proposals under the ordinary legislative procedure, albeit, here, only a majority of the votes allocated to the national parliaments will trigger it.[83] Under this 'orange card' mechanism, the Commission's justification for maintaining the proposal, as well as the reasoned opinions of the national parliaments, will be submitted to the Union legislator. The latter will then have to consider whether the proposal is compatible with the principle of subsidiarity. Where one of its chambers finds that the proposal violates the principle of subsidiarity, the proposal is rejected.[84]

With its adoption of the yellow (orange) card mechanism, the Lisbon Protocol has thus not followed the idea of a 'red card' mechanism. The rejection of a hard procedural solution has been bemoaned by some, who have argued that the chosen control method would 'add very little' to the political control of the Union legislator.[85] Others have—rightly—greeted the fact that the established mechanism leaves the political decision on subsidiarity ultimately to the European legislator. '[T]o give national parliaments what would amount to a veto over proposals would be incompatible with the Commission's constitutionally protected independence.'[86] Indeed, 'a veto power vested in national Parliaments would distort the proper distribution of power and responsibility in the EU's complex but remarkably successful system of transnational governance by conceding too much to State control'.[87] To have made national parliaments 'co-legislators' in the making of European law would have aggravated the 'political interweaving' of the European and the national level and thereby further deepened joint-decision traps.[88]

---

[82] Protocol (No. 2) 'On the Application of the Principles of Subsidiarity and Proportionality' (n 76) Art 7(2). The threshold is lowered to a quarter for European laws in the area of freedom, security and justice.

[83] Protocol (No. 2) 'On the Application of the Principles of Subsidiarity and Proportionality' (n 76) Art 7(3).

[84] Protocol (No. 2) 'On the Application of the Principles of Subsidiarity and Proportionality' (n 76) Art 7(3)(b) 'if, by a majority of 55 per cent of the members of the Council or a majority of the votes cast in the European Parliament, the legislator is of the opinion that the proposal is not compatible with the principle of subsidiarity, the legislative proposal shall not be given further consideration'.

[85] Thirty-third Report of House of Commons European Scrutiny Committee: Subsidiarity, National Parliaments and the Lisbon Treaty (http://www.parliament.the-stationery-office.com/pa/cm200708/cmselect/cmeuleg/563/563.pdf), para 35).

[86] A. Dashwood, 'The Relationship between the Member States and the European Union/Community' (2004) 41 *Common Market Law Review* 355 at 369.

[87] S. Weatherill, 'Using National Parliaments to Improve Scrutiny of the Limits of EU Action' [2003] 28 *EL Rev* 909 at 912.

[88] On the concept and shortfalls of *Politikverflechtung*, see F.W. Scharpf, 'The Joint-Decision Trap: Lessons from German Federalism and European Integration' (1988) 66 *Public Administration* 239.

V. Proportionality: Safeguarding Liberal (and Federal) Values

The principle of proportionality is one of the oldest constitutional principles of the Union legal order.[89] It began its career as an *unwritten* principle of Union law that prohibits the use of excessive power to achieve a desired end. The prohibition against the use of disproportionate power here applies to Union as well as Member State action. Since the 1992 Maastricht Treaty, the proportionality principle has been—partially—codified in Article 5(4) TEU. The provision states:

Under the principle of proportionality, the content and form of Union action shall not exceed what is necessary to achieve the objectives of the Treaties.[90]

Unlike the unwritten general principle, the codified version is thus narrower: it only applies to *Union* measures—and not national measures.[91] The proportionality review of Union measures however covers—in contrast to a subsidiarity review—*all* Union actions and thus includes Union measures adopted under an exclusive competence. And unlike the principle of subsidiarity, the proportionality principle is conceived as a *judicial* safeguard that is not complemented by a political control mechanism.[92]

1. Proportionality Review: Two Constitutional Functions

(a) Protecting Liberal Values: Fundamental Rights

The traditional function of the proportionality principle in the review of Union acts has been to protect liberal values because the prohibition against the use of excessive public power principally developed in the context of European fundamental

---

[89] An implicit acknowledgement of the proportionality principle can already be found in Case 8/55, *Fédération Charbonnière de Belgique v High Authority of the ECSC*, [1955] ECR (English Special Edition) 245 at 306: 'not exceed the limits of what is strictly necessary.'

[90] The provision continues: 'The institutions of the Union shall apply the principle of proportionality as laid down in the Protocol on the application of the principles of subsidiarity and proportionality.'

[91] The review of national law against the principle of proportionality cannot be rooted in Art 5(4) TEU but must be found in the unwritten general principle. For an express exclusion of this unwritten principle to certain national actions, see Art 276 TFEU.

[92] While the second indent of Art 5(4) TEU refers to the Protocol 'On the Application of the Principles of Subsidiarity and Proportionality', the *political* safeguards of federalism discussed above only apply to the subsidiarity principle—not the proportionality principle. On this point, see F. Fabrini and K. Kranat, 'Yellow Card, but no Foul' (n 81). The Protocol imposes a number of *justificatory* obligations on the Union institutions to explain the proportionality of the Union measure, yet, since these justificatory obligations are ultimately enforced by the Court, they are subject to judicial safeguards.

rights. The Union has here recognized that each restriction of a fundamental right must be 'proportionate' in relation to the public interest pursued.[93]

The application of the proportionality principle as a constitutional safeguard of liberalism emerged in *Internationale Handelsgesellschaft*.[94] The case involved the review of a Union measure that stipulated the forfeiture of a financial deposit for an import/export licence. Was this a disproportionate interference with the fundamental freedom of trade? The Court found that this was not the case. The intervention constituted a method that was 'both necessary and appropriate to enable the competent authorities to determine in the most effective manner their interventions on the market'; and the 'costs involved in the deposit [did] not constitute an amount *disproportionate* to the total value of the goods in question'.[95] Nonetheless, the Court had expressed a general principle: any Union act had to be proportionate in the light of affected private interests, and in particular, fundamental rights.[96]

This function of the proportionality principle as a constitutional safeguard of liberalism finds a special expression today in the EU Charter of Fundamental Rights. Article 52 of the Charter here states: 'Subject to the principle of proportionality, limitations [on the rights and freedoms recognized by this Charter] may be made only if they are necessary and genuinely meet objectives of general interest recognized by the Union or the need to protect the rights and freedoms of others.'[97]

(b) Protecting Federal Values: National Autonomy

The Maastricht Treaty and the introduction of Article 5(4) TEU have been said to add a federal dimension to the proportionality principle.[98] Following this view, the proportionality inquiry within Article 5(4) TEU is—partly or even exclusively—concerned with limiting the intensity of Union intervention in order to protect *national* regulatory autonomy. Despite arguments to the contrary,[99] the Court indeed—often—analyses the second 'subsidiarity' aspect within the context of the proportionality principle.[100]

---

[93] Case 44/79, *Hauer v Rheinland-Pfalz*, Case 44/79, [1979] ECR 3727, para 23.

[94] Case 11/70, *Internationale Handelsgesellschaft mbH v Einfuhr- und Vorratsstelle für Getreide und Futtermittel*, [1970] ECR 1125.

[95] *Internationale Handelsgesellschaft mbH* (n 94) paras 12–16 (emphasis added).

[96] See also *Nold v Commission*, Case 4/73, [1974] 491, ECR para 14; and *Hauer v Rheinland-Pfalz* (supra n 93), para 23.

[97] Art 52 (1) EU Charter.

[98] T. Tridimas, *The General Principles of EU Law*, (2007), 138 and 176: 'Art 5[4] was included in the Treaty primarily with a view to protecting the interests of Member States rather than the interests of the individual . . . This is not to say that the protection of rights of the individual is excluded from the scope of Art 5[4].'

[99] For my own arguments, see R. Schütze, *From Dual to Cooperative Federalism* (n 37), 263ff but see also: G. Davies, Subsidiarity: 'The Wrong Idea, in the Wrong Place, at the Wrong Time' (2006) 43 *Common Market Law Review* 63.

[100] Case C-84/94, *United Kingdom of Great Britain and Northern Ireland v Council* (n 8), para 47: 'The argument that the Council could not properly adopt measures as general and mandatory as

According to Article 5(4) TEU, the degree of Union intervention may thereby be limited with regard to the 'content *or form of* Union action'.[101] The former refers to the substance of the act, while the latter refers to the legal instrument of Union intervention.

With regard to the *substantive* intensity of Union intervention, we saw above, in our discussion of the subsidiarity principle, that the Court generally offers the Union legislator a wide margin of appreciation for (discretionary) policy choices. 'Judicial review of the exercise of that discretion must therefore be limited to examining whether it has been vitiated by manifest error or misuse of powers, or whether the institution concerned has manifestly exceeded the limits of its discretion'.[102] This constitutional choice in favour of low judicial scrutiny has been confirmed in *Germany v Parliament & Council (Deposit Guarantees)*.[103] The plaintiff had here argued that a Union directive violated the principle of proportionality, as it did 'not leave any room for the Member States to adopt "different approaches" in regard to the application of the Directive'.[104] The Court bluntly rejected the argument by simply pointing to the political decision to establish a particular level of (minimum) harmonization within the Union.[105]

What about the *form* of Union intervention mentioned in Article 5(4) TEU? The general proportionality reference in Article 5(4) TEU now finds a specific expression in Article 296 TFEU, which states: 'Where the Treaties do not specify the type of act to be adopted, the institutions shall select it on a case-by-case basis, in compliance with the applicable procedures *and with the principle of proportionality*.'[106] And while the proportionality principle is here theoretically free to operate as a liberal or federal safeguard, the federal aspect has dominated past discussions on the use of a 'proportionate' Union instrument.[107]

There is however little jurisprudence on the application of the proportionality principle with regard to the Union's choice of legal instrument. In *Portuguese Republic v Commission*,[108] a national decree had provided that certain airport charges were to

those forming the subject-matter of the directive will be examined below in the context of the plea alleging infringement of the principle of proportionality'.

[101] Art 5(4) TEU (emphasis added).   [102] Case C-84/94 (n 8), para 58.
[103] Case C-233/94, *Germany v Parliament and Council* [1997] ECR 2405.
[104] *Germany v Parliament and Council* (n 103) para 77.
[105] *Germany v Parliament and Council* (n 103) paras 82–84.
[106] Art 296 TFEU—first indent.
[107] The federal aspect of the principle of proportionality was expressly acknowledged in the Amsterdam Protocol on Subsidiarity and Proportionality. The relevant Art 6–7 read: 'The [Union] shall legislate only to the extent necessary. Other things being equal, directives should be preferred to regulations and framework directives to detailed measures . . . Regarding the nature and the extent of [Union] action, [Union] measures should leave as much scope for national decision as possible, consistent with securing the aim of the measure and observing the requirements of the Treaty. While respecting [Union] law, care should be taken to respect well established national arrangements and the organisation and working of Member States' legal systems. Where appropriate and subject to the need for proper enforcement, [Union] measures should provide Member States with alternative ways to achieve the objectives of the measures.'
[108] *Portuguese Republic v Commission*, Case 163/99, [2001] E.C.R. 2613.

be determined by a public undertaking on the basis of maximum take-off weight. The discriminatory pricing policy amounted to a state measure within the meaning of Article 106 TFEU and the Commission had issued a decision condemning the Portuguese system under Article 106(3) TFEU. Portugal brought an action for annulment of the State-addressed decision, alleging a violation of the principle of subsidiarity-proportionality: 'The Portuguese Republic contends that the Commission infringed the principle of proportionality laid down in [Article 5(4) TEU] by choosing from among the courses of action open to it that which was the least appropriate and the most onerous.'[109]

The Court was however not swayed. For it found that the Commission enjoyed a wide discretion in matters covered by Article 106 TFEU 'as regards both the action which it considers necessary to take and the means appropriate for that purpose'.[110] The following constitutional guidelines were nonetheless given for the choice between a directive and a decision:

[T]he choice offered by [Article 106(3)] of the Treaty between a directive and a decision is not determined, as the Portuguese Republic contends, by the number of Member States which may be concerned. The choice depends on whether the Commission's objective is to specify in general terms the obligations arising under the Treaty, or to assess a specific situation in one or more Member States in the light of [Union] law and determine the consequences arising for the Member State or States concerned.[111]

These were indeed not very clear constitutional guidelines; and we shall have to wait for better criteria on the application of the proportionality principle with regard to the choice of legal instrument.

2. Proportionality Review: Test(s) and Standard(s)

The idea of proportionality presupposes the existence of a test and a standard. The proportionality test comprises a number of questions as to the balance of values behind the Union measure, while the review standard represents the degree of judicial 'curiosity' with which that balance is questioned. These two dimensions of the proportionality inquiry are—relatively—independent.[112]

What is the Union's proportionality test? In its most elaborate form, the Court has used a tripartite test.[113] It analyses the suitability, necessity, and proportionality

---

[109] *Portuguese Republic v Commission* (n 108) paras 16–17.

[110] *Portuguese Republic v Commission* (n 108) para 20.

[111] *Portuguese Republic v Commission* (n 108) para 28 (emphasis added).

[112] After all, the fact that a student is asked three instead of two questions during an exam will tell us little about the rigour with which the separate answers are to be assessed.

[113] See Case C-331/88, *The Queen v Minister of Agriculture, Fisheries and Food and Secretary of State for Health, ex p Fedesa and others* [1990] ECR I-4023, para 13: '[T]he principle of proportionality is one of the general principles of [Union] law. By virtue of that principle, the lawfulness of the

(in the strict sense) of a Union act.[114] Within its suitability review, the Court explores whether the European measure was suitable for achieving a given objective. The measure must thus be in a 'causal' relationship with its desired aim. This is often straightforward.[115] The necessity test, on the other hand, is more demanding. The Union will here have to show that the act adopted represents the *least restrictive means* to achieve a given Union objective. This second prong of the proportionality test thus examines the *formal* 'excessiveness' of a Union measure. For in accepting the substantive degree of Union intervention, it formally enquires only whether the Union end could have been achieved by a less restrictive means. The third part of the proportionality test finally scrutinizes the substantive degree of Union intervention by reviewing whether the Union disproportionately interferes with—say—fundamental rights of Union citizens. Proportionality in a strict sense thus asks whether the Union end imposes *substantively* excessive burdens on individuals.

What standard of scrutiny does the Court apply to these questions? A court's capacity to review the exercise of legislative or executive power ranges from classifying it as a non-justiciable (political) question to fully substituting a political compromise with a judicial solution.[116] In between these two extremes exists a number of distinct review standards for particular contexts, such as external relations. For the Union legal order, the European Courts have traditionally distinguished between a soft and a strict(er) review standard depending on whether the Union enjoys a sphere of discretion. The legality of a discretionary act will indeed only be affected, where its disproportionality is 'manifest'.[117] The 'manifestly inappropriate' standard thereby cuts across the entire proportionality test. This can be seen in *Fedesa*,[118] where the European Court was called to review the legality of a Directive prohibiting the use of hormonal substances in livestock farming. The latter was attacked as an unsuitable, unnecessary, and disproportionate Union act; and the Court examined each single element of the tripartite proportionality test against its manifestly inappropriate standard.

---

prohibition of an economic activity is subject to the condition that the prohibitory measures are appropriate and necessary in order to achieve the objectives legitimately pursued by the legislation in question; when there is a choice between several appropriate measures recourse must be had to the least onerous, and the disadvantages caused must not be disproportionate to the aims pursued.'

[114] However, the Court does not always distinguish between the second and third prong, cf Case C-233/94, *Germany v Parliament and Council (Deposit Guarantee Scheme)* (n 103) para 54.

[115] For a rare example, where the test is not satisfied, see Case C-368/89, *Crispoltoni v Fattoria autonoma tabacchi di Città di Castello*, [1991] ECR I-3695, esp. para 20.

[116] For the various review standards developed by the US Supreme Court, see Footnote 4 of *United States v Carolene Products Company*, 304 U.S. 144 (1938), as well as L. Lusky, 'Footnote Redux: A "Carolene Products" Reminiscence' (1982) 82 *Columbia Law Review* 1093.

[117] See Case C-122/95, *Germany v Council (Bananas)*, [1998] ECR I-973, para 79.

[118] Case C-331/88, *The Queen v Minister of Agriculture, Fisheries and Food and Secretary of State for Health, ex p Fedesa and others* [1990] ECR I-4023.

(Under the 'manifestly inappropriate' standard the European Court rarely finds a Union measure to be disproportionate) Yet we can find an illustration of such a disproportionate Union act—even in the context of external relations—in *Kadi*.[119] In its fight against international terrorism, the Union had adopted a Regulation freezing the assets of people suspected to be associated with Al-Qaeda. The applicant alleged, inter alia, that the Union act disproportionately restricted his right to property. Finding that 'the exercise of the right to property may be restricted', the Court nonetheless insisted that 'those restrictions in fact correspond to objectives of public interest pursued by the [Union] and do not constitute, in relation to the aim pursued, a disproportionate and intolerable interference, impairing the very substance of the right so guaranteed'.[120] This required that 'a fair balance has been struck between the demands of the public interest and the interest of the individuals concerned'.[121] In the present case, this fair balance had not been struck for the applicant.[122]

VI. Conclusion

The European Union is not a sovereign state. (Its competences are limited competences, which must be conferred on it by the Member States.) This principle of conferral has nonetheless been dramatically softened in the Union legal order. For the Union is—within some political and constitutional limits—able to determine the scope of its competences itself. Teleological interpretation, in particular of its general competences, has thus provided it with a partial competence-competence. The erosion of the principle of conferral has however been partly compensated by the invention of various competence types that limit the Union's legal power—even if the precise constitutional contours of coordinating and complementary competence still need to be defined.

Article 5 TEU recognizes two additional constitutional principles that govern the *exercise* of Union power. (The principle of subsidiarity is designed to limit the exercise of non-exclusive Union competences to situations where the Union can demonstrate to be better able to solve a social problem.) The subsidiarity test provided in Article 5(3) TEU has however proven difficult to apply by the European Courts. In the absence of an objective definition, the Union legal order has tried

---

[119] Case C-402/05P, Kadi Council and Commission (n 49).
[120] Kadi Council and Commission (n 49) para 355.
[121] Kadi Council and Commission (n 49) para 360.
[122] Kadi Council and Commission (n 49) para 371.

to rely on the (subjective) political views of national parliaments. The principle of proportionality, by contrast, has had a distinctive judicial career. Designed as a judicial limit to excessive Union intervention, it has been developed into a constitutional safeguard of liberalism and federalism.

BIBLIOGRAPHY

G. Berman, 'Taking Subsidiarity Seriously: Federalism in the European Community and the United States' (1994) 94 *Columbia Law Review* 331

A. von Bogdandy and J. Bast, 'The European Union's Vertical Order of Competences: The Current Law and Proposals for its Reform' (2002) 39 *Common Market Law Review* 227

C. Calliess, *Subsidiaritäts- und Solidaritätsprinzip in der Europäischen Union* (1999)

V. Constantinesco, *Compétences et pouvoirs dans les Communautés européennes: Contribution a l'étude de la nature juridique des Communautés* (1974)

G. Davies, Subsidiarity: 'The Wrong Idea, in the Wrong Place, at the Wrong Time' (2006) 43 *Common Market Law Review* 63

G. de Búrca, 'The Principle of Proportionality and its Application in EC Law' (1993) 13 *Yearbook of European Law* 105

E. Ellis (ed), 'The Principle of Proportionality in the Laws of Europe' (1999)

R. Schütze, *From Dual to Cooperative Federalism: The Changing Structure of European Law* (2009)

R. Schütze, *European Constitutional Law* (2012)

A. Tizzano, 'The Powers of the Community' in Commission of the European Communities (ed), *Thirty Years of Community Law* (1981), 43

T. Tridimas, *The General Principles of EU Law* (2006)

CHAPTER 5

LEGAL ACTS AND HIERARCHY OF NORMS IN EU LAW

DEIRDRE CURTIN AND
TATEVIK MANUCHARYAN

I. INTRODUCTION

PRIOR to the Treaty of Lisbon, there was no formal hierarchy between the various acts of the European Union. Hierarchy is a ranking of acts according to 'the democratic legitimacy of their respective authors and adoption procedures'.[1] In other words, it is the supremacy of legislative over executive acts in case of conflict.[2] This chapter outlines the history and the objectives of the hierarchy of norms, which is now incorporated into the text of the Lisbon Treaty. It highlights the key legal issues that arise in relation to the current typology and ranking of the legal acts of the Union, especially in the light of the aims pursued by the Convention on the Future of Europe. Section II of this chapter focuses on the origins of the current hierarchy of norms. Section III provides an overview of the legal instruments

[1] Koen Lenaerts and Marlies Desomer, 'Towards a Hierarchy of Legal Acts in the European Union? Simplification of Legal Instruments and Procedures' (2005) 11 *European Law Journal* 744, 745.
[2] Lenaers and Desomer (n 1) 745.

of the Union in their pre- and post-Lisbon forms. Sections IV to VII discuss the three main categories of legal acts, along with a fourth category that appeared in the Constitutional Treaty but did not make its way into the Lisbon Treaty. Section VIII examines the extent to which the key objectives of the Treaty revision were achieved.

II. Hierarchy of Norms: Origin and Objectives

Proposals for the establishment of a hierarchy of norms in the Union legal order date as far back as the 1984 draft Treaty on European Union.[3] Those proposals resulted in Declaration No 16 which was annexed to this Treaty and provided that the 1996 Intergovernmental Conference (IGC) would examine the possibility of establishing a hierarchy between various categories of act.[4] The reports[5] of the Reflection Group preparing the 1996 IGC highlight the tensions that have characterized the debate on hierarchy of norms in the EU ever since. The reports indicate the division between two opposing camps. Those in favour of a hierarchy propose a ranking of acts based on their source of origin: constitutional, legislative, and implementing acts, as well as a clear division between the legislative and executive functions of the Community institutions. The main argument of those who oppose this hierarchical system is that it is 'based on the idea of separation of powers within a State, since this approach would transform the Council into a second legislative chamber and the Commission into the European executive'.[6] This second group favours maintaining the existing system of acts: Regulations, Directives, Decisions, and Recommendations. Thus, since the 1990s, debates on the applicability of the principle of separation of powers to the Union institutions have been closely tied to the discussion on the categorization and the ranking of Union acts.

The current hierarchy of norms in the EU legal order is primarily the product of the work done by the Convention on the Future of Europe (hereafter the Convention) between 2002 and 2003. Within the Convention, Working Group IX on Simplification focused on the simplification of the Union's instruments and

---

[3] Roland Bieber and Isabelle Salomé, 'Hierarchy of Norms in European Law' (1996) 33 *Common Market Law Review* 907, 921.

[4] Bieber and Salomé (n 3) 922, 907.

[5] Progress Report from the Chairman of the Reflection Group on the 1996 Intergovernmental Conference, SN 509/1/95 of 1 September 1995; Final Report of 5 December 1995.

[6] Final Report of the Reflection Group (n 5), Second Part, point 126.

procedures and the ranking of norms. The Working Group defined simplification as making the EU legal order more comprehensible to the citizens of the Union and providing 'a guarantee that acts with the same legal/political force have the same foundation in terms of democratic legitimacy'.[7] With regard to the question of how to simplify the Union legal instruments, the Working Group consulted three experts: Michel Petite, Director General of the Commission Legal Service; Koen Lenaerts, at the time, a judge at the Court of First Instance; and Jean-Claude Piris, Legal Adviser and Director General of the Council Legal Service. The final report of the Working Group was very much in line with the recommendations of Koen Lenaerts.[8] Lenaerts' view was that the distinction between legislative and executive acts

based not on the identity of the author of the act, but on the type of procedure followed for its adoption, is not so much inspired by the principle of separation of powers in a Union based on the rule of law, as it is concerned with the necessity to identify, in a transparent way, the procedure which is best suited—in terms of legitimacy and efficiency—for the exercise of the legislative and executive functions of the institutions of the Union.[9]

In accordance with Lenaerts' suggestions,[10] the Group proposed a hierarchy of acts based on adoption procedures rather than the identity of the authors of the acts; the classification of legislative acts as those which contain the essential elements of an area or, as Lenaerts termed it, 'basic policy choices'; and finally, the division of executive acts into two categories—delegated and implementing.[11] The outcome was the creation of three levels of hierarchy: legislative, delegated, and implementing acts.[12]

The hierarchy established in the Draft Constitutional Treaty[13] (hereinafter DCT) adopted by the Convention was very much in line with the recommendations of the Working Group—with one highly significant exception: in addition to Article 33 on legislative acts, Article 35 on delegated regulations, and Article 36 on implementing acts, the text of the DCT included a fourth category—Article 34 on non-legislative acts adopted by the European Council, the Council, the Commission, and the European Central Bank directly on the basis of the Constitution. This category also appears in the Constitutional Treaty[14] (hereinafter CT) in the form of Article I-35, yet it is entirely absent from the Lisbon Treaty. Given that non-legislative acts adopted directly on the basis of the Lisbon Treaty constitute a big proportion of the

---

[7] Final Report of Working Group IX on Simplification, CONV 424/02, 29 November 2002, 2.

[8] Carl Bergström, *Comitology: Delegation of Powers in the European Union and the Committee System* (2005) 339–340.

[9] Koen Lenaerts, 'How to Simplify the Instruments of the Union,' Working Group IX Working Document 07, 6 November 2002, 2.

[10] Lenaerts (n 9) 2–3, 5.   [11] Bergström (n 8) 339–340.

[12] Final Report of Working Group IX on Simplification (n 7) 9.

[13] Draft Treaty establishing a Constitution for Europe, CONV 850/03, 18 July 2003.

[14] Treaty establishing a Constitution for Europe [2004] OJ C310/01.

acts adopted by the Union institutions, the failure to include an explicit reference to this category of act is significant. It means that the hierarchy of acts in the Lisbon Treaty, unlike the one found in the CT, is incomplete as it fails to account for this second type of non-legislative act.[15] Apart from that, the ranking of legal acts in the Lisbon Treaty is largely the same as the one in the CT, with the categories of legislative, delegated, and implementing acts—in descending hierarchical order.[16]

The Convention's rationale behind this hierarchy of norms can be narrowed down to three key aims: simplification, democratic legitimacy, and separation of powers.[17] This is why a distinction was made between legislative and executive acts (through the introduction of the category of legislative acts) and why implementing acts were split into two distinct types (through the introduction of delegated acts). The question as to whether the aims of simplification, democratic legitimacy, and separation of powers are achieved is addressed in Section VIII.

III. Forms of Legal Acts of the Union

Article 249 EC listed the legal acts of the Community in the pre-Lisbon legal order. Its successor in the Lisbon Treaty is Article 288 TFEU. A comparison between the two shows that the *substance* of the new provision on legal instruments of the Union is not much different from that of its predecessor. The definitions of Regulations and Directives, Recommendations, and Opinions are exactly the same in both Articles. The only substantial change is in relation to Decisions.[18] In the pre-Lisbon legal regime, a second type of Decision (in addition to the one listed in Article 249 EC) was created. This was the *sui generis* Decision—without an addressee—also known by its German name *Beschluss*.[19] It was used for 'detailed institutional arrangements in the internal operation of the European Union, such as in laying down rules of procedure or setting up new committees or new administrative bodies . . .

---

[15] See Bruno de Witte, 'Legal Instruments and Law-Making in the Lisbon Treaty' in Stefan Griller and Jacques Ziller (eds), *The Lisbon Treaty: EU Constitutionalism without a Constitutional Treaty?* (2008) 79, 100–102.

[16] Paul Craig and Gráinne de Búrca, *EU Law: Text, Cases and Materials* (5th ed, 2011) 103. It must be noted that the *complete* hierarchy of norms (in descending order) is as follows: the constituent Treaties and the Charter of Fundamental Rights of EU; general principles of law; legislative acts; delegated acts; and implementing acts.

[17] Paul Craig, *The Lisbon Treaty, Revised Edition: Law, Politics, and Treaty Reform* (2013) 247.

[18] Edward Best, 'Legislative Procedures after Lisbon: Fewer, Simpler, Clearer?' (2008) 15 *Maastricht Journal of European and Comparative Law* 85, 87.

[19] Best (n 18) 87.

the adoption of the budget . . . as well as the multi-annual action programmes adopted in all kinds of policy areas'.[20] Article 288 TFEU now takes into account the existence of this second type of Decision: by referring to 'a decision which specifies those to whom it is addressed' it makes clear that there are also Decisions which do not have specific addressees. Thus, the new legal definition of a Decision actually includes two different instruments, which, while sharing the same name, perform quite different functions.[21] De Witte argues that this 'has rendered the instrument called "decision" more fuzzy by mixing together legal instruments which have little to do with one another'.[22] More specifically, he identifies two problems with this arrangement: the fact that the distinction between this new type of addressee-less Decision and a Regulation is not quite clear and the fact that it is uncertain whether this Decision is the same as the one used in the context of the Common Foreign and Security Policy (hereinafter CFSP).[23] As de Witte notes, this is probably not the case because Decisions within the meaning of Article 288 TFEU can have direct effect in the national systems—something that would not be desirable in the area of CFSP from the perspective of the Treaty drafters.[24] Moreover, were the alternative to be true, we would have acts with three different functions covered by the umbrella term 'Decision'!

The *number* of instruments, as listed under Articles 249 EC and 288 TFEU, has also remained the same. The issue, however, lies not in the instruments listed in these articles, but the ones that are utilized by the Union institutions without being expressly acknowledged in the provisions on legal acts. The *sui generis* Decision is one such act, which has now (somewhat problematically) found its way into Article 288 TFEU, yet the wide range of unlisted acts has been an issue since pre-Lisbon times, as illustrated in the following statement by the Convention Praesidium:

A range of more than 30 different types of act is the outcome of the addition to the initial catalogue in Article 249 of the TEC (decision, regulation, directive, recommendation and opinion) of a whole series of other instruments (guidelines, framework programme, implementing decision, etc.) to be found elsewhere in the Treaties. Yet more (decision as a general rule, declarations, resolutions, conclusions, etc.) have been added in practice. The pillar structure has also contributed to the proliferation of instruments by introducing types of act specific to foreign policy (common strategy, common position, joint action, etc.) and to cooperation in criminal matters (decision, framework decision, etc.).[25]

Although this description applied to the system under Article 249 EC, a close look at the text of the Lisbon Treaty reveals that the issue of unlisted acts persists. While the legal instruments of the former Third Pillar (now the Area of Freedom, Security and Justice) have been abolished and replaced by the 'mainstream legal

---

[20] De Witte (n 15) 82.   [21] De Witte (n 15) 95.   [22] De Witte (n 15) 104.
[23] De Witte (n 15) 96.   [24] De Witte (n 15) 90.
[25] Mandate of Working Group IX on the simplification of legislative procedures and instruments, CONV 271/02, 6.

instruments' of Regulations, Directives, and Decisions,[26] the same did not happen in relation to the former Second Pillar, ie the area of CFSP today. The 'Decision' within the meaning of Article 288 TFEU is (most likely) not the same instrument as the one used in the context of CFSP. Moreover, the CFSP Decision is an umbrella term, which covers a wide range of instruments applied in that area under the pre-Lisbon legal regime. In that sense, 'the terminological simplification is somewhat deceptive'.[27]

Finally, Regulations, Directives, and Decisions may take the form of legislative, delegated and implementing acts.[28] It follows that there are nine basic categories of binding legal acts (although the Treaty acknowledges other forms of binding acts, such as inter-institutional agreements under Article 296 TFEU, international agreements under Article 216 TFEU, and specific forms of act, such as the ones for budget matters under Article 313 TFEU).[29]

IV. LEGISLATIVE ACTS

Article 289 TFEU is the Lisbon Treaty provision on legislative acts of the Union. This category was first introduced in the DCT, in line with the recommendations of the Working Group IX on Simplification. Article 289(1) TFEU defines the ordinary legislative procedure (OLP), stating that the procedure is defined in Article 294 TFEU. Article 289(2) TFEU provides a basic definition of the special legislative procedure (SLP). It is notable that, unlike the ordinary legislative procedure, the special legislative procedure is not defined in detail in the Treaty. This is perhaps due to the fact that, in reality, it is not one procedure, but a collection of procedures.[30] The definition in 289(2) is far from clear: according to that article, '[i]n the specific cases provided for by the Treaties, the adoption of a regulation, directive or decision by the European Parliament with the participation of the Council, or by the latter with the participation of the European Parliament, shall constitute a special legislative procedure'. First of all, the term 'participation' in this article is not very telling. An examination of the Treaty provisions which provide for the SLP shows that what 'participation' really stands for is the 'consultation' or the 'consent' of the EP to be obtained by the Council or the 'consent' of the Council to be obtained by

---

[26] De Witte (n 15) 88–89.   [27] De Witte (n 15) 90.   [28] Craig and de Búrca (n 16) 104.

[29] Herwig Hofmann, 'Legislation, Delegation and Implementation under the Treaty of Lisbon: Typology Meets Reality' (2009) 15 *European Law Journal* 482, 486.

[30] According to Best, there are seven different kinds of special legislative procedure. See Best (n 18) 95.

the EP. It must be noted that in the majority of cases, the SLP entails adoption of acts *by the Council* after *consultation* of the EP[31]—something that is far from obvious based on the wording of Article 289(2).

The phrase 'in the specific cases provided for by the Treaties' also deserves special attention, as it gives rise to a very complex issue. The problem lies in the fact that there are numerous provisions in the Treaty, which provide for a procedure very similar to the SLP—without an explicit reference to a 'special legislative procedure'. Since Article 289(2) refers to 'specific cases provided for by the Treaties', the procedure in those Articles which do not refer to the SLP does not constitute a special legislative procedure.[32] To understand why this is very problematic, we must look at Article 289(3) TFEU, which defines legislative acts: 'Legal acts adopted by legislative procedure shall constitute legislative acts.' As is evident from the language of the article, the definition of legislative acts is very formal: they are defined in relation to their adoption procedure—not their content.[33] The two forms of legislative procedure applicable in this case are the ordinary and the special legislative procedures. Accordingly, Article 289(3), read in conjunction with 289(2), leads to the situation where an act adopted according to one of those provisions of the Treaty which do not explicitly refer to the 'special legislative procedure' cannot be classified as a legislative act.[34] This issue arises in the area of competition law: as the procedure prescribed by Article 103 TFEU is neither an ordinary nor a special legislative procedure, this leads to the problem of legal acts under Article 103 TFEU, such as Regulation 1/2003, not being viewed as legislative acts, even though they may be legislative in content.[35] The same problem arises in relation to Article 109 TFEU on state aid.[36]

The wording of the final paragraph of Article 289 is not as controversial as the ones discussed above. Nonetheless, it grants powers of initiating legislation to a group of Member States, the European Parliament, the European Central Bank, the Court of Justice, and the European Investment Bank. The Commission is no longer the sole initiator of legislation.

A second major issue in relation to legislative acts arises due to the fact that acts adopted under the special legislative procedure are categorized as legislative acts. Given that in most cases the SLP entails the adoption of acts by the Council, with mere *consultation* of the EP, these acts cannot be considered truly legislative—in the sense of the term used on the national level. Acts made under the ordinary

---

[31] Alexander Türk, 'Lawmaking after Lisbon' in Andrea Biondi, Piet Eeckhout, and Stefanie Ripley (eds), *EU Law after Lisbon* (2012) 62, 69.

[32] Craig (n 17) 257–258; Michael Dougan, 'The Convention's Draft Constitutional Treaty: Bringing Europe Closer to its Lawyers?' (2003) 28 *European Law Review* 763, 784; De Witte (n 15) 100.

[33] Craig (n 17) 256.   [34] De Witte (n 15) 100; Craig (n 17) 257.

[35] This example was first used by Dougan (n 32) 784; later, in relation to the Lisbon Treaty, by De Witte (n 15) 100; Craig (n 17) 257.

[36] De Witte (n 15) 101; Craig (n 17) 258.

legislative procedure are worthy of that name.[37] When an act is adopted by the Council based on the special legislative procedure that requires the *consent* of the Parliament, and when it is adopted by the EP with the consent of the Council, it may be called a legislative act. However, an act adopted by the Council only with *consultation* of the EP cannot be considered truly legislative[38] from the perspective of democratic legitimacy.

A related issue is the question of whether legislative acts are regulatory acts within the meaning of Article 263(4) TFEU. The current view of the Court is that they are not: this is reflected in *Inuit Tapiriit Kanatami and others v Parliament and Council*,[39] an action for annulment brought by Inuit seal hunters and trappers, organizations representing their interests, and individuals and companies involved in the processing of seal products.[40] The contested decision was Regulation (EC) No 1007/2009 on trade in seal products, which according to the applicants, was a regulatory act within the meaning of Article 263(4) TFEU. The General Court held that the meaning of 'regulatory act' for the purposes of Article 263(4) TFEU was 'all acts of general application apart from legislative acts'[41] and that the 'categorisation [of an act] as a legislative act or a regulatory act according to the FEU Treaty is based on the criterion of the procedure, legislative or not, which led to its adoption'.[42] It went on to dismiss the action as inadmissible on the ground that the contested Decision was not a regulatory but a legislative act, and that the applicants did not satisfy the requirement of individual concern. The order of the General Court was appealed,[43] but the ECJ dismissed the appeal confirming the judgement of the General Court. The fact that *all* legislative acts, regardless of their adoption procedure, do not constitute regulatory acts and, accordingly, cannot be challenged under Article 263(4) is problematic because legislative acts that are adopted according to the SLP with the *consultation* of the European Parliament are not 'functionally equivalent to national legislation'.[44] In the words of Türk: 'Acts of general application adopted in the special legislative procedure in which one branch of the legislative authority is merely consulted cannot occupy . . . a privileged position and should therefore be considered as regulatory acts within the meaning of Article 263(4) TFEU.[45]

---

[37] Türk (n 31) 69.   [38] Türk (n 31) 69–70.

[39] Case T-18/10 *Inuit Tapiriit Kanatami and others v Parliament and Council* [2011] ECR II-05599.

[40] Steve Peers and Marios Costa, 'Court of Justice of the European Union (General Chamber), Judicial review of EU Acts after the Treaty of Lisbon; Order of 6 September 2011, Case T-18/10 Inuit Tapiriit Kanatami and Others v. Commission & Judgment of 25 October 2011, Case T-262/10 Microban v. Commission' (2012) 8 *European Constitutional Law Review* 82, 87.

[41] Case T-18/10 *Inuit* (n 39) para 56.   [42] Case T-18/10 *Inuit* (n 39) para 65.

[43] Case C-583/11 P *Inuit Tapiriit Kanatami and others v Parliament and Council*, judgment of 3 October 2013.

[44] Türk (n 31) 73.   [45] Türk (n 31) 73.

V. Delegated Acts

As mentioned earlier, the category of delegated acts was one of the novelties introduced by the European Convention. Prior to the Treaty of Lisbon, no distinction was made between different types of executive act, ie 'delegation of normative powers and implementation in the sense of execution'.[46] Instead, legal acts were classified either as 'primary' legal acts or as 'secondary' legal measures that implemented the primary measures.[47] The key provision with regard to executive rule making was Article 202 EC, which provided for the conferral of implementing powers by the Council on the Commission under the control of the Council. It also stated that in specific cases the Council had the right 'to exercise directly implementing powers itself'. The new articles governing executive acts in the Union—290 and 291 TFEU—are quite different from the system under Article 202 EC.

Article 290(1) TFEU states: 'A legislative act may delegate to the Commission the power to adopt non-legislative acts of general application to supplement or amend certain non-essential elements of the legislative act.' First of all, it is clear from the wording of the article that delegated acts may be based only on *legislative* acts. Next, it is evident from the specific reference to the Commission that the Council can no longer enact acts of quasi-legislative nature, and that this is the prerogative of the Commission. This reflects the objective of separation of powers pursued by the European Convention.[48] Third, the meanings of 'supplement' and 'amend' and 'non-essential elements' are of particular interest to us as their ambiguity has led to a number of legal debates and disputes. The meaning of 'amend' and 'supplement' is important for the purposes of distinguishing between delegated and implementing acts.[49] The term 'amend' is clearer than 'supplement'; therefore, it is the latter term that will be a determining factor for the distinction between the two forms of act.[50] Based on the application of these terms in the 1999 Comitology Decision[51] and the 2006 amended Decision,[52] it can be argued that 'amend' is the deletion of non-essential elements, while 'supplement' is the addition of non-essential elements to a legislative act.[53] However, scholars question the purpose of 'supplement' given that the term 'amend' may cover both additions and deletions.[54]

---

[46] Opinion of AG Jääskinen of 12 September 2013 in Case C-270/12 *United Kingdom v Council and Parliament*, footnote 98 of the Opinion.

[47] Craig and de Búrca (n 16) 114.   [48] Bergström (n 8) 345.   [49] Craig (n 17) 276.

[50] Craig (n 17) 276.

[51] Council Decision 1999/468/EC laying down the procedures for the exercise of implementing powers conferred on the Commission [1999] OJ L184/23.

[52] Council Decision 2006/512/EC amending Decision 1999/468/EC laying down the procedures for the exercise of implementing powers conferred on the Commission [2006] OJ L200/11.

[53] Craig (n 17) 276.   [54] Craig (n 17) 276.

With respect to 'non-essential elements' and 'essential elements' in the first and second paragraphs of Article 290(1) TFEU, the *Köster* line of case law[55] is relevant.[56] More recently, a certain degree of clarification was provided in the case *Parliament v Council*.[57] This was an action for annulment brought by the European Parliament against the Council. The measure to be annulled was Council Decision 2010/252/EU supplementing the Schengen Borders Code (SBC). The EP argued that the contested Decision went beyond the limits of the implementing powers laid down in Article 12(5) of the Borders Code. The Court annulled the Decision in its entirety 'because it [contained] essential elements of the surveillance of the sea external borders of the Member States which [went] beyond the scope of the additional measures within the meaning of Article 12(5) of the SBC, and only the European Union legislature was entitled to adopt such a decision'.[58] Even though the facts of that case took place prior to the entry into force of the Lisbon Treaty, it is considered relevant for the interpretation of Article 290(1) TFEU.[59] In *Parliament v Council*, the Court tied 'essential elements' to 'political choices' that involve reconciliation of conflicting interests.[60] In the Court's view, a measure entails political choices when it is liable to interfere with 'the sovereign rights of third countries' or the fundamental rights of persons.[61] The Court's reference to the 'extent' of interference with fundamental rights indicates that the assessment of the essentiality of an element may depend on the level of interference.[62] All of these observations may shed light on the meaning of 'non-essential elements' and 'essential elements' in the context of Article 290(1).[63]

The effectiveness of the *ex ante* and *ex post* controls (over powers delegated to the Commission) contained in Article 290(1) and (2) TFEU are also subject to considerable debate in the legal literature. Regarding the *ex ante* control mechanism, Article 290(1) provides that '[t]he objectives, content, scope and duration of the delegation of power shall be explicitly defined in the legislative acts'. As to the *ex post* controls, Article 290(2) states that:

---

[55] In particular, Case 25/70 *Einfuhr und Vorratsstelle v Köster* [1970] ECR 1161; Case C-240/90 *Germany v Commission* [1992] ECR I-5383; and Case C-417/93 *Parliament v Council* [1995] ECR I-1185.

[56] Opinion of AG Mengozzi of 17 April 2012 in Case C-355/10 *Parliament v Council*, footnote 32 of Opinion.

[57] Case C-355/10 *Parliament v Council*, judgment of 5 September 2012.

[58] Case C-355/10 *Parliament v Council* (n 57) para 84.

[59] Maarten den Heijer and Eljalill Tauschinsky, 'Where Human Rights Meet Administrative Law: Essential Elements and Limits to Delegation: European Court of Justice, Grand Chamber C-355/10: European Parliament v. Council of the European Union' (2013) 9 *European Constitutional Law Review* 513, 514; Merijn Chamon, 'How the Concept of Essential Elements of a Legislative Act Continues to Elude the Court. Parliament v. Council' (2013) 50 *Common Market Law Review* 849.

[60] Case C-355/10 *Parliament v Council* (n 57) para 76.

[61] Case C-355/10 *Parliament v Council* (n 57) paras 76–78; see also den Heijer and Tauschinsky (n 59) 526–527.

[62] Den Heijer and Tauschinsky (n 59) 527.

[63] For a view that the Court did not add much clarity to the concept of essential elements, see Chamon (n 59) 858–859.

Legislative acts shall explicitly lay down the conditions to which the delegation is subject; these conditions may be as follows: (a) the European Parliament or the Council may decide to revoke the delegation; (b) the delegated act may enter into force only if no objection has been expressed by the European Parliament or the Council within a period set by the legislative act.

Since in the pre-Lisbon legal order, there was no distinction between delegated and implementing acts, what are now delegated acts, just like purely implementing measures, were subject to the comitology controls. As comitology procedures are no longer applicable in relation to delegated acts, the major question is whether the current system of *ex ante* and *ex post* controls is more or less effective than the controls under the comitology system. Opinions vary with regard to the discontinuance of comitology in this area.

Craig views it as a negative development because he doubts the efficiency of the current controls.[64] According to him, the comitology system 'allowed for regularized, general and detailed input into the content of [delegated] norms by Member State representatives, with increasing control exercised by the EP, more especially since the 2006 reforms'.[65] In contrast, the *ex ante* controls provided in Article 290 TFEU may be difficult to exercise, in practice because the Council and the European Parliament 'will often have neither the knowledge, nor the time to delineate precise parameters for the exercise of delegated regulatory choices in the legislative act'.[66] According to this perspective, comitology committees served as very important sources of information both for the Council and the EP.[67] Now that they can no longer serve this function, the Council and the EP will have instead to rely on information indirectly obtained from expert groups—advisory bodies, which will provide technical knowledge to the Commission in the drafting of delegated acts.[68] However, with these advisory bodies 'there is no certainty that the EP would be able to access any information about the content of the delegated act in the manner that it has done hitherto'.[69] Another compelling argument brought forward by Craig is that under Article 202 EC, comitology was primarily used for acts that would be the equivalent of *delegated* rather than implementing acts.[70] However, at the Convention on the Future of Europe, an important shift occurred: comitology procedures were no longer conceived as control mechanisms in the making of delegated acts although this would have been 'the true analogy with the status quo ante'.[71] Instead, comitology controls were to be exercised only in relation to

[64] Paul Craig, 'The Role of the European Parliament under the Lisbon Treaty' in Stefan Griller and Jacques Ziller (eds), *The Lisbon Treaty: EU Constitutionalism without a Constitutional Treaty?* (2008) 109, 115–119.

[65] Craig (n 64) 115.   [66] Craig (n 17) 267.   [67] Craig (n 64) 118.

[68] For the Commission's statement regarding the consultation of expert groups, see: Communication from the Commission to the European Parliament and the Council 'Implementation of Article 290 of the Treaty on the Functioning of the European Union' Brussels 9.12.2009 COM(2009) 673 final, 6–7.

[69] Craig (n 64) 118.   [70] Craig (n 64) 124.   [71] Craig (n 64) 124.

implementing acts 'even though this was in stark contrast to the circumstances where Comitology [applied at the time]'.[72]

Peers and Costa also find the current control mechanisms more problematic than the previous comitology system.[73] According to them, accountability problems arise from the fact that expert groups have replaced comitology committees as sources of expertise for the Commission and as suppliers of information (required effectively to control delegated rule making by the Commission) for the Council and the EP.[74] While expert groups do not have any formal voting powers and function only as advisory bodies, they play a crucial role in the making of draft delegated acts 'by providing the essential scientific knowledge and expertise required for preparing the Commission's proposals'.[75] Yet the delegated acts procedure does not function within a predefined framework as is the case with implementing acts—adopted according to the rules of the Comitology Regulation[76] now enacted jointly by the Council and the EP.[77] The Common Understanding—negotiated between the Commission, the EP and the Council—does govern certain practical aspects of the delegated acts procedure, yet it only refers to the expert groups in passing, simply stating that '[t]he Commission . . . will . . . carry out appropriate and transparent consultations well in advance, including at expert level'.[78] Thus, unlike comitology committees, expert groups are not subject to any transparency or accountability standards, and very little is known about their exact number, composition, and meetings.[79] This is unacceptable, especially in view of 'serious allegations of a systemic corporate bias in the membership of [these] groups'[80] and in view of the Commission's intention to continue consulting expert groups in the important field of financial services.[81]

On the opposite end of the spectrum is Ponzano, who argues that even though the comitology system was efficient, from the point of view of democracy this 'anomaly' in the Union's decision making had to be modified.[82] According to

[72] Craig (n 64) 125.

[73] Steve Peers and Marios Costa, 'Accountability for Delegated and Implementing Acts after the Treaty of Lisbon' (2012) 18 *European Law Journal* 427, 455, 460.

[74] Peers and Costa (n 73) 453.   [75] Peers and Costa (n 73) 454.

[76] Regulation (EU) No 182/2011 of the European Parliament and of the Council laying down the rules and general principles concerning mechanisms for control by Member States of the Commission's exercise of implementing powers [2011] OJ L55/13.

[77] Peers and Costa (n 73) 448.

[78] Common Understanding: Delegated Acts, Council doc. 8753/11, 10 April 2011, point 4.

[79] Peers and Costa (n 73) 454.   [80] Peers and Costa (n 73) 454–455.

[81] Communication from the Commission (n 68) 7; see also Declaration on Article 290 of the Treaty on the Functioning of the European Union, Declarations Annexed to the Final Act of the Intergovernmental Conference which Adopted the Treaty of Lisbon, signed on 13 December 2007 [2012] OJ C326/352.

[82] Paolo Ponzano, '"Executive" and "Delegated" Acts: The Situation after the Lisbon Treaty' in Stefan Griller and Jacques Ziller (eds), *The Lisbon Treaty: EU Constitutionalism without a Constitutional Treaty?* (2008) 135, 141.

Ponzano, when the executive acts in the area of competence of the legislator, 'legislative delegation' is the right choice. More specifically, '[i]t would be a shame if the
loss of the previous system [ie comitology] is regretted on the basis that it was more
efficient the moment the Lisbon Treaty changes the Comitology system making it
more transparent and "democratic"!'.[83]

Another major debate in relation to Article 290(2) TFEU is whether the controls
provided in it are exhaustive or illustrative.[84] The provision states that the conditions to which the delegation is subject *'may* be as follows' (emphasis added). The
ambivalence regarding the list of conditions being open or closed is due to this
wording. In the legal literature, there are arguments in favour of both.[85] The institutions also have divergent views on this: the Commission, in its Communication
on the implementation of Article 290 TFEU, appears to favour a closed list of
control mechanisms, as is evident from its repeated references to *'the two* conditions to which the legislator may subject the delegation of power'.[86] In contrast, the
European Parliament, in its resolution of 5 May 2010 on the power of legislative
delegation, expressed the view that the control mechanisms were non-exhaustive.[87]
Yet the practice of the institutions, particularly that of the Council, seems to point
towards a non-exhaustive list. The picture that emerges from an examination of a
number of post-Lisbon legislative acts[88] is that the Council tends to reserve solely
for itself the power to control delegation whenever an act is adopted based on the
special legislative procedure with mere consultation of the EP. Since Article 290
TFEU does not explicitly provide for divergences in control mechanisms depending on the legislative procedure used, the practice of the Council would have been
unlawful if the only applicable control mechanisms were the two mentioned in the
said Article.[89]

The Common Understanding on delegated acts[90] negotiated between the EP, the
Council, and the Commission in 2011 at the request of the European Parliament,[91]
also points towards a non-exhaustive list of control mechanisms. The Common

---

[83] Ponzano (n 82) 141.   [84] Craig (n 17) 268.

[85] Hofmann (n 29) 493 (presents both views). For an argument that the list is exhaustive, see
Robert Schütze, '"Delegated" Legislation in the (new) European Union: A Constitutional Analysis'
(2011) 74 *Modern Law Review* 661, 685–686. Also, Lenaerts and Desomer (n 1) 755. For an argument
that the list is non-exhaustive, see Peers and Costa (n 73) 443–444; Dougan, (n 32) 785, also refers to
the controls as non-exhaustive.

[86] Communication from the Commission (n 68) 7 (emphasis added).

[87] European Parliament Resolution of 5 May 2010 on the Power of Legislative Delegation, [2011]
OJ C81 E/6.

[88] For instance, Council Regulation (EU) No 973/2010 of 25 October 2010 temporarily suspend-
ing the autonomous Common Customs Tariff duties on imports of certain industrial products into
the autonomous regions of the Azores and Madeira [2010] OJ L 285/4, Arts 6-10; Council Decision
of 3 December 2013 establishing the specific programme implementing Horizon 2020 [2013] OJ L
347/965, Art 11.

[89] Peers and Costa (n 73) 444.   [90] Common Understanding (n 78).

[91] European Parliament Resolution of 5 May 2010 (n 87), point 10.

Understanding regulates practical matters with regard to the adoption of dele-gated acts.[92] Of special interest, for the present purposes, is point 3 of the Common Understanding, which provides: 'The Institutions concerned, *depending on the proced-ure for the adoption of the basic act*, undertake to refer as far as possible to the standard clauses annexed to this Common Understanding when proposing or making delega-tions of power under Article 290 TFEU' (emphasis added). It must be pointed out that the standard clauses annexed to that document provide for control by both the EP and the Council. Accordingly, the qualification provided in point 3, with regard to the adoption procedures, suggests that there is an understanding between the Union institutions that whenever the special legislative procedure requires only EP consult-ation, the Council will exercise control over delegation on its own.

In this connection the link between the procedure specified in Article 290 TFEU and the regulatory procedure with scrutiny (RPS), which operated under the pre-Lisbon comitology system, is relevant. The delegated acts procedure is the successor of the RPS, the difference between the two procedures being that the delegated acts proced-ure can apply to *all* legislative acts—whether adopted under the ordinary or the spe-cial legislative procedure—while the RPS applied only to those acts that were adopted according to the co-decision procedure.[93] However, the distinction between the RPS and the delegated acts procedure may not be that great after all: as noted above, in practice, the Council acts on its own whenever an act is adopted according to the SLP with EP consultation, and the latter is the predominant variety of the SLP.[94]

Yet another issue is that Article 290(2) requires the EP to act by 'a majority of its component members' for the purposes of exercising the *ex post* control mecha-nisms. According to some commentators, this is a much heavier voting rule than the 'majority of the votes cast' requirement, which is prescribed by the Treaty as the default voting rule (Article 231 TFEU).[95] That voting requirement is one of the reasons why some scholars question the ability of the EP effectively to control del-egated decision making by the Commission.[96] In contrast, the Council will act by qualified majority—which means that it will be easier for the Council than for the EP to exercise the *ex post* control mechanisms under Article 290(2) TFEU.[97]

The final paragraph of Article 290 TFEU mandates the insertion of the adjective 'delegated' in the title of delegated acts. The explicit reference to 'delegated' in these acts makes it easier for the reader immediately to identify the executive nature of the measure.

---

[92] Thomas Christiansen and Mathias Dobbels, 'Non-legislative Rule Making after the Lisbon Treaty: Implementing the New System of Comitology and Delegated Acts' (2013) 19 *European Law Journal* 42, 49–50.

[93] Peers and Costa (n 73) 441–442.   [94] Türk (n 31) 69.

[95] Lenaerts and Desomer (n 1) 755.

[96] Joana Mendes, 'Delegated and Implementing Rule Making: Proceduralisation and Constitutional Design' (2013) 19 *European Law Journal* 22, 38.

[97] Lenaerts and Desomer (n 1) 755.

VI. Implementing Acts

Article 291(1) TFEU, the provision on implementing acts, begins with the reaffirmation of the fact that implementation of EU acts is primarily the responsibility of the Member States. However, according to Article 291(2), 'where uniform conditions for implementing legally binding Union acts are needed', the Commission and occasionally the Council can exercise implementing powers. Some commentators have questioned the clarity of this provision, wondering exactly how 'uniform' conditions would have to be in order for the Commission (or the Council), rather than the Member States, to exercise implementing powers.[98] Moreover, unlike delegated acts, implementing acts entail execution without supplementation or amendment of the legislative act.[99] This is true at least in theory. However, some scholars assert that by specifying uniform conditions of implementation, an implementing act is bound to add something to the legislative or delegated act, and that it is difficult to distinguish between this type of 'addition' and the one that is only permissible under Article 290 TFEU.[100] The difference between the two may be based on the addition of 'new' non-essential elements (which could be done only through delegated acts).[101] However, as Craig rightly observes, 'There will inevitably be instances where juxtaposition of acts will reveal scant reason as to why the "supplementation" of the legislative act in the one instance should be regarded as a "new" non-essential element, such that a delegated act is required, while in other instances this is not so, such that an implementing act can be used.'[102]

The reference to 'legally binding Union acts' in this Article shows that implementing acts can be made pursuant to a legislative *or a delegated act*.[103] The fact that implementing legislation can be enacted based on a delegated act means that the Commission might be able to sub-delegate implementing powers to itself through delegated rule making.[104] A related issue is that the Treaty is silent on the question of whether implementing acts can supplement or amend a *delegated* act.[105] Since the Treaty does not contain an explicit prohibition, in principle this could be the case. Yet another ambiguous point in this provision is the reference to 'duly justified specific cases' in which the Council may implement Union acts.[106] Not only is it unclear what is meant by this phrase, but according to some commentators the sheer preservation of the Council's ability to implement Union legislation runs contrary to the logic behind the changes made in the Lisbon Treaty, namely the attainment of a better separation of powers.[107] Also noteworthy is that pursuant to

---

[98] Dougan (n 32) 786. Note: Dougan is discussing the Constitutional Treaty. However, the wording of that Treaty is the same as that of the Lisbon Treaty for this particular paragraph.

[99] Craig (n 17) 271–272.   [100] Craig (n 17) 277.   [101] Craig (n 17) 277–278.

[102] Craig (n 17) 278.   [103] Craig and de Búrca (n 16) 115.   [104] Hofmann (n 29) 502.

[105] Craig (n 17) 274.   [106] Dougan (n 32) 786.   [107] Lenaerts and Desomer (n 1) 756.

Article 291(2), the Council has implementing powers under Articles 24 and 26 TEU as well—in the area of the CFSP.

Article 291(3) provides that 'the European Parliament and the Council, acting by means of regulations in accordance with the ordinary legislative procedure, shall lay down in advance the rules and general principles concerning mechanisms for control by Member States of the Commission's exercise of implementing powers'. This paragraph is significant because, by calling for the ordinary legislative procedure, it places the European Parliament on the same footing as the Council, thus giving it a voice in the enactment of the new rules governing comitology—for the first time since the inception of that system. The aim was to ensure a better separation of legislative and executive powers whereby 'control of the executive was no longer a matter for the Council alone but for the "legislature"'.[108] This achievement is overshadowed by the preservation of some executive powers ('in duly justified specific cases') for the Council under Article 291(2) TFEU.[109] Moreover, although the new rules were adopted according to the ordinary legislative procedure, the EP did not have a real input in their formation, as the negotiations were primarily dominated by the Council and the Commission.[110]

Regulation 182/2011[111] entered into force on 1 March 2011. Unlike the previous comitology regime, it entails only two—the advisory and the examination—procedures.[112] More importantly, in line with the objective of separation of powers, the new rules do not entail any *formal* involvement of the Council in the comitology procedures. However, in practice, 'channels of communication' between Member States' representatives on comitology committees and their representatives in the Council are likely to contribute to the *indirect* control of implementing acts by the Council.[113]

Going back to the wording of Article 291 TFEU, the fourth and final paragraph of that provision mandates the insertion of the word 'implementing' in the title of implementing acts, thus making those acts easily cognizable.

One final question is whether implementing acts are regulatory acts within the meaning of Article 263(4) TFEU. Since the General Court ruled that regulatory acts are 'all acts of general application apart from legislative acts',[114] and since implementing acts can be both of individual and of general application, they can, in principle, be regulatory acts. In *Microban v Commission*,[115] the General Court held that a Decision

---

[108] Bergström (n 8) 346.   [109] Lenaerts and Desomer (n 1) 756.

[110] Thomas Christiansen and Mathias Dobbels, 'Delegated Powers and Inter-Institutional Relations in the EU after Lisbon: A Normative Assessment' (2013) 36 *West European Politics* 1159, 1166.

[111] Reg (EU) No 182/2011 (n 76).

[112] For a detailed analysis of the provisions of the new Regulation and an argument that the Regulation in reality entails more than two procedures, see Paul Craig, 'Delegated Acts, Implementing Acts and the New Comitology Regulation' (2011) 36 *European Law Review* 671, 677–687.

[113] Craig (n 112) 686.

[114] Case T-18/10 *Inuit* (n 39) para 56.

[115] Case T-262/10 *Microban International and Microban (Europe) v Commission* [2011] ECR II-07697.

that was an implementing act adopted by the Commission constituted 'a regulatory act of direct concern to the applicants, which [did] not entail any implementing measures'.[116] Thus, if the implementing act is of general application, is of direct concern to the individual, and does not entail implementing measures, it satisfies the conditions laid out in Article 263(4) TFEU.[117]

VII. Non-Legislative Acts Adopted Directly on the Basis of the Treaty

A comparison between the section of the Lisbon Treaty on the legal acts of the Union and the corresponding section of the DCT is striking. The section on legal acts under the Lisbon Treaty includes only three main categories of legal act—legislative, delegated, and implementing. The CT and DCT included a fourth category—that of 'non-legislative acts'—placed between the provisions on legislative and delegated acts. The latter category should not be confused with delegated and implementing acts: non-legislative acts, within the meaning of Article I-35 CT[118] and Article 34 DCT, are binding legal acts adopted by the European Council, the Council, the Commission, or the European Central Bank directly on the basis of the Constitution (under the current legal order—the Lisbon Treaty). In contrast, delegated and implementing acts are non-legislative acts adopted on the basis of other acts. The omission of an explicit reference to the former category of act from the text of the Lisbon Treaty is very significant. This is because non-legislative acts directly based on the Treaty make up a significant proportion of rules actually adopted by the institutions of the Union.

Best has identified 19 different procedures (a total of 28 different TFEU legal bases) of this kind for the Council and the Commission alone.[119] What is striking is that these types of non-legislative act are used in a variety of fields of EU law—not just in the sensitive areas of EU activity. Lenaerts and Desomer refer to these acts as 'autonomous regulations'[120] and argue that while their use in the areas of foreign policy and freedom, security and justice are warranted, their application in certain other fields 'seems primarily motivated by the intention to evade the ordinary legislative procedure'.[121] Indeed, the difference between most of these non-legislative

---

[116] Case T-262/10 *Microban* (n 115) para 39.   [117] See Peers and Costa (n 40) 90–91.
[118] Note that only the third paragraph of Article I-35 has made it into the Lisbon Treaty in the form of Article 292 TFEU.
[119] Best (n 18) 93–95.
[120] Lenaerts and Desomer (n 1) 753.   [121] Lenaerts and Desomer (n 1) 754.

acts of the Council and the ones it adopts under the SLP is simply the absence of an explicit reference to the 'special legislative procedure'. The distinction lies mainly in wording rather than any material dissimilarity between the procedures. Jürgen Bast also argues that '[i]n drawing the line between legislative and non-legislative powers of the Council, the Lisbon Treaty has perpetuated the Constitutional Treaty's dishonesties. Important provisions of the TFEU are classified as non-legislative on an opportunistic basis'.[122] However, even if the non-legislative acts of the Council listed by Best were to be somehow included within the scope of the categorization of legal acts under Articles 289, 290, and 291 TFEU, *other* non-legislative acts would still be adopted by the European Council, the Commission, and the ECB. That is why the exclusion of this category of act from the text of the Lisbon Treaty is so disconcerting.

VIII. Discussion

The overview of the hierarchy of norms established by the Treaty of Lisbon calls for an evaluation of this hierarchy in the light of the objectives behind the Treaty revision—simplification, democratic legitimacy, and separation of powers.

1. Simplification

At first sight, the progress made by the framers of the Lisbon Treaty seems quite impressive. One of the primary aims of simplification was to make the system more comprehensible to Union citizens. The number of legal instruments has been reduced and the distinction between them has been clarified. First, in relation to the number of acts, all former Third Pillar instruments have been abolished and replaced by the 'mainstream' Union instruments. As to the former Second Pillar, the default instrument here has become the Decision. Second, with regard to the distinction between acts, Article 202 EC on implementing measures has been succeeded by three categories of act, clearly arranged according to their legislative (Article 289 TFEU) or executive (Articles 290 and 291 TFEU) nature. Moreover, executive acts have been split into two: those that have a quasi-legislative nature and those that are meant for implementation *stricto sensu*. Finally, the requirement to insert the adjectives 'delegated' and 'implementing' in the titles of executive

---

[122] Jürgen Bast, 'New Categories of Acts after the Lisbon Reform: Dynamics of Parliamentarization in EU Law' (2012) 49 *Common Market Law Review* 885, 898.

acts, makes it easier for the Union citizens to distinguish between legislative and non-legislative acts.

The issues relating to the simplification of instruments become apparent only after a close examination of text of the Lisbon Treaty. From this examination, first, it becomes clear that Article 288 TFEU, just like its predecessor, does not reflect the whole range of instruments used by the Union institutions. Moreover, the only instrument that was incorporated into the framework of Article 288 TFEU—the *sui generis* Decision—is combined with the regular Decision (within the meaning of Article 249 EC) in a way that is rather problematic since these two acts served entirely different functions under the pre-Lisbon regime. Adding to that the Decision which is used in the area of CFSP results in the term 'Decision' being used for three entirely different types of act.

With respect to the distinction between legislative and non-legislative acts, in other words the ranking of norms, the choice was made to differentiate them predominantly according to their adoption procedures, not their content. This resulted in the difference between legislative and executive acts being purely one of form rather than of substance. Thus, delegated acts may be quite legislative in terms of their content, yet they may be viewed as non-legislative. Conversely, some acts classified as legislative—such as the ones based on Article 82(1) TFEU providing for European judicial training programmes—can be quite administrative in nature.[123] Though it might seem otherwise at first sight, the division lines between legislative and executive acts are far from straightforward.

The same issue arises in relation to the distinction between the two forms of executive act, which is dependent on obscure criteria such as 'essential and non-essential elements' and 'supplementation'. Moreover, the entirely different control mechanisms and power dynamics attached to Articles 290 and 291 TFEU give rise to divergent incentives for the institutions of the Union to opt for one procedure over the other. Thus, the Commission and the EP may be more in favour of delegated acts as they enjoy greater powers in the enactment of those acts, while the Council may prefer implementing acts under which Member States (even if outside the framework of the Council) exercise greater control through comitology. The increasing number of inter-institutional disputes brought before the CJEU over the choice between delegated and implementing acts[124] is indicative of the fact that the division line between the two types of executive acts is not so simple and clear.

---

[123] De Witte (n 15) 92.

[124] Such as Case C-427/12 *Commission v Parliament and Council*, judgment of 18 March 2014; Case C-65/13 *Parliament v Commission*, judgment of 15 October 2014; Case C-679/13 *Parliament v Council*, application (OJ) of 7 February 2014.

2. Democratic Legitimacy

The Lisbon provisions on legal acts of the Union have substantially increased the democratic legitimacy of the EU in the sense that they give greater powers to the EP in relation to legislative, delegated, and implementing acts. However, when looking at the details of the provisions on these three categories of act, the advances made through the Treaty revision seem more modest. First, with regard to legislative acts, the extension of the ordinary legislative procedure to many new areas has made it the primary form of decision making in the Union. However, acts adopted under the special legislative procedure are also considered legislative acts even though in most cases of SLP, the EP is merely consulted. Given this observation, the fact that acts adopted according to the SLP with consultation are considered 'legislative' is highly problematic from the perspective of democratic legitimacy. Not only are these acts shielded from real parliamentary scrutiny, but they also do not qualify for easier access to judicial review under Article 263(4) TFEU.

Second, with regard to delegated acts, it would seem that the EP is finally placed on the same footing with the Council since now *both* of these institutions exercise control over the delegated powers of the Commission. However, we saw that when it comes to legislative acts adopted by the Council under the special legislative procedure with *consultation* of the EP, control over these types of act is exercised only by the Council. Moreover, due to voting rules, time constraints and insufficient information, it will be difficult for the EP to effectively make use of this power.

Third, as regards implementing acts, neither the EP nor the Council exercises control over them, as this has now become the prerogative of the Member States only. The adoption of the new comitology regulation according to the ordinary legislative procedure is also a major victory for the EP. However, as noted in Section VI, in practice, the EP was sidelined in the formation of the new rules. In addition, implementing acts may be adopted pursuant to legislative acts enacted according to the SLP with consultation of the EP or pursuant to non-legislative acts adopted directly on the basis of the Treaty, and this means that the Council may be able to adopt an act on its own and then confer implementing powers on itself without any democratic control over it whatsoever.

Last but not least, as Section VII made clear, the framers of the Lisbon Treaty have made the highly contentious choice of simply omitting any explicit reference to the category of non-legislative acts adopted by the Council, the European Council, the Commission, and the ECB directly on the basis of the Treaty. The seriousness of this omission from the perspective of transparency, accountability, and in broader terms democratic legitimacy cannot be overstated.

3. Separation of Powers

The effort by the Convention to achieve a certain degree of separation of legislative and executive powers in the Union is evident from the control mechanisms with regard to delegated and implementing acts, and more specifically, from the complete disengagement of the Council from the comitology procedures. First, the control on the part of the Council over quasi-legislative acts under the comitology system was replaced by *ex ante* and *ex post* controls *jointly* exercised by the EP and the Council.[125] However, this is not always the case, since for acts adopted according to the SLP with consultation of the EP, the Council controls delegated powers on its own. Second, even though comitology was maintained for implementing acts, the Council again does not play any formal role in these controls as, under the new comitology regulation, Member States act outside its institutional framework. Yet, as stated in Section VI, due to the close communication between Member State representatives in comitology committees and the colleagues in the Council, the latter may still be able indirectly to influence these procedures. Lastly, 'The fact that an implementing role for the Council is being maintained in "duly justified specific cases" . . . is . . . to be considered as an anomaly in the overall picture of separation of functions.'[126] In sum, the attempt to draw a clearer separation of legislative and executive powers in the EU is far from successful.

IX. Conclusion

A careful examination of the Treaty leads to the conclusion that the ambitious language of the provisions on the legal acts of the Union does not correspond to reality. The reality is that under the Lisbon Treaty there is an incomplete list of legal instruments in Article 288 TFEU and an incomplete hierarchy of legal acts as embodied by Articles 289, 290, and 291 TFEU. While it may be argued that the system has been rendered simpler and more comprehensible to the citizens of the Union, the changes seem rather superficial. The instruments missing from Article 288 TFEU; the omitted category of non-legislative acts adopted directly on the basis of the Treaty; and the hazy lines dividing legislative and executive acts, on the one hand, and delegated and implementing acts, on the other hand, make for a inadequate typology and hierarchy of legal acts. In short, the clarity, transparency and,

---

[125] See Bergström (n 8) 345.   [126] Lenaerts and Desomer (n 1) 756.

in a broader sense, the democratic legitimacy of the Union's new framework on legal acts leaves much scope for further reform.

BIBLIOGRAPHY

Jürgen Bast, 'New Categories of Acts after the Lisbon Reform: Dynamics of Parliamentarization in EU Law' (2012) *49 Common Market Law Review* 885

Carl Bergström, *Comitology: Delegation of Powers in the European Union and the Committee System* (Oxford University Press, 2005) Ch 5

Edward Best, 'Legislative Procedures after Lisbon: Fewer, Simpler, Clearer?' (2008) *15 Maastricht Journal of European and Comparative Law* 85

Roland Bieber and Isabelle Salomé, 'Hierarchy of Norms in European Law' (1996) *33 Common Market Law Review* 907

Merijn Chamon, 'How the Concept of Essential Elements of a Legislative Act Continues to Elude the Court: Parliament v. Council' (2013) *50 Common Market Law Review* 849

Thomas Christiansen and Mathias Dobbels, 'Non-legislative Rule Making after the Lisbon Treaty: Implementing the New System of Comitology and Delegated Acts' (2013) *19 European Law Journal* 42

Thomas Christiansen and Mathias Dobbels, 'Delegated Powers and Inter-Institutional Relations in the EU after Lisbon: A Normative Assessment' (2013) *36 West European Politics* 1159

Paul Craig, 'Delegated Acts, Implementing Acts and the New Comitology Regulation' (2011) *36 European Law Review* 671, 677–687

Paul Craig, 'The Role of the European Parliament under the Lisbon Treaty' in Stefan Griller and Jacques Ziller (eds), *The Lisbon Treaty: EU Constitutionalism without a Constitutional Treaty?* (Vienna: Springer, 2008) 109

Paul Craig, *The Lisbon Treaty, Revised Edition: Law, Politics, and Treaty Reform* (Oxford University Press, 2013)

Michael Dougan. 'The Convention's Draft Constitutional Treaty: Bringing Europe Closer to its Lawyers?' (2003) *28 European Law Review* 763

Maarten den Heijer and Eljalill Tauschinsky, 'Where Human Rights Meet Administrative Law: Essential Elements and Limits to Delegation: European Court of Justice, Grand Chamber C-355/10: European Parliament v. Council of the European Union' (2013) *9 European Constitutional Law Review* 513

Herwig Hofmann, 'Legislation, Delegation and Implementation under the Treaty of Lisbon: Typology Meets Reality' (2009) *15 European Law Journal* 482

Koen Lenaerts and Marlies Desomer, 'Towards a Hierarchy of Legal Acts in the European Union? Simplification of Legal Instruments and Procedures' (2005) *11 European Law Journal* 744

Joana Mendes, 'Delegated and Implementing Rule Making: Proceduralisation and Constitutional Design' (2013) *19 European Law Journal* 22

Steve Peers and Marios Costa, 'Accountability for Delegated and Implementing Acts after the Treaty of Lisbon' (2012) *18 European Law Journal* 427

Steve Peers and Marios Costa, 'Court of Justice of the European Union (General Chamber), Judicial review of EU Acts after the Treaty of Lisbon; Order of 6 September 2011,

Case T-18/10 Inuit Tapiriit Kanatami and Others v. Commission & Judgment of 25 October 2011, Case T-262/10 Microban v. Commission' (2012) *8 European Constitutional Law Review* 82

Paolo Ponzano, '"Executive" and "Delegated" Acts: The Situation after the Lisbon Treaty' in Stefan Griller and Jacques Ziller (eds), *The Lisbon Treaty: EU Constitutionalism without a Constitutional Treaty?* (Vienna: Springer, 2008) 135

Robert Schütze, '"Delegated" Legislation in the (new) European Union: A Constitutional Analysis' (2011) *74 Modern Law Review* 661

Alexander Türk, 'Lawmaking after Lisbon' in Andrea Biondi, Piet Eeckhout, and Stefanie Ripley (eds), *EU Law after Lisbon* (Oxford University Press, 2012) 62

Bruno de Witte, 'Legal Instruments and Law-making in the Lisbon Treaty' in Stefan Griller and Jacques Ziller (eds), *The Lisbon Treaty: EU Constitutionalism without a Constitutional Treaty?* (Vienna: Springer, 2008) 79

CHAPTER 6

....

ACCESSION AND
WITHDRAWAL IN
THE LAW OF THE
EUROPEAN UNION

....

CHRISTOPHE HILLION[*]

THE Treaty on European Union (TEU) contains two procedures that make it possible for a European state respectively to become, and to cease to be, a member of the EU. Since the establishment of the European Communities, the entry device (currently provided in Article 49 TEU) has been used many times,[1] whereas no member has yet initiated the EU exit clause (Article 50 TEU).

The provisions outlining how states enter and how they could leave the Union offer some insight into the notion of EU membership, and more generally into the nature of the EU legal order. State-centred mechanisms, located at the intersection of EU and international law, the two procedures are also firmly embedded in the

  [*] Author note: many thanks to Tony Arnull, Steven Blockmans, and Anne Myrjord for all their helpful comments. All mistakes are mine.
  [1] On successive waves and ongoing processes of EU enlargement: http://ec.europa.eu/enlargement/index_en.htm; Bart Van Vooren and Ramses Wessel, *EU External Relations Law* (2014), Ch 5; Allan Tatham, *Enlargement of the European Union*, (2009).

system of the EU treaties, normatively determined by the integration goal that the latter pursue, and thus an integral part of the constitutional order they underpin.

After an analysis of the EU law of accession and withdrawal (I), this chapter attempts to expound its rationale by reference to the EU's aspiration to 'ever closer union' (II).

I. ACCESSION, WITHDRAWAL, AND THE EU LEGAL ORDER

The EU accession and withdrawal provisions govern the *state* configuration of the Union: they determine which state is in (1), and which state is out (2).

1. EU Accession Process

At its heart, the EU accession procedure is a process between states (a). However, it has gradually evolved into an enlargement *policy* driven mainly by EU institutions (b), a development which has led Member States to reassert their control (c).

(a) *The EU Legal Basis for Accession: Article 49 TEU*

Article 49 TEU establishes a two-stage process whereby a European state may become a member of the Union. The aspirant country must first send its application to the EU Council, which decides by unanimity on the admissibility of the request, after having consulted the Commission and received the consent of the European Parliament.

Such admissibility depends on the aspirant's fulfilment of the condition of statehood, and on its European identity ('Any European State'), as well as on its respect for and commitment to promote the EU values enshrined in Article 2 TEU. Article 49 TEU also refers to additional 'conditions of eligibility agreed upon by the European Council [, which] shall be taken into account'. These conditions were codified in 1993, when the EU acknowledged the membership prospect of central and east European countries (CEECs). According to what have become known as the 'Copenhagen criteria', EU membership requires the candidate country to demonstrate: (i) the stability of institutions guaranteeing democracy, the rule of law, human rights, and respect for and protection of minorities; (ii) the existence of a functioning market economy, as well as the capacity to cope with competitive pressure and market forces within the Union; and (iii) the ability to take on the obligations of membership, including adherence to the aims of political, economic and monetary union.[2] Subsequently elaborated,[3] the Copenhagen criteria have become standard accession conditions,[4] and progressively, if only partly, constitutionalized through various treaty revisions.[5] They also constitute the normative basis of the EU enlargement policy, which will be discussed below.

Should the application be deemed admissible, the accession process may then begin in the form of the negotiation of a treaty between the Member States and the candidate country, the purpose of which is to agree on 'the conditions of admission and the adjustments to the Treaties on which the Union is founded' (Article 49(2) TEU).[6] The ensuing accession treaty is an international agreement concluded between Member States and the applicant country, and ratified by all states concerned according to their constitutional requirements. It belongs to EU primary law, together with the EU founding treaties, which it is meant to modify to make accession legally possible.[7] As such, the accession treaty may be interpreted and enforced by the European Court of Justice, but not declared invalid.[8]

While occasionally revised by the EU *pouvoir constituant*, the succinct procedure of Article 49 TEU has been articulated through incremental practice, notably to adapt it to the specific needs of each enlargement episode. In this exercise, EU institutions have played a sizable role alongside Member States.

---

[2] Presidency Conclusions, Copenhagen European Council, 21–22 June 1993. Further on the Copenhagen criteria: Marise Cremona, 'Accession to the European Union: Membership Conditionality and Accession Criteria' (2001) 25 *Polish Yearbook of International Law* 219; Frank Hoffmeister, 'Earlier Enlargements' in Andrea Ott and Kirstyn Inglis (eds) *Handbook on European Enlargement* (2002) 90; Christophe Hillion, 'The Copenhagen Criteria and their Progeny' in Christophe Hillion (ed), *EU Enlargement: A Legal Approach* (2004) 17.

[3] eg Presidency Conclusions, Madrid European Council, 15–16 December 1995; Presidency Conclusions, Helsinki European Council, 10–11 December 1999; 'Thessaloniki Agenda for the Western Balkans: Moving towards European Integration', June 2003. Further: Steven Blockmans, 'Raising the Threshold for further EU Enlargement: Process, and Problems and Prospects' in Andrea Ott and Ellen Vos (eds) *Fifty Years of European Integration—Foundations and Perspectives* (2009).

[4] eg Commission Opinion on Iceland's application for membership of the European Union; COM(2010) 62.

[5] On the latest formulation of the accession procedure: eg the amendments proposed to Art 57 on the 'Conditions and procedure for applying for Union membership' at the European Convention on the future of Europe: http://european-convention.europa.eu/EN/amendments/amendments7b33. html?content=43&lang=EN.

[6] Case 93/78 *Mattheus v Doego* [1978] ECR 2203. On 'adjustments to the Treaties' contained in accession treaties and their limits: eg Case C-413/04 *European Parliament v Council* [2006] ECR I-11221, and Case C-414/04 *European Parliament v Council* [2006] ECR I-11279; and annotation by Kirsty Inglis, (2009) 46 *CMLRev* 641.

[7] On such treaties: eg Adam Lazowski, 'And then they were Twenty-seven . . . A Legal Appraisal of the Sixth Accession Treaty' (2007) 44 *CMLRev* 401; Christophe Hillion, 'The European Union is dead. Long live the European Union . . . A Commentary on the Accession Treaty 2003' (2004) 29 *ELRev* 583.

[8] eg Case C-31 and 35/86 *LAISA et al. v Council* [1988] ECR I-2285.

(b) From a Member-State-Driven Procedure
to an EU Member-State-Building Policy

The drafters of the 1957 Treaties of Rome crafted a classic state-centred accession procedure inspired by the canons of international institutional law,[9] which appears to endure in its essentials. Thus both the start and finalization of the process still depend on a unanimous approval by the Member States, while the terms of accession to the Union are in principle negotiated between them and the candidate, rather than determined by the EU itself.[10] In that, the EU procedure differs from the US accession clause, which provides for a new state being admitted to the Union by the Congress.[11] In practice and in law however, all EU political institutions have become more actively involved in the admission of new states to the Union, thus mitigating, at least to some extent, its original inter-state character.[12]

Legally, the accession procedure was first altered to involve the European Parliament. Since the Single European Act, admission of new states no longer depends solely on the Member States' will, but equally requires the consent of a majority of the component members of the European Parliament.[13] As evoked above, the Lisbon Treaty also codified the role of the European Council, confirming that it may adapt the normative framework of accession and adjust the terms of EU membership. Whilst it represents Member States' interests in this exercise, the European Council nevertheless acts as an EU institution, whose powers are governed by the rules of the EU legal order.[14]

In practice too, EU institutions have exerted considerable influence in the operation of the accession procedure. In addition to giving its opinion on the application, an opinion that is procedurally mandatory but non-binding in its substance,[15] the Commission has always played an active role notably in the preparation of the negotiations foreseen in Article 49(2) TEU.[16]

---

[9] In this respect: Henry G Schermers and Niels Blokker, *International Institutional Law* (2003) 70ff.

[10] Art 98 ECSC however foresaw that the Council as such, and not the Member States, had to 'determine the terms of accession' to the ECSC Treaty. Art 116(1) of the stillborn European Political Community Treaty also envisaged accession based on an instrument drawn up by its own institutions. Further: Christophe Hillion, 'EU Enlargement' in Paul Craig and Grainne de Búrca (eds), *The Evolution of EU Law* (2011) 187.

[11] See Art IV, section 3, US Constitution, and its interpretation by the Supreme Court in eg *Coyle v Smith* (1911) 221 US 559.

[12] Final Communiqué of the Hague Summit, 2 December 1969. See also Jean-Pierre Puissochet, *L'Elargissement des Communautés Européennes* (1974).

[13] Art 8 SEA, which provided that the European Parliament was to act by an absolute majority of its component members.

[14] Art 13(1) TEU. It was the Lisbon Treaty that formally included the European Council in the list of EU institutions.

[15] Thus, the initial negative opinion of the Commission on Greece's application (COM (76) 30 final, 20 January 1976) was ignored, and so was its positive *Avis* on the first British application for membership.

[16] Puissochet (n 12), see also the 1961 exchange of letters between the then President of the Commission and the President of the Council on the technical arrangements for accession negotiations (Ref. P 6323-E).

Moreover, the EU 'pre-accession strategy' launched in 1994 to prepare for EU enlargement to include the CEECs[17] considerably increased the institutions' involvement.[18] In particular, the European Council asked the Commission to elaborate the substance of the Copenhagen criteria,[19] and to report back to it on the candidates' progress in meeting them, so as to decide on their ability to start accession negotiations.[20] Through the ensuing *enlargement policy*, EU institutions have actively contributed to transforming applicant states into operating members of the Union, in constitutional, administrative and judicial terms, thereby articulating the attributes of EU membership.[21]

This input was further bolstered following the 'New Consensus for Enlargement',[22] adopted by the European Council in the aftermath of the so-called 'big bang' enlargement of 2004, and while the EU was preparing to admit Bulgaria and Romania.[23] One of the key features of the New Consensus was the introduction of conditionality in accession negotiations themselves, notably to enhance the candidate's preparation for membership. Thus, the opening and closing of several chapters of negotiation are dependent on the candidate's preliminary fulfilment of 'opening' and 'closing benchmarks', which are pre-defined and monitored by the Commission with the approval of Member States.

Of particular significance in the post-'New Consensus' practice is the negotiation of two specific chapters headed 'Judiciary and Fundamental Rights' (Chapter 23), and 'Justice, Freedom and Security' (Chapter 24). Based on lessons learned from Croatia's accession process, and considering the importance of these chapters for

---

[17] Presidency Conclusions, Essen European Council, 9–10 December 1994.

[18] Further: eg Marc Maresceau, 'Pre-accession' in Marise Cremona (ed) *The Enlargement of the European Union* (2003) 9.

[19] The Commission already had a significant influence on the elaboration of the Copenhagen criteria: Report by the Commission to the European Council, Edinburgh, 11–12 December 1992, 'Towards a closer association with the Countries of Central and Eastern Europe', SEC (92) 2301 final; Communication by the Commission to the Council, in view of the meeting of the European Council in Copenhagen, 21–22 June 1993, 'Towards a closer association with the countries of central and eastern Europe', SEC(93) 648 final. Further: Alan Mayhew, *Recreating Europe. The European Union's Policy towards Central and Eastern Europe* (1998); Karen Smith, 'The Evolution and Application of EU Membership Conditionality' in Cremona (n 18) 105 at 113. Marc Maresceau, 'Quelques réflexions sur l'origine et l'application des principes fondamentaux dans la stratégie d'adhésion de l'UE' in *Le droit de l'Union européenne en principes—Liber Amicorum en l'honneur de Jean Raux* (2006) 69.

[20] eg Presidency Conclusions, Luxembourg European Council, 12–13 December 1997 (pt 29).

[21] The term 'Member State building' was invented by Gerald Knaus and Marcus Cox, 'The "Helsinki Moment" in Southeastern Europe' (2005) 14 *Journal of Democracy* 39; see also Steven Blockmans, 'EU Enlargement as a Peacebuilding Tool' in Steven Blockmans, Jan Wouters and Tom Ruys (eds) *The European Union and Peacebuilding* (2010) 77. Further on Europeanization in the context of EU enlargement: eg Heather Grabbe, 'A Partnership for Accession? The Implications of EU Conditionality for the Central and East European Applicants' *European University Institute Working Papers* RSC no 99/12 [1999]; Frank Schimmelfennig and Ulrich Sedelmeier (eds), *The Europeanization of Central and Eastern Europe* (2005).

[22] Presidency Conclusions, European Council, Brussels, 15 December 2006.

[23] Hillion (n 10) 187.

the implementation of the whole EU *acquis*, the Commission suggested a 'New Approach' to invigorate the candidates' absorption of the norms related to them.[24] They are henceforth opened early, and closed late in the negotiations so as to allow maximum time for the candidates to establish the necessary legislation, institutions and track record of implementation,[25] and thus demonstrate that new norms are entrenched in their constitutional fabric, prior to admission. In addition, EU 'screening reports', which generally establish possible gaps between EU law and the candidates' legislation over the whole range of accession chapters, now provide specific EU guidance in relation to the two chapters.[26] Candidate state's authorities are thus given explicit tasks, such as the establishment of 'related timetables and resource implications, setting out clear objectives, quantifiable indicators as appropriate, and the necessary institutional set up', in the process of adopting EU standards.[27] Moreover, the New Approach includes a system of sanctions, in the form of possible 'corrective measures'. Thus, according to the negotiating framework for Serbia:

Given the link between the chapters 'Judiciary and fundamental rights' and 'Justice, freedom and security' and the values on which the Union is founded, as well as their importance for the implementation of the acquis across the board, should progress under these chapters significantly lag behind progress in the negotiations overall, and after having exhausted all other available measures, the Commission will on its own initiative or on the request of one third of the Member States propose to withhold its recommendations to open and/or close other negotiating chapters, and adapt the associated preparatory work, as appropriate, until this imbalance is addressed. The Council will decide by qualified majority on such a proposal and on the conditions for lifting the measures taken.[28]

The elaboration of benchmarking following the 'New Approach' has entailed further articulation of EU standards, sometimes even *beyond* the obligations binding Member States themselves.[29] The means to achieve their assimilation have also been beefed up, through a considerably strengthened EU monitoring, notably by the Commission. More generally, the development of the EU enlargement policy

---

[24] Communication from the Commission to the European Parliament and the Council, 'Enlargement Strategy and Main Challenges 2011–2012', COM(2011) 666 final, 12.10.2011, 5. The 'New Approach' was later endorsed by the Council (General Affairs Council Conclusions on enlargement and stabilisation and association process, 5 December 2011, pt 4) and the European Council (Conclusions, European Council, December 2011).

[25] eg General EU position—ministerial meeting opening the Intergovernmental Conference on the Accession of Montenegro to the European Union (AD 23/12, 27 June 2012).

[26] eg 'Outcome of Screening on Chapter 23 for Montenegro: Judiciary and Fundamental Rights' (doc. 17785/12, 14 December 2012).

[27] 'Outcome of Screening' (n 26).

[28] Para 24, General EU Position, Ministerial meeting opening the Intergovernmental conference on the accession of Serbia to the European Union (AD 1/14, 12).

[29] On this discrepancy: eg Christophe Hillion, 'Enlarging the European Union and its Fundamental Rights Protection' in Inge Govaere, Erwan Lannon, Peter van Elsuwege and Stanislas Adam (eds) *The European Union in the World—Essays in Honour of Marc Maresceau* (2013) 557.

has meant that accession negotiations proceed not only on the basis of settlements between the parties as regards 'the conditions of admission and the adjustments to the treaties . . . which such admission entails', but also, if not primarily, in view of the candidate's ability to meet the targets set by the Union. Combined with the key accession condition that the candidate has to accept the whole EU *acquis* (cf third Copenhagen criterion), the extensive use of conditionality and the ensuing involvement of EU institutions have partly eroded the significance of the negotiations of the accession treaty foreseen in Article 49(2) TEU. For the terms of accession are set by the Union, understood as Member States and institutions, and marginally bargained between the parties to the negotiations.[30]

(c) Nationalization of EU Enlargement Policy

The *EU member-state-building policy* evoked above has become a standard facet of the EU accession process.[31] As suggested, the latter is far more than the inter-state bargaining that Article 237 EEC originally envisaged. Yet, faced with the increasing unpopularity of enlargement, partly due to deficiencies in its preparations,[32] Member States have reasserted their control over various phases of the accession process, notably when negotiations were being opened with Croatia and Turkey in 2005.

At EU level, the role of the Council, as agent of the Member States, has been reaffirmed. In particular, instances of unanimous decision-making, and thus of veto opportunities have multiplied well beyond the requirements of Article 49 TEU. Contrary to what a literal reading of paragraph 1 would suggest, the Council does not automatically transmit the candidate's application to the Commission. Rather, it first *decides* to implement the procedure of Article 49 TEU, thereby acquiring the ability to assess the admissibility of the application, *before* the Commission and indeed the Parliament have had a chance to voice their views. As a result, the Commission does not provide or even prepare its opinion without having first been requested to do so by the Council. While the practice had hitherto been to decide to invite the Commission to start to prepare its opinion by simple majority, it now appears that single Member States feel entitled to block, or at least hold up, the Council's request to the Commission.

For example, the Commission's invitation to prepare an Opinion on Albania's application was withheld as a result of the German Government's intention first to

[30] A phenomenon that Marc Maresceau had already pointed out in eg 'Pre-Accession Strategies: A Political Analysis' in Marc Maresceau and Erwan Lannon (eds) *The EU's Enlargement and Mediterranean Strategies—A Comparative Analysis* (2001) 3.

[31] Thus, despite its high degree of integration with the EU, notably through the EEA and the Schengen agreements, Iceland as a candidate has also been subject to the EU pre-accession regime.

[32] eg Christophe Hillion, 'The Creeping Nationalisation of the EU Enlargement Policy' (2010) *SIEPS Report* 6/2010.

consult its parliament on the matter, in application of the revised Lisbon ratification law, adopted following the *Lisbon* judgment of the German Constitutional Court.[33] The procedure of Article 49 TEU was only resumed after the German approval, six months later, when the Council eventually '*decided* to implement the proce-dure laid down in Article 49 [TEU]. Accordingly, the Commission [was] *invited* to submit its opinion' (emphasis added).[34] In effect, the duplication of the Council's *unanimous* decisions has weakened the role of the other EU political institutions and, *de facto*, changes the nature of the procedure of Article 49(1) TEU: in principle inter-institutional, in practice intergovernmental.

Member States also appear to be tempering the EU fundamental freedoms and principles with domestic concerns, as epitomized by the EU negotiating frame-work for Turkey.[35] The document envisages that the Accession Treaty could include 'permanent safeguard clauses' with respect notably to movement of persons, agri-cultural and structural policies. As suggested elsewhere, such clauses would put at risk the functioning of the internal market and could, more generally, strike at the heart of the EU legal order,[36] and particularly at the principle of equality of EU citizens and states.[37]

At Member States' level too, control over the procedure has been equally tight-ened, especially by tweaking the national 'constitutional requirements' to ratify accession treaties. The most conspicuous example in this respect is the principle introduced in 2008 in France's constitution that future accession treaties be rati-fied by referendum. Parliamentary ratification is the exception, and would require a three-fifths majority in Parliament convened in Congress [ie the meeting of the two chambers].[38] The revamped French constitutional requirement thus deliber-ately makes future accessions to the Union more uncertain.[39]

Member States have also tightened their control on other phases of the pro-cedure. For example, the amended German ratification law evoked above[40]

---

[33] *Lissabon-Urteil*, Judgment of 30 June 2009 (BVerfGE 123, 267).

[34] 16 November 2009; 15913/09 (Presse 328).

[35] 'Negotiating Framework', 3 October 2005.

[36] Christophe Hillion, 'Negotiating Turkey's Membership to the European Union—Can Member States do as they Please?' (2007) 3 *European Constitutional Law Review* 269.

[37] Case 231/78 *Commission v UK* [1979] ECR 1447, para 9. This principle of equality is enshrined in Art 4(2) TEU.

[38] See first paragraph of new Art 88–5 of the French Constitution, which came into effect upon the coming into force of the Treaty of Lisbon, in accordance with Art 2 of Constitutional Act no. 2008-103 of February 4, 2008 and Art 47 of Constitutional Act no. 2008-724 of July 23, 2008.

[39] Other Member States have been considering new constitutional requirements for ratify-ing accession treaties in the form of, eg, a two-thirds qualified majority in parliament (eg The Netherlands, see Kamerstukken TK 30874, nrs 1-3), or referendum (eg Austria, see Government Programme 2007–2010: http://www.austria.gv.at/DocView.axd?CobId=19542 at 8).

[40] *Gezets zur Änderung des Gesetzes über die Zusammenarbeit von Bundesregierung und Deutschem Bundestag in Angelegenheiten der Europäischen Union* (EuZBBG; available at http://www.bundesrat.de/nn_8396/SharedDocs/Beratungsvorgaenge/2009/0701-800/715-09.html).

explicitly requires that the German government seek the Bundestag's opinion on the *opening* of accession negotiations.[41] Yet, this requirement has been invoked at other stages of the enlargement procedure too, as for instance in the case of the Albanian application, referred to above, in which the law was brought into play prior to requesting an opinion from the Commission. While the government is not bound by the opinion of the Bundestag, in the specific field of enlargement, they are explicitly asked to seek a common position.[42] Thus, were the German Parliament to give a negative opinion on the matter, EU enlargement could be stalled.

The above analysis of its legal basis and practice suggests that the EU accession mechanism includes both strong (inter-)state and EU components. The relative weight of the two appears to vary depending on the political context, and in particular as a function of Member States' intentions. The stronger the latter's political will to allow further accession, the more extensive the EU's institutions influence over the process. While legally acknowledged by Treaty provisions, Member States' discretion, bolstered in recent years, remains constrained by the discipline deriving from their EU membership, including in the context of Article 49 TEU. Indeed, excessive national interference with the application of the EU accession procedure[43] could in principle be contested before the European Court of Justice. The latter could thus be called upon to restore the delicate balance the procedure foresees between the state and EU dimensions,[44] and to preserve its integrity,[45] particularly in view of its function in the system of the treaties, as argued below, after a detour through the withdrawal procedure.

Prior to the judgment, the Bundestag had already proposed that the German Government seek its approval before the start of new accession negotiations, as recalled in the House of Lords, 'The Further Enlargement of the EU: Threat or Opportunity?' European Union Committee, 53rd Report of Session 2005–06, 20.

[41] §3(1)2 EuZBBG.   [42] This is provided for in §10(2) EUZBBG.

[43] This phenomenon is also typified by the increasing impact of bilateral issues on the accession process, noted by the Commission's recent enlargement reports (see eg COM(2013) 700, 2). A particularly glaring example is the name issue between Greece and (the former Yugoslav Republic of) Macedonia. The dispute has prevented the opening of accession negotiations with Skopje, despite regular favourable recommendations in this sense from the Commission.

[44] Christophe Hillion, 'Enlarging the Constitutional Order of States' in Anthony Arnull, Catherine Barnard, Michael Dougan and Eleanor Spaventa (eds) *A Constitutional Order of States—Essays in EU Law in Honour of Alan Dashwood* (2011) 485. The Court's jurisdiction in relation to EU primary-law-making procedures was confirmed in Case C-370/12 *Pringle*, judgment of 27 Nov 2012.

[45] A new discussion about the scope of application of Art 49 TEU, and its integrity has been triggered by the question of whether an independent Scotland could be Member State of the Union without having to apply on the basis of Art 49 TEU. See in particular: *White Paper on Scottish Independence* (2013) Annex 5, esp. 86; cf Kenneth Armstrong, Memorandum on Scottish Membership of the European Union, submitted as Written Evidence to the European and External Relations Committee, Scottish Parliament, *CELS Working Paper*, New Series, No.2/2014.

2. EU Withdrawal Law

In contrast to the accession procedure, the EU exit mechanism has not been put to the test. And yet, it has already been subject to considerable scholarly scrutiny.[46] This stems not only from its recent (and controversial) inclusion in EU primary law,[47] but also from the possible UK referendum on EU membership that could lead to its first ever use.[48] A common critique in the literature is that the procedure of Article 50 TEU is formulated in an 'incomplete',[49] 'unclear',[50] if not 'cryptic'[51] fashion, thus generating 'uncertainty'.[52] Indeed, akin to the accession procedure, the TEU only sets out the rudiments of the withdrawal process. Hence, if triggered, the procedure would most likely be supplemented by ad hoc arrangements the way the accession process has been elaborated. Having recalled the key elements of the procedure (a), this section will speculate on the way they could be interpreted (b).

(a) The EU Legal Basis of Withdrawal: Article 50 TEU

The EU withdrawal procedure set out in Article 50 TEU is activated when a Member State 'decides to withdraw from the Union in accordance with its own constitutional requirements' (para 1), and accordingly notifies the European Council

---

[46] eg Raymond J. Friel, 'Providing a Constitutional Framework for Withdrawal from the EU: Art 59 of the Draft European Constitution' (2004) 53 *ICLQ* 407; Laurent Grosclaude, 'La clause de retrait du Traité établissant une Constitution pour l'Europe: réflexions sur un possible marché de dupes', (2005) 41 *RTDEur*; Florentinas Harbo, 'Secession Right—An Anti-Federal Principle? Comparative Study of Federal States and the EU' (2008) 1 *Journal of Politics and Law* 132; Jochen Herbst, 'Observations on the Right to Withdraw from the European Union: Who are the "Masters of the Treaties"?' (2005) 6 *GLJ* 1755; Hannes Hofmeister, '"Should I Stay or Should I Go?"—A Critical Analysis of the Right to Withdraw From the EU' (2010) 16 *ELJ* 589; Adam Lazowski, 'Withdrawal from the European Union and Alternatives to Membership' (2012) 37 *ELRev* 523; Susanne Lechner and Renate Ohr, 'The Right of Withdrawal in the Treaty of Lisbon: A Game Theoretic Reflection on Different Decision Processes in the EU' (2011) 32 *Eur J Law Econ* 357-375; Jean-Victor Louis, 'Le droit de retrait de l'Union Européenne' (2006) *CDE* 293; Rostane Medhi, 'Brèves observations sur la consecration constitutionnelle d'un droit de retrait volontaire' in Paul Demaret, Inge Govaere, and Dominik Hanf (eds), *30 Years of European Legal Studies at the College of Europe / 30 ans d'études juridiques européennes au Collège d'Europe: Liber Professorum 1973/74—2003/04* (2005); Phedon Nicolaides, 'Withdrawal from the European Union: A Typology of Effects' (2013) 20 *MJ* 209; Jean-Luc Sauron, 'L'appartenance à l'Union européenne (article 7, 49 et 50 du Traité sur l'Union européenne)' *Gazette du Palais*, 19 juin 2008, n°171, 15; Allan Tatham, '"Don't Mention Divorce at the Wedding, Darling!" EU Accession and Withdrawal after Lisbon' in Andrea Biondi, Piet Eeckhout, and Stefanie Ripley (eds), *EU Law after Lisbon* (2012) 128; Alexis Vahlas, 'Souveraineté et droit de retrait au sein de l'Union européenne' (2005) 6 *Revue du Droit Public* 1565.

[47] See further Section II.

[48] Art 50 TEU has also been evoked in the context of the discussion surrounding Scottish independence and the relation between a potentially independent Scotland and the EU: see eg David Edward, 'EU Law and the Separation of Member States' (2013) 36 *Fordham International Law Journal* 1151 at 1164.

[49] Hofmeister (n 46).   [50] Friel (n 46).   [51] Lazowski (n 46).

[52] Nicolaides (n 46).

'of its intention' (para 2). Once notified, the latter has to agree on the guidelines for the negotiations between the Union and the withdrawing Member State. An agreement is thus to be negotiated by the EU, in accordance with the procedure of Article 218(3) TFEU. It is concluded by the Council, using qualified majority voting in accordance with Article 238(3)(b) TFEU, having obtained the consent of the European Parliament. Article 50(3) TEU then foresees that the EU treaties would cease to apply to the withdrawing state as soon as the withdrawal agreement enters into force, or absent such accord, two years after the European Council has been notified. It is also foreseen that the state having withdrawn would have to apply on the basis of Article 49 TEU, should it want to re-join the Union.

(b) A Tentative Reading

Article 50 TEU recognizes the right of any Member State to decide to withdraw, under its own constitutional rules. The terminology of the provision suggests, however, that it is *not* an absolute and immediate right.[53] For, only the *decision to depart* is taken in accordance with the state's domestic law, whereas withdrawal itself is determined by EU law.[54] The EU procedure is therefore not premised on a 'state primacy' conception of the right.[55] Indeed, in speaking of 'any Member State', rather than using the notion of the 'High Contracting Parties' contained Article 1 TEU,[56] paragraph 1 embeds the withdrawal process in the EU legal order, rather than outside it. The success of a withdrawal initiative therefore depends not only on the Member State's intention, but also on the fulfilment of the procedural and substantive requirements of Article 50 TEU, and more generally on its compliance, qua Member State, with rules and principles underpinning the EU legal order, under the control of the European Court of Justice.

Indeed, Article 50 TEU indicates that the *decision* to withdraw, and its *notification* to the European Council are both subject to conditions. While each Member State is free to set out its own constitutional requirements for the purpose of Article 50(1) TEU, as for ratifying accession treaties, this freedom might be circumscribed in at least two possible ways. First it has been suggested, referring to the literature on secession, that the decision to withdraw ought to be subject to a constraining internal procedure in terms, particularly, of democratic accountability, for instance in the form of a super qualified majority in the national parliament.[57]

---

[53] Friel (n 46) 425.   [54] Lazowski (n 46) 527.

[55] Friel (n 46) 422, Tatham (n 46), referring (at 147) to the proposal put forward by the 'Cambridge group': A. Dashwood; M. Dougan; C. Hillion; A. Johnson; and E. Spaventa; 'Draft Constitutional Treaty of the European Union and related Documents' (2003) 28 *ELRev* 3.

[56] On the notion of Member States, see eg Christopher Bickerton, *European Integration: From Nation-States to Member States* (2012).

[57] eg Tatham (n 46) 149.

Secondly, and in connection with this first point, the reference in Article 50(1) TEU to the withdrawing state's 'constitutional requirements' could indicate that EU law has no bearing on the way in which the decision to withdraw is taken, also in view of the provisions of Article 4(2) TEU. The application of domestic constitutional requirements is however premised on the assumption, deriving from that state's membership, that these conform to the general requirements of EU law, and notably to the EU values of Article 2 TEU.[58] If the decision to withdraw was taken in the midst of a domestic constitutional turmoil, that assumption could arguably be rebutted. In particular, the question could be raised as to whether mere compliance with domestic constitutional requirements would suffice to validate the initial withdrawal decision if doubts existed as to the appropriateness of such requirements in relation to EU rule of law standards,[59] particularly in view of the implications of such a decision for the state concerned, its people, and for the rest of the Union and other EU citizens.[60]

It is thus contended that the domestic *decision to withdraw* is implicitly subject to EU requirements too, notably that it conforms to the values of Article 2 TEU,[61] and primarily the rule of law. In practical terms, the European Council, to which the decision has to be notified, should ascertain that such standards are respected to consider the notification valid.[62] Indeed, it is only when this notification is acknowledged as such that the process begins and, in particular, that the clock starts ticking for the purpose of terminating the application of the treaties to the withdrawing state in accordance with Article 50(3) TEU. It has even been pointed out that since Article 50 TEU 'would be justiciable by the ECJ, this insertion [ie constitutional requirements] has catapulted that court into the role of final arbiter of a significant issue of national constitutional law'.[63]

---

[58] Recall that, according to Art 49 TEU, membership is based on the respect and promotion of the values of Art 2 TEU.

[59] The rule of law is increasingly subject to EU oversight. See, in this respect, the Commission's Communication, 'A New EU Framework to Strengthen the Rule of Law' COM(2014) 158. Also: Carlos Closa and Dimitry Kochenov, 'Reinforcing Rule of Law Oversight in the European Union' *EUI Working Papers*, RSCAS 2014/25; Anthony Arnull, 'The Rule of Law in the European Union' in Anthony Arnull and Daniel Wincott (eds) *Legitimacy and Accountability in the European Union* (2002) 239.

[60] The 'all-affected' dimension of withdrawal has been underlined by Tatham, (n 46); cf Herst (n 46) and Lazowski (n 46).

[61] Tatham, (n 46) is also of the view that the withdrawing state is 'still bound by Union values in the manner of its withdrawal. In particular, it could be argued that the values of democracy, the rule of law, freedom, solidarity and equality –Arts 2 and 49 TEU– are equally applicable to withdrawal'.

[62] In view of Art 7 TEU, there might be an EU interest in seeing a Member State leaving the Union if its constitutional evolution were at odds with the requirements of membership. However, it may be wondered whether a state that violates the values of Art 2 TEU could be sanctioned under Art 7 TEU to the effect that its membership rights, including the right to withdraw, could be suspended. The rationale being again that withdrawal affects not only the state concerned but also other Member States and EU citizens, and may thus only be admissible under EU law if initiated in accordance with EU principles.

[63] Friel (n 46) 425.

To be sure, a degree of formalism might be warranted, particularly to reduce the Member States' temptation to instrumentalize the exit threat and acquire bargaining power in the EU decision-making process.[64] This point raises another question, namely that of the implications of the notification for the participation of the withdrawing state in the EU decision-making process. The notification does not of itself have a terminating effect.[65] Article 50(3) TEU provides that the Treaties 'cease to apply' only when the withdrawal agreement enters into force, or 'failing that, two years after the notification . . . unless the European Council, in agreement with the Member State concerned, unanimously decides to extend the period'. This does not mean, however, that the notification is devoid of legal implications: paragraph 4 stipulates that the member of the European Council or of the Council representing the withdrawing state will not participate in the discussions of these institutions for the purpose of Article 50(2) and (3) TEU, or 'in decisions concerning it'.

Such an arrangement is logical in view of the roles of the European Council and of the Council in the withdrawal process: the former determines the guidelines for negotiating the withdrawal agreement with the state concerned, while the latter concludes it. Conversely, it indicates that citizens of the withdrawing state who work for the same institutions, though at administrative levels, or who are members of other EU institutions, such as the Commission (including the High Representative for Foreign affairs and Security Policy and Vice-President of the European Commission), the European Parliament and the Court, not to mention agencies, bodies and other working groups, would not be immediately affected by this exclusion.[66] While this may be justified given that they do not formally represent their state, some of these citizens might nevertheless be more amenable to defending their state's interests in the extraordinary context of withdrawal, and the ensuing job relocation that it entails. They could use their influence accordingly, for instance within the Commission, if and when taking a legislative initiative that might be of significance to the withdrawing state.[67]

Indeed, if interpreted *a contrario*, the phrase 'in decisions concerning it' of paragraph 4 could indicate that the withdrawing state is allowed, somewhat paradoxically, to take part in Council and European Council discussions about decisions *not* 'concerning it'. While such a participation may be defensible given that the state formally remains a 'Member State' until its effective withdrawal under the terms of paragraph 3, it is questionable whether it should nevertheless be entitled to influence EU decisions that might never apply to it, or indeed use its position to

---

[64] eg A. Buchanan, 'Secession' in Edward N. Zalta (ed) *The Stanford Encyclopedia of Philosophy* (2013); Andrew Shorten, 'Constitutional Secession Rights, Exit Threats and Multinational Democracy' (2014) 62 *Political Studies* 99; Harbo (n 46).

[65] Herbst (n 46) 1756.

[66] Schermers and Blokker (n 9) at 93, footnote 193, Friel (n 46) 426, Herbst (n 46) 1747, Lazowski (n 46) 530.

[67] Tatham (n 46) 151.

obtain concessions in the context of the withdrawal negotiations—even if arguably, its actual influence might have diminished as a result of its precarious position
in the system. While Article 50 TEU does not readily provide a legal basis for an
outright suspension of the withdrawing state's decision-making rights as soon as
the exit process is formally initiated, the notion of 'decisions concerning it' could
nevertheless be construed broadly enough so as to limit its weight in the Council
and European Council. The ensuing *partial* suspensive effects of the notification,
foreseen in paragraph 4, would thus circumscribe the withdrawing state's influence on the production of EU norms that would not affect it as Member State.[68]

After all, the interests of that state's *people* would still be taken care of, particularly in the European Parliament, where its MEPs would in principle still be
sitting until formal withdrawal.[69] Should there be an interval between the signature of the withdrawal agreement and its conclusion, the former could trigger a pre-withdrawal phase which, akin to the signature of a treaty of accession,
grants the state concerned 'observer' status, notably in the Council and European
Council, rather than a fully-fledged voting right, until the entry into force of the
agreement.[70] Or else, the withdrawing state would have more influence than a state
about to become member.

The notification, if deemed admissible by the European Council, triggers an
obligation to negotiate an agreement with the departing state to carve out the
arrangements for its withdrawal. This obligation is only addressed to the Union.
By contrast, paragraph 4 allows the candidate to wait until the end of the two-year
period for its departure to become effective, even in the absence of an agreement.
In other words, Article 50 TEU does not require a *negotiated* withdrawal,[71] but only
appears to establish an obligation of conduct.[72] The negotiations only depend on
the departing state's willingness to discuss although, as a Member State, it remains
bound by the principle of sincere cooperation, and therefore by the duty to help the
Union carry out its tasks, including that of negotiating an agreement, until effective departure.

Whether the principle could have any bearing on the situation is moot. Indeed,
in suggesting that the arrangements be set out with the withdrawing state 'taking
account of the framework for its future relation with the EU' (paragraph 2), the

---

[68] It should nevertheless not be construed too broadly so as not to make it too difficult for the
state concerned to change its mind before the completion of the process, eg following a change of
government.

[69] Arguably withdrawal would concern not only MEPs of the nationality of, and elected in, the
withdrawing state, as well as MEPs of the nationality of a different Member State elected in the withdrawing state, but also MEPs of the withdrawing state's nationality elected in another Member State.

[70] Case C-413/04 *European Parliament v Council* [2006] ECR I-11221, and Case C-414/04 *European
Parliament v Council* [2006] ECR I-11279, Case C-273/04 *Poland v Council* [2007] ECR I-8925.

[71] Hence it is considered by some as an '*unfettered* right to *unilateral* withdrawal': Hofmeister
(n 46) 592; also Tatham (n 46) and Herbst (n 46).

[72] Medhi (n 46).

procedure recognizes that the terms and implications of withdrawal will depend heavily on the specific circumstances and the atmosphere in which a possible negotiation would take place. In practical terms, the degree of interdependence created by membership would nonetheless push both parties to address the complex implications of their separation in a cooperative fashion, particularly for EU citizens,[73] since the absence of an agreed settlement might otherwise open the floodgates to legal claims, especially against the withdrawing state.

That a settlement should not be made exceedingly difficult is reflected by the procedural arrangements for the conclusion of the withdrawal agreement. First, in referring to Article 218(3) TEU, Article 50 TEU indicates that exit ought to be arranged by EU institutions through an *EU external agreement*, rather than through an inter-state process and treaty, as in the accession context. Secondly, the Council has to conclude the ensuing agreement by qualified majority voting, irrespective of whether its content could suggest otherwise. Thus, no Member State is in principle able to veto the conclusion of the EU agreement, in stark contrast to an accession treaty. One may indeed wonder whether the conclusion by the Council, and the absence of any reference to Member States' ratification of the agreement also entails that mixity is in principle excluded.[74] Since the EU treaties are rather explicit about when Member States must ratify specific agreements (eg accession treaties under Article 49 TEU, or an accession agreement to the ECHR, under Article 218(8) TFEU), the silence of Article 50 TEU could indeed be read as precluding their participation, however surprising that may be in view of the possible comprehensive scope of the agreement, and considering the (case) law on EU external competence.[75] That the Member States do not have to conclude the agreement would be consistent with the apparent intention to facilitate its entry into force, and to prevent its ratification lingering on in view of the disruptive effects it may have on the functioning of the Union. In short, once agreed, 'exit' would be procedurally easier than 'entry'.[76]

The procedure envisaged by Article 50(2) TEU could also mean that the agreement might not contain far reaching EU commitments in terms of future cooperation with the withdrawing state, and be limited to setting out the 'arrangements for [the] withdrawal' of a technical nature, possibly to areas where the EU has exclusive powers, such as trade. If so, further articulation of the 'framework of the future relation' referred to in paragraph 2, would be left for a more comprehensive agreement, to be negotiated at a later date. On the other hand, the arrangements for the withdrawal, however technical, might nevertheless entail policy choices, and thus

---

[73] As pointed out by Lazowski (n 46), Medhi (n 46), and Edward (n 48).

[74] cf Lazowski (n 46).

[75] eg Allan Rosas, 'Exclusive, Shared and National Competence in the Context of EU External Relations: Do Such Distinctions Matter?' in Govaere et al. (n 29) 17.

[76] Nicolaides (n 46).

the exercise of a competence. A case in point would be the movement and treatment of citizens from the withdrawing state, and of citizens from other Member States resident in that state.[77] One could hardly imagine that the borders would be shut down completely as a result of separation.[78]

That a Member State's exit might entail further agreements also results from the fact that the withdrawal agreement, as an EU external agreement, could not in itself modify EU primary law, though such modification would be necessary. For instance, the list of contracting parties included in the Preamble(s) of the Treaties, Article 52 TEU, the geographical references for example in Article 355 TFEU, and, where applicable, protocols may all have to be amended or repealed. The amendments necessitated by withdrawal would thus have to be introduced through, or in the context of, another treaty based on Article 48 TEU, or possibly on Article 49 TEU,[79] *viz* a treaty of accession concluded with another state.

It remains the case that Article 50 TEU itself makes it possible to alter the legal borders and territory of the EU, as well as its state composition, without the formal approval of all its Member States. Indeed, if negotiated, the terms of withdrawal would in principle reflect the interests of the Union,[80] rather than those of the Member States as such. The reference to Article 218(3) TFEU indicates that, alongside the European Council, the Commission would be involved in drafting the negotiating mandate,[81] and possibly entrusted with the task of negotiating the withdrawal agreement. For its part, the European Parliament, representing the interests of other EU peoples, would have to give its consent before the conclusion of the agreement, and could thus influence its content. Incidentally, the question may be raised as to how possible institutional divergence as regards the content and nature of the agreement would be addressed. Given the integration aim of the Union, including in relation to its neighbourhood,[82] and out of practical necessity, the Commission and the Parliament might seek an agreement that is more integrative than the Council would wish. The legal nature and basis of the agreement might also raise disputes. The *renvoi* in Article 50 TEU to Article 218 TFEU opens the possibility of the European Court of Justice intervening, either by way of an advisory opinion based on Article 218(11) TEU, in order to establish the agreement's compatibility with the Treaty, or by controlling the lawfulness of the decision to conclude it, either through Article 263 TFEU or indirectly through

---

[77] On the possible substance and shape of this agreement, see eg Lazowski (n 46) 528.

[78] Further: Edward (n 48) 1164.

[79] Bruno De Witte, 'Treaty Revision Procedures after Lisbon' in Biondi, Eeckhout, and Ripley (n 46) 107 at 125.

[80] cf Nicolaides (n 46).

[81] Although the participation of the High Representative should not be excluded at that stage, it is unlikely that s/he would negotiate the agreement as a whole, as it is unlikely to be considered as relating principally or exclusively to the CFSP.

[82] See further, Section II.

the preliminary ruling procedure (Article 267 TFEU). Indeed, unlike the accession agreement based on Article 49 TEU, the jurisdiction of the Court over the withdrawal agreement does not seem to be restricted.

The above discussion confirms that, like the accession procedure, the TEU only sets out the basic elements of the withdrawal process. Much would remain to be clarified if and when it were activated. That the new procedure is not more detailed may seem paradoxical. After all, its very insertion in EU law was meant to establish in advance the specific steps to be taken in the event of a separation, a situation in which ad hoc procedural arrangements are perhaps less easy to agree upon.[83] That said, the imperfection of the procedure reflects the uncertainty about the implications of exit, and the necessity of leaving room to cater for the particular needs of the situation. Perhaps the lack of clarity is also a way to avoid making the clause too user-friendly and thereby encouraging its use.

To be sure, it appears that, albeit to varying degrees, neither accession nor withdrawal can be approached as state-centred processes. More than international law inspired procedures, they both provide for a significant input from EU institutions, including the Court, and for the application of EU rules. This tends to indicate that both procedurally and substantively, the two procedures are deeply integrated in the system established by the Treaties. This seems all the more the case since, as the next section argues, they both fulfil a function in relation to the EU objective of ever closer union.

II. Accession, Withdrawal, and the European Integration Process

The previous section showed that the EU was conceived as an *open* regional organization. The Treaties on which it is founded may not only be adhered to by third European states, Member States can also leave it. This openness stems from, and epitomizes, the notion that participation in the European integration process is voluntary. While membership is the most advanced expression of such participation (1), the latter may also take other forms. It is perhaps from this perspective that withdrawal, as an *EU* procedure, may be reconciled with the integration purpose of the Treaties (2).

---

[83] Medhi (n 46).

1. Accession as an Instrument of European Integration

Enlargement to additional states (and peoples) has been regarded as instrumental to the realization of European integration (a). Yet, the interaction between accession and integration has evolved (b), paving the way for making withdrawal conceptually logical.

(a) The Continental Vocation of the European Integration Process

In introducing 'the first concrete foundation of a European federation indispensable to the preservation of peace', the 1950 Schuman Declaration spoke of 'an organization open to the participation of the other countries of Europe'.[84] This open-door conception was then couched in *legal* language, both in the initial Treaty of Paris and in the subsequent Community and then Union Treaties.[85] Expounding the accession procedure discussed above, the preamble of the 1957 Treaty of Rome underlined that Member States were 'Resolved by thus pooling their resources to preserve and strengthen peace and liberty, and *calling upon the other peoples of Europe who share their ideal to join in their efforts*' (emphasis added).

The persistence of the call may be explained by the function that accession is held to fulfil in relation to the integration process. This function is apparent in the excerpt from the preamble mentioned above, today included in the TFEU: the 'pooling their resources' formula is structurally connected to the realization of the primary ambition to 'strengthen peace and liberty' and to the 'call . . . upon the other peoples of Europe'. Membership of additional states is thereby conceived as a means to achieving the essential goal of *European* integration. As aptly put by Tatham: 'EEC (and later EU) enlargement is a natural corollary of [the] continent-wide vocation' of the integration process.[86] It is noticeable in this respect that the Schuman Declaration evoked above uses the definite article 'the' when referring to 'other countries of Europe' to which the organization should be open.[87]

The continental vocation of the integration process, and the function of enlargement in relation to it, has pervaded the discourse of EU institutions and Member States to varying degrees,[88] particularly, since the EU started enlarging to admit CEECs. Hence, on the occasion of the tenth anniversary of the EU's inclusion of

---

[84] The Declaration can be found here: http://europa.eu/about-eu/basic-information/symbols/europe-day/schuman-declaration/index_en.htm.

[85] eg Hillion (n 10).   [86] Tatham (n 1) 1.

[87] Similarly, the original French version speaks of 'une organisation ouverte à la participation *des autres* pays d'Europe', rather than '*d'autres* pays d'Europe' (emphases added).

[88] Conclusions of the Heads of State or Government meeting in The Hague in 1969. In the same vein see the letter of application for Membership in the EEC of M. Harold Macmillan, Prime Minister of the United Kingdom of Great Britain and Northern Ireland, to M. Ludwig Erhard, President of the EEC Council, August 9th, 1961. Additional explanations of enlargement are explored by Helene Sjursen, 'Why Expand?' (2002) 40 *JCMS* 491.

central and eastern Europe, then enlargement Commissioner, Štefan Füle, declared that 'enlargement is in Europe's DNA. It is a key EU policy. It is the most powerful instrument of transformation—it serves as a strong incentive for reforms. Enlargement is also the most effective and powerful tool we have for strengthening security. Together—in a united Europe—we can better face the consequences of globalization, the financial crisis or climate change'.[89] Marc Maresceau also recalls that 'it is the EU's official position that enlargement, after all, is vital to achieving the ideals of prosperity, peace and security in Europe as a whole'.[90] In the same vein, the Presentation Speech by the Nobel Peace Price Committee Chairman paid particular attention to successive EU enlargement episodes, and their significance from a peace-making perspective. It notably suggested that 'The paramount solution [to the remaining unresolved conflict in the Balkans] is to extend the process of integration that has applied in the rest of Europe'.[91] In sum, accession of additional European states has been instrumental to furthering the European integration process, and particularly to fulfilling its peace-making objectives.[92]

(b) Accession and EU Integration Capacity

The umbilical link between accession and integration as peace making has however been questioned. In practice, enlargement has not systematically defused tensions among Member States nor prevented them from getting involved in armed conflicts, albeit not among themselves, but domestically, or outside the Union.[93] Indeed, recent enlargement episodes have been seen as putting a strain on relations between the EU and its main eastern neighbour: while the accession of the Baltic States did not immediately contribute to pacifying their relations with the Russian Federation, the prospect of closer EU relations with other post-Soviet states, such as Ukraine, has considerably heightened tensions with it. It would thus appear that the contribution of enlargement to the peace-making aims of the European integration process is primarily *internal*.

The instrumental role of accession in relation to European integration has also been challenged in principle. Rather than a contribution to it, enlargement has occasionally been regarded as a hindrance to integration. This view became particularly strong in the context of the EU admission of CEECs in the 1990s.

---

[89] http://europa.eu/rapid/press-release_STATEMENT-14-143_en.htm?locale=en; also eg Council conclusions of 14 December 2010: 'Enlargement reinforces peace, democracy and stability in Europe'.

[90] Marc Maresceau, 'Foreword' in Ott and Inglis (n 2) V.

[91] http://nobelpeaceprize.org/en_GB/laureates/laureates-2012/presentation-2012/;   also   http://ec.europa.eu/enlargement/pdf/publication/2014/infographic_02_en.pdf; Steven Blockmans, 'The EU as a Global Peacemaker' inaugural speech accepting the appointment as Professor of EU External Relations Law and Governance, University of Amsterdam (2014).

[92] Further: eg Maresceau (n 30) 3.

[93] Recall the lingering conflict in Northern Ireland, or the dispute over Gibraltar. Also, France was at war in Algeria when the EEC was created.

Having established the Copenhagen criteria, the European Council insisted that any enlargement was to be decided taking account of 'the Union's capacity to absorb new members, while maintaining the momentum of European integration in the general interest of both the Union and the candidate countries'.[94]

The notion of 'absorption capacity' is not entirely new. Even on the occasion of the first expansion of the EEC it was made clear that enlargement should not hamper the objectives of integration.[95] Ever since the 'widening' of the integration process was effectively envisaged, the notion of 'deepening' has emerged to offset its possible weakening effect.[96] The constitutive elements of such capacity have however proliferated in recent years, albeit remaining chronically hazy. Initially concerned with the ability of EU institutions to function effectively,[97] absorption capacity is also contingent on the degree of public support for enlargement and on the financial sustainability of further EU expansion.[98] The most recent definition of the concept was given by the Commission in a special report on the Union's capacity to integrate new members, annexed to its 2006 Enlargement Strategy.[99] According to the report, enlargement should not hamper the EU's capacity to maintain the momentum of integration, which entails that institutions must continue to act effectively, that policies must meet their goals, and that the budget is commensurate with its objectives and its financial resources.

The enlargement–integration nexus has therefore evolved significantly. While conceptually contributing to fulfilling its continental vocation, enlargement is increasingly perceived as a possible threat to the Union's integration objective.[100] This evolution has

---

[94] Presidency Conclusions, Copenhagen European Council, 21–22 June 1993.

[95] Aurélien Hassin, 'La capacité d'intégration de l'UE—prérequis politique ou alibi technique?' *Les Brefs de Notre Europe*, 2007/06.

[96] The Hague Communiqué (n 12).

[97] eg Presidency Conclusions, European Council, Corfu, 24–25 June 1994, Presidency Conclusions, European Council, Luxembourg, 12–13 December 1997. Geoffrey Edwards, 'Reforming the Union's Institutional Framework: A New EU Obligation?' in Christophe Hillion (ed), *EU Enlargement: a Legal Approach* (2004) 23. See Alexander Stubb, EP Plenary, December 2006 available at http://www.youtube.com/watch?v=oidLHjHhCqM; see also his interview on 'The EU's integration capacity': http://www.euractiv.com/en/enlargement/interview-eu-integration-capacity/article-158959.

[98] COM(2006) 649, 2–3 and 5.

[99] COM(2006) 649; Annex 1: 'Special Report on the EU's capacity to integrate new members'. The report was drawn up at the behest of the European Council, and following various studies from the European Parliament. See eg the Stubb Report on the institutional aspects of the European Union's capacity to integrate new Member States, A6-0393/2006 (16.11.2006). The report was subsequently endorsed by the European Council: Presidency Conclusions, European Council, Brussels, 14–15 December 2006, pts 6 and 9.

[100] See, in this respect, the Coalition Agreement of the previous CDU-CSU-FDP German Government, http://www.cdu.de/doc/pdfc/091215-koalitionsvertrag-2009-2013-englisch.pdf 167. Also: Fabian Amtenbrink, 'On the European Union's Institutional Capacity to Cope with Further Enlargement' in Steven Blockmans and Sacha Prechal (eds), *Reconciling 'Deepening' and 'Widening' of the European Union* (2008) 111; Michael Emerson, Senem Aydin, Julia De Clerck-Sachsse, and Gergana Noutcheva, 'Just What is this "Absorption Capacity" of the European Union?' (2006); *CEPS*

however attracted criticism, for example from the House of Lords EU Committee, which has considered 'the debate about the absorption capacity . . . harmful since the term is inherently vague and is interpreted by many in the candidate countries as an excuse for closing the Union's doors'.[101] To be sure, the evolution points towards the notion that the number of Member States ought to be controlled, if not limited, if integration is to be pursued. It is against such a backdrop, that the rationale for the inclusion of the express right for Member States to withdraw from the Union may be examined. While it seemingly flies in the face of 'ever closer union', it may also be apprehended through the prism of the Union's integration capacity.

2. Accepting Withdrawal and Maintaining the Momentum of Integration?

It is only since the entry into force of the Lisbon Treaty in 2009 that EU primary law has explicitly acknowledged the right of Member States to leave the Union. Finding its origins in Article I-60 of the Treaty establishing a Constitution for Europe, this recent addition to the Treaties raises the question of whether such an exit was previously precluded (a) and if so, whether its introduction into EU primary law alters the nature of the Treaties and of the legal order they establish (b).[102]

(a) A New Right for Member States?

According to one view, leaving the Union had always been conceivable, both legally and practically, despite the Treaties' silence on the matter. In particular, like any other international treaty, those founding the EU could be left by any of its contracting parties,[103] based on the application of public international law, *viz* the Vienna Convention on the Law of Treaties (VCLT), or customary international norms for those states that have not ratified the Convention. To be sure, the absence of such a withdrawal clause in the statute of an international organization does not in itself prevent withdrawal by its participating states,[104] and it is precisely because the EC/EU Treaties lacked specific provisions to that effect that the above *lex generalis* would apply. On that view, a Member State could always invoke eg a 'fundamental

---

Policy Brief nr 113; Adam Lazowski, 'Treaty of Lisbon and EU's Absorption Capacity' (2011) 19 *Polish Quarterly of International Affairs* 56.

[101] House of Lords Report (n 40).

[102] In this sense see: Harbo (n 46), who suggests that it 'gives a new face to the EU'.

[103] While the Court of Justice has conceived of the EC treaty as constituting the Constitutional charter of the Community, it has also consistently admitted that it remains an international agreement (notably in Case 6/64 *Costa v ENEL* [1964] ECR 1251 and Opinion 1/91 *EEA I* [1991] ECR I 6079).

[104] As Lazowski aptly recalls, the absence of such a clause in the UN Charter did not prevent Indonesia from withdrawing (n 46) 526; also Schermers and Blokker (n 9).

change of circumstances', ie the *rebus sic stantibus* clause (Art 62 VCLT) to terminate its participation in the Treaties, under the (strict) conditions of Arts 54 and
56 VCLT.[105]

Indeed, even if conceived as the constitutional charter for the Union, the
pre-Lisbon EU primary law's silence on withdrawal would not necessarily preclude
it either. After all, the absence in the Canadian constitution of the right of provin-
cial secession did not prevent the Canadian Supreme Court from considering such
secession conceivable, albeit under certain conditions of clarity, and provided it
was negotiated with the rest of Canada.[106] Even the 'unlimited', 'indissoluble',[107] or
'perpetual'[108] characterization of a Union may not in itself guarantee its everlast-
ing existence. Hence, despite its Article 1 stipulating that 'the Two Kingdoms of
Scotland and England shall upon the 1st May next ensuing the date hereof, *and
forever after*, be United into One Kingdom by the name of Great Britain' (emphasis added), the 1706 Treaty of the Union between England and Scotland is today
deemed reversible.

The notion that withdrawal from the Community/Union has always been plausible was epitomized in practice by the nation-wide referendum held in the UK in
June 1975. Then, the British people were asked whether 'the UK should stay in the
European Community (Common Market)', implying that there was no doubt, at
least in the UK, that a Member State could always leave.[109] It has also been suggested
that withdrawal partly occurred in the case of Greenland, though in the specific
context of devolution within Denmark's constitutional system,[110] and when Algeria
became independent from France, thereby leaving the Community's territory.[111]

In sum, the absence of an exit clause in the EU founding treaties, whether
approached as international treaties or as the constitutional charter of the Union,

[105] This proposition is supported in the literature: eg Mehdi (n 46) who recalls (at 6) that the
Praesidium of the Convention made a link between the EU provision and the VCLT); Lazowski
(n 46) 525; it was also the view of some of the *conventionnels* (eg proposal for amendment of Art I-59
by Mr Lopes and Mr Lobo Antunes), though criticized by, eg, Hofmeister (n 46) footnotes 12–14 (and
literature mentioned).

[106] Reference *re Secession of Quebec*, [1998] 2 S.C. 217, which led to the adoption of Bill C-20,
'An Act to give effect to the requirement for clarity as set out in the opinion of the Supreme Court
of Canada in the Quebec Secession Reference', 2nd. sess., 36th Parliament, 1999 (first reading,
December 13, 1999).

[107] The term featured in the defunct Treaty establishing a European Political Community
(available at: http://aei.pitt.edu/991/1/political_union_draft_treaty_1.pdf).

[108] The notion featured in the *Articles of Confederation and Perpetual Union*, but not explicitly
in the US constitution, which replaced them. However, see US Supreme Court in *Texas v White*, 74
(1869) US 700.

[109] Recall also the ambition of the Labour party for Britain to leave the EC without referendum in
1981 on the basis of international law. The PASOK in Greece had similar intentions in 1981.

[110] Interestingly, this was done by relying on Art 48 TEU (OJCE 1985 L29). Further: Friel
(n 46) 409ff.

[111] Tatham (n 46) 142ff.

did not make withdrawal impossible. It was even contended during the Convention drafting the Constitutional Treaty that this addition might simply be superfluous.[112]

According to the other view, leaving the Union was not plausible prior to the inclusion of Article 50 TEU, given the specific features of the EU legal order. In particular, the notion that the EC Treaty was concluded for 'unlimited duration',[113] 'creating a Community of [equally] unlimited duration',[114] aimed at 'an ever closer union', precluded Member States' unilateral withdrawal, including through the means of international law. It has particularly been questioned whether the strict conditions for termination based on a change of circumstances could ever be met by a Member State in view of the original 'ever closer union' purpose of the Treaties to which all had to subscribe, and considering that any significant modifications, for example of the treaties. requires unanimous approval.[115] The supremacy of Community law, the enforceable rights it confers directly on Member States and individuals, its institutions endowed with sovereign rights and entitled to deal with economic, social and political issues, and its compulsory system for the judicial resolutions of disputes, have also been invoked to submit that, at the very least, 'Member States were not entitled *unqualifiedly* to revoke their membership'[116] (emphasis added). The inclusion of an exit clause in the Treaty establishing a Constitution for Europe was thus regarded as contravening the commitment to an ever closer union that States take on when they become members,[117] and the underlying general principles of loyalty and solidarity to which they are thereby committed.[118]

(b) A Logical Move?

It may indeed be wondered whether the exit clause now included in EU primary law can be reconciled with the canons of the EU legal order. For it does raise the question of how, legally, an explicit right to depart, even if always conceivable, fits with the system of the Treaties, designed as it is to fulfil the EU's 'ever closer union' objective. The question is all the more acute since the withdrawal procedure involves EU institutions. How could they be empowered by the Treaties to act against the Union's integration aim, in view of the provisions of Article 13 TEU? To be sure, such a right has a centrifugal force: it represents a risk for the very functioning of the EU in that it becomes a bargaining chip with distorting effects on the EU decision making,[119]

---

[112] Suggestion for amendment of Art I-59 DCT by Mr Ernâni Lopes and Manuel Lobo Antunes; http://european-convention.europa.eu/docs/Treaty/pdf/46/46_ArtI%2059%20Lopes%20EN.pdf.

[113] Art 53 TEU and Art 356 TFEU.

[114] Case 6/64 *Costa v ENEL* [1964] ECR 1251, 1269–1271.

[115] Further: Herbst (n 46) 1755; Jean Paul Jacqué, *Droit institutionnel de l'Union européenne* (2006) 115.

[116] Koen Lenaerts and Piet van Nuffel, *Constitutional Law of the European Union* (2005) 363.

[117] Friel (n 46), Harbo (n 46).   [118] cf Medhi (n 46) 3, Herbst (n 46) 1756.

[119] Friel then speaks of a 'system of delayed withdrawal [that] threatens both the withdrawing state and the stability of the Union' (n 46) 427.

particularly in the hands of bigger states.[120] And, once used, it could encourage other Member States to leave.

The broader (legal and political) context in which the clause was introduced may be of significance in addressing these questions, and in apprehending its meaning and possible function. It should first be recalled that the withdrawal procedure finds its birthplace in the defunct Treaty establishing a Constitution for Europe (TCE). As such, it was an integral part of the EU constitutional(izing) package, rather than an element of the de-constitutionalization course instigated by the 2007 Intergovernmental Conference, following the rejection of the Constitutional Treaty.[121] From this constitutional perspective, the inclusion of the clause in the TCE, first, reflects the intention to submit it to the canons of the EU legal order, instead of leaving it to the vicissitudes of international law, should withdrawal ever occur.[122] As Article 50 TEU is the *lex specialis*, any withdrawal of a Member State would henceforth have to take place within the framework of EU law, rather than outside it.

Secondly, the acknowledgement of the right to withdraw can be, at least partly, expounded by the *constituants'* intention to maintain, if not to bolster the dynamic of the 'ever closer union'. The right to withdraw was thus understood as a safety valve to reassure Member States[123] who would always be allowed to leave, should they be(come) unwilling to pursue the enhanced integration path incarnated in the Constitutional Treaty.[124] In the initial context of the constitutionalization of the EU Treaties, and of the strengthened commitment to integration that it argu-ably entailed, the inclusion of the exit would therefore be a quid pro quo.[125] For the Member States' choice *not* to leave arguably entails a firm pledge to pursue the 'ever closer union' goal, in line with the principle of sincere cooperation, now enshrined in Article 4(3) TEU. Conversely, the latter principle could be construed as entic-ing, though not obliging, the recalcitrant Member State to consider withdrawal, to allow the Union to fulfil its tasks and pursue its integration objectives—instead of allowing that state to obtain the dilution, or deletion of the aim of ever closer union.[126]

The right to withdraw may thereby be interpreted as the ultimate elaboration of the constitutional devices, *viz* the subsidiarity principle, enhanced cooperation,

---

[120] Tatham (n 46), Medhi (n 46) 151, and literature on secession referred to above (n 64).

[121] Pt 3 of IGC 2007 Mandate (11218/07, 26 June 2007).   [122] Medhi (n 46).

[123] See Shorten, 'a pressure valve that deflates full blown secessionist politics' (n 64).

[124] Jacqué (n 115), Medhi (n 46).

[125] eg Harbo (n 46) 42. To be sure, the then president of the European Convention had in mind that withdrawal would be open to those states that would not ratify the constitution, so as not to prevent the latter's ultimate entry into force. Beyond the question of the legal validity of such an approach, the clause was in the event not used to allow France and the Netherlands to leave the Union, follow-ing their rejection of the Constitutional Treaty (CT). In the absence of the CT, the Treaties contained no procedure for withdrawal.

[126] 'UK Keen to Delete "Ever Closer Union" from EU Treaty', http://euobserver.com/political/121607.

opt-outs and Article 4(2) TEU, deemed to cater for the needs of less integration-ist states. By the same token, it confirms that participation in the European integration process is essentially voluntary, and that the continental vocation of 'ever closer union' cannot trump its democratic foundations encapsulated in the notion that only European peoples who 'share [this] ideal' may take part.[127]

Indeed, the preamble's notions of 'shar[ing] their ideal' and 'join[ing] in their efforts' may take several forms, of which membership is only but one, particularly in view of the changing conception of the accession-integration nexus evoked above. Hence non-membership does not mechanically result in non-participation in, let alone rejection of, the European integration process. The network of EU association agreements with other European states *not* seeking membership, such as the EEA, or the EU bilateral arrangements with Switzerland, is a useful reminder of this point.[128]

The introduction of Article 8 TEU by the Treaty of Lisbon should also be mentioned in this context. Building upon the ad hoc European Neighbourhood Policy,[129] the provision establishes a specific mandate for the EU to develop a 'special relationship' with neighbouring states, aimed at establishing an area of prosperity and stability based on EU values, and involving 'the possibility of undertaking activities jointly'.[130] Read in the light of Article 21(1) TEU, Article 8 suggests that the post-Lisbon integration goal transcends the legal boundaries of the Union, and of its constituent states.[131]

By definition, the withdrawing state would become a (European) neighbour of the Union and would fall within the ambit of Article 8 TEU, as a state with which the EU would be bound to engage.[132] This provision thus not only bolsters the normative

---

[127] See, in this respect, pt 27 of the conclusions of the European Council of 27 June 2014.

[128] Consider Norway's current position in relation to the EU, as thoroughly exposed in Fredrik Sejersted et al., *Utenfor of innenfor—Norges avtaler med EU* (2012); contributions in Isabelle Bosse-Platière et Cécile Rapoport (eds), *L'Etat tiers en droit de l'Union européenne* (2014); consider also the status of 'associate membership' envisaged by The Spinelli Group, *A Fundamental Law of the European Union* (2013) 20 and 93; and Adam Lazowski, 'Enhanced Multilateralism and Enhanced Bilateralism: Integration without Membership' (2008) 45 *CMLRev* 1433.

[129] Van Vooren and Wessel (n 2) 536ff, Steven Blockmans, 'Friend or Foe? Reviewing EU Relations with its Neighbours Post Lisbon' in Panos Koutrakos (ed), *The European Union's External Relations A Year After Lisbon*, CLEER Working Papers 2011/3, 113, Marise Cremona and Christophe Hillion, 'L'Union fait la force? Potential and Limits of the European Neighbourhood Policy as an Integrated EU Foreign and Security Policy', *European University Institute Law Working Paper* No 39/2006.

[130] Further on Art 8 TEU: Peter van Elsuwege and Roman Petrov, 'Article 8 TEU: Towards a New Generation of Agreements with the Countries of the European Union?' (2011) *ELRev* 688; Dominik Hanf, 'The ENP in the light of the new "neighbourhood clause" (Article 8 TEU)', *College of Europe, Research Paper in Law—Cahiers juridiques* No 2 / 2011; Christophe Hillion, 'The EU Neighbourhood Competence under Article 8 TEU' in Elvire Fabry (ed) *Thinking Strategically about the EU's External Action* (2013) 204.

[131] eg Sandra Lavenex and Frank Schimmelfennig (eds), *EU External Governance. Projecting EU Rules Beyond Membership* (2010); Anne Myrjord, 'Governance Beyond the Union: EU Boundaries in the Barents Euro-Arctic Region' (2003) 8 *EFARev* 239.

[132] Whether this provision was ever envisaged as a post-membership device is a moot point. Suffice to recall that in its initial formulation in the draft Treaty establishing a Constitution for Europe,

basis for a *negotiated* withdrawal, it also points towards a strong post-withdrawal engagement by the Union with the former Member State. The withdrawing state's legal system might not be entirely shielded from the influence of EU law as a result.

Indeed, while enlargement is an EU foreign policy, aimed at transforming a third state into an operational member, withdrawal too is part of EU foreign policy.[133] It is a process whereby a member is to become a third state with which the Union is expected to entertain relations. Withdrawal thus entails the production of new post-membership external devices that are all the more pressing given the degree of interaction and interdependence that is created in the context of membership.[134] To be sure, the concerns of Union citizens living and working in the withdrawing state ought to be addressed,[135] particularly in view of the first EU mission which, according to Article 3(1) TEU, is to ensure the well-being of its 'peoples'.

III. Concluding Remarks

Accession to, and withdrawal from, the Union primarily involve a choice by (Member) States, thus epitomizing the original international law character of the EU legal order. A close look at the nitty-gritty of the two procedures however reveals that the freedom Member States enjoy in determining the terms of accession and withdrawal of a state, and thus the state composition of the Union as well as the notion of membership, is nevertheless constrained by the *rule of EU law*. It thereby uncovers the degree to which the EU has been de-internationalized. Both procedures involve EU institutions, albeit in dissimilar ways, and set in motion the norms of the EU legal order in which they are included. Indeed, more than simply governing the entry into, and exit from the Union by states, the accession and withdrawal clauses have a specific function in relation to, and may be explained by, the integration goal of the Union. As such, they are fully embedded in the system of the treaties, and an integral part of the evolving EU constitutional structure they underpin.

---

the withdrawal clause was inserted in Title IX together with the accession and suspension clauses respectively, which followed Title VIII on the EU's relation with its neighbourhood.

[133] The two processes also have consequences for the rest of the world. Thus, accession entails that the acceding states renounce agreements in areas where the EU is exclusively competent. Conversely, the withdrawing state has to (re)establish agreements both with third states and the EU in those very areas, once outside the Union.

[134] Edward (n 48) 1164; Adam Lazowski, 'How to Withdraw from the European Union? Confronting Hard Reality' (2013) *CEPS Commentary*.

[135] Herbst (n 46) 1755.

BIBLIOGRAPHY

Steven Blockmans, 'EU Enlargement as a Peacebuilding Tool' in Steven Blockmans, Jan Wouters & Tom Ruys (eds) *The European Union and Peacebuilding* (2010) 77

Marise Cremona, 'Accession to the European Union: Membership Conditionality and Accession Criteria' (2001) 25 *Polish Yearbook of International Law* 219

Raymond J. Friel, 'Providing a Constitutional Framework for Withdrawal from the EU: Article 59 of the Draft European Constitution' (2004) 53 *ICLQ* 407

Heather Grabbe, 'A Partnership for Accession? The Implications of EU Conditionality for the Central and East European Applicants' (1999) *European University Institute Working Papers* RSC no 99/12

Laurent Grosclaude, 'La clause de retrait du Traité établissant une Constitution pour l'Europe: réflexions sur un possible marché de dupes' (2005) 41 *RTDEur* 533

Florentinas Harbo, 'Secession Right—An Anti-Federal Principle? Comparative Study of Federal States and the EU' (2008) 1 *Journal of Politics and Law* 132

Jochen Herbst, 'Observations on the Right to Withdraw from the European Union: Who are the "Masters of the Treaties"'? (2005) 6 *GLJ* 1755

Christophe Hillion, 'EU Enlargement' in Paul Craig and Grainne de Búrca (eds), *The Evolution of EU Law* (2011) 187

Frank Hoffmeister, 'Earlier Enlargements' in Andrea Ott and Kirstyn Inglis (eds) *Handbook on European Enlargement* (2002) 90

Hannes Hofmeister, '"Should I Stay or Should I Go?"—A Critical Analysis of the Right to Withdraw From the EU' (2010) 16 *ELJ* 589

Adam Lazowski, 'Withdrawal from the European Union and Alternatives to Membership' (2012) 37 *ELRev* 523

Jean-Victor Louis, 'Le droit de retrait de l'Union Européenne' (2006) *CDE* 293

Marc Maresceau, 'Pre-accession' in Marise Cremona (ed) *The Enlargement of the European Union* (2003) 9

Rostane Medhi, 'Brèves observations sur la consecration constitutionnelle d'un droit de retrait volontaire' in Paul Demaret, Inge Govaere, and Dominic Hanf (eds), *30 Years of European Legal Studies at the College of Europe/30 ans d'études juridiques européennes au Collège d'Europe: Liber Professorum 1973/74—2003/04* (2005)

Phedon Nicolaides, 'Withdrawal from the European Union: A Typology of Effects' (2013) 20 *MJ* 209

Jean-Pierre Puissochet, *L'Elargissement des Communautés Européennes* (1974)

Helene Sjursen, 'Why Expand' (2002) 40 *JCMS* 491

Karen Smith, 'The Evolution and Application of EU Membership Conditionality' in Marise Cremona (ed) *The Enlargement of the European Union* ()

Allan Tatham, *Enlargement of the European Union* (2009)

Allan Tatham, '"Don't Mention Divorce at the Wedding, Darling!" EU Accession and Withdrawal after Lisbon' in *EU Law after Lisbon* (2012) 128

Alexis Vahlas, 'Souveraineté et droit de retrait au sein de l'Union européenne' (2005) 6 *Revue du Droit Public* 1565

CHAPTER 7

THE COURT OF JUSTICE OF THE EUROPEAN UNION

MICHAL BOBEK

I. Introduction

The Court of Justice of the European Union is one of the institutions of the Union. Praised by some as the relentless and steady motor of European integration and attacked by others as an example of a clearly biased institution, more ink has perhaps been spilled over the years on discussing the (de)merits of the Court of Justice than any other Union institution. In face of such considerable literature coming from legal, political science, sociological, and more recently also historical quarters, this chapter cannot but scratch the surface of the vast topic by providing a concise introduction to selected institutional themes in a legal[1] and, where possible, diachronic perspective: the structure of the Union courts located in Luxembourg; basic information about the type of judicial business the Court of Justice carries out; the composition of the Court of Justice, including the recent changes made to the way in which Judges and Advocates General are selected; the often discussed style and structure of the judgments; and, finally, the even more frequently discussed and recurring question of the legitimacy of the Court of Justice.

---

[1] For an introduction into the political science debate on the ECJ, see eg Alec Stone Sweet, 'The European Court of Justice' in P. Craig and G de Búrca (eds), *The Evolution of EU Law* (2nd ed, 2011).

II. STRUCTURE

When thinking of the structure of a judicial system, the image that usually comes to a national lawyer's mind is one of a *pyramid*. There is the base formed by a number of first instance courts. On it rests the middle, already narrower, appellate level. At the very top, located under the roof, is the supreme jurisdiction. In this regard, it is no accident that judicial systems are sometimes portrayed as buildings,[2] each level fulfilling a different role within the structure, but synergic and complementary to the others.

The logic of the structure of the Union courts located and concentrated in Luxembourg is, however, rather one of an internal *suspension*, carried out over the years somewhat mechanically within the limits of the politically possible. There is the Court of Justice in the narrow sense, also called the European Court of Justice (ECJ), to which attached (or from which suspended) is the General Court (GC), to which attached again (or from which suspended again) is so far the only specialized court, the Civil Service Tribunal (CST). All three judicial instances put together form one institution called the Court of Justice of the European Union.[3]

1. Evolution: The Politics of Gradual Suspension

The explanation for such a singular judicial structure lies in the evolution of the Luxembourg courts. It did not follow the logic of the gradual building up of a fully fledged 'federal' judiciary, but one of de-burdening by internal delegation/suspension. When, by 1988, the average length of procedure in the then one EC jurisdiction, the ECJ, had reached 18 months for a preliminary ruling and 24 months for a direct action,[4] it was deemed necessary to unburden the ECJ by attaching the Court of First Instance (CFI) to it.[5] As its original name indicated, the first instance decisions of the CFI could be made subject to appeal to the ECJ on points of law only. The initially narrow jurisdiction of the CFI has been enlarged step by step,[6] turning it gradually into a genuine 'General Court' of EU law, a functional shift eventually recognized by the Treaty of Lisbon, which changed the name from the CFI to the GC.

---

[2] Unless in case of buildings which might be said to be slightly out of proportion, such as the Brussels *Palais de justice*, one building in itself is able to personify the entire judicial system. In general, the structure and the design of a judicial building can tell a great deal about the type of court it harbours.

[3] Art 19(1) TFEU.   [4] A. Arnull, *The European Union and its ECJ* (2nd ed, 2006) 25.

[5] Council Decision 88/591/ECSC, EEC, Euratom of 24 October 1988 establishing a Court of First Instance of the European Communities [1988] OJ L319/1.

[6] Further eg H.G. Schermers and D.F. Waelbroeck, *Judicial Protection in the European Union* (6th ed, 2001) 755–758 or L. Neville Brown and T. Kennedy, *The ECJ of the European Union* (5th ed, 2000) 75–81.

When already some ten years after its creation, the then CFI was facing an increasing workload, the solution adopted was to replicate the same formula as in 1988, this time one level down. The Nice Treaty opened the way for 'specialized courts', previously referred to as 'judicial panels', to be attached to the CFI itself, thus creating a third level (jurisdiction) of the Luxembourg judiciary. As we have seen, the only so far established specialized court is the CST.[7] In a similar vein, the decisions of the CST, or of any other future specialized court, may be subject to appeal to the GC, and, very exceptionally, when specific conditions are met, also reviewed by the ECJ.

The problem that the evolution of EU courts poses may by now be evident: the problems of narrow straits, in which demand exceeds capacity, is not genuinely resolved, but just internally suspended onto a new, lower level, but technically speaking within the same institution (the Court of Justice of the EU). The emerging picture is thus not one of a judicial pyramid with stable foundations, but rather one of a tall skyscraper with a somewhat shaky basis, regularly threatening to tip over.

The greatest structural instability can currently be located in the middle of the Luxembourg judicial edifice: the GC ceased to be able to dispose of its case load or 'docket' in what might be considered a reasonable time. For example, in recent years, the average length of procedure in a state aid case has been about three years. A competition law case took almost four years to decide.[8] Such alarming figures[9] and the apparent inability of the Member States' governments to agree on at least the mechanical increase of the number of judges for the GC,[10] may cast doubts as to the future viability of the current EU judicial architecture. In addition, in view of the contemplated EU accession to the European Convention on Human Rights, the time might be ripe for (re) considering the Union judicial structure in broader terms, allowing for a more durable solution than the patchwork of successive suspensions that defer but do not really tackle structurally the problem of an ever increasing and more and more diverse docket.[11]

---

[7] Council Decision 2004/752/EC, Euratom of 2 November 2004 establishing the European Union Civil Service Tribunal [2004] OJ L333/7.

[8] Cf. *ECJ of the EU Annual Report for 2012* (2013) 189. Between 2008 and 2012, a competition law case in the GC took 46.2 months on average. A state aid case took some 39 months.

[9] For instance, in Joined Cases C-40/12 P, C-50/12 P, and C-58/12 P, *Gascogne and others,* judgment of 26 November 2013, the ECJ concluded that the length of proceedings before the GC in the appealed cases (five years and nine months) amounted to a violation of the Charter (Art 47—right to a fair trial within reasonable period of time) and could trigger liability of the EU.

[10] Since March 2011, the Council has not been able to agree on the increase of the number of judges in the GC proposed by the Court of Justice. See further eg A.W.H. Meij, 'Courts in Transition: Administration of Justice and How to Organize It' (2013) 50 *Common Market Law Review* 1, 6–9 and more recently 'Amendments adopted by the European Parliament on 12 December 2013 on the draft regulation of the European Parliament and of the Council amending the Protocol on the Statute of the Court of Justice of the European Union by increasing the number of Judges at the General Court' (02074/2011—C7-0126/2012—2011/0901B(COD)) http://www.europarl.europa.eu/sides/getDoc.do?pubRef=-//EP//TEXT+TA+P7-TA-2013-0581+0+DOC+XML+V0//EN.

[11] Critically J.P. Jacqué and J.H.H. Weiler, 'On the Road to European Union—A New Judicial Architecture: An Agenda for the Intergovernmental Conference' (1990) 27 *Common Market Law*

2. The Internal Structure: The Courts within the Court

In parallel to the process of jurisdictional suspension, the expansion of the ECJ itself has been equally significant: from the seven judges and two Advocates General that met for the first time in the Villa Vauban in 1952,[12] through a bigger but still arguably cosy family of some 250 people in the 1980s,[13] to 28 judges, nine Advocates General and an overall staff of over 2000 people in 2013, spread across a number of buildings. As captured by Sacha Prechal, today herself a judge but previously a legal secretary at the ECJ in the late 1980s and early 1990s, the institution has evolved from a 'bit of a family', to 'a bit of a factory'.[14]

That evolution has had considerable impact on the internal structure and the working methods of the ECJ. In 1995, in anticipation of future enlargements, the ECJ diplomatically stated that 'any significant increase in the number of judges might mean that the plenary session of the Court would cross the invisible boundary between a collegiate court and a deliberative assembly. Moreover, as the great majority of cases would be heard by chambers, this increase could pose a threat to the consistency of the case-law'.[15] The ECJ crossed this boundary in 2004 at the latest, when the number of its judges increased from 15 to 25. Today, with 28 judges, the ECJ is structurally a 'civilian' court.[16] The plenary court virtually never sits.[17] The vast majority of all cases is decided by smaller formations: either by the 'default' chambers of five judges or, if the case is believed to be a straightforward application of the existing case law, by a small chamber

Review 185. For further past discussions, see eg A. Dashwood and A. Johnston (eds), *The Future of the Judicial System of the European Union* (2001) or more recently 'Editorial Comments—Delivering Justice: Small and Bigger Steps at the ECJ' (2011) 48 *Common Market Law Review* 987.

[12] P. Mathijsen, 'Le début: la Cour CECA' in M. Lagrange, *La Cour de justice des Communautés européennes 1952–2002: Bilan et perspectives* (2004) 4.

[13] Ole Due, 'Looking Backwards and Forwards' in M. Lagrange, *La Cour de justice des Communautés européennes 1952–2002: Bilan et perspectives* (2004) 26. See also Ditlev Tamm, 'The History of the Court of Justice of the European Union Since its Origin' in *The Court of Justice and the Construction of Europe: Analyses and Perspectives on Sixty Years of Case-law* (2013).

[14] 'Interview with Judge Sacha Prechal of the European Court of Justice: Part I: Working at the CJEU' of 18 December 2013 http://europeanlawblog.eu/?p=2115.

[15] Report of the ECJ on certain aspects of the application of the Treaty on European Union [16], restated by the ECJ in The Future of the Judicial System of the European Union (Proposals and Reflections), Ch IV. 1. (i), reprinted in Dashwood and Johnston (n 11) 131.

[16] Further M. Bobek, 'Learning to Talk: Preliminary Rulings, the Courts of the New Member States and the ECJ' (2008) 45 *Common Market Law Review* 1611, 1637–1639. More generally on the structural differences between 'civilian' and 'common law' supreme jurisdictions, see J.A. Jolowicz, 'The Role of the Supreme Court at the National and International Level' in Yessiou-Faltsi (ed), *The Role of the Supreme Courts at the National and International Level: Reports for the Thessaloniki International Colloquium* (1998).

[17] Except for cases foreseen in Art 16(4) of the Statute (mandatory cases) or if the ECJ decides that a case is of 'exceptional importance' and must therefore be heard by the plenary Court pursuant to Art 16(5) of the Statute and Art 60(2) of the Rules of Procedure (discretionary cases). A rare recent example in the latter category is Case C-370/12 *Pringle*, judgment of the plenary court of 27 November 2012.

of three judges.[18] The body entrusted to assume the coherence of the case law and also to further develop the law is the Grand Chamber, composed of 15 judges, including the president of the Court, the vice-president, and three presidents of chambers of five judges.[19]

Looking at the ECJ and its operation today, it might be more appropriate not to talk of 'a court', but rather a number of 'courts within the Court' with the Grand Chamber being '*the* court within the Court', or, if its unification of case law agenda were at the forefront, 'the court of courts'. The rise of the Grand Chamber as the most important formation within the ECJ after 2004 is, however, not attributable to any effort to marginalize some judges.[20] It is rather the only way in which a body of 28 judges can reasonably operate without becoming entirely a 'deliberative assembly'. Thus, in a way, ten years after the 2004 'big bang enlargement', the pre-1995 ECJ composed of 15 judges is functionally still there. It is just called the 'Grand Chamber' now, and it is hidden within a larger structure.

A similar structure brings about different internal dynamics and working methods. Perhaps similarly to 'civilian' supreme jurisdictions, but certainly not on the same scale, preserving the unity and coherence of the case law has become an important concern for the ECJ.[21] New types of problem need to be tackled, previously unknown to a smaller, collegiate court: a five-judge chamber creating its own case law in a given area, heading off unchecked by others; emerging inconsistency across chambers' decisions, making the stepping in of the Grand Chamber necessary; even worse, modification or even silent departure of a later five-judge-chamber decision from the previous Grand Chamber ruling—to name just a few. Correspondingly, the readers of the decisions of the ECJ are becoming perhaps more circumspect with respect to the individual decisions of 'mere' chambers, unless and until they are confirmed by either the Grand Chamber or by further decisions coming from other chambers. This is, however, a logical externalization of the internal structural change: in civilian systems, it is the 'established case law' rather than a single precedent that is considered to form the (case) law.

---

[18] The 2012 Annual Report (n 8) 11 and 96 indicates that in 2012, chambers of five judges dealt with 54 per cent of cases, chambers of three judges with 34 per cent of cases and roughly 9 per cent of cases have been assigned to the Grand Chamber.

[19] Art 27(1) of the Rules of Procedure. It ought to be added, however, that the establishment of the Grand Chamber has also been accompanied by some 'soul-searching' as to what precisely that body should represent. Originally composed of only 13 judges who were mostly presidents of chambers, the membership has now been increased to 15 judges with greater participation of elected members who are not presidents of chambers. Thus, it could be suggested that the rationale has moved from a more 'unity in case law' driven composition of the Grand Chamber to perhaps more 'representative' and 'democratic' considerations.

[20] Critically H. Rasmussen, 'Present and Future European Judicial Problems after Enlargement and the Post-2005 Ideological Revolt' (2007) 44 *Common Market Law Review* 1661, 1670–1675.

[21] Further eg E. Carpano (ed), *Le revirement de jurisprudence en droit européen* (2012).

III. Docket

Function-wise, the current work of the ECJ may be roughly divided into three main categories:

1. *References for a preliminary ruling*—are submitted in most cases pursuant to Article 267 TFEU by national courts that seek either the interpretation or the assessment of the validity of an EU act. A decision rendered by the ECJ forms part of the national proceedings and will be applied by the referring court, as well as later on by other courts in the Member States.

2. *Judicial review*—within this functional category, the ECJ reviews, directly or more frequently today on appeal, the legality of acts of Union institutions (Article 263 TFEU). The remedy sought is the annulment of the Union act challenged. Jurisdiction falling under this head includes actions brought by the Member States directly to the ECJ, appeals against first instance decisions of the GC in cases of all other applicants,[22] as well as incidental review of legality of EU acts emerging from other types of proceeding.

3. *(Inter-)Institutional disputes*—re-groups types of action that oppose primarily Union institutions and/or the Member States, including infringement proceedings (Article 258 TFEU and its extension in Article 260 TFEU) and actions for failure to act (Article 265 TFEU). The remedy sought is the ECJ's declaration that a Member State or an EU institution failed to act or acted in violation of the Treaties.

This division illustrates the different type of work carried out by the ECJ, but is naturally not the only or the necessary division. Apart from the three main categories, there is also the 'left-over' jurisdictional category that cannot be put under either of the main headings outlined above. The most notable amongst these other tasks of the ECJ are opinions rendered pursuant to Article 218 (11) TFEU. In an opinion, the ECJ is called to assess the compatibility with the Treaties of a contemplated international agreement the EU wishes to sign.

The individual types of jurisdiction are the subject of detailed discussion elsewhere in this volume.[23] On the whole, however, the order in which the three main types of ECJ activity have been set out reflects how strongly each category is represented within the overall docket of the ECJ today. In the course of the last decade, there has been a distinct rise in the number of preliminary rulings and a decline in direct actions. In the past three years, about two-thirds of all cases decided by the ECJ were requests for a preliminary ruling.[24] In a way, a transformation of the

---

[22] Art 256 TFEU and its (partial) derogation in Art 51 of the Statute.

[23] Preliminary rulings in Ch 11; infringement proceedings in Ch 16; and judicial review in ch. 17.

[24] The 2012 Annual Report (n 8) 94 and 110.

ECJ into a supreme jurisdiction largely shielded from direct, first instance actions, and concerned primarily with preliminary rulings and appellate review, may have occurred. However, as outlined in Section II, the price paid for such docket 'dislocation' is becoming painfully apparent in the GC today.

Subject-wise, the ECJ remains an essentially economic court. Browsing through the court reports of the past years, most judicial attention was devoted to the same 'usual suspects', namely taxation; intellectual property; competition; state aid; internal market (free movement of goods retreating and making way for services and persons); agriculture; public procurement; and customs. However, newer areas are certainly on the rise: judicial cooperation in civil, administrative and criminal matters, in particular the fleshing out of a number of horizontal mutual recognition regimes; consumer protection law; environment; social policy and non-discrimination; and the various external dimensions of the Union and EU law.

Even if the ECJ remains predominantly an economic court as far as the overall subject matter of its docket is concerned, there has been a considerable change as to how such economic issues have been discussed in the recent case law. In 2009, the Lisbon Treaty elevated the Charter of Fundamental Rights to the status of binding primary law. Since then, the Charter has exercised a distinct *centripetal effect* on the entire EU law discourse and the reasoning of the ECJ. Problems and issues put before the ECJ have started being (also or predominantly) framed as fundamental rights issues. To be clear: the subject matter remained the same; it is just the language that has changed.

Similar effects of a human rights charter are not that surprising. In a way, they follow the same logic of the evolution in legal discourse in a number of national legal systems in Europe. Since the introduction of a powerful bill of rights and constitutional review after the fall of undemocratic regimes, be it after the Second World War in Germany, in the 1980s or 1990s in Southern or Central and Eastern Europe, but arguably also since the entry into force of the 1998 Human Rights Act in the UK, the discourse in these legal systems gradually refocused from 'mere' legality to fundamental rights protection and constitutionality. In a way, any legal problem can be translated into and put as a fundamental rights issue.[25]

Realistically speaking, the Charter or any other fundamental rights catalogue do not make the analytical tools for solving cases any sharper. With most of the fundamental rights provisions indeterminate and vague, any difficult case eventually ends up in some kind of proportionality or balancing exercise, which in itself is essentially a value judgment, just hidden somewhat behind mathematical-styled algorithms or tests. The changes are rather ideological: with the Charter, individuals and their legal protection have been put structurally to the centre of legal discourse and judicial reasoning. It could naturally be said that protection of fundamental rights was already provided for before the Charter, which is certainly

---

[25] Generally eg R. Alexy, *A Theory of Constitutional Rights* (2010).

correct. There is, however, a slight difference in such protection being a sort of a 'by-product' of other provisions or litigation strategies or the protection being the 'product' in itself.

In a number of areas, the influx of Charter-invoking cases since Lisbon has not changed much in the actual outcome. It has just added an additional discursive layer. Thus, for instance, the fact that consumer protection cases are now argued also in terms of Article 38 of the Charter ('Union policies shall ensure a high level of consumer protection'), and not just in terms of interpretation of consumer Directives, appears to have changed little in the overall approach of the ECJ.[26] On the other hand, there are also areas in which the existence of a vague 'umbrella' provision in the Charter seems to be changing the interpretation of pre-existing secondary law, such as apparently the 'freedom to conduct business' in Article 16 of the Charter for some areas of EU law.[27] Whether eventually, under the Charter and its authority, the ECJ might exercise its judicial review of the validity of EU secondary legislation more assertively than before remains to be seen.[28] There is some ground for moderate optimism in this regard.[29]

Finally, *length-wise*, the ECJ of the past years has been able to dispose of its docket within reasonable time. The average length of proceedings has been roughly one and a half years for both preliminary rulings as well as appeals. This is certainly an admirable result, taking into account that at its peak in 2003, the average length of procedure on preliminary rulings was almost 26 months, with 29 months for appeals.[30] The results have been achieved by a number of successive reforms of the rules of procedure and internal changes at the ECJ, aiming at speeding up the various stages of the procedure.[31]

A more sceptical way of looking at the same results, praiseworthy as they are, might be that the reduction in the length of proceedings since 2004 has been achieved only because the ECJ has been living on borrowed time. Following the 2004 and the 2007 enlargements of the EU, the number of judges almost doubled: from 15 to 25 and 27 respectively, with a corresponding rise in the ECJ's judicial

---

[26] Most recently eg Case C-470/12, *Pohotovosť*, judgment of 27 February 2014.

[27] See eg Case C-426/11, *Mark Alemo-Herron*, judgment of 18 July 2013, interpreting 'freedom to conduct business' in quite a sweeping manner.

[28] For a post-Lisbon case law review, see eg S. Iglesias Sánchez, 'The Court and the Charter: The Impact of the Entry into Force of the Lisbon Treaty on the ECJ's Approach to Fundamental Rights' (2012) 49 *Common Market Law Review* 1565 or Daniel Sarmiento, 'Who is Afraid of the Charter? The Court of Justice, National Courts and the New Framework of Fundamental Rights Protection in Europe' (2013) 50 *Common Market Law Review* 1267.

[29] See eg Joined Cases C-92/09 and C-93/09, *Schecke and Eifert* [2010] ECR I-11063; Case C-236/09, *Test-Achats* [2011] ECR I-773; and most recently Joined Cases C-293/12 and C-594/12, *Digital Rights Ireland*, judgment of 8 April 2014.

[30] Annual Report of the Court of Justice for 2003 (2004) 174.

[31] Further eg F.G. Jacobs, 'Recent and Ongoing Measures to Improve the Efficiency of the European Court of Justice' (2004) 29 *European Law Review* 823 or V. Skouris, 'Self-conception, Challenges

staff. At the same time, in its *Ynos* decision,[32] the ECJ stated that for a request for a preliminary ruling from a new Member State to be admissible in Luxembourg, the facts of the original case before the national court must have occurred after the accession. With the ECJ later silently departing from this requirement,[33] the *Ynos* decision nonetheless effectively discouraged requests for preliminary rulings from the new Member States. This created a window of opportunity to cut back on the deadlock. After the initial settling in of the new staff, the capacity of the institution to dispose of cases has increased without there being a corresponding increase in the amount of new cases yet.

This post-accession window of opportunity has now been closing for three reasons. First, the purely post-accession cases have by now made their way through the national judicial systems in the new Member States, with a corresponding increase, moderate but steady, in the amount of preliminary rulings arriving before the ECJ. Second, the already mentioned Charter-driven transformation of the EU law discourse has also had some impact on the number of cases being submitted to the ECJ after Lisbon. New cases may perhaps have been sent to Luxembourg because it might have been thought that the Charter had changed the legal situation, and a national court or a litigant might wish to 'test' new grounds. A number of such 'Charter-driven' cases might eventually be considered inadmissible because they are outside the scope of EU law,[34] but such cases consume judicial resources nevertheless. Third, in 2014, the transitional provision that so far limited the possibility of lower national courts to request preliminary rulings relating to the former Third Pillar measures (police cooperation and judicial cooperation in criminal matters) lapsed.[35] There might, perhaps, not be that many new criminal cases coming in from lower national courts at once. However, if they concern a person in custody, they will have to be dealt with pursuant to Article 267(4) TFEU 'with the minimum of delay', thus likely to trigger the urgent preliminary rulings procedure. This will naturally push back the 'normal' docket and distort the internal workflow.[36]

and Perspectives of the EU Courts' in I Pernice, J. Kokott, and C. Saunders (eds), *The Future of the European Judicial System in a Comparative Perspective* (2006).

[32] Case C-302/04 *Ynos kft* [2006] ECR I-371.

[33] See in particular Case C-64/06 *Telefónica O2* [2007] ECR I-4887; Case C-168/06 *Ceramika Paradyż* [2007] ECR I-29; Case C-96/08 *CIBA* [2010] ECR I-2911. Critically Bobek (n 16) 1616–1620 or Nina Półtorak, 'Ratione Temporis Application of the Preliminary Rulings Procedure' (2008) 45 *Common Market Law Review* 1373.

[34] In particular as far as the member states' compliance with the Charter is concerned. Most recently see eg Case C-206/13, *Cruciano Siragusa*, judgment of 6 March 2014, applying Case C-617/10, *Åkerberg Fransson*, judgment of 26 February 2013.

[35] Art 10(1) and (3) of the Protocol No 36 on Transitional Provisions attached to the Treaty of Lisbon (published in OJ C 83/322 of 30 March 2010).

[36] Being in turn later on translated into a rise in the overall length of procedure, even if the urgent preliminary rulings procedure itself will naturally lower the statistics a bit, but it will delay

In sum, it will soon become apparent whether and how far the smaller scale procedural efficiency oriented measures, adopted at the ECJ since 2004, may provide for a durable solution. In 2011 and 2012, the number of new requests for a preliminary ruling had risen to over 400 for the first time, in contrast to the over 200 requests of a few years before.[37] It is likely that the increase will continue. This starts creating backlogs that may, in the not so distant future, become apparent in the overall length of procedure. Reforms aiming at 'margin squeeze' within the established system are always practicable only up to a certain point. Beyond that point, the question of deeper structural changes needs to be addressed as well. It appears likely that in few years' time, structural questions relating to the Luxembourg courts might be posed again, not only because of the GC effectively drowning in its docket, but also because of the ECJ likely facing more difficult times as well.

IV. COMPOSITION

Even though we tend to refer to a court as 'it', a court is always 'they'. In the case of the ECJ the 'they' are Judges, Advocates General, legal secretaries, and other staff. Both the ECJ and the GC are currently composed of 28 judges. Ever since the Coal and Steel Community Court, the convention has been that the number of judges is either equal to the number of Member States, or, in the periods when the number of Member States was even, a second judge from one Member State would be appointed to make the number of judges odd.[38] As the protracted discussions concerning the increase in the number of judges of the GC evidence,[39] parting from this convention appears politically very difficult.

There is certainly some virtue to the system of one state, one judge. All legal systems of the Union are represented. 'Fall-back' knowledge of each of them is available. Apart from being beneficial for the ECJ internally, the one state, one judge convention may also generate external legitimacy by representation. Each Member

---

the processing of all other cases. Generally on the urgent preliminary ruling procedure, see eg C. Barnard, 'The PPU: Is It Worth the Candle? An Early Assessment' (2009) 34 *English Law Review* 281.

[37] The 2012 Annual Report (n 8) 110. Moreover, according to the provisional annual report for 2013, 450 new requests for a preliminary ruling were submitted in 2013, which represents the highest number ever submitted.

[38] Tom Kennedy, 'Thirteen Russians! The Composition of the European Court of Justice' in A.I.L. Campbell and M. Voyatzi (eds), *Legal Reasoning and Judicial Interpretation of European Law: Essays in Honour of Lord Mackenzie-Stuart* (1996) 69.

[39] Above (n 10).

State feels that 'our' judge was present, even though judges naturally exercise their mandate in full independence of their Member States and in most cases will not be present when a case originating from their Member State is being decided. On the other hand, the price paid for such representation is that presently with 28 judges, the ECJ has moved more in the direction of a 'deliberative assembly', or, as already explained above, towards a 'civilian' court in its internal functioning.

There are only two instances in which the Union courts have so far moved beyond the one state, one judge convention. First, the so far only specialized court, the CST, is composed of seven members. Its members are selected in a Europe-wide open competition. Any Union citizen whose independence is beyond doubt and who possesses the ability required for appointment may submit an application. The (pre)selection is carried out by a committee which proposes the names of at least twice as many candidates as there are judges to be appointed by the Council. The appointment and the ultimate selection is done by the Council which is instructed to 'ensure a balanced composition of the Tribunal on as broad a geographical basis as possible from among nationals of the Member States and with respect to the national legal systems represented'.[40] Second, as there are only nine, soon to be increased to 11,[41] Advocates General, their appointment is also governed by different considerations than one state, one Advocate General.[42]

1. The Selection of Judges and Advocates General

Even if the conventional composition of the ECJ has remained the same, the way in which judges and Advocates General are selected has changed considerably with the Treaty of Lisbon. Traditionally, it was for the respective national government to select a candidate internally. Once nominated by a Member State, a judge or an Advocate General was then appointed by the common accord of the governments.

---

[40] Art 3(1) of the Annex I to the decision establishing the CST, above (n 7), now re-enacted as Annex I to the Protocol No 3 to the Lisbon Treaty on the European Civil Service Tribunal, OJ [2010] C 83/226. Further see Leif Sevón, 'The Procedure for Selection of Members of the Civil Service Tribunal: A Pioneer Experience', speech given at the celebration of the fifth anniversary of the Civil Service Tribunal http://curia.europa.eu/jcms/upload/docs/application/pdf/2010-10/5anstfp_sevon_en.pdf. Interestingly, the freshly established Administrative Tribunal of the European Stability Mechanism is modelled on the CST. Art 3 of the Statute of the ESM Administrative Tribunal provides that its five members are selected by a committee following an open competition.

[41] Council Decision 2013/336/EU of 25 June 2013 increasing the number of Advocates-General of the Court of Justice of the European Union [2013] OJ L179/92.

[42] There are six AG seats permanently allocated to the larger Member States (Germany, UK, France, Spain, Italy, and since 2013 Poland) with the three (as from October 2015 five) remaining seats rotating amongst the other 22 Member States, for which today any convincing structural explanation (with the exception of blunt power politics) is lacking. Critically see R. Greaves, 'Reforming Some Aspects of the Role of Advocates General' in A. Arnull et al (eds), *A Constitutional Order of States? Essays in EU Law in Honour of Alan Dashwood* (2011) 161, 171–175.

In practice, the entire selection process was somewhat opaque. With selection criteria on the national level often unclear and selection procedures in most Member States non-transparent, it was typically not a job for which one could openly apply. Moreover, the 'common accord' stage on the EU level was rather formal, with the national governments mutually confirming their own candidates without ever questioning them, at least openly.[43]

With the quantitative expansion of the ECJ and GC after 2004, the question of the quality of appointments became arguably more acute. The Lisbon Treaty therefore established a new body that was called to give an opinion on a candidate's suitability to perform the duties of judge or Advocate General of the ECJ and the GC, now known as 'the 255 Panel' because it is provided for in Article 255 TFEU. Attached to the Council, the 255 Panel gives opinions on the suitability of individual candidates proposed by a Member State to the representatives of the governments of the Member States.[44] Thus, the Panel intervenes after a Member State has nominated a candidate but before the government representatives decide by 'common accord'.

As far as can be assessed after four years of the operation of the 255 Panel, its advent has considerably but positively changed the way in which judicial selections to the ECJ and the GC are carried out. In its first four years, the 255 Panel examined 67 candidatures. Thirty-five of the candidatures concerned the renewal of the term of office of a previously already sitting judge. Thirty-two candidatures concerned a first term of office. Out of those 32 'first-timers', the 255 Panel issued a negative opinion with respect to seven candidates. This means that the 255 Panel effectively blocked about one in five candidates.[45] Although formally the 255 Panel gives non-binding opinions, all of those opinions were so far followed by the governments of the Member States. The reason for this, apart from the unquestionable expertise of the 255 Panel members and ensuing authority, might be quite simply unanimity. To depart from the opinion of the 255 Panel and to appoint a candidate previously not recommended by the 255 Panel, all Member States would have to agree, as their 'common accord' is required. Effectively, unanimity is required to overrule a formally 'non-binding' opinion of the 255 Panel.

The advent of the 255 Panel thus started generating different institutional dynamics on the EU level as well as in the Member States. Three of them may be outlined briefly.[46] First, the six requirements set out by the 255 Panel[47] that a candidate should

---

[43] Critically eg Arnull (n 4) 23–24.

[44] See Council Decision 2010/124/EU relating to the operating rules of the panel provided for in Art 255 TFEU [2010] OJ L50/18.

[45] Third Activity Report of the Panel provided for by Art 255 TFEU, report published 13 December 2013, SN 1118/2014, 8–9.

[46] In greater detail see the individual chapters in M. Bobek (ed), *Selecting Europe's Judges: A Critical Review of Appointment Procedures to the European Courts* (2015).

[47] According to the 3rd Activity Report (n 45) 17, these are: legal expertise, including basic knowledge of EU law; professional experience; ability to perform the duties of a judge; language skills;

meet clearly set the benchmark higher than the Article 253 TFEU-based 'qualifications required for appointment to the highest judicial offices [. . .] or [. . .] jurisconsults of recognised competence'. Thus, in spite of the Panel formally insisting that it only made the Treaty criteria 'more clearly and precisely explained',[48] additional, more demanding criteria have in fact been added.

Second, the seven-member Panel consists of a majority of senior national judges.[49] The composition of the 255 Panel therefore sensibly allows for greater involvement of national judges in selecting Europe's judges. This may generate legitimizing potential for Union courts within the national judiciaries, in the eyes of which the previous system might have appeared too political, government-driven, and determined in some Member States without any representative involvement of the national judiciary in the nomination process.

Third, the European changes in both procedure as well as substance of nominations influence both of these elements on the national levels. One may notice an example of a spillover from the EU to national level. First, since the 255 Panel also enquires into the national process that led to the nomination of the proposed candidate, Member States might be more inclined than in the past to make the national selection subject to an open competition.[50] Second, as the national governments are by now aware that the 255 Panel is likely to block candidates who clearly fail to meet its criteria, they started incorporating those criteria into their own assessment on the national level.

In sum, the changes in judicial selections to the Union courts since the Lisbon Treaty have been progressive and beneficial, certainly in terms of ensuring greater quality of candidates. However, as most of these processes happen behind closed doors,[51] they represent a sort of 'progress by stealth'. They encapsulate the EU's overall predicament well known from a number of other areas of European governance: the dominance of quality but technocratic output over democratic input.

---

aptitude for working as part of a team in an international environment in which several legal systems are represented; guarantees as to impartiality and independence.

[48] 3rd Activity Report (n 45) 17. See also J.M. Sauvé, 'Le rôle du comité 255 dans la sélection du juge de l'Union' in *The Court of Justice and the Construction of Europe* (n 13) 99, 111.

[49] Within both, the first 255 Panel (with the term of office 2010–2014) as well as the second (2014–2018). See the Council Decision of 25 February 2010 [2010] OJ L50/20 and the Council Decision of 11 February 2014 [2014] OJ L41/18.

[50] The Czech national selection process established in July 2011 may serve as an example in this regard: see the Decision of the Czech Government No 525 of 13 July 2011 establishing the 'Rules for the Selection of Candidates to the Office of the Judge at the Court of Justice of the European Union' https://kormoran.vlada.cz.

[51] Operating Rules of the 255 Panel in Annex to the Council Decision 2010/124/EU provide that the deliberations of the 255 Panel take place behind closed doors and hearings of candidates take place in private. Furthermore, the (final) opinion of the 255 Panel is confidential, transmitted only to the representatives of the Member States. On the other hand, the 255 Panel sought to alleviate the

2. Inside the Factory: Judges, Advocates General, and Ghost-Writers

In contrast to the American realist tradition, EU legal scholarship does not dwell much on who the individuals are behind the 'it' of an impersonal high jurisdiction. In the ECJ, judicial individuality is suppressed. There are no dissenting opinions. No personalized style of drafting individual judgments. No individual judicial faces emerge from the collegiate court, at least in the judicial capacity. Still, who are the 'factory workers',[52] at least within the highest of the European jurisdiction, the ECJ?

Remaining on a general level,[53] to a national judge or practitioner, the ECJ may appear distinctly 'academic'. It is composed of high-profile experts with chiefly academic, not necessarily judicial, professional backgrounds. From within the present 37 members of the ECJ (28 judges and 9 Advocates General combined), 11 mention in their official biographies online at least some judicial experience in national ordinary courts prior to their appointment. A further three members of the ECJ, although they come from primarily academic professional backgrounds, have had judicial experience in national constitutional courts. The majority of current members have, however, no prior national judicial experience. They have either an academic or a civil service background, or frequently both.

The more 'academic' tone in the composition of the ECJ can be justified both functionally as well as culturally, naturally provided that it does not lead to the ECJ losing touch with the reality of national judicial function(s).[54] *Functionally*, the abstract law making carried out by the ECJ, in particular within the preliminary rulings procedure, requires analytical minds that are able to rise above a single case and a national judicial routine, and able to see the bigger European picture. A similar mindset can certainly come from both sides: from the side of a theorizing practitioner as well from a practically minded academic. *Culturally* and historically, insisting on a higher court being composed of (mainly or

---

secrecy concerns by publishing regular reports of its activity that contain general (and anonymized) information on its activities—see Council Document No 6509/11 of 17 February 2011; No 5091/13 of 22 January 2013; and No SN 1118/2014 of 13 December 2013. All of the reports are available online at http://curia.europa.eu/jcms/jcms/P_64268.

[52] Reusing the already quoted expression by Justice Prechal (above n 14). See also P. Mbongo and A. Vauchez (eds), *Dans la fabrique du droit européen: scènes, acteurs et publics de la Cour de justice des Communautés européennes* (2009).

[53] For more individualized judicial portraits, see eg Brown and Kennedy (n 6) 58–63.

[54] See generally M. Bobek, 'Of Feasibility and Silent Elephants: The Legitimacy of the Court of Justice through the Eyes of National Courts' in M. Adams, H. de Waele, J. Meeusen, and G. Straetmans (eds), *Judging Europe's Judges: the Legitimacy of the Case Law of the European Court of Justice* (2013) 197, 227–229. Critically P.J. Wattel, 'Köbler, CILFIT and Welthgrove: We Can't Go On Meeting Like This' (2004) 41 *Common Market Law Review* 177.

wholly) senior judges who are believed to be the only competent persons to understand the business of judging is the reflection of one particular legal tradition within the Union. Conversely, other legal traditions within the Union are much more open towards higher courts also being composed of academics. Succinctly put in the way of a historical parallel: is the preliminary ruling procedure at the end of the day that much different from the seventeenth- or eighteenth-century practice of *Aktenversendung*, by which any German court could have requested a legal opinion on a complex case from a *Spruchkollegium* of esteemed law professors?[55]

There are, apart from judges, other members of the ECJ: the Advocates General. In spite of having equal status with judges, they are not judges. To capture succinctly the role of an Advocate General is difficult. Article 252 TFEU states that Advocates General deliver in open court, with complete impartiality and independence, reasoned submissions on cases that are submitted to the ECJ. Since the Treaty of Nice, however, the involvement of the Advocate General is not required in every case. Today, the majority of the decisions of the ECJ are reached without requesting the Opinion of the Advocate General.[56] The fact of the Advocate General being heard only in a minority of cases, together with the fundamental rights challenges to this office,[57] may have contributed to the ongoing questions concerning their role. In contrast to the past, when the Advocate General would be heard in every case and provided a second pair of eyes and analytical layer overall, her role today has shifted perhaps more in the direction of an 'expert advisor' to the ECJ. She will be called upon only in the more complex cases, invariably a Grand Chamber case or some of the five-judge chamber ones. Within these complex cases, the Advocate General is expected not only succinctly to present the extant law and propose a solution to the case on its basis, but ideally also to provide a broader and critical analysis of the ECJ's case law in the area.

In this way, the Advocate General brings into play critical and discursive elements to the decision making at the ECJ, which to the outside world might appear somewhat magisterial. On the other hand, the critical and potentially 'dissenting' mirror held up by the Advocate General reflects only the case law of the ECJ in general. In contrast to a popular myth, the Opinion of the Advocate General can hardly serve as a 'dissenting opinion' to the judgment of the ECJ

[55] See eg S. Vogenauer, 'An Empire of Light? Learning and Lawmaking in the History of German Law' (2005) 64 *Cambridge Law Journal* 481, 486.

[56] Annual Report 2012 (n 8) 11. In 2012, 53 per cent of the judgments were delivered without an Opinion (compared with eg 50 per cent in 2010; 41 per cent in 2008; 33 per cent in 2006; or 30 per cent in 2004).

[57] Further eg N. Burrows and R. Greaves, *The Advocate General and EC Law* (2007) or M. Bobek, 'A Fourth in the Court: Why are there Advocates-General in the Court of Justice?' (2012) 14 *Cambridge Yearbook of European Legal Studies* 529.

in which it was issued, for the simple reason that the Advocate General drafts her Opinion months before the final judgment of the ECJ will even be deliberated. Thus, the judgment can position itself vis-à-vis the Opinion, but not vice versa. However, in contrast to the somewhat anonymous, collegiate bench, the Advocate General is always an 'I'. Although their influence on the ECJ might be open to debate,[58] their opinions, written in the first-person singular, are out in the open. Thus, they add a distinctly individual level to the more collegiate and anonymous bench.

Finally, somewhat hidden in the shadows of the collegiate bench or the individual Advocates General are the legal secretaries, or in French the *référendaires*. They are not members of the ECJ or the GC; they are *just* assisting individual judges or Advocates General. What precisely 'assisting' means will depend on the individual court member and the working habits within the respective judicial chambers. In practical terms, 'assisting' may mean anything between researching the case law and writing memoranda and acting as a fully-fledged ghost writer, drafting but never signing a judgment or Opinion. Whatever the case may be, it is clear that writing a judicial decision, especially at the supreme level, is nowadays a collective enterprise, both across the individual chambers as well as within.

Who are the *référendaires*? If it was previously stated that 'judicial biographies' of the members of the Union courts were so far subject to little sustained research, this is even more applicable to the level of legal secretaries.[59] This is regrettable, taking into account the hardly deniable fact that legal secretaries do exercise intellectual influence over the judicial decision making of the ECJ, coupled with the fact that a number of past legal secretaries have later became members of one of the Union courts,[60] or had illustrious careers in legal academia or practice.

---

[58] Apart from the individual studies in Burrows and Greaves (n 57) see more recently eg C. Ritter, 'A New Look at the Role and Impact of Advocates-General—Collectively and Individually' (2005–2006) 12 *Columbia Journal of European Law* 751 or I. Solanke, '"Stop the ECJ"? An Empirical Analysis of Activism at the Court' (2011) 17 *European Law Journal* 764.

[59] For a notable recent exception in this regard see S. Gervasoni, 'Des référendaires et de la magistrature communautaire' in *Etat souverain dans le monde d'aujourd'hui: Mélanges en l'honneur de Jean-Pierre Puissochet* (2008) 105. The author suggested that the community of legal secretaries at all Union courts today would be quite professionally diverse, coming from other Union institutions, legal practice, or academia. An increasing number of legal secretaries is likely to stay for longer periods, with the average age of a référendaire being about 39. Finally, around one half of all the legal secretaries would be of French or Belgian nationality.

[60] In both dimensions: past legal secretaries later becoming members of the ECJ or current legal secretaries, in particular from the ECJ, becoming judges at either the GC or the CST. By way of illustration: five out of seven current members of the CST were previously legal secretaries at the ECJ. Critically on this phenomenon see G. Vandersanden, 'The Real Test—How to Contribute to a Better Justice' in Bobek (n 46) 89–90.

V. JUDGMENT

After having introduced the 'factory workers' and their selection, the attention of this section turns to the ultimate 'product' of the assembly line: the judgment. The factory metaphor gains renewed pertinence with respect to the judgment of the ECJ, as some of the more recent changes to the structure and style of the decisions were motivated by streamlining and increasing the overall 'production' of judgments.[61]

Opening the European Court Reports from the 1960s or the 1970s and reading through the decisions of the ECJ, the inspiration of the French drafting style is readily apparent: the *attendu que* of the original French version of the early judgments assembled in a succinct, syllogistic structure, with a dry tone and abstract style. The judgments were also quite short, with most of the facts and details being confined to the separately printed 'report for the hearing'. From the 1980s onwards, the style became slightly more relaxed, gradually abandoning the 'grammatical strait-jacket of a single sentence'.[62]

Today, it is difficult to put the style of the ECJ's judgment into a particular cultural box. The drafting style could still be said to be 'civilian' in nature, but only to a certain extent. The by now distinct judicial style of the ECJ today is characterized by (1) abstract and deductive reasoning; (2) relatively succinct judgments, at least when seen from the common law world; (3) immutable and fixed structure of the judgments; and (4) the absence of any dissenting or concurring opinions.

In a decision rendered by the ECJ on a preliminary ruling, the solution adopted will frequently be 'announced' rather than discussed in great depth. The reasoning starts with the statement of one or more broad principles, with the solution adopted flowing, sometimes more, sometimes less apparently, from those principles. The language is dry and technical. Ethical, moral, and other value choices that necessarily had to be made when deciding the case will not be openly discussed.[63]

The reasoning tends to be concise, with a fixed and immutable structure. This immutability operates with respect to both the overall structure of the judgment (macro-level) as well as on the level of particular expressions, phrases, or even entire paragraphs (micro-level). Each judgment opens with a short summary of the

---

[61] Above (n 31).   [62] Brown and Kennedy (n 6) 55.

[63] Contrast eg the style and tone of reasoning by the ECJ in Case C-423/04 *Richards* [2006] ECR I-3585 with the reasoning of the ECtHR in *Christine Goodwin v the UK*, GC judgment of 11 July 2002, No 28957/95. Both cases concerned a similar factual situation—a transsexual who has undergone a gender reassignment operation sought the award of her retirement pension in accordance with her new sex. However, whereas the ECtHR would in its reasoning openly acknowledge and discuss the deeper and conflicting moral choices, the ECJ presented the (same) answer as 'naturally following' from a number of quite abstract and technical general principles of EU law and the Directive in question.

case, followed by the legal framework of the Union; national law; facts, procedure, and questions referred; arguments of the parties; the ECJ's appraisal; all neatly packed in paragraphs and numbered. At the same time, within the fixed structure, the ECJ extensively uses what could be called 'cluster citations'. It reproduces sentences or entire paragraphs from its own previous decisions, sometimes copying them verbatim, sometimes slightly changing the content of the 'cluster'.

'Cluster citations' are a distinct feature of a number of the highest Continental courts that are obliged to dispose of a number of (often parallel and similar) cases. Within the ECJ, the frequency of cluster citations may be attributed, certainly originally, rather to the issue of language and the need for a standardized text for translations. A side effect of cluster citations is the enhanced normativity of the ECJ's case law and what to a common lawyer might seem a surprising degree of 'case textualism' or 'case positivism'.[64] Decisions of the ECJ are not being primarily approached as precedents, tied to a specific case, and interpreted in its context, but viewed as a collection of normative sentences that have universal validity. In future cases, such normative sentences or propositions will be applied similarly to legal provisions, unrestrained by the context of a concrete case.

The outlined structural immutability on both a macro- as well as a micro- level further enhances the sensation of 'inevitability' as to the results reached by the ECJ. It appears that the ECJ just puts together parts of the law that were already there. Naturally, such an illusion might dissipate quite quickly if a curious reader inspects more closely the references to previous decisions employed in a judgment. As the ECJ would typically not canvass its own previous decisions in any depth, with the references having more of a 'bibliographical' value, if a reader takes the effort and tracks back all the references made, she might soon find out that some references are more appropriate than others. Some might indeed point back to clear and rich established case law, whereas others would only point to rich but not really established case law. Eventually, there may also be references pointing just to the pious wishes of the ECJ that it had said something before, typically introduced by an enigmatic 'see in this sense'.[65]

Whatever formation of the ECJ decided a case, the outcome will always be a single, collegiate judgment. This may regressively influence the reasoning of the ECJ. If no dissent is allowed, a court may prefer to reach unanimity, even at the cost of making compromises. Alternatively, even if eventually outvoted, the minority might be successful in introducing some of their ideas into the judgment, even if the majority solution stands. This is how gaps in the reasoning of the ECJ may

---

[64] A feature previously observed with respect to the work with highest courts' case law in a number of civilian systems in N. MacCormick and R.S. Summers (eds), *Interpreting Precedents: A Comparative Study* (1997). Further see also J. Komárek, 'Reasoning with Previous Decisions: Beyond the Doctrine of Precedent' (2013) 61 *American Journal of Comparative Law* 149.

[65] Further see eg M.A. Jacob, *Precedent and Case-based Reasoning in the European Court of Justice: Unfinished Business* (2014).

appear. A reader of a judgment may sometimes have the impression that 'there is something missing here'. There is a 'non sequitur' in the flow of the argument. In extreme cases, collegiality might even lead to almost no reasons at all, in particular in some exceptional Grand Chamber cases.[66]

Whether the format and style of judgments sketched above are appropriate for a European court to adopt may naturally be open to debate. The more vocal critiques of the judicial style of the ECJ came in the past, in particular from Anglo-American legal commentators. The ECJ was said to be 'simply oracular and almost apocryphal'.[67] It was suggested that the ECJ should 'abandon the cryptic, Cartesian style [. . .] and move to the more discursive, analytic, and conversational style associated with the common law world'.[68]

Two elements essential for the discussion ought to be clearly articulated: the practical and the normative. On the *practical* level, a working environment predetermines the judicial style. If there is an international, multilingual court the decisions of which are to be translated into a further 23 languages and the task of which is to provide, certainly on preliminary rulings, general statements of the law and not to solve concrete cases, then having decisions that are rather abstract, succinct, with a fixed structure, and speaking with one voice can hardly be said to be that shocking. It would be rather surprising if a court working within such an environment indulged in passing detailed, lengthy, discursive, and conversational judgments in the form of a bundle of individual judicial opinions that concur in part and dissent in the rest, and which one has to disentangle first, in order to understand what may be the opinion of the court.

This is certainly not to state that there is 'no choice left' with respect to how the judgment of the ECJ might look. However, how such a choice should be exercised is then the question of the *normative* vision of how a court ought to reason and for whom. Who is the audience and what do they expect? Academic expectations might be different from judicial ones. What an English judge might consider 'simply oracular' may appear a decently reasoned decision to some of her Continental colleagues. Yet again, after 2004, not only did the ECJ become a 'civilian' court as to its internal structure and working method, the vast majority of its 'judicial clients' are now also in fact Continental judges.[69]

In sum, over the years, the ECJ developed a singular way of reasoning its judgments. Originally inspired by the French tradition, the style has by now grown into a distinct style in its own right. Although it may be subject to critique on a number of grounds, with particular cultural/professional traditions in the background or

---

[66] Cf eg Case C-34/09 *Ruiz Zambrano* [2011] ECR I-1177.
[67] Lord Melville quoted by Brown and Kennedy (n 6) 55.
[68] J.H.H. Weiler, 'Epilogue: The Judicial Après Nice' in G. de Búrca and J.H.H. Weiler (eds), *The European Court of Justice* (2001) 225.
[69] Further Bobek (n 54). Generally also Arnull (n 4) 9–14.

driven by a particular normative agenda, the overall outcome is perhaps not as problematic as is sometimes portrayed. This does not preclude, as in any system, individual lapses in which the ECJ offers questionable reasons in a decision[70] or hardly any reasons at all.[71] Nevertheless, the performance of a factory ought to be assessed as to its overall output, of which the amount of rejects is just one of the factors to be taken into consideration.

VI. Legitimacy

There is hardly any other issue relating to the operation of the Court of Justice of the EU and the ECJ in particular that would give rise to such heat and passion—the legitimacy of what the ECJ has been doing and how it has been doing it. Perhaps the problem starts at the definition level. Legitimacy is a hopelessly indeterminate notion. When is an institution such as a court legitimate? Who assesses what with respect to what constituency or respondents (general public, professional public, other specific group or constituency)?[72] What precisely is being looked at (an institution as a whole, staff, procedures, reasoning, standards of written decisions, etc)?[73] Against what criteria is the output of the institution measured (legal (textual), sociological, moral)?[74] Finally, precisely what level of legitimacy debate is one engaging in? General or overall legitimacy or support for an actor or institution or specific legitimacy or support for a concrete policy or decision?

Much of the disagreement as to whether the ECJ is 'legitimate' might thus perhaps have been caused by the initial divergence in approach and yardstick. Whatever approach might eventually be chosen, the overall debate concerning the

---

[70] An example in this category might be provided by a three paragraph 'reasoning' together with a reference to an impertinent previous decision, while completely omitting to mention a number of other, pertinent previous decisions, but saying actually the contrary, in Case C-302/04 *Ynos* [2006] ECR I-71.

[71] See eg the already quoted *Ruiz-Zambrano* (n 66) or Case C–273/04 *Poland v Council* [2007] ECR I-8925. In such cases, the ECJ can be said to give 'a circumloquacious statement of the result, rather than a reason for arriving at it'—see S. Weatherill, 'The Court's Case Law on the Internal Market: "A Circumloquatious Statement of the Results, Rather than a Reason for Arriving at It"?' in Adams, de Waele, Meeusen, and Straetmans (n 54) 87.

[72] See eg G.A. Caldeira and J.L. Gibson, 'The Legitimacy of the Court of Justice in the European Union: Models of Institutional Support' (1995) 89 *American Political Science Review* 356.

[73] Cf Nick Huls, 'Introduction: From Legitimacy to Leadership' in Nick Huls, Maurice Adams, and Jacco Bomhoff (eds), *The Legitimacy of Highest Court's Rulings: Judicial Deliberations and Beyond* (2009) 3, 13–18.

[74] See R.H. Fallon, Jr, 'Legitimacy and the Constitution' (2005) 118 *Harvard Law Review* 1787.

legitimacy of the ECJ today has become perhaps more critical and richer than in the past.[75] This might be due not only to ongoing Euro-fatigue and omnipresent 'crisis-talk', but also perhaps to the fact that courts in general are being scrutinized more critically, on the international as well as on the national levels.[76]

Within the 'legal' strand of the legitimacy debate, as opposed to the more political science or sociological approaches, there is one issue that stands out: the question of the 'proper' reasoning method[77] to be followed by the ECJ. In the European positivist tradition, lawyers tend to assert that there is a proper, 'scientific' method for a court, and hence also for the ECJ, to reason. Implicitly or even explicitly, if the ECJ departs from such 'proper' ways of interpretation, its decisions are illegitimate.[78]

The corresponding debate is one of legal 'activism', 'self-restraint', and the limits of legal reasoning for the ECJ. A recurring and major theme in these debates is a certain 'pro-Union' interpretative tendency in the reasoning of the ECJ. This may be called an interpretative 'meta-rule', a *communautaire* tendency', just a collision rule of *in dubio pro integratione*, or dismissed as 'pro-EU interpretative bias' on the part of the ECJ. Stated in very simplistic terms, the ECJ is said to favour the interpretative approach and outcome that enhance further integration.

The abstract issue of this 'pro-Union interpretative tendency' can be further teased out on the basis of the examples of two arguably problematic areas: first, how far can a court override relatively clear legislation? Second, can EU law be further developed in sensitive areas (criminal law, tax law, areas of judicial cooperation) to the detriment of the individual? Whereas the first type of case is questionable in terms of the principle of separation of powers, the second type encounters problems with the rule of law.

More recent examples falling into the first category might include *Mangold*,[79] *Sturgeon*,[80] and, in a lesser way, also perhaps *Pringle*.[81] Naturally, the inclusion of

---

[75] For a succinct recent review of the English literature up to 2012, see Gerard Conway, *The Limits of Legal Reasoning and the European Court of Justice* (2012) 52–85. From the most recent contributions, see for instance: M. Adams, H. de Waele, J. Meeusen, and G. Straetmans (n 54); M. Dawson, B. de Witte, and E. Muir (eds), *Judicial Activism at the European Court of Justice* (2013). See also Thomas Horsley, 'Reflections on the Role of the Court of Justice as the "Motor" of European Integration: Legal Limits to Judicial Lawmaking' (2013) 50 *Common Market Law Review* 931.

[76] Cf eg the critical analysis offered by C. Schönberger, M. Jestaedt, O. Lepsius, and C. Möllers in *Das entgrentzte Gericht: Eine kritische Bilanz nach sechzig Jahren Bundsverfassungsgericht* (2011), which challenges on many levels the icon of the German post Second World War constitutional system: the Federal Constitutional Court.

[77] See in general also Ch 2 in this volume on Legal Reasoning in the EU.

[78] Recently put forward eg by Roman Herzog and Ludwig Gerken in 'Stoppt den Europäischen Gerichtshof' published in the *Frankfurter Allgemeine Zeitung* of 8 September 2008, in English translation accessible online at http://www.cep.eu. See also the Editorial Comments 'The Court of Justice in the Limelight—Again' (2008) 45 *Common Market Law Review* 1571.

[79] Case C-144/04 *Mangold* [2005] ECR I-9981.

[80] Joined cases C-402/07 and C-432/07 *Sturgeon* [2009] ECR I-10923.

[81] Case C-370/12 *Pringle*, judgment of the Full Court of 27 November 2012.

these cases into such a category might be contested.[82] However, for the sake of the argument, one may suggest that in *Mangold*, the ECJ effectively overwrote the legislative choice of both the Union legislator as well as the German legislator, conjuring out of thin air a questionable general principle of EU law. In *Sturgeon*, the ECJ disregarded fairly clear categories established by the EU legislation, an interpretative approach that at least according to its own Advocate General[83] was not appropriate for a 'court' to take.[84] Lastly, whether the ECJ went too far in *Pringle* and effectively overwrote or just 'distinguished' categories created by primary law may perhaps be open to debate.[85] However, in terms of clear expression of legislative will, *Pringle* is perhaps the most 'restrained' amongst the illustrative triplet mentioned here.

The second category unites the examples in which the ECJ, in the interest of further development of EU law in a specific area, may appear to have disregarded area-specific principles that call for caution or restrictive interpretation in matters of, for instance, criminal law, tax law, or administrative sanctions. In general terms, these principles favour legal certainty and the protection of rights of the individual over 'effective enforcement of the law' by introducing principles like *nullum crimen, nulla poena sine lege*; the requirement of clarity and foreseeability of criminal or tax legislation; the requirement for a proper and clear statutory basis for the imposition of obligations or fines; or access to effective review and judicial remedies. If in these areas, the sweeping purposive reasoning that presumably favours unity and effective enforcement of EU law is applied, the ECJ might end up imposing *de facto* sanctions without a proper legal basis, or denying legal protection to persons who are lost in between legal systems.

Examples in this category might include *Halifax* in the area of value added tax, where the ECJ concluded that abusive practice might be also an activity that is in fact not expressly prohibited by legislation, but 'the transactions concerned [. . .] notwithstanding formal application of the conditions laid down by the relevant provisions of the Sixth Directive [. . .] result in the accrual of a tax advantage the grant of which would be *contrary to the purpose* of those provisions'.[86] In the subsequent case of *R.*, the issue of criminal legality is picked up and discussed by AG Cruz Villalón, leading him to the conclusion that criminal law sanctions imposed on the basis of

---

[82] Cf the opposing views on these and other recent cases of Koen Lenaerts and J.H.H. Weiler in Adams, de Waele, Meeusen, and Straetmans (n 54.)

[83] Cf the Opinion of AG Sharpston of 2 July 2009 in *Sturgeon* 91–97.

[84] Thus prompting also the singular request for a preliminary ruling by the *Landgericht Köln* in reaction to *Sturgeon* that inquired, in a nutshell, whether the ECJ has heard of the principle of separation of powers—see Case C-413/11 *Germanwings*, judgment of 18 April 2013.

[85] A debate that is not over, taking into account the recent first ever request for a preliminary ruling submitted to the ECJ by the German Federal Constitutional Court (BVerfG of 14 January 2014, 2 BvR 2728/13 www.bverfg.de), in which a number of issues addressed in *Pringle* are likely to be tackled again.

[86] Case C-255/02 *Halifax* [2006] ECR I-1609, 86, author's emphasis.

'teleological' reading of VAT legislation are not possible.[87] Again, the Grand Chamber appeared not to be impressed by such arguments and affirmed the possibility of criminal sanctions in similar cases.[88] In *Estonia v Commission*, the EU courts found no difficulty in confirming a fine imposed on Estonia, the legal basis for which was very questionable, again essentially approving a legal sanction based on the aim and purpose of a provision.[89] In a rule-of-law-based system, can one impose restrictions or sanctions on the basis of judicially or administratively conjured purpose without proper legal basis in the law itself?

Finally, the recent spree of horizontal cooperation mechanisms in criminal and administrative matters meant that the ECJ entered an area where a restrictive, rights-protecting approach may be deemed more appropriate than EU-enhancing, sweeping *effet utile* assertions, which may appear further to develop European integration, but also leave the individual in question without an effective remedy. The Opinion of AG Mazák in *Kyrian*[90] is a vivid example of such an approach: the full effectiveness of horizontal mutual assistance for the recovery of levies and tax cannot be called in question and must be asserted, even if the procedural system established by the Directive is clearly deficient,[91] and leaves the individual without any possibility of judicial review of an administrative decision in the adoption of which he did not participate in the requesting state, and which was served on him in a foreign language in his home state.[92]

With respect to examples in both of the categories as well as others, the discussion whether or not it is correct for a court to reason in this way and to arrive at such conclusions is a normative debate on the 'proper' method to be adopted by the ECJ and its limits. It is essentially a value judgment about the boundaries of the judicial function, often heavily determined by the personal and social background of the author. The important point is nonetheless that in terms of 'legal' analysis, the debate on method glides over into the discussion of the legitimacy of the ECJ: can a body consistently deciding in one direction be perceived as an independent and impartial court?

At the root of the social legitimacy of courts is arguably their impartiality: a court is called to decide because it is the independent third. That is why it was created and

---

[87] Opinion of 29 June 2010 in Case C-285/09 *Criminal proceedings against R* [2010] ECR I-12605, in particular 48–56.

[88] Case C-285/09 *Criminal proceedings against R* [2010] ECR I-12605.

[89] Case T-324/05 *Estonia v Commission* [2009] ECR II-3681, 116 and 119, confirmed on appeal in Case C-535/09 P, *Republic of Estonia v European Commission* [2011] ECR I-34.

[90] Opinion of AG Mazák of 15 September 2009 in Case C-233/08 *Kyrian* [2010] ECR I-177. It ought to be added that the ECJ did not follow the Advocate-General.

[91] Council Dir 76/308/EEC of 15 March 1976 on mutual assistance for the recovery of claims resulting from operations forming part of the system of financing the European Agricultural Guidance and Guarantee Fund, and of the agricultural levies and customs duties [1976] OJ L73/18.

[92] Further examples A. Albi, 'An Essay on How the Discourse on Sovereignty and the Co-operativeness of National Courts Has Diverted Attention from the Erosion of Classic Constitutional Rights in the EU' in M. Claes, M. De Visser, P. Popelier, and C. van de Heyning (eds), *Constitutional Conversations in Europe: Actors, Topics and Procedures* (2012).

that is also why disputes keep being submitted to it. However, can a 'biased' institution be called a court? The legitimacy debate shifts its focus from the method to its outcomes. The chief challenge becomes not (just) that the ECJ is perceived to have stepped over the boundaries of 'proper' judicial reasoning, in either of the two or more categories outlined above, but that it does so instrumentally and asymmetrically in one and only one direction: to further enhance integration. Even a more assertive court that is generally believed to have sometimes stepped over the boundaries of 'proper' judicial reasoning might still be perceived as impartial and thus somewhat legitimate, because it does so indiscriminately to the benefit/detriment of all actors.

If pushed even further, it may be suggested that the approach that once moved the ECJ forward and allowed it to make its distinct imprint on the process of European integration has now become an obstacle to its further evolution within a changed social context. Today, the ECJ arguably has the ambition to become more than a 'one-sided economic court'. Taking into account the spread of issues and areas coupled with the rise of the Charter already discussed and the overall re-focusing of the legal discourse in EU law, the ECJ is on the verge of becoming a genuine Supreme Court of the Union. The strength and legitimacy of a genuine supreme court lies, however, in its impartiality and independence. The source of its legitimacy rests less in substance (result or outcome) and more in the process itself. A genuine supreme court in a larger federal unity ought to decide even-handedly in favour as well as against the federation. Such a court draws its legitimacy from the impartial judicial process itself, not from one-sided 'corruption by rights' for the individuals coupled with messianic[93] promises of a 'Community of Destiny' to come.[94]

Should this be the next step for the ECJ? If yes, would this also herald the evolution of the Union into a more stable and matured community that does not see a mere annulment of one or more legislative adventures to be a life-threatening disaster? Equally, maturity of a political community might mean the maturing of its scholarship, which may become more ready to accept that the criticism of some or even all aspects of the method of the ECJ or any other EU institution does not necessarily mean an attack on the very idea of European integration. There might be persons criticizing the style of reasoning of the ECJ that are, in their political convictions, ardent European federalists. They may just not believe that noble political ends should be allowed to justify any judicial means.

Eventually, as already explained, at the heart of the debates concerning the 'proper' judicial method to be employed by the ECJ and spilling over into the debates concerning its legitimacy will always be a further non-reducible judgment

---

[93] Further J.H.H. Weiler, 'The Political and Legal Culture of European Integration: an Exploratory Essay' (2011) 9 *International Journal of Constitutional Law* 678, 682.

[94] Further M. Bobek, 'Van Gend +50: The Changing Social Context of Direct Effect' in Court of Justice of the European Union, *50th Anniversary of the Judgment in Van Gend en Loos 1963–2013: Conference Proceedings* (2013) 181, 183–186.

call. The ongoing debates concerning the legitimacy of the ECJ offered in the closing section of this chapter, together with the institutional and structural changes the institution has been facing since 2004, and the current omnipresent 'Euro-crisis' and ensuing 'Euro-fatigue' indicate that there are interesting times ahead for the Court of Justice of the European Union.

BIBLIOGRAPHY

M. Adams, H. de Waele, J. Meeusen, and G. Straetmans (eds), *Judging Europe's Judges: the Legitimacy of the Case Law of the European Court of Justice* (2013)

A. Arnull, *The European Union and its Court of Justice* (2nd ed, 2006)

L. Azoulai and R. Dehousse, 'The European Court of Justice and the Legal Dynamics of Integration' in E. Jones, A. Menon, and S. Weatherill (eds), *The Oxford Handbook of the European Union* (2012)

G. de Búrca and J.H.H. Weiler (eds), *The European Court of Justice* (2001)

N. Burrows and R. Greaves, *The Advocate General and EC Law* (2007)

A.I.L. Campbell and M. Voyatzi (eds), *Legal Reasoning and Judicial Interpretation of European Law: Essays in Honour of Lord Mackenzie-Stuart* (1996)

Court of Justice of the EU, *50th Anniversary of the Judgment in Van Gend en Loos 1963–2013: Conference Proceedings* (2013)

Court of Justice of the EU, *The ECJ and the Construction of Europe: Analyses and Perspectives on Sixty Years of Case-law* (2013)

A. Dashwood and A. Johnston (eds), *The Future of the Judicial System of the European Union* (2001)

M. Dawson, B. de Witte, and E. Muir (eds), *Judicial Activism at the European Court of Justice* (2013)

R. Dehousse, *La Cour de Justice des Communautés européennes* (2nd ed, 1997)

M. Lagrange, *La Cour de justice des Communautés européennes 1952–2002: Bilan et perspectives* (2004)

L. Neville Brown and T. Kennedy, *The Court of Justice of the European Communities* (5th ed, 2000)

I. Pernice, J. Kokott, and C. Saunders (eds), *The Future of the European Judicial System in a Comparative Perspective* (2006)

H. Rasmussen, *On Law and Policy in the European Court of Justice* (1986)

H.G. Schermers and D.F. Waelbroeck, *Judicial Protection in the European Union* (6th ed, 2001)

A. Stone Sweet, 'The European Court of Justice' in P. Craig and G. de Búrca (eds), *The Evolution of EU Law* (2nd ed, 2011)

House of Lords European Union Committee, 'Workload of the Court of Justice of the European Union'—report of 29 March (2011) http://www.publications.parliament.uk/pa/ld201011/ldselect/ldeucom/128/12802.htm

House of Lords European Union Committee, 'Workload of the Court of Justice of the European Union: Follow-Up Report' of 29 April (2013) http://www.publications.parliament.uk/pa/ld201213/ldselect/ldeucom/163/16302.htm

CHAPTER 8

THE PRIMACY OF EU LAW IN EUROPEAN AND NATIONAL LAW

MONICA CLAES

I. INTRODUCTION

SINCE the Court of Justice first established it in *Costa v ENEL*, primacy continues to be one of the core principles of EU law, and is without a doubt one of the most fundamental characteristics that make EU law unprecedented and unique to this day.[1] No other body of international law has managed to become so deeply immersed and so effective in the domestic legal orders of its Member States. The EU principle of primacy claims that *all* EU law has absolute and unconditional precedence and should always be given precedence over *all* conflicting provisions of national law. The latter can therefore never be invoked to escape the application of EU law. This obligation to award priority to EU law applies to all state bodies, legislative, executive, and judicial.

Nevertheless, for all its uniqueness and despite the fact that most legal actors have accepted it to a large extent, primacy remains sensitive and contested. This is witnessed by the fact that the attempt to codify it in the Constitutional Treaty failed.

---

[1] Note that Declaration 17 to the TEU uses the term 'primacy', not 'supremacy'. The Court seems to use interchangeably the terms 'priority', 'primacy', and 'precedence', but not 'supremacy'.

Primacy was eventually omitted from the main body of the Lisbon Treaty, as part of the 'de-constitutionalization' operation, along with the Union's flag and anthem, its Minister of Foreign Affairs, its 'laws' and its constitutional appearance. In the Lisbon Treaty, the principle has been relegated to Declaration 17, and essentially remains judge-made.

The absolute and unconditional version of the principle of primacy is only the EU version of primacy: it is the position as a matter of EU law. It has not been accepted unconditionally in the Member States. Indeed, since the principle has to be given effect in the domestic legal order by national authorities over which the EU institutions have no direct say, the actual acceptance and compliance by these authorities is crucial. And in response, they have formulated their own conceptualization of the relationship between national and European law and of primacy which does not always overlap with the EU version. Accordingly, the reality of the primacy of EU law is two-dimensional:[2] there is an EU principle of EU law, and there are national conceptions of the primacy of EU law. As Lord Reed JSC recently explained in *HS2* with respect to the UK, any question about the relationship between EU and national law 'cannot be resolved simply by applying the doctrine developed by the Court of Justice of the supremacy of EU law, since the application of that doctrine in our law itself depends upon the 1972 Act'.[3] A complete understanding of the *actual* relationship between national and European law as it operates in practice thus requires an inquiry both into the EU and the national perspectives.

While these national versions of the primacy of EU law vary between themselves, a number of common trends can be discerned. First, virtually all of them seek the foundation of the primacy of EU law in the national constitution rather than in the nature of EU law as an autonomous new legal order. As it is national law that serves as the basis for the application of EU law in the domestic legal order, it also determines the conditions and limits of such application. Second, while most national conceptions generally accept the primacy of EU law over national legislation, the same is not true for primacy over (parts of) the national Constitution. In other words, primacy is not unconditional, but hinges on the compliance of the relevant EU law with the core principles of the national Constitution.

The principle of primacy is one of the oldest and most basic principles of EU law. Yet since it was first introduced, the European Union and EU law have changed dramatically. Is the principle still the same as when it was developed in the cases *Costa v ENEL*,[4] *Internationale Handelsgesellschaft*,[5] *Simmenthal*,[6] and *IN.CO.GE*?[7] Or has it changed, and is there now a softer, more 'pluralist' principle of primacy

---

[2] Bruno De Witte, 'Direct Effect, Primacy and the Nature of the Legal Order' in Gráinne de Búrca and Paul Craig (eds), *The Evolution of EU Law* (2011) 323, 356.

[3] *UK Supreme Court*, judgment of 22 January 2014 *R (on the application of HS2 Action Alliance Limited) v The Secretary of State for Transport and another* [2014] UKSC 3; [2014] 1 WLR 324.

[4] Case 6/64 *Costa v ENEL* [1964] ECR 595.

[5] Case 11/70 *Internationale Handelsgesellschaft* [1970] ECR 1125.

[6] Case 106/77 *Simmenthal* [1978] ECR 629.

[7] Joined Cases C-10/97 to C-22/97 *IN.CO.GE '90* [1998] ECR 6307.

that is no longer unconditional and permits exceptions? And *should* the principle continue to exist in its absolute form, or should a mature EU be able to accept unilateral national exceptions to EU law, in order to sanction the existing value plurality and national diversity existing in the EU?[8] The position defended in this chapter is that the principle of primacy in EU law is essentially exactly the same as before, and that it has not changed its meaning of absolute and unconditional primacy. Despite the inclusion of a national identity clause in Article 4(2) TEU, despite Article 53 of the Charter, the success of the 'pluralist movement', and talk of judicial deference and dialogue, EU law still does not permit Member States to unilaterally decide to override EU obligations and give precedence to measures of national law, however framed. Nevertheless, the contours of the principle of primacy have changed, because the context within which the principle applies today is different, and EU law itself allows for more flexibility. However, this does not inherently change the principle and its operation.

This chapter will proceed as follows. The second section focuses on the EU perspective and explains the principle as a matter of EU law. The subsequent section then moves on to discuss the national perspective and sets out the main trends in the case law of national courts on the primacy of EU law. The fourth section addresses the newer developments that presumably modify the absolute nature of primacy to conclude that while the context within which it applies is different, the principle of primacy in EU law is still the same as it was when it was first formulated in *Costa*.

II. The Principle of Primacy in EU Law

1. The Origins of Primacy

While it may be true that the extent to which the EU is able to give effect to the primacy of EU law is unparalleled, and in a sense also distinguishes it from most other treaty organizations, this is not to say that primacy is unknown to general international law.[9] Indeed, it is a general principle of international law that international treaties take precedence over national law and that national law cannot

---

[8] For a lucid normative account of value diversity in the EU, see Floris De Witte, 'Sex, Drugs and EU Law: The Recognition of Moral and Ethical Diversity in EU Law' (2013) 50 *Common Market Law Review* 1545.

[9] For an 'international reading' of the EU principle of primacy, see Bruno De Witte, 'Retour à Costa'—La primaute du droit communautaire a la lumière du droit international' (1984) *Revue trimestrielle de droit europeéen* 425 and more recently by the same author 'The European Union

be invoked to prevail over international treaties.[10] Yet this primacy is situated at the international plane and does not concern the domestic effect of such treaties in the national legal orders. In principle, states are free to decide how to give effect to international treaty obligations in their domestic legal order and whether or not to award them priority. The EU Treaty, however, does not, according to the Court, leave its Member States such freedom. In *Costa v ENEL*, the Court, interpreting the Treaties in light of their terms and spirit, held that it was impossible for the Member States to accord precedence to a unilateral and subsequent measure over a legal system accepted by them on a basis of reciprocity. National measures could not therefore be inconsistent with that legal system.[11] *Costa* was soon considered a revolutionary decision which, together with its twin *Van Gend en Loos*, forever changed the EU, constitutionalizing the Treaties and transforming the EU from 'international' to 'constitutional'.[12] The jury is still out as to whether *Costa* was really a juridical *coup d'état* or not.[13] And while some perceive primacy as the main characteristic that distinguishes EU law from 'classic international law', others propose an alternative reading, explaining primacy as a 'creative development of international law'.[14] But in the classic EU narrative, *Costa* and primacy are cornerstones of EU law without which the EU would never have become what it is today.

In *Costa*, the Court based primacy mainly on the autonomous nature of EU law, resulting from the transfer of competences or limitations of sovereignty by the Member States. The reasons as to *why* EU law should be given precedence are palpable and have been repeated on and on: the coherence, unity, and effectiveness

---

as an International Legal experiment' in Gráinne de Búrca and J.H.H. Weiler (eds), *The Worlds of European Constitutionalism* (2012) 19.

[10] See already *Permanent Court of International Justice*, Advisory Opinion of 31 August 1930, PCIJ, Series B, No 17, p. 32 *(Greek and Bulgarian Communities)*.

[11] Case 6/64 *Costa v ENEL* [1964] ECR 585 at 594; for a short historical account see JHR and MC, 'For History's Sake: On *Costa v. ENEL*, André Donner and the Eternal Secret of the Court of Justice's Deliberations' (2014) 10 *European Constitutional Law Review* 191; Morten Rasmussen, 'From *Costa v ENEL* to the Treaties of Rome: A Brief History of a Legal Revolution' in Miguel Poiares Maduro and Loïc Azoulai (eds), *The Past and Future of EU Law* (2010) 69; and see A Antoine Vauchez, 'The Transnational Politics of Jurisprudence. *Van Gend en Loos* and the Making of EU Polity' (2010) 16 *European Law Journal* 1.

[12] Eric Stein, 'Toward Supremacy Of Treaty-Constitution By Judicial Fiat: On The Margin Of The Costa Case' (1964–1965) 63 *Michigan Law Review* 491; Eric Stein, 'Lawyers, Judges, and the Making of a Transnational Constitution' (1981) 75 *American Journal of International Law* 1; J.H.H. Weiler, 'The Transformation of Europe' (1991) 100 *Yale Law Journal* 2403.

[13] See eg Morten Rasmussen, 'Revolutionizing European Law: A History of the van Gend en Loos judgment' (2014) 12 *ICON* 136; Anne Boerger and Morten Rasmussen, 'Transforming European Law: The Establishment of the Constitutional Discourse from 1950 to 1993' (2014) 10 *European Constitutional Law Review* 199; Alec Stone Sweet, 'The Juridical *Coup d'État* and the Problem of Authority' (2007) 8 *German Law Journal* 915 and responses in the same special issue; Gerard Conway, *The Limits of Legal Reasoning and the European Court of Justice* (2012).

[14] So Bruno De Witte, 'EU Law: Is It International Law?' in Catherine Barnard and Steve Peers (eds), *European Union Law* (2014), Ch 7, 187.

of EU law. But the Court still does not seem to have an overall theoretical vision on primacy and how it is to be construed.[15] What seems to matter most for the Court is the result: that EU law is effectively applied, that Member States cannot get away with non-compliance (this is related also to the equality of the Member States, now laid down in Article 4(2) TEU) and that individuals are not unequally affected by such non-compliance (this is related to the principle of non-discrimination in Article 18 TFEU). But it seems to leave the Member States free to construe it and to arrive at the result required.

2. The Meaning of Primacy—the EU Perspective

Primacy is not necessarily to be seen as a 'hierarchical' *supremacy* ('higher law') in the sense that the validity of national law would depend on its compliance with EU law. For instance, while the principle of primacy does impose an obligation on the national legislature to refrain from adopting laws that are inconsistent with EU law and a duty to modify laws that are so inconsistent, it does not automatically render such conflicting national measures invalid or non-existent.[16] Rather, primacy imposes an obligation on all national authorities to 'set aside conflicting national measures' and leave them inapplicable; hence the emphasis, in German parlance, on the fact that EU primacy concerns only *Anwendungsvorrang* and not *Geltungsvorrang*. The EU principle of primacy is a conflict rule, indicating which norm should be applied where two inconsistent norms collide.

In this respect, the EU version of primacy differs from similar principles in federal states such as the German *Bundesrecht bricht Landesrecht* laid down in Article 31 Basic Law and the *Supremacy Clause* under Article 6, Clause 2 of the US Constitution. The EU principle of primacy affects only the *applicability* of the conflicting national provision, not its *validity*, on which the EU has no direct say. In 'truly federal systems' the federal organs and especially the federal courts do have a direct say on conflicting acts of the federated entities. The EU and its Court do not have such jurisdiction: they can only declare them in breach of EU law, and oblige national authorities to leave them inapplicable to the extent of their inconsistency with EU law. Accordingly, the EU is highly dependent on the cooperation of the national authorities to heed and actually set aside inconsistent measures of national law. To what extent they actually do take up this mandate will be discussed in the third section of this chapter.

---

[15] On the lack of a consistent theory of primacy see eg Michal Dougan, 'When Worlds Collide! Competing Visions of the Relationship between Direct Effect and Supremacy' (2007) 44 *Common Market Law Review* 931.

[16] Joined Cases C-10/97 to C-22/97 *IN.CO.GE '90* [1998] ECR 6307.

At this point, it is important to point to two further issues relating to the operation of the principle, one concerning the relationship between primacy and direct
effect, and the other concerning the obligations primacy entails for national
authorities.

First, primacy is most effective in connection with direct effect. Where EU law
lacks such direct effect, EU law may have primacy, but this carries less weight.
Depending on the nature of the measure involved and the obligations it imposes,
primacy may then result in an obligation of consistent interpretation, liability for
infringement of a Treaty obligation, and possibly also in the setting aside of inconsistent national law. The exact link between direct effect and primacy is still not
entirely clear. Some defend the view that non-directly effective provisions do not
actually have primary effect. The duty to consistent interpretation would result
from the requirements of effectiveness of EU law rather than primacy. While
this may in many cases remain an academic discussion, it is highly relevant with
respect to framework decisions whose direct effect the Member States had explicitly excluded in the former Article 34 of the EU Treaty. This exclusion arguably
remains valid as long as framework decisions continue to exist under the Lisbon
regime. Now while direct effect of framework decisions was explicitly excluded,
the Treaty said nothing about their primacy. Some authors have argued, on the
basis of a 'radiation effect', that framework decisions should carry similar effects,
leading, for instance, to accepting the exclusionary effect of framework decisions.[17]
The question has never been answered conclusively by the Court and it seems to
have faded from the debate. It is striking therefore, that the issue did not even come
up in *Melloni*, which concerned a conflict between the European arrest warrant
(EAW) framework decision and the Spanish Constitution.[18]

The obligation to leave conflicting measures aside is addressed to the Member
States, and thus to all national authorities. It concerns not only courts but affects all
state authorities, which thus all have ensuing obligations depending on the powers
and responsibilities in the domestic legal order. (Constitutional) national legislatures are under an obligation to remove inconsistent legislation from the law books
to the extent that it is inconsistent, and not to enact new laws that are incompatible
with EU law. Administrative authorities are precluded from applying inconsistent
national law in the same way as courts are.[19] They are often reluctant to do so, as

---

[17] Koen Lenaerts and Tim Corthaut, 'Of Birds and Hedges: The Role of Primacy in Invoking Norms
of EU Law' (2006) 31 *English Law Review* 287; Christian Timmermans, 'The Constitutionalization
of the European Union' (2001–2002) 21 *Yearbook of European Law* 1; contra Alicia Hinarejos, 'On
the Legal Effect of Framework Decisions and Decisions: Directly Applicable, Directly Effective,
Self-executing, Supreme?' (2008) 14 *European Law Journal* 620.

[18] But see Leonard Besselink, 'The Parameters of Constitutional Conflict after *Melloni*' (2014)
European Law Review 531.

[19] Case 103/88 *Fratelli Costanzo* [1989] ECR 1839; Case C-224/97 *Ciola* [1999] ECR I-2517. See
Maartje Verhoeven, *The Costanzo Obligation. The Obligations of National Administrative Authorities*

they feel bound by the rule of law, and they usually do not have such competence in the national context. Finally, all courts are under an obligation to set aside conflicting national law. What 'setting aside' means in a concrete case depends on the type of case, and on their jurisdiction, and is decided ultimately by national law.[20] Moreover, 'setting aside' is only a minimum obligation and does not restrict the power of the competent national courts to apply, from among the various procedures available under national law, those which are appropriate for protecting the individual rights conferred by EU law.[21] Thus, administrative courts having jurisdiction to annul administrative decisions for breach of higher law will also have to do so for breach of EU law. Courts that do not have jurisdiction to annul primary legislation should not be so competent for EU law, but they must leave the law inapplicable. Courts that *are* so competent, however, should also annul such legislation for infringement of EU law. This follows from the principle of equality.[22]

Finally, primacy also has a structural element. The duty to set aside does not only apply to national measures that are substantively inconsistent with EU law, but also to those provisions of national law that would prevent a court from setting aside the conflicting provisions. Cases in point are *Simmenthal* (the national rule that obliges the national court to refer the case to the constitutional court to declare the inconsistent provision unconstitutional must be set aside), *Factortame* (a national court that, in a case before it concerning EU law, considers that the sole obstacle which precludes it from granting interim relief is a rule of national law must set aside that rule), and *Lucchini* (the provision on *res judicata* must be set aside insofar as the application of that provision prevents the recovery of state aid found to be incompatible with the common market in a decision of the Commission that has become final).[23] Again, the rationale is full and immediate effect of EU law in the domestic legal order, effectiveness or *effet utile*. The Court has little sympathy for national judicial settings. Thus, primacy may upset the hierarchy of courts, as lower courts are no longer bound by decisions of higher courts on points of EU law.[24] Primacy requires that national courts should always be free to make a reference for preliminary ruling that it considers necessary, at whatever stage of the proceedings it considers appropriate, even at the end of an interlocutory procedure for the review of constitutionality, including in those countries where national law gives priority to references to the constitutional court.[25]

---

in the Case of Incompatibility between National Law and European Law (2011), and Monica Claes, *The National Courts' Mandate in the European Constitution* (2006), Ch 10.

[20] See also Case C-314/08 *Filipiak* [2009] ECR I-11049.

[21] Joined Cases C-10/97 to C-22/97 *IN.CO.GE '90* [1998] ECR 6307, at para 21.

[22] See on this issue Monica Claes, *The National Courts' Mandate in the European Constitution* (2006).

[23] Case C-119/05 *Lucchini*.

[24] Case C-173/09 *Elchinov* [2011] ECR; Case C-210/06 *Cartesio* [2008] ECR.

[25] Joined Cases C-188/10 and C-189/10 *Melki and Abdeli* [2010] ECR I-05667; on this issue see Marc Bossuyt and Willem Verrijdt, 'The Full Effect of EU Law and of Constitutional Review in Belgium and France after the Melki Judgment' (2011) 7 *European Constitutional Law Review* 355.

The primacy of EU law obliges the national court to refuse application of conflicting national provisions, irrespective of a judgment of the national constitutional court which has deferred the date on which those provisions, held to be unconstitutional, are to lose their binding force.[26]

3. Absolute and Unconditional: EU Primacy and National Constitutions

As Stephen Weatherill has famously stated, 'even the most minor piece of techni-cal Community legislation ranks above the most cherished constitutional norm'.[27] In *Internationale Handelsgesellschaft*, the Court confirmed that the validity of EU law or its effects within a Member State can only be judged in the light of EU law itself and cannot be affected by allegations that it runs counter to either funda-mental rights as formulated by the constitution of that state or the principles of a national constitutional structure.[28] The rationale for the insistence on the absolute character of primacy is, again, the coherence, efficacy, and uniformity of EU law.[29] Primacy thus disregards the role of these constitutional principles as expressions of the fundamental values prevailing in these Member States and their societies, and is therefore a rather blunt and ruthless instrument. Indeed, the fact that cer-tain norms are given constitutional form is an expression of their importance for a particular state and society. Nevertheless, until this day, the Court has regularly repeated its stance and emphasized the need for absolute and unconditional pri-macy to secure the effectiveness of EU law.[30]

This effect resembles standing case law on state defences to justify non-compliance with obligations: Member States cannot invoke provisions, practices, or situations present in their domestic legal order (including those resulting from their consti-tutional arrangements) to escape EU law obligations or justify failures to comply with those obligations under EU law.[31] While this is not strictly speaking an appli-cation of the principle of primacy understood as pertaining to the domestic effect

---

[26] Case C-314/08 *Filipiak* [2009] ECR I-11049 and Case C-409/06, *Winner Wetten* [2010] ECR I-08015.

[27] Stephen Weatherill, *Law and Integration in the European Union* (1995) 106.

[28] Examples of cases where national courts are asked to set aside constitutional law include C-285/98 *Tanja Kreil* [2000] ECR I-00069 and C-213/07 *Michaniki* [2008] I-09999. In those cases, the Court paid little attention to the fact that these norms were of a constitutional nature.

[29] See eg Case C-409/06, *Winner Wetten* [2010] ECR I-08015 para 61: 'Rules of national law, even of a constitutional order, cannot be allowed to undermine the unity and effectiveness of Union law.'

[30] See eg Case C-409/06 *Winner Wetten* [2010] ECR I-8015; Case C-399/11 *Melloni* [2013] ECR Case C-409/06.

[31] Examples include Case 102/79 *Commission v Belgium*; Case 87/02 *Commission v Italy* [2004] ECR I-5975; Case C-70/06 *Commission v Portugal*; C-288/12 *Commission v Hungary*, decision of 8 April 2014.

of EU law, it does follow from the same basic idea—which is also a principle of international law—that a Member State cannot invoke provisions prevailing in its domestic legal system, even of a constitutional nature, to justify a failure to observe obligations arising under EU law.

There are a number of principles and mechanisms, however, that may take off the sharp edges of EU primacy and to some extent even out the ruthlessness of the principle. First, primacy is not the only principle that regulates the relations between national and EU law. Primacy should be read together with other principles that often—in contrast with primacy—have found a place in the TEU: the principles of loyalty, respect for national identities of the Member States, national constitutional autonomy, procedural autonomy, the principle of conferral, respect for the principles of constitutionalism in Articles 2 and 6 TEU, and respect for the Charter. In other words, under the EU Treaties, secondary EU law must also comply with constitutional principles in order to be valid.

Second, from the very beginning, *Internationale Handelsgesellschaft* came with a promise: while it was impossible to invoke *national* fundamental rights, the Court must review whether general principles of *EU law* had been disregarded, including fundamental rights. The promise served to convince the constitutional courts of Italy and Germany to accept the principle of primacy unconditionally and to give up their objections. It could not, however, prevent the Italian *Corte costituzionale* shortly after-wards from developing the position that in exceptional cases European law would not be applicable in Italy, namely if it were to conflict with the basic principles of the Constitution (*i principi fondamentali del nostro ordinamento costituzionale, o i diritti inalienabili della persona umana*).[32] In similar vein, the *Bundesverfassungsgericht*, in the same case, *Internationale Handelsgesellschaft*, came up with its *Solange I* formula, stating that EU law would not be applicable in Germany if it conflicted with consti-tutional rights, which were considered to be an inalienable essential feature of the Constitution and part of its identity.[33] However, since then, these European general principles have been gradually developed, on the basis of common constitutional tra-ditions, and with reference to the ECHR, 'translated' and incorporated in European law, and now under the Charter, and are used to assess the validity of EU law. Most national courts have adjusted their positions, and have retreated to a large extent for the benefit of EU law and the ECJ in the area of fundamental rights, while retain-ing the competence to intervene in exceptional circumstances. While the Court has been criticized for merely paying lip-service to fundamental rights and not taking them sufficiently seriously, the post-Lisbon case law on the Charter shows signs of a Court of Justice that is more aware of its responsibility.[34] In any case, the injection of

---

[32] *Corte costituzionale*, decision 183/73 *Frontini* [1974] 2 CMLR 372.
[33] *Bundesverfassungsgericht*.
[34] Case C-236/09 *Tests-Achats* [2011] ECR I-00773; Joined Cases C-92/09 and C-93/09 *Schecke* [2010] ECR I-11063; Joined Cases C-293/12 and C-594/12 *Digital Rights Ireland*, judgment of 8 April 2014.

fundamental values and principles at EU level should serve to temper the effects of the primacy principle, as these should ensure that EU law complies with constitutional standards.

Another element that 'softens' the harshness of the principle of primacy is that EU law often provides for other tools and mechanisms to take account of national values. In other words, there is room for these values not qua national constitutional principles, but for instance, as public policy or mandatory requirements allowing for derogations under EU law, such as in *Omega*. Finally, EU legislation may explicitly make room for national constitutional concerns. A prominent example is Article 1(7) of the Services Directive,[35] which states that '[t]his Directive does not affect the exercise of fundamental rights as recognized in the Member States and by Community law'. To conclude: while the EU principle of primacy may be ruthless, EU law itself can give room to the constitutional concerns of the Member States.

Finally, primacy only applies in so far as secondary law has been validly adopted, and is *intra vires*. European Union law that is *ultra vires* cannot claim primacy over national law. However, and contrary to what national courts have stated,[36] under EU law it is only for the CJEU alone to declare EU secondary law invalid or inapplicable, including also for infringement of the limits of EU competences. Therefore, under EU law, it is for the CJEU to decide on the validity of EU law and define the scope within which it is to have precedence.

III. The Primacy of EU Law in National Law

Accepting the primacy of EU law implies admitting that the state cannot *unilaterally* withdraw from its obligations under EU law, and that any attempt to do so by adopting laws, acts, or measures conflicting with these obligations should not carry any effect. The principle of primacy thus touches on sovereignty understood as a power legally unconstrained by others to make decisions independently. Moreover, primacy comes with the mandate for all national courts to set aside inconsistent national law, including primary legislation, which in similar national circumstances is immune to constitutional review or can only be reviewed by

---

[35] Dir 2006/123 on services in the internal market, OJ 2006, L 376/36.

[36] For instance the German *Bundesverfassungsgericht*, decision of 30 June 2009, BVerfGE 123, 267 (*Lisbon*); decision of 6 July 2010, BVerfG 126, 286 (*Honeywell*); the Czech *Ustavni Soud*, decision of 31 January 2012, Pl. ÚS 5/12 (*Slovak pensions*); Polish *Trybunał Konstytucyjny*, decision of 24 November 2010, K 32/09 (*Lisbon*).

a constitutional court. As a result, the acceptance of primacy has not been easy in many Member States. In order to structure the discussion, a distinction can be made between 'ordinary primacy' (the priority of EU law over ordinary, ie non-constitutional law, including primary legislation) and the priority of EU law over (parts of) constitutional law. While the former has by and large been accepted in all Member States, the latter is accepted in very few, or perhaps none, of the Member States.

1. Accepting 'Ordinary Primacy'

There are several ways to construe the primacy of EU law and to achieve the result requested by the ECJ, namely that conflicting provisions of national legislation are set aside and that EU law is effectively applied. The first is the easiest, because it is unequivocal and leaves little to be decided by the courts: national law explicitly provides for the primacy of EU law. In some Member States, the constitution awards precedence to *all* international treaty provisions[37] over conflicting provisions of national law in the domestic legal order. In those systems, the fact that EU law claims primacy over national law neatly fits in the general approach to international treaty law. The Netherlands is the most well-known example. The primacy of international treaty provisions that are 'binding on anyone' was confirmed in the text of the Constitution in 1953 and 1956.[38] Since then, with a couple of later adaptations, international treaty provisions and decisions of international organizations that have been duly published take immediate effect in the Dutch legal order and take precedence over conflicting provisions of national law. Remarkably, since the mid-1980s, a considerable number of Dutch constitutional lawyers have begun holding the view that the constitutional provisions do not govern the effect of EU law in the national legal order. The status and rank of EU law are, according to this view, governed by EU law itself, as established in *Van Gend and Loos* and *Costa v ENEL*, which in their view entails the exclusion of any possible function of Articles 93 and 94 Constitution. Therefore, in a Member State with the ideal fertile ground to incorporate EU primacy in the Constitution and thus combine the primacy of EU law with the supremacy of the Constitution, the Constitution is considered irrelevant in this context.

---

[37] Usually, the Constitution imposes some conditions, restricting this effect, for instance, to treaty provisions that have been duly published, that are directly effective, or perhaps also only on the condition of reciprocity. The reference here to *all* treaty provisions is meant to distinguish those Member States where primacy is awarded only to EU law and not to other treaty provisions.

[38] According to most commentators, the monism of the Netherlands Constitution is only declaratory, and existed before the constitutional amendments of 1953 and 1956, which merely confirmed it.

Constitutional provisions awarding primacy to treaty law also exist in the Constitutions of *Poland*[39] and *Bulgaria.*[40] In those countries, the position of EU law is not very different, in this respect, from that of other treaties. In *Estonia*,[41] the Constitution equally prescribes the precedence of treaty provisions. Nevertheless, Estonia adopted the Constitution of the Republic of Estonia Amendment Act (CREAA) when it was preparing for EU membership.[42] That Act is now considered to govern the effect of EU law in the Estonian legal order, and to 'suspend' the application of the Constitution within the scope of EU law.[43] The Estonian courts are to enforce the primacy of EU law in accordance with the requirements of EU law.[44]

Nevertheless, a constitutional provision awarding primacy to treaties has not always proven sufficient to convince courts that they actually have jurisdiction to review inconsistent legislation and set it aside. Article 55 of the French Constitution has stated since 1958 that 'Treaties or agreements duly ratified or approved shall, upon publication, prevail over Acts of Parliament, subject, with respect to each agreement or treaty, to its application by the other party'. While it was generally agreed that the provision confirmed that EU law and international treaty law should be awarded precedence, it was not clear who should enforce the constitutional requirement that treaties should prevail, and whether the ordinary courts had any role in this. The courts were reluctant to grant priority to treaty provisions, as they considered the consistency of primary legislation with treaty provisions to be an issue that affected the constitutionality of the relevant legislation, which was a matter for the legislature and the *Conseil constitutionnel*, not for the courts. It was only after the *Conseil constitutionnel* had declared that *conventionnalité* (the consistency with treaty provisions) and *constitutionnalité* (consistency with the Constitution) were distinct issues and that an act inconsistent with a treaty provision was not for that matter unconstitutional, that the ordinary courts changed their position.[45] Since it is not a matter of constitutionality, it is not the business of the *Conseil constitutionnel*. Things appeared in a different light when the constitutional legislature inserted a Europe clause in Article 88-1 of the Constitution. That

[39] Art 91(2) of the Constitution provides that '[a]n international agreement ratified upon prior consent granted by statute shall have precedence over statutes if such an agreement cannot be reconciled with the provisions of such statutes'.

[40] Art 5 (4) of the Bulgarian Constitution states: 'International treaties which have been ratified in accordance with the constitutional procedure, promulgated and having come into force with respect to the Republic of Bulgaria, shall be part of the legislation of the State. They shall have primacy over any conflicting provision of the domestic legislation.'

[41] Art 123, second sentence of the Constitution reads: 'If laws or other legislation of Estonia are in conflict with international treaties ratified by the *Riigikogu*, the provisions of the international treaty shall apply.'

[42] Constitution of the Republic of Estonia Amendment Act (CREAA) of 14 December 2003.

[43] Constitutional Review Chamber of the Supreme Court, Opinion 3-4-1-3-06 of 11 May 2006.

[44] Constitutional Review Chamber of the Supreme Court, decision 3-4-1-5-08 of 26 June 2008.

[45] *Cour de cassation*, decision of 25 May 1975 (*Jacques Vabre*) and *Conseil d'État*, decision of 20 October 1989 (*Nicolo*).

provision is now considered to include a constitutional duty to implement EU law and now functions as the basis for the primacy of EU law in the French legal order. Ensuring the primacy of EU law is largely the responsibility of the ordinary courts rather than of the *Conseil constitutionnel*.[46] The *Conseil* will only review the compatibility with EU law of a parliamentary act implementing a directive when there is a *manifest* inconsistency with the underlying directive. For the remainder, it is for the ordinary courts to enforce the primacy of EU law.

In other Member States, the legal system does not give priority to treaties over national law, and hence, the acceptance of primacy required a specific solution for EU law. In other words, EU law has to be distinguished from classic international law.

Several Member States' Constitutions thus make explicit provision for the primacy of EU law over national legislation, while other treaties do not carry such effects. The Slovakian Constitution, for instance, provides for the primacy of EU law in its Europe clause,[47] as does Article 2 of the Lithuanian Constitutional Act on Membership of the Republic of Lithuania in the EU.[48] Similar constitutional amendments have also been introduced in Member States that do recognize the primacy of international treaty law, such as Estonia, to remove all possible doubt.

There is a group of Member States that have ensured primacy in the act of approval, rather than in the constitutional text. In Finland,[49] Ireland, and the United Kingdom—countries with a strong dualist tradition—the acts which serve to approve the Treaties and incorporate EU law in the domestic legal orders contain a *renvoi* to EU law concerning the effect of EU law in the domestic legal order. For instance, Section 2 of the Irish EC Act 1972 reads: 'from the 1st day of January, 1973, the treaties governing the European Communities and the existing and future acts adopted by the institutions of those Communities shall be binding on the State and shall be part of the domestic law thereof under the conditions laid down in those treaties.' And after some initial hesitation as to the consequences of EU membership for the fate of inconsistent legislation, the House of Lords in *Factortame* also

---

[46] *Conseil constitutionnel*, decision 2006-540 DC of 27 July 2006 (*Loi relative au droit d'auteur et aux droits voisins dans la société de l'information*).

[47] Art 7(2) reads: 'The Slovak Republic may, by an international treaty ratified and promulgated in a manner laid down by law, or on the basis of such treaty, transfer the exercise of a part of its rights to the European Communities and European Union. Legally binding acts of the European Communities and European Union shall have primacy over the laws of the Slovak Republic.'

[48] Art 2 of the Constitutional Act on Membership of the Republic in the EU, No. IX-2343, 13 July 2004: 'The norms of the European Union law shall be a constituent part of the legal system of the Republic of Lithuania. Where it concerns the founding Treaties of the European Union, the norms of the European Union law shall be applied directly, while in the event of collision of legal norms, they shall have supremacy over the laws and other legal acts of the Republic of Lithuania.' According to Art 150 of the Constitution, the Act forms an integral part of the Constitution.

[49] Tuomas Ojanen, 'The EU at the Finnish Constitutional Arena' (2013) 4 *Tijdschrift voor Constitutioneel Recht* 242; Juha Lavapuro, Tuomas Ojanen, and Martin Scheinin, 'Rights-based Constitutionalism in Finland and the Development of Pluralist Constitutional Review' (2011) 9 *International Journal of Constitutional Law* 505.

arrived at the conclusion that EU law can prevail over incompatible domestic legislation, and that UK courts can disapply Acts of Parliament in the event of such incompatibility. Referring to Section 2(4) of the EC Act 1972, Lord Bridge held that any limitation upon parliamentary sovereignty brought about by EU membership was necessarily a limitation that Parliament had accepted on an 'entirely voluntary' basis. Opinions are still divided on what this means for parliamentary sovereignty, and whether it was the 1972 Parliament or the courts who changed the old rule that courts could never set aside parliamentary acts. But what is clear today is that British courts can set aside Acts of Parliament for breach of EU law.[50]

Where the Constitution or accompanying acts are not explicit about the effect of EU law in the domestic legal order and EU law cannot be given primacy as treaty law, the courts have had to develop their own understanding of the effect and status of EU law. A typical constitutional foundation for primacy of EU law has been the constitutional transfer of powers or limitation of sovereignty clause, which serves as the constitutional authorization of membership. In one of the early cases concerning EU law, the German *Bundesverfassungsgericht* did not hesitate to use Article 24 of the Basic Law as the basis for the primacy of EU law. That provision for transfer of powers implied not only that membership was constitutional, but also that 'the sovereign acts of its organs, in this case the ECJ, are to be recognised as deriving from an original and exclusive sovereign authority'. Accordingly, provisions of EU law were to be applied with direct effect and given primacy in accordance with the case law of the European Court.[51] It took the *Italian Corte costituzionale* much longer to develop a similar conceptual view on the basis of the Italian constitutional provision authorizing such transfer, and to accept primacy and the ensuing competence of ordinary Italian courts to set aside conflicting primary legislation. In the end, it followed an approach that resembles the German one, based on the limitation of sovereignty clause in Article 11 of the Italian Constitution.

Finally, in a few countries, the courts have come up with a new conceptualization of the relationship between treaty law and national law in the absence of any constitutional provisions dealing with the issue. Thus, the Belgian *Cour de cassation* has accepted the primacy of EU law on the basis of the very nature of treaty law.[52] It goes beyond *Costa v ENEL* since it accepted the primacy of all treaty law, but its argumentation comes closest to that of the Court of Justice, as it does not link this primacy to any constitutional provision, but argues on the basis of the 'very nature of international treaty law'.

---

[50] See eg NW Barber, 'The Afterlife of Parliamentary Sovereignty' (2011) 9 *International Journal of Constitutional Law* 144 and other contributions to Symposium: The Changing Landscape of British Constitutionalism in that same issue; Mark Elliott, 'Constitutional Legislation, European Union Law and the Nature of the United Kingdom's Contemporary Constitution' (2014) 10 *European Constitutional Law Review*, forthcoming.

[51] *Bundesverfassungsgericht*, decision of 9 June 1971, BVerfGE 31, 145 (*Lütticke*).

[52] *Cour de cassation*, decision of 27 May 1971, Pas. 1971, I, 886 (*Fromagerie franco-suisse Le Ski*).

So, by and large, and using different techniques and the tools available in national law, the Member States have achieved acceptance of ordinary primacy and the ensuing jurisdiction of all courts to disapply inconsistent national legislation.

An important caveat is still in place. While it is fair to say that 'national courts have embraced their European mandate',[53] their acceptance of primacy in doctrinal terms does not imply that they regularly act on it to set aside inconsistent legislation. The actual practice shows a much more nuanced and sober picture. Courts often avoid setting aside conflicting national legislation, and they tend to prefer interpreting national law in conformity with EU law. This is not problematic in itself, as the ultimate aim—that EU law is given effect—is achieved. In other cases, courts choose to decide the case on the basis of domestic law, rather than EU law. Again, as long as the result complies with what the EU demands, there is no real problem. But it does mean that in actual practice, primacy is not as blunt and ruthless as it appears at first sight, and that EU law may not be so different from international treaties.

The reasons why courts often choose not to go the whole way are in part to be found in the constitutional setting that is not used to having courts question legislative acts. This is in a national context often the prerogative of a constitutional court. Asking the ordinary courts to award primacy to EU law brings them in direct competition with the constitutional courts, especially now that EU law is increasingly becoming more important in issues which have traditionally been the province of constitutional courts: fundamental rights protection in areas such as criminal law, and asylum and immigration. Judicial empowerment has often been used to explain why national courts have heeded and accepted primacy.[54] However, it may also be a reason for ordinary courts to be careful not to interfere with the business of constitutional courts. And in Belgium and France, this inter-court competition has led to reforms to salvage the constitutional courts as crucial actors in the national setting.[55]

In several states, for instance in the Nordic countries and the Netherlands, which do not possess a constitutional court, the prevailing notions of parliamentary sovereignty and democracy and the more restrictive conception of the role of courts in society have resulted in the courts shying away from setting aside conflicting legislation.[56] In Central and Eastern European countries, it is the formalist

---

[53] Monica Claes, *The National Courts' Mandate in the European Constitution* (2006).

[54] See eg Karen J. Alter, *Establishing the Supremacy of European Law. The Making of an International Rule of Law in Europe* (2003).

[55] The *question prioritaire de constitutionnalité*. On the consequences in the context of EU law, see Marc Bossuyt and Willem Verrijdt, 'The Full Effect of EU Law and of Constitutional Review in Belgium and France after the Melki Judgment' (2011) 7 *European Constitutional Law Review* 355, and various contributions in Monica Claes, Maartje de Visser, Patricia Popelier, and Catherine van de Heyning (eds), *Constitutional Conversations in Europe* (2012).

[56] For the situation in the Netherlands see Leonard Besselink, 'Constitutional Adjudication in the Era of Globalization: The Netherlands in Comparative Perspective' (2012) 18 *European Public Law* 231;

tradition that is said to be hindering the smooth acceptance of the European mandate of courts.[57]

But there are also other, more mundane reasons for the non-application of the
primacy of EU law: lack of knowledge of EU law, lack of time and resources, the fact
that arguments from EU law are not brought before the court, and so forth. This
has important implications: if national courts do not really act on their European
mandate to give effect to EU law with precedence over inconsistent national law,
the decentralized judicial system of EU law is only a virtual reality.[58] The reality of
the principle of primacy may be less of a success story than the narrative of acceptance suggests.[59]

2. The Primacy of EU Law and National Constitutional Law

While primacy over ordinary national legislation is now by and large accepted, at
least doctrinally, the same cannot be said for primacy over national constitutional
law. Here, the trend goes in the opposite direction, as more and more Member
States make the application of EU law conditional on its compliance with fundamental principles of the national constitution and hence introduce exceptions to

on the Nordic countries, see Juha Lavapuro, Tuomas Ojanen, and Martin Scheinin, 'Rights-based
Constitutionalism in Finland and the Development of Pluralist Constitutional Review' (2011) 9
International Journal of Constitutional Law 505. See also the first question in the reference of the
Swedish court in *Åkerberg Fransson*, pointing to the rule contained in Swedish law that a Swedish
court may disregard the application of a Swedish statute adopted by the Riksdag or the government
only if the error is 'manifest', and asking whether this condition complies with the primacy of EU
law. The condition of manifest error has been deleted from the text of Art 11:14 of the Instrument of
Government, but it is still present in the minds of the judges.

[57] Zdenek Kühn, 'Worlds Apart: Western and Central European Judicial Culture at the Onset
of the European Enlargement' (2004) 52 *American Journal of Comparative Law* 531; Siniša Rodin,
'Discourse and Authority in European and Post- communist Legal Culture' (2005) 1 *Croatian
Yearbook of European Law and Policy* 1; see however Jan Komárek, 'The Struggle for Legal Reform after
Communism. A review of Zdeněk Kühn, *The Judiciary in Central and Eastern Europe: Mechanical
Jurisprudence in Transformation?*' LSE Law, Society and Economy Working Papers 10/2014.

[58] See eg the so-called Wallis report, European Parliament (Committee on Legal Affairs), Report
on the Role of the National Judge in the European Judicial System of 4 June 2008 (A6-0224/2008), and
ensuing initiatives such as Commission, 'Judicial Training in the European Union' (Communication)
COM (2006) 356 final of 29 June 2006. More generally on this point see M. Claes, M. de Visser,
and M. de Werd, 'Operationalizing the European Mandate of National Courts: Insights from the
Netherlands', forthcoming in B. De Witte, M. Wind, J.A. Mayoral, U. Jaremba, and K. Podstawa
(eds), *National Courts and EU Law: New Issues, Theories and Methods* (2015); Sacha Prechal, 'National
Courts in EU Judicial Structures' (2006) 25 *Yearbook of European Law* 429.

[59] See also Michal Bobek, 'Of Feasibility and Silent Elephants: The Legitimacy of the Court of
Justice through the Eyes of National Courts' in Maurice Adams, Johan Meeusen, Gert Straetmans,
and Henri de Waele (eds), *Judging Europe's Judges: The Legitimacy of Case Law of the European Court
of Justice Examined* (2013) 197.

the primacy of EU law. Since constitutional law is, in the domestic legal system, the supreme norm of the land, it should not come as a surprise that the absolute and unconditional version of primacy over and above the national constitution is almost nowhere actually accepted in its fullest sense, even if some states go a long way.

In the Netherlands, Articles 93 and 94 of the Constitution have been interpreted as applying to constitutional law as well, so that treaties also take precedence over inconsistent provisions of constitutional law. As some support the view that the constitutional provisions do not even apply in the context of EU law, and that the latter has primacy on the basis of the case law of the ECJ, the Dutch version of the primacy of EU law is certainly an absolute and unconditional version. However, even in the Netherlands, there is the notion that in the case of a conflict between EU law and fundamental rights protected in other international treaties, the latter would have to be awarded precedence because in the case of treaty conflict, the courts tend to give priority to the human rights treaty. This situation, however, has not yet occurred in practice.[60]

In Estonia, the Amendment Act (CREAA) suspends the application of the Constitution: only those parts of the Constitution which are in conformity with EU law or which fall outside the scope of EU law are still applicable; the applicability of all other constitutional provisions is suspended.[61] In practical effect, therefore, the Constitution Amendment Act guarantees the primacy of EU law over the national Constitution.[62]

Article 29.4.6 of the Irish Constitution grants constitutional immunity to European law and to Irish laws enacted, acts done, and measures adopted that are necessitated by the obligations of membership.[63] The provision intends to

---

[60] Leonard Besselink, Constitutional Adjudication in the Era of Globalization: The Netherlands in Comparative Perspective' (2012) 18 *European Public Law* 231.

[61] *Constitutional Review Chamber of the Supreme Court* of 11 May 2006, Opinion 3-4-1-3-06, paras 14–16: as such, only that part of the Constitution is applicable which is in conformity with European Union law or which regulates the relationships that are not regulated by European Union law. The effect of those provisions of the Constitution that are not compatible with European Union law and thus inapplicable is suspended. This means that within the spheres that are within the exclusive competence of the European Union or where there is a shared competence with the European Union, European Union law shall apply in the case of a conflict between Estonian legislation, including the Constitution, with European Union law.

[62] Julia Laffranque, 'A Glance at the Estonian Legal Landscape in View of the Constitution Amendment Act' (2007) 12 *Juridica International* 55.

[63] The provision has been copied almost literally in the Cyprus Constitution. Art 1A reads: 'No provision of this Constitution shall be considered as invalidating laws enacted, acts done or measures adopted by the Republic necessitated by its obligations as a Member State of the European Union or shall prevent Regulations, Directives or other acts or binding measures of a legislative character adopted by the European Union or by the European Communities or by their institutions or by their competent bodies under the provisions of the treaties founding the European Communities or the European Union, from having legal effect in the Republic,' and Art 179 adds: 'Without prejudice to the provisions of article 1A, the Constitution shall be the supreme law of the Republic . . .'

limit the reach of the Constitution, and prevents the courts from reviewing the constitutionality of EU law, and of Irish law necessitated by the obligations of membership, thus ensuring the primacy of EU law over the Irish Constitution. Nevertheless, in *SPUC v Grogan,* a case concerning the particularly sensitive issue of abortion, Walsh J stated in the High Court that 'it cannot be one of the objectives of the European Communities that a Member State should be obliged to permit activities which are clearly designed to set at nought the constitutional guarantees for the protection within the State of a fundamental human right'. So despite the constitutional immunity granted to EU law in the constitutional texts, courts feel uneasy about actually awarding primacy to EU law in cases where it appears to be at odds with fundamental values protected in the Constitution, such as fundamental rights.

The same argument is even more persuasively and more effectively put forward in those countries where the primacy of EU law is not built on an explicit constitutional authorization, but on a reinterpretation of the existing text of the Constitution, usually a transfer of powers or limitation of sovereignty clause. These clauses are to be interpreted in context with the rest of the Constitution, which will typically be seen as restricting the extent of the transfer or limitation. These transfers themselves have to be constitutional, and so does the law ensuing from them. Take for example the Italian case. When the *Corte costituzionale,* after initial hesitation, accepted the primacy of EU law over ordinary legislation, and the jurisdiction of the ordinary courts to set aside inconsistent legislation, it did so only insofar as EU law does not violate the fundamental principles (*i principi fondamentali*) of the Italian constitutional order or the inalienable rights of the human person (*i diritti inalienabili della persona umana*).[64] Accordingly, the limitation to national sovereignty to which the legislature agreed when joining the EU implies that within the areas 'vacated' for the benefit of the EU institutions, the Italian authorities are no longer sovereign and EU law applies. However, this limitation of sovereignty is itself limited by the core principles of the constitution, which are known as *controlimiti* or counterlimits.

The case law of the German *Bundesverfassungsgericht* is based on a similar line of argument. It began in the 1970s, focusing on fundamental rights protection. In the absence of a European system of fundamental rights protection, and given the low credentials of the EU with regard to democracy and

---

This amendment was introduced after the Cypriot Supreme Court had held in its EAW decision (Supreme Court of Cyprus, decision of 7 November 2005, *Attorney General of the Republic v Costas Constantinou* (2005) 1 C.L.R. 1356) that the EAW framework decision could not prevail over the provisions of Art 11(2) of the Constitution.

[64] *Corte costituzionale,* decision n. 183/73 of 27 December 1973, 2 CMLR [1974] 372(*Frontini*); decision170/84 of 8 June 1984, CMLRev (1984) 756 (*Granital*).

legitimacy, the *Bundesverfassungsgericht* was not prepared to accept the primacy of EU law over the German Basic Law and to restrict its own powers to ensure that fundamental rights were protected in the land. Accordingly, in its *Solange I* case—the same case in which the ECJ had rendered its *Internationale Handelsgesellschaft* judgment a few years before—the *Bundesverfassungsgericht* identified fundamental rights as pertaining to the identity of the Basic Law and not giving way to EU law. While Article 24 of the Basic Law did authorize the transfer of sovereign rights to interstate institutions, the provision must be understood in the overall context of the whole Basic Law. Accordingly, it cannot open the way to amending the basic structure of the Basic Law, which forms the basis of its identity, without a formal amendment to that Basic Law. The part dealing with fundamental rights is an inalienable, essential feature of the German Basic Law and forms part of its constitutional structure. To the extent that EU law would infringe constitutional rights, it would not be applicable in Germany. The German Basic Law therefore puts conditions on the primacy of EU law.

The position of the *Bundesverfassungsgericht* that in the context of European integration the core principles of the Constitution should not be infringed has since been incorporated in the text of the Basic Law. At the signing of the Maastricht Treaty, Article 24 of the Basic Law was no longer considered to be an appropriate basis for membership of the EU, and a new 'Europe clause' was inserted in Article 23. That provision now explicitly points to the requirements German Basic Law imposes on the EU in terms of compliance with 'democratic, social and federal principles, to the rule of law, and to the principle of subsidiarity, and that guarantees a level of protection of basic rights essentially comparable to that afforded by this Basic Law'.

Over the years, and as a consequence of the development of EU fundamental rights jurisprudence and the expansion of EU law into ever wider fields, the focus of the *Bundesverfassungsgericht* has gradually shifted away from fundamental rights[65] and turned to the issue of competences (*ultra vires* control, since Maastricht) and constitutional identity review (since Lisbon).[66]

Many Member States have adopted a similar approach, indicating limits to the primacy of EU law in the text of their Constitution, and imposing conditions on EU integration. Such conditions have for instance been included in the Europe

---

[65] *Bundesverfassungsgericht*, decision of 22 October 1986, BVerfGE 73, 339 (*Solange II*).

[66] See on this evolution among many others eg Mehrdad Payandeh, 'Constitutional Review of EU Law after Honeywell, 'Contextualizing the relationship between the German Constitutional Court and the EU Court of Justice' (2011) 48 *Common Market Law Review* 9; Mattias Wendel, *Permeabilität im europäischen Verfassungsrecht. Verfassungsrechtliche Integrationsnormen auf Staats- und Unionsebene im Vergleich* (2011); special issues of the *German Law Journal* on the Lisbon decision (2009) and on the OMT reference (2014).

clauses in Sweden,[67] in Portugal,[68] and in Lithuania.[69] More often still, there has been the implicit assumption that the Constitution remains the supreme norm of the land,[70] and that membership of the EU does not allow a deviation from the most fundamental principles of the Constitution. These core principles of the Constitution are considered to be so fundamental that they cannot be affected by European integration. Accordingly, the European Treaties are reviewed in the light of these core principles at 'constitutional moments' such as accession and amendment. Treaties infringing upon these core principles cannot be ratified. In some countries, this simply means that the Constitution must be amended before the Treaty can be ratified, as is the case in France, where the *Conseil constitutionnel* has held that Treaties infringing upon the French Constitution or the *conditions essentielles de l'exercice de la souveraineté nationale* can only be ratified upon constitutional amendment. It would seem, therefore, that in this respect an infringement of the constitutional core does not differ much from a violation of other provisions of the Constitution: in both cases, the constitutional legislature can amend the Constitution and France can ratify the relevant Treaty.

In other Member States, however, the 'constitutional core' is immutable and hard and cannot be affected even by the constitutional legislature. The constitutional hard core (sometimes referred to as the 'constitutional identity') thus constitutes an almost absolute limit to further integration, and going beyond this limit requires stepping outside the prevailing Constitution—requires, in other words, a constitutional revolution, or a return to the original holder of sovereignty understood as *pouvoir constituant*.[71]

However, these situations do not actually concern the principle of primacy: in the situation depicted above, the Treaty is not yet in force and so does not yet claim primacy under EU law. This is different for secondary EU law that has been

[67] Art 6 of Chapter 10 of the Instrument of Government: 'Within the framework of European Union cooperation, the *Riksdag* may transfer decision-making authority which does not affect the basic principles by which Sweden is governed. Such transfer presupposes that protection for rights and freedoms in the field of cooperation to which the transfer relates corresponds to that afforded under this Instrument of Government and the European Convention for the Protection of Human Rights and Fundamental Freedoms.'

[68] Art 7(6) of the Portuguese Constitution: 'Subject to reciprocity and to respect for the fundamental principles of a democratic state based on the rule of law and for the principle of subsidiarity, and with a view to the achievement of the economic, social and territorial cohesion of an area of freedom, security and justice and the definition and implementation of a common external, security and defence policy, Portugal may enter into agreements for the exercise jointly, in cooperation or by the Union's institutions, of the powers needed to construct and deepen the European Union.'

[69] See the preamble to the Constitutional Act of the Republic of Lithuania on Membership of the Republic of Lithuania in the European Union.

[70] The Constitution may state this explicitly, eg Art 8(1) of the Polish Constitution and Art 3 of the Portuguese Constitution.

[71] Thus also the Estonian *Riigikohus*, Judgment of 12 July 2012—3-4-1-6-12—sec no 128, 223 (*ESM Treaty*).

validly adopted under EU law. In these cases too, many national courts have held that where EU law should infringe the core principles of the Constitution (sometimes referred to as constitutional identity—*Identität der geltenden Verfassung; Grundstruktur der Verfassung*), such EU law would not be applicable in the land, and the national authorities could not constitutionally participate in the execution and application of such provisions. There is thus an exception to the primacy of EU law, since parts of the national constitution can be invoked to block the application of EU law—contrary to what the EU principle of primacy requires.

The examples are numerous and they are increasing: in addition to the German and the Italian constitutional courts, the Spanish *Tribunal constitucional*,[72] the Danish *Højesteret*,[73] and the Polish *Trybunal Konstytucyjny*[74] have announced that in exceptional circumstances, where EU law interferes with fundamental principles of the Constitution, it will not be applicable.[75] Most courts do indicate that they will only act in exceptional cases and often only upon a reference to the ECJ. Certainly, the number of constitutional courts that has made references to the ECJ on sensitive issues of a constitutional nature has increased. This is a welcome evolution, since the constitutional principles that these courts aim to protect are also shared constitutional values that bind the EU itself (Articles 2 and 6 TEU and the Charter). At the national level, it is the constitutional courts that are confronted with allegations that EU law or national law implementing it infringes constitutional principles, such as fundamental rights. By making a preliminary reference, these courts can offer the Court of Justice the opportunity to protect these principles for the entire EU, and further to develop the values of constitutionalism at the European level.[76] In doing so, the Court can contribute to shaping EU law in accordance with the values of constitutionalism. Unilateral derogations from EU law and national exceptions to the primacy of EU law may then no longer be necessary. The recent Data Retention Directive saga provides an excellent illustration. The constitutional and supreme courts of Romania, Germany, Cyprus, and the Czech Republic,[77] and several

---

[72] *Tribunal Constitucional*, Declaration of 13 December 2004, DTC 1/2004 (*Constitutional Treaty*).

[73] *Hojesteret*, decision of 6 April 1998—I 361/1997 (*Maastricht*).

[74] *Trybunal Konstytucyjny*, decision of 24 November 2010, K 32/09 (*Lisbon Treaty*) and decision of 16 November 2011 SK 45/09 (*Re Brussels Regulation—Council Regulation (EC) No 44/2001*).

[75] For comparative overviews see Julio Baquero Cruz, 'The Legacy of the Maastricht-Urteil and the Pluralist Movement' (2008) 14 *European Law Journal* 389; Monica Claes, *The National Courts' Mandate in the European Constitution* (2006).

[76] See eg Marta Cartabia, 'Europe and Rights: Taking Dialogue Seriously' (2009) 5 *European Constitutional Law Review* 5–31.

[77] Romanian *Constitutional Court*, decision 1258 of 8 October 2009 (*dataretention*); *Bundesverfassungsgericht*, decision of 2 maart 2010 (*dataretention*); *Supreme Court of Cyprus*, decision 65/2009 of 1 februari 2011 (*dataretention*); Czech *Ustavni Soud*, decision of 22 maart 2011, Pl. ÙS 24/10 (dataretention); see Eleni Kosta, 'The Way to Luxemburg: National Court Decisions on the Compatibility of the Data Retention Directive with the Rights to Privacy and Data Protection' (2013) 10 *SCRIPTed* 339.

Parliaments were struggling with the directive, which they considered to be at odds with fundamental rights. Their attempts to salvage these rights were limited to trying to use the discretion provided by the directive in accordance with national constitutional rights. It was only when the Irish Supreme Court and the Austrian *Verfassungsgerichtshof* made references to the ECJ challenging the validity of the directive itself that the Court of Justice was able actually to declare the directive invalid on the basis of the Charter.[78] The decision of the Court illustrates that using the EU system involving the Charter and preliminary references to the European Court can be more effective in protecting fundamental rights than procedures challenging the primacy of EU law before national courts based on national Constitutions. It also shows how the 'self-cleansing' capacity of the EU legal system in terms of fundamental rights protection can operate.

(At this point in the discussion, we can conclude that the national versions of the primacy of EU law are very diverse, and that there are as many conceptions of primacy as there are Member States. However, virtually no Member State unconditionally accepts the principle of primacy as propounded by EU law. As a result, both continue to claim the ultimate authority, and to claim that the other will eventually have to give way. Thus, the current reality is that there is a plurality of conceptions as to how they interrelate and how conflicts are to be resolved. There is not *one* principle of primacy, but many in operation.)

IV. THE PRINCIPLE OF PRIMACY IN EU LAW—STILL THE SAME AFTER ALL THESE YEARS?

So, then, has nothing changed since the Court of Justice introduced the absolute and unconditional principle of the primacy of EU law in *Costa v ENEL*, *Internationale Handelsgesellschaft*, and *Simmenthal*? The ensuing section examines a number of more recent developments that may have an impact on the principle of primacy in EU law. Some have argued that primacy in EU law is no longer as absolute and unconditional as it once was, and that the contemporary principle is much more flexible than previously.

---

[78] Joined Cases C-293/12 and C-594/12 *Digital Rights Ireland*, judgment of 8 April 2014.

1. Codification and Non-codification: Does It Make a Difference?

Primacy remained a judge-made principle until the Convention that drew up the Constitutional Treaty proposed to include it in the text of the Treaty.[79] The proposed Article I-6 TEU read: 'The Constitution and law adopted by the institutions of the Union in exercising competences conferred on it shall have primacy over the law of the Member States.' The provision caused quite a stir among both the conventioners and the general public. In order to convince them that such primacy was in fact only the confirmation of the existing situation, a Declaration was added to the Treaty, stating that Article I-6 reflected the existing case law of the Court and did not essentially alter the existing situation. The provision played an important role in the decisions of both the French and the Spanish constitutional courts on the Constitutional Treaty. Both discussed the provision as one of the elements of the Treaty that might change the nature of the Union and make it unconstitutional for the state to adhere to such a Treaty. Both arrived at the conclusion that it did not and that the provision did not alter the nature of the Treaty or the status of the national Constitution as the supreme norm of the land. Both courts also paid particular attention to the national identity clause immediately preceding the primacy provision in Article I-5 to arrive at that conclusion. The French *Conseil constitutionnel*, moreover, emphasized that the scope of the principle remained the same and was duly accepted by Article 88-1 of the Constitution. The Spanish *Tribunal constitucional* insisted on the difference between the supremacy of the Constitution and the primacy of EU law. Effectively, both courts opined that Article I-6 did not change the nature of the Union.

Or did it? Would the inclusion of a primacy provision in the body of the Treaty not make any difference?[80] It could be argued that the inclusion of the provision would weaken the position of those national courts that have argued that the primacy of EU law could only apply and have primacy to the extent that it was constitutional. A reservation of this kind would go against the explicit text of the Treaty, which imposes primacy of *all* EU law. To then hold that such primacy only applies under national conditions—even if constitutional—seems much less convincing than when EU primacy was a judge-made principle that, so it was argued, was

---

[79]   Note, however, that until then, the principle had not been challenged by the Member States in the consecutive Treaty amendments. And while the direct effect of framework decisions had been explicitly excluded in the Treaty of Amsterdam, primacy was not mentioned.

[80]   Mattias Kumm and Victor Ferreres Comella, 'The Primacy Clause of the Constitutional Treaty and the Future of Constitutional Conflict in the European Union' (2005) 3 *International Journal of Constitutional Law* 473.

never explicitly agreed to. Moreover, while the principle might be the same, its scope would be different, as the principle prior to 2004 applied only to Community law, while its application to the then second and third pillars was disputed.[81] The Constitutional Treaty did away with the distinction between the pillars, so the scope of application of the principle would be different, even if its essence remained the same.

In the Lisbon Treaty, primacy was deleted from the body of the Treaty and relegated to Declaration 17, annexed to the Treaty, in which the Conference confirms the primacy of EU law under the conditions laid down by the case law of the ECJ. It also attached as an annex to the Final Act an Opinion of the Council Legal Service on the primacy of EC law, stating that the fact that the principle of primacy was not included in the treaty should not in any way change the existence of the principle and the existing case law.

The gist of the message is clear: the principle of primacy continues to apply and its non-codification does not in itself affect the principle in any way and should not be seen as a rejection of that principle. Nevertheless, the technique is rather clumsy: a (non-binding) Declaration that in turn refers back to the case law of the ECJ and an Opinion of the Council Legal Service. The legal effect of the Declaration is very limited. Moreover, the Opinion of the Legal Service was drafted in 2007 and speaks of 'Community law', which no longer exists. This leaves open the question as to whether primacy should also apply to what was then second and third pillar law. This is a question that had been left open, and that the declaration does not address.

On the other hand, while primacy has been left out, the new and improved version of the national identity clause, which the Spanish and French constitutional courts had picked up on, has remained. It is no longer 'balanced out' by a reference to primacy, and now receives all judicial and academic attention.

The Declaration does not seem to have had an impact on the case law of national courts on the primacy of EU law, as is evident for instance from the Lisbon decision of the Danish *Højesteret*:

The fact that it was stated in Declaration 17 to the Lisbon Treaty that the Conference recalls the case law of the Court of Justice of the European Union regarding the primacy of EU law, and the fact that an Opinion from the Council Legal Service was attached to this Declaration, does not change the Supreme Court's conclusion on the Danish courts' testing of the constitutionality of acts and EU acts.[82]

[81] Christian Timmermans, 'The Constitutionalization of the European Union' (2001–2002) 21 *Yearbook of European Law* 1.

[82] *Hojesteret*, decision 199/2012 of 20 February 2013 (*Lisbon*). On the decision Helle Krunke, 'The Danish Lisbon Judgment' (2014) *European Constitutional Law Review*, forthcoming.

2. The 'Pluralist Movement' and the Principle of Primacy

The discussion so far has shown that there is not one principle of primacy but many, European and national. There is therefore no shared rule of conflict and no encompassing, external perspective or 'law of laws' on the basis of which it can be decided what provision or standard should give way in a concrete case. The issue of primacy therefore remains unsettled and contested. A number of scholars often referred to as the 'constitutional pluralists' have tried to develop criteria on the basis of which it would be possible to decide whether national courts would have valid and legitimate grounds to give precedence to national rather than EU law.[83] Mattias Kumm, for instance, takes recourse to 'cosmopolitan values', a set of overarching constitutional principles and values of constitutionalism such as the protection of fundamental rights, democracy, and the principle of subsidiarity (the 'better placed' argument).[84] Miguel Maduro has attempted to give guidelines to courts, directing the respective courts to mutual engagement and dialogue in order to prevent conflict.[85]

Yet none of these authors has been able to formulate a convincing alternative overarching rule of conflict which would help to decide which norm should be awarded precedence in case of dispute. To put it bluntly, the pluralist movement has failed to solve the conundrum it tried to resolve: 'constitutional pluralists give up precisely where an answer is most needed, namely when a constitutional conflict cannot be prevented or solved.'[86] The movement cannot escape the fact that both legal systems are autonomous and self-referential, and that each has its own

[83] Overviews of the various pluralist approaches can be found in eg Matej Avbelj and Jan Komárek (eds), *Constitutional Pluralism in the European Union and Beyond* (2012); see also, among many others, Nico Krisch, *Beyond Constitutionalism: The Pluralist Structure of Postnational Law* (2010); Neil Walker, 'The Idea of Constitutional Pluralism' (2002) 65 *Modern Law Review* 317.

[84] See for instance his 'The Moral Point of Constitutional Pluralism. Defining the Domain of Legitimate Institutional Civil Disobedience and Conscientious Objection' in Julia Dickson and Pavlos Eleftheriadis (eds), *Philosophical Foundations of European Union Law* (2012) 216; 'The Jurisprudence of Constitutional Conflict: Constitutional Supremacy in Europe before and after the Constitutional Treaty' (2005) 11 *European Law Journal* 262; 'The Cosmopolitan Turn in Constitutionalism: On the Relationship between Constitutionalism in and beyond the State' in Jeffrey L. Dunoff and Joel P. Trachtman (eds), *Ruling the World: International Law, Global Governance, Constitutionalism* (2009).

[85] See eg his 'Interpreting European Law: Judicial Adjudication in a Context of Constitutional Pluralism' (2007) 1 *European Journal of Legal Studies*; 'Contrapunctual Law: Europe's Constitutional Pluralism in Action' in Neil Walker (ed), *Sovereignty in Transition* (2003) 502.

[86] Alexander Somek, 'Monism: A Tale of the Undead?' in Avbelj and Komárek (n 83) 343–379; critiques of the pluralist movements can be found also in Martin Loughlin, 'Constitutional Pluralism: An Oxymoron?' 3 *Global Constitutionalism* (2014) 9; Piet Eeckhout, 'Human Rights and the Autonomy of EU Law: Pluralism or Integration?' (2013) 66 *Current Legal Problems* 169; René Barents, 'The Precedence of EU Law from the Perspective of Constitutional Pluralism' (2009) 5 *European Constitutional Law Review* 421–446.

points of reference and conflict rules. 'Constitutional pluralism' operates on the basis of principles that are indeed shared, but they are so broad and vague that they are not helpful in answering concrete conflicts or in balancing competing values. This tends to be the problem in concrete cases of conflict between EU law and national constitutional law: not that a particular value or principle does not exist at either level, or that it is completely overlooked, but that the balance is struck differently by actors belonging to different legal systems. Reasonable authorities acting on the basis of the same values of constitutionalism can reasonably disagree over whether priority should be given to one principle, value, or interest over another. What seems more legitimate to one may not seem so to another.

More recently, actors operating within each of the systems, national and European, have also spoken the language of constitutional pluralism. For instance, Judge Koen Lenaerts, member of the ECJ, has agreed to a version of constitutional pluralism, stating that:

For general principles, a moderate discourse on 'constitutional pluralism' would posit that beyond a core nucleus of shared values where the ECJ must ensure uniformity, the *ius commune europaeum* resulting from the application of general principles cannot disregard the cultural, historical and social heritage that is part and parcel of national constitutional traditions.[87]

Yet the type of constitutional pluralism embraced by Lenaerts was very limited and does not seem to amount to much more than an attitude of sensitivity to national values: 'However, the ECJ must still guarantee a core nucleus of shared values vital to the integrity of the EU legal order. In relation to those values, the ECJ has no choice but to follow a hierarchical approach.'[88]

This 'degree of judicial deference', aiming to be responsive to constitutional traditions of the Member States touching upon sensitive areas of national constitutional law, is of course very welcome and to be applauded, but it fits perfectly within an approach based on the principles of autonomy and primacy. In other words, it does not question primacy, but should be part and parcel of EU law and of the EU approach to national constitutions. It is now explicitly provided for in Article 4(2) TEU, as well as in Article 52 of the Charter.

Andreas Voßkuhle, President of the German Federal Constitutional Court, has also replaced the concept of hierarchy with the non-hierarchical handling of constitutional issues, conceptualizing the relationship between the courts as a *Verbund*.[89] In his view, this concept makes it possible to do without 'oversimplistic spatial and hierarchic concepts such as 'superiority' and 'subordination'.[90] Instead, it opens up

---

[87] Koen Lenaerts and José A Guttiérez Fons, 'The Constitutional Allocation of Powers and General Principles of EU Law' (2010) 47 *Common Market Law Review* 1629, at 1663.

[88] Lenaerts and Fons, 1664.

[89] Andreas Voßkuhle, 'Multilevel Cooperation of the European Constitutional Courts: Der Europäische Verfassungsgerichtsverbund' (2010) 6 *European Constitutional Law Review* 175.

[90] Voßkuhle (n 89) at 183–184.

the possibility of a differentiated description on the basis of different systematic aspects such as unity, difference and diversity, homogeneity and plurality, delimitation, interplay, and involvement.' In this 'multilevel cooperation of the European constitutional courts' (*europäischer Verfassungsgerichtsverbund*), constitutional courts operating in different contexts and pertaining to different legal orders cooperate and handle multilevel constitutional issues in a non-hierarchical fashion. Thus, there is a composite multilevel structure of constitutional jurisdictions entertaining complementary and cooperative relationships. Rather than 'superiority or subordination', it is about appropriately sharing and assigning responsibilities in a complex multilevel system. Ultimately, however, both judges stick to less fluid, more old-fashioned conceptions of that relationship, placing each court firmly in its own legal order, and maintaining a more radical principle of primacy.

 'Constitutional pluralism' has not changed the EU principle of primacy. This is exemplified by the recent case law of the Court of Justice in cases such as *Melloni*: the primacy, effectiveness, and unity of EU law must not be endangered by national constitutions. Conversely, national constitutional courts 'stick to their guns' and leave open the possibility of making exceptions to primacy in certain cases. Nevertheless, the 'pluralist movement' has contributed to increasing awareness of the existing value plurality among Member States, as well as the need for dialogue and careful mutual consideration of and responsiveness to these values.[91]

3. National Identity: An Exception to Primacy of EU Law?

Several authors and constitutional courts have presented the identity clause of Article 4(2) TEU as an exception to primacy confirming the *controlimiti* case law of the national constitutional courts.[92] According to this view, Article 4(2) is the

[91] See eg the contributions in Monica Claes, Maartje de Visser, Patricia Popelier, and Catherine van de Heyning (eds), *Constitutional Conversations in Europe* (2012); Marta Cartabia, 'Europe and Rights: Taking Dialogue Seriously' (2009) 5 *European Constitutional Law Review* 5–31; Aida Torres Pérez, *Conflict of Rights in the European Union: A Theory of Supranational Adjudication* (2009).

[92] Armin von Bogdandy and Stephan Schill, 'Overcoming Absolute Primacy: Respect for National Identity under the Lisbon Treaty' (2011) *Common Market Law Review* 1417–1453. To be sure, the authors do stress that it does not give national courts a *carte blanche*. The balancing of national identity and the concern for uniform application is rather seen as a common endeavour of the ECJ and national constitutional courts. Nevertheless, they accept that under Art 4(2) TEU the national courts can unilaterally detract from EU law. For similar approaches see Leonard F.M. Besselink, 'National and Constitutional Identity before and after Lisbon' (2010) 6 *Utrecht Law Review* 36; Ingolf Pernice, 'Der Schutz nationaler Identität in der Europäischen Union' 136 *Archiv des öffentlichen Rechts* (2011), 185. *Bundesverfassungsgericht*, decision of 30 June 2009, BVerfGE 123, 267 (*Lisbon*); Polish *Trybunał Konstytucyjny*, decision of 24 November 2010, K 32/09 (*Lisbon Treaty*); Constitutional Court of Latvia, Decision of 7 April 2009 in Case No. 2008-35-0.

European recognition of national exceptions to the absolute primacy of EU law. However, that is not how the provision was intended and it is not the way in which it has been applied by the ECJ.[93] The provision makes explicit that the EU must respect the self-determination of the Member States as to their fundamental structures, political and constitutional, and must respect their essential state functions. National identity as laid down in Article 4(2) TEU can be understood as selfhood,[94] as the continuing ability of the Member States to define and organize themselves within the evolving process of European integration.[95] The text does not seem intended to refer to fundamental substantive *values*, but was quickly interpreted to include a duty to respect constitutional traditions and fundamental values, such as language diversity or the values of republicanism and its consequences for the nobility and their names.[96]

Article 4(2) TEU is an expression of the plurality of political and constitutional orders and of a 'value diversity' beyond the nucleus of shared values expressed in Article 2 TEU. Yet this concern for diversity remains under the control of the Court. A claim based on national identity will only be effective under EU law if it is accepted by the ECJ. While the Court recognizes that particular national (constitutional) interest or institutional circumstances may justify *derogations* from EU law, they may do so only as a matter of EU law, and under the supervision of the European Court. It does not allow the Member States or national courts to deviate unilaterally from EU law and escape EU obligations, and it does not provide an exception to primacy.

In its reference in the *OMT* case, however, the *Bundesverfassungsgericht* made it clear that the concept of 'national identity' protected in Article 4(2) TEU is very different from 'the constitutional identity of the German Basic Law', which sets an ultimate limit to European integration and cannot be balanced against other legal interests. Hence, the protection of the German constitutional identity is a task for the German Constitutional Court alone and cannot be left to the ECJ. Where the *Bundesverfassungsgericht* finds a provision of EU law to infringe Germany's

---

[93] Barbara Guastaferro, 'Beyond the Exceptionalism of Constitutional Conflicts: The Ordinary Functions of the Identity Clause' (2012) *Yearbook of European Law* 263–318 and Monica Claes, 'National Identity: Trump Card or Up for Negotiation?' in Alejandro Saiz Arnaiz and Carina Alcoberro Llivina, *National Constitutional Identity and European Integration* (2013) 109–140.

[94] So Julien Sterck, 'Expressing Sovereignty in the European Union: An Irish Perspective on Constitutional Identity', UCD Working Papers in Law, Criminology & Socio-Legal Studies Research Paper No.03/2014.

[95] On the origins of Art 4(2) TEU see Barbara Guastaferro, 'Beyond the Exceptionalism of Constitutional Conflicts: The Ordinary Functions of the Identity Clause' (2012) *Yearbook of European Law* 263–318 and Monica Claes, 'National Identity: Trump Card or Up for Negotiation?' in Alejandro Saiz Arnaiz and Carina Alcoberro Llivina (eds), *National Constitutional Identity and European Integration* (2013) 109–140.

[96] See eg Case C-391/09 *Runevič-Vardyn*; Case C-208/09 *Ilonka Sayn-Wittgenstein*, Case C-473/93 *Commission v Luxembourg* [1996] ECR I-03207 (with reference to Art 4(2) TEU's predecessor Art 6 of the TEU).

'constitutional identity', German authorities may not take part in those measures. This applies to all constitutional organs, authorities, and courts. It results from the constitutional principles of democracy (Article 20(1) and (2) of the Basic Law) and the rule of law (Article 20(3) of the Basic Law), as well as from Article 23(1) of the Basic Law, and is safeguarded under EU law by the principle of conferral (Article 5(1) and (2) TEU) and the obligation of the European Union to respect the national identities of the Member States (Article 4(2) TEU).[97]

Some have argued that 'national identity' functions as a bridge to expressing national constitutional values at the EU level and to 'deconstructing' absolute primacy in favour of a constitutional body of values and principles.[98] Certainly, recourse to national or constitutional identity should be taken seriously, in the sense that it is a signal that a Member State feels that its most fundamental principles and values, its selfhood, are at stake, something that the EU has a duty to respect. It is an argument that the Court would be wise to engage with. If the EU does infringe the national identities of its Member States, it infringes the obligation that the TEU imposes. But it does not alter the principle of primacy in EU law.

4. Article 53 Charter: An Exception to the Primacy of EU Law?

Another post-Lisbon provision that has been seen by some to restrict the primacy of EU law is Article 53 of the Charter. According to the Explanations the provision is intended to maintain the level of protection currently afforded within their respective scope by Union law, national law, and international law. Owing to its importance, mention is made of the ECHR. The text is reminiscent of Article 53 ECHR, a non-regression clause that is usually understood as implying that the ECHR offers only a minimum level of protection and that the Contracting Parties are free to offer higher protection, except where conflicting considerations—the rights of others—oblige states to limit them.[99] At the same time, it prevents states from diminishing or deviating from higher national and international protection: the ECHR may not be used as a pretext to diminish national protection. From its inception, it has been debated whether Article 53 Charter implies in a similar

---

[97] *Bundesverfassungsgericht*, decision of 14 January 2014, 2 BvR 2728/13 (*OMT*); for an analysis see the special issue of the *German Law Journal* (2014).

[98] François-Xavier Millet, *L'Union européenne et l'identité constitutionnelle des États membres* (2013).

[99] 'Nothing in this Convention shall be construed as limiting or derogating from any of the human rights and fundamental freedoms which may be ensured under the laws of any High Contracting Party or under any other agreement to which it is a Party.' See also Art 5(2) of the UN CESC and Art 5(2) of the UN CCPR. On Art 53 ECHR see eg Jonas Christoffersen, *Fair Balance. Proportionality, Subsidiarity and Primarity in the European Convention on Human Rights* (2009).

vein that national Constitutions may always offer a higher level of protection and that in those circumstances the Charter must give way to national Constitutions.[100] On that interpretation, Article 53 would create an exception to the primacy of EU law and detract from *Internationale Handelsgesellschaft* because, in some cases, national constitutional provisions *could* as a matter of EU law be invoked to block the application of EU law, namely when they offer higher protection. In fact, it could even be difficult to maintain *Internationale Handelsgesellschaft*, since the cases in which Constitutions are invoked to block EU law are precisely those where the Constitution offers protection that is not available under EU law.

Nevertheless, despite the similarities between the texts of both Articles 53 and their shared aim of preventing a devaluation of the protection of the rights the relevant document seeks to protect, there are important differences between them as well. Article 53 Charter contains the illusive but important phrase '*in their respective fields of application*'. According to the Explanations to the Charter, the provision was intended to maintain the level of protection already afforded *within their respective scope* by Union law, national law, and international law. Presumably, therefore, the provision was meant merely to confirm that the Charter should not lead to a devaluation of the level of protection each of these systems allowed *in their own field of application*. This is trivial: where EU law does not apply, neither does the Charter, so it cannot lower (or indeed increase) the standard of protection.[101] The problem, of course, is that the fields of application often overlap: when EU law is implemented and applied by the Member States, the Member States are bound by the Charter, but their respective constitutions also continue to apply. This is known as the problem of multiple standards.[102] It is here that conflicts may arise, specifically when the Charter allows certain EU measures that could be considered unconstitutional under the national constitution. This is exactly the situation that occurred in *Melloni*, which will be discussed further below.

In addition, the context and the system within which both Articles 53 apply are very different. The ECHR is exclusively concerned with human rights, and the Strasbourg machinery offers only subsidiary supervision and a minimum level of protection. In addition, it does not require a specific method of implementation or domestic effect, but is concerned with the end result. EU law is different in all these respects: it pursues not only the protection of fundamental rights but also the

---

[100] Jonas Bering Liisberg, 'Does the EU Charter of Fundamental Rights Threaten the Supremacy of Community Law?' (2001) 38 *Common Market Law Review* 1171–1199; Leonard Besselink, 'The Member States, the National Constitutions and the Scope of the Charter' (2001) 8 *Maastricht Journal* 68; Stefan Griller, 'Der Anwendungsbereich der Grundrechtscharta und das Verhältnis zu sonstigen Gemeinschaftsrechten, Rechten aus der EMRK und zu verfassungsgesetzlich gewährleisteten Rechten' in Alfred Duschanek and Stefam Griller (eds), *Grundrechte für Europa* (2002) 163–182.

[101] Case C-206/13 *Siragusa* [2014] ECR I-00000.

[102] See eg Federico Fabbrini, *Fundamental Rights in Europe* (2014); Aida Torres Pérez, *Conflict of Rights in the European Union: A Theory of Supranational Adjudication* (2009).

attainment of a host of other objectives. This may restrict the margin of manoeuvre on the part of national authorities in the choice of methods to protect fundamental rights and balance them with other interests. While EU fundamental rights do accept some variation and diversity in local or national protection in the context of EU law, this is not unlimited and is defined by EU law. Moreover, the Court of Justice operates in a different institutional environment than the ECtHR, and deals not only with the Member States (vertically), but also with the EU legislature (horizontally). Finally, EU law does impose a particular method of implementation and effectiveness on the domestic legal orders via the direct effect and primacy of EU law, which the ECHR does not.

In *Melloni*, the Court of Justice rejected the view that Article 53 Charter can be read as a general authorization to a Member State to apply the higher national constitutional standard of protection and to give it priority over the application of provisions of EU law, because this would undermine the principle of the primacy of the EU. These, of course, were the questions to be answered: whether the ECJ would reconsider the relationship between EU law and national constitutional law, and whether Article 53 of the Charter did or did not introduce an exception to primacy.[103] The Court's answer is circular —Article 53 Charter does not contain an exception to primacy because of the primacy of EU law.[104] However, in the Court's view, Article 53 of the Charter confirms that national fundamental rights continue to apply when Member States implement EU law, subject to two conditions: first, the application of the national constitution may not lower the level of protection offered by the Charter as interpreted by the Court, and, second, it may not compromise the primacy, unity, and effectiveness of EU law. Consequently, Member States cannot avail themselves of Article 53 Charter to set aside an obligation under EU law.

Two situations can thus be distinguished. Where EU law leaves a margin of discretion to the Member States, they remain free to apply their constitutions in addition to the Charter, and offer more protection, within the space left by EU law. This is evident and does not require the permission of Article 53 Charter: where EU law leaves the Member States a choice between two options, one of which would be unconstitutional and the other constitutional, it is evident that EU law does not preclude a choice for the constitutional option. Take for example the decision of the German *Bundesverfassungsgericht* in which it annulled the German implementation of the Data Retention Directive because the legislature had not sufficiently used the discretion left in the Directive to

---

[103] If the first two questions had been answered in the affirmative, namely if indeed the protection under the framework decision was such that it did not allow the courts to impose the condition on retrial, and second, if the framework decision was not invalid for infringement of the Charter.

[104] For arguments as to why Art 53 Charter should not be read as restricting the primacy of EU law, see Bruno De Witte, 'Article 53' in Steve Peers, Tamara Hervey, Jeff Kenner, and Angela Ward (eds), *The EU Charter of Fundamental Rights—A Commentary* (2014), 1523–1538.

choose an implementation that was in conformity with the Basic Law.[105] This is perfectly in line with EU law, as was also stated in *Åkerberg Fransson*, decided on the same day, in which the Court held that national fundamental rights may serve as a standard of review to be used by national courts when 'the action of the Member States is not entirely determined by EU law', subject to the conditions mentioned above. It could even be argued that Article 53 Charter imposes an obligation *under EU law* to maintain the 'higher' national level of protection in such cases. Of course, this would be an obligation that would be difficult to enforce by the EU institutions.

Where, on the other hand, EU law does not leave any discretion to the Member States and the national constitution offers a higher level of protection, the latter cannot be invoked against EU law. The level of protection is then defined exclusively by EU law, more specifically by the Charter and EU general principles. Common traditions of the Member States and the ECHR inform these EU fundamental rights under Article 52 Charter,[106] and hence contribute to defining the EU level, but a state cannot unilaterally invoke its national standard to escape from the duty to comply with obligations of EU law. If it were to do so, it would infringe EU law and fail to award it primacy, and Article 53 cannot be used as a justification. In these cases, the Charter has the effect of harmonizing fundamental rights in the scope of EU law, and Member States are not allowed under Article 53 to deviate from the common standard. They can, however, have recourse to other techniques and mechanisms offered by EU law to derogate from EU obligations. The famous *Omega* case illustrates this nicely. In this case, the ECJ permitted derogation from the rules of free movement because the protection of fundamental rights was considered a legitimate interest capable of justifying the restriction of the obligations imposed by EU law. The harmonizing effect of EU fundamental rights is thus not absolute, and is subject to exceptions, insofar as allowed under EU law.

This harmonizing effect of the Charter imposes a great responsibility on the Court of Justice, in view of the promise contained in *Internationale Handelsgesellschaft*

---

[105] *Bundesverfassungsgericht*, decision of 2 March 2010 *(dataretention)*, see Anna-Bettina Kaiser, 'German Federal Constitutional Court—German Data Retention Provisions Unconstitutional in their Present Form: Decision of 2 March 2010' (2010) *European Constitutional Law Review* 503–517. See also the decision of the Czech constitutional court, decision of 22 March 2011, Pl. ÚS 24/10 *(data retention)* with references to the German, Romanian, Bulgarian, and Cypriot constitutional courts which had similarly annulled the implementing legislation, and, strikingly, a reference to Joined Cases C-92/09 and C-93/09 *Schecke and Eifert*, where the Court emphasized the necessity to provide, in a manner as stringent as possible, the guarantees and instruments for protecting the fundamental rights of individuals when handling their personal data generated in course of electronic communications.

[106] See also the suggestion of Mr Justice Hogan in his reference to the ECJ in Case C-326/14 *Schrems v Data Protection Commissioner*, currently pending before the ECJ, see *Schrems v Data Protection Commissioner* [2014] IEHC 310.

that EU law would, in place of the national courts protecting national constitutional rights, ensure such protection on the basis of general principles of EU law. If the Court offers to replace the constitutional courts, it must take its role of guardian of fundamental rights seriously. And it is here that the decision in *Melloni* is most disappointing. The Court rejected the application of the Spanish standard on the ground that the framework decision reflected 'the consensus reached by all the Member States regarding the scope to be given under EU law to the procedural rights enjoyed by persons convicted in absentia who are the subject of a European arrest warrant'. This, however, is not the point: it is the mission of the Court to review whether the consensus reached by the Member States[107] in a legislative document complies with the fundamental EU rights as laid down in the Charter, protected under general principles and as informed by the ECHR. To state that the Member States have consented is hardly convincing. The real question was whether they were allowed to do so under the Charter. This is a different question, as it relates to the EU standard of protection, and not to the case of one Member State offering a higher standard. Furthermore, the Court should have reiterated that when executing an EAW, the Member States are implementing EU law and hence are bound to respect fundamental rights (Articles 6 TEU and 51(2) Charter), which was the case here. More specifically with respect to the position of the Spanish constitutional court, it is disappointing that the Court did not show awareness of the problem the referring court was confronted with and did not engage with its arguments.

The *Tribunal constitucional* has accepted the decision and went along with the Court, albeit having 'translated' the ECJ approach to the Spanish context with the Spanish Constitution as the focal point. As a result, it lowered the standard that used to be applicable, even for extradition to non-EU countries. Rather than framing its decision in terms of the primacy of EU law, the Tribunal reinterpreted the Constitution in line with the case law of the ECJ.[108]

Of course, the decision in *Melloni* concerns only the perspective of EU law, and most likely will not affect the position of national courts that, in exceptional cases, EU law will have to give way to national constitutional rights; in other words, that the principle of EU primacy is not absolute.[109]

---

[107] Or rather: the EU legislature, in which the Member States' governments play a crucial role. However, it is important to stress here that the Member States are represented in the Council by their governments. The Spanish government voted in favour of a framework decision that infringed the constitutional rights as expounded by its constitutional court. See on this point Leonard F.M. Besselink, 'The Parameters of Constitutional Conflict after *Melloni*' (2014) *European Law Review*, forthcoming 531–552.

[108] Aida Torres Pérez, '*Melloni* in Three Acts: From Dialogue to Monologue' (2014) *European Constitutional Law Review*, forthcoming.

[109] See section III above.

CONCLUSION

This chapter has demonstrated that the EU principle of the primacy of EU law is as absolute and unconditional as it was when it was first developed by the Court in the 1960s and 1970s. Recent developments, such as the planned codification and eventual non-codification, alleged paradigm shifts in the understanding of the EU and the legal relationships between national and European law ('constitutional pluralism), the identity clause of Article 4(2) TEU and Article 53 of the Charter, have not essentially altered the principle. However, what has changed is EU law itself: the expansion of the EU into areas touching upon the most sensitive issues of life has forced it to find ways to accommodate the diversity of values and cultural and societal differences in the Union. EU law has developed strategies to accommodate the deep-seated concerns of its Member States, but the principle of primacy is not one of them.

At the same time, the EU principle is not the only version of primacy. Each of the Member States has developed its own understanding of the primacy of EU law, usually on the basis of its constitution, indicating exceptions to the primacy of EU law as a matter of national constitutional law.

The dynamics resulting from the co-existence of these competing versions of primacy call for careful consideration of and responsiveness to the concerns of 'the other', and take away some of the sharpest edges of the principle of primacy.

BIBLIOGRAPHY

Julio Baquero Cruz, 'The Legacy of Maastricht-Urteil and the Pluralist Movement' (2008) 4 *European Law Journal* 389

Michal Bobek, 'Of Feasibility and Silent Elephants: The Legitimacy of the Court of Justice through the Eyes of National Courts' in Maurice Adams, Johan Meeusen, Gert Straetmans and Henri de Waele (eds), *Judging Europe's Judges: The Legitimacy of Case Law of the European Court of Justice Examined* (2013) 197

René Barents, 'The Precedence of EU Law from the Perspective of Constitutional Pluralism' (2009) 5 *European Constitutional Law Review* 421

Monica Claes, *The National Courts' Mandate in the European Constitution* (2006)

Gráinne de Búrca and J.H.H. Weiler, *The Worlds of European Constitutionalism* (2012)

Bruno De Witte, 'Direct Effect, Primacy and the Nature of the Legal Order' in Gráinne de Búrca and Paul Craig (eds), *The Evolution of EU Law* (2011) 323

Michal Dougan, 'When Worlds Collide! Competing Visions of the Relationship between Direct Effect and Supremacy' (2007) 44 *Common Market Law Review* 931

Adam Lazowksi (ed), *The Application of EU Law in the New Member States. Brave New World* (2012)

Koen Lenaerts and Tim Corthaut, 'Of Birds and Hedges: The Role of Primacy in Invoking Norms of EU Law' (2006) 31 *English Law Review* 287

Franz C. Mayer, 'Supremacy—Lost?' (2005) 6 *German Law Journal* 1497–1505

CHAPTER 9

EFFECTIVENESS OF EU LAW BEFORE NATIONAL COURTS

DIRECT EFFECT, EFFECTIVE JUDICIAL PROTECTION, AND STATE LIABILITY

DOROTA LECZYKIEWICZ

I. Introduction

THE chapter considers the doctrines developed by the Court of Justice of the EU in order to ensure effectiveness of norms belonging to the EU legal order before national courts. It examines the development of these doctrines, how their recognition was justified by the Court, and how they made it possible for the body of rules found in the Treaty establishing the European Economic Community (EEC Treaty) and the subsequent Treaties, as well as in acts adopted by institutions of the Community and then the Union, to constitute a new legal order, semi-autonomous from the legal orders of the Member States.[1] The chapter explains why the

[1] Eric Stein, 'Lawyers, Judges and the Making of a European Constitution' (1981) 75 *American Journal of International Law* 1; Joseph H.H. Weiler, 'The Transformation of Europe' (1991) 100 *Yale*

theoretical rationalization of the legal phenomena hidden behind the described doctrines is difficult. The case law of the Court of Justice does not allow us to construct a coherent picture of when EU norms should be effective before national courts. The chapter attempts, however, to explain the considerations that played a role in the judicial development of the doctrines, and to formulate the rules that could be derived from the Court's case law.

II. Direct Effect and the Case of *Van Gend en Loos*

'Direct effect' is a structural principle of EU law and it is the justification supporting it (the principle of effectiveness or *effet utile*) that explains why its significance could not be restricted to just one Treaty provision or only a set of provisions displaying similar characteristics.[2] Another important factor is the method of precedent applied by the Court of Justice of the EU. While in the common law systems the case has to be significantly similar on facts to be relevant for deciding another case, the Court of Justice makes connections between cases at a much higher level of abstraction. This enables the Court to move freely between formal sources of law and sectors of Union law. Because ensuring effectiveness of EU law is always a relevant consideration, judgments that rely on this justification have a potentially limitless scope of application as precedents for future cases. It should also be recognized that the doctrine of direct effect was unlikely to develop had it not been for the preliminary ruling procedure, which enabled national courts to refer questions of interpretation of Community/Union provisions to the Court of Justice.

The *Van Gend en Loos* case[3] concerned incorrect classification by a Dutch tax authority of a product imported into the Netherlands from Germany. The tariff applied was incorrect in the light of Article 12 EEC, which provided that Member States should refrain from introducing between themselves any new customs duties

---

Law Journal 2403; Paul Craig, 'Once upon a Time in the West: Direct Effect and the Federalisation of EEC Law' (1992) 4 *Oxford Journal of Legal Studies* 453; Bruno de Witte, 'Direct Effect, Primacy, and the Nature of the Legal Order' in Paul Craig and Gráinne De Búrca (eds), *The Evolution of EU Law* (2nd edn, 2011) 323.

[2] On the constitutional implications of effectiveness, see Malcolm Ross, 'Effectiveness in the European Legal Order(s): Beyond Supremacy to Constitutional Proportionality' (2006) 31 *European Law Review* 476.

[3] Case 26/62 *NV Algemene Transport- en Expeditie Onderneming van Gend & Loos v Netherlands Inland Revenue Administration* [1963] ECR 3.

on imports or exports or any charges having equivalent effect, and from increasing those they had already applied in trade with each other. The Dutch administrative tribunal asked the Court of Justice whether Article 12 EEC had 'direct application within the territory of a Member State'. The question defined 'direct application' as involving the capacity of nationals of a given State to 'lay claim to individual rights', on the basis of the Article in question, which the national courts were under obligation to protect. The Court's reply was positive. Article 12 EEC had 'direct application' because of the Treaty's spirit (the establishment of a Common Market and of institutions with sovereign rights). According to the Court, the functioning of the Common Market was 'of direct concern to interested parties in the Community', which implied that the Treaty was 'more than an agreement which merely create[d] mutual obligations between the contracting states'.[4] The Treaty was held to be able to confer rights on individuals.[5] Article 12 EEC in particular conferred rights because: (1) the provisions contained a clear and unconditional prohibition which was not a positive but a negative obligation; (2) the obligation was not qualified by any reservation on the part of the states which would make its implementation conditional upon a positive legislative measure enacted under national law; (3) the implementation of Article 12 EEC did not require any legislative intervention on the part of the states.

Only a year after the *Van Gend en Loos* judgment the Court decided another fundamental case, *Costa v ENEL*,[6] which addressed directly the question of the relationship between a Treaty provision relied on by an individual and a national measure that violated the prohibition imposed on the Member States by that provision. The Court held that 'the EEC Treaty ha[d] created its own legal system which, on the entry into force of the Treaty, became an integral part of the legal systems of the Member States and which their courts are bound to apply'.[7] The *Costa v ENEL* judgment did not clearly resolve the issue of the relationship between the principle of Community law precedence, or primacy, as it later became to be called, and the producing of direct effects by a particular provision of Community law. This has led to a persisting uncertainty over that relationship. Primacy is a principle of a higher level of generality and with potentially broader implications. Protection of individual rights is not, unlike in the context of direct effect, the primary concern. The doctrine of primacy is focused on the objective effectiveness of Community law stemming from the need to respect the reciprocal arrangement in which the Member States have entered, and the ability of the organization they created, ie the Community or the Union, to achieve its objectives.[8] These considerations could in principle justify the introduction of other doctrines, which, alongside direct effect,

---

[4] *Van Gend & Loos* (n 3) 12.   [5] *Van Gend & Loos* (n 3) 12 (emphasis added).

[6] Case 6/64 *Flaminio Costa v E.N.E.L.* [1964] ECR 1141, English version: [1964] ECR 585.

[7] *Costa* (n 6) 593.

[8] Effectiveness is often considered to have two guises, a subjective and an objective one. Subjective effectiveness is oriented towards ensuring effective protection of individual rights conferred by Union law. Objective effectiveness concerns efficient operation of regimes created by Union law,

would contribute to the effectiveness of Community/Union law, independently of whether they are also demanded by the need to protect individual rights.

In a number of cases following *Van Gend en Loos* the Court was given the opportunity to embed the doctrine of direct effect into Community law in the face of variations in the cases' factual circumstances. Direct effect was possible also when the applicant relied on a Treaty provision that envisaged a transitional period,[9] or when a Treaty provision was elaborated by a Directive.[10] In *Reyners*,[11] the Court held that even a Treaty provision envisaging the adoption by the Community of further measures was directly effective at the end of the transitional period. In *Grad*,[12] the applicant was allowed to rely on a Decision, an act of Community secondary law. In this way the path was opened for Directives, another type of Community secondary law, to be recognized to produce 'direct effects'. This recognition would have to overcome the wording of Article 189 EEC (now Article 288 TFEU), which stated: 'Directives shall bind any Member State to which they are addressed, as to the result to be achieved, while leaving to domestic agencies a competence as to form and means.' In *van Duyn*,[13] the Court held that:[14]

[i]t would be incompatible with the binding effect attributed to a directive by Article 189 to exclude, in principle, the possibility that the obligation which it imposes may be invoked by those concerned. In particular, where the Community authorities have, by directive, imposed on Member States the obligation to pursue a particular course of conduct, the useful effect of such an act would be weakened if individuals were prevented from relying on it before their national courts and if the latter were prevented from taking it into consideration as an element of Community law.

The Court also began to develop the doctrine of horizontal direct effect of Treaty provisions. In *BRT v SABAM*,[15] the Court held that it was clear from the wording of Articles 85(1) and 86 (now Article 101(1) and 102 TFEU) that they were intended to regulate relations between private parties, and therefore that these provisions produced direct effects between individuals. In *Walrave and Koch*,[16] the Court extended horizontal direct effect onto Treaty articles concerning free movement of workers and services, which were addressed only to the Member States. The Court reasoned that the private rules challenged under the provisions on free movement of workers

such as the Common Market, regardless of whether, or beyond the extent to which, they create individual rights.

[9] Case 13/68 *SpA Salgoil v Italian Ministry of Foreign Trade, Rome* [1968] ECR 661.

[10] Case 33/70 *SpA SACE v Finance Minister of the Italian Republic* [1970] ECR 1213.

[11] Case 2/74 *Jean Reyners v Belgian State* [1974] ECR 631.

[12] Case 9/70 *Franz Grad v Finanzamt Traunstein* [1970] ECR 825.

[13] Case 41-74 *Yvonne van Duyn v Home Office* [1974] ECR 1337.

[14] *Van Duyn* (n 13), para 12.

[15] Case 127/73 *Belgische Radio en Televisie and société belge des auteurs, compositeurs et éditeurs v SV SABAM and NV Fonior* [1974] ECR 51.

[16] Case 36/74 *B.N.O. Walrave and L.J.N. Koch v Association Union cycliste internationale, Koninklijke Nederlandsche Wielren Unie and Federación Española Ciclismo* [1974] ECR 1405.

and services were 'regulating in a collective manner gainful employment'.[17] Their arguable 'public law' character justified subjecting them to review against the relevant Treaty provisions. It was *Defrenne*[18] that enabled review against the Treaty of individual private contracts.[19] The case concerned Article 119 EEC (now Article 141 TFEU) on equal pay for equal work between men and women. The Court hesitated the longest to recognize the horizontal direct effect of the free movement of goods provisions (now articles 34 and 35 TFEU). In *Sapod*, the Court held that contractual provisions cannot be regarded as barriers to trade because they were not imposed by a state but agreed between individuals.[20] However, in *Fra.bo* the Court tentatively allowed horizontal application of Article 34 TFEU (then Article 28 EC) on the ground that the private body against whom the provision was invoked in reality held 'the power to regulate the entry into the German market of products . . . at issue'.[21] Article 34 TFEU has not been so far used to review the content of a private contract.

III. DIRECT EFFECT AND ENFORCEABILITY
OF NATIONAL MEASURES

The early judgments of the Court about direct effect did not elucidate whether 'producing direct effect' entailed some specific legal consequence which the national court had to recognize and implement in its decision. The *Simmenthal* judgment clarified that the obligation of the national court stemming from the doctrine of direct effect is to disapply or set aside conflicting national rules. This obligation flows directly from the principle of primacy of Community/Union law.[22] One of the persisting questions of EU law is whether this obligation of the national courts is dependent on the provision

---

[17] *Walrave and Koch* (n 16), para 17. See also Case C-415/93 *Union royale belge des sociétés de football association ASBL v Jean-Marc Bosman* [1995] ECR I-4921; Case C-438/05 *International Transport Workers' Federation and Finnish Seamen's Union v Viking Line ABP and OÜ Viking Line Eesti* [2007] ECR I-10779; Case C-341/05 *Laval un Partneri Ltd v Svenska Byggnadsarbetareförbundet* [2007] ECR I-11767

[18] Case 43/75 *Gabrielle Defrenne v Société anonyme belge de navigation aérienne Sabena* [1976] ECR 455.

[19] *Defrenne* was followed, among others, in Case C-281/98 *Roman Angonese v Cassa di Risparmio di Bolzano SpA* [2000] ECR I-4139 and Case C-94/07 *Andrea Raccanelli v Max-Planck-Gesellschaft zur Förderung der Wissenschaften eV* [2008] ECR I-5939.

[20] Case C-159/00 *Sapod Audic v Eco-Emballages SA* [2002] ECR I-5031, para 74.

[21] Case C-171/11 *Fra.bo SpA v Deutsche Vereinigung des Gas- und Wasserfaches eV (DVGW)— Technisch-Wissenschaftlicher Verein*, judgment of 12 July 2012, para 31.

[22] Case 35/76 *Simmenthal SpA v Ministero delle Finanze italiano* [1976] ECR 1871, para 17.

conferring rights on the individual. Individuals may benefit from inapplicability of conflicting national law also when they have not been granted any rights by the invoked provisions of Union law. For example, if their conduct was prohibited by some national rule, excluding its application would enable individuals to claim that their conduct was legal and avoid punishment. The conferral of rights is not necessary because in many such situations individuals will argue that they were free to act as they did because of *absence of regulation* (when national rules are disapplied), and not because they had a legal right. Such a situation arises also when it is a Directive with which national rules are incompliant. In *Ratti*,[23] the Court held with respect to Directives[24]:

[A] Member State which has not adopted the implementing measures required by the directive in the prescribed periods may not rely, as against individuals, on its own fail-ure to perform the obligations which the directive entails. It follows that a national court requested by a person who has complied with the provisions of a directive not to apply a national provision incompatible with the directive not incorporated into the internal legal order of a defaulting Member State, must uphold that request if the obligation in question is unconditional and sufficiently precise.

The obligation not to apply a national provision incompatible with a Directive arises after the expiry of the Directive's transposition period. After that date, a Member State 'may not apply its internal law—even if it is provided with penal sanctions—which has not yet been adapted in compliance with the directive, to a person who has complied with the requirements of the directive'.[25]

The view that a Member State which has not implemented a Directive can never apply national rules incompliant with the Directive against an individual whose conduct is illegal only because of these rules, has become known as the 'estoppel argument'. The direct effect of the Directive is here a sanction imposed on the state which failed to implement the Directive. An individual is given the *right to rely* on a Directive when its provision is unconditional and sufficiently precise and therefore enables the assessment of the national rules' (in)compatibility with the Directive. For this function of direct effect, it is irrelevant whether the individual was conferred a substantive right by the Directive. This is visible in *Becker*,[26] where the Court disa-greed with the German government that only provisions that were enacted in the interest of the individual, and were clear and unconditional on their introduction, could be directly effective.[27] The Court's approach is not, however, uniform. *Ratti* and *Becker* can be contrasted with *Enichem Base*,[28] where the Court held that the appli-cants could not rely on a Directive to set aside a decision of a local authority because on its proper construction the Directive in question did not give individuals a right.[29]

---

[23] Case 148/78 *Criminal proceedings against Tullio Ratti* [1979] ECR 1629.
[24] *Ratti* (n 23), para 22.   [25] *Ratti* (n 23), para 23.
[26] Case 8/81 *Ursula Becker v Finanzamt Münster-Innenstadt* [1982] ECR 53.
[27] *Becker* (n 26), para 30.
[28] Case 380/87 *Enichem Base and others v Comune di Cinisello Balsamo* [1989] ECR 2491.
[29] *Enichem Base* (n 28), para 11.

IV. The Doctrine of Consistent Interpretation

In the cases at which we have looked so far it was sufficient for the applicant to succeed if the national court disapplied conflicting national law or if it recognized and protected, using national procedural mechanisms, a right that was conferred on the applicant by a provision of Union law. Clearly, there are also cases where an individual is able to argue that EU law creates rights that the national court must protect, but the remedial and procedural protection offered by national law is ineffective. Does EU law require national courts to do more than they would under national law in order fully to remedy a breach of an individual Union right? In the early 1980s this was a contentious issue that led to the creation of another doctrine of Union law, frequently called the doctrine of 'indirect effect'.

The case *Von Colson*[30] concerned interpretative obligations stemming for national courts from Community/Union provisions. Under German law, the only compensation which the applicants unlawfully rejected as candidates for a job because of their sex could receive was reimbursement of their travelling expenses (damages were restricted only to the losses 'incurred by the worker as a result of his reliance on the expectation that the establishment of the employment relationship would not be precluded by...a breach' of the prohibition of discrimination). The right to equal treatment between women and men in employment was guaranteed in Community law by Directive 76/207.[31] Article 6 of the Directive required Member States to introduce into their national legal systems such measures as were necessary 'to enable all persons who consider themselves wronged by discrimination to pursue their claims by judicial process', but left it to the Member State to choose the precise form of the remedy. The Court held that despite this discretion the sanctions that were required by the Directive had to be 'sufficiently effective' to achieve the objective of the Directive. They had to guarantee 'real and effective judicial protection' and act as 'a real deterrent effect on the employer'.[32] It followed that where a Member State chose to sanction the breach of the prohibition of discrimination by the duty to compensate, the level of compensation had to be 'adequate in relation to the damage sustained'.[33] National courts had a duty 'effectively' to transpose a Directive in the event when the national legislator had failed to enact provisions which achieved the objective of imposing an effective sanction. The

---

[30] Case 14/83 *Sabine von Colson and Elisabeth Kamann v Land Nordrhein-Westfalen* [1984] ECR 1891.

[31] Council Dir No 76/207/EEC of 9 February 1976 on the implementation of the principle of equal treatment for men and women as regards access to employment, vocational training and promotion, and working conditions (Official Journal 1976, L39, p 40) ('The Equal Treatment Directive').

[32] *Von Colson* (n 30), para 23.   [33] *Von Colson* (n 30), para 23.

Court held that national courts were required to interpret national law in the light of the wording and the purpose of the Directive in order to achieve the result of its implementation.[34] This obligation became known as the doctrine of consistent interpretation, described also, very confusingly, as the doctrine of 'indirect effect' merely because it created another possibility for EU provisions to generate some effect before national courts.

The doctrine of consistent interpretation enabled insufficiently precise and conditional provisions of a Directive to produce some effects in national law. So in *Von Colson*, the task of the German court was to ensure that substantial compensation was available to the claimants by the appropriate interpretation of national law. The Court thus expected the national court, where effectiveness of Union law so required, to change the traditional interpretation of national provisions so as to comply with the Directive's wording and purpose. What it meant in practice was that the national court had to comply with the Court's interpretation of the Directive. In *Von Colson*, the Court did not specify when the obligation of interpreting national law in the light of the Directive would be discharged. The exact limits of the obligation of consistent interpretation were explored in later cases, many of which involved attempts by individuals to rely on Directives against employers, commercial partners, and traders, and thus related to the question of horizontal effect of Union provisions.[35]

V. Directives and Obligations
of Private Parties

We have seen that in *Defrenne* the Court held that a Treaty provision guaranteeing the right to equal pay was applicable 'horizontally'. An individual was able to rely on this provision against their employer regardless of whether it was a private or a public entity. *Von Colson* concerned applicability of the equal treatment principle against an employer, but this time the principle was laid down not by the Treaty but by a Directive. Another case which concerned the same Directive was *Marshall*.[36] The UK Court of Appeal asked the Court of Justice whether

---

[34] *Von Colson* (n 30), para 26.

[35] On the role of the doctrine of consistent interpretation in enhancing effectiveness of EU social policy, see Leone Niglia, 'Form and Substance in European Constitutional Law: The "Social" Character of Indirect Effect' (2010) 16 *European Law Journal* 439.

[36] Case 152/84 *M. H. Marshall v Southampton and South-West Hampshire Area Health Authority (Teaching)* [1986] ECR 723.

the Equal Treatment Directive could be relied upon before the national court by Ms Marshall notwithstanding the inconsistency between the Directive and the UK Sex Discrimination Act, which permitted discrimination by employers when it related to pensions. The employer and the UK argued that a Directive could never impose obligations directly on individuals and that it could only have direct effect against a Member State qua public authority, and not against a Member State qua employer. The Court first dealt with the argument that a Directive could never impose obligations directly on individuals. It held that:[37]

according to Article 189 of the EEC Treaty the binding nature of a directive, which constitutes the basis for the possibility of relying on the directive before a national court, exists only in relation to 'each Member State to which it is addressed'. It follows that *a directive may not of itself impose obligations on an individual and that a provision of a directive may not be relied upon as such against such a person.*

However, where the applicant was able to rely on a Directive as against the State, they could do so regardless of the capacity in which the latter was acting. So even when the state acted merely as an employer an individual could rely on a directly effective provision of the Directive against it.[38] While the Court did not say it explicitly, the judgment strongly suggested that it was the estoppel argument which had been *the* justification for the effect of an unimplemented Directive's provisions before national courts, and therefore Directives could be effective also in quasi-horizontal situations, where the state acted as a mere employer. However, due to the fact that the estoppel argument worked only against a state, Directives could not be effective in purely horizontal situations, ie between two private parties.

On the facts, this was confirmed in *Faccini Dori*.[39] The Court was asked to interpret a Directive that created rights for consumers and was clearly sufficiently precise and unconditional to produce direct effect.[40] Under the Directive, a consumer had a right of withdrawal from a contract concluded away from the business' premises but the Directive was not implemented in Italy. The trader brought proceeding before the

---

[37] *Marshall* (n 26), para 48 (emphasis added), hereinafter: 'the *Marshall* prohibition'.

[38] *Marshall* (n 26), para 49. This means that provisions of a Directive could be relied on not only against tax authorities (*Becker*), local or regional authorities (Case 103/88 *Fratelli Costanzo v Comune di Milano* [1989] ECR 1839), but also against constitutionally independent authorities responsible for the maintenance of public order and safety (Case 222/84 *Johnston v Chief Constable of the Royal Ulster Constabulary* [1986] ECR 1651) and public authorities providing public health services (*Marshall*) acting as employers. In Case C-188/89 *A. Foster and others v British Gas plc* [1990] ECR I-3313, para 20, the Court held that 'a body, whatever its legal form, which has been made responsible, pursuant to a measure adopted by the State, for providing a public service under the control of the State and has for that purpose special powers beyond those which result from the normal rules applicable in relations between individuals is included in any event among the bodies against which the provisions of a directive capable of having direct effect may be relied upon'.

[39] Case C-91/92 *Paola Faccini Dori v Recreb Srl* [1994] ECR I-3325.

[40] Council Dir 85/577/EEC, concerning protection of the consumer in respect of contracts negotiated away from business premises (OJ 1985 L372, p 31)

Italian court against Ms Faccini Dori for the agreed sum with interest and costs, which she had refused to pay. Despite the criticism of its earlier rejection of the horizontal direct effect of Directives, the Court maintained its ruling as to the Directive's impossibility of imposing obligations on an individual.[41] The Court explained that it was clear from the *Marshall* judgment and the case law on the possibility of relying on Directives against a State that under Article 189 EEC a Directive was binding only 'in relation to "each Member State to which it [was] addressed"'.[42] The judgment listed two further possibilities for ensuring that individual rights conferred by a Directive were made effective. The first was the doctrine of consistent interpretation and the second—the state's obligation to make good damage caused to the individual through the failure to transpose the Directive, which I will discuss in Section VI.

In *Arcaro*,[43] the Court treated the *Marshall* prohibition as a more general principle which underpinned not only the doctrine of direct effect but also that of consistent interpretation. As a result, if the changed interpretation of national law demanded by the requirement of ensuring the Directive's objective led to the imposition of a new obligation on a private party, the national court was not obliged to adopt this interpretation.[44] AG Jacobs in *Centrosteel*[45] argued that *Marshall* did not require such a general constraint on horizontal effectiveness of Directives.[46] Directives could create obligations for individuals, just not 'by themselves'.[47] It was, however, difficult to reconcile this proposition with a view that a Directive's effect before national courts stemmed from the estoppel argument. In particular, it would go against its precepts to allow unimplemented Directives to produce effects through the doctrine of consistent interpretation in inverse vertical cases, where Directives were invoked by the state *against* an individual. This concern explains the judgment in *Kolpinghuis Nijmegen*, where the Court held that a Directive could not 'of itself and independently of a law adopted for its implementation, have the effect of determining or aggravating the liability in criminal law of persons who act in contravention of the provisions of that directive'.[48] A less strict version of this restriction applies in taxation cases, where

---

[41] *Faccini Dori* (n 39), para 20.

[42] *Faccini Dori* (n 39), para 24. In Case C-201/02 *The Queen, on the application of Delena Wells v Secretary of State for Transport, Local Government and the Regions* [2004] ECR I-723, para 56, the Court explained that it is the principle of legal certainty which prevents Directives from creating obligations for individuals.

[43] Case C-168/95 *Criminal proceedings against Luciano Arcaro* [1996] ECR I-4705.

[44] *Arcaro* (n 43), para 42.

[45] Case C-456/98 *Centrosteel Srl v Adipol GmbH* [2000] ECR I-6007, Opinion of AG Jacobs of 16 March 2000.

[46] *Centrosteel* (n 45), para 34 of the Opinion.

[47] *Centrosteel* (n 45), para 35 of the Opinion: 'While that process of interpretation cannot, of itself and independently of a national law implementing the directive, have the effect of determining or aggravating criminal liability, it may well lead to the imposition upon an individual of civil liability or a civil obligation which would not otherwise have existed.'

[48] Case 80/86 *Criminal proceedings against Kolpinghuis Nijmegen BV* [1987] ECR 3969, para 14.

the Court accepted that a Member State could impose 'directive-compliant interpret-ation' of national law on individuals, but the national law under interpretation had to be sufficiently precise and clear so that the persons concerned could in advance know the full extent of their rights and obligations.[49] It seems that when this requirement is not met the obligation of consistent interpretation does not apply, which in practice means that also in taxation cases the doctrine of indirect effect cannot lead to the imposition of new obligations on individuals.

But conversely to inverse vertical cases, in horizontal cases the Court gradually did accept far-reaching effects of Directives brought about by the doctrine of con-sistent interpretation. In *Marleasing*,[50] a company incorporated under Spanish law was entitled to rely on a Directive[51] against another company in order to exclude application of the provisions of the Spanish civil code that enabled the latter to challenge on the grounds of lack of cause the validity of the contract establish-ing the first company. The Court repeated its ruling in *Marshall* that 'a direct-ive may not of itself impose obligations on an individual and, consequently, a provision of a directive may not be relied upon as such against such a person', but claimed that the national court was in fact asking whether in a case falling within the scope of the Directive it was required to interpret its national law in the light of the wording and the purpose of that Directive 'in order to preclude a declaration of nullity of a public limited company on a ground other than those listed in Article 11 of the directive'.[52] Thus, in *Marleasing*, the Court broke the link between the limits of the obligation of consistent interpretation and the prohib-ition against allowing Directives to impose obligations on individuals. Moreover, the *Marshall* prohibition was no longer presented as related to the limits of the estoppel argument. Instead, it was interpreted independently and applied *a con-trario*, as permitting other ways in which a Directive could affect the outcome of a case before a national court. Both national provisions adopted in order to implement a Directive and those which were adopted before or after the Directive for other reasons than its implementation were covered by the obligation of con-sistent interpretation.[53] Moreover, the Court asked the national court to interpret national provisions 'as far as possible' 'in order to achieve the result pursued by [the Directive] and thereby comply with the third paragraph of Article 189 of the Treaty' (the state's obligation to implement Directives).[54] In some cases, including

---

[49] Case C-321/05 *Hans Markus Kofoed v Skatteministeriet* [2007] ECR I-5795, paras 44–45.

[50] Case C-106/89 *Marleasing SA v La Comercial Internacional de Alimentacion SA* [1990] ECR I-4135

[51] First Council Dir 68/151/EEC of 9 March 1968 on coordination of safeguards which, for the pro-tection of the interests of members and others, are required by Member States of companies within the meaning of the second paragraph of Art 58 of the Treaty, with a view to making such safeguards equivalent throughout the Community (OJ 1969 L65, p 8).

[52] *Marleasing* (n 50), para 13.   [53] *Marleasing* (n 50), para 8.

[54] *Marleasing* (n 50), para 8.

Marleasing, the Court was even prepared to declare which interpretation of national provisions was precluded by the obligation of consistent interpretation. This shows that the doctrine of consistent interpretation could in fact substitute for direct effect where the latter was not applicable.

The Court's judgment in *Pfeiffer*[55] could be taken as evidence that the *Marshall* prohibition, on its post-*Marleasing* interpretation, in no way restricts the effectiveness of Directives in horizontal situations. The case concerned compatibility of German law with the Working Time Directive.[56] German law made it possible to extend the weekly working time beyond 48 hours and accepted consents given in the form of collective agreements. The Court of Justice had to determine whether the workers' agreement had to be given by each worker individually. It concluded that each worker should have the benefit of an upper limit on weekly working time and minimum rest periods, and that German legislation was incompatible with the Directive.[57] Yet in order for the Directive to affect individual contracts, the Court needed to make it possible for the claimants to rely on the Directive against their employer. The Court found the relevant provision of the Directive direct effective, but did not want to overrule *Marshall* and allow the Directive's *horizontal* direct effect.[58] Instead, it focused on the doctrine of consistent interpretation.[59] It held that it was 'the responsibility of the national courts in particular to provide the legal protection which individuals derive from the rules of Community law and to ensure that those rules are fully effective'.[60]

The judgment lays down three interpretational instructions to national courts, whose observance entails that they have properly discharged the obligation of consistent interpretation. First, all national provisions have to be used in the interpretation process so as to avoid a result contrary to that sought by the Directive.[61] Second, the scope of application of national provisions should be restricted by applying them only insofar as they are compatible with the Directive concerned.[62] Third, the national court must do whatever lies within its jurisdiction to ensure compatibility with the Directive.[63] The judgment in *Pfeiffer* shows that the doctrine of consistent interpretation enables an employee to rely on an EU right created by a Directive against another private party to alter the content of an employment contract. The effect is arguably achieved by means of interpretation of national law, but it is indistinguishable from ascribing the Directive 'horizontal direct effect'. Craig argues that in the light of the

---

[55] Joined cases C-397/01 to C-403/01 *Bernhard Pfeiffer v Deutsches Rotes Kreuz, Kreisverband Waldshut eV* [2004] ECR I-8835.

[56] Council Dir 93/104/EC of 23 November 1993 concerning certain aspects of the organization of working time (OJ 1993 L307, p 18).

[57] *Pfeiffer* (n 55), para 100.   [58] *Pfeiffer* (n 55), paras 106 and 108.

[59] *Pfeiffer* (n 55), paras 112–113.

[60] *Pfeiffer* (n 55), para 111.   [61] *Pfeiffer* (n 55), para 115.   [62] *Pfeiffer* (n 55), para 116.

[63] *Pfeiffer* (n 55), para 119.

Pfeiffer judgment, it is no longer tenable to deny Directives such effect, and concludes that legal certainty would be enhanced by abolishing the *Marshall* prohibition.[64]

The continuing ambiguity concerns the content of the obligation of consistent interpretation. What exactly does the national court have to do to fulfil the obligation? In *Pupino* the Court held that:[65]

[t]he obligation on the national court to refer to the content of a framework decision when interpreting the relevant rules of its national law ceases when the latter cannot receive an application which would lead to a result compatible with that envisaged by that framework decision. In other words, the principle of conforming interpretation cannot serve as the basis for an interpretation of national law *contra legem*. That principle does, however, require that, where necessary, the national court consider the whole of national law in order to assess how far it can be applied in such a way as not to produce a result contrary to that envisaged by the framework decision.

In *Adeneler*, the obligation of consistent interpretation was extended temporarily onto the time after the Directive's entry into force but before the expiry of its transposition deadline.[66] During this time national courts were imposed an obligation to refrain as far as possible from interpreting domestic law in a manner which might seriously compromise, after the period for transposition had expired, attainment of the objective pursued by that Directive.[67] In *Impact*,[68] the Court considered a situation where national provisions belatedly implementing a Directive excluded their retrospective effect because, under a rule of that legal system, retrospective application of legislation required a clear and unambiguous indication in the law in question. The Court held that the obligation of consistent interpretation was limited by general principles of law, particularly those of legal certainty and non-retroactivity, and that this obligation could not serve as the basis for interpreting the national law *contra legem*.[69] The Court left it for the national court to ascertain

---

[64] Paul Craig, 'The Legal Effect of Directives: Policy, Rules and Exceptions' (2009) 34 *European Law Review* 349. The author is sceptical about the importance that is attached in the Court's case law on the horizontal effect of Directives to 'the humble pronoun "itself"'. One of the reasons why before the Lisbon Treaty the Court was reluctant to extend the doctrine of direct effect onto cases subjected to the doctrine of consistent interpretation stemmed from the pre-Lisbon wording of Art 34 TEU, setting out the measures which the Union could adopt in the field of Police and Judicial Cooperation in Criminal Matter (the Third Pillar). This provision stated that framework decisions, one of the possible measures, could not entail direct effect. In *Pupino*, the Court held that this was no obstacle to imposing on national courts the obligation of consistent interpretation. Case C-105/03 *Criminal proceedings against Maria Pupino* [2005] ECR I-5285, para 60.

[65] *Pupino* (n 64), para 47. In Case C-212/04 *Konstantinos Adeneler and others v Ellinikos Organismos Galaktos (ELOG)* [2006] I-6057, para 112, the Court applied this principle to Directives.

[66] *Adeneler* (n 65), para 121. The Member States to which the Directive is addressed must refrain from taking any measures liable seriously to compromise the attainment of the result prescribed by it already after the Directive's entry into force but before its deadline for implementation.

[67] *Adeneler* (n 65), para 123.

[68] Case C-268/06 *Impact v Minister for Agriculture and Food* [2008] ECR I-2483.

[69] *Impact* (n 68), para 100.

whether domestic law included a provision that enabled retrospective application of the implementing measure, but, in the absence of such a provision, the national court was released from the obligation to give effect to the Directive.[70] However, as the Court explained in *Mono Car Styling*:[71]

If the application of interpretive methods recognised by national law enables, in certain circumstances, a provision of domestic law to be construed in such a way as to avoid conflict with another rule of domestic law or the scope of that provision to be restricted to that end by applying it only in so far as it is compatible with the rule concerned, the national court is bound to use those methods in order to achieve the result sought by the directive at issue.

VI. The Principle of Member State Liability

Liability in damages is a universal enforcement mechanism, which in principle could attach to any form of irregular behaviour. The *Faccini Dori* judgment made it clear that Community law did not possess a perfect system of enforcement. The doctrine of direct effect had significant limitations, some of which stemmed from the requirement of sufficient precision and unconditionality, and some of which arose from the *Marshall* judgment, which excluded the operation of the doctrine of direct effect in horizontal cases. Unimplemented Directives creating obligations for non-state actors or those that could not be invoked against states because of their insufficient clarity and precision would remain ineffective, and no sanction, apart from the Commission starting proceedings against the non-complying state, would be available. As we have seen, the Court extended the doctrine of direct effect onto provisions which left discretion to the Member States. It also developed the doctrine of consistent interpretation. In the line of cases described below it created yet another possibility for individuals to rely on unimplemented Directives.

In *Francovich*,[72] a group of employees brought proceedings against Italy for its failure to implement a Directive guaranteeing a minimum level of protection in the event of the employer's insolvency.[73] The remedies sought included the recovery of unpaid

---

[70] *Impact* (n 68), paras 102–103.

[71] Case C-12/08 *Mono Car Styling SA, in liquidation v Dervis Odemis* [2009] ECR I-6653, para 63.

[72] Joined cases C-6/90 and C-9/90 *Andrea Francovich and Danila Bonifaci v Italian Republic* [1991] ECR I-5357.

[73] Council Dir 80/987/EEC of 20 October 1980 on the approximation of the laws of the Member States relating to the protection of employees in the event of the insolvency of their employer (Official Journal 1980 L283, p 23).

wages or, in the alternative, compensation. The Court found that the rights of employees under the Directive were not unconditional and sufficiently precise because the provisions left the Member States a broad discretion with regard to the organization, operation, and financing of the guarantee institutions. This meant that the relevant provisions of the Directive were not directly effective and the employees could not simply receive the outstanding wages.[74] As a result, the Court of Justice had to focus on the question of the state's liability in damages. It observed that the issues had to be considered 'in the light of the general system of the Treaty and its fundamental principles'. At paragraph 33 the Court held: 'The full effectiveness of Community rules would be impaired and the protection of the rights which they grant would be weakened if individuals were unable to obtain redress when their rights are infringed by a breach of Community law for which a Member State can be held responsible.'

The principle that a Member State is liable for loss and damage caused to individuals as a result of a breach of Community law was held to be 'inherent in the system of the Treaty'.[75] As for conditions, the Court did not refer the Italian courts to their own rules on compensating for damage caused by illegal conduct. Instead, the conditions were set out in the judgment (the granting of rights to individuals, the possibility of identifying the content of those rights on the basis of the provisions of the unimplemented Directive, and the existence of causal link between the state's failure to implement and the loss or damage suffered). These conditions were held to be sufficient to give rise to a right to reparation.[76] However, while national courts were not entitled to use additional conditions of liability, they were permitted to use national rules concerning the designation of competent courts, detailed procedural rules,[77] and arguably also concerning the remaining substantive issues, such as the level of compensation and the sufficiency of the causal connection.[78]

The conditions of Member State liability were further spelt out in the *Brasserie du Pêcheur/Factortame III* judgment of the Court.[79] The two cases each concerned liability of a Member State for a breach of Community law. The Court held that the right to reparation was 'the necessary corollary of the direct effect of the Community provision whose breach caused the damage sustained'.[80] It submitted

---

[74] *Francovich* (n 72), paras 25–26.   [75] *Francovich* (n 72), para 35.

[76] *Francovich* (n 72), para 41.

[77] Such as eg, those concerning the length of the limitation period to bring the *Francovich* cause of action. See Case C-261/95 *Rosalba Palmisani v Istituto nazionale della previdenza sociale (INPS)* [1997] ECR I-4025.

[78] Case C-140/97 *Walter Rechberger, Renate Greindl, Hermann Hofmeister and others v Republik Österreich* [1999] ECR I-3499. In Case C-94/10 *Danfoss A/S and Sauer-Danfoss ApS v Skatteministeriet* [2011] ECR I-9963, the Court held that the national legal system could not interpret the condition of a direct causal link in such a way as to make it virtually impossible or excessively difficult to obtain compensation for the damage suffered (para 36).

[79] Joined cases C-46/93 and C-48/93 *Brasserie du Pêcheur SA v Bundesrepublik Deutschland and The Queen v Secretary of State for Transport, ex p Factortame Ltd* [1996] ECR I-1029.

[80] *Brasserie du Pêcheur/Factortame* (n 79), para 22.

that creation of the *Francovich* remedy was legitimate as an 'interpretation of the Treaty'.[81] Just as in the process of creating the 'general principles of law', also here the Court was invoking the fact that its jurisdiction covered the duty to ensure that law was observed, and the 'generally accepted methods of interpretation' permitted the Court to refer to 'general principles common to the legal systems of the Member States'.[82] It found evidence to the effect that liability in damages of public institutions was indeed common to the laws of the Member States in Article 215 EEC (now Article 340 TFEU), which mentioned the laws of the Member States as the basis for the non-contractual liability of the Community for damage caused by its institutions.[83] The principle of state liability was held to apply to 'any case in which a Member State breaches Community law, whatever be the organ of the State whose act or omission was responsible for the breach', including the national legislature.[84]

The negative effect of linking *Francovich* liability with Article 215 EEC Treaty was the pressure to unify the conditions of liability applying to Community institutions and to Member States.[85] Because the Community had immunity from liability unless its institutions manifestly and gravely disregarded the limits on the exercise of its powers, the Court introduced a similar requirement with respect to claims brought by individuals against the states. The scope of the state's discretion under Community law became the crucial issue. Member States have no discretion as to whether to implement Directives, but in individual sectors of Community/ Union law they are often left with much autonomy. The Court held that in such circumstances the Member States should be liable only where their breach was 'sufficiently serious'.[86] According to the Court,[87]

[t]he factors which the competent court may take into consideration include the clarity and precision of the rule breached, the measure of discretion left by that rule to the national or Community authorities, whether the infringement and the damage caused was intentional or involuntary, whether any error of law was excusable or inexcusable, the fact that the position taken by a Community institution may have contributed towards the omission, and the adoption or retention of national measures or practices contrary to Community law.

The important ingredient in the decision as to whether the breach was sufficiently serious was the Court's own case law, especially when the Court's judgment had already found the state to be in breach. The conditions set out in the *Brasserie du Pêcheur/Factortame III* judgment were clearly only the minimum conditions of the right to reparation. The state could incur liability under less strict conditions on the basis of national law,[88] but

---

[81] *Brasserie du Pêcheur/Factortame* (n 79), para 25.
[82] *Brasserie du Pêcheur/Factortame* (n 79), para 27.
[83] *Brasserie du Pêcheur/Factortame* (n 79), para 28.
[84] *Brasserie du Pêcheur/Factortame* (n 79), paras 32 and 36.
[85] *Brasserie du Pêcheur/Factortame* (n 79), para 42.
[86] *Brasserie du Pêcheur/Factortame* (n 79), para 51.
[87] *Brasserie du Pêcheur/Factortame* (n 79), paras 55–56.
[88] *Brasserie du Pêcheur/Factortame* (n 79), para 66.

no more onerous conditions were allowed.[89] That meant that it was not permissible for English courts to use the conditions of the tort of misfeasance in public office to impose liability on the UK government. When it came to the condition of fault, only certain factors that are traditionally examined by reference to this concept were accepted as playing a role in deciding on the seriousness of the state's breach.[90] The condition of fault as a separate requirement could not be applied, which was a very sensible dictum given the divergent understandings of this concept in the laws of the Member States. The Court also provided some guidance as to what items of loss were recoverable in a *Francovich* claim. In principle, compensation should be commensurate with the loss or damage sustained. However, the claimant would not obtain full compensation if some losses they incurred could have been avoided if they had acted diligently, or if they had availed themselves in time of all the legal remedies available.[91] Lost profits were held to be recoverable but national rules were to regulate precisely which heads of damage should be compensated, what was required as a matter of proof, and how damages were to be calculated.[92]

The Court's relaxation of the conditions of liability under *Francovich*, in particular the inclusion among them of the requirement of serious breach in situations where the Member States had some discretion, largely disabled the remedy as a method of improving compliance and protecting individual rights.[93] In *British Telecommunications*,[94] the Court held that the UK could not be liable under *Francovich* because the relevant provision of the Directive in question[95] was imprecisely worded and therefore could reasonably bear the meaning accorded to it by the UK government, especially in the light of the fact that no guidance was available in the case law of the Court on how the provision should be interpreted.[96] In *Hedly Lomas*,[97] on the other hand, where the

---

[89] *Brasserie du Pêcheur/Factortame* (n 79), paras 70–74.

[90] *Brasserie du Pêcheur/Factortame* (n 79), paras 78–79. See also Case C-140/09 *Fallimento Traghetti del Mediterraneo SpA v Presidenza del Consiglio dei Ministri* [2010] ECR I-5243 and Case C-429/09 *Günter Fuß v Stadt Halle* [2010] ECR I-12167.

[91] *Brasserie du Pêcheur/Factortame* (n 79), paras 82–84. See Case C-445/06 *Danske Slagterier v Bundesrepublik Deutschland* [2009] ECR I-2119. Cf Joined cases C-397/98 and C-410/98 *Metallgesellschaft Ltd, Hoechst AG and Hoechst (UK) Ltd v Commissioners of Inland Revenue and HM Attorney General* [2001] ECR I-1727 and Case C-118/08 *Transportes Urbanos y Servicios Generales SAL v Administración del Estado* [2010] ECR I-635.

[92] See Case C-66/95 *The Queen v Secretary of State for Social Security, ex p Eunice Sutton* [1997] ECR I-2163, para 34.

[93] Takis Tridimas, 'Liability for Breach of Community Law: Growing Up and Mellowing Down?' (2001) 38 *Common Market Law Review* 301. Cf Carol Harlow, '*Francovich* and the Problem of the Disobedient State' (1996) 2 *European Law Journal* 199.

[94] Case C-392/93 *The Queen v H.M. Treasury, ex p British Telecommunications plc* [1996] ECR I-1631.

[95] Council Dir 90/531/EEC of 17 September 1990 on the procurement procedures of entities operating in the water, energy, transport and telecommunications sectors (OJ 1990 L297, p 1).

[96] *British Telecommunications* (n 94), paras 43–44.

[97] Case C-5/94 *The Queen v Ministry of Agriculture, Fisheries and Food, ex parte Hedley Lomas (Ireland) Ltd* [1996] ECR I-2553.

Community enacted a Directive harmonizing national measures necessary to achieve the objective which previously could justify a derogation from a free movement provision, the mere infringement of Community law was sufficient to establish a sufficiently serious breach. In *Dillenkofer*,[98] the Court made it clear that mere non-implementation of the Directive was sufficient to constitute serious breach.[99] It also reconciled a slight difference in the formulation of conditions of liability between *Francovich* and *Brasserie*. According to the Court, while the requirement of serious breach was not mentioned in *Francovich*, it was 'evident from the circumstances of the case'.[100]

The *Francovich* liability underwent two further major developments. Chronologically, first came its extension onto violations of Community law committed by private parties. In *Courage*,[101] the Court was asked whether a party to a contract liable to restrict or distort competition within the meaning of Article 85 EC Treaty (now Article 101 TFEU) could rely on the breach of that provision before a national court to obtain 'relief' from the other contracting party. In particular, the case concerned the right to compensation enforceable against another private party in the situation where under domestic (English) law the claim would be barred by the defence of illegality. The Court held:[102]

The full effectiveness of Article 85 of the Treaty and, in particular, the practical effect of the prohibition laid down in Article 85(1) would be put at risk if it were not open to any individual to claim damages for loss caused to him by a contract or by conduct liable to restrict or distort competition.

The *Courage* remedy, while similar in content (it offers compensation for loss caused by a breach of Community/Union law), should in fact be seen as independent from *Francovich*. This is evident in the Court's reasoning in *Courage*. Instead of relying on *Francovich*, the Court returned to the argument from the creation of the Community's own legal order. It discussed extensively the special importance of Article 85 EC Treaty and its recognized horizontal direct effect. The right to compensation enforceable against the claimant's contracting party was created because it 'strengthens the working of the Community competition rules and discourages agreements or practices, which are frequently covert, which are liable to restrict or distort competition'.[103] The national court was asked to take into account the economic and legal context of the parties' situation, in particular their respective bargaining powers. In addition, no statement in the judgment supports the conclusion

---

[98] Joined cases C-178/94, C-179/94, C-188/94, C-189/94, and C-190/94 *Erich Dillenkofer, Christian Erdmann, Hans-Jürgen Schulte, Anke Heuer, Werner, Ursula and Trosten Knor v Bundesrepublik Deutschland* [1996] ECR I-4845.

[99] *Dillenkofer* (n 98), para 26.   [100] *Dillenkofer* (n 98), para 23.

[101] Case C-453/99 *Courage Ltd v Bernard Crehan and Bernard Crehan v Courage Ltd* [2001] ECR I-06297.

[102] *Courage* (n 101), para 26.

[103] *Courage* (n 101), para 27. See also Joined cases C-295/04 to C-298/04 *Vincenzo Manfredi v Lloyd Adriatico Assicurazioni SpA, Antonio Cannito v Fondiaria Sai SpA and Nicolò Tricarico and Pasqualina Murgolo v Assitalia SpA* [2006] ECR I-6619.

that the Court was introducing a general principle of private party liability for breach of EU law comparable to Member State liability under *Francovich*.[104]

The second major development related to the possibility of Member State liability for a judicial breach of Community/Union law. Judicial breach can consist in an incorrect application or failure to apply EU law, a failure to interpret national law consistently with EU law, a failure to set aside conflicting national provisions, a failure to provide effective remedies to those whose EU rights were violated, or, finally, a failure to refer a preliminary ruling question to the Court of Justice of the EU. Member State liability for judicial breach was recognized by the Court in the judgment in *Köbler*,[105] in response to a reference sent by a Regional Civil Court in Vienna. The Court of Justice held:[106]

In the light of the essential role played by the judiciary in the protection of the rights derived by individuals from Community rules, the full effectiveness of those rules would be called in question and the protection of those rights would be weakened if individuals were precluded from being able, under certain conditions, to obtain reparation when their rights are affected by an infringement of Community law attributable to a decision of a court of a Member State adjudicating at last instance.

The conditions of liability were held to be the same as those set out in *Brasserie du Pêcheur/Factortame III*. The most difficult was the question of the appropriate assessment of the condition of the sufficiently serious nature of the breach. The Court took it upon itself to assess whether the Austrian Supreme Administrative Court deciding in the first proceedings committed a serious breach by withdrawing a preliminary ruling reference. The factors that the Court took into account shed some light on what considerations should play a role in deciding on that condition. The Court observed that Community law did not expressly cover the legal point in issue and no reply could be found in the Court's case law.[107] The national court's decision not to maintain a preliminary ruling request arose from an incorrect reading of the judgment of the Court, and for this reason it could not be regarded as a manifest error. The Court did not say, however, as it did in *British Telecommunications* with respect to an incorrect implementation of a Directive, whether the 'incorrect' reading was reasonably justified by the wording of the judgment. In the following judgment, *Traghetti del Mediterraneo*,[108] the Court was

[104] See Dorota Leczykiewicz, 'Private Party Liability in EU Law: In Search of the General Regime' (2009) 12 *Cambridge Yearbook of European Legal Studies* 257.

[105] Case C-224/01 *Gerhard Köbler v Republik Österreich* [2003] ECR I-1239.

[106] *Köbler* (n 105), para 33.

[107] *Köbler* (n 105), para 118. This links Member State liability for judicial breach with the *CILFIT* criteria for when the national court from whose judgment there is no further remedy is permitted not to make a reference to the Court of Justice. See Case 283/81 *Srl CILFIT and Lanificio di Gavardo SpA v Ministry of Health* [1982] ECR 3415.

[108] Case C-140/09 *Fallimento Traghetti del Mediterraneo SpA v Presidenza del Consiglio dei Ministri* [2010] ECR I-5243

asked to assess Italian rules that excluded all state liability for damage caused to individuals by an infringement of Community law committed by a national court adjudicating at last instance, where that infringement was the result of an interpretation of provisions of law or of an assessment of the facts and evidence carried out by that court. The Court rejected the possibility of any general exclusionary rule such as the one existing under Italian law. Furthermore, it recalled the relevance of its own case law in determining the correct reading of Union and national law. In practice, state liability for judicial breach is bound to be rare, especially given the imprecise nature of the Court's case law. While absence of 'settled' case law is a sufficient reason for holding that the national court infringed Union law by not referring the case to the Court of Justice, at the same time it makes it possible to conclude that the failure and the resulting incorrect application of Union law did not constitute a manifest error, or sufficiently serious breach, the finding of which is necessary to impose liability under *Francovich*.

VII. Incidental Effect of Directives

Despite the doctrines of direct effect and consistent interpretation there still remained a question as to whether Directives could generate any other effects. There were three directions of the possible more extensive effect of Directives. First, Directives could be used as general criteria of national law's compatibility with EU law (regardless of their precision and unconditionality and regardless of whether they conferred rights on individuals). Second, Directives could be used as grounds of review of private contracts to the extent that their use would not lead to the imposition of a new obligation on an individual. Third, Directives could be used as grounds of review of national administrative decisions.

The first type of situation arose in the case *CIA Security*.[109] The dispute before the national court concerned the cessation of unfair trading practices in the form of marketing alarm systems which did not meet the requirements of Belgian law. The law, which imposed requirements as to the marketing of alarm systems in Belgium, had not been notified to the Commission, as envisaged by Directive 83/189 (the Notification Directive).[110] The Belgian court established that it was the defendant in

---

[109] Case C-194/94 *CIA Security International SA v Signalson SA and Securitel SPRL* [1996] ECR I-2201.

[110] Council Dir 83/189/EEC of 28 March 1983 laying down a procedure for the provision of information in the field of technical standards and regulations (OJ 1983 L109, p 8), as amended by Council Dir 88/182/EEC of 22 March 1988 (OJ 1988 L81, p 75).

the proceedings, the firm CIA Security, which had breached Belgian law, but was unsure whether the national provisions should at all be used in assessing the practices of the parties involved given the fact that as technical regulations they should have, but were not, notified to the Commission. Could the Notification Directive be directly effective to exclude application of the Belgian unnotified technical regulation?

To answer this question, the Court assessed unconditionality and the level of precision of the Directive's provisions imposing the obligation to communicate technical regulations. It held that they laid down 'a precise obligation on Member States to notify draft technical regulations to the Commission before they are adopted. Being, accordingly, unconditional and sufficiently precise in terms of their content, those articles [could] be relied on by individuals before national courts'.[111] This shows that the doctrine of direct effect is the primary gatekeeper of the Directive's applicability. But then the Court, separately from the issue of direct effect, discussed the legal consequences to be drawn from the Member States' failure to notify the technical regulation. The legal consequence to which the Court referred was 'inapplicability' of national rules understood as unenforceability against individuals.[112] The Court recalled that the aim of the Directive was to protect freedom of movement for goods by means of preventive control and that the obligation to notify was essential for achieving such Community control. Once again, it is the argument from effectiveness which provided the main justificatory ground:[113]

The effectiveness of Community control will be that much greater if the directive is interpreted as meaning that breach of the obligation to notify constitutes a substantial procedural defect such as to render the technical regulations in question inapplicable to individuals.

The horizontal dimension of the case is invisible in the judgment. The Court is not concerned with the fact that unenforceability of the technical regulation against an individual meant that they were able to succeed in a lawsuit against other private parties. Yet these other parties, in compliance with the narrow reading of *Marshall*, had no obligations imposed on them by means of the Directive. They simply had to tolerate the activities of CIA Security as legal, which probably led to some indirect negative consequences for them in the form of smaller profits from the sale of alarm systems. The application of the Directive to make Belgian technical regulations unenforceable had therefore 'incidental effect' for private parties. In the constellation set out by the Court of Justice, they became 'third parties' because the Court was more concerned about the vertical relationship between the state that breached Community law by failing to notify a technical regulation and the party whose conduct would be characterized as illegal should the unnotified technical regulation apply to them.

---

[111] *CIA Security* (n 109), para 44.
[112] *CIA Security* (n 109), para 45.   [113] *CIA Security* (n 109), para 48.

The broad and unyielding judgment of the Court in *CIA Security* caused problems at two levels. At the conceptual level it was difficult to reconcile it with the logic of the *Marshall* and *Faccini Dori* judgments, which aimed at protecting individuals from the effects of unimplemented Directives. At the practical level, the unlimited invocability of Directives, leading to the exclusion of application of incompliant national rules, had undesirable consequences. For example, in *Lemmens*,[114] the person charged with driving a vehicle while under the influence of alcohol argued that the administrative rules which specified how the testing of the alcohol content of the driver's breath should be carried out was an unnotified technical regulation. The Court needed to determine whether, if the obligation to notify a technical regulation on breath-analysis apparatus had been infringed, the effect of the Directive was that evidence obtained by means of the apparatus authorized in accordance with the unnotified regulation, could not be relied upon against an individual charged with driving while under the influence of alcohol.[115] To avoid this absurd result, the Court imposed an additional requirement on when the Notification Directive could lead to disapplication of national rules: not only should the rules constitute technical regulations which have not been notified to the Commission but their application has to be liable to create an obstacle to trade.[116]

The relationship between the obligations stemming for the Member States from Directive 83/189 and the free movement of goods in the context of the Directive's horizontal invocability was further explored in the case of *Unilever*.[117] The case concerned a contractual arrangement between Central Foods, which ordered extra virgin olive oil, and Unilever, which delivered the right quantity of oil but in packaging which did not comply with Italian law on the labelling of olive oil. A draft of that law was communicated to the Commission but, in breach of the standstill obligation, Italy proceeded with its adoption. Unilever argued that the law which was adopted in violation of the standstill obligation was affected by the same substantial procedural defect which rendered the Belgian law inapplicable in the case *CIA Security*. Central Foods, on the other hand, maintained that the contract had not been performed because the labelling of the olive oil was not compliant with Italian law, and refused to pay for the delivery.

AG Jacobs delivered a powerful opinion in the case, underlining its context, that of civil proceedings between individuals arising from a contract.[118] He argued that it was not necessary to permit individuals to rely on Directive 83/189 when the

---

[114] Case C-226/97 *Criminal proceedings against Johannes Martinus Lemmens* [1998] ECR I-3711.

[115] *Lemmens* (n 114), para 27.

[116] *Lemmens* (n 114), paras 34–35; confirmed in Case C-443/98 *Unilever Italia SpA v Central Food SpA* [2000] ECR I-7535, para 8.

[117] *Unilever* (n 116).

[118] *Unilever* (n 116), Opinion of 27 January 2000.

interest of the Community was sufficiently served by the possibility to rely on the Treaty provision on the free movement of goods.[119] Unenforceability of unnotified technical regulations was, according to the Advocate General, justified by the need to ensure the effectiveness of the control mechanism under the Directive, and the Court could not have intended in *CIA Security* that this sanction should apply in all proceedings between individuals.[120] This view was supported by two arguments; the argument from the principle of legal certainty and the argument from injustice. AG Jacobs pointed out that trade required certainty as to which regulations apply to the sale of goods and in the light of the transparency problems in the Directive's control mechanism it would be difficult for individuals to know which laws applied. The Advocate General also submitted that it would be unfair to allow that an individual lost a case not because of their own failure but because of the failure of the Member State. The Advocate General then attempted to distinguish *CIA Security* on the ground that it concerned unfair trading practice proceedings, which although initiated by a private party, the defendant's competitor, were not very different in nature from state enforcement activities.[121] Lastly, he distinguished the notification obligation from the standstill requirement on the ground that its violation did not pose the same threat to the effectiveness of Community control under the Directive.[122] At paragraph 108 AG Jacobs implicitly asked the Court to observe the principle of proportionality in its rulings about the legal consequences stemming from the desire to ensure the effectiveness of the Directive. It claimed that in the circumstances he outlined the sanction of unenforceability would be 'disproportionately severe'.

The Court's judgment in *Unilever* does not engage with the very convincing arguments of AG Jacobs. The national court's obligation to refuse to apply a technical regulation is extended to a situation where the Member State notified its draft but failed to comply with the standstill requirement. This extension is justified solely by the fact that in the *CIA Security* judgment the Court discussed this requirement in conjunction with the notification obligation.[123] The Court did raise as a separate issue the question of whether inapplicability of technical regulations could be invoked in civil proceedings between individuals concerning contractual rights and obligations. Yet, it took the *CIA Security* judgment to have established that inapplicability of technical regulation could be invoked in proceedings between individuals, regardless of their character. So, while the Advocate General maintained that in *CIA Security*, exceptionally, the legal consequence of inapplicability was permitted *despite* the horizontal nature of the proceedings before the national court, the Court held that it was precisely *because* the earlier case had been

---

[119] *Unilever* (n 118), para 86 of the Opinion. However, at the time, the *horizontal* direct effect of the free movement of goods provisions had not been yet recognized.

[120] *Unilever* (n 118), paras 88 and 97 of the Opinion.

[121] *Unilever* (n 118), para 98 of the Opinion.   [122] *Unilever* (n 118), para 106 of the Opinion.

[123] *Unilever* (n 116), para 44 of the Opinion.

horizontal that inapplicability of national provisions could be demanded in another horizontal case had been, namely *Unilever*. As a result of the Italian law's inapplicability, Central Food was legally obliged to pay Unilever for the delivery of the oil.[124] It could be argued, of course, that this obligation arose out of the contract and a general rule of national law about enforceability of contractual promises. But it is undisputable that without the Directive's invocability, Central Foods could claim non-performance by Unilever and refuse to pay for the delivery. Thus, it would have possessed powers, liberties, or rights that were removed by Unilever's ability to invoke the Directive. Does this then mean that the *Unilever* judgment implicitly recognizes the horizontal direct effect of Directives, prohibited by *Marshall* and *Faccini Dori*?

The attempts to solve the conflict between *Unilever* and *Marshall/Faccini Dori* have generally focused on two questions. The first concerned the impact of direct effect, on the one hand, and of the *CIA Security/Unilever* doctrine, on the other, on national rules. If national rules were merely excluded by the application of a Directive (the invocability of exclusion), the direct effect was arguably not triggered and therefore, even in a horizontal case, we could not speak of a violation of the *Marshall* prohibition, which was considered to concern only 'horizontal direct effect'. The *Marshall* judgment could be reinterpreted to exclude only the invocability of substitution, ie a situation where a Directive substitutes for the incompatible national rule and constitutes the legal basis for the judgment of the national court, but allow of the invocability of exclusion—the so-called theory of exclusionary effect.[125] The second attempt to solve the conflict focused on the nature of direct effect. Direct effect was linked with the protection of individual rights. Whenever a Directive did not confer any such rights we could not speak of its horizontal 'direct effect' even if the Directive was applied in a horizontal case.[126] The principle of primacy arguably made it possible to use any norm of EU law as a ground of review of national law regardless of the character (vertical or horizontal) of the case. Naturally, neither of these two solutions actually solves the problem posed by the *CIA Security* and *Unilever* judgments. As explained by Arnull,[127] claiming

---

[124] For comment, see Stephen Weatherill, 'Breach of Directives and Breach of Contract' (2001) 26 *European Law Review* 177.

[125] The distinction was first introduced by AG Léger in Case C-287/98 *Grand Duchy of Luxemburg v Berthe Linster, Aloyse Linster and Yvonne Linster* [2000] ECR I-6917. He argued that the effectiveness of the Directive is subject to different requirements depending on the type of effect which is being sought by the parties. See also Pablo V. Figueroa Regueiro, 'Invocability of Substitution and Invocability of Exclusion: Bringing Legal Realism to the Current Developments of the Case-Law of "Horizontal" Direct Effect of Directives' Jean Monnet Working Paper 7/02.

[126] Koen Lenaerts and Tim Corthaut, 'Of Birds and Hedges: The Role of Primacy in Invoking Norms of EU Law' (2006) 31 *European Law Review* 287, 304–305. According to the authors, direct effect should be restricted only to cases where individuals claim rights directly from a Directive, a situation which does not obtain when rights are being created by the principle of the binding effect of contracts or the general terms of national legislation.

[127] Anthony Arnull, *The European Union and its Court of Justice* (2nd edn, 2006) 241–243. The author also observes that the theory of exclusionary effect would render the principle of consistent

that all cases in which the desired consequence was disapplicaiton of national law could be justified by the theory of exclusionary effect, and not direct effect, would require a retrospective rejection of a lot of the Court's case law in which it was the doctrine of direct effect that generated this consequence. More fundamentally, the criterion of distinction between the two types of invocability does not clarify why the requirements to which the effectiveness of Directives is subjected should differ depending on how (directly or by a mere exclusion of national rules) an individual is imposed an obligation as a result of the Directive's invocability. The same objection should be voiced against the second solution; restricting the meaning of direct effect to Union provisions that created individual rights. Moreover, the second solution does not offer an explanation as to why the removal of an existing right (eg not to pay for a contractual delivery) should be treated differently from the imposition of a new obligation. After all, in *Faccini Dori*, the defendant also wanted only to remove her obligation to pay and yet the Court excluded that possibility as incompliant with the permitted scope of the Directive's effectiveness. The argument that in *Unilever* the Court did not actually review the content of a private contract is equally unconvincing given the fact that it was an (implied) term of the contract that the goods to be delivered by Unilever conformed to the law.

The opportunity to reconcile the traditional concerns of contract law, such as legal certainty and the binding effect of contracts, with the desire to ensure effectiveness of the control mechanism under Directive 83/189 came with the case *Sapod Audic*.[128] The dispute concerned payment for disposal of waste carried out in accordance with French provisions implementing the Community Waste Directive.[129] Sapod claimed that the French provisions were technical regulations within the meaning of Directive 83/189, which had not been notified to the Commission, and which could not therefore be relied upon against them. The Court first held that it was for the national court to determine whether the provisions in question constituted technical regulations[130] and proceeded to examine what consequences should follow if the national court decided that the French law in question was a technical regulation, given the fact that it had not been notified to the Commission. It relied on *CIA Security* and *Unilever* to hold that if the national court interpreted French law as establishing an obligation to apply a mark or label, and therefore constituted a technical regulation, 'it would be incumbent on that court to refuse to apply that provision in the main proceedings'.[131] But the Court continued that:[132]

interpretation redundant because the provision of national law in its incompliant interpretation could simply be disapplied (at 243). The Court of Justice has never endorsed the distinction between the exclusionary and the substitutive effect and its implications, and could even be regarded to have implicitly rejected it in *Pfeiffer* (n 55).

[128] Case C-159/00 *Sapod Audic v Eco-Emballages SA* [2002] ECR I-5031.
[129] Council Dir 75/442/EEC of 15 July 1975 on waste (OJ 1975 L194, p 39), as amended by Council Dir 91/156/EEC of 18 March 1991 (OJ 1991 L78, p 32).
[130] *Sapod Audic* (n 128), paras 29–32.   [131] *Sapod Audic* (n 128), para 51.
[132] *Sapod Audic* (n 128), para 53.

the question of the conclusions to be drawn in the main proceedings from the inapplicability of [the French law in question] as regards the severity of the sanction under the applicable national law, such as nullity or unenforceability of the contract between Sapod and Eco-Emballages, is a question governed by national law, in particular as regards the rules and principles of contract law which limit or adjust that sanction in order to render its severity proportionate to the particular defect found.

The ruling in *Sapod Audic* should be interpreted as permitting the national court to enforce a contractual obligation that referred to national rules constituting technical regulations which should have been notified to the Commission under Directive 83/189. Review of the content of private contracts is not permitted unless the EU provision has 'horizontal direct effect' (as in *Defrenne*), which means that a Directive could never serve as the ground of such review.

The exception to this rule is the case of *Ruiz Bernáldez*.[133] In issue were three Directives relating to insurance against civil liability in respect of the use of motor vehicles.[134] Mr Ruiz Bernáldez caused a road accident while driving intoxicated. The Spanish court ordered him to make reparation for damage to property he had caused, but absolved the insurance company because Spanish law excluded from the insurance policy cover damage to property caused by an intoxicated driver. An appeal was brought by the victim of the property damage, who argued that Spanish law could not be interpreted as releasing the insurance company from the obligation to pay compensation.

The Court held that it stemmed from the Directives in question that:[135]

a compulsory insurance contract may not provide that in certain cases, in particular where the driver of the vehicle was intoxicated, the insurer is not obliged to pay compensation for the damage to property and personal injuries caused to third parties by the insured vehicle. It may, on the other hand, provide that in such cases the insurer is to have a right of recovery against the insured.

The Directive was then allowed to have a direct bearing on the content of a private insurance contract. If the Court had intended to comply with the rule that (unimplemented) Directives should not serve as grounds of review of private contracts, it should have held that the Directive precluded national law which removed from the contract the obligation of the insurance company to compensate the victim of property damage where the insured person who caused the damage through their driving was intoxicated. Alternatively, it should have stated that national law

---

[133] Case C-129/94 *Criminal proceedings against Rafael Ruiz Bernáldez* [1996] ECR I-1829.

[134] Council Dir 72/166/EEC of 24 April 1972 on the approximation of the laws of the Member States relating to insurance against civil liability in respect of the use of motor vehicles, and to the enforcement of the obligation to insure against such liability (OJ, English Special Edition 1972(II), 360), the Second Council Dir 84/5/EEC of 30 December 1983 (OJ 1984 L8, 17), and the Third Council Dir 90/232/EEC of 14 May 1990 (OJ 1990 L129, 33).

[135] *Bernáldez* (n 133), para 24 (emphasis added).

should be interpreted in the light of the Directive's objective, and could not invalidate a contractual term which offered insurance cover for the situation in question. However, such rulings would not have brought about the result compliant with the Directive (availability of the insurance cover) if the contract itself excluded from the policy property damage caused by an intoxicated driver. This perhaps explains why the Court addressed the insurance contract directly and held what it could not provide. The Directive was thus permitted to create a new legal obligation for a private insurance company, an obligation that did not exist under the contract or the national law.

The case that evades both rationalizations of the conflicting strands of the Court's case law on the effect of Directives (the invocability of exclusion theory and the narrow understanding of the direct effect) is *Wells*.[136] It concerned the obligation to carry out an environmental impact assessment imposed by a Directive.[137] The UK Secretary of State issued a planning permission for quarrying activities without examining whether it was necessary to carry out an environmental impact assessment. Ms Wells requested that the Secretary of State revoke or modify the planning permission. The UK High Court of Justice was unsure whether Ms Wells could rely on the Directive or should be prevented in doing so due to the limitations imposed on the doctrine of direct effect. On the superficial understanding, the *Wells* case should obviously be seen as vertical and not raising any difficult issues. The applicant invoked a Directive against a state body. However, the applicant's aim was not to exclude application of the national law, but to subject authorities taking planning permissions directly to the requirements stemming from the Directive.[138] It follows that the Directive is used as a standard of the legality of a national administrative decision, which happens to guarantee certain rights to a third party, a private entity.

The Court's reasoning implies that applicability of Directives before national courts to review national administrative decisions depends on their 'direct effect'.[139] Sufficient precision and unconditionality of the relevant provisions of the Directive were not considered in the judgment, probably because they were presumed to be present.[140] It is clear that their direct effect could not

---

[136] Case C-201/02 *The Queen, on the application of Delena Wells v Secretary of State for Transport, Local Government and the Regions* [2004] ECR I-723.

[137] Council Dir 85/337/EEC of 27 June 1985 on the assessment of the effects of certain public and private projects on the environment (OJ 1985 L175, p 40).

[138] Such cases are sometimes described as 'direct review' cases, where Union law serves as a standard of review and where the legal consequence, in the event of the national measure's incompatibility, is its disapplication. See Angela Ward, *Judicial Review and the Rights of Private Parties in EU Law* (2nd edn, 2007) 69–71.

[139] In Case 103/88 *Fratelli Costanzo SpA v Comune di Milano* [1989] ECR 1839 the Court held that 'when the conditions under which the Court has held that individuals may rely on the provisions of a directive before the national courts are met, all organs of the administration, including decentralized authorities such as municipalities, are obliged to apply those provisions'.

[140] See Case C-244/12 *Salzburger Flughafen GmbH v Umweltsenat*, judgment of 21 March 2013.

have been taken for granted if the doctrine had been understood to require a conferral of a substantive right on the individual who invoked the Directive. An important step in the Court's reasoning was the discussion of the *Marshall* prohibition, which was held to lay down a rule that for individuals 'the provisions of a directive [could] only create rights'. 'Consequently,' the Court continued, 'an individual may not rely on a directive against a Member State where it is a matter of a State obligation directly linked to the performance of another obligation falling, pursuant to that directive, on a third party'.[141] The *Marshall* prohibition was thereby extended to cases where a third (private) party would be imposed an obligation because of the applicant's reliance on the Directive against the state. 'Obligations' were, however, contrasted with 'mere adverse repercussions on the rights of third parties', which the Court did not regard as problematic. If a third (private) party were to suffer 'mere adverse repercussions', individuals were to be permitted to rely on a Directive.[142] In *Wells*, the fact that the mining operations would have to be halted to await the results of the impact assessment, constituting the belated performance of that state's obligations, did not justify an exception to the Directive's effectiveness.

The insistence on the Directive's effectiveness despite the negative consequences for a private party was counterbalanced by the Court's acceptance of the national courts' discretion in determining what measures were necessary to ensure that projects were subjected to impact assessment. The Court held that they 'included', but not 'entailed', revocation or suspension of a consent already.[143] It then held that:[144]

it is for the national court to determine whether it is possible under domestic law for a consent already granted to be revoked or suspended in order to subject the project in question to an assessment of its environmental effects, in accordance with the requirements of Directive 85/337, or alternatively, if the individual so agrees, whether it is possible for the latter to claim compensation for the harm suffered.

The only logical interpretation of this paragraph is that the Court contemplated the possibility that a planning permission granted without the required environmental impact assessment would be neither suspended nor revoked, and instead the individual who relied on the Directive would obtain compensation for the harm suffered. The Court stated that the choice and the availability of particular remedies were to be governed by domestic law. Thus, it seems to be saying that in the case of national remedies the principle of effectiveness, acting here as a limitation on national procedural autonomy, would be satisfied if, with her consent,

[141] *Wells* (n 136), para 56.   [142] *Wells* (n 136), para 57.
[143] *Wells* (n 136), para 65.   [144] *Wells* (n 136), para 69.

Ms Wells was granted only compensation, and the defective planning permission remained in force. So the possibility to rely on a Directive to instigate a review of a national administrative decision does not necessarily entail under the EU law the possibility of obtaining its revocation.

VIII. Enforceability of Directives through General Principles

Despite various inroads into the prohibition of the horizontal direct effect of Directives, it still remains the case that in principle Directives cannot 'of themselves' impose obligations on private parties. Weatherill has pointed out that this creates a situation of 'remedial imbalance', whereby economically focused Treaty provisions are to a large extent enforceable against private parties, while more socially focused Directives are not.[145] This observation overlooks the fact that the two of the most broadly horizontally enforceable provisions of the Treaty are Article 141 TFEU on equal pay for women and men, and Article 18 TFEU and the principle of non-discrimination on the ground of nationality. It is difficult to perceive these two provisions as protecting merely economic interests. It is also clear that Directives are often used in commercial disputes.

The Court has found a way of improving enforceability of 'social' Directives by relying on the concept of 'general principles'. General principles of law were first introduced by the Court of Justice into Community law as a way of incorporating into that law a fundamental rights review. Initially, that review was directed against Community acts, although in practice Community acts were rarely found invalid due to their incompatibility with general principles of fundamental rights. Member States were also bound by general principles when they acted with the scope of Community law. Some general principles of fundamental rights were expressed already in the Treaties, such as the aforementioned principles of non-discrimination between women and men with respect to pay or on the grounds of nationality. However, general principles could not themselves generate rights for individuals enforceable against the state or a private party.[146] They required

---

[145] Stephen Weatherill, 'Addressing Problems of Imbalanced Implementation in EC Law: Remedies in an Institutional Perspective' in Claire Kilpatrick, Tonia Novitz, and Paul Skidmore (eds), *The Future of Remedies in Europe* (2000) 87.

[146] Case 149/77 *Gabrielle Defrenne v Société anonyme belge de navigation aérienne* [978] ECR 1365, paras 26–29.

legislative implementation, usually in the form of Directives, which at the expiry of their transposition period become enforceable against the state, but have only limited enforceability against private parties via the doctrine of consistent interpretation.

All these tenets were put in doubt with the Court's judgement in *Mangold*.[147] The Court allowed an employee to rely directly on a general principle of non-discrimination on the ground of age to disapply national provisions enabling the employer to conclude a fixed-term contract with an individual who was 52 years old or older. After the Court had established that Germany had breached its obligation under a Directive[148] progressively to take concrete measures for the purpose of approximating its legislation to the result prescribed by the Directive,[149] it focused on the final question of the German court concerning the legal consequences which should be drawn from the German legislation's incompatibility with the Directive. Here the Court observed that:[150]

Directive 2000/78 does not itself lay down the principle of equal treatment in the field of employment and occupation. Indeed, in accordance with Article 1 thereof, the sole purpose of the directive is 'to lay down a general framework for combating discrimination on the grounds of religion or belief, disability, age or sexual orientation', the source of the actual principle underlying the prohibition of those forms of discrimination being found, as is clear from the third and fourth recitals in the preamble to the directive, in various international instruments and in the constitutional traditions common to the Member States.

According to the Court, two consequences followed from that fact. Because observance of the general principle of equal treatment, in particular in respect of age, was not as such conditional upon the expiry of the period allowed the Member States for the transposition of a Directive, the individual could rely on the principle, as concretized in the Directive, already before the end of the transposition period.[151] Second, the Court held that national courts were under an obligation to ensure that the principle was 'fully effective' by setting aside any provision of national law that might conflict with Community law, even where the period prescribed for transposition of the Directive had not yet expired.[152]

It is important to note two points about the *Mangold* judgment. Just as in *CIA Security* and *Unilever*, the national court is asked only to *disapply* national law which has been found incompatible with Community/Union law. However, the incompatibility is here substantive in nature. Moreover, the individual clearly derives a right from the general principle of non-discrimination on the grounds of

---

[147] Case C-144/04 *Werner Mangold v Rüdiger Helm* [2005] ECR I-9981.

[148] More specifically, under Clauses 2, 5, and 8 of the Framework Agreement on fixed-term contracts concluded on 18 March 1999 and put into effect by Council Dir 1999/70/EC of 28 June 1999 concerning the framework agreement on fixed-term work concluded by ETUC, UNICE, and CEEP (OJ 1999 L175, p 43), and of Art 6 of Council Dir 2000/78/EC of 27 November 2000 establishing a general framework for equal treatment in employment and occupation (OJ 2000 L303, p 16).

[149] *Mangold* (n 147), paras 72–73.   [150] *Mangold* (n 147), para 74.

[151] *Mangold* (n 147), para 76.   [152] *Mangold* (n 147), paras 77 and 79.

age and the existence of this right, as well as the need to ensure its effective judicial protection, is mentioned by the Court as a justification for the national court's obligation to disapply national law. Is it horizontal direct effect of Directives through the back door? Yes, if one believes that direct effect is about giving individuals the possibility to invoke a Directive that creates rights for them.[153] A contractual term is reviewed against a general principle that is taken to have the same substantive content as a Directive. But just as in *Unilever*, the source of the rights and obligations is technically speaking not the Directive but the contract between the parties and the remaining body of national law. This might explain why for many commentators what was most problematic about the *Mangold* judgment was not the expansion of horizontal enforceability of Directives but the surprising invention of the principle of non-discrimination on the grounds of age as a 'general principle of Community law'.[154]

The *Mangold* judgment was confirmed in the *Kücükdeveci* case.[155] It reinforced the significance of the principle by pointing to the fact that discrimination on the ground of age is prohibited by Article 21(1) of the EU Charter of Fundamental Rights. The reference to the Charter of Fundamental Rights in the *Kücükdeveci* judgment opened up debate about the potential horizontal applicability of this document, either independently or as an expression of 'general principles' of Union law.[156] Horizontal applicability of the Charter, within limits, has now been confirmed in a Grand Chamber judgment of the Court of Justice in *Association de médiation sociale (AMS)*.[157] The case concerned the Employees' Consultation Directive,[158] which gives workers the right to be informed and consulted about certain circumstances concerning their establishment, and for this purpose to be represented, as provided by national law. Workers have the right to be represented and consulted also under the Charter (Article 27) 'under the conditions provided for by Union law and national laws and practices'. The AMS was an association promoting reintegration into working life of unemployed persons or persons with social and professional difficulty in gaining access to employment. When a representative of a trade union was

---

[153] See Editorial, 'Horizontal Direct Effect—A law of Diminishing Coherence?' (2006) 43 *Common Market Law Review* 1 and Alan Dashwood, 'From Van Duyn to Mangold via Marshall: Reducing Direct Effect to Absurdity? (2006–2007) 9 *Cambridge Yearbook of European Legal Studies* 81.

[154] Case C-411/05 *Félix Palacios de la Villa v Cortefiel Servicios SA* [2007] ECR I-8531, Opinion of AG Mazák of 15 February 2007, para 94. The *Honeywell* decision of the German Federal Constitutional Court, BVerfG, 6 July 2010, 2 BvR 2661/06, NJW 2010, 3422.

[155] Case C-555/07 *Seda Kücükdeveci v Swedex GmbH & Co. KG* [2010] ECR I-365.

[156] Dorota Leczykiewicz 'Horizontal Application of the Charter of Fundamental Rights' (2013) 38 *European Law Review* 479.

[157] Case C-176/12 *Association de médiation sociale v Union locale des syndicats CGT*, judgment of 15 January 2014.

[158] Dir 2002/14/EC of the European Parliament and of the Council of 11 March 2002 establishing a general framework for informing and consulting employees in the European Community (OJ 2002 L80, p 29).

appointed to the AMS, the association challenged this appointment. It argued that it had no duty to offer workers representation because in accordance with French law certain categories of workers employed by the AMS, for example those with 'assisted' contracts, which were necessary to make up the minimum number of employees that created the duty, were excluded from the calculation. Horizontal direct effect of Article 27 of the Charter would make it possible to exclude this rule of French law and include workers with 'assisted' contracts in the calculation.

The Court of Justice first interpreted the Directive and ruled that it precluded a national provision, such as that of the French Labour Code, under which workers with 'assisted' contracts were excluded from the calculation of staff numbers in the undertaking when determining the legal thresholds for setting up bodies representing staff.[159] Then the Court assessed whether the relevant provision of the Directive was directly effective due to its unconditionality and sufficient precision, and came to the conclusion that it was.[160] However, the Court recalled that 'even a clear, precise and unconditional provision of a directive seeking to confer rights or impose obligations on individuals cannot of itself apply in proceedings exclusively between private parties'.[161] From this it followed that the other parties could not rely on the Directive against an association governed by private law, such as the AMS. Because it was clear that the French provisions could not be interpreted 'consistently' with the Directive, the Court proceeded to assess whether 'the situation in the case in the main proceedings [was] similar to that in the case which gave rise to *Kücükdeveci*'.[162] *Kücükdeveci* was thus taken to introduce a new doctrine into EU law, by which Charter provisions 'could be invoked in a dispute between individuals in order to preclude the application of the national provision'.[163] What the *AMS* judgment clarified is that in a horizontal case the Charter right would not always trigger the application of the Directive. The Court took a close look at Article 27 of the Charter and observed that it subjected the right to information and consultation to the conditions provided for by EU law and national laws and practices. From this the Court concluded that the provision 'must be given more specific expression in European Union or national law' before it becomes 'fully effective'.[164] It seems that the Court accepted that the Directive could in principle constitute such a more specific expression of Article 27 of the Charter, but the minimum content of the legal rule would nevertheless have to be inferable from the wording of Article 27 and the Charter's Explanations.[165] The *Kücükdeveci* doctrine was not applicable because, unlike the

---

[159] *Association de médiation sociale* (n 157), para 29.
[160] *Association de médiation sociale* (n 157), para 35.
[161] *Association de médiation sociale* (n 157), paras 36–37.
[162] *Association de médiation sociale* (n 157), para 41.
[163] *Association de médiation sociale* (n 157), para 41.
[164] *Association de médiation sociale* (n 157), paras 44–45.
[165] Explanations relating to the Charter of Fundamental Rights (OJ 2007 C303, p 2). This seems to be the only possible interpretation of the following cryptic paragraph in the judgment (*Association*

principle of non-discrimination on grounds of age laid down in Article 21(1) of the Charter, Article 27 was not sufficient to confer an individual right. The *AMS* judgement can be seen as introducing into EU law the concept of the 'horizontal direct effect' of the Charter. This effect is not possible if the Charter provision is conditional upon further legislative implementation and the right or the prohibition, on which a party before the national court relies, cannot be inferred directly from the Charter. And in a horizontal case, the Directive that concretises the Charter provision cannot be invoked to supply the missing elements because this would amount to the circumvention of the *Marshall* prohibition.[166]

IX. Conclusion: Complementarities or Contradictories?

In this chapter we looked at the fundamental doctrines regulating the effect of EU law before national courts. From this perspective these doctrines appear to complement each other in the effort to achieve the broadest possible enforceability of EU norms, and in this way contribute to the attainment of the EU's objectives. More locally, the doctrines complement each other in the protection of individual rights and in the creation of incentives for the Member States to fulfil their obligations under Union law. From the perspective of the judicial function, the doctrines described in this chapter do not all operate at the same stage of the legal process. We have noticed that the doctrine of direct effect is addressed not only to courts but also to administrative authorities and that it enables a provision of EU law to act as the source of a legal norm to which facts are subsumed, and thus to regulate in substance the particular situation. The doctrine of consistent interpretation retains the national rule as the law applicable to the facts of the case, but with a changed content. *Francovich* is a remedial rule concerned with a situation in which an individual has suffered a loss as a result of the state's breach of Union law. *Courage* is also a remedial rule suspended between national private law and the standards set out by the Court in the judgment. Thus, it would be wrong to look for much coherence

---

de médiation sociale (n 157), para 46): 'It is not possible to infer from the wording of Art 27 of the Charter or from the explanatory notes to that article that Art 3(1) of Dir 2002/14, as a directly applicable rule of law, lays down and addresses to the Member States a prohibition on excluding from the calculation of the staff numbers in an undertaking a specific category of employees initially included in the group of persons to be taken into account in that calculation.'

[166] See also, Case C-282/10 *Maribel Dominguez v Centre informatique du Centre Ouest Atlantique and Préfet de la région Centre*, judgment of 24 January 2012, para 42.

between direct effect and consistent interpretation, on the one hand, and *Francovich* and *Courage*, on the other. The direct effect of a particular Union law provision should not entail the necessary existence of a compensatory remedy under that law. This is particularly true where the defendant is a private party. An EU provision's enforceability against individuals and the right to compensation should be seen as distinct questions governed by different policy rationales.[167]

If we focus just on the doctrines aimed at invocability of EU law by individuals before national courts, we can legitimately ask whether they paint a coherent picture. In this context, we face a number of incoherencies, especially in the context of Directives. If legal certainty prevents Directives from imposing of themselves obligations on individuals, why doesn't it prevent other negative consequences for individuals, such as when the Directive's application leads to the removal of a liberty, power, or right under national law? And if legal certainty is the most important concern in horizontal cases, how can one explain the very extensive effect of the obligation of consistent interpretation? Finally, if individuals should not be imposed obligations by EU law against the wording of national law, why is such an effect permitted where the obligation is contained in a general principle of Union law or a Charter right? In legal reasoning we are, of course, also concerned about values other than legal certainty. We ask about fairness between the parties and social justice. This is a type of reasoning which the Court does not use very often. It does not ask when it is 'fair' to interfere into the content of a private contract. Its rulings are sometimes justified by the need to protect the weaker party, but the horizontal effects of Directives go beyond the range of instances which could be justified by that rationale, as evidenced by such cases as *CIA Security* and *Unilever*. Neither can these two judgments be explained by social justice considerations, in particular the perceived problem of remedial imbalance in EU law.

The literature on direct effect and invocability of Directives has traditionally regarded the estoppel argument to be the most convincing. The state in breach of Union law should be neither entitled to rely on their conflicting laws nor use their conflicting laws as a defence against arguments based on Union law. The justificatory force of the estoppel argument has led some authors to the conclusion that problematic judgments, such as *CIA Security, Unilever, Marleasing, Pfeiffer*, or *Mangold*, might in fact be explained as 'disguised' vertical cases, as cases with a public law dimension arising from the state's administrative failure.[168] Regrettably,

[167] Dorota Leczykiewicz, 'Private Party Liability in EU Law: In Search of the General Regime' (2009) 12 *Cambridge Yearbook of European Legal Studies* 257. Cf. Sara Drake, 'Scope of Courage and the Principle of "individual liability" for Damages: Further Development of the Principle of Effective Judicial Protection by the Court of Justice' (2006) 26 *European Law Review* 841.

[168] Michael Dougan, "The "Disguised" Vertical Direct Effect of Directives?" (2000) 59 *Cambridge Law Journal* 586; 'In Defence of *Mangold*?' in Anthony Arnull, Catherine Barnard, Michael Dougan, and Eleanor Spaventa (eds), *A Constitutional Order of States?* (2011) 219 and 'The Application of General Principles of EU Law to Horizontal Relationships' in Dorota Leczykiewicz and Stephen Weatherill (eds), *The Involvement of EU Law in Private Law Relationships* (2013) 71.

this explanation is not supported by an argument of principle. Member States may breach EU law in various ways, including by failing to provide adequate protection against the rights-violating conduct of private parties, or by failing to provide access to effective remedies. While these failures add a 'public law dimension' to the cases, the Member States' misconduct is not normally taken to justify the imposition on individuals of negative consequences (the 'disguised' vertical effect). It is true that individuals should be discouraged from exploiting the fact of a Member State's breach to their advantage (what Dougan calls 'opportunistic behaviour'), but it cannot be assumed that every employer or trader who relies on incorrect national law is doing so with the intention of benefiting from the fact that the state failed to fulfil its obligations under EU law. While various cases show that the private party's opportunistic behaviour could be one of the implicit motivations of the Court's decision to allow a Directive to produce effects before national courts, the judgments do not go so far as to inquire about the quality of the defendant's conduct as a way of justifying horizontal enforceability.

The doctrines developed by the Court of Justice to ensure effectiveness of Union law raise also the issue of the limits of judicial power and of the role of unrepresentative institutions in transforming the status of the provisions of a legal system of which they form part. We have seen that the textual basis for the doctrine of direct effect and for the obligation of consistent interpretation is very thin. But convincing substantive arguments are available. In the case of the *CIA Security* doctrine, on the other hand, the only substantive argument that can be discerned from the judgment is that without the national provision's unenforceability the practical effect of the control mechanisms established by the Directive would be weakened. The Court's motivation is thus to contribute, through its case law, to the functioning of the internal market. The only way in which the Court can make this contribution is by making legal acts intended to realize the internal market objective more effective. The EU is an entity created by law and acting primarily through law.[169] The principle of primacy arguably provides an explanation for why potentially all national measures, legislative, administrative, or judicial, in all situations falling within the scope of EU law should be subjected to review against that law.[170] Dougan has called it a 'primacy' model of the relationship between EU law and national law.[171] The alternative model, the 'trigger' model, makes direct effect a pre-condition of EU law's cognizability or justiciability before national courts.

---

[169] Mauro Cappelletti, Monica Seccombe, and Joseph Weiler (eds), *Integration through Law. Vol 1: Methods, Tools and Institutions. Book 1* (1986).

[170] Koen Lenaerts and Tim Corthaut, 'Of Birds and Hedges: The Role of Primacy in Invoking Norms of EU Law' (2006) 31 *European Law Review* 287. According to the authors, horizontal cases display an indirect review situation but are in principle no different from the direct review situations present in vertical cases.

[171] Michael Dougan, 'When Worlds Collide! Competing Visions of the Relationship between Direct Effect and Supremacy' (2007) 44 *Common Market Law Review* 931.

The 'trigger' model leaves in an uncertain place the doctrine of consistent interpretation, which, according to some authors, and now also in the Court's view, should be given priority among the judicial methods of ensuring effectiveness of EU law.[172] In the model that gives priority to the obligation of consistent interpretation, EU law and national law are in dialogue, inspiriting each other in the construction of their respective content. Moreover, a theory that governs the questions discussed in this chapter should also explain the place of individuals vis-à-vis EU law, when they act both as beneficiaries and as burden-bearers of its rules. Constructing such a theory, in particular in relation to the democratic accountability of Union institutions, is a task that still lies before the scholars of EU law.

BIBLIOGRAPHY

Anthony Arnull, *The European Union and its Court of Justice* (2nd ed, 2006)

Paul Craig, 'Once upon a Time in the West: Direct Effect and the Federalisation of EEC Law' (1992) 4 *Oxford Journal of Legal Studies* 453

Paul Craig, 'The Legal Effect of Directives: Policy, Rules and Exceptions' (2009) 34 *European Law Review* 349

Bruno de Witte, 'Direct Effect, Primacy, and the Nature of the Legal Order' in Paul Craig and Gráinne De Búrca (eds), *The Evolution of EU Law* (2nd edn, 2011) 323

Michael Dougan, 'When Worlds Collide! Competing Visions of the Relationship between Direct Effect and Supremacy' (2007) 44 *Common Market Law Review* 931

Michael Dougan, 'The "Disguised" Vertical Direct Effect of Directives?' (2000) 59 *Cambridge Law Journal* 586

Michael Dougan, 'In Defence of *Mangold*?' in Anthony Arnull, Catherine Barnard, Michael Dougan, and Eleanor Spaventa (eds), *A Constitutional Order of States?* (2011) 219

Pablo V. Figueroa Regueiro, 'Invocability of Substitution and Invocability of Exclusion: Bringing Legal Realism to the Current Developments of the Case-Law of "Horizontal" Direct Effect of Directives' Jean Monnet Working Paper 7/02

Carol Harlow, '*Francovich* and the Problem of the Disobedient State' (1996) 2 *European Law Journal* 199

Dorota Leczykiewicz, 'Private Party Liability in EU Law: In Search of the General Regime' (2009) 12 *Cambridge Yearbook of European Legal Studies* 257

[172] Sacha Prechal, 'Direct Effect, Indirect Effect, Supremacy and the Evolving Constitution of the European Union' in Catherine Barnard (ed), *The Fundamentals of EU Law Revisited: Assessing the Impact of the Constitutional Debate* (2007) 35. Dougan argues that the doctrine of consistent interpretation should be seen as flowing from the direct effect of Art 4(3) (previously Art 10 EC) laying down the principle of sincere cooperation. See Dougan (n 171). In Case C-282/10 *Maribel Dominguez v Centre informatique du Centre Ouest Atlantique and Préfet de la région Centre*, judgment of 24 January 2012, para 23, the Grand Chamber of the Court held that 'the question whether a national provision must be disapplied in as much as it conflicts with European Union law arises only if no compatible interpretation of that provision proves possible'.

Dorota Leczykiewicz 'Horizontal Application of the Charter of Fundamental Rights' (2013) 38 *European Law Review* 479

Koen Lenaerts and Tim Corthaut, 'Of Birds and Hedges: The Role of Primacy in Invoking Norms of EU Law' (2006) 31 *European Law Review* 287

Leone Niglia, "Form and Substance in European Constitutional Law: The 'Social' Character of Indirect Effect"(2010) 16 *European Law Journal* 439

Sacha Prechal, 'Direct Effect, Indirect Effect, Supremacy and the Evolving Constitution of the European Union' in Catherine Barnard (ed), *The Fundamentals of EU Law Revisited: Assessing the Impact of the Constitutional Debate* (2007)

Mattias Ruffert, 'Rights and Remedies in European Community Law: A Comparative View' (1997) 34 *Common Market Law Review* 307

Malcolm Ross, 'Effectiveness in the European Legal Order(s): Beyond Supremacy to Constitutional Proportionality (2006) 31 *European Law Review* 476

Francis Snyder 'The Effectiveness of European Community Law: Institutions, Processes, Tools and Techniques' (1993) 56 *Modern Law Review* 19

Takis Tridimas, 'Liability for Breach of Community Law: Growing Up and Mellowing Down?' (2001) 38 *Common Market Law Review* 301

Angela Ward, *Judicial Review and the Rights of Private Parties in EU Law* (2nd edn, 2007)

Stephen Weatherill, 'Breach of Directives and Breach of Contract' (2001) 26 *European Law Review* 177

Stephen Weatherill, 'Addressing Problems of Imbalanced Implementation in EC Law: Remedies in an Institutional Perspective' in Claire Kilpatrick, Tonia Novitz, and Paul Skidmore (eds), *The Future of Remedies in Europe* (2000) 87

CHAPTER 10

....

HUMAN RIGHTS
IN THE EU

....

ANDREW WILLIAMS

I. INTRODUCTION

....

WOULD it be an odd claim to make that the Court of Justice of the European Union (CJEU) is a reactionary, self-preserving, and ultimately conservative institution when it comes to promoting human rights? There can be little doubt that many commentators would agree with this statement. There is a history of such a critique in European Union studies stretching back at least to Coppell and O'Neill's article in 1992.[1]

Would it then be strange to assert that, in comparison, the European Commission may be *the* radical human rights institution in the EU, in Europe, and perhaps even globally: a potent, if flawed, force for the promotion of human rights, an antagonistic counterweight to the CJEU and the overburdening reactionary judicialization of fundamental rights? It is by no means certain that so many would support such a view.

But contrary, perhaps, to received wisdom, these two propositions are arguably and necessarily mutually supporting. Any evaluation of the CJEU and its human

---

[1] I. Coppell and A. O'Neill, 'The European Court of Justice: Taking Rights Seriously?' (1992) 29:4 *Common Market Law Review* 669–692, which set in train a consistent critique against the ECJ (as it then was). For a more contemporary account of the failings of the Court, see Grainne de Burca, 'After the EU Charter of Fundamental Rights: The Court of Justice as a Human Rights Adjudicator?' (2013) 20:2 *MJ* 168–184.

rights record is sharpened when compared with the other significant actors in this EU field. Taken in isolation, the Court's judgments can easily be dissected and assessed for error or achievement, determined to be logically sound or of diseased thinking. Much of this analysis can be undertaken by reference to some perceived understanding of human rights standards. We may find it difficult to agree on what these may be (do we refer to the EU Charter or the European Convention on Human Rights or the UN Conventions or the panoply of Council of Europe human rights related instruments?) but in theory at least this can be a worthwhile endeavour.

If we are to assess more fully the value of the EU institutions in human rights terms, then some comparative work is necessary. Of course, a dry itemization of the activities or decisions of the Court, the Commission, the Council, the Parliament, and perhaps those accompanying parasitical bodies (such as the Fundamental Rights Agency) could provide something of a holistic picture. That lies beyond the scope of this chapter. However, a more limited comparison of the CJEU with the Commission is possible and is indeed my aim here. It is premised on the appreciation that these two institutions are the most practically influential in terms of human rights development *within* the EU.[2] And by focusing on them, we might attain a better and deeper understanding of where the best prospects for human rights within the EU may lie.

The sting in the tail of this comparison is that neither the Commission nor the Court is a creature of human rights: neither was constructed with the realization of human rights as a constituting principle; and neither are credible institutions for the fulfilment of human rights. The human rights role they have adopted have evolved over a long period of time, haphazardly and with other goals in mind.

This is hardly revelatory. The EU institutions were conceived as administering a project of economic cooperation *not* social justice. Why should they have had a proactive remit when it came to human rights and their realization? Who could have identified all the rights to be fulfilled with certainty in any case? Although it may have quickly become apparent that 'fundamental rights' could not be ignored without undermining the whole project's legitimacy, human rights *within the Union* remained of peripheral concern.[3] Only in the latest constitutional iteration (the Lisbon Treaty) have both institutions become enveloped by the requirement

---

[2] For the purposes of this chapter I do not consider the roles of the Parliament or the Council. Both are significantly less influential *within* the EU in terms of active development or enforcement or promotion of human rights internally.

[3] I do not intend to examine the history of human rights promotion externally. The Court has little if any role to play here and the Commission's is limited too. A wholly different critique becomes evident when we do look at the role and impact of the EU in human rights terms globally. See, for instance, my *EU Human Rights Policies: A Study in Irony* (2004), which although ten years old remains apposite as far as the EU's approach to human rights externally is concerned.

that the EU must *promote* 'respect for human rights'. Whether even this dictate has really changed the landscape is open to doubt.

So, when embarking on a comparison of the relative merits of the Commission and the Court we should have in mind their relative shortcomings too. That is, if the evaluation is to be based on human rights 'fulfilment' rather than simply their 'respect'.

To address these matters, the chapter is divided into four sections. First, there is a quick sketch of the constituting arrangements that have developed over the past half-century of the EU's history. These set the parameters for defining those expectations which might realistically be assumed vis-à-vis human rights fulfilment by the EU institutions.

Second, the Court's achievements over recent years are reviewed. This is not to ignore the deeper historical significance of its judgments. But any court's value never rests solely on its past. Current practices, recent decisions, observable trends of omission as much as commission provide a more relevant impression. I leave the historical view to those many worthwhile textbooks available.

Within this contemporary assessment of the Court, the charge of conservatism is drawn a little more fully. But as I have said, the claim possesses far greater weight when the comparatively more radical approach of the Commission is presented alongside it.

The third section thus turns its focus on the Commission's recent role in the EU's human rights narrative. By examining the nature and scope of the Commission's work here, my proposition that this institution is the more valuable from a human rights perspective is substantiated.

Finally, in Section IV, I place the comparative analysis in some kind of perspective. Looking at the failures of human rights by the EU as a whole will shed some light on whether I have only been comparing relative failure rather than success. Is the EU congenitally ill-disposed towards realizing human rights? Or have its institutions done enough to suggest that the failure to date is but a reflection of practice not matching design?

II. A Sketch of Human Rights and the EU

The story of human rights in the EU may be complex, but it has a surprisingly familiar set of coordinates. It only requires a short introduction to set the context for the remainder of this chapter.

In the beginning, silence in relation to human rights in the original EEC Treaty was accompanied by a vague rhetoric of values that were concerned with promoting the project's credentials as a system for capitalist free market economic cooperation. The rhetoric began to change towards the end of the 1960s when the move towards closer integration of Member States' economies threw up the danger of individuals' rights, otherwise protected at national level, being affected adversely by measures introduced through the EEC (as it then was).

This slight change in appreciation was prompted by the ECJ's determination that EU law should have supremacy over national law and that EU legislation should have direct effect in the laws of Member States without intervention by national legislatures. In order to assuage the concerns of national courts arising because of the potential imposition of rights-breaching EU legislation or decisions, the ECJ held, reasonably early in its life, that fundamental rights 'were enshrined in the general principles of Community law'. As Advocate General Maduro more recently and eloquently put it,

respect for fundamental rights is intrinsic in the EU legal order and that, without it, common action by and for the peoples of Europe would be unworthy and unfeasible. In that sense, the very existence of the European Union is predicated on respect for fundamental rights. Protection of the common code of fundamental rights accordingly constitutes an existential requirement for the EU legal order.[4]

The juridical infusion of principle into the institutional philosophy of the EU was therefore more about 'respect' than 'fulfilment' or 'promotion'. It was a negatively oriented position, whereby the Union became committed *not* to breach fundamental rights of individual persons (legal or natural).[5] The only exception was in the pursuit of obligations imposed on the EU institutions through the constituting Treaties. So, the EU could address limited human rights when framing social and economic policy, concerning equal pay for instance, but it could not introduce legislation designed to promote human rights per se. The ECJ made clear in *Opinion 2/94* that no 'Treaty provision confers on the Community institutions any general power to enact rules on human rights'.[6] There was an 'absence of express or implied powers for this purpose'.[7] Neither the EEC Treaty of 1957 nor its successors contained general powers to enact legislation to develop human or fundamental rights.

---

[4] Case C-380/05 *Centro Europa 7 Srl v Ministero delle Comunicazioni e Autorità per le garanzie nelle comunicazioni and Direzione generale per le concessioni e le autorizzazioni del Ministero delle Comunicazioni*, [2008] ECR I-349 Opinion of Mr Advocate General Poiares Maduro delivered on 12 September 2007 para 19.

[5] The rights were largely but not exclusively defined by the European Convention on Human Rights.

[6] *Re the Accession of the Community to the European Human Rights Convention (Opinion 2/94)* [1996] 2 CMLR 265 [27].

[7] *Re the Accession of the Community to the European Human Rights Convention (Opinion 2/94)* (n 6) [28].

This landscape changed potentially with the amendments to the Treaty of European Union by the Lisbon Treaty. Article 2 TEU now reads that the EU is

. . . founded on the values of respect for human dignity, freedom, democracy, equality, the rule of law and respect for human rights, including the rights of persons belonging to minorities. These values are common to the Member States in a society in which plural-ism, non-discrimination, tolerance, justice, solidarity and equality between women and men prevail.

This is complemented by Article 3 TEU, which maintains that the Union's aim is 'to promote peace, its values and the well-being of its peoples'. In human rights terms, the value remains related to 'respect'. But internally, the provision goes on to demand that the EU shall 'offer its citizens an area of freedom, security and justice without internal frontiers', shall 'combat social exclusion and discrimination', shall 'promote social justice and protection, equality between women and men, solidar-ity between generations and protection of the rights of the child', and 'economic, social and territorial cohesion, and solidarity among Member States'. Although not entirely without ambiguity, the requirement to 'promote' now suggests a more positive and proactive institutional commitment.

The pledge to respect the EU Charter on Fundamental Rights lends weight to the overall impression that human rights have attained much greater consti-tutional presence in the EU and that this demands a similarly greater degree of attention by the EU's institutions. The Charter's legally binding status has indeed produced some changes to practical procedures so that proposed legislation is at least reviewed to ensure compliance with its articles.[8] But there is a great difference between avoiding the breach of human rights and seeking to enhance respect for human rights *through* policy development.

The question then is to what extent, if at all, the EU has adopted a proactive stance towards realizing, promoting and protecting human rights in accordance with this new constitutional framework. As the EU exists through its institutions, examining the current record of the Court and the Commission should provide something of an answer. It has to be accepted that these institutions do not operate in isolation, and that the Council is the main determiner of policy. But both the decisions of the Court and the proposals and practices of the Commission illustrate how deeply and in what ways, the EU is moving forwards practically in terms of human rights protection *and* promotion. It might also provide clues as to whether we are seeing a revised philosophy of EU law develop in this respect.[9]

---

[8] See Israel De Jesus Butler, 'Ensuring Compliance with the Charter of Fundamental Rights in Legislative Drafting: The Practice of the European Commission' (2012) *ELR* 397–418.

[9] See my essays on the desirability of a revised philosophy: 'Taking Values Seriously: Towards a Philosophy of EU Law' (2009) 29:3 *Oxford Journal of Legal Studies* 549–577; and 'Promoting Justice after Lisbon: Groundwork for a New Philosophy of EU Law' (2010) 30:4 *Oxford Journal of Legal Studies* 663–694.

III. Human Rights and the CJEU:
In the Beginning was the Word

No doubt some would argue that the judiciary of the CJEU are in an invidious position: if they seek to promote human rights as of paramount concern in any effective way through opinion or judgment then they may be condemned as interfering in the political imagination of the Union. If they react to cases before them in a restrained manner, judging cases individually without recourse to any grand ethical picture, they may be condemned as operating with undue constraint and without proper regard to the importance of fundamental rights. Of course, between these ends of the spectrum there is always scope for judicial invention, the insertion of a political flavour to a legal decision. Individual judgments could thus be crafted so as to fulfil the paramountcy of human rights whilst couching the decisions in a vocabulary of traditional precepts. The reverse may also be true.

In a fluid or free judicial environment, one might expect a considerable variance of tone and philosophy over time. Different judges will imprint different approaches upon their judgments. But the CJEU and the judicial structures operating in the Union have not been particularly effective in allowing individuality to develop. Even without recent studies into the means by which judgments are constructed, it has not been difficult to tell that a sort of iron straitjacket has embraced the *process* and the language, if not substance, of final decisions. One only has to read the repetitive nature of Court judgments to sense this control. Nonetheless, within her study into the multilingual jurisprudence of the CJEU, Karen McAuliffe shows how constrained the process of judgment writing is in practice.[10] She reports on how the judge's *référendaire*, who perhaps unsurprisingly writes the initial draft judgment, is tightly bound by the strict precedent of both decision *and* language. One *référendaire* is quoted as saying, 'maybe once in five or six years a case will come along that might have one single paragraph saying something completely new or different'.[11] Only in the Advocate General's office are the apparent shackles released somewhat and creativity and critique are allowed to invade the style and vocabulary presented.

Albeit of anecdotal value, McAuliffe's research supports the sense of a bureaucratic approach to judgment that focuses on a consistency of form. Of course, the rationale for this approach may be to reduce confusion arising from the necessity of maintaining coherent translation into multiple languages. But it

---

[10] Karen McAuliffe, 'Language and Law in the European Union: The Multilingual Jurisprudence of the ECJ' in Lawrence M. Solan and Peter M. Tiersma (eds), *The Oxford Handbook of Language and Law* (2012)

[11] McAuliffe (n 10).

might also be interpreted plausibly as a strategy for sustaining a credible authority for the Court through tightly controlled repetition of thought and judgment.

The question is, though, whether the constraints on the language of final judgments of the CJEU and the AGs are so ingrained, and the slavish adherence to the exact wording of a few old decisions so prevalent (perhaps a necessity in the early life of the EU to establish authority), that any creative interpretation of the requirement to promote respect for human rights under the recent constitutional realignment is, and will continue to be, absent. In other words, does the traditional construction of judgments militate, for whatever reason, against (*inter alia*) human rights development?

This danger, as some might see it, could be reinforced if the Court continued to use the language and method of legal interpretation enshrined in pre-Lisbon Treaty jurisprudence. *Cilfit v Ministero della Sanità* held that

every provision of Community law must be placed in its context and interpreted in the light of the provisions of Community law as a whole, regard being had to the objectives thereof and to its state of evolution at the date on which the provision in question is to be applied.[12]

One consistent critique of the CJEU has been its tendency to see every case through the lens of this position, whereby the central objective was always closer integration *through* law. Although not precluding preserving the rights of individuals (indeed the brilliant sleight of hand devised by the Court has been the incorporation of individual rights into the very idea of the market), those individual rights have been read in this light. Therefore, in judgments that reportedly advanced human rights, such as *Omega*[13] and *Schmidberger*,[14] the language of preserving the integrity of this philosophy (namely the coherence of the internal market as the focus of integration and thus law) lies at the root of decisions.

Omega is typical. Much has been made of the Court's supposed enhancement of the right to human dignity in its consideration of the lawfulness of the Bonn police authority banning the use of premises for a laser-simulated killing game. But no such right was established by the decision, at least not one that might have wider application. The only principles that were reaffirmed were those of proportionality and necessity. At heart, the question addressed was: Did the Bonn authority's ban amount to an unjustifiable restriction of the freedom to provide services? In other words, could the 'rule' of market freedom be overridden by the 'exception' of protection of a fundamental value—in this case respect for human dignity enshrined in the German Basic Law? In essence, the referred question and the decision represents a reaffirmation of the EU's ranking of value, in that those seeking to protect

---

[12] Case C-283/81, *Cilfit v Ministero della Sanità*, [1982] ECR 3415, para 20.
[13] Case C-36/02 *Omega v Bonn* [2004] ECR I-9609.
[14] Case C-112/00 *Schmidberger v Austria* [2003] ECR I-5659.

a fundamental right have to convince the Court that the act restricting a commercial interest is both necessary (cannot be attained by other less restrictive means) and proportionate (those means employed are no more restrictive than required to achieve the protection desired). The value of market freedom is the primary consideration, *subject to* but not unseated by a fundamental right. Thus whether the national authority decision in *Omega* went 'beyond what is necessary in order to attain the objective pursued' was the critical issue. It was not whether the protection of human dignity was considered worthy of protection per se. That was taken as a given. But there was no acceptance that the protection of human dignity was in any way paramount, a right so fundamental that its violation was clear through the act of simulating a killing. If that were the case, then would not the CJEU be obliged to accept an outright ban by an authority of a Member State on *all* video games of violence (including those ubiquitous and graphic computer games) on the grounds that they offended human dignity regardless of the impact on trade and business?

Such a decision, however, would not be countenanced. The Court made clear in *Omega* that it would interpret any derogation from the free movement principles (which the Bonn ban allegedly accomplished) strictly 'so that its scope cannot be determined unilaterally by each Member State without any control by the Community institutions'.[15] This sting in the tail emphasizes the Court's sense of priorities and indeed its sense of who is best placed to determine the value of values.

On the face of it, *Schmidberger* perhaps suggests a different approach. There, the Court was confronted with examining the decision of the Austrian authorities in allowing a demonstration by an environmental group on the Brenner Pass motorway, closing the route to all traffic for some thirty hours and thus interfering with the applicant's international transport business. The Court referred to both the rights to freedom of expression and association, on the one hand, and the free movement of goods, on the other, as equal 'interests'. And it confirmed that 'the interests involved must be weighed having regard to all the circumstances of the case in order to determine whether a fair balance was struck between those interests'.[16] The Court accepted that the national authorities enjoyed a wide margin of discretion in determining that balance. But it was for the Court to decide whether national actions that restricted intra-Community trade were 'proportionate in the light of the legitimate objective pursued, namely, in the present case, the protection of fundamental rights'.[17] In other words, the protection of rights could only be properly assessed in terms of the freedoms associated with the functioning of the single market. Its analysis indeed focused on the value of the national authority's actions in *limiting* the impact of the demonstration. And to emphasize the fact, the Court noted that 'the competent national authorities must endeavour

---

[15] See *Omega* (n 13) at para 30. See also Case 41/74 *Van Duyn v Home Office* [1974] ECR 1337 at para 18 and Case 30/77 *Bouchereau* [1977] ECR 1999 at para 33.

[16] *Schmidberger* (n 14) at para 81.   [17] *Schmidberger* (n 14) at para 82.

to limit as far as possible the inevitable effects upon free movement of a demonstration on the public highway'.[18] Though recognizing the importance of the right to protest and giving it a value that *should* be considered when assessing restrictions on intra-state trade, the reference point remained the sanctity of the market and the freedoms that defined it.

In this sense, both *Omega* and *Schmidberger* reflect an eerie and perhaps surprising echo of international humanitarian law. Whether the killing of civilians as 'collateral damage' is proportionate or not is determined not in terms of the value of human life (or any fundamental right to life) but in terms of the military advantage planned.[19] Similarly, for the CJEU, questions of respect for human rights are conditional on the market rather than the other way around. This, I suggest, can be plausibly construed as a natural consequence of ignoring any positive obligation to *promote* human rights.

The conditional nature of commitment to human rights applied by the Court can also be seen in more recent judgments. So, in the 2014 decision in *Cruciano Siragusa v Regione Sicilia—Soprintendenza Beni Culturali e Ambientali di Palermo*, the Court made explicit that the objective of protecting fundamental rights in EU law was 'to ensure that those rights are not infringed in areas of EU activity, whether through action at EU level or through the implementation of EU law by the Member States'.[20] The reason for this is then expressed as 'the need to avoid a situation in which the level of protection of fundamental rights varies according to the national law involved in such a way as to undermine the unity, primacy and effectiveness of EU law'.[21] Of course, EU law has been set to include respect for fundamental rights as a general principle. But the scope of this obligation was determined more than forty years ago when the constituting environment (not to mention the political, sociological, technical and economic) was very different from today. That contemporary judgments retain adherence to the exact terminology adopted decades ago is troublesome should one be looking for an evolutionary approach to rights within EU law.

Certainly, the CJEU and the Advocates General have not taken the opportunity to adopt a different view now that the Treaty of Lisbon is in force. Recent matters involving the operation of the Framework Decision 2002/584 and the European Arrest

---

[18] *Schmidberger* (n 14) at para 90.

[19] See Art 57(2)(iii) of General Protocol I Additional to the Geneva Conventions of 1949 and Relating to the Protection of Victims of International Armed Conflicts 1977, which states that in the conduct of military operations precautions must be taken to 'refrain from deciding to launch any attack which may be expected to cause incidental loss of civilian life. . . . which would be excessive in relation to the concrete and direct military advantage anticipated'.

[20] Case C-206/13 *Cruciano Siragusa v Regione Sicilia—Soprintendenza Beni Culturali e Ambientali di Palermo* at para 31 6 March 2014, not yet reported. In making this appraisal the Court followed Case 11/70 *Internationale Handelsgesellschaft* [1970] ECR 1125, para 3, and Case C-399/11 *Melloni* [2013] ECR I-000, para 60.

[21] *Siragusa* (n 20) para 32.

Warrant (EAW) provide something of a litmus test for this proposition.[22] This controversial piece of legislation is symbolic of the tensions between human rights and the EU as a system of rules that requires perpetual legitimation by reference to the system itself. The case of *Radu* illustrates the underlying conservatism of the judiciary.[23]

The CJEU explained in that case that the purpose of the EAW was 'to replace the multilateral system of extradition between Member States with a system of surrender, as between judicial authorities, of convicted persons or suspects for the purpose of enforcing judgments or of conducting prosecutions, that system of surrender being based on the principle of mutual recognition'.[24] The rationale for the procedure was to establish a 'new simplified and more effective system for the surrender of persons convicted or suspected of having infringed criminal law, to facilitate and accelerate judicial cooperation with a view to contributing to the objective set for the European Union to become an area of freedom, security and justice by basing itself on the high degree of confidence which should exist between the Member States'.[25] The Court acknowledged that Member States may refuse to execute a warrant but only in the 'cases of mandatory non-execution provided for in Article 3' of the Framework Decision. In effect it confirmed that the whole system would fail if challenged on human rights grounds that related to the details of national criminal prosecution procedures. Indeed, the Framework Decision reinforced this tangentially by declaring its 'implementation may be suspended only in the event of a serious and persistent breach by one of the Member States of the principles set out in Article 6(1) of the Treaty on European Union, determined by the Council pursuant to Article 7(1) of the said Treaty with the consequences set out in Article 7(2)'.[26] The likelihood of this happening is miniscule, but given that the rationale for the Decision already contemplates differences across Member States, there is certainly no prospect of challenging a warrant merely on inherent features of a national legal system.

Nonetheless, the CJEU's approach in *Radu* is more instructive by what it does not say. There is a complete absence of critique in relation to the EAW operation. This is so even though it has been accepted that the system has structural and operational flaws.

The European Parliament noted many of these in Sarah Ludford's recent report, including: the absence of an explicit ground for warrant refusal where the execution would be incompatible with Charter rights; disproportionate use of the EAW for petty offences; and the absence of 'minimum standards to ensure effective

---

[22] Council Framework Decision 2002/584/JHA on the European arrest warrant and surrender procedure between Member States of 13 June 2002 ('the Framework Decision' or 'the decision') [2002] OJ L190, 1). The decision has been amended by Council Framework Decision 2009/299/JHA of 26 February 2009 [2009] OJ L81, 24).

[23] Case C-396/11 *Ciprian Vasile Radu,* not yet reported.

[24] *Ciprian Vasile Radu* (n 23) para 33.   [25] *Ciprian Vasile Radu* (n 23) para 34.

[26] Council Framework Decision (n 22) preamble para 10.

judicial oversight of mutual recognition measures which has led to inconsistent Member State practices in regard to legal safeguards and protections against fundamental rights violations'.[27] The Commission too has identified 'the systematic issue of EAWs for the surrender of persons sought in respect of often very minor offences' thus contradicting one of the underlying motives for the Decision in the first place as a tool to be used against serious crime.[28] But none of this was reflected in the Court's judgment. Instead, the preservation of the system was the mainstay of its reasoning. There was no mention of the critical hinterland on the EAW issue.

Such judicial blinkers reinforce the proposition that human rights remain of secondary concern. The maintenance of the grand system of a single market is reflected in the maintenance of sub-systems of inter-state cooperation: the philosophy remains unaltered and seemingly unalterable.

Given what has been noted in relation to the less inhibited approach of the AG's office in its deliberations, it makes sense to consider the opinion delivered in *Radu*. Did AG Sharpston, who was assigned the case, adopt a different approach? She certainly considered whether the human rights regime of the Union had now changed. Prompted by the application, she noted that 'Mr Radu appears to claim that the coming into force of the Treaty of Lisbon brought with it a fundamental change in the manner in which fundamental rights and principles fell to be applied in the Union'.[29] Her answer was conservative.

I do not believe so. It seems to me that Article 6(1) and (3) TEU merely represents what the United Kingdom terms in its observations a 'codification' of the pre-existing position. They encapsulate, to put it another way, a political desire that the provisions they seek to enshrine and to protect should be more visible in their expression. They do not represent a sea change of any kind. For that reason, I see any argument that the provisions of the Framework Decision must be given a different interpretation with their coming into force as being bound to fail.[30]

Interestingly, Sharpston supported her interpretation even whilst acknowledging some hint of a counterview in another EAW case. Her footnote 27 declared,

I should refer for the sake of completeness to the Opinion of Advocate General Cruz Villalón in Case C-306/09 I.B. [2010] ECR I-10341, where he said 'the need to interpret the Framework Decision in the light of fundamental rights has become more imperative since the entry into force of the Charter of Fundamental Rights' (point 44). While that may, at

---

[27] Committee on Civil Liberties, Justice and Home Affairs 'Report with recommendations to the Commission on the review of the European Arrest Warrant' (2013/2109(INL)) 28.1.2014 preamble para F.

[28] Report from the Commission to the European Parliament and the Council on the implementation since 2007 of the Council Framework Decision of 13 June 2002 on the European arrest warrant and the surrender procedures between Member States COM(2011) 175 final.

[29] Opinion of Advocate General Sharpston delivered on 18 October 2012 Case C-396/11 *Ministerul Public—Parchetul de pe lângă Curtea de Apel Constanţa v Ciprian Vasile Raduat* at para 47.

[30] Sharpston, *Ciprian Vasile Raduat* (n 29) para 51.

first glance, appear to suggest the need for a different interpretation of the Framework Decision following the coming into force of Article 6(1) TEU, I do not consider that it was in that spirit that the observation was made. Rather, I see it as emphasising the strength of the political desire for visibility to which I have referred above.[31]

This is a highly conventional interpretation of the politics. It would seem visibility is the substitute for substantive improvement. This may indeed be a reasonable interpretation of both the Council's and national sensibilities. But that is not the point. The door was opened a crack with the change of language in the TEU, but no attempt to push at that door has been entertained.

The reasoning for Sharpston's conclusion was based on the standard mantra of the EU judiciary. In the beginning was the word:

As long ago as 1969, the Court held in *Stauder* that 'fundamental human rights [are] enshrined in the general principles of Community law and protected by the Court'. That case-law, initially embryonic, has been applied and developed through leading judgments such as *Internationale Handelsgesellschaft* and *Nold* through to the present day. In *Kadi* and *Al Barakaat*, the Court roundly stated that 'measures incompatible with respect for human rights are not acceptable in the Community'.[32]

And the word was good and regardless of any political or social development, that is how it remains. More particularly, the word was not transformed by Lisbon. Sharpston chose not to make reference to the identification of values as having any influence whatsoever on her thinking or the constitutional environment of the Union as a whole. Perhaps this was sensible for a member of an institution that has always been intent on preserving its legitimacy through the restatement of a general principle. But the opportunity to give some recognition to Articles 2 and 3 TEU demonstrates the persistent myopia when it comes to realizing and *promoting* rather than simply protecting human rights through legal judgment.

Nonetheless, in terms of the substance of *Radu*, Sharpston did at least reference the problems with the EAW and the Commission's critical report, which she went out of her way to accept.[33] And she also accepted that the Framework Decision does not remove the obligation to respect fundamental rights and principles, that 'the duty to respect those rights and principles permeates the Framework Decision', and that it 'is implicit that those rights may be taken into account in founding a decision not to execute a warrant'.[34] She stated, '[t]o interpret Article 1(3) [of the Decision] otherwise would risk its having no meaning—otherwise, possibly, than

---

[31] Sharpston, *Ciprian Vasile Raduat* (n 29) footnote 27.
[32] Sharpston, *Ciprian Vasile Raduat* (n 29) para 49.
[33] Sharpston, *Ciprian Vasile Raduat* (n 29) paras 60 and 61.
[34] Sharpston, *Ciprian Vasile Raduat* (n 29) para 70. Support for her view is provided not by case law but by AG Cruz Villalón's Opinion in Case C-306/09 *I.B.* [2010] ECR I-10341.

as an elegant platitude', a charge that might also be assigned to Articles 2 and 3 TEU given their complete absence within Sharpston's general analysis.

Sharpston did then set out a suggested basis for a series of tests that could be deployed by Member States' courts in trying to determine whether or not to refuse a warrant on fair trial rights grounds. But, this was wholly ignored by the CJEU, belying the idea that there might be any meaningful role played by the AG when it comes to influencing systemic change to the human rights landscape.

No doubt some would argue that the Court has been responsible for entrenching and making more visible the importance of respecting human rights in the EU. And some would no doubt argue that without its intervention relatively early in the EU's life, human rights issues would not have developed as a concern for the other institutions, particularly the Commission. In both respects, one can see the value in the judicial role. But there is no suggestion at present that the Court feels able to contribute to the further promotion of human rights in the Union. Its task is reactive; as many believe it should be. Apply the law as it stands, do not make law, would be the position, one identified, if not justified, as being either a functional or teleological interpretative method.[35]

The problem with this approach is that there is therefore little point in looking to the Court for inspiration when it comes to evolving human rights across the EU. There may be a limited protective role, but this is entirely dependent on individual actions appearing before it. Even then, the opportunity to use such occasions for a form of constitutional justice is highly unlikely to occur in practice.

This raises an additional concern. When accession to the ECHR is finally resolved, will the ECtHR fill that void? If its growing predilection for constitutional rather than individual justice is anything to go by, then there may likely develop a dual track approach to human rights. Those enshrined in the ECHR may be policed by the ECtHR with an eye to setting down principles that can then guide the EU and its Member States in the legal promotion of those rights. But given that the EU Charter contains a spread of rights far beyond the ECHR, any issues relating to these other rights will be determined by the Union's judiciary in terms of its current constrained philosophy. Rather than serve to promote human rights more widely there is a danger that an environment of legal confusion will arise.

---

[35] And as such would conform to Bengoetxea's categorization of methods of legal interpretation adopted by the Court generally. A functional interpretation would operate so as to give effect to any piece of legislation (thus focusing on the individual set of rules). A teleological approach would potentially favour the goals and purposes of the grander constitutional design (the formation of a single market most prominently). See J. Bengoetxea, *The Legal Reasoning of the European Court of Justice: Towards a European Jurisprudence* (1993).

IV. Human Rights and the Commission

If the judiciary is beset by a conservative tendency, how does the Commission fare? The proposition raised at the beginning of this chapter was that in comparison it was significantly more effective than the Court has proven to be. That might not be particularly praiseworthy.

However, the language of promotion has at least been embraced by the Commission in looking to implement the EU Charter, which is now legally binding. In the Commission's 2010 published strategy for implementation, the Lisbon amendments are interpreted as having turned an acknowledged commitment (to respect the Charter) into a determination to *implement* and *promote* it.[36] In contrast to AG Sharpston's analysis in *Radu*, the Commission begins with the philosophy that here is a 'new legal environment'.[37] It demands that the EU be exemplary in making 'the Charter as effective as possible' and aims to focus on its 'effective implementation' by strengthening and promoting a 'culture of fundamental rights' within its own work. The Charter is supposed to be a primary reference point in the legislative process. And the Commission adopts a commitment to 'enforce fundamental rights' in Member States where EU law has application, through monitoring and infringement procedures.

Much of this is rhetoric. One would not expect more in a fourteen-page strategy document. But language is important. It sets an institutional tone. There, nonetheless, needs to be some assessment of whether this tone has been accompanied by practice that fulfils the linguistic intent. The absence of a legislative or policy strategy would place the rhetoric in the largely reactive rather than proactive camp.

What has been seen over the last three to four years is a willingness to produce rights-promoting legislation *as well as* rights monitoring *of* legislation. So, in its 2012 Annual Report, the Commission claims the former is being realized through a 'major reform of the EU's rules on the protection of personal data',[38] a 'proactive approach to accelerate progress towards a better gender balance' on the boards of listed corporations,[39] and the safeguarding of 'procedural rights' in

[36] Communication from the Commission 'Strategy for the effective implementation of the Charter of Fundamental Rights by the European Union' COM(2010) 573 final.

[37] COM(2010) 573 final (n 36) 3.

[38] The legislation includes Communication on Safeguarding Privacy in a Connected World—A European Data Protection Framework for the 21st Century, COM (2012) 09 final; Proposal for a Regulation of the European Parliament and of the Council on the protection of individuals with regard to the processing of personal data and on the free movement of such data, COM (2012) 11 final; and Proposal for a Directive on the protection of individuals with regard to the processing of personal data by competent authorities for the purposes of prevention, investigation, detection or prosecution of criminal offences or the execution of criminal penalties, and the free movement of such data, COM(2012) 10 final.

[39] The document referred to is the Proposal for a Directive on improving the gender balance among non-executive directors of companies listed on stock exchanges and related measures, COM (2012) 614 final.

criminal cases across EU Member States.[40] In its enforcing role as guardian of the Treaties it reports variously on: infringement (and other persuasive) procedures against Hungary following controversial constitutional changes there; engagement with France about its dismantling of Roma settlements; and legal action against Malta in relation to free movement rules in particular as they applied to same-sex spouses. These are the highlights.

It is clear, though, that the Commission has acted on a broad range of rights-related initiatives. From anti-trafficking to new rules on equal treatment, from the promotion of the rights of the child to establishing minimum standards for the rights of victims of crime, there is claimed to be an almost dizzying amount of human rights work being undertaken or in the pipeline. And that does not even include the external remit (which lies outside the focus of this chapter). So, the Commission's analysis of the application of the Charter is able to proceed through the six chapters of rights in methodical fashion, itemizing each article and right and demonstrating some valuable progression with regard to rights of individuals.

Even if one strips away the inevitably self-congratulatory nature of much of the Commission's reportage on its recent record, there is still much for human rights activists to applaud. The package of proposals produced to standardize rights in criminal proceedings could even be seen as a response to the Court's inability to look behind the EAW and its assumption that all Member States respect fair trial and pre-trial rights.[41] There might be suggestions to improve the proposals, but the underlying response is positive and supportive.[42] The Commission has embarked on a process of human rights promotion that would have been unthinkable ten years ago and certainly could not have been contemplated as a result of judicial interference.

But is all this activity a veneer, behind which lies as much of a traditional prop for the institution of the European Union as the Court provides? Does the sweep of interest in individual rights identified in the Charter detract from any coherent sense of purpose in realizing human rights across Europe? In other words, is the Commission afflicted by not seeing the wood for the trees, more concerned with tactical responses to particular rights than developing a strategy for fulfilling all rights as an integral value for the future of the Union and its people?

---

[40] Commission 2012 Report on the Application of the EU Charter of Fundamental Rights available at http://ec.europa.eu/justice/fundamental-rights/charter/application/index_en.htm. Further details of the legislation aiming to establish procedural rights in criminal cases are considered below.

[41] The package includes the presumption of innocence and the right to be present at trial (COM(2013) 821/2), procedural safeguards for children (COM(2013) 822/2) and vulnerable persons (COM(2013) 8178/2), and legal aid (COM(2013) 824 and COM(2013) 8179/2).

[42] See for instance the largely supportive Meijers Committee report to the European Parliament Committee on Civil Liberties, Justice and Home Affairs 18 March 2014 available at http://www.commissie-meijers.nl/assets/commissiemeijers/CM1402%20Note%20on%20the%20Package%20of%20Fair%20Trial%20Rights.pdf.

Perhaps the best place to examine this is not at the margins of procedure, but at the heart of crisis. Economic downturn and the re-emergence of austerity as a seemingly unassailable (albeit perhaps temporary) condition has placed something of a spotlight on the underlying position of the Commission vis-à-vis human rights. If in these times there is an intent to promote human rights then the otherwise busy Commission might demonstrate that other 'interests' (in the parlance of the Court) are not necessarily (and always) the more important concern.

Claus Offe has considered the territory in a recent logical and lucid flow of consciousness.[43] He recognizes the crisis as producing a 'remedial responsibility' that 'the less an agent (Member State and its economy) has suffered as a consequence of the mistakes collectively made or the more it even has benefitted from them having been made (through interest rates which are lower than they otherwise would be, and external exchange rates of the Euro more favourable), the greater the share of the burdens the agent must shoulder in compensating others for adverse consequences resulting from the original mistake'.[44] It is a 'moral duty' that coincides with the long-term interests of the benefactors (mainly, if not exclusively, Germany). But Offe's most apt point (for this chapter at least) is his assertion of a complete absence of the voice of the Commission in this crisis. According to him, the Commission, along with the Court, is 'completely depoliticised', incapable of constructing policy that will deal with the misery induced by austerity measures.

If Offe is right, individual or even collective rights do not figure here where they might otherwise bite the hardest. And indeed, there is a case to be answered that the focus of the Commission has been to see rights as an ameliorating rather than directive force faced by institutional financial measures and budget cuts. The latter policy is hardly challenged, if at all: austerity is taken as necessary. 'Sustainable, smart and inclusive economic growth' is therefore the mantra promulgated at a very public level.[45] Sustainable public finances are demanded and policies that seek to grow economies out of difficulty are the solution. Fundamental rights are only mentioned in the context of reducing the effects of this approach, not central to its construction. So the aim of the Commission's 'European Platform against Poverty' is quoted as 'to ensure economic, social and territorial cohesion . . . so as to raise awareness and recognise the fundamental rights of people experiencing poverty and social exclusion, enabling them to live in dignity and take an active part in society'.[46] Such 'awareness' and 'recognition' may be necessary but they are hardly

[43] Claus Offe 'Europe Entrapped: Does the EU have the Political Capacity to Overcome its Current Crisis?' (2013) 19:5 *ELJ* 595–611.

[44] Offe (n 43) 605.

[45] It was introduced in the Commission's Communication 'Europe 2020: A strategy for smart, sustainable and inclusive growth' COM(2010) 2020 final.

[46] COM(2010) 2020 final (n 45) 19.

sufficient in the context of the scale of economic catastrophe and transformation that the Commission reports as having taken place.

The failure of its approach is particularly reflected in the Commission's own review of progress, carried out in March 2014.[47] Its goal of lifting at least 20 million people out of the risk of poverty and social exclusion looks optimistic. The Commission says the 'EU has drifted further away from its target . . . and there is no sign of rapid progress to remedy this situation'. Instead the number of those at risk of financial poverty, experiencing material deprivation or living in jobless households is reported as having increased from 114 million in 2009 to 124 million in 2012.[48]

Looking also at the Commission's 2012 Report on the application of the EU Charter, one can see that fundamental rights' measures taken in the context of austerity are viewed as merely a *response* to the 'economic crisis'.[49] And even then, only some limited consequences of the crisis are noted. These are almost exclusively in terms of undermining further the right to equality. There is no analysis of the impact on individual or collective rights of the cuts that have been made. Where indeed, in this respect, is the application of in-depth human rights impact assessments that are supposed to be one of the Commission's significant tools for supporting human rights?

Admittedly, the Commission is little different from many national governmental bureaucracies. But this is beside the point. For the Commission to be treated seriously as a promoter and protector of human rights, it has to demonstrate that commitment at the most vulnerable of times and for the most vulnerable of people within its territory. Otherwise we are seeing little more than an institution playing on the side-lines of justice rather than getting its hands dirty with the business of protecting the massive human rights issues across (and not simply in) European society.

One indication that it *could* develop this role lies in the history of its anti-discrimination policy. Over many years, the Commission has maintained a commitment to counter racism and xenophobia. Its approach is typified in its report on the Council Framework Decision 2008/913/JHA (on combating certain forms and expressions of racism and xenophobia by means of criminal law) in January 2014, where it noted that the fight 'must be framed within a fundamental rights context' and based on 'the need to protect the rights of individuals, groups and society at large'.[50] But the only balance to be struck here is with individual freedoms of association and expression, a predictable human rights related dilemma. Nonetheless, the Commission's understanding of the 'fundamental rights context'

---

[47] Communication from the Commission, 'Taking stock of the Europe 2020 strategy for smart, sustainable and inclusive growth' COM(2014) 130 final/2.

[48] COM(2014) 130 final/2 (n 47) 14.   [49] 2012 Report (n 40).

[50] Report from the Commission to the European Parliament and the Council on the implementation of Council Framework Decision 2008/913/JHA on combating certain forms and expressions of racism and xenophobia by means of criminal law COM(2014) 27 final.

demonstrates a willingness to see human rights issues as societal and not purely individual concerns. Seeing the strategic as well as the tactical benefit of pursuing justice through rights, thus marks the Commission out as a body capable of promoting human rights *tout court*.

Unfortunately, the economic crisis of the past few years has seen a relative *inability* of the Commission to see matters of justice in rights terms. The survival of the Union, and particularly the Eurozone, has taken precedence. The stark contrast to anti-racism measures has been highlighted in the Council of Europe's report, 'Safeguarding human rights in times of economic crisis' produced in 2013.[51] This not only identifies a catalogue of austerity measures, implemented in part by the Commission, as causing significant impact on all forms of social protection, but it also shows how the most vulnerable are the worst hit, with disproportionate impacts being recorded on 'disadvantaged and marginalised groups of people'.[52] The poor, the disabled, migrants, asylum seekers, women, the young, are all noted as suffering structural inequalities that have been increased as a result of action to reduce social protection and cut budgets.

These effects are interpreted in specific human rights terms: for instance, the Commission's demand for public spending on health in Greece not to exceed 6 per cent GDP is described as having 'a potentially long-term impact on public health'. And, indeed, when one examines the Commission's communications and literature on its interventions into Member States' fiscal affairs, the words 'fundamental rights' or 'human rights' do not appear.[53]

Not only is the Commission seen as complicit in applying or enforcing these measures but also deficient in monitoring the human rights impact of cuts it has policed. The report states that while 'the European Commission and the IMF conduct annual economic evaluations of many European countries to assess and enforce their compliance with fiscal rules, no such arrangement exists to systematically monitor the human rights consequences of economic policies'.[54] Nor is the Commission seen to have much to say about responses to resistance to austerity that have arisen in certain Member States. Spain's laws restricting the right to protest, for instance, are marked as a consequence of an overarching belief that there

[51] Council of Europe, Commissioner for Human Rights 'Safeguarding human rights in times of economic crisis' November 2013 available at https://wcd.coe.int/com.instranet. InstraServlet?command=com.instranet.CmdBlobGet&InstranetImage=2429572&SecMode=1&Do cId=2099360&Usage=2.

[52] 'Safeguarding human rights' (n 51) 22.

[53] See, for instance, Communication from the Commission to the Council Follow-up to the Council Decision 2011/734/EU of 12 July 2011 addressed to Greece, with a view to reinforcing and deepening fiscal surveillance and giving notice to Greece to take measures for the deficit reduction judged necessary to remedy the situation of excessive deficit 9 March 2012 COM(2012) 117 final.

[54] COM(2012) 117 final (n 53) 40.

is no alternative. Thus, protest can only be a detrimental distraction rather than a democratic benefit.

The lack of reflection on the effect of fiscal measures promoted by the Commission is particularly evident in relation to social protection. The whole 'excessive deficit procedure', which the Commission launches should the deficit of any Member State exceed 3 per cent GDP (a frequent occurrence), seems to do its best to avoid mentioning rights language whatsoever. The Commission has been engaged in many such procedures, all of which are aimed at reducing the deficit in a relatively short time. Even the Fundamental Rights Agency, which normally avoids political comment, produced a working paper in 2010 warning 'there is at least a possibility that the Member State can only achieve the deficit reduction over the required timescale by reducing social security expenditures to such an extent that social protection is adversely affected'.[55] It recommended that 'clear and transparent information' on the impact on vulnerable groups was necessary. But why should the Commission need to be reminded of such an obligation?

The combination of direct involvement in the imposition of austere measures, the failure to properly consider the effects of those measures, and the relative silence evident when faced by the social decay that results, places the Commission in a peculiarly ambivalent position vis-à-vis human rights. On the one hand, it sits as a guardian of the Treaties and thus the values espoused therein; on the other, it must carry out the political strategies that are devised by the Council and the powerful Member States for the continuing survival (as it might be seen) of the European polity as a whole. These are not necessarily mutually exclusive. However, in human rights development terms, it can be (and is, in this current period of economic crisis) problematic. The pre-Lisbon Treaty approach, whereby fundamental rights were largely contained within a limited number of particular rights categories (anti-discrimination, equal pay, freedom of movement) has been hard to dislodge. Though the advent of the Charter in 2000 may have placed greater emphasis on individual rights across a broad range of freedoms and rights, any concerted effort to develop human rights *tout court* within the Union remains very tightly constrained. Whenever the economy rises as the salient issue, rights take a distant second place.

And it is not a tendency that waits for crisis to be reinvigorated. As already mentioned, the EU records the high, and increasing, level of those in or at risk of poverty. 24.2 per cent of the EU's population were in this category according to the 2011 *eurostat* analysis. In 2010 it was 23.6 per cent. This figure is only an average across the Union but it is getting worse. In Romania, Bulgaria and Latvia it was more than 40 per cent in 2011 compared with 15 per cent in the Netherlands. Unemployment

---

[55] EU FRA Protecting fundamental rights during the economic crisis' Working Paper December 2010 available at http://www.europarl.europa.eu/meetdocs/2009_2014/documents/peti/dv/working-paper-fundrgts_crisis_/working-paper-fundrgts_crisis_en.pdf at 39.

in Greece ran at 26.8 per cent in March 2013 but was only 5.3 per cent in Germany.[56] Although the Commission is keen to stress the importance of growth in resolving these atrocious statistics, it does not seek to frame any parallel or perhaps balancing response in rights terms. This belies the notion that the promotion of human rights rests at the centre of the Commission's thinking, at least when it comes to economic affairs.

V. A Failure of Practice or Design

Undoubtedly, many will see the criticisms I have levelled against the Court and the Commission as indicative not simply of a human rights failure but of a deeper and broader failure of justice.[57] This may be true. Seeing the EU incapable of confronting the inequities and inequalities of Europe—seeing it even contribute to them through valuing the market and the continuing existence of the Union above all other considerations—might well lend weight to such an overarching critique.

However, if some consideration is to be given to the EU's performance vis-à-vis its response to its own stated value and objective regarding respect for human rights, then assessing its record and future potential in this narrower aspect is necessary. It may also be true that the CJEU is more constrained in its approach to the subject than the Commission. But both institutions are afflicted with the same systemic problem: taking human rights seriously from a strategic perspective does not come naturally to them. That is the appearance given, despite the varying personnel who will work there, whose integrity should not be doubted. The matter is not one of individual ethics but institutional ethos. That has been framed by an economic functionality where the integrated and single market is its founding precept. Though fundamental rights can be interpreted to form a component part, they cannot be allowed to challenge it. If they did to any appreciable degree, then the whole edifice would be undermined.

To avoid such a calamity, the Commission and the Court (albeit in different ways) have adopted contingent responses to the demands of fundamental rights. On the one hand, the rhetoric of respect can be shored up by testing any decision or

---

[56] For latest data see *Eurostat,* 'People at Risk of Poverty or Social Exclusion' available at http://epp.eurostat.ec.europa.eu/statistics_explained/index.php/People_at_risk_of_poverty_or_social_exclusion

[57] For a varied and extensive review of the EU's justice deficit, see Grainne de Burca, Dimitry Kochenov and Andrew Williams (eds) *Europe's Justice Deficit* (2014 forthcoming).

piece of legislation against individually articulated rights (now helpfully listed in the Charter). On the other, any attempt to alter the general sense of economic priority or to develop strategies that might question the efficacy of the market to address social inequalities, will not be countenanced in human rights terms. Instead, the retreat to some social conditioning (with marginal and generally derided efforts coordinated through the European Social Fund or Cohesion policy) is the preferred option. And this approach is not couched with rights in mind other than in very peripheral terms. The latest iteration of the European Regional Development Fund makes one reference in its preamble:

(13) In the context of its effort to increase economic, territorial and social cohesion, the Union should, at all stages of implementation of the ESI Funds, aim at eliminating inequalities and at promoting equality between men and women and integrating the gender perspective, as well as at combating discrimination based on sex, racial or ethnic origin, religion or belief, disability, age or sexual orientation as set out in Article 2 of the Treaty on the European Union (TEU), Article 10 TFEU and Article 21 of the Charter of Fundamental Rights of the European Union, taking into account in particular accessibility for persons with disabilities, as well as Article 5(2) of the Charter of Fundamental Rights stating that no one is to be required to perform forced or compulsory labour.[58]

Nowhere is consideration given to the mosaic of fundamental rights that might be engaged in pursuing a 'strategy for smart, sustainable and inclusive growth'. Only the anti-discrimination agenda is capable of standing within the expenditure initiative, an important, even vital, aim but hardly all-encompassing from a human rights perspective.

At the beginning of this chapter, two queries were raised: is the EU congenitally ill-disposed towards realizing human rights? Or have its institutions done enough to suggest that the failure to date is but a reflection of practice not matching design?

From the review conducted above of the practices and rhetoric of both the Court and the Commission (the latter marginally less ineffective than the former), there is strong reason to remain sceptical about the EU's ability to do justice to human rights within its borders.[59] And there is little evidence to suggest the systemic predisposition is under threat.

---

[58] Regulation (EU) No 1303/2013 of the European Parliament and of the Council of 17 December 2013, laying down common provisions on the European Regional Development Fund, the European Social Fund, the Cohesion Fund, the European Agricultural Fund for Rural Development and the European Maritime and Fisheries Fund and laying down general provisions on the European Regional Development Fund, the European Social Fund, the Cohesion Fund and the European Maritime and Fisheries Fund and repealing Council Regulation (EC) No 1083/2006 preamble paragraph (13).

[59] And nothing has been said about the EU's operations on and beyond its borders in this evaluation. That, of course, demands further and separate consideration.

BIBLIOGRAPHY

Philip Alston and Olivier de Schutter (eds), *Monitoring Fundamental Rights in the EU: The Contribution of the Fundamental Rights Agency* (2005)

J. Bengoetxea, *The Legal Reasoning of the European Court of Justice: Towards a European Jurisprudence* (1993)

I. Coppell and A. O'Neill, 'The European Court of Justice: Taking Rights Seriously?' (1992) *Common Market Law Review* 29:4 669–692

Grainne de Burca, 'After the EU Charter of Fundamental Rights: The Court of Justice as a Human Rights Adjudicator?' (2013) 20:2 *Maastricht Journal of European and Comparative Law* 168–184

Israel de Jesus Butler, 'Ensuring Compliance with the Charter of Fundamental Rights in Legislative Drafting: The Practice of the European Commission' (2012) *European Law Review* 397–418

Sybe de Vries, Ulf Bernitz, and Stephen Weatherill (eds), *The Protection of Fundamental Rights in the EU After Lisbon* (2013)

Claus Offe, 'Europe Entrapped: Does the EU have the Political Capacity to Overcome its Current Crisis?' (2013) 19:5 *ELJ* 595–611

Steve Peers, Tamara Hervey, Jeff Kenner, and AngelaWard (eds), *The EU Charter of Fundamental Rights* (2014)

Takis Tridimas, *The General Principles of EU Law: 2nd Edition* (2007)

Andrew Williams, *The Ethos of Europe: Values, Law and Justice in the EU* (2010)

Andrew Williams, 'Promoting Justice after Lisbon: Groundwork for a New Philosophy of EU Law' (2010) 30:4 *Oxford Journal of Legal Studies* 663–694

Andrew Williams, 'Taking Values Seriously: Towards a Philosophy of EU Law' (2009) 29: 3 *Oxford Journal of Legal Studies* 549–577

Andrew Williams, *EU Human Rights Policies: A Study in Irony* (2004)

CHAPTER 11

EXTERNAL ACTION

COMMON COMMERCIAL POLICY, COMMON FOREIGN AND SECURITY POLICY, COMMON SECURITY AND DEFENCE POLICY

PANOS KOUTRAKOS

I. Introduction

THE European Union is active on the international scene in a number of policy areas. Originally, its primary rules referred only to two such areas, namely external trade[1] and international agreements establishing an association between the EU and one or more states or international organizations.[2] However, over the years, Treaty amendments and the assertive practice of its institutions have given rise to the Union's increasingly ambitious international role, which is governed by a dense set of rules and procedures.[3]

This chapter will focus on three policies which appear to share a fundamental characteristic and yet are divided in both legal and policy terms. The Common

---

[1] Now Art 207 TFEU.   [2] Now Art 217 TFEU.
[3] For a general analysis, see P. Eeckhout, EU External Relations Law (2nd ed, 2011) and P. Koutrakos, *EU International Relations Law* (2nd ed 2015).

Commercial Policy (CCP), the Common Foreign and Security Policy (CFSP) and the Common Security and Defence Policy (CSDP) are the only external policies which are defined in the Treaties as 'common'. The adjective they share appears to connote a commonality of purpose and a degree of institutional and substantive integration which would aim to enhance their effectiveness. It is recalled that, from the establishment of the European Economic Community, the term 'common policies' has been used to describe only policies where the EU exercises regulatory intervention to a quite intrusive degree.[4] And while one may be tempted to explain this description of the Union's external policies as a relic from the Union's past, it is noteworthy that the Common Security and Defence Policy has only been thus described since the entry into force of the Lisbon Treaty.

And yet, a closer examination of CCP, CFSP, and CSDP suggests that there are fundamental differences both in the logic underpinning their legal framework as well as in the various factors which shape their implementation. The starting point for these differences is the fundamentally distinct character of the subject matter of the policies under discussion: external trade is an area that is traditionally viewed as ideally suited to supranational cooperation, whereas foreign policy, security, and defence are deemed so close to the core of national sovereignty that they are more suited to inter-governmental cooperation. The development of the Union legal order and the structure set out in the Lisbon Treaty may appear to challenge this dichotomy by providing a constitutional space where these policies may be carried out as a part of a coherent whole. In examining the law and practice of these policies, this chapter will offer a snapshot of the wide range of areas covered by the Union's external action.

II. The Organization of the Common External Policies

The organization of the policies examined in this chapter is couched distinctly in the language of integration. This is illustrated in different ways. Reference has already been made to the adjective 'common' used to describe policies at the opposite ends of the supranationalism–inter-governmentalism spectrum. In the same vein, these policies are all part of what the Treaties describe as the Union's 'external action'.[5] Terms such as 'external policies' or 'actions' are avoided. Instead,

---

[4] See the common transport policy (Arts 90–100 TFEU) and the common agricultural and fisheries policies (Arts 38–44 TFEU).
[5] See Ch 2 TEU and Title II of Part V TFEU.

the choice of reference to 'external action' signifies the design of the EU's foreign affairs as a coherent whole.

The language of integration is also reflected in the organization of the legal rules applicable to the EU's external action as well as their overarching principles and objectives. In terms of the former, the CCP is grouped together with the provisions governing the other external economic and social policies of the Union.[6] In addition, and for the first time since the establishment of the European Economic Community, a common set of principles and objectives whose overarching scope covers all the EU's external action is set out in the TEU. This covers the entire range of the Union's external trade, economic, and political relations.[7] These principles are laid down in Article 21(1) TEU and include 'democracy, the rule of law, the universality and indivisibility of human rights and fundamental freedoms, respect for human dignity, the principles of equality and solidarity, and respect for the principles of the United Nations Charter and international law', as well as commitment to effective multilateralism.

The objectives of the Union's external action are set out in Article 21(2) TEU and their content varies, as they are:

- political (safeguarding the EU's values, and fundamental interests, the consolidation and support of democracy and the rule of law, the promotion of an international system based on stronger multilateral cooperation and good global governance);
- security-related (preservation of peace and prevention of conflicts);
- development-related (fostering of the sustainable economic, social and environmental development of developing countries);
- economic (encouragement of the integration of all countries into the world economy);
- environmental (assistance to the sustainable management of global natural resources);
- social (assistance to regions confronting natural or man-made disasters).

The above categorization is somewhat artificial, as the whole point of grouping together these objectives is that they all relate to each and every aspect of what the Union does in the world. In accordance with Article 21(3) TEU, the 'Union shall respect the principles and pursue the objectives set out in paragraphs 1 and 2 in the development and implementation of the different areas of the Union's external action covered by this Title and by Part Five [TFEU], and of the external aspects of its other policies'. This is an important feature of the Union's external action. In

---

[6] See Part V, Title II V TEU which includes CCP (Arts 206–207 TFEU), development cooperation (Arts 208–211 TFEU), economic, financial and technical cooperation with third countries (Arts 212–213 TFEU), humanitarian aid (Art 214 TFEU), and sanctions (Art 215 TFEU).

[7] Arts 205 TFEU and 24(2) TEU.

constitutional terms, it brings together different strands of activity, which, due to their differing political sensitivity, had been subject to drastically different sets of rules and procedures.

By defining principles and objectives common to all of them, their diverse subject matter notwithstanding, the Lisbon Treaty shapes a legal order which appears homogeneous and integrated. In policy terms, this function of the organization of the Union's common external policies is highlighted by the duty of consistency. This is laid down in Article 21(3) subparagraph (2) TEU which applies 'between the different areas of [the Union's] external action and between these and its other policies' and compliance with which is entrusted to the Council and the Commission, assisted by the High Representative of the Union for Foreign Affairs and Security Policy. Therefore, in the light of the design of the Union's external action under the Treaties, common principles and objectives ensure that the various strands of the Union's external action, different though they are in their implications, political sensitivity, and applicable procedures, are consistent and coherent.

This dimension of the relevant primary rules becomes clearer if viewed in the context of the abolition of the much-maligned and complex pillar structure. Introduced by the Maastricht Treaty, it had been viewed as largely responsible for conveying the impression that the EU legal order was both convoluted and detrimental to the effectiveness of the Union's international policies. In this context of de-pillarization, the reorganization of the relevant rules, the mainstreaming of their principles and objectives, and, in the case of the CSDP, even the change of the policy's title reflect the emphasis of the Treaties on unity and coherence.

This language of integration must be understood in the broader political context that shaped the drafting and negotiation of the Treaty Establishing a Constitution for Europe and, following its long and painful death, the negotiation of the Lisbon Treaty. The international role of the Union and its effectiveness were central in these processes. For instance, the Laeken Declaration on the Future of the European Union, which initiated the process of reform of the Union's Treaties in December 2001, referred prominently to 'Europe's new role in a globalised world' and raised the following question: 'Does Europe not, now that is finally unified, have a leading role to play in a new world order, that of a power able both to play a stabilising role worldwide and to point the way ahead for many countries and peoples?' The role it envisaged was directly linked to 'its responsibilities in the governance of globalisation' which 'Europe needs to shoulder'.[8] Therefore, the general tenor of the organizing principles that govern the conduct of CCP, CFSP, and CSDP within the overall structure of the Union's external action reflects the policy imperative and ambition which prevailed at the time of the drafting of the Treaties.

---

[8] European Council, December 14–15, 2001, 2.

However, the language of integration described in this section is by no means the only analytical tool to enable one to understand the nature and conduct of CCP, CFSP, and CSDP. Within the reorganized contours of the Union's external action in the Treaties, there are clear reminders of the distinctiveness of these policies. This theme will be examined further in Sections IV and V. At this juncture, suffice it to point out these are not random indications that there is something unique about CFSP and CSDP that distinguishes them from the other external policies in general and CCP in particular. In fact, the institutional setup of these policies, their procedural mechanisms and substantive rules, as well as their conduct all illustrate their distinct position within the Union's constitutional architecture. Therefore a nuanced picture emerges. The language of integration underpinning the logic of the organization of the Union's external action in the Treaties co-exists with clear indications of the legal and policy distinctiveness that characterizes the different strands of this action.

III. Common Commercial Policy

The CCP is the oldest external policy of the Union. It is also a policy which, well before the entry into force of the Lisbon Treaty, was described as 'representing the [EU] at the height of its legal powers, control and supremacy over the member states'.[9] Such a statement may be explained on the basis of two factors. The first is the exclusive nature of the Union's competence in the area, introduced by the Court of Justice early on in the 1970s[10] and formalized at Lisbon in Article 3(1)(e) TFEU. The second factor is procedural and is about the qualified majority voting in the Council pursuant to which most CCP measures are adopted.[11]

1. Scope

The CCP covers unilateral measures and international agreements in the area set out in Article 207(1) TFEU. The definition of the CCP has been a contentious issue since its inception. The Court of Justice ruled in the 1970s that it should be construed broadly in order to be able to adjust to the development of the international economic arena, as otherwise it would face irrelevance.[12] Long and protracted

---

[9] D. McGoldrick, *International Relations of the European Union* (1997) 70.
[10] See Opinion 1/75 [1975] ECR 1355, 1364 and Case 41/76 *Donckerwolcke* [1976] ECR 1921, para 33.
[11] See Art 297(2) TFEU for unilateral measures and Art 207(4) TFEU for international agreements.
[12] See Opinion 1/75 (n 10) and Opinion 1/78 [1979] ECR 2871.

disputes ensued between the Commission and the Council about the outer limits of the policy, centred on, but by no means confined to, questions about services and intellectual property rights.[13] Following two Treaty amendments which first provided for qualified expansion (at Amsterdam) and then set out a highly convoluted set of rules (at Nice), the Lisbon Treaty simplifies the scope of the policy in the current version of Article 207 TFEU. It reads as follows:

The common commercial policy shall be based on uniform principles, particularly with regard to changes in tariff rates, the conclusion of tariff and trade agreements relating to trade in goods and services, and the commercial aspects of intellectual property, foreign direct investment, the achievement of uniformity in measures of liberalisation, export policy and measures to protect trade such as those to be taken in the event of dumping or subsidies. The common commercial policy shall be conducted in the context of the principles and objectives of the Union's external action.

The above provision makes it clear that the activities referred to therein are non-exhaustive. Of these, foreign direct investment is included for the first time. The outcome of a long and complex dialogue between the EU institutions, the Court of Justice, and the Member States,[14] the current version of Article 207(1) TFEU still raises questions about the scope of the CCP. The definition of the commercial aspects of intellectual property, for instance, is left open. In its recent judgment in *Daiichi Sankyo*, the Court held that this term covers the entire scope of the Agreement on Trade Related Aspects of Intellectual Property Rights (TRIPS) concluded in the framework of the World Trade Organization.[15]

However, it is the reference to foreign direct investment which gives rise to considerable debate. Foreign direct investment refers to the establishment of a lasting interest from an investor based in one state for a company in another state. Therefore, it suggests that indirect investment would be excluded. This would cover portfolio investment, that is holdings of equity, bonds, stocks, or other financial assets which do not entail managerial control over the company concerned. In the light of the exclusive competence of the Union over the CCP and the apparent intention of the drafters of the Treaties to exclude certain aspects of foreign investment from its scope, the reference to foreign direct investment in Article 207 TFEU has considerable practical and legal implications.

In this respect, two issues are worth raising. The first issue is about the reach of the Union's foreign investment policy. Differing views have been put forward. The Commission argues that the Union is exclusively competent to adopt measures on all matters relating to foreign investment, that is both foreign direct investment

[13] See Opinion 1/94 [1994] ECR I-5267.
[14] See G. De Baere and P. Koutrakos, 'The Interactions between the European Court of Justice and the Legislature in the European Union's External Relations' in P. Syrpis (ed), *The Relationship between the Judiciary and the Legislature in the Internal Market* (2012) 243.
[15] Case C-414/11, judgment of 14 July 2013.

and portfolio investment. This is based on its view that the former is covered by CCP and the latter is implied by Article 63 TFEU, which provides that the movement of capital between Member States and third countries must be free of restrictions. This approach is based further on Article 3(2) TFEU, which provides that the EU's external competence is exclusive in cases where an international agreement 'may affect common rules or alter their scope'. According to the Commission, any rules included in an investment treaty would apply to portfolio investment as well, and might, therefore, affect the common rules on capital movement adopted under Article 63 TFEU.[16] On the other hand, the Council and the Member States argue that the Union's exclusive competence is confined to foreign direct investment under Article 207(1) TFEU, and that any other investment measures, such as those related to portfolio investment, dispute settlement, property and expropriation, are covered by competence that is shared between the EU and the Member States.[17]

The second issue raised by the reference to foreign direct investment in Article 207 TFEU is the fate of the existing Bilateral Investment Treaties (BITs) which Member States have concluded with third countries. More than 1200 such treaties exist. As the entry into force of the Lisbon Treaty deprived the Member States of the power to conclude such agreements insofar as they refer to direct investment, their continuing existence may be viewed as a violation of EU law. However, the negotiation and conclusion of international agreements is a long and complex process the outcome of which depends on a range of political, economic, practical, and legal considerations. The emergence of the Union's exclusive competence on 1 December 2009 in the area by no means entailed the automatic emergence of an EU investment policy.[18] It was for this reason that the Council and the Parliament established a procedural framework which required that Member States notify all their existing BITs to the Commission, while enabling national authorities to retain, apply, and renegotiate them in close contact with the Commission.[19] This procedural mechanism suggests that the Union's exclusive competence does not necessarily rule out action by Member States provided that this is carried out within a

---

[16] See COM (2012) 335 final *Proposal for a Regulation of the European Parliament and of the Council establishing a framework for managing financial responsibility linked to investor-state dispute settlement tribunals established by international agreements to which the European Union is party* (Brussels, 21 June 2012) 3–5.

[17] See the negotiating Directives issued by the Council for the negotiation of trade agreements with Canada, India, and Singapore which were leaked by this non-governmental organization: http://www.s2bnetwork.org/themes/eu-investment-policy/eu-documents/text-of-the-mandates.html. See C. Brown and M. Alcover-Llubia, 'The External Investment Policy of the European Union in the Light of the Entry into Force of the Treaty of Lisbon' (2010–2011) *Yearbook on International Investment Law and Policy* 145 and A. Dimopoulos, *EU Foreign Investment Law* (2011).

[18] See COM (2010) 343 final *Towards a Comprehensive European International Investment Policy* (Brussels, 7 July 2010) 4.

[19] Reg 1219/2012 establishing transitional arrangements for bilateral investment agreements between Member States and third countries [2012] OJ L351/40.

predetermined EU framework that provides for close interaction between national and EU authorities.[20]

However, it is not only the policy areas mentioned in Article 207(1) TFEU that raise questions about the application of the CCP rules. External trade is intrinsically linked with other areas of economic activity, such as development and environment, and distinguishing between them is by no means without problems. Nevertheless, the distinction between such policies may have significant legal implications, not least because the Union's competence to carry out its CCP is exclusive, whereas development cooperation and environmental policies are covered by shared competence.[21] The Court has stressed 'the constitutional significance' of the choice of the appropriate legal basis and has ruled that 'to proceed on an incorrect legal basis . . . is liable to invalidate the act concluding the agreement and so vitiate the Community's consent to be bound by the agreement it has signed'.[22] In this vein, the Commission and the Council have fought intensely over the years about the legal basis of measures with both trade and environmental implications. These inter-institutional disputes have given rise to a body of case law[23] which is not easy either to follow or to apply[24] and which has not dissipated the appetite of the institutions and Member States for legal basis disputes.

2. Decision Making

In accordance with Article 207(2) TFEU, the Council and the European Parliament follow the ordinary legislative procedure in order to adopt 'the measures defining the framework for implementing the common commercial policy'. Such measures are to be distinguished from the specific acts which apply them to a given case and which are viewed as implementing acts adopted by the Commission under Article 291(2) TFEU, albeit under the control of the Member States pursuant to Regulation 182/2011.[25] In 2014, the Council adopted a new Regulation ('Omnibus I Regulation')

---

[20] See also, in other contexts, Council Reg 847/2004/EC on the negotiation and implementation of air services agreements between Member States and third countries [2004] OJ L157/7, Reg 662/2009 on agreements concluded by Member States on particular matters concerning the law applicable to contractual and non-contractual obligations [2009] OJ L200/25, and Reg 664/2009 on agreements by Member States on jurisdiction, recognition and enforcement of judgments and decisions in matrimonial matters, parental responsibility and applicable law in matters relating to maintenance obligations [2009] OJ L200/46.

[21] Art 4(2)(e) and (4) TFEU.   [22] Opinion 2/00 [2001] ECR I-9713, para 5.

[23] See Opinion 2/00 [2001] ECR I-9713; Case C-281/01 *Commission v Council* [2002] ECR I-12049; Case C-94/03 *Commission v Council* [2006] ECR I-1; Case C-178/03 *Commission v Parliament and Council* [2006] ECR I-107; and Case C-411/06 *Commission v Council and Parliament* [2009] ECR I-7585.

[24] See P. Koutrakos, 'Legal Basis and Delimitation of Competence in EU External Relations' in M. Cremona and B. De Witte (eds), *EU Foreign Relations Law: Constitutional Fundamentals* (2008) 171.

[25] Regulation of the Parliament and the Council 182/2011 laying down the rules and general principles concerning mechanisms for control by Member States of the Commission's exercise of implementing powers [2011] OJ L55/13 (adopted under Art 291(3) TFEU).

which brings the decision making procedures in a host of CCP areas in line with Regulation 182/2011.[26]

As far as CCP international agreements are concerned, and in deviation from the general decision making procedure governing international agreements as laid down in Article 218 TFEU, a special procedure applies. It is set out in Article 207(3) TFEU and involves a clear division of functions between the Commission and the Council: the former negotiates and the latter concludes the agreement. The negotiation of agreements is carried out on the basis of a proposal by the Commission and following authorization by the Council. During the negotiations, the Commission must follow any Directives that the Council may issue and must also consult with a committee comprising national experts. Furthermore, the Commission must report to the Parliament on the progress of the negotiations. In authorizing the negotiation of the agreement, as well as concluding it, the Council acts by qualified majority. The Parliament is also involved: it must give its consent under Article 218(6)(a)(v) TFEU.

The decision making procedure set out in Article 207 TFEU differs drastically from that which applied in the first 50 years of European integration. Its central innovation consists of the considerable power it offers to the Parliament. The latter has now become a co-legislator in this area.[27] This development becomes all the more significant given that neither the original Treaty of Rome nor its subsequent amendments referred to the Parliament at all in the context of CCP. Given the emphasis of the current public discourse on democratic legitimacy, it may seem extraordinary that this significant part of the Union's activities should have been carried out in the absence of any input by the only directly elected institution of the Union. However, as the years went by, the Union institutions developed informal arrangements pursuant to which the Parliament was consulted on CCP matters as a matter of practice.[28]

It becomes apparent from the above that CCP decision making is characterized by a significant supranational characteristic, namely majority voting in the Council. This was the principle since the establishment of the European Economic Community. However, Article 207(4) TFEU introduces an exception and requires unanimity for the negotiation and conclusion of international agreements in three cases:

- in the field of trade in services and the commercial aspects of intellectual property, as well as foreign direct investment, where such agreements include provisions for which unanimity is required for the adoption of internal rules;

---

[26] Reg 37/2014 amending certain regulations relating to the common commercial policy as regards the procedures for the adoption of certain measures [2014] OJ L18/1. Under its provisions, specific anti-dumping measures are no longer adopted by the Council, but by the Commission and under the supervision of a committee of representatives of the Member States acting under qualified majority voting.

[27] See R. Passos, 'The European Union's External Relations a Year after Lisbon: A First Evaluation from the European Parliament' in P Koutrakos (ed), *The European Union's External Relations a Year after Lisbon* (2011).

[28] See Koutrakos (n 3) Ch 4.

- in the field of trade in cultural and audiovisual services, where these agreements risk prejudicing the Union's cultural and linguistic diversity;
- in the field of trade in social, education and health services, where these agreements risk seriously disturbing the national organization of such services and prejudicing the responsibility of Member States to deliver them.

Of the above exceptions to the principle of qualified majority voting, the first aims to prevent the decision making rules set out in Article 207 TFEU from being relied upon in order to circumvent the procedural constraints imposed elsewhere in the TFEU for the adoption of internal measures. This seems to refer to a risk that was raised in Opinion 1/94 in the context of TRIPS. The Court held that the conclusion of the latter under CCP rules (hence by qualified majority voting) would harmonize fully intellectual property law in the EU, even though the Treaty provides that internal harmonization rules should be introduced pursuant to procedures different from those governing the CCP.[29] Such an outcome would not be tolerated as it would render internal decision making rules irrelevant.

The latter two exceptions from the qualified majority voting rule in Article 207 (4)(b) and (c) TFEU apply to areas of considerable political sensitivity. This is also reflected by the opaque wording in which the conditions for the application of the exceptions are couched. The negotiations for the Transatlantic Trade and Investment Partnership between the EU and the USA illustrate clearly the issues underpinning the unanimity exceptions. In the discussions in the Council about the content of the Directives pursuant to which the Commission would negotiate the agreement, the French Government was adamant that the regulation of trade in cultural and audiovisual services should be excluded from the negotiations. The issue attracted considerable publicity. Quite how emotive this issue is was illustrated by a statement made by Wim Wenders, the celebrated German cinema director, who argued that dropping the cultural exception would be tantamount to 'burning our books, closing our museums, cutting our thumbs, sacrificing our first-born, rebuilding the Berlin Wall'.[30] A compromise was finally reached in June 2013 according to which audiovisual services would not be part of the mandate, but it would be possible for the Commission to request additional negotiating Directives from the Council at a later stage.[31] The seriousness of the French commitment to protect the cultural exception becomes all the more apparent in the light of the considerable importance which both the EU and the US leadership attach to the successful

---

[29] Opinion 1/94 (n 13).

[30] 'Charlemagne: L'exception française' *The Economist*, 14 June 2013, 38.

[31] After the text of the Directives was leaked by an NGO, and following a accusations about lack of transparency in the negotiations, the Commission declassified the negotiating Directives and made them available here: http://data.consilium.europa.eu/doc/document/ST-11103-2013-DCL-1/en/pdf.

conclusion of the Agreement—so much so, that United States President Barack Obama referred to it expressly and in strong terms in his 2013 State of the Union Address.[32]

IV. Common Foreign and Security Policy

The position of the CFSP within the Union's constitutional architecture has evolved over the years. Originally, there were no provisions in primary law related to foreign policy. But in the late 1960s, the Member States initiated a process of cooperation, partly in response to the tendency of third countries to view them as a coherent group and partly reflecting the culture of cooperation followed in the then Community legal order. Their cooperation in foreign policy was first informal and then carried out on the basis of reports submitted by their foreign ministers. These reports formed the basis of European Political Cooperation (EPC), that is, the precursor to CFSP.[33] Providing for procedures which would enhance consultation between the Member States, they set out a non-binding framework within which the Member States gradually fostered a culture of cooperation.

This process acquired Treaty status in the Single European Act. This included a set of freestanding provisions on EPC which set out cooperation procedures at a clearly inter-governmental level and construed the role of Member States in very wide terms. The Treaty of Maastricht replaced EPC with CFSP, a tighter set of rules and procedures that was set out as a distinct framework (or 'pillar') within the emerging constitutional structure of the Union. However, the inter-governmental nature of this framework was still the main feature of CFSP and was maintained by the subsequent amendments at Amsterdam and Nice.[34]

It becomes apparent that the DNA of CFSP is characterized by two main features. The first is its dynamic and incremental development, shaped by practical considerations, emerging informally and then formalized and consolidated to adjust to any considerable amendment of the Union's constitutional structure.

---

[32] See http://www.whitehouse.gov/state-of-the-union-2013. However, political will about the conclusion of the Agreement seemed to wane later on. The negotiations covered a number of controversial issues, such as an investor-State arbitration clause, and provoked considerable reaction in both some governments and civil society.

[33] On EPC, see S. Nuttall, *European Political Co-operation* (1992).

[34] See E. Denza, *The Intergovernmental Pillars of the European Union* (2002).

The second feature is its distinct position in the EU's legal order. Defined in clearly inter-governmental terms, reflected notably by its exclusion from the jurisdiction of the Court of Justice and the dominant role of unanimous voting, the CFSP was carried out over the years on the basis of legal rules and procedures which differed from those governing the other strands of the Union's activities.

1. The Language of Integration and the Distinct Character of the CFSP

The scope of CFSP is broad and covers 'all areas of foreign policy and all questions relating to the Union's security, including the progressive framing of a common defence policy that might lead to a common defence'.[35] The duties imposed on Member States are also broad and reminiscent of the general duty of cooperation.[36] They are set out in Article 24(3) TEU, which reads as follows:

The Member States shall support the Union's external and security policy actively and unreservedly in a spirit of loyalty and mutual solidarity and shall comply with the Union's action in this area.

The Member States shall work together to enhance and develop their mutual political solidarity. They shall refrain from any action which is contrary to the interests of the Union or likely to impair its effectiveness as a cohesive force in international relations.

It was mentioned above that the revamping of the Union's external policies under the Lisbon Treaty is defined by the language of integration, the de-pillarization of the constitutional order being a case in point. In this vein, the definition of a common set of principles and objectives pursuant to which the Union would carry out all the strands of its external action was also mentioned. Both these developments seem to recast the CFSP legal framework in terms that would bring it closer to the mainstream of the Union's constitutional order.

While it is mainly in terms of the constitutional position of the CFSP that the language of integration is notable, it is also apparent in relation to specific rules and procedures governing the EU's foreign policy. For instance, the main instruments on the basis of which the Union carries out its foreign and security policy are decisions,[37] a type of measure relied upon in all other areas of EU law. Introduced at Lisbon, the provision for decisions replaces the previous provision

---

[35] Art 24(1) TEU.   [36] Art 4(3) TEU.

[37] Art 25 TEU which, in addition to decisions, refers to other instruments of CFSP, namely general guidelines which are defined by the European Council and the strengthening of systematic cooperation between the Member States in the conduct of policy. The Union makes frequent use of declarations and statements (these appear at http://eeas.europa.eu/ashton/index_en.html).

for CFSP-specific measures defined as joint actions, common positions, and common strategies.

CFSP decisions are still adopted mainly by unanimous voting under Article 31(1) TEU. However, this rule has been relaxed. The Lisbon Treaty provides for qualified majority voting in two cases: where a decision is adopted in order to define a Union action or position on a proposal which the High Representative has presented following a specific request by the European Council, the latter made either on its own initiative or that of the High Representative;[38] and where the European Council decides unanimously that the Council may act by qualified majority.[39]

These are added to the exceptions that had already been introduced prior to Lisbon. The first is about abstentions, as they may not prevent the adoption of a decision.[40] This provision has only been relied upon once, by Cyprus in relation to the decision establishing an EU police mission in Kosovo in 2008.[41] A Member State may qualify its abstention by making a formal declaration, in which case it will not be obliged to apply the decision, but should accept that the decision commits the Union and should refrain from any action likely to conflict with or impede Union action based on that decision. However, if a large number of Member States make such a declaration (one-third of the Member States representing one-third of the Union population), the decision may not be adopted. The second exception applies to decisions that may be adopted by the Council by qualified majority in cases where they implement another decision that has already been adopted unanimously.[42]

Finally, while the CFSP has been traditionally excluded from the jurisdiction of the Court of Justice,[43] two exceptions were introduced at Lisbon. The first is about competence: the Court is responsible for monitoring compliance with Article 40 TEU, hence ensuring that a measure which ought to be adopted under the CFSP rules is in fact adopted under them.[44] The second exception is about the rights of individuals: the Court has jurisdiction to review the legality of decisions providing for restrictive measures against natural or legal persons adopted by the Council under the CFSP rules.[45]

The language of integration in which certain provisions about the constitutional position and conduct of the CFSP are couched ought to be assessed against the clear indications of the distinct nature of the CFSP. First, the CFSP rules are not set out in the TFEU along with the provisions governing all the other strands of external action. Instead, they are laid down in the TEU. In fact, along with the CSDP, it is the only substantive policy whose provisions are set out in the TEU.

---

[38] Art 31(2) TEU.   [39] Art 31(3) TEU.   [40] Art 31(1) TEU.
[41] Joint Action 2008/124/CFSP [2008] OJ 42/92.   [42] Art 31(2) TEU.
[43] Art 24(1) subpara (2) TEU.   [44] Art 24(1) subpara (2) TEU.
[45] Art 24(1) subpara (2) TEU and Art 275 TFEU.

Second, the Union's competence in the area of CFSP is distinguished from the other EU competences and is not included in Article 2 TFEU and, therefore, may not be characterized as either exclusive, shared, coordinating, supporting, or supplementing. Instead, it is listed separately in Article 2(4) TEU. Similarly, Article 24(1) subparagraph (2) TEU states that the CFSP 'is subject to specific rules and procedures'.

Third, Article 40 TEU, which refers to the relationship between the CFSP rules and the rest of the primary rules governing the Union's action, underlines further the distinct legal position of CFSP rules. It reads as follows:

> The implementation of the common foreign and security policy shall not affect the application of the procedures and the extent of the powers of the institutions laid down by the Treaties for the exercise of the Union competences referred to in Articles 3 to 6 of the Treaty on the Functioning of the European Union.
>
> Similarly, the implementation of the policies listed in those Articles shall not affect the application of the procedures and the extent of the powers of the institutions laid down by the Treaties for the exercise of the Union competences under this Chapter.

The thrust of the first paragraph of Article 40 TEU predates the Lisbon Treaty, whereas the second paragraph was added at Lisbon. This suggests that the integrity of CFSP as a distinct set of rules within the Union's architecture is not only maintained but also worthy of protection from any attempt to undermine it by over-reliance on the rules governing the other strands of the Union's external action. As mentioned above in this section, compliance with this provision is a matter for the Court.

Fourth, the exceptions to the principle of unanimity introduced at Lisbon are of limited significance. This is not because of the 'emergency break' set out in Article 31(2) TEU. It is partly because their exercise depends on the prior adoption of a unanimous CFSP measure and partly because they are entirely consistent with the logic of the pre-existing exceptions. The prevailing role of unanimity and the limited function of qualified majority voting may be viewed as undermining the ability of the Union to act effectively and swiftly, and therefore may be considered difficult to reconcile with one of the objectives of the Union, namely to 'reinforc[e] the European identity and its independence in order to promote peace, security and progress in Europe and in the world'.[46] In this vein, it may be recalled that decision making procedures are central to the pace of integration achieved in other areas of EU action. It is often recalled, for instance, that a major factor in the success of the establishment of the internal market was the introduction of qualified majority voting for the adoption of harmonizing legislation by the Single European Act.[47] However, while important, the decision making rules laid down in Title V TEU ought to be placed in their proper political and international context. As CFSP

---

[46] TEU preamble.   [47] Art 114 TFEU.

activities are carried out in the sphere of high politics, law is only one of the factors that determine policy—and quite often it is not even the most important factor. There is an inherent limit to what procedural rules may contribute: they may facilitate the adoption of efficient action but they cannot substitute for substantive policies in areas at the core of national sovereignty, where it is notoriously difficult to attract broad agreement.

Finally, the extension of the jurisdiction of the Court of Justice under Article 24(1) subparagraph (2) TEU by no means changes fundamentally the main premise of the role of the Court of Justice in the CFSP. For instance, the delimitation between the pillars, in the pre-Lisbon constitutional constellation, has always been part of the Court's jurisdiction.[48]

2. Institutional Structure: High Representative and EEAS

Even when its constitutional distinctiveness was more pronounced and illustrated by the pillar structure of the EU, the CFSP was carried out by the institutions that were responsible for all the other activities of the Union. Articulated in the pre-Lisbon era with reference to 'a single institutional framework',[49] this is still the case, albeit with the variations necessary to reflect the underpinning sensitivity of the scope of the CFSP. Therefore, the role of the European Council is pronounced[50] and, in contrast with the considerable powers in external relations with which it has been endowed by the Lisbon Treaty,[51] the European Parliament is marginalized.[52]

The main institutional feature of the CFSP, introduced at Lisbon, is the post of the High Representative of the Union for Foreign Affairs and Security Policy. This is, in all but name, the post of the Foreign Affairs Minister established under the ill-fated Constitutional Treaty. The choice of this rather inelegant name reflects the concern of the Member States to avoid any connotation of aspiration to statehood. The first High Representative was Baroness Catherine Ashton, who was appointed in November 2009. In August 2014, the then Italian Foreign Affairs Minister Federica Mogherini was appointed by the European Council as the Union's second High Representative.

Appointed by the European Council by a qualified majority,[53] the High Representative occupies a unique position in the Union's institutional constellation: on the one hand, she is a Vice President of the European Commission,[54] and, on the other hand, she presides over the Foreign Affairs Council.[55] The mandate of the High Representative reflects the dual institutional status of the post: she 'shall

---

[48] See Case C-170/96 *Commission v Council* [1998] ECR I-2763 and Case C-91/05 *Commission v Council* [2008] ECR I-3651.

[49] Ex Art 3 TEU.   [50] Art 26(1) TEU.   [51] See Arts 207 and 218 TFEU.

[52] Art 36 TEU.   [53] Art 18(1) TEU.   [54] Art 18(4) TEU.   [55] Art 18(3) TEU.

conduct the Union's common foreign and security policy[56] and will be responsible within the Commission for 'external relations and for coordinating other aspects of the Union's external action'.[57]

In essence, the introduction of the post of High Representative aims to achieve two main objectives. The first is external: it is to provide the Union's international role with a face, hence facilitating the contacts of the Union with its international partners, and ultimately raising its profile. The second objective is internal: it is about ensuring greater interdependence and coherence in external policy by bringing together the different threads that underpin the various strands of the Union's external policies.[58]

The brief is broad. The High Representative is involved in decision making, as she enjoys the right of initiative that she shares with the Member States.[59] She also enjoys executive powers, as she is entrusted with the implementation of the CFSP, carrying out the policy as mandated by the Council, whose decisions, along with those of the European Council, she is responsible for implementing by relying on national and Union resources.[60] The High Representative is also responsible for the international representation of the Union, carrying out political dialogue with third countries and international organizations on the Union's behalf, and expressing the Union's position in international organizations and at international conferences.[61] Crucially, the High Representative, along with the Council, is responsible for ensuring 'the unity, consistency, and effectiveness of action by the Union'.[62]

The introduction of the post of High Representative at Lisbon was heralded as an innovation central to the effectiveness of EU foreign policy. Expectations were high. For instance, in August 2008, the then French President Nicolas Sarkozy argued during the Russia–Georgia war that, had the Lisbon Treaty been in force, the Union would have had the institutions and tools to act decisively and exert its influence.[63]

However, in legal terms, while construing the High Representative's mandate broadly, there is very little in Title V TEU about its scope. The actual portfolio is determined in practice in the light of various considerations, not least practical (the portfolio of the High Representative must be manageable by one holder of the post) and political (it must reflect the understanding of the President of the Commission and take into account the interests of the Member States). The latter

---

[56] Art 18(2) TEU.

[57] Art 18(4) TEU.

[58] On coherence on the basis of the Lisbon arrangements, see M. Cremona, 'Coherence in EU Foreign Relations Law' and S. Duke, 'Consistency, Coherence and EU External Action: The Path to Lisbon and Beyond' in P. Koutrakos, *European Foreign Policy: Legal and Political Perspectives* (2011) 55 and 15 respectively.

[59] Art 30(1) TEU. This is a right which he shares with any Member State. This right is also set out in the context of CSDP (Art 42(4) TEU).

[60] Art 26(3) TEU.   [61] Art 27(2) TEU.   [62] Art 26(2) subpara (2) TEU.

[63] *Le Figaro*, 18 August 2008.

factors are in themselves subject to continuous redefinition, as they reflect shifts in political power in both the EU institutions and the Member States.

As for the institutional affiliations of the High Representative, their legal implications are not without problems. The issue of international agreements is a case in point. This is an instrument on which the Union has relied considerably in the CFSP area generally and in the CSDP in particular.[64] Article 218(3) TFEU provides that the High Representative, rather than the Commission, would recommend that the Council authorize the opening of negotiations on international agreements in areas where the subject matter of the agreements relates exclusively or principally to the CFSP. However, this new provision of the Lisbon Treaty by no means makes it easier to determine whether an agreement is principally about the CFSP, or whether it is about other aspects of the Union's external action, albeit with peripheral CFSP implications. In fact, the very question of the delimitation between the CFSP and other external policies has given rise to considerable inter-institutional disputes.[65] It is regrettable (though predictable given the sensitivity of the issue in inter-governmental negotiations) that a post intended to bring clarity and coherence to the EU's external policies should be defined in such unclear terms as to feed further the inter-institutional tensions which have marred these policies.

Against this somewhat vague framework set out by primary law, any assessment of the contribution of the post of High Representative to the effectiveness and coherence of EU foreign policy ought to take into account two factors. The first is the ability and willingness of the post holder to delineate her role in the area of foreign policy. The second is the extraordinary complexity in which the function of this post is shrouded, and the often diverging interests of Member States in the conduct of foreign policy.[66]

The High Representative is assisted by the European External Action Service (EEAS), the establishment of which was viewed at the time as 'one of the most significant changes introduced by the Treaty of Lisbon'.[67] Aiming to work in cooperation with the diplomatic services of the Member States, the EEAS consists of Commission

---

[64] See Koutrakos, *The EU Common Security and Defence Policy* (2013) Ch 7 and D. Thym, 'Piracy and Transfer Agreements Concluded by the EU' in P. Koutrakos and A. Skordas (eds), *The Law and Practice of Piracy at Sea: EU and International Perspectives* (2014) 167.

[65] See Case C-91/05 *Commission v Council (re: ECOWAS)* [2008] ECR I-3651, and Case C-403/05 *Parliament v Commission (re: Philippines borders)* [2007] ECR I-19045. See Koutrakos (n 64) 229ff, and C. Hillion and R.A. Wessel, 'Competence Distribution in EU External Relations after *ECOWAS*' (2009) 46 *Common Market Law Review* 551. See also Case C-658/11 *European Parliament v Council* ECLI:EU:C:2014:2025 about the EU-Mauritius transfer agreement (where its adoption under CFSP rules was not disputed) and Case C-263/14 *European Parliament v Council* (pending) where the legality of the adoption of the EU-Tanzania transfer agreement under CFSP rules is challenged.

[66] See A. Menon, *Europe: The State of the Union* (2008) 195 where he wonders: 'who really believes that particularly the larger member states would call this individual prior to dealing with Washington or Beijing?'

[67] Council Conclusions of 26 April 2010 (8967/10) 8.

and Council officials, as well as diplomats seconded from the Member States.[68] The introduction of the EEAS was not uncontroversial—in the UK, for instance, the then Conservative Shadow Foreign Secretary William Hague (later Foreign Secretary) saw it as yet another illustration of 'a power grab by the EU'.[69] In order to dispel such scepticism, the establishment of the EEAS was mentioned in Declaration 13 on the CFSP as one of the developments that 'do not affect the responsibilities of the Member States, as they currently exist, for the formulation and conduct of their foreign policy nor of their national representation in third countries and international organisations'.

However, not for the first time, the Lisbon Treaty was silent on the specifics about the Service's function: the distribution of posts among the Council, the Commission and the Member States, the scope of the policies it oversees, the definition of the lines of authority between the Union institutions involved, and its precise role in the conduct of the Union's foreign affairs were all left for subsequent resolution among the Member States and the institutions.

Against this blank canvas, the process of the organization and management of the EEAS provided the playground for the kind of inter-institutional disputes that its establishment had purported to address. The Commission was concerned to maintain its control over development cooperation and the various financing instruments which it covers,[70] and the Parliament was keen to exercise control over the functioning of the Service. The outcome of this process is Council Decision 2010/427/EU establishing the organization and functioning of EEAS.[71] It seeks to strike a balance between interacting institutions' competing claims to influence by setting out complex arrangements couched in vague language. Furthermore, the High Representative adopted a Declaration on political accountability in which she sets out the practicalities of her interactions with the Parliament.[72]

The benefits from the EEAS may be both tangible (to facilitate the gathering of information, streamline the conduct of different external activities, enhance coordination between both the EU services and national administrations and increase coherence between the relevant policies[73]) and intangible (to foster a culture of cooperation between officials from Member States and the EU institutions, and establish a framework within which a common language will be gradually developed and shared). The effective functioning of the Service is a process that is bound to take time and constant adjustment.[74] However, the legal and policy issues

---

[68] Art 27(3) TEU.   [69] *The Daily Telegraph*, 3 May 2008.

[70] See H. Merket, 'The European External Action Service and the Nexus between CFSP/CFSP and Development Cooperation' (2012) 17 *European Foreign Affairs Review* 625.

[71] [2010] OJ L201/30.   [72] [2010] OJ C210/1 and [2010] OJ C217/12.

[73] See S. Duke, 'The European External Action Service: Antidote against Incoherence?' (2012) 17 *European Foreign Affairs Review* 45 and B Van Vooren, 'A Legal-institutional Perspective on the European External Action Service' (2011) 48 *Common Market Law Review* 475.

[74] See S. Blockmans, *The European External Action Service One Year On: First Signs of Strengths and Weaknesses*, CLEER Working Papers 2012/12, 37.

that its functioning raises within the multi-layered system of foreign affairs set out in the Union's primary rules are formidable.[75]

Following the first two years of its operation, and in accordance with Council Decision 2010/470/EU,[76] Baroness Ashton carried out a review of the Service. In July 2013, she made a number of short- and medium-term recommendations, some of which are a matter of administrative practice while others require a broader amendment of existing legal rules.[77]

V. COMMON SECURITY
AND DEFENCE POLICY

Security and defence are policies that are associated with the core of national sovereignty and linked to the most traditional and fundamental function of states. It is, therefore, somewhat ironic that the very genesis of European integration should lie in a failed attempt by European countries to establish supranational structures in this area. The European Defence Community Treaty was signed by West Germany, France, Italy, and the Benelux countries in 1952, only to be voted down by the French Parliament in 1954. Since then, security and defence policy issues have been addressed by the Member States cautiously, first within EPC and then within the CFSP framework.

Following a joint British–French initiative in St Malo in 1998, security and defence became an area on which the Member States focused with renewed energy. Presidency Reports were drafted, Conclusions on security and defence were adopted by the European Council on many occasions, and the ultimate goal for the policy was defined in very ambitious terms in 1999, aiming to enable the Union to 'deploy rapidly and then sustain forces . . . in operations of up to corps level (up to 15 brigades or 50,000–60,000 persons)'.[78] That this goal has not been achieved has not prevented the Union institutions from designing their strategic approach

---

[75] For a negative assessment, see A.E. Juncos and K. Pomorska, 'Manufacturing Esprit de Corps: The Case of the European External Action Service' (2014) 52 *Journal of Common Market Studies* 302.

[76] Art 13(3) of Council Decision 2010/428/EU.

[77] See EEAS Review, July 2013 http://eeas.europa.eu/library/publications/2013/3/2013_eeas_review_en.pdf. See also S. Blockmans and C. Hillion (eds), *EEAS 2.0* (2013) (http://www.sieps.se/sites/default/files/EEAS%202%200%20.pdf) and S. Duke, 'Reflections on the EEAS Review' (2014) 19 *European Foreign Affairs Review* 23.

[78] Helsinki European Council (10–11 December 1999), Presidency Conclusions, Annex: Progress Report on Strengthening the Common European Policy on Security and Defence.

to security and defence. The European Security Strategy was adopted in 2003. It defined the security challenges facing the Union and articulated the role of the Union in grand, if vague, language: 'Europe should be ready to share in the responsibility for global security and in building a better world.'[79]

The European Security and Defence Policy was mentioned in primary law in the context of the CFSP but in a rather cursory manner. Following the entry into force of the Lisbon Treaty, this policy appears to have become more prominent: not only has its name been changed to suggest a tighter and more integrated policy (Common Security and Defence Policy, CSDP), but its rules and procedures are also set out in a separate section in the TEU (Section 2 of Chapter 2 in Title V).

The CSDP is about providing the Union 'with an operational capacity drawing on civilian and military assets' which may be used 'on missions outside the Union for peace-keeping, conflict prevention and strengthening international security in accordance with the principles of the United Nations'.[80] It is not about the Union's defence, even though, in legal terms, it might develop in this direction in the future.[81]

The Treaty shows deference to the security and defence policies of the Member States: alluding to the neutral countries, it states that the CSDP 'shall not prejudice the specific character of the security and defence policy of certain Member States',[82] it also makes it clear that it 'shall respect the obligations of certain Member States, which see their common defence realised in [NATO]'.[83]

Article 43(1) TEU provides a list of CSDP activities including:

- joint disarmament operations;
- humanitarian and rescue tasks;
- military advice and assistance tasks;
- conflict prevention and peace-keeping tasks;
- tasks of combat forces in crisis management, including peace-making and post-conflict stabilization.

All the above tasks may contribute to the fight against terrorism, including by supporting third countries in combating terrorism in their territories.[84]

Decisions in this area are adopted by the Council unanimously—it is recalled that the exceptions to this principle do not apply to decisions with security and defence implications.[85]

---

[79] *A Secure Europe in a Better World: European Security Strategy* (Brussels, 12 December 2003) 1. See also *Providing Security in a Changing World: Report on the Implementation of the European Security Strategy* (Brussels, 11 December 2008).

[80] Art 42(1) TEU.

[81] Art 42(2) TEU provides that the 'common security and defence policy shall include the progressive framing of a common Union defence policy. This will lead to a common defence, when the European Council, acting unanimously, so decides'.

[82] Art 42(2) TEU.   [83] Art 42(2) TEU.   [84] Art 43(1) TEU.   [85] Art 31(4) TEU.

1. Legal Framework

The CSDP is 'an integral part of the common foreign and security policy',[86] and therefore the general duty of Member States under Article 24(3) TEU applies here too. There are also more specific duties which, reflecting the increasing significance of this policy, were articulated at Lisbon for the first time.

The first duty is about capabilities. Article 42(3) TEU requires that Member States 'make civilian and military capabilities available to the Union for the implementation of the common security and defence policy, to contribute to the objectives defined by the Council'. This is coupled with the duty of Member States to 'undertake progressively to improve their military capabilities'.[87] These provisions appear to enhance the ability of the Union to carry out CSDP missions. Nevertheless, their function is bound to be rhetorical at best. The choices of Member States about their capabilities are determined on the basis of multifarious factors extraneous to the legal provisions set out in the Treaty, including, but by no means confined to, internal political developments, economic exigencies, the geopolitical environment, and the security approach of actors such as the USA. The premise that a primary law provision would marginalize such factors and determine the political assessment of national authorities ignores the realities of security and defence policy. In fact, the Union's military missions have been marred by the unwillingness of the Member States to commit personnel and resources, a problem which the provisions of Article 42(3) TEU have not solved.

The second specific duty is laid down in a mutual assistance clause in Article 42(7) TEU, which includes the following provision: 'If a Member State is the victim of armed aggression on its territory, the other Member States shall have towards it an obligation of aid and assistance by all the means in their power, in accordance with Article 51 of the United Nations Charter.' The existence of this clause is significant as it suggests that the CSDP is not only about missions around the world, but it is also relevant to the security of each Member State.

However, compliance with this clause cannot but depend on the subjective assessment of a Member State as to how best it may assist a State which is a victim of armed aggression on its territory. Such assessment is bound to be subject to inherently indeterminate considerations of a political and economic nature which do not lend themselves to a rigorous mechanism of verification or control. In any case, the means of assistance, while construed broadly in Article 42(7) TEU, are entirely to be determined by the political authorities of each Member State. After all, the EU is not a military alliance—and the mutual assistance clause cannot make it become one.[88]

---

[86] Art 42(1) TEU.   [87] Art 42(3) subpara (2) TEU.
[88] See J.-C. Piris, *The Lisbon Treaty* (2010) 275.

The legal duties in the CSDP area are articulated against an institutional framework characterized by considerable density and complexity. The roles of the High Representative and the EEAS were outlined above. These operate alongside a number of administrative bodies. The Political and Security Committee consists of senior diplomats from the Member States and is responsible for monitoring the international situation, and exercising political control and strategic direction of crisis management operations.[89] The Military Committee is composed of the Chiefs of Defence of the Member States and provides the Political and Security Committee with advice on military matters.[90] The Military Staff is composed of military experts seconded to the Council by the Member States, and carries out early warning situation assessment and strategic planning for CSDP tasks, including the identification of European national and multinational forces.[91]

To the above, the Lisbon Treaty adds the European Defence Agency (EDA), an inter-governmental body tasked with fostering cooperation between Member States and rationalization of their defence industries.[92] Whilst provided for in the Lisbon Treaty, the EDA was in fact established in 2004.[93]

So far the analysis of the CSDP rules suggests that they are set out in a framework which is legally tighter than in the past and which is also considerably process-oriented. This is confirmed by another innovation introduced at Lisbon, that is, the provision for flexibility in the conduct of the Union's military operations and civilian missions. This may take different forms. The first is laid down in the 'willing and able' clause pursuant to which the Union may entrust the execution of a task to a group of countries 'in order to protect the Union's values and serve its interests'.[94] This is agreed upon by the Council unanimously, provided that the Member States involved are willing to implement the task in question and have the necessary capabilities. The second form of flexibility is 'permanent structured cooperation' and involves groups of Member States that meet certain criteria and have made certain substantive commitments.[95] These are set out in a Protocol annexed to the Treaty and are about military capabilities.

Enhanced cooperation in the area of the internal market has been a feature of the Union legal order for some time (even though the relevant arrangements have only been relied upon very sparingly). The Lisbon Treaty for the first time

---

[89] Art 38 TEU and Council Decision 2001/78/CFSP [2001] OJ L27/1. Under the Political Security Committee, the Civilian Planning and Conduct Capability plans and carries out the civilian missions of the Union. In addition, and within the EEAS structure, the Crisis Management and Planning Directorate is responsible for ensuring the coherence of the military operations and civilian missions with the other strands of the Union's external action.

[90] Council Decision 2001/79/CFSP [2001] OJ L27/4.

[91] Council Decision 2001/80/CFSP [2001] OJ L27/7, amended by Council Decision 2005/395/CFSP [2005] OJ L132/1.

[92] Art 45 TEU.   [93] Joint Action 2004/551/CFSP [2004] OJ L245/17.

[94] Arts 42(5) and 44 TEU.   [95] Arts 42(6) and 46 TEU.

extended this possibility to the area of security and defence policy. From a pragmatic point of view, this is sensible, given that the defence capabilities of Member States differ widely, and only in the case of a handful are they robust enough to carry out their internal security function and be deployed in different areas in the context of multinational operations simultaneously. Therefore, the mechanisms set out in the Treaty may enhance the Union's ability to assert its identity on the international scene.

However, the criteria set out in the Treaty about permanent structured cooperation are extremely vague. In effect, it is entirely up to the Member States to choose what these mean and how to apply them in a given case. This vagueness highlights a theme which emerges in most EU legal arrangements that govern security and defence: they appear merely to set out the broad parameters within which the Member States and the Union's institutional actors may determine how to proceed, at what pace and in which direction. This is borne out entirely by the extremely limited progress in collaboration between Member States in the area of armaments.[96]

In any case, flexibility in this area has always prevailed as a matter of practice. For instance, not all Member States participate in all operations. Another case in point is the existence of battlegroups. This is an initiative focused on the swift deployment of 'effective, credible and coherent' rapid reaction units. Declared operational in 2007, battlegroups consist of 1500 troops each which should be deployable at 15 days' notice and sustainable for at least 30 days. Each battle group is led by a Member State which acts as the lead nation and provides the assets either on its own or with the contribution of other states. No primary rules were required for the establishment of such forces—and the absence of a detailed procedural framework for them by no means prevented their establishment (and neither can it explain the fact that no battlegroup has yet been deployed as a matter of practice).

Therefore, while increased legalization appears to be the pattern governing the CSDP framework, the relevance of the applicable rules and procedures is by no means apparent. After all, in the area of security and defence, a great deal hinges on practical considerations: the defence capabilities of Member States, their willingness to deploy them, their ability to pay for them, the political capital which such choices would entail for the government of the day. There is very little that heavily proceduralized legal mechanisms may do to address them. This is also borne out by the Member States' record in armaments collaboration and the decidedly modest record of the EDA.[97] Viewed from this angle, a paradox emerges: the legal framework governing the policy becomes denser and tighter, while its impact remains negligible in practical terms.

---

[96] There was some discussion amongst Member States in the latter part of 2010, and a German–Swedish proposal for closer military cooperation (http://www.robert-schuman.eu/doc/actualites/papsweallpoolsharingnot.pdf) was also discussed but to no apparent effect.

[97] See Koutrakos (n 64) Ch 9.

2. CSDP Practice

In the context of the CSDP, the Union has acted over the years in Europe, Asia, and Africa. Its initiatives may be divided into the following categories.

First, the EU has carried out the following military operations:

- in the Former Yugoslav Republic of Macedonia (EUFOR Concordia) in 2003;[98]
- in the Democratic Republic of Congo (Operation Artemis) in 2003[99] and then in 2006 (EUFOR RD Congo);[100]
- in Bosnia and Herzegovina (EUFOR ALTHEA) since 2004;[101]
- in Darfur in Western Sudan (EU Support to AMIS Action) (2005–2007);[102]
- in Tchad and the Central African Republic (EUFOR Tchad/RCA) (2008–2009)[103] and, more recently, in the Central African Republic (EUFOR RCA) since 2014;[104]
- off the coast of Somalia (EUNAVFOR Somalia—Operation Atalanta) since 2008;[105]
- in Somalia (EUTM Somalia) (2010–2012);[106]
- in Libya (EUFOR Libya) (decided in 2011 but never deployed);[107]
- in Mali (EUTM Mali) since 2013.[108]

Second, the Union has carried out a number of civilian missions. These include police missions:

- in Bosnia and Herzegovina (EUPM BiH) (2003–2012);[109]
- in FYROM (EUPOL Proxima) (2003–2005)[110] and EUPAT FYROM (2005–2006);[111]

---

[98] Joint Actions 2003/202/CFSP [2003] OJ L76/43 and 2003/563/CFSP [2003] OJ L190/20.
[99] Joint Action 2003/423/CFSP [2003] OJ L143/50.
[100] Joint Action 2006/319/CFSP [2003] OJ L116/98.
[101] Joint Action 2004/570/CFSP [2004] OJ L252/10.
[102] Joint Actions 2005/557/CFSP [2005] OJ L188/46, 2007/245/CFSP [2007] OJ L106/65 and 2007/887/CFSP]2007] OJ L346/28.
[103] Joint Actions 2007/677/CFSP [2007] OJ L279/21, 2008/101/CFSP [2008] OJ L34/39, and 2009/795/CFSP [2009] OJ L283/61.
[104] Council Decision 2014/73/CFSP [2014] OJ L40/59.
[105] Joint Action 2008/851/CFSP [2008] OJ L301/33, Council Decision 2010/766/CFSP [2010] OJ L327/49 2012/174/CFSP.
[106] Council Decision 2010/96/CFSP [2010] OJ L44/16.
Council Decision 2010/197/CFSP [2010] OJ L87/33, Council Decision 2011/484/CFSP [2011] OJ L198/37.
[107] Council Decision 2011/210/CFSP [2011] OJ L89/17, Council Decision 2011/764/CFSP [2011] OJ L314/35.
[108] Council Decision 2013/34/CFSP [2013] OJ L14/19, Council Decision 2013/87/CFSP [2013] OJ L46/27, Council Decision 2013/729/CFSP [2013] OJ L332/18.
[109] Joint Action 2002/210/CFSP [2002] OJ L70/1, amended a number of times, finally by Council Decision 2010/755/CFSP [2010] OJ L320/10.
[110] Joint Actions 2003/681/CFSP [2003] OJ L249/66, 2004/87/CFSP [2004] OJ L21/31, and 2004/789/CFSP [2004] OJ L348/40.
[111] Council Joint Action 2005/826/CFSP [2005] OJ L307/61.

- in Democratic Republic of Congo (EUPOL Kinshasa) (2005–2007),[112] and then EUPOL RD Congo since 2007;[113]
- in the Palestinian territories (EUPOL COPPS) since 2006;[114]
- in Afghanistan (EUPOL AFGHANISTAN) since 2007.[115]

Security sector reform missions:

- in Democratic Republic of Congo (EUSEC RD CONGO) since 2005;[116]
- in Guinea-Bissau (EU SSR GUINEA_BISSAU) (2008–2010).[117]

Monitoring missions:

- in Aceh, Indonesia (AMM) (2005–2006);[118]
- in Georgia (EUMM CEORGIA) since 2008;[119]
- in Libya (EUBAM Libya) since 2013.[120]

Rule of law missions:

- in Georgia (EUJUST THEMIS) (2004–2005);[121]
- in Iraq (EUJUST LEX) (2005–2013);[122]
- in Kosovo (EULEX KOSOVO) since 2008.[123]

There has also been a border mission in the Rafah Crossing Point (EUBAM RAFAH) since 2005.[124]

---

[112] Joint Action 2004/847/CFSP [2004] OJ L367/30, amended a number of times, finally by Joint Action 2006/868/CFSP [2006] OJ L335/50.

[113] Joint Action 2007/405/CFSP [2007] OJ L151/46, amended a number of times, more recently by Council Decision 2012/514/CFSP [2012] OJ L257/16.

[114] Joint Action 2005/797/CFSP [2005] OJ L300/65 amended a number of times, more recently by Council Dec. 2013/354/CFSP L185/12.

[115] Joint Action 2007/369/CFSP [2007] OJ L139/33, amended more recently by Council Decision 2012/391/CFSP [2012] OJ L187/47.

[116] Council Joint Action 2005/355/CFSP [2005] OJ L112/20, amended a number of times, more recently by Council Decision 2013/468/CFSP L252/29.

[117] Council Joint Action 2008/112/CFSP [2008] OJ L40/11, amended a number of times, more recently by Council Decision 2010/298/CFSP [2010] OJ L127/16.

[118] Council Joint Action 2005/643/CFSP [2005] OJ L234/13, amended a number of times, finally by Council Joint Action 2006/607/CFSP [2006] OJ L246/16.

[119] Joint Action 2008/760/CFSP [2008] OJ L259/16 amended a number of times, more recently by Council Decision 2013/446/CFSP [2013] OJ L240/21.

[120] Council Decision 2013/233/CFSP [2013] OJ L138/15.

[121] Joint Action 2004/523/CFSP [2003] OJ L228/21, amended by Joint Action 2004/638/CFSP [2004] OJ L291/7.

[122] Joint Action 2006/413/CFSP [2006] OJ L163/17, amended a number of times, finally by Decision 2012/372/CFSP [2012] OJ L179/22.

[123] Joint Action 2008/124/CFSP [2008] OJ 42/92 amended a number of times, more recently by Council Decision 2012/291/CFSP [2012] OJ L146/46.

[124] Council Joint Action 2005/889/CFSP [2005] OJ L327/28, amended a number of times, more recently by Council Decision 2013/355/CFSP [2013] OJ L185/16.

Finally, the EU has carried out other missions:

- in South Sudan (EUNAVSEC—South Sudan) since 2012;[125]
- in Niger (EUCAP Sahel Niger) since 2012;[126]
- in the Horn of Africa (EUCAP NESTOR) since 2012.[127]

A detailed analysis of the CSDP practice is beyond the scope of this contribution.[128] Suffice it to make four points. First, whilst the range and territorial scope of the Union's activities is broad, the overall size of the operations and missions is rather small. Writing in 2008, Nick Witney, the first Chief Executive of the European Defence Agency, estimated that 'the total number of troops deployed today . . . constitutes less than one third of one percent of European military manpower'.[129] Things have not changed since.

Second, the mandate of the operations and missions is narrow and the terrain in which they are deployed largely safe. The hard security questions have already been addressed prior to EU deployment by either NATO or the United Nations. The EU operations have a limited and clearly defined task to perform which, whilst worthwhile and useful in itself, constitutes only a small part of a wide and complex problem.

Third, a characteristic which all military operations share is the unwillingness of the Member States to provide the troops necessary for deployment. It is by no means uncommon for the number of troops actually deployed to be lower than that originally envisaged by the EU bodies as necessary and, hence to undermine the conduct of the operation (in Operation Artemis, for instance, there was no reserve force even though the Political and Security Committee had deemed one necessary). In relation to the capabilities upon which the operations rely on the ground, there have been consistent shortfalls and problems. It is noteworthy, for instance, that in its military operation in Tchad, the EU relied on Russian helicopters and Ukrainian aircraft.

Fourth, considerable time and energy is spent in coordination and turf wars between the personnel deployed in CSDP operations and missions and other EU actors both on the ground and in Brussels. This is partly due to the interdependence between security and defence policy and other external policies, in particular development policy.

The CSDP record so far appears somewhat lacking in ambition. This, in itself, may not be necessarily problematic. After all, the problems which the EU seeks to address have been complex, long-standing and serious, and no international actor

---

[125] Council Decision 2012/312/CFSP [2012] OJ L158/17.
[126] Council Decision 2012/392/CFSP [2012] OJ L187/48.
[127] Council Decision 2012/389/CFSP [2012] OJ L187/40.
[128] See Koutrakos (n 64) Chs 5–8.
[129] Nick Witney, *Re-energising Europe's Security and Defence Policy* (2008) 7.

on its own has managed to solve them. However, the lack of ambition is striking in the light of the very considerable ambition which oozes from every statement made by EU officials in the area and which has shaped the drafting of the relevant primary rules. It is also striking in the light of the density of the evolving legal framework that governs the CSDP.

The CSDP record ought to be assessed against the divergent views of Member States about the reach of the CSDP. This becomes apparent not only from the lack of progress on the practical underpinnings of defence, but also by what Member States do beyond the Union framework. A case in point is Libya. In March 2011, a coalition of various states initiated a military operation against Libya under the authorization of United Nations Security Council Resolution (2011) 1973. This operation consisted of the enforcement of a no-fly zone and a naval blockade and led, controversially but inevitably, to strikes against forces remaining loyal to Gaddafi. The operation was not carried out by the EU, but by a number of individual states, most of which were European, led by the UK and France, whilst the USA was for political reasons content to play second fiddle. It is worth noting that Germany abstained at the UN Security Council vote on SC Resolution 1973, in the company of China and Russia. It is also interesting that, in relation to this operation, British Prime Minister David Cameron, US President Barack Obama, and French President Nicolas Sarkozy wrote an article in *The Times*[130] in which there was no reference to the Union at all.

Quite apart from the serious problem facing Libya following the operation, this episode is interesting for various reasons. First, it suggests differing political assessments amongst Member States of what may be done by the EU, the CSDP legal framework notwithstanding. Second, it highlights the considerable capabilities shortfalls even of the most serious defence actors amongst the Member States. The UK, for instance, contributed about a dozen fighter aircraft, a couple of frigates, and a submarine, and yet its military chiefs suggested that no more was possible and that they would have had serious problems had the operation lasted into the autumn. France faced similar problems.[131] Even though the operation was not US-led, the USA provided 70 per cent of all air support sorties. Third, these shortfalls did not go unnoticed. In a speech he gave in June 2011, outgoing US Defense Secretary Gates highlighted the perilous state of European military capabilities with brutal honesty.[132] All in all, this episode suggests clearly that the relevance of the rules and procedures set out in Title V TEU depend entirely on the political, economic, and practical factors on the basis of which Member States shape their security and defence policy.

---

[130] 15 April 2011, 25.   [131] *The Financial Times*, 25 March 2011, 13.

[132] Speech delivered on 10 June: http://blogs.wsj.com/washwire/2011/06/10/transcript-of-defense-secretary-gatess-speech-on-natos-future/.

VI. Conclusion

Now that the EU is positively middle-aged, its external relations are considered an integral part of its identity. Their conduct features prominently in primary law, there is a considerable body of practice across a wide range of policy areas, and the EU's international posture occupies a central place in public debate about the role and direction of the Union. This chapter highlighted the legal and policy issues which are raised by the efforts of the Union to be a global actor in areas as diverse as trade, foreign and security policy, and defence.

The legal framework examined in this chapter was designed at a time when the Union was ambitious about its external role, which it articulated in bold terms. Yet it is now applied at a time of financial crisis, the political repercussions of which have placed the EU in the midst of an existential crisis. According to an editorial in the *Financial Times*, 'the EU's effectiveness as an international actor has been battered by the Eurozone crisis, its political will sapped by economic austerity and by growing public disaffection with the entire European project'.[133]

EU decision makers may ignore the implications of the internal difficulties of the EU for its international role at their peril. The Union's external policies developed organically from the success of its internal market, which they were designed to complement and enhance. These policies emerged in the context of a prosperous, growing, and vibrant Union. Therefore the negotiating position of the Union in the area of economic relations is affected directly by the manner in which the EU institutions and the Member States tackle the sovereign debt crisis and the rigour with which they choose to enforce and expand the internal market.

Two further considerations are also central to the effectiveness of the ways in which the Union relates to the rest of the world. First, in the area of security and defence, the impact of legal rules is in direct correlation to the will of the Member States to commit the political capital, energy, and resources to addressing the problems of military capabilities as a matter of urgency. The financial crisis has made Member States slash their defence budgets farther, focus all their energies on averting financial catastrophe, and become less interested in security and defence operations and missions. It also makes the economic case for joint initiatives on addressing the problems of capabilities all the more compelling. Consequently, the economic rationale could give rise to developments that political considerations had overlooked.

The second consideration is about the inherent limits of legal rules and procedures in the area of security and defence policy. Legal rules in themselves do not make for an effective security and defence policy. Otherwise we risk misunderstanding the peculiarities of security and defence, overestimating the function of

---

[133] *The Financial Times*, 23 February, 2014.

law, ignoring the complexities of the various challenges in the area, and overlooking the lessons that emerge from existing practice.[134]

BIBLIOGRAPHY

S. Blockmans and C. Hillion (eds), *EEAS 2.0* (2013) http://www.sieps.se/sites/default/files/EEAS%202%200%20.pdf

S. Blockmans, *The European External Action Service One Year On: First Signs of Strengths and Weaknesses*, CLEER Working Papers 2012/12 http://www.asser.nl/upload/documents/1272012_11147cleer2012-2web.pdf

C. Brown and M. Alcover-Llubia, 'The External Investment Policy of the European Union in the Light of the Entry into Force of the Treaty of Lisbon' (2010–2011) *Yearbook on International Investment Law and Policy* 145

M. Cremona, 'Coherence in EU Foreign Relations Law' in P. Koutrakos, *European Foreign Policy—Legal and Political Perspectives* (2011) 55

G. De Baere and P. Koutrakos, 'The Interactions between the European Court of Justice and the Legislature in the European Union's External Relations' in P. Syrpis (ed), *The Relationship between the Judiciary and the Legislature in the Internal Market* (2012) 243

E. Denza, *The Intergovernmental Pillars of the European Union* (2002)

A. Dimopoulos, *EU Foreign Investment Law* (2011)

S. Duke, 'Consistency, Coherence and EU External Action: The Path to Lisbon and Beyond' in P. Koutrakos, *European Foreign Policy: Legal and Political Perspectives* (2011)

S. Duke, 'The European External Action Service: Antidote against Incoherence?' (2012) *17 European Foreign Affairs Review* 45

S. Duke, 'Reflections on the EEAS Review' (2014) *19 European Foreign Affairs Review* 23

P. Eeckhout, *EU External Relations Law* (2nd ed, 2011)

C. Hillion and R.A. Wessel, 'Competence Distribution in EU External Relations after ECOWAS' (2009) *46 Common Market Law Review* 551

P. Koutrakos, *EU International Relations Law* (2nd ed, 2015)

P. Koutrakos, 'Legal Basis and Delimitation of Competence in EU External Relations' in M. Cremona and B. De Witte (eds), *EU Foreign Relations Law—Constitutional Fundamentals* (2008) 171

P. Koutrakos, *The EU Security and Defence Policy* (2013)

H. Merket, 'The European External Action Service and the Nexus between CFSP/CFSP and Development Cooperation' (2012) *17 European Foreign Affairs Review* 625

R. Passos, 'The European Union's External Relations a Year after Lisbon: A First Evaluation from the European Parliament' in P. Koutrakos (ed), *The European Union's External Relations a Year after Lisbon* (2011)

D. Thym, 'Piracy and Transfer Agreements concluded by the EU' in P. Koutrakos and A. Skordas (eds), *The Law and Practice of Piracy at Sea: EU and International Perspectives* (2014)

B. Van Vooren, 'A Legal-institutional Perspective on the European External Action Service' (2011) *48 Common Market Law Review* 475

---

[134] These ideas are explored in Koutrakos (n 64).

PART III

MAKING AND ADMINISTERING EU LAW

CHAPTER 12

....

THE DEMOCRATIC AMBIGUITY OF EU LAW MAKING AND ITS ENEMIES

....

DAMIAN CHALMERS

I. Democratic Ambiguity and the Democratic Dilemmas of EU Law Making

....

EU law making sits on the horns of an irresolvable dilemma. The question of its democratic calibre presents a choice between parameters that set out a false characterization of the Union and parameters that carry no democratic authority. Domestic parameters of democracy thus cannot be readily transferred to it because the Union is a different type of beast from the nation state. It would be difficult to imagine, for example, that most EU citizens would accept as a solution to the Union's democratic deficit a single Union Parliament based on universal suffrage, with all votes weighted equally, which would have a monopoly over Union law making.[1] To argue, however,

[1] For various reasons why the fit does not work see Ben Rosamond 'Open Political Science,

that EU law making should be judged by its own standard of democracy is to beg the riposte that this standard is simply not democracy as we know it.[2] And this riposte matters because any democracy must have resonance for its citizens. This dilemma is further compounded by a threshold issue caused by the co-presence of domestic democratic processes. Insofar as EU laws conflict with laws adopted through processes with stronger democratic credentials, it would be insufficient for EU law making to assert that it was democratic to secure its authority; it would have to show a quality of democracy not matched by the domestic process.

It is best to see Union law making, therefore, as enjoying democratic ambiguity. There is a Union commitment to democracy[3] and much of its settlement can only be explained by reference to that commitment. However, the meaning of this commitment can only ever be obscure. This ambiguity is destabilizing for those wishing a powerful post-national system as it suggests that its authority will always be questionable. However, democratic ambiguity bears exploring not only because it is the hallmark of the Union but also because it contains considerable potential. This lies, on the one hand, in its granting EU law making certain democracy-affirming qualities without which it would be unambiguously undemocratic. It lies, on the other, in its reminder that EU law making does not have the pedigree to supplant domestic democratic processes. Instead, its value lies in its bringing its democracy-affirming qualities to bear to complement these processes or to offer them where they cannot be supplied by domestic processes.

These qualities are most difficult to contest where they are immanent to the law making process itself as law making has democratic advantages over other forms of rule, whatever the polity. Law making can, first, mediate plurality more easily than other processes of government. Legislatures comprise, typically, more decision makers (ie MPs), and their membership is often more heterogeneous. Second, procedures for initiating, reviewing and adopting legislation allow for a detailed and unique form of reflection. Elements of the proposal can be withdrawn, added to, or amended in a transparent manner that does not take place elsewhere. Finally, the legislature enjoys a greater panorama over a wider array of interests, values, and possibilities than other processes. It is not confined, unlike courts, by the terms of the dispute or the boundaries of the legal text. Equally, unlike government

Methodological Nationalism and European Union Studies' (2008) 43 *Government and Opposition* 599; Stefano Bartolini, 'The Nature of the EU Legitimacy Crisis and Institutional Constraints: Defining the Conditions for Politicisation and Partisanship' in Olaf Cramme (ed), *Rescuing the European Project: EU Legitimacy, Governance and Security* (2009); Giandomenico Majone, 'Transaction-cost Efficiency and the Democratic Deficit' (2010) 17 *Journal of European Public Policy* 150.

[2] Thomas Zweifel, '. . . Who is without Sin Cast the First Stone: The EU's Democratic Deficit in Comparison' (2002) 9 *Journal of European Public Policy* 812; Myrto Tsakatika, 'Governance vs. Politics: The European Union's Constitutive 'Democratic Deficit'' (2007) 14 *Journal of European Public Policy* 867.

[3] Art 10(1) TEU.

agencies, it does not operate under a doctrine of delegated powers.[4] These qualities of accommodation of pluralism, reflection, and panoramic vista can also be better supplied by EU legislative processes than national legislative processes. By dint of their scale, they can accommodate a wider array of interests. The requirement for EU law making to show added value over national law and the number of different institutions involved both act as pressures for reflection in a way that do not have ready counterparts in most Member States. Finally, the integration process can be seen as a commitment to open up state vistas and continually to reconsider the horizons of problem solving and political community.

If these elements are insufficient to convince citizens fully of EU law making's democratic calibre, this insufficiency can amplify the potential of democratic ambiguity. It can lead to greater self-questioning by EU law makers as uncertainty about the democratic credentials of the laws enacted can increase concern about what more could have been done. It can also increase politicization as the weaker democratic authority of EU laws leads to their being challenged and debated more. This self-questioning and politicization can, in turn, stimulate the accommodation of pluralism, reflection, and panorama by fostering an anxiety that EU law making will be particularly exposed if it fails on these counts.

Attempts to resolve this ambiguity through proposing reforms that will some-how render EU law making unambiguously democratic have not only been for-lorn but have also neglected those structures which foster EU law making's democracy-affirming qualities. This chapter is concerned with detailing how this has taken place within the EU legislative process.

The presence of a democratic compass is central to a legislature's capacity to mediate pluralism, the first of the values mentioned above. This compass indicates when collective action should be taken and whether legislation rather than other forms of rule should be adopted as that collective action. The compass is weak in EU law making given the paradox that EU legislation is often adopted when sig-nificant numbers of groups are opposed to it whilst, other forms of EU measure are used excessively at its expense. There are parallel challenges with the EU legis-lature's capacity to secure effective review, the second quality mentioned. Review relies on a series of autonomous stages that allow for reflection, internal debate, and actors representing different interests to exercise voice. This is marred within EU law making by the problem of democratic multiplicity. Insufficient attention is given to the challenges of multiple points of review: be it arbitrage between these, capture of these, or the development of mutual mistrust so that review is replaced by unnecessary oppositionalism. Finally the wide panoramas of EU law makers are often curtailed by democratic fluidity. In the name of legislative efficiency, EU law making has increasingly become dominated by informal practices which

---

[4] On these qualities see Jeremy Waldron, 'The Dignity of Legislation' (1995) 54 *Maryland Law Review* 633, 654ff.

concentrate decision making in a limited number of actors, curtail discussion, and undermine the formal structures intended to secure a balance between policy vision and interest mediation.

II. The Neglected Democratic Compass of EU Law Making

The diversity of the EU legislative settlement is evidenced in the number of institutional actors involved, the internal diversity of these institutions, and the plurality of actors in the surrounding public sphere.

The three main Union legislative processes—the ordinary legislative, the consent and consultation procedures—involve three EU institutions: the Council, the Commission, and the European Parliament. Notwithstanding the significant differences between the procedures,[5] all institutions have significant powers within each of them. The weakest general power enjoyed by any is that of the European Parliament within the consultation procedure, where it only has the right to be consulted on a legislative proposal. However, even there, it submits high numbers of amendments to about 54 per cent of proposals and a considerable proportion, about 19 per cent, are accepted.[6] Each of these institutions represents different interests: national governments with the Council, the European citizen with the Parliament, and the wider public Union interest within the Commission.[7] The institutional settlement has, furthermore, pluralized beyond these three institutions. There is provision for widespread consultation of both the Committee of the Regions and the Economic and Social Committee. Since the Treaty of Lisbon, national Parliaments are tightly associated with the legislative process, both through being consulted by the Commission on any significant proposal[8] and through their power to review legislative proposals against the subsidiarity and proportionality principles.[9]

---

[5] The formal details of the procedures will not be set out in this chapter. These can be found at Damian Chalmers, Gareth Davies, and Giorgio Monti *European Union Law* (3rd ed, 2014) 117–128.

[6] Raya Kardasheva, 'The Power to Delay: The European Parliament's Influence in the Consultation Procedure' (2009) 47 *Journal of Common Market Studies* 385, 392–394.

[7] With regard to the Council and Parliament see Art 10(2) TEU. On the Commission see Art 17(1) TEU.

[8] Protocol on the role of national parliaments in the European Union, Art 1.

[9] Protocol on the application of the principles of subsidiarity and proportionality, Arts 6 and 7.

This diversity is amplified by significant pluralism within many of these institutional actors. The Council sits at the apex of an extensive system of over 150 Working Committees or preparatory bodies of national civil servants which agree positions or set out differences to be taken up within the Council.[10] The European Parliament is a large parliament, comprising 766 MEPs. It is also ideologically diverse. Within the 2009 to 2014 Parliament, there were seven groupings with the centre left, centre right, and greens all split into more than one grouping. In addition, there were 32 non-attached members, most of whom represented radical right parties.[11] Different chambers within national Parliaments, rather than simply national Parliaments qua institutions, are given the possibility to express their positions individually:[12] something taken up by all Member States other than Bulgaria.

EU law making is not merely marked by institutional pluralism but also by the scale of its public sphere. In March 2014, 6493 groups involved with EU policy making had registered with the European Transparency Register, the central register governing the activities of such groups. If groups representing trade or corporate interests accounted for about 62 per cent, the registration of 2481 representing other interests signifies a considerable non-corporate presence. There is also diversity within this non-corporate sphere: 1665 NGOs are represented, 471 think tanks, 36 religious communities and 307 public authorities.[13] If democracy is about bringing together communities of strangers to recognize their interdependence and consequent need to respect the standpoint of others in order to bring about mutual solutions then the Union is successful in this. This plurality has also led to high levels of contestation.[14] However, lobbyists are rarely able to secure influence by simply banging the drum for their narrow interest. Instead, they have to reach out to other actors to build coalitions which will be of sufficient value to secure influence with the EU institutions, often through the provision of expertise not otherwise possessed, a level of citizen support for the initiative and a sense that it will accepted by industry.[15]

The mediation of this pluralism is, finally, served well by the highly sequential structure of the EU law making process. There is no agora where legislation emerges from the tumult of a debate in which all institutional actors participate

[10] These are set out in Council of the European Union, *List of Council Preparatory* Bodies, Council Doc 5312/14. On these see Frank Häge, *Bureaucrats as Law-makers: Committee Decision-Making in the EU Council of Ministers*, (2013).

[11] On the spectrum of views see Gail McElroy and Ken Benoit, 'Policy Positioning in the European Parliament' (2012) 13 *European Union Politics* 150.

[12] http://www.europarl.europa.eu/meps/en/map.html.

[13] http://ec.europa.eu/transparencyregister/public/consultation/statistics.do?locale=en&action=prepareView.

[14] Heike Klüver, *Lobbying the European Union: Interest Groups, Lobbying Coalitions and Policy Change* (2013) 136–138.

[15] Heike Klüver, 'Lobbying as a Collective Enterprise: Winners and Losers of Policy Formulation in the European Union' (2013) 20 *Journal of European Public Policy* 59.

simultaneously with the most forceful winning the day. Instead, there is a series of steps: the pre-legislative step of the publication of Green Papers, White Papers, and impact assessment, the initial formal proposal, consideration by the national Parliaments, hearings by the European Parliament and consideration by the Committee of Permanent Representatives (COREPER), and then hearing within the Council.[16] Each of these steps grants the institutional actor in question a space for internal debate and contestation, and creates an opportunity for non-institutional actors best served by it to make their point to it. If this secures the autonomy of the different institutional actors, the process is also one where each new perspective elaborates on the previous one, reinforcing points where there is agreement whilst sharpening issues for contention by setting out points of amendment. Parties are incentivized to incorporate different perspectives because of difficulties in enforcement if laws are adopted against strong national opposition,[17] and by awareness that trampling over one party today might leave them similarly exposed on another issue in the future. A culture of decision making by consensus has thus emerged in the Council[18] as has a pattern of legislation taking longer to adopt with the increase in states acceding to the Union.[19]

One curiosity of such a pluralistic legislative process is the opposition to its scale and scope. In terms of the scale of EU law, at the end of 2012 there were 9576 Regulations and 1989 Directives in force.[20] Since the mid 1990s, between 40 and 60 Directives and 160 and 220 Regulations have been adopted per median year, with this having dropped to about 30 Directives and 75 to 100 Regulations per

---

[16] The number of times the matter is considered by the European Parliament and Council will vary according to the procedure, with these hearing the matter up to three times in the ordinary legislative procedure.

[17] On the relationship between opposition in the Council and poor application of EU law see Thomas König and Brooke Luetgert 'Troubles with Transposition? Explaining Trends in Member State Notification and the Delayed Transposition of EU Directives' (2009) 39 *British Journal of Political Science* 163; Bernard Steunenberg and Dimiter Toshkov, 'Comparing Transposition in the 27 Member States of the EU: The Impact of Discretion and Legal Fit' (2009) 16 *Journal of European Public Policy* 951.

[18] George Tsebelis, 'Bridging Qualified Majority and Unanimity Decision-making in the EU' (2013) 20 *Journal of European Public Policy* 1083. Since 2009, 65 per cent of measures subject to QMV have been adopted by consensus. This is lower than the figure for the previous five-year period of 82 per cent. This is largely a consequence of more aggressive voting by the United Kingdom. Votewatch Europe, *Agreeing to Disagree: The Voting Records of EU Member States in the Council since 2009* (2012) Figure 3. Mikko Mattila, 'Voting and Coalitions in the Council after Enlargement' in Daniel Naurin and Helen Wallace (eds), *Unveiling the Council of the European Union: Games Governments Play in Brussels* (2008).

[19] Edward Best and Paolo Settembri, 'Legislative Output after Enlargement: Similar Number, Shifting Nature' in Edward Best, Thomas Christiansen, Pierpaolo Settembri (eds), *The Institutions of the Enlarged European Union: Change and Continuity* (2008).

[20] European Commission, *30th Annual Report on the Monitoring the Application of EU Law 2012* COM (2013) 726, 2. For annual adoption levels see House of Commons Library, *How Much Legislation Comes from Europe?* (2010, Research Paper 10/62) 12. It is not clear in either case how much of this is legislation and how much implementing or delegated measures.

year since the coming into force of the Lisbon Treaty.[21] This is seen as too intrusive. Seventy-four per cent of Union citizens believe that the Union generates too much 'red tape',[22] and the Commission is committed to reviewing the entire legislative *acquis* for inconsistencies, burdens, gaps, and ineffective measures.[23] Concerns about the scope of Union legislation were conveyed most saliently by the subsidiarity review of the Dutch government of June 2013[24] and the speech of the British Prime Minister David Cameron pressing for renegotiation of the Treaties.[25] However, the most extensive constraints have been put in place by domestic constitutional courts. Certain fields of domestic policy are protected from significant encroachment by EU legislation.[26] Alongside this, in fields where it enjoys more open-ended competences, most notably with regard to measures adopted under Article 352 TFEU, the provision which allows laws to be adopted to realize Union objectives where there is no legislative competence, EU laws may only be adopted in some states when the national Parliament has also ratified the legislation.[27]

If pluralism were mediated effectively, these tensions would not exist. The failure lies in the Union having an insufficiently finely tuned democratic compass. This compass goes to how to marry the presence of plural interests with the possibility of collective action. Simple juxtaposition of the two is insufficient; they must be organized in such a way as to secure pluralism through the legislative process. There are two dimensions to this. First, the incorporation of plural views into the legislation must be allowed for. Secondly, it must protect plural interests from legislation. If the former goes to the distribution of benefits and burdens of collective

---

[21] On Directives see Dimiter Toshkov, 'Public Opinion and Policy Output in the European Union: A Lost Relationship' (2011) 12 *European Union Politics* 169, 177. On Directives and Regulations see Damian Chalmers and Mariana Chaves, 'EU Law-making and the State of European Democratic Agency' in Olaf Cramme and Sara Hobolt (eds), *Democratic Politics in a European Union under Stress* (2014).

[22] European Commission, *Regulatory Fitness and Performance (REFIT): Results and Next Steps*, COM (2013) 685, 1.

[23] European Commission (n 22) 3.

[24] Ministerie van Buiterlandse Zaken, 'Testing European Legislation for Subsidiarity and Proportionality—Dutch List of Points for Action', 21 June 2013, Recommendation 1 http://www.government.nl/documents-and-publications/notes/2013/06/21/testing-european-legislation-for-subsidiarity-and-proportionality-dutch-list-of-points-for-action.html.

[25] https://www.gov.uk/government/speeches/eu-speech-at-bloomberg.

[26] On national constitutional court case law on this see Damian Chalmers, 'European Restatements of Sovereignty' in Richard Rawlings, Peter Leyland, and Alison Young (eds), *Sovereignty and the Law* (2013) 186, 195–198.

[27] In Germany see most recently 2 BvR 1390/12 *ESM Treaty (Temporary Injunctions)*, judgment of 18 March 2014, paras 159–175 (German Constitutional Court). On the parliamentary arrangements put in place after the Treaty of Lisbon see Davor Jančić, 'Caveats from Karlsruhe and Berlin: Whither Democracy after Lisbon' (2009) 16 *Columbia Journal of European Law* 337, 371–380. In the United Kingdom, any use of Art 352 TFEU requires British parliamentary ratification except in limited circumstances, European Union Act 2011, section 8.

action, the latter goes to questioning the need for collective action or its scope and suggests that pluralism may, in certain circumstances, require no laws or that they do not apply to the activities of certain actors.

The structured sequential nature of EU law making outlined above secures the first of these dimensions, the incorporation of plural views. However, the other dimension, freedom from legislation, is largely neglected. In national settlements, citizens are protected from legislation by the presence of elections. These typically require manifestos to be presented that set out a limited range of proposals, aware that excessive law making may be poorly regarded by the electorate. Proposals are time-limited. They will only be enacted during that government and there is no sense that they can persist beyond it. Elections are also immediate, times when different groups can campaign both for new legislation and the repeal of existing legislation. Parties are sensitive to this, aware that a failure to show responsiveness may play badly with swing voters.

There are, of course, no such elections based on manifestos within a Union context. This allows proposals to remain on the books until there is a window of opportunity for success, provides no incentives for an economy of law making,[28] and creates no moment when EU decision makers must be responsive to stakeholders not directly involved with the law making process. This is not the only difference. To be repealed or amended, national legislation requires only a majority. EU law making, by contrast, requires a super-majority, most notably Qualified Majority Voting (QMV) or unanimity in the Council and the assent of the Commission. This has the effect of protecting incumbent legislation from repeal.[29]

The absence of elaborate political mechanisms to protect diverse groups from EU legislation has led to the central legal instrument, the subsidiarity principle, becoming overloaded. In areas which do not fall within its exclusive competence, that principle requires the Union to act only if the objectives of the proposed action cannot be sufficiently achieved by the Member States but can be better achieved at Union level.[30] Irrespective of the institutional mechanism deployed to protect it, subsidiarity does not address the concerns of the democratic compass directly, as it does not consider the balance between those that wish to be free from Union legislation and those that wish such legislation to be adopted or retained. In a multilevel system such as the Union's, this should be addressed by weighing up the difference between the value attached to the EU law by its supporters against the value of the laws or legal freedoms superseded by it to those who support the latter. There is

---

[28] There are numerous examples of proposals just being left dormant until there is a moment for their reactivation of which the most salient is the European Company Statute, which was first proposed in 1989 and only formally adopted in 2001, Reg 2157/2001 on the Statute for a European company (SE), OJ 2001, L 294/1.

[29] Famously, Fritz Scharpf, 'The Joint-Decision Trap Revisited' (2006) 44 *Journal of Common Market Studies* 845.

[30] Art 5(2) TEU.

currently no principle which grants voice to the latter concerns. They are treated as deadweight.[31] Consequently, the subsidiarity principle requires the Union measure only to show some notional added value measured against a single objective chosen by the legislature for collective action to be justified, with no weight attached to existing countervailing values, decision making structures, or traditions that might be harmed by this.[32]

The other aspect of the democratic compass goes not to whether there should be collective action but to what form the collective action should take. In most constitutional democracies, this revolves around debates between majoritarian and non-majoritarian possibilities. Majoritarian processes, such as legislation, have the advantages of greater electoral accountability. Non-majoritarian processes protect interests or values historically poorly served by electoral politics, be these fundamental rights, diffuse interests, minority interests, or the interests of future generations. The EU to some extent acknowledges this. It contains fundamental rights protections and the pursuit of certain of its activities; notably, the economic freedoms and equal opportunities law are developed mainly through courts rather than the legislature. Furthermore, non-majoritarian institutions, in the form of the European Central Bank (ECB) and the European Commission, govern monetary and competition policy.

This distinction is, however, not fully elaborated in democratic terms because choice of the form of Union rule is above all governed by regulatory politics. The regulatory imperative requires the EU to legislate only where necessary and to use alternate methods of regulation where possible.[33] This substitutability of EU law for regulation grants EU law a strongly instrumental flavour. An economy of rule is developed in which EU legislation must 'be ever more effective and efficient in achieving its public policy objectives: demonstrating clear added value, delivering full benefits at minimum cost'.[34] Unnecessary cost and intrusiveness are not justified by anybody. Making this a central narrative of EU law making cannot, therefore, be about refuting arguments that waste or intrusion are desirable. It is rather deployed to characterize EU law making as something that carries high risks of

[31] One way of resolving this would be to allow an EU law to be adopted only if two-thirds of national Parliaments vouched that the benefits to collective Union action outweighed the democratic costs; Damian Chalmers, *Democratic Self-government in Europe* (2013) 4–5.

[32] Gareth Davies 'Subsidiarity: The Wrong Idea, in the Wrong Place, at the Wrong Time' (2006) 43 *Common Market Law Review* 63. It might be argued that the requirement of impact assessment is meant to address these. It does not. It requires more elaborate assessment of projected notional impacts when measured against a current 'base line scenario'. This scenario considers, inter alia, national laws and policies but these are measured against how effectively they pursue the Union legislative objective identified by the Commission. There is no requirement to look at other values, benefits, or traditions these institutionalize. European Commission, *Impact Assessment Guidelines* (2009) Ch 5.3.

[33] Inter-institutional Ageement, *Better Law-Making*, OJ 2003, C 321/1, para 16.

[34] European Commission, *EU Regulatory Fitness*, COM (2012) 746, 3.

intrusiveness and waste, and to ensure that these risks are given strong priority relative to other values that could be realized through EU legislation.

Legislative acts adopted through EU legislative procedures constitute, as a consequence, only a small proportion of the instruments of Union rule.[35] Since the mid 1990s, soft law, measures with no direct binding effects, such as Recommendations, Guidelines, Action Plans, or Resolutions, is estimated to have been adopted at twice the rate of Regulations and Directives.[36] Alongside this, the number of Commission implementing measures dwarfs legislative output, with 1625 and 1657 measures adopted in 2011 and 2012 respectively.[37] Of particular concern is the ease with which non-legislative procedures can be substituted for legislative procedures. Two examples will suffice. Non-legislative procedures govern, for example, important aspects of fiscal and welfare policy[38], intellectual property,[39] and education law[40] at the expense of legislative measures in fields where the Union undoubtedly has law making competence.

A choice to deploy non-legislative processes over legislative procedures reflects a prioritization of certain democratic values over others. Non-legislative procedures rarely have the transparency, respect for institutional process, pluralism, representative qualities, or levels of public debate enjoyed by legislative processes. However, traditionally EU law says little about when each should be deployed. For implementing measures, only the 'basic elements' of any activity needed to be addressed directly by legislation.[41] This allows the substance of any matter to be governed by the implementing measures and there was, prior to 2012, not a single instance of the legislature having been found to have transferred unduly wide implementing

---

[35] On this see Art 289(3) TFEU.

[36] Jørgen Christensen, 'EU Legislation and National Regulation: Uncertain Steps towards a European Public Policy' (2010) 88 *Public Administration* 3, 12. This only includes data until the end of 2005.

[37] European Commission, *Report from the Commission on the Working of the Committees During 2011*, COM (2012) 685, 8; European Commission, *Report from the Commission on the Working of the Committees During 2012*, COM (2013) 701, 6–7.

[38] The most draconian example is the European Stability Mechanism Treaty 2012, which governs the conditions under euro area states experiencing financing difficulties which can secure public finances from other euro area states, http://www.esm.europa.eu/pdf/ESM%20Treaty%20consolidated%2013-03-2014.pdf. This was agreed by international agreement and is not seen as EU law, Case C-370/12 *Pringle v Government of Ireland*, judgment of 27 November 2012. However, it covers measures that are now governed by an EU Regulation, Reg 472/2013/EU on the strengthening of economic and budgetary surveillance of Member States in the euro area experiencing or threatened with serious difficulties with respect to their financial stability, OJ 2013, L 140/1, Art 7.

[39] The Lisbon Treaty introduced Art 118 TFEU to allow for centralized intellectual property arrangements. To avoid the constraints imposed by Opinion 1/09 *Creation of a unified patent litigation system* [2011] ECR I- 1137, the Member States used an international agreement. Agreement on a Unified Patent Court, OJ 2013, C 175/01.

[40] On this in this field see Sascha Garben, 'The Bologna Process: From a European Law Perspective' (2010) 16 *European Law Journal* 186.

[41] Case 25/70 *Einfuhr- und Vorratsstelle für Getreide und Futtermittel v Köster* [1970] ECR 1161.

powers to the Commission. In its *Border Surveillance* decision, the Court stated, however, that matters to be reserved to the legislature included those that involved the weighing of political choices and those that interfered significantly with the fundamental rights of individuals.[42] If the mood music of the judgment suggests a recalibration whereby more is done by legislation, the division is crude. Reserving legislation only for important measures begs questions as to what is considered to be important, and skates over the relative qualities and limits of each procedure. The relationship between legislation and soft law is even less structured. Procedures for legislation and soft law can be used interchangeably.[43] In many instances, the scope of soft law exceeds that of legislation. This not only raises questions about creeping competences but results in soft law providing the context against which legislation is adopted, applied, and interpreted. It might be countered that these soft law procedures cannot generate binding instruments. However, these instruments would not be adopted if it was not intended that they have some effects.[44]

III. The Multiplicity
of Democratic Review

The review of legislative proposals comprises the power to examine and propose amendments. It falls short of a formal power of veto. A feature of Union legislative procedures is the presence of multiple reviewing processes. This multiplicity, unique to the Union legislative process, can be a source of democratic value.[45] If each reviewing process is more accessible to different interests, it allows different perspectives to have voice within the process. Conversely, to be successful, any reviewing process cannot appeal only to parochial interests as this will be highlighted by the other reviewing processes. It must also appeal to other interests and values. However, there

---

[42] Case C-355/10 *Parliament v Council*, judgment of 5 September 2012.

[43] Art 293 TFEU.

[44] The results of the European Semester are therefore to feed into national budgets in the following year, Reg 473/2013/EU on common provisions for monitoring and assessing draft budgetary plans and ensuring the correction of excessive deficit of the Member States in the euro area, OJ 2013, L 140/11, Art 4(1).

[45] Richard Bellamy, 'An Ever Closer Union Among the Peoples of Europe: Republican Intergovernmentalism and Democratic Representation within the EU' (2013) 35 *Journal of European Integration* 499; Francis Cheneval and Frank Schimmelfennig, 'The Case for Democracy in the European Union' (2013) 51 *Journal of Common Market Studies* 334; Kalypso Nicolaidis, 'European Democracy and its Crisis' (2013) 51 *Journal of Common Market Studies* 351.

are dangers in this multiplicity.[46] More specialized processes can be more easily cap-tured by narrow interests[47] or can identify themselves by their difference and, thus, antagonism towards other processes. Powerful actors can arbitrage between processes to maximize their advantage at the expense of actors who do not have this mobility. The extent to which these risks can be averted depends on a transparency across the process, which allows arbitrage, sectionalism, or capture to be identified. Such trans-parency would include publication of the organizations that have lobbied actors in the different reviewing processes; the publication of internal dissents within the review-ing process; and the provision of detailed reasons for each amendment.

There are three main processes of review within EU law making: the first read-ing of a legislative proposal by the European Parliament;[48] the preparation of the Council meeting by COREPER; and the Early Warning Mechanism (EWM), where national Parliaments review the proposal for its compliance with the subsidiarity principle.

1. The European Parliament's First Reading

Under the consultation procedure, the European Parliament is consulted upon Commission proposals, but there is no duty on the Council to accept its amendments or even to give detailed reasons for rejecting them. Under the ordinary legislative procedure a similar process takes place at first reading. The Parliament proposes amendments to the Commission proposal. These do not have to be accepted by the Council nor does it have to give reasons for rejecting them, though it does have to give reasons for its own position.[49] As mentioned earlier, about 19 per cent of Parliament amendments made under the consultation procedure are accepted.[50] The number is lower, but not outrageously so, than the number of those accepted under the ordinary legislative procedure, which, on admittedly dated analysis, was about 27 per cent.[51] It is easy to see why amendments might be accepted under the latter procedure. There is the shadow of the possibility of a European Parliament veto, albeit one rarely exercised.[52] Furthermore, it is easier for the Council to accept

---

[46] Jose de Areilza, 'Enhanced Cooperation in the Treaty of Amsterdam: Some Critical Remarks', *Jean Monnet Working Paper 13/98*.

[47] On this within the European Parliament see David Marshall, 'Who to Lobby and When: Institutional Determinants of Interest Group Strategies in European Parliament Committees' (2010) 11 *European Union Politics* 553.

[48] This is the only reading in the case of the consultation process unless significant amendments are made by the Council. In such a case the Parliament must be reconsulted.

[49] Art 294(6) TEU.   [50] Kardasheva (n 6).

[51] Amy Kreppel, 'Moving Beyond Procedure: An Empirical Analysis of European Parliament Legislative Influence' (2002) 35 *Comparative Political Studies* 784.

[52] Between 1 May 1999 and 1 January 2013, a veto was exercised in five out of 1166 procedures http://www.consilium.europa.eu/policies/ordinary-legislative-procedure/other-information?lang=en.

Parliament amendments, which it can do by QMV (if the Commission agrees with them), than propose its own, which it must do by unanimity.[53] Within the consultation procedure, in some instances, the Parliament can tie its amendments to proposals under the ordinary legislative procedure in which it has a veto. In others, notwithstanding the illegality of this practice, it may secure leverage by threatening to delay the proposal.[54] Furthermore, even within the consultation procedure Parliament is the only plausible alternate agenda setter to the Commission in that it has a credibility not possessed by national governments to act on behalf of the collective interest.

The European Parliament's power of review should benefit from its being an ideologically and territorially diverse body in terms of the plurality that it can bring to the process. This is curtailed to some extent by the Parliament's working methods. Parliamentary amendments, whilst voted on by the plenary session, are drafted by Committees, and it is here that they are debated at most length. The most influential person within the Committee is the rapporteur, who writes the report on the proposal that will act as the basis for discussions and, often, recommendations. This MEP also presents the Committee's findings to the plenary session and negotiates with the other institutions.[55] For the consultation procedure, evidence suggests that level of expertise and loyalty to party groups are the central determinants in allocation of these posts.[56] However, once chosen, the reports of rapporteurs tend to be closer to the preferences of their national government.[57] The process is thus a highly managed one with long-term observers bemoaning the bureaucratization of the Parliament at the expense of its role as a place of contestation and debate.[58] This centralization of power within the Parliament has had a further effect. It has rendered the Parliament more exposed to external pressures, as the key players are very identifiable to outside parties. Furthermore, MEPs, unlike the Commission, do not disclose with whom they have had meetings. Lobbying can therefore take place in a hidden way. This is so commonplace that there is considerable obscurity about the provenance of many parliamentary amendments; it is not always clear whether

[53] Art 294(8) and (9) TFEU. This possibility exists only at second reading, but awareness of this shapes institutional dispositions at first reading. On the requirement of unanimity for autonomous Council amendments see Art 293 TFEU.

[54] Kardasheva (n 6).

[55] On the power of this position see Giacomo Benedetto, 'Rapporteurs as Legislative Entrepreneurs: The Dynamics of the Codecision Procedure in Europe's Parliament' (2005) 12 *Journal of European Public Policy* 67.

[56] Nicoleta Yordanova, 'Inter-institutional Rules and Division of Power in the European Parliament: Allocation of Consultation and Co-decision Reports' (2011) 34 *West European Politics* 97.

[57] Rory Costello and Robert Thomson, 'The Policy Impact of Leadership in Committees: Rapporteurs' Influence on the European Parliament's Opinions' (2010) 11 *European Union Politics* 219.

[58] Katrin Huber and Michael Shackleton, 'Codecision: A Practitioner's View from Inside the Parliament' (2013) 20 *Journal of European Public Policy* 1040, 1044–1045.

they did, in fact, originate within the Parliament or whether an MEP was persuaded to introduce them on behalf of other actors, notably but not exclusively, national governments.[59]

2. The Preparation of Council Decision Making by COREPER

The formal duty of COREPER, the committee of permanent representatives and deputy permanent representatives of each Member State, is to prepare the work of the Council.[60] It has no power to take formal decisions on anything of a legislative substance.[61] Its power of review lies instead in the division of agenda items for Council meetings into 'A' and 'B' items, with the former seen as non-controversial matters on which there is agreement and which can be nodded through the Council without any discussion. This forecloses debate by leading, typically, to only 15–30 per cent of the items on any Council agenda being discussed by ministers.[62] It also opens out debate as COREPER, rather than debating internally, instigates debate between national administrations through the establishment of Working Groups of national civil servants who do review the legislative proposals.

COREPER secures national government buy-in to proposals and sharpens agreement (if possible) on points outstanding between these governments. Beyond this, it brings a level of expertise and national scrutiny to the legislative process which would otherwise not be possible. This scrutiny allows the possibility of including other domestic stakeholders within the process. Representatives indicate, therefore, the presence of parliamentary reserves that set out domestic parliamentary opposition to a proposal, and this will often result in more time being given to see if a solution can be found.[63] Finally, COREPER brings a practical rationality to the process by calibrating what is to be prioritized politically. This takes place not simply through the division into 'A' and 'B' items but through briefings within national ministries, with some evidence that ministers are usually consulted on matters of political salience before civil servants commit themselves.[64]

---

[59] Simon Hix and Bjørn Høyland, 'Empowerment of the European Parliament' (2013) 16 *Annual Review of Political Science* 171, 176.

[60] Art 16(7) TEU, Art 240(1) TFEU.

[61] Case C-25/94 *Commission v Council* [1996] ECR I-1469.

[62] Frank Häge, 'Politicising Council Decision-Making: The Effect of European Parliament Empowerment' (2011) 34 *West European Politics* 18, 33–34.

[63] On this practice see Katrin Auel, Olivier Rozenberg, and Anja Thomas, 'Lost in Translation? Parliamentary Reserves in EU Bargains' *OPAL Online Paper 10/2012*, 17–21.

[64] Frank Häge, *Bureaucrats as Law-makers: Committee Decision-Making in the EU Council of Ministers* (2013) especially Chs 13 and 14.

As a review process, the central challenge with COREPER is its lack of structure. Discussions of permanent representatives and Working Parties are not published nor are links with lobbyists disclosed. This might have to be revised in the light of the *Access Info Europe* judgment. Prior to this judgment, the Council refused access to information about the discussions and documents of Working Parties on the grounds that this would undermine the decision making of the institution.[65] The ECJ found no evidence that this was generally the case, and, in the absence of such evidence, held that individuals had a right to information both about documents supplied to the Working Parties and about the identity of those supplying the documents.[66] Even if increased transparency emerges, other concerns remain. The engagement of national civil servants with domestic civic society or national Parliaments is unclear, and there are currently no structures in place to facilitate this. Indeed, the absence of these structures allows governments to agree positions for which it would be impossible to secure domestic legislative agreement. This issue is particularly challenging because of the dual role played by national civil servants within this process, where they both have to represent national positions and secure pan-Union consensus.[67] The autonomy enjoyed by civil servants accentuates the tensions between these roles with the corresponding danger that they can either overstate a national position or agree too readily to a common Council position.

3. National Parliaments and the Early Warning Mechanism

Under the EWM, the Commission must review a proposal if one-third (one-quarter in the field of the area of freedom, security, and justice) of parliamentary chambers[68] issue opinions that it violates the subsidiarity principle.[69] The Commission must provide reasons if it decides to maintain, withdraw, or amend the proposal. If a majority of national parliamentary chambers issues opinions that a proposal made under the ordinary legislative procedure violates the subsidiarity principle and the Commission decides to maintain the proposal, it must send a reasoned

---

[65] Reg 1049/2001 regarding public access to European Parliament, Council and Commission documents, OJ 2001, L 145/43, Art 4(3).

[66] Case C-280/11P *Council v Access Info Europe*, judgment of 17 October 2013.

[67] Frank Häge, 'Committee Decision-making in the Council of the European Union' (2007) 8 *European Union Politics* 299.

[68] Each national Parliament is granted two votes which may be allocated between national parliamentary chambers as it sees fit, Protocol on the Application of the principles of subsidiarity and proportionality, Art 7(1).

[69] Protocol on the Application of the principles of subsidiarity and proportionality, Art 7(2). This is informally described as the yellow card procedure.

opinion setting out why it believes the measure complies with the principle as well as the positions of the national Parliaments to the Council and Parliament. Before the first reading, these must consider whether the proposal does comply with that principle. If 55 per cent of members of the Council or a majority of votes cast in the Parliament vote that it does not, the measure will be dropped.[70]

The procedure acts as a form of review because parliamentary opinions are rarely confined to analysis of the subsidiarity principle but rather discuss the merits of the proposal.[71] Furthermore, though there is no formal power of veto, the EWM grants national Parliaments a relatively strong institutional position, as it is difficult to see a national government voting for a measure which its Parliament has opposed. By March 2014, two yellow cards had been shown. One proposal, on the right to collective action, was withdrawn.[72] The Commission refused to withdraw the other, a proposal establishing a European Public Prosecutor's Office, but indicated that it would make significant amendments to meet the stated concerns.[73] This informal power to thwart or radically alter a Commission proposal has led to a claim that national Parliaments now exist as a third chamber within the EU legislature, supplementing those of the Council and the European Parliament.[74] This is a slight overstatement as much will depend on how authoritatively the position of national Parliaments is treated by the other institutions. The EWM's source of 'added value' also lies in the democratic pedigree of national Parliaments and the experience of review many parliamentary chambers can bring to bear as historical reviewing chambers. Perhaps most importantly, national Parliaments can act as access points for voices and perspectives beyond those represented by governments, thus allowing national positions to be presented in a more differentiated way.

The process is constrained, however, in a number of ways. First, the period for review, eight weeks, is insufficient for national Parliaments to gather the views of stakeholders and reflect on their contributions. Twenty-four national parliamentary chambers have indicated that the period for the EWM is too short.[75] Second,

---

[70] Protocol on the Application of the principles of subsidiarity and proportionality, Art 7(3). This is informally described as the orange card procedure.

[71] Katarina Granat and Federico Fabbrini, ' "Yellow Card, but no Foul": The Role of the National Parliaments under the Subsidiarity Protocol and the Commission Proposal for a Right to Strike' (2013) 50 *Common Market Law Review* 115.

[72] European Commission, *Commission Decision to Withdraw the Proposal for a Council Regulation on the Exercise of the Right to Take Collective Action within the Context of the Freedom of Establishment and the Freedom to Provide Services*, COM (2012) 130; European Commission, *On the Review of the Proposal for a Council Regulation on the Establishment of the European Public Prosecutor's Office with Regard to the Principle of Subsidiarity*, COM (2013) 851.

[73] COM (2013) 851, 11–13.

[74] Ian Cooper, 'A "Virtual Third Chamber" for the European Union? National Parliaments after the Treaty of Lisbon' (2012) 35 *West European Politics* 441; Ian Cooper, 'Bicameral or Tricameral? National Parliaments and Representative Democracy in the European Union' (2013) 35 *Journal of European Integration* 531, 536–539.

[75] COSAC, *Sixteenth Bi-annual Report: Developments in European Union Procedures and Practices Relevant to Parliamentary Scrutiny* (2011) 7.

the threshold for when leverage is exerted through either of the procedures is too high. Most parliamentary chambers express opinions only occasionally, with the amount of legislative opinions submitted rising from less than 1.5 per cent of the potential total in 2010 to about 3.25 per cent in 2013.[76] If the threshold of opposition for the yellow card has been met only twice in 2011 and 2012 alone, nine proposals received three or more opposing opinions, four received five or more opinions and one nine opinions. None of these proposals was withdrawn.[77] These difficulties have been exacerbated by coordination between different national parliamentary chambers being limited, with such contacts as take place usually being between officials rather than parliamentarians, and the weak organizational capacities of some chambers.[78] The prevailing modus operandi is thus asymmetric uncoordinated intervention from individual chambers—a very unstructured form of review.

Notwithstanding the above shortcomings, a strong case can be made that the cup of the EU legislative process is at least half full. Few national processes can point to three moments of review, each representing different interests, accessible to different actors and with a different perspective. Cumulatively, it might be imbalanced, with some processes having more time and influence, but for all that there is an abundance of review. If space is allowed for each of these processes, this can only be a good thing. The central challenge emerges, however, from each process being seen as insufficiently significant to be subject to EU constitutional disciplines. There are no general rules on maintaining an arms-length relationship with lobbyists; no ethics codes for lobbyists; no duties for national Parliaments to give sufficiently detailed reasons for their positions. Individual MEPs are not required to declare their meetings with non-institutional actors. Indeed, until very recently, the Conference of Community and European Affairs Committees of Parliaments of the European Union (COSAC) had been allowed to operate under a veil of complete secrecy. This culture allows arbitrage by powerful actors between different review processes to secure with one what they were unable to obtain through another. It is a context where capture is easier. Finally, it creates a context in which there is more likely to be institutional mistrust as the goings on surrounding one process are not always fully disclosed to other processes.

---

[76] Katjana Gattermann and Claudia Hefftler 'Political Motivation and Institutional Capacity: Assessing National Parliaments' Incentives to Participate in the Early Warning System' *OPAL Online Working Paper Series 15/2013*, 13.

[77] European Commission, *Annual Report 2012 on Relations between the European Commission and National Parliaments*, COM (2013) 565, 9–10. European Commission, *Annual Report 2011 on Relations between the European Commission and National Parliaments*, COM (2012) 375, 11.

[78] Thomas Christiansen, Anna-Lena Högenauer, and Christine Neuhold, 'National Parliaments in the post-Lisbon European Union: Bureaucratization rather than Democratization?' *Opal Online Working Paper Series 11/2012*, 11.

IV. Democratic Fluidity and the Foreclosing of Legislative Panoramas

The grant of the power of legislative initiative to the Commission is controversial as it is a non-elected actor, and the power to propose is arguably as central to law making as the power to adopt legislation, as it is the power to decide what is decided. Its vesting in a non-elected actor, it is argued, reduces political accountability, allows political drift, and results in reduced citizen engagement in EU legislative politics.[79] The counter-argument for the Commission's power of initiative is that it secures a panorama for the legislature which no other actor could secure.[80] Freed from national territorial constraints or electoral pressures, the Commission can think in a more imaginative manner about the needs across the Union and in the long term.[81] On its own terms, such an argument is challenged by the centralization of decision making within the Commission. Usually, a lead Directorate General will be given the task of drafting the proposal. Adoption by the Commission will be subject either to the written procedure, where the proposal is circulated around the Cabinets of Commissioners and adopted if there is no objection, or the oral procedure, where adoption follows a short meeting of the Cabinets to iron out any differences. Both procedures leave the power of the lead Directorate General largely untouched. In addition to drafting the initial proposal, it can decide how to incorporate suggestions, and when to put the proposal forward.[82]

Awareness of this constraint has led to two strategies by the Commission: responsiveness to external proposals and stronger structuring of the pre-legislative process leading up to the formal adoption of the legislative proposal. With regard to the former, a study of initiatives in 1998 found that the impetus for only 5 per cent of Commission proposals lay with the Commission itself. Other drivers were international obligations, requests from other EU Institutions, Member States, or other actors, or adaptation of EU law to new social, technological, and economic data.[83] To

---

[79] Andreas Follesdal and Simon Hix, Why There is a Democratic Deficit in the EU: A Response to Majone and Moravcsik (2006) 44 *Journal of Common Market Studies* 533, 554ff.

[80] On the history of this see Kevin Featherstone, 'Jean Monnet and the "Democratic Deficit" in the European Union' (1994) 32 *Journal of Common Market Studies* 149, 154–155.

[81] On whether this is sufficient in today's European Union see Giandomenico Majone, *Dilemmas of European Integration: The Ambiguities and Pitfalls of Stealth by Integration* (2005) 51–53.

[82] Miriam Hartlapp, Julia Metz, and Christian Rauh, 'Linking Agenda Setting to Coordination Structures: Bureaucratic Politics inside the European Commission' (2013) 35 *Journal of European Integration* 425.

[83] Initially provided as evidence to the *Future of Europe* Convention, this data can now be found in the House of Lords European Union Committee, *Initiation of EU Legislation* (2008, 2nd Report) para 23.

these must now be added the Citizens' Initiative, which requires the Commission to consider petitions from one million citizens from more than eight states.[84]

The Commission is centrally, therefore, a gatekeeper of initiatives to which it gives formal blessing. This counters concerns about lack of expertise within the Commission or possibly excessive concentration of decision making within it. However, it raises questions about the population of interests to which the Commission is responsive and the style of relations it has with them. This has been addressed through extensive structuring of the pre-legislative process. There are demanding duties of transparent consultation on the Commission prior to any significant legislative initiative. Consultation must involve adequate coverage of those affected by the policy, involved in its implementation or in stated objectives which give them a direct interest in it. The consultation period should be for at least eight weeks with written public consultations. Memoranda accompanying legislative proposals must set out how the consultation was carried out, its results, and how these were taken into account in the proposal.[85] The Commission is also required to assess the social, economic, and ecological impacts of any proposal,[86] as well as to review it against the EU Charter of Fundamental Rights and the proportionality and subsidiarity principles.[87] Alongside this, strong incentives are imposed on non-institutional actors involved in the law making process to register with the European Transparency Register, because, whilst registration is voluntary, non-registration might limit the extent to which an actor is consulted.[88] This register imposes ethical obligations on these by setting out a Code of Conduct requiring them, inter alia, to be transparent about the interests they represent and not to induce either EU staff to contravene any rules or former EU staff to violate confidentiality requirements.[89]

National Parliaments are also to be involved at the pre-legislative stage through political dialogue. Begun as the Barroso initiative in 2006,[90] all Commission

---

[84] Art 11(4) TEU. Reg 211/2011 on the citizens' initiative, OJ 2011, L 65/1, Art 5(2). There must also be a minimum number of signatories from each state equating to 750 times that state's number of MEPs.

[85] European Commission, *General Principles and Minimum Standards for Consultation of Interested Parties by the Commission*, COM (2002) 704.

[86] European Commission, *Impact Assessment Guidelines*, SEC (2009) 92.

[87] European Commission, *Strategy for the Effective Implementation of the Charter of Fundamental Rights by the European Union*, COM (2010) 573; European Commission, *Annual Report 2012 on Subsidiarity and Proportionality*, COM (2013) 566.

[88] Agreement between the European Parliament and the European Commission on the establishment of a transparency register for organizations and self-employed individuals engaged in EU policy-making and policy implementation, OJ 2011, L 191/29.

[89] The Secretariat has raised questions about how well the Code is observed. Joint Transparency Register Secretariat, *Annual Report on the operations of the Transparency Register 2012*, 9–10. This is available at http://ec.europa.eu/transparencyregister/info/about-register/reportsAndPublications.do?locale=en.

[90] European Commission, 'A Citizens' Agenda: Delivering Results for Europe' COM (2006) 211, 9. On this see Davor Jančić, 'The Barroso Initiative: Window Dressing or Democracy Boost?' (2012) 8 *Utrecht Law Review* 78.

consultation documents, annual legislative programmes, as well as 'any other instrument of legislative planning or policy' are forwarded to national Parliaments at the same time as to the European Parliament and the Council.[91] National Parliaments can express their observations on these, and the Commission will respond to each observation it receives. This is less successful than other elements of the pre-legislative process with national Parliament take-up uneven and upper chambers, such as the British House of Lords or Senate in France, Italy, and the Czech Republic, tending to be more involved than lower chambers.[92] There are no formal requirements imposed on the Commission as to how it handles national parliamentary observations. Commission replies are often brief,[93] and it is very unclear how far national parliamentary observations shape policy.

In toto, the range of inputs and their structured organization allow for quite wide-ranging legislative panoramas to be secured at the pre-legislative stage. A broad number of interests will have been considered and the Commission will have to project in a detailed manner possible consequences of the legislation. To be sure, the process is asymmetric in that those not benefitting from Union action may be less likely to organize at a pan-Union level and influence decision making, and the subsidiarity principle fails to value sufficiently existing legal traditions. However, once again, if compared against domestic pre-legislative structures, it is not clear that the Union fares badly. It is, however, undermined severely by the problem of democratic fluidity.

Democratic fluidity involves the establishment of practices that curtail formal legislative procedures and telescope decision making. Their rationale is to avoid the complications of negotiating between so many different actors and to shorten decision making times. Insofar as they take place outside formal decision making structures and can radically revisit what was proposed, they can foreclose the legislative panoramas just described and destabilize the balances established within them. There are three examples of democratic fluidity: legislative package deals, the commitment to secure deals at first reading, and, most importantly, the trilogue.

Kardasheva found that about 25 per cent of all EU legislation is subject to package deals in which a number of legislative proposals are bundled together. Typically, consultation procedure proposals were bundled with ordinary legislative procedure proposals as this allowed the European Parliament through assertion of its powers under the latter to secure sway under the former.[94] Such horse-trading

---

[91] Protocol on the Role of National Parliaments in the European Union, Art 1.

[92] There were 663 opinions given in 2012. Of the 13 chambers which gave ten or more opinions, nine were the upper chamber and three the lower chamber. There was in addition the Bulgarian National Assembly which is a unicameral legislature, European Commission, *Annual Report 2012 on Relations between the European Commission and National Parliaments*, COM (2013) 565, 9.

[93] The replies are on the Commission website. For the replies to the British Parliament, see eg http://ec.europa.eu/dgs/secretariat_general/relations/relations_other/npo/united_kingdom/2011_en.htm.

[94] Raya Kardasheva, 'Package Deals in EU Legislative Politics' (2013) 57 *American Journal of Political Science* 858.

is problematic. It is unstructured and not carried out in any transparent manner. Otherwise unrelated interests are treated as substitutable for one another. Furthermore, it can only occur where significant concessions are made in each piece of legislation, as something of value has to be offered, with the consequence that balances between interests in original proposals are discarded and clear policy horizons altered in quite unpredictable ways.

There is a commitment between EU institutions to secure agreement at first reading wherever possible within the ordinary legislative procedure.[95] This commitment has been highly successful. Between 1 July 2004 and 31 December 2012, 577 out of 726 legislative dossiers (79.5 per cent) were agreed at first reading.[96] Consequently, the overwhelming majority of legislative procedures share a similar pattern. There is a Commission proposal, followed by a Parliament opinion, and then a final decision, whether shared by the Council and the Parliament in the case of the ordinary legislative procedure, made usually by both the Council and the Parliament, albeit separately, in the case of the consent procedure, or made by the Council exclusively in the case of the consultation procedure.

As the first reading now brings the legislative process to an end, the time between the formal start of the process, with the Commission proposal, and its conclusion is much shorter. This can lead to actors not directly involved becoming less engaged, because they believe that the time for giving voice has passed them by. A study of British and Dutch parliamentary activity found far less involvement on the part of both Parliaments when the matter was resolved at first reading than when procedures continued beyond that.[97] Alongside this, the shortening of the legislative stage increases the relative importance of the pre-legislative stage. It has already been said that, as a process for envisioning the legislative terms of debate the pre-legislative process works pretty well. This is different, when it becomes the main sphere of action, with the legislative process little more than a process that reviews and formally ratifies the pre-legislative process. In this context, both the Commission and its surrounding stakeholders acquire too much power.

The most dramatic example of democratic fluidity is the trilogue. Instigated initially in the late 1990s,[98] the trilogue takes place most commonly before the Council has adopted a formal position and after the first reading of the European Parliament.[99] Comprising a small number of representatives from the Commission, MEPs from the

---

[95] Joint Declaration on Practical Arrangements for the Codecision Procedure (Art 251 EC Treaty), OJ 2007, C 145/2, para 11.

[96] http://www.consilium.europa.eu/policies/ordinary-legislative-procedure/other-information?lang=en accessed 30 March 2014.

[97] Rik de Ruiter, 'Under the Radar? National Parliaments and the Ordinary Legislative Procedure in the European Union' (2013) 20 *Journal of European Public Policy* 1196.

[98] On its emergence see Michael Shackleton, 'The Politics of Codecision' (2000) 38 *Journal of Common Market Studies* 325, 334–336.

[99] The basis for the trilogue is formalized in the Joint Declaration on Practical Arrangements for the Codecision Procedure (Art 251 EC), OJ 2007, C145/2, paras 4, 7–9, and 11. The literature is

Parliamentary Committee which considered the proposal, and civil servants from the state holding the Council presidency, the aim of the trilogue is to secure legislative agreement. In many ways, it can be seen as a legislative body in its own right, as any such agreement is seen as binding on Union institutions and national governments. It can also be seen as possibly the most powerful legislative body as it governs the over-whelming majority of legislative procedures.

The trilogue's attraction to the Council and Parliament lies in its countering the Commission's right of initiative. As any amendment can be proposed and decided within the trilogue, it is offered a universe of alternatives beyond simply deciding whether to adopt (or veto) a Commission proposal because it is less bad than the sta-tus quo. The quid pro quo for the Commission is that it acquires greater say over the review and adoption of the proposal as, within the trilogue, it enjoys an equal say with the Council and the Parliament.

The trilogue reshapes relations within the institutions and re-styles the manner of decision making. Within the trilogue, Parliament and COREPER act as genuine joint decision takers. Within the Council, this enhances the power of national civil serv-ants at the expense of ministers. It also has more subversive effects. Research suggests that ministers involve themselves less in negotiations leading up to the trilogue, as they know it is likely to be resolved by civil servants, with a corresponding weakening of ministerial accountability.[100] Within the Parliament, a concern emerged that tri-logues would enhance the power of the *relais*, the Parliament representatives, and the interests these stand for.[101] This has been mitigated by party groupings and different committees sending representatives to oversee the negotiations. Nevertheless, parties poorly represented in the European Parliament committees still feel bypassed.[102]

The most obvious concerns with the trilogue lie in its centralization of power and, prior to the *Access Info Europe* judgment, the secrecy surrounding discussions within it. However, more pervasively, it unpacks existing legislative procedures and checks and balances. It pre-empts subsequent debate. The value of more considered deliberation in the second and third readings of the ordinary legislative procedure is lost. It is difficult for stakeholders to raise points to counter amendments raised

considerable. Christine Reh, Adrienne Héritier, Edoardo Bressanelli, and Christel Koop, 'The Informal Politics of Legislation: Explaining Secluded Decision Making in the European Union' (2013) 46 *Comparative Political Studies* 1112; Anne Rasmussen and Christine Reh, 'The Consequences of Concluding Codecision Early: Trilogues and Intra-institutional Bargaining Success' (2013) 20 *Journal of European Public Policy* 1006.

[100] Frank Häge and Daniel Naurin, 'The Effect of Codecision on Council Decision-making: Infor malization, Politicization and Power' (2013) 20 *Journal of European Public Policy* 953.

[101] David Judge and David Earnshaw, '"Relais actors" and First-reading Agreements in the European Parliament: The Case of the Advanced Therapies Regulation' (2011) 18 *Journal of European Public Policy* 53.

[102] Charlotte Burns, 'Consensus and Compromise Become Ordinary—But at What Cost? A Critical Analysis of the Impact of the Changing Norms of Codecision upon European Parliament Committees' (2013) 20 *Journal of European Public Policy* 988.

at first reading and just before the trilogue. The sense of the legislative procedure as an ongoing review which folds perspectives into one another is lost. However, it also forecloses debate and panoramas prior to the trilogue. There are disincentives for parties to engage with the pre-legislative process organized by the Commission, when what really matters is whether a point can be raised in a trilogue, where it will not have to mediate so many other perspectives or be subsequently exposed by counter-arguments. The power of the Commission's proposal previously was that it was difficult to amend. In the ordinary legislative procedure, without Commission approval, it requires European Parliament agreement and unanimity in the Council. Long-term visions or wider panoramas therefore had a stickiness that was difficult to avoid. As there are no limits on the trilogue's scope to amend and no constraints on how this is done (the Commission will, if these amendments are very extensive, simply reissue a proposal), it can make the Commission proposal unrecognizable. It merely becomes one institutional bid to be placed alongside the other institutional bids.

V. Democratic Ambiguity and Democratic Maturity

For much of its life the EU has been a political and legal settlement in development. It has benefitted from that but there have also been costs—in particular, a tendency to believe that if democratic authority were not sufficiently forcefully asserted, the project would collapse. However, as this chapter has shown, the EU involves an established political settlement with a large public sphere which produces significant amounts of laws. This maturity should allow a less shrill and less aspirational approach which focuses on those democratic qualities possessed by the Union that cannot be enjoyed by national settlements, whilst freely acknowledging that the converse is also the case. In that regard, to suggest that EU law making could have qualities of pluralism, reflection, and breadth of panorama that national settlements cannot have is not only true, but also presents a vision which is less mission-dependent and less wrapped in the mystique of post-national romanticism. To be sure, these qualities may, in many cases, be insufficient to grant EU law making greater democratic authority than national processes because the latter may possess more valued democratic qualities which can simply not be present to the same extent in EU law making. However, they create a valuable democratic ambiguity. National processes are induced to reconsider their democratic performance: namely whether do they realize the democratic qualities that they claim to uphold and whether they are sufficiently sensitive to the democratic quali-ties embodied in EU law making? Converse responsibilities apply to the EU law making process. It has to evaluate its own performance and be sensitive to national democratic traits. If such ambiguity suggests neither law making procedure has the democratic authority to prevail in all cases of conflict, this mutual questioning generates a democratic virtue that is unique to the EU.

BIBLIOGRAPHY

Ian Cooper, 'A "Virtual Third Chamber" for the European Union? National Parliaments after the Treaty of Lisbon' (2012) 35 *West European Politics* 441

Frank Häge, *Bureaucrats as Law-makers: Committee Decision-Making in the EU Council of Ministers* (2013)

Frank Häge and Daniel Naurin, 'The Effect of Codecision on Council Decision-making: Informalization, Politicization and Power' (2013) 20 *Journal of European Public Policy* 953

Andreas Follesdal and Simon Hix, 'Why There is a Democratic Deficit in the EU: A Response to Majone and Moravcsik' (2006) 44 *Journal of Common Market Studies* 533

Katarina Granat and Federico Fabbrini, ' "Yellow Card, but no Foul": The Role of the National Parliaments under the Subsidiarity Protocol and the Commission Proposal for a Right to Strike' (2013) 50 *Common Market Law Review* 115

Miriam Hartlapp, Julia Metz, and Christian Rauh, 'Linking Agenda Setting to Coordination Structures: Bureaucratic Politics inside the European Commission' (2013) 35 *Journal of European Integration* 425

Katrin Huber and Michael Shackleton, 'Codecision: A Practitioner's View from Inside the Parliament' (2013) 20 *Journal of European Public Policy* 1040

Davor Jančić, 'The Barroso Initiative: Window Dressing or Democracy Boost?' (2012) 8 *Utrecht Law Review* 78

Raya Kardasheva, 'The Power to Delay: The European Parliament's Influence in the Consultation Procedure' (2009) 47 *Journal of Common Market Studies* 385

Raya Kardasheva, 'Package Deals in EU Legislative Politics' (2013) 57 *American Journal of Political Science* 858

Kalypso Nicolaidis, 'European Democracy and its Crisis' (2013) 51 *Journal of Common Market Studies* 351

Anne Rasmussen and Christine Reh, 'The Consequences of Concluding Codecision Early: Trilogues and Intra-institutional Bargaining Success' (2013) 20 *Journal of European Public Policy* 1006

Christine Reh, Adrienne Héritier, Edoardo Bressanelli, and Christel Koop, 'The Informal Politics of Legislation: Explaining Secluded Decision Making in the European Union' (2013) 46 *Comparative Political Studies* 1112

Fritz Scharpf, 'The Joint-Decision Trap Revisited' (2006) 44 *Journal of Common Market Studies* 845

Myrto Tsakatika, 'Governance vs. politics: The European Union's Constitutive "Democratic Deficit" ' (2007) 14 *Journal of European Public Policy* 867

CHAPTER 13

....

COMITOLOGY

....

ALEXANDER TÜRK

I. INTRODUCTION

....

CONCEIVED as a temporary compromise between centralized and decentralized forms of Union administration, comitology has become an integral feature of the Union's legal system. Its enduring appeal can perhaps best be explained by its capacity for integrating national administrations and the European Commission within an organizational framework for the adoption of implementing acts at Union level. The comitology system has thereby led the Member States to sanction the delegation of considerable powers to the Commission while at the same time allowing them to retain a varying degree of control over the exercise of those powers. The cooperation between national civil servants and the Commission behind closed doors, under the shadow of a possible referral to the Council, provided a forum for consensual problem solving and could be said to have contributed to greater efficiency of the Union's implementation process. At the same time, with the ever-expanding use of comitology within Union law and the politically sensitive nature of its output, the exclusivity and closed nature of its operation have raised political tensions and concerns about its legitimacy and accountability.

The evolution of the Union's legal system generally, and in particular its move towards greater parliamentarization had a profound impact on the comitology system. Its enhanced position in the Union's legislative process in the reforms of the 1990s has allowed the European Parliament to pursue its demands for greater involvement in the comitology regime with more vigour culminating in the rearrangement of the process for the adoption of non-legislative acts in the Lisbon

Treaty. At the same time, an increasing demand for and reliance on technical scientific expertise at Union level led to a remarkable expansion of European agencies, which complement and, in a few areas, have now replaced comitology committees in the implementation of Union law. Finally, the drive to enhance the Union's democratic legitimacy through greater transparency and better opportunities for participatory mechanisms in the adoption of implementing acts will further shape the comitology regime.

While these developments have constrained its scope of application and mode of operation, comitology is still pivotal to the Union's administrative decision making process. According to a recent study, in 2011 almost 50 per cent of the Commission's legal acts, which constitute the vast majority of Union legal acts, were adopted after a committee, composed of civil servants of the Member States, had given its opinion on a draft act presented by the Commission.[1] The comitology process involves around 270 committees, which in 2012 collectively issued almost 2000 opinions in close to 800 meetings leading to the adoption of 1657 legal acts.[2] Such implementing measures cover a wide range of activities[3] and deal with important policy issues that go well beyond the merely technical regulation of the internal market.[4]

It was, however, not until the inter-institutional conflict in the 1990s about the comitology process, which brought to the fore the practical importance and politically sensitive nature of its output, that political scientists and legal scholars really took notice of the comitology phenomenon.[5] While some have concentrated on the formal procedures, which are designed to allow the Member States control over the exercise of the Commission's implementing powers, others have found that it is its practical operation as an integrated organizational structure that raises difficult questions as to the nature and function of comitology and comitology committees

---

[1] Gijs J. Brandsma, *Controlling Comitology—Accountability in a Multi-level System* (2013) 23.

[2] See European Commission, *Report from the Commission: On the Working of Committees During 2012*, COM (2013) 701 final 3–7. See also the pre-2012 statistics in Brandsma (n 1) Ch 2.

[3] Such activities include rule application (eg the granting of marketing authorizations for veterinary or medicinal products), approval of funds (eg management of specific research and development programmes and economic aid), the extension/new specification of funding programmes, rule interpretation, and information management.

[4] Implementing measures must, however, respect the legislative prerogative of adopting the 'essential rules governing the matter in question', see Case C-355/10 *European Parliament v Council*, judgment of 5 September 2012, para 64.

[5] See Robin Pedler and Guenther F. Schaefer (eds), *Shaping European Law and Politics: The Role of Committees and Comitology in the Political Process* (1996); Christian Joerges and Ellen Vos (eds), *EU Committees: Social Reg, Law and Politics* (1999); Thomas Christiansen and Emil Kirchner (eds), *Committee Governance in the European Union* (2000); Mads Andenas and Alexander Türk (eds), *Delegated Legislation and the Role of Committees in the EC* (2000). On earlier works, see Sabino Cassese, *The European Administration* (1987); Claude Bluman, 'Le pouvoir exécutif de la Commission à la lumière de l'Act unique européen' (1988) 24 *Revue trimestrielle de droit européen* 23; Kieran Bradley, 'Comitology and the Law: Through a Glass Darkly' (1992) 29 *Common Market Law Review* 693.

as fora for such interaction. In particular, it is the argument that the comitology regime as a non-hierarchical governance form with the capacity of deliberative problem solving could be perceived as particularly suitable for the Union's transnational governance regime[6] that has sparked controversial debates in political and legal science. These debates have far transcended the narrow confines of comitology committees. Comitology has hereby become a useful prism through which wider questions of European integration and law can be debated, and new theoretical and normative arguments be pursued.

II. History of Comitology

The origins of the comitology system can be found in the establishment of the first common agricultural policy regimes in the 1960s.[7] Even though formally entrusted with the law making function, the Council of Ministers was not itself in a position to adopt all necessary rules. The dilemma for the Member States consisted in the fact that while not willing to concede the Council's rule making function to the Commission, a decentralized arrangement risked the unravelling of bargains struck in the Council. From among the various options debated in the Council emerged a compromise solution,[8] which foresaw that the Council would confer on the Commission implementing powers to adopt the necessary measures for the management of the various agricultural regimes subject to the supervision of management committees, comprised of national representatives. Even though these committees did not have any decision making powers, the Commission had to refer any draft measure which received a negative opinion[9] in the committee to Council, which could take a different decision within a specified time limit.

The comitology system soon became a permanent feature not only in the agricultural sector, but in other areas as well. It allowed the Council to subject the Commission's exercise of implementing powers to controls of varying intensity depending on the importance of those powers. For politically sensitive decisions,

---

[6] See Christian Joerges and Jürgen Neyer, 'From Intergovernmental Bargaining to Deliberative Political Processes: The Constitutionalisation of Comitology' (1997) 3 *European Law Journal* 273.

[7] On the history of comitology, see Carl F. Bergström, *Comitology—Delegation of Powers in the European Union and the Committee System* (2005).

[8] Bergström (n 7) 46–53.

[9] A negative opinion required a qualified majority of the committee members against the Commission's draft implementing measure. Notwithstanding the negative opinion, the Commission could adopt the measure and apply it. While it allowed the Commission to adopt the necessary measures without delay, it preserved the possibility for the Council to intervene in controversial cases.

the regulatory procedure was employed, which required the Commission to present a proposal to the Council in case it could not obtain a qualified majority for its draft measures in the committee. In certain areas, the Commission could adopt the measures where the Council failed to adopt the proposal by qualified majority within a specified time (*filet*). In other areas, mainly concerned with public health, Community legislation was to provide that the Council, by simple majority, could prevent the Commission from acting altogether, even if the Council could not muster a qualified majority for the adoption of the Commission's proposal (*contrefilet*).

The European Parliament followed the development of the comitology system with suspicion from the beginning.[10] Its exclusion from the implementation process deprived the European Parliament of the consultative role it enjoyed in the legislative process. Moreover, the involvement of national representatives in the comitology procedures diminished the accountability of the Commission vis-à-vis the European Parliament. Apart from its budgetary powers, which included the power to block or freeze expenditure for committees, the European Parliament lacked any political or legal means to tilt the balance of power in its favour.

Moreover, the Court sanctioned the existing comitology regime in its *Köster*[11] ruling. The Court held that 'both the legislative scheme of the Treaty, reflected in particular by the last indent of Article 155 [EEC Treaty], and the consistent practice of the Community institutions establish a distinction, according to the legal concepts recognized in all the Member States between measures directly based on the Treaty itself and derived law intended to ensure their implementation'.[12] Moreover, the Council was entitled to make the powers it delegated to the Commission in a basic act subject to certain requirements. The Court also considered the 'management' committee procedure as legitimate since the committee had no decision making power. *Köster* thereby helped to pave the way for, and foreshadowed, the introduction of Article 145 (Article 202 EC), third indent, EEC as formal legal basis for the comitology regime.[13]

The Single European Act (SEA) considerably expanded the areas in which the Council could decide by qualified majority and also gave the European Parliament a greater say in the legislative process. Therefore, comitology offered the Member States compensation for the loss of influence in the legislative process. With an increase of implementation measures due to the Internal Market programme, Member States considered it necessary to put the comitology regime on a sound

---

[10] See European Parliament Resolution of 17 October 1967 [1967] OJ 268/7; EP Resolution of 3 October 1968 [1968] OJ C108/37.

[11] Case 25/70 *Köster* [1970] ECR 1161.   [12] *Köster* (n 11) para 6.

[13] See Alexander Türk, 'The Role of the European Court of Justice in the Area of Comitology' in Thomas Chrstiansen and Torbjörn Larsson (eds), *The Role of Committees in the Policy-Process of the European Union* (2007) 227.

constitutional basis. A new third indent of Article 145 EEC provided for the conferral of implementing powers to the Commission, and allowed the Council to impose restrictions on the exercise of such powers through the use of comitology procedures. However, as such procedures had to be laid down in advance, in 1987 the Council adopted the first Comitology Decision,[14] which codified the main types of existing comitology procedures.[15] But the Decision did not contain any criteria as to which procedure had to be chosen in a legislative act and omitted any rules which would have aligned the existing procedures with the new regime. In addition, it did not provide for any involvement of the European Parliament. It therefore fell considerably short of what the European Parliament and even the Commission had expected.[16]

The introduction of the co-decision procedure in the Maastricht Treaty finally granted the European Parliament an opportunity to pursue its demands more vigorously in the political process. The European Parliament's position was not entirely homogeneous and certainly evolved over time, but at its core was the desire to protect the Parliament's legislative power and its prerogative to hold the Commission to account, both of which the comitology process threatened to undermine.[17] While the Member States were not prepared to concede a greater role in the comitology process to the European Parliament, the Parliament's legal, budgetary, and political powers made a reform of the comitology regime inevitable. After concluding a temporary compromise in 1994 (*modus vivendi*), the Member States agreed to a modest reform, which found its expression in the second Comitology Decision in 1999.[18] But while it simplified the existing procedures,[19] enhanced the transparency of the implementation process, and entrusted the European Parliament with specific information rights and a limited right of intervention where the Commission intended to adopt implementing acts that exceeded the legislative act adopted under

[14] Council Decision 87/373 laying down the procedures for the exercise of implementing powers conferred on the Commission [1987] OJ L197/33.

[15] Bergström (n 7) 189 states that until the Comitology Decision 1987 (n 14), it was said that around 30 different comitology procedures existed. The Council decision established five comitology procedures and two safeguard procedures. In addition to the advisory procedure, the Decision also contained the management committee procedure with two variants. The regulatory committee procedure with its *filet* and *contrefilet* variants was also included.

[16] A challenge brought by the European Parliament before the Court for review of the Comitology Decision was declared inadmissible. See Case 302/87 *European Parliament v Council* [1988] ECR 5615. The European Parliament merely obtained commitments from the Commission to forward certain documents sent to comitology committees to the European Parliament as well.

[17] See Resolution of the European Parliament on questions of comitology relating to the entry into force of the Treaty on European Union of 16 December 1993 [1994] OJ C20/176.

[18] Council Decision 1999/468 laying down the procedures for the exercise of implementing powers conferred on the Commission [1999] OJ L184/23.

[19] The Decision provided for an advisory, a management, a regulatory, and a safeguard procedure without variants.

co-decision,[20] the Decision fell short of establishing the European Parliament as equal partner in the implementation process. Fundamental opposition to the existing comitology regime was also voiced by the Commission in 2001 in its White Paper on European Governance,[21] which argued that, as the Union's executive, the Commission should be freed from management and regulatory committee procedures. The supervision of the Commission's executive powers should be entrusted to the Council and the European Parliament on equal terms.

It was not, however, until the Lisbon Treaty that the Union's implementation process was fundamentally modified and the inter-institutional conflict resolved.[22] Based on the changes in the Constitutional Treaty, the Lisbon Treaty provides for the partial abolition of the comitology regime. Article 290 TFEU stipulates that legislative acts can delegate to the Commission the power to adopt delegated acts to 'supplement or amend certain non-essential elements' of legislative acts. The supervision of the exercise of such powers is entrusted to the Council and the European Parliament on equal terms, including the right by either institution to revoke the delegation or object to the entry into force of the delegated act. But while the Commission has committed itself to consulting expert committees,[23] a comitology mechanism *strictu senso* is no longer foreseen. The comitology system has, however, been maintained for implementing acts under Article 291 TFEU,[24] albeit with certain modifications. As implementing measures are considered to be within the competence of the Member States, a Union act can confer powers for the adoption of implementing measures to the Commission, or exceptionally the Council only where uniform conditions of implementation are necessary. Article 291(3) TFEU makes it clear that a comitology regulation, even though adopted by the Council and the European Parliament, will be limited to setting out in advance mechanisms of control by the Member States of the exercise of such powers.

[20] See also Agreement between European Parliament and the Commission on procedures for implementing Council Decision 1999/468/EC of 28 June 1999 laying down the procedures for the exercise of implementing powers conferred on the Commission, [2000] OJ C339/270.

[21] COM (2001) 428.

[22] After the failed ratification of the Constitutional Treaty, the Council had to concede the establishment of a 'regulatory procedure with scrutiny' designed to provide the legislative authority (European Parliament and Council) with the right to oppose implementing measures of general scope designed to amend non-essential elements of a basic instrument adopted under the co-decision procedure. See Council Decision 2006/512 amending Decision 1999/468/EC laying down the procedures for the exercise of implementing powers conferred on the Commission [2006] OJ L200/11.

[23] See point 4 of the Common Understanding between the European Parliament, the Council of Ministers, and the Commission, Council doc 8640/11, Annex, of 4 April 2011.

[24] On the relationship between Arts 290 and 291 TFEU, see Case C-427/12 *Commission v European Parliament and Council*, judgment of 18 March 2014. See also the contribution by Damian Chalmers, this volume.

III. COMITOLOGY PROCEDURES

The 'mechanisms of control' of the Member States have been enshrined in Regulation 182/2011[25] in the form of procedural arrangements that formally govern the Commission's exercise of implementing powers.[26] The Regulation contains two main procedures: the advisory and the examination procedure. In addition, it provides for a specific procedure for the adoption of immediately applicable acts.[27]

For the application of the advisory and the examination procedures the Regulation contains criteria, which are drafted in more mandatory, but still vaguer, terms than the 1999 Comitology Decision. Article 2(1) provides that the nature and impact of the implementing act are to guide the choice of procedure more generally. In order to limit the considerable discretion in the selection of the adequate comitology procedure granted by this provision, Article 2(2) requires that the examination procedure apply to the making of implementing acts of general scope[28] or relating to areas having a certain political sensitivity.[29] The term 'in particular' used in this provision indicates, however, that the list of measures in the provision is not exhaustive. All the same, situations in which the examination procedure can be applied beyond the instances enumerated in Article 2(2) should be regarded as exceptional. Otherwise, the scope of the advisory procedure, according to Article 2(3), applicable to implementing acts 'not falling within the scope of paragraph 2', would be undermined. Moreover, Article 2(3) allows, 'in duly justified cases', for the application of the advisory procedure, even for the adoption of implementing acts referred to in Article 2(2).

All procedures have in common that they are initiated by the Commission through the submission of draft implementing measures to the relevant committee members, comprised of national officials and chaired by the Commission. The advisory procedure (Article 4) requires the Commission merely to consult the

---

[25] Reg 182/2011 of the European Parliament and the Council laying down the rules and general principles concerning mechanisms for control by Member States of the Commission's exercise of implementing powers [2011] OJ L55/13Reg 182/2011. As a consequence of the requirement in Art 291(3) TFEU for such rules and general principles to be adopted 'in advance', the Reg has a quasi-constitutional status, as it has to be observed by other Union acts, including legislative acts conferring implementing powers to the Commission. See Case C-378/00 *Commission v Parliament and Council* [2003] ECR I-937, paras 40 and 42.

[26] For a better understanding of these procedural arrangements, Reg 182/2011 (n 25) has to be read in conjunction with the Rules of Procedures of each committee, which are to be based on the Standard Rules of Procedure, OJ [2011] C206/6. See Art 9(1) of Reg 182/2011 (n 25).

[27] The procedure in Art 8 of Reg 182/2011 (n 25) replaces the old safeguard procedure.

[28] Art 2(2)(a) of Reg 182/2011 (n 25).

[29] Art 2(2)(b) of Reg 182/2001 (n 25) refers to programmes with substantial implications; the common agricultural and common fisheries policies; the environment, security and safety or protection of the health or safety of humans, animals or plants; the common commercial policy; and taxation.

committee and 'take utmost' account of its opinion, which does therefore not have binding force. It can be argued, however, that where the Commission intends to depart from the committee's opinion, it is under an obligation to give reasons in the implementing act.[30]

In contrast, the examination procedure (Article 5), merging as it does the previous management and regulatory procedures, provides the Member States with greater control. The Commission adopts implementing measures which receive a qualified majority in the committee (positive opinion). On the other hand, the Commission cannot adopt implementing measures which the committee rejects by qualified majority (negative opinion). Two variants exist where the Commission obtains neither a positive nor a negative opinion in the committee (no opinion). Generally, in this case, the Commission has discretion to adopt these implementing measures.[31] This variant therefore corresponds to the old management procedure.[32] However, in certain instances set out in Article 5(4)(2), the Commission is prevented from adopting such measures. This variant applies where (1) the matter falls within certain subject matter areas (taxation, financial services, public health, and multilateral safeguard measures), or (2) where the basic act so determines, or (3) where a simple majority of the committee opposes the Commission's draft implementing measure.[33] This procedure therefore resembles the most stringent variant of the old regulatory procedure.[34] Even where the Commission is not allowed to adopt a draft act because of either a negative opinion or no opinion, in the instances set out in Article 5(4)(2), it can resubmit an amended draft to the committee or take its measure to the appeal committee.[35] The appeal committee is an innovation of the Comitology Regulation and is in effect a substitute for the Council. At the appeal stage, the Commission is only prevented from adopting its measures if it receives a negative opinion, but not in case of a positive or no opinion.[36]

The Comitology Regulation also provides for the adoption of immediately applicable acts under the regime set out in Article 8, which replaces the safeguard procedure of the 1999 Comitology Decision.[37] Where a basic act on duly justified

---

[30] In any event, Art 3(4) of Reg 182/2011 (n 25) requires the Commission to inform the committee as to how it has taken the opinion into account.

[31] Art 5(4)(1) of Reg 182/2011 (n 25).

[32] This is also clear from the alignment provision in Art 13(1)(b) of Reg 182/2011 (n 25).

[33] Art 5(5) of Reg 182/2011 (n 25) applies different rules for draft definitive anti-dumping or countervailing measures, in case the committee delivers no opinion, but a simple majority of its members oppose the draft measures.

[34] See also Art 13(1)(c) of Reg 182/2011 (n 25).

[35] Alternatively, the Commission can use the urgency procedure in Art 7 of Reg 182/2011 (n 25).

[36] In 2012 the appeal committee had to discuss six draft implementation measures referred to it by the Commission. It delivered 'no opinion' on each of them allowing the Commission to adopt the acts. Similarly, in 2013 each of the eight draft implementing measures referred to the appeal committee received 'no opinion'.

[37] Art 13(1)(e) of Reg 182/2011 (n 25).

grounds of urgency so provides, the Commission adopts acts which are to apply immediately and remain in force for not more than six months, unless the basic act stipulates otherwise. The Commission has to refer such acts, no later than 14 days after their adoption, to the relevant committee in order to obtain its opinion. Where the committee in the examination procedure delivers a negative opinion, the Commission must repeal such acts immediately. This procedure applies also where the Commission adopts provisional anti-dumping or countervailing measures.[38] In this case, the Commission has to consult or, in cases of extreme urgency, inform the Member States.

In Article 13, the Regulation automatically aligns the old comitology procedures with the new procedures, the exception being the regulatory procedure with scrutiny, set out in Article 5a of Regulation 1999/468 (as amended), which continues to be applied for a transitional period, where basic acts adopted prior to the entry into force of the Lisbon Treaty refer to it. Most, but arguably not all, implementing acts adopted under this procedure will ultimately fall within the scope of Article 290 TFEU. Similarly, certain basic acts whose reference to the old regulatory procedure is now to be understood to refer to the examination procedure might have to be brought under the regime of delegated acts in Article 290 TFEU.

It seems to be clear from this overview that the new Comitology Regulation failed to achieve any simplification of the previous comitology procedures. The criteria for application remain vague, and the procedures are by and large similar to those used in the 1999 Comitology Decision. Worse, the drafting has become ever more complex with rules being subjected to exceptions, which are themselves subject to counter-exceptions. While this provides for a finely tuned balance of power between Commission and Member States, it does not create an intelligible set of rules. What is more, the comitology procedures have to be situated in the wider context of the Union's procedures for the adoption of implementing acts. They are often an integral part of what can be termed 'composite' procedures.[39] Such procedures integrate Member State authorities, Union agencies, comitology committees, and the Commission into a single procedural framework, prescribed by Union law. Such multi-level procedures often require a sequence of procedural steps, designed to gather information, evaluate scientific evidence, and engage the participation of third parties. The comitology process often constitutes the final procedural component before the adoption of any Union implementing acts by the Commission. In some instances, agencies carry out tasks which precede and often considerably constrain the comitology process.[40] This is in particular the case where agencies

---

[38] Art 8(5) of Reg 182/2011 (n 25).

[39] See Herwig C.H. Hofmann, Gerard Rowe, and Alexander Türk, *Administrative Law and Policy of the European Union* (2011) 405–410.

[40] Madalina Busuioc, 'Rule-making by the European Financial Supervisory Authorities: Walking a Tight Rope' (2013) 19 *European Law Journal* 111.

provide scientific opinions that constitute an essential procedural requirement for the adoption of implementing acts,[41] or have been entrusted with the submission of draft implementing acts, which cannot be amended without prior coordination with the agency.[42] And in case of the adoption of implementing technical standards by the Commission on the basis of a draft by the European Financial Supervisory Authorities, the involvement of comitology committees has been dispensed with altogether.[43]

IV. Comitology as Organizational Structure

Comitology procedures matter, as they provide the formal rules of the comitology process. It is therefore not surprising that the interaction between the Commission and the national representatives is often assessed in purely formal terms as being determined by the procedures which the Commission has to follow for the adoption of implementing acts.[44] Empirical research seems, however, to suggest that the applicable procedure is only one factor in the relationship between the Commission and national representatives[45] and therefore provides only a limited insight into the actual functioning of the comitology system. A fuller understanding can only be gained when we perceive comitology as an organizational structure, which provides for the interaction between the Commission and the Member States in the adoption of Union implementing acts. In this organizational arrangement,

---

[41] See Art 5(2) of Regulation 726/2004 of the European Parliament and of the Council of 31 March 2004 laying down Community procedures for the authorization and supervision of medicinal products for human and veterinary use and establishing a European Medicines Agency [2004] OJ L136/1.

[42] See Art 17(2)(b) of Reg 216/2008 of the European Parliament and of the Council of 20 February 2008 on common rules in the field of civil aviation and establishing a European Aviation Safety Agency [2008] OJ L79/1. See also Art 15(1)(7) of Reg 1093/2010 of the European Parliament and of the Council of 24 November 2010 establishing a European Supervisory Authority (European Banking Authority), [2010] OJ L331/12.

[43] See eg Art 15 of Reg 1093/2010 (n 42).

[44] See Adrienne Héritier, Catherine Moury, Carina Bischoff, and Carl F. Bergström, *Changing Rules of Delegation—A Contest for Power in Comitology* (2013) 13–14.

[45] See Christian Joerges and Jürgen Neyer, 'Transforming Strategic Interaction into Deliberative Problem-solving: European Comitology in the Foodstuffs Sector' (1997) 4 *Journal of European Public Policy* 609; Jarle Trondal, 'EU Committee Governance and the Multilevel Community Administration' in Herwig C.H. Hofmann and Alexander Türk (eds), *EU Administrative Governance* (2006); Brandsma (n 1) 94–101.

the Commission is formally in charge of the proceedings.[46] It is entrusted with the convening of the committees,[47] the preparing of the agenda, the submission of draft implementing acts, the chairing of the meetings, the obtaining of the committee's opinion, and the adoption of the final act. The decisive role within the Commission is played by the policy units, even though the adoption of the final act is a matter for the College of Commissioners. In contrast, the Member States seem to play a more reactive role. The opinion of the committee on the Commission's implementing draft is formally the main contribution that the representatives of the Member States make. The Member States can, however, shape the Commission's draft act by making suggestions for amendments, which the Commission is obliged to consider.[48] Member States are represented by the policy experts from the national administrations and often have considerable discretion in the formulation of the national position.[49] This discretion is constrained on the one hand by the expectation of committee members of a rational discourse based on policy expertise and on the other hand by the expectations of their national supervisors. It is only at the level of the appeal committee that Member States are represented at a more senior level, mainly through representatives of the Member States' permanent representations. The Council, but also the European Parliament, play no formal role in the proceedings, but are merely informed by the Commission and can exercise an *ultra vires* power.[50] All the same, organizationally the appeal committee provides for all intents and purposes the link with the Council, as its composition seems to overlap largely with that of the COREPER.

In practice, the relationship between the Commission and national representatives is largely based on cooperation, which is facilitated by the consensual approach of the Commission and the tendency of national representatives to perceive their role as contributing to the discussion as policy experts.[51] It is therefore more appropriate to consider the interaction between the Commission and the Member States in comitology as a form of 'joint decision making'.[52] The integration of the Commission and Member States within this organizational arrangement has proven to be an effective way to accommodate the different interests between the Commission and the Member States and between the Member States themselves in the adoption of Union implementing acts.[53] Comitology as an organizational form

---

[46] The Commission's tasks can be found in Reg 182/2011 (n 25) and the Rules of Procedure of the committees.

[47] In duly justified cases, the Commission can proceed by written procedure. See Art 3(5) of Reg 182/2011 (n 25).

[48] See Art 3(4) of Reg 182/2011 (n 25).   [49] See Brandsma (n 1) 120ff.

[50] See Arts 10 and 11 or Reg 182/2011 (n 25).

[51] The attitude of national representatives is, however, ambiguous. On the one hand, their expertise should contribute to a good decision, but on the other, they are formally expected to protect the national interest in the decision making process.

[52] Brandsma (n 1) 119.

[53] Herwig C.H. Hofmann and Alexander Türk, 'The Development of Integrated Administration in the EU and its Consequences' (2007) 13 *European Law Journal* 253.

of EU administrative law has thereby acquired a distinctive character that sets it apart from other organizational structures of the Union. It does not fit into the dichotomy of centralized[54] and decentralized[55] administration that has often been used to characterize the Union's administrative structure.[56] Comitology also differs from agency and network structures, which are regarded as atypical forms of administrative integration in the EU.[57]

V. COMITOLOGY COMMITTEES AS CONTROL MECHANISMS FOR MEMBER STATES?

While the preceding discussion focused on the formal procedures which govern the comitology process and on the functioning of comitology as organizational structure within the Union's legal system, this section will examine in more detail the stipulation in Article 291(3) TFEU, read in conjunction with Regulation 182/2011, that comitology committees constitute a control mechanism for Member States on the Commission's exercise of implementing powers. It will be argued that this formulation raises a number of difficult questions about the function and nature of comitology committees when assessed in the wider constitutional context of Article 291 TFEU.

As a first point, the function of comitology committees, according to Article 291 TFEU, to provide a control mechanism for *Member States* differs from the pre-Lisbon regime, which considered comitology committees as a control mechanism that would allow the *Council* as delegating authority to guide the Commission, and intervene instead of the Commission if necessary.[58] However, the congruence of the views of committee representatives with those of Council members which this mechanism assumed has been shown to be empirically questionable.[59]

---

[54] In contrast to centralized administration, comitology is characterized by a formal and systematic cooperation between the Commission and the Member States, which have a constitutionally protected position in the control of the Commission's exercise of implementing powers.

[55] Comitology differs from decentralized or shared forms of Union administration, in that the Commission and the Member States do not pursue distinct administrative tasks, but are integrated into an organizational and procedural framework in pursuance of the same task, namely the adoption of Union implementing acts.

[56] For a typology of centralized and shared administration, see P. Craig, *EU Administrative Law* (2nd ed, 2012) 27–33.

[57] See Merijn Chamon, 'Transforming the EU Administration: Legal and Political Limits to Agencification' (2015) PhD thesis, Gent University, 73 (on file with author).

[58] *Köster* (n 11), para 9.

[59] See Brandsma (n 1) 68 and Chs 5 and 6. See also Trondal (n 45) 391.

The dual position of committee members as national representatives and technical policy experts distinguishes their engagement with the Commission from that of the more politically minded members of Council.[60] Moreover, the cooperative interaction between the Commission and national civil servants has led in practice to a very limited number of referrals to the Council.[61] While from a formal point the committees would not take any decisions themselves, the close interaction between the Commission and the committees and the potential for divergent positions of the committee members and the Council made debatable the Court's argument that the comitology arrangement did not distort 'the Community structure and the institutional balance'.[62]

In contrast, the new regime under Article 291 TFEU is based on the premise that implementing powers are in principle to be exercised by the Member States, which therefore should have the power to control the exercise of the Commission's implementing powers. While it reflects a more realistic understanding of the function of comitology committees, on further reflection, this premise is constitutionally questionable. The assumption that the Commission's exercise of implementing powers under Article 291 TFEU takes place within a constitutionally assigned area of Member State competence is not sustainable. Article 291(2) TFEU makes it mandatory for the Union to delegate implementing powers to the Commission (exceptionally to the Council), where uniform conditions for implementation are needed. This implies with necessity that such implementing powers are within the Union's exclusive competence and not the competence of the Member States. Article 291(1) and Article 291(2) TFEU therefore assign mutually exclusive competence areas to the Member States and Union institutions, respectively, for the adoption of implementing acts.[63]

This has important consequences for the function and legal nature of comitology committees. As they exercise their powers in the sphere of Union (and not Member State) competence, comitology committees cannot be said to act in protection of any national prerogative, but as an integral part of the organizational structure established by Union law for the adoption of Union implementing acts. In this view, the representation of Member States in the decision making processes of the Union is an important functional element of the EU legal order. In

---

[60] This is at least the case as far as COREPER and the ministerial formations are concerned.

[61] See eg the number of referrals in 2010 in European Commission, *Commission Staff Working Paper 'Presentation of Committee Activities in 2010 by policy sectors' Accompanying Document to the Report from the Commission: On the Working of Committees During 2010* COM (2011) 879 final.

[62] Case 25/70 *Köster* [1970] ECR 1161, para 9.

[63] Art 291 TFEU can therefore not be considered as a shared competence. In contrast to shared competences, which provide the Union with a facultative option to exercise its competence, Art 291(2) TFEU contains a mandatory requirement for conferral to the Commission or Council. On the relationship between Art 291(1) and (2) TFEU, see also Robert Schütze, 'From Rome to Lisbon: "Executive Federalism" in the (New) European Union' (2010) 47 *Common Market Law Review* 1385, 1398.

the Union's multi-level system of governance, it is important that the impact of binding Union acts on the Member States is considered and taken into account. The application of such measures by the Member States, which are constitutionally obliged to execute them, and their acceptance within the national legal orders can be seen as the *quid pro quo* for the involvement of the governments of the Member States in the Union's decision-making process. This, and not the protection of a national prerogative, justifies the involvement of the Member States in the process for the adoption of Union implementing acts.

The argument that comitology committees operate in the sphere of Union competence also has consequences for the assessment of their legal nature. While comitology committees are obviously not Union institutions in the meaning of Article 13(1) TEU, it is argued that comitology committees should be considered to be Union bodies. It is true that in *Rothmans*[64] the General Court stated that, since the Customs Code committee, a comitology committee, did not have 'its own administration, budget, archives or premises, still less of an address of its own',[65] it could not be regarded as 'Community institution or body'.[66] The General Court found that, as the committee was also not 'a natural or legal person, a Member State or any other national or international body',[67] or a working party in Council, it had to be regarded as coming under the Commission. This assessment, which was primarily concerned with the then applicable access to documents rules,[68] was questionable at the time[69] and is even more so post Lisbon. The participation of comitology committees is governed by Union legislation, which, by virtue of Regulation 182/2011, endows them with certain autonomous powers of action vis-à-vis the Commission. Moreover, the governments of the Member States determine their representation independently of the Commission. This means that comitology committees are neither functionally nor organizationally subordinate to the Commission. Comitology committees are, however, not merely bodies of the Member States. They are formally established by Union law, which entrusts them with a specific task to be carried out in the sphere of Union law, and to that end they are endowed with the power independently to formulate opinions that are formally attributed to them and binding on the Commission.[70] They therefore have the legal capacity, albeit rather limited, by virtue of Union law to act as an

---

[64] Case T-188/97 *Rothmans v Commission* [1999] ECR II-2463. See also Case T-111/00 *BAT v Commission* [2001] ECR II-2997, para 37.

[65] *BAT* (n 64) para 58.   [66] *BAT* (n 64) para 59.   [67] *BAT* (n 64) para 59.

[68] The assessment has to be seen in the context of the difficulties posed to access to documents by the authorship rule in the Code of Conduct adopted by Decision 94/90 on public access to Commission documents [1994] OJ L46/58.

[69] Kieran Bradley, 'Comitology and the Courts: Tales of the Unexpected', in Herwig Hofmann and Alexander Türk (eds), *EU Administrative Governance* (2006) 417, 437–440.

[70] See also Case T-411/06 *Sogelma v EAR* [2008] ECR II-2771, paras 50–56. Cf Case T-395/11 *Elti v Delegation of the European Union to Montenegro*, judgment of 4 June 2012.

independent body of Union law. Hence, they should be regarded as Union bodies. This is not altered by the fact that, together with the Commission, they form an integral part of the organizational structure established by Union law for the adoption of Union implementing acts, since within that structure they carry out their Union tasks in full independence from the Commission.

A second point that needs to be addressed in this context concerns the question as to what extent comitology committees act as mechanisms of *control*. A purely formal view would suggest that comitology committees merely provide opinions, which permit or prohibit the Commission to proceed with the adoption of implementing acts. This could be considered as an *ex post* form of control. As discussed in Section III, this would, however, not be an adequate representation of what actually happens in comitology committees. Committee members are often involved in the drafting of Union implementing acts, but in this case not in their formal capacity as members of comitology committees, but rather as national policy experts. When the Commission then formally presents its draft, committee members discuss the text in detail and make suggestions for amendments, leading to a cooperative form of decision making.[71] The dual position of committee members as policy experts and national representatives here comes to the fore. The ambiguity of the involvement of national representatives has also led to different assessments as to whether comitology constitutes a forum for deliberation or for the aggregation of national interests. This debate, which will be explored in more detail in Section VI, is not only relevant for an accurate description of comitology, but from a normative perspective also raises the question as to what the true purpose of comitology committees should be.

VI. COMITOLOGY AS FORUM FOR DELIBERATION OR BARGAINING

Following the discussion above, we could define comitology as a formally established organizational arrangement of the Union for the interaction between the Commission and the Member States in the exercise of a Union competence (the adoption of Union implementing acts) following prescribed procedural arrangements. Comitology committees provide the institutionalized forum, in which this interaction takes place, and which, as Union bodies, allow Member States, formally to express opinions, the legal effects of which are determined by Union law, on

---

[71] Brandsma (n 1) 94–101.

draft implementing acts submitted by the Commission. The interaction between the Commission and national representatives within the comitology process has, however, led to widely different views amongst academic scholars as to what the purpose of such interaction should be. This is not merely a debate as to what scholars believe they can empirically observe in comitology committees, but rather a debate about the normative purpose of the comitology process itself.

Weiler's observation in 1999 that 'comitology is not a discreet phenomenon which occurs at the end of the decision-making process' but—like the discovery of a new sub-atomic particle—calls 'for a rewriting of the entire decision-making field because of the importance of the committee particle in all its stages'[72] still captures the challenge posed for any evaluation of comitology. His own suggestion to consider comitology as a form of infranationalism seems to have been chiefly designed to convey the point that the reality of comitology does not easily fit the supranational-intergovernmental paradigms of European governance and to accentuate the challenges comitology poses to our understanding of constitutionalism and democracy.

All the same, the supranational-intergovernmental framework is still influential in the academic debates on comitology. Rational choice institutionalism, which argues that actors use institutions to maximize their influence, sees comitology as an instrument of the Member States to exercise control over power delegated by them to the Commission.[73] Its analysis of comitology is based on the principal-agent model. Comitology in this view ensures that the Commission as supranational agent does not deviate from the preferences of the Member State principals. Comitology committees act as fora in which national representatives articulate the preferences of their Member States and seek to maximize their positions through a process of bargaining.[74] Comitology procedures are commensurate with the interests of the Member States in the control of the Commission. Rational choice institutionalism has to be seen as a reaction to a more transformative conceptual framework for comitology, which considers comitology to be a supranational forum for deliberative problem solving at European level. Deliberative supranationalism[75] does not merely attempt to give

---

[72] Joseph Weiler, 'Epilogue: "Comitology" as Revolution—Infranationalism, Constitutionalism and Democracy', in Joerges and Vos (n 5).

[73] Fabio Franchino, 'Control of the Commission's Executive Functions: Uncertainty, Conflict and Decision Rules' (2000) 1 *European Union Politics* 63; Mark A. Pollack, *The Engines of Integration, Delegation, Agency and Agenda Setting in the EU* (2003) 75–154; Adrienne Héritier, 'Institutional Change in Europe: Co-decision and Comitology Transformed' (2012) 50 *Journal of Common Market Studies* 38; Jens Blom-Hansen, 'Legislative Control of Powers Delegated to the Executive: The Case of the EU' (2013) 26 *Governance* 425.

[74] See Héritier, Moury, Bischoff, and Bergström (n 44).

[75] Joerges and Neyer (n 6); Joerges and Vos (n 5); Christian Joerges, 'Deliberative Political Processes' Revisited: What Have we Learnt About the Legitimacy of Supranational Decision-making' (2006) 44 *Journal of Common Market Studies* 779; Ellen Vos, '50 Years of European Integration, 45 Years of Comitology' (2009) *Maastricht Faculty of Law Working Paper* 2009-3.

a descriptive account of comitology, it also seeks to provide a normative framework that respects the constitutional legitimacy of national democracies while
imposing a supranational discipline on the harmful tendency of Member States
to pursue self-interested policies.[76] Comitology, in this view, avoids the legitimacy problems of centralized executive decision making by the Commission,
while at the same time offering a deliberative style of policy making disciplining the interactions of the Member States.[77] Comitology as a non-hierarchical
transnational governance structure is thereby thought to fit best the Union's *sui
generis* nature.

Despite their differences, rational choice institutionalism and deliberative
supranationalism models share certain premises. While they disagree on the
mode of decision making in comitology (interest bargaining v deliberative
problem solving), both theories take it for granted that the Member States are
central to the decision making process at Union level and that decisions which
emanate from this process derive their legitimacy from the participation of
the Member States. Both theories assume, for different reasons, that the position of national officials in comitology committees is sufficiently representative of the national interest. This is problematic, as empirical work suggests
that members of comitology committees often have considerable discretion in
what they perceive the national interest to be, as they often have only vague or
no instructions from their national departments.[78] They are frequently instrumental in shaping the national positions. Moreover, while there are some issues
in comitology, such as genetically modified foodstuffs, that are sufficiently
controversial to have led to national positions being formally adopted by
national governments or even national Parliaments, often interest formation is
mostly less legitimized and, if it takes place at all, results from positions taken
within the national administrations themselves.[79] Finally, there is considerable
empirical evidence that the national identity of committee officials is affected
by a socialization effect in committees that creates 'supranational' commitments to a common interest developed by the group.[80] A further weakness of
the centrality of the Member States in the comitology process, on which both
theories are premised, is that it marginalizes the contribution of other actors.
The Commission's role is reduced to that of a coordinating body, while the
European Parliament and public participation are regarded as impracticable
or, worse, undesirable.[81] This raises concerns about the legitimacy of comitology, in particular its accountability.

---

[76] Joerges and Neyer (n 6) 294; Joerges (n 75) 789.   [77] Joerges and Neyer (n 6) 298.
[78] See Brandsma (n 1) Ch 6.   [79] See Brandsma (n 1) Ch 6.
[80] Jarle Trondal, 'Beyond the EU Membership–Non-membership Dichotomy? Supranational
Identities among National EU Decision-makers' (2002) 9 *Journal of European Public Policy* 468.
[81] See Craig (n 56) 122–124.

VII. Legitimacy of Comitology

It is generally acknowledged that the EU suffers from weak input legitimacy given that the representation of the Union's citizens in the Union's majoritarian institutions is far more limited than in its Member States. Despite the protestations of Article 10 TEU to the contrary, this is not only because of institutional weaknesses of the European Parliament[82] and the still dominant role of the European Council and the Council of Ministers, but also because of the 'thinness of the communicative processes that articulate citizen ideas and concerns in the European public sphere'.[83] Moreover, the constitutional imperative for institutional balance and the institutional desire for consensus weaken the impact of Union citizens in European politics. From this perspective, Article 291 TFEU, in contrast to Article 290 TFEU, compounds this problem by restricting the role of majoritarian institutions in the comitology process.

In contrast, the contribution of comitology to output legitimacy within the EU has been viewed more favourably. The capacity of comitology for problem solving has been seen as its primary rationale.[84] Rational choice institutionalists would consider comitology to be a mechanism for ensuring that the preferences of Member States, and indirectly their citizens, are delivered by the Commission. However, the largely integrated and autonomous nature of comitology committees based on intense cooperative interaction between the Commission and the Member States' representatives has not been matched by adequate control by the Member State governments.[85] The limited control of national governments over their representatives in comitology committees also weakens any argument that the deliberative quality of discussions between Commission and Member States in comitology enhances its output legitimacy.[86] The decisional autonomy of comitology also undermines the argument that the structural checks and balances inherent in comitology justify its output legitimacy. While the committees certainly impose a check on the Commission, the structural checks and balances on comitology decisions as a product of intensive cooperation between the Commission and national

---

[82] The European Parliament suffers from an unequal system of representation of Union citizens. Its elections are often regarded as second-order elections and turnout is usually low. Moreover, European parties are often considered weak and need to cater for a broad spectrum of opinion.

[83] Vivien A. Schmidt, 'Democracy and Legitimacy in the European Union Revisited: Input, Output and "Throughput"' (2013) 61 *Political Studies* 2, 13.

[84] Mark Rhinard, 'The Democratic Legitimacy of the European Union Committee System' (2002) 15 *Governance* 185, 188.

[85] Weiler (n 72), 342. Brandsma (n 1) Ch 6.

[86] The danger is that national positions merely reflect whatever the civil servant in the comitology committee believes it to be rather than the reflected and coordinated position of the national government.

civil servants are rather weak.[87] Conversely, while the relative independence of its activities might be employed as an argument that its problem solving capacity would be enhanced by insulation from political input,[88] comitology, with its considerable social, economic, and political consequences, cannot simply be reduced to mere regulatory functions, which should escape majoritarian control.

The legitimacy of comitology has therefore also to consider the legitimacy of the decision making process itself. This seems all the more important as the *sui generis* nature of the Union makes national standards for democratic legitimacy less appropriate. While different views exist as to how such process legitimacy could be conceptualized,[89] the following can be regarded as essential[90]: the process needs to be intelligible, in the sense that citizens can understand what decisions are made and how they are made; it needs to have a deliberative quality, allowing access of diverse public interests and the fair consideration of such interests; and it needs to provide for accountability. Comitology has responded to these challenges to a different degree.

As regards the intelligible nature of the process, over the years comitology has certainly become a more formalized and transparent process. All the same, while the statutory provisions on comitology procedures, and the criteria for their application, have reached a baffling complexity,[91] informal practices continue and often deviate from the constitutionally designed rules.[92] At the same time, while the information that the public receives via the comitology register, about agendas of meetings, draft acts, summary records of meetings, and so on, has been beneficial, it is still considered insufficient.[93] Similarly, while the Union's access-to-documents regime applies also to comitology documents,[94] the Union institutions frequently invoke its exceptions to deny access. In respect of its deliberative qualities, it is now widely acknowledged that the decision making process is more deliberative than rational choice institutionalists predicted. However, while deliberation seems to be the predominant mode of behaviour in committees, in many cases bargaining

---

[87] Generally, on structural checks and balances as basis for output legitimacy, see Andrew Moravcsik, 'Reassessing Legitimacy in the European Union' (2002) 40 *Journal of Common Market Studies* 603.

[88] The argument has been used by Giandomenico Majone, 'Europe's Democratic Deficit' (1998) 4 *European Law Journal* 5 to make the case for regulatory agencies.

[89] See Schmidt (n 83), on 'throughput' legitimacy as normative criterion for democratic legitimacy of the EU.

[90] See also Rhinard (n 84) 190–192.

[91] So Section III. See also Paul Craig, 'Delegated Acts, implementing acts and the new Comitology Regulation' (2011) 36 *European Law Review* 671, 684–685.

[92] Brandsma (n 1) 162.

[93] Gijs J. Brandsma, Deirdre Curtin, and Albert Meijer, 'How Transparent are EU "Comitology" Committees in Practice?' (2008) 14 *European Law Journal* 819.

[94] See Art 9(2) of Reg 182/2011 (n 25), which makes applicable Reg 1049/2011 of the European Parliament and the Council regarding public access to European Parliament, Council and Commission documents [2001] OJ L145/43.

can be found alongside deliberation.[95] And while it can reduce sectarian power, the possibility, though it is as yet unsubstantiated, that committees' deliberations are conditioned by the social background and biases of their privileged members is of concern.[96] This raises questions about the inclusiveness of the process of different public-interest conceptions and their fair consideration.[97] In this respect, citizens have only limited participation rights granted in statutory provisions or in the case law of the CJEU.[98] In practice, however, the participation of interested parties is increasingly dependent on the statutory provisions and practices of agencies, which have come to dominate the procedural phase preceding the deliberation of implementing acts in comitology committees.[99] This is even more important, as the technical and scientific expertise of agencies can impose considerable constraints on the deliberations of the comitology process.[100]

The conundrum that the comitology process faces is that its (traditional) ideal of expert-led deliberations between national and supranational administrations, preferably behind closed doors, is in tension with the Union's ambition and constitutional demand for a more democratic and open decision making process. How, and perhaps even whether, this tension can be resolved is a key challenge for the comitology regime.[101] Similar problems also arise in respect of its accountability.[102] The complexity of the comitology process and its multi-level nature pose considerable difficulties for political and judicial accountability.[103] In a recent study on the political accountability of comitology, Brandsma proposes a disaggregated framework of analysis of comitology as a multi-level governance process, where each actor is accountable to a forum for its own input.[104] In this view, accountability requires a focus on the constitutional design of the comitology system, the daily operation of the comitology process at the committee level, and the contribution

---

[95] Brandsma (n 1) 96.   [96] See Weiler (n 72) 348.

[97] Denis J. Calligan, *Due Process and Fair Procedures: A Study of Administrative Procedures* (1996).

[98] Joana Mendes, *Participation in EU Rule-making: A Rights-based Approach* (2011), Ch 4.

[99] Hofmann, Rowe, and Türk (n 39) 304–307.

[100] Such constraints do not merely exist de facto, but can also be the result of case law of the CJEU (see Case T-70/99 *Alpharma v Commission* [2002] ECR II-3495; Case T-240/10 *Hungary v Commission*, judgment of 13 December 2013) and of Union legislation (see Art 15 of Reg 1093/2010 (n 42)).

[101] See also Michelle Egan and Dieter Wolf, 'Reg and Comitology: The EC Committee System in Regulatory Perspective' (1998) 4 *Columbia Journal of European Law* 499.

[102] Accountability is defined here as 'a relationship between an actor and a forum, in which the actor has an obligation to explain and justify his or her conduct; the forum can post questions and pass judgment, and the actor may face consequences'; see Mark Bovens, 'Analysing and Assessing Accountability: A Conceptual Framework' (2007) 13 *European Law Journal* 447, 450.

[103] See Steve Peers and Marios Costa, 'Accountability for Delegated and Implementing Acts after the Treaty of Lisbon' (2012) 18 *European Law Journal* 427; Brandsma (n 1). On the difficult questions which external accountability can raise, see Grace Skogstad, 'Contested Accountability Claims and GMO Reg in the European Union' (2011) 49 *Journal of Common Market Studies* 895.

[104] Brandsma (n 1) 148.

of Member State civil servants at participant level. Accountability, he argues, needs to be tailored to the 'jurisdictional boundaries to which the accountability relationships are subject'.[105] This means that accountability for final decisions is located at supranational level, while accountability at national level considers the input of the national representatives. The main accountability deficit that emerges from his study is the weakness of the forum—at supranational level the European Parliament and at national level the officials supervising the national representatives.[106] While providing a valuable framework of analysis and important insights into actor–forum relationships in the practice of comitology, the approach falls short in one important respect, namely that national representatives in the committee should face accountability only at national level, leaving the Commission responsible for what is essentially a collective output in comitology.[107] It is submitted that this approach ignores the legal and political importance of comitology committees as *Union* bodies.

While the CJEU has played a crucial role in shaping the constitutional framework of comitology, the integrated nature of the comitology process also poses a considerable challenge to judicial supervision.[108] First, the dictum of the Court in *Köster* that committees do not pose a challenge to the institutional balance, as they have no decision making power,[109] has always been empirically questionable in light of the cooperative nature of the comitology process. With the elimination of the Council from the decision making process, it is no longer legally tenable. In certain instances, committees, even in the narrow legal sense, do make decisions that bind the Commission. A negative opinion of the committee precludes the Commission from adopting an implementing act,[110] and a negative opinion at appeal level constitutes a binding, and final, rejection of a Commission draft.[111] The committees' power is entirely negative, but in the case of an application for a marketing authorization a negative opinion by the committee is *de facto* determinative of the outcome of the procedure. Legal fiction, and the right to an effective remedy, demands that the Commission adopt the final act, but this should not obscure the binding nature of the opinion of committees.[112] This raises uncomfortable questions. Should committees be required to give reasons for their opinions? Can the CJEU review the procedural and substantive legality of the opinion?[113] The nature of comitology

---

[105] Brandsma (n 1) 161.   [106] Brandsma (n 1) 162–163.   [107] So Brandsma (n 1) at 148.

[108] See Weiler (n 72) 343–346   [109] *Köster* (n 11), para 9.

[110] Art 5(3)(1) of Reg 182/2011 (n 25).

[111] Art 6(3)(3) of Reg 182/2011 (n 25). See, however, Case T-301/12 *Laboratoires CTRS v Commission*, judgment of 4 July 2013, where the Commission had resubmitted a draft implementing act despite a negative opinion of the appeal committee. The General Court did not discuss the issue, but annulled the Commission act on different grounds.

[112] The committee's opinion has legally binding effects only for the Commission, but not third parties, and therefore in strict legal terms does not constitute a reviewable act in the meaning of Art 263(1) TFEU.

[113] This questions has been answered affirmatively by the Court for agency opinions: see Joined Cases T-74/00 etc *Artegodan and others v Commission* [2002] ECR II-4945.

committees as Union bodies and their judicial accountability would demand as much. Second, the CJEU has been asked to play a more active role in granting process rights to applicants. By strengthening the right of access to documents,[114] the CJEU has no doubt contributed to a more transparent decision making process in comitology. The danger that sensitive issues will be pushed to the margins of the meetings is real, but has to be viewed in light of the need for enhanced legitimacy of comitology committees. This is even more so because the participation rights of citizens in the comitology process are limited. However, this should not lead to the conclusion that the CJEU should widen the scope of participation rights[115] beyond the considerations of individualization and adverse effects that currently underpin the right to be heard.[116] It is submitted that the responsibility for such action, however necessary it might be to enhance the legitimacy of the process, rests with the Union legislator and not the Union courts.[117] Third, the question can be asked as to whether the right to an effective remedy is infringed where private parties have to rely, often successively, on Article 265 TFEU to force a reluctant Commission to proceed through the various stages of the comitology process.[118]

BIBLIOGRAPHY

Carl F. Bergström, Comitology—Delegation of Powers in the European Union and the Committee System (2005)

Gijs J. Brandsma, *Controlling Comitology—Accountability in a Multi-level System* (2013)

Thomas Chrstiansen and Torbjörn Larsson (eds), *The Role of Committees in the Policy-process of the European Union* (2007)

Paul Craig, *EU Administrative Law* (2nd ed, 2012), Ch 5 Comitology 109

Adrienne Héritier, Catherine Moury, Carina Bischoff, Carl F. Bergström, *Changing Rules of Delegation—A Contest for Power in Comitology* (2013)

Herwig Hofmann, Gerard Rowe, and Alexander Türk, *Administrative Law and Policy of the European Union* (2011), Chs 9B Comitology 264 and 11C Comitology 386

Christian Joerges and Jürgen Neyer, 'From Intergovernmental Bargaining to Deliberative Political Processes: The Constitutionalisation of Comitology' (1997) 3 *European Law Journal* 273

Christian Joerges and Ellen Vos (eds), *EU Committees: Social Regulation, Law and Politics* (1999)

---

[114] See Hofmann, Rowe, and Türk (n 39) 402–403.

[115] Mendes (n 98); Craig (n 56) 290–298.

[116] Alexander Türk, 'The Concept of Legislation and Participation Rights in EU Law' (2013) 6 *Indian Journal of Constitutional Law* 79, 89–94.

[117] Türk (n 116) 114–116.

[118] For an instructive example, see Case T-164/10 *Pioneer Hi-Bred v Commission*, judgment of 26 September 2013. See also John Temple Lang and Colin Raftery, 'Remedies for the Commission's Failure to act in "Comitology" Cases (2011) 36 *European Law Review* 264.

Mark Pollack, *The Engines of Integration, Delegation, Agency and Agenda Setting in the EU* (2003), Ch 2 The Commission as an Agent: Delegation of Executive Power in the European Union 75

Mark Rhinard, 'The Democratic Legitimacy of the European Union Committee System' (2002) 15 *Governance* 185

Jarle Trondal, 'Beyond the EU Membership–Non-membership Dichotomy? Supranational Identities among National EU Decision-makers' (2002) 9 *Journal of European Public Policy* 468

CHAPTER 14

......

THE EVOLUTION OF INFRINGEMENT AND SANCTION PROCEDURES

OF PILOTS, DIVERSIONS, COLLISIONS, AND CIRCLING

......

MELANIE SMITH

I. INTRODUCTION

......

THERE are multiple ways to enforce EU law in national courts.[1] The centralized enforcement provisions are the method by which the Commission provides overall supervision, or guardianship, over the Union Treaties and the rule of law in the Union.[2] The centralized enforcement provisions are Article 258 and Article 260 TFEU, commonly referred to as the infringement procedure and the financial sanction. This chapter will consider the evolution of these two articles over the last decade or so, examining the changes in law and administrative practice that have

---

[1] Paul Craig and Gráinne de Búrca, *EU Law: Text, Cases and Materials* (5th ed, 2011) Ch 13–17; this volume, Chs 8, 11, 17.

[2] Art 17(1) TEU.

occurred, as well as the evolving approach in the academic literature. These legal provisions are pivotal to a Union based on the rule of law[3] as they ensure *post hoc* adherence to policies agreed at the political and institutional levels of the EU. To imagine these provisions simply as blunt legal instruments designed to force compliance, however, is to underestimate the administrative and political complexity that characterize the infringement and sanction processes and the extent to which resort to these instruments is avoided wherever possible.

The evolution of these two sister provisions has been radically different. The infringement process is perpetually grounded, unable to take flight and realize its full potential. In contrast, the sanction process has been dynamic, a legal provision able to launch from its original tightly circumscribed legal language and become a reasonably effective sanction against infracting Member States. Why have there been such different evolutions of these two intertwined and originally virtually indistinguishable provisions? What can we learn from examining the political, administrative, and legal interactions behind them? How will the centralized enforcement mechanism develop in the future? Section II of this chapter will briefly examine the basic legal framework of the infringement and sanction procedures. It will comment on the academic literature in this area, questioning why this is one of the most under-researched areas of EU law. Section III will discuss the current practice with regard to the operation of the infringement procedure and financial sanction, and finally the chapter will conclude by looking toward the future development of these two important policy areas.

II. Two Articles with Different Trajectories

The infringement and sanction processes are often treated in the literature as quite separate entities, despite the obvious interdependence and similar legal language. They are both expressions of the Commission's duty as guardian of the treaties. They are both concerned, broadly speaking, with compliance with norms and legal judgments. A richer understanding of the centralized enforcement process can really only be gained when looking at these provisions of policy, law, and administration in conjunction, not least because the apparent surface similarities belie huge political, administrative, and operational differences, which, it might be argued, highlight the deficiencies of one and celebrate the achievements of the other.

---

[3] Art 2 TEU.

1. The Infringement Procedure in Article 258 TFEU: Failure to Launch?

Article 258 TFEU is one of the few relatively static provisions in the Treaties. It is remarkable for its total lack of legal dynamism and unchanging dogma over the last 50 or so years. Its text has survived unchanged, save for a technical change brought about by the collapsing of the 'pillars' in the Lisbon Treaty,[4] since the original Treaty of Rome in 1957. This provision sets out the Commission's power to bring Member States into compliance with EU law. Where Member States have 'failed to fulfil their obligations' under EU law, the Commission may refer them to the European Court of Justice (ECJ) to obtain a judgment against them. Failure to fulfil obligations has been interpreted widely to include acts and omissions of the state and state actors, including failure to transpose part or all of a Directive, failure to implement a Decision or Regulation, failure of the administration (including the courts) to implement EU law, and failure to notify the Commission of transposition where this is required.[5] This judgment states whether a breach has occurred, and if so, the Member State must remedy the infringement to the Commission's satisfaction.[6] The process contains several official steps, known as the letter of formal notice (or formal letter), reasoned opinion, and referral to ECJ. The case law relating to these steps confers broad discretion on the Commission to do whatever it sees fit, whilst attempting to protect Member States' limited rights of defence.[7] The Commission must not deviate from the case it initially sets out in the formal letter and reasoned opinion, although it is allowed to adduce new evidence.[8] It must not give too short a period of time for the Member State to respond to its enquiries, although the ECJ has not set definitive timescales for action.[9] However, until the ECJ actually hears the case, the Commission may withdraw or stop proceedings at any time without explanation.

---

[4] Steve Peers, 'Sanctions for Infringements of EU Law after the Treaty of Lisbon' (2012) 18 *European Public Law* 33.

[5] Non-notification is an infringement in itself as it is normally an obligation of the Member State under the Directive concerned. This means that, even if the Member State has transposed the Directive, it will be in breach of its obligations if it has not notified the Commission or responded to Commission enquiries about transposition. It also includes failure to uphold Treaty principles including the failure to observe the duty of sincere cooperation contained in Art 4(3) TEU. For more detail see Damian Chalmers, Gareth Davies, and Giorgio Monti (eds), *European Union Law* (2010) Ch 8.

[6] If the Member State does not remedy the infringement the Commission may refer the state to the ECJ for a second time under Art 260 TFEU to obtain a financial sanction, see below.

[7] Craig and de Búrca (n 1) 429–431.

[8] Case C-371/04 *Commission v Italy* [2006] ECR I-10257; Case C-494/01 *Commission v Ireland* [2005] ECR I-3331; Case C-11/95 *Commission v Belgium* [1996] ECR I-4115.

[9] Case C-350/02 *Commission v Netherlands* [2004] ECR I-6213. What is a reasonable time depends on the facts of each case.

In legal terms, there are no other recognized parties in the infringement process besides the Member State and the Commission.[10] Third parties are unable to compel a prosecution or obtain access to infringement files, as the Court has recognized the process of negotiation between the parties as confidential.[11] This wide discretion compounded by the lack of judicial oversight by the ECJ has created a space of interaction that is characterized by secrecy and a lack of accountability on the part of the Commission.[12] The approach of the ECJ is remarkable for its lack of 'teleological' interpretation so prevalent throughout the rest of the Treaties and the development of the EU legal system. It has bled through into the institutional attitude of the Commission and the Member States when it comes to developing the infringement procedure. Article 258 TFEU has yet to get off the ground from a legal perspective; it is rarely a focus for discussion at inter-governmental conferences or conventions[13] as the main players (the Commission and Member State) have no interest in changing the status quo from which they both benefit in different ways.

From the 1950s until the new millennium, this rigid case law also filtered through to the scholarship (or lack thereof) on the infringement process. Legal scholarship in particular, save a few notable exceptions,[14] was rather doctrinal and anaemic in nature. It concentrated upon the precise meaning of each word in the Treaty text and reported upon any particularly controversial judgments or any perceived expansion or deviation from the jurisprudence of the Court, which generally were few and far between.[15] This approach to infringements was, and continues to be, a

---

[10] Case 48/65 *Lütticke v Commission* [1966] ECR 19; Case 47/87 *Star Fruit v Commission* [1989] ECR 291.

[11] This has been a particularly tortuous legal saga where incremental gains are made and then lost. Case T-105/95 *WWF UK v Commission* [1997] ECR II-313; Case T-309/97 *Bavarian Lager Company v Commission* [1999] ECR II-3217; Case T-191/99 *Petrie and others v Commission* [2001] ECR-II 3677. In Case T-194/04 *Bavarian Lager v Commission* [2007] ECR II-4523, the Court confirmed that documents relating to a case that had been closed six years previously could be released in certain circumstances and in Case C-514/07 *API and Sweden v Commission* [2010] ECR I-8533, that documents would not be protected once the ECJ had handed down a judgment on that case.

[12] In principle, the Commission as an institution is accountable to the European Parliament but when it comes to infringements this really doesn't operate very well in practice; see Melanie Smith, 'Accountability in Issue: The European Parliament, the Commission and Enforcement of EU Obligations' (2015) forthcoming.

[13] See Jonas Tallberg, *European Governance and Supranational Institutions: Making States Comply* (2003), which traces the discussions throughout various Treaty negotiations in relation to the enforcement provisions.

[14] H.A.H. Audretsch, *Supervision in European Community Law* (2nd ed, 1986); Richard Rawlings, 'Engaged Elites: Citizen Action and Institutional Attitudes in Commission Enforcement' (2000) 6 *European Law Journal* 4.

[15] Eg A.C. Evans, 'The Enforcement Procedure of Art 169 EEC: Commission Discretion' (1979) *European Law Review* 442; Ulrich Everling, 'The Member States of the European Community before their Court of Justice' (1984) 9 *European Law Review* 215; Ami Barav, 'Failure of Member States to Fulfil their Obligations under Community Law' (1975) *Common Market Law Review* 369; Alan Dashwood and Robin White, 'Enforcement Actions under Arts 169 and 170 EEC' (1989) 14 *European Law Review* 388.

disservice to what is a fascinating legal, political, and administrative space of interaction, and much more than a staid legal process. The real interest in Article 258 TFEU is not what happens in the Court (not much does) but rather all the points in the process before a judgment is handed down. The characterization of Article 258 TFEU as a unique space of interaction between many different stakeholders (including the Ombudsman, complainant, and European Parliament) is a more rounded view of what actually happens in infringement cases. It facilitates interesting research questions about the nature of the polity, how bureaucratic entities cope with political change, and how executive power is wielded in the name of upholding the rule of law but without any apparent adherence to the concept itself. It has been described as having as many as five functions: a constitutional mechanism of enforcement; an executive policy choice; a forum for citizen–institution interaction; a regulatory/administrative tool; and an inter-institutional forum for debate, control, and accountability. Seen in this way it requires us to ask what meaning the concepts of transparency, accountability, and legitimacy have in a policy area devoid of such notions.[16] Building on this more complex characterization, other scholars have introduced different facets into the analysis, recognizing the potential of political discourse available in this space that might lead to greater democratic and regional interaction with EU norms, which may in turn allow for more sensitive enforcement policies.[17]

Beyond the narrow interpretative doctrinal confines this area of law has much to offer multiple disciplines as a case study or as a source of data. Indeed, much of the rich research into infringements has taken place in political science referencing the data produced by the infringement process, for example in studies on international relations theory[18] or compliance theory.[19] Such studies, however, might be perceived as necessarily limited when they rely on statistics derived from the Commission reports without having any reference to the complex processes that drive the production of these statistics and perpetuate the inaccuracies contained therein. In contrast, studies which seek to source data themselves are faced with the sheer numbers of instruments, countries/administrations, and languages which make individual data collection problematic, and so necessarily restrict themselves to pilot or (relatively) small sample studies.[20] All these studies are focused on the behaviour of the Member State rather than the behaviour of the Commission, and this should not

---

[16] Melanie Smith, *Centralised Enforcement, Legitimacy and Good Governance in the EU* (2009) Ch 1.

[17] Chalmers, Davies, and Monti (n 5).

[18] For a typical example, see Tania A. Börzel, Tobias Hofmann, Diana Panke, and Carina Sprungk, 'Obstinate and Inefficient: Why Member States Do Not Comply with European Law' (2010) 43 *Comparative Political Studies* 1363. Even here, where the research team had unique access to the Commission NIF database rather than the annual monitoring report, the case remains the same.

[19] Gerda Faulkner and Oliver Treib, 'Three Worlds of Compliance or Four? The EU-15 Compared to the New Member States' (2008) 46 *Journal of Common Market Studies* 293.

[20] See in this vein a study of over a 1000 instruments across eight policy sectors and five member states: Markus Haverland, Bernard Steunenberg, and Frans van Waarden, 'Sectors at Different

really surprise us. It is the secretive nature of infringements (policy and administration) that on the one hand prompts fascinating research questions but on the other makes investigation into those research questions highly problematic.

2. The Sanction Procedure in Article 260 TFEU: Onwards and Upwards, Chocks Away!

The sanction procedure could not be more different in nature than Article 258 TFEU. First of all, it has seen three major Treaty changes in its history and behind this legal architecture some dynamic and at times surprising jurisprudence from the ECJ. The sanction procedure began merely as an opportunity for the Commission to obtain a second judgment from the Court should it decide to refer Member States who had not implemented the first judgment handed down against them. It mirrored the infringement procedure in that there were the same legal stages involved: a formal letter, a reasoned opinion, and then referral to the Court. It had the same extensive executive discretion attached to the infringement procedure. It was widely acknowledged that, as sanctions go, this was less than persuasive and it was neither efficient nor effective.[21] Accordingly, at Maastricht, the Treaties were amended to include the possibility of a financial sanction being imposed on Member States. The sanction would consist of either a lump sum or a penalty payment.

Despite this amendment there was no reason to suggest that the sanction procedure, being almost identical in wording to the infringement procedure (and arguably much more controversial), would evolve any differently. In other words there was every indication that it would be an arduous, inefficient, and non-transparent mechanism bogged down in judicial dogma similar to its sister provision. The reality could not be more different. Although initially slow to utilize this sanction, the Commission eventually brought the first case against Greece in 2000[22] and the rate at which cases are referred has steadily increased since then.[23] Once the Court was allowed to become involved through the hearing of the first case, it became its best 'teleological' self, by completely disregarding the Commission's suggestion as to what the appropriate amount of penalty should be without explanation. It carried on with this interpretative dynamism in the now infamous fisheries case against

Speeds: Analysing Transposition Deficits in the European Union' (2011) 49 *Journal of Common Market Studies* 265.

[21] Anne Bonnie, 'Commission Discretion under Article 171(2) EC' (1998) 23 *European Law Review* 537; Anne Bonnie, 'The Evolving Role of the European Commission in the Enforcement of Community Law: From Negotiating Compliance to Prosecuting Member States?' (2006) 1 *Journal of Contemporary European Research* 39; Maria Mendrinou, 'Non-compliance and the European Commission's Role in Integration' (1996) 3 *Journal of European Public Policy* 1.

[22] Case C-387/97 *Commission v Greece* [2000] ECR I-5047.

[23] Until 2010 the Commission had brought only 11 cases before the ECJ.

France,[24] where, contrary to the clear wording of the Treaty provision (*either* a penalty payment *or* a lump sum), the Court decided both sanctions could be imposed in a single case.

This judicial dynamism bled through once again into the Treaty amendment process. Article 258 TFEU might appear untouchable but that did not stop the Lisbon Treaty making two changes to Article 260 TFEU. The first change was to dispense with the requirement for a reasoned opinion[25] in order to make the formal process more efficient by reducing the time given to Member States to comply. This means that once a formal letter has been sent to the infracting Member State, if the state does not satisfy the Commission it has complied with the judgment, the Commission may refer the state to the ECJ immediately. The second amendment was curious at least as to its physical positioning. Article 260(3) enables the Commission to dispense with a second judicial process (that is Article 260(2)) in relation to cases of non-notification of national measures transposing Directives. In other words, it amends Article 258 by including in this procedure the possibility of the Commission requesting a financial sanction (penalty payment or lump sum) for non-notification that a Directive has been transposed into national legislation. Unlike the traditional Article 260 actions, it is the Commission that can set the outer limit of the sanction rather than the Court, which can reduce but not increase the Commission's tariff. This appears to be an amendment to Article 258 and thus ought to have been placed in that text but such is the sensitivity regarding this provision that it ended up elsewhere. Nonetheless, this new mechanism has been embraced with vigour by the Commission and, if previous inter-institutional dialogue between the Court and Commission sets a precedent, it will in turn probably encourage similar judicial dynamism.[26]

III. Administration of the Infringement and Sanction Procedure

The way in which the Commission has internally managed these two processes of enforcement has been quite distinct. Since the infringement process has been in the Treaties since 1957, it has had time to mature and lay down roots in a quite

---

[24] Case C-304/02 *Commission v France* [2005] ECR I-6263.

[25] A long-held ambition of the Commission in previous Treaty negotiations, see Tallberg (n 12).

[26] For detailed analysis of this relationship see Melanie Smith, 'Inter–institutional Dialogue and the Establishment of Enforcement Norms: A Decade of Financial Penalties under Article 228 EC (now 260 TFEU)' (2010) 16 *European Public Law* 547.

different political, financial, and legal environment from today—one that was concerned with secrecy, diplomacy—an elite club with its attendant small membership. In support of this approach to enforcement the Commission has elaborated several compliance-promoting tools that seek to buttress and entrench the *status quo* and much administrative resource has been dedicated to 'pre-infringement' enforcement techniques carried out under the banner of guardian of the Treaties. In contrast, the sanction process is a relatively new invention (getting 'newer' at each revision of the Treaties) and accordingly has grown up in a more modern administrative and political environment, one more concerned with transparency and accountability. The following sections will explore the changes that have occurred in the administration of the infringement and sanction processes, and question what has prompted the various innovations in practice to emerge.

1. The Administration of Infringements: Brakes On, Forward Momentum, Dead Stop

(a) Brakes On

From the early days of the EEC the approach of the Commission to how it discharged its duty as guardian of the Treaties was set in stone both philosophically and operationally. It was conceived as a largely diplomatic process conducted by negotiation, and operationally relied on secrecy and a fairly small number of people (the Commissioners) taking decisions about whether to advance a potential infringement case through the formal steps identified in the Treaty. Each formal step requires the College of Commissioners to assent to the continuance of the case and this is still the procedure today.[27] This process is derived from the Treaty itself, which has been interpreted to refer to the College as a whole as opposed to Directorate Generals (DGs), officials, or even individual Commissioners. Again what seemed manageable and sensible with six Member States is still trying to cope with 28 Member States in a different political environment with a vastly increased and more complex legislative output.

Behind this formal process the picture was a little more complicated, and early on attention was devoted to avoiding infringements before the formal Treaty process was engaged. This pre-formal notice phase, particularly from the 1980s onwards, had its own set of mechanisms dedicated to the early resolution of potential infractions: so-called 'package meetings' and 'Committees'.[28] These forums for dispute

---

[27] For a detailed overview of this process and its implications, see Smith *Centralised Enforcement* (n 16) Ch 4. The only change to the organization of this procedure came in January 2008 when these Commissioner meetings took place monthly as opposed to every three months in the old system.

[28] See Audretsch (n 14). Latterly these have been expanded to include stakeholder representations and expert networks, see below. Package meetings are informal arrangements of single member

resolution remain extremely opaque to those outside the process, but they are composed of Member State officials or stakeholders with specific sectoral interests or expertise. Their aim is to work with the Commission to resolve application or transposition difficulties in much the same spirit that influenced the jurisprudence of the ECJ and the administration of infringements since the beginning: the watchwords are diplomacy, secrecy, and a total lack of accountability or transparency.

The practice in infringements overall has barely changed over the last 16 years. In 2012, the Commission received 3141 new complaints.[29] The top three Member States subject to these complaints were Italy, Spain, and France, and the top three sectors were environment, justice,[30] and the internal market. 791 investigations were launched on the Commission's own initiative against Italy, Spain, and France, but in slightly different sectors to those represented by complaints (the environment, the internal market, and transport).[31] The Commission closed 1062 infringement cases in 2012,[32] with the Court handing down 46 judgments, 91 per cent in favour of the Commission. Belgium, Portugal, the Netherlands, and France had the most cases against them before the ECJ. The top three sectors in Court were the environment, tax, and the internal market. Whatever new strategies are deployed, whatever changes in administration occurs, the practice in prosecutions remains quite stable.

(b) Forward Momentum?

The good governance agenda announced in the Commission's White Paper on Governance[33] was intended to be a philosophical change in how the EU, and in particular the Commission, would pursue different policy objectives. There was even a brief flirtation with the idea that the sacred ground of infringements might not escape contamination from the principles of effectiveness, openness, coherence, accountability, and participation. A tiny paragraph or two in the main document led to a rare Communication on the topic of the application of EU law.[34] Unfortunately, analysis of what seemed like forward momentum only revealed the opposite; a brief emblematic foray into the land of good governance yielded little

State officials and commission officials but Committees are formal mechanisms that are mandated by a particular legislative instrument and comprise a group of Member State officials and Commission officials.

[29] Report from the Commission '30th Annual Report on Monitoring the Application of EU Law' (2012) COM (2013) 726.

[30] Justice is a relatively recent addition to these statistics which over the last decade or so have seen environment, internal market, and energy/transport regularly take the top three positions.

[31] These sectors have consistently been the focus of Commission enforcement before the Court.

[32] 661 after the formal letter, 359 cases after the reasoned opinion stage and 42 withdrawn from the Court after referral, 30th Annual Report (n 29) 13.

[33] European Governance: A White Paper COM (2001) 428.

[34] The first ever in fact, Commission Communication 'Better Monitoring of the Application of Community Law' COM (2002) 725 final.

information and no actual changes in practice. To be fair, there was a brief outline of the strategy the Commission would adopt when pursuing infringements as, for the first time, it announced priority criteria consisting of 'undermining the rule of law', 'undermining the functioning of the legal system', and incorrect transposition of or failure to transpose a Directive. However, cursory analysis of these reveals that they are pretty nonsensical: for example, each infringement undermines the rule of law and the functioning of the legal system.[35] What was important here was not what the Commission actually said, but that they attempted or felt compelled to say anything at all. This indeed was forward momentum in a policy area that had not seen change or even an attempt at explanation since inception. This tentative step in the direction of communicating about the administration and policy of infringements nonetheless left a glaring gap. The Union was just about to expand by ten Member States and the Commission had said nothing about how it would handle this huge increase in potential infringement workload. Its second Communication announced the first real change in the administration of infringements—the EU Pilot. This would replace the rather mysterious practice of sending administrative letters, which formed the negotiation and investigation phase of infringements.

(c) Of Pilots and Bureaucratic Imperatives

The Commission launched its first (public) attempt at reorganizing the way in which it managed potential infringements in its 2007 Communication 'A Europe of Results'.[36] This Communication initially announced a new way of handling the complaints it received in relation to potential Member State infractions: the EU Pilot. Complaints make up a huge element of the Commission's workload, accounting for 49 per cent of infringement investigations. As the name indicated, the project began as a pilot in April 2008 and originally involved only 15 Member States.[37] Ostensibly, the new working method paid homage to the good governance agenda as its main objective was 'for any problems in the application of EU law to be corrected as quickly and effectively as possible'.[38] In reality, it had many more practical implications, with several different motivations underpinning the design and implementation of the new system. The Commission reiterated the importance of the confidential and close relationship with the Member State and noted that the 'objective of the EU Pilot is to achieve speedier results and to find solutions compatible with EU law for citizens and business through better cooperation between the Member States and the Commission without the need to launch infringement procedures'.[39]

---

[35] For a detailed critique of this, see Smith, *Centralised Enforcement* (n 16) Ch 5.
[36] Commission Communication 'A Europe of Results—Applying Community Law' COM (2007) 502 final.
[37] Austria, Czech Republic, Denmark, Germany, Finland, Hungary, Ireland, Italy, Lithuania, Netherlands, Portugal, Slovenia, Sweden, Spain, and the UK.
[38] Report from the Commission 'EU Pilot Evaluation Report' (2010) COM 70 final.
[39] Report from the Commission 'Second Evaluation Report of EU Pilot' SEC (2011) 1629/2, 4.

The EU Pilot would also deliver internal management benefits: the Secretariat General would be able to set benchmarks and so be able effectively to monitor the performance of each DG on its infringement work.[40] Since the initial construction of the EU Pilot, which came in for some criticism,[41] the Commission has refined and expanded its original design. The Pilot now includes 27 Member States with Luxembourg and Malta having recently joined the system in 2012. The significant alterations are that the Commission no longer expects to outsource its responsibility as guardian of the Treaty, for it no longer requires the Member State to remedy the infraction by communicating directly with the complainant. The system will henceforth not only be used for complaints/enquiries relating to the application of EU law but will also include the Commission's own investigation files into infractions. This is now the go-to process for all this activity across the Commission, with one big exception—the non-notification of transposition of Directives, which is handled by a separate database.[42] This is a major omission since this type of infraction has a high priority in the Commission's enforcement strategy. The EU Pilot process as it now stands is detailed in Figure 14.1.[43]

The first key change shown in Figure 14.1 is that all correspondence coming to the Commission in relation to the application of EU law is classified as either a complaint or an enquiry, registered in CHAP,[44] and entered into the Pilot system. If the Commission decides the complaint has some merit and cannot answer the problem because it requires further clarification of factual or legal circumstances from the Member State concerned, the Commission contacts the Member State, setting out the issues. The Member State then has a target of ten weeks in which to respond. Although the IT platform of Pilot only envisaged this single back-and-forth consultation between the Commission and Member State, it seems that in fact this can be repeated several times until the Commission is clear it is getting no further.[45] This has

---

[40] Second Evaluation Report (n 39) 4. On the resentment this has caused see the European Parliament Study (n 57) 71.

[41] Melanie Smith, 'Enforcement, Monitoring, Verification, Outsourcing: The Decline and Decline of the Infringement Process' (2008) 33 *European Law Review* 777, European Parliament Resolution of 25 November 2010 on the 26th Annual Report on Monitoring the Application of European Union Law (2008) (2010/2076) P7_TAPROV (2010)0437.

[42] The Asmodée II database.

[43] The Commission's flow chart looks nothing like this as it presents a rather idealized version of (Commission) reality and one in which the complainant is not mentioned; see Commission Staff Working Document, Accompanying Document to the Report from the Commission, EU Pilot Evaluation Report SEC (2010) 182, 19.

[44] CHAP is the Commission's internal database for registering correspondence. On receipt of a complaint, the Commission has two weeks to register it if it decides it qualifies as a complaint, and one month to open a file in EU Pilot. CHAP is managed by the Secretariat General and begins the timeline contained in the soft law guidelines as to how the Commission manages relations with complainants, Commission Communication 'Updating the Handling of Relations with the Complainant in Respect of the Application of Union Law' COM (2012) 154.

[45] Commission Staff Working Document (n 43) 9.

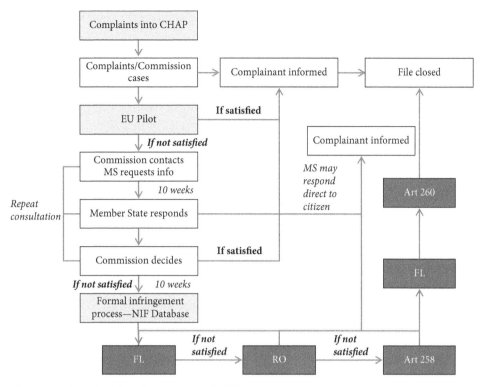

Figure 14.1 The administrative operation of EU Pilot

two implications—it requires further amendment to the IT system to accommodate the extra documentation and somewhat undermines the proposed ten-week deadline. Once in receipt of its response, the Commission is now committed to a ten-week deadline for its own services to make a decision.

If the Commission is satisfied by the Member State's response, the Commission will send its conclusions to the complainant and close the file.[46] The Member State is free to respond directly to the complainant (with its own opinion but not the Commission's) but it appears that the Commission will not communicate the Member State's response to the complainant. Where the outcome is not satisfactory for the Commission, it may decide to launch formal infringement proceedings as defined in the Treaty; that is, the formal letter, reasoned opinion, and referral to the ECJ.[47] The Commission is committed to a 12-month period between receiving a complaint/opening a file and closing it, or sending a formal letter.[48] As noted above, the formal Treaty

---

[46] The Commission has committed in its soft law code to providing four weeks for the complainant to respond before closing the file (n 44).

[47] This formal treaty process is managed through yet another database, the Commission internal NIF database which holds the files and all the steps in relation to formal infringement processes.

[48] As stated in the Communication on relations with the complainant (n 44).

process then has no defined time periods for action and is at the complete discretion of the Commission.

Although the name has stuck, the moniker is rather disingenuous as this Pilot is here to stay. For better or worse it has become a fully fledged administrative process. It was declared a success almost immediately by the Commission, and it certainly has achieved many of the outcomes it was originally designed for. It forced creation of a Contact Point in each Member State and has made communication between the Commission and the relevant officials much more efficient.[49] It also has the internal management benefits that were the drive behind its creation as the Secretariat General has much more control over the relevant DGs, which no longer operate as individual satellites but have a clear line of accountability as to how they perform individually. This was a genuine problem with the old system, which saw infringement work as virtually invisible within a DG, generating low prestige and little acknowledgment or reward internally.[50] The fragmented approach to the administration of infringements led to multiple complaints to the Ombudsman who alongside Parliament noted the inconsistent application of the soft law code for processing complaints.[51] Love it or hate it, the EU Pilot has brought some daylight to the way in which the Commission conducts its affairs in what was the 'administrative letter' or investigation phase. This in itself should be a cause for celebration.

(d) Practice in Pilot: Turbulence Ahead

Besides these internal bureaucratic drivers for change, the much publicized purpose was to increase efficiency and effectiveness, and to ensure that infringements were rectified as soon as possible. Not content with the simple assertions that things would just be better under the new system, Parliament insisted the Commission provide some initial public evaluations,[52] and so in 2010 and 2011 the Commission reported. In the period 2008–2011, a total of 2121 files were submitted to the EU Pilot. Of these 1410 completed the process (defined as obtaining Member State responses and analysis by the Commission). Of these 1410 files 80 per cent were deemed 'successful'; that is, after an answer from the Member State, the Commission closed the file. The remaining 20 per cent of files (303) went on to the formal infringement procedure.

The files submitted reflected the same statistics that are present in the formal infringement procedure in terms of sector representation: 33 per cent environmental issues; 15 per cent internal market; 11 per cent taxation; 8 per cent mobility

[49] Second Evaluation Report (n 39) 6.   [50] Smith, *Centralised Enforcement* (n 16) Ch 5.

[51] See eg European Parliament Resolution of 21 October 2008 on monitoring the application of Community law—24th annual report from the Commission (2008/2046) P6_TA(2008)0494.

[52] Report of the European Parliament Legal Affairs Committee Report on the 26th annual report from the Commission on monitoring the application of Community law (2008) and Report from the Commission EU Pilot Evaluation Report, Rapporteur Eva Lichtenberger 22 October 2010. A7-0291/2010.

and transport; and 6 per cent health and consumer protection. Of the 2121 files 49 per cent originated from complaints while 7 per cent were classed as enquiries or business related, and 44 per cent were the Commission's own initiative files.[53] The Commission measured its 'success' rate over the two periods: 85 per cent in 2008–2010 and 80 per cent in 2010–2011.[54] According to the Commission, since 2010, the original volunteer Member States have experienced a reduction in the volume of new infringement proceedings launched against them, and the remaining 12 have also enjoyed a reduction albeit to a lesser extent. By the end of 2012, the Commission had opened 1405 new files in the EU Pilot: 621 new complaints and 784 new own initiative files. Most of the open files were addressed to Italy, Spain, and Greece, with environment (400), internal market (176), and justice and fundamental rights (125) the top three sectors of concern. In 334 files, a satisfactory solution could not be found within the Pilot and formal infringement proceedings were then launched, again with Italy, France, and Spain being the Member States that had the highest conversion to infringements (29, 28, and 26 files, respectively). In only two cases did the Commission not use the EU Pilot and immediately start infringement proceedings (both against Hungary).[55]

One of the main initial questions surrounding the use of the Pilot was the concern over efficiency; that is, how could adding another step into the prosecution of infringements speed up what was already a lengthy and unwieldy process? However, the results in the Pilot have been surprisingly positive. The average time taken by Member States to respond to the Commission is 67 days, which is in line with the putative ten-week deadline.[56] From the Commission's perspective, this is a huge improvement on what was an indeterminate amount of time under the 'administrative letter' procedure. However, less encouraging is the practice of the Commission itself, where the average time taken to respond to Member States is 102 days, which significantly exceeds the ten-week deadline.

The Commission defends this on the basis that two factors cause delay: where the services need to request additional information from Member States, the need for translation; and where particularly complex issues are at stake. This information is important in two respects. First, it to some degree debunks the myth that the Member States are most culpable when it comes to delay in processing infringement files. Second, it speaks to the internal management of individual file handlers and DGs by the Secretariat General. Although no breakdown of performance between DGs is provided, it is clearly now available. The legal unit in DG

[53] Second Evaluation Report (n 39) 5.   [54] Second Evaluation Report (n 39) 6.

[55] 30th Annual Report on monitoring the application of EU Law (n 29) 10–12. This is perfectly acceptable as the Commission states in its EU Pilot guidelines that in exceptional circumstance requiring swift intervention there will be no recourse to Pilot, but instead immediate infringement proceedings will be launched. One case against Hungary concerned serious incidents of undermining the rule of law: Case C-286/12 *Commission v Hungary*, 6 November 2012.

[56] Second Evaluation Report (n 39) 5.

Environment (typically one of the slowest moving DGs in infringement cases) has recently been disbanded.[57] It is reasonable to assume this innovation in internal management has at least partly contributed to that decision, although it is also a fact that environmental infringements are often the most technically complex to pursue.

The mere existence of the EU Pilot and the subsequent reports regarding its operation have brought into the light a previously closed process of negotiation, albeit to a limited degree. This was not the intention of the Commission but it has been the effect. As is the nature of things, a little information only creates greater clamour for more, and the lack of access to the EU Pilot by outsiders (complainants, stakeholders, even researchers) has started to become increasingly contentious, resulting in a call to reappraise the purpose of the Pilot. A recent study funded by the European Parliament looked into the effectiveness of the tools for ensuring the implementation and application of EU law.[58] One part of this study was dedicated to infringements and the EU Pilot. The study drew connections between the effectiveness of the current administrative and executive practices, and the lack of transparency that prevented the complainant from becoming more involved. In essence, it identified that greater involvement in enforcement beyond the Commission and Member State would increase the effectiveness of the compliance mechanisms, providing concrete examples of where this had occurred. One example of this was in relation to the Pilot and access to documents therein.

The Commission asserts that there is no access to documents within the confidential database it maintains for its purpose of communication with Member States, and has a number of arguments as to why this is the case. It asserts, for example, that the case law on access to infringement documents is clear (there is no access); however, the study questions this assertion since by definition the Pilot is not part of the official infringement proceeding. The Commission asserts that releasing its interaction with the Member State to the complainant would undermine the purpose of the process—negotiation conducted in partnership and in confidence[59]—but it could not offer any evidence for this assertion. On the contrary, the study offered instances where Member States, in accordance with their own transparency laws or decided practice, had released all the documents in the Pilot and this had led to swifter and better problem solving, and increased the trust of stakeholders and citizens in the entire process. Indeed, 'Swedish law offers complainants a privileged participation in the dialogue between the Commission and Member State authorities, and thus a better integration of their expectations and points of view.'[60]

---

[57] European Parliament Study: Directorate General for Internal Policies, Policy Department C: Citizens Rights and Constitutional Affairs 'Tools for ensuring Implementation and Application of EU Law and Evaluation of their Effectiveness' PE 493.014.108.

[58] European Parliament Study (n 57).

[59] European Parliament Study (n 57) 75.   [60] European Parliament Study (n 57) 73.

The recommendations of the study claim that greater transparency would be the preferred model, not only of stakeholders but in fact also of some of the Member States surveyed (eg Germany).[61] The study cites actual examples where the involvement of the complainant has led to better outcomes,[62] and where Member States have taken the initiative to create their own national databases which are partly accessible by the public.[63] Despite such evidence, the Commission remains resolute and, in typical graceless fashion, denied access to the Pilot by the researchers engaged in the study, and instructed all DGs not to talk to the researchers on the topic of the Pilot.[64]

The study also canvassed the views of Member State officials, which largely confirmed the Commission's view that the Pilot had definitely led to 'smooth interaction' with the Commission and that their overriding concern was 'satisfying the Commission to avoid infringement proceedings', and that it was certainly preferable to the administrative letter which was seen as more confrontational in nature.[65] The views of the complainants and NGOs were markedly different, and in some ways their responses were quite surprising. For instance, one of their main objections was the Commission's measure of 'success' (closure of files). They saw this as quite different from providing effective solutions to potential infractions of EU law, but if one is charitable one might assume that the Commission closes the file only when it is satisfied there is no longer an infraction, ergo solving the problem. There seems to be a longing to turn the EU Pilot into SOLVIT,[66] which it most definitely is not, and was never meant to be. It is difficult to accept that closing files and thereby avoiding infringement proceedings is not a good measure of success, as claimed by the Commission, which has repeatedly stated that infringement proceedings before the Court are a last resort. The study also repeatedly asserted there was no legal basis for the Pilot, which again seems patently incorrect as the Commission is free to organize itself as its sees fit in its role as guardian of the Treaties.[67]

The study has several recommendations in relation to the EU Pilot going forward. These can all be placed rather loosely in the box of 'transparency', and involve the opening up of the EU Pilot to other actors besides the Commission and Member State, including access to the files and a greater role for the complainant.

---

[61] Although the study also notes that the same Member States emphasized the confidential nature of the database and saw no apparent contradiction to expressing the view that complainants should be party to the process.

[62] European Parliament Study (n 57) 104, citing the Clean Air London (CAL) organization being able to communicate directly with DEFRA and the Commission as a result of DEFRA including them in the conversation.

[63] eg Italy and Hungary; European Parliament Study (n 57) 104.

[64] Only two designated Secretariat General officials were allowed to communicate with the researchers. European Parliament Study (n 57) 104.

[65] European Parliament Study (n 57) 70.

[66] SOLVIT is the online problem-solving forum created for offering solutions to complainants in the area of the internal market http://ec.europa.eu/solvit/site/about/index_en.htm#how.

[67] European Parliament Study (n 57) 65.

The study recommended binding legal rules relating to infringements outside of the Pilot; access of the European Parliament to the files and data in order to increase Parliament's effectiveness at monitoring the Commission; and adjusting the way in which 'success' is measured.[68] These recommendations broadly align with the overall message of the study which is that greater participation in enforcement brings better results—more efficient and effective investigations and prosecutions resulting in better application of EU law. In short, the Commission has finite resources and opening up the process only assists it in its duty as guardian of the Treaty. It seems that the Commission may experience some turbulent times ahead if NGOs and Parliament begin to challenge the purpose, legal basis, and transparency of the EU Pilot.

(e) Databases, Diversions, and Circling

It should be clear by now that the Commission favours managing enforcement via database. There is Asmodée, NIF, CHAP, and now the Pilot. The obsession with these bureaucratic management techniques has led to a somewhat skewed enforcement policy with an over-concentration in some areas and a lack of attention to others, with the result that it appears that enforcement strategy is dictated by what the Commission can put into a database. Elements that cannot be managed in this technocratic fashion are left untended. The range of compliance tools at the Commission's disposal might be described as shown in Table 14.1.

Enforcement by database lends itself to a particular type of infringement, and this has resulted in the Commission pursuing late transpositions of Directives as a major strategic focus, as illustrated by Table 14.1. To achieve better results on transposition the Commission constructed a database that automatically flags up non-notification of measures of transposition from Member States. Not content with this automation, the Commission then expended energy on a further mechanism to tackle this type of infringement, which would incentivize Member States into transposing Directives on time in the Treaty of Lisbon.

This new regime only applies to infringements caused by non-notification of national measures implementing Directives. In contrast with the sanction under Article 260(2) TFEU, the Commission has embraced this particular sanction with some enthusiasm and it is already delivering tangible results; late transpositions are falling rapidly with 1185 in 2011 but only 447 recorded in 2012. There has also been an increase in the efficiency of processing these cases with a 45 per cent decrease in open cases between 2011 and 2012. Cases of late transposition do not necessarily reflect the general trend in infringement cases across the board when it comes to sector representation, since the main sectors are transport, health and consumers, then environment and the internal market. The Commission prosecution

---

[68] European Parliament Study (n 57) 106–109.

Table 14.1 **The compliance promoting toolkit**

Type of mechanism	When it occurs	Focus of compliance
Correlation Tables	Ex ante and ex post	Transposition
Scoreboards	Ex post	Transposition
Networks/stakeholders	Ex post and ex ante	Transposition/application/implementation
Conformity checking	Ex post	Transposition
Package meetings	Ex ante/ex post	Transposition/application
Implementation plans/guidelines	Ex ante	Application
Inspections/investigations	Ex post	Application/enforcement
Fitness checks	Ex post	Evaluation

strategy is quite different from before as the Commission now favours prosecution across the Member States per Directive. For example, the Commission launched proceedings against 24 Member States for the late transposition of the Directive on buildings' energy performance.[69] This strategy was repeated in relation to several different instruments and is of course particularly suited to late transposition cases, since the Commission has no need to perform any resource-consuming investigation or examination of multiple Member States.

When it comes to the somewhat trickier business of incorrect transposition, non-implementation, and bad application of EU laws (that is principles, Regulations, Directives, and Decisions), the Commission appears to be going round in circles. Where databases do not work, the Commission turns back to the beginning of its enforcement activity: small elite clubs, non-transparent, and unaccountable mechanisms (elite negotiation). Bad application or implementation cannot be detected by bureaucratic automation, but requires either a resource-intensive Commission own initiative investigation, or information from and the involvement of a complainant. Conformity checking studies, meetings with stakeholders, and expert networks and package meetings are all types of elite negotiation. These avenues exclude 'outsiders' and usage is not reported or documented systematically. Even these non-database mechanisms are dedicated mainly to transposition of Directives, strengthening this singular enforcement design.

The Commission has expended a good deal of energy on the issue of correlation (or concordance) tables that it sees as vital to its role as guardian of the Treaties and the proper enforcement of EU law. A correlation table is a piece of information in tabular form provided by the Member State on transposition of a Directive which

---

[69] Dir 2010/31/EU on the energy performance of buildings OJ L153/13; see 30th Annual Report on Monitoring the Application of EU Law (n 29) 4.

lists where each provision has been transposed in national law, enabling a swift reconciliation by the Commission services to verify that transposition has not only occurred, but been executed properly. The Member States in the form of the Council have strenuously opposed this obligation in various fora from the negotiation of individual Directives to a wholesale legislative requirement across the board. With the assistance of Parliament, it seemed some headway had been made in the 2010 inter-institutional agreement[70] regarding the provision of 'explanatory documents' that 'may take the form of correlation tables'.

In the absence of correlation tables, in order check not just transposition but implementation, the Commission might outsource a conformity-checking study. These are expensive and time-consuming exercises undertaken by third-party contractors and in general are not open to public scrutiny.[71] Package meetings with Member State officials might be used to discuss *ex post* problems with implementation but these obstacles must first be uncovered by the Commission or a complainant. Elite networks or stakeholders are helpful when discussing potential or actual implementation problems of EU law mechanisms, and inspections by Commission officials (for example in environment and fisheries) are critical compliance tools aimed at the implementation of norms.

Implementation plans (TIPS) and fitness checks are relatively new phenomena that have materialized from the Commission's Smart Regulation and REFIT agenda.[72] The Commission had been silent on the relationship between its main mechanism of enforcement and other interconnecting policy initiatives, in particular the advent of 'Smart Regulation' and latterly its Regulatory Fitness and Performance Programme (REFIT). It is now beginning to appreciate the important linkages between improving legislation and effective *post hoc* evaluation of which implementation (or difficulties therein) play a significant role. The latest Communication on REFIT states that 'Recurrent problems in the application of law (reflected by complaints or case law, for example) should be part of this evaluation process. The Impact Assessment Board will systematically consider the use of evaluation results in its quality reviews.'[73] In the latest annual report, the Commission does make brief mention of these different policy strands, branding the EU Pilot as part of its Better Regulation initiative. It also promises a more systematic, risk-based conformity checking of national implementing rules, and

---

[70] Framework Agreement on relations between the European Parliament and the European Commission OJ L304/10 s 44.

[71] Although DG Environment has made some available on its website. This DG leads the way on enforcement practices and is probably the most transparent of all the DGs; see its website http://ec.europa.eu/environment/legal/implementation_en.htm.

[72] See http://ec.europa.eu/smart-regulation/.

[73] Communication from the Commission to the European Parliament, the Council, the European Economic and Social Committee and the Committee of the Regions 'Regulatory Fitness and Performance (REFIT): Results and Next Steps' (2013) COM 685, 11.

enhanced assistance in transposing EU Directives through the use of implementation plans,[74] acknowledging that 'proper implementation is an indispensable ingredient in regulatory fitness and performance'.[75]

All of these mechanisms have a few things in common: they are not transparent and they lock the complainant, NGOs, and other public interest representations out of enforcement. For all the supposed innovation of some of these new mechanisms, this appears suspiciously like circling back to the good old days of elite negotiation and not the realization of the promise that the 'Treaty marks a new stage in the process of creating an ever closer union among the peoples of Europe, in which decisions are taken as openly as possible and as closely as possible to the citizen.'[76]

It seems that with shrinking resources and an expanding Union the Commission might want to utilize all the help it can get in the enforcement of EU law but this would require a radical shift of thinking: from secrecy to transparency, from elite negotiation to collaboration with complainants and others.[77]

2. The Administration of Sanctions: Dialogue, Collisions, and Increased Velocity

When it came to the administration of the financial sanction the Commission inexplicably opted for transparency. Perhaps it was because of the controversial nature of imposing sanctions (although clearly agreed to by all the Member States at Maastricht) or perhaps the sanction has simply evolved in a more modern era. The Commission's actual policy on the use of Article 260 TFEU has changed little since it produced its first statement in a Memorandum in 1996,[78] which it followed up with a lengthier Communication a year later.[79] The Commission clearly believed it was duty bound to state the criteria that it would apply when pursuing Member States for the purposes of obtaining a financial penalty against them. It would explain its reasons for the type of financial penalty chosen (ie a periodic penalty payment or a lump sum), and in doing so it would identify the types of case it considered serious enough for the imposition of a financial penalty. In addition, it would explain the method of calculation of that sanction. The three criteria that it uses to determine the level of financial penalty it will request the Court to impose are: the seriousness of the infringement; the duration of the infringement; and the need to ensure that the

---

[74] 30th Annual Report on monitoring the implementation of EU law (n 55) 14.

[75] 30 Annual Report on monitoring the implementation of EU law (n 55) 15.

[76] Art 1 TEU.

[77] Assessing the relative effectiveness of these compliance-promoting tools is outside the scope of this chapter but conclusions on this can be found in the European Parliament Study (n 57) 96–100.

[78] Memorandum on applying Article 171 of the EC Treaty OJ C242/96.

[79] Method of calculating the penalty payments provided for pursuant to Article 171 of the EC Treaty OJ C63/97.

penalty is a deterrent to further infringements. Each of these elements is explained in great detail, with examples given to show how the Commission would exercise its discretion.[80] These two initial documents were updated by a third Communication on the application of Article 260, published in 2005.[81] On a practical level the Commission thought it necessary to update its method of calculation and 'adapt it to the enlargement of the Union' and to reflect the changing jurisprudence from the ECJ, which enabled dual penalties. Finally, after Lisbon, the Commission issued a further three Communications on this subject, first in 2010[82] to update the criteria used in the basic formula, then in 2011[83] to explain the innovations of Lisbon and the operation of Article 260(3), and then in 2013[84] to update the criteria again.

This more open approach has been hugely significant in the evolution of financial sanctions. Transparency has created a dialogue with other actors besides the Member State. The Commission and ECJ working together have crafted the operation of the sanction. This interaction has led to each institution having to state and re-state its position. For example, there have been power struggles and collisions between the Court and Commission over who sets the financial penalty, and this inter-institutional dialogue[85] has taught the Commission some lessons. When negotiating the Treaty amendment at Lisbon, the Commission made sure that the text stated unequivocally that it was responsible for setting the outer limit of the penalty under Article 260(3). This is not coincidental but a direct result of what happened in the first case against Greece, when the Commission had essentially stated that it was responsible, only for the Court to impose its authority instead. The Court again took the lead (contrary to the policy stated in the Commission Communications) on the imposition of the dual penalty. This open dialogue between the institutions and to some extent the Commission and the Member States has led to a more effective, dynamic, and efficient sanction procedure.

(a) Practice under Article 260 TFEU: A Steep Ascent

The Commission was slow to utilize the mechanism, taking nearly a decade to bring the first case. Between that case and 2010, only 11 judgments were handed down by the ECJ. Since then, however, there has been a steep increase in cases and by 2011 the Commission had 77 sanction cases open under Article 260(2) TFEU, with 11 referred to the Court.

---

[80] See Ian Kilbey, 'Financial PENALTIES under Article 228(2) EC: Excessive Complexity?' (2007) 44 *Common Market Law Review* 743 and Peers (n 4).

[81] Commission Communication 'Application of Article 228 of the EC Treaty' SEC (2005) 1658.

[82] Commission Communication 'Application of Article 260 of the Treaty on the Functioning of the European Union: Updating of data used to calculate lump sum and penalty payments to be proposed by the Commission to the Court of Justice in infringement proceedings' SEC (2010) 923/3.

[83] Commission Communication 'Implementation of Article 260(3) of the Treaty' OJ C12/1.

[84] Commission Communication 'Updating of data used to calculate lump sum and penalty payments to be proposed by the Commission to the Court of Justice in infringement proceedings' C (2013) 8101 final.

[85] Smith 'Inter-institutional Dialogue' (n 26).

Most of the cases concerned Greece, Italy, and Spain and, mirroring the practice under Article 258 TFEU, the top sectors were environment, internal market, and transport. The Court managed to hand down only two judgments that year.[86]

By the end of 2012 the Commission had 128 open sanction procedures with Portugal, Greece, and Spain now the biggest offenders in environment, internal market, and tax. Of the 128 cases, 11 had already been referred to the ECJ for a penalty or lump sum under Article 260(2). Three court judgments were given in 2012, two against Ireland and one against Spain.[87] The judgments against Ireland concerned environmental and waste Directives and the Commission notes in its annual report that the Court took into account the economic situation and in particular recent trends in inflation and GDP . . . when calculating the penalty'.[88] The judgment against Spain was in relation to non-compliance with a judgment handed down in 2002 on state aid.[89]

The position of the Court in the case against Ireland is the first indication of some attempt to ameliorate the effects of the sanction against the backdrop of an economic collapse and financial austerity. Ireland has suffered financially more than most, having to be bailed out partly by the EU. Despite this economic reality, the Commission has not significantly amended its formula, which showed only a tiny alteration since 2005.[90] When the enforcement policy is examined in the round, the same states (Greece, Ireland, Spain, Italy) that are in most financial difficulty are the ones that are being prosecuted regularly under Article 258 and the financial sanction.[91] There is no suggestion that such states be 'let off' their obligations but an amendment to the formula might have been one way to mitigate the imposition of further financial pressure. It was once again left to the Court to depart from the Commission suggestion to alter the fine, but this seems to be rather late in the day as there is no indication of this practice before 2012, with Ireland exiting the financial bailout package in 2013.[92]

The practices under Article 260 TFEU have been more transparent in the sense that the Commission articulates a reasonably clear policy on the types of case it will pursue and its proposed time limit for action. Certainly, it had the ambition that sanction cases would take between eight and 18 months (in the 2005 Communication) and by 2011 it was hoping that the Lisbon amendments would

---

[86] Case C-407/09 *Commission v Greece* [2011] ECR I-2467 (lump sum of €3,000,000) and Case C-496/09 *Commission v Italy* [2011] ECR I-11483 (lump sum of €30,000,000), Report from the Commission '29th Annual Report on Monitoring the Application of EU Law' (2011) COM (2012) 714.

[87] Case C-374/11 *Commission v Ireland* 19 December 2012; Case C-279/11 *Commission v Ireland* 19 December 2012; Case C-610/10 *Commission v Spain* 11 December 2012.

[88] 30th Annual Report (n 54) 31.

[89] The fine was €20 million lump sum and a daily penalty of €50,000 until compliance.

[90] In 2005 Ireland's 'n' factor was 2.84 and in 2012 it was 2.60, 'n' representing that state's ability to pay. The last Communication has Ireland at 2.61.

[91] Although it is tempting to assume direct correlation between austerity and the inability to fulfil obligations, these same States had a relatively poor record before the economic downturn.

[92] Financed by the so-called Troika of the EU, the IMF, and the European Central Bank.

significantly reduce this with the dispensation of the reasoned opinion stage, although a cursory glance at the Spanish case on state aid reveals that it took from 2002 to 2012 to bring it to judgment. No real explanation is provided on the extensive period given to Spain to comply. So although many things are in the open, the same problems present themselves here: why does the Commission decide not to prosecute some cases and why does it take so long to bring them? There is no equivalent of the EU Pilot for financial sanctions with the administration of this stage of the enforcement cycle lacking administrative transparency.[93]

As noted above, the Lisbon Treaty revised Article 260 TFEU by enabling the Commission to bring a case for a sanction without first obtaining a judgment from the Court under Article 258 in the case of failure to notify timeously measures transposing Directives. The purpose of this, according to the Commission, is 'to give stronger incentive to Member States to transpose directives within the deadlines laid down by the legislator'.[94] In contrast to earlier practice under Article 260(2) TFEU, the Commission has been swift to operationalize its new mechanism and it brought the first late transposition sanction cases in 2011. In total, nine cases were brought against five Member States: Austria, Germany, Greece, Italy, and Poland. In 2012, the Commission increased its activity and took 35 cases under this mechanism against 12 Member States,[95] with the proposed daily penalties ranging from €5909.40 to €315 036.54. As per the Commission's stated policy, lump sum payments were not requested. A separate section is now dedicated to this practice in the annual monitoring reports, with the Commission highlighting 'good' and 'bad' Member States.

The opening up of the sanction process began with the Commission choosing to explain its policy but that was not the most significant factor. The role played by the ECJ has been teleological and dynamic, and affords the Commission less executive power. This interaction between the institutions legitimizes the Commission's power and renders the process more transparent. From the same legal language as Article 258 totally different behaviour has emerged.

IV. Concluding Remarks

Infringements and sanctions are intimately linked but operate quite differently. The infringement process has evolved in a way that has stifled creativity. The lack of

---

[93] Presumably these cases are retained in the NIF database, although this has never been made clear by the Commission.

[94] 30th Annual Report (n 54) 8.

[95] Poland, Slovenia, the Netherlands, and Finland had the most cases against them.

inter-institutional dialogue with the Court, which has chosen to award unlimited discretion to the Commission, has encouraged an inward-looking administration which balks at any suggestion of transparency. This in turn has presented many obstacles to effective and efficient enforcement, with the dominant approaches being bureaucratic oversight (database enforcement) and circling back to elite negotiation. Whilst many internal management benefits might be derived from database enforcement, this approach definitely has its limits. A lack of access to information for outsiders (complainants, interest groups, and others) removes a vital avenue of enforcement for the Commission, which has limited resources and lacks knowledge of particular types of infringement, ie all those that are not concerned with the transposition of Directives. Whatever policy, administration, or compliance-promoting tools are employed, the practice of prosecuting infringements remains unchanged.

This lack of inter-institutional dialogue has stunted the development of infringements, and there appears to be administrative stalemate or coasting in this area, brought on in part by excluding other actors from the process, although latterly the European Parliament is attempting to fill the void left by the Court. New initiatives like REFIT are welcome additions to a more holistic approach to enforcement and there surely must be something to learn from the feedback provided by the infringement process, particularly when the Commission is launching wholesale infraction cases against 23 or more Member States in respect of one instrument. So far, however, REFIT seems to fit more into the inward-looking bureaucratic approach, with limited reporting and little to no involvement of other institutional actors.

The financial sanction has been more dynamic in its evolution and a great deal has been achieved in terms of transparency. The involvement of other actors in the process has legitimized and energized the sanction mechanism, leading to multiple amendments of the Treaty that assist the Commission in keeping up with an expanding Union. It appears that involvement of other actors has not destroyed Commission decision making or the Commission–Member State relationship (as is so often claimed would happen under Article 258). However, the sanction mechanism is far from perfect. There is still little explanation regarding cases that take 10 years to come to Court. On the other hand, the sanction mechanism faces unique challenges in relation to efficacy and flexibility in an era of austerity. Can the Commission continue to pursue sanctions as an (increasingly) automatic recourse against those States which can ill afford the costs of the legislation or the costs of the fine?

Looking to the future, the Commission faces multiple challenges in its role as guardian of the Treaties. There are possibly turbulent times ahead over the purpose of, and access to, the EU Pilot. These challenges will not only come from complainants and NGOs, and the Parliament in its role as supervisor of the Commission, but also from the Member States themselves. Different States have different constitutional traditions in relation to transparency and some are already granting access that the Commission firmly denies.[96]

The Parliament's interest is intensifying when it comes to the matter of supervising the Commission's guardian function. Besides public and private hearings, working groups, reporting duties, resolutions, and independent studies into the Commission's performance, it is also trying to develop legislative instruments that would overturn the Commission (and Court) position on the administration of infringements. Parliament has proposed an administrative Regulation which contains certain basic administrative principles that all EU institutions should abide by in any area of administration, including the infringement process.[97] These principles chime with the calls to give basic procedural rights to complainants in the administration of infringements that the Commission has consistently rejected.

The Commission faces challenges of its own making, namely developing an enforcement strategy that is not database dependent and can detect all manner of infringements besides non-transposition of Directives. It also requires greater devotion of resources to infringement activity across the DGs, more so if its new REFIT idea is to make any impact. This type of innovation and institutional learning is difficult to develop when processes and information remain closed off to outsiders.

Finally, there are challenges to the Commission's role of guardian of the Treaties in relation to upholding the rule of law and in particular fundamental rights and democratic principles across the Member States. According to Justice Commissioner Reding, recent events have posed serious questions in relation to the ability of the Commission to police fundamental Treaty provisions such as Article 2 TEU.[98] DG Justice has launched a consultation on the development of future mechanisms dedicated to upholding the rule of law in the EU. In this sense, the Commission is talking about the rule of law with its constituent parts of respect for democracy and fundamental rights.[99] The infringement process was acknowledged in this discussion but surprisingly it was quickly dismissed as 'inappropriate', although not because the Commission discharges its current duty as guardian without transparency, accountability, or legitimacy.[100]

---

[96] The Commission maintains that EU Pilot files are covered by the exception relating to investigations in Reg 1049/2001 regarding public access to European Parliament, Council and Commission documents OJ L145/43, which covers all documents held by the Commission in relation to ongoing formal infringement procedures.

[97] European Parliament Resolution of 15 January 2013 with recommendations to the Commission on a Law of Administrative Procedure of the European Union (2012/2024(INI)).

[98] http://europa.eu/rapid/press-release_SPEECH-13-677_en.htm.

[99] It acknowledges the contested notion of the rule of law whilst defining the EU version.

[100] It is surprising because at least one of these recent events cited, the Hungarian crisis, in which wholesale replacement of parts of the judiciary via compulsory retirement was put in place by the new ruling party, was in fact dealt with by infringement proceedings.

The central purpose of enforcement of EU law is to enable citizens to enjoy their EU rights by upholding the rule of law in the very general sense of ensuring that Member States comply with their obligations. It does not require new mechanisms dedicated to ensuring compliance with the values in Article 2 TEU, but rather the appropriate use of the infringement mechanism itself, which can arguably perform this task already. Upholding the rule of law requires consistency, transparency, and a certain legitimacy of action, and the Commission must strive to discharge its own power according to these principles before attempting to hold Member States to these exacting standards.

BIBLIOGRAPHY

H.A.H. Audretsch, *Supervision in European Community Law* (2nd ed, 1986)

Damian Chalmers, Gareth Davies, and Giorgio Monti (eds), *European Union Law* (2010)

Paul Craig and Gráinne de Búrca, *EU Law: Text, Cases and Materials* (5th ed, 2011)

Ulrich Everling, 'The Member States of the European Community before their Court of Justice' (1984) 9 *European Law Review* 215

Gerda Faulkner and Oliver Treib, 'Three Worlds of Compliance or Four? The EU-15 Compared to the New Member States' in (2008) *46 Journal of Common Market Studies* 293

Markus Haverland, Bernard Steunenberg, and Frans van Waarden, 'Sectors at Different Speeds: Analysing Transposition Deficits in the European Union' (2011) 49 *Journal of Common Market Studies* 265

Ian Kilbey, 'Financial Penalties under Article 228(2) EC: Excessive Complexity?' (2007) *44 Common Market Law Review* 743

Steve Peers, 'Sanctions for Infringements of EU Law after the Treaty of Lisbon' (2012) *18 European Public Law* 33

Richard Rawlings, 'Engaged Elites: Citizen Action and Institutional Attitudes in Commission Enforcement' (2000) 6 *European Law Journal* 4

Melanie Smith, 'Enforcement, Monitoring, Verification, Outsourcing: The Decline and Decline of the Infringement Process' (2008) *33 European Law Review* 777

Melanie Smith, *Centralised Enforcement, Legitimacy and Good Governance in the EU* (2009)

Melanie Smith, 'Inter-institutional Dialogue and the Establishment of Enforcement Norms: A Decade of Financial Penalties under Article 228 EC (now 260 TFEU)' (2010) *16 European Public Law* 547

Jonas Tallberg, *European Governance and Supranational Institutions: Making States Comply* (2003)

CHAPTER 15

....

JUDICIAL REVIEW IN THE EUROPEAN UNION

....

ANTHONY ARNULL[*]

I. Introduction

....

THIS chapter is concerned with the mechanisms available under the European Union Treaties for providing judicial review of acts adopted by the Union's institutions and other bodies. It focuses particularly on acts of general application. The central argument will be that the capacity of judicial review to enhance the Union's legitimacy has been undermined by the reluctance of the Court of Justice to rectify shortcomings in the action for annulment and its increasing reliance on the preliminary rulings procedure in its stead.

The discussion is structured as follows. Section I considers briefly the place of the action for annulment and the preliminary rulings procedure in the remedial framework of the Treaties. Section II reviews some of the extensive Anglo-American literature on the legitimacy of judicial review. The essential problem addressed by that literature is whether, and if so how, strong judicial review can be reconciled with democracy. Sections III and IV trace the evolution of the action for annulment before and after the Treaty of Lisbon. They concentrate on the standing requirements applicable to claims brought by natural and legal persons for the annulment

* The comments of Albertina Albors-Llorens, Damian Chalmers, and Graham Gee on some of the issues discussed in this chapter are gratefully acknowledged, with the usual disclaimer.

of acts of general application and the Court's growing emphasis on the remedies available in national courts. Section V offers some reflections on the rationale for the Court's current approach and the effectiveness of the Union's contemporary system of remedies.

II. The Union's System of Remedies

In *Les Verts* v *Parliament*,[1] the Court of Justice boldly asserted: '. . . the European Economic Community is a Community based on the rule of law, inasmuch as neither its Member States nor its institutions can avoid a review of the question whether the measures adopted by them are in conformity with the basic constitutional charter, the Treaty.' The Court referred in particular to the action for annulment under what is now Article 263 TFEU; the plea of illegality under what is now Article 277 TFEU; and the preliminary rulings procedure established by what is now Article 267 TFEU. By those provisions, the Court declared, 'the Treaty established a complete system of legal remedies and procedures designed to permit the Court of Justice to review the legality of measures adopted by the institutions'.[2]

Of the remedies mentioned by the Court, the authors of the EEC Treaty clearly saw the action for annulment and the preliminary rulings procedure as the principal mechanisms by which judicial review of Union acts would be ensured.[3] Article 263 TFEU sets out four grounds on which annulment proceedings may be brought: lack of competence; infringement of an essential procedural requirement; infringement of the Treaties or of any rule relating to their application; and misuse of powers. Those grounds, heavily influenced by French administrative law,[4] to a large extent overlap and the Court does not draw technical distinctions between them. It has been remarked that 'they encompass amongst themselves almost all conceivable cases of illegality'.[5] Article 267 TFEU does not specify the grounds on

---

[1] Case 294/83 [1986] ECR 1339, para 23. See also Case C-50/00 P [2002] *Unión de Pequeños Agricultores v Council (UPA)* [2002] ECR I-6677, para 40; Case C-199/11 *Otis and others* [2013] 4 CMLR 4, para 56; Joined Cases C-584/10 P, C-593/10 P and C-595/10 P *European Commission and others v Yassin Abdullah Kadi*, judgment of 18 July 2013, para 66.

[2] *Les Verts* (n 1). See generally Paul Craig, *EU Administrative Law* (2nd ed, 2012); Herwig Hofmann, Gerard Rowe and Alexander Türk, *Administrative Law and Policy of the European Union* (2011).

[3] See Albertina Albors-Llorens, 'Remedies Against the EU Institutions After Lisbon: An Era of Opportunity?' (2012) 71 *Cambridge Law Journal* 507, 510–512.

[4] See A.G. Lagrange in Case 3/54 *Assider v High Authority* [1954–56] ECR 63, 75.

[5] See Akos Toth, *The Oxford Encyclopedia of European Community Law, Vol I* (1990) 282.

which the validity of a Union act may be challenged in reference proceedings, but in practice they are the same as those applicable in annulment proceedings.[6]

In due course, the preliminary rulings procedure seemed to fall out of favour as a means of reviewing the validity of Union acts. This was underlined in two cases where the Court modified its operation in ways which were hard to reconcile with the language of the Treaty. First, it held in *Foto-Frost* v *Hauptzollamt Lübeck-Ost*[7] that national courts had to refer to the Court any challenge to a Union act which they thought might be well founded and could not (except in interlocutory proceedings[8]) declare such an act invalid themselves. The Court did not dispute the importance of allowing the validity of Union acts to be questioned in national courts. It argued, however, that since it had exclusive jurisdiction to entertain actions for the annulment of such acts, the 'coherence of the system of judicial protection established by the Treaty'[9] would be undermined if the power to declare such acts invalid when they were challenged in national proceedings was shared with national courts. Secondly, the Court ruled in *TWD Textilwerke Deggendorf*[10] that the validity of a Union act could not be challenged in national proceedings by an applicant who could clearly have contested it in annulment proceedings but had failed to do so within the time limit laid down in the Treaty. The Court may therefore have to consider in reference proceedings whether a party contesting the validity of a Union act would indisputably have had standing to challenge it directly had annulment proceedings been brought in good time.[11]

The result seemed to be to elevate the action for annulment to pride of place among the remedies which permitted the Court to review the legality of measures adopted by the institutions. It was, after all, the only procedure to allow an applicant to challenge the validity of a Union act directly before a specialized court. The plea of illegality, the third avenue mentioned by the Court in *Les Verts*, is by definition collateral, merely permitting an applicant, unable to challenge an act of general application directly, to contest its validity in other proceedings before the Union Courts.[12] It does not constitute a remedy in its own right. It is true that the

---

[6] See David Anderson and Marie Demetriou, *References to the European Court* (2nd ed, 2002) 78–79; Alexander Türk, *Judicial Review in EU Law* (2009) 227; Trevor Hartley, *The Foundations of European Union Law* (7th ed, 2010) 417–418.

[7] Case 314/85 [1987] ECR 4199. See Miguel Poiares Maduro and Loïc Azoulai (eds), *The Past and Future of EU Law: The Classics of EU Law Revisited on the 50th Anniversary of the Rome Treaty* (2010) Pt V.

[8] See further Case C-465/93 *Atlanta Fruchthandelsgesellschaft and others (I) v Bundesamt für Ernährung und Forstwirtschaft* [1995] ECR I-3761.

[9] Case 314/85 [1987] ECR 4199, para 16.

[10] Case C–188/92 [1994] ECR I–833. See also Case 370/12 *Pringle v Government of Ireland*, judgment of 27 November 2012, paras 38–42. For criticism, see Derrick Wyatt, 'The Relationship Between Actions for Annulment and References on Validity after *TWD Deggendorf*' in Julian Lonbay and Andrea Biondi (eds), *Remedies for Breach of EC Law* (1997) Ch 6; AG Tesauro in Case C–408/95 *Eurotunnel and others v SeaFrance* [1997] ECR I–6315, 63C8.

[11] See eg Case C-550/09 *E and F* [2010] ECR I-6213, paras 45–52.

[12] eg Case T-13/11 *Post Bank Iran v Council*, judgment of 6 September 2013, paras 37–39.

action for damages against the Union under Article 340 TFEU (not mentioned by the Court in *Les Verts*) may, where successful, lead to a result similar to annulment. However, the action for damages 'was introduced as an autonomous form of action, with a particular purpose to fulfil within the system of actions and subject to conditions on its use dictated by its specific nature'.[13] Those conditions are not easy to satisfy. Moreover, the Court has held that an action for damages may not be brought if it is designed to nullify the legal effects of a measure which has become definitive.[14] Only in limited circumstances can that action therefore offer a genuine alternative to annulment proceedings.

As we shall see, subsequent developments in the case law and amendments to the Treaties displayed renewed confidence in the capacity of national courts, described in Opinion 1/09[15] as ' "ordinary" courts within the European Union legal order', to assist in dealing with challenges to the validity of Union acts. That trend has been accompanied by the progressive marginalization of the action for annulment in cases involving challenges by private applicants to measures of general application. These developments raise questions about the effectiveness of the system of judicial review now in place and whether the case law is underpinned by a coherent theory of judicial review and the place of the citizen in the European polity. More broadly, they prompt reflection on the capacity of the Court to help rebuild the Union's crumbling legitimacy.

III. JUDICIAL REVIEW AND DEMOCRACY

American constitutional theorists have agonized over the legitimacy of strong judicial review, such as that practised in the United States and the European Union, which enables courts to quash primary legislation. Weaker forms of judicial review, such as those practised in many of the Member States,[16] including the United Kingdom, as well as Canada and New Zealand,[17] raise the issue of legitimacy

---

[13] Case 5/71 *Zuckerfabrik Schöppenstedt v Council* [1971] ECR 975, para 3. See further Case C-352/98 P *Bergaderm and Goupil v Commission* [2000] ECR I-5291.

[14] Case 175/84 *Krohn v Commission* [1986] ECR 753, para 30; Case T-514/93 *Cobrecaf and others v Commission* [1995] ECR II-621, paras 59–60.

[15] [2011] ECR I-1137 'Creation of a Unified Patent Litigation System', para 80.

[16] See Case C-583/11 P *Inuit Tapiriit Kanatami and others v Parliament and Council*, judgment of 3 October 2013, Opinion of AG Kokott, para 38.

[17] Jeremy Waldron, 'The Core of the Case Against Judicial Review' (2005–06) *115 Yale Law Journal* 1346, 1355–1357.

less starkly, while there seems to be general agreement that judicial review of executive and administrative action is in principle appropriate.

The basic problem with strong judicial review is the so-called counter-majoritarian difficulty.[18] As John Hart Ely put it,[19] 'a body that is not elected or otherwise politically responsible in any significant way is telling the people's elected representatives that they cannot govern as they'd like'. A particularly trenchant attack on the legitimacy of strong judicial review was mounted by Jeremy Waldron,[20] who argued that judges have no special insight into great substantive constitutional dilemmas. The quality of parliamentary debates, he maintained, made 'nonsense of the claim that legislators are incapable of addressing such issues responsibly—just as the liberal outcomes of those proceedings cast doubt on the familiar proposition that popular majorities will not uphold the rights of minorities'.[21] Outcome-related arguments in favour of judicial review were therefore in his view unpersuasive. Furthermore, process-related reasons militated unequivocally in favour of legislative decision-making. Advocates of judicial review frequently painted an unrealistic picture of what judicial decision-making was like in multi-member courts, where the outcome was often determined by simple majority voting. Waldron argued that there was no moral basis for allowing a majority decision by a small number of unelected judges to trump a majority decision by a much larger number of directly elected representatives. The idea that issues 'present themselves to judges in the form of flesh-and blood individual situations' was 'mostly a myth. By the time cases reach the high appellate levels . . . almost all trace of the original flesh-and-blood right holders has vanished, and argument . . . revolves around the abstract issue of the right in dispute'.[22] Moreover, in dealing with that issue, courts were liable to be distracted by legal technicalities, while legislators tended to go 'directly to the heart of the matter'.[23]

For all its panache, the scope of Waldron's argument was limited. He did not seek to show that judicial review of legislation was always inappropriate. Instead he invited us to imagine a society with democratic and judicial institutions in reasonably good order; a commitment to individual and minority rights which have been enshrined in a bill of rights of some kind; and good-faith disagreement about rights among its members.[24] Where these assumptions could not be made, he said,

---

[18] That term was coined by Alexander Bickel: see *The Least Dangerous Branch: The Supreme Court at the Bar of Politics* (2nd ed, 1986) 16. (The first edition was published in 1962.)

[19] John Hart Ely, *Democracy and Distrust: A Theory of Judicial Review* (1980) 4–5. See Paul Cox, 'John Hart Ely, *Democracy and Distrust: A Theory of Judicial Review*' (1981) 15 *Valparaiso University Law Review* 637; Michael Dorf, 'The Coherentism of *Democracy and Distrust*' (2005) 114 *Yale Law Journal* 1237.

[20] Waldron (n 17). See also Jonathan Sumption, 'Judicial and Political Decision-Making: The Uncertain Boundary' (the 2011 FA Mann Lecture) http://www.legalweek.com/digital_assets/3704/MANNLECTURE_final.pdf (accessed 28 June 2013). For an overview of the debate on the basis for judicial review in the United Kingdom, see Paul Craig, *Administrative Law* (6th ed, 2008) Ch 1.

[21] Waldron (n 17) 1346.   [22] Waldron (n 17) 1379.   [23] Waldron (n 17) 1384.

[24] Waldron (n 17) 1360.

his argument against judicial review would fail.[25] Moreover, he made it clear that he was concerned exclusively with 'primary legislation enacted by the elected legislature of a polity',[26] not with executive or administrative action.

A detailed rebuttal of Waldron's thesis was provided by Aileen Kavanagh.[27] Kavanagh argued that judicial review should be seen, not as an alternative to, but as an element of democratic government and that it can be 'a valuable channel of political participation'.[28] She maintained that 'the justice of the outcomes of political decisions' is the 'fundamental criterion for judging political institutions and it determines what political procedures we choose'.[29] Although there is 'more to the justification of political authority than good results, there is also more to it than the participatory nature of the procedure'.[30] Kavanagh insisted that, since courts are only to a limited extent politically accountable, they

can provide an impartial forum in which the issues can be decided in light of constitutional principles. This procedure is preferable precisely because judges are not directly affected by their own decision. As unelected officials, they can provide a corrective to some of the energies which animate normal politics, such as those of political interest and power.[31]

She pointed out that the weak may be disenfranchized by normal politics and that a mechanism that can be activated by those who feel their rights have been infringed can be useful in bringing such infringements to light and prompting parliament to rectify legislative shortcomings. Political participation, she said, is 'dependent on the possession of political, financial and organizational resources'.[32] Just giving people 'the right to vote and participate in democratic politics' does not mean 'that everyone will be able to get their voice heard . . .'[33] Judicial review 'involves a distribution of political power in society, such that those who might otherwise be effectively disenfranchised in the political system can press their claim in the public life of their country'.[34] It can be 'a way of empowering citizens to assert, publicise and ultimately enforce their rights in the public forum'.[35]

Ronald Dworkin maintained that '[d]emocracy does not insist on judges having the last word, but it does not insist that they must not have it'.[36] He argued that the controversy is not about how far democracy can be reconciled with other

[25] Waldron (n 17) 1402. He insisted, however, that even where his assumptions failed there might be other good arguments against judicial review.

[26] Waldron (n 17) 1354.

[27] Aileen Kavanagh, 'Participation and Judicial Review: A Reply to Jeremy Waldron' (2003) 22 *Law and Philosophy* 451. See also Richard Fallon, 'The Core of an Uneasy Case for Judicial Review' (2007–08) 121 *Harvard Law Review* 1693; Alon Harel and Adam Shinar, 'Between Judicial and Legislative Supremacy: A Cautious Defense of Constrained Judicial Review' (2011) *International Journal of Constitutional Law* 950; Dimitrios Kyritsis, 'Constitutional Review in Representative Democracy' (2012) 32 *Oxford Journal of Legal Studies* 297.

[28] Kavanagh (n 27) 453.   [29] Kavanagh (n 27) 462.   [30] Kavanagh (n 27) 464.

[31] Kavanagh (n 27) 472.   [32] Kavanagh (n 27) 480.   [33] Kavanagh (n 27) 480.

[34] Kavanagh (n 27) 483.   [35] Kavanagh (n 27) 484.

[36] Ronald Dworkin, *Freedom's Law: The Moral Reading of the American Constitution* (1996) 7.

values, but what democracy actually is. Dworkin described democracy as 'government subject to conditions . . . of equal status for all citizens'. When majoritarian institutions fail to respect those conditions, he maintained, 'there can be no objection in the name of democracy, to other procedures that protect and respect them better'.[37] Francis Jacobs went so far as to suggest that the very notion of the rule of law should nowadays be understood as embodying the supremacy of the law, which binds all public authorities and parliament itself. 'This will imply', he wrote, 'extensive judicial review including limited review of parliamentary legislation, based on a constitution or quasi-constitutional texts; but also based on certain fundamental values, especially fundamental rights.'[38]

It will be clear from what has been said so far that the strongest case against judicial review concerns rights-based challenges to primary legislation where a court is being asked to overturn the conclusion reached by a democratically elected legislature. Judicial review to protect what Richard Fallon called 'structural constitutional norms'[39] (such as rules governing the separation of powers) or secondary legislation is less controversial. Questions of legitimacy may arise where the courts appear to substitute their own views on matters of policy for those of the primary decision-maker,[40] though there will nearly always be room for argument over whether this has occurred in any particular case.[41] On the other hand, judicial review may offer the weak and marginalized a stake in the political system which the democratic process denies them because of their inability to compete with more powerful groups. It can help to bring unpredicted infringements of individual rights to the notice of the legislature and limit the consequences of misguided or immoral legislation. It may be considered compatible with democracy properly understood or as integral to the rule of law. As Fallon observed, political legitimacy may derive from several sources. So '. . . a shortfall. . . in democratic legitimacy may ultimately be outweighed, as a matter of overall legitimacy, by the contribution that judicial review can make to the protection of individual rights'.[42]

There is therefore a close link between judicial review and democracy. The more effectively the principles of democratic government are observed in a political system, the more strong judicial review is likely to attract criticism as illegitimate. Conversely, where the democratic process in a political system is in some way deficient, then the need for strong judicial review is more likely to be accepted because of its capacity to uphold individual rights and give a voice to those who find themselves excluded from the political process.[43] Waldron assumed, for the purposes

---

[37] Dworkin (n 36) 17.

[38] Francis Jacobs, *The Sovereignty of Law: The European Way* (2007) 49.

[39] Fallon (n 27) 1729.   [40] See Sumption (n 20).

[41] See Stephen Sedley's response to Sumption (n 20) in the *London Review of Books* (23 February 2012, 15–16).

[42] Fallon (n 27) 1735. cf Kavanagh (n 27) 454.

[43] Cf Walter van Gerven, *The European Union: A Polity of States and Peoples* (2005) 63.

of his thesis, a society 'in which its laws are made and its public policies are set by the people and their representatives working through elective institutions'.[44] That society has 'a broadly democratic political system with universal adult suffrage, and it has a representative legislature, to which elections are held on a fair and regular basis'. The legislature is used to dealing with difficult and important issues, which sometimes touch on sensitive questions of justice and social policy. Waldron referred to law-making procedures which are 'elaborate and responsible' and which incorporate various safeguards: links with wider debates in society; the way in which legislators think of themselves; the existence of political parties. He spoke of 'a culture of democracy, valuing responsible deliberation and political equality'.

Can the European Union be considered democratic for these purposes? Article 2 TEU says that 'democracy' is one of the values on which the Union is founded. Title II of the TEU is headed 'Provisions on Democratic Principles' and contains four articles elaborating on the various means by which democracy may be said to be embedded in the governance of the Union. Notwithstanding those provisions, it is widely accepted that the Union suffers from a democracy deficit. The outlines of the argument are familiar.[45] The Union has a process of governance but no identifiable government. As the Bundesverfassungsgericht put it in its *Lisbon* judgment,[46] the Union lacks 'a system of organisation of political rule in which a European majority will carries the formation of the government sustained by free and equal electoral decisions . . .' This means that there is never an opportunity for voters 'to throw the scoundrels out', in Joseph Weiler's memorable phrase.[47] Weiler points out that there have been 'some spectacular political failures of European governance', but that these have not led 'to any measure of political accountability, of someone paying a political price for their failure, as would be the case in national politics'.[48] Moreover, the influence wielded by national governments in the decision-making process of the Union, and the difficulties national parliaments frequently encounter in monitoring and controlling the conduct

[44] Waldron (n 17) 1361. Cf Ely (n 19) 4–7. For discussion of what Ely meant by 'democracy', see Cox (n 19) 641–644.

[45] See Paul Craig, 'Integration, Democracy, and Legitimacy' in Paul Craig and Gráinne de Búrca, *The Evolution of EU Law* (2nd ed, 2011) 13, 28–31; Damian Chalmers, Gareth Davies and Giorgio Monti, *European Union Law* (2nd ed, 2010) 125–136; Vivien Schmidt, 'Democracy and Legitimacy in the European Union' in Erik Jones, Anand Menon and Stephen Weatherill, *The Oxford Handbook of the European Union* (2012) 661. Cf Koen Lenaerts, 'The Principle of Democracy in the Case Law of the European Court of Justice' (2013) 62 *International and Comparative Law Quarterly* 271; Andrew Moravcsik, 'In Defence of the "Democratic Deficit": Reassessing Legitimacy in the European Union' (2002) 40 *Journal of Common Market Studies* 603. On the implications for democracy of the Union's response to the euro crisis, see Mark Dawson and Floris de Witte, 'Constitutional Balance in the EU after the Euro-Crisis' (2013) 76 *Modern Law Review* 817.

[46] [2010] 3 CMLR 13, para 256.   [47] Joseph Weiler, *The Constitution of Europe* (1999) 266.

[48] Joseph Weiler, 'Deciphering the Political and Legal DNA of European Integration: An Exploratory Essay' in Julie Dickson and Pavlos Eleftheriadis (eds), *Philosophical Foundations of European Union Law* (2012) 137, 140–141.

of national ministers in that process, enhance the power of national executives at the expense of national legislatures. Although directly elected, the European Parliament has not solved the problem. It is not, as the Bundesverfassungsgericht has pointed out, 'a representative body of a sovereign European people'.[49] Despite successive increases in its formal powers and hampered by its split location,[50] it has failed to connect with the European electorate. This is reflected in the decline in voter turnout at every European election since the first in 1979. Moreover, in the 2014 election there was an influx of members hostile to the Union.[51] Weiler concludes[52] that 'the two most primordial norms of democracy, the principle of accountability and the principle of representation, are compromised in the very structure and process of the Union'.

Against that background, robust and effective judicial review can be seen as an essential element of the Union's claim to overall political legitimacy. It is a fundamental safeguard of the democratic bargain struck by Member States with their electorates whenever they ratify a Union Treaty, that the institutions of the Union will observe the law in discharging their responsibilities. It can help reinforce the right of Union citizens to participate in the democratic life of the Union.

IV. The Evolving Scope of the Action for Annulment Before Lisbon

Given the importance of judicial review in a system of conferred powers,[53] the place accorded to the action for annulment in the scheme of the EEC Treaty may readily be understood. The current text of Article 263 TFEU is radically different from—and in some respects markedly better than—that of Article 173 EEC.[54] Two particular classes of difference are worth noting here.

---

[49] *Lisbon* judgment (n 46), para 256. See also Michael Dougan, 'What Are We To Make of the Citizens' Initiative?' (2011) 48 *Common Market Law Review* 1807, 1814.

[50] Protocol No 6 on the Location of the Seats of the Institutions and of Certain Bodies, Offices, Agencies and Departments of the European Union, annexed at Lisbon to the TEU, TFEU and EAEC Treaty.

[51] See http://www.europarl.europa.eu/elections2014-results (accessed 9 March 2015). The picture is more nuanced than the bald figures make it appear because of the growth in the number of Member States.

[52] Weiler (n 48) 142.

[53] In *Federalist No 78*, Alexander Hamilton described the courts as 'the bulwarks of a limited Constitution against legislative encroachments'.

[54] Anthony Arnull, *The European Union and its Court of Justice* (2nd ed, 2006) 54–56.

Article 173 envisaged only two possible defendants: the Council and the Commission. Article 263 TFEU adds the European Parliament as well as certain institutional newcomers: the European Central Bank; the European Council; and bodies, offices and agencies of the Union. Furthermore, Article 173 included only the Member States, the Council and the Commission in the list of so-called privileged applicants who could bring proceedings without needing to establish their standing to do so. Article 263 TFEU includes the European Parliament in that list. It also reflects changes in the Union's institutional architecture by recognizing a class of so-called semi-privileged applicants comprising the Court of Auditors, the European Central Bank and the Committee of the Regions. These may bring proceedings 'for the purpose of protecting their prerogatives'.

The second paragraph of Article 173 was concerned with the circumstances in which natural or legal persons (so-called non-privileged or private applicants) could launch annulment proceedings. Such applicants may range from individuals to powerful corporations, but all contribute to the good governance of the Union by seeking to vindicate their rights, whether in the national courts through the doctrine of direct effect or the principle of state liability or in the Union Courts through the action for annulment. While we should acknowledge the revolutionary character of 'the very notion of an individual having independent standing to sue before an international tribunal . . .',[55] the right of action conferred on private applicants appeared rather limited, being confined initially to three categories of act only. These were decisions addressed to the applicant; decisions disguised as ('in the form of') regulations, which were of direct and individual concern to the applicant; and decisions addressed to third parties but which were of direct and individual concern to the applicant. Unlike privileged applicants, private applicants were apparently to have no right to challenge genuine regulations or directives even if directly and individually concerned by them. The position under Article 263 TFEU is markedly different, as we shall see.

1. Reviewable Acts and the Status of the European Parliament

As the case law developed, the text of Article 173 became less and less reliable as a statement of the law. The process began with the *ERTA* case,[56] where the Court held that the action for annulment was not confined, as Article 173 EEC seemed to imply, to acts of the types described in Article 189 EEC (now 288 TFEU) but extended to 'all measures adopted by the institutions, whatever their nature or form, which are

---

[55] Eric Stein and G. Joseph Vining, 'Citizen Access to Judicial Review of Administrative Action in a Transnational and Federal Context' (1976) 70 *American Journal of International Law* 219, 222.
[56] Case 22/70 *Commission v Council* [1971] ECR 263.

intended to have legal effects'. While the Court's conclusion involved accepting that legal effects might be produced by steps taken by the institutions which did not fit the mould of Article 189 EEC, it also ensured that such steps would be subject to judicial review. Had the Court ruled otherwise, a class of acts of uncertain status might have developed outside its control.

The Court's ruling in the *ERTA* case was not incompatible with the rather imprecise wording of the first paragraph of Article 173. Whether the same can be said of its later case law on the status of the European Parliament is more doubtful. The absence of any reference to that institution in the original text of Article 173 began to seem anomalous with the advent of the first set of direct elections in 1979. The lacuna was filled by two momentous decisions of the Court. The first was *Les Verts*,[57] where it was held that 'an action for annulment may lie against measures adopted by the European Parliament intended to have legal effects *vis-à-vis* third parties'. The second was *Chernobyl*,[58] where it was held that the Parliament had the right to bring annulment proceedings where the purpose was to protect its prerogatives.

The Member States amended Article 173 at Maastricht to reflect those decisions but they remain among the most controversial ever delivered by the Court, attacked by critics for rewriting the Treaty[59] and lauded by defenders for their contribution to the Union's system of judicial protection.[60] There is room for argument about whether the line taken by the Court was justified, but what cannot be denied is that each decision involved a *contra legem* reading of the Treaty, which made it quite clear that the European Parliament could neither sue nor be sued in annulment proceedings. Indeed, the Court had concluded shortly before *Chernobyl*, in a case known as *Comitology*,[61] that the Treaty did not enable it 'to recognize the capacity of the European Parliament to bring an action for annulment'. The Court had assumed in that case that the Commission could be relied on to protect the Parliament's prerogatives, but the validity of that assumption was thrown into doubt in *Chernobyl*, where the Commission and the Parliament were at odds with each other. In a remarkable act of judicial sleight of hand, the Court expressly endorsed its recent conclusion in *Comitology* on the interpretation of Article 173[62] but sought to circumvent it by creating a new right of action, parallel to but separate from proceedings under Article 173, so that it could ensure respect for the prerogatives of the Parliament.[63] This amounted to an acknowledgment by the Court that the outcome could not be reconciled with the strict terms of the Treaty.[64]

---

[57] *Les Verts* (n 1) para 25.   [58] Case C-70/88 *Parliament v Council* [1990] ECR I-2041.

[59] See eg Hartley (n 6) 72–73; Patrick Neill, 'The European Court of Justice: A Case Study in Judicial Activism' (European Policy Forum, 1995).

[60] See eg Maduro and Azoulai (n 7) Pt VIII.

[61] Case 302/87 *Parliament v Council* [1988] ECR 5615, para 28.

[62] *Chernobyl* (n 58) paras 13 and 24.   [63] *Chernobyl* (n 58) para 27.

[64] As we have seen, the device of confining the right to bring annulment proceedings to cases involving the 'prerogatives' of the applicant would later be extended, but the European

2. The Standing of Private Applicants

The Court's approach to the interpretation of the standing rules that private applicants must normally satisfy to access the action for annulment has been more nuanced. Direct concern, which concerns the immediacy of the contested measure's impact on the applicant, did not generally prove problematic.[65] It acquired increased prominence following the amendments introduced by the Treaty of Lisbon, as we shall see in the next section. More troublesome were the distinction between regulations and decisions, and the meaning of individual concern.

In practice, it proved very difficult to persuade the Court that a measure labelled a regulation was in reality a decision, even where it affected only a small number of traders whose identity was known or could be established.[66] Apparently to avoid unfairness, the Court would sometimes decide the question of admissibility on the basis of direct and/or individual concern without reference to the requirement of a decision.[67]

Individual concern proved an even more significant barrier to the admissibility of actions brought by private applicants.[68] It has been evident from the outset that the action for annulment was not intended to be an *actio popularis* and that, to establish standing, a private applicant would generally need to show that the contested act had a more particular effect on him or her than it did on others. But the notion of individual concern is self-evidently an open-textured one, capable of being understood in a number of different ways,[69] so the extent and nature of the particularity it required was for the Court to decide. In 1963, it nailed its colours to the mast in *Plaumann*,[70] an action for the annulment of a

Parliament now has an untrammelled right to bring annulment proceedings: Art 263 TFEU, para 2.

[65] Cases where direct concern was decisive include Case T-96/92, *CCE de la Société générale des grandes sources and others v Commission* [1995] ECR II-1213 and Joined Cases T-172/98, T-175/98 to T-177/98 *Salamander and others v Parliament and Council* [2000] ECR II-2487.

[66] See eg Joined Cases 789 and 790/79 *Calpak v Commission* [1980] ECR 1949.

[67] See eg Case 100/74 *CAM v Commission* [1975] ECR 1393; Case C-152/88 *Sofrimport v Commission* [1990] ECR I-2477.

[68] Private applicants must also show that they have an interest in the annulment of the contested measure: see eg Joined Cases T-480/93 and T-483/93 *Antillean Rice Mills and others v Commission* [1995] ECR II-2305, paras 59–60; Case T-102/96, *Gencor Ltd v Commission* [1999] ECR II-753, paras 40–41; Case C-239/12 P *Abdulrahim v Council and Commission* [2013] 3 CMLR 41. That requirement is not expressly laid down in the Treaty and does not apply to privileged applicants: see Case C-355/10 *Parliament v Council*, judgment of 5 September 2012, para 37; Case C-583/11 P *Inuit Tapiriit Kanatami and others v Parliament and Council*, judgment of 3 October 2013, para 53.

[69] See A.G. Jacobs in *UPA* (n 1) para 75; Case T-177/01 *Jégo-Quéré v Commission* [2002] ECR II-2365, para 49.

[70] Case 25/62 *Plaumann v Commission* [1963] ECR 95, 107.

Commission decision addressed to the Federal Republic of Germany brought by a private applicant. The Court declared:

Persons other than those to whom a decision is addressed may only claim to be individually concerned if that decision affects them by reason of certain attributes which are peculiar to them or by reason of circumstances in which they are differentiated from all other persons and by virtue of these factors distinguishes them individually just as in the case of the person addressed.

That famously restrictive formula has cast its shadow over the case law ever since and severely limited private applicants' access to the Court.[71]

Two cases decided in the early 1990s seemed to portend a change of direction. In *Extramet Industrie v Council* and *Codorniu v Council*,[72] the Court was persuaded to accept that 'the requirement of a decision does not exist independently of the requirement of individual concern'[73] and that true regulations could be challenged by private applicants if they could show direct and individual concern. It was later conceded that directives could also be challenged by private applicants in these circumstances.[74] The Court also accepted that individual concern might be shown where a measure affected a trader's ability to compete effectively, as in *Extramet*, or to exploit a long-held intellectual property right, *as in Codorniu*. Together with *TWD*, decided less than three months before *Codorniu*, these developments in the case law seemed to make the action for annulment the principal remedy for challenging the validity of Union acts.[75]

The requirement of a decision was abolished at Lisbon, Article 263 TFEU confirming, through the use of the term 'act', that true regulations and directives may in principle be challenged by private applicants. However, individual concern in its *Plaumann* incarnation has been one of Union law's great survivors. In the *Greenpeace* case in the late 1990s, Advocate General Cosmas cautioned against overstating '[t]he significance and extent of mitigation by the Court, in *Extramet* and *Codorniu*, of the rigour of the case-law [on individual concern]'[76] and the *Plaumann* formula reasserted itself.

---

[71] Anthony Arnull, 'Private Applicants and the Action for Annulment under Article 173 of the EC Treaty' (1995) 32 *Common Market Law Review* 7.

[72] Case C-309/89 [1994] ECR I-1853.

[73] AG Jacobs in Case C-358/89 *Extramet Industrie v Council* [1991] ECR I-2501, para 53 of the Opinion.

[74] See Joined Cases T-172/98 and T-175/98 to T-177/98 *Salamander AG and others v Parliament and Council* [2000] ECR II-2487; Joined Cases T-125/96 and T-152/96 *Boehringer v Council and Commission* [1999] ECR II-3427; Case T-135/96 *UEAPME v Council* [1998] ECR II-2335; Case C-408/95 *Eurotunnel and others v SeaFrance* [1997] ECR I-6315; Case C-10/95 P *Asocarne v Council* [1995] ECR I-4149; Case C-298/89 *Gibraltar v Council* [1993] ECR I-3605.

[75] Anthony Arnull, 'Private Applicants and the Action for Annulment since *Codorniu*' (2001) 38 *Common Market Law Review* 7.

[76] Case C-321/95 *Greenpeace Council and others v Commission* [1998] ECR I-1651, 1689.

The case law on individual concern came under renewed scrutiny in *UPA*,[77] where Advocate General Jacobs urged the Court to adopt a new, more liberal, test under which a person would be regarded as individually concerned by a Community measure 'where, by reason of his particular circumstances, the measure has, or is liable to have, a substantial adverse effect on his interests'.[78] Before the Court gave judgment in *UPA*, the General Court gave judgment in *Jégo-Quéré v Commission*.[79] Citing with approval the Opinion of Advocate General Jacobs in *UPA*, the General Court declared that a private applicant should be considered individually concerned where a measure affected his legal position 'in a manner which is both definite and immediate, by restricting his rights or by imposing obligations on him'.[80] When the Court gave judgment in *UPA*, however, it reaffirmed the existing case law and declared that reform of the system currently in force would require an amendment to the Treaty.[81]

The Court acknowledged in *UPA* that individuals were 'entitled to effective judicial protection of the rights they derive from the Community legal order'.[82] However, it sought to show that the Treaty provided various means of challenging the validity of Community acts, devoting particular attention to the preliminary rulings procedure. The Court declared that it was the responsibility of the Member States 'to establish a system of legal remedies and procedures which ensure respect for the right to effective judicial protection'.[83] In particular, national courts were required,

> so far as possible, to interpret and apply national procedural rules governing the exercise of rights of action in a way that enables natural and legal persons to challenge before the courts the legality of any decision or other national measure relative to the application to them of a Community act of general application, by pleading the invalidity of such an act.[84]

When it later set aside the General Court's judgment in *Jégo-Quéré*,[85] the Court effectively acknowledged that the existing case law might in some cases deprive applicants of their right to effective judicial protection. The Court made it clear that, where the test of individual concern was not satisfied, it was not prepared to allow a private applicant to seek the annulment of a measure of general application, even if the individual concerned was unable to contest the validity of that

---

[77] *UPA* (n 1).

[78] *UPA* (n 1) para 60 of the Opinion.   [79] Case T-177/01 [2002] ECR II-2365.

[80] *Jégo-Quéré* (n 79) para 51 of the judgment.   [81] *UPA* (n 1) para 45 of the judgment.

[82] *UPA* (n 1) para 39.   [83] *UPA* (n 1) para 41.

[84] *UPA* (n 1) para 42. Cf Case C-106/89 *Marleasing* [1990] ECR I-4135.

[85] Case C-263/02 P *Commission v Jégo-Quéré* [2004] ECR I-3425. The European Court of Human Rights later gave the case law of the Court of Justice a qualified blessing: *Bosphorus Hava Yollari Turizm ve Ticaret Anonim Şirketi v Ireland* [GC], no 45036/98, ECHR 2005-VI. On the compatibility of the Treaty standing rules with the Aarhus Convention on Access to Information, Public Participation in Decision-Making and Access to Justice in Environmental Matters, [2005] OJ L124/4, see Peter Oliver, 'Access to Information and to Justice in EU Environmental Law: The Aarhus Convention' (2013) 36 *Fordham International Law Journal* 1423, 1468–1469.

measure in the national courts without first contravening it.[86] This was a situation the General Court had sought to avoid[87] and which the Court of Justice later conceded was unacceptable.[88]

V. The Lisbon Reforms
to the Standing Rules

1. Background

The *UPA* judgment amounted to a public invitation to the Convention on the Future of Europe, which was sitting when the case was decided, to consider whether the action for annulment, and particularly the standing rules applicable to private applicants, should be reformed. That issue was considered by the Discussion Circle on the Court set up by the Convention.[89] The Discussion Circle was divided on the question whether any such reform was desirable.

One group of members favoured underlining the duty of Member States and national courts to ensure effective protection of the rights enjoyed by individuals under Union law. That view is now reflected in the second subparagraph of Article 19(1) TEU, which provides: 'Member States shall provide remedies sufficient to ensure effective legal protection in the fields covered by Union law.'

Another group proposed that the fourth paragraph of Article 230 EC should be amended to read as follows: 'Any natural or legal person may . . . institute proceedings against an act addressed to that person or which is of direct and individual concern to him, and against [an act of general application] [a regulatory act] which is of direct concern to him without entailing implementing measures.'[90]

That proposal is now reflected in the fourth paragraph of Article 263 TFEU. Implementing measures are regarded as entailed for these purposes where the provisions in dispute of the parent act do not define their 'specific consequences' for the applicant, a somewhat amorphous notion.[91] Where such measures are envisaged, it is they that should be challenged by the applicant rather than the parent

---

[86] Case C-263/02 P, para 34.

[87] *Jégo-Quéré* (n 79) para 45.   [88] Case C-432/05 *Unibet* [2007] ECR I-2271, para 64.

[89] CONV 636/03.   [90] CONV 636/03, 7 (square brackets in the original).

[91] See Case C-274/12 P *Telefónica v Commission*, judgment of 19 December 2013, para 35. Cf Case C-132/12 P *Stichting Woonpunt and others v Commission*, judgment of 27 February 2014, para 53. The relationship between the presence or absence of implementing measures and direct concern (see text at n 65) will no doubt be clarified as the case law develops. See the Opinions of AG Kokott in

act. If those measures are to be adopted at Union level, this would be done before the Union Courts, where the illegality of the parent act may be pleaded under Article 277 TFEU. If national implementing measures are required, such a challenge would be brought before the courts of the Member State concerned.

The authors of Article 263 preferred the term 'regulatory act' to 'act of general application'. The absence of a Treaty definition of the former term prompted much speculation about what it might mean.[92] That question was addressed for the first time by the General Court and, on appeal, by the Court of Justice in *Inuit Tapiriit Kanatami and others v European Parliament and Council*, a case that merits detailed discussion.

2. The *Inuit* Case

(a) The Judgment of the General Court

The *Inuit* case involved an action for the annulment of a regulation on trade in seal products[93] brought by a number of private applicants. Citing the *travaux préparatoires* relating to the Constitutional Treaty, the General Court[94] maintained that the point of the new addition to the fourth paragraph of Article 263 was to avoid a situation in which a private applicant affected by an act of general application could only have access to a court by infringing the law. It concluded that the term 'regulatory act' covered 'all acts of general application apart from legislative acts'.[95] Having been adopted under the ordinary legislative procedure, the regulation at issue in *Inuit* constituted a legislative act, not a regulatory act.

The General Court then considered whether the applicants were directly concerned. It observed that 'the contested regulation directly affects only the legal situation of those of the applicants who are active in the placing on the market of the European Union of seal products'.[96] The possible economic consequences of the regulation for other applicants did not affect their legal situation, only their factual situation. This

---

Case C-274/12 P *Telefónica*, paras 35–42, and A.G. Wathelet in Case C-132/12 P *Stichting Woonpunt*, paras 69–76; Albors-Llorens (n 3) 526–528.

[92] See Stephan Balthasar, 'Locus Standi Rules for Challenges to Regulatory Acts by Private Applicants: The New Article 263(4) TFEU' (2010) 35 *European Law Review* 542; Réné Barents, 'The Court of Justice After the Treaty of Lisbon' (2010) 47 *Common Market Law Review* 709, 724–726; Paul Craig, *The Lisbon Treaty: Law, Politics and Treaty Reform* (2010) 130–131; Koen Lenaerts, 'Le traité de Lisbonne et la protection juridictionnelle des particuliers en droit de l'Union' (2009) 45 *Cahiers de Droit Européen* 711, 725–728; Türk (n 6) 166–169.

[93] Reg 1007/2009 [2009] OJ L286/36.   [94] Case T-18/10 [2011] ECR II-5599.

[95] Case T-18/10 (n 94) para 56 of the Order. See further Alexander Türk, 'Oversight of Administrative Rulemaking: Judicial Review' (2013) 19 European Law Journal 126.

[96] Para 75 of the Order (n 95).

was not enough to establish direct concern.[97] It therefore concluded that only some of the applicants were directly concerned by the contested regulation, but they were in any event unable to establish individual concern. The action was therefore dismissed as inadmissible.

(b) The Opinion of Advocate General Kokott

On appeal, Advocate General Kokott endorsed the conclusion of the General Court.[98] Referring to the drafting history of the fourth paragraph of Article 263 TFEU and the Lisbon Intergovernmental Conference (IGC) mandate, the reinforcement of the remedies available in national courts by Article 19(1) TEU and 'the particularly high democratic legitimation of parliamentary legislation',[99] she concluded that the General Court had interpreted the term 'regulatory act' correctly. She proceeded to endorse the conclusions of the General Court on direct and individual concern, rejecting any suggestion that the *Plaumann* formula should be abandoned on the basis that the authors of the Treaty had decided 'not to revise the criterion of individual concern . . .'.[100] Advocate General Kokott insisted that there was 'no reason to fear a gap in the legal remedies available to individuals against European Union legislative acts'.[101] Where, for example, it fell to the national authorities to monitor compliance with a legislative act, any individual could write to such an authority requesting confirmation that the act concerned did not apply to him or her. A negative decision would have to be open to review in the national courts, which would be able to ask the Court for a preliminary ruling on the act's interpretation or validity.[102] By relegating the action for annulment to a supporting role behind the preliminary rulings procedure in providing judicial review of Union acts, Advocate General Kokott's Opinion reflected the general trend of the case law since at least *UPA*, a trend now partly endorsed by Article 19(1) TEU. However, her reasoning was not wholly convincing.

The suggestion that the extent to which an applicant should enjoy standing might depend on the democratic legitimacy of the contested act is unsound. If this characteristic were important, some degree of correspondence might be expected between the democratic credentials of the contested act and those of the applicant seeking to challenge it. This would imply the imposition of restrictions on the standing of, for example, the Commission. Instead, a right of action has been conferred on the Court of Auditors, the European Central Bank and the Committee of the Regions, none of which has any democratic legitimacy of its own. That step was

---

[97] The possibility that the test for direct concern under the final clause of the fourth paragraph of Art 263 was not the same as the test for direct concern under the preceding clause was rejected in Case T-262/10 *Microban International and Microban (Europe) v Commission* [2011] ECR II-7697, para 32. See also the Opinions of A.G. Kokott in *Inuit* (n 68) paras 68–69 and *Telefónica* (n 91) para 59.

[98] Case C-583/11 P *Inuit* (n 68).   [99] *Inuit* (n 68), Opinion, para 38.

[100] *Inuit* (n 68), Opinion, para 90.   [101] *Inuit* (n 68), Opinion, para 115.

[102] *Inuit* (n 68), Opinion, para 120.

taken on the basis, not of the quality of the contested act, but of the nature of its effect on the applicant. In any event, the democratic legitimacy of the contested act has no bearing on the Court's jurisdiction to review its validity under the preliminary rulings procedure.

The term 'legislative acts' includes not just acts adopted under the ordinary legislative procedure but also acts adopted under special legislative procedures.[103] It has been pointed out that, 'from the point of view of process, many "special legislative procedures" (based on a Commission proposal, unanimity or QMV in Council, and consultation with or the consent of the European Parliament) appear identical to non-legislative procedures conducted in the same manner'.[104] Moreover, several special legislative procedures involving consultation of the European Parliament differ from non-legislative procedures which also involve consultation of the European Parliament only in the way in which the Council votes: by unanimity in the case of the former and QMV in the case of the latter.[105] Whether this affects the democratic legitimacy of the process in any real sense is a moot point.

Article 81(3) TFEU exemplifies the disjuncture between the democratic legitimacy of a procedure and its classification as special or non-legislative. The second sub-paragraph of that provision allows the Council, acting unanimously 'on a proposal from the Commission' and after consulting the European Parliament, to adopt decisions specifying aspects of family law with cross-border implications which may be the subject of acts adopted by the ordinary legislative procedure. By virtue of the third sub-paragraph, the Council may act only in the absence of opposition from any national parliament. The involvement of the national parliaments might be thought to confer enhanced democratic legitimacy on the procedure, but it is technically non-legislative in character.[106] So the distinction between legislative and non-legislative acts is purely formal (or pragmatic) rather than qualitative. There is therefore merit in Advocate General Wathelet's conclusion in *Stichting Woonpunt*[107] that regulatory acts should be defined as acts of general application, whether legislative or not. An alternative might be to regard the term regulatory acts as embracing any act of general application which gives effect to rules or principles laid down elsewhere, for example in the Treaties or a parent act. This approach would not, however, have benefited the

---

[103] Art 289 TFEU.

[104] Alan Dashwood, Michael Dougan, Barry Rodger, Eleanor Spaventa and Derrick Wyatt, *Wyatt and Dashwood's European Union Law* (6th ed, 2011) 85; Albors-Llorens (n 3) 524. See also Michael Dougan, 'The Treaty of Lisbon 2007: Winning Minds, Not Hearts' (2008) 45 *Common Market Law Review* 617, 678–679; Steve Peers and Marios Costa, 'Judicial Review of EU Acts after the Treaty of Lisbon' (2012) *European Constitutional Law Review* 82, 94–95. Compare eg Arts 23 and 74, and 21(3) and 349 TFEU.

[105] Compare eg Arts 21(3) and 22(1) and (2) TFEU with Arts 74 and 78(3) TFEU.

[106] If the procedure were legislative, the express reference to a proposal from the Commission would not be necessary: Art 17(2) TEU. Cf Art 81(3) TFEU, first sub-paragraph.

[107] *Stichting Woonpunt* (n 91), para 65 of the Opinion.

applicants in *Inuit*, since the regulation being challenged in that case envisaged the adoption of implementing measures by the Commission.[108]

In *Inuit*, Advocate General Kokott was doubtless thinking mainly of acts adopted under the ordinary legislative procedure. The democratic legitimacy of such acts may be greater than that of Union acts adopted under other procedures in which the European Parliament plays a less influential role, but it remains limited and does not match that of primary legislation adopted in all (or nearly all) of the Member States. Indeed, from the perspective of democratic legitimacy, the Court's case law according primacy to all rules of Union law over conflicting rules of national law *of whatever status* is hard to justify.[109]

In referring, like the General Court, to the *travaux préparatoires* of the Convention on the Future of Europe, Advocate General Kokott did not seem troubled by the fact that this was a body with no legal basis and limited democratic credentials. Moreover, there are concerns about the manner in which its proceedings were conducted. Paul Magnette and Kalypso Nicolaïdis observed[110] that the muscular role played by the Convention's chairman, aided and abetted by the Praesidium, rendered the consensus ultimately arrived at a fragile one[111] and deprived it of 'the kind of legitimacy that a more thoroughly negotiated text' might have enjoyed.[112] A similar view was reflected in a highly critical account of the working methods of the Convention and the Praesidium given by the British MP Gisela Stuart, who was a member of both.[113]

More significantly, the product of the Convention was decisively rejected by referendums held in two of the founding Member States and plunged the Union into a prolonged constitutional crisis (one of the 'spectacular political failures of European governance' referred to by Joseph Weiler,[114] though they have all now been overshadowed by the eurozone débâcle[115]). The process which led to the signing

---

[108] A Commission implementing regulation was the subject of annulment proceedings in Case T-526/10 *Inuit Tapiriit Kanatami and others v Commission*, judgment of 25 April 2013. Those proceedings were dismissed by the General Court as unfounded. Unusually the General Court expressly declined to rule on the admissibility of the action. An appeal to the Court of Justice is pending at the time of writing: see Case C-398/13 P.

[109] See eg Case C-399/11 *Melloni* [2013] 2 CMLR 43.

[110] Paul Magnette and Kalypso Nicolaïdis, 'The European Convention: Bargaining in the Shadow of Rhetoric' (2004) 27 *West European Politics* 381, 391. See also Alan Dashwood, 'The Draft EU Constitution—First Impressions' (2002-03) 5 *Cambridge Yearbook of European Legal Studies* 395, 396–398.

[111] Magnette and Nicolaïdis (n 110).   [112] Magnette and Nicolaïdis (n 110) 398.

[113] Gisela Stuart, *The Making of Europe's Constitution* (2003) 19–21. See also 'Alternative Report: The Europe of Democracies' annexed to the report of the Presidency of the Convention to the President of the European Council (CONV 851/03, 18 July 2003).

[114] Weiler (n 48), 141.

[115] Cf Dariusz Adamski, 'National Power Games and Structural Failures in the European Macroeconomic Governance' (2012) 49 *Common Market Law Review* 1319.

of the Treaty of Lisbon was shrouded in secrecy,[116] offering outside observers and even national governments little opportunity to digest and analyse what was being proposed.[117] The British House of Commons European Scrutiny Committee revealed in a report published in October 2007[118] that the Presidency circulated the draft IGC mandate for the first time at 5 p.m. on 19 June, little more than 48 hours before the start of the European Council meeting at 5.30 p.m. on 21 June, where the convening of the IGC and its mandate were agreed.[119] No draft text had been provided or discussed previously. The consultations that had taken place with the Member States had not involved any negotiations, merely statements of each country's position.[120] In its conclusion, the Committee referred to 'an essentially secret drafting process conducted by the Presidency, with texts produced at the last moment before pressing for agreement'. It added that the compressed timetable 'could not have been better designed to marginalise' the role of national parliaments.[121]

Although these criticisms do not seem to have directly implicated the work of the Discussion Circle, it is hard to know how much influence its report on the Court ultimately had on the Treaty of Lisbon. By Advocate General Kokott's own admission,[122] the wording of the Treaty for 'regulatory act' differs from that of the Constitutional Treaty in five language versions and in 10 language versions it is unclear whether that term was intended to exclude legislative rule making. Perhaps the Member States did not give the matter any serious attention or were content to leave the ambiguity to be resolved by the Court. Had there been a consensus on the issue, it could have been settled simply by replacing the term regulatory act with 'non-legislative act', a term used elsewhere in the Treaty of Lisbon.[123]

Advocate General Kokott dealt in some detail with an argument of the applicants that the approach of the General Court deprived them of their right to an effective remedy, which the Court has recognized as a general principle of law and which is now enshrined in Article 47 of the Charter of Fundamental Rights. Although the Charter has Treaty status,[124] the Advocate General maintained that

---

[116] See Anthony Arnull, 'Europe's Nemesis? The Long Road to the Lisbon Treaty' in Henning Koch, Karsten Hagel-Sørensen, Ulrich Haltern and Joseph Weiler (eds), *Europe: The New Legal Realism. Essays in Honour of Hjalte Rasmussen* (2010) 11.

[117] See Paul Craig, 'The Treaty of Lisbon: Process, Architecture and Substance' (2008) 33 *European Law Review* 137, 139; Gráinne de Búrca, 'Reflections on the Path from the Constitutional Treaty to the Lisbon Treaty' (*Jean Monnet Working Paper* No 03/08, http://centers.law.nyu.edu/jeanmonnet/papers/08/080301.html) 7, 30–1.

[118] House of Commons European Scrutiny Committee, 'European Union Intergovernmental Conference', 35th Report of Session 2006-07, HC1014 (9 October 2007).

[119] House of Commons European Scrutiny Committee (n 118), para 11.

[120] House of Commons European Scrutiny Committee (n 118), para 10.

[121] House of Commons European Scrutiny Committee (n 118), para 71.

[122] *Inuit* (n 68), nn 25 and 26 of the Opinion.

[123] See Arts 16(8) TEU and 290(1) and 297(2) TFEU; A.G. Wathelet in *Stichting Woonpunt* (n 91) para 57; Peers and Costa (n 104) 91–92.

[124] See Art 6(1) TEU.

'it has not changed the substance of the fundamental right to an effective remedy recognized at EU level'.[125] This, she said, was clear from the explanations relating to the Charter, to which the Court is required by Article 6(1) TEU to have regard in interpreting it. The Advocate General pointed out that, according to that provision, the Charter was not to extend the competences of the Union as defined in the Treaties. It followed that the Charter

cannot be invoked in support of categorising legislative acts as regulatory acts . . . or relaxing the requirements governing whether legislative acts are of direct and individual concern to individuals . . . Such an interpretation would amount to an extension of the competences of the Union . . . or more precisely an extension of the judicial competences of the Court of Justice of the European Union . . .[126]

The same conclusion followed, she maintained, from Article 51(2) of the Charter.

The explanation of Article 47 of the Charter of Fundamental Rights is inconclusive. It states that Article 47 is not intended 'to change the system of judicial review laid down by the Treaties, and particularly the rules relating to admissibility for direct actions before the Court of Justice of the European Union'. However, it goes on to acknowledge that the Union's system of judicial review has been changed 'as to certain respects', referring specifically to the fourth paragraph of Article 263. It does not offer any guidance on the meaning of the term 'regulatory act' or seek to constrain the Court's freedom to interpret that term as it thinks fit. The explanations do not in any event purport to be legally binding. Article 47 of the Charter is based on Articles 6 and 13 ECHR, which only lay down a minimum standard.[127] The Advocate General accepted this, but insisted that 'due regard must be had to the intention of the authors of the Treaty . . .'[128] Even if that were true, their intention is obscure.[129]

Advocate General Kokott maintained that it would require a Treaty amendment to modify fundamentally the requirements of direct and individual concern in relation to legislative acts,[130] thereby seeming to suggest that the Court had lost the freedom it previously enjoyed to interpret and reinterpret the Treaty dynamically in accordance with changing circumstances. It would be an unwelcome new departure if an amendment to part of a Treaty provision were to deprive the Court of ultimate responsibility for deciding on its meaning or that of related provisions

---

[125] *Inuit* (n 68), Opinion, para 109. Here she is presumably referring to the direct actions available before the Union Courts, for the Charter has undoubtedly affected the duty of national courts to ensure effective judicial protection of the rights enjoyed by litigants under Union law. See below.

[126] *Inuit* (n 68), Opinion, para 112.

[127] See Art 52(3) of the Charter. Cf Art 53 ECHR; *Bosphorus Hava Yolları Turizm ve Ticaret Anonim Şirketi v Ireland* (n 85).

[128] *Inuit* (n 68), Opinion, para 111.

[129] See further, George Letsas, 'Strasbourg's Interpretive Ethic: Lessons for the International Lawyer' (2010) 21 *European Journal of International Law* 509, 536–538.

[130] *Inuit* (n 68), Opinion, para 114.

or ossify the case law as it stood immediately before the amendment was made. This would be inconsistent with the Court's duty to ensure that the law is observed in the interpretation and application of the Treaties, a duty retained and given increased prominence by the Treaty of Lisbon.[131]

(c) The Judgment of the Court of Justice

Disappointingly, but perhaps unsurprisingly, the Court followed the Opinion of its Advocate General and dismissed the appeal. Observing that the 'origins of a provision of European Union law may . . . provide information relevant to its interpretation',[132] the Court said that the conclusion of the General Court on the meaning of the term 'regulatory act' was supported by the *travaux préparatoires* relating to Article III-365(4) of the Constitutional Treaty.[133] There was no evidence that the authors of the Treaty of Lisbon had intended to alter the conditions of admissibility previously laid down in the fourth paragraph of Article 230 EC. The Court therefore endorsed the General Court's finding on individual concern[134] (though it saw no need to consider its finding on direct concern[135]). Although the corresponding conditions in Article 263 TFEU had to 'be interpreted in the light of the fundamental right to effective judicial protection' embodied in Article 47 of the Charter of Fundamental Rights, 'such an interpretation could not have the effect of setting aside the conditions expressly laid down in that Treaty . . .'.[136] Article 47 was not intended to alter the Treaty system of judicial review, particularly the rules on the admissibility of direct actions. This was apparent from the explanation of Article 47, which the Court was required to take into consideration. Article 47 certainly did not require individuals to be given 'an unconditional entitlement' to seek the annulment of legislative acts in the Union Courts.[137] Responsibility for ensuring observance of the law in the interpretation and application of the Treaties lay with both the Union Courts and the national courts.[138] It was 'therefore for the Member States to establish a system of legal remedies and procedures which ensure respect for the fundamental right to effective judicial protection . . .'.[139] That obligation was reaffirmed by the second paragraph of Article 19(1) TEU. It might in exceptional

---

[131] See Art 19(1) TEU.

[132] *Inuit* (n 68), judgment, para 50. See Case C-370/12 *Pringle*, judgment of 27 November 2012, para 135, referring to 'the preparatory work relating to the Treaty of Maastricht . . .'.

[133] The Parliament, the Council and the Commission pointed out before the Court that the number of acts embraced by the term as interpreted by the General Court was very large: see *Inuit* (n 68), para 41 of the judgment.

[134] Cf *Stichting Woonpunt* (n 91) paras 62–63.   [135] *Inuit* (n 68) judgment, para 74.

[136] *Inuit* (n 68) judgment, para 98. See *UPA* (n 1) para 41; *Jégo-Quéré* (n 85) para 31.

[137] *Inuit* (n 68) judgment, para 105. The appellants do not seem to have claimed any such entitlement.

[138] See *Inuit* (n 68), Opinion 1/09 (n 15) paras 66 and 69.

[139] *Inuit* (n 68), judgment, para 100.

cases require new national remedies to be created,[140] though it was not necessary for individuals to be given a right to bring actions in the national forum against legislative acts of the Union 'as their primary subject matter'.[141]

This was a remarkable judgment for a court not generally noted for its restraint. Absent was any trace of the spirit that animated *Van Gend en Loos*[142] and its progeny. The Court could have taken as its starting point the observation of the General Court in *Microban*[143] that the final clause of Article 263 'pursues an objective of opening up the conditions for bringing direct actions . . .'. Instead it resorted to a narrow conservatism jerry-built on the presumed intentions of the authors of the Treaty of Lisbon, the explanations accompanying the Charter and the *travaux préparatoires* of the Convention on the Future of Europe. Whether this approach will be applied in other areas of Union law remains to be seen.[144] In the present context, it led the Court to a conclusion which it accepted might sometimes prove inadequate to guarantee respect for the fundamental right to effective judicial protection, a general principle of law having constitutional status.[145] The result was to leave the Union dependent on the national courts to ensure full respect for that principle, one which seems to impose greater burdens on them than it does on the Union Courts. It is potentially more intrusive than the older principles of national procedural autonomy, effectiveness and equivalence, which it shows signs of superseding.[146]

VI. The Judicial Reconstruction of the Union's System of Remedies

The drawbacks of a system of judicial review that relies so heavily on the national courts emerge clearly if the action for annulment is compared directly with the

---

[140] See *Unibet* (n 88) paras 41 and 64. Cf. Case 158/80 *Rewe v Hauptzollamt Kiel* [1981] ECR 1805, para 44.

[141] *Inuit* (n 68), judgment, para 106.

[142] Case 26/62 [1963] ECR 1.   [143] *Microban* (n 97) para 32.

[144] Cf. Francis Jacobs, 'The Lisbon Treaty and the Court of Justice' in Andrea Biondi, Piet Eeckhout, and Stefanie Ripley, *EU Law After Lisbon* (2012) 197, 201.

[145] See Case C-101/08 *Audiolux and others* [2009] ECR I-9823, para 63; Case C-174/08 *NCC Construction Danmark* [2009] ECR I-10567, para 45.

[146] See eg Joined Cases C-317/08, C-318/08, C-319/08 and C-320/08 *Alassini and others* [2010] ECR I-2213; Case C-279/09 *DEB* [2010] ECR I-13849; Case C-199/11 *European Community v Otis and others* [2013] 4 CMLR 4; A.G. Jääskinen in Case C-536/11 *Bundeswettbewerbsbehörde v Donau Chemie AG and others* [2013] 5 CMLR 19, para 47 of the Opinion; Anthony Arnull, 'Remedies Before National

preliminary rulings procedure.[147] The action for annulment involves adversarial proceedings against the author of the contested measure before a court (initially the General Court in the case of a private applicant) with jurisdiction to rule on its validity. It must be brought within a reasonable time of the adoption of the measure concerned and will be based on a full exchange of pleadings.[148] If interim measures are required, they will in principle apply across the Union as a whole. The preliminary rulings procedure, on the other hand, is 'not a remedy available to individual applicants as a matter of right'.[149] The applicant must first bring proceedings in a national court, which may have little or no experience of dealing with claims based on Union law. That court will not itself have jurisdiction to declare the contested act invalid. Proceedings might not commence until a considerable period has elapsed since the act was adopted. The author of the act is unlikely to be a party. The applicant must base his or her claim on a national cause of action and persuade the national court that a ruling on the validity of the contested act is necessary to enable it to give judgment.[150] There may be disputes over the extent to which procedural rules can be interpreted and applied in accordance with the principle of effective judicial protection. If the national court takes the view that the act is valid, the applicant must appeal, perhaps until he or she reaches a top court that is in principle obliged to refer (though that obligation is in practice virtually unenforceable).[151] If a reference is made, the national court's questions may not capture accurately the nature and scope of the challenge and there will not be a full exchange of pleadings before the Court of Justice.[152] Should interim measures be required, they will be granted by the national court and will apply only within its own territorial jurisdiction. Interim protection elsewhere will have to be sought from the courts of the state or states concerned. The attitude of national courts to many of these issues may vary from state to state.[153]

Courts' in Takis Tridimas and Robert Schütze (eds), *Oxford Principles of European Union Law* (Volume 1) (forthcoming).

[147] See Arnull (n 54) 129–131.

[148] Court of Justice, Rules of Procedure, Title IV, Chapter 2; General Court, Rules of Procedure, Title 2, Chapter 1.

[149] A.G. Jacobs in *UPA* (n 1) para 42.

[150] The duty of national courts to refer when it considers a challenge to a Union act to be well founded was reemphasized in *Inuit* (n 68) para 96 of the judgment.

[151] Franz Mayer, 'Multilevel Constitutional Jurisdiction' in Armin von Bogdandy and Jürgen Bast (eds), *Principles of European Constitutional Law* (2nd edn, 2010) 399, 402–403. In theory breaches of the obligation to refer may be the subject of actions for damages and infringement proceedings: see Case C-224/01 *Köbler* [2003] ECR I-10239; Case C-173/03 *Traghetti del Mediterraneo* [2006] ECR I-5177; Case C-129/00 *Commission v Italy* [2003] ECR I-14637; Maciej Taborowski, 'Infringement Proceedings and Non-Compliant National Courts' (2012) 49 *Common Market Law Review* 1881.

[152] Statute of the Court of Justice of the European Union, Art 23. The General Court is not involved as it does not currently have jurisdiction to give preliminary rulings.

[153] Cf Morten Broberg and Niels Fenger, 'Variations in Member States' Preliminary References to the Court of Justice—Are Structural Factors (Part of) the Explanation?' (2013) 19 *European Law Journal* 488.

Of course this is not a zero sum game and both avenues should be available to applicants, as the authors of the Treaty originally intended. But it is clear that, as a mechanism for protecting both public and private interests, the action for annulment is more direct and more effective than proceedings in the national courts,[154] offering review by a specialized administrative court in the form of the General Court with the possibility of an appeal. This level of expert scrutiny is simply not available in reference proceedings. Why, then, did the Court seek to decentralize responsibility for judicial review in a way that tends to undermine rather than reinforce effective judicial protection?[155] Why did it impose duties on national courts, of respect for the principle of effective judicial protection and consistent interpretation, which it was not prepared to assume itself? The Court is not an institution plagued with doubts about its own legitimacy and has in the past been willing to interpret previous versions of Article 263 *contra legem* in the interests of the rule of law. It is not therefore uncomfortable with the notion of judicial review per se and there is no counter-majoritarian difficulty[156] in the Union because of its persistent democracy deficit. Indeed, there is a danger that the voices of minorities (even substantial ones) may be drowned out by the very size of the Union.

The origin of the problem is *Plaumann*, a jurisprudential changeling whose malefic character was only thinly disguised. That case was decided less than six months after *Van Gend en Loos*, where the Court had made much of the rights conferred on individuals as part of their legal heritage by the new legal order of international law constituted by the Community. In *Plaumann* itself, the Court declared that 'provisions of the Treaty regarding the right of interested parties to bring an action must not be interpreted restrictively'.[157] However, in the early 1960s the main problem was holding the Member States to their Treaty commitments. The risk of backsliding was underlined by the Fouchet Plan of 1961–62[158] and by the Luxembourg Compromise of 1966,[159] which was to have such a baleful effect on the decision-making process of the Community. We may regret that the Court did not set an example by ensuring that individuals could easily hold the institutions to account if they acted unlawfully. However, it might have seemed prudent, especially to judges unaccustomed to strong judicial review, to offer the still fragile Community some protection from private litigants. By the time the effect of the Luxembourg Compromise began to wane in the 1980s, the pattern had been set. The developments in the case law which occurred in the early to mid 1990s may perhaps be explained by optimism about the effect the establishment of the General Court would have on the Court's case load. That optimism faded

---

[154] See A.G. Wathelet in *Stichting Woonpunt* (n 91) para 78; van Gerven (n 43) 115.
[155] See Arnull (n 54) 92–94.   [156] On this see text at n 18.   [157] *Plaumann* (n 70) 107.
[158] Anthony Teasdale and Timothy Bainbridge, *The Penguin Companion to European Union* (4th ed, 2012) 462–469.
[159] Teasdale and Bainbridge (n 158) 565–572.

as it became clear that managing the case load of both Union Courts was likely to be a permanent preoccupation. Routeing challenges to the validity of Union acts through the national courts in the knowledge that some would be filtered out before they reached the Union Courts might from that perspective have seemed a useful technique of case management.

But important though it undoubtedly is, the Court should not allow case management to take precedence over the rule of law in the Union and the need to bolster the Union's legitimacy.[160] Instead it should exploit the vigilance of Union citizens[161] in order to help police the boundaries of the ever-wider fields in which the Member States have limited their sovereign rights.[162] This will mean restoring the action for annulment to its rightful place at the heart of the Union's system of remedies and enlarging access to private applicants through interpreting and reinterpreting key terms, such as individual concern and regulatory act. The review conducted by the Court should be both substantive and procedural, paying particular attention to structural constitutional norms, such as conferral, subsidiarity and proportionality.[163] If it is thought necessary to distinguish between different acts according to the extent to which they may be considered democratically legitimated, this should be done coherently, not through the rules on standing, but through the intensity of the review of their legality conducted by the Union Courts.[164]

Bibliography

Albertina Albors-Llorens, 'Remedies Against the EU Institutions After Lisbon: An Era of Opportunity?' (2012) 71 *Cambridge Law Journal* 507

Anthony Arnull, 'Europe's Nemesis? The Long Road to the Lisbon Treaty' in Henning Koch, Karsten Hagel-Sørensen, Ulrich Haltern and Joseph Weiler (eds), *Europe: The New Legal Realism. Essays in Honour of Hjalte Rasmussen* (2010) 11

Paul Craig, 'Integration, Democracy, and Legitimacy' in Paul Craig and Gráinne de Búrca, *The Evolution of EU Law* (2nd ed, 2011) 13

Michael Dougan, 'The Treaty of Lisbon 2007: Winning Minds, Not Hearts' (2008) 45 *Common Market Law Review* 617

---

[160] See AG Jacobs in *UPA* (n 1) para 77. Cf Christoph Werkmeister, Stephan Potters and Johannes Traut, 'Regulatory Acts within Article 263(4) TFEU—A Dissonant Extension of Locus Standi for Private Applicants' (2010-11) 13 *Cambridge Yearbook of European Legal Studies* 311, 332.

[161] Cf *Van Gend en Loos* (n 142) 13.

[162] Cf Opinion 1/09 'Creation of a Unified Patent Litigation System' (n 15) para 65.

[163] Art 5 TEU.

[164] Albertina Albors-Llorens, 'Edging Towards Closer Scrutiny? The Court of Justice and its Review of the Compatibility of General Measures with the Protection of Economic Rights and Freedoms' in Anthony Arnull, Catherine Barnard, Michael Dougan and Eleanor Spaventa (eds), *A Constitutional Order of States? Essays in EU Law in Honour of Alan Dashwood* (2011) 245; Craig (n 2) Ch 15; Kyritsis (n 27) 316–318; Türk (n 95). Cf *European Commission and others v Yassin Abdullah Kadi* (n 1).

Ronald Dworkin, *Freedom's Law: The Moral Reading of the American Constitution* (1996)

John Hart Ely, *Democracy and Distrust: A Theory of Judicial Review* (1980)

Richard Fallon, 'The Core of an Uneasy Case for Judicial Review' (2007–08) 121 *Harvard Law Review* 1693

Alon Harel and Adam Shinar, 'Between Judicial and Legislative Supremacy: A Cautious Defense of Constrained Judicial Review' (2011) *International Journal of Constitutional Law* 950

Francis Jacobs, *The Sovereignty of Law: The European Way* (2007).

Aileen Kavanagh, 'Participation and Judicial Review: A Reply to Jeremy Waldron' (2003) 22 *Law and Philosophy* 451

Dimitrios Kyritsis, 'Constitutional Review in Representative Democracy' (2012) 32 *Oxford Journal of Legal Studies* 297

Koen Lenaerts, 'The Principle of Democracy in the Case Law of the European Court of Justice' (2013) 62 *International and Comparative Law Quarterly* 271

George Letsas, 'Strasbourg's Interpretive Ethic: Lessons for the International Lawyer' (2010) 21 *European Journal of International Law* 509

Andrew Moravcsik, 'In Defence of the "Democratic Deficit": Reassessing Legitimacy in the European Union' (2002) 40 *Journal of Common Market Studies* 603

Steve Peers and Marios Costa, 'Judicial Review of EU Acts after the Treaty of Lisbon' (2012) *European Constitutional Law Review* 82

Eric Stein and G. Joseph Vining, 'Citizen Access to Judicial Review of Administrative Action in a Transnational and Federal Context' (1976) 70 *American Journal of International Law* 219

Alexander Türk, 'Oversight of Administrative Rulemaking: Judicial Review' (2013) 19 *European Law Journal* 126

Walter van Gerven, *The European Union: A Polity of States and Peoples* (2005).

Jeremy Waldron, 'The Core of the Case Against Judicial Review' (2005–06) 115 *Yale Law Journal* 1346

Joseph Weiler, 'Deciphering the Political and Legal DNA of European Integration: An Exploratory Essay' in Julie Dickson and Pavlos Eleftheriadis (eds), *Philosophical Foundations of European Union Law* (2012) 137

CHAPTER 16

THE ECJ AND THE NATIONAL COURTS

DIALOGUE, COOPERATION, AND INSTABILITY

TAKIS TRIDIMAS

I. THE EU AND ITS JUDICIAL UNIVERSE

ALTHOUGH the development of EU law is the result of the interaction of many political and institutional actors, no other relationship is perhaps as important as that between the ECJ and the national courts.[1] Their interaction is dialectical,

---

[1] For previous contributions, see among others, A. Arnull, 'Judicial Dialogue in the European Union' in J. Dickson and P. Eleftheriadis (eds), *The Philosophical Foundations of European Union Law* (2012) 109; E. Cloots, 'Germs of Pluralist Judicial Adjudication' (2010) 47 *Common Market Law Review* 645; P. Craig, 'The ECJ, the National Courts and the Supremacy of Community Law' http://www.ecln.net/elements/conferences/bookrome/craig.pdf; M. Kumm, 'The Jurisprudence of Constitutional Conflict' (2004) 11 *European Law Journal* 262; N. Walker, 'The Idea of Constitutional Pluralism' (2002) 65 *Modern Law Review* 317; G. de Búrca and J.H.H. Weiler (eds), *The European Court of Justice* (2001); A.-M. Slaughter, A. Stone Sweet and J.H.H. Weiler (eds), *The European Courts and National Courts, Doctrine and Jurisprudence* (1998); T. Tridimas, 'Knocking on Heaven's Door: Fragmentation, Efficiency and Defiance in the Preliminary Reference Procedure' (2003) 40 *Common Market Law Review* 9.

full of circumspection and deference, albeit occasionally tense, and based on an incomplete and somewhat unstable political bargain. This chapter seeks to explore some recent trends in this intra-judicial dialogue. It looks at the attributes of the interaction between the ECJ and the national courts, the centralized constitutional model favoured by the ECJ case law, and the vexed issue of *Kompetenz-Kompetenz*. Finally, it explores some recent judgments which suggest uneasiness and even open defiance on the part of some the national supreme jurisdictions.

The EU legal order is rights-based and owes as much to the adjudication process as to political negotiations. This is partly by treaty design but mostly self-generated by the judiciary. The EU legal system is based on a decentralized system of justice where national courts are the primary venue for the assertion of EU rights. The preliminary reference procedure establishes paths of dependency that elevate the national courts to key interlocutors. But treaty design did not predetermine the constitutional character of the interaction or the way it would develop. Through the articulation of the principles of primacy and direct effect, the ECJ began to create 'constitutional law by the common law method',[2] a process that national courts embraced and encouraged, albeit with varying degrees of enthusiasm. National courts are the most important interlocutors for two reasons. Their cooperation is essential for the initiation of the preliminary reference dialogue, the enforcement of the ECJ's rulings, and more generally the application of EU law in national proceedings. In addition, crucially, they provide the most effective oversight over the ECJ's activist tendencies. If the ECJ were to overstep its powers, Member States could envisage a number of measures but all of them would be subject to important limitations. It would be difficult to reach agreement, they would take a long time to bear fruit, and their effect would be indirect and uncertain. By contrast, if national courts were to withdraw their cooperation, that would have a more immediate and direct impact on the ECJ. Viewed in that perspective, a successful relationship between the ECJ and the national courts is the key that unlocks the integration door. The importance of the dialogue has been emphasized both judicially and extra-judicially by members of the ECJ and the national courts.[3] Interaction occurs both directly and indirectly. Direct dialogue takes place through the preliminary reference procedure. Indirect dialogue takes

---

[2] See R. Posner, *Law and Legal Theory in the UK and the USA* (1996) 14.

[3] See eg Opinion 1/09 [2011] ECR I-1137; Case 283/81 *CILFIT* [1982] ECR 3415; in *HS2* Lord Neuberger and Lord Mance viewed the 'all important dialogue' as having a 'vital role of interpreting and consolidating the role of European law' (see *R (on the application of HS2 Action Alliance Limited) v Secretary of State for Transport* [2014] UKSC 3, para 173); Judge Rosas states that the EU and national courts 'work together, being complementary parts in a shared legal sphere': see A. Rosas, 'The National Judge as EU Judge: Opinion 1/09' in P. Cardonnel, A. Rosas, and N. Wahl (eds), *Constitutionalising the EU Judicial System: Essays in Honour of Pernilla Lindh* (2012) 105. This is echoed by Judge Sajan in M. Safjan and D. Düsterhaus, 'A Union of Effective Judicial Protection: Addressing a Multi-level Challenge through the Lens of Article 47 of the EU Charter' (2014) 33 *Yearbook of European Law* doi: 10.1093/yel/yeu015.

place, more generally, through the process of adjudication. A national court may pronounce on the relationship between EU law and national law in national proceedings or apply or refuse to apply EU law without making a reference. Similarly, the ECJ establishes important principles concerning competence, institutional powers, and rights in direct proceedings where there is no direct interlocution with national judicial actors. This dispersed body of case law establishes principles, draws boundaries, and determines the dialectical relationship between national and EU law through which EU law is shaped.

How has the interaction between the ECJ and the national courts changed over the years? One could identify the following trends. First, in terms of subject matter, there has been a shift of emphasis from issues of economic integration to themes of governance and constitutionalism. The most remarkable development in the case law over the last ten years has perhaps been the way the ECJ has broadened and deepened its jurisdiction on fundamental rights. Second, the dialogue is conducted in the shadows of a centralized constitutional model. The ECJ is willing to embrace national constitutional traditions but not at the expense of the coherence of the EU legal order. Third, the expansion of EU competence beyond negative integration to economic and social regulation and justice and home affairs has coincided with greater engagement by the national supreme courts.[4] This in turn has given rise to new developments. National courts appear to have become more assertive and the debate is less about fundamental rights and more about democracy and national constitutional identity. Finally, the ECJ's reasoning has become more expansive although, by common law standards, its use of precedent is somewhat less articulate.

II. Attributes of the Relationship

The dialogic interaction has many distinct features. The intention here is not to make an exhaustive analysis but highlight selected aspects.[5] The interaction is democratic, it has in-built flexibility, and combines both cooperative and hierarchical

---

[4] References have been made in recent years, among others by the French Conseil d'Etat (Joined Cases C-188 and C189/10 *Melki and Abdeli* [2010] ECR I-5667), the French Constitutional Court (Case C-168/13 PPU *Jeremy F v Premier ministre*), the Czech Supreme Administrative Court (see *Landtová case* discussed below) the UK Supreme Court (*HS2* n 3), the Spanish Constitutional Court (*Melloni*, discussed below), and now the German Federal Constitutional Court in the *OMT* case, discussed below.

[5] For a discussion, see among others, the contributions referred to in n 1 and M. Broberg and N. Fenger, *Preliminary References to the European Court of Justice* (2nd ed, 2010).

elements. It is dialogue conducted in the context of a centralized constitutional model, which, however, is malleable and in some respects inherently unstable, being based on an incomplete political bargain. It takes place in a background contoured by Strasbourg case law, which operates as a further force of convergence.

1. Democracy

The preliminary reference procedure is democratic in that direct dialogue with the ECJ is open to all courts whatever their status in the national judicial hierarchy. Such a wide constituency enhances judicial independence and serves the rule of law. The potential omnipresence of EU law in the national adjudication process enables it to permeate national law and facilitates the litigation before the ECJ of novel or sensitive points which might not have reached it if higher courts had the monopoly of reference.[6] Indeed, the power of a lower national court to make a reference serves as the most effective enforcement mechanism of the obligation of a last instance court to do so. Even if a court covered by Article 267(3) refuses to uphold EU law, a lower national court may in a future case refer the same point, thus giving to the ECJ the opportunity to correct the mistake.[7] The broad constituency of interlocutors results in the dispersal of judicial power and may lead to tense intra-judicial competition at the national level.[8] The democratic character of the procedure is enhanced by the lax admissibility requirements. The ECJ remains an open and welcoming court operating on a strong presumption that it is for the referring court to decide whether to make a reference.[9]

2. Hierarchy and Cooperation

The relationship between the ECJ and the national courts has both cooperative and hierarchical elements. With some exceptions, the model has been successful in that it has avoided rebellion by national courts whilst accommodating the symbiosis of different judicial outlooks on constitutional supremacy.[10] The relationship

---

[6] See eg 6/64 *Costa v ENEL* [1964] ECR 585; C-60/00 *Carpenter v Secretary of State for the Home Department* [2002] ECR I-6279.

[7] See eg Case C-285/98, *Kreil* [2000] ECR I-69; C-224/01*Köbler v Austria* [2003] I-10239.

[8] See eg the *Landtová case* discussed below.

[9] See eg Case C-466/04 *Acereda Herrera* [2006] ECR I-5341, para 47; Case C-379/98 *PreussenElektra* [2001] ECR I-2099, para 38. The ECJ may refuse to give an answer only if it considers that the question referred in hypothetical or if the referring court has failed to define adequately the factual and legislative context of the dispute or where the issues of EU law on which the referring court seeks guidance bear no relation to the actual nature of the case or to the subject matter of the main action. See eg Case C-83/91 *Meilicke* [1992] ECR I-4871; Case C-343/90 *Lourenço Dias* [1992] ECR I-4673; Joined Cases 320-322/90 *Telemarsicabruzzo SpA v Circostel* [1993] ECR I-393.

[10] See below.

is cooperative in that it is based on a carefully crafted division of competences that requires the close cooperation of the two interlocutors and promotes a model of dual judicial sovereignty. Thus, it is the ECJ which, subject to the *CILFIT*[11] doctrine, has the final say on interpretation of EU law. By contrast, the ECJ does not have jurisdiction to decide on questions of national law or the application of EU law to specific facts. Such issues fall within the exclusive jurisdiction of the national court,[12] although in some cases the distinction between interpretation and application of law becomes difficult to draw. The national courts also act as gatekeepers since it is for them to decide whether to make a reference and the questions to be referred, as well as to apply the judgment of the ECJ on the facts of the dispute. Time and again the ECJ has emphasized that the dialogue is conducted in 'a spirit of cooperation' based on the allocation of separate tasks to the respective courts.[13]

There is, however, no doubt that the relationship also incorporates elements of hierarchy and compulsion. These are inherent in a governance model premised on supremacy. Thus, failure of a national court to abide by EU law may give rise to an enforcement action by the Commission against the Member State concerned.[14] Notably, under *Köbler*,[15] the failure of the national judiciary to comply with EU law may give rise to a right to reparation. *Köbler* highlights the dual perception of national courts. On the one hand, the ECJ views them as an integral part of the judicial branch, a source of power outside the national governments whose oversight they help to ensure. On the other hand, they remain part of the state imperium and thus institutionally subordinate in relation to EU law. In the EU's judicial universe, cooperation and hierarchy coexist and many aspects of the interaction between the ECJ and the national courts incorporate elements of both. National courts must employ a number of techniques to ensure primacy including the doctrine of direct effect, the doctrine of consistent interpretation, and the principle of effectiveness.[16] In applying those doctrines, however, they acquire a formative influence in the development of EU law. The interaction is as constraining as it is empowering, the national court acquiring the role of EU law apostles.

---

[11] Case 283/81 *CILFIT v Ministry of Health* [1982] ECR 3415.

[12] According to established case law, the Court does not have jurisdiction to: (1) rule upon the compatibility of a national measure with European Union law; (2) give a ruling on the facts in an individual case; or (3) apply the European Union law rules which it has interpreted to national measures or situations. Those issues are matters for the exclusive jurisdiction of the national court (see eg Case C-140/09 *Traghetti del Mediterraneo SpA v Presidenza del Consiglio dei Ministri (Traghetti II)*, judgment of 10 June 2010, para 22; Case C-118/08 *Transportes Urbanos y Servicios Generales* [2010] ECR I-635, para 23; Case C-451/03 *Servizi Ausiliari Dottori Commercialisti* [2006] ECR I-2941, para 69.

[13] See eg Case C-212/04 *Adeneler* [2006] ECR I-6057, para 42; Case C- 571/10 *Kamberaj v IPES*, judgment of 24 April 2012, para 41.

[14] Case C-154/08 *Commission v Spain*, judgment of 12 November 2009.

[15] Case C-224/01 *Köbler v Austria* [2003] ECR I-10239.

[16] See Monica Claes, 'Primacy and the National Reaction', this volume; Dorota Leczykiewicz, 'Direct Effect, Effective Judicial Protection and State Liability', this volume.

Although there is an inherent tension between cooperation and hierarchy, it is best to view the relationship between the ECJ and the national courts under the prism of cooperative supranationalism. They fulfil distinct but complementary functions based on 'interaction, dialogue and compromise'.[17] There is a strong awareness that they are both bound by 'a common judicial enterprise'[18] to the success of which they are both committed. As stated above, without the national courts, the ECJ could not have achieved the constitutionalization of the Treaties. The EU legal system has distinct, quasi-federal elements which have been built primarily by case law. Those were by no means predetermined[19] and they could not have been achieved without the encouragement, tolerance, or acquiescence of national courts.

3. Dialectics, Discretion, and the Flow of Judicial Power

In conducting the dialogue, the ECJ grants itself broad discretion. It has leeway with regard to the provisions of EU law on which it may offer guidance. Thus, it may recast the questions referred or examine issues which have not specifically been asked by the national court.[20] It may even give a ruling on the interpretation of an EU measure other than that to which the order of reference refers if, in the light of the factual and legal background, it considers it helpful for the national court in order to decide the case.[21] Such flexibility is justified by the nature of the preliminary reference procedure which is intended to facilitate a judicial dialogue rather than reassert the parties as masters of the litigation.

Furthermore, the ECJ also enjoys significant discretion as regards the specificity of its ruling.[22] It may be concrete and prescriptive or leave margin for input by the referring court. This aspect of its jurisdiction operates as a constitutional valve: it regulates the flow of judicial direction and determines whether review of national choices is carried out solely by the ECJ or shared with the national judiciaries. One may distinguish three categories of case depending on the specificity of the ruling. The ECJ may give an answer so specific that it leaves the referring court no margin for manoeuvre and provides it with a ready-made solution to the dispute (*outcome*

---

[17] Arnull (n 1) 119.

[18] A.-M. Slaughter, 'A Global Community of Courts' (2003) 44 *Harvard International Law Journal* 191, 193.

[19] Arnull (n 1) 119.   [20] See eg Case C-67/89 *Berkenheide* [1990] ECR I- 2615, para 16.

[21] See eg Case C-315/92 *Verband Sozialer Wettbewerb v Clinique Laboratories and Estée Lauder* [1994] ECR I-317. For an interesting example of a difference in view between the Court and the Advocate General as to the provisions of EC law applicable in the case, see Case 367/89 *Richardt* [1991] ECR I-4621.

[22] See T. Tridimas, 'Constitutional Review of Member State action: The virtues and vices of an incomplete jurisdiction' (2011) 9 *International Journal of Constitutional Law* 737.

cases); it may, alternatively, provide the referring court with guidelines as to how to resolve the dispute (*guidance cases*); finally, it may answer the question in such general terms that, in effect, it defers to the national judiciary on the point in issue (*deference cases*).[23] Guidance and deference may be seen as illustrations of judicial subsidiarity: the ECJ appoints national courts as its agents and asks them to fulfil their part of the bargain. The outcome approach may be seen as a sign of leadership although leadership and activism may be pursued also through deference.[24] The choice of each approach is not random but depends on a series of factors not overtly articulated in the judgments of the ECJ.[25]

One way by which the ECJ promotes dialogue is through the use of abstract and imprecise tests to determine the compatibility of national action with EU law. Such tests offer opportunities to citizens and invite responses by lawyers. Because of their indeterminate nature, they open the way to the incremental development of the law and maximize the gatekeeping function of the national courts. The ECJ draws the contours of a future direction often with deliberate imprecision and leaves the national courts the task of initiating further dialogue through the preliminary reference procedure. The use of such tests has an experimental value and can be seen as invitations to the national governments to renegotiate authority. A common pattern of their development is that they are introduced in cases with strong facts, involve new areas of the law where the constraints of existing authority are relatively weak, and initiate a judicial debate with no predetermined ideas as to their outer limits or their destination. A prime example of such a test is the *Zambrano* formula.[26] In that case, reiterating that citizenship of the Union is intended to be the fundamental status of nationals of the Member States, the ECJ held that Article 20 TFEU precludes national measures which have the effect of depriving citizens of the Union of the genuine enjoyment of the substance of their rights as Union citizens.[27] Although the Court referred to *Rottman*[28] as authority for that finding, the truth is that it introduced a new and broader principle. The judgment expands the substantive content of citizenship and brings within the ambit of EU law situations which do not involve inter-state movement. Its importance lies in that it

---

[23] The Court might use different approaches in response to different questions in the same case; see eg Case C-341/08 *Petersen*, judgment of 12 January 2010.

[24] Tridimas, above n 22, 740.   [25] Op. cit., 749ff.

[26] Case C-34/09 *Zambrano* v *Office national de l'emploi* [2011] ECR I-1177. For other such tests, see eg the test governing the scope of application of Article 34 TFEU (Joined cases C-267/91 and C-268/91 *Keck* [1993] ECR I-6097 and its progeny); the conditions governing state liability (commencing with Joined Cases C-6/90 and C-9/90 *Francovich and others* [1991] ECR I-5357 and Joined Cases C-46 and 48/93 *Brasserie du Pêcheur v Germany and the Queen v Secretary of State for Transport ex p Factortame* [1996] ECR I-1029); and the test governing the scope of application of EU fundamental rights and the Charter (Case C-260/89 *ERT* [1991] ECR I-2925; Case C-617/10 *Åklagaren v Hans Åkerberg Fransson*, judgment of 26 February 2013).

[27] *Zambrano* (n 26) para 42.

[28] Case C-135/08 *Rottmann v Freistaat Bayern* [2010] ECR I-1449.

marked a departure, albeit hesitant and qualified, from the internal market model of European integration to a citizenship paradigm. *Zambrano* sent shockwaves to the home offices of the Member States but, in subsequent cases, the ECJ signalled a narrow understanding of the genuine enjoyment test, stating that it applies only where a Union citizen would be forced to leave the EU territory as a whole, detaching it from economic welfare,[29] and subordinating EU citizenship rights to state citizenship.[30] In many cases, indeterminate tests go through corrective readjustments in the light of subsequent references before reaching a stage of relative stability. National courts have important input in deciding whether to make a reference, in applying the guidance offered by the ECJ and in highlighting possible problems arising from the ECJ's case law.

The decision to refer should be understood as the result of a cost-benefit analysis where the referring court considers that its notion of justice is best served by making a reference.[31] Beyond that, one could distinguish here several patterns of judicial behaviour. A national court may relish the conversation, viewing it as a form of empowerment.[32] It may disagree with the ECJ's previous case law but, in a spirit of cooperation, explain why it is problematic and invite the ECJ to reconsider. There are many examples of such protest through cooperation.[33] A national court may sometimes express open defiance.[34] In some cases, the reference may be the result of disagreement among the members of the national court as to the outcome.[35] In such cases, it would perhaps be best for the ECJ to engage at length with both the majority's and the minority's arguments providing detailed reasoning in its judgment.

An interesting development in recent years is that the growth of EU legislation in diverse areas accompanied by the proliferation of constitutional rights protected

---

[29] Case C-434/09 *McCarthy v Secretary of State for the Home Department,* judgment of 5 May 2011; Case C-256/11 *Dereci v Bundesministerium für Inneres,* judgment of 15 November 2011.

[30] Case C-86/12 *Alokpa and Moudoulou,* judgment of 10 October 2013.

[31] As Arnull argues, the 'legalistic approach' provides at least to a good extent an explanation why national courts embraced the preliminary reference procedure: it provided the most cost-effective way to resolve the dispute and appealed to the professional instincts of judges to do their best to find a solution in conformity with the applicable rules. Seen from that perspective, the decision as to whether to make a reference is less the result of a strategic vision and more the response to ad hoc legal issues. Arnull (n 1) 120–122.

[32] See eg *Carpenter* (n 6); *Melki* (n 4).

[33] See eg the cases on Greek corporate law: Joined Cases C-19 and 20/90, *Karellas* [1991] ECR I-2691; Case C-381/89 *Syndesmos Melon tis Eleftheras Evangelikis Ekklisias and others* [1992] ECR I-2111; Joined Cases C-134 and 135/91 *Kerafina-Keramische und Finanz-Holding and Vioktimatiki* [1992] ECR I-5699; Case C-367/96 *Kefalas and others v Greek State* [1998] ECR 1-2843; C-373/97 *Diamandis v Elliniko Domosio* [2000] ECR 1-1705. See further Case C-54/90 *Paletta I* [1992] ECR I-3458; Case C-206/94 *Paletta II* [1996] ECR I-2382.

[34] See below the *Landtová* and *OMT* cases.

[35] See eg Case C-81/09 *Idryma Typou AE v Ypourgos Typou kai Meson Mazikis Enimerosis* [2010] I-10161.

at EU level has resulted in EU norms addressing a wider spectrum of interests. This has had an impact on the judiciary. Whilst in earlier years, judicial balancing involved compromising an EU interest vis-à-vis a state interest, it now increasingly involves balancing diverse EU interests. The juxtaposition, in other words, has become somewhat more horizontal and less vertical. The role of national courts remains crucial here. They must carry out an assessment which allows a fair balance to be struck between the various fundamental rights and freedoms protected by the EU legal order.[36]

4. From Dialogue to Trialogue: The Role of Strasbourg

The dialogue between the ECJ and the national courts takes place in a background contoured by Strasbourg case law which operates as a further force of convergence. Despite the fact that EU law does not govern the effect of the ECHR in the domestic legal orders of the Member States,[37] the affinity with Convention rights is very close and the impact of the Convention permeating and extensive. Strasbourg and Luxembourg are in a mood of convergence. In line with Article 6(3) TEU and Articles 52 and 53 of the Charter, the ECJ is committed to upholding Convention standards. It regularly refers to Strasbourg case law[38] and has reminded national courts that the Convention operates as a minimum.[39] Indeed, landmark cases where the ECJ has deferred to the constitutional standards of Member States or annulled EU measures for breach of fundamental rights[40] can be seen as gestures of reconciliation towards national courts and an attempt to pre-empt the ECtHR by projecting Luxembourg as a one-stop venue. The higher the protection of fundamental rights offered by the ECJ, the less the need to go to Strasbourg. The interaction between the ECJ and the ECtHR, as that between the ECJ and the national courts, is one of mutual respect and deference. The ECtHR has reciprocated by granting the ECJ more leeway than it appears to be prepared to grant to national courts, perhaps too much leeway. Thus, in *Bosphorus*, the ECtHR held that since the EU offers standards for the protection of fundamental rights that are equivalent to those of the Convention, the ECtHR would not intervene unless in the

---

[36] See Case C-544/10 *Deutsches Weintor*, judgment of 6 September 2012, para 47; Case C-275/06 *Promusicae* [2008] ECR I-271, paras 65 and 66; Case C-12/1131 *McDonagh v Ryanair Ltd*, judgment of 31 January 2013.

[37] Case C- 571/10 *Kamberaj v IPES*, judgment of 24 April 2012.

[38] See eg Case C-300/11 *ZZ*, judgment of 4 June 2013.   [39] See *Dereci* (n 29).

[40] C-112/00 *Schmidberger* [2003] ECR I-5659; Case C-36/02 *Omega* [2004] ECR I-9609, the Kadi litigation (Joined Cases C-402/05 P and C-415/05 P *Kadi and Al Barakaat International Foundation v Council and Commission* [2008] ECR I-6351 and Joined Cases C-584/10 P, C-593/10 P, and C-595/10 P *Commission et al v Kadi*, judgment of 18 July 2013) and the retention of data cases: Joined Cases C-293/12 and C-594/12 *Digital Rights Ireland Ltd v Minister for Communications*, judgment of 8 April 2014; Case C-131/12 *Google Spain v AEPD*, judgment of 13 May 2014.

circumstances of a specific case, the protection of Convention rights was 'manifestly deficient'.[41] Given the impending accession of the EU to the Convention, it may be questioned why the ECJ should continue to benefit from the *Bosphorus* presumption of compatibility. In addition, the ECtHR has notably recognized the importance of the dialogue between the national courts and the ECJ for the development of EU law and has sought to encourage it and even reinforce it.[42]

III. A CENTRALIZED CONSTITUTIONAL MODEL

The interaction between the ECJ and the national courts occurs in the shadow of a centralized constitutional model with some strong federal elements. This model is powered by the principles of primacy and direct effect, and includes, among others, the following features: an expansive interpretation of EU competence, a relatively narrow conception of national constitutional autonomy, and strong reliance on the principle of effectiveness.

One of the main ways in which the ECJ has contributed to integration is through an expansive interpretation of EU competence. The Court has been activist by being passive in the exercise of its power of judicial review of EU measures.[43] A prime example is provided by the interpretation of the internal market harmonization clause. Although in the first *Tobacco Advertising* case,[44] the ECJ annulled a policy measure adopted under Article 114 TFEU for the first time, this was an aberration. Subsequent case law suggests that the Court is minded to facilitate rather than question the exercise of EU competence adopting an expediency rationale.[45] Most recently, in the

---

[41] Judgment of 30 June 2005 in *Bosphorus Hava Yollari Turizm ve Ticaret AS v Ireland*, application no. 45036/98.

[42] In *Pafitis v Greece*, judgment of 26 February 1998, the ECtHR held that the time during which the national proceedings were stayed pending a reference for a preliminary ruling to the ECJ could not be taken into account in assessing whether the length of proceedings ran counter to Article 6(1) as that would adversely affect the system instituted by Article 234 TFEU. More recently in *Dhahbi v Italy*, judgment of 8 April 2014, the ECtHR held that the refusal of a national court to consider a request for a preliminary reference may amount to a violation of Article 6 ECHR and found such a violation. But note now Opinion 2/13 of 18 December 2014 where the ECJ found the draft Treaty of EU Accession to the Convention to be incompatible with EU law. The Court's ruling was delivered after the manuscript was sent for production.

[43] See H. Rasmussen, in D. O'Keeffe and A. Bavasso (eds), *Judicial Review in European Union Law, Liber Amicorum in Honour of Lord Slynn* (2000) below, note 69.

[44] Case C-376/98 *Germany v Parliament and Council (Tobacco case)* [2000] ECR I-8419.

[45] See eg C-210/03 *The Queen on the Application of Swedish Match AB v Secretary of State for Health* [2004] ECR I-11893; Case C-380/03 *Federal Republic of Germany v European Parliament and Council of the European Union* [2006] ECR I-11573 (*Second Tobacco Advertisement Directive*

ESMA case,[46] it held that Article 114 can be used to endow an EU agency with regulatory powers over undertakings adopting a narrow understanding of the *Meroni* doctrine.[47] An expansive interpretation of EU competence maximizes the effect of primacy. The *ESMA* judgment sanctions the increasing presence of EU law and institutions in the field of enforcement and supervision. One of the most notable effects of the 2008 financial crisis and the subsequent Eurozone crisis has been the increase in direct involvement of the EU in monitoring compliance and enforcement of EU law. The transition of the EU from law maker to supervisor signals a stepping up of the integrative process, a more advanced form of federalism, and, perhaps, a less romantic and more threatening view of EU integration.

The bias in favour of a centralized constitutional model is also illustrated by *Melloni*.[48] In that case, the Court subordinated Article 53 of the Charter to the primacy of EU law and found that that provision does not preclude a maximalist interpretation of the Charter. Article 53 of the Charter provides that nothing in the Charter is to be interpreted as restricting or adversely affecting human rights and fundamental freedoms as recognized, in their respective fields of application, among others, by the Member States' constitutions. *Melloni* is a judgment of constitutional importance both because of the subject matter of the case and the parties to the judicial dialogue. It was the first ever reference made by the Spanish Constitutional Court. There was also previous case law of that court which appeared to support the opposite conclusion from that reached by the ECJ. The case concerned the compatibility of Article 4a of the Framework Decision on the European Arrest Warrant (EAW) with the right to a fair trial. Article 4a provides in essence that if a person convicted *in absentia* was properly informed of the scheduled trial and chose not to appear, the executing judicial authority would be required to surrender him and could not make surrender subject to there being an opportunity for a retrial. The ECJ held that Article 4a was compatible with the right to an effective remedy and the right to a hearing as provided in the Charter. It then held that that interpretation foreclosed the possibility of a Member State refusing to execute the warrant on the ground that the standard of protection of the right to a fair trial is higher under the national constitution.

Melloni projects an inclusive, centralized approach to the protection of fundamental rights placing the Charter at the apex of the edifice. It interpreted Article 53 as a soft conciliation clause but with little bite to restrict the interpretation of EU law by the ECJ. This interpretation is correct. Once the Court decided that Article 4a did not

---

case); Case C-301/06 *Ireland v Parliament and Council* [2009] ECR I-593; Case C-58/08 *The Queen, Vodafone Ltd v Secretary of State for Business, Enterprise and Regulatory Reform* [2010] ECR I-04999.

[46] Case C-270/12 *UK v Council* (*ESMA case*), judgment of 22 January 2014.

[47] Case 9/56 *Meroni v High Authority* [1958] ECR 133. In that case, the ECJ imposed strict limitations on the power of the EU institutions to delegate their powers, and held that they could not delegate discretionary powers to other agencies established at EU level.

[48] Case C-399/11 *Melloni v Ministerio Fiscal*, judgment of 26 February 2013.

breach the right to a fair trial as guaranteed by the Charter, it would make little sense to allow a Member State to condition that interpretation to national constitutional requirements. As the Court stated, that would cast doubt on the uniformity of the standard of protection as defined in EU law and undermine the principle of mutual recognition. Viewed in that light, *Melloni* is merely a reiteration of *Internationale Handelsgesellschaft*.[49] Behind the clinical language of the Court and the cold logic of primacy, however, lies a choice of a centralized constitutional model in which the capacity of Article 53 to protect national constitutional standards is severely impaired.[50] The problem does not lie with *Melloni*, but perhaps in the earlier judgments where the ECJ upheld the validity of the EAW, giving the green light to the model of mutual recognition without prior harmonization of substantive criminal law.[51]

Finally, the principle of effectiveness has been used by the Court with creativity to enhance the binding effect of directives and more generally buttress EU norms. Effectiveness has been used, for example, to provide for the immediate protection of EU rights, minimum standards of remedies, or even new 'hybrid' remedies and the procedural prioritization of EU law over national constitutional law.[52] Effectiveness

---

[49] Case 11/70 [1970] ECR 1125.

[50] For an interesting contrast in the US context see, *State of Wisconsin v Knapp* 2005 WI 127, 285 Wis. 2d 86, 700 N.W.2d 899 (2005) (*Knapp II*). In that case, the Supreme Court of Wisconsin held that the right against self-incrimination as protected by the Constitution of Wisconsin went further than the same right as guaranteed by the US Constitution, and prohibited the prosecution from taking into account not only statements but also physical evidence collected without the accused having been read his rights. The case provides an interesting example of constitutional conversation between State courts and the US Supreme Court. In *Knapp I* (*State v Knapp* 2003 WI 121, 265 Wis. 2d 278, 666 N.W.2d 881), the Wisconsin Supreme Court had interpreted the US Constitution as requiring the suppression of physical evidence obtained as a direct result of the violation of the right against self-incrimination when the violation was an intentional attempt to prevent the suspect from exercising his due process rights. When the Supreme Court disagreed (*US v Patane* 542 U.S. 630), the judgment of the Wisconsin Supreme Court in *Knapp I* was vacated and the case was remanded to it for further consideration. In *Knapp II*, the Wisconsin Court found again for the defendant relying this time on the Wisconsin Constitution. The court acknowledged that giving the Wisconsin Constitution an interpretation no broader than that of the US Constitution promoted uniformity in the law, which was advantageous but not indispensable. It would not 'be bound by the minimums which are imposed by the Supreme Court of the United States if it is the judgment of this court that the Constitution of Wisconsin and the laws of this state require that greater protection of citizens' liberties ought to be afforded' (para 59). Recalling its previous case law, the Wisconsin Court held as follows: 'While this results in a divergence of meaning between words which are the same in both federal and state constitutions, the system of federalism envisaged by the United States Constitution tolerates such divergence where the result is greater protection of individual rights under state law than under federal law' (para 61). *Knapp II*, however, can be distinguished from *Melloni* in that, unlike the latter, which concerned the application of an EU measure, the former did not involve the interpretation of a federal enactment. The constitutional framework was different and there was no suggestion that, by following a broader interpretation of state rights the court was violating the US Constitution.

[51] See Case C-303/05 *Advocaten voor de Wereld VZW v Leden van de Ministerraad* [2007] ECR I-3633.

[52] See Case 92/78 *Simmenthal v Commission* [1979] ECR 777.

has evolved to being the gold standard, the overarching touchstone for determining the EU credentials of national rules and remedies. It is a more articulate proxy than primacy and direct effect, and, as such, corresponds to a more advanced stage of the federalization process.

An interesting illustration of the impact of effectiveness on national constitutional norms is provided by *Melki*.[53] The case concerned a French constitutional amendment introduced in 2008 which granted the *Conseil Constitutionnel* jurisdiction to rule on the compatibility of legislation with fundamental rights guaranteed by the Constitution. By introducing a system of concrete a posteriori constitutional review, the amendment signalled a major change from the 1958 constitutional model which had given to the *Conseil* only power of *ex ante* review. The French law implementing the constitutional amendment provided that, where the compatibility of a French law with the Constitution and with EU law was questioned, a French court had to give priority to initiating the procedure for constitutionality review. The court had to stay the proceedings and await the decision of the *Conseil* except in cases of urgency or where the liberty of the individual was at stake. The *Cour de cassation* considered that such priority might interfere with its ability to make a preliminary reference under Article 267 TFEU and referred the matter to the ECJ.

Melki is important because it brought to the fore the interaction between EU obligations and national constitutional norms. The French law implementing the constitutional amendment did not intend to question the primacy of EU law but give priority to constitutional review over review of compatibility with international treaties, thus reiterating that the constitution was at the apex of the national legal system. Its compatibility with the strict requirements of *Simmenthal*,[54] however, was far from clear.[55] When the law was being debated, many considered that an exception to the priority rule should be introduced in relation to issues pertaining to compatibility with EU law but the French Parliament eventually decided not to do so. One of the reasons appears to have been a fear that with the expansion of EU law and the EU Charter acquiring the same status as primary EU law, the exception would become very broad and make review of constitutionality of lesser importance.[56] *Melki* is also important for another reason. It reveals a conflict between the *Cour de cassation* and the *Conseil Constitutionnel*. The former was keen to advance an interpretation of the implementing law which made it incompatible with the principle of primacy and to test its EU law credentials via the preliminary reference procedure despite the fact that a reading of the priority rule compatible with EU law was possible.

---

[53] Joined Cases C-188 and C189/10 *Melki and Abdeli* [2010] ECR I-5667.

[54] *Melki and Abdeli* (n 53).

[55] See R. Medhi, 'French Supreme Courts and European Union Law: Between Historical Compromise and Accepted Loyalty' (2011) 48 *Common Market Law Review* 439, 464–465.

[56] Medhi (n 55) 459, where further bibliography is given.

The ECJ was sensitive to the constitutional conflict but gave little ground. It held that a Member State might not reserve to a constitutional court the power to examine the compatibility of national law with EU law or to make a preliminary reference. Thus, if the French law was interpreted to mean that it was for the *Conseil Constitutionnel* to assess compatibility with EU law as part of reviewing constitutionality, that would be incompatible with the Treaties. It would mean that the court ruling on the substance could not rule on the compatibility with EU law or make a reference to the ECJ before submitting the case for constitutionality review. In addition, if the *Conseil Constitutionnel* were to find the legislation in question compatible with EU law, the court ruling on the substance could not, after the *Conseil's* decision, refer a question to the ECJ. Such a system would be incompatible with the principle of primacy.[57] This, however, was not the only interpretation of the French law. An EU law compatible interpretation could not be ruled out and it was for the national court to interpret the law, as far as possible, in a manner which accorded with EU law.[58] The Court went on to reiterate the procedural attributes of primacy.[59] The judgment is somewhat ambiguous. It appears to provide Member States with more leeway than the strict application of *Simmenthal* in that it recognizes the possibility that the court hearing the substance of the case may be prevented from disapplying immediately a national norm incompatible with EU law. There is however no breach of effectiveness in that, in those circumstances, the national court must be able to order provisional protection. The bottom line appears to remain the same as that in *Simmenthal*.

Notably, following the judgment of the ECJ, the *Cour de cassation* went on to deliver a pro-EU primacy judgment. It acknowledged that EU law took priority even over national constitutional norms and applied the *Simmenthal* principle unconditionally holding that, for procedural reasons, it did not have power to order interim relief.[60] *Melki* also opened the way for a direct dialogue between the ECJ and the *Conseil Constitutionnel*.[61] The effect of *Melki* is that the Court reversed the priorities: instead of EU primacy accommodating the national system of constitutionality review, the latter had to fit in with EU primacy. *Melki* accords with

---

[57] Para 47.   [58] Para 50.

[59] It held that, where an obligation to initiate an interlocutory procedure for constitutionality review prevented a court from immediately disapplying a national provision which it considered to be contrary to EU law, that court must be free to provide interim protection for EU rights and also disapply, at the end of the interlocutory procedure, that national provision contrary to EU law: see para 53.

[60] *Cour de cassation*, judgment of 29 June 2010.

[61] See the subsequent reference in Case C-168/13 PPU *F v Premier ministre*, judgment of 30 May 2013, which pertained to the interpretation of the Framework Decision on the European Arrest Warrant. For a case where the *Cour de cassation* made a preliminary reference after raising a constitutionality question with the *Conseil Constitutionnel*, see Case C-176/12 *AMS v Union locale des syndicats CGT*, judgment of 15 January 2014.

Kücükdeveci.[62] There, the Court held that the power of a national court to disapply a provision which it considers to be incompatible with EU law cannot be restricted by a rule of national law which makes the setting aside of national legislation subject to a declaration of unconstitutionality by the *Bundesverfassungsgericht*. Nor can such a rule oblige a non-final national court to make a reference to the ECJ. The discretion to refer cannot be turned into an obligation by the need to temper the effects of primacy on national procedures for constitutionality review. The Court understands effectiveness as empowering any national court to disapply national legislation which it considers to be contrary to EU law without necessarily invoking the assistance of the preliminary reference procedure.[63]

It would be wrong, however, to consider that these federal elements leave no room for national constitutional standards. In fact, the case law on fundamental rights, in contrast to the case law on EU competence, shows a strong tendency for activism and for embracing the national constitutional traditions. Judgments such as *Schmidberger, Omega, Kadi*, and, more recently, activist case law in the field of data retention[64] suggest that EU standards capture and reflect the national constitutional pulse.

IV. The Conundrum
of *Kompetenz-Kompetenz*

Which authority has ultimate competence to define the outer boundaries of EU law? This is an issue on which the ECJ and the national judiciaries differ and which marks the fault line of the EU edifice. There is essentially no ecumenical understanding of EU law primacy.

According to the established case law of the ECJ, national courts do not have power to determine the validity of EU law.[65] That power belongs exclusively to the ECJ. If it were otherwise, the uniform application of EU law would be prejudiced and legal certainty would suffer. It would be possible, for example, for a German

---

[62] Case C-555/07 *Kücükdeveci v Swedex*, judgment of 19 January 2010, paras 53–54; for further confirmation of *Melki*, see Case C-457/09 *Chartry v Belgium*, order of 1 March 2011.

[63] In addition, a lower national court is not bound by the judgment of a higher national court, which is inconsistent with EU law: see Case C-396/09 *Interedil Srl v Fallimento Interedil Srl*, judgment of 20 October 2011, para 37; Case C-173/09 *Elchinov* [2010] ECR I-0000, para 30.

[64] See above n 40.

[65] See Case 314/85 *Foto-Frost v Hauptzollamt Lübeck-Ost* [1987] ECR 4199 and Case C-461/03 *Gaston Schul Douane-expediteur* [2005] ECR I-10513.

court to decide that an EU regulation was valid and for a French court to decide that the same regulation was invalid. That would give rise to legal uncertainty and lead to distortions in the conditions of competition. Understood in that way, uniformity and internal market go hand in hand. Exclusivity is not necessary to satisfy an abstract notion of unity but instrumental to economic expectations. It is also closely related to primacy. If national courts could unilaterally determine the validity of EU acts, primacy would essentially become a dead letter since whether EU law could override national norms would depend on the decision of the national judiciaries. In the Court's instrumental rationale, the EU is a closed system in which the protection of national interests is channelled through the institutional framework of the Union. Member States can influence policies through their participation in the EU decision-making process and safeguard the rules of the bargain through the process of adjudication before the EU judiciary.

National courts, on the other hand, start from a different premise. The EU is based on a transfer of sovereignty from the nation states to the Union. A national government, however, may not surrender more power than it possesses under the national constitution. This is a fundamental principle of any legal system based on the rule of law. To establish therefore if the exercise of EU competence exceeds the powers surrendered to the EU, one has to look at the national constitution of which the national supreme judiciary is the only rightful exponent. It is inevitable therefore that national courts must have the ultimate say.

Essentially, the problem of *Kompetenz-Kompetenz* receives a different answer depending on the underlying premise of one's reasoning. Successive Treaty revisions have not sought to provide an answer. There is, in effect, a tacit agreement to disagree, leading to a constitutional symbiosis which lies at the heart of the EU construct and makes the cooperation of the EU and the national judiciaries essential. Although it represents the fault line of the EU system, a head-on clash has so far been avoided subject to limited exceptions.[66] Whilst the post nation state constitutional paradigm remains unstable, there is a direct or indirect and often coded and nuanced judicial dialogue through which the basic terms of the bargain morph. The threat of rebellion by the national courts provides a powerful control mechanism over the activism of the ECJ. But the conversation is respectful and disciplined, and centres on boundaries rather than outcomes. To use a biblical analogy, the ECJ and the national judiciaries tend to differ on the first commandment, namely, what is the source of authority, rather than substantive rules of conduct. Given how fluid the EU construct is, such symbiosis is a constitutional imperative. It enables the EU and the national legal orders to coexist in a state of creative disagreement.

---

[66] See the *Landtová* litigation, discussed below.

Whilst, with limited exceptions, the judiciaries of the Member States have embraced the primacy of EU law as espoused by the ECJ, they have done so on the basis that primacy derives from the dispositions of national law on the incorporation of EU law into domestic legal systems, and not from EU law itself.[67] In ways reminiscent of that of the *Bundesverfassungsgericht*,[68] they reserve to themselves the power to test *in extremis* the outer boundaries of EU competence by reference to their national constitutional principles.[69]

V. CONFLICT AND REBELLION

It is interesting to examine at this juncture three judgments which manifest different visions of the relationship between the ECJ and national courts but all of which suggest a more confrontational approach. They originate from the Czech Constitutional Court, the *Bundesverfassungsgericht*, and the UK Supreme Court, and illustrate respectively defiance, a dialogue of conflict, and a more subtle exercise in circumspection and warning.

---

[67] See the overview provided in the House of Lords, European Union Committee Sixth Report of Session 2003–04, 2 March 2004, Ch 3, paras 64ff. The courts which have perhaps come closest to endorsing an unqualified view of primacy are the Belgian courts.

[68] In a series of cases, the *Bundesverfassungsgericht* has held that it guarantees the essential content of fundamental rights and the tenets of the German Constitution not only against German authorities but also against the EU, but that it does so in a relationship of cooperation with the Court of Justice. It retains residual jurisdiction to control the compatibility of EU law with those principles but will only find that an EU measure is *ultra vires* if the EU has manifestly exceeded its competence. The evolution of its case law can be traced by reference to the *European Union Treaty* case (*Bundesverfassungsgericht*, judgment of 12 October 1993, 2 BvR 2134/92 and 2159/92, 89 BverfGE 155, [1993] 1 *Common Market Law Reports* 57), the *Lisbon Treaty case* (9BVerfG, 2 BvE 2/08, 30 June 2009 http://www.bverfg.de/entscheidungen/es20090630_2bve000208en.html), and *Honeywell* (BVerfG, 2 BvR 2661/06, 6 July 2010 http://www.bverfg.de/entscheidungen/rs20100706_2bvr266106en.html). In *Honeywell*, the *Bundesverfassungsgericht* held that it will only find that an EU measure is *ultra vires* if the EU has exceeded its competence in a way which is 'sufficiently qualified', ie sufficiently serious. This will be the case where the EU act in question is manifestly in breach of the competences of the EU and 'is highly significant in the structure of competences between the Member States and the Union', ie leads to a structurally significant shift to the detriment of the Member States. The judgment appeared to grant more deference to the ECJ than previous judgments had suggested.

[69] For a prominent example, see the Danish Supreme Court Maastricht judgment: *Hanne Norup Carlsen and others v Prime Minister Poul Nyrup Rasmussen* [1999] 3 *Common Market Law Review* 854, judgment delivered on 6 April 1998, UfR 1998.800. For a discussion, see, among others, H. Rasmussen, 'Confrontation or Peaceful Coexistence? On the Danish Supreme Court's Maastricht Ratification Judgment' in D. O'Keeffe and A. Bavasso (eds), *Judicial Review in European Union Law* (2000) 377.

1. Defiance

A head-on collision occurred in *Landtová*, a case that concerned the allocation of pension liabilities in the aftermath of the dissolution of Czechoslovakia.[70] Following dissolution, a treaty concluded between the Czech and the Slovak Republics determined that responsibility for payment of pensions rested with the state where the employer had its establishment on the date of the dissolution. Following separation, however, the economic development of the two republics was uneven and Slovak pensions soon became lower than Czech ones. This created unfairness in relation, in particular, to Czech citizens who had worked in Czech territory but were paid lower pensions because the formal place of business of their employer was on Slovak soil. To redress the perceived inequality, the Czech authorities provided supplements, but disagreement emerged between the administrative courts and the Constitutional Court (CC) as to their legality and the categories of persons who were entitled to them.

The CC considered that, under the principle of equality, all Czech citizens were entitled to receive equal pensions irrespective of the place of business of their employer, since they were part of the same pre-dissolution pension system.[71] The Supreme Administrative Court took the opposite view considering the payment of supplements to be contrary to the bilateral treaty and also Regulation 1408/71.[72] The CC insisted on its interpretation and quashed the judgment of the Supreme Administrative Court, which sought to move the war theatre to Luxembourg. On a reference from it, the ECJ found that the payment of supplements did not run counter to Regulation 1408/71 but that the approach of the CC 'incontrovertibly' discriminated.[73] By providing for payment of the higher Czech pension solely to Czech nationals residing in the territory of the Czech Republic, it involved both direct and indirect discrimination on grounds of nationality. The ECJ held that, as long as measures reinstating equal treatment had not been adopted, the principle of non-discrimination required that the higher pension should be paid to all citizens from other Member States who worked in Czechoslovakia before dissolution and were in the same position.[74]

---

[70] For a detailed discussion, see R. Zbíral, 'Czech Constitutional Court, Judgment of 31 January 2012, Pl. ÚS 5/12. A Legal Revolution or a Negligible Episode? Court of Justice Decision Proclaimed Ultra Vires' (2012) 49 *Common Market Law Review* 1475.

[71] Judgment 405/02, 3 June 2003.

[72] Regulation No 1408/71 on the application of social security schemes to employed persons, to self-employed persons and to members of their families moving within the Community, as amended by Regulation No 118/97 (OJ 1997 L 28, 1) and Regulation No 629/2006 (OJ 2006 L 114, 1).

[73] Case C-399/09 *Landtová v Česká správa sociálního zabezpečení*, judgment of 22 June 2011, para 43.

[74] *Landtová* (n 73), paras 51–53. This followed from previous case law; see Case C-18/95 *Terhoeve* [1999] ECR I-345, para 57.

In subsequent proceedings, the CC refused to follow the *Landtová* judgment.[75] It considered that employment in Slovakia prior to dissolution could not be equated with employment in another Member State and that, in the absence of an inter-state element, Regulation No 1408/71 was not applicable.[76] It also held that, because the contested provisions of the bilateral treaty were referred to in Annex III of Regulation 1408/71, that treaty applied and the CC was entitled to interpret it in accordance with its own case law. The CC's reasoning has been persuasively criticized.[77] Its approach seems to be flawed both in substance and in process since, at the very least, it ought to have made a reference to the ECJ. The CC's defiance was not the end of the matter. Its judgment was followed by a further preliminary reference made by the Supreme Administrative Court in which the latter essentially asked the ECJ to rule on the compatibility of the CC's views with regard to EU law but the reference was subsequently withdrawn.[78]

The CC's rebellion, whilst startling and dangerous, is limited in scope. First, it related to a specific issue connected with the dissolution of Czechoslovakia and pension rights that accrued before accession to the EU. Second, it did not question the exercise of EU competence by the EU legislative bodies. Third, it occurred against the background of strong intra-judicial competition at the national level and in the context of a preliminary reference made by a rival court which offended the CC.[79] Defiant as it was, the judgment did not raise strategic issues of European integration.

2. The Dialogue of Conflict

Such strategic issues, however, are raised by the OMT case. In 2014, the German Federal Constitutional Court (FCC) made its first preliminary reference asking a number of questions concerning the validity of the OMT decision of the European Central Bank (ECB).[80] In September 2012, the Governing Council of the ECB adopted a decision on Technical Features of Outright Monetary Transactions

---

[75] Pl. ÚS 5/12, Judgment of 31 January 2012.   [76] Zbíral (n 70) 1482.

[77] Zbíral (n 70) 1484.   [78] Case C-253/12 *JS*, Order of 27 March 2013.

[79] A highly unusual aspect of the case is that, following the reference to the ECJ by the Supreme Administrative Court, the CC sent a letter to the ECJ explaining the pension system under the bilateral treaty. In accordance with the ECJ's rules of procedure, however, that letter was not part of the case file. See Zbíral (n 70) 1483.

[80] BVerfG, 2 BvR 2728/13, 14 January 2014 http://www.bverfg.de/entscheidungen/rs20140114_2bvr272813en.html. For commentary, see, among others, the contributions published in the special issue of the (2014) 15 *German Law Journal* 2, including F.C. Mayer, 'Rebels without a Cause? A Critical Analysis of the German Constitutional Court's OMT Reference' (2014) 15 *German Law Journal* 111; U. di Fabio, 'Karlsruhe Makes a Referral' (2014) 15 *German Law Journal* 107; J. Bast, 'Don't Act Beyond Your Powers: The Perils and Pitfalls of the German Constitutional Court's *ultra vires* Review' (2014) 15 *German Law Journal* 167. See also C. Gerner-Beuerle, E. Kücük, and E. Schuster, 'Law Meets Economics in the German Federal Constitutional Court' (2014) 15 *German Law Journal* 281.

(OMT). The OMT decision essentially authorizes the ECB to make, as an emergency measure and subject to strict conditionality, unlimited purchases of government bonds of Member States who are in financial difficulties when they are unable to obtain sustainable interest rates in the open financial markets. The ECB may make such purchases only on condition that the state in question agrees to participate in a reform programme agreed under the auspices of the EFSF or the ESM.[81] The decision itself provides only an authorization and has not yet been put into effect. But it did have an impact as the mere publication of the ECB's intention was sufficient to calm down the financial markets.

The FCC questioned the compatibility of the OMT decision with the treaty provisions which restrict the mandate of the ECB in the field of monetary policy (Articles 119, 127 TFEU) and prohibit the monetary financing of national budgets (Article 123 TFEU). The FCC considered that the purchase of government bonds appeared to be an economic rather than a monetary policy measure for a number of reasons. First, because of its objective, which was to neutralize the spreads of government bonds. Second, because of its selectivity: it authorized purchases of bonds of only selected Member States whilst monetary policy was intended to be uniform throughout the EU. Finally, because of its affinity to financial rescue programmes. It was intended to provide relief to Member States in difficulties and therefore it was the functional equivalent of a financial assistance measure. Those characteristics also suggested that the OMT programme was intended to circumvent Article 123(1) TFEU which prohibits the ECB and the national central banks from providing overdraft facilities to Member States and purchasing directly debt instruments of Member States.

Applying the *Honeywell* standard,[82] the FCC considered that, unless interpreted restrictively, the OMT decision would manifestly exceed EU competences and bring about a structural shift in the balance of competences. It held that if the OMT decision is to be qualified as an independent act of economic policy, it manifestly violates this distribution of powers.[83] It would also be structurally significant because the OMT decision is functionally equivalent to a financial assistance measure but not subject to the same safeguards. Rescue programmes, owing to 'their significant financial scope and general political implications, belong to the core aspects of the Member States' economic policy responsibilities'.[84] The FCC noted that the choice of instruments for the stabilization of monetary union depends on the democratic process in the Member States. Whilst German participation in the ESM bodies must first be cleared by the *Bundestag*, the ECB's decision to intervene under the OMT scheme is not subject

---

[81] The EFSF (European Financial Stability Facility) and the ESM (European Stability Mechanism) are two of the mechanisms set up by the Member States to provide financial assistance to Eurozone Member States encountering solvency and liquidity problems.

[82] For the *Honeywell* standard, see above, n 68.   [83] Para 39.   [84] Para 40.

to parliamentary approval.[85] In short, the ECB's action was functionally equivalent to the ESM but was not subject to the same safeguards and therefore usurped the national Parliaments' powers and did away with the national democratic processes.[86] The OMT intervention was structurally significant especially because it led to a considerable redistribution between the budgets and the taxpayers of the Member States, and thus amounted to fiscal redistribution that runs counter to Article 125 TFEU.[87]

The FCC held that, unless interpreted restrictively, the OMT decision would also violate Article 123(1) TFEU. Such violation would be manifest because Article 123(1) TFEU stipulates an explicit prohibition of monetary financing of the budget. It would also be structurally significant because the prohibition of monetary financing of the budget is one of the fundamental rules that guarantee the design of the monetary union as a 'community of stability' and safeguards the overall budgetary responsibility of the German *Bundestag*.[88]

The FCC outlined in detail the conditions to be fulfilled to rescue the validity of the OMT decision. It would not be incompatible with EU primary law if it could be interpreted in such a way as not to undermine the conditionality of the financial assistance programmes agreed under the EFSF and the ESM and as being ancillary to economic policy. This would require excluding the acceptance of a debt cut, not permitting the purchase of an unlimited amount of bonds, and avoiding interference with price formation on the market. Those conditions have been viewed with scepticism on the ground that they would undermine the effectiveness of the ECB's intervention and effectively cripple the OMT programme.[89] Still, they may be more malleable than their first reading suggests.[90]

The OMT reference is important for a number of reasons. Being the first reference by the FCC, it marks the transition from indirect to direct dialogue. Second, it is important because of its subject matter: the FCC is concerned not about human rights but about majoritarianism and the intrusion of the EU on basic state functions. It builds on its previous judgments on the powers of the *Bundestag*. Third, it is significant because it illustrates a more assertive understanding of the *Honeywell* test than previous judgments of the FCC might have led one to believe. Finally, it is notable because the order for reference contains detailed guidance as to how the OMT decision must be interpreted in order to rescue its validity.[91] The tenor of

---

[85] See para 78.   [86] See para 40.

[87] Para 41. Article 125 TFEU prohibits the direct or indirect common liability of the Member States for government debts.

[88] Para 42.

[89] Mayer (n 80) 114, 120; C. Gerner-Beuerle, E. Küçük, and E. Schuster (n 80).

[90] Mayer (n 80) 120.

[91] Although this may be said to be in line with a more general practice of German courts when making references.

the judgment is such that one might be excused for thinking that it is less a genuine request for guidance and more an invitation to repent.

Interestingly, the reference was not made without dissent. What the majority of the FCC considered as a likely manifest violation was seen by the minority as transgression of the judicial province and an extension of the FCC's earlier case law.[92] The minority heeded the ECB's claim that the OMT was an instrument of monetary policy and considered that, in view of its political nature, the issue was not appropriate to judicial determination. Whilst a number of commentators have criticized the ruling as aggrandizement of the FCC or inept in the specific case,[93] and even as exceeding the powers of a judicial body because the questions involved are highly political,[94] others have seen it as a natural or at least a reasonable consequence of the national courts' mandate to respect the limits on government power posed by the national constitution.[95]

Undoubtedly, the OMT reference poses a challenge to the ECJ and may potentially open a systemic rift. If the ECJ endorsed the interpretation of the FCC, it would avoid an intra-judicial crisis but would also store up trouble for the future as the FCC and other courts might find it easier in the future to make demands. If the ECJ upheld the validity of the OMT decision, it would make conflict inevitable. There might be intermediate solutions.[96] Be that as it may, and irrespective of the ECJ's response, it is unlikely that the future evolution of EMU will be directed solely by the judiciary and without the participation of political actors. The ECJ may depend more on the self-restraint of national courts in the future, but compelling reasoning and circumspection by both interlocutors rather than intransigence will show the way forward. The system should be strong enough to absorb the shock. Viewed in that light, the OMT decision may be seen as contributing to the new public law that the EU's presence in economic governance demands.[97] As the *Pringle* judgment shows, this is a troublesome area where the ECJ has had to engage in some complex judicial acrobatics.[98]

---

[92] The reference was made by a majority of four to two with Judge Lübbe-Wolffe and Judge Gerhardt, the two most senior judges, dissenting.

[93] C. Gerner-Beuerle, E. Kücük, and E. Schuster (n 80).   [94] Mayer (n 80) at 115.

[95] Di Fabio (n 80).

[96] Conceivably, the ECJ could decide that the OMT decision does not create any legal effects in EU law until it is actually applied and that, if it has any effects in German law, it is for German courts to decide on those effects and their interpretation. Note, however. that the FCC left itself little scope for manoeuvre posing a number of alternative questions to the ECJ in the event that the latter were to decide that it was not appropriate to decide the principal set of questions on the ground that the OMT decision has not yet been implemented.

[97] See D. Chalmers, 'The European Redistributive State and a European Law of Struggle' (2012) 18 *European Law Journal* 667.

[98] Case C-370/12 *Pringle v Government of Ireland*, judgment of 27 November 2012, is the only case so far where the Court sat as a Full Court. In a seminal judgment, it held that the establishment of a stability mechanism enabling the granting of financial assistance to a Member State fell within the ambit of economic policy and not monetary policy, and that Member States could establish the ESM Treaty without breaching their obligations under EU law. The judgment is an exercise

3. Circumspection and Warning

A more critical stance towards EU law is also evinced by the judgment of the UK Supreme Court in the *HS2* case.[99] The appellants, a group of local authorities, had applied for judicial review of the government's decision to promote a high-speed train line. The government outlined its strategy in a command paper, in which it stated that it intended to obtain development consent through hybrid bills in Parliament. The appellants argued that the decision should have been preceded by a strategic environmental assessment under Directive 2001/42[100] and that the hybrid bill procedure did not comply with the environmental impact assessment directive (EIA Directive).[101] The case brought to the fore not an issue of substantive normative conflict but the compatibility with EU law of the parliamentary process, and, in dismissing the claim, the Supreme Court made some important pronouncements concerning the relationship of EU law with domestic law.

Article 1(4) of the EIA Directive excludes from its scope of application projects the details of which are adopted by a specific act of national legislation. The ECJ has interpreted that provision to mean that the exclusion applies only where the objectives of the Directive are fulfilled by the legislative process. Thus, a pre-condition for exclusion is that the legislative process must satisfy certain conditions.[102] The applicants argued that the hybrid bill procedure[103] did not meet those standards because it provided limited opportunity for debate in Parliament and because the parliamentary system of whips effectively foreclosed substantive discussion.

The Supreme Court found that the envisaged parliamentary procedure did not conflict with the requirements of the Directive. As Lord Reed noted, the submission that members of Parliament must act without the Parliament whip and not be influenced by parliamentary politics misunderstood the role of the legislature and ran counter to the separation of powers, parliamentary democracy, and the role of political parties, which are themselves principles of EU law.[104] The Supreme Court noted that, if the argument of the appellants was well founded, it would raise the issue of judicial scrutiny of parliamentary procedure and thus a conflict between the

---

in constitutional containment: the Court's interpretation contrasts sharply with its classic approach to the division of competence between the EU and the member states. Ironically, the Court facilitates further integration by following a narrow interpretation of EU competence.

[99] *R (on the application of HS2 Action Alliance Limited) v Secretary of State for Transport* [2014] UKSC 3.

[100] Directive 2001/42 on the assessment of the effects of certain plans and programmes on the environment, OJ 2001 L197/30.

[101] Directive 2011/92 on the assessment of the effects of certain public and private projects on the environment, OJ 2012, L 26/1.

[102] Those conditions regard eg the information that must be available to the legislature, the elements of the project, the reasons for the legislation, and the powers of judicial scrutiny.

[103] A hybrid bill procedure combines elements of a public and a private bill. It consists of three readings but contains an additional select committee stage after the second reading.

[104] Paras 102 et seq.

obligation to comply with EU law and the principle laid down in Article 9 of the Bill of Rights, which enshrines the freedom of speech and debate in Parliament. If such a conflict arose, it could not be resolved solely by reference to the principle of primacy since that principle itself derives from the European Communities Act 1972. It would be for the domestic courts to determine whether the intention of the Parliament in adopting the 1972 Act was to abrogate the conflicting principle of domestic law.[105]

There is in fact no surprising element in this pronouncement, which reflects the established approach of UK courts to the primacy of EU law. Primacy is endogenous to domestic law and thus conditional on the intention of Parliament. As Craig points out, the crucial issue is to determine what Parliament must do to persuade the courts that it does not intend EU law to take precedence.[106]

Lord Neuberger and Lord Mance acknowledged that there may well be some fundamental constitutional principles, established by statute and common law, of which Parliament 'did not contemplate or authorize the abrogation' when it enacted the European Communities Act 1972.[107] They left open the question of how such a conflict would be resolved but left no doubt that sovereignty lies with Parliament and that the domestic courts are the masters of the constitutional game. Lord Reed embedded the principles of EU law and the EU Charter in a constitutional discourse framed by national law, reaching a solution in conformity with EU values. Given that EU law itself embraced parliamentary democracy, acknowledged the importance of political parties, and respected the national constitutional identity, the Directives could not be interpreted as intending to scrutinize the adequacy of parliamentary procedures. Such a solution would run counter to the principle of mutual trust which underpins the Union.[108]

The *HS2* case brought to the fore some fundamental issues on the relationship between EU and national law and the ECJ's approach to construction. In determining the compatibility of national law with EU law, the ECJ takes into account the constitutional dimension of the case, ie whether the conflict raises an issue of constitutional importance for the Member State concerned. It does not, however, employ a presumption of compatibility or constitutionality in favour of national law. There is, in other words, no general principle of interpretation to the effect that EU legislation is presumed not to intend to trump national constitutional principles unless there is a clear indication to that effect. Rather, the constitutional significance of the national interest at stake is part of the mix of factors which overtly or covertly the Court takes into account in deciding the dispute. The orthodox EU view would suggest that a presumption of compatibility of the type described above would run counter to the principle of primacy and hold EU law hostage to

---

[105] Per Lord Reed, at para 79; per Lords Neuberger and Mance, para.
[106] See P.P. Craig, United Kingdom Sovereignty after Factortame (1991) 11 YEL 221 at 252.
[107] Para 207.   [108] Per Lord Neuberger and Lord Mance, at para 202.

national priorities. The tenor of the case law is, in fact, the opposite. The interpretation of EU law and its constraining effect on national choices is guided by the principle of effectiveness, which has a pro-integration bias.

There is a second reason why the presumption of compatibility in favour of national constitutions cannot work. How would the ECJ be able to assess objectively the constitutional value of the national interest at stake? On the basis of what criteria could it determine its constitutional importance for the polity concerned? In this respect, the judicial dialogue that takes place through the preliminary reference procedure has the capacity to provide an efficient and accurate mechanism of information flow, a constitutional messaging service. Rather than employing a general presumption in favour of state interests, the reference mechanism enables national courts to voice their concerns, point to adjustments, and indicate red lines. Such yellow or red cards can be shown to the ECJ not only in references but also in judgments where no reference is made. In this respect, the *HS2* case is as interesting as the case law of the FCC. Lord Neuberger and Lord Mance elevated the issue to one of principle. Even though they accepted that the Directives as interpreted by the ECJ did not require setting aside the hybrid bill procedure, they nonetheless took the opportunity to engage in a wider critique of the purposive interpretation followed by the ECJ.

They considered that an interpretation guided too much by the objectives of the statute and insufficiently grounded on the text would be impregnated with risks. If EU legislation was not given its 'intended and obvious effect', there would be a risk of loss of confidence in EU law and a risk of impairment of the dialogue between national courts and the ECJ.[109] National courts would find it much more difficult to decide whether a point of EU law is *acte clair* or not. That, in turn, would lead to the risk of the ECJ becoming over-loaded with references and the litigation becoming more protracted and expensive for the parties.[110] Furthermore, it would make it more difficult to draft EU legislation and, more importantly, achieve agreement on it in the future. Unpredictability about the meaning of measures would also make it more difficult for Member States with an opt-out to decide whether to opt in.[111] One could add to that list of evils. Unwarranted activism, and the ensuing unpredictability of the law, would not only be costly for the parties and lead to legal uncertainty but risk loss of confidence in the judgments of the ECJ, weaken its legitimacy, and lead to a rebellion by national courts. The paradox is that the critique was not directly relevant to the case in issue. Lord Neuberger and Lord Mance expressed disagreement both with the way the ECJ has interpreted Article 1(4) of the EIA Directive and its approach to Article 2(a) of the Strategic Assessment Directive.[112] It is, however, an open question as to whether the case law under those

---

[109] Para 172.   [110] Para 173.   [111] Para 174.

[112] The Lords took issue, in particular, with the interpretation provided by the ECJ in Case C-567/10 *Inter-Environnement Bruxelles Asbl v Région de Bruxelles-Capitale*, judgment of 22 March 2012.

provisions exceeds the limits of acceptable teleology. Both are provisions on the interpretation of which reasonable minds may differ. In any event, as the Supreme Court unanimously held, the case law of the ECJ did not result in accepting the interpretation proposed by the appellants. The issue therefore was more theoretical than real.

Be that as it may, the Lords' critique evinces that the Supreme Court and the ECJ take different views on the scope of their role and the limits of the judicial province. Imbued by teleology, the ECJ sometimes appears to distrust the legislative process and considers it to be within its powers to supplement legislation with the assistance of indeterminate objectives. A startling example is provided by *Sturgeon*.[113] The case concerned the right of air passengers to compensation in the event of a flight delay under Regulation No 261/2004.[114] The Regulation seeks to protect air passengers in the event that a flight is delayed or cancelled and provides for various forms of assistance and redress. The Court interpreted it as meaning that passengers are entitled to compensation not only where a flight is cancelled, which is expressly provided in Article 5, but also where a flight is delayed despite the absence of an express provision to that effect. It came to that conclusion on the ground that, in view of the objective of the regulation which was to strengthen passenger protection, situations covered by it must be compared by reference to the type and extent of the various types of inconvenience and damage suffered by the passengers concerned. In the light of the principle of equal treatment, it would be unjustifiable to offer compensation to passengers whose flights were delayed where they suffered a similar loss to those whose flights were cancelled.

In *Sturgeon*, as in other cases,[115] the Court understood equal treatment as going well beyond a negative constitutional stipulation which constrains legislative discretion. It used the principle to promote specific policy outcomes in the economic and social sphere based on the putative intentions of the legislature rather than its actual dispositions. Showing constitutional empathy, the Court sees its role as being to contribute to the realization of substantive values. But as Lord Neuberger and Lord Mance pointed out, there is a limit as to how far objectives can be relied upon beyond the text of the law. '[L]egislators cannot always agree everything that the most ardent supporters of its general objectives would like them to have achieved.'[116] Relying too much on objectives entails taking liberties, which strains the judicial function. The ECJ's approach to interpretation is characterized by a distrust towards the legislative process which is difficult to reconcile with the majoritarian instincts of Anglo-American common law. But why such distrust?

---

[113] Joined Cases C-402/07 and C-432/07 *Sturgeon v Condor Flugdienst GmbH* [2009] ECR I-10923.

[114] Regulation No 261/2004 establishing common rules on compensation and assistance to passengers in the event of denied boarding and of cancellation or long delay of flights (OJ 2004 L 46/1).

[115] See eg C-236/09 *Association Belge des Consommateurs Test-Achats*, judgment of 1 March 2011; C-144/04 *Werner Mangold v Rüdiger Helm* [2005] ECR I-9981.

[116] *HS2* (n 99) para 186.

There are a number of reasons for this. The loose drafting of EU measures, which tend to be less precise than common law statutes, the Continental judicial culture which, bred in a civil law tradition, accords a more prominent role to purposive interpretation, the enhanced role that the founding treaties grant to judicial oversight, and the deficient democratic credentials of the EU, whose decision-making processes lack thoroughbred parliamentary features, can all be viewed as explaining, if not legitimating, the ECJ's more active approach.

In any event, the ECJ's taste for teleology is sometimes exaggerated. The ECJ is certainly no stranger to a literal interpretation and a close analysis of the text in the light of many language versions.[117] Sometimes, it might be said, it pushes literal interpretation in support of its reasoning to the extreme.[118]

In *HS2*, the Supreme Court reserved itself the power to test the compatibility of EU with domestic constitutional principles but, in contrast to the FCC, it did not articulate any specific standard, such as manifest breach, that would trigger its intervention. It left its power of residual control vague. In addition, although Lord Neuberger and Lord Mance considered that the ECJ's interpretation of the Strategic Assessment Directive gave it a meaning which 'the European legislature clearly did not intend',[119] they stopped short of advocating rebellion pointing out instead that, if the issue were material, they would invite the ECJ to reconsider hoping that the Grand Chamber would be more accommodating.[120] The judgment is cautious, full of caveats and circumspection but also subtle warnings and has all the features of a constructive judicial dialogue.

VI. Conclusion: It's All About Democracy

The EU construct is fundamentally open-ended and capable of accommodating diverse preferences. Given the incomplete character of the underlying political bargain, relations between institutions are of cardinal importance.[121] This is especially so with regard to the relations between the EU and the national courts. Within the uncertain jurisdictional boundaries of the EU judicial universe, there is a constant

---

[117] See eg Case C-340/08 *The Queen, on the application of M and others v Her Majesty's Treasury* [2010] ECR I-3913.

[118] See eg the Court's interpretation of Article 125 TFEU (the 'no bail out' clause) in *Pringle* (n 98) at paras 131–132.

[119] Para 189.   [120] Para 189.

[121] See K. Culver and M. Guidice, *Legality's Borders: An Essay in General Jurisprudence* (2010).

renegotiation of authority.[122] The contribution of national courts is a *sine qua non* to the success of the integration through law paradigm. It is circumspection, flexibility, and power of reasoning that can provide the answers.

As the EU integration project expands in scope and intensity so will, inevitably, the engagement of national constitutional courts. Recent cases discussed above suggest that national courts are becoming less tolerant and more assertive. The judgment of the Czech Constitutional Court in *Landtová* and the OMT reference go beyond the protest through cooperation paradigm and illustrate a mood for direct conflict. Whether they will herald, more generally, a more confrontational approach towards the ECJ remains to be seen. One might expect a more reflective attitude towards the ECJ. In this respect, the reference of the FCC is particularly important. Being the first, it carries a symbolic value. It also carries an export value as the FCC is influential.

There appears to be growing disagreement between the ECJ and some national courts about what and how much can be done on the basis of the Treaties. It is perhaps no accident that the OMT decision and the *HS2* judgment relate to issues of democracy and governance and not directly to issues of fundamental rights. The ECJ has established a track record in taking fundamental rights seriously but less so in controlling the expansion of EU competence. The two are inextricably linked but, whilst the ECJ has won the battle on human rights supremacy, it risks losing the battle over the dynamics of competence. The key to resolving the pluralism conundrum might be in the ECJ taking a more reflective view of EU competence.

---

[122] See, in a different context, the excellent analysis of J. Resnik, 'Federalism(s)'s Forms and Norms: Contesting Rights, De-Essentializing Jurisdictional Divides, and Temporizing Accommodations' in J. Fleming (ed), *Nomos LV: Federalism and Subsidiarity* (2014) http://ssrn.com/abstract=2284200.

CHAPTER 17

......

ACCOUNTABILITY

......

PAUL CRAIG

I. Introduction

......

THIS chapter is concerned with accountability, a topic on which there is a large literature.[1] This chapter is not, however, a literature review, nor is it possible within the word confines to consider all aspects of the topic as it applies to all EU institutions and the Member States. The chapter addresses three central aspects of accountability—political, legal, and financial—which are integral to the analysis and which interrelate. The overall discussion is informed by Mark Bovens' conception of accountability, which is a relationship between an actor and a forum,

---

[1] See eg Anthony Arnull and Daniel Wincott (eds), *Accountability and Legitimacy in the European Union* (2002); Carol Harlow, *Accountability in the European Union* (2002); Richard Mulgan, *Holding Power to Account: Accountability in Modern Democracies* (2003); Elizabeth Fisher, 'The European Union in the Age of Accountability' (2004) 24 *Oxford Journal of Legal Studies* 495; Vernon Bogdanor, *Legitimacy, Accountability and Democracy in the European Union* (2007); Mark Bovens, 'Analysing and Assessing Accountability: A Conceptual Framework' (2007) 13 *European Law Journal* 447; Deirdre Curtin, *Executive Power of the European Union: Law, Practices and the Living Constitution* (2009); Sverker Gustavsson, Christer Karlsson, and Thomas Persson (eds), *The Illusion of Accountability in the European Union* (2009); Mark Bovens, Deirdre Curtin, and Paul 't Hart, 'Towards a More Accountable EU: Retrospective and Roadmap', ACELG 2010-4; Mark Bovens, 'Two Concepts of Accountability: Accountability as a Virtue and as a Mechanism (2010) 33 *West European Politics* 946; Mark Bovens, Deirdre Curtin, and Paul 't Hart (eds), *The Real World of EU Accountability: What Deficit?* (2010); Madalina Busuioc, *European Agencies: Law and Practices of Accountability* (2013).

in which the actor has an obligation to explain and to justify his or her conduct; the forum can pose questions and pass judgement, and the actor may face consequences.[2]

The theme that runs throughout the analysis is that proper consideration must be given to each facet of accountability as it applies to the EU institutions and to the Member States. This may seem obvious, and so it should be, but it is nonetheless often not done. The nature of this inquiry should be made clear at the outset. A proper discourse about Member State accountability means not simply consideration of the way in which national representatives in the Council or European Council do and should behave. It captures equally, if not more importantly, the nature of the political, legal, and financial accountability that rests, or should rest, on the Member States qua contracting parties to the EU.

II. Political Accountability

1. EU Political Accountability

Three principal dimensions shape discourse on political accountability and serve to explain the diversity of views on this topic. The intellectual frame for consideration of political accountability is provided by the normative dimension of the subject. This connotes the fundamental value assumptions against which the accountability of a particular institution is judged. Thus, EU accountability may be viewed against the postulate that the allocation of institutional power should ensure that a body with democratic credentials exercises control over the direction of EU policy for which it can be held accountable to the electorate through the democratic process.

The normative dimension is then tested through evaluation of the positive legal rules enshrined in the constituent Treaties and regulations made thereunder. This is the second dimension. The object is to decide whether these rules enable the institutions to perform their assigned role as indicated by the normative frame, and to criticize the system if this is not possible. This entails identification of the relevant legal rules in order to determine whether, for example, they attribute power to institutions that possess democratic credentials, the supposition being that the principal accountability mechanism is democratic accountability through the vote.

---

[2] Bovens 'Analysing and Assessing Accountability' (n 1) 450.

The third dimension is empirical. The inquiry focuses on whether the positive legal rules do what the legal text suggests, or whether the *modus operandi* of a particular institution reveals that real-world disposition of power is very different from that suggested by the black letter legal, with the consequence that assumptions as to whether the normative dimension of accountability is working as it should are thereby undermined. Thus, our vision of agency accountability may be predicated on certain hypotheses as to how the decision making process therein works, which may be undermined if they are falsified by empirical revelation of the true workings of power within an agency.

Most, if not all, differences concerning EU accountability turn on disagreement about one or more of these three dimensions. There is significant divergence of view at the normative level as to the framework against which EU accountability should be judged. There can be real dispute as to what the positive legal rules prescribe, which can shape different conclusions as to whether the normative vision, whatsoever it might be, is properly reflected in the legal rules. There are differences yet again at the empirical level, as to whether the legal rules, given their natural textual interpretation, capture the reality of how the institutions operate in practice, with consequential implications for assessment of accountability. This analysis can be briefly exemplified by the way in which we consider political accountability of the principal EU institutions, but the same type of analysis could be applied to, for example, comitology past and present, and EU agencies.

It is not fortuitous that discourse concerning EU political accountability rapidly shades into discussion of democracy,[3] the latter providing the normative frame for debate about the former. The disjunction between power and electoral accountability is the most potent aspect of the democracy deficit argument. It is axiomatic within national systems that the voters can express their dislike of the incumbent party through periodic elections. Governments can be changed if they incur electoral displeasure. In the EU, legislative power is divided between the Council, European Parliament, and Commission, with the European Council playing a significant role in shaping the overall legislative agenda. The voters therefore have no direct way of signifying their desire for change in the legislative agenda. European elections can alter the complexion of the European Parliament, but it is only one part of the legislative process. The Commission, Council, and European Council have input into the legislative agenda, but they cannot be voted out by the people. The fact that the European Parliament exerts real influence over the choice of the Commission President alleviates but does not cure the problem, in part because the other Commissioners remain national government appointees, and in part

---

[3] Joseph Weiler, Ulrich Haltern, and Franz Mayer, 'European Democracy and its Critique' in J. Hayward (ed), *The Crisis of Representation in Europe* (1995); Andreas Follesdal and Simon Hix, 'Why there is a Democratic Deficit in the EU: A Response to Majone and Moravcsik' (2006) 44 *Journal of Common Market Studies* 533.

because the European Parliament's power in this respect does not touch the considerable role played by the Council and European Council in the EU decision making process.

Some such as Moravcsik seek to affirm political accountability, notwithstanding the absence of direct electoral accountability analogous to national legal regimes. He contends that 'constitutional checks and balances, indirect democratic control via national governments, and the increasing powers of the European Parliament are sufficient to ensure that EU policy-making is, in nearly all cases, clean, transparent, effective and politically responsive to the demands of European citizens'.[4] For Moravcsik, this is more especially so given that the EU only undertakes a 'modest subset of the substantive activities pursued by modern states',[5] and the EU's ability to act 'is constrained by institutional checks and balances, notably the separation of powers, a multi-level structure of decision-making and a plural executive',[6] thereby rendering arbitrary action less likely. He contends, moreover, that there are mechanisms for direct and indirect democratic accountability in the EU, via the European Parliament, the Council, and European Council.[7] For Moravcsik democratic accountability is important, but it is conceived in terms of the prevention of arbitrary and corrupt power being exercised by the state. Judged by this criterion, Moravcsik concludes that there is sufficient democratic and political accountability in the EU, because of the multiple constraints, substantive, administrative, and procedural, on the scope of EU power.

This normative frame from within which to consider political accountability has been contested by those who regard electoral accountability as central to conceptions of democracy. Checks and balances are indeed part of the standard fare of democratic politics, but the justification for democracy at its most fundamental is that it allows participatory input to determine the values on which people within that polity should live. Thus, conceptions of democracy are premised on input by those entitled to vote, who then choose those who should govern for a period of time, and make that choice in the light of policy choices presented by rival political parties. It is not therefore surprising that Moravcsik's thesis has been challenged by writers such as Weiler,[8] and Follesdal and Hix.[9] They contend that a democratic polity requires contestation for political leadership and over policy, this being an essential element of even the 'thinnest' theories of democracy, and that it is absent in the EU. Thus, on this view, real political accountability is lacking for the very reason that there is no direct democratic accountability through which the voters can express their view as to the direction of EU policy and who should be charged with delivering it. There is scant opportunity to present an alternative set of policy outcomes to those currently espoused by the

---

[4] Andrew Moravcsik, 'In Defence of the "Democratic Deficit": Reassessing Legitimacy in the European Union' (2002) 40 *Journal of Common Market Studies* 603, 621.

[5] Moravcsik (n 4) 606.   [6] Moravcsik (n 4) 609.   [7] Moravcsik (n 4) 609–610.

[8] Weiler (n 3).   [9] Follesdal and Hix (n 3).

Commission, Council, and European Parliament, and EU elections tend moreover to be second-order national contests, 'fought by national parties on the performance of national governments, with lower turnout than national elections'.[10] The 2014 EP elections did however alleviate this problem by increasing the linkage between the choice of Commission President and the dominant party in the EP.

2. Member State Political Accountability

The richness of the literature on EU political accountability stands in stark contrast to the paucity of material that addresses such accountability from the perspective of the Member States. I am not referring here to accountability insofar as it concerns national representatives in the Council, or that of heads of state within the European Council, on which there is indeed considerable discussion. I am referring rather to the way in which we think more generally about the political accountability of Member States themselves as contracting parties to the EU. It is the very nature of the political obligations that flow from the legal maxim *pacta sunt servanda* that are of interest here. The response might well be that there are no distinctly political obligations that can be cast in terms of Member State political accountability, and that the legal dimension of *pacta sunt servanda* exhausts the meaning of this precept. This does not withstand examination, and reflects the very fact that consideration of national political accountability is under-theorized. Consider three applications of such accountability.

(a) Political Accountability, Member States, and Inter-institutional Division of Power

Consider first the issue examined above, that of democracy deficit and the implications that this has for EU political accountability. Note that this is presented as a critique of the EU. It is the EU qua real and reified entity that suffers from this infirmity, the corollary being that blame is cast on it. The EU is of course not blameless in this respect, but nor are the Member States, viewed collectively and individually. The present disposition of EU institutional power is the result of successive Treaties in which the principal players have been the Member States. There may well be debate as to the relative degree of power wielded by Member States and the EU institutions in the shaping and application of EU legislation, but there is greater consensus on the fact that Member States tend to dominate at times of Treaty reform. The inter-institutional distribution of power is the result of hard-fought battles, the results of which are embodied in Treaty amendment. Thus insofar as the present arrangements divide EU policy making de facto and de jure

---

[10] Follesdal and Hix (n 3).

between the Commission, Council, European Parliament, and European Council, this is reflective of power balances that the Member States were willing to accept.

This point can be reinforced by considering the reforms that would be required to alleviate the democratic deficit. The European Parliament has been further empowered by the Lisbon Treaty through extension of what is now the ordinary legislative procedure to new areas, and it has greater control over the appointment of the Commission President than hitherto. Thus, while the European Council retains ultimate power over the choice of Commission President, it will not force a candidate on the European Parliament that is of a radically different persuasion from the dominant party or coalition. A formal linkage between the dominant party/coalition in the European Parliament and the appointment of the Commission President serves to strengthen the connection between policy and party politics, thereby alleviating the disjunction of political power and political responsibility that has underpinned previous critiques of the EU. This linkage was further increased in the 2014 EP elections, where the rivals for Commission President campaigned expressly as the candidates for the main political groupings in the EP.

There are nonetheless obstacles that subsist to a closer link between policy and politics in the EU, even after the Lisbon Treaty reforms. The EU policy agenda is not exclusively in the hands of the European Parliament and/or Commission. The Council and the European Council have input both de jure and de facto. Thus even if the European Parliament and Commission President are very closely allied in terms of substantive policy for the EU, the policy that emerges will necessarily also bear the imprint of the political vision of the Council and European Council. Moreover while the President of the Commission may well be *primus inter pares*, he or she is still only one member of the Commission team. The other Commissioners will not necessarily be of the same political persuasion as the President or the dominant party in the European Parliament.

It would in theory be possible to have a regime in which the people voted directly for two constituent parts of the legislature, the European Parliament and Council, and for the President of the Commission and the President of the European Council. The political reality is that radical change of this kind will not happen, and it will not happen because the Member States will not accept such a disposition of power. It was not even on the political agenda during the extensive negotiations concerning institutional power that led to the Constitutional Treaty, later taken over into the Lisbon Treaty. The diminution of state power in the Council and European Council that would be entailed by such change would not be tolerated and would lead to the charge that the EU was truly becoming a super-state. Such change would still not ensure that the people could exercise electoral control over the direction of EU policy, since the European Council would still be populated by heads of state, who would continue to have a marked influence over the policy agenda, and members of the Commission, with diverse political views, would still be chosen by the Member States.

The preceding argument does not mean that the present disposition of institutional power is 'wrong'. It does mean that the consequential implications for EU democracy cannot be simply laid at the feet of the EU. The Member States are polit-ically accountable for the choices that they have made, individually and collectively, in shaping EU decision making. Insofar as there is a democratic deficit of the kind considered in Section II.1, political responsibility cannot simply be 'offloaded' by the Member States to the EU.

(b) Political Accountability, Member States, and Substantive Treaty Provisions

Member State political accountability is also relevant in relation to substantive Treaty provisions. This can be exemplified by the financial crisis and the consequential ascrip-tion of accountability, in which blame has been laid principally at the door of the EU itself. There is little doubt that the EU bears responsibility in this regard, but so too do the Member States, both collectively and individually. The Treaty provisions on economic and monetary union were crafted in the Maastricht Treaty. Insofar as there was an asym-metry between EU power over monetary as opposed to economic union, this reflected what Member States were willing to accept. This is readily apparent when one considers the architecture of the EMU Treaty provisions and the Stability and Growth Pact.[11]

Monetary union was all about the single currency and the Treaty articles were powerfully influenced by German ordo-liberal economic thought, which demanded independence of the European Central Bank, governance by experts, and the pri-macy of price stability. These foundational precepts were embodied in the primary Treaty Articles.[12] It was integral to the Maastricht settlement that monetary policy was Europeanized. This was reinforced by the Lisbon Treaty provisions on compe-tence, which stated that monetary policy for those countries that subscribed to the euro was within the exclusive competence of the EU.[13] This was further strengthened by mandatory Treaty provisions precluding instructions or interference from any out-side party, whether that was a nation state or another EU institution.[14]

The Maastricht settlement in relation to economic policy was markedly different. It was built on two related assumptions: preservation of national authority and pres-ervation of national liability. The former was reflected in the fact that Member States retained fiscal authority for national budgets, subject to limited oversight and coordin-ation from the EU designed to persuade Member States, with the ultimate possibility of sanctions, to balance their budgets and not run excessive deficits. The latter, pres-ervation of national liability, was the quid pro quo for the former, which found its most powerful expression in the no bail-out provision.[15] While there was some limited

---

[11] Council Reg (EC) 1466/97 of 7 July 1997 on the strengthening of the surveillance of budgetary positions and the surveillance and coordination of economic policies [1997] OJ L209/1; Council Reg (EC) 1467/97 of 7 July 1997 on speeding up and clarifying the implementation of the excessive deficit procedure [1997] OJ L209/6.

[12] Arts 127, 130, 282(3) TFEU.   [13] Arts 2(1), 3 TFEU.   [14] Art 130 TFEU.

[15] Art 125(1) TFEU.

qualification to this precept,[16] the message was nonetheless that national governments retained authority over national economic policy, subject to the Treaty rules designed to persuade them to balance their budgets, the corollary being that if they did not do so then the consequential liabilities would remain at the door of the nation state.

Oversight of national economic policy was weakened in subsequent years through Member State unwillingness to subscribe to the rules, which led to their modification, the effect of which was to weaken centralized EU control.[17] The Maastricht 'deal' was nonetheless left largely unaltered in the Lisbon Treaty. The Member States recognized the proximate connection between economic and monetary policy. They understood that the economic health of individual Member State economies could have a marked impact on the valuation of the euro, hence the need for some oversight and coordination of national economic policy. They were, however, mindful of the policy decisions made in and through national budgets, including those of a redistributive nature, and were unwilling to accord the EU too much control over such determinations. It was only when the financial crisis hit the EU that the Member States were willing to accept that greater control over national economic policy was a necessary condition for monetary union. This led to the plethora of measures enacted to tighten centralized control over national budgets and national banks. While the EU should properly be held accountable for the way in which it dealt with the financial crisis, the Member States cannot escape political accountability in this regard either. They had a major role in shaping the Maastricht architecture on EMU and determined how it was applied in the years thereafter.

(c) Political Accountability, Member States, and EU Legislation

It is also interesting to reflect on what Member State political accountability connotes when we think of the shaping of, and compliance with, EU legislation. It may be helpful to contrast two possible positions, while being mindful that there may well be more nuanced variations.

Member State political accountability might be regarded as coterminous with legal accountability. Thus, on this view, it is legitimate for Member States to behave as 'rational actors' when EU legislation is made, in the sense that resources will be deployed to ensure that the legislation best meets the needs of that particular state. The same approach will shape attitudes to compliance. The state accepts the consequences of non-compliance with EU legislation, whether cast in terms of state

---

[16] Art 122(2) TFEU.

[17] Case C-27/04 *Commission v Council* [2004] ECR I-6649; Imelda Maher, 'Economic Policy Co-ordination and the European Court: Excessive Deficits and ECOFIN Discretion' (2004) 29 *European Law Review* 831; Council Regulation (EC) 1055/2005 of 27 June 2005 amending Reg 1466/97 [2005] OJ L174/1; Council Regulation (EC) 1056/2005 of 27 June 2005 amending Reg 1467/97 [2005] OJ L174/5.

liability in damages, Commission action for breach of EU law, or direct effect of Directives. This is, however, conceived for what it is: legal accountability when one breaks the rules. It does not undermine the foundational precept that the state will act as a rational actor seeking to maximize the returns and minimize the costs of EU membership. It is integral to this approach that the state will regard it as politically 'natural' and normatively 'uncontroversial' to offload blame for failures to the EU itself, rather than accept that the states individually or collectively bear responsibility in this regard. The rational state actor as thus conceived describes not only how states behave in relation to the EU, but also sets the normative boundaries for their politically accountability.

Member State political accountability might, alternatively, be conceptualized more broadly, to include, but also go beyond the limits of legal accountability. The principle of sincere cooperation, whereby it is incumbent on the EU and Member States in full mutual respect to assist each other in carrying out tasks that flow from the Treaties, is central to this alternative vision.[18] So too is the remainder of this Treaty provision, which enjoins the Member States to take any appropriate measure to ensure fulfilment of the obligations arising out of the Treaties, or resulting from acts of the EU institutions, and requires Member States to facilitate achievement of the EU's tasks and refrain from any measure which could jeopardize the attainment of the EU's objectives.[19] This Treaty obligation can be used as part of the foundation for more discrete legal obligations, as exemplified by its deployment in the jurisprudence on state liability in damages.[20] It is, however, integral to this second vision that Member State political accountability is not exhausted by the legal dimension to the principle of sincere cooperation. It also has a distinctly political dimension that is expressive most fundamentally of the positive side of the maxim *pacta sunt servanda*, irrespective of whether it is capable of being embodied in a legally enforceable norm.[21] Thus the principle of sincere cooperation could provide the basis for an obligation of political good faith engagement by Member States in ensuring that Treaty obligations are fulfilled efficaciously; the injunction on Member States to take any appropriate measure to ensure fulfilment of Treaty obligations could generate a political obligation on states to be proactive in thinking about the best way to achieve Treaty imperatives; and the duty to refrain from behaviour that could jeopardize attainment of EU objectives could provide the foundation for a political obligation not to offload blame to the EU when this is unwarranted.

---

[18] Art 4(3) TEU.   [19] Art 4(3) TEU.

[20] Cases C-6 and 9/90 *Francovich and Bonifaci v Italy* [1991] ECR I-5357.

[21] What has been termed here the positive side of *pacta sunt servanda* may have legal implications. The point being made here is that even if this is not so there may still be the foundations for political obligation and political accountability.

Some may well disagree with this broader formulation of state political accountability, but that is equally true of the narrower formulation. What is important is that the alternatives are placed on the table and openly assessed, rather than conclusions being drawn from assumptions that are often implicit and untested.

III. Legal Accountability

There are chapters of this Handbook dealing with judicial review and other related legal concepts.[22] Discussion of law is nonetheless necessary here, because it is an important facet of accountability, and interrelates with the political and financial dimensions of accountability. The focus will perforce be on foundational precepts, not detail. Three such precepts are apposite for the present analysis: availability of judicial review, access to judicial review, and monetary relief. Legality review and damages actions are two complementary methods of securing legal accountability within any legal system. These precepts will be considered in relation to the EU and Member States.

1. EU Legal Accountability: Foundational Precepts

(a) Legality

It is fitting to begin with the availability of judicial review, since this is clearly central to legal accountability. From the outset, the Community fared well in this regard, insofar as Article 173 EEC made express provision for judicial oversight by the European Court of Justice (ECJ), and post the Single European Act 1986 by the Court of First Instance (CFI). The Lisbon Treaty made further changes in Article 263 TFEU, formally rendering EU bodies, offices, and agencies amenable to judicial review in relation to acts intended to produce legal effects vis-à-vis third parties.

The CFI had however already filled this gap in the *Sogelma* case.[23] The applicant sought judicial review of a decision by the European Agency for Reconstruction, which claimed that it was not susceptible to review under Article 230 EC, since agencies were not listed in Article 230(1). The CFI acknowledged this, but held that

---

[22] See in particular the chapters by Arnull and Leczykiewicz.
[23] Case T-411/06 Sogelma—Societá generale lavori manutenzioni appalti Srl v European Agency for Reconstruction (AER) [2008] ECR II-2771. See also, Case C-15/00 Commission v EIB [2003] ECR I-7281, para 75; Case C-370/89 SGEEM and Etroy v EIB [1992] ECR I-6211, paras 15–16.

the Agency was nonetheless subject to judicial review, drawing on the principle in *Les Verts*[24] to the effect that the Community was based on the rule of law and therefore that a direct action should be available against all measures adopted by the institutions intended to have legal effects, including in that case the European Parliament, even though it was not at the time listed as amenable to review under Article 173 EEC. The CFI reasoned by analogy and held that 'the situation of Community bodies endowed with the power to take measures intended to produce legal effects vis-à-vis third parties is identical to the situation which led to the *Les Verts* judgment: it cannot be acceptable, in a Community based on the rule of law, that such acts escape judicial review'.[25] The decision represented an example of teleological judicial reasoning in anticipation of Treaty amendment.

The decision also avoided what would have been an unwarranted asymmetry between the reviewability of national agencies applying EU law and EU agencies themselves. National agencies applying EU law are indirectly reviewable through Article 267 TFEU, and it would therefore have been very odd if EU agencies were not also subject to judicial review. National regulatory agencies are commonly integral to EU administration, since shared administration is the standard method of policy delivery in areas as diverse as agriculture, customs, the structural funds, telecommunications, and utilities regulation.[26] It will be the national agency, using that term in a broad sense, that is responsible for delivery of EU policy. A claimant can argue that a national regulatory agency charged with applying EU regulations at national level has misinterpreted the relevant Union provisions and hence that its decision should be set aside. A national court can make a reference under Article 267 TFEU if it feels this is necessary, or it may alternatively decide the matter without the need for a reference if, for example, there is existing case law.

(b) Access

If the amenability of EU institutions to judicial review is one foundational precept of legal accountability, access to judicial review by aggrieved individuals is another. The EU courts have however been considerably less willing to exercise creativity in relation to standing, which prior to the Lisbon Treaty reforms was regulated by Article 230(4) EC. The ECJ's oft-repeated statement that the Treaties provided a complete set of legal protection through the combination of direct and indirect challenge, such that there was no pressing need for reform of the standing rules, was repeatedly criticized.[27] The ECJ was equally insistent that any such reform was

---

[24] Case 294/83 *Les Verts v Parliament* [1986] ECR 1339, para 23.

[25] *Les Verts* (n 24) para 37.   [26] Paul Craig, *EU Administrative Law* (2nd ed, 2012) Ch 4.

[27] See eg Case C-50/00 P *Unión de Pequeños Agricultores v Council* [2002] ECR I-6677, AG Jacobs; Anthony Arnull, 'Private Applicants and the Action for Annulment under Article 173 of the EC Treaty' (1995) 32 *Common Market Law Review* 7; Paul Craig, 'Standing, Rights and the Structure of Legal Argument' (2003) 9 *European Public Law* 493; Takis Tridimas and Sarah Poli, '*Locus Standi*

beyond the purview of legitimate judicial interpretation and would have to come through Treaty amendment.[28] This reasoning was unconvincing, since the wording of Article 230(4) could clearly accommodate an interpretation of the term 'individual concern' other than that given in *Plaumann*.[29] This conclusion concerning the limits of judicial interpretive capacity was, moreover, difficult to sustain, given the judicial approach to other provisions in the very same Treaty article. It was, after all, the ECJ that engaged in creative Treaty interpretation as to who can sue and can be sued within the confines of Article 230 EC.

The reasoning in such cases followed the same pattern. There was open recognition that the Treaty had not, at the time, provided for the relevant capacity to sue or be sued. The ECJ and CFI felt that it was legitimate to fill this gap by resort to normative principle. In the case of the European Parliament's capacity to defend its prerogatives, the ECJ's reasoning was premised on institutional balance, the role afforded to the European Parliament in the legislative process, and the fact that this could not be adequately protected unless it was given the ability to bring an action in its own name.[30] In relation to the case law rendering the European Parliament and agencies susceptible to judicial review, it was the rule of law that provided the meta-principle driving the legal reasoning, the ECJ and CFI concluding that it would be inconsistent with a Community based on the rule of law for there to be institutions that were not amenable to judicial review.[31] If resort to background normative principle were legitimate in relation to creative construction of Article 230(1)–(3), it was unclear as to why this should not also be so in relation to Article 230(4). It cannot plausibly be maintained that 'more' was required to transform Article 230(4) than Articles 230(1)–(3). This does not withstand examination, given that more judicial creativity was needed in relation to Article 230(1)–(3) than in relation to Article 230(4), the latter being capable of being read in a variety of ways. The ECJ nonetheless favoured a narrow reading and held that any change would have to be by way of Treaty amendment, refusing to have recourse to background normative precepts concerning access to justice that could have been used to broaden the construction of individual concern.

(c) *Damages*

The ECJ was, by way of contrast, willing to exercise considerable creativity in relation to the third foundational precept relating to legal accountability, viz that concerning the criteria for damages liability. This is unsurprising given that

under Article 230(4): The Return of Euridice?' in Anthony Arnull, Piet Eeckhout, and Takis Tridimas (eds), *Continuity and Change in EU Law: Essays in Honour of Sir Francis Jacobs* (2008) Ch 5.

[28] *Unión de Pequeños Agricultores* (n 27) paras 44–45.
[29] Case 25/62 *Plaumann & Co v Commission* [1963] ECR 95.
[30] Case C–70/88 *European Parliament v Council* [1990] ECR I–2041.
[31] Case 294/83 *'Les Verts'* (n 24); Case T-411/06 *Sogelma* (n 23).

Article 215(2) EEC presented the ECJ with a clean slate on which to craft principles of non-contractual liability, stating only that these should be devised in accordance with the general principles common to the laws of the Member States. Notwithstanding the fact that some prominent Member States regarded damages liability as flowing from a finding of illegality, the ECJ nonetheless crafted a more limited test for recovery in cases where the political institutions made discretionary determinations, requiring the claimant to show that a sufficiently flagrant violation of a superior rule of law for the protection of the individual has occurred.[32] The concept of a superior rule of law was itself interpreted in various ways, on some occasions connoting 'important', on others being equated with a more formalistic conception of one rule being hierarchically superior to another. The principal hurdle to recovery in the early case law was the difficulty of proving a 'flagrant violation', which required the claimant to show that the loss was sufficiently serious[33] and also that the breach itself was serious, recovery on occasion being denied because the claimant could not show that the institutional error verged on the arbitrary.[34]

The test is now interpreted less restrictively, although it is still not easy to win. The major shift came in *Bergaderm*.[35] When considering state liability in damages, the ECJ in *Brasserie du Pêcheur/Factortame*[36] held that the test should not be different from that used to determine the EU's liability under Article 340(2) TFEU. This cross-fertilization between the test for the EU's damages liability and that of the Member States was carried further in *Bergaderm*, where the ECJ completed the circle by explicitly drawing on the factors mentioned in *Brasserie du Pecheur/Factortame* to determine the meaning of flagrant violation for the purposes of liability under Article 340(2). Thus in *Bergaderm*, the ECJ held that the rules for liability under Article 340(2) take account, as do those in relation to state liability in damages, of 'the complexity of situations to be regulated, difficulties in the application or interpretation of the texts and, more particularly, the margin of discretion available to the author of the act in question'.[37] It affirmed that the test for damages liability was in general the same irrespective of whether the Union or the Member State inflicted the loss: the rule of law infringed must be intended to confer rights on individuals; there must be a sufficiently serious breach; and there had to be a direct causal link between the breach and the damage. This means

---

[32] Case 5/71 *Aktien-Zuckerfabrik Schöppenstedt v Council* [1971] ECR 975, para 11; Case C-352/98 P *Laboratoires Pharmaceutiques Bergaderm SA and Goupil v Commission* [2000] ECR I-5291, para 46; Case C-472/00 P *Commission v Fresh Marine A/S* [2003] ECR I-7541, para 27.

[33] Cases 83, 94/76, 4, 15, and 40/77 *Bayerische HNL Vermehrungsbetriebe GmbH & Co KG v Council and Commission* [1978] ECR 1209.

[34] Cases 116 and 124/77 *Amylum NV and Tunnel Refineries Ltd v Council and Commission* [1979] ECR 3497, para 19.

[35] *Laboratoires Pharmaceutiques Bergaderm* (n 32).

[36] Cases C–46 and 48/93 *Brasserie du Pêcheur SA v Germany; R v Secretary of State for Transport, ex p Factortame Ltd* [1996] ECR I–1029.

[37] *Laboratoires Pharmaceutiques Bergaderm* (n 32) para 40.

that under Article 340(2), the seriousness of the breach will be dependent upon factors articulated in the case law on state liability, such as the relative clarity of the rule which has been breached; the measure of discretion left to the relevant authorities; whether the error of law was excusable or not; and whether the breach was intentional or voluntary. Where the Member State or the EU institution has only considerably reduced, or even no discretion, the mere infringement of EU law may be sufficient to establish the sufficiently serious breach. The decisive issue for the purposes of damages liability is not the individual or general nature of the act adopted, but the discretion available to the institution when it was adopted.

2. Member State Legal Accountability: Foundational Precepts

(a) Legality

Member States have been amenable to judicial oversight since the outset of the Community legal order, even though this might not have been so readily foreseen by the Treaty framers. The key building blocks in this respect were direct effect, supremacy, and the preliminary ruling procedure. The latter is justly recognized as the jewel in the crown of the EU courts' jurisdictional regime. It constitutes the procedural mechanism through which direct effect and supremacy take effect in the national legal order.[38] The very existence of this procedure was part of the justificatory argument for the existence of direct effect, the Court opining that the 'the task assigned to the Court of Justice under Article 177, the object of which is to secure uniform interpretation of the Treaty by national courts and tribunals, confirms that the states have acknowledged that Community law has an authority which can be invoked by their nationals before those courts and tribunals'.[39] This argument is not absolutely secure in terms of strict logic, but it nonetheless has considerable force, since if the preliminary ruling procedure could not be invoked by an individual then it would mean that it was only available to a public entity, and there is nothing in its wording to indicate that this should be so.

It is therefore unsurprising that the ECJ should choose to play this 'winning card' once again, when constructing the argument for extension of direct effect to Directives. The justificatory argument cast in terms of rendering Directives more effective if they could be enforced by private individuals through direct effect was reinforced by the Court emphasizing the textual generality of Article 177 EEC.

---

[38] Federico Mancini and David Keeling, 'From *CILFIT* to *ERT*: The Constitutional Challenge Facing the European Court' (1991) 11 *Yearbook of European Law* 1, 2–3.

[39] Case 26/62 NV *Algemene Transporten Expeditie Onderneming van Gend en Loos v Nederlandse Administratie der Belastingen* [1963] ECR 1.

It held that: 'Article 177, which empowers national courts to refer to the Court questions concerning the validity and interpretation of all acts of the Community institutions, without distinction, implies furthermore that these acts may be invoked by individuals in the national courts.[40]

Direct effect, whereby individuals could bring actions in their own names in national courts to vindicate rights secured by the Treaty, Regulations, Directives, or Decisions, constituted private enforcement of EU law. It was used to supplement public enforcement, which was the method expressly provided in Article 169 EEC, whereby Member States were to be rendered legally accountable for breach of Community law by an action brought by the Commission. While this public enforcement was innovative it nonetheless had limitations, which were alleviated or resolved through private enforcement via direct effect. Thus public enforcement placed the entire burden on the Commission, since one Member State rarely sued another under Article 170 EEC, whereas private actions through direct effect, complemented the Commission's role by sanctioning claims brought by individuals in their own capacity; public enforcement is only available against a Member State, whereas private enforcement through direct effect can be used vertically or horizontally; and the remedial regime attendant on public enforcement was weak for the first thirty-plus years of the Community's existence, whereas the remedies that could be secured via direct effect in national courts were significantly stronger, more especially because the ECJ, while leaving some choice to the national courts, made it clear that the remedy must provide an effective protection for the right in question, which often meant that national courts should, in effect, treat as done what ought to be done. Thus if, for example, a state imposed a tariff inconsistent with EU law and levied money pursuant thereto, then the national court should treat the tariff as invalid and return the money.

The preliminary ruling procedure was moreover the mechanism through which the supremacy doctrine was 'nationalized',[41] since its very structure meant that the case began and ended in the national courts. The principle that any national court must be able to invoke the supremacy of EU law, which could not be the exclusive preserve of a national constitutional court, was an equally important part of this 'nationalization' process.[42] This principle meant that the supremacy of EU law penetrated throughout the national legal system and was to be applied by all national courts in cases that fell within their jurisdiction. This was important in practical terms, obviating the need for an individual to fight a case to the national Constitutional Court in order to invoke the full force of EU law, since the national court seised of the dispute could itself refuse to apply provisions of national law

[40] Case 41/74 *Van Duyn v Home Office* [1974] ECR 1337, para 12.
[41] Case 6/64 *Costa v ENEL* [1964] ECR 585.
[42] Case 106/77 *Amministrazione delle Finanze dello Stato v Simmenthal SpA* [1978] ECR 629.

that conflicted with EU law.[43] It was also important in more 'political terms', since it meant that the effect of EU law within a national legal order could not be shaped solely by the predisposition of the top court to the reception of EU law.

(b) Access

It is important to disaggregate two different issues when thinking about legal accountability and access via Article 267 TFEU.

It clearly provides a broad gateway through which individuals can vindicate their rights against the Member States. Direct effect is liberally construed by the EU courts, with the consequence that a broad group of people will be regarded as having rights flowing from a provision of EU law, and any such person can seek a reference for a preliminary ruling where he or she feels that the national government has failed to comply with the requirements of EU law.

Article 267 clearly also provides a mechanism for indirect challenges to the validity of EU norms where non-privileged applicants cannot satisfy the standing criteria under Article 263 TFEU. Here the picture on access is more nuanced, since the individual who seeks to challenge EU law in this manner faced the hurdles charted most authoritatively by AG Jacobs.[44] There was, moreover, a perverse institutional consequence of the restrictive standing rules limiting access under Article 263, insofar as it compelled applicants to use Article 267, since this further overburdened the ECJ with cases that would otherwise have been heard by the General Court in a direct action.

(c) Damages

The EU courts were at the forefront of the third facet of legal accountability insofar as it relates to Member States, damages liability, via the seminal decision in *Francovich*.[45] The ECJ's reasoning was grounded in conceptions of effectiveness and good faith enforcement of EU law. It held that although the Directive lacked sufficient precision to be directly effective, it was nevertheless intended to confer rights on individuals, and stated that 'the full effectiveness of Community rules would be impaired and the protection of the rights which they grant would be weakened if individuals were unable to obtain compensation when their rights are infringed by a breach of Community law for which a Member State can be held responsible'.[46] The principle of state monetary liability was said to be inherent in the system of the Treaty,[47] and grounded also in what was Article 10 EC, requiring

---

[43] See eg Case C-314/08 *Krzysztof Filipiak v Dyrektor Izby Skarbowej w Poznaniu* [2009] ECR I-11049; Cases C-188 and C-189/10 *Melki and Abdeli* [2010] ECR I-5667.

[44] *Unión de Pequeños Agricultores* (n 27).

[45] Cases C–6/90 and C–9/90 *Francovich and Bonifaci v Italy* [1991] ECR I–5357.

[46] Cases C–6/90 and C–9/90 *Francovich and Bonifaci* (n 45) para 33.

[47] Cases C–6/90 and C–9/90 *Francovich and Bonifaci* (n 45) para 35.

Member States to take all appropriate measures to ensure fulfilment of their EU obligations, including 'the obligation to nullify the unlawful consequences[48] of a breach of EU law.

It was left to the ECJ in *Brasserie du Pêcheur/Factortame*[49] to develop the criteria for state liability, emphasizing that the right to reparation was a corollary of direct effect and that liability could be imposed irrespective of which state organ was responsible for the breach: the legislature, the executive, or the judiciary. The Court held that the conditions for state liability should cohere with the Article 340 TFEU case law, since the criteria for protection should not vary depending on whether a national authority or an EU institution was responsible for the breach. The rule of law infringed must therefore have been intended to confer rights on individuals, the breach of this rule of law must have been sufficiently serious, and there had to be a causal link between the breach and the subsequent damage. The finding of serious breach turned on whether the Member State had manifestly and gravely disregarded the limits of its discretion, in relation to which the following factors would be relevant: the clarity and precision of the rule breached; the measure of discretion left by the rule to the national or EU authorities; whether the breach and consequential damage were intentional or voluntary; whether any error of law was excusable or inexcusable; whether the position adopted by an EU institution contributed to the act or omission causing loss committed by the national authorities; and whether on the facts the national measures had been adopted or retained contrary to EU law. A breach of EU law would be sufficiently serious where the state persisted in its behaviour, notwithstanding an ECJ judgment finding an infringement, or where there was settled ECJ case law from which it was clear that the Member State action was in breach of EU law.

IV. FINANCIAL ACCOUNTABILITY

The discussion thus far has been concerned with central precepts of political and legal accountability. The EU's institutional history has however been markedly shaped by concerns with financial accountability, which led to the fall of the Santer Commission and subsequent reform. The subsequent discussion will be informed by the same sense of accountability as the earlier analysis.

---

[48] Cases C–6/90 and C–9/90 *Francovich and Bonifaci* (n 45) para 36.
[49] Cases C–46 and 48/93 *Brasserie du Pêcheur SA v Germany, R v Secretary of State for Transport, ex p Factortame Ltd* [1996] ECR I-1029.

There are two dimensions of financial accountability that are especially interesting. There is the issue as to the optimal way to secure EU financial accountability for the projects and expenditure that it undertakes. Thinking in this respect has evolved considerably since the inception of the EEC, with the major change occurring at the beginning of the new millennium. There is also a second dimension to financial accountability, which is the optimal way to ensure that Member States are financially accountable for the very considerable sums of money that they disburse in pursuit of EU programmes, in particular those undertaken through shared administration. It is significant in this respect that Article 325 TFEU imposes obligations on both the EU and Member States to combat fraud that affects the financial interests of the EU, and to cooperate when doing so.

1. EU Financial Accountability: Crisis and Reform

There had been concern throughout the 1980s and 1990s about fraud and mismanagement, particularly in the context of the Common Agricultural Policy, which consumed such a large part of the Community budget. This culminated in 1999 in the setting up of a Committee of Independent Experts convened by the European Parliament and the Commission.[50] Its first report found instances of mismanagement by the Commission and criticized it for failing to take responsibility for the errors. This had the dramatic consequence that the Santer Commission resigned en bloc, which some might regard as 'jumping' before it was 'pushed'.[51] The Committee produced a more far-reaching report six months later,[52] which examined in greater depth the causes of the malaise uncovered in its initial inquiry.

Romano Prodi, the new President of the Commission, lost no time in introducing reforms designed to restore faith in the Commission, which included a new Code of Conduct for Commissioners,[53] and new Commission Rules of Procedure.[54] These initiatives were followed by the establishment in October 1999 of the Task Force for Administrative Reform (TFRA) for which Neil Kinnock was given responsibility. This led to an important White Paper on Commission reform,[55] which was heavily influenced by the Second Report of the Committee of Independent Experts.

---

[50] Committee of Independent Experts, First Report on Allegations regarding Fraud, Mismanagement and Nepotism in the European Commission (15 March 1999).

[51] Paul Craig, 'The Fall and Renewal of the Commission: Accountability, Contract and Administrative Organisation' (2000) 6 *European Law Journal* 98.

[52] Committee of Independent Experts, Second Report on Reform of the Commission, Analysis of Current Practice and Proposals for Tackling Mismanagement, Irregularities and Fraud (10 September 1999).

[53] *Formation of the New Commission*, 12 July 1999.

[54] *Operation of the Commission*, 12 July 1999.

[55] Reforming the Commission, COM (2000) 200.

A central theme of the White Paper was that the Commission should concentrate more on core functions such as policy conception, political initiative, and enforcing Community law, with the execution of Community programmes undertaken by other bodies, albeit under the overall control of the Commission.[56] The modern Commission should be independent, responsible, accountable, efficient, and transparent.[57] This entailed the efficient use of resources, human resources policy, and the overhaul of financial management, the last of which is of particular importance for the present discussion.

The Committee of Independent Experts was critical of the regime for financial management. The authorization of expenditure and collection of revenue were both in the hands of the Financial Controller of each EU institution, who gave the 'visa' authorizing the expenditure, and collected the revenue.[58] There was also a separation of function between the authorizing officer and the accounting officer. The former entered into the financial commitments, subject to the grant of a 'visa' by the Financial Controller, and the latter actually carried out the relevant operation. The 'visa' system was designed to ensure that proposals for expenditure were in conformity with the appropriate rules. It was not however effective, and many items of expenditure for which a visa had been granted were later found to be illegal. The system displaced responsibility for financial regularity from the person managing the expenditure onto the person approving it, with the consequence that no-one was ultimately responsible.

The Committee recommended that the authorizing officer should bear responsibility for proposals which he authorized, as opposed to validation by a separate, central authority of the kind hitherto undertaken by the Financial Controller.[59] It also favoured creation of an independent Internal Audit Service, which should report directly to the President of the Commission.[60]

The White Paper adopted this reasoning. It recognized that the centralized 'visa' system of control had not worked and accepted that the position of the Financial Controller, who was responsible for the *ex ante* visa, and the *ex post* audit, could give rise to a conflict of interest.[61] Financial responsibility should be allocated to authorizing officers within departments. There would in addition be an Internal Audit Service and each department would have its own specialized audit capability.

---

[56] Reforming the Commission (n 55) Part I, 2.

[57] Reforming the Commission (n 55) Part I, 3–4.

[58] Financial Regulation of 21 December 1977 applicable to the general budget of the European Communities [1977] OJ L356/1, Art 24.

[59] Committee of Independent Experts, Second Report (n 52) Vol 1, paras 4.7, 4.18.1.

[60] Committee of Independent Experts, Second Report (n 52) Vol 1, paras 4.13, 4.18.2.

[61] Reforming the Commission (n 55) Part I, 17.

2. EU Financial Accountability: The Financial Regulation

The reforms in the White Paper were carried through by an admixture of formal legislation, soft law, and internal administrative reform.[62] Many of the precepts concerning financial accountability were embodied in a new Financial Regulation in 2002. The previous Financial Regulation dated from 1977.[63] Regulation 1605/2002[64] was a complete overhaul of the previous regime, and was extended to agencies.[65] It provided a legal framework for EU administration, including rules on financial accountability that sought to effectuate the proposals in the White Paper. There were also significant organizational changes as a result of the Financial Regulation. An Independent Internal Audit Service[66] was established in July 2001, and there are specialized audit services within each Directorate General, which report directly to the Director General or head of department.[67] Regulation 1605/2002 has now been replaced by Regulation 966/2012, which made some amendments to the earlier provision and updated it in the light of the Lisbon Treaty.[68]

The Financial Regulations of 2002 and 2012 gave legal force to the ideas advanced by the Committee of Independent Experts and the Commission White Paper. The duties of the authorizing officer and the accounting officer are separated.[69] The latter is responsible for payments, collection of revenue, keeping the accounts, and the like.[70] It is however the authorizing officer that is central to the whole scheme. Each institution 'performs' the duties of authorizing officer.[71] The authorizing officer to whom power has been delegated makes the budget and legal commitments, validates expenditure, and authorizes payments.[72] The provisions on expenditure reinforce the centrality of the authorizing officer. Every item of expenditure must

---

[62] Progress Review of Reform, COM(2003) 40 final; Completing the Reform Mandate: Progress Report and Measures to be Implemented in 2004, COM(2004) 93 final; Paul Craig, *EU Administrative Law*, (2nd ed, 2012) Ch 2.

[63] Financial Regulation of 21 December 1977 Applicable to the General Budget of the European Communities [1977] OJ L356/1.

[64] Council Regulation (EC, Euratom) 1605/2002 of 25 June 2002 on the Financial Regulation applicable to the general budget of the European Communities [2002] OJ L248/1, as amended by Council Reg 1995/2006 [2006] OJ L390/1.

[65] Commission Delegated Reg (EU) No 1271/2013 of 30 September 2013 on the framework financial regulation for the bodies referred to in Art 208 of Regulation (EU, Euratom) No 966/2012 of the European Parliament and of the Council [2013] OJ L328/42, replacing Commission Reg (EC, Euratom) 2343/2002 [2002] OJ L357/72.

[66] http://ec.europa.eu/dgs/internal_audit/index_en.htm.

[67] http://ec.europa.eu/budget/explained/reports_control/audits/audits_en.cfm.

[68] Reg (EU, Euratom) No 966/2012 of the European Parliament and of the Council of 25 October 2012 on the financial rules applicable to the general budget of the Union and repealing Council Regulation (EC, Euratom) No 1605/2002 [2012] OJ L291/1.

[69] Reg 966/2012 (n 68) Art 64.   [70] Reg 966/2012 (n 68) Art 68.

[71] Reg 966/2012 (n 68) Art 65(1).   [72] Reg 966/2012 (n 68) Art 66(3).

be committed, validated, authorized, and paid.[73] The budget commitment consists of making the appropriation necessary to cover a legal commitment. The legal commitment is the act whereby the authorizing officer enters into an obligation to third parties, which results in expenditure being charged to the budget. The same authorizing officer undertakes the budget and legal commitment,[74] and the former must precede the latter.[75] It is for the authorizing officer, when adopting a budget commitment, to ensure that the appropriations are available, that the expenditure conforms to the relevant legal provisions, and that the principles of sound financial management are complied with.[76] It is the authorizing officer that is responsible for validation of expenditure: the creditor's entitlement to payment, and the conditions on which it is due.[77] The onus is also on the authorizing officer to authorize the expenditure through the issuance of a payment order for expenditure that has been validated.[78] These rules are designed to 'give authorizing officers the entire responsibility for the internal controls in their departments and for the financial decisions they take in the exercise of their functions'.[79]

3. Member State Financial Accountability: Rules and Incentives

It is common to regard issues of accountability as pertaining solely or principally to the EU institutions. This is mistaken. Member States have responsibility, direct and indirect, for the disbursement of large amounts of EU funding. There must therefore be effective mechanisms to ensure that the Member States remain accountable in this respect.

It is necessary to understand the 'back story' in order to appreciate the new provisions introduced by Regulation 966/2012. The legislative history of much shared administration in areas such as the Common Agricultural Policy and the Structural Funds is explicable in terms of the EU seeking improvements in the ways that Member States disbursed EU funds through shared administration.[80] This often took the form of requirements directed towards audit and control at national level, with increasingly tough obligations imposed on national administrations to reduce the fraud oft attested to by the Court of Auditors. This Court kept pressure on the EU institutions by refusing to attest that Community accounts were satisfactory when it was dissatisfied with the financial control mechanisms,

---

[73] Reg 966/2012 (n 68) Art 84(1).   [74] Reg 966/2012 (n 68) Art 85(1).
[75] Reg 966/2012 (n 68) Art 86(1).   [76] Reg 966/2012 (n 68) Art 87.
[77] Reg 966/2012 (n 68) Art 88.   [78] Reg 966/2012 (n 68) Art 89.
[79] Proposal for a Council Regulation on the Financial Regulation Applicable to the Reg 966/2012 (n 68) Budget of the EC, COM (2000) 461 final, Explanatory Memorandum, 17.
[80] Craig (n 62) Ch 4.

and also published special reports that subjected a particular sectoral area to a harsh spotlight in terms of financial accountability broadly conceived. There was, however, no general control and audit obligation. It existed only by and through sector-specific legislation. The need for tougher obligations was highlighted by the Committee of Independent Experts, which noted that even where formal law imposed obligations on Member States they were often flouted.

Regulation 966/2012 made significant changes in this respect, by introducing a new transversal obligation on Member States when they disburse the EU budget in the context of shared administration. Recital 25 stated the need for a more general control and audit obligation, which would set out a coherent framework for all policy areas subject to shared management, but which could be modified where needed in sector-specific provisions. The substance of the new obligation is contained in Article 59(2), which provides that 'when executing tasks relating to the implementation of the budget, Member States shall take all the necessary measures, including legislative, regulatory and administrative measures, to protect the Union's financial interests'. Article 59 embodies a two-pronged approach.

It is for the Member States to prevent, detect, and correct irregularities and fraud.[81] Article 59(2) stipulates that in order to protect the EU's financial interests, Member States shall, while respecting proportionality, 'and in compliance with this Article, and the relevant sector-specific rules, carry out ex ante and ex post controls including, where appropriate, on-the-spot checks on representative and/or risk-based samples of transactions'. The Member States must recover funds unduly paid, and impose effective, dissuasive, and proportionate penalties where provided for in sector-specific rules and in specific provisions in national legislation.

It is also for the Member States to ensure that actions financed from the budget are implemented correctly and effectively, and in accordance with applicable sector-specific rules to designate national supervisory bodies responsible for the management and control of Union funds.[82] If audit and control results show that the designated bodies no longer comply with the criteria in the sector-specific rules, Member States shall take the measures necessary to ensure that these deficiencies are remedied. The role played by such designated bodies is addressed in more detail in Article 59(4). Thus they must set up and ensure the functioning of an effective and efficient internal control system; use an accounting system that provides accurate, complete, and reliable information in a timely manner; provide the information required under Article 59(5); and ensure publication of information on recipients of payments. Article 59(5) further requires that designated bodies must provide the Commission in the following financial year with: their accounts on expenditure in execution of their tasks that was presented to the

---

[81] Reg 966/2012 (n 68) Art 59(2)(b).   [82] Reg 966/2012 (n 68) Art 59(2)(a).

Commission for reimbursement, including a declaration that the expenditure was used for its intended purpose, and that the requisite control systems were in place to give the necessary guarantees concerning the legality and regularity of the transactions; and an annual summary of the final audit reports and of controls carried out, including analysis of errors and weaknesses identified in systems, as well as corrective action taken or planned. These accounts must be verified by an independent audit body. It is then for the Commission to decide whether to accept the accounts, and it has power, where provided in sector-specific rules, to suspend payments.[83] The Commission is more generally charged with risk assessment of the management and control systems of Member States, in accordance with sector-specific rules.[84]

The changes made by Regulation 966/2012 in terms of Member State financial accountability are important. The establishment of a transversal obligation that is applicable to all instances of shared administration, but which can be adapted to the needs of sector-specific areas, ensures that basic precepts of good financial accounting are applicable across all areas, and that EU legislators do not have to rethink the issue afresh when they are drafting new legislation.

V. CONCLUSION

There will be no attempt to précis the preceding analysis. Suffice it to say the following. It is axiomatic that accountability is central to the legitimacy of any polity, and that is no less true of the EU than other forms of political organization. It is also axiomatic that accountability is to some extent always a 'work in progress', marked by new challenges and the need to learn from past mistakes. The challenges posed by securing political, legal, and financial accountability in an EU of 28 Member States are very considerable, and greater than those that exist within nation states even where they have a federal structure. It should also be acknowledged that the EU has been willing to admit mistakes and learn from them, as attested to by the reforms enacted in the wake of the resignation of the Santer Commission. The argument of this chapter has, however, been that we must also systematically consider the political, legal, and financial accountability of Member States as contracting parties within the EU, in order to gain a rounded picture of the subject of our inquiry.

---

[83] Reg 966/2012 (n 68) Art 59(6).   [84] Reg 966/2012 (n 68) Art 59(2).

BIBLIOGRAPHY

Anthony Arnull and Daniel Wincott (eds), *Accountability and Legitimacy in the European Union* (2002)

Vernon Bogdanor, *Legitimacy, Accountability and Democracy in the European Union* (2007)

Mark Bovens, 'Analysing and Assessing Accountability: A Conceptual Framework' (2007) *13 European Law Journal* 447

Mark Bovens, Deirdre Curtin, and Paul 't Hart (eds), *The Real World of EU Accountability: What Deficit?* (2010)

Madalina Busuioc, *European Agencies: Law and Practices of Accountability* (2013)

Deirdre Curtin, *Executive Power of the European Union. Law, Practices and the Living Constitution* (2009)

Elizabeth Fisher, 'The European Union in the Age of Accountability' (2004) *24 Oxford Journal of Legal Studies* 495

Andreas Follesdal and Simon Hix, 'Why there is a Democratic Deficit in the EU: A Response to Majone and Moravcsik' (2006) *44 Journal of Common Market Studies* 533

Sverker Gustavsson, Christer Karlsson, and Thomas Persson (eds), *The Illusion of Accountability in the European Union* (2009)

Carol Harlow, *Accountability in the European Union* (2002)

Andrew Moravcsik, 'In Defence of the "Democratic Deficit": Reassessing Legitimacy in the European Union' (2002) *40 Journal of Common Market Studies* 603

Richard Mulgan, *Holding Power to Account: Accountability in Modern Democracies* (2003)

Joseph Weiler, Ulrich Haltern, and Franz Mayer, 'European Democracy and its Critique' in J Hayward (ed), *The Crisis of Representation in Europe* (1995)

PART IV

THE ECONOMIC
CONSTITUTION
AND THE CITIZEN

CHAPTER 18

THE FREE MOVEMENT OF WORKERS IN THE TWENTY-FIRST CENTURY

ELEANOR SPAVENTA

THE free movement of workers is one of the cornerstones of the original European integration project: it pursued a variety of different, if interrelated, aims. It allowed for the efficient allocation of resources, by allowing labour to move from areas with high unemployment to areas of under-employment, which in turn enhanced the quality of life of its beneficiaries and the reduction in the welfare expenditure of the Member States; and creating new opportunities for business and workers alike allowing talent to move and employers to benefit from a workforce with more diverse skills and, at times (and crucially), a higher motivation to succeed. The free movement of workers also allowed individuals to expand their experience, opening up new opportunities as well as the markets. In order to make the right to move fully effective, the legislature and the Court ensured that workers would be treated primarily as individuals, rather than merely as agents of integration. For this reason, the legislative framework, interpreted generously by the Court, ensured that migrants would be treated fairly. This meant not only providing a right to equal treatment well beyond that usually afforded to immigrants, but also equipping the migrant worker with generous family rights, allowing them to have their families with them regardless of whether such family was formed before or after migration. The migrant worker also enjoyed full equal treatment in relation to most social

and tax advantages, even (and especially) when the income earned through economic activity fell below the minimum considered sufficient to survive. As a result,
part-time workers as well as low-earners are eligible for the same social protection
(from income support to housing benefits) that is afforded to the host state's own
nationals.

The European ambition in establishing the free movement of workers was (and
to a certain extent still is) great: it not only eliminated immigration restrictions
in the participating Member States, but it also deprived Member States of direct
control over fluctuations in their labour market, so that protectionist and ad hoc
policies could no longer be adopted at the expense of EU migrants. In this way,
one of the most effective instruments for sustaining employment during economic
downturns, the creation of jobs in the public sector or through public procurement
in the private sector, lost some of its attractiveness. On the other hand, the eradi-
cation of the barriers to migration amongst Member States means that whilst the
Member States cannot (by and large) adopt protectionist policies, individuals are
able to react to economic conditions and move accordingly.[1]

Up until the first big enlargement, migration was not at the centre of the political debate about the EU; if anything, the lack of migration raised concerns as to
the proper functioning of the internal market. However, the enlargement in 2004,
when ten new Member States joined the EU at once, had a more profound effect, if
not on migration patterns, certainly on the debate about migration.[2]

First of all, the paradigm of the 'fundamental freedom' was shaken to its core
by the transitional arrangements: here Member States were allowed, without
having to justify their decision in relation to any factual evidence,[3] to delay the
migration flow of workers from eight of the ten acceding countries.[4] The derogation from one of the cornerstones of European integration was (allegedly)

---

[1] Although intra-EU mobility remains very low and therefore the corrective effect of migration on
labour market conditions is equally very limited. See D. Holland and P. Paluchowski, 'Geographical
Labour Mobility in the Context of the Crisis' (ad hoc report prepared at the request of the European
Employment Observatory), June 2013, available at www.eu-employment-observatory.net/resources/
reports/ESDE-SynthesisPaper-June2013-Final.pdf. They conclude that 'free movement of workers
within the EU does not appear to be acting as a significant shock absorber against the widening
economic asymmetries between Core and Periphery within the EU' (page 20).

[2] For an interesting historical juxtaposition of migration from the East of Europe to the UK in
the aftermath of WWII, and then after enlargement, see L. McDowell, 'Old and New European
Economic Migrant: Whiteness and Managed Migration Policies' (2009) 35 *Journal of Ethnic and
Migration Studies* 19.

[3] It should be remembered that the first Eastern enlargement took place in times of economic
boom. The accession of Bulgaria and Romania took place in 2007, just before the start of the recession in 2008. Thus, even for Bulgaria and Romania, the transitional arrangements were prepared and
adopted in rosier economic circumstances.

[4] For a critical appraisal of this decision from an economic perspective, see Frigyes Ferdinand
Heinz and Melanie E. Ward-Warmedinger, 'Cross-Border Labour Mobility within an Enlarged EU'
(October 2006), *ECB Occasional Paper* No 52, available at SSRN http://ssrn.com/abstract=923371.

justified by the need to avoid serious disturbances in the labour markets of the existing Member States: after all the sheer scale of the enlargement coupled with the substantial difference in the economic conditions of the acceding Member States made this threat a very 'real' one.[5] And yet, it is important to bear in mind that only workers were prevented from moving: self-employed and non-economically active individuals could still move unhindered from new to 'old' Member States. The same arrangements were put into place for the accession of Romania and Bulgaria in 2007, an enlargement on a much lesser scale, and Croatia in 2013.[6]

Secondly, the economic crisis which erupted in 2008 led to a re-emergence of protectionist talk, at least in some Member States and most notably the United Kingdom. Here the anti-migration rhetoric has found fertile ground in the euro-sceptic roots of the country.

The combination of these factors, enlargement and economic crisis, have had a significant effect on the debate and practice surrounding the free movement of workers. Thus, whilst the legislative provisions have not changed much, what is changing is the reception of these provisions at national level, with an indication by at least two of the big Member States of a desire to tighten up their legislation so as to ensure that migrant workers are not treated more generously than need be.[7] It is important to note that this move towards a less generous (and more legalistic) treatment of the EU migrant seems not to be justified by recent data that suggests reliance by migrant workers (and non-workers) on welfare provision in the host State to be negligible.[8] This goes then to indicate that one of the cornerstones of EU integration has become fraught with controversy, so much so that it is now a legitimate target for political point scoring.

In this contribution, I will recall the main features of the free movement of workers regime and then focus on more problematic aspects, in particular on the workers who are excluded, such as unpaid workers and workers from acceding countries. I will then try to draw some conclusions as to what those exclusions tell us about EU integration.

---

[5] Whether there was a real 'threat' or rather a real 'fear' of impact on Western labour markets is debatable. *Ex post facto* reports seems to indicate the absence of a threat, see eg Dawn Holland, Tatiana Fic, Ana Rincon-Aznar, Lucy Strokes, and Pawel Paluchowski, *Labour Mobility within the EU—The Impact of Enlargement and the Functioning of The Transitional Arrangements,* (report on behalf of the European Social Affairs and Inclusion Directorate General of the European Commission), July 2011, available on ec.europa.eu/social/BlobServlet?docId=7191&langId=en. This study is particularly interesting as it also includes country-specific reports, including for the United Kingdom.

[6] See below Section III.2.   [7] See text and footnotes at the end of Section III.2.

[8] See L. Andor (Commissioner for Employment, Social Affairs and Inclusion), 'Labour Mobility in the EU—The Inconvenient Truth', Lecture at the University of Bristol delivered on 10 February 2014, Speech /14/115, available on http://europa.eu/rapid/press-release_SPEECH-14-115_en.htm.

I. The Free Movement of Workers: Who is Protected?

1. Workers

Article 45 TFEU, and the legislation adopted to give it effect,[9] guarantee freedom of movement for workers, as well as the right not to be discriminated against on grounds of nationality. It also provides for the ability of the Member States to impose limits justified on grounds of public policy, security and health; and for a general exemption for employment in the public sector. The Court has always given a broad and teleological interpretation to Article 45 TFEU. For this reason, it has clarified that the term 'worker' should be given a uniform European Union meaning,[10] and that a substantive, rather than formal, assessment should be carried out in order to determine whether someone is to be qualified as a worker. Accordingly, a worker is defined as someone who for a certain period of time performs services for and under the direction of someone else in return for remuneration.[11] The amount of remuneration is immaterial, provided that the economic activity is 'genuine and effective'.[12] As a result, part-time workers benefit from the Treaty freedom, and crucially, from equal access to social and tax advantages regardless of the amount earned and provided that their activity is not on such a small scale as to be purely 'marginal and ancillary'. If these conditions are satisfied, it is immaterial whether the worker draws on public funds to supplement her income[13]; or whether the worker works only a few hours a week.[14]

According to the case law, work is considered 'effective and genuine' only if the activity in question is capable of being regarded as forming part of the normal labour market: work that is undertaken as part of a social re-integration programme is normally not so considered.[15] On the other hand, the reason why a person has decided to take up employment is immaterial to her status as a worker—thus, for

---

[9] Dir 2004/38 on the right of the citizens of the Union and their family members to move and reside freely within the territory of the Member States [2004] OJ L 158/77; Regulation 883/2004 on the coordination of social security systems [2004] OJ L 166/1, implemented by Regulation 987/2009 {2009} OJ L 284/1; Reg 482/2011 on freedom of movement for workers [2011] L 141/1; Dir 2014/54 on measures facilitating the exercise of rights conferred on workers in the context of the freedom of movement for workers [2014] OJ L 128/8.

[10] Case 75/63 *Hoekstra* [1964] ECR 1771; Case 53/81 *Levin* [1982] ECR 1035.

[11] Case 66/85 *Lawrie-Blum* [1986] ECR 2121; in Case C-94/07 *Raccanelli* [2008] ECR I-5939, the Court has indicated that doctoral researchers might also be qualified as workers if the conditions of remuneration and subordination are satisfied.

[12] Case 53/81 *Levin* [1982] ECR 1035; case C-413/01 *Ninni-Orasche* [2003] ECR I-13187.

[13] Case 139/85 *Kempf* [1986] ECR 1741.   [14] Case C-357/89 *Raulin* [1992] ECR I-1027.

[15] Case C-456/02 *Trojani* [2004] ECR I-7573.

instance, it is irrelevant that the only reason that led a person to move and work in another Member State is to obtain a residence permit for her spouse[16]; or that a student might have taken up employment also so as to benefit from equal treatment in relation to maintenance aid for her studies.[17]

The concept of 'remuneration' is also given a fluid interpretation: it is not limited to a monetary transaction; rather it can take the form of a quid pro quo,[18] so that schemes whereby work is provided in exchange for board and lodging fall also within the scope of the free movement of workers provisions.[19] However, when work is done without remuneration of any kind, it does not fall within the protection of the Treaty. As we shall see in more detail below, this means, for instance, that work done within a religious organization is most likely to be covered by the Treaty, whilst work done on a voluntary basis is more likely to fall outside the scope of the free movement of workers provisions. Furthermore, the focus on remuneration, rather than on the economic value of the services provided, means that care and housework done within the family ambit is also not taken into account in European law.[20]

2. Workseekers

Rather more contested, at least politically,[21] is the situation concerning workseekers. Article 45 TFEU refers to the freedom of movement for *workers*, as well as the right to take up offers of employment *already made*; however, it does not mention the possibility of moving in order to secure a job.[22] Given the fact that the free movement rights would have been rather ineffective had individuals not been able

---

[16] Case C-109/01 *Akrich* [2003] ECR I-9607.

[17] Eg Case C-46/12 *L.N. v Styrelsen for Videregående Uddannelser og Uddannelsesstøtte*, judgment of 21 February 2013. It is unclear whether this ruling represents a rethinking of the obiter dictum in C-413/01 *Ninni-Orasche* [2003] ECR I-13187, where the Court indicated that taking up short-term employment with the sole aim of benefitting from student assistance in the host Member State might constitute an abuse of the right to free movement. In any case, if the work is purely marginal and ancillary, the Union citizen will not benefit from equal treatment in relation to maintenance grants; see Case 197/86 *Brown* [1988] ECR 3205.

[18] Case 196/87 *Steymann* [1988] ECR 6159.

[19] In relation to au pairs (in the context of the Turkey Association Agreement but of broader relevance), see Case C-294/06 *Payir and others* [2008] ECR I-203.

[20] See eg Louise Ackers, 'Citizenship, Migration and the Evaluation of Care in the European Union' (2004) 30 *Journal of Ethnic and Migration Studies* 373.

[21] See eg D. Cameron letter to the *The Daily Telegraph*, 15 March 2014, where he advocates 'the free movement to take up work, not free benefits'.

[22] That said, Article 5 of Reg 1612/68 [1968] OJ Sp. Ed. L257/2 p. 475 (now Article 5 Regulation 482/2011 on freedom of movement for workers [2011] L 141/1) provided that a national of a Member State *seeking* employment in the territory of another Member State was eligible to the same assistance as host nationals. On this point, see also Case C-292/89 *ex p Antonissen* [1991] ECR I-745, para 14.

to move in order to look for a job, the Court struck a compromise between the two conflicting interests: ensuring the full effectiveness of the Treaty whilst at the same time sheltering the welfare systems of the Member States from claims by those who were yet to secure employment. As a result, the Court originally held that workseekers enjoyed the right to move to another Member State to look for a job and stay there for a reasonable time,[23] but they did not enjoy a right to equal treatment in relation to social and tax advantages.[24]

With time, the exclusion of workseekers from the right to equal treatment had to be revisited in the light of the introduction of Union citizenship: given that in the rulings in *Martínez Sala* and *Grzelzyck*, the Court had found that migrant Union citizens benefited from a right not to be discriminated against on grounds of nationality,[25] it was difficult to justify a different regime for those who moved in search of a job. Accordingly, in *Collins*,[26] the Court brought its case law on workseekers into line with that on Union citizenship by declaring that Union citizens looking for employment in another Member State would benefit from the right not to be discriminated against in relation to all matters falling within the scope of the Treaty (including social advantages). For this reason, if a Member State restricts access to welfare benefits that facilitate access to the employment market, such as a jobseeker allowance, it must justify such a limitation as being pursuant to a public interest and choose the most proportionate and least restrictive means to do so. The Court then found that, at least in theory, a Member State is allowed to curtail eligibility to a job seeker allowance to ensure that there is a real link between workseeker and employment market. For this reason a minimum residence requirement was in principle justified.

Whilst the *Collins* case was pending, the institutions were in the process of negotiating the citizenship Directive (which was then adopted as Directive 2004/38).[27] Article 12(4) of Directive 2004/38, codifying the case law before *Collins*, provides that workseekers have a right to stay in the host country beyond the initial three months of unconditional residence bestowed on any Union citizen, provided that they are still looking for a job and have a genuine chance of securing employment. However, Article 24(2) of the same instrument provides that Member States are not obliged to confer entitlement to social assistance on workseekers. The ruling in *Collins* then seemed incompatible with the provisions of the Directive. In order to reconcile the two, in *Vatsouras*,[28] the Court found that the definition of social assistance should be interpreted narrowly so that benefits intended to facilitate access

---

[23]   Case C-292/89 *ex p Antonissen* [1991] ECR I-745.

[24]   Case 316/85 *Lebon* [1987] ECR 2811.

[25]   Case C-85/96 *Martínez Sala* [1998] ECR I-2691; Case C-184/99 *Grzelczyck* [2001] ECR I-6193.

[26]   Case C-138/02 *Collins* [2004] ECR I-2703.

[27]   Directive 2004/38 on the right of the citizens of the Union and their family members to move and reside freely within the territory of the Member States [2004] OJ L 158/77.

[28]   Joined Cases C-22 and C-23/08 *Vatsouras and Koupatantze* [2009] ECR I-4585.

to the labour market are not to be considered social assistance for the purposes of Article 24(2).[29] As a result, and provided the workseeker has a genuine link with the host employment market,[30] benefits which facilitate access to the labour market are available also to those who are looking for a job.

The fact that the Court did not overrule the ruling in *Collins* raises some interesting theoretical questions in relation to the debate about EU migration and access to benefits: whilst Article 24(2) could be tightened so as to explicitly exclude workseekers from *any* welfare benefit, as advocated in some quarters of the British political establishment, such a modification would do little without a change in the interpretation of Article 45 TFEU. If the latter protects workseekers and guarantees their equal treatment, the amendment of Directive 2004/38 would be redundant, indeed it would risk infringing the Treaty provisions.

3. Migration, Purely Internal Situations, and Family Rights

In order to be protected by the Treaty free movement of workers provisions, the claimant must establish some migration 'credentials'. Thus, a worker is always protected in the territory of a Member State of which she is not a national; moreover, workers are also protected when they return to the Member State of nationality after having moved,[31] and when they work in a Member State and reside in another one (frontier workers). In relation to the latter, the most complex questions relate to the allocation of welfare responsibility between Member State of residence and Member State of employment—those are determined mainly by Regulation 883/2004 on the coordination of social security systems.[32] In relation to returning workers, the Court has held that returning migrants must be treated at least as favourably as migrants from other Member States: this means, for instance, that they enjoy a general right not to be penalized because of their movement,[33] including in relation to experience

---

[29] A slightly different interpretation is given to 'social assistance' in the context of Article 7(1)(b) Dir 2004/38, in relation to the right of residence of economically inactive Union citizens. See Case C-140/12 *Brey*, judgment of 16 September 2013, nyr.

[30] See Case C-138/02 *Collins* [2004] ECR I-2703 and, more recently, Case C-367/11 *Prete* [2012] ECR I-0000.

[31] Case C-370/90 *Singh* [1992] ECR I-4265; Case C-419/92 *Scholz* [1994] ECR I-505; Case C-443/93 *Ioannis Vougioukas* [1995] ECR I-4033.

[32] [2004] OJ L166/1. On the difficult interaction between Reg 883/2004 (and its previous incarnation as Reg 1408/71 on the application of social security schemes to employed persons, to self-employed persons and to members of their families moving within the Community [1971] OJ L149/2) and Art 45 TFEU, see eg Case C-352/06 *Bosmann* [2008] ECR I-3827, and R Babayev, 'Exploring the fate of the *lex loci laboris* rule and its exclusive effect under Reg 883/2004: annotation to Case C-352/06 *Bosmann* [2008] ECR I-3827' (2011) 1 *European Journal of Social Law* 76. See generally Frans Pennings, *European Social Security Law,* (2010).

[33] Eg Case C-19/92 *Dieter Kraus* [1993] ECR I-1663.

acquired in another Member State.[34] It also, and more controversially, means that returning and frontier workers might enjoy family reunification rights against their Member State of origin.[35] It should be noted that those rights originate directly from the Treaty, since Directive 2004/38 cannot be invoked against the Member State of origin;[36] and that a link with a migratory element is always required so that purely internal situations are not protected by EU law.[37]

This said, it is fairly easy to establish an intra-EU element: the provision of services abroad, in a self-employed or employed capacity, is sufficient to obtain protection from the Treaty against one's own Member State.[38] In the case of *S and G* the Grand Chamber examined the case of two Dutch nationals who were claiming family rights in the Netherlands on the basis of the fact that they travelled to another Member State for work: Mr S only once a week; Mr G every day. The Court clarified that whilst the intra-Union element is established by frontier workers, in order to obtain residency rights for the family on the basis of the Treaty, the claimant has to show that refusal of such rights would entail an interference with her right to move.[39] The Court also acknowledged that the fact that the family member is taking care of the Union citizen's children might be a relevant consideration, but only insofar as the children are looked after by the spouse. The mere desirability of children being cared for by their grandparents is not in itself sufficient to have a dissuasive effect on the right to move.

The ruling in *S and G* sought to clarify, and possibly curtail, the effect of the prior ruling in *Carpenter*,[40] and yet, it demonstrates the aleatory nature of the Court's

---

[34] Eg Case C-419/92 *Scholz* [1994] ECR I-505; Case C-443/93 *Ioannis Vougioukas* [1995] ECR I-4033.

[35] See eg Case C-370/90 *Singh* [1992] ECR I-4265. The *Singh* ruling was confirmed, and explained, in Case C-456/12 *O and B*, judgment delivered on 12 March 2014, where the Court clarified that, pursuant to Article 21(1) TFEU (right to move of Union citizens), returning migrants should be treated, in relation to their families, exactly the same as migrants covered by Directive 2004/38. However, the Court added a caveat: it is only when the migrant has resided in the host State pursuant to Article 7 Directive 2004/38, beyond the initial three months and (presumably) having satisfied the conditions of economic activity or economic independence in the host country, that the refusal of the Member State of origin to grant residence rights to family members would be construed as a barrier to movement. In relation to frontier workers, see Case C-457/12 *S and G.*, judgment delivered 12 March 2014, discussed further below.

[36] Art 3(1) Dir 2004/38; see eg Case C-434/09 *McCarthy* [2011] ECR I-3375. In Case C-456/12 *O and B*, judgment of 12 March 2014, the Court held that Art 21 (1) TFEU requires the provisions of Dir 2004/38 concerning family rights to be applied by analogy to the returning migrant.

[37] Eg Case C-434/09 *McCarthy* [2011] ECR I-3375.

[38] Case C-60/00 *Carpenter* [2002] CR I-6279; see also Case C-109/01 *Akrich* [2003] ECR I-9607.

[39] As mentioned in n 35, in *O and B* the Court held that if the migrant has resided in another Member State satisfying the conditions set out in Art 7(1) Dir 2004/38, then an obstacle to movement will be presumed; see generally E Spaventa 'If only I could be a fly on that wall ... the ECJ, own nationals and their spouses, Annotation of Case C-456/12 *O v Minister voor Immigratie, Integratie en Asiel* and *Minister voor Immigratie, Integratie en Asiel v B* and Case C-457/12 *S v Minister voor Immigratie, Integratie en Asiel and Minister voor Immigratie, Integratie en Asiel v Si'* forthcoming CMLREv.

[40] It might be recalled that in that case Mr Carpenter, a British citizen residing in the UK and providing services in other Member States where he occasionally travelled, successfully argued that the

interpretation: after all, it is difficult to gauge the extent to which the refusal of a right to reside for a family member might deter Union citizens from exercising their right to move; rather, if anything, it might encourage them to transfer their residence abroad so as to gain full EU rights and be able to care more easily for their children.[41] The Court's ruling then entails a degree of legal fiction that might be considered regrettable not only because it makes the rules unpredictable but also because it leaves the door open to preconceptions about family structures and dynamics. For instance, the ruling in *S and G* seems to imply a premium for the parent carer that cannot but reinforce prejudices about the role of women within the family unit (would the working spouse of a frontier worker obtain residence rights?). Whilst it could be argued that both *Carpenter* and *S and G* are cases concerning the right to family life, rather than the right to move, and therefore the treatment of grandparents is necessarily different from that of parents or main carers, the gender implications of the rulings are disappointing. Furthermore, the same gender stereotyping is to be found in the *Dereci* ruling, in the context of Union citizenship, where the Court implied that the presence of fathers within the territory of the EU is merely 'desirable' and that a Union citizen's children would not leave the territory of the EU in order to be able to have closer links with their fathers.[42] In this way, once again the Court reinforces the traditional family paradigm where the mother is the main carer (emotionally and factually) and the father is the breadwinner, whose main role is to support the family financially rather than playing a crucial role in the children's upbringing.[43]

But the ruling in *S and G* also highlights, and originates from, another problem which plagues the free movement and citizenship case law: the inequality arising from the case law on purely internal situations. Here, the combined effect of the limited application of Directive 2004/38, which as mentioned above only applies in a country different from that of nationality,[44] and of national rules which can be very restrictive in relation to family reunification rights, give rise to discrimination against a State's own citizens which from the citizen's perspective might appear wholly irrational and unjust, if not altogether cruel. Cases like *Carpenter* and *S and G*

---

removal of his wife from the UK was a barrier to his freedom to provide services in that it was 'detrimental to their family life and, therefore, to the conditions under which Mr Carpenter exercises a fundamental freedom'. Since the free movement provisions were engaged, EU fundamental rights applied and the Court found that deportation would have been a disproportionate interference with the Carpenters' rights to family life.

[41] Advocate General Sharpston suggested in her Opinion in *O and B* and *S and G* that Article 45 TFEU should be interpreted as encompassing also a right not to be forced to move. The Court did not take on board this suggestion.

[42] Some other, rather random, assumptions were also made in Case C-86/12 *Alokpa*, 10 October 2013.

[43] It should be noted also that Art 13 (d) Dir 2004/38 provides that parents who have a right of access to a minor child have the right to reside in the host Member State.

[44] And in Case C-434/09 *McCarthy* [2011] ECR I-3375, the Court found that Dir 2004/38 does not apply to a citizen who has dual nationality and has never exercised her right to move.

then seem to seek to reduce this inequality; and yet it should be remembered that most Union citizens are static and no matter how generous the Court's interpretation of the intra-Union link needed to trigger the Treaty, still fall outside the scope and benefits granted by EU free movement law. Furthermore, *S and G* appear to reinforce the premium enjoyed by those who are economically active: in *Alokpa*,[45] the Court found that the third country national mother of EU children could not rely on the citizenship provisions to obtain the right to stay and work in the host country since it 'might be possible' for mother and children to go back to the children's country of nationality.[46]

II. The Right Not to be Discriminated Against and Barriers to Movement

It has been indicated above that workers and workseekers have a right to move and reside in any Member State. This right is unconditional, meaning that workers (and workseekers) do not have to satisfy any criterion besides establishing an economic link. As a result, they do not need comprehensive health insurance and sufficient resources.[47]

Workers enjoy a broad right to equal treatment so that they have equal access to almost all employment,[48] benefits, and welfare provision, as well as tax advantages. The scope of the equal treatment right has been very broadly interpreted so that direct as well as indirect advantages accruing to workers are covered by the prohibition on discrimination.[49] Article 45 TFEU can be invoked also by employers

---

[45] Case C-86/12 *Alokpa*, 10 October 2013.

[46] Cp Case C-200/02 *Chen* [2004] ECR I-9925, where the Chinese mother of a baby with Irish nationality, acquired by virtue of being born in Northern Ireland, and with no other link to Ireland or the EU, was granted residency rights in the UK in order to ensure the full effectiveness of the baby's EU citizenship. The two cases differ because in *Chen*, the claimants were wealthy and therefore automatically satisfied the conditions in Article 7 1(b) of Dir 2004/38. In *Alokpa*, the mother of the Union citizens children needed to work in order to sustain herself and her family. Whether this difference in treatment, where wealthy people are awarded more rights than those who need to work to earn their keep, is defensible is another matter.

[47] See Article 7(1) of Dir 2004/38 for the different types of residence.

[48] With the exception of employment in the 'public service' which has however been narrowly defined so as to cover only those posts that involve direct or indirect participation in powers conferred by public law and presume a 'special relationship of allegiance' to the State. See eg Case 149/79 *Commission v Belgium (no. 2)* [1980] ECR 3881; and more recently, see Case C-47/02 *Anker* [2003] ECR I-10447.

[49] Recently, see eg Case C-208/05 *ITC Innovative Technology Center GmbH v Bundesagentur für Arbeit* [2007] ECR I-181, where the Court found that a Member State could not limit the payment of a fee to an employment agency for work found, *de facto*, within the national territory.

to challenge rules that limit (directly or indirectly) their ability to employ migrant workers.[50]

Furthermore, migrant workers also enjoy rights as Union citizens: this means that restrictions to the enjoyment of benefits which were previously excluded from the scope of the Treaty might now fall within its scope by virtue of the Citizenship provisions: this is particularly the case in relation to residence requirements that prevent claimants from residing in a country different from that awarding the benefit. Those requirements must now be justified. In some cases, such as instances where the authorities need to be able to perform spot checks on continued eligibility,[51] such a requirement will be easily justifiable. In other cases, where once the benefit is granted there are no continuing eligibility criteria to be satisfied, such as a civilian war victim pension, a residence criterion might be very difficult to justify.[52]

Beside a right not to be discriminated against, workers also enjoy a right to access the employment market in other Member States without facing undue barriers. Again, the concept of barrier is broadly interpreted, so that any rule which impedes the free movement of workers, especially (but not exclusively[53]) by directly affecting access to the labour market, falls within the scope of the Treaty.[54] In practice however, very few cases concern truly non-discriminatory barriers.[55]

Workers also enjoy the right to have their family with them; and family members (in particular spouses) derive not only a right of residence from the worker, but also a right to work as if they were Union nationals (including rights not to be discriminated against on grounds of nationality[56]). Finally, the right not to be discriminated against can be invoked also against private parties.[57]

Whilst the rights of migrant workers and their families are extensive, in practice the effective exercise of these rights is still a challenge.[58] In particular, the lack of awareness of those rights, together with the more vulnerable position faced by migrants, have been identified by the Commission as barriers to the effective functioning of an integrated Union labour market. To address the gap between the 'law and its application', Parliament and Council adopted Directive 2014/54 aimed at

---

[50] Eg Case C-350/96 *Clean Car* [1998] ECR I-2521; Case C-202/11 *Anton Las v PSA Antwerp NV*, judgment of 16 April 2013.

[51] Eg Case C-406/04 *De Cuyper* [2006] ECR I-6947.

[52] Eg C-192/05 *Tas-Hagen and Tas* [2006] ECR I-10451.

[53] Eg Case C-202/11 *Anton Las v PSA Antwerp NV* [2013] ECR I-0000.

[54] Case C-415/93 *Bosman* [1995] ECR I-4921. See also Case C-18/95 *F.C. Terhoeve* [1999] ECR I-345; Case C-109/04 *Kranemann* [2005] ECR I-493; Case C-208/05 *ITC Innovative Technology Center GmbH v Bundesagentur für Arbeit* [2007] ECR I-181; Case C-325/08 *Olympique Lyonnais SASP v Bernard* [2010] ECR I-2177; Case C-18/95 *F.C. Terhoeve* [1999] ECR I-345. Case C-109/04 *Kranemann* [2005] ECR I-493.

[55] On the limit of *Bosman*, see eg Case 190/98 *Graf* [2000] ECR I-493.

[56] See Art 23 and 24(1) of Dir 2004/38.

[57] Case C-281/98 *Angonese* [2000] ECR I-4139; Case C-94/07 *Raccanelli* [2008] ECR I-5939.

[58] See Preamble to Dir 2014/54 on measures facilitating the exercise of rights conferred on workers in the context of the freedom of movement for workers [2014] OJ L 128/8.

facilitating the exercise of migrant workers rights. This Directive, following the trend started by the services Directive,[59] requires Member States to establish national bodies (contact points) entrusted with the promotion, analysis, monitoring and support of equal treatment of Union workers and their family members. The contact points will provide independent legal and/or other assistance to Union workers, act as a contact point for equivalent bodies in other Member States, and be entrusted with data collection and analysis in relation to restrictions to the free movement of workers as well as with the publication of independent reports to that effect.

The adoption of Directive 2014/54 highlights the limits of negative integration: whilst the case law paints a rosy and progressive picture of the rights of Union migrant workers and their family members, especially given the generous and teleological interpretation adopted by the Court, the reality on the ground is rather different and barriers to movement are still rife in all of the Member States. The gap between law and practice in this area is, in some ways, confirmed by data gathered not only in relation to the practices of the Member States,[60] but also by eurobarometer,[61] which indicates that only 43 per cent of Union citizens feel they know their rights, at least to a certain extent (but on the upside 59 per cent they would like to know more).

III. The Limits to the Free Movement of Workers—Challenges for the Future

Having briefly recalled the framework of the free movement of workers it is now time to provide a more critical analysis; in particular, it will be argued that even after Union citizenship, workers are still protected primarily within a market paradigm, as a tool of market integration.

---

[59] Dir 2006/123 on services in the internal market [2006] OJ L 376/36 requires Member States to introduce points of single contact where economic operators can complete the requirements necessary to carry out an economic activity; Reg 764/2008 laying down procedures relating to the application of certain national technical rules to products lawfully marketed in another Member State and repealing Decision No 3052/95/EC [2008] L 218/21 also requires Member States to establish products contact points with the aim of providing information about technical rules applicable to goods, the details of the authorities responsible and information about remedies.

[60] See generally, European Parliament's report on 'Problems and prospects concerning European Citizenship' (P6-TA-2009-204) available on http://www.europarl.europa.eu/sides/getDoc.do?pubRef=-//EP//NONSGML+TA+P6-TA-2009-0204+0+DOC+WORD+V0//EN; on the UK see J. Shaw and N. Miller, 'When Legal Worlds Collide: an Exploration of what Happens when EU Free Movement Law meets UK Migration Law' (2013) ELRev 137.

[61] Autumn 2013.

1. The Excluded Workers

(a) 'Genuine' Activity and Drug Addicts

It has been mentioned above that the Court adopted a generous and purposive interpretation of the definition of worker within the context of the Treaty free movement provisions; thus, for instance, it has included part-time workers (even when the hours worked are minimal) as well as workseekers. Yet, and perhaps surprisingly, in *Bettray*, the Court excluded work undertaken in the context of a social reintegration or rehabilitation scheme from the scope of the Treaty, even when such work is paid.[62] *Bettray* was confirmed in *Trojani*.[63] Here the national court enquired whether Mr Trojani could be considered a worker given that he performed about 30 hours work per week for the Salvation Army in return for which he received benefits in kind and pocket money. Whilst the two constituent elements (remuneration and subordination) of an employment relationship were satisfied, the Court found that the work could only be considered *genuine* for the purposes of Article 45 TFEU if it formed part of the 'normal labour market'. In order to determine the latter, the national court would have to take account of the 'status and practices of the hostel, the content of the social integration programme, and the nature and details of performance of the services'.[64]

The exception, according to which the social integration aim of the work is a relevant consideration when assessing the existence of an employment relationship for the purposes of Article 45 TFEU, is surprising for two different reasons. First of all, the Court has consistently held that the reasons that led someone to seek employment are immaterial to the qualification of the relationship in EU law. One would have therefore expected that the reasons that lead an employer to employ someone would be similarly immaterial; and, beside social reintegration, they probably are immaterial. Thus, in *Birden*,[65] in the context of the Turkish Association Agreement, the Court held that the ruling in *Bettray* was confined to the facts of that particular case and could not therefore be extended to a State sponsored working scheme aimed at (re-)introducing those in receipt of social assistance to the employment market. It is, therefore, unclear how central to the definition of worker is the existence of a genuine economic link: when the employer is not interested in pursuing economic gains, but rather is moved by other (non economic) considerations, is the worker protected by Article 45 TFEU? For instance, would work tailored to the

---

[62] Case 344/87 *Bettray* [1989] ECR 1641.   [63] case C-456/02 *Trojani* [2004] ECR I-7573.

[64] case C-456/02 *Trojani* [2004] ECR I-7573, para 24. The *Bettray/Trojani* case law is also at odds with the ruling in Case 196/87 *Steymann* [1988] ECR 6159, where the Court accepted that members of a religious community whose work was compensated by non-monetary means, and regardless of the amount of work actually performed, fell within the scope of the Treaty. In *Steymann*, the Court therefore focused on the nature of the 'work' rather than on the economic link between employer and employee.

[65] Case 1/97 *Birden* [1999] ECR I-7747.

specific abilities of a person with disability be counted as 'employment' within the EU framework? After all, much as it was the case in *Bettray* and in *Trojani*, such work does not form part of the normal employment market and is 'adapted to the physical and mental possibilities of each person',[66] so that it is not the candidate who is chosen to perform a job but a job that is chosen to suit the candidate. If such work is not to be included in the definition of employment for the purposes of the Treaty, then the exclusion of people with disabilities from the benefits accruing from EU membership would be even greater than it is in any event, not least since health insurance for many people with disabilities is prohibitively expensive, making it very difficult, if not impossible, to move as an economically inactive person. Yet, if work-schemes for the disabled are to be included in the definition of employment, the *Bettray/Trojani* case law would imply a difference in treatment which would appear to be based solely on the nature of the problem addressed by the socio-integration programme (drug addiction) rather than on the nature of the work itself. It is then to be queried whether there is an additional 'qualitative' dimension to the enjoyment of the Treaty freedoms so that less 'attractive' Union citizens might enjoy, for that reason only, fewer rights than others.[67]

(b) Non-Remunerated Work

As mentioned above, the focus on 'remuneration' rather than on the economic value of the work performed has the effect of excluding from the scope of the Treaty free movement provisions work done within the context of family relationships (house work and care work), as well as work done on a voluntary and/or unpaid basis. Whilst the Court's interpretation might have been understandable in the light of the predominantly market ethos of the European Economic Community, it is debatable whether it can still be defended post-citizenship, not least since carers and stay at home individuals tend to be female, so that this interpretation inevitably has discriminatory effects. This said, it must be recognized that the extensive interpretation of the rights of workers and citizens has resulted in more extensive rights for parents (and presumably, by analogy, for carers). So, for instance, in the context of the education rights of workers' children, the Court has found that the parent of a child of a worker who is in education in the host country derives residence rights from the child even after the child has reached the age of majority,[68] and regardless of whether the parent claiming the right is a third country national and/or is still in a relationship with the worker, and of whether the worker is still

---

[66] Case 344/87 *Bettray* [1989] ECR 1641, para 17.

[67] On the introduction of a qualitative assessment, not contained in Dir 2004/38, in relation to residence rights and to the enhanced protection provided for long term residents, see Case C-378/12 *Onuekwere*, judgment delivered on 16 January 2014, nyr; Case C-400/12 *M. G.*, judgment delivered on 16 January 2014, nyr.

[68] Eg Case C-480/08 *Texeira* [2010] ECR I-1107.

in the host country.[69] This, in practice means that the parent of a worker's child is protected by EU law and does not have to satisfy the requirements contained in Article 7(1) Directive 2004/38.[70] Furthermore, the above-mentioned ruling in *S and G* also ensures that the parent/carer might derive a right to reside in the Member State of nationality of her spouse by virtue of her parental/caring role.

A further problem with the Court's approach arises in relation to voluntary and unpaid work (such as internships). Much as in the case of parenting and caring, the former is work of value not only to the organization for which it is performed but usually also to society at large. Furthermore, voluntary work might be a valuable step towards entering the paid labour market. On the other hand, unpaid work might be, depending on the conditions of the labour market and the economy more generally, the only work available and the only way individuals might increase their chances of getting paid employment by developing skills and experiences of value to employers. In the context of part time and fixed term contracts,[71] in providing a generous interpretation to Article 45 TFEU, the Court relied also on the asymmetry inherent in the employment market, where the worker often does not have a choice as to the conditions under which she is employed. It is to be hoped that, should the need arise, the Court will accept that unpaid work forms part of the employment market and that, therefore, those performing work of actual economic value to the employer should be protected in the same way as their luckier remunerated peers. Similarly, it is to be hoped that atypical contracts which subject the worker to a duty to be available for work at the request of the employer (so called zero-hours contracts) will be considered as employment contracts, even before the employer has actually requested the services of the worker, and therefore before the worker has been actually remunerated. This of course increases the possibility of abuse, as those contracts could in theory just be entered into so as to provide the worker with rights of residence and welfare. And yet that is an argument in support of increasing guarantees for those subject to these types of contracts, rather than in favour of excluding migrants from any supplementary protection.

2. Accession Workers

As mentioned above, workers from acceding Member States are seeing their right to access the employment market of other Member States limited for a maximum of seven years (2+3+2). In the first five years, the limitation on the movement of

---

[69] Eg Case C-413/99 *Baumbast and R* [2002] ECR I-7091; Case C-310/08 *Ibrahim* [2010] ECR I-1065.

[70] But periods of residence which have been carried out without satisfying the conditions contained in Art 7(2), 12 or 13 of Dir 2004/38, as the case might be, do not count towards the five years for permanent residence. See C-529/11 *Alarape and Tijani* [2013] ECR I-0000.

[71] Case C-413/01 *Ninni Orasche* [2003] ECR I-3187, paras 42 and 43.

workers does not need to be justified whilst an extension of further two years must be justified by serious disturbances, or threats thereof, to the functioning of the labour market.[72]

The transitional arrangements in relation to workers were first imposed in relation to the big enlargement of 2004. The sheer scale of that enlargement, when the population of the EU increased at once by almost 75 million people, together with the differences in economic performance between the old and the new countries,[73] justified—at least politically if not factually—the imposition of transitional measures on all acceding member States bar Malta and Cyprus. The same measures were then also imposed at the accession of Romania and Bulgaria (2007) and, more recently, at the accession of Croatia (2013).[74]

The standardization of the transitional measures is interesting for a number of reasons. First of all, it should be noted that Member States are not required to justify the imposition of restrictions for the first five years: this means that there might be no real threat to the host labour market, and yet workers might see their right to free movement considerably limited. In this way, whilst foreign entrepreneurs are able to access the new Member States' market, and therefore exploit the differences in living standards to reduce labour costs, workers are not allowed to take advantage of higher salaries in the 'old' Member States, regardless of whether there is an actual threat to the host State's employment market.

Secondly, the evidence from the 2004 enlargement is that the transitional arrangements have a negative effect on at least some of the labour markets. This is so since the limitations apply only to the free movement of workers and

---

[72] Annexes V to XV of the Treaty of Accession of the Czech Republic, Estonia, Cyprus, Latvia, Lithuania, Hungary, Malta, Poland, Slovenia and Slovakia [2003] OJ 236/803ff; Annexes VI and VII of the Treaty of Accession of the Republic of Bulgaria and Romania [2005] OJ L 157/104ff; Annex V of the Treaty of Accession of Croatia [2013] OJ L 112/67; for extension of the restrictions in relation to Bulgaria and Romania beyond the initial five years, see Council of the EU *Information from the Commission—Transitional Arrangements regarding the free movement of workers of Bulgarian and Romanian nationality* 6651/13, SOC 113, MI 119; for the UK report see *Review of the Transitional Restrictions on Access of Romanian and Bulgarian Nationals to the UK Labour Market*, Report Prepared by the Migration Advisory Committee, November 2011, available on https://www.gov.uk/government/uploads/system/uploads/attachment_data/file/257232/transitional-restrictions.pdf. The report concludes that at the time (2011) there was a serious disturbance of the UK labour market (it being still deep in recession); that maintaining restrictions would assist in addressing such labour market disturbance but it found that the *extent* to which maintaining restrictions would assist in addressing such disturbance to be uncertain.

[73] The difference in GDP per capita varied at the moment of accession between 35 per cent (Latvia) to 74 per cent (Slovenia) of the EU15 average, source Eurostat; see the Commission's Communication *More Unity and More Diversity. The Europe Union's Biggest Enlargement* (NA-47-02-389-EN-C) (http://www.europa.eu.int/comm/publications/booklets/move/41/index_en.htm).

[74] Fourteen out of the 27 Member States of the EU have not imposed restrictions on the free movement of Croatian workers.

not to the free movement of self-employed or Union citizens. As a result, the effect of the transitional arrangements can be to drive labour underground, so that accession workers are employed unlawfully, thus risking exploitation because of the lack of legal protection in terms of salary and working conditions, and undercutting the lawful labour market. Furthermore, the actual effect of restrictions on the movement of workers cannot be assessed in the abstract, since migration flows will respond also to the restrictions imposed by each EU country: the fewer countries allow migration of workers, the greater the impact on those who do permit migration (provided the country is 'attractive'). Therefore, the transitional arrangements, which are decided on a country by country basis without the knowledge of what other Member States will be doing, seem not entirely rational, at least if the aim of the arrangements is to protect the home employment market, rather than making enlargement politically more acceptable.

Thirdly, the transitional arrangements were (allegedly) originally justified by the scale of enlargement and the differences in economic performance. The accession of Bulgaria and Romania might have presented similar challenges since their population is sizeable (approximately 9 million and 21.7 million, respectively) and their economic performance considerably weaker than the EU's average, both at the time of accession and now.[75] However, these considerations do not seem to apply to Croatia. Whilst the latter's per capita GDP is significantly inferior to the EU average,[76] its population, with less than five million inhabitants, is comparatively small. It is therefore difficult to believe that the restrictions on the free movement of Croatian workers are actually necessary to protect the employment markets in the other Member States. By means of comparison, take the accession of Portugal in 1986: its population was just under 10 million,[77] so both in real and in relative terms considerably larger than Croatia's population. Portugal's economic performance was lower than that of the big Member States and, roughly speaking, comparable to that of Croatia. Thus, in 1985, the year preceding accession, Portugal's per capita GDP was about 53.9 per cent of Germany's and 59.45 per cent of Italy's,

---

[75] In 2006, the year before accession, the GDP per capita in PPS (purchasing power standard, ie the difference in cost of living, is taken into account so that price level differences are eliminated) of Romania and Bulgaria was 38 per cent of the EU average, it is now 50 and 47 per cent, respectively; source Eurostat http://epp.eurostat.ec.europa.eu/tgm/table.do?tab=table&plugin=1&language=en&pcode=tec00114.

[76] Most recent statistics put it at 62 per cent of EU average, with both Romania (50 per cent) and Bulgaria (47 per cent) significantly lower, Latvia a bit above at 64 per cent; and Poland and Hungary at 67 per cent; source Eurostat data from Nov 2013 http://epp.eurostat.ec.europa.eu/tgm/table.do?tab=table&plugin=1&language=en&pcode=tec00114.

[77] It was 9 833 014 in the 1981 census; and 9 862 540 in the 1991 census, source eurostat http://epp.eurostat.ec.europa.eu/portal/page/portal/population/data/database. The population of the EEC in 1981 was just above 271 million; so, in a very approximate way, Portugal's population was 3.7 per cent of the EEC, whilst Croatia is about 1 per cent of the EU at the time of joining.

whilst in 2012 Croatia's per capita GDP was 49.84 per cent of Germany's and 61.32 per cent of Italy's.[78]

Seen in this light, the imposition of a transitional period for the free movement of Croatian workers seems due more to political considerations than to economic ones, and might indicate a shift in the perception of the importance of the free movement of workers for the European project. In this respect, one might also recall the direct attacks on the very principle of the free movement of workers mounted by Mr David Cameron, among others. The British Prime Minister has openly called for more limits on future acceding countries, as well as more severe checks on eligibility for welfare provision for existing migrants.[79] Whilst there seems to be little appetite in the rest of the EU for restrictions on the free movement of workers beyond the transitional period,[80] the 'welfare tourism' rhetoric seems to be spreading.[81] And yet, there is no evidence that benefit tourism is a problem within the European Union: rather all the evidence seems to point to a net fiscal benefit for Member States of destination of EU migrants.[82]

---

[78] This data is rather rough and by way of indication only since, unfortunately, data about the EEC economic performance for 1985 could not be found. For this reason, I took two large Member States: Germany and Italy. Germany alone could not be used as a comparator since the difference in performance during the recent recession from other Member States was too great; Italy has therefore been selected as a medium low performer. The data is taken from two different sources: the OECD tables for the 1985 data; and eurostat for the 2012 data. The need to rely on two different data sets is due to the fact that the OECD does not provide data for Croatia; and eurostat does not provide data before 1991. That said, there is a positive element in comparing data with countries that have always been Member States since it allows us to compare the economy of two potential receiving countries with that of acceding Member States. The sizeable disparity amongst the performance of some of the new Member States relative to old Member States not only brings the EU average performance down, but also means that the less strong Member States are less likely to be the target of migration from new acceding States.

[79] D. Cameron, Letter to the *Financial Times*, 26 November 2013; on the same lines Mr Cameron's letter to the *The Daily Telegraph*, 15 March 2014, although possibly a bit more cautious given the rather cold reception to his ideas see 'Cameron Faces EU Isolation on EU Anti-immigration Stance' *Financial Times,* 19 January 2014.

[80] Mr Renzi, at the time of writing Italian Prime Minister, has set out an ambitious agenda for the incoming Italian Presidency; see M Renzi, speech at the State of the Europe Conference, *EUI,* 9 May 2014; reported http://www.euractiv.com/sections/eu-elections-2014/italian-pm-vows-push-united-states-europe-during-presidency-302048.

[81] See 'German Conservatives Stir up "Welfare Tourism" Row' *EUobserver.com* 4, December 2013; 'Merkel Considers Restrictions on Unemployed EU Migrants', *Financial Times,* 26 March 2014; 'EU Migration. The Gates are Open' *The Economist,* 4 January 2014; 'Belgium Sends 'Burden' EU Citizens Letters Asking them to Leave the Country' *EUobserver.com*, 30 January 2014.

[82] Slightly more complex is the situation for the 'exporting' Member States, those who are seeing their young workers emigrate as well as facing a brain drain. Both problems can surely not be addressed by limiting the free movement of workers; rather they need to be addressed through targeted and general policies, sustaining research and employment. See eg Commission's Press Release IP/14/538, 8 May 2014, 'Reversing the Brain Drain: Major Investment for EU Scientific Research Hub in Hungary Gets Go Ahead'.

IV. Conclusions

It cannot be denied that the free movement of workers was an ambitious aim and that the EU institutional actors, both Court and legislature, have done much to ensure its realization and full effectiveness. And yet, post-Citizenship, the practice of free movement of workers seems still very much anchored in its market roots. This can be seen in the persisting discrimination against non-migrant workers; in the exclusion of work done in the context of social rehabilitation; in the exclusion of non-remunerated work from the scope of the Treaty. Furthermore, the standardization of transitional arrangements for acceding countries, not linked to any economic assessment, together with emerging rhetoric about the 'problems' arising from the free movement provisions (also not supported by any available data) seem to indicate a shift in the foundational nature of the free movement of workers for the EU integration project. In the context of an economic crisis which was not created by workers, this seems particularly distasteful: it is therefore to be hoped that the Court (and the EU institutions) will return to a progressive interpretation of the Treaty—protecting workers as individuals rather than as mere agents of integration.

Bibliography

L. Andor, 'Labour Mobility in the EU—The Inconvenient Truth', Lecture at the University of Bristol delivered on 10 February 2014, Speech/14/115, available at http://europa.eu/rapid/press-release_SPEECH-14-115_en.htm

Catherine Barnard, *The Substantive Law of the EU. The Four Freedoms* (4th ed, OUP 2013)

Frigyes Ferdinand Heinz and Melanie E. Ward-Warmedinger, 'Cross-Border Labour Mobility within an Enlarged EU' (October 2006), *ECB Occasional Paper* No 52, available at SSRN http://ssrn.com/abstract=923371

Dawn Holland, Tatiana Fic, Ana Rincon-Aznar, Lucy Strokes and Pawel Paluchowski, *Labour Mobility within the EU—The Impact of Enlargement and the Functioning of The Transitional Arrangements* (report on behalf of the European Social Affairs and Inclusion Directorate General of the European Commission), July 2011, available at http://ec.europa.eu/social/BlobServlet?docId=7191&langId=en

D. Holland and P. Paluchowski, *Geographical Labour Mobility in the Context of the Crisis* (ad hoc report prepared at the request of the European Employment Observatory), June 2013, available at http://www.eu-employment-observatory.net/resources/reports/ESDE-SynthesisPaper-June2013-Final.pdf

Paul Minderhoud and Nicos Trimikliotis (eds), *Rethinking the Free Movement of Workers: the European Challenges ahead* (2009)

Niamh Nic Shuibhne, *The Coherence of EU Free Movement Law. Constitutional Responsibility and the Court of Justice* (2013)

Siofra O'Leary, 'Free Movement of Persons and Services' in Paul Craig and Gráinne De Búrca *The Evolution of EU Law* (2nd ed, 2011)

Frans Pennings, *European Social Security Law* (5th ed, 2010)

Jo Shaw and N. Miller, 'When Legal Worlds Collide: An Exploration of what Happens When EU Free Movement Law Meets UK Migration Law' (2013) 38 *ELRev* 137

Henrik Skovgaard-Petersen, 'There and Back Again: Portability of Student Loans, Grants and Fee Support in a Free Movement Perspective' (2013) 38 *ELRev* 783

Eleanor Spaventa, *Free Movement of Persons: Barriers to Movement in their Constitutional Context* (2007)

CHAPTER 19

THE DEVELOPING LEGAL DIMENSIONS OF UNION CITIZENSHIP

NIAMH NIC SHUIBHNE

I. INTRODUCTION

THE framework of Union citizenship introduced by the Maastricht Treaty has become, in the interim decades, a complex ecology of legal rights and implementation practices. It is a dynamic status that has generated significant legislation and an extensive body of case law, as well as a rich and often challenging academic literature—producing an integrated process that has been described as having 'actively coshaped the Union and its citizenship'.[1] It is important to acknowledge that Union citizenship has captured and sustained the imagination of disciplines beyond law.[2] But even from within that perspective in a more isolated sense, citizenship has both enriched pre-existing EU rights and established

[1] D. Kochenov, 'The Essence of EU Citizenship Emerging from the Last Ten Years of Academic Debate: Beyond the Cherry Blossoms and the Moon?' (2013) 62 *International and Comparative Law Quarterly* 97, 98.
[2] See eg A. Wiener, *European Citizenship Practice: Building Institutions of a Non-State* (1999), and the essays in J. Shaw, R. Bellamy, and D. Castiglione (eds), *Making European Citizens* (2006); for inter-disciplinary perspectives on citizenship more generally, see J. Shaw and I. Štiks (eds), *Citizenship Rights* (2013).

novel dimensions of the scope of EU law more autonomously beyond the threshold of economic activity—and even, in exceptional circumstances, beyond the conventional free movement law threshold of cross-border connections. Its intersection with questions of a constitutional nature about sovereignty, rights, and the boundaries between EU and state competences means that the development of citizenship law represents, in several respects, a microcosm of the development of EU law more generally. In addition, its acute resonance with broader debates on identity, migration, and social priorities underscores its critical role, both actual and potential, in current disputes about the role and even the future of the EU.

Bearing this complex and dynamic character in mind, and aiming to complement work that evaluates the evolution of conceptual thinking on citizenship in a more longitudinal sense,[3] this chapter seeks to present a current snapshot of the developing legal dimensions of Union citizenship, emphasizing two streams of development in particular. Following an overview of the applicable legal framework, its implementation, and key activities, as well as challenges related to its enforcement (Section II), the discussion then evaluates how central concepts of citizenship legislation are being interpreted at present (Section III.1). In large part, the process of applying and interpreting Directive 2004/38 drives the development of this dimension.[4] The emerging scope of the concept of dependency and the distinctive right of permanent residence are focused on in particular.

As a point of contrast, the continuing scope and significance of the primary rights conferred directly by the Treaty are examined in Section III.2. The controversial role of EU law in situations that are purely internal to a Member State are noted here. But this part of the chapter also aims to shed light on the application of the Treaty in other instances where the Directive does not apply directly either: EU rights that stem from lawful residence in a host state that is based on national law; and the legal situation of returning migrant citizens when back in their home states.

The chapter concludes by reflecting on the broader dimensions of citizenship, arguing that the relative thinness of Union citizenship beyond law is uncomfortably exemplified at present in widespread and challenging debates on intra-EU migration.

---

[3] See eg D. Kostakopolou, "European Union citizenship: Writing the future' (2007) 13 *European Law Journal* 623; J. Shaw, 'Citizenship: Contrasting Dynamics at the Interface of Integration and Constitutionalism' in P. Craig and G. De Búrca (eds) *The Evolution of EU Law* (2nd ed, 2011) 575; and Kochenov (n 1).

[4] Dir 2004/38/EC on the right of citizens of the Union and their family members to move and reside freely within the territory of the Member States [2004] OJ L158/77.

II. Foundational Legal Dimensions: The Framework of Union Citizenship Law

1. The Treaty Framework

Union citizenship was introduced by the Maastricht Treaty, reflecting proposals that had been developed and debated since the 1970s, building on legislation and case law that regulated the right to move and reside in other states for the purposes of economic activity (whether work, establishment, or services), and introducing a distinctive new set of political rights.[5]

Union citizens are now referred to in several of the Treaties' framing provisions. In the preamble to the TEU, for example, the resolution of the signatories 'to continue the process of creating an ever closer union among the peoples of Europe' is characterized explicitly as one 'in which decisions are taken as closely as possible to the citizen in accordance with the principle of subsidiarity'.[6] More concretely, the Lisbon Treaty effected amendments to the TEU that emphasize the role played by citizens in the Union's governance structures. Article 10 TEU outlines the links between citizenship and both participatory and representative political processes. On the theme of openness and transparency,[7] Article 11(4) introduces the citizens' initiative, ie an organizing mechanism through which citizens can contribute to the shaping of Union policy: 'Not less than one million citizens who are nationals of a significant number of Member States may take the initiative of inviting the European Commission, within the framework of its powers, to submit any appropriate proposal on matters where citizens consider that a legal act of the Union is required for the purpose of implementing the Treaties.' Legislative competence to establish the necessary procedures and conditions for the running of the initiative is provided by Article 24 TFEU.

The Lisbon Treaty also forged a direct link between non-discrimination and Union citizenship by bringing both sets of provisions together as Part Two of the TFEU. Article 20(1) TFEU 'establishes' citizenship of the Union, provides that every person holding the nationality of a Member State is a Union citizen, and confirms that Union citizenship is 'additional to and [shall] not replace national citizenship'. Article 20(2) TFEU then lists the basic framework of citizenship rights:

---

[5] On the shaping of Union citizenship pre-Maastricht, see S. O'Leary, *The Evolving Concept of Community Citizenship: From the Free Movement of Persons to Union Citizenship* (1996).

[6] See similarly eg Arts 3(2) (area of freedom, security and justice) and 3(5) (relations with the wider world) TEU.

[7] See relatedly, Art 15(3) TFEU and Art 42 of the Charter of Fundamental Rights.

Citizens of the Union shall enjoy the rights and be subject to the duties provided for in the Treaties. They shall have, inter alia:

(a) the right to move and reside freely within the territory of the Member States;[8]
(b) the right to vote and to stand as candidates in elections to the European Parliament and in municipal elections in their Member State of residence, under the same conditions as nationals of that State;[9]
(c) the right to enjoy, in the territory of a third country in which the Member State of which they are nationals is not represented, the protection of the diplomatic and consular authorities of any Member State on the same conditions as the nationals of that State;[10]
(d) the right to petition the European Parliament, to apply to the European Ombudsman, and to address the institutions and advisory bodies of the Union in any of the Treaty languages and to obtain a reply in the same language.[11]

These rights shall be exercised in accordance with the conditions and limits defined by the Treaties and by the measures adopted thereunder.

Finally, Article 25 TFEU imposes a reporting obligation on the Commission ('every three years on the application of the provisions of this Part'), and enables the Council (acting unanimously under the special legislative procedure, after obtaining the consent of the European Parliament) to 'adopt provisions to strengthen or to add to the rights listed in Article 20(2)'.

Four features of the Treaty framework can be noted at this stage. First, while Article 20 TFEU refers to 'the duties provided for in the Treaties', this idea has not (yet) been developed in a functional or recognizably legal sense.[12] Second, citizenship rights are not intended to be absolute. Rather, they are subject to 'the conditions and limits defined by the Treaties and by the measures adopted thereunder'. For the right to move and reside within the territory of the Member States, conditions and limits include derogations on the basis of public policy, public security, or

---

[8] Repeated in Art 21 TFEU, but qualified there with slightly different phrasing ('subject to the limitations and conditions laid down in the Treaties and by the measures adopted to give them effect'); Arts 21(2) and (3) outline related legislative procedures, the latter provision focusing explicitly on 'measures concerning social security or social protection'.

[9] Art 22 TFEU makes it clearer that these rights apply in situations where the citizen is residing 'in a State of which he is not a national' and outlines relevant legislative procedures.

[10] See also Art 23 TFEU.

[11] See also Art 24 TFEU. The first two rights—ie to petition the Parliament and to apply to the Ombudsman—are also enjoyed by natural and legal persons residing or having their registered office in a Member State; see respectively, Arts 227 and 228 TFEU. The wider scope of these rights is confirmed in Arts 43 and 44 of the Charter.

[12] For further discussion of this point, see D. Kochenov, 'EU Citizenship without Duties', (2014) 20 *European Law Journal* 482; see also D. Kostakopoulou 'European Union Citizenship Rights and Duties: Civil, Political and Social' in E. Isin and P. Neyers (eds), *Global Handbook of Citizenship Studies* (2014).

public health—ie the grounds specified in Articles 45 and 52 TFEU—and, for situations that do not involve direct discrimination against Union citizens, the more flexible objective justification framework based on legitimate and proportionate public interest arguments.[13] It also includes conditions and limits contained in legislation, such as those specified in Directive 2004/38. In that context, the conditions linked to the financial self-sufficiency of migrant Union citizens in Article 7 of the Directive—and the implications of *not* meeting them alluded to in Article 14(1)—mark a point of tension with the rule in free movement law more generally that states cannot be excused of their obligations under the Treaty on purely economic grounds,[14] a point also expressed in Article 27 of the Directive. The provisions of the Directive are discussed in more detail in Section III.1. But the Court has emphasized that while legislative limits placed on the primary citizenship rights conferred by the Treaty can regulate the exercise of those rights, they cannot go so far as to negate their existence; therefore such conditions are subject to judicial review.[15]

Third, it is important to acknowledge the role that the general principles of EU law play in the interpretation of citizenship rights, especially the requirements of proportionality and respect for fundamental rights.[16] Relatedly, fourth, some of the provisions of the Charter of Fundamental Rights specify that *only* Union citizens come within their scope.[17] This example of the *exclusionary* as well as *privileged* character of citizenship is also a useful reminder of its limits as an instrument of change, a theme picked up again in Sections III and IV.

2. Implementing Treaty Rights

As noted in Section I, the right to move and reside within the territory of the Member States is regulated by Directive 2004/38, a comprehensive measure that

---

[13] See eg Case C-220/12 *Thiele Meneses*, judgment of 24 October 2013, para 29.

[14] See eg Case C-35/98 *Verkooijen* [2000] ECR I-4071, para 48: '[A]ims of a purely economic nature cannot constitute an overriding reason in the general interest justifying a restriction of a fundamental freedom guaranteed by the Treaty.'

[15] Case C-413/99 *Baumbast and R* [2002] ECR I-7091, paras 84–86. Relatedly, the convention that residence cards or permits are reflective rather than constitutive of residence rights is normally beneficial to the citizen (see eg Case C-459/99 *MRAX* [2002] ECR I-6591, para 74). However, in the context of accruing periods of lawful residence in a host state to acquire permanent residence there under Art 16(1) of Dir 2004/38, the decision in *Dias* provides an interesting—and disadvantageous—twist (Case C-325/09 *Dias* [2011] ECR I-6387, paras 53–55). The right of permanent residence is discussed more fully in Section III.1(b).

[16] See eg *Baumbast*, para 91 (proportionality); Case C-391/09 *Runevič-Vardyn and Wardyn* [2011] ECR I-3787, para 43 (respect for fundamental rights).

[17] See Arts 15(2) (freedom to seek employment, to work, to exercise the right of establishment and to provide services in any Member State); 39 (right to vote and stand as a candidate in European Parliament elections); 40 (right to vote and stand as a candidate in municipal elections); 45 (right to move and reside); and 46 (diplomatic and consular protection in third countries) of the Charter.

amended parts of what is now Regulation 492/2011 on the free movement of work-ers,[18] and replaced nine other Directives and Regulations entirely. The main objec-tive of the Directive is 'to simplify and strengthen the right of free movement and residence of all Union citizens' (recital 3 of the preamble), irrespective of the activ-ity or purpose underlying the exercise of that right. The scope of this Directive and its interpretation in the case law to date are discussed in detail in Section III.1.

Additionally, several measures have been adopted (or proposed) in order to implement the political rights conferred on Union citizens. First, two Directives were adopted in the 1990s to implement the right to vote in European Parliament elections and in municipal elections, respectively.[19] These measures also specify permitted limitations and exceptions.[20] Elections to the European Parliament have twice been addressed in proceedings before the Court of Justice. In *Spain v United Kingdom*, Spain unsuccessfully challenged the extension of the right to vote and stand as a candidate in these elections by the UK to Commonwealth citizens resid-ing in Gibraltar.[21] In *Eman and Sevinger*, concerning electoral rights restrictions placed on nationals of the Netherlands who resided in Aruba, the Court confirmed that while the Member States may define, in accordance with EU law:

the conditions of the right to vote and to stand as a candidate in elections to the European Parliament by reference to the criterion of residence in the territory in which the elec-tions are held, the principle of equal treatment prevents, however, the criteria chosen from resulting in different treatment of nationals who are in comparable situations, unless that difference in treatment is objectively justified.[22]

Second, following the publication of an Action Plan in 2007 and a Communication on consular protection in March 2011,[23] the Commission eventually published (at the end of 2011) its proposal for a Directive to implement this right.[24] Finally,

---

[18] Council Regulation (EEC) No 492/2011 of 5 April 2011 on freedom of movement for workers within the Union, [2011] OJ L141/1.

[19] Council Dir 93/109/EC of 6 December 1993 laying down detailed arrangements for the exercise of the right to vote and stand as a candidate in elections to the European Parliament for citizens of the Union residing in a Member State of which they are not nationals [1993] OJ L329/34; and Council Dir 94/80/EC of 19 December 1994 laying down detailed arrangements for the exercise of the right to vote and to stand as a candidate in municipal elections by citizens of the Union residing in a Member State of which they are not nationals [1994] OJ L368/98.

[20] See eg Art 5(3) of Dir 94/80 provides that: 'Member States may provide that only their own nationals may hold the office of elected head, deputy or member of the governing college of the executive of a basic local government unit if elected to hold office for the duration of his mandate.'

[21] Case C-145/04 *Spain v United Kingdom* [2006] ECR I-7917.

[22] Case C-300/04 *Eman and Sevinger* [2006] ECR I-8055, para 61.

[23] Effective consular protection in third countries: the contribution of the European Union—Action Plan 2007–2009 C (2007) 5841 final; and Consular protection for EU citizens in third countries: State of play and way forward, COM (2011) 149 final.

[24] Proposal for a Council Directive on consular protection for citizens of the Union abroad COM (2011) 881 final; the legislative process for the adoption of this measure was still ongoing at the time of writing.

Regulation 211/2011 establishes the framework of operation for the citizens' initiative.[25] It codifies administrative requirements for the organizers and signatories of an initiative, procedures for registration and for the collection of signatures, and detailed thresholds on the minimum number of signatories needed—at least one million eligible signatories must be collected from at least one-quarter of the Member States, which must in turn comprise at least the minimum number of citizens specified for each state in Annex 1 of the Regulation (eg 74250 for Germany; 16500 for Hungary; and 24750 for Romania). On 23 December 2013, the Commission confirmed that it had 'officially received the first ever successful European Citizens' Initiative, with properly validated support from at least one million European citizens in at least seven Member States'.[26]

The 'Let Me Vote' Initiative—which had just closed at the time of writing—is an important proposal important to flag against the limited framework of electoral rights provided for in the Treaty. This initiative sought '[t]o strengthen the rights listed in article 20(2) TFEU by granting EU citizens residing in another Member State the right to vote in all political elections in their country of residence, on the same conditions as the nationals of that State'.[27] Progress on the sensitive question of disenfranchisement that results directly from the exercise of free movement rights is clearly gaining momentum. Tackling the problem from the other direction—the responsibilities of the *home* state—the Commission confirmed in its 2013 Report on Citizenship that it would 'propose constructive ways to enable EU citizens living in another EU country to fully participate in the democratic life of the EU by maintaining their right to vote in national elections in their country of origin'.[28] In January 2014, it published a Communication and a Recommendation,[29] on the basis that 'disenfranchisement practices are . . . at odds with the founding premise of EU citizenship which is meant to give citizens additional rights, rather than depriving them of rights'.[30] But the extent to which these developments will actually change state practices remains to be seen.

---

[25] Reg (EU) No 211/2011 of the European Parliament and of the Council of 16 February 2011 on the citizens' initiative [2011] OJ L65/1.

[26] See Press Release at http://europa.eu/rapid/midday-express-23-12-2013.htm; for further information on the Initiative (Right2Water), see http://ec.europa.eu/citizens-initiative/public/initiatives/finalised/details/2012/000003.

[27] See further http://www.letmevote.eu/en/.

[28] 'EU Citizenship Report 2013 EU citizens: your rights, your future' COM (2013) 269 final, p 25 (Action 12). For academic conceptualization of exclusion from national elections as a restriction of free movement rights, see D. Kochenov, 'Free Movement and Participation in the Parliamentary Elections in the Member State of Nationality: An Ignored Link?' (2009) 16 *Maastricht Journal of Europea and Comparative Law* 197.

[29] Commission Communication addressing the consequences of disenfranchisement of Union citizens exercising their right to free movement COM (2014) 33; Commission Recommendation addressing the consequences of disenfranchisement of Union citizens exercising their right to free movement C (2014) 391.

[30] See Press Release at http://europa.eu/rapid/press-release_IP-14-77_en.htm.

3. Supporting Implementation

The Commission plays a central role in supporting—and monitoring—the application and implementation of the Treaties. In the area of citizenship, its reporting obligations under Article 25 TFEU were noted briefly in Section II.2. The Commission has produced two EU Citizenship Reports to date,[31] as well as a series of supplementary[32] and issue-specific texts. For example, in 2012, the Commission reported on the application of Directive 94/80 on municipal elections,[33] and it also issues communications both before[34] and after[35] European Parliament elections. In 2008, it published a stinging report on the problematic implementation of Directive 2004/38,[36] leading to a communication on 'guidance for better transposition and application' in 2009.[37] Its pursuit of infringement proceedings against Member States for failure to respect their obligations under EU law is another important limb of its enforcement role, but this work is an intensive and iterative process. To date, just two successful cases have been concluded judicially in connection with the implementation of Directive 2004/38.[38] The prospect of further litigation continues to be raised,[39] but it should be remembered too that the Commission manages to resolve the majority of infringements before recourse to the Court actually becomes necessary.[40]

Alongside the formal supervisory role carried out by the Commission, less obvious examples of enforcement *practice* illustrate the breadth of activities that feed into the monitoring of citizenship rights. Statistics on complaints made at EU level in connection with the implementation of citizenship rights raise questions about the degree of divergence between the *centralized* legal framework of Union citizenship and its realization through *decentralized*

---

[31] In 2010 (http://ec.europa.eu/justice/citizen/files/com_2010_603_en.pdf) and 2013 (http://ec.europa.eu/justice/citizen/files/2013eucitizenshipreport_en.pdf). The preparation of both reports involved processes of public consultation, see eg 2013 Report, p 4.

[32] See eg the Commission's report on 'progress towards effective EU Citizenship 2011–2013' COM (2013) 270 final; and its 2013 Communication on 'Free movement of EU citizens and their families: five actions to make a difference' COM (2013) 837 final.

[33] COM (2012) 99 final.

[34] See eg 'Preparing for the 2014 European elections: further enhancing their democratic and efficient conduct' COM (2013) 126 final; see also, Commission Recommendation on enhancing the democratic and efficient conduct of the elections to the European Parliament C (2013) 1303 final.

[35] See eg 'Report on the election of Members of the European Parliament [and] on the participation of European Union citizens in elections for the European Parliament in the Member State of residence (Dir 93/109/EC)' COM (2010) 603 final.

[36] COM (2008) 840 final.   [37] COM (2009) 313 final.

[38] Against Austria (Case C-75/11, judgment of 4 October 2012) and Luxembourg (Case C-294/07, [2007] ECR I-192* [unpublished decision]).

[39] See eg the press releases at http://europa.eu/rapid/press-release_IP-13-475_en.htm (the UK) and http://europa.eu/rapid/press-release_IP-12-646_en.htm (Austria, Germany, and Sweden).

[40] See eg the data presented in an August 2011 press release http://europa.eu/rapid/press-release_IP-11-981_en.htm?locale=fr.

national practices.[41] The Council flagged this theme in its own conclusions on the Commission's 2013 Citizenship Report.[42] In particular, however, the importance of the review of Member State practices that takes place through the preliminary rulings procedure cannot be overstated. As will become apparent in Section III, the broader legal contribution made by citizens trying to enforce their own rights has been extraordinary. But the cases that make it to Luxembourg (or any EU institution) will, of course, constitute only the barely visible tip of a national implementation iceberg. Projects that aim to track national practices on a more systemic scale add considerable value in this respect. For example, research initiatives that collate information on citizenship rights include the EUDO Observatory on Citizenship, which also hosts the FRACIT project on access to electoral rights in the EU.[43] On this dimension of Union citizenship law, however, much work can still be done.

III. Developing Legal Dimensions

The right to move and reside within the territory of the Member States is the most developed legal dimension of the Union citizenship framework. In this section, two case studies are presented in order to examine the substance of this right in a rounded way. First, in Section III.1, the emerging content and outer boundaries of specific citizenship concepts found in Directive 2004/38 are traced. The interpretation of these provisions is the most active strand of citizenship case law at the Court of Justice at present, as national authorities try to make sense of how the Directive should

---

[41] Eg in its 30th Annual Report on Monitoring the Application of EU Law (http://ec.europa.eu/eu_law/docs/docs_infringements/annual_report_30/sg_annual_report_monitoring_eu_law_131023.pdf), the Commission noted that '[t]here were 491 complaints concerning justice in 2012 (433 in 2011). Most concerned the free movement of people, citizenship rights, various forms of discrimination, fundamental rights, civil justice and consumer law' (57); the Commission noted on the same page that it had sent reasoned opinions to six Member States (Austria, the Czech Republic, Germany, Lithuania, Sweden, and the UK) 'because of their incomplete implementation' of Dir 2004/38/EC. Similarly, in its 2012 Report on the activities of the Committee of Petitions (A7-0299/2013), it was observed that '[p]etitions give evidence that citizens in the European Union continue to face barriers to exercising their freedom of movement as individuals, workers, and also as providers and consumers of goods and services' and that 37 per cent of all petitions received in connection with the internal market concerned the free movement of persons (23).

[42] See http://www.consilium.europa.eu/uedocs/cms_data/docs/pressdata/en/jha/139959.pdf. In the preamble, the Council notes 'gaps between the applicable legal rules and the reality confronting citizens in their daily lives'; see also, para 24.

[43] See http://eudo-citizenship.eu/ and http://eudo-citizenship.eu/about/fracit, respectively. See also eg http://beucitizen.eu and https://sites.google.com/a/york.ac.uk/eurightsproject.

be applied in an inevitable multitude of factual circumstances. But the Directive does not capture the full reach of free movement rights. In Section III.2, the scope—and independent significance—of the primary rights conferred directly by the Treaty is therefore outlined.

Linking both case studies together, it will become apparent that the legal dimensions of citizenship are being shaped at present by an increasingly atomistic case law. We now see a less strident emphasis on rights expansion as well as, relatedly, a tamer release of the path-breaking force of EU law—in contrast to the pioneering judicial confidence with which we had perhaps become more familiar.

1. Animating the Concepts of Union Citizenship Legislation

It was noted in Section II.2 that Directive 2004/38 was intended to have *both* simplifying or consolidating and rights-strengthening purposes. Examples of the latter objective include the enhanced protection established for the family members of Union citizens in situations of the death of the citizen or his/her departure from a host state (Article 12) as well as in cases of divorce, annulment of marriage, or termination of a registered partnership (Article 13). The rights-strengthening impulse of the Directive reflected a dynamic that was clearly evident in case law on the free movement of persons more generally. For example, reflecting the Union's incrementally deepening concern for the protection of fundamental rights, respect for the family life of Union citizens had become a powerful source of material rights in the case law—whether the applicant was engaged in economic activity[44] or not.[45] More generally, the Court has consistently stressed that the provisions of the Directive should not be interpreted restrictively.[46] It has also continued to require that qualitative, case-by-case assessments of individual situations must be made when the determination of eligibility for EU rights protection is at stake.[47]

Case law on the interpretation of the Directive has focused primarily on two sets of its provisions. First, several cases explore rights that originated in repealed legislative measures and are now reconfigured (normally expanded) in the Directive. For example, the provisions that regulate expulsion from the Member States pull

---

[44] See eg Case C-60/00 *Carpenter* [2002] ECR I-6279.

[45] See eg *MRAX* (n 15); confirming this approach after the adoption of the Directive, see eg Case C-127/08 *Metock and others* [2008] ECR I-6241.

[46] See eg *Metock* (n 45) para 84.

[47] An example of this approach can be seen in case law on maintenance aid for studies. Art 24(2) of the Directive derogates from the principle of equal treatment by confirming that Member States are not under an obligation to extend such assistance to migrant students unless the latter are economically active, family members of an economically active migrant citizen, or permanently resident in the host state. However, where national rules fall outwith this threshold, they can still be subjected

together not only the baseline premises that were scattered across different legislative measures, but also the interpretative scaffolding layered onto those rights by principles and tests developed through case law.[48] But the Directive innovates too. In the context of expulsion, two stronger tiers of protection that go beyond the pre-existing norm were created: 'serious' grounds of public policy or public security in Article 28(2)—applicable when Union citizens or their family members have the right to permanent residence—and 'imperative' grounds of public security in Article 28(3), applicable when Union citizens have resided in a host state for ten years or are minors (unless expulsion is necessary in their best interests).[49] The interpretation of the Article 7(1) conditions on comprehensive sickness insurance and sufficient resources—introduced in three Directives adopted in the 1990s and applicable when migrant citizens are not workers or self-employed—provides another example of this set of cases.[50] The example used as a case study here concerns the definition of 'other' family members and partners for the purposes of Article 3(2), noting the volume of case law appearing on this provision already.

The second main theme of litigation addresses the meaning and scope of rights created by the Directive for the first time, of which the right of permanent residence is an important example. Both of these case studies will now be looked at in turn, linked through a shared objective of identifying broader themes of interpretation as well as spikes of interpretative concern.

(a) Article 3 of the Directive: The Relationships that Matter (in Law)

It has long been provided for in free movement law that certain family members accompanying or joining migrant Member State nationals acquire through that connection a series of derivative rights in the host Member State. Article 3 of the Directive effects two different levels of protection in this respect. Article 3(1) links back to the family members specified in Article 2(2)—ie spouses; registered partners if the partnership was contracted on the basis of the legislation of a Member State and the legislation of the host Member State treats registered partnerships as equivalent to marriage; direct descendants of the Union citizen (or their spouse

---

to review against the 'genuine link' integration test developed before the entry into force of the Directive in Case C-209/03 *Bidar* [2005] ECR I-2119; see eg Joined Cases C-523/11 & C-585/11 *Prinz and Seeberger*, judgment of 18 July 2013.

[48] Eg the statement in Art 27 of the Directive that '[t]he personal conduct of the individual concerned must represent a genuine, present and sufficiently serious threat affecting one of the fundamental interests of society' can be traced back to eg Case 67/74 *Bonsignore* [1975] ECR 297, para 7 and Case 30/77 *Bouchereau* [1977] ECR 1999, para 35.

[49] On the scope of Art 27, see Case C-33/07 *Jipa* [2008] ECR I-5157, Case C-430/10 *Gaydarov* [2011] ECR I-11637, and Case C-300/11 *ZZ*, judgment of 4 June 2013; on Art 28, see Case C-145/09 *Tsakouridis* [2010] ECR I-11979, Case C-348/09 *PI*, judgment of 22 May 2012, and Case C-400/12 *MG*, judgment of 16 January 2014.

[50] See eg Case C-46/12 *LN*, judgment of 21 February 2013; Case C-140/12 *Brey*, judgment of 19 September 2013; and Case C-507/12 *Saint Prix*, judgment of 19 June 2014.

or registered partner) under 21 or dependent; and dependent direct relatives in the ascending line of the Union citizen (or their spouse or partner). Article 3(1) states simply that the Directive 'shall apply' to these family members—extending to them, in effect, the rights associated with movement and residence, including the right to work. However, Article 3(2) requires that a host Member State need only 'in accordance with its national legislation, facilitate entry and residence' for two other categories of persons:

(a) any other family members, irrespective of their nationality, not falling under the definition in [Article 2(2)] who, in the country from which they have come, are dependants or members of the household of the Union citizen having the primary right of residence, or where serious health grounds strictly require the personal care of the family member by the Union citizen;
(b) the partner with whom the Union citizen has a durable relationship, duly attested.

Article 3(2) also requires that the host state 'shall undertake an extensive examination of the personal circumstances and shall justify any denial of entry or residence to these people'.

Some of the distinctions drawn in Article 3 have their origins in previous legislation or case law. For example, Article 10(2) of Regulation 1612/68 provided that: 'Member States shall facilitate the admission of any member of the family not coming within the provisions of paragraph 1 if dependent on the worker referred to above or living under his roof in the country whence he comes.' Similarly, the reciprocal significance of host state partnership recognition can be traced to the Court's decision in *Reed*, which concerned a right of residence for the partner of a British national working in the Netherlands.[51] Classifying that right as a 'social advantage' within the meaning of Article 7(2) of the Regulation, the Court then applied equal treatment reasoning and held that: 'a Member State which permits the unmarried companions of its nationals, who are not themselves nationals of that Member State, to reside in its territory cannot refuse to grant the same advantage to migrant workers who are nationals of other Member States.'[52]

But the extended framework created by Article 3 is not straightforward innovation. It is not clear, for example, what the position of same-sex *spouses*—ie spouses rather than 'registered partners' under the legislation of the state in which the marriage took place—actually is. Surely they should be fully recognized as spouses under Article 3(1) rather than partners in a durable relationship under Article 3(2)(b)— irrespective of how (or whether) same-sex partnerships are regulated under host state law? To conclude otherwise would exclude such spouses from the statement in Article 3(1) that the Directive 'shall apply' to them and require, instead, that a host Member State would merely have to 'facilitate' their entry and residence should they

---

[51] Case 59/85 *Reed* [1986] ECR 1283.   [52] *Reed* (n 51) para 29.

wish to accompany or join their Union citizen spouse there. How could that outcome be defended in a Union that commits, in Article 21(1) of the Charter, to a prohibition of discrimination on grounds of sexual orientation? AG Mengozzi has remarked that:

The fact that the rights granted to family members are only derived rights highlights the fundamental objective pursued by Directive 2004/38, which is not family reunification, or respect for the private and family life of Union citizens, but rather those citizens' 'primary and individual right to move and reside freely within the territory of the Member States' . . . The preservation of the unity of the family group was not overlooked by the European Union legislature, but it was not its principal concern.[53]

But even bearing that context in mind, it does not follow that a Directive regulating citizenship rights should hold quite so much potential for *unequal* treatment within it.

The legislature's reluctance to take a more direct stance on the rights of same-sex partners lies in the argument that social mores evolve at different paces in different States.[54] Directive 2004/38 is not about forcing states to change their own partnership recognition laws (though this may happen in some states where there is an obligation under national law to avoid situations of reverse discrimination against home state nationals). Rather, the Directive seeks to ensure that migrant Union citizens are not disadvantaged in such a fundamental way if they do make the choice to move. At the time of writing, seven Member States provide for same-sex marriage and a further eight for registered partnerships.[55] This means that the majority of the substantive rights provided for by Directive 2004/38 will not be conferred on the registered partners of nationals of the latter set of eight Member States in almost half of the Union's other Member States. And yet, ironically, the Union's commitment to prohibiting discrimination based on sexual orientation is repeated in recital 31 of the preamble. The position of same-sex partnerships thus raises questions about the limits of law generally, but also about situations that sit perhaps at the boundary between *equal* treatment in a host state and *special* treatment there.

Article 3 also creates the possibility of disparities across states on the meaning of dependency and of the durability of relationships—something that again sits uneasily with the EU's legal lodestar of equal treatment, since it indicates that a not inconsequential set of apparently *acceptable* differences in treatment are condoned by the Directive. The Commission's 2009 guidance on the implementation of the Directive suggested that durable partners seeking the facilitation of their entry to

[53] AG Mengozzi in Case C-423/12 *Reyes*, judgment of 16 January 2014, para 32 of the Opinion.

[54] Commenting on the scope of the Directive on this point prior to its adoption, the Council decided that 'when contained in a [Union] act the notion of "spouse" has to be interpreted by reference to the situation in the large majority of Member States, meaning spouse of the opposite sex in the framework of the traditional marriage' (Doc 12218/03, 5 September 2003, p 3, cited in M. Meduna with N. Stockwell, F. Geyer, C. Adamo, and P. Nemitz, 'Union Citizenship: Development, Impact and Challenges' (Institutional Report prepared for FIDE 2014 http://fide2014.eu/) at 26).

[55] Meduna et al. (n 54) 27.

and residence in a host state 'may be required to present documentary evidence that they are partners of an EU citizen and that the partnership is durable' and that related national rules 'can refer to a minimum amount of time as a criterion for whether a partnership can be considered as durable. However, in this case national rules would need to foresee that other relevant aspects (such as for example a joint mortgage to buy a home) are also taken into account'.[56]

These examples demonstrate a starting point of *loosely* drawn outer limits vis-à-vis the concepts codified in Article 3, and so it is unsurprising that the European Court of Justice is being consistently asked to clarify the scope of the discretion conferred on the Member States by several parts of the provision. Looking first at Article 3(1), a fundamental finding in the *Metock* case was that

Directive 2004/38 precludes legislation of a Member State which requires a national of a non-member country who is the spouse of a Union citizen residing in that Member State but not possessing its nationality to have previously been lawfully resident in another Member State before arriving in the host Member State, in order to benefit from [its] provisions.[57]

The Court confirmed in *Sahin* that third-country national spouses of migrant Union citizens benefit from the Directive 'irrespective of when and where their marriage took place and of how the national of a non-member country entered the host Member State', which includes situations where the family member arrived in the host state independently of the Union citizen.[58]

In *McCarthy*, the Court emphasized that a Union citizen who has 'never exercised his right of free movement and has always resided in a Member State of which he is a national . . . is not covered by the concept of "beneficiary" for the purposes of Article 3(1)', even if that citizen also holds the nationality of another Member State too and excluding their spouse, in turn, from the scope of the measure.[59] The pre-Directive status afforded to spouses who have separated from Union citizens was confirmed in *Iida*, with the Court holding that 'a marital relationship cannot be regarded as dissolved as long as it has not been terminated by the competent authority, and that is not the case where the spouses merely live separately, even if they intend to divorce at a later date, so that the spouse does not necessarily have to live permanently with the Union citizen in order to hold a derived right of residence'.[60] But the Court qualified the scope of that finding:

while he may be regarded as a 'family member' of his spouse within the meaning of Article 2(2)(a) of Directive 2004/38, he cannot be classified as a '*beneficiary*' of that directive, as

---

[56] COM (2009) 313 final, para 2.1.2.

[57] *Metock* (n 45) para 80; contra the earlier decision (on workers) in Case C-109/01 *Akrich* [2003] ECR I-9607.

[58] Case C-551/07 *Sahin* [2008] ECR I-10453, paras 32–33.

[59] Case C-434/09 *McCarthy* [2011] ECR I-3375, paras 39–41.

[60] Case C-40/11 *Iida*, judgment of 8 November 2012, para 58, referring to Case 267/83 *Diatta* [1985] ECR 567, paras 20 and 22.

Article 3(1) . . . requires that the family member of the Union citizen moving to or residing in a Member State other than that of which he is a national should *accompany or
join* him.[61]

However, the latter condition does not require more than residence in the same
state as the Union citizen.[62]

Second, the criterion of dependency has generated several preliminary rulings
to date. Looking first at Article 2(2), AG Sharpston has contrasted the 'automatic'
derived rights granted to a 'select group of family members' (spouses, registered
partners, and children under 21) with those subject to a requirement of dependency, ie direct descendants over 21 and direct relatives in the ascending line.[63] She
argues that, in the context of the Directive:

[D]ependency has been interpreted narrowly so as to focus on whether an EU citizen materially supports these family members. Whilst such dependency undoubtedly can be highly
indicative of the extent to which denying residence interferes with the exercise of rights of
free movement and residence, the Court has indicated—outside the context of Directive
2004/38—that dependency can also be measured using indicators of legal or emotional ties
or that it can be relevant that an EU citizen is dependent on a third country national family
member ('reverse dependency').[64]

Situations 'outside the context of the Directive' will be considered in Section III.2.
In *Iida*, interpreting the meaning of dependency within Article 2(2) of the Directive,
the Court confirmed that it 'is the result of a factual situation characterised by the
fact that *material support* for the family member is provided by the holder of the
right of residence'.[65] In *Reyes*, the Court added that a descendant over 21 does not
need 'to establish that he has tried without success to find work or obtain subsistence support from the authorities of his country of origin and/or otherwise
tried to support himself', and, moreover: 'the fact that a relative—due to personal
circumstances such as age, education and health—is deemed to be well placed to
obtain employment and in addition intends to start work in the Member State
does not affect the interpretation of the requirement in that provision that he be a
"dependant".'[66]

For family members that fall within the scope of Article 3(2)(a), however, the situation is more complicated. The provision itself introduces the additional prospect of
physical as well as material dependence, noting the possibility of establishing a claim

---

[61] *Iida* (n 60) para 61 (emphasis added).   [62] *Iida* (n 60) paras 62–64.

[63] AG Sharpston in Case C-456/12 *O* and Case C-457/12 *S*, judgments of 12 March 2014, para 48 of
the joint Opinion.

[64] AG Sharpston in *O* and *S*, ibid, para 48 of the joint Opinion.

[65] *Iida* (n 60) para 55 (emphasis added), affirming the pre-Directive position established in eg Case
C-1/05 *Jia* [2007] ECR I-1, para 35. The Court therefore inferred that the third country national father
in *Iida* could not be 'dependent' on his Union citizen child, referring to paras 43 and 44 of its earlier
ruling in Case C-200/02 *Zhu and Chen* [2004] ECR I-9925.

[66] *Reyes* (n 53) paras 25 and 33.

on 'serious health grounds strictly requir[ing] the personal care of the family member by the Union citizen'. However, the Directive seems to ignore the possibility that a Union citizen may have the same kind of relationship of care with a non-relative, a point picked up again below. Article 2(2) does not make it clear whether physical dependency applies to, for example, ascending relatives or descendants over 21, and there has been no case law on the point to date. To complicate matters, recital 6 of the Directive's preamble seems to suggest that the criteria that are specified do not necessarily amount to an exhaustive list: 'taking into consideration their relationship with the Union citizen *or any other circumstances, such as* their financial or physical dependence on the Union citizen' (emphasis added).

In *Rahman*, the first comprehensive analysis of Article 3(2), the Court pointed out that:

it follows both from the wording of Article 3(2) . . . and from the general system of the directive that the European legislature has drawn a distinction between a Union citizen's family members as defined in Article 2(2) . . . who enjoy . . . a right of entry into and residence in that citizen's host Member State, and the other family members envisaged in Article 3(2) of the Directive, whose entry and residence has only to be facilitated by that Member State.[67]

The Court did not accept the argument that an obligation of facilitation created a 'presumption of admission',[68] but did characterize it as 'impos[ing] an obligation on the Member States to confer a certain advantage, compared with applications for entry and residence of other nationals of third states, on applications submitted by persons who have a relationship of particular dependence with a Union citizen', which requires states to base such decisions on 'an extensive examination of their personal circumstances' and to ensure that refusals are 'justified by reasons'.[69]

The Court then articulated the parameters of state discretion under Article 3(2) in more detail. First, when examining the personal circumstances of an applicant, states should 'take account of the various factors that may be relevant in the particular case, such as the extent of economic or physical dependence and the degree of relationship between the family member and the Union citizen whom he wishes to accompany or join'.[70] This passage, which had been framed by direct reference to recital 6 of the preamble, conveys openness to a broad understanding of dependency. The same impression of expansiveness is seen in paragraph 32 of the judgment:

as follows from recital 6 . . . the objective of [Article 3(2)] is to 'maintain the unity of the family in a broader sense' by facilitating entry and residence for *persons* who are not

---

[67] Case C-83/11 *Rahman*, judgment of 5 September 2012, para 19.

[68] AG Bot in *Rahman* (n 67) para 59 of the Opinion, referring to written observations submitted in the case by the Centre for Advice on Individual Rights in Europe (AIRE Centre).

[69] *Rahman* (n 67) para 22; in para 25, the Court also confirmed an applicant's entitlement to judicial review of a refusal decision.

[70] *Rahman* (n 67) para 23.

included in the definition of family member of a Union citizen contained in Article 2(2) of Directive 2004/38 but who nevertheless maintain *close and stable family ties* with a Union citizen *on account of specific factual circumstances, such as* economic dependence, *being a member of the household* or serious health grounds (emphasis added).

Perhaps it is not entirely clear after all, then, if the concept of 'family member' has to be premised only on an objective, ie blood relationship. This is an important point that needs to be clarified in future case law.

The Court also acknowledged, noting the reference to 'national legislation' in Article 3(2), that 'each Member State has a wide discretion as regards the selection of the factors to be taken into account'.[71] In that context, a Member State may include in its rules 'particular requirements as to the nature and duration of dependence, in order in particular to satisfy themselves that the situation of dependence is genuine and stable and has not been brought about with the sole objective of obtaining entry into and residence in the host Member State'.[72] Reflecting the distinction between the existence and the exercise of Treaty rights drawn in Section II.1: 'the host Member State must ensure that its legislation contains criteria which are consistent with the normal meaning of the term "facilitate" and of the words relating to dependence used in Article 3(2), and which do not deprive that provision of its effectiveness.'[73] Finally, the Court held that 'the situation of dependence must exist in the country from which the family member concerned comes, at the very least at the time when he applies to join the Union citizen on whom he is dependent'.[74]

Overall, it is important first to recognize that the framework created by Articles 2 and 3 of the Directive clearly strengthens the rights of family members when compared to the rules that applied before the Directive's adoption. However, signs of unequal treatment do tarnish the picture now in place. The fact that the concept of dependency seems to mean different things for Articles 2 and 3 of the Directive is an example of unnecessary complication. Additionally, notwithstanding the objective of maintaining the 'unity of the family in a broader sense' in recital 6, there is evidence of a sliding scale of rights that is partly based more on the form than the meaningfulness of the relationship at stake. The potential for different outcomes in different states is amplified by, in particular, the discretion that states retain not only with respect to recognition of same-sex partnerships but also in the *substantiation* of concepts such as dependency and durability.

On one view, this position accords with the notion that migrant citizens are not entitled to special treatment in host states above and beyond the rules applicable to home state nationals. But the value judgments about different kinds of families and different kinds of relationships—even if implicit—that the Directive reflects sit

---

[71] *Rahman* (n 67) para 24.   [72] *Rahman* (n 67) para 38.
[73] *Rahman* (n 67) para 34.   [74] *Rahman* (n 67) para 35.

uneasily with the qualities of dignity and tolerance that should guide the development of citizenship law. Notably, in *Rahman*, the Court did not repeat a point made by AG Bot in his Opinion: that 'the margin of discretion enjoyed by the Member States is limited by the obligation to respect the right to private and family life, enshrined in Article 7 of the Charter'.[75] In fact, there is no mention of either respect for family life or the Charter more generally in any part of the judgment at all.

(b) Article 16 and the Right of Permanent Residence

Permanent residence is one of the most important innovations of the Directive. Recital 17 of the preamble asserts that the status 'would strengthen the feeling of Union citizenship and is a key element in promoting social cohesion'. Article 16(1) confers a right of permanent residence on Union citizens 'who have resided legally for a continuous period of five years in the host Member State'. Article 16(2) extends the right to third-country national family members who meet the same criteria—in effect, shifting their situation at this point from derived towards more autonomous rights. Conditions regarding permitted interruptions to continuity of residence are outlined in Article 16(3), and, according to Article 16(4), the right will be lost only through absence from the host state for a period exceeding two consecutive years. Articles 17 and 18 set out a series of exemptions and other conditions, for example on the acquisition of the right before five years in certain cases, and Articles 19–21 outline relevant administrative formalities.

As mentioned previously, Article 28(2) provides for greater protection from expulsion. Article 16(2) establishes another concrete privilege: that the conditions outlined in Chapter III of the Directive—including the financial self-sufficiency criteria—cease to apply.[76] Recital 18 explains that this limb of permanent residence seeks to ensure that it will 'be a genuine vehicle for integration into the society of the host Member State'. The derogation from equal treatment outlined in Article 24(2) sets out the converse position, enabling host states to restrict access to certain benefits before the right is acquired.[77]

Early case law concerned whether or not periods of legal residence completed in states prior to the expiry of the transposition period,[78] or prior to the accession of the host state to the Union,[79] could be counted towards the acquisition of

---

[75] AG Bot in *Rahman* (n 67) para 70 of the Opinion.

[76] See further, Case C-46/12, *LN*, judgment of 21 February 2013, paras 34–35.

[77] The particularity of jobseeker's allowance, given that it is tied to Art 45 as well as Art 21 TFEU, has been taken out of Art 24(2) altogether through case law; see Joined Cases C-22/08 and C-23/08 *Vatsouras and Koupatantze* [2009] ECR I-4585.

[78] Case C-162/09 *Lassal* [2010] ECR I-9217. The Court also confirmed that absences from the host Member State of less than two consecutive years that occurred before 30 April 2006 but following a continuous period of five years' legal residence completed before that date do not affect the acquisition of permanent residence.

[79] Joined Cases C-424/10 and C-425/10 *Ziolkowski and Szeja*, judgment of 21 December 2011; Joined Cases C-147/11 and C-148/11 *Czop and Punakova*, judgment of 6 September 2012.

permanent residence—with both points ruled on positively by the Court of Justice on the basis that concluding otherwise would deprive the rights included in the Directive of their effectiveness. The meaning of 'legal' residence has been focused on in more recent case law, as national authorities seek to understand when periods of residence can be *excluded* from consideration. In *Ziolkowski and Szeja*, it was noted that 'the wording of [Article 16(1)] of Directive 2004/38 does not give any guidance on how the terms "who have resided legally" in the host Member State are to be understood' but that, equally, the Directive 'does not contain any reference to national laws as regards the meaning of those terms either'.[80] The Court thus reasoned that legal residence must be considered as 'an autonomous concept of European Union law which must be interpreted in a uniform manner throughout the Member States'.[81] Drawing from the general scheme of the Directive,[82] the Court then held:

[T]he concept of legal residence implied by the terms 'have resided legally' in Article 16(1) . . . should be construed as meaning a period of residence which complies with the conditions laid down in the Directive, in particular those set out in Article 7(1). Consequently, a period of residence which complies with the law of a Member State but does not satisfy the conditions laid down in Article 7(1) of Directive 2004/38 cannot be regarded as a 'legal' period of residence within the meaning of Article 16(1).[83]

AG Bot took a different view. In line with the approach applied in citizenship case law more generally, he argued that legal residence under *either* EU law or national law should be taken into account.[84] The distinction brought about by the Court's judgment privileges a more uniform compliance with the conditions laid down in the Directive, at one level; but it does leave the case law on residence acquired through national law out on a limb. That result does not quite align with the broader statement that 'the aim of Directive 2004/38 is to leave behind a sector-by-sector piecemeal approach to the right of freedom of movement and residence'.[85]

The Court was careful to point out that its approach to legal residence does not preclude the application of more favourable national provisions.[86] But it did prefer the stricter of the two interpretations that could feasibly have been applied.[87] The repercussions can be illustrated with reference to case law in which it was

---

[80] *Ziolkowski and Szeja* (n 79) para 33.   [81] *Ziolkowski and Szeja* (n 79) para 33.

[82] And noting, in particular, Arts 1, 7, 12, 13, 14, and 18, as well as several recitals of the preamble.

[83] *Ziolkowski and Szeja* (n 79) paras 46–47.

[84] AG Bot in *Ziolkowski and Szeja* (n 79) para 36ff. This view aligns with eg Case C-85/96 *Martínez Sala* [1998] ECR I-2691 and Case C-456/02 *Trojani*. These cases are discussed in Section III.2.

[85] Case C-529/11 *Alarape and Tijani*, judgment of 8 May 2013, para 36.

[86] *Ziolkowski and Szeja* (n 79) paras 48–50.

[87] Cf reasoning based more explicitly on respect for family life, in the specific context of the Directive, with the EFTA Court holding that 'an EEA national with a right of permanent residence, who is a pensioner and in receipt of social welfare benefits in the host EEA State, may claim the right to family reunification even if the family member will also be claiming social welfare benefits' (Case E-4/11 *Clauder*, judgment of 8 April 2013, para 50).

confirmed, first, that children of migrant workers in host state education have a right to reside there (under Regulation 492/2011) in order to complete their education and, second, that the parent who is their primary carer—irrespective of nationality—has a derived right to reside there with them.[88] On the second point, since these residence rights stem from the Regulation and not Directive 2004/38, there is no obligation on either the citizen or their carer to meet the Directive's conditions on self-sufficiency, whether through the exercise of economic activity or the holding of independent resources. But periods in which those conditions are not met cannot then be counted towards the acquisition of permanent residence.[89] This result advances a very particular understanding of the 'social cohesion' referred to in recital 16: what could be termed 'sub-Directive residence rights' might be recognized in certain situations, but the beneficiaries will not be 'rewarded' with an outcome of permanent residence.

A second dimension of the same issue concerns whether or not periods of imprisonment in the host state can be counted towards permanent residence. In *Onuekwere*, the Court answered the question in the negative for third-country national family members of Union citizens. First, it reasoned that the acquisition of permanent residence in these circumstances

is dependent . . . not only on the fact that the Union citizen himself satisfies the conditions laid down in Article 16(1) . . . but also on the fact that those family members have resided legally and continuously 'with' that citizen for the period in question, the word 'with' reinforcing the condition that those family members must accompany or join that same citizen.[90]

It is not altogether clear if the Court is backtracking here from the 'in the same State' understanding of 'with' noted earlier. If it were, then all kinds of other situations outwith the specificities of imprisonment would be similarly excluded.

Adding another (and presumably cumulative) interpretative layer, however, and reflecting the ideas captured by recital 17 of the preamble, the Court went on to emphasize integration into host state society as a 'precondition' (para 25) for acquiring permanent residence rights:

Such integration . . . is based not only on territorial and temporal factors *but also on qualitative elements*, relating to the level of integration in the host Member State . . . to such an extent that the undermining of the link of integration between the person concerned and the host Member State justifies the loss of the right of permanent residence *even outside the circumstances mentioned in Article 16(4) of Directive 2004/38* . . . The imposition of a prison sentence by the national court is such as to show the non-compliance by the person concerned with the values expressed by the society of the host Member State in its criminal law, with the result that the taking into consideration of periods of imprisonment for the

---

[88] Case C-310/08 *Ibrahim* [2010] ECR I-1065; Case C-480/08 *Teixeira* [2010] ECR I-1107.
[89] *Alarape and Tijani* (n 85) paras 35–37.
[90] Case C-378/12 *Onuekwere*, judgment of 16 January 2014, para 23.

purposes of the acquisition by family members of a Union citizen who are not nationals of a Member State of the right of permanent residence ... would clearly be contrary to the aim pursued by [Directive 2004/38] in establishing that right of residence.[91]

We can assume that the same analysis would apply if the applicant were a Union citizen.[92]

The Court expressly admits that its integration test falls 'outside the circumstances mentioned in Article 16(4) of the Directive'. At a basic level, another value judgment is being made here: permanent residence is again conceived of as a 'reward' and certain citizens are excluded from attaining it.[93] But within the text extracted, there is also, as pointed out above, the potential for other restrictions to be placed on the acquisition of permanent residence, ie for understanding imprisonment as just one example of a situation that 'undermines the link of integration'. An example was provided by one of the questions forwarded by the High Court in Ireland for a preliminary ruling:

Can it be said that the spouse of an EU national who was not at the time himself a national of a Member State has 'legally resided with the Union citizen in the host Member State for a continuous period of five years' for the purposes of Article 16(2) of Directive 2004/38/EC2, in circumstances where the couple had married in May 1999, where a right of residency was granted in October 1999 and where by early 2002 at the absolute latest the parties had agreed to live apart and where both spouses had commenced residing with entirely different partners by late 2002?[94]

Wisely, the Court of Justice ruled that 'Article 16(2) of Directive 2004/38 must be interpreted as meaning that a third-country national who, during a continuous period of five years before the transposition date for that directive, has resided in a Member State as the spouse of a Union citizen working in that Member State, must be regarded as having acquired a right of permanent residence under that provision, even though, during that period, the spouses decided to separate and commenced residing with other partners, and the home occupied by that national was no longer provided or made available by his spouse with Union citizenship' (para 47).

The right to permanent residence is a significant innovation that brings novel rights with it. So it is hardly unreasonable to ensure that its acquisition is

---

[91] *Onuekwere*, paras 25–26 (emphasis added); the Court also clarified that imprisonment interrupts the 'continuity of residence' demanded by Art 16(2) and (3) of the Directive.

[92] On the application of the reasoning in *Onuekwere* to Art 28(3)(a) of the Directive—special protection against expulsion—in a case involving a Portuguese national residing in the UK, see Case C-400/12 *MG*, judgment of 16 January 2014.

[93] In the context of expulsion but developing the same theme of conceptualizing integration in this way, see D. Kochenov and B. Pirker, 'Deporting Citizens within the European Union: A Counter-intuitive Trend in Case C-348/09 PI *v Oberbürgermeisterin der Stadt Remscheid*' (2013) 19 *Columbia Journal of European Law* 369.

[94] Case C-244/13 *Ogieriakhi*, judgment of 10 July 2014, para 27.

clearly—and carefully—delineated. However, we see here the recurrence of some themes also identified in the discussion on Article 3: a splintering of approaches and/or concepts, and the making of stricter choices when more than one route might be legally feasible. At one level, the case law on Directive 2004/38 represents a *settling* phase, focused on concepts and tests within individual provisions, being applied by national authorities in discrete sets of circumstances. But this means that the case law has also become more *atomistic* and it raises a question about whether a coherent vision still underpins the bigger picture of citizenship law—analogous to the 'fundamental status' idea or the focus on respect for family life that dominated from the early to mid 2000s. In Section III.2, case law on the primary rights of citizenship is explored in order to pursue that quest, on the basis of testing the extent to which a 'bigger' citizenship project can be detected outwith the detail of the Directive.

2. The Scope and Persisting Significance of Primary Citizenship Rights

Directive 2004/38 was a milestone in Union citizenship law but it does not absorb the legal dimensions of entry and residence rights absolutely. Essentially, three types of situation continue to necessitate direct recourse to the primary rights conferred by the Treaty: the application of equal treatment to citizens who reside in a host state on the basis of national law; situations that are purely internal to a Member State; and situations where citizens rely on Union law against their own Member States after returning there from another state.

(a) Lawful Residence beyond EU Law

The legal basis on which a Member State national resides in a host state can be linked to Union law where the individual meets the conditions of Directive 2004/38, including the requirement of either economic activity or financial self-sufficiency in accordance with Article 7. Conversely, where a condition required by the Directive is *not* fulfilled, an EU basis for lawful residence cannot normally be claimed. However, as the Court emphasized in *Martínez Sala*, Member State nationals might be lawfully resident in a host state on the basis of national law. In such cases, they fall within the *personal* scope of Articles 20 and 21 TFEU and the host state is, in consequence, bound by the requirements of non-discrimination on the grounds of nationality for any related claims that fall within the *material* scope of EU law.

The implications of this reasoning were developed further in *Grzelczyk* and *Trojani*.[95] In both cases, the referring courts queried the eligibility of the applicants,

---

[95] Case C-184/99 *Grzelczyk* [2001] ECR I 6193; *Trojani* (n 84).

neither of whom was economically active, for the Belgian *minimex* (a subsistence allowance). In *Grzelczyk*, the Court acknowledged that a Member State was not precluded by EU law from 'taking the view that a student who has recourse to social assistance no longer fulfils the conditions of his right of residence or from taking measures, within the limits imposed by [Union] law, either to withdraw his residence permit or not to renew it' so long as such a measure was not the *automatic* consequence of the applicant's application to the state's social assistance system.[96] Where a state did not contest the lawfulness of that citizen's residence within their territory, however, s/he 'can rely on Article [18 TFEU] in all situations which fall within the scope *ratione materiae* of Community law'.[97] The underpinning vision was stated explicitly: 'Union citizenship is destined to be the fundamental status of nationals of the Member States, enabling those who find themselves in the same situation to enjoy the same treatment in law irrespective of their nationality, subject to such exceptions as are expressly provided for'[98]—a sentence repeated by the Court in several judgments in the area of citizenship law afterwards, but one that appears less frequently in more recent judgments.

The same approach was taken in *Trojani*, where another point made by the Court is worth reflecting on, however: 'Mr Trojani is lawfully resident in Belgium, *as is attested by the residence permit* which has in the meantime been issued to him by the municipal authorities of Brussels.'[99] Lawful residence in a host state under national law is not, therefore, an accidental status that can be derived from failure to deport.

However, the recent ruling in *Dano* – in which the Court focused exclusively on the limits to equal treatment set out in *secondary* law – casts serious doubt on the continuing force of equal treatment as a *primary* right for Union citizens.[100]

(b) Purely Internal Situations

The Court has consistently confirmed that the material scope of the Treaty cannot be extended to 'internal situations which have no link with [Union] law'.[101] This does not mean that situations that are purely internal to one state can never come within the scope of the Treaty. But it does mean that a 'link' with Union law must be established. For citizenship law, a *cross-border* connection normally provides the relevant link—usually, but not necessarily,[102] through the exercise of movement.

---

[96] *Grzelczyk* (n 95) paras 42–43.   [97] *Grzelczyk* (n 95) para 32.
[98] *Grzelczyk* (n 95) para 31.   [99] *Trojani* (n 84) para 37 (emphasis added).
[100] "Case C-333/13 *Dano*, judgment of 11 November 2014. See further, N. Nic Shuibhne, 'State-less' (2014) 39 ELRev 751."
[101] Case C-499/06 *Nerkowska* [2008] ECR I-3993, para 25.
[102] See eg holding the passport of a Member State other than the state against which the material claim is being made can be sufficient, even if the claimant has never been in (ie moved to) the former State; see *Zhu and Chen* (n 65) paras 36–41.

However, the Court established in *Ruiz Zambrano* that 'Article 20 TFEU precludes national measures which have the effect of *depriving citizens of the Union of the genuine enjoyment of the substance of the rights* conferred by virtue of their status as citizens of the Union'.[103] Applying that test to the facts of the case, the Court held that '[a] refusal to grant a right of residence to a third country national with dependent minor children in the Member State where those children are nationals and reside, and also a refusal to grant such a person a work permit, has such an effect' on the basis that 'such a refusal would lead to a situation where those children, citizens of the Union, would have to leave the territory of the Union in order to accompany their parents'.[104] Any rights granted to family members on this basis are, like those codified in the Directive, derivative in nature.[105]

The Court had not used the language of 'genuine enjoyment of the substance' of citizenship rights before *Ruiz Zambrano*, but it did reference its earlier decision in *Rottmann* on this point. There, the Court held that, first, determining the conditions for acquisition and loss of nationality falls within the competence of the Member States; second, the Member States must nevertheless have 'due regard' to EU law in situations falling within its scope; and therefore, third, that:

[T]he situation of a citizen of the Union who, like the applicant in the main proceedings, is faced with a decision withdrawing his naturalisation, adopted by the authorities of one Member State, and placing him, after he has lost the nationality of another Member State that he originally possessed, in a position capable of causing him to lose the status conferred by Article [20 TFEU] and the rights attaching thereto falls, by reason of its nature and its consequences, within the ambit of European Union law.[106]

This is the specific paragraph to which the Court referred in *Ruiz Zambrano* as supporting authority for the genuine enjoyment of rights test. Mr Rottmann had moved from Austria to Germany, but this did not seem to be a material factor in the Court's substantive finding that national authorities should take decisions on the withdrawal of nationality in light of EU proportionality requirements.

Although referring to the family reunification cases rather than to *Rottmann*, a point made by the Court in *Ymeraga* better reflects the thread between both sets of cases: 'The common element . . . is that, although they are governed by legislation which falls a priori within the competence of the Member States . . . they none the less have an intrinsic connection with the freedom of movement of a Union citizen.'[107]

---

[103] Case C-34/09 *Ruiz Zambrano* [2011] ECR I-1177, para 42 (emphasis added).

[104] *Ruiz Zambrano* (n 102) paras 43–44; in para 44, the Court added that '[s]imilarly, if a work permit were not granted to such a person, he would risk not having sufficient resources to provide for himself and his family, which would also result in the children, citizens of the Union, having to leave the territory of the Union. In those circumstances, those citizens of the Union would, in fact, be unable to exercise the substance of the rights conferred on them by virtue of their status as citizens of the Union.'

[105] *Iida* (n 60) para 67.   [106] Case C 135/08 *Rottmann* [2010] ECR I-1449, para 42.

[107] Case C-87/12 *Ymeraga*, judgment of 8 May 2013, para 37.

When national authorities make decisions that either withdraw Union citizenship altogether, or force a Union citizen to live outwith the EU territory, the resulting implications are so serious, in other words, that the purely internal boundary is necessarily and rightly displaced by the very status, and associated rights, conferred by Article 20. But nothing short of this *level* of interference will suffice.

Questions of dependency can also play a role in the context of forced departure, as indicated in Section III.1.i. In *Dereci*, AG Mengozzi considered that 'the refusal to grant a residence permit to a national of a non-member country on whom one of his or her parents, who is a Union citizen, is economically *and/or* legally, administratively and emotionally dependent, could expose that citizen to the same risk of no longer being able to rely on his or her status and of having to leave the territory of the Union'.[108] But he also appeared to confine this perspective to situations involving the dependency of minor children only.[109] In *O and S*, both AG Bot's Opinion and the judgment of the Court went further. AG Bot suggested that situations of forced departure in the context of dependency might additionally 'concern adult children on whom a parent is dependent because of an illness or a disability'.[110] In its judgment, the Court referred to 'persons on whom those citizens are legally, financially or emotionally dependent'.[111]

In *Rahman*, AG Bot wrote that the significance of the genuine enjoyment test lies in the fact that it 'bring[s] within the protective scope of EU law situations which, in the absence of any cross-border element, would normally be excluded from it'.[112] That shift caused a profound constitutional change, and it rightly generated strong academic reactions that assessed the indelibly altered character of Union citizenship.[113] However, it is important also to emphasize that the steep benchmark of *forced* departure from the Union is what has been consistently emphasized in subsequent case law.[114] The constitutional shift is thus deep but narrow—at least for now. The Court has been especially reluctant to engage in substantive discussions of respect

---

[108] AG Mengozzi in Case C-256/11 *Dereci*, judgment of 15 November 2011, para 48 of the View (emphasis added).

[109] AG Mengozzi in *Dereci* (n 108) para 36 of the View.

[110] AG Bot in Joined Cases C-356/11 and C-357/11 *O and S*, judgment of 6 December 2012, paras 44–45 of the Opinion.

[111] *O and S* (n 110) para 56 (emphasis added). Cf AG Tizzano in *Chen* (n 65) para 84 of the Opinion; and fn 15 of the Commission's 2009 Communication on Better Transposition of Dir 2004/38 (n 37).

[112] AG Bot in *Rahman* (n 67) para 69 of the Opinion.

[113] See eg K. Hailbronner and D. Thym, 'Comment on Case C-34/09 Ruiz Zambrano' (2011) 48 *Common Market Law Review* 1253; D. Kochenov and R. Plender, 'EU Citizenship: From an Incipient Form to an Incipient Substance? The Discovery of the Treaty Text' (2012) 37 *European Law Review* 369; H. van Eijken and S.A. dee Vries, 'A New Route into the Promised Land? Being a European Citizen after *Ruiz Zambrano*' (2011) 36 *European Law Review* 704; and F. Wollenschläger, 'A New Fundamental Freedom beyond Market Integration: Union Citizenship and its Dynamics for Shifting the Economic Paradigm of European Integration' (2011) 17 *European Law Journal* 34.

[114] *McCarthy* (n 59) paras 49–50; *Dereci* (n 108) paras 64–67; *Iida* (n 60) para 71; *O and S* (n 110) paras 47–48; *Ymeraga* (n 107) paras 35–40.

for family life in more recent case law—no reference to that right is made in the *Ruiz Zambrano* ruling; and subsequent judgments stress the proviso in Article 51(2) of the Charter that '[t]his Charter does not establish any new power or task for the Community or the Union, or modify powers and tasks defined by the Treaties'. The downplaying of fundamental rights in this way reflects a similar finding made in Section III.1 in connection with case law interpreting the Directive. But if that trend leads also to a downplaying of substantive protection, it should be resisted.

(c) Returning Home

The third set of cases based traditionally on the primary rights of Union citizenship relates to situations where a Member State national seeks to rely on EU law against *her or his own* state when s/he returns there *having already exercised* free movement rights. The idea that past movement could be legally relevant in those circumstances was established before the genesis of Union citizenship. In *Singh*, the Court developed this reasoning in the context of derivative residence for family members of economically active Member State nationals:

A national of a Member State might be deterred from leaving his country of origin in order to pursue an activity as an employed or self-employed person . . . in the territory of another Member State if, on returning to the Member State of which he is a national in order to pursue an activity there as an employed or self-employed person, the conditions of his entry and residence were not at least equivalent to those which he would enjoy under the Treaty or secondary law in the territory of another Member State. He would in particular be deterred from so doing if his spouse and children were not also permitted to enter and reside in the territory of his Member State of origin under conditions at least equivalent to those granted them by Community law in the territory of another Member State.[115]

That logic has left a significant impression on the development of citizenship rights too. In *Eind*, the Court reframed the *Singh* principle in the language of both general free movement rights and respect for fundamental rights.[116] The principle extends into other aspects of citizenship too. In *D'Hoop*, for example, the *Singh* case was applied to a question about access to a tideover allowance, which had been denied to the applicant in her home state (Belgium) because she had completed her secondary education in another Member State (France). The Court again considered that the opportunities offered by freedom of movement 'could not be fully effective if a national of a Member State could be deterred from availing himself of them by obstacles raised on his return to his country of origin by legislation penalising the fact that he has used them'.[117]

Two parallel frameworks had therefore developed: Directive 2004/38 covers situations where a Union citizen has moved to/is residing in another Member State;

---

[115] Case C-370/90 *Singh* [1992] ECR I-4265, paras 19–20.
[116] Case C-291/05 *Eind* [2007] ECR I-10719, paras 35–38 and 44.
[117] Case C-224/98 *D'Hoop* [2002] ECR I-6191, para 31.

but Articles 20 and 21 TFEU are the relevant legal pivots when the applicability of the Directive is ruled out, whether for reasons connected to (the absence of) self-sufficiency, or the fact that the exercise of free movement was in the past (or is still potential,[118] or is in fact non-existent[119]). An important question decided very recently by the Court is the extent to which these two rights tracks have the potential to *overlap*—in particular, do the conditions governing residence rights that apply in situations covered by the Directive apply to situations *outside* the scope of the Directive too?

This question connects back to the point that the rights conferred directly by Articles 20 and 21 TFEU are made expressly subject to limitations and conditions both in the Treaty itself *and* in measures adopted thereunder. Questions referred to the Court also raised another legal dimension of primary rights: situations that do involve *movement* to another state but *not* residence there. In that situation, and focusing in the first instance on the scope of the Directive directly, AG Sharpston pointed out that '[o]nly those provisions . . . regarding entry and exit will then apply. In principle, third country nationals cannot derive from EU law a right of residence in a Member State if their family member who is an EU citizen does not claim a right of residence and does not reside there'.[120] Noting that past movement does, however, trigger the relevance of Article 21 TFEU, she went on to argue that 'the conditions and limitations set out in Directive 2004/38 *also indirectly apply* to EU citizens returning to their home Member State'.[121] On this point, the Court ruled:

Even though Directive 2004/38 *does not cover* such a return, *it should be applied by analogy* to the conditions for the residence of a Union citizen in a Member State other than that of which he is a national, given that in both cases it is the Union citizen who is the sponsor for the grant of a derived right of residence to a third-country national who is a member of his family.[122]

In the same case, the Court also imposed, in effect, a *minimum duration* for the exercise of free movement rights that needs to be met before the protective EU shield can be generated by aligning the idea of 'genuine residence' (the first time that the Court has used this phrase in its citizenship case law) with residence established under Article 7(1)—and not Article 6(1)—of the Directive, ie residence for more than three months.[123]

The exercise of free movement does generate a sustained shield of protection in these situations, in other words, but it is not obligation free. This finding again reflects a theme that links recent case law on the interpretation of the Directive and

---

[118] See eg Case C-148/02 *Garcia Avello* [2003] ECR I-11613.
[119] See eg *McCarthy* (n 59) esp paras 43–44.
[120] AG Sharpston in *O* and *S* (n 63) para 71 of the joint Opinion.
[121] AG Sharpston (n 63) para 95 of the joint Opinion (emphasis added).
[122] *O* (n 63) para 50 (emphasis added).
[123] *O* (n 63) esp paras 52–53.

on the interpretation of primary rights. The legal dimensions of citizenship have shifted palpably towards a dynamic of rights *limiting*; accordingly, the complexity of the balance of interests between Union and state actors, and between rights and responsibilities, is increasingly apparent. While we might perceive that, overall, the extraordinary edifice of citizenship rights that grew from the Maastricht and *Martínez Sala* starting points is still legally solid, that does not mean that it goes far enough.[124] Neither does it convey a *truly* bigger picture of Union citizenship beyond the law. Section IV reflects in more detail on this second point.

IV. Conclusion: Broader Dimensions

The year 2013 was designated as the European Year of Citizens. However, in that initiative's closing conference, the European Ombudsman stated plainly that 'we must confront the reality . . . that "EU citizenship is now in crisis" '.[125] The reporting of certain states' concerns about the expiry in January 2014 of transitional arrangements that had been in place for Bulgarian and Romanian nationals is a particularly acute example in this context—and for that reason, it also represents a particularly low point in the progression of the EU as a fulcrum of integration more generally. For example, an opinion piece written by the British Prime Minister David Cameron for the *Financial Times* in November 2013 was entitled 'Free Movement within Europe Needs to be Less Free' on the basis that, primarily since the 2004 EU enlargement, 'things have gone wrong'.[126]

But that attitude is not by any means confined to the UK.[127] The result of the Swiss referendum on free movement restrictions in February 2014 provides powerful evidence of a far more widespread disconnect between the *vision* of an area without frontiers underpinned by free movement rights and perceptions of what that vision

---

[124] For a recent critique of how we conceptualize Union citizenship, see C. O'Brien, 'I Trade Therefore I Am: Legal Personhood in the European Union' (2013) 50 *Common Market Law Review* 1643. Cf N Nic Shuibhne, 'The Resilience of EU Market Citizenship', (2010) 47 *Common Market Law Review* 1597.

[125] The full text of the Ombudsman's speech, delivered on 13 December 2013, is available at http://www.ombudsman.europa.eu/en/activities/speech.faces/en/52763/html.bookmark.

[126] See http://www.ft.com/cms/s/0/add36222-56be-11e3-ab12-00144feabdc0.html#axzz2tmIoI8NT.

[127] For details of a letter sent by ministers from Austria, Germany, the Netherlands, and the UK to the EU Presidency in April 2013 on 'systematic and frequent abuse of the right to free movement by certain EU citizens' and 'the strain placed on host societies by EU citizens who allegedly move to other Member States to claim benefits and called for immediate measures to combat fraud and systematic abuse', see http://ymlp.com/z1Mumiú.

actually looks and feels like in reality. The implications of the Swiss result are only beginning to unfold.[128] However, the thinness of transnational solidarity has also been widely exposed through the prolonged pain of the euro zone crisis.[129]

What is particularly concerning in recent migration debates is that the lack of a credible empirical evidence base that might actually validate concerns about so-called welfare tourism has made little difference.[130] In response to figures provided by his own government that presented a broadly balanced inflow/outflow pattern vis-à-vis the UK and the rest of the EU, an elected British MP commented that '[t]hese [figures] are not like for like: Lots of Brits abroad are successful people living in second homes in Spain or France. Most Brits living abroad are not aggressive beggars or sleeping rough on the streets: just comparing headline figures doesn't tell the whole story.'[131] Statements of that kind are inexcusable. What they also show is that political and public debate on *intra* EU migration has intensified to the point where a basic question needs to be asked: what role does the concept of Union *citizenship* contribute in all of this? Has the legal animation of citizenship left any imprint, in other words, beyond the confines of case law and academic comment?

The pan-EU responses provoked by current inflammations of migration fear do remind us that the narrowing of citizenship rights is not the preoccupation of all EU Member States at present.[132] For example, a letter sent in January 2014 to the *Financial Times* from ministers in Finland, Norway, and Sweden stands out in this context; its opening line—'[f]ree movement of persons is the essence of European citizenship'—provides welcome relief from the political scaremongering outlined above.[133] The letter goes on to argue that 'the only actual problem is the "widespread belief that EU migrants are a burden". Prejudiced arguments have no place in political debate. EU migrants who work and contribute financially to building our societies should not be made scapegoats for loopholes in national benefit schemes.'

But do the principles established for EEC6 still hold for EU28? This is another difficult question to ask, and a difficult question to discuss in a balanced and sensible

---

[128] See eg the reports at http://www.reuters.com/article/2014/02/16/us-swiss-eu-croatia-idUSB REA1FoX420140216; http://www.bbc.co.uk/news/world-europe-26214138.

[129] For a sobering analysis, see F. Amtenbrink, 'Europe in Times of Economic Crisis: Bringing Europe's Citizens Closer to One Another?' in M. Dougan, N. Nic Shuibhne, and E. Spaventa (eds), *Empowerment and Disempowerment of the European Citizen* (2012) 171.

[130] 'Two Million British People Emigrated to EU, Figures Show', 10 February 2014 http://euobserver.com/social/123066.

[131] 'EU Migrants Moving to UK Balanced by Britons Living Abroad', 10 February 2014, *Financial Times* http://www.ft.com/cms/s/0/21f36df8-6c01-11e3-a216-00144feabdco.html#axzz2tmIoI8NT.

[132] See eg 'Poland Attacks Cameron View on Migrants', 23 December 2013, *Financial Times* http://www.ft.com/cms/s/0/21f36df8-6c01-11e3-a216-00144feabdco.html#axzz2tmIoI8NT; 'Roma Are EU Citizens too, Romanian President Says', 31 January 2014 http://euobserver.com/social/122960.

[133] 'In Times of Crisis, We Must Safeguard Free Movement', 16 January 2014, *Financial Times* http://www.ft.com/cms/s/0/c13711ee-7ec6-11e3-8642-00144feabdco.html#axzz2tmIoI8NT.

way, but it is also a question that has to be asked. Commission President Barroso continued to reconfirm the expected response: that the principle of free movement is non-negotiable.[134] Addressing the April 2013 letter on welfare tourism concerns, noted above, the Council responded that free movement was a 'core value of the European Union'.[135] However, it also invited the Commission to issue guidance on fighting abuse of those rules—guidance that was published in September 2014.[136] Once again, this example illustrates that rights come with certain responsibilities, and that reflecting on that dimension of things is not inherently reductive of the rights in question.[137] But the gap between the legal dimensions of Union citizenship and its broader dimensions at present does suggest a worrying point of frailty—one that is being stretched because of, rather than against, the prevailing political momentum. A basic message of the European Ombudsman's 'citizenship in crisis' warning should thus be heeded: Union citizenship has failed, so far at least, to transcend the fundamental 'them' and 'us' dichotomy that Member State nationals still *feel*. That is why it is so difficult to have a balanced and sensible discussion on more challenging aspects of Union citizenship. But law will not change that in isolation.

BIBLIOGRAPHY

F. Amtenbrink, 'Europe in Times of Economic Crisis: Bringing Europe's Citizens Closer to One Another?' in M. Dougan, N. Nic Shuibhne, and E. Spaventa (eds), *Empowerment and Disempowerment of the European Citizen* (2012) 171

M. Dougan, 'The Constitutional Dimension to the Case Law on Union Citizenship' (2006) 31 ELRev 613

D. Kochenov, 'The Essence of EU Citizenship Emerging from the Last Ten Years of Academic Debate: Beyond the Cherry Blossoms and the Moon?' (2013) 62 *International and Comparative Law Quarterly* 97

D. Kostakopoulou, 'Ideas, Norms and European Citizenship: Explaining Institutional Change' (2005) 68 *Modern Law Review* 233

N. Nic Shuibhne, 'The Resilience of EU Market Citizenship', (2010) 47 *Common Market Law Review* 1597

---

[134] See eg http://www.europeanvoice.com/article/2014/february/free-movement-non-negotiable-barroso-tells-swiss/79697.aspx.

[135] See the press release at http://www.consilium.europa.eu/ueDocs/cms_Data/docs/pressData/en/jha/137407.pdf

[136] See http://europa.eu/rapid/press-release_IP-14-1049_en.htm.

[137] For another example of acknowledgement of problems within free movement law—the issue of *uneven* migration flows between States in the context of attending university—see the Opinion of AG Sharpston in Case C-73/08 *Bressol and others and Chaverot and others v Gouvernement de la Communauté française* [2010] ECR I-2735, paras 141–154 of the Opinion.

S. O'Leary, *The Evolving Concept of Community Citizenship: From the Free Movement of Persons to Union Citizenship* (1996)

S. O'Leary, 'The Past, Present and Future of the Purely Internal Rule in EU Law' in M. Dougan, N. Nic Shuibhne, and E. Spaventa (eds), *Empowerment and Disempowerment of the European Citizen* (2013) 37

J. Shaw, *The Transformation of Citizenship in the European Union: Electoral Rights and the Restructuring of Political Space* (2007)

E. Spaventa, 'Seeing the Wood Despite the Trees? On the Scope of Union Citizenship and its Constitutional Effects' (2008) *45 Common Market Law Review* 13

P. van Elsuwege and D. Kochenov, 'On the Limits of Judicial Intervention: EU Citizenship and Family Reunification Rights' (2011) *13 European Journal of Migration and Law* 443

F. Wollenschläger, 'A New Fundamental Freedom beyond Market Integration: Union Citizenship and its Dynamics for Shifting the Economic Paradigm of European Integration' (2011) *17 European Law Journal* 34

CHAPTER 20

···

GOVERNING GOODS

CONTENT AND CONTEXT

···

KENNETH ARMSTRONG

I. INTRODUCTION

···

THE law relating to the free movement of goods holds an iconic place in EU legal studies. It is often the starting point for an exploration of the law of the internal market more generally, with the judgments of the European Court of Justice occupying a near mythical status. It is also a vehicle for understanding the nature of the EU legal order and its capacity for enforcement in national courts.[1] Indeed, such is the iconic status of this area of law that articles devoted to its study have been written by many of the leading EU law scholars writing in the English language. For students of EU law, an understanding of the free movement of goods—and more particularly the scope of Article 34 of the TFEU which prohibits 'quantitative restrictions' on imports and 'measures having equivalent effect'—forms an important part of the teaching curriculum. A fairly non-scientific illustration of the enduring status and importance attached to understanding EU law through the lens of the free movement of goods is the statistic that out of the top ten articles of the *European Law Review* accessed via Westlaw in 2013, four analysed the scope of application of Article 34 TFEU.

·····

[1] Case 26/62, *Van Gend en Loos v Nederlandse Administratie der Belstingen* [1963] ECR 1.

Icons serve as focal points. Our gaze is framed and drawn towards the object to be studied. In so doing, certain vantage points, interpretations, and perspectives are privileged. As lawyers, we often start with the legal text—primarily the substantive law now found in the TFEU—and then proceed rapidly to its authoritative interpretation by courts. Given that the wording of the relevant Treaty provisions has barely, if at all, changed since adoption in the Treaty of Rome of 1957, it is not surprisingly to the courts that we look to reveal the law. There are, however, two risks associated with the adoption of this perspective. The first risk is that we pay insufficient attention to the full range of locations in which the law relating to goods is promulgated, interpreted, and, importantly, applied in operations associated with the production, marketing, distribution, and sale of goods. The second danger is that, ironically, we lose sight of goods and trade in goods themselves, preferring instead to invest our intellectual resources in understanding the role of the courts and of legal doctrine almost abstracted from the subject matter of the disputes that have created the litigation in the first place.

The strategy adopted for this chapter is to examine some specific examples of goods and their legal treatment in EU law. In part, this is an illustrative device with the aim being to highlight the diverse forms of legal intervention applicable to goods. But it is also an approach that draws attention to the quality of the legal regimes applicable to particular types of goods, the aim being to examine how legal regimes balance competing pressures in specific ways depending upon the goods themselves. This approach seeks to draw attention to the range of EU legal instruments; the diverse sources of norms—international, EU, and national—applicable to the movement of goods; and the different institutional locations responsible for facilitating free movement.

Typically, the adjudicative function of courts in removing national barriers to the free movement of goods—often referred to as *negative* integration—is contrasted with the legislative function of EU institutions in the adoption of common rules, compliance with which allows goods to be placed on the European Single Market—the realm of *positive* integration. Understanding the relationship between 'normative' and 'decisional' supranationalism[2] is certainly an important dimension to be explored. On the one hand, there might be an optimal relationship between the legal interventions of courts and legislatures to ensure an appropriate balance between national and EU regulatory competence, and between market integration and market regulation. On the other hand, there could be a sub-optimal relationship such as that depicted by Scharpf's 'joint decision trap', in which negative integration reaches further into national political autonomy in a way that cannot be rebalanced by the coordinative capacity

---

[2] Joseph Weiler, 'The Community System: The Dual Character of Supranationalism' (1981) 1 *Yearbook of European Law* 267.

of political actors to adopt joint rules at EU level.[3] Institutional constraints on EU legislative action—for example, the applicable voting rules in the Council of Ministers—together with the diversity of national regulatory policies, shape and frame the dynamics of EU action.

In addition to the role played by courts and the EU legislature, there is a complex world of European 'administration' that impacts upon the intra-EU movement of goods. At its simplest, rule making powers are frequently delegated to the European Commission in elaboration or implementation of EU legislative rules. Yet even this depiction is incomplete given that the executive power of the European Commission is subject to direct and indirect influence from a variety of other institutional actors in the form of working groups, committees, networks of national administrations, and European agencies.[4] Any account of the institutional forms of legal intervention has to have regard to this diverse normative ecosystem.

Finally, there is a realm of private governance beyond 'public' regulation. That goods can circulate freely across borders often owes much to the development by industry of common standards and specifications that ensure that a washing machine will fit in a kitchen in Birmingham or Bilbao. Technical innovation, particularly in areas like electronic goods, raises issues of compatibility and interoperability across products which technical standardization by representatives of industry may seek to address. Private standards setting can also serve public functions, including facilitating compliance with EU law itself in terms of the 'new approach' to harmonization.[5] But the realm of transnational private regulation remains important in its own right as a form of normative order that impacts on the regulation of goods.[6]

The structure of this chapter is as follows. To orient the discussion, the analysis begins by considering the scale and nature of the trade in goods. Attention then turns to what constitutes a 'good' from the perspective of EU law. The circumstances in which the supervisory jurisdiction of the Court is triggered, and the analytical/normative foundations for this jurisdiction are then explored before turning to a wider analysis of the legal frameworks applicable to three specific goods: alcohol, tobacco, and chemicals.

---

[3] Fritz W. Scharpf, 'The Joint-Decision Trap Revisited' (2006) 44 *Journal of Common Market Studies* 845.

[4] Deirdre Curtin, *Executive Power of the European Union: Law, Practices, and the Living Constitution* (2009).

[5] Michelle P. Egan, *Constructing a European Market: Standards, Regulation, and Governance* (2001); Harm Schepel, *The Constitution of Private Governance: Product Standards in the Regulation of Integrating Markets* (2005); Dagmar Schiek, 'Private Rule-making and European Governance—Issues of Legitimacy' (2007) 32 *European Law Review* 443.

[6] Colin Scott, Fabrizio Cafaggi, and Linda Senden, *The Challenge of Transnational Private Regulation: Conceptual and Constitutional Debates* (2011).

II. Trade in Goods

It is worth reflecting for a moment on the scale and nature of the trade in goods within the EU and between the EU and non-Member States. The aim is not simply to provide epiphenomenal 'context' but also to get a sense of the significance of trade in different sorts of goods. That we know anything about patterns of trade between states is itself a product of international and European law. It is well known that the European Economic Community (EEC) Treaty of 1957 established a customs union as part of its aim of facilitating the free movement of goods. However, ten years previously, 13 European states had formed a study group on customs union out of which developed the Customs Co-operation Council (CCC) established by a Convention of the 13 contracting states.[7] In order to establish a common statistical system for the collection of data concerning the movement of goods, the 1950 Convention on Nomenclature for the Classification of Goods was adopted, and entered into force in 1959. The influence of this Convention on what was then European Community law was identified in proceedings before the ECJ in 1970.[8] As the Court noted, Council Regulation 950/68 on the common customs tariff[9] is based on the 1950 Convention Nomenclature. In the absence of any specific EEC instrument, the interpretation afforded by explanatory notes prepared by a nomenclature committee established under the Convention constituted an authoritative source for the interpretation of the common customs tariff. Over time the system has evolved and now the EU's 'Combined Nomenclature',[10] used for the classification of goods and for data on their movement, is based on the Harmonized System of the World Customs Organization (the successor to the CCC). It is on the basis of the classification of goods for customs purposes that we can obtain a picture of the scale and types of good moving across the EU frontier.

Nonetheless, the paradox of the removal of frontier controls on the movement of goods within the EU could have been that we would simply have little idea of what goods were in free circulation within the EU, and their respective departure and arrival destinations. As such, important information about intra-EU trade flows—information that is relevant to national and EU policy makers—could have been lost. To avoid this problem, EU law puts in place extensive reporting requirements. For trade between EU Member States, a uniform system of reporting is

---

[7] The 1950 Convention establishing a Customs Co-operation Council entered into force in 1952, and was signed by Belgium, Denmark, France, Germany, Greece, Iceland, Italy, Luxembourg, the Netherlands, Norway, Portugal, Sweden, and the United Kingdom.

[8] Case 14/70 *Deutsche Bakels Gmbh v Oberfinanzdirektion München* [1970] ECR 1001.

[9] [1968] OJ L172/1.

[10] See Council Regulation (EEC) No 2658/87 on the tariff and statistical nomenclature and on the Common Customs Tariff: [1987] OJ L256/1, as amended.

created by Regulation 638/2004.[11] In general, goods are classified using the same Combined Nomenclature that is used for the purposes of external trade. This also makes sense given that once goods have legitimately entered the EU, they also enter into free circulation and, in that sense, lose their identity as 'imports' into the EU. Using this coding, together with country codes for the dispatch and arrival of goods, national authorities collect and report data in a system known as INTRASTAT. The primary legal duty to report this information falls on EU VAT-registered businesses, and so forms an important part of the legal environment in which businesses engage in cross-border trade.

Eurostat data suggests that manufactured goods are the primary form of goods moving between EU Member States. Machinery and transport equipment account for the largest group of dispatches. Within this, motor vehicles are a particularly large sub-group of goods circulating within the EU, accounting for over 10 per cent of dispatches from one EU state to another. Industrial and electrical machinery followed by movements of telecommunications, sound and television equipment combine to form around 14 per cent of dispatches. Around 15 per cent of dispatches relate to the movement of chemicals. Food and energy each account for roughly 6–8 per cent of dispatches with clothing, bags, and footwear taking just over 3 per cent.

Patterns of trade between EU states vary enormously. This has wider significance for the European economy and for its economic governance. Germany's very significant trade surplus globally, and more particularly with regard to its European partners, has raised concerns internationally and at European level. With Germany the primary EU destination for the exports of most EU countries, low levels of domestic demand in Germany have an impact on the capacity of other EU states to fuel export-led economic growth. Using the new 'macroeconomic imbalance procedure' introduced to enhance European economic governance following the financial and economic crisis that materialized in 2008,[12] the European Commission launched an investigation into the destabilizing effects of Germany's high trade surplus. Policy recommendations addressed to Germany in 2013 highlighted that enabling wage growth could help support domestic demand. In this way, we can see how patterns of trade between Member States are connected to the wider macroeconomic environment. Trade patterns are also linked to the wider politics of European integration. Over half of the UK's trade exports are now to EU Member States, representing 15 per cent of national income, with some economists suggesting that a UK withdrawal from the EU could result in a loss equivalent to 2.2 per cent of GDP. Therefore, an understanding of trade in goods is relevant to a much broader appreciation of the relationship between the economics of the Single Market and its constitutional and political implications.

---

[11] Regulation (EC) 638/2004 of the European Parliament and of the Council on Community statistics relating to the trading of goods between Member States: [2004] OJ L102/1.

[12] Regulation 1176/2011/EU on the prevention and correction of macroeconomic imbalances: [2011] OJ L306/25.

III. Characterizing Goods

Taking goods seriously requires us to consider what it is that makes something generally a 'good' from the point of view of EU law. A useful illustration of the point is the enforcement action brought by the European Commission against Italy in respect of an Italian law that subjected the export of articles of an artistic, historical, archaeological, or ethnographic nature to a tax.[13] The issue was whether this law violated provisions of the Treaty establishing the customs union by prohibiting the imposition of customs duties and charges having an equivalent effect, including charges of a fiscal nature (now Article 30 TFEU). The Italian government objected that such articles did not constitute 'goods' in the sense of being consumer goods or ordinary merchandise. In finding the Treaty rules applicable to the situation, the Court of Justice defined 'goods' as 'products which can be valued in money and which are capable, as such, of forming the subject of commercial transactions'. Yet it is also clear that while it is true that goods can be valued in money and be the subject of commercial transactions, so can the provision of services and the movement of capital. For example, should a fishing permit or licence—a tangible object with a monetary value that is capable of being exchanged—be considered to be a good, or, as the Court concluded, the provision of a service?[14]

Indeed, it may not always be immediately apparent which provisions of EU law are applicable to a particular situation given certain difficulties of characterization. The boundary between goods and services can be a particularly difficult one to draw but, as the Court pointed out in its *Omega* ruling—concerned with German restrictions on a laser game—goods and services are covered by different provisions of the Treaty.[15] As the Court identified in that judgment, an economic activity will generally only be assessed in the light of one of the fundamental freedoms where the exercise of the other is secondary in relation to the first. Thus, while goods would be provided as part of the laser game, the Court concluded that this was secondary to the provision of a service. Nonetheless, it is evident that economic activities often involve the simultaneous provision of both goods and services. A really clear example of this is digital television broadcasting, where the provision of broadcast services is reliant upon consumers purchasing equipment including digital decoders. Given that important areas of economic activity like telecommunications and broadcasting engage issues both of goods and services, the Court's approach is to consider national rules in light of both provisions of

---

[13] Case 7/68 *Commission v Italy* [1968] ECR 423.

[14] Case C-97/98 *Peter Jägerskiöld v Torolf Gustafsson* [1999] ECR-7319.

[15] Case C-36/02 *Omega Spielhallen- und Automatenaufstellungs-GmbH v Oberbürgermeisterin der Bundesstadt Bonn* [2004] ECR I-9609. Similarly in respect of lotteries see Case C-275/92 *Schindler* [1994] ECR I-1039.

the Treaties.[16] Conversely, the finding by the Court that rules governing the days or times at which goods are sold fall beyond the scope of the Treaty rules on free movement of goods did not incline the Court towards considering whether such rules also inhibited freedom of establishment.[17]

The sale of certain products may, of course, be prohibited. This is particularly the case with regard to narcotic drugs, the sale of which—other than for specific medicinal or scientific purposes—is prohibited and subject to criminal penalties.[18] Thus, in litigation concerning measures taken by the Municipal Council of Maastricht to prevent non-Dutch residents obtaining cannabis in Dutch 'coffee houses', the Court reasoned that as narcotic drugs were prohibited for sale, a coffee shop owner could not rely on the free movement of goods as a basis for challenging the local authority restriction.[19] Sometimes EU law treats something as a good in a way that is not necessarily intuitive. While we typically think of 'waste' as an environmental issue, it is, of course, also a good.[20] Energy has also been treated as a good for the purposes of the application of Article 34 TFEU.[21]

IV. JURISDICTIONAL TRIGGERS

The sequence of judgments of the Court of Justice defining the circumstances that trigger the jurisdiction of the Court to assess the compatibility of measures with Article 34 TFEU forms the genetic code that has given this iconic area of law its particular shape and form.[22] Typically, such measures are public in origin, reflecting

---

[16] Case C-390/99 *Canal Satélite Digital SL v Adminstración General del Estado, and Distribuidora de Televisión Digital SA (DTS)* [2002] ECR I-607.

[17] In its ruling in Joined Cases C-69/93 and C-258/93 *Punto Casa and PPV* [1994] ECR I-2355, the ECJ held that national rules that mandated that certain retail establishments remain closed on Sundays and certain other days fell outside the scope of Art 34 TFEU. In a preliminary reference from the same court in a materially similar case, the Court dismissed the suggestion that such rules might also impact on the freedom of establishment of such retailers: Case C-418/93 *Semeraro Casa Uno Srl v Sindaco del Comune di Erbusco* [1996] ECR I-2975. On which see: Mike Pullen and M.T. Paola Caputi Jambrenghi, 'The Use of Arts 30 and 52 to Attack Barriers to Market Access: An Overview of the ECJ's Case Law' (1996) 17 *European Competition Law Review* 388.

[18] Framework Decision 2004/757/JHA laying down minimum provisions on the constituent elements of criminal acts and penalties in the field of illicit drug trafficking: [2004] OJ L335/8. See also the proposal for a Directive to amend this Framework Decision: COM (2013) 618 final.

[19] Case C-137/09 *Josemans v Burgemeester van Maastricht* [2010] ECR I-13019.

[20] Case C-2/90 *European Commission v Belgium (Wallonia Waste)* [1992] ECR I-4431.

[21] C-573/12 *Ålands Vindkraft AB v Energimyndigheten (Swedish Energy Agency)* [2014] ECR I-000.

[22] My thanks to Joanne Scott for making me think about jurisdictional 'triggers': Joanne Scott, 'The New EU "Extraterritoriality"' (2014) 51 *Common Market Law Review* 1343. The focus of the

the division of labour between the competition law provisions of the Treaty applicable to private market behaviour and the role of Article 34 TFEU in controlling market-partitioning exercises of state power.[23] Nonetheless, the state can itself assume responsibility for the behaviour of private parties—including behaviour it has either induced[24] or done nothing to prevent[25]—while conversely, the activities of private bodies that effectively regulate market entry can trigger the jurisdiction of the Court under Article 34 TFEU.[26]

Having adopted in *Dassonville* a potentially very wide definition of the scope of a 'measure having equivalent effect' to a quantitative restriction,[27] the Court signalled an enhanced capacity for adjudication to scrutinize a wide range of national measures that might impact on free movement. In subsequent rulings, the Court made clear that it was the effect of a measure on free movement and not its form that mattered. Thus, any regulatory norm that conditioned the placing of a good on a market, even if it applied without distinction between domestic and imported goods, could fall within the scope of Article 34 TFEU. Analytically, the focus then shifted to whether such a measure could be permitted because of its pursuit of a non-economic and legitimate public interest. In addition to those interests recognized as derogations under Article 36 TFEU,[28] the Court permitted objective justification where the measure was indistinctly applicable. Finally, the Court insisted that, to be lawful, any interference with the fundamental freedom had to be the least restrictive having regard to its legitimate public interest goal: an application of the proportionality principle.

As is well known, the Court, in its ruling in *Keck*, sought to limit its supervisory jurisdiction by taking 'selling arrangements' outside of the scope of Article 34 TFEU.[29] Such rules, which remain within the regulatory competence of the

analysis here is on Art 34 TFEU applicable to the import of goods rather than Art 35 TFEU, which applies to exports, not least because the former has generated far more case law and significantly more academic commentary than the latter, but see: Marek Szydlo, 'Export Restrictions within the Structure of Free Movement of Goods. Reconsideration of an Old Paradigm' (2010) 47 *Common Market Law Review* 753.

[23] See Joined Cases 177-178/82 *Van de Haar* [1984] ECR 1797.

[24] Case 249/81 *Commission v Ireland ('Buy Irish')* [1982] ECR 4005.

[25] Case C-265/95 *Commission v France (Strawberries)* [1997] ECR I-6959.

[26] Case C-171/11 *Fra.bo SpA v Deutsche Vereinigung des Gas- und Wasserfaches eV (DVGW)* [2012] ECR I-453.

[27] 'All trading rules enacted by Member States which are capable of hindering, directly or indirectly, actually or potentially, intra-Community trade are to be considered as measures having an effect equivalent effect to quantitative restrictions': Case 8/74 *Procureur du Roi v Dassonville* [1974] ECR 82.

[28] Art 36 TFEU: 'The provisions of Articles 34 and 35 shall not preclude prohibitions or restrictions on imports, exports or goods in transit justified on grounds of public morality, public policy or public security; the protection of health and life of humans, animals or plants; the protection of national treasures possessing artistic, historic or archaeological value; or the protection of industrial and commercial property. Such prohibitions or restrictions shall not, however, constitute a means of arbitrary discrimination or a disguised restriction on trade between Member States.'

[29] Joined Cases C-267, 268/91 *Keck and Mithouard* [1993] ECR I-6097.

host state, only give rise to scrutiny where they demonstrably discriminate against imported goods by preventing or restricting their capacity to penetrate the national market. In situations covered by other economic freedoms, the Court has resisted attempts to develop similar *Keck*-style exclusions.[30] In this way, the *Keck* formula is limited to the realm of goods, although, as Spaventa argues, even within the free movement of goods, the significance of *Keck* may have been limited by subsequent cases which have either found that rules were not covered by the *Keck* exception or have been found to fall within the scope of Article 34 TFEU because of their impact on market access.[31]

V. ANALYTICAL FRAMEWORKS AND NORMATIVE FOUNDATIONS

As described in the previous section, the ECJ has adopted an effects-based approach to when national measures limit free movement and trigger judicial scrutiny, combined with a proportionality-based approach to when national measures may legitimately interfere with free movement. As will be apparent from other chapters, it is also an analytical framework that has application to the other economic freedoms promoted by the treaties. However, there is a deeper debate about the conceptual and normative foundation underpinning the free movement provisions in general, and free movement of goods in particular.

The Court's approach has looked beyond direct forms of discrimination and instead considers the effect of national rules in preventing or impeding the free circulation of goods within the European market. Nonetheless, often these 'indistinctly applicable' rules—rules that seek to regulate the market without distinguishing directly between domestic and imported goods—will act as forms of indirect discrimination.[32] The discrimination paradigm and the approach that demands objective justification for indirect discrimination does a significant amount of

---

[30] Eg Case C-384/93 *Alpine Investments BV v Minister van Financien* [1995] ECR I-1141. See generally Wulf-Henning Roth, 'The European Court of Justice's Case Law on the Freedom to Provide Services: Is *Keck* Relevant?' in Mads Andenas and Wulf-Henning Roth (eds), *Services and Free Movement in EU Law* (2003).

[31] Eleanor Spaventa, 'Leaving Keck Behind? The Free Movement of Goods after the Rulings in Commission v Italy and Mickelsson and Roos' (2009) 34 *European Law Review* 914.

[32] Nicolas Bernard, 'Discrimination and Free Movement in EC Law' (1996) 45 *International & Comparative Law Quarterly* 82, Niamh Nic Shuibhne, 'The Free Movement of goods and Article 28 EC: An Evolving Framework' (2002) 27 *European Law Review* 408.

analytical work in the realm of goods as well as other economic freedoms, where what may be demanded is equal treatment.[33]

Nonetheless, when we look beyond goods, it is evident that the Court's jurisdiction can be triggered by 'restrictions' that hinder or render less attractive the exercise of economic freedoms. In these cases, it is often said that it is the prevention or restriction of 'market access' that is the jurisdictional trigger. Yet even in these cases, as Davies argues, it is the effect of national rules in creating an inequality in the position of different market actors that makes market access harder.[34] In this way, the opposition between jurisdictional triggers based on discrimination rather than market access may simply be a mis-characterization of what's at stake.

The extent to which legal discourse on the free movement of goods has become preoccupied with whether the concept of preventing or impeding market access ought to provide a normative basis for Article 34 TFEU cannot be ignored.[35] Certainly, discontent with the judgment in *Keck* and its bifurcated approach to jurisdiction premised on a distinction between product/production requirements and *Keck*-style 'selling arrangements' fuelled the search for a more encompassing rationale for jurisdiction under Article 34 TFEU to be triggered. Inspired not least by Advocate General Jacobs—whose Opinions revealed a desire to move beyond the apparent limits of a discrimination-based approach to free movement—attention began to focus on an alternative basis for the Court's supervisory jurisdiction based on whether a measure prevents or restricts market access. Although the Court of Justice has indeed appeared to embrace the concept as one means of defining that scope, instead of adopting a singular jurisdictional trigger replacing all others, it has produced a tripartite jurisdictional approach.[36] Thus, where a measure does not on its face directly discriminate against imported goods but is instead indistinctly applicable, it will only fall within the *Dassonville* conceptualization of a measure having equivalent effect if any of the following hold true:

1. It is a 'dual burden' rule in the sense of imposing requirements relating to the product or its production process which are additional to those imposed in the Member State where the good is produced.

---

[33] See also, Daniel Wilsher, 'Does *Keck* Discrimination Make any Sense? An Assessment of the Non-discrimination Principle within the European Single Market' (2008) 33 *European Law Review* 3.

[34] Gareth Davies, 'Understanding Market Access: Exploring the Economic Rationality of Different Conceptions of Free Movement Law' (2010) 11 *German Law Journal* 671.

[35] Max S. Jansson and Harri Kalimo, 'De minimis Meets "Market Access": Transformations in the Substance—and the Syntax—of EU Free Movement Law?' (2014) 51 *Common Market Law Review* 523; Jukka Snell, 'The Notion of Market Access: A Concept or a Slogan?' (2010) 47 *Common Market Law Review* 437.

[36] Case C-110/05 *European Commission v Italy (Motorcycle Trailers)* [2009] ECR I-519; Case C-142/05 *Åklagaren v Mickelsson and Roos* [2009] ECR I-4273 discussed in Stefan Enchelmaier, 'Moped Trailers, *Mickelsson & Roos, Gysbrechts*: The ECJ's Case Law on Goods Keeps on Moving' (2010) 29 *Yearbook of European Law* 190.

2. It is a measure which is apparently a 'selling arrangement' but which through its restriction of the method of retail, advertising, marketing, or promotion demonstrably prevents or restricts the capacity of an imported good to penetrate the national market.

3. It is any other measure that demonstrably hinders the access of goods produced in other Member States to the market of a Member State.[37]

Framed in this way, measures that prevent or restrict 'market access' are just one source of jurisdictional trigger alongside more established triggers where the philosophy and analytical framework remain linked to the concept of discrimination.

It has not been the intention of this analysis to explore in detail every aspect and nuance of the scholarly debates that are well rehearsed in the literature.[38] Rather, it provides both an overview of the issues and a basis for developing the analysis in some more particular contexts. Indeed, the more substantive analysis that follows returns us to some of the foundational judgments of the Court on the free movement of goods, but viewed less abstractly and more concretely in terms of the particularities of the goods under examination. Accordingly, our exploration of the law on the free movement of goods considers three areas: alcohol, tobacco, and chemicals.

VI. Types of Goods and their Regulatory Regimes

The analysis below explores the legal treatment of different goods within EU law. The aim is to highlight not only the range of forms of legal intervention but also their evolution over time. Other areas could be examined, such as foodstuffs or cosmetics or motor vehicles, each of which would add something to the overall picture. But for simplicity, and to give an appropriate level of analytical depth, the discussion focuses on alcohol, tobacco, and chemicals as examples of the EU and Member States' approaches to 'risk regulation'. Whereas alcohol and tobacco represent 'lifestyle risks',[39] chemicals regulation illustrates the environmental and health and safety risks that chemicals—and their movement—may present.

---

[37] This jurisdictional trigger was used in the cases cited at n 36 to bring certain rules limiting 'product use' within the scope of Art 34 TFEU.

[38] See the Bibliography.

[39] See generally Alberto Alemanno and Amandine Garde, 'The Emergence of an EU Lifestyle Policy: The Case of Alcohol, Tobacco and Unhealthy Diets' [2013] 50 *Common Market Law Review* 1.

1. Alcohol

One might be forgiven for thinking that much, if not all, of the salient aspects of free movement of goods law can be gleaned from an understanding of how that law relates to alcohol. In an EU of different social practices around food and drink, a variety of social and legal norms have developed that relate not just to the intrinsic qualities of alcoholic beverages but also to their retail and marketing. In some instances, these social and legal practices become synonymous with the cultural identity of a state. Such was the status of its sixteenth-century beer purity laws, the German authorities even sought—unsuccessfully—to claim that 'Bier' was not a generic term but in fact one synonymous with a beverage produced only in accordance with German beer purity laws and that to accept any other product as beer would be likely to generate confusion among German consumers.[40] The beer purity case is just one of many cases that illustrate the breadth of the scope of the prohibition which is now found in Article 34 TFEU on measures having equivalent effect to quantitative restrictions. That said, the analysis explores a number of different dimensions of the legal regulation of the sale of alcohol.

Like tobacco and petroleum products, alcohol is subject to national rules imposing excise duties. The taxation of alcohol serves an important revenue-raising function and to some degree also pursues public health goals insofar as higher rates of taxation are intended also to curb consumption. Member States have a significant degree of fiscal autonomy, and, not surprisingly, different taxation policies across the Member States risk creating obstacles to free movement or distortions to competition. Article 110 TFEU, therefore, prohibits Member States from using their competence in internal taxation to either discriminate—directly or indirectly—against imported goods that are 'similar' to domestic goods (Article 110(1) TFEU), or otherwise to protect domestic goods from competition from imported products that, while not similar, are, nonetheless, substitutable (Article 110(2) TFEU). Cases involving alcoholic beverages feature prominently in the case law relating to Article 110 TFEU.

Take, for example, the issue of whether wine made from grapes and wine made from other fruits should be considered to be 'similar'. The Commission brought legal action against Denmark for imposing a higher rate of tax on wine from grapes than wine made from other fruit, arguing that this was indirect discrimination against wines made from grapes that were exclusively imported, while national wines were often made from other fruit.[41] The Danish government objected that fruit wines were classified differently under the Common Customs Tariff, had different alcoholic strengths (with alcohol typically added to fruit wines to increase their strength), and had different production processes. The Court noted that in

---

[40] Case 178/84 *Commission v German (Beer Purity)* [1987] ECR 1227.
[41] Case 106/84 *Commission v Denmark (Fruit Wine)* [1986] 833.

order to be 'similar', products need not be identical. Rather, what was relevant was, first, their origin, method of manufacture, and intrinsic qualities such as taste and alcohol content, and, second, whether the products to be compared met the same need from the point of view of the consumer. In finding both types of wine to be similar, the Court noted that Member States were free to conduct their fiscal policies in a manner that differentiated even between similar goods, provided the difference was based on objective factors relating to the conduct of taxation policy and provided that it did not result in discrimination between imported and domestic goods. Given that wines made from grapes were exclusively imported, there was no objective justification for their discriminatory tax treatment.

It is readily apparent that even if goods are not considered to be similar, they still fall to be analysed under Article 110(2) TFEU in terms of whether national tax rules have a protective effect for national products in competition with imported goods. A very useful illustration of the point is if we consider national rules that tax beer and wine differently. The Commission brought infringement proceeding against the UK for the differential tax treatment of beer and wine. As is clear from the earlier discussion, there is nothing in principle objectionable to such a differential treatment provided it is based on objective factors. The analytical issue under Article 110(2) TFEU is whether there is a protective effect for domestic products. The Court concluded that in imposing a higher rate of tax for wine, the national authorities had in effect stamped wine 'with the hallmarks of a luxury product' in a manner that clearly favoured domestically produced beer.

Of course, one obvious solution to such problems would be to take advantage of the legislative competence conferred on the EU to approximate the excise duties of the Member States (Article 113 TFEU). Yet it is also the differences in their national treatment, the differences in approach across alcohol products, and the need for unanimity under Article 113 TFEU which make approximation difficult, as was recognized by the European Commission in its 1985 White Paper on *Completing the Internal Market*.[42] The Commission's strategy was to propose a gradual approximation of excise rates through adoption of minimum rates of duty, with Member States retaining fiscal sovereignty above this floor. Two Directives were adopted in 1992: one setting out a common structure for the application of excise duties to alcohol, and another establishing the minimum rates of duty.[43] Interestingly, the latter Directive established differential minimum rates of duty as between beer and wine. In proceedings brought before the French courts, the validity of the

[42] COM (1985) 310.

[43] Council Dir 92/83/EEC on the harmonization of the structures of excise duties on alcohol and alcoholic beverages [1992] OJ L316/21; Council Dir 92/84/EEC on the approximation of the rates of excise duty on alcohol and alcoholic beverages [1992] OJ L316/29. In addition to the sectoral Directives that apply to alcohol, tobacco (see below) and petroleum products, there is also a 'horizontal' Council Dir 2008/118/EC concerning the general arrangements for excise duty [2009] OJ L9/12.

EU legislation was challenged, arguing that it created discrimination contrary to the Treaty, highlighting again that provisions of the Treaty condition not only the legality of Member State action, but also the exercise by the EU legislator of its legislative competence.[44] However, the Court held that a Directive would not infringe the Treaty if it left a sufficiently wide discretion to the Member States to transpose the Directive into national law in a manner that was compatible with the Treaty. Given that the Directive only attempted a minimum and gradual harmonization, Member States retained a significant level of fiscal autonomy in their implementation of the Directive.

Notwithstanding the intervention of the EU legislature, there remain significant disparities in the excise duties applied and revenues obtained across Member States. Provided local rules are applied in a non-discriminatory manner, and given that duties are payable in the state of destination at rates applicable in that state, obstacles to free movement and distortions to competition may in practice be avoided. In short, it may be possible to live with quite different approaches to the taxation of alcohol products across the Member States. As the Commission itself conceded in a review of the legislative framework a decade after its introduction, 'the politically sensitive aspects of the issue', combined with 'regional, rural and cultural factors', did not warrant further EU legislative activity.[45]

In the earlier discussion, the capacity of Article 34 TFEU to tackle obstacles to trade in general was highlighted. Here, we consider its specific application to alcohol. Quantitative restrictions in the form of specific quotas on the amount of a particular good that may be imported tend not to be of enduring relevance within the European Single Market. Nonetheless, issues relating to a hard-core quantitative restriction—a total ban or restriction on the import of certain goods—have arisen. The case of *Rosengren* illustrates the point while highlighting the very restrictive retail conditions that apply to the sale of alcohol in some EU states. At issue was an effective ban on the importation of alcohol by individuals into Sweden other than that transported directly by an individual for personal consumption. Systembolaget Aktiebolag possessed a retail monopoly on the sale of alcohol to consumers, and processed requests by individuals for the import of specific alcoholic beverages. Applying the Swedish law on alcohol, Swedish authorities impounded cases of wine imported from Spain pursuant to contracts entered into directly with consumers resident in Sweden. Determining that the situation did not directly concern the operation of a 'monopoly of a commercial character' governed by what is now Article 37 TFEU, the Court did, however, conclude that the restriction at issue constituted a quantitative restriction on imports.[46]

---

[44] Case C-166/98 *Société critouridienne de distribution (Socridis) v Receveur principal des douanes* [1999] ECR I-3791.

[45] European Commission, *Report on the Rates of Excise Duties Applied to Alcohol and Alcoholic Beverages* COM (2004) 223.

[46] C-170/04 *Rosengren and others v Riksåklagaren* [2007] ECR I-313. Similar sorts of retail monopoly apply to the sale of tobacco in other Member States. In an analogous case, the Court found

Aside from such bans on the importation of goods, restrictions on the importation of alcohol can constitute 'measures having equivalent effect' to quantitative restrictions ('MEQRs'). It is, again, in the context of alcohol that we find the Court of Justice's seminal definition of an MEQR in its *Dassonville* judgment.[47] The issue concerned whether a demand that imports of Scotch be accompanied by a certificate of authenticity could constitute an MEQR. Concluding that such a requirement did have an impact on the free movement of goods, the Court defined MEQRs as 'all trading rules enacted by Member States which are capable of hindering directly or indirectly, actually or potentially intra-Community trade'. In so doing, the Court signalled its apparent intention to adopt a wide definition of an MEQR based on the effect of the measure on intra-EU trade. All of which leads us to the Court's judgment in *Cassis de Dijon*.[48]

It is difficult to imagine how litigation relating to German restrictions on the marketing of a French liqueur could have produced a judgment that is known not only by legal cognoscenti but also within European studies more generally. Nonetheless, the judgment is used and abused within the literature in a variety of ways. It is important to be clear about what was decided and what implications this had both for our understanding of the scope of Article 34 TFEU and its wider impact on the European integration process.

In comparison to more contemporary judgments of the Court which—albeit without a formal system of precedent—tend to refer back to previous judgments, the ruling in *Cassis* belongs to an older style of short judgments and terse judicial reasoning with no other judgments—including *Dassonville*—cited. The Court's starting point was that in the absence of common rules adopted at EU level, it was for the Member States 'to regulate all matters relating to the production and marketing of alcohol and alcoholic beverages'. Nonetheless, the Court recognized that disparities between the laws of the Member States relating to alcohol might create obstacles to trade, notwithstanding that the rule at issue applied without distinction between domestic and imported goods ('indistinctly applicable'). The Court does not explain precisely why disparities per se create such obstacles. Yet it is apparent that if each Member State were to insist on the application of its local rules on minimum alcohol content—the point at issue in *Cassis*—the result would be either that production costs would rise as the goods were adapted for each local market or that goods would be denied access to such

that the Spanish tobacco retail monopoly had the effect of hindering the access of imported tobacco products: Case C-456/10 *Asociación Nacional de Expendedores de Tabaco y Timbre (ANETT) v Administración del Estado* [2012] ECR I-241.

[47] Case 8/74 *Procureur du Roi v Dassonville* [1974] ECR 837.

[48] Case 120/78 *Rewe-Zentral AG v Bundesmonopolverwaltung für Branntwein* ('*Cassis de Dijon*') [1979] ECR 649. See Nick Bernard, 'On the Art of Not Mixing One's Drinks: *Dassonvile* and *Cassis de Dijon* Revisited' in Miguel Poiares Maduro and Loïc Azoulai, *The Past and Future of EU Law: The Classics of EU Law Revisited on the 50th Anniversary of the Rome Treaty* (2010).

markets. However, the Court accepted that obstacles arising from such disparities had to be accepted insofar as necessary to satisfy mandatory requirements
of the importing state relating to the public interest. Analytically, the focus of
attention turned away from the threshold question of why something might
constitute an obstacle to trade and towards the issue of whether the importing
state had a good reason to insist on the application of its local rules. Having
canvassed the justifications presented in terms of risk to consumer protection
and public health, and having found such arguments to be either implausible
or at least their regulatory consequences to be disproportionate to their aim,
the Court concluded that Germany could not insist on the application of its
own rules.

The judgment was clearly significant insofar as it tended to see disparities between
local laws as inherently likely to trigger Article 34 TFEU, but then balanced this by
an acknowledgment that, at least in principle, Member States retained capacity to
regulate their local markets in pursuit of public interest goals, which, in the case
of measures that were indistinctly applicable, went beyond those derogations formally recognized in Article 36 TFEU. In practice, judicial scrutiny of such 'mandatory requirements' and derogations has often closed down the regulatory space
open to Member States,[49] not least where regulatory objectives lack coherence and
consistency,[50] or fail the test of proportionality,[51] or otherwise appear to lack an evidential basis.[52] The exercise of this national regulatory competence is also framed
by the need generally to comply with other general principles of EU law including
respect for fundamental rights.[53]

The Court's judgment in *Cassis* also had implications for the development of
EU harmonization policy and these were laid out by the European Commission
in an unprecedented communication aimed at explaining how the Commission
intended to utilize the ruling.[54] Indeed, the European Commission's willingness
to exploit the potential of the judgment is itself indicative of the interplay between
the EU Courts and the European Commission in both its enforcement and its

---

[49] Catherine Barnard, 'Derogations, Justifications and the Four Freedoms: Is State Interest Really
Protected?' in Catherine Barnard and Oke Odudu (eds), *The Outer Limits of European Union Law*
(2009); Eleanor Spaventa, 'On Discrimination and the Theory of Mandatory Requirement' (2002) 3
Cambridge Yearbook of European Legal Studies 457.

[50] Gjermund Mathisen, 'Consistency and Coherence as Conditions for Justification of Member
State Measures Restricting Free Movement' (2010) 47 *Common Market Law Review* 1021.

[51] Wolf Sauter, 'Proportionality in EU Law: A Balancing Act?' (2013) 15 *Cambridge Yearbook of
European Legal Studies* 439.

[52] Niamh Nic Shuibhne and Marsela Maci, 'Proving Public Interest: The Growing Impact of
Evidence in Free Movement Case Law' (2013) 50 *Common Market Law Review* 965.

[53] Sybe A. de Vries, 'Balancing Fundamental Rights with Economic Freedoms According to the
European Court of Justice' (2013) 9 *Utrecht Law Review* 169.

[54] European Commission, Communication from the Commission concerning the consequences of the judgment given by the Court of Justice on 20 February 1979 in case 120/78 ('Cassis de
Dijon'): [1980] OJ C256/2.

legislation-initiating roles.[55] Nonetheless, the significance of the judgment and its impact on harmonization policy rather depends on how we understand the nature and extent of the 'mutual recognition' principle with which *Cassis* has become so closely associated even without the Court ever using the term in the case.

Having established that the measure at issue was an obstacle to free movement and having determined that the public interest justifications advanced by the German authorities were insufficiently convincing, instead of simply declaring a rule of such a type to be incompatible with the Treaties, the Court went on to state: 'There is therefore no valid reason why, provided that they have been lawfully produced and marketed in one of the Member States, alcoholic beverages should not be introduced into any other Member State.'

In one sense, this could be taken simply to be the Court's summing up of what it had just determined. But it could be—and was taken to be—the articulation of a wider idea that once goods are lawfully placed on the market in one Member State they should be permitted free movement: a statement of the underlying philosophy of an internal market in which the primary locus of regulatory responsibility rests with the Member State in which the goods are first placed on the EU market. The allocation of regulatory responsibility to the state of origin is known as the principle of home country control or the country of origin principle. In turn, this principle is often conceptualized as being synonymous with the concept of 'mutual recognition'.

The difficulty, however, is that it is self-evident—not least from *Cassis* itself—that the allocation of primary regulatory competence to the country of origin does not wholly pre-empt the regulatory capacities of Member States into whose markets goods are imported. Indeed, the importing state may seek to impose its own mandatory requirements. The issue, therefore, is how to manage this relationship between home and host state regulation. What *Cassis* does is to establish a rebuttable presumption in favour of the country of origin. Analysis then needs to turn to the factors and legal principles discussed earlier which in practice restrict the capacity of the host state to exercise its regulatory competence. What the principle of mutual recognition does is demand particular consideration of the regulatory history of the good and the application of regulatory controls applied in the state of production. It is this need to recognize the regulatory history of a product that may be better captured by the principle of mutual recognition rather than a rather blunt conflation of it with a principle of country of origin.[56]

If we consider *Cassis* itself, the Court concluded that while the protection of public health and consumer protection were legitimate mandatory requirements,

[55] Karen Alter and Sophie Meunier-Aitsahalia, 'Judicial Politics in the European Community: European Integration and the Pathbreaking Cassis de Dijon Decision' (1994) 26 *Comparative Political Studies* 535.

[56] Kenneth Armstrong, 'Mutual Recognition' in Catherine Barnard and Joanne Scott (eds), *The Law of the Single European Market: Unpacking the Premises* (2002)

the German authorities had failed to show why the rules on minimum alcohol content were suitable for or proportionate to achieving those goals and that 'therefore' there was no valid reason why an alcohol lawfully marketed in another Member State should be denied access to the German market. While the Court was allocating primary regulatory responsibility to the French authorities, it was not demanding that the German authorities recognize a specific regulatory process or outcome carried out in another Member State. In that sense, in *Cassis*, we arrive at the presumed authority of the country of origin to regulate without actually engaging any substantive mutual recognition analysis.

Be that as it may, certainly, the European Commission took from this judgment the idea that decentralized application of Article 34 TFEU could do much of the work of removing obstacles to free movement without the need for it to initiate detailed harmonization legislation. Indeed, a 'new approach' to harmonization was announced which would combine limited legislative harmonization of 'essential requirements' related to the public interest with processes of private European standardization supported through mutual recognition of testing and certification.[57] While this approach has been applied to placing toys, medical devices, recreational craft, and other technical products onto the EU market, it is has not been applied to alcoholic beverages.[58]

Like tobacco, the sale of alcohol is permitted but may be subject to restrictions in respect of marketing, promotion, and advertising addressed either to ultimate consumers or to other businesses. As illustrated by the judgment of the Court in *Keck*, national measures relating to marketing, promotion, and advertising may constitute 'selling arrangements' which fall outside the scope of Article 34 TFEU, leaving Member States free to adopt their own attitude towards marketing, promotion, and advertising activities. That said, insofar as business-to-consumer advertising falls within the scope of the Unfair Commercial Practices Directive, this is now fully harmonized at EU level, with certain unfair practices falling within the scope of Annex I to the Directive, prohibited across the EU.[59] Otherwise, unfair practices must be assessed on a case-by-case basis in line with criteria set out in the Directive. However, the scope of application of the Directive is without prejudice to national rules relating to the health and safety aspects of products, which may result in national measures being considered in the light of Article 34 TFEU directly. This may well cover aspects of the advertising of alcoholic products. As the case of *Gourmet* usefully highlights, national measures restricting the advertising

---

[57] See generally, Harm Schepel, *The Constitution of Private Governance: Product Standards in the Regulation of Integrating Markets* (2005).

[58] See more generally http://www.newapproach.org.

[59] Dir 2005/29/EC concerning unfair business-to-consumer commercial practices in the internal market: [2005] OJ L149/22. That the Directive is one of total harmonization that leaves no scope for discretion by the Member States to adopt rules including those of a stricter standard was affirmed in Case C-261/07 *VTB-VAB NV v Total Belgium NV* [2009] ECR I-2949.

of alcoholic beverages may not meet the preconditions established by the Court for a measure to be considered to be a selling arrangement beyond the scope of Article 34 TFEU.[60]

The *Gourmet* case concerned Swedish law restricting advertising of alcoholic beverages. The Swedish Consumer Ombudsman sought an injunction against Gourmet—the publisher of a magazine aimed principally at traders and retailers and with a small number of consumer subscribers—for publishing certain advertisements of alcoholic beverages. *Gourmet* sought to challenge the legality of the Swedish law in light of Article 34 TFEU. If we recall the earlier discussion about the Swedish alcohol retail system, where consumers buy alcohol from, or request the acquisition of particular products by, a monopoly retailer, it is apparent why restrictions on advertising to consumers might create unequal conditions of competition between familiar local producers and out-of-state producers of alcohol. As the Court concluded:

in the case of products like alcoholic beverages, the consumption of which is linked to traditional social practices and to local habits and customs, a prohibition of all advertising directed at consumers in the form of advertisements in the press, on the radio and on television, the direct mailing of unsolicited material or the placing of posters on the public highway is liable to impede access to the market by products from other Member States more than it impedes access by domestic products, with which consumers are instantly more familiar.

In using the language of an impediment to market access, the Court found that the non-discrimination requirement laid down in *Keck*—that the provision 'affect in the same manner, in law and in fact, the marketing of domestic products and of those from other Member States'—was not fulfilled. In this way, it becomes apparent that the preoccupations of a 'discrimination' and a 'market access' analytical framework may in fact be the same.

The capacity of advertising rules to either constitute selling arrangements or to in fact impact on the free movement of goods, highlights a particular conceptual difficulty with whether the scope for harmonization merely mirrors the scope of Article 34 TFEU. If measures fall outside the scope of Article 34 TFEU because they are not intrinsically likely to create obstacles to free movement, then is there any reason for the EU legislator to seek to harmonize such rules under Article 114 TFEU? As the example of tobacco advertising– discussed below—illustrates, the Court has insisted that harmonization aimed at advertising must genuinely contribute to the functioning of an internal market by removing barriers to trade and/or distortions to competition. It might be argued that insofar as selling arrangements do not create obstacles to free movement there is no legal basis for their harmonization.

---

[60] Case C-405/98 *Konsumentombudsmannen (KO) v Gourmet International Products AB (GIP)* [2001] ECR I-1795.

As Davies has highlighted, the issue of EU legislative competence to harmonize advertising prompts us to reflect more widely on the relationship between 'negative' and 'positive' integration, as well as the scope of EU competence to adopt legislation aimed at protecting consumers.[61] After all, one of the aims of the Unfair Commercial Practices Directive is to address the effects of disparities in the national laws concerning misleading advertising.[62] For Davies, the scope of legislative competence under Article 114 TFEU and the supervisory jurisdiction of the Court under Article 34 TFEU need not be symmetrical, not least because the former has a different—albeit imperfect—basis for its legitimacy. That said, the Court has somewhat shackled itself insofar as it has stated that Article 114 TFEU does not provide a general legal basis for regulating the internal market and the preconditions for its use tend to refer back to whether or not a measure creates barriers to trade despite the fact that the presence of a distortion to competition would also be sufficient to establish legislative competence.

Advertising of alcoholic products is big business in Europe. However, harmonization of rules at EU level is relatively limited. Indeed, aside from rules relating to misleading advertising and rules primarily concerned with labelling of foodstuffs (typically related to information about alcohol strength),[63] the main restriction on alcohol advertising is with respect to television advertising.[64] Recommendations have been adopted which focus particularly on alcohol and youth. More generally, this is an example of an area where self-regulation by industry itself is intended to operate. As such, and given the global nature of the business, initiatives for self-regulation have extended beyond Europe. In 2014, the International Chamber of Commerce published a *Framework for Responsible Marketing Communications of Alcohol*, setting out general principles for adoption by industry in their advertising and marketing strategies. This is one example of the use of transnational private governance to secure public interest goals in ways that impact on both the movement of goods (alcohol) and the provision of services (advertising).[65]

2. Tobacco

There are similarities between the regulation of alcohol and tobacco across EU Member States. In principle, the sale of such products is lawful albeit that national

---

[61] Gareth Davies, 'Can Selling Arrangements be Harmonised?' (2005) 30 *European Law Review* 371

[62] Above n 58.

[63] See Dir 2000/13/EC on the approximation of the laws of the Member States relating to the labelling, presentation and advertising of foodstuffs (as amended): [2000] OJ L109/29.

[64] See Art 22 of Dir 2010/13/EU on the coordination of certain provisions concerning the provision of audiovisual media services: [2010] OJ L95/1.

[65] For a more extensive discussion and analysis see: Paul Verbruggen, 'Enforcement of Transnational Private Regulation of Advertising Practices: Decentralization, Mechanisms and Procedural Fairness' in Fabrizio Cafaggi (ed), *Enforcement of Transnational Regulation: Ensuring Compliance in a Global World* (2012) 302

rules do place controls on their manufacture and presentation—particularly their packaging—and on the time, place, and manner of their marketing and retailing. Excise duties and taxation of alcohol and tobacco are important sources of revenue for Member States. At the same time, increasing levels of duties, in combination with restrictions on product packaging and on retailers, are intended to deter consumption on grounds of public health. As with alcohol regulation, it is the different approaches of Member States to the control of tobacco that give rise to potential distortions to competition and barriers to free movement within the Single Market.

As is clear from earlier discussion, free movement law involves trade-offs and balances along two central dimensions: the relationship between national and EU-level regulation; and the relationship between market liberalization and market regulation. The control of tobacco and related products highlights the tensions within each of these dimensions as illustrated in particular by their effects on EU harmonization policy. The analysis begins by considering the relationship between exercises of national and EU competence with a particular focus on minimum harmonization as a technique within the internal market. Subsequently, attention turns to the tensions between the market liberalization and public health objectives of EU policy, and their implications for the choice of legal basis for EU legislation.

There is an inherent difficulty with strategies of minimum harmonization within the internal market. After all, the typical justification for a resort to the EU's legislative powers is that disparities between the laws of the Member States may create obstacles to free movement or distortions to competition between the Member States. An approach based on minimum harmonization necessarily assumes that certain disparities will remain. Yet for policy reasons, minimum harmonization may be desirable at least as part of a process of gradually bringing about a convergence in the approaches of Member States to the regulation of tobacco.

It is useful to illustrate the role that minimum harmonization plays by first considering its application to the taxation of tobacco products. For example, Council Directive 72/464/EEC was adopted with the aim of developing a process for the staged harmonization of excise duties.[66] It had a dual legal basis of Articles 99 and 100 EEC, reflecting the close connection between tax harmonization and the harmonization of laws relating to goods. The legislation adopted some common definitions of the tobacco products that fell within its scope. It also initiated a process for setting a minimum level of excise duty applicable to products within its scope. The legislative framework was subsequently amended, extended, and codified with a view to approximating national laws on the taxation of tobacco products albeit within a minimum harmonization approach.[67]

---

[66] Council Dir 72/464/EEC on taxes other than turnover taxes which affect the consumption of manufactured tobacco: [1972] OJ L303/1.

[67] Council Dir 2011/64/EU on the structure and rates of excise duty applied to manufactured tobacco: [2011] OJ L176/24.

While EU harmonization has placed a common floor under the taxation of tobacco, this has not prevented states from imposing higher levels of tax. This can encourage both legitimate and illegitimate behavior, both of which can circumvent higher tobacco taxes. For example, consumers may themselves legitimately choose to purchase lower taxed and cheaper tobacco products in other Member States in exercise of their rights of free movement. Conversely, tobacco products may be illegally imported and avoid the imposition of local taxes beyond the minimum required under EU law. Thus, in a review of the legislative framework, the European Commission concluded that the existing minimum level of duty was not sufficient to bring about harmonization in retail prices for tobacco products, with the result that distortions in the internal market remained.[68] While levels and method of calculation of the minimum level of duty have been changed, EU harmonization remains premised on a minimum harmonization approach, though the level of the floor rises over time.

The minimum harmonization approach has also been applied to the packaging of tobacco products. In 1989, the Council adopted Directive 89/622/EEC on the approximation of the laws, regulations, and administrative provisions of the Member States concerning the labelling of tobacco products.[69] The aim of the Directive was to lay down common minimum requirements regarding the size and scale of warnings and information about tar and nicotine content to be provided on the packaging of tobacco products. Member States were, in principle, free to adopt stricter rules. Yet, as is well established in the case law of the Court of Justice, the application of local rules on product packaging, in addition to rules on packaging applicable in the state in which the goods are manufactured, is liable to create barriers to trade even if the rules also apply to domestically produced goods.[70] In its *Gallaher* ruling, the Court of Justice made clear that provided a product was manufactured in conformity with the minimum requirements of the Directive, it had to be permitted free movement.[71] In other words, stricter local rules could not be imposed on imported goods. Conversely, a Member State was free to impose stricter rules on tobacco products manufactured within its territory. While the Court recognized that this would result in domestic goods receiving less favourable treatment, it noted that 'those consequences are attributable to the degree of harmonization sought by the provisions in question'.

---

[68] Report from the European Commission to the European Parliament and Council on the structure and rates of excise duty applied on cigarettes and other manufactured tobacco products: COM (2008) 460/2.

[69] [1989] OJ L359/1.

[70] See eg Case C-470/93 *Verein gegen Unwesen in Handel und Gewerbe Köln e.V. v Mars GmbH* [1995] ECR I-1923.

[71] Case C-11/92 *R v Secretary of State for Health ex p Gallaher Ltd, Imperial Tobacco Ltd and Rothmans International Tobacco (UK) Ltd* [1993] ECR I-3545.

In addition to the rules on tobacco packaging and labelling, Directive 90/239/EEC established certain maximum limits on tar yields. Directives 89/622/EEC and 90/239/EEC were replaced by Directive 2001/37/EC approximating the laws on the manufacture, presentation, and sale of tobacco products. The aim of the Directive was to tackle the barriers to trade and distortions to competition arising from different national rules, particularly those relating to product composition and labelling. Not only did it have a legal basis in then Article 95 EC (now 114 TFEU), its reference to Article 133 EC highlighted the relationship between the liberalization of internal and external trade. However, in a legal challenge to the Directive,[72] the Court of Justice held that the extra-EU effects of the Directive—the requirement that tobacco products for export outside the EU must also comply with the Directive in order to limit the illegal re-importation of non-compliant goods—could be managed within the scope of Article 95 EC and that there was no need to include Article 133 EC as a legal basis. That conclusion did not, however, affect the validity of the Directive.

Policy, and the legal framework, has continued to evolve as the market, scientific knowledge, and public attitudes to tobacco have changed. New products and retail methods have emerged that have provoked domestic responses with consequential demands for EU-wide harmonization. As with earlier regulatory interventions, harmonization has also resulted in litigation by tobacco companies. For example, attempts to control the marketing of a novel oral form of tobacco in the UK resulted in a legal challenge to the validity of Article 8 of Directive 2001/37/EC.[73] This provision replicated the earlier restrictions on oral tobacco found in Directive 89/622/EEC (as amended), and the Court dismissed the challenge to the use of Article 95 EC as a legal basis for its regulation. More recently, the invention of 'e-cigarettes'—battery-operated devices that release a vapour which may or may not contain nicotine—has increased demands for their EU-wide regulation. Combined with other issues such as the use of the Internet as a retail method, the European Commission proposed a revision of the legal regime and, in December 2013, the EP and Council reached agreement on a new Directive to replace Directive 2001/37/EC.[74] The freedom given to Member States under the Directive to enact stricter rules on tobacco packaging, including mandating 'plain' packaging, is likely to give rise to further litigation by tobacco companies.

It will, therefore, be apparent, that tobacco as a product is highly regulated within the EU and subject to continual adaptation of the legislative framework. Article 114 TFEU (ex Article 95 EC) does a lot of work in providing a legal basis for such legislative interventions. Yet it is also clear that litigation has sought to define and confine the scope of application of Article 114 TFEU. Most famously, it was in the context of a legal challenge to Directive 98/43 approximating the laws relating

---

[72] Case C-491/01 *The Queen v Secretary of State for Health, ex p British American Tobacco (Investments) Ltd and Imperial Tobacco Ltd* [2002] ECR I-11453.

[73] Case C-201/03 *The Queen on the application of Swedish Match AB and Swedish Match UK Ltd v Secretary of State for Health* [2004] ECR I-11893.

[74] Dir 2014/40/EU: [2014] OJ L127/1.

to tobacco advertising and sponsorship that the Court of Justice stated that what is now Article 114 TFEU does not give the EU a general competence to regulate the internal market.[75] In this way, the approximation of laws relating to tobacco as a good can be viewed as a wider illustration of the problems of regulating an internal market in an EU with only a conferred and shared competence, where Member States wish to retain a degree of regulatory autonomy. The interpretations which the Court has given in the course of litigation over the scope of Article 114 TFEU have wider implications, and the effects of these rulings are felt, for example, in litigation over aspects of the EU's response to the financial crisis.[76] But as important as the wider constitutional principles are, it is important not to lose sight of the specificity of the context of tobacco, its regulation and litigation fuelled as they are by vested interests including the tobacco companies themselves.

3. Chemicals

Amid the hyperbole, mythology, and celebration that attend recitation of the judgment of the Court of Justice in *Van Gend en Loos*, it is easy to forget that at its heart is the story of a company engaging in the cross-frontier trade of goods, including the movement of chemicals. At issue was the imposition of a customs duty—contrary to what is now Article 30 TFEU—applied to the importation of urea formaldehyde. Of course, there is little in the case that really turns on the nature of the good being imported, and, not surprisingly, it was the direct effect of the Treaty that was of real interest.

Nonetheless, the relationship between the constitutional dimension of enforcement and the EU's approach to harmonization in the area of chemicals turns out to be of some significance. It is again in the context of chemicals that the Court expanded on the scope of direct effect, particularly the idea that the direct effect of a Directive may not be relied upon until the expiry of the transposition period. The Court made this point in its ruling in *Ratti* concerning EU legislative intervention relating to the classification, packaging, and labelling of dangerous preparations (solvents) and the classification, packaging and labelling of paints, varnishes, inks, and adhesives.[77] As early as 1967, the EEC had begun to approximate the laws of the Member States relating to the classification, packaging, and labelling of dangerous

---

[75] Case C-376/98 *Germany v EP and Council (Tobacco Advertising)* [2000] ECR I-8419. It is worth noting that the directive adopted in 2014 replacing Directive 2001/37/EC is the subject of a legal challenge alleging the inappropriate use of Art 114 TFEU as a legal basis for certain provisions of the directive, as well as breaches of the principles of proportionality and subsidiarity: Case C-358/14, *Poland v EP and Council (Tobacco)* (pending).

[76] Eg Case C-270/12, *United Kingdom v EP and Council (Short Selling)*, judgment of 22 January 2014.

[77] Case 148/78, *Pubblico Ministero v Tullio Ratti* [1979] ECR 1629.

substances. This legislative activity continued throughout the 1970s, with the aim of putting in place common European frameworks to prevent obstacles to trade arising from the sort of national rules on packaging and labelling at issue in *Ratti*. Ensuring that this legislation was in principle directly effective and therefore substitutive for incompatible rules of national law was aimed at ensuring the effectiveness of this legal regime.

The legislative framework of the 1970s was amended and then repealed in the 1980s, amended and then repealed in the 1990s until finally, in the mid 2000s, the legal framework was recast. If the hidden story of *Ratti* was one of chemicals regulation based on harmonizing national laws through Directives and decentralized administration, in 2007 and 2008 the regime took a more centralized turn. First, the framework of Directives was replaced by Regulation 1272/2008 on the classification, labeling, and packaging of substances and mixtures.[78] This new regime—effective from 1 June 2015—is contained in a regulation whose annexes alone run to over 1300 pages. It establishes a general legal framework of application where no more specific legislation applies, for example EU rules on cosmetics and foodstuffs. It is particularly noteworthy—returning to an earlier theme about the importance of global rules—that the regulation is as much focused on external as internal trade in its adoption of a classification system developed by the UN: the Globally Harmonized System of Classification and Labelling of Chemicals (GHS). The Regulation places obligations on manufacturers and importers to classify products in accordance with the Regulation and only to place goods on the market that are labelled accordingly. It is also worth noting that this evolution in the legislative framework from one based on Directives—with subsequent amending Directives—to one based on a Regulation has parallels in other regulatory regimes such as that applicable to cosmetics.[79]

Second, the 'REACH' regulation entered into force on 1 June 2007.[80] The aim of the regulation is to seek a balance between managing risks and permitting the operation of a market which, as indicated above, represents around 15 per cent of 'dispatches' in intra-EU trade. Certainly a key concern for industry prior to the adoption of REACH was that any centralized regime also had to promote competitiveness and innovation in the European chemicals market, not least to ensure that the system did not, paradoxically, make it harder for new products to enter the market compared to the advantage in favour of older and potentially more risky chemicals with which the industry was already familiar. The Regulation places duties on manufacturers and importers that supply chemicals of more than 1 tonne per year to provide data regarding these substances through a registration process

---

[78] [2008] OJ L353/1.   [79] See Reg 1223/2009 on cosmetic products: [2009] OJ L342/59.
[80] Reg 1907/2006 concerning the Registration, Evaluation, Authorisation and Restriction of Chemicals (REACH), establishing a European Chemicals Agency: [2007] OJ L136/3.

with the European Chemicals Agency (ECHA). Without registering, goods cannot be placed on the market. It is fundamentally for market actors to assess the risks associated with their products and, through the registration process, to demonstrate how such risks are managed in the context of goods circulating within the internal market. ECHA carries out evaluations of the dossiers submitted by market actors to ensure conformity with registration requirements. In cooperation with national authorities, ECHA also carries out certain substance evaluations where there is a risk to health or the environment. Once registered, chemicals can be placed on the market. Where substances are of high concern, they may be made subject to a centralized EU authorization procedure based on risk assessment carried out by ECHA's scientific committee, with authorization decisions made on the basis of a comitology procedure. If centralized authorization is not required, the placing of certain chemicals on the market can, nonetheless, be made subject to EU-wide restrictions.

There is much that can be said, about REACH.[81] For some, the EU model may have a wider global influence on the design of systems of transnational risk regulation.[82] While instruments such as 'association agreements' can formally extend the reach of the EU's free movement *acquis* beyond the territorial borders of the EU, in a more subtle way, European regulatory models may be emulated or mimicked beyond European frontiers. As was noted in respect of the classification and labelling of chemicals, European norms develop in an increasingly international context, including UN-sponsored harmonization initiatives. In this way, a regulatory regime such as that developed to regulate the movement of chemicals within the European internal market is nested within a broader and more international normative landscape.[83]

Specific regimes have developed in respect of particular chemicals of which biocidal products are especially noteworthy. Biocides have a very wide range of domestic and commercial uses as disinfectants, insecticides, and fungicides. Their use has typically been subject to a requirement of prior authorization by national authorities. This is an area where the principle of mutual recognition can play a role in the manner suggested earlier. In other words, while

---

[81] See generally, Joanne Scott, 'REACH: Combining Harmonization and Dynamism in the Regulation of Chemicals' in Joanne Scott (ed), *Environmental Protection: European Law and Governance* (2009)

[82] Marco de Morpurgo, 'The European Union as a Global Producer of Transnational Law of Risk Regulation: A Case Study on Chemical Regulation' (2013) 19 *European Law Journal* 779; Veerle Heyvaert, 'Regulating Chemical Risk: REACH in a Global Governance Perspective' in Johan Eriksson, Michael Gilek, and Christina Ruden (eds), *Regulating Chemical Risks* (2010) 217.

[83] For a provocative evaluation of how governance in the global order is being reshaped by new and experimental forms of governance see: Graínne De Búrca, Robert O. Keohane, and Charles Sabel, 'New Modes of Pluralist Global Governance' (2013) 45 *New York University Journal of International Law & Politics* 723.

Member States are in principle competent to impose local regulatory require-ments, they must have regard to the regulatory history of a product, including whether a biocide has already been authorized in another Member State and what regulatory procedures have been applied to it, including chemical analy-ses and tests.[84]

Directive 98/8/EC was adopted to regulate the placing of biocides on the EU market. It combined a centralized process for determining a positive list of active substances that could be used in biocidal products with a decentral-ized process of market authorization by national authorities. Using the prin-ciple of mutual recognition, such national authorizations were intended to ensure market access for biocidal products while keeping the locus of regula-tory activity close to the small and medium-sized enterprises that are active in this market. However, consistent with the trend identified above of moving the EU regulatory framework away from Directives that require transposition to directly applicable Regulations, Directive 98/8/EC was repealed and replaced by Regulation 528/12 concerning the making available on the market and use of biocidal products,[85] applicable as of September 2013. Its aim is to involve ECHA in establishing positive lists of active substances; to improve the operation of the mutual recognition of authorizations; and to provide for EU authorization of certain products in certain circumstances. Consistent with the analysis above, when we consider how chemicals, including biocides, are regulated within the EU, whether through labelling and classification, or through registration and authorization, the provision of information and data, together with scientific testing and evaluation, is at the core of how EU law governs the free movement of chemicals.

If we often fail to pay sufficient attention to the 'goods' in free movement of goods, then we may also risk ignoring the legal regulation of 'movement' itself. The movement of chemicals is likely to trigger legal regimes applicable to the movement of hazardous or dangerous materials by different forms of transport: road, rail, air, or waterway. Not surprisingly, these regimes rely heavily on the harmonized classifications described earlier and on international norms that recognize that transportation is a global, not merely a European, phenomenon. In this way, UN Recommendations on the transportation of dangerous goods have been translated into international agreements, which, in turn, are given effect through specific EU instruments. In the mid 2000s the EU legal framework was recast to consolidate mode-specific legal instruments into a single legal framework based on Directive 2008/68/EC.[86]

---

[84] Case 272/80 *Frans-Nederlandse Maatschappij voor Biologische Producten* [1981] ECR 3277; Case C-293/94 *Brandsma* [1996] ECR I-3159.
[85] [2012] OJ L167/1.   [86] [2008] OJ L260/13.

VII. Conclusions

The analysis presented here has not sought to be iconoclastic as far as the voluminous case law of the ECJ is concerned. But there is a challenge for any author writing on the free movement of goods seeking simultaneously to do justice to this much-analysed area of judicial governance and at the same time aspiring to draw in wider perspectives. Focusing on particular types of goods can certainly perform an illustrative function, and indeed we can learn much about the evolution not just of litigation but also of the legislative and administrative frameworks that together form specific regimes applicable to different types of good. Beyond the realm of alcohol, tobacco, and chemicals explored here there are other regimes—medicines, automotives, cosmetics, foodstuffs—that each present their own characteristics in terms of the relationship between EU and national regulatory authority, and in terms of their reconciliation of the aims of market integration and market regulation. There is much to be appreciated and understood by starting with the particularities of specific goods and considering the full range of norms and institutional locations—national, EU, and international, public and private—that condition their free movement within the Single Market.

Bibliography

Kenneth A. Armstrong, 'Mutual Recognition' in Catherine Barnard and Joanne Scott (ed), *The Law of the Single European Market. Unpacking the Premises* (2002) 225.

Catherine Barnard, *The Substantive Law of the EU: The Four Freedoms* (4th ed, 2013)

Damian Chalmers, Gareth T. Davies, and Giorgio Monti, *European Union Law: Cases and Materials* (3rd ed, 2014) Ch 17

Paul Craig and Gráinne de Búrca, *EU Law: Text, Cases and Materials* (5th ed, 2011) Chs 18–19

Gareth Davies, 'Understanding Market Access: Exploring the Economic Rationality of Different Conceptions of Free Movement Law' (2010) 11 *German Law Journal* 671

Michael Dougan, 'Minimum Harmonization and the Internal Market' (2000) 37 *Common Market Law Review* 853

Laurence W. Gormley, *EU Law of Free Movement of Goods and Customs Union* (2009)

Panos Koutrakos, 'On Groceries, Alcohol and Olive Oil: More on Free Movement of Goods after Keck' (2001) 26 *European Law Review* 391

Miguel Poiares Maduro, *We, the Court: the European Court of Justice and the European Economic Constitution: A Critical Reading of Article 30 of the EC Treaty* (1998)

Peter Oliver (ed), *Oliver on Free Movement of Goods in the European Union* (5th ed, 2010)

Niamh Nic Shuibhne, *The Coherence of EU Free Movement Law: Constitutional Responsibility and the Court of Justice* (2013)

Jukka Snell, 'The Notion of Market Access: A Concept or a Slogan?' (2010) 47 *Common Market Law Review* 437

Eleanor Spaventa, 'On Discrimination and the Theory of Mandatory Requirement' (2002) *3 Cambridge Yearbook of European Legal Studies* 457

Alina Tryfonidou, 'Further Steps on the Road to Convergence among the Market Freedoms' (2010) *35 European Law Review* 36

Stephen Weatherill, 'Limits of Legislative Harmonization Ten Years after *Tobacco Advertising*: How the Court's Case Law has Become a Drafting Guide' (2011) *12 German Law Journal* 827

Joseph H.H. Weiler, 'The Constitution of the Common Market Place: Text and Context in the Evolution of the Free Movement of Goods' in Paul Craig and Gráinne de Búrca (eds), *The Evolution of EU Law* (1999)

CHAPTER 21

......

FREEDOM OF ESTABLISHMENT AND REGULATORY COMPETITION

......

ZOE ADAMS AND SIMON DEAKIN[*]

I. INTRODUCTION

......

FEW areas of European Union law have given rise to as much controversy as the case law on freedom of establishment. Since the early 1990s, a broad 'market access' test has displaced the discrimination and 'double burden' approaches to defining a market restriction.[1] The Court has gone down this path, however, without clearly enunciating what it means for market access to be 'restricted'. It has veered between two extreme positions: on the one hand, treating formal market access as sufficient;[2] and, on the other, regarding national regulatory requirements, often imposed equally on domestic and foreign providers, as obstacles to free movement.[3] In the context of the right of

---

[*] We are grateful to the editors and to Julian Ghosh for comments on an earlier draft.

[1] C. Barnard and S. Deakin, 'Market Access and Regulatory Competition', in C. Barnard and J. Scott (eds) *The Law of the Single Market: Unpacking the Premises* (2001).

[2] Joined Cases 267/91 and 268/91 *Keck and Mithouard* [1993] I-ECR 6097 (goods).

[3] Case C-76/90 *Sager v Dennemeyer & Co* [1991] ECR 1-4221 (services); Case C-55/94 *Gebhard v Consiglio dell'Ordine degli Avvocati e Procuratori di Milano* [1995] ECR I-4165 (establishment); Case

establishment, new avenues for judicial review of company, labour and tax laws have been opened up,[4] and novel forms of liability attached to private regulatory behaviour.[5] Freedom of establishment has evolved into a meta-law for the governance of the internal market, setting the limits of state capacity and private power in the regulation of economic activity.

In this chapter, we will argue that freedom of establishment needs to be understood in the context of a larger debate about the appropriate sphere of state autonomy in the emerging constitutional polity of the European Union. The issue is no longer whether a transnational economic space is to be created, but how that space is to be constituted and governed. Depending on the Court's analysis of freedom of movement, the nature and effects of regulatory competition will vary, with implications for the content of economic regulation within and across Member States.

We begin by taking a step back from the case law to consider the principles underlying economic governance in multi-level jurisdictional entities. Section II accordingly provides an outline of the theory of regulatory competition in federal jurisdictions (or quasi-federal ones such as the European Union) and considers its relevance to the law on freedom of movement. Sections III–V look in more detail at the development of the market access test in the context of freedom of establishment and analyse its application in the substantive areas of company law, tax law and labour law. Section VI provides an assessment and conclusion.

II. The Theory of Regulatory Competition and the Concept of a 'Market Restriction'

It was recognized prior to the foundation of the European Economic Community that the creation of a common market, within which economic resources would be free to move across national borders, would have implications for the regulation of economic activity not just between but also within the Member States. Concerns over regulatory arbitrage or a 'race to the bottom' were expressed in

---

415/93 *Union Royale Belge des Sociétés de Football Association ASBL v Bosman* [1995] ECR I-4921 (workers); Case C-112/05 *Commission v Germany (Volkswagen)* [2007] ECR I-8995 (capital).

[4] Case C-212/97 *Centros Ltd v Erhvervs-og Selskabsstyrelsen* [1999] ECR I-1459 (company law); Case C-438/05 *International Transport Workers' Federation v Viking Line ABP* [2007] ECR I-10779 (labour law); Case C-446/03 *Marks & Spencer plc v Halsey (Inspector of Taxes)* [2005] ECR I-10837.

[5] C-438/05 *Viking* [2007] ECR I-10779.

the debates that preceded the conclusion of the Treaty of Rome. The Ohlin[6] and Spaak[7] reports took the view that labour market standards would 'level up' as workers migrated to states with higher levels of wages and social protection. Since wages mostly reflected productivity, capital flight, it was thought, would not be a problem for high-wage states, whose industries were also the most efficient and developed.[8] Differences in competitiveness across states would be naturally offset by exchange rate fluctuations.[9] Harmonization of regulatory standards would only be necessary in cases where exchange rates could not cancel out the effects of 'artificial' economic advantages such as those stemming from gender discrimination.[10] This thinking led to the adoption of the Treaty provisions on equal pay between women and men,[11] but also, conversely, to the rejection of any more extensive harmonization of labour laws, a position which is still reflected in the relatively limited contents of the TFEU's Social Policy Title.[12]

The decision to insert into the Rome Treaty legal protections for the 'fundamental freedoms'[13] and a competition law designed to prevent partitioning of the market, while rejecting harmonization of regulatory standards, was consistent with the theories of regulatory competition which were predominant at that time. The 'pure theory' of fiscal federalism, associated with Tiebout's paper of 1956,[14] predicted that competition between local government units over the levels and incidence of taxation would lead to an efficient (welfare-maximizing) result in a context where citizens were free to choose where to locate. A two-tier jurisdictional structure was needed, with the higher level (federal) rule maker ensuring that lower level units (states) complied with the condition of allowing free entry and exit to economic actors. As long as this condition was met,[15] spending decisions could be devolved

---

[6] International Labour Office, 'Social Aspects of European Economic Cooperation' (1956) 74 *International Labour Review*, 99–278.

[7] Comité Intergouvernemental créé par la conférence de Messine, *Rapport des Chefs de Délégation aux Ministres des Affaires Etrangères (Spaak)*, Brussels, 21.4.1956, reproduced in part in *Political and Economic Planning* (1956), no. 405.

[8] ILO (n 6) 102; Spaak, (n 7) 233.   [9] ILO (n 6) 107.

[10] ILO (n 6) 108.   [11] Originally Article 119 TEEC, currently Article 157 TFEU.

[12] On the economic reasoning used in the Ohlin and Spaak reports to justify the limited scope for harmonization in what is now Article 152 TFEU, see S. Deakin, 'Labour Law as Market Regulation: The Economic Foundations of European Social Policy', in P. Davies, A. Lyon-Caen, S. Sciarra, and S. Simitis (eds) *Principles and Perspectives on EC Labour Law: Liber Amicorum for Lord Wedderburn* (1996); S. Giubboni, *Social Rights and Market Freedom in the European Constitution. A Labour Law Perspective* (2006).

[13] These provisions now form Title IV of the TFEU. Freedom of establishment is governed by Articles 49–55. The core right of establishment is set out in Article 49. Article 54 extends the right to companies and Article 55 sets out a non-discrimination rule.

[14] C. Tiebout, 'A Pure Theory of Local Expenditures' (1956) 64 *Journal of Political Economy* 416–424.

[15] 'If consumer-voters are fully mobile, the appropriate local governments, whose revenue-expenditure patterns are set, are adopted by the consumer-voters': Tiebout (n 14) 424.

to local level without loss of welfare. An 'optimal' degree of local expenditure and related provision of public goods would emerge through decentralized decision making. The result would not necessarily be a uniform system of rules across economic space of the larger (federal) unit. On the contrary, there would be diversity, based on the matching of agents' heterogeneous preferences to distinct mixes of taxation and public expenditure at local level.[16]

Tiebout's theory applies not just to taxation but to regulatory aspects of law more generally since legal regulations, like government services, are examples of 'indivisible' public goods, which, because of their non-excludable character, are most effectively organized via the political process. There is nothing in the 'pure theory' of regulatory competition flowing from Tiebout's model to justify the federal rule maker—whether legislator *or court*—in doing anything more than guaranteeing formal conditions of market entry and exit. In his model, differences in the regulatory standards set by states are not simply tolerated, they are to be encouraged. The contents of state-level laws should reflect local preferences as expressed through the political process at that level, in order for diversity of interests to be respected and aggregate welfare to be maximized.[17] A second, 'dynamic' argument is that preserving diversity in the regulatory solutions offered by states allows for experimentation and learning to be optimized at the level of the federal unit as a whole.[18] The idea that regulatory divergences at local level might in and of themselves constitute 'barriers to entry' or equivalent obstacles to free movement, however else it might be explained, finds no justification in the Tieboutian model of economic governance in a federal polity.

The Tieboutian model is of course just that, a formal model which makes assumptions about the efficiency of decentralized decision making which may not be borne out in practice.[19] Without an effective layer of federal regulation governing competition between them to attract goods and resources, states may find themselves in a prisoner's dilemma, that is, a situation in which it would not be in the interests of any one of them, individually, to avoid a race to the bottom, even if, collectively, they would be better off observing at least a certain minimum threshold of regulation.[20] This 'collective action' problem necessitates some form of centralized

---

[16] 'Each locality has a revenue and expenditure pattern that reflects the desires of its residents': Tiebout (n 14) 420.

[17] 'The solution, like a general equilibrium solution for a private spatial economy, is the best that can be obtained given preferences and resource endowments': Tiebout (n 14) 424. To the same effect is Spaak (n 7) 230.

[18] 'The greater the number of communities and the greater the variance among them, the closer the consumer will come to fully realizing his preference position': Tiebout (n 14) 418. See, in the European context, the analysis of K.-H. Paqué, 'Does Europe's common market need a social dimension?' in J. Addison and W.S. Siebert (eds) *Labour Markets in Europe: Issues of Harmonisation and Regulation* (1997).

[19] It is an 'extreme model': Tiebout, (n 14) 19.

[20] R. Revesz, 'Rehabilitating Interstate Competition: Rethinking the Race to the Bottom Rationale for Federal Environmental Regulation' (1992) 67 *New York University Law Review* 1210–1254. Revesz

coordination or regulation of state-level law making. Thus, there is scope, for example, for Directives which set minimum standards across the Member States to prevent a welfare-reducing erosion of regulatory standards, while allowing them leeway to customize centralized regulation to meet local conditions ('reflexive harmonization').[21] Permitting diverse local solutions to be adopted above the floor of rights is also consistent with a learning model that is biased towards the strengthening or improvement of regulatory standards over time. Federal 'preemption', setting both a floor and a ceiling to state level laws would, however, be discouraged under this approach, as would Directives in general which set uniform standards, since in both cases the higher-level measure would have the effect of closing off regulatory options and reducing the scope for learning.[22]

The theory of regulatory competition abstracts from the institutional detail of the rules needed to make market access effective in practice. To that extent, it does not rule out a version of the mutual recognition principle. Viewed through the lens of regulatory competition theory, mutual recognition is a principle according to which states are required to accept as legitimate the regulatory decisions taken by other units within the federal space, at least in contexts where inter-state trade or mobility of resources is at stake.[23] However, it would still be consistent with the principles underlying the regulatory competition model for the federal rule maker to place limits on mutual recognition in order to prevent a mutually-destructive race to the bottom of the kind which can occur in a prisoner's dilemma. Thus a state engaging in a deregulatory strategy that imposed significant external costs on to its neighbours—social or environmental 'dumping'—should not be able to insist on the application of the mutual recognition principle to validate its regulatory choices.[24]

---

discusses various theoretical models of the 'race to the bottom' before concluding that none of them justifies harmonizing regulation, but as he also accepts, the question of whether such harmonization is needed is ultimately an empirical one. For discussion in the European context, see C. Barnard, 'Social Dumping Revisited: Lessons from Delaware' (2000) 25 *European Law Review* 57–80.

[21] S. Deakin, 'Regulatory Competition versus Harmonisation in European Company Law', in D. Esty and D. Geradin (eds) *Regulatory Competition and Economic Integration: Comparative Perspectives* (2001), and Two Types of Regulatory Competition: Competitive Federalism versus Reflexive Harmonisation. A Law and Economics Perspective on *Centros*' (1999/2000) 2 *Cambridge Yearbook of European Legal Studies*, 231–260; S. Mock, 'Harmonization, Regulation and Legislative Competition in European Corporate Law' (2002) 3 *German Law Journal*, available at http://www.germanlawjournal.com/index.php?pageID=11&artID=216; M. Dougan, *National Remedies Before the Court of Justice* (2004) 187–190; R. Rogowski, *Reflexive Labour Law in the World Society*, (2013) p. 212

[22] S. Deakin, 'Regulatory Competition after Laval' (2008/9) 10 *Cambridge Yearbook of European Legal Studies* 581–609.

[23] R. Van den Bergh, 'The Subsidiarity Principle in European Community Law: Some Insights from Law and Economics' (1994) 1 *Maastricht Journal of European & Comparative Law* 337–366.

[24] S. Deakin (1999), 'Two Types of Regulatory Competition: Competitive Federalism versus Reflexive Harmonisation. A Law and Economic Perspective on *Centros*' *Cambridge YB European Legal Studies* 2, 231–260.

Following the adoption of the Rome Treaty, the Court's free movement jurisprudence was initially based on the idea that a Member State would be required to justify a
restriction on free movement only where it was either discriminatory in law or fact, or
imposed a 'double burden' on the foreign entity or provider. Compliance with cumulative regulatory burdens imposed by both the home and host state was interpreted
as a restriction in the mutual recognition cases deriving from the *Cassis de Dijon*[25]
judgment. However, in the 1990s the Court shifted its position, in *Säger*,[26] *Gebhard*,[27]
and *Bosman*,[28] to focusing on the *effect* the measure had on market access.[29] The Court
now regularly applied the *Gebhard* formulation: 'measures liable to hinder or make
less attractive the exercise of the fundamental freedoms' constituted restrictions and
to be lawful had to be applied in a non-discriminatory manner, justified by imperative
requirements in the general interest, suitable to achieve the objective which they pursued, and go no further than is necessary to achieve the objective. As a result, a wider
range of measures potentially affecting the exercise of free movement was opened up
to scrutiny. This development was problematic since the Court not only failed to give
definitive guidance on what a restriction on market access meant, it failed also to take
a consistent line on the content of the market access test across the different freedoms,
despite suggestions in *Gebhard*[30] that this would be the case. Thus the narrow reading
given to market access in *Keck*[31] was not replicated beyond the case law on free movement of goods. This had far-reaching consequences for national regulatory capacity in
the areas of company, tax, and labour law, which we will now consider.

III. Company Law: Delaware Comes
to Europe?

1. Delaware as a Model for a Market for Incorporations

The threat of a 'race to the bottom' in company law as a result of the progressive establishment of the Common Market was a concern of European law

---

[25] Case 120-78 *Rewe-Zentral AG v Bundesmonopolverwaltung für Branttwein* [1976] ECR 649.
[26] C-76/90 [1991] ECR I-4221.   [27] Case C-55/94 [1995] ECR I-4165.
[28] Case 415/93 [1995] ECR I-4921.
[29] For a view that the scheme of the Treaty provisions on freedom of establishment (and other
freedoms) all along implied two distinct aspects of protection under which the host state should
first guarantee market access and *then* avoid discrimination, see I.J. Ghosh, *Principles of the Internal
Market and Direct Taxation* (2007) 48.
[30] Case C-55/94 [1995] ECR I-4165.   [31] Joined Cases 267/91 and 268/91 [1993] ECR-I 6097.

makers in the 1960s and 1970s. Averting a European version of the 'Delaware' effect was a principal motivation behind the adoption of the first company law Directives,[32] which, however, were only able to address a number of fringe issues, partly because political agreement on the content of a more comprehensive set of common rules could not be reached. Meanwhile, views on the Delaware effect began to shift on both sides of the Atlantic. The view that migration of companies to Delaware had brought about a deterioration in the protections afforded to shareholders was challenged by law-and-economics analyses, which questioned why shareholders, where they had the power to do so, would not have blocked reincorporations which diminished their legal rights.[33] Gradually, the view took hold that a 'market for incorporations' was at work, with the Delaware courts and legislature adjusting the content of state law to reflect actors' preferences; as such, the results should, presumptively at least, be regarded as welfare-maximizing.[34]

A more nuanced and historically-grounded account of the Delaware effect would have emphasized that the 'market for incorporations' was not a spontaneous or 'natural' phenomenon but an institutional construct which depended on the interaction of state and federal law at a number of levels. The US Supreme Court decided in the late nineteenth century, under the case law on the 'internal affairs' doctrine, that a company incorporated in one state was entitled to be recognized as validly constituted in that state by the courts of another, regardless of the physical location of its operations. Delaware's pre-eminence as the favoured state of incorporation, however, began several decades later, as a reaction to the adoption in the early 1900s of Progressive-era antitrust legislation, which aimed to disperse and fragment the power of large corporate groups, in New York and New Jersey.[35] These had been the preferred states of incorporation for large, quoted companies up to that point.

Delaware was initially chosen as the alternative to its larger neighbours for contingent reasons. In particular, it had no sizable urban population, and so was relatively unaffected by Progressive politics of the kind that tended to lead state legislatures to adopt antitrust laws. Once Delaware was established as the state of choice, its legislators and courts adjusted corporate law with a view to maintaining this position. Over time, Delaware came to provide advantages associated with specialization and agglomeration effects: its position was locked in by virtue of the

---

[32] C. Schmitthoff, 'The Future of the European Company Law Scene', in C. Schmitthoff (ed) *The Harmonisation of European Company Law* (1973).

[33] R. Winter, 'State law, Shareholder Protection, and the Theory of Corporations' (1977) 6 *Journal of Legal Studies* 251–292.

[34] R. Romano, *The Genius of American Corporate Law* (1993).

[35] On the contingent relationship between the development of the internal affairs doctrine and the later rise of Delaware as preferred state of incorporation, see F. Tung, 'Before Competition: Origins of the Internal Affairs Doctrine' (2006) 32 *Journal of Corporation Law* 33–101.

advisory and judicial expertise that it could offer, making it relatively immune to attempts by rival states to undercut its position.[36]

Given its particular history, the Delaware experience arguably has limited relevance to the European context. However, against the background of the continuing failure of the Member States in the 1990s to agree a common approach to the issue of cross-border incorporations,[37] the Court opened the way to a European version of the Delaware effect by ruling, in *Centros*,[38] that state-level restrictions on the choice of the national law applicable to a company could amount to an infringement of freedom of establishment.

2. The Effects of *Centros* and *Cartesio*

The immediate issue in *Centros* was the effect of the refusal of the Danish company law authorities to register a branch of an English company in Denmark, thereby denying it the capacity to conduct its business there. Viewed this way, *Centros* looks like a straightforward case in which a company based in one Member State was denied access to the territory of another. In fact, Centros Ltd had been set up by two Danish citizens, Mr. and Mrs. Bryde, and incorporated under English law in order to avoid a Danish regulation on minimum capital requirements which had no counterpart in the UK. It was the Brydes' aim of avoiding the Danish law on creditor protection which led the Danish company registrar to reject their application to register a branch of Centros Ltd in Denmark.

The company's operations appear to have been based in Denmark throughout and there was no cross-border movement of corporate assets. There was no physical relocation of the company's business; it never traded in the UK (had it done so, the Danish authorities would have registered its presence in their jurisdiction). The company's owner-managers were seeking to opt out of Danish jurisdiction in favour of the lighter-touch UK regulatory regime. In so far as there was any cross-border transfer of resources it took the form of the purchase of the services of UK-based legal advisers (those supplying the means to incorporate overseas companies under English law) in preference to Danish ones, and the extra work created for the UK's regulatory authorities (the UK's company registrar, Companies House).

The Court's discussion of this point had a circular air to it—*once* it was accepted that *Centros* was validly established under English law, it was *necessarily* an

---

[36] D. Charny, 'Competition Among Jurisdictions in Formulating Corporate Law Rules: An American Perspective On The "Race To The Bottom" in the European Communities' (1991) 32 *Harvard International Law Journal* 422–456; M. Roe, 'Delaware's Politics', in M. Blair (ed) *The Deal Decade* (1993)

[37] See V. Edwards, *European Company Law* (1999).   [38] Case C-212/97 [1999] ECR I-1459.

infringement of its establishment rights for it to be denied a Danish presence—but it did have the merit of getting to the nub of the core issue, for internal market law, of whether the mutual recognition principle applied to incorporations. *Centros* decided that it did: the host state had to recognize an incorporation which was valid under the laws of the company's home state, subject to a justification defence. The later judgments of *Inspire Art, Überseering,* and *Sevic* Systems confirmed this approach, and also cemented in place a restrictive approach to the proportionality test: national courts would have little leeway in cases where domestic laws denied recognition to a validly constituted foreign company or one seeking access to the host state via reincorporation.[39]

The possibility of a justification defence should mean that in a case where the home state's incorporation requirements are too lax, in the sense of allowing welfare-reducing (negative) externalities to be displaced on to third parties, the host state can in principle refuse to accept the incorporation as valid. In *Centros* itself, the defence failed since the Court took the view that less restrictive means had been available for protecting the rights of creditors. The Court dismissed the defences put forward by the Danish authorities in barely a sentence. Nor did it accept that this was an appropriate case for the notion of 'abuse' of the right of establishment to be applied, although without clearly saying why, or when, in general, that notion would apply.

As it turned out, allowing small-firm start-ups in mainland Europe to evade minimum capital requirements by incorporating under English law did have negative effects: German and Dutch firms taking the English route to incorporation were more likely to fail than equivalents incorporated under the laws of the host state, and a significant proportion of them failed to file accounts with the UK authorities, creating a gap in regulatory coverage.[40] There is also evidence that the *Centros* judgment led to the weakening of creditor protection laws in several Member States,[41] an outcome that can be interpreted as a 'race to the bottom'. The generally deregulatory bias of the Court's intervention is clear in this instance.[42]

Centros has, however, not quite led to the demise of the 'real seat' theory according to which the applicable law of a company is determined, at least in part, by reference to the location of its headquarters and/or main site of operations, rather

---

[39] Case C-208/00 *Überseering v Construction Company Baumanagement GmbH (NCC)* [2002] ECR-I Case; C-167/01 *Kamer van Koophandel en Fabrieken voor Amsterdam v Inspire Art Ltd.* [2003] ECR-I 10115; Case C-411/03 *Sevic Systems* [2005] ECR I-10805.

[40] M. Becht, C. Mayer and H. Wagner, 'Where do Firms Incorporate? Deregulation and the Cost of Entry (2008) 14 *Journal of Corporate Finance* 241–256.

[41] W. Bratton, J. McCahery and E. Vermeulen, 'How Does Corporate Mobility Affect Lawmaking? A Comparative Analysis' (2009) 57 *American Journal of Comparative Law* 347–386.

[42] It should be noted, however, that the deregulatory effect of *Centros* seems to be confined, so far, to incorporations and reincorporations affecting smaller firms and start ups: Bratton et al. (n 41).

than the state of its incorporation. Most, although not all, civil law countries follow the real seat principle, and it was observed in a majority of Member States prior to *Centros*. The real seat principle is not entirely dead, as it remains open to a Member State, under the establishment case law, to determine the 'connecting factor' that identifies a company as subject to its own jurisdiction. Thus in *Daily Mail*,[43] the UK was not acting in breach of the freedom of establishment by preventing a company transferring its residence for tax purposes to another country, while retaining its UK incorporation; similarly, in *Cartesio*,[44] the Hungarian authorities could refuse to acknowledge the transfer of a company's seat to Italy while that company continued to be governed by Hungarian company law.

The UK follows the incorporation theory while Hungary follows the real seat theory, so the common outcome to these decisions suggests that the critical issue is not a given country's choice of conflict of law rule. Instead, they illustrate a wider principle according to which a Member State is entitled to set the conditions under which a company can incorporate *under its own jurisdiction*: it can insist on the company retaining a tax presence (*Daily Mail*) or physical presence (*Cartesio*) in the home state. In these cases, as long as national and foreign companies are treated in the same way, no issue of freedom of establishment arises. The effect is to allow a Member State to take steps to ensure the viability of its tax base and regulatory capacity, at least to the extent of attaching to incorporation certain mandatory fiscal and regulatory requirements.

However, a Member State cannot, subject to the justification test, prevent one of its own companies from exiting its jurisdiction, where the company meets the conditions for reincorporation in the 'entry' state. This is the implication of the Court's statement in *Cartesio* that the 'freedom of the "exit state" to regulate the real seat of a company' is not unlimited. Thus the exit state would not be able to insist on the liquidation of a company as a precondition for its reincorporation under the law of the entry state. As we shall see below, the application of this principle has had repercussions for tax law.

It further follows that the 'entry' state cannot, in principle, refuse to accept a foreign company which seeks access to its jurisdiction by converting its legal form in accordance with the entry state's own rules, where domestic companies would be allowed to do so. This is the effect of the Court's ruling in *VALE*.[45] That decision, however, does not signify the end of the real seat principle, since the company in that case was seeking to end its operations in the exit state (Italy) and transfer them to the entry state (Hungary). *VALE* can be understood as turning on the presence

[43] Case 81-97 *R v HM Treasury, ex p Daily Mail* [1988] ECR 5483.
[44] Case C-210/06 *Cartesio Oktato es Szolgaltato bt* [2008] ECR I-9641.
[45] Case C-378/10 *VALE Epitesi kft* [2012] 3 CMLR 41.

of discrimination, since Hungarian law treated foreign and domestic companies differently for the purposes of conversion.

The upshot of the post-*Centros* case law, then, is that while Member States retain the capacity to tax and regulate companies falling under their own jurisdiction, they may not prevent them leaving for other jurisdictions which offer a different mix of regulatory controls; nor may they refuse to admit foreign companies which meet local conditions for incorporation. As a result, the European Union has moved several steps closer to realizing the conditions for a market for incorporations. It does not follow that the Delaware experience will be replicated in Europe. As we have seen, Delaware's position as the favoured state of incorporation for US companies owes much to factors specific to its particular history and institutional context.

Moreover, the conditions for the replication of a Delaware effect in Europe have not been completely met. The justification defence, even if it is of limited and uncertain scope, qualifies the mutual recognition principle in a way that has no equivalent in the US context. Where companies seek to relocate in order to avoid mandatory requirements operating for the benefit of third parties, such as codetermination laws that protect worker interests, it is at least arguable that the exit state would be entitled to place limits on reincorporations, and to refuse to recognize the law of the entry state as applicable. It has to be acknowledged, however, that an argument of precisely this kind failed in *Centros*, where the interests of other third parties (creditors) were at stake. It remains to be seen if Member States' codetermination laws would meet a similar fate.

The effect of *Cartesio* is that a company must accept the package of regulatory norms which are attached to incorporation in a given Member State: it can only escape them by exiting the jurisdiction entirely. However, given this exit option, many regulations will become at best semi-mandatory 'default rules'. A degree of 'negative harmonization' can be expected to follow. With a wide market access test, the justification test becomes critical, but the strictness of the proportionality principle in this context implies a further deregulatory bias. Whether the Court is the right institution to decide the future of a complex socio-political compromise such as codetermination is open to question.

3. Legislative Encouragement of Regulatory Competition in Company Law

Alongside the developing case law of the Court, a number of Directives have addressed the issue of regulatory competition in company law. The Societas

Europaea (SE) Statute, adopted in 2001,[46] was an exercise in legislative compromise. By building in a menu of options over the configuration of the SE, the Regulation intended to leave room for experimentation within mutually accepted parameters. The issue of employee participation was dealt with in a Directive informed by the same experimentalist approach.[47] The SE statute facilitated cross-border mobility for SE companies through two mechanisms: a cross-border merger mechanism, and a power of relocation. In this way, the statute is an experiment in regulatory competition. Provided that certain minority shareholder, worker and creditor rights are protected, it offers competitive advantages to the SE company by providing a mechanism through which it can choose the national regulatory regime applicable to it. It should thereby stimulate regulatory competition, with Member States competing to attract SE companies. This effect of the SE Statute is limited, however, by the attachment of procedural conditions to cross-border relocations, and by Article 7 of the Regulation, which requires territorial correspondence between the head and registered offices of an SE and the state of its incorporation. This in effect requires an SE company to elect for the 'real seat' doctrine. In practice, there is little evidence of the SE Directive leading to more regulatory competition.[48]

Potentially more significant is the Tenth Company Law Directive on Cross-Border Mergers, adopted in 2005.[49] The CBM Directive provides a mechanism for reincorporation by merger with a company in another jurisdiction that is not limited to SEs. This mechanism is similar to the basis for re-incorporations in the USA but is differentiated by the inbuilt protections for stakeholder interests. In common with the SE Directive, the CBM Directive contains provisions designed to preserve codetermination rights in companies undergoing trans-border mergers, while also limiting the export of two-tier board structures to jurisdictions where they are not recognized. The 'no escape' principle is, in practice, less than complete, since holding company structures and serial reincorporations could be used to deprive workers of board-level participation rights under the terms of the CBM Directive.[50]

---

[46] Council Regulation (EC) No 2157/2001 of 8 October 2001 on the Statute for a European company (SE), OJ 2001 L294/1.

[47] Council Directive 2001/86/EC of 8 October 2001 supplementing the Statute for a European company with regard to the involvement of employees, OJ 2001 L294/22.

[48] Bratton et al. (n 41).

[49] Directive 2005/56/EC of the European Parliament and of the Council of 26 October 2005 on cross-border mergers of limited liability companies, OJ 2005 L310; M. Pannier, 'The EU Cross Border Merger Directive—A New Dimension for Employee Participation and Company Restructuring; (2006) 16 *European Business Law Review* 1424–1442.

[50] H. Eidenmüller, L. Hornuf, and M. Reps, 'Contracting Employee Involvement; An Analysis of Bargaining over Employee Involvement Rules for a Societas Europaea' (2012) 12 *Journal of Corporate Law Studies*, 201–235. On the prospects for a Directive on the transfer of the seat, see M. Krarup, '*VALE*: Determining the Need for Amended Regulation Regarding Free Movement of Companies Within the EU' (2013) 24 *European Business Law Review* 691–698.

IV. Tax Law: Tax Avoidance
and Fiscal Competition

Tax systems consist of a complex web of rules on direct taxation, deferrals and reliefs. Independent scrutiny of individual tax measures, taken in isolation, threatens the internal coherence of these systems. The Member States' taxation powers are exclusive, but they are also subject to internal market law.[51] The existence of multiple tax jurisdictions makes the interplay between direct taxation and the right of establishment particularly complex.[52] Tax treaties are concluded in order to allocate the taxing rights regarding specific incomes between contracting States and to avoid double taxation, and the Court has sometimes embraced the principles of these treaties in its reasoning.[53] However, the scope and effect of these treaties, in the context of the EU, is limited.

Cross-border capital movement inevitably enhances the risks to Member States of a loss of revenue through tax avoidance. Schemes aimed at tax avoidance through deferral are common among Member States, and have been positively encouraged by the OECD.[54] However, anti-avoidance measures have themselves been categorized by the Court as 'restrictions' on freedom of establishment.

1. Exit Taxes

Daily Mail was one of the earliest cases to address the issue of the application of the internal market provisions to Member State fiscal regimes, which seek to tax latent profits at the point at which a taxpayer leaves the Member State's jurisdiction. The company wanted to transfer its central management and control to the Netherlands while remaining incorporated under UK law. UK capital gains tax would no longer be chargeable once the company became non-resident, and the transfer required the consent of the UK government. This was granted on the basis that the company sold part of its assets before emigrating. The effect of this would be to realize the gains on these assets and so make them liable to tax in the UK. The Court did not find a restriction in this case, which was initially interpreted as ruling that the requirement to obtain Treasury Consent, dependent on realizing

---

[51] See generally Ghosh (n 29) Ch 3.

[52] L. Faulhaber, 'Sovereignty, Integration and Tax Avoidance in the European Union: Striking the Proper Balance' (2009) 48 *Columbia Journal of Transnational Law* 177–241.

[53] K. Cejie, 'Emigration taxes—Several Questions, Few Answers: From Lasteyrie to *National Grid Indus* and Beyond' (2012) 40 *Intertax* 382–399.

[54] Faulhaber, (n 52); common provisions include Controlled Foreign Corporation Rules, Foreign Personal Holding Company Rules, and Passive Foreign Investment Rules.

a charge to tax, did not fall within the scope of freedom of establishment at all. However, it later appeared that the crux of the case was the company's decision to remain incorporated under UK law. The absence of harmonization of company law throughout the Union meant that the internal market provisions were not breached by the United Kingdom's demand that a United Kingdom incorporated company obtain prior Treasury Consent before moving its seat to a different jurisdiction. But it does not follow that a Member State may place fiscal restraints on cross-border reincorporations.[55]

In two cases which did consider exit taxes, *Lasteyrie*[56] and *N*,[57] the Court held that exit taxes on latent income did fall under the free movement rules. In both cases, national rules meant that unrealized gains of individuals were taxed at the moment of exit. The Court accepted that the objective, of allocating tax jurisdiction between states, was legitimate, but ruled that the measures were not proportionate. The national measures should have provided for deferral without restriction: the exit state could not require a bank guarantee as a condition for deferral, nor refuse to take account of decreases in value occurring after emigration when calculating the tax.

The same issue came before the Court in a corporate context in *National Grid Indus*.[58] Dutch law required the immediate payment of capital gains tax on a company's exit. The measures came into effect by virtue of the Double Taxation Treaty between the UK and the Netherlands, the effect of which was that the right to tax built-in gains switched to the UK automatically on transfer of the company. Unlike in *Daily Mail*, the contested rule had no bearing on the legal status of the company.[59] This time, the Court found a restriction: immediate taxation imposed a cash-flow disadvantage on a company exercising freedom of establishment, which was not imposed on non-moving companies. The Court again accepted as legitimate the aim of maintaining a proper balance between taxation powers of Member States but, modifying its line in *Lasteyrie* and *N*, indicated that exit taxes might satisfy the proportionality test. While immediate recovery was not normally proportionate, it could be, in certain cases, when accompanied by an option to defer. Such an option could also, the Court said, be accompanied by an interest charge or a bank guarantee requirement. It additionally stated that post-emigration decreases in value need not be taken into account by the exit state in calculating the value of the tax. How far *National Grid Indus* has made a

---

[55] S. Peeters, 'Exit Taxation on Gains in the European Union: A Necessary Consequence of Corporate Relocation?' (2013) 10 *European Company and Financial Law Review* 507–522.

[56] Case C-9/02 *Lasteyrie du Saillant v Ministère de l'Economie* [2004] ECR I-2409.

[57] Case C-470/04 *N v Inspecteur van de Belastingdienst Oost/kantoor Almelo* [2006] ECR I-7409.

[58] Case C-371/10 *National Grid Indus BV v Inspecteur van de Belastingdienst Rijnmond/Kantoor Rotterdam* [2011] ECR I-12273.

[59] A relevant factor was that the Netherlands followed the incorporation principle: *National Grid Indus* (n 58) paras 22–33.

material change to the law on exit taxes is unclear; in practice, the conditions for meeting the proportionality test remain strict.[60]

2. Tax Reliefs

In *Marks & Spencer*[61] it was argued that UK group loss relief rules, which allowed parent companies to off-set losses incurred by domestic subsidiaries but not foreign ones, hindered the exercise of the parent company's freedom of establishment by deterring it from setting up subsidiaries in other Member States. The Court found a restriction, but this aspect of its reasoning is highly questionable. There is a strong argument to the effect that the UK had simply not exercised jurisdiction in this case.[62] UK tax law does not extend its group loss relief to foreign subsidiaries precisely because those subsidiaries fall within the tax jurisdiction of the state of establishment. The principle of territoriality, so conceived, is fundamental to the prevention of double taxation. It is why the UK does not tax the *profits* of foreign subsidiaries.[63]

Having found that there was a restriction without much discussion, the Court devoted most of its judgment to applying the *Gebhard* proportionality test. It held that the loss relief rules could be justified by the need to maintain a balanced allocation of taxation powers between Member States, to avoid double loss recovery, and to prevent tax avoidance. However, the particular measures were not proportionate: group loss relief had to extend to foreign subsidiaries where the company could show that those losses had not, and could not, be taken into account elsewhere. Furthermore, as Ghosh has argued, the Court made the application of the justification and proportionality tests contingent upon how another state's tax regime

---

[60] See Cejie (n 53); Peeters (n 55); O. Thömme, and A. Linn, 'Deferment of Exit Taxes after *National Grid Indus*: Is the Requirement to Provide a Bank Guarantee and the Charge of Interest Proportionate? (2012) 40, *Intertax* 485–493; K. von Brocke and S. Müller, 'Exit Taxes: the *Commission v. Denmark* Case Analysed against the Background of the Fundamental Conflict in the EU: Territorial Taxes and an Internal Market without Barriers' (2013) 22 *EC Tax Review* 299–304.

[61] Case C-446/03 [2005] ECR I-10837.

[62] Ghosh (n 29) 81–85; P. Martin, 'The Marks & Spencer EU Group Relief Case—a Rebuttal of the "Taxing Jurisdiction" Argument' (2005) 14 *EC Tax Review*, 61–68.

[63] On the purposes of the UK's group loss relief measures, see the Inland Revenue in their Press Release REVBN2A (21 March 2000) announcing changes to the Finance Act 2000 following the decision in Case C-264/96, *ICI plc v Colmer* [1998] ECR I-4695: group relief allows a company to claim the benefit of trading losses and certain other reliefs of another company if both companies are members of the same group. Its objective is to make the tax treatment of a group carrying on a variety of activities through different companies closer to what it would have been if those activities had been carried on by a single company. For discussion of the interaction of the internal market rules in this context with the Parent-Subsidiary Directive (Council Directive 90/435/EEC of 23 July 1990 on the common system of taxation applicable in the case of parent companies and subsidiaries of different Member States), see D. Gutmann, 'The *Marks & Spencer* Case: Proposals for an Alternative Way of Reasoning' (2003) 12 *EC Tax Review* 154–158; Martin (n 62).

operates. The acceptance of a state's justification, and the assessment of its proportionality, thus depends upon the operation of other Member States' tax regimes. This is tantamount to applying the principle of mutual recognition not only at the breach stage—as in the free movement of goods case law—but also at the justification stage.[64]

The problem with the Court's approach is that the corporate income tax systems of the Member States are not harmonized.[65] The issues raised in the *Marks & Spencer* case were addressed, at least in part, by the 1990 draft Cross-Border Relief Directive which, however, had to be abandoned in the absence of political agreement. In effect, the Court is using the proportionality test not to combat tax avoidance, as courts in other jurisdictions have done,[66] but to *limit* the extent to which the Member States can address the issue of corporate tax avoidance through legislation.

3. Tax Avoidance and Abuse of Rights

In *Cadbury-Schweppes*[67] there was a challenge to the UK rules on foreign-controlled companies (CFCs), which are measures of a kind adopted by many states to combat tax avoidance via deferral schemes. The UK CFC rules included a 'motive test', which sought to determine whether the purpose of the transaction and the existence of non-resident subsidiaries was to reduce UK income tax. The Court held that the CFC rules did amount to a restriction, rejecting an 'abuse' argument as it had in *Centros*. At the justification stage of the argument it accepted the legitimacy of the aim of preventing tax avoidance, but proceeded to outline criteria for when such rules would be sufficiently *limited* to be proportionate. The CFC rules could *only* apply to 'wholly artificial arrangements'. This meant that it was insufficient for the CFC rules to refer to the subjective motive of the taxpayer: there was also a requirement for an absence of 'economic reality' in the transaction. The Court came close to saying that if cross-border migration in search of a lighter tax regime were the motive, the arrangement could not be wholly artificial:[68] bootstrap reasoning of the kind it had used in *Centros* to expand the right of establishment. Rules aimed at combating tax avoidance through deferral schemes, which were widespread prior

---

[64] J. Ghosh, 'A Tax Law Perspective on the Internal Market: A Critique of a "Two Country" Approach to Mutual Recognition' CELS Seminar, 14 May 2014, University of Cambridge.

[65] G. Meussen, 'The *Marks & Spencer* Case: Reaching the Boundaries of the EC Treaty' (2003) 12 *EC Tax Review* 144–148.

[66] Faulhaber (n 52), discussing the US 'economic substance' doctrine.

[67] Case C-196/04 *Cadbury Schweppes plc v Inland Revenue Commissioners* [2006] ECR I-7995.

[68] See R. Karimeri, 'A Critical Review of the Definition of Tax Avoidance in the Case Law of The European Court of Justice' (2011) 39 *Intertax* 296–316.

to *Cadbury-Schweppes*, have since been restricted in several Member States, in response to the Court's decision and in particular the narrowness of the concept of 'wholly artificial arrangements'.[69]

V. Labour Law: Between Social Regulation and Market Rights

1. The Background: Limited Harmonization in Social Policy

Under the Treaty on the Functioning of the European Union (TFEU), social policy is a matter of shared competence between the Union and the Member States, but even with some limited powers for the Union, the provisions of the Social Policy Title fall a long way short of providing a comprehensive transnational floor of rights in labour law, let alone a European labour code. Certain collective labour law matters, including freedom of association and the right to take industrial action, are explicitly excluded from the scope of the principal legal source of the Union's powers to adopt Directives in the social policy field, Article 152 (formerly Article 137 TEC). The rationale for limiting the harmonization of social policy goes back to the Ohlin and Spaak reports[70] of the mid-1950s and their view that since a race to the bottom would not ensue from the establishment of the common market, such harmonization was generally not needed.[71] As we have seen,[72] this analysis turned in part on the preservation of separate national currencies and the related macroeconomic policy flexibility which this gave the Member States. It was also buttressed by the strong political support given by each of the founding Member States to the protection of worker rights, including collective rights, which a majority of them recognized as entitled to constitutional protection. By the late 1990s, these conditions no longer held: the gradual implementation of the currency union was removing the flexibility previously provided by adjustable exchange rates, while the political consensus on the importance of strong welfare states and collective wage determination systems had fragmented under the pressure of deregulatory arguments and policies.[73] Nevertheless, the Union's approach to social policy at this point could be justified on the grounds that allowing Member States autonomy to

---

[69] These include Denmark, Germany and Sweden: Faulhaber (n 52).
[70] See above, Section II.   [71] Deakin, (n 12).   [72] See Section II.
[73] Giubboni, (n 12).

frame their own responses to the issues raised by labour market regulation, within the broad parameters of Union law, was preferable to imposing uniform rules. Member State capacity to make social policy was the other side of the coin of limited harmonization.

2. The Concept of 'Restriction' in *Viking* and *Laval*

This precarious compromise was shaken by the judgments in *Viking*[74] and *Laval*.[75] *Viking* raised an issue of establishment and *Laval* one of services, but the two decisions took a similar route in defining the relationship between the fundamental freedoms and social policy, and should be considered together when assessing the implications of freedom of establishment for labour law.

In *Laval*, the Court ruled that there had been a restriction on market access in the context of the freedom to provide services where industrial action to enforce the terms of a sectoral collective agreement in the host state (Sweden) increased the costs associated with the completion of a public works contract. The contract had been entered into by the locally-based (Swedish) subsidiary of the home-state (Latvian) company, using the labour of workers posted from the home state.[76]

In *Viking*, the restriction took the form of industrial action organized across several Member States including the home and host states (Finland and Estonia respectively), for the purpose of preventing the reflagging of a commercial vessel under the law of the host state being used as a pretext for reducing the wages of the crew. In neither case was there any formal barrier to the cross-border movement of economic resources. There would have been no strike action in *Laval* if the local collective agreement had been observed, while in *Viking* the unions' negotiating position was not that the reflagging should not take place, simply that it should not entail negative consequences for the crew of the ship.

These actions only became 'restrictions' because they made it more difficult for the employers concerned to access jurisdictions with lower regulatory requirements and, relatedly, lower direct wage costs. According to the Court in *Laval*, it '[had to be] pointed out' that the imposition of a collective agreement through strike action

---

[74] Case C-438/05 [2007] ECR-I 10779 (*Viking*).

[75] Case C-341/05 [2007] ECR I-11767 (*Laval*).

[76] *Laval* was argued as a services case, but it could equally well have been presented in terms of the right of establishment, and perhaps should be have been on its facts, since the company which was affected by the strike action was Laval's Swedish subsidiary. If there was no genuine issue of cross-border services in *Laval* (see Deakin (n 22)), there could have been an issue of secondary establishment, in which case the same questions concerning the nature of a 'restriction' and the scope of the proportionality defence would have arisen, since the *Gebhard* test applies to both establishment and services (see above).

was 'liable to make it less attractive, or more difficult'[77] for foreign service providers to carry out construction work in Sweden, without exactly saying why. Advocate General Mengozzi referred more explicitly to the 'significant costs for the foreign service provider'[78] of complying with the local agreement.[79] For the Court in *Viking*, 'it [could not] be disputed' that there was a restriction where the industrial action had prevented Viking and its Estonian subsidiary from 'enjoying the same treatment in the host member state as other operators established in that state',[80] without saying exactly what this was. Advocate General Poiares Maduro was more explicit: an issue of establishment arose 'because the possibility for a company to relocate to a Member State where its operating costs will be lower is pivotal to the pursuit of effective intra-Community trade'.[81]

Repeated references to a restriction on free movement being indisputable or beyond doubt mask the very real doubts which were present in these decisions. There was no bar on or hindrance to market entry or exit except to the extent that different Member States were operating different labour market rules. The idea that cross-state differences in labour standards could amount, in and of themselves, to a distortion of competition in the common or internal market had been (correctly) rejected in the Ohlin and Spaak reports,[82] and the Court itself, in *Graf*,[83] had earlier rejected the same proposition in the context of free movement of workers. In *Graf*, the claim that labour laws should be *levelled up* so that workers would be not disadvantaged when moving from high-regulation labour law states to lower-regulation ones was rejected.[84] This is the precise converse of the claim, in *Viking* and *Laval*, that enterprises are entitled to have the labour laws of high-costs states disapplied in their favour if cross-state mobility is

---

[77] *Laval*, (n 75), Judgment, at para 99.   [78] *Laval*, (n 75) Opinion, at para 233.

[79] See also Case C-346/06 *Rüffert v Land Niedersachsen* [2008] ECR I-1989 in particular the Opinion of the Advocate General, at paras 102–103.

[80] *Viking* (n 74) Judgment, at para 72.   [81] *Viking* (n 74) Opinion, at para 57.

[82] See above, Section II.

[83] Case C-190/98 *Graf v Filzmoser Maschinenbau GmbH* [2000] ECR I-493.

[84] See the Opinion of Advocate General Fennelly at paras 31–33. He considers whether it would be possible to 'treat as restrictions on the exercise of freedom of movement neutral national rules which allegedly preclude, deter, impede, hinder or render less attractive such exercise simply by raising material barriers, for example, by establishing commercial and regulatory conditions in the market in question which are less enticing than in other Member States, or by offering benefits which would be lost in the event that a worker changed employment, those criteria could not be applied in the same way as in the case of a formal condition'. A restriction cannot be presumed, he argues, 'where an alleged obstacle to freedom of movement does not result from a formal condition of market participation but is instead alleged to arise from some neutral material barrier or disincentive deriving from national regulations' (para 31); there must be something more, namely a 'material barrier' to market access (para 32). The Court dismissed the case on the ground that entitlement to compensation on termination of employment is not dependent on the worker's choosing whether or not to stay with his current employer but on a future and hypothetical event, namely the subsequent termination of his contract 'without such termination being at his own initiative or attributable to him' (Judgment, para 24). However, this is no less a 'cost' to the worker than there was a 'cost' to the employer of conforming to local labour laws in *Laval*.

not to be inhibited. The failure of the Court to apply a uniform analysis across the different freedoms suggests that there is more to these cases than meets the eye.

This impression is reinforced when it is borne in mind that the regime governing free movement of workers operates in an internally inconsistent way in the case of cross-border postings: posted workers are entitled to access the territory of the host state, thanks to the rules on free movement, but, once there, as a result of the Court's ruling in *Finalarte*,[85] are not entitled to equal treatment with the home state workforce. Were the rules on free movement of workers to be applied consistently to level up the conditions of employment of posted workers, the argument that application of the host state's labour law rules to posted workers amounts to a 'restriction' would disappear.

Viking is the labour law equivalent to *Centros*, in the sense that it validates the right of exit in the specific sense of a right to seek out an alternative, low-cost jurisdiction. As in *Centros*, in *Viking* there was no physical change of establishment, and no cross-border movement of economic resources: the ownership and management of the company stayed in Denmark, in one case, and Finland, in the other, at all stages. However, according to the Court in *Viking*, this did not matter: it was precisely the union policy of opposing *virtual* changes of establishment—using a 'flag of convenience' to escape a high-regulation regime—that triggered the application of internal market law.[86] In *Centros*, it was accepted that regulatory arbitrage of this kind might be grounds for applying an (admittedly narrow) concept of 'abuse' of the right of establishment. In *Viking*, the Court went a step further in asserting that encouraging regulatory arbitrage was the *purpose* of the internal market laws.

Laval marks a yet further development of internal market law, since the effect of that case is to allow a foreign service provider to retain the benefit of the (less regulatory) home state regime when operating on the territory of the (more regulatory) host state. This principle prevents a Member State from applying its labour laws consistently to enterprises present on its territory. Since labour laws generally apply on a territorial basis, this is a fundamental challenge to the regulatory capacity of Member States. It goes a step beyond the position in company law and tax law where, as we have seen, a Member State can still insist that a company incorporated under its laws satisfies conditions relating to its registered office (*Cartesio*) and residence (*Daily Mail*). Put slightly differently: a Member State can apply its tax and company laws across the board to enterprises subject to its jurisdiction, but is unable to do so in the case of labour law. This is not *permitting* regulatory arbitrage, so much as *mandating* it.

---

[85] Case C-49/98 *Finalarte Sociedade de Construcao Civil Lda v Urlaubs- und Lohnausgleichskasse der Bauwirtschaft* [2001] ECR I-7831.
[86] *Viking* (n 74), Judgment, at para 73.

In this context, the interaction between the different freedoms is a further factor which tends towards deregulatory outcomes. As the right of establishment
has been interpreted, over time, as a right to access a given jurisdiction regardless
of the need for an enterprise to have a physical presence in the relevant Member
State, the scope to avoid national regulatory requirements through protection of
the right to provide services has been expanded. Given the narrowness of the
'abuse' principle as set out in *Centros*, there is little to stop an enterprise reincor-
porating, or setting up a subsidiary which counts as a secondary establishment,
in another Member State, for reasons related to regulatory arbitrage. By using
its new form, or its foreign subsidiary, as a vehicle to provide services in the exit
state, it can access a lower cost labour law regime without changing the physical
location of its activities. The rules on free movement for workers are no barrier to
this process, since migrant workers cannot argue for levelling up, following *Graf*,
and, in the context of the cross-border provision of services, posted workers cannot argue that they are entitled to equal treatment with workers of the host state,
after *Finalarte*.[87]

3. Justification and Preemption

The destabilizing effects of the *Viking* and *Laval* rulings, which included extending
the scope of free movement law to cover private action by trade unions,[88] might
have been reduced had the Court given Member States more leeway to reconcile
economic and social interests through the application of their own labour laws. In
Viking, the Court had the opportunity to allow a similar degree of autonomy for
labour law within the framework of internal market law, but rejected it, declining
to follow the lead set by its earlier *Albany*[89] decision in the context of competition
law. Having held that private action which was liable to hinder the right of establishment fell within the scope of Union law, the Court went on to define a restrictive
approach to the proportionality test, according to which a national court applying
Union law would have the power to determine that industrial action was unlawful
where it was not a proportionate means of achieving the goal of protecting workers'
interests. This move renders the 'right to strike' recognized by the Court in *Viking*
as a general principle of Union law of little importance in practice. Partly because

---

[87] It is an open question how far the use of 'letterbox companies' to avoid labour law obligations
in the context of the transborder assignment of workers might be limited by the provisions of the
so-called Posted Workers Enforcement Directive, Directive 2014/67/EU.

[88] On this see D. Wyatt, 'Horizontal Effect of Fundamental Freedoms and the Right to Equality
after *Viking* and *Mangold*, and the Implications for Community Competence (2008) 4 *Croatian
Yearbook of European Law and Policy* 1–48.

[89] *Case* C-67/96) [1999] ECR I-5751.

the precise contours of the proportionality test are difficult to discern, *Viking* has had a chilling effect on collective industrial action aimed at mitigating the effects of cross-border relocations.[90]

In *Laval*, the issue of justification was complicated by the presence of the Posting Directive, which the Court interpreted as concretizing the proportionality test implied by its own interpretation of internal market law. Having established that the Directive should be read as allowing a space for Member State autonomy in the application of labour law rules to posted workers, the Court then proceeded to give a remarkably narrow reading to its terms, interpreting provisions which had been drafted in terms which *required* Member States to observe certain minimum protections for workers as *permitting* them to do so only up that point. In this way, minimum standards, on which Member States could build, were turned into maxima, and the Directive was generally given a preemptive effect, reducing the scope for national measures to be tailored to local circumstances. This too has had a chilling effect on worker protection, with several German Länder reducing the level of protection for social interests in the law governing procurement contracts.[91]

VI. Assessment and Conclusion

The case law on establishment has evolved to the point where cross-state differences in laws and regulation affecting business enterprises have come to be seen as potential obstacles to free movement. This situation has come about because the Court has expanded the notion of a restriction on market access to include legal and regulatory barriers which are thought likely to hinder corporate migration. Specifically, laws in 'high regulation' host states are characterized as restrictions where it is costly, in comparative terms, for enterprises seeking entry from 'low-regulation' home states to comply with them (*Laval*). Host state laws, where they fail a justification test which is increasingly narrow, will be disapplied in favour of the incoming enterprise (*Centros, Laval*). Conversely, home states may not prevent enterprises from leaving their jurisdiction to seek out low-regulation jurisdictions

---

[90] K. Apps, 'Damages Claims against Trade Unions after *Viking* and *Laval*' (2009) 34 *European Law Review* 141–154.

[91] M. Blauberger, 'With Luxembourg in Mind . . . the Remaking of Policies in the Face of ECJ Jurisprudence' (2012) 19 *Journal of European Public Policy*, 109–126; D. Sack, 'Europeanisation through Law, Compliance, and Party Differences—The ECJ's *Rüffert* Judgment (C-346/06) and Amendments in German Federal States' (2012) 34 *Journal of European Integration* 241–260.

(*Centros, Cartesio, Viking*). So far, the right of the home state to impose fiscal and regulatory conditions on companies which remain subject to its jurisdiction—an aspect of the 'real seat' rule for determining the applicable law of the company and of certain principles of fiscal competence—has just about remained intact (*Daily Mail, Cartesio*). However, the capacity of states to regulate businesses as a condition of granting them the right to operate within their jurisdiction is coming under severe pressure. Fiscal measures premised on the notion of state autonomy in the taxation field are being characterized as restrictions where they impact on the costs of incorporation (*Cadbury-Schweppes*). In the field of labour law, thanks to the interaction of the rules on establishment and with those of services, national measures for the protection of workers can no longer be applied consistently with the principle of territoriality (*Laval, Rüffert*). While companies can invoke free movement rights to access the laws of low-regulation jurisdictions outside the territory of the state where the work is being carried out, the converse process of accessing a more protective labour law regime on a similar non-territorial basis is not available to workers via their free movement rights (*Graf*).

As the scope of right of establishment has been extended, so the power of the Court to determine the legitimate content of state laws regulating business firms has grown. The Court regularly pronounces on the content of laws in the areas of corporate governance, worker protection and tax avoidance. It applies a strict proportionality test that puts the onus on Member States to defend the aims of national measures and the means used to achieve them. Decisions which would once have been within the exclusive domain of national parliaments have been transferred to a transnational court exercising a quasi-constitutional jurisdiction to review the legitimacy of legislation and to channel the law-making process.

This trend is often presented as the inevitable, and by implication, desirable effect of the completion of the internal market.[92] Economic integration has become identified with rules for business which are uniform and, moreover, have an inbuilt deregulatory bias. This is far removed from the original conception of the internal market as an economic space within which wages and social standards would naturally 'level up'. It also has little in common with the idea of the internal market as a space for experimentation and learning. It has more to do with the idea of labour and fiscal regulation as a restraint on 'doing business',[93] associated with

[92] 'Workers throughout Europe must accept the recurring negative consequences that are inherent to the common market's creation of increasing prosperity' (Advocate General Poiares Maduro in *Viking* (n 74), Opinion, para 59).

[93] See the annual *Doing Business Reports* of the World Bank, discussed in S. Lee, D. McCann and N. Torm, 'The World Bank's "Employing Workers" Index: Findings and Critiques—A Review of Recent Evidence' (2008) 147 *International Labour Review*, 416–432. Cf Advocate General Poiares Maduro: 'Member State authorities are generally in a position that enables them to intervene in the functioning of the common market by restricting the activities of market participants'. Viking (n 74), Opinion, at para 34.

World Bank policy for 'emerging' markets, but now transferred to the 'advanced' economies of Europe.

The goal of regulatory competition is not an aim of the Union, but it is an unavoidable consequence of rules designed to promote cross-border economic mobility. This was recognized at the outset of the European project in the 1950s, and safeguards built into the institutional design of what eventually became the Union, in the form of limited but significant powers to harmonize national laws. Those safeguards are no longer effective in the face of free movement jurisprudence which elevates Treaty-based economic rights above legislation at both federal and state level, and which override social protections even when they too are expressed as fundamental rights. A focus on regulatory competition as the inevitable by-product of free movement law would help to clarify these issues. Then there could at least be a more focused debate about the merits of a policy of treating laws for worker and fiscal protection as a restraint on enterprise.[94]

BIBLIOGRAPHY

C. Barnard, 'Social Dumping Revisited: Lessons from Delaware' (2000) 25 *European Law Review* 57–80

C. Barnard and S. Deakin, 'Market Access and Regulatory Competition', in C. Barnard and J. Scott (eds) *The Law of the Single Market: Unpacking the Premises* (2001)

D. Charny, 'Competition among Jurisdictions in Formulating Corporate Law Rules: an American Perspective on the "Race to the Bottom" in the European Communities' (1991) 32 *Harvard International Law Journal* 422–456

G. Davies, 'The Court's Jurisprudence on Free movement of Goods: Pragmatic Presumptions, not Philosophical Principles' (2012) *Business Law Review* 705, 760

S. Deakin and F. Wilkinson, 'Rights v. Efficiency? The Economic Case for Transnational Labour Standards' (1994) 23 *Industrial Law Journal* 289–310

S. Deakin, 'Labour law as Market Regulation: The Economic Foundations of European Social Policy' in P. Davies, A. Lyon-Caen, S. Sciarra, and S. Simitis (eds) *Principles and Perspectives on EC Labour Law: Liber Amicorum for Lord Wedderburn* (1996)

S. Deakin, 'Two Types of Regulatory Competition: Competitive Federalism versus Reflexive Harmonisation. A Law and Economic Perspective on Centros' (1999) *Cambridge YB European Legal Studies* 2 231–260

S. Deakin, 'Regulatory Competition versus Harmonisation in European Company Law' in D. Esty and D. Geradin (eds) *Regulatory Competition and Economic Integration: Comparative Perspectives* (2001)

S. Deakin, 'Regulatory Competition after Laval' (2007) *Cambridge Yearbook of European Legal Studies*, 10(1) 581–609

---

[94] On which, see S. Deakin and F. Wilkinson. 'Rights v. Efficiency? The Economic Case for Transnational Labour Standards' (1994) 23 *Industrial Law Journal* 289–310.

S. Enchelmaier, 'Always at Your Service (Within Limits): The ECJ's Case Law on Article 56 TFEU (200611)' (2011) *European Law Review*, (5) 615–650.

L. Faulhaber, 'Sovereignty, Integration and Tax Avoidance in the European Union: Striking the Proper Balance' (2009) 48 *Columbia Journal of Transnational Law* 177–241

I.J. Ghosh, *Principles of the Internal Market and Direct Taxation* (2007)

J.L. Hansen, 'The Vale Decision and the Court's Case Law on the Nationality of Companies' (2013) *European Company and Financial Law Review*, *10*(1) 1–17

R. Karimeri, 'A Critical Review of the Definition of Tax Avoidance in the Case Law of the European Court of Justice' (2011) 39 *Intertax* 296–316

M. Krarup, 'VALE: Determining the Need for Amended Regulation Regarding Free Movement of Companies within the EU' (2013) *European Business Law Review*, *24*(5) 691–698

S. Lombardo, 'Regulatory Competition in Company Law in the European Union after Cartesio' (2009) *European Business Organization Law Review*, *10*(4) 627

S. Peeters, 'Exit Taxation on Capital Gains in the European Union: A Necessary Consequence of Corporate Relocations?' (2013) *ECFR 507*, 522

W. G Ringe, 'Company Law and Free Movement of Capital' (2010) *Cambridge Law Journal 69*, 378

A. M Sachdeva 'Regulatory Competition in European Company Law' (2010) *European Journal of Law and Economics*, *30*(2) 137–170

J. Snell, 'The Notion of Market Access: A Concept or a Slogan?' (2010) 47 *Common Market Law Review*, Issue 2 437–472

E. Spaventa, 'From *Gebhard to Carpenter*: Towards a (Non-) Economic European Constitution' (2004) 41 *CML Rev*, *41* 743

C. Tiebout, 'A Pure Theory of Local Expenditures' 64 *Journal of Political Economy* 416–424

R. Van den Bergh, 'The Subsidiarity Principle in European Community Law: Some Insights from Law and Economics' (1994) 1 *Maastricht Journal of European & Comparative Law* 337–366

D. Wyatt, 'Horizontal Effect of Fundamental Freedoms and the Right to Equality after Viking and Mangold, and the Implications for Community Competence' (2008) *Croatian Yearbook of European Law and Policy*, *4*(4) 1–48

CHAPTER 22

THE LAW ON THE FREE MOVEMENT OF SERVICES

POWERFUL, BUT NOT ALWAYS PERSUASIVE

GARETH DAVIES

I. INTRODUCTION

THE law on the free movement of services is perhaps the most sensitive and important area of free movement law. Services are the larger part of modern economies, but are relatively under-represented in international trade. To some extent this is because of the local nature of many services, but it is widely suggested that it is also because barriers to cross-border trade in services continue to exist to a greater extent than is the case for goods, and perhaps even for establishment or capital.

One reason why states and other lobbies may resist cross-border service trade is that where service competition is possible, it may often be particularly effective. A large part of the cost of many services is labour, and labour costs vary a great deal within the EU. The craftsman and the posted worker, the transport firm, and the IT specialist are examples of providers of services whose livelihoods depend to a large extent on their relative cost in the marketplace. If, through the physical movement of service providers or clients, or the cross-border movement of services themselves, the costs of the eastern part of the EU can be brought to the western part, then a dramatic shake-up of industries is likely, with social consequences that may call the legitimacy of the very EU into question, as debate about the services Directive showed.

Other reasons to resist the liberalization of service markets are less to do with protectionism and more about other norms: services are often politically and socially sensitive, touching on aspects of national identity, organization, and morality. One may think of medical, educational, and sexual services, but also of cultural institutions and their activities. The opening of these to foreign competition is not merely a technical matter. Other services are highly complex, and part of the infrastructure of society or the economy. Examples are telecoms, water provision, or financial services. Any attempts to open these markets cannot be carried out with the blunt instrument of judicial abstraction, but require sector specific regulation. There is much of this.

This chapter will, however, focus on the general, Court-created principles underlying the free movement of services. Partly this is for reasons of length, but it is also because these basic principles, derived from the Treaty, continue to provide the conceptual framework for many disputes. Even within the sphere of the services Directive, briefly discussed in Section V below, the relevant terms and ideas are all derived from the case law and will inevitably be interpreted in its light. Moreover, the Court has consistently attempted to interpret services, establishment, workers, and capital in parallel, using similar formulae. To grasp successfully a part of the internal market through this case law is to a large extent to grasp the whole.

1. Defining a Service: The Distinction Between Services and Other Freedoms

Services are not goods, and they are not capital, but these distinctions are rarely troublesome—although it may surprise some that electricity is a good and that e-books are a service.[1] The distinction appears to turn on tangibility, in the dictionary sense of 'detectable by touch'. More challenging is the distinction between the provision of services in another Member State and establishment there. The Court has maintained that this is a case-specific judgment, in which common sense factors such as the degree of time spent in the state, the frequency of visits, and the extent to which the service provider has an infrastructure there are all relevant, without there being any fixed lines.[2] Is it the case, on all the facts, that the service provider is 'based' in the state in question, or is he just a visitor whose base is elsewhere?

---

[1] Case 155/73 *Giuseppe Sacchi* [1974] ECR 409; Case C-403/08 *Football Association v QC Leisure* [2011] ECR I-9083; Case C-379/98 *PreussenElektra* [2001] ECR I-2099.

[2] Case C-215/01 *Schnitzer* [2003] ECR I-14847; Case 2/74 *Reyners v Belgium* [1974] ECR 631; Case C-55/94 *Gebhard* [1995] ECR I-4165.

2. The Economic Nature of Services: Remuneration

Determining the economic nature of the services is considerably more complicated and troublesome. Article 57 TFEU provides that the free movement of services only applies to services provided 'normally for remuneration'. The Court has said that remuneration is consideration, or payment,[3] making clear that the free movement of services is about those services that are the subject of market-like transactions, rather than those provided charitably or merely in the hope of gifts,[4] albeit that the word 'normally', which has never been explained, might well have the effect of bringing give-away services within the Treaty if they were, for example, part of a commercial promotion, and could be said to be 'normally' for sale.

(a) Socially Important Services as Economic Activities

Knowing that services must be paid for, however, leaves many questions unanswered. Who must pay for them, and precisely how? The ways in which service providers may earn their money vary greatly. The Court found early on that payment need not come from the service recipient, a finding that has mundane but common sense importance, in preventing services bought as gifts from suddenly falling outside the market, but also systemic social importance, by potentially including services paid for by insurance companies or even the state.[5] Healthcare, education, and unemployment and other forms of social insurance are all services that are certainly paid for in some sense, since the providers receive money to carry out their tasks, albeit not necessarily directly or entirely, from the recipients.

One reason to think that Article 56 will not apply to such services is their social importance, and the fact that they are typically provided by the state, or guaranteed by the state, in a way involving considerable cross-subsidy. They do not take place on a normal market. Yet arguments along these lines were put forward by the Member States in *Kohll*, the first case where medical services were found to fall within the Treaty, and the Court offered a riposte which it has since often repeated: the 'special nature' of certain services does not remove them from the scope of the Treaty.[6] All the social interests that may be affected by applying free movement law are to be addressed at the stage of justifications and derogations, but the existence of such interests does not exclude the application of the Treaty a priori.

That might seem clear, if controversial, but it is not immediately easy to reconcile with other statements of the Court, notably its finding in *Humbel* that where the

---

[3] Case 263/86 *Humbel v Belgium* [1988] ECR 5365.

[4] See Case C-16/93 *Tolsma v Inspecteur der Omzetbelastingen Leeuwarden* [1994] ECR I-743, on Dir 77/388/EEC [1977] OJ L145/1, which is similarly worded to Art 57.

[5] Joined Cases C-51/96 and C-191/97 *Deliège v Asbl Ligue Francophone de Judo* [2000] ECR I-2549.

[6] Case C-158/96 *Kohll v Union des Caisses de Maladie* [1998] ECR I-1931, para 20.

state funded higher education this was not to be seen as remunerating universities for educational services, but rather as the state fulfilling its responsibilities to its public.[7] To oppose remuneration to responsibility in this way seems to be directly opposite in philosophy, if not quite in the letter, to the approach taken in *Kohll*, suggesting implicitly that the special nature of education actually does take it outside Article 56 by making the money received in order to supply that education something nobler and different than mere payment.

Yet this is not the case: there are other cases where education, both in universities and even primary schools, has been found to be an economic service.[8] These have concerned publicly owned as well as private institutions. What engages Article 56, the Court found in these cases, is that the education is primarily paid for by the student or their parents.[9]

(b) State Payments for Services as Remuneration

This distinction between payment by the recipient and the state is quite odd. It is established that third parties are allowed to pay for services without taking them outside Article 56. Is state payment different, so that when a state pays for a service on behalf of a member of its population this fact makes the payment something other than remuneration? It is suggested that as a rule this is implausible. In *Watts* the British (state-funded) National Health Service was asked to pay for medical care provided abroad precisely on the basis that this care was a Treaty service.[10] It would be paradoxical if an agreement by the state to assume the bill—as the Court insisted it must—suddenly had the effect of taking that very care outside of the Treaty.

(c) The Relationship between the Payer and Provider: The Difference Between Market-like Transactions and Internal Payments

Rather, it seems to be the case that the state certainly may, in some circumstances, buy economic services for remuneration, but in other circumstances giving money to a service provider will not be seen as remuneratory. The difference between these circumstances cannot lie purely in the fact that the state has a 'responsibility', contrary to the abbreviated reasoning in *Humbel*, because it also has responsibilities regarding healthcare, and indeed, arguably, to guarantee efficient and accessible public transport and other services, which are unquestionably economic. On the contrary, there must be something in the mechanism of payment, in the

---

[7] *Humbel* (n 3) para 18.
[8] Case C-56/09 *Zanotti* [2010] ECR I-4517; Case C-318/05 *Commission v Germany* [2007] ECR I-6957; Case C-76/05 *Schwarz and Gootjes-Schwarz* [2007] ECR I-6849.
[9] *Schwarz* (n 8); Case C-109/92 *Wirth* [1993] ECR I-6447.
[10] Case C-372/04 *Watts v Bedford Primary Care Trust* [2006] ECR I-4325.

institutional arrangements, in *Humbel* which makes it reasonable to categorize the educational services in question as non-economic.[11]

There are a number of factors which often characterize state financing of public service institutions. It is often done in a way which seems to break the link between a particular service, the cost of that service, and the financing of that service. There may be yearly budgets, rather than payments per service, and there may be standardized payments linked to, for example, the number of patients or students enrolled, without taking account of how many services they actually use. Both of these might make the state financing look less like consideration in a traditional sense. Yet neither of these factors is really unique to public services. Market actors may buy bundles of services for a fixed price, providers may charge standard fees even though different clients actually use different amounts of service, and some clients may in fact cross-subsidize others. Mobile telephony contracts contain all these elements, and are more commonly criticized as being over-commercial than uneconomic.

Rather, what is distinctive about the state financing of a state-owned university is likely to be the fact that the university, the service provider, is not an autonomous market actor. They are not competing for different purchasers, of which the state is but one. They are not in a position to prefer some other purchaser to the state, if that other offers a better price. The university is essentially an entity within the sphere of the state, rather than existing within the sphere of a market, and payments are better characterized as internal accounting phenomena than as consideration resulting from an agreement between two autonomous parties.

Thus it is suggested that it is the relationship between the provider, and their client and payer, which makes a transfer of money into remuneration or not. To sell a service implies a degree of autonomy, and location within at least some kind of market.[12] It implies that the parties to the transaction could be different ones, without that changing the very nature of what the transaction is.

This would mean that, for example, if the state issued vouchers worth €20 000 for higher education to all those graduating from high school, allowing students to choose their course and college on the (regulated) higher education marketplace, then the services offered to those students, in return for the vouchers, which would be cashed by the state, would be likely to fall within Article 56. This situation would be precisely analogous to healthcare insurance and services.

On the other hand, if the state creates, runs, and finances educational or healthcare or other institutions, to which it admits those living in its territory, then there is no market-like transaction between authentically separate parties taking place, and the financing process will not be remuneration.

---

[11] See Gareth Davies, 'Welfare as a Service' (2002) 29 *Legal Issues of Economic Integration* 27.

[12] Davies (n 11).

The difficulty is that in between these situations there is a continuum, and the complexity of public services is such that more or less all points along that continuum are likely to be occupied by some feature of the welfare state of some Member State. Some states may own and run childcare institutions, others may outsource the provision to the private sector, others may use public-private legal constructions to create childcare providers, others may issue parents vouchers to use for private childcare, others may expect parents to pay up front but reimburse them at the end of the year, others may reimburse those costs partially via the tax system. The distinction between each step can seem like a formal one, unworthy to found a policy distinction, yet the situations at the two extremes are different in genuine ways, and on the basis of the existing case law there must be some point where Article 56 begins to apply. The core question, it is suggested, is whether the provider is autonomous of the state in its decisions about what, and whom, to supply.

If so, this is very relevant to social insurance and pensions. In some systems the state is the provider of these, while in others it is an intervener in the market, compelling individuals to purchase from certain private service providers—suggesting the application of Article 56. If the recipient is compelled by law to buy a service, is their payment still remuneration, or is it more like extortion, or at least some other category? In *Freskot*, the Court found that a compulsory agricultural insurance scheme was outside Article 56 for what appeared to be two reasons: those engaged in the relevant activities were compelled by law to participate in the insurance scheme, and they all paid a fixed price, even though they represented different degrees of risk.[13]

The latter reason is an odd one: few insurance companies have truly personalized premiums, and almost entirely depersonalized ones are quite common, for example for travel insurance. The fact that this means that there is cross-subsidy between clients is not shocking: there are few industries where this is not so, and some, like the airline industry, with its sophisticated pricing schemes that extract the maximum from each passenger and ensure a wide variety in prices for essentially the same product, are the very embodiment of the Marxist principle of 'from each according to his abilities'. There is little sense in making personalized pricing a key indicator of economic character. Indeed, it is far more a characteristic of non-commercial activities that the price is rigidly fixed to the cost, since the principle there is more one of reimbursement than profit making. By contrast, market actors will tend to try and get whatever they can from each customer.

The suggestion that where individuals are compelled to buy a service by law this makes their payment something other than remuneration is more interesting. In *Freskot*, the Court repeated a phrase it has often used, that a characteristic

---

[13] Case C-355/00 *Freskot* [2003] ECR I-5263.

of remuneration is that it is normally agreed between provider and recipient.[14] If by this is meant that the degree of remuneration is agreed, then this is of course pure fantasy. There are relatively few market transactions that are the outcome of anything that might be called a negotiation. However, the consumer agrees in the sense that he has the option of walking away, and that option is removed by a compulsion to purchase. Similarly, in *Humbel*, one wonders whether the state-owned universities had the capacity to refuse to offer education to the students of that state, perhaps if they were not satisfied with the price paid. It seems unlikely.

This would be an important principle. It might mean that, for example, the provision of medical insurance is not an economic service in states where it is compulsory to have such insurance, a result that would be counter-intuitive in states where such insurance is provided by vigorously competing private providers. However it is more likely that the point in *Freskot* was precisely that there was no choice of provider, that the individuals were compelled to purchase from the particular fund in question so that one could not speak of a market for agricultural insurance on which the fund was operating. This means that *Freskot* is close to the interpretation of remuneration suggested above—that it is essentially a phenomenon of the right kind of relationship between payer and provider. The fund in *Freskot* had been set up by the state, which owned and, in substance, controlled it, and which collected the payments into it via its tax authority. The payments were essentially just taxes, akin to those paid to local authorities for waste collection and other infrastructural services. The state is capable, in principle, of offering services for remuneration, but then it must offer them, that is to say that the customer must have the chance to look elsewhere. A certain degree of voluntarism is inherent in markets.

(d) The Deregulatory Mechanism of Article 56: Policy Pressure Between States

Despite the limits represented by *Humbel* and *Freskot*, the Court's approach to defining a service is probably over-inclusive in comparison with the intentions of those involved in originally crafting what is now Article 56. That Article was intended, like the other free movement Articles, to ensure that markets are free and open, but not to create markets where they do not exist. The role of the remuneration condition is as a proxy for the existence of a market.

The problem with this approach is that finding economic services to be present, so that Article 56 applies, does not just result in obligations on the service provider. Free movement law, in contrast to competition law, concerns itself primarily not with the economic actor but with those who stand in his way. Thus the act of offering an economic service creates rights, rather than obligations, for the provider,

---

[14] eg Case C-372/09 *Peñarroja Fa* [2011] ECR I-1785; Case C-169/08 *Presidente del Consiglio dei Ministri* [2009] ECR I-10821; *Wirth* (n 9).

the obligations being imposed on states whose rules might make it harder for those services to be bought.

The paradox which this creates is that even if a state chooses to organize a sector in an entirely non-economic way, so that its institutions do not offer Treaty services, it does not thereby escape the effects of Article 56, since if some actor in another Member State does offer such services for sale this creates an obligation on the state to facilitate defection of clients from the public system to the foreign private one: precisely the story in the healthcare cases, where the non-economic British, and arguably Dutch, healthcare systems were forced to finance patients wishing to go and receive economic services abroad.[15] The case that displayed this for the first time was *Geraets-Smits*.[16] In this case, a Dutch patient, insured within a Dutch medical system that was arguably non-economic in character given the relationships between the state and the institutions involved, received treatment abroad and was refused reimbursement. It was argued that the Dutch system did not provide services within Article 56, because of the way it was organized, and the case is often cited for the proposition that the Court rejected this, ruling that all medical services fall within the Treaty. This is wrong. It did not say that at all. Instead it took the far more radical and alarming position that even though it was possible that medical care in the Netherlands was not a Treaty service, this did not mean that it escaped Article 56: since the treatment abroad was undoubtedly paid for, *it* was unquestionably a Treaty service—and this was accepted by all parties—which meant that aspects of the Dutch system that discouraged patients from receiving such services amount to restrictions on free movement.[17] The aspects that had this effect were, however, precisely those closely linked to the non-economic character of the Dutch system—the fact that there was no mechanism for remunerating care, and hence for paying for treatment abroad. A state thus has considerably more chance of violating Article 56 if its institutions do not offer economic services than if they do, since the failure to have payment mechanisms makes it particularly hard for clients to go abroad. This aspect of *Geraets-Smits* has since been re-argued, and

---

[15] eg Case C-157/99 *Geraets-Smits v Stichting Ziekenfonds* [2001] ECR I-5473; Case C-385/99 *Müller-Fauré* [2003] ECR I-4509; Case C-372/04 *Watts v Bedford Primary Care Trust* [2006] ECR I-4325. For discussion see Vassilis Hatzopoulos, 'Killing National Health and Insurance Systems but Healing Patients? The European Market for Health Care Services after the Judgments of the ECJ in *Van Braekel and Peerbooms*' (2002) 39 *Common Market Law Review* 683; Gareth Davies, *The Process and Side-effects of Harmonisation of European Welfare States*,, Jean Monnet Working Paper No 2/06 (2006); Christopher Newdick, 'Citizenship, Free Movement and Healthcare: Cementing Individual Rights by Corroding Social Solidarity' (2006) 43 *Common Market Law Review* 1645. See now also Dir 2011/24 on the Application of Patients' Rights in Cross-Border Healthcare [2011] OJ L88/45; Stephane de la Rosa, 'The Directive on Cross-border Healthcare or the Art of Codifying Complex Case Law' (2012) 49 *Common Market Law Review* 15; Miek Peeters, 'Free Movement of Patients: Directive 2011/24 on the Application of Patients' Rights in Cross-Border Healthcare' (2012) 19 *European Journal of Health Law* 29.

[16] *Geraets-Smits* (n 15).   [17] *Geraets-Smits* (n 15) para 55.

re-judged in exactly the same way, in the context of the UK system, in *Watts*.[18] Paragraph 55 of *Geraets-Smits*, in which the interaction between an economic provider in one state and a non-economic public service system in another is exposed with some nonchalance, is as follows:

With regard more particularly to the argument that hospital services provided in the context of a sickness insurance scheme providing benefits in kind, such as that governed by the ZFW, should not be classified as services within the meaning of Article [56] of the Treaty, it should be noted that, far from falling under such a scheme, the medical treatment at issue in the main proceedings, which was provided in Member States other than those in which the persons concerned were insured, did lead to the establishments providing the treatment being paid directly by the patients. It must be accepted that a medical service provided in one Member State and paid for by the patient should not cease to fall within the scope of the freedom to provide services guaranteed by the Treaty merely because reimbursement of the costs of the treatment involved is applied for under another Member State's sickness insurance legislation which is essentially of the type which provides for benefits in kind.

As a result, states exert considerable policy pressure on each other. If an Austrian hospital or university offers services to the nationals of other Member States for payment—even if most of its services are not offered in this way—then it will be systems in other Member States who will pay the price for this, being compelled to engage with the market despite their own conscious policy decision not to do so. For this reason, the suggestion that Article 56 only 'applies' to economic services is rather misleading. It only grants rights to those buying or selling economic services, but it applies to all states and systems who may stand in their way, for their market avoidance is likely to be a 'restriction' on movement, and such restrictions, not the services, are the true subject of application of Article 56. They are also the subject of Section II.

However, a final note may be made on two other apparent exclusions from Article 56: services that are offered by not-for-profit organizations, and services that are within the sphere of 'official authority'.

3. Non-profit Organizations and Free Movement of Services

The apparent exclusion of non-profit organizations from the sphere of services arises from Article 54 TFEU, which extends Article 56 to cover not just natural persons but also companies or firms and other legal persons 'save for those which are non-profit-making'. It may be assumed that the intention here is to exclude only the deliberately non-profit making rather than also firms suffering a dip in their fortunes, but even this narrower definition is hard to fit into the existing case law.

---

[18] *Watts* (n 10) para 89.

The fact is that in deciding whether services fall within Article 56, the Court has never shown interest in whether the legal person providing or purchasing them was profit making. Where this has been put forward by states as a necessary criterion it has been explicitly rejected. In the precedent-setting *Geraets-Smits and Peerbooms*, a number of governments intervened, and as the Court put it 'some of those governments also maintain . . . that a further condition to be satisfied before a service can constitute an economic activity within the meaning of Article [56] of the Treaty is that the person providing the service must do so with a view to making a profit'. The Court however found that the argument could 'not be upheld' without further explanation.[19] It appears that the last phrase of Article 54 has been the object of a judicial assassination and effectively no longer exists.

4. Official Authority

The second, more substantial, exclusion from Article 56 is for services that fall within official authority. This is provided for in Articles 51 and 62 TFEU. For such services it is quite irrelevant whether they are provided for payment, for profit, or for free: they simply do not fall within the Treaty.

States have often tried to push the limits of this derogation, suggesting that it should apply to all services that are provided by the state or its agents or contractees.[20] The Court is somewhat stricter: it does in fact apply only to activities undertaken using 'privileges of official power or powers of coercion'.[21] The service provider must be sharing in some small way in the state's monopoly of violence to benefit from the definition. AG Mancini's metaphorical description is still unequalled: those who 'don full battle-dress' in the service of the state,[22] engaging in activities which the Court has described, in the context of the free movement of workers, where a public service exemption applies which is interpreted similarly to that of official authority, as presuming 'the existence of a special relationship of allegiance to the State and reciprocity of rights and duties which form the foundation of the bond of nationality'.[23] The police, judges, and more senior civil servants might all fall within this. It was recently necessary for the Court to explain that ambulance services did not.[24] The rights to bear a blue flashing light and to break the speed limit are indeed privileges, but they do not comprise state-backed power over others—or at least not enough.[25]

---

[19] *Geraets-Smits* (n 15) paras 50–52.

[20] Case 149/79 *Commission v Belgium (No. 2)* [1982] ECR 1845; Case C-54/08 *Commission v Germany* [2011] ECR I-4355.

[21] Case C-160/08 *Commission v Germany (Ambulance Services)* [2010] ECR I-3713, para 79.

[22] Case 307/84 *Commission v France* [1986] ECR 1725, para 5 of the Advocate General's Opinion.

[23] *Commission v Belgium* (n 20) para 10.

[24] *Ambulance Services* (n 21).   [25] *Ambulance Services* (n 21) paras 81–82.

II. Defining a Restriction on the Cross-Border Provision of Services

Article 56 only applies where there is a restriction on the movement of services, but the notion of a restriction is far from self-explanatory. Indeed, there is considerable academic literature on what 'restriction', in the context of all the freedoms, does or should mean, with debate focusing on a suggested opposition between discrimination or protectionism on the one side, and market access on the other.[26] One argument is that Article 56 should be used to remove discrimination against service providers established in other states, or to remove protectionist measures, while another point of view is that it should be used to remove barriers to market access. A particularly frustrating aspect of this literature is that there is no commonly accepted definition for either of the key terms—discrimination or market access—often making it unclear what the agreement is precisely about, or indeed whether there is in fact substantive disagreement at all or merely a preference for different terms.[27]

A second reason for the relative fruitlessness of the academic discussion on this topic is that the Court resolutely refuses to enter the fray. While it has a small portfolio of descriptions of a restriction that it draws upon in the judgments, these are without exception brief and pithy rephrasings of Article 56, which do not decisively resolve the various ambiguities about how a restriction is to be identified in practice.[28]

Partly this is because the Court does not appear to be primarily concerned with the macro-economic logic of Article 56 so much as with its consequences for a real or imagined individual litigant. It does not appear to ask itself the question 'What does this measure do to the market as a whole?' so much as the question 'What does this measure mean for an individual trying to offer his services in this state while established in another Member State?' While the two questions are very closely related they are not the same, and the individually oriented, rights-based approach of the Court lends itself to a different kind of language and reasoning

---

[26] eg Eleanor Spaventa, 'From Gebhard to Carpenter: Towards a (Non)-Economic European Constitution' (2004) 41 *Common Market Law Review* 743; Stephen Weatherill, '*After Keck*: Some Thoughts on How to Clarify the Clarification' (1996) 33 *Common Market Law Review* 885; Catherine Barnard, 'Fitting the Remaining Pieces into the Goods and Persons Jigsaw' (2001) 26 *European Law Review* 35; Jukka Snell 'The Notion of Market Access: A Concept or a Slogan?' (2010) 47 *Common Market Law Review* 437; Gareth Davies 'Understanding Market Access: Exploring the Economic Rationality of Different Conceptions of Free Movement Law' (2010) 11 *German Law Journal* 671.

[27] Davies (n 27).

[28] For a thorough discussion, see Stefan Enchelmaier, 'Always at Your Service (within Limits): The ECJ's Case Law on Article 56 TFEU (2006–11)' (2011) 36 *European Law Review* 615.

than the macro-policy of the commentators. The more legal attitude of the Court does, however, have the considerable advantage that free movement law in general, and free movement of services in particular, have been spared the fuss of economic analysis that bedevils competition law.

This is despite the fact that the Court adopts effects-based reasoning. Although it is tempting to try and structure the kind of measures that might restrict free movement, and build up some kind of scheme of legality and illegality, the Court does not do this. Distinctions between measures applying to the provider and to the service itself and to the method of bringing the service to the market, for example, have not been important to the law.[29] Nor have distinctions between measures imposing financial conditions on a service activity, administrative conditions, or conditions to do with qualifications, for example. By contrast, it is quite clear that the group of measures that may comprise a restriction on free movement is an open-ended one, defined not by any particular form or method, but by the measures' effect. This is captured most clearly in one of the most cited and influential re-statements of Article 56, that found in *Gebhard*, where the Court said that any measure which was 'liable to hinder or make less attractive the exercise of a fundamental freedom' (including services) was to be seen as a restriction on movement.[30] It is equally evident in a more recent, but increasingly cited, re-statement, found in *Commission v Italy*.[31] Having repeated *Gebhard*, the Court went on: 'the concept of restriction covers measures taken by a Member State which, although applicable without distinction, affect access to the market for undertakings from other Member States and thereby hinder intra-Community trade'.[32]

Although the latter definition appears at first glance to be a little more concrete, both of these fail to tell the reader when a measure will be considered to make movement less attractive, or when it will be considered to affect market access. That is a considerable problem because it is at least arguable that almost all regulation, tax, and other cost burdens affecting a market and the actors in that market make it, to some extent, less attractive to enter that market. These cases suggest that the mere fact that a person involved in cross-border services is subject to law that is in some sense burdensome engages Article 56.[33]

[29] Wolf-Henning Roth, 'The European Court of Justice's Case Law on Freedom to Provide Services: Is *Keck* Relevant?' in Mads Andenas and Wolf-Henning Roth (eds), *Services and Free Movement in EU Law* (2002) 1; Vassilis Hatzopoulos, 'Annotation of *Alpine Investments*' (1995) 29 *Common Market Law Review* 1427.

[30] Case C-55/94 *Gebhard* [1995] ECR I-4165, para 37. See also Joined Cases C-369/96 and C-376/96 *Arblade* [1999] ECR I-8453.

[31] Case C-518/06 *Commission v Italy* [2009] ECR I-3491.

[32] *Commission v Italy* (n 31) para 64.

[33] Spaventa (n 26).

Other cases, however, suggest limits. Most clearly, in *Mobistar*, the Court dismissed the idea that a tax on mobile phone pylons was a restriction on services by saying:

the Court has already held that Article [56 TFEU] precludes the application of any national rules which have the effect of making the provision of services between Member States more difficult than the provision of services purely within one Member State.

By contrast, measures, the only effect of which is to create additional costs in respect of the service in question and which affect in the same way the provision of services between Member States and that within one Member State, do not fall within the scope of Article [56 TFEU].[34]

This is rarely cited, but that is probably because almost all the cases before the Court involve situations that in fact affect cross-border services more than they affect intra-state trade rather than because it is no longer good law. Moreover, other cases do fit the view it takes. *Commission v Italy*, noted above, concerned an Italian obligation on motor insurers to accept all customers.[35] This was disturbing for those whose business practice was to target certain population groups. The Court found that the measure was a restriction on market access, but the reasons it gave for this are significant, emphasizing that the company would be required to change its business model, which would lead it to incur additional costs, which would reduce its ability to compete with undertakings already established on the Italian market.[36]

The changes and costs which the Court refers to would arise where an insurer was established in a different Member State, where it was able to operate in a different way. As in *Mobistar*, the Court appears to be suggesting that a restriction on free movement of services occurs where a measure has specific cross-border effects. It must not just affect trade, it must also affect cross-border trade more than domestic trade. In the language of market access, it must affect market access for out-of-state actors more than it does for domestic market entrants.

The approach taken in *Mobistar* is conceptually clear, and corresponds to the policy goals of Article 56. It locates free movement law clearly in the wider internal market logic of a level playing field for all economic actors within the EU.[37] It is essentially the same approach as taken in the free movement of goods, where *Keck* exempts a category of measures which the Court considers, like the cost burden in *Mobistar*, to have no trade-diverting effect.[38] Just as *Keck* modifies (or interprets), the apparently all-encompassing language of *Dassonville*, *Mobistar* and phrases such as that in *Commission v Italy* give nuance to the apparent breadth of *Gebhard*.[39]

---

[34] C-544/03 *Mobistar v Commune de Fléron* [2005] ECR I-7723, paras 30–31.
[35] *Commission v Italy* (n 31).   [36] *Commission v Italy* (n 31) paras 66–70.
[37] Davies (n 26).
[38] Joined Cases C-267/91 and C-268/91 *Keck and Mithouard* [1993] ECR I-6097. Cf Henning-Roth (n 29).
[39] Case 8/74 *Procureur du Roi v Benoît and Gustave Dassonville* [1974] ECR 837.

The great problem with this approach is the issue of evidence. Distinguishing between protectionist and non-protectionist restrictions on market access as a matter of economic reality is likely to be difficult, and contested. However, it is made much easier as a matter of law by the fact that the Court has been much more concerned with mechanisms of effect than with economic evidence. Where a party successfully argues that a restriction on movement within Article 56 exists, this is because it has shown how that measure interacts with their particular situation to make market access harder. It is this classically legal cause-and-effect reasoning that has been at the heart of the case law rather than dossiers of market analysis and empirical data. If that means that the outcomes of the cases do not necessarily entirely match the conceptual framework around them, then this should be understood to be the price paid for having workable rules rather than law which is no more than the enactment of an economic idea in all its empirical indeterminacy.

Thus although one can theorize about the difficulties of identifying restrictions which have a greater specifically cross-border effect, in practice it has not been difficult. The cases referred to the Court typically display fact sets which clearly show how the problem of movement or market access is a result of the cross-border situation. Moreover, the Court typically makes this fact a part of its reasoning.

The most extreme examples of this are cases where a state actually requires a person to be established in their jurisdiction in order to provide certain services there, as happened in the well-known *van Binsbergen*.[40] Such a restriction is essentially a denial of the very possibility of cross-border service provision. Yet less extreme examples involve situations where a state makes cross-border services less advantageous than domestic ones, as in the many healthcare cases where national rules had the effect of encouraging patients to seek medical care in their own state rather than abroad.[41] The statement that Article 56 prohibits rules which make cross-border service provision harder than purely domestic transactions is often repeated in the case law, for the reason that it is a very common practice among the Member States to do exactly this.[42]

Yet other cases involve situations where the essence of the problem is that domestic law fails to take account of the situation in the state of origin. This occurred in *Cipolla*, where minimum fees for lawyers ran the risk of undoing a competitive advantage that service providers located in cheaper Member States might have.[43] This is similar to *Commission v Italy* in that both measures prevented businesses from carrying on business in a host state in the same way as they do at home, requiring them to adapt their business plan and competitive techniques.

---

[40] Case 33/74 *Van Binsbergen* [1974] ECR 1299.

[41] See n 15; Case C-211/08 *Commission v Spain* [2010] ECR I-5267; Case C-512/08 *Commission v France* [2010] ECR I-8833; Case C-8/02 *Leichtle v Bundesanstalt für Arbeit* [2004] ECR I-2641.

[42] See Enchelmaier (n 28) 621.

[43] Joined Cases C-94/04 and C-202/04 *Cipolla* [2006] ECR I-11421.

This idea that a business should be able to do business abroad as if it were at home is behind the principles of mutual recognition and the country of origin rule. These core elements of free movement law provide that—as a general, pre-sumptively applicable, rule—an economic actor should be regulated by their state of establishment, and provided they comply with the laws in that state they should be able to export their goods and services without fear of regulation in the states of destination.[44] Were this not the case then providers would have to comply with multiple sets of laws, which in practice would make cross-border trade very dif-ficult indeed. While the Court allows in principle that a host state may apply its laws where the interests at stake are not sufficiently protected by the regulation of the home state, it tests such application so strictly that lawfulness is the exception rather than the rule.[45]

While not often discussed in such explicit terms by the Court, these ideas are staples of every textbook and it is not controversial to suggest that they underlie the judgments in the many cases in which a destination state attempts to play the role of regulator and subject a service provider to its domestic rules. The requirement in *Webb* that a service provider undergo a police check, irrespective of whether such a check had been done in the home state, or the requirement in *Corsten* that all artisans be registered with the chamber of commerce, or the requirement in *Säger* that a patent lawyer possess qualifications equivalent to a domestic patent agent before offering patent services all fall within this group.[46] While some of these rules might eventually have been justified—for the country-of-origin princi-ple is not absolute—they were all examples of a state acting as an extra regulator, in addition to the home state, and the particular market access problems caused are specific to the cross-border situation. It is quite evident that a requirement to have local qualifications, register with local authorities, or undergo local police checks are all likely to have a far less deterrent effect on a local provider wanting to enter the market than on a foreign provider who has already had to comply with the regulations and requirements at home. This is even more so because the essence of service provision is that it is temporary and to some extent incidental, meaning that such requirements are relatively more burdensome than they will be for a ser-vice provider established in that state.

---

[44] Case 279/80 *Webb* [1981] ECR 3305; Case C-458/08 *Commission v Portugal* [2010] ECR I-11599; Case C-212/11 *Jyske Bank*, judgment of 25 April 2013. See generally Rachel Craufurd Smith, *Old Wine in New Bottles? From the 'Country of Origin Principle' to 'Freedom to Provide Services' in the European Community Directive on Services in the Internal Market* Mitchell Working Paper No 6/2007 (2007).

[45] See Vassilis Hatzopoulos and Thien Uyen Do, 'The Case Law Of the ECJ Concerning the Free Provision of Services: 2000–2005' (2006) 43 *Common Market Law Review* 923; Vassilis Hatzopoulos, 'The Court's Approach to Services (2006–2012): From Case Law to Case Load?' (2013) 50 *Common Market Law Review* 459.

[46] *Webb* (n 44); Case C-58/98 *Corsten* [2000] ECR I-7919; Case C-76/90 *Säger v Dennemeyer* [1991] ECR I-4221.

In short, while the Court regularly speaks in the wide language of *Gebhard* and its ilk, as if burdensome regulation was subject to Article 56, the facts of the cases tell a different story, about specifically cross-border problems, and in the rare situations where no such story can be found the Court in fact fails to find that a restriction exists. This is even true of cases that fit into no obvious pattern or category, such as *Carpenter* and *Alpine Investments*.[47] In the first of these, a British attempt to deport the illegally present non-European wife of a British citizen failed, because without her presence he would be unable to travel to other Member States to provide services: she looked after the children while he was away. While often discussed as a controversial, even strange, judgment, the case displays two things. The judgment displays clearly how it is not the form of the measure, but its effect on cross-border movement—in this case probably quite dramatic—which counts. More relevant here, *Carpenter* is a case where it was the specifically cross-border nature of the movement which was the issue. There was no claim that he would have to give up work if his wife was deported, but that he would not be able to go on longer business trips, which in practice means generally foreign ones. The British action would have changed Mr Carpenter from an internationally oriented businessman into a domestic one.

Alpine is also a case where it was the home state creating the problem, rather than the state of destination. The Netherlands refused to allow cold calling to sell financial services, claiming that such practices undermined the reputation of the Dutch financial industry. What was controversial was that it applied this rule to Dutch institutions wanting to cold call to Germany, where the practice was legal. Surely it was for the German government to protect the German consumer? It is true that the Dutch government could hardly be accused of discrimination against foreigners here, or of protectionism: it was restraining its own industry. However, what it was doing was putting its business at a disadvantage on the German market, so that the case is another example of how the national laws often, even without being intended to, have the effect of keeping markets divided along national lines. This is what Article 56 aims to redress, and what the cases, without exception, are about.

III. Justifications and Derogations

Articles 52 TFEU, applied to services by Article 62 TFEU, provides that Article 56 shall not prejudice measures providing for special treatment for foreign nationals on grounds of public policy, public security, or public health. This apparently

---

[47] Case C-60/00 *Carpenter v Secretary of State for the Home Department* [2002] ECR I-6279; Case C-384/93 *Alpine Investments v Minister van Financiën* [1995] ECR I-1141.

rather narrow derogation from the free movement of services is complemented by an open-ended category of Court-created justifications: as in the other freedoms, measures that restrict free movement will be acceptable to the Treaty provided they are equally applicable, pursue a legitimate goal, and pass the test of proportionality.[48] These justifications are commonly referred to as mandatory requirements, a rather unhappy name in English which has nevertheless stuck.

In adjudicating these derogations the core issue is usually proportionality. It is rare for a Member State to fail to produce at least some legitimate goal that it is pursuing, so that the dispute is usually about whether it is doing so in the least restrictive way, or whether it is necessary to pursue that goal via restrictive measures at all.

Decisions on these questions can be very controversial. The services sector encompasses many activities which are socially and politically sensitive: abortion, sexual services, trade union rights, gambling, war games, and public provision of health and education have all been the subject of litigation. Member state legislation in these areas often reflects specific cultural sensitivities, traditions, and institutional commitments, so that deciding what is 'necessary' is far from a technical issue. It is not just concrete policy goals that are at issue, but the values and history that are embedded in existing ways of doing things. The fact that the case law tends not to discuss these amorphous issues, but to treat proportionality in a largely practical way, is one reason why it has often been controversial: the reasoning in decisions does not fully reflect their social import, inviting public dissatisfaction.[49]

Proportionality is further complicated by the division of functions between the national court and the Court of Justice in the preliminary reference procedure. Formally it is for the Court to interpret the Treaty, and the referring court to apply this to the facts and national law.[50] As a result, the Court can never actually rule that a national measure is disproportionate, because this would involve taking a stance on the content and effects of that measure in its national context, which is outside the Court's jurisdiction. Rather, the Court can only provide guidelines to help the national judge take the final decision.

In practice, neither the European Court of Justice nor national judges would be enthusiastic about strict adherence to this doctrine.[51] National judges are not particularly served by abstract explanations of proportionality, but want concrete guidance on whether they should set aside a specific measure or not. The Court will have views on the national measure, and whether it is legitimate or not, and will want to ensure

---

[48] *Gebhard* (n 2).

[49] Gareth Davies 'Democracy and Legitimacy in the Shadow of Purposive Competence. European Law Journal' (2015) 21 *European Law Journal* 2.

[50] Case 6/64 *Costa v Enel* [1964] ECR 585.

[51] See generally Anthony Arnull, 'The Past and Future of the Preliminary Rulings Procedure' (2002) 13 *European Business Law Review* 183; Gareth Davies 'The Division of Powers between the European Court of Justice and National Courts', ConWEB Paper 2004/3 (2004).

that its judgment leads to the right result, something which it cannot be sure about if it simply provides an abstract interpretation of proportionality. Yet at the same time, there are cases in which it genuinely does require a deep understanding of the national legal and factual context in order to rule on the proportionality of a measure, so that a coercive ruling by the European Court of Justice would be inappropriate.

As a result of these factors one sees great variability in how derogations are adjudicated.[52] In some cases, the Court effectively rules on proportionality, while in others it emphasizes that it is for the national judge to consider and decide this. Increasingly, in recent years, it has attempted to find a constructive middle way by taking a procedural approach, judging Member State action primarily on whether the relevant interests appear to have been taken into account, the relevant facts investigated, and so on.[53]

The central concept relied upon is consistency: if a state claims that a restriction on services is necessary to serve some goal then the Court will consider whether other policy actions taken by the state support the claimed commitment to the goal. Consistency is thus used as a proxy for genuineness, the presumption being that inconsistent behaviour indicates opportunistic market closure, probably for illegitimate reasons.

Consistency has a long history in free movement law, going back to early goods and workers cases, and in the field of services being present in the well-known *Adoui and Cornuaille*.[54] Here two French women were accused of being prostitutes in Belgium, but an attempted Belgian expulsion on grounds of public policy failed because the Court found that repressive measures were not being taken against Belgian prostitutes. In the light of this, its claim that prostitution was a threat to policy could not be accepted.

The advantage of a focus on consistency is that it does seem to allow respect for diverse values: one state may tolerate prostitution, or war games, while another may not, and the law can cope with this easily, neither needing a uniform European conception of public policy, nor accepting legal fragmentation, but rather relying on the common EU rule that state goals must be pursued in a consistent and non-discriminatory way. However, the reality of policy making is often somewhat more complex than can be summarized in a brief judgment, so that there is a risk that nuance is lost and legitimate measures become the victim of a stylized

---

[52] Davies (n 51).

[53] Sacha Prechal, 'Free Movement and Procedural Requirements: Proportionality Reconsidered' (2008) 35 *Legal Issues of Economic Integration* 201; Constance Semmelman, 'The European Union's Economic Constitution under the Lisbon Treaty: Soul Searching among Lawyers Shifts the Emphasis to Procedure', (2010) 35 *European Law Review* 516.

[54] Case 121/85 *Conegate v Customs and Excise Commissioners* [1986] ECR 1007; Case 34/79 *R v Henn and Darby* [1979] ECR 3975; Case 41/74 *Van Duyn v Home Office* [1974] ECR 1337; Joined Cases 115/81 and 116/81 *Adoui and Cornuaille v Belgian State and City of Liège* [1982] ECR 1665; see also Case C-268/99 *Jany v Staatssecretaris van Justitie* [2001] ECR I-8615.

consistency test. *Adoui* may well be an example of this: there are many reasons to treat foreign prostitutes differently from domestic ones. Repression in the form of expulsion may be an effective measure, from a state point of view, while the kinds of repressive measures which can be imposed on nationals—imprisonment, fines—probably bring a higher human cost with less effectiveness.[55] Additionally, there is the issue of trafficking, which is a problem specifically for non-nationals. These arguments could have been made, but where the Court's central analytic tool is comparison between the domestic and cross-border, an argument that such comparison is misplaced will in practice have presumptive hurdles to overcome.[56]

A more recent, and clearer, example of the difficulties of consistency is *Carmen Media*.[57] German measures restricting betting services were found to contravene the Treaty because other kinds of gambling, notably casinos, were enjoying a period of government-supported expansion. The goals of the restrictions, preventing crime and gambling addiction, were quite legitimate and the measure would probably have been accepted were it not for the contrary behaviour towards other gambling. This suggested, to the Court, that the government could not be said to be pursuing its goals in a 'consistent and systematic' way, which meant that its measures would not be effective, and were therefore disproportionate.[58]

Yet the restrictive policy and the policy of expansion came from different levels of government, which under the German constitution enjoyed different and independent competences. Neither could tell the other what to do. The Land in question, Schleswig-Holstein, may have been quite consistent in its gambling policy but was the victim of the fact that the federal government was taking a different line. To this argument the Court merely responded that internal matters cannot justify non-compliance with EU law, a statement not without irony; it is only because the Court chose to engage with, and take a view on, those internal matters that it found there to be a violation. This is not a case of a state arguing internal matters to justify Treaty violations, but a case of the Court finding internal politics to be part of what defines such violations in the first place.

The problem here is that the reality of politics and multi-level governments means that very few policy areas will be marked by true consistency, nor should one expect them to be: if different governmental levels were all expected to agree on everything there would be not much point in having them. While consistency is a useful and potentially powerful concept, it will need to be employed in a more detailed and careful way than is evident in *Carmen Media* if it is not to be a bull in the china shop of national political compromise.

---

[55] See *Van Duyn* (n 54).   [56] See *Jany* (n 54).

[57] Case C-46/08 *Carmen Media* [2010] ECR I-8149.

[58] *Carmen Media* (n 57) para 64. See also Case C-169/07 *Hartlauer* [2009] ECR I-1721; Case C-500/06 *Dermoestetica* [2008] ECR I-5785; Case C-570/07 *Blanco Perez* [2010] ECR I-4629; Case C-470/11 *Garkalns*, Judgment of 19 July 2012 Case C-212/08 *Zeturf* [2011] ECR I-5633; Case C-316/07 *Stoß* [2010] ECR I-8069.

IV. Horizontal Effect of Article 56

It is long established that Article 56 applies not just to public measures, but also to private bodies who regulate a sector of economic activity, such as the international cyclists' union which was at issue in *Walrave and Koch* and the many other international sporting federations which have since felt the bite of free movement law.[59] However, in *Viking Line*, the Court appeared to extend this, ruling that the obligation to respect freedom of establishment was not confined to public bodies, or private regulators, or quasi-legislative bodies, and did, for example, apply to trade unions.[60] There is no reason to expect that the situation would be any different for services.

The case was one of two fiercely controversial judgments concerning Scandinavian trade unions. *Viking Line* concerned the reflagging of ships to enable crews to be employed on cheaper Estonian terms and conditions, while *Laval* was about Swedish companies using cheaper Baltic posted workers.[61] In both cases, trade unions took industrial action and the companies claimed that as a result they were prevented from carrying out their plans, with the result that free movement of services and freedom of establishment were hindered.

Although the judgments were nuanced, and left room for industrial action, and for state action to protect national employment conditions, this did not satisfy critics, for whom the very fact that Article 56 was applied was a problem: to say that the freedom to take industrial action was subject to the economic freedom of employers was to put the cart before the horse, and reverse the very principles upon which (historically hard-won) trade union freedoms had been founded.[62] More practically, the possibility of justifying trade union action was not enough. The reality of free movement law is that it is far from settled and certain, and subjection to Article 56 means that trade unions are exposed to legal risk each time they organize action. That risk could ultimately lead to damages which might bankrupt them. Article 56, it could be argued, can now be used to intimidate unions which threaten to strike.

---

[59] Case 36/74 *Walrave and Koch v Association Union Cycliste Internationale* [1974] ECR 1405; Case C-176/96 *Lehtonen* (FRBSB) [2000] ECR I-2681; Case T-313/02 *Meca Medina and Majcen v Commission* [2004] ECR II-3291; Joined Cases C-51/96 and C-191/97 *Deliège v Asbl Ligue Francophone de Judo* [2000] ECR I-2549.

[60] Case C-438/05 *International Transport Workers' Federation and Finnish Seamen's Union v Viking Line ABP* [2007] ECR I-10779, paras 64–65.

[61] Case C-341/05 *Laval* [2007] ECR I-11767.

[62] See eg Catherine Barnard, *Employment Rights, Free Movement under the EC Treaty and the Services Directive*, Mitchell Working Paper No. 5/08 (2008); Jonas Malmberg and Tore Sigeman, 'Industrial Actors and EU Economic Freedoms: The Autonomous Collective Bargaining Model Curtailed by the European Court of Justice' (2008) 43 *Common Market Law Review* 1115; Alan Dashwood, '*Viking* and Laval: Issues of Horizontal Direct Effect' (2008) 10 *Cambridge Yearbook of European Legal Studies* 525; Tonia Novitz, 'A Human Rights Analysis of the Viking and *Laval* Judgments' (2008) 10 *Cambridge Yearbook of European Legal Studies* 541.

It is difficult to know precisely what the scope of horizontal effect now is.[63] Trade unions are, as the Court pointed out in *Viking*, involved in collective negotiations, and therefore have a role in what can be described as a regulatory process.[64] Extending free movement law to them does not necessarily mean that it applies to every private person or body. And yet the reasoning behind applying the Treaty to private actors has always been that otherwise the law would become ineffective, as private barriers would arise to replace prohibited public ones—something emphasized in *Laval*.[65] That would suggest that the true message of *Viking Line* is that it is not the form or function of the body which counts, but the effect of its actions on free movement. If they restrict it, then they will be subject to the Treaty, whoever they may be.

Does this mean that a company decision to use local sub-contractors or an individual's choice to go to a compatriot hairdresser are now restrictions on movement? It seems unlikely that these contractual preferences would be caught by Article 56. In the case law on goods, services, and establishment, restrictions on movement have always been third-party actions interfering with the contracts of others: the situation where a state or private body prevents two other parties from contracting.[66] Yet the free movement of workers does prohibit discriminatory preferences as such, and the line between employment and a service contract is a fine one, with the Court often speaking as if the same principles apply. In releasing Article 56 from its previously stable limitation to private regulators, the Court opens a door to a passageway whose length and destination is not immediately clear.

V. The Services Directive

The services Directive, adopted in 2006, was an attempt finally to open up services markets by legislation, which tends to be taken more seriously and more fully implemented in many states than is case law. As a result of a very contentious legislative process many of the economically and socially most sensitive services were removed from its scope, such as financial and health services, and it

---

[63] See for discussion Harm Schepel, 'Constitutionalising the Market, Marketising the Constitution, and to Tell the Difference: On the Horizontal Application of the Free Movement Provisions in EU Law' (2012) 18 *European Law Journal* 177.

[64] *Viking Line* (n 60) para 65.   [65] *Laval* (n 61) para 98.

[66] Gareth Davies, 'Freedom of Movement, Horizontal Effect, and Freedom of Contract' (2012) 20 *European Review of Private Law* 805.

primarily applies to what one may describe as the small business sector or the artisan service provider: from consultants to estate agents to personal trainers and so on.[67]

The Directive performs three functions: one part of the Directive contains administrative provisions, which attempt to make it easier for service providers, and those wishing to establish in a state, to comply with whatever formalities may still be legitimately applicable.[68] Another part provides for better cooperation between regulatory bodies in different states, to avoid supervisory gaps and bottlenecks.[69]

However the most obscure part, and thus the most interesting for a lawyer, are the substantive provisions on free movement, of which the most relevant here is Article 16(1), which provides that Member States shall not impose any obligations on a service provider unless these are non-discriminatory; necessary for public policy, public security, public health, or the protection of the environment; and proportionate. This is largely a repetition of the case law, except that the legitimate reasons for restrictive measures now seem to be exhaustively covered by policy, security, health, and the environment, and the open class of mandatory requirements appears to have been abolished. Indeed, the specific mention of one mandatory requirement, the environment, could be argued to emphasize the absence and by implication the exclusion of the others.[70]

This would be of some symbolic significance, although the relatively low success rate of states who attempt to rely on mandatory requirements may put its practical import in perspective. However, it is not certain that it is the correct reading of Article 16. The Treaty itself only allows derogations on public policy, security, and health grounds, but the Court was able to find that other legitimate reasons nevertheless could justify measures, this being somehow implicit. It is hard to see what textual reason prevents it doing precisely the same again. It is therefore quite possible that Article 16 will not be understood to abolish mandatory requirements but simply to be an enactment of the case law as it stands. The one case on this point so far, *Commission v Portugal*, contains comments from the Court suggesting that this is the case.[71]

---

[67] See Dir 2006/123 on services in the internal market [2006] OJ L376/36; generally Craufurd Smith (n 44); Bruno de Witte, *Setting the Scene: How Did Services Get to Bolkestein and Why?* Mitchell Working Paper No 3/2007 (2007); Markus Klamert, 'Of Empty Glasses and Double Burdens: Approaches to Regulating the Services Market à propos the Implementation of the Services Directive' (2010) 37 *Legal Issues of Economic Integration* 111; Catherine Barnard, 'Unravelling the Services Directive' (2008) 41 *Common Market Law Review* 323.

[68] Dir 2006/123/EC, Arts 5–10.   [69] Dir 2006/123/EC, Arts 28–36.

[70] I am grateful to Anthony Arnull for pointing out this argument to me.

[71] Case C-458/08 *Commission v Portugal* [2010] ECR I-11599.

VI. Conclusion

This chapter has necessarily been an overview of some of the key issues and cases in the free movement of services. If there is a theme, it is that an adherence to flexible and open-textured doctrine has allowed this freedom to grow into a powerful tool of social engineering, whose reach extends from the welfare state to sport, via most aspects of the modern economy. In services, more than in any other freedom, it becomes apparent that de-nationalizing markets is quite inseparable from restructuring social institutions, with all the attendant cost and controversy this brings. The great weakness of the law on services to date is the failure fully to absorb this into the doctrine. It is not that the judgments lack coherence on their own free movement terms, but that these terms are too dominant in the reasoning, which fails to engage with, or even acknowledge, the wider impact of the law.

Bibliography

Catherine Barnard, 'Unravelling the Services Directive' (2008) *41 Common Market Law Review* 323

Catherine Barnard, *Employment Rights, Free Movement under the EC Treaty and the Services Directive*, Mitchell Working Paper No 5/08 (2008)

Rachel Craufurd Smith, *Old Wine in New Bottles? From the 'Country of Origin Principle' to 'Freedom to Provide Services' in the European Community Directive on Services in the Internal Market*, Mitchell Working Paper No. 6/2007 (2007)

Alan Dashwood, '*Viking and Laval*: Issues of Horizontal Direct Effect' (2007–2008) *10 Cambridge Yearbook of European Legal Studies* 525

Gareth Davies, 'Welfare as a Service' (2002) *29 Legal Issues of Economic Integration* 27

Gareth Davies 'The Division of Powers between the European Court of Justice and National Courts', ConWEB Paper 2004/3 (2004)

Gareth Davies, *The Process and Side-effects of Harmonisation of European Welfare States*, Jean Monnet Working Paper No 2/06 (2006)

Gareth Davies, 'Freedom of Movement, Horizontal Effect, and Freedom of Contract' (2012) *20 European Review of Private Law*, 805

Gareth Davies 'Democracy and Legitimacy in the Shadow of Purposive Competence. European Law Journal' (2015) *21 European Law Journal* 2

Stefan Enchelmaier, 'Always at Your Service (within Limits): The ECJ's Case Law on Article 56 TFEU (2006-11)' (2011) *36 European Law Review* 615

Vassilis Hatzopoulos, 'Annotation of *Alpine Investments*' (1995) *29 Common Market Law Review* 1427

Vassilis Hatzopoulos, 'Killing National Health and Insurance Systems but Healing Patients? The European Market for Health Care Services after the Judgments of the ECJ in *Van Braekel* and *Peerbooms*' (2002) *39 Common Market Law Review* 683

Vassilis Hatzopoulos and Thien Uyen Do, 'The Case Law of the ECJ Concerning the Free Provision of Services: 2000–2005' (2006) *43 Common Market Law Review*, 923

Vassilis Hatzopoulos, 'The Court's Approach to Services (2006–2012): From Case Law to Case Load?' (2013) *50 Common Market Law Review* 459

Markus Klamert, 'Of Empty Glasses and Double Burdens: Approaches to Regulating the Services Market à propos the Implementation of the Services Directive' (2010) *37 Legal Issues of Economic Integration* 111

Jonas Malmberg and Tore Sigeman, 'Industrial Actors and EU Economic Freedoms: The Autonomous Collective Bargaining Model Curtailed by the European Court of Justice' (2008) *43 Common Market Law Revew* 1115

Christopher Newdick, 'Citizenship, Free Movement and Healthcare: Cementing Individual Rights by Corroding Social Solidarity' (2006) *43 Common Market Law Review* 1645

Tonia Novitz, 'A Human Rights Analysis of the *Viking* and *Laval* Judgments' (2008) 10 *Cambridge Yearbook of European Legal Studies* 541

Miek Peeters, 'Free Movement of Patients: Directive 2011/24 on the Application of Patients' Rights in Cross-border Healthcare' (2012) *19 European Journal of Health Law* 29

Stephane de la Rosa, 'The Directive on Cross-border Healthcare or the Art of Codifying Complex Case Law' (2012) *49 Common Market Law Review* 15

Harm Schepel, 'Constitutionalising the Market, Marketising the Constitution, and to Tell the Difference: On the Horizontal Application of the Free Movement Provisions in EU Law' (2012) *18 European Law Journal* 177

Constance Semmelman, 'The European Union's Economic Constitution under the Lisbon Treaty: Soul Searching among lawyers Shifts the Emphasis to Procedure' (2010) *35 European Law Review* 516

Jukka Snell 'The Notion of Market Access: A Concept or a Slogan?' (2010) *47 Common Market Law Review* 437

Eleanor Spaventa, 'From Gebhard to Carpenter: Towards a (non)-Economic European Constitution' (2004) *41 Common Market Law Review* 743

Bruno de Witte, *Setting the Scene: How Did Services Get to Bolkestein and Why?* Mitchell Working Paper No 3/2007 (2007)

PART V

REGULATION OF THE MARKET PLACE

CHAPTER 23

THE COMPLEX WEAVE OF HARMONIZATION

LOÏC AZOULAI

THE European Union can be defined in a number of ways. It may be envisaged as a power or as a market, as a union of states or as a federation, as a special mode of governance or as a community of values. The EU Treaties themselves offer a more neutral and basic definition. The European Union is an institutional arrangement, which allows for the development of a set of policies and the regulation of a broad range of economic, social and legal relationships. The harmonization of national laws is a prominent instrument for achieving this goal of policy development and regulation. It and its synonyms are frequently referred to by the Treaties.[1] At the

---

[1] The general bases of harmonization of national laws for the functioning of the internal market are to be found in Title VII, Chapter 3 of the TFEU under the title 'Approximation of laws' (Arts 114 to 118). Specific harmonization provisions relying on market integration include Art 46 TFEU (free movement of workers), Art 48 TFEU (certain aspects of social security), Art 50 TFEU (freedom of establishment and company law), Art 53 TFEU (regulation of activities of self-employed persons), Art 59 TFEU (liberalisation of services), and Art 64 TFEU (free movement of capital). Other legal bases not explicitly tied to the internal market include Art 18 TFEU (rules designed to prohibit discrimination on grounds of nationality), Art 21 TFEU (citizenship rights), Art 43 TFEU (common agricultural policy Art 78 TFEU (asylum policy), Art 79 TFEU (immigration policy), Art 81 TFEU (civil matters), Art 83 TFEU (criminal matters), Arts 91 and 100 TFEU (transport policy), Art 106 TFEU (public undertakings), Art 113 TFEU (indirect taxation), Art 153 TFEU (social policy), Art 157 TFEU (equal treatment of men and women), Art 169 TFEU (consumer protection), and Art 192 TFEU (environmental protection).

same time, its basis has evolved over time, both in scope and in substance. This is reflected in the two main references juxtaposed in Article 3 TEU.

The first and still dominant reference is to the establishment of a European internal market mentioned in Article 3(3). Before the advent of the European Communities, Europe was essentially perceived as a collection of closed national markets. European integration has been a conscious effort aimed at creating interconnections between domestic markets. It first materialized in the idea of establishing a common mode of production and a more efficient allocation of resources in certain sectors, then developed as a means to 'merge the national markets into a single market bringing about conditions as close as possible to that of a genuine internal market'.[2] The Treaties contain two possible routes to creating the internal market: one is that of negative integration, relying on provisions contained in the Treaties prohibiting restrictions on trade; the other is positive integration which tries to establish common rules for regulating the market. The latter is what is usually broadly referred to as harmonization.[3]

The other reference in Article 3(2) is to the area of freedom, security and justice (AFSJ). Although its definition draws heavily on the definition of the internal market introduced by the Single European Act (now to be found in Article 26 TFEU), it now comes first in the Treaties. The AFSJ is defined as 'an area without internal frontiers' in which the free movement of persons is ensured in conjunction with policies concerning migration and the prevention of crime. This area is 'offered' as Union citizens' own place. A sense of identification with the Union is thus brought about. With the AFSJ, one is led to think of the Union not simply as a technical construction concerned mainly with interstate economic harmony but as a personal engagement of individual citizens with an area to circulate in and to occupy under the protection of common values. To be sure, the enforcement mechanisms of these values are not quite perfect. Still, there is a clear shift in the rhetoric of the Treaties, from the building of an economic union to the establishment of a new social space structured around a set of shared values. Harmonization of national laws may also be a useful tool in this regard.[4]

A familiar narrative presented by the EU institutions suggests that the AFSJ is a logical extension to the establishment of the internal market. The abolition of internal borders within the Union would call for an intensification of cooperation in civil and criminal matters, the development of common controls at the external borders as well as European cooperation in the field of migration. Moreover,

---

[2] Case 15/81 *Schul* [1982] ECR 1409, para 33.

[3] See initially Raymond Vander Elst, 'Les notions de coordination, d'harmonisation, de rapprochement et d'unification du droit dans le cadre juridique de la Communauté économique européenne' in *Les instruments du rapprochement des législations dans la Communauté économique européenne* (1976) 1.

[4] As demonstrated by Art 83(2) TFEU which provides a legal base for the approximation of criminal laws under certain conditions.

the AFSJ is often presented as a tentative response to the general crisis affecting the European project where the grand market, long associated with the success of European integration, is now perceived as a source of cultural standardization and social commodification. However a more detailed look at the legal picture reveals a different story. To a large extent internal market law anticipated the realization (and the shortcomings) of the AFSJ. What appears to the lawyer is a process of market integration largely informed by the defining features of the AFSJ. This is reflected in the nature of harmonization.

I. Harmonization in a Changing Legal Context

The evolution of the law of the internal market has brought about three interrelated features which bring it closer to the way we usually define AFSJ law: we shall call them the personalization, the re-valuation and the fragmentation of the law. First of all, individual rights were not the main concern of the EEC Treaty drafters. The focus was on ensuring the rational distribution of production and the circulation of products as well as factors of production. A significant change took place in 1963 when the ECJ made clear that it was individuals who engage in the market, who develop transnational activities and who trigger cross-border exchanges.[5] However, as has been pointed out, 'if the internal market comprises not just the Member States but also consumers (defined in as broad a sense as possible) as well as traders and industries, then its regulation must accomplish a fragile balance between protection and empowerment'.[6] Internal market law is intended to elaborate on individual rights as well as on the social and personal conditions that structure and foster the development of trade.[7] Indeed, that is how Union citizenship was discovered. This rights-based approach has led to uncertainty regarding the sense of this law. On the one hand, it can be seen as a deregulatory device in the hands of free movers, transformed into free-riders seeking personal advantage to the detriment of regulatory systems and welfare structures of Member States. On the other hand, it can be seen

[5] Case 26/62 *Van Gend en Loos* [1963] ECR 7.

[6] Niamh Nic Shuibhne, 'Introduction' in Niamh Nic Shuibhne (ed), *Regulating the Internal Market* (2006) 9.

[7] Case 186/87 *Cowan* [1989] ECR 195; Case C-60/00, *Carpenter*, [2002] ECR I-6279. See generally Eleanor Spaventa, 'From *Gebhard* to *Carpenter*: Towards a (Non-)Economic European Constitution' (2004) 41 *Common Market Law Review* 743.

as a means of re-embedding the market by granting an economic and social status to European citizens.[8]

Secondly, there has been shift from fact to values. The internal market has long been presented as a matter of facts. It has been conceived as a rational and volitional exercise, endorsed by the main players of European integration, to construct a level playing field in the area of trade. The main job of the Court was one of supporting this exercise through a constructive interpretation of the law. As has been pointed out by a perceptive observer, the Court relied on the assumption that the common market is 'a fact, of the existence of which it takes judicial notice and from which observation it draws the necessary consequences'.[9] The granting of rights to individuals as market participants mirrored a general commitment to market integration principles that were broadly agreed amongst Member States, even when the vindication of these rights in individual cases conflicted with their self-interest, narrowly conceived. This commitment can no longer be taken for granted. It is difficult to view the internal market today as a consensual institutional fact concentrating on trade. As was made clear by the Court in the recent *Demirkan* case, internal market law cannot be reduced to a law which 'pursues an essentially economic purpose'.[10] It addresses issues which inextricably affect market and non-market interests such as consumption habits, the regulation of gambling activities, drugs policies, healthcare, data protection, the patentability of biotechnological inventions, social rights and so on. By extending far beyond its origins in commercial activities, the internal market has entered a new era where value conflicts arise, ideological differences emerge and political choices are to be made. Viewed in this way, it is no surprise that it has to cope with a new set of difficulties relating to the recognition of social, moral and ethical diversity.[11]

The third and final change comes from our having to give up the holistic and uniform picture of the internal market that was until recently taken for granted. The European Community and its market were usually seen as forming 'a system, that is it say, a structured, organized and finalized whole'.[12] This assumption was manifested legally through 'the perspective of the unity of market' adopted by European institutions. It was through this perspective that the legal principles governing the establishment of the internal market were given maximum coverage and it led to the notion that these principles have to be applied and interpreted in a

---

[8] On this debate see recently Martin Höpner and Armin Schäfer, 'Embeddedness and Regional Integration: Waiting for Polanyi in a Hayekian Setting' (2012) 66 *International Organization* 429.

[9] Roger-Michel Chevallier, 'Methods and Reasoning of the European Court in its interpretation of Community Law' (1965) 2 *Common Market Law Review* 21.

[10] Case C-221/11 *Demirkan*, judgment of 24 September 2013.

[11] Floris de Witte, 'Sex, Drugs & EU Law: The Recognition Of Moral And Ethical Diversity In EU Law' (2013) 50 *Common Market Law Review* 1545.

[12] Pierre Pescatore, *The Law of Integration. Emergence of a New Phenomenon in International Relations Based on the Experience of the European Communities* (1974) 41.

uniform manner across all relevant sectors and in all Member States. This however soon gave rise to a form of legal centralism that was perceived as threatening diversity. Already in 1974 the Commission stated that its objective was 'to make it possible for producers and consumers to benefit fully from trade liberalization', but not to 'eliminate from the market diverse local products which help maintain the originality of the various Member States'.[13] To respond more generally to this concern, an element of differentiation was incorporated into the operation of internal market law. Some states were provisionally exempted from its application while others were granted derogations.[14] Seen in this way, internal market law was historically as much a field of differentiation as current AFSJ law, if to a more limited extent. However, differentiated integration has recently expanded in the internal market context. This raises serious issues concerning not only the institutional dynamic of the EU but also for the very meaning of the project of creating a 'single' market.[15]

These three broad features of personalization, re-valuation, and fragmentation, are reflected in the way harmonization is currently developing in the EU. The first of these concerns the scope of harmonization. Internal market law goes far beyond the completion of the customs union and the removal of obstacles to trade. It is as much concerned with the institutional, the social, and the moral infrastructure of the market. Harmonization measures are designed to deal not only with the nature, composition, and control of specific products, services, sectors, or professions, but also address the conditions under which these products are traded, these services provided, these sectors structured and the professions exercised. They seek to ensure the smooth functioning of the internal market by opening up new opportunities for businesses, but also to protect the non-market interests that are deemed to be essential to the pursuit of European integration, such as the safety of workers, the security of the populations, the protection of environment and public health, or the preservation of welfare structures in Member States. As a result, the harmonization process that is founded on an internal market legal base may give rise to the liberalization of network industries and services as well as the strengthening of workers', consumers' or patients' rights.[16]

Second, it is not only the scope but also the quality of harmonization that has changed. Quality refers to the fact that fundamental rights and values are present

---

[13] *Seventh General Report on the Activities of the European Communities* (1974) 130. In its more recent *Green Book on the Promotion of Regional Products* of 2011, the Commission states again that 'regional and local markets are an essential meeting place for producers and consumers'.

[14] Gráinne de Búrca, 'Differentiation within the Core: The Case of the Common Market' in Gráinne de Búrca and Joanne Scott (eds), *Constitutional Change in the EU. From Uniformity to Flexibility?* (2000) 133.

[15] Editorial comments, 'What do we want? "Flexibility! Sort of. . . ." When do we want it? "Now! Maybe. . . ."' (2013) 50 *Common Market Law Review* 673.

[16] Daniel Kelemen, 'The EU Rights Revolution: Adversarial Legalism and European Integration' in Tanja A. Börzel and Rachel A. Cichowski (eds), *The State of the European Union. Law, Politics and Society* (2003) 222.

in the harmonization process. References are now frequently found to the safe-guarding of fundamental rights of individuals as one of the manifold objectives of harmonization or to fundamental values which apply despite the pursuit by the harmonization measure of an objective of market integration.[17] As part of the har-monization process, the EU institutions may have to give meaning to the 'dignity and integrity' of a regulated profession;[18] or they may be involved in difficult issues concerning the 'dignity and integrity of the person' such as the definition of the concept of human embryo.[19] Harmonization is not simply the regulation of mar-ket activities—it does not simply influence the lifestyle of European populations through the regulation of environmental and public health risks, but it directly affects the basic ethical and social conditions of human life as well as incidentally those of animal welfare.[20]

Finally, since the new approach to technical harmonization, endorsed by the Council and the Commission in 1985 with a view to completing the internal mar-ket by 1992, flexibility is an integral part of the EU approach to harmonization. In the context of an expansion in the scope of the Union's competence combined with rather limited administrative and enforcement capacities and an enlarged and ever less homogeneous Union where the concerns of Member States regarding the preservation of national and local diversity are ever more pressing, flexibility becomes a kind of magic formula. Through it one can address the conundrum of maintaining the dynamic of integration whilst at the same time accounting for its practical limits and allowing for the possibility of granting some leeway to the Member States. Flexibility takes various forms in EU legislation: the use of minimum harmonization clauses whereby Member States are allowed to maintain or to introduce more stringent standards than those required by the harmoniza-tion measure;[21] the limitation of harmonization to essential substantive standards coupled with mutual recognition clauses whereby Member States are required to

---

[17] See for instance Dir 95/46 on the protection of individuals with regards to the processing of personal data and on the free movement of such data [1995] OJ L 281/31 and Dir 98/44 on the legal protection of biotechnological inventions [1998] OJ L 213/13.

[18] Case C-119/09 *Société fiduciaire nationale d'expertise comptable* [2011] ECR I-2551 interpreting Art 24 of Dir 2006/123 on services in the internal market [2006] OJ L 376/36.

[19] Case C-34/10 *Brüstle* [2011] ECR I-2821.

[20] See eg Reg 1007/2009 on trade in seal products [2009] OJ L 286/36. In the proposal leading to this regulation, the Commission argued that the Treaty 'does not provide for a specific legal basis allowing the Community to legislate in the field of ethics as such. However, where the Treaty empowers the Community to legislate in certain areas and that the specific conditions of those legal bases are met, the mere circumstance that the Community legislature relies on ethical considera-tions does not prevent it from adopting legislative measures. It should be noted, in that respect, that the Treaty enables the Community to adopt measures aimed at establishing and maintaining an internal market, which is a market without internal frontiers according to Art 14 of the Treaty' (COM (2008) 469 final, p. 3).

[21] Michael Dougan, 'Minimum Harmonization and the Internal Market' (2000) 37 *Common Market Law Review* 853.

rely on legal situations established in other Member States;[22] the combination of limited harmonization with forms of coordination of national legislation whereby Member States retain competence to enact rules regarding the substantive aspects of the matter covered.[23] More recently, however, flexibility has developed unexpectedly. It has freed harmonization from the traditional institutional framework of the EU. Thus, the creation of unified patent protection and the financial transaction tax are the subjects of enhanced cooperation regimes involving only a limited number of Member States.[24] Even more striking is the new instrument of the banking union, the Single Resolution Mechanism, which is adopted partly as an intergovernmental agreement concluded by the eurozone Member States outside the EU institutional framework. It may appear paradoxical to seek to complete the internal market through means that fail to establish a uniform legal field. However, this seems to be the price to be paid for accommodating tensions, resistances and calls for autonomy amongst the Member States whilst helping to establish a framework of cooperation between businesses and public administrations.

II. Unbound Harmonization

The question of the limits to harmonization has long been neglected. From the outset, the Community was said to operate on the basis of the broad objective of establishing a common market that in turn was considered by the Court as one of the 'most fundamental objectives of the Community'. Hence, although it was originally conceived of as 'partial' in nature and restricted to the socioeconomic sphere, market integration was construed as a 'non-specific' legal project capable of embracing a wide range of sectors and interests.[25] The EU legislator and the Court accepted that any disparity between legislation that may affect the current or future functioning of the common market justified harmonization. That the Member States were content with this construction was made clear at the Paris

---

[22] See eg Case C-241/97 *Skandia* [1999] ECR I-9821 and generally Christine Janssens, *The Principle of Mutual Recognition in EU Law* (2013).

[23] Examples include pieces of legislation as diverse as Reg 883/2004 on the coordination of social security systems [2004] OJ L 166/1 and Dir 2000/31 on electronic commerce [2000] OJ L 178/1.

[24] Reg 1257/2012 implementing enhanced cooperation in the area of the creation of unitary patent protection [2012] L 361/1 and Council Decision 2013/52 authorising enhanced cooperation in the area of financial transaction tax [2013] OJ L 22/1.

[25] Opinion of AG Fennelly in Case C-376/98 *Germany v Parliament and Council (Tobacco Advertising)* [2000] ECR I-8419, para 62 and Opinion of AG Tesauro in Case C-300/89 *Commission v Council (Titanium Dioxide)* [1991] ECR I-2867, para 10.

Summit of 1972 where the Member State heads of government agreed to extend the scope of the powers of the Community. From then on the former Article 100 of the EEC Treaty and later Article 100a of the EC Treaty were interpreted so as to include both market and non-market activities within the ambit of the Community.[26] It amounted to a general power to regulate the internal market.

This framework was acceptable so long as two conditions were met: harmonization measures were to be agreed by the Council acting unanimously in the form of directives and the Common Market was perceived and even appropriated by the main EU players as a key element of the success of European integration, able to deliver long-term socioeconomic gains. These conditions ceased to apply following the introduction of Article 114 TFEU by the Single European Act requiring the use of qualified majority instead of unanimity and the growth of discontent surrounding the alleged benefits delivered by the dynamic of market integration. The question of the limits to harmonization then emerged as part of a broader debate pointing to a 'competence problem' in the EU.[27] This debate ended up reaching the Court, which had built its position and legitimacy on the functional and holistic consolidation of the internal market. In the famous *Tobacco Advertising* case of 2000, it finally delivered a message which had a clear constitutional resonance: just as there are limits to deregulation on the basis of the free movement Treaty provisions, made clear in the *Keck and Mithouard* case, so there are limits to the power to regulate contained in the general legal base for harmonization. Article 114 TFEU can no longer be construed as 'as meaning that it vests the [Union] legislature a general power to regulate the internal market'.[28] A mere finding of a disparity between national rules is not sufficient to trigger the harmonization legislative competence. The disparity must be such as to create 'likely' obstacles to trade or 'appreciable' distortions of competition.

Where none of the judicial tests are met, recourse to Article 114 as a legal base is not justified, and another legal base needs to be found in the TFEU. However, account should now be taken of the limits placed on other legal bases by the Treaty. Many of the specific legislative competences explicitly exclude, in part or in full, the harmonization of national laws.[29] Moreover, a new subsidiarity mechanism was

---

[26] Bruno de Witte, 'A Competence to Protect: The Pursuit of Non-Market Aims Through Internal Market Legislation' in P. Syrpis (ed), *The Judiciary, the Legislature and the EU Internal Market* (2011) 25.

[27] René Barents, 'The Internal Market Unlimited: Some Observations on the Legal Basis of Community Legislation' (1993) 30 *Common Market Law Review* 85; Loïc Azoulai (ed), *The Question of Competence in the European Union* (2014).

[28] C-376/98 *Germany v Parliament and Council* (*Tobacco Advertising*) [2000] ECR I-8419, para 83.

[29] This is the case in Art 19(2) TFEU (the combat against discrimination), Art 79(4) TFEU (integration of third country nationals), Art 84 TFEU (crime prevention), Art 149 TFEU (employment), Art 153 (2)(a) (specific actions related to social policy) and, according to Art 2(5) TFEU, in all areas where the Union has competence to support, coordinate or supplement the actions of the Member States (health protection, industry, culture, tourism, education, vocational training, youth and sport, civil protection, and administrative cooperation).

introduced by the Lisbon Treaty empowering national parliaments to exercise an *ex ante* control over proposed EU legislation. Thus, even though the broad competence conferred on the Union legislature on the basis of Article 114 TFEU has not been affected by subsequent amendments to the Treaties, restrictive judicial formulas and political safeguards are in place.

Whether this is sufficient to turn the idea of limits into an effective reality remains to be seen. In practice, the implementation of the criteria set out by the Court amounts to little more than a rejection of the total elimination of trade barriers as a goal of harmonization. In the *Tobacco Advertising* case, the Court accepted that a Directive prohibiting the advertising of tobacco products could be adopted. It objected to a measure that amounted to an outright obstacle on trade affecting all kinds of products, but it accepted that any other measure which restricts particular forms of trade by relying on non-trade objectives would be legitimate.[30] As has been noted, the outcome of the new judicial tests is simply 'to serve as a "drafting guide" which readily enables the legislative institutions to comply with the principle of conferral'.[31] As a matter of fact, in exercising its review, the Court is principally engaged in a careful reading of the preambles of the EU legislative acts and the explanatory memorandums to the legislative proposals issued by the Commission in order to identify arguments that support the adoption of the challenged measure. This leads it to accept, for instance, acts of harmonization adopted not to approximate existing national measures but to 'forestall [national] measures which would probably have been taken by the Member States' or acts that provide for the setting up of a European agency which may act under certain circumstances in addition to (not in lieu of) existing national authorities.[32] The internal market harmonization clause of the Treaty continues to contain a number of heterogeneous forms of action.

Strict judicial review of harmonization measures by the Court still seems far off. The judicial control lies essentially in a cautious use of the principle of proportionality. The Court sees its main task as imposing a duty on the legislature to give careful prior consideration and to conduct an assessment of all relevant economic and scientific data justifying the adoption of a measure.[33] In fact, this form of review transposes to the legislative sphere an obligation that was traditionally imposed on the EU administration as a 'duty of diligence' and is now reflected in Article 41(1)

---

[30] Case C-210/03 *Swedish Match* [2004] ECR I-11893 and Case T-526/10 *Inuit Tapiriit Kanatami and others v Commission*, judgment of 25 April 2013.

[31] Stephen Weatherill, 'The Limits of Legislative Harmonization Ten Years after *Tobacco Advertising*: How the Court's Case Law has become a "Drafting Guide"' (2011) 12 *German Law Journal* 827.

[32] Case C-58/08 *Vodafone and others* [2010] ECR I-4999, para 43; Case C-270/10 *United Kingdom v Parliament and Council (ESMA)*, judgment of 22 January 2014, para 115.

[33] Koen Lenaerts, 'The European Court of Justice and Process-oriented Review' (2013) 32 *Yearbook of European Law* 3.

of the EU Charter.[34] The idea is to ensure that the political discretion granted to the EU institutions is exercised in a rational manner. Discretion still applies however, and renders any real engagement by the Court with the principle of subsidiarity unlikely. As a matter of fact, under the subsidiarity review, the Court has generally failed to clearly differentiate the reason for granting a competence to the Union and the reason for exercising that competence at the EU level.[35] The former seems to imply the latter. Such a control does not set any serious limits to EU legislative action.

Nor do political safeguards. True, there are clauses inserted in the Treaties to protect the powers of Member States in relation to sensitive areas. But the legislature has not been put under strong pressure by the Court to opt for specific legal bases or to make a clear choice between the various legal bases available. The fact that a measure is to a large extent inspired by objectives which relate to an area of competence in which harmonization is excluded or limited to minimum standards, is not considered by either the Union legislature or the Court as an overriding reason to exclude the use of Article 114 TFEU as a legal base.[36] More often than not, a measure which pursues inextricably associated market and non-market objectives will be based on several legal bases, including Article 114 TFEU.[37] As for the political mechanism of subsidiarity, it is widely acknowledged that it has had but a limited impact on the dynamic of the harmonization process thus far.[38]

It follows that few constraints exist on harmonization under EU law. Once this is recognized, it may be argued that there is virtually no limit to harmonization. That however would be a mistake. Certainly, the categorical and economic approach consisting in excluding harmonization in certain areas and subjecting it to a market-making test has failed. Formal textual exclusions of harmonization do not work and the tests established in the *Tobacco Advertising* case are rather loose. This does not however mean that the idea of limits does not hold. It is still there and manifests itself in a variety of forms, sometimes pathological. For many important actors it remains a source of concern.

Once we have admitted that harmonization has both market integration and regulatory goals, perhaps the real test should not be confined to assessing its

---

[34] Loïc Azoulai and Laure Clément-Wilz, 'La bonne administration' in Jean-Bernard Auby and Jacqueline Dutheil de la Rochère (dir.), *Traité de droit administratif européen* (2014) 671.

[35] Case C-58/08 *Vodafone* (n 32) para 78.

[36] Case C-376/98 *Tobacco Advertising* (n 27) paras 78–79.

[37] A good illustration of these multi-based acts is Reg 178/2002 laying down the general principles and requirements of food law, establishing the European Food Safety Authority and laying down procedures in matters of food safety [2002] OJ L 31/1.

[38] There has been only one Commission's proposal withdrawn under the pressure of national parliaments so far and it concerned the regulation of the exercise to take collective action within the context of internal market law.

contribution to trade or competition. Beyond this test, a deeper justification for harmonization is required, which must be derived from its added value with respect to national regulatory processes.[39] The EU legislator is a 're-regulator'.[40] The current legal and political discourse lacks a set of clear justifications for engaging in this re-regulation, as well as a set of criteria to measure the appropriateness of the justification in each individual case. The arguments used or implied in the current practice are often not clearly identified and remain under-debated. The first is that national action alone is incapable of dealing with large-scale processes that may adversely affect Member States' structures or interests. A good example is money laundering on a global scale. It may be argued that isolated actions on a national level are likely to be insufficient to deal with this phenomenon or cause helpless fragmentation. A second oft-heard argument refers to local phenomena or activities which have cross-border effects. A classic example is pollution. In such a case, it is evident that purely national initiatives make little if any sense. The third argument is that, irrespective of global processes or cross-border externalities, the Union may be better placed to deal with certain structural failures or biases on the part of states, such as natural monopolies.

Unbound harmonization is not necessarily irresponsible or unresponsive harmonization. In every case, it would be important to show that the Union's action is not detrimental to nationally sensitive interests and values. Internal market harmonization has to be rethought as an area sufficiently wide to take into account the heterogeneity of regulatory ends involved in each particular context, but one within which the degree of harmonization may vary, different values may be expressed, and involving the different levels of responsibilities.

III. Embedded Harmonization

EU harmonization law is a 'world of its own'.[41] While drawing on the experience of harmonization at the international level, it goes far beyond the mere approximation of diverse legal sources. It not only aims to bring national laws together and putting them into a single rational scheme. It aims at achieving the project of

---

[39] Miguel Poiares Maduro, 'Three Claims of Constitutional Pluralism' in Matej Avbelj and Jan Komárek (eds), *Constitutional Pluralism in the European Union and Beyond* (2012) 67.

[40] Stephen Weatherill, 'Supply of and Demand for Internal Market Regulation: Strategies, Preferences and Interpretation' in Niamh Nic Shuibhne (ed), *Regulating the Internal Market* (2006) 29, 53.

[41] cf Pescatore (n 12) 77.

market integration.[42] This presupposes that EU harmonization measures should strive to be legally perfect, substantively complete, socially effective and applied in a uniform manner.[43] Now, this is just what EU law, relying on political compromises during the legislative process and on the support of domestic remedies and enforcers at the stage of application, is incapable of being. To keep up with this project, the law of harmonization has been construed as a closed system, standing on its own and keeping the connections to external legal sources to a minimum. This is reflected in two general assumptions. The first is that harmonization law should be more or less immune from the effect of the non-market provisions of the Treaties, including the reference to fundamental rights. The second is that reference to national law should be minimized. To be sure, these assumptions still generally hold and continue to impact on legal practice. However, a look at recent legislation and case law suggests a more complex and nuanced legal picture. There is evidence of an increasing interplay between harmonization law and external legal sources. Harmonization measures are being articulated in light of the fundamental and horizontal provisions of the Treaties as well as fundamental conceptions enshrined in national law. This is for two reasons. First of all, by giving consideration to concerns different from the ones it outlines itself, internal market harmonization gains a wider basis of legitimation. Second and perhaps more clearly, it may be a way of protecting diversity and local autonomy.

1. Harmonization and EU Constitutional Law

Free movement law has experienced a process of transformation through case law in the last ten years.[44] Market freedoms have been put in touch with non-market values. The internal market provisions of the Treaties have been embedded in an interpretive framework which allows for the possibility of reconciling free movement and contradictory requirements of equal constitutional value that arise out of EU and national constitutional law. Until recently, the law of harmonization seemed to be immune from this evolution. There may be two main reasons for this. The first is that when a harmonization measure is adopted it is somehow assumed that the goal of market integration is achieved. The threat to interstate trade is then

---

[42] Jérôme Porta, *La réalisation du droit communautaire. Essai sur le gouvernement juridique de la diversité* (2007) 303–325.

[43] Opinion of AG Ruiz-Jarabo Colomer in Case C-374/05 *Gintec* [2007] ECR I-9517, § 30: 'there is nothing to support the argument that, in fulfilling their commitment under Arts 95 and 152 EC to safeguard that collective interest, the Community institutions can adjust downwards and accommodate each Member State's particular requirements, which, as the EU legislature points out, hinders the achievement of the project'.

[44] Starting with Case C-112/00 *Schmidberger* [2003] ECR I-5659 and Case C-36/02 *Omega Spielhallen* [2004] ECR I-9609.

regarded as removed. As a consequence, the confrontation with superior rules of the Treaties other than the underlying economic freedoms is deemed unnecessary. The second reason has to do with a desire to defend the integrity of EU legislation. If recourse to EU constitutional grounds were openly permitted, the possibility they could be relied upon before national courts to challenge national legislation implementing harmonization measures, in turn challenging the underlying EU harmonization measure, would be endless.

This may change as the result of two main developments. The first concerns the place of harmonization in the system of EU norms. Treaty provisions are conditions of the validity of EU legislative norms. Harmonization norms are no exception to this. The Court has repeatedly held that free movement provisions apply 'not only to national measures but also to measures adopted by the Community institutions'.[45] At the same time, it is generally acknowledged that judicial review of harmonization measures has been rather soft. By assuming that the EU legislature 'must be allowed a broad discretion which entails political, economic and social choices on its part', the Court considers that 'the legality of the measure can be affected only if it is manifestly inappropriate having regard to the objective which the legislature is seeking to achieve'.[46] In the case of potential conflicts with the economic freedoms, the Court has usually opted for a constructive reading of the measure so as to save it from being declared invalid. A similar technique has been used when fundamental rights or values were invoked.[47] However, the entry into force of the Lisbon Treaty including the Charter and the perspective of accession to the ECHR has made it harder to maintain this approach. Evidence of a stricter approach appears in recent case law.[48] Regardless of the outcome of each individual case, what is striking is the way the Court has become increasingly familiar with addressing the challenge. Far from assuming that the harmonization measures are designed exclusively to meet the needs of economic integration, it focuses the review on their non-market objectives.[49] The reference to fundamental rights is used to widen the framework in which the measure is to be interpreted and to give

[45] Case C-15/83 *Denkavit* [1984] ECR 2171, para 15. Kamiel Mortelmans, 'The Relationship between the Treaty Rules and Community Measures for the Establishment and Functioning of the Internal Market. Towards a Concordance Rule' (2002) 39 *Common Market Law Review* 1303.

[46] Joined Cases C-154 and C-155/04 *Alliance for Natural Health v Secretary of State for Health* [2005] ECR I-6451, para 52. See Kosmas Boskovits, *Le juge communautaire et l'articulation des compétences normatives entre la Communauté européenne et ses Etats membres* (1999) 725–733.

[47] Antoine Bailleux, *Les interactions entre libre circulation et droits fondamentaux dans la jurisprudence communautaire. Essai sur la figure du juge traducteur* (2009) 321–326.

[48] See Cases C-293/12 & C-594/12 *Digital Rights Ireland*, judgment of 8 April 2014.

[49] See eg Case C-51/93 *Meyhui* [1994] ECR I-3879 para 20; Case C-245/01 *RTL Television* [2003] paras 62-70; Case C-210/03 *Swedish Match* (n 29), para 74; Joined Cases C-154 and C-155/04 *Alliance for Natural Health v Secretary of State for Health* (n 45), para 152; Case C-479/04 *Laserdisken* [2006] ECR I-8089, para 65; Case C-544/10 *Deutsches Weintor*, judgment of 6 September 2012, paras 42-60; Case C-283/11 *Sky Österreich*, judgment of 22 January 2013.

effect within the area of harmonization to the pluralism of interests and values protected by EU law.

The second development concerns the place of harmonization with respect to negative integration. The former is traditionally seen as supporting and completing the latter. Ever since the introduction of the so-called 'new approach', harmonization is the classic response to national measures that are seen as restrictions to trade but are justified on the basis of a recognized non-market public interest. Triggered by the application of the free movement rules, harmonization applies independently of it.[50] This holds true as regards the scope of application of harmonized law: recourse to the internal market legal base 'does not presuppose the existence of an actual link with free movement between Member States in every situation referred to by the [harmonization] measure'.[51] This also applies to substance: internal market legislation has long pursued non-market aims. This has only been reinforced by the introduction of qualified majority voting in the Council.[52] However, the traditional model of harmonization remains firmly committed to the idea of building a cross-border market.

The recent institutional practice bears witness to a two-way and somewhat paradoxical trend. On the one hand, a growing amount of legislation conforms to the conditions for the application of the free movement provisions. Some harmonization measures are designed to be applicable to cross-border situations only. Others incorporate a clause directly referring to primary internal market law.[53] This 'light touch' approach may be the price to be paid for the continuous expansion of the harmonization programme to fields that are heavily regulated at the national level. At the same time, it raises issues as to the real impact of harmonization. On the other hand, however much free movement law may endow the legislation with its market integration rationale, there is still a possibility of recognizing other values flowing from the overriding objectives pursued by the Union. The legislature may be encouraged in this by the numerous horizontal clauses introduced by a series of amendments of the Treaties since the Single European Act, making it legitimate to take into consideration gender inequality, social protection, health and environmental protection, consumer protection, animal welfare or social and territorial cohesion when adopting harmonization measures (Articles 8 to 14 TFEU). A good

---

[50] Pedro Caro de Sousa, 'Negative and Positive Integration in EU Economic Law: Between Strategic Denial and Cognitive Dissonance' (2012) 13 *German Law Journal* 979.

[51] Joined Cases C-465/00, C-138/01 and C-139/01 *Rechnungshof and others* [2003] ECR I-4989, para 41.

[52] Bruno de Witte, 'Non-Market Values in Internal Market Legislation' in Niamh Nic Shuibhne (ed), *Regulating the Internal Market* (2006) 61.

[53] The Directive on electronic commerce (n 23) and the services Directive (n 18) are two prominent examples of the use of this technique. See also Case C-108/09 *Ker Optica* [2010] ECR I-12213 paras 75–76. On this technique see Marc Fallon, '1992–2012: Etat des lieux et enjeux du droit du marché intérieur' in Valérie Michel (dir.), *1992–2012: 20 ans de marché intérieur* (2014) 17.

example is provided by the Directive on the application of patients' rights. Building upon the application of free movement principles developed by the Court on a case-by-case basis, it recognizes the importance of state health systems as contributing to social cohesion and social justice, and as 'part of the wider framework of services of general interest'.[54] This is a means of re-embedding internal market harmonization in the wider scheme of the Treaties. Arguably, this move responds to the perceived need to grant more leeway to the Member States in sensitive fields covered by harmonization. It may then in turn inform the way free movement law itself is applied.[55]

2. Harmonization and National Law

The initial picture looks pretty much the same regarding the interaction between harmonization and national law. Although Article 114 TFEU does not specify the type of harmonization to be attained, a vague assumption exists that, if not otherwise stated, complete harmonization entailing comprehensive displacement of domestic law is the best way to achieve the internal market.[56] Complete harmonization does not necessarily mean that national variation is not permitted. Indeed, the legislature may provide for specific derogations, options or references to national law. However, the room for manoeuvre allowed Member States under these provisions is strictly delimited.[57] In particular, a Member State is not allowed to rely on grounds different from those governing harmonization.[58] More generally, the Court has consistently held that where EU legislation provides for the protection of various public interests, derogations by Member States based on grounds of public interest referred to in the Treaties (especially Article 36 TFEU) are no longer admissible.[59] In other words, harmonization excludes reliance by Member States on the Treaty based public interest exceptions. National measures must be adopted within the framework outlined by harmonized law. This doctrine presupposes

---

[54] Dir 2011/24 on the application of patients' rights in cross-border healthcare [2011] OJ L 88/45 (preamble, recital 3).

[55] See with respect to posted workers, Opinion of AG Cruz Villalón in Case C-515/08 *Palhota* [2010] ECR I-9133.

[56] This is clearly reflected in Opinion of AG Ruiz-Jarabo Colomer in Case C-374/05 *Gintec* (n 42) paras 22–40.

[57] Case C-52/00 *Commission v France* [2002] ECR I-3827. But this is without prejudice to the boundaries which affect the scope of harmonized law: 'complete harmonization' is not to be conflated with 'exhaustive harmonization' as made clear in Case C-285/08 *Leroy Somer* [2009] ECR I-4733.

[58] Case C-540/08 *Mediaprint* [2010] ECR I-10909 (concerning a national measure justified on the ground of the protection of media pluralism). See also Case C-512/12 *Octapharma France*, judgment of 13 March 2014, paras 42–46.

[59] See eg Case 28/84 *Commission v Germany* [1985] ECR 3097.

that the policy concerns as well as fundamental rights concerns of Member States have been exhaustively addressed by the EU legislature.[60] This doctrine fits poorly with the notion that harmonized law is part of a wider legal and constitutional framework.

True, Article 114 TFEU provides for mechanisms to derogate from harmonization. This provision is partly the outcome of a concession made to Member States who expressed reservations on the adoption of qualified majority voting during the negotiations for the Single European Act. In response to these concerns, it was decided to insert paragraphs 4 to 9 allowing for the possibility of derogation. However, this possibility is subject to strict interpretation and has been used very little in practice.[61] On the other hand, it is still possible for the legislature to insert a safeguard clause pursuant to Article 114(10) or to opt for minimum harmonization using a distinct legal base[62] thereby allowing for the possibility of maintaining or introducing more stringent national measures justified by the protection of public interests.[63] This does not however mean total freedom and it should be pointed out that these national measures remain subject to free movement provisions.[64]

In the end, there seems to be a very limited scope for there to be exemptions from harmonization in the internal market framework. This stands in contrast to the evolution of free movement law. In this domain, the Court has reintroduced a preoccupation for the wider constitutional and social context, resulting in more leeway for the Member States. In *Sayn Wittgenstein*, for instance, the Court stated that the objective of observing the principle of equal treatment, as enshrined in Austrian constitutional law, reflects an important value that should be recognized as a general principle guiding the interpretation of free movement law and ultimately restricting its application.[65] It expressly referred to the EU Charter and to Article 4(2) TEU, the national identities clause introduced by the Lisbon Treaty.

However, it seems that, in some instances at least, the Court is now capable of demonstrating the same awareness of national interests in the field of harmonization. In doing so it employs different techniques. Relying on the flexibility offered

---

[60]   Regarding fundamental rights concerns Georgios Anagnostaras, 'Balancing conflicting fundamental rights: the Sky Östereich paradigm' (2014) 39 *European Law Review* 111.

[61]   Isodora Maletić, *The Law and Policy of Harmonisation in Europe's Internal Market* (2013).

[62]   eg in contrast to Art 114 TFEU, Art 193 TFEU leaves untouched the Member States' power to adopt more stringent protective measures. However, it is clearly stated that 'such measures must be compatible with the Treaties' and notably the free movement provisions. See further Nicolas de Sadeleer, *EU Environmental Law and the Internal Market* (2014).

[63]   An example is to be found in the field of consumer law in Art 8 of Dir 2006/114 concerning misleading and comparative advertising [2006] L 376/21.

[64]   Case C-309/02 *Radlberger* [2004] ECR I-11763, paras 56–57; Case C-12/00 *Commission v Spain (Chocolate)* [2003] ECR 459, para 97.

[65]   Case C-208/09 *Sayn-Wittgenstein* [2010] ECR I-13693, para 89.

by some Directives, it grants national authorities a margin for manoeuvre to apply the provisions of these directives in a way which sets a fair balance between the applicable fundamental rights. The Court offers the Member States the opportunity to interpret these provisions in a manner consistent with EU fundamental rights where the protection of these rights reflects a domestic constitutional concern.[66] This is one way of responding to the legitimate concerns of Member States without destabilizing EU legislation. In relation to the Directive on television without frontiers, it finds that the Directive grants the Member States a broad discretion to determine the events which are of major importance for society, taking account of social and cultural particularities in the Member State concerned, with the result that this designation will lead to 'inevitable' obstacles to trade.[67] To that end, it finds support in Article 11 of the EU Charter guaranteeing the freedom to receive information in a democratic and pluralistic society. In the realm of consumer law, the Court resorts to a new category of principles, the 'general principles of civil law', in order to correct the application of EU directives, reading them in light of core values underlying the national legal orders.[68] In all of these cases, the connection to fundamental rights or general principles is a way of placing the harmonization measure in the context of Member States' own understandings of the factual, legal, social or ethical environment in which they operate. If not the letter, at least the spirit of the duty to respect the national identities of the Member States enshrined in their political, civil and social constitution now seems to operate in harmonization law.

Harmonization law began as a self-sufficient and comprehensive legal regime for a particular economic project. As it extends and affects ever larger areas of national law and deeper sets of socioeconomic relationships, it becomes apparent that it cannot rely solely on its own resources and its own limited goals. It must now be seen within a wider constitutional and pluralist context, dealing with external references and competing rationales while keeping in mind the broad market-building project pursued by the Union.

---

[66] Case C-101/01 *Lindqvist*, [2003] ECR I-12971, paras 83–87 (data protection). Case C-314/12 *UPC Telekabel*, judgment of 27 March 2014, para 46. See more generally in that connection, Case C-377/98 *Netherlands v Commission* [2001] ECR I-7079.

[67] Case C-201/11 P *UEFA*, judgment of 18 July 3013, paras 10–21. Compare this to the case law of the Court in the context of primary law: C-67/96 *Albany* [1999] ECR I-5751; Joined Cases C-51/97 and C-191/97 *Deliège* [2000] ECR I-2549; Case C-309/99 *Wouters* [2002] ECR I-1577. See further on primary law, Loïc Azoulai, 'The European Court of Justice and the duty to respect sensitive national interests', in Mark Dawson, Bruno de Witte and Elise Muir (eds), *Judicial Activism at the European Court of Justice* (2013) 167.

[68] See eg Case C-412/06 *Hamilton* [2008] ECR I-2383. Stephen Weatherill, 'Interpretation of the Directives: The Role of the Court' in Arthur Hartkamp et al. (eds), *Towards a European Civil Code* (2011) 185.

IV. Managed Harmonization

Harmonization law is not made according to a single and coherent plan run by an institution driven by clear and consistent ideas. It is not a perfect set of texts smoothly received and uniformly applied. On the contrary, it appears as a complex set of actions based on sectoral programmes, as the outcome of institutional initiatives, political compromises, and civil society inputs, as a set of networks involving EU and national public and private actors, as a mix of divergent elements and tendencies expressed in different areas of EU law, all interpenetrating each other and leading to a rather fragmented body of law. The result is a constant concern about coherence and a recent focus on management and monitoring.

As the harmonization programme gathered pace in the aftermath of the Single European Act, attention shifted to setting up governance mechanisms to improve the functioning of the internal market.[69] There has been a focus on the implementation of and compliance with harmonization rules, sometimes expressed in the motto: 'less regulation, better implementation' and captured by the Commission in a communication entitled, *A Europe of Results—Applying Community Law.*[70] Instead of intensifying the production of legislation, it was decided to 'extensify' it. The idea was to limit the adoption of new legislative texts while streamlining the decision-making process and enhancing the monitoring and surveillance of the application of existing legislation. Whether this has been a success is far from certain, but it has resulted in a broad structure of governance involving three distinct layers of actors and responsibilities: Union institutions and bodies, Member States and private actors.

1. The Responsibilities of Union Bodies

The Union's responsibilities are mainly of a political and administrative nature. Harmonization clearly entails a shift from the judiciary entrusted with the task of applying the free movement rules to the legislature and the administration. This shift is, however, reversible. Ambiguous or imprecise texts as well as texts filled with broad clauses or general principles inevitably lead to re-empowering the judicial process, giving the Court the opportunity to decide on how harmonization is to be applied. In fact, the special character and the many flaws of the Union

---

[69] Kenneth Armstrong and Simon Bulmer, *The Governance of the Single European Market* (1998); Michelle Egan, *Constructing a European Market* (2001); Shawn Donnelly, *The Regimes of European Integration: Constructing Governance in the Single Market* (2010).

[70] COM (2007) 512 final. And see recently Commission's proposal, 'Better Governance for the Single Market' (COM (2012) 259 final).

decision-making process make the Court a powerful actor in fashioning the harmonization programme.[71]

The process of setting harmonization standards involves a multiplicity of actors.
Member States participate in this process alongside the European legislature, ie
the Commission, the Council and the Parliament, which are assisted by a myriad
of committees and expert networks. This process entails a form of competition
of state as well as non-state interests and regulatory models.[72] In some cases, it
may not be too hard to trace the models relied upon during the drafting process
by looking at the broad and consensual recitals of the preamble of a legislative
act. More often than not, harmonization measures are based on a complex and
imperfect combination of different models. This is also the reason why numerous
pieces of legislation undergo adaptations and revisions after some years. This process of revision may result, depending on the context and the political balance, in
an exercise of deepening market integration through the elimination of obstacles
or distortions of competition that may have remained or emerged, as well as in a
strengthening of the level of protection of health or environment.

Under Article 114(3) TFEU, the legislature is required to aim for a high level of
protection as far as health, safety, environmental protection and consumer protection are concerned. However, the Court has made clear that the level of protection
does not necessarily have to be the highest possible. It is sufficient to show that this
aim has been taken into consideration in a serious manner.[73] The same broad discretion characterizes the choice of harmonization technique. This is particularly the
case in specific fields where the proposed approximation requires a highly technical
analysis or implies sensitive issues. The Court has therefore accepted that Article
114 could be used for establishing a complete regulatory infrastructure under which
a Union body would be granted the power to take decisions directed at individuals and to adopt measures that prevail over measures taken by specialized national
authorities.[74] Accordingly, a specific administrative system of intervention entailing
the replacement of national decision making may count as harmonization.

In *A Europe of Results*, the role of the Commission is crucial in ensuring that
internal market rules are applied and enforced. Accordingly, it has been provided
with a plethora of supervisory instruments. These mainly consist in obligations to

[71] See eg in relation to the protection of social rights, Claire Kilpatrick, 'Internal Market
Architecture and the Accommodation of Labour Rights: As Good as it Gets?' (2011) *EUI Working
Papers LAW* No. 2011/04.
[72] Adrienne Héritier, 'The Accommodation of Diversity in European Policy Making and its
Outcomes: Regulatory Policy as a Patchwork' (1996) n° 96/2 *European University Institute Working
Paper SPS*.
[73] Case C-233/94 *Germany v Parliament and Council* [1997] ECR I-2405, para 48.
[74] Case C-58/08 *ESMA* (n 31), paras 102-103; Case 66/04 *United Kingdom v Parliament and Council*
[2005] ECR I-10553, para 44; Case C-217/04 *United Kingdom v Parliament and Council* (2006) ECR
I-3771, para 44.

inform that is imposed on Member States, a power to request that Member States take all necessary measures, and investigation and prosecution powers against recalcitrant Member States through infringement proceedings.[75] The responsibilities clearly lie principally on the Member States.

2. Member States' Obligations

The first responsibility of the Member States is of course to correctly implement Union legislation. This may prove to be a burdensome exercise. Thus, for instance, in 2007 the Commission felt it necessary to publish a handbook on the implementation of the services Directive in order to give Member States technical assistance in the implementation process.[76] This text is a proper 'discourse on the method' amounting to a set of practical exercises. Part of these consists in screening thousands of domestic laws to assess their compatibility with the Directive's provisions or engaging in a 'mutual evaluation' exercise in cooperation with other Member States. This does not ensure that implementation is done perfectly. Incorrect implementation or failure to notify transposing measures of a Directive to the Commission may lead to the Member State being sanctioned under Article 260 TFEU.

National authorities are also under an obligation to inform the Commission of the introduction of new norms or standards which may have a restrictive effect on trade.[77] This obligation is justified by the idea that this information may supply the Commission with a possible basis for developing harmonization. Accordingly, the Court has famously stated that a failure to notify a draft technical standard renders the technical regulation adopted by the Member State concerned inapplicable.[78] This obligation to notify extends to national measures maintained or introduced after the adoption of a harmonization measure. This may be provided by individual directives[79] and a notification procedure is laid down in Article 114(6) for derogating national provisions justified on specific non-market grounds.

Finally, Member States are under an obligation, increasing in both intensity and scope, to cooperate and exchange mutual information.[80] Again, the services Directive provides an excellent example. It is arguable that the main added value of this legislation consists in establishing a system of mutual assistance by

---

[75] See eg Reg 2679/98 on the functioning of the internal market in relation to the free movement of goods among the Member States [1998] OJ L 337/8.

[76] COM (2012) 261 final.

[77] Dir 98/34 laying down a procedure for the provision of information in the field of technical standards and regulations [1998] OJ L 204/37.

[78] Case C-194/94 *CIA Security International* [1996] ECR I-2201.

[79] An example is given by Dir 2001/95 on general product safety [2002] L 11/4.

[80] Commission's Working Document, 'Administrative Cooperation in the Single Market' (SEC(2009) 881).

obliging Member States and their administrations to establish contact points and a European network of competent authorities, which may even include an exchange of officials. Cooperation and mutual assistance is aimed at facilitating access to service activities, promoting the quality of service provision and ensuring the supervision of providers and services. Furthermore, Member States must encourage the involvement of private actors in the regulatory process.[81]

3. The Role of Private Actors

Harmonization is addressed to Member States as regulators. It is an attempt to provide market participants and citizens with a legal environment in which production, trade, consumption, and all other sorts of activities are made secure and effective. Harmonized law is not supposed to directly involve or target private actors and relations. Market participants and citizens are supposed to enjoy the benefits of the internal market and to trust the effective collaboration of EU and national regulatory authorities.[82] And yet it is quite clear that private actors are deeply involved in harmonization. They are included in this exercise as co-regulators or efficient monitors of the smooth functioning of the market.

Firstly, under the new approach to harmonization, regulatory tasks have been delegated by the Union legislature to private European standardization bodies.[83] These bodies have been entrusted with the responsibility of managing the process for the elaboration of national and European technical standards. Co-regulation, whereby private parties are associated to the formation or implementation of rules, and self-regulation, whereby they are exclusively responsible for the elaboration of regulatory standards, have also been promoted in various sectors.[84] Secondly, private actors are in some cases assigned a major role in monitoring and ensuring that the regulatory objective incorporated in the harmonization measure is met. For instance, under the regulation on food law and food safety, food and feed operators are required, while being monitored by competent national authorities and subject to liability, to produce safe food, inform consumers and withdraw unfit food.[85] Other examples include the outstanding responsibility of data controllers

---

[81] See Art 37(1) of the services Directive (n 18).

[82] It follows in particular that Member States are bound to respect the freedom granted to private parties by the EU legislature (Case C-639/11, *Commission v Poland*, judgment of 20 March 2014, para 38).

[83] Jacques Pelkmans, 'The New Approach to Technical Harmonization and Standardization' (1987) 25 *Journal of Common Market Studies* 249.

[84] See eg in the sectors of services Vassilis Hatzopoulos, *Regulating Services in the European Union* (2012) 290–306.

[85] Reg 178/2002 on food law (n 37).

under the data protection Directive or the obligation on private actors to pass on information to Member States authorities.[86]

In the *Vodafone* case about roaming, Advocate General Poiares Maduro proposed to go one step further and to accept that harmonization may directly address and regulate the behaviour of private parties restricting free movement.[87] The Court rejected this proposal. This may be justified by the letter of Article 114 TFEU and more generally by the stance that harmonized law does not directly impact on private relationships but leaves it to national law to organize the enforcement of the rights and obligations provided for in EU law. However, it is quite evident that there are cases, such as the roaming case, in which the Member States have no clear interest in regulating and yet nonetheless require the intervention of the EU regulator. More generally, and despite the recurring statements to the contrary by the Commission, it must be acknowledged that EU harmonized law has profound consequences for large sectors of private relationships and, as a consequences, for all branches of national private law.[88] In fact this is a matter of real concern for private lawyers and for those concerned with the integrity of national legal systems.

In a ruling of 1985, the Court suggested that harmonization aims at bringing about a new era in which the population will become 'fully conscious' of the reality and the benefits of the common market.[89] How emphatic—indeed, optimistic—these words appear in today's context, in the aftermath of the financial crisis, in the middle of the Eurozone crisis, in light of the shortcomings of the harmonization *acquis*, with the lingering fragmentation of the internal market, and the widespread perception that the internal market is a place of desocialization and discrimination in favour of the mobile and the wealthy. But these words still make sense as a point of reference, as a welcome counter-point to institutional constructions which view the harmonization process as simply a form of management targeting the 'happy few' engaged in transnational activities.

What is harmonization? It is an enterprise in trade liberalization as well as a form of re-regulation, a set of standard legal formulas inseparable from a case-by-case analysis, an unbound and still poorly justified mode of action, a complex weave of legislative choices and constitutional requirements, a quest for uniformity and coherence anxious to accommodate plurality and diversity, a complex form of governance involving a bundle of various actors and layers of responsibility, and finally a combination of diligent management and genuine commitment. It

---

[86] See eg Case C-131/12 *Google Spain*, judgment of 13 May 2014 (data protection); Case C-40/04 *Yonemoto* [2005] ECR I-7755 (machinery); Case C-305/05, *Ordre des barreaux francophones et germanophone and others* [2007] ECR I-5305 (fight against money laundering).

[87] Opinion of AG Poiares Maduro in Case C-58/08 *Vodafone and others* (n 32), paras 19–21.

[88] Hugh Collins, *The European Civil Code. The Way Forward* (2008).

[89] Case 54/84 *Michael Paul* [1985] ECR 920, para 15.

is in light of these contradictions that harmonization emerges, an insuperable yet imperative task—a symbol of Europe's condition.

Bibliography

Antoine Bailleux, *Les interactions entre libre circulation et droits fondamentaux dans la jurisprudence communautaire. Essai sur la figure du juge traducteur* (2009)

Bruno de Witte, 'A Competence to Protect: The Pursuit of Non-Market Aims Through Internal Market Legislation' in P. Syrpis (ed), *The Judiciary, the Legislature and the EU Internal Market* (2011) 25

Michael Dougan, 'Minimum Harmonization and the Internal Market' (2000) 37 *Common Market Law Review* 853

Christine Janssens, *The Principle of Mutual Recognition in EU Law* (2013)

Isodora Maletic, *The Law and Policy of Harmonisation in Europe's Internal Market.* (2013)

Niamh Nic Shuibhne (ed), *Regulating the Internal Market* (2006)

Jacques Pelkmans, 'The New Approach to Technical Harmonization and Standardization' (1987) 25 *Journal of Common Market Studies* 249

Jérôme Porta, *La réalisation du droit communautaire. Essai sur le gouvernement juridique de la diversité* (2007)

Stephen Weatherill, 'Why Harmonise?' in Takis Tridimas and Paolo Nebbia (eds), *European Union Law for the Twenty-First Century: Rethinking the New Legal Order* (2003) 11

Stephen Weatherill, 'The Limits of Legislative Harmonization Ten Years After *Tobacco Advertising*: How the Court's Case Law has become a "Drafting Guide"' (2011) 12 *German Law Journal* 827

CHAPTER 24

··

COMPETITION AND MERGER LAW AND POLICY

··

OKEOGHENE ODUDU

I. Introduction

··

THE EU Treaties provide a system for the governance of competition within the European Union. This system is crafted from Articles 101 and 102 TFEU. Further important components of the system are contained in Regulation 139/2004, known as the European Merger Regulation (EUMR). Whilst the original text of the 1957 Treaties remains largely unchanged, a new understanding of competition law and of its role within the EU Treaties has emerged.[1] 'Modernization' re-orientates EU competition law to focus on the control of market power. A number ways in which problems of market power manifest themselves and the ways in which EU competition law can be, and has been, marshalled to address those problems are the subject of this chapter. This chapter covers the unilateral abuse of market power; cooperation or coordination giving rise to market power; and the control of durable changes in market structure that would otherwise give rise to market power.[2]

[1] Modernization is catalysed by B.E. Hawk, 'System Failure: Vertical Restraints and EC Competition Law' (1995) 32 *Common Market Law Review* 973 with the first shift being seen in Green Paper on Vertical Restraints in EC Competition Policy COM (96) 721 final.

[2] This chapter does not cover the licensing of intellectual property or procurement rules. Enforcement and state aid are the subject of chapters 26 and 27 in this volume.

II. The Concern with Market Power

The understanding of what it is necessary, possible, and desirable for the Treaties' competition provisions to achieve has evolved over time.[3] In the pre-modernization era EU competition law had been understood as orientated to achieve the Union objective of market integration.[4] This orientation was necessary at time when it was recognized that non-state actors may impede market integration. Market integration is advanced via the Treaties rules on free movement, but the extent to which the rules on free movement impose obligations on entities other than state actors and the nature of any obligation imposed has remained uncertain.[5] EU competition law was thus interpreted in a manner preventing non-state actors creating or maintaining impediments to market integration.[6] This understanding is clearly present in *Consten & Grundig*, it being considered that:

an agreement . . . which might tend to restore the national divisions in trade between Member States might be such as to frustrate the most fundamental [objectives] of the Community. The Treaty, whose preamble and content aim at abolishing the barriers between states, and which in several provisions gives evidence of a stern attitude with regard to their reappearance, could not allow undertakings to reconstruct such barriers. Article [101(1)] is designed to pursue this aim.[7]

---

[3] See David J. Gerber, *Law and Competition in Twentieth Century Europe: Protecting Prometheus* (2001).

[4] Albertina Albors-Llorens, 'Competition Policy and the Shaping of the Single Market' in Catherine Barnard and Joanne Scott (eds), *The Law of the Single European Market* (2002) 311; Ian S. Forrester, 'Competition Law Implementation at Present' in Claus Dieter Ehlermann and Laraine L. Laudati (eds), *European Competition Law Annual 1997: The Objectives of Competition Policy* (1998) 359; David J. Gerber, 'The Transformation of European Community Competition Law?' 35 *Harvard International Law Journal* (1994) 97; and Giuliano Marenco, 'The Birth of Modern Competition Law in Europe' in A. von Bogdandy, P.C. Mavroidis, and A. Mény (eds), *European Integration and International Co-ordination* (2002).

[5] Case 8/74 Procureur du Roi v Benoît and Gustave Dassonville [1974] ECR 837, para 5; Joined Cases 177/82 and 178/82 Criminal Proceedings against Jan van de Haar and Kaveka de Meern BV [1984] ECR 1797, para 12; Case 311/85 VZW Vereniging van Vlaamse Reisbureaus v VZW Sociale Dienst van de Plaatselijke en Gewestelijke Overheidsdiensten [1987] 3801, para 30; Case C-159/00 Sapod Audic v Eco-emballages SA [2002] ECR I-5031, para 74; Kamiel Mortelmans 'Towards Convergence in the Application of the Rules on Free Movement and on Competition?' (2001) 38 *CML Rev* 613–649 at 622–623, 635–636; Stefaan Van den Bogaert 'Horizontality: The Court Attacks?' in Catherine Barnard and Joanne Scott (eds) *The Law of the Single European Market Hart*, 2002) 123–152; and Michelle Cini, and Lee McGowan, *Competition Policy in the European Union* (Macmillan, 1998), 11, 32–33.

[6] Joseph J.A. Ellis, 'Source Material for Article 85(1) EEC' (1963) 32 *Fordham Law Review* 247, 248–265; Giuliano Marenco, 'Competition between National Economies and Competition between Businesses—a Response to Judge Pescatore' (1987) 10 *Fordham International Law Journal* 420, 429–430; Green Paper on Vertical Restraints in EC Competition Policy COM (96) 721 Final [1997] 4 CMLR 519, paras 70–84; OECD, 'Complementarities between Trade and Competition Policies' COM/TD/DAFFE/CLP(98)98/Final (1999), 5; and Guidelines on Vertical Restraints [2000] OJ C291/1, para 7.

[7] Cases 56 and 58/64 Établissements Consten Sàrl and Grundig-Verkaufs-Gmbh v Commission [1966] ECR 299, 340.

Once the internal market was formally completed the conception of competition law as a tool of market integration began to wane.[8] At this point, a conception of competition law that differed from free movement began to emerge.[9] As AG Capotorti had earlier noted: 'There is a distinction between Articles [34] and [35] on the one hand and Articles [101] and [102] on the other, not only with regard to those subject to the prohibitions but also with regard to the nature of the behaviour which is prohibited.'[10]

If 'modernization' does not reinvent or repurpose EU competition law, at the very least it re-imagines, refocuses, and redirects EU competition law towards a concern with market power.[11] This modern concern is reflected in the new style of block exemption Regulations; the Commission's package of Guidelines and soft law instruments that set out how competition law ought to be applied; and revised modes of enforcement that place greater emphasis on the role of private parties, national courts, and national competition authorities.[12]

---

[8] Julio Baquero Cruz, *Between Competition and Free Movement: The Economic Constitutional Law of the European Community* (2002) 100–101; David J. Gerber, 'The Transformation of European Community Competition Law?' (1994) 35 *Harvard International Law Journal* 97, 143–145; and Rein Wesseling, *The Modernisation of EC Antitrust Law* (2000) 48–50. Though see Cases C-403 and 429/08 Premier League Ltd v QC Leisure and Murphy v Media Protection Services Ltd, 4 October 2011, para 139 (Art 101); Cases C-468–478/06 Sot. Lélos kai Sia EE v GlaxoSmithKline AEVE Farmakeftikon Proïonton [2008] ECR I-7139, paras 65–66 (Art 102), indicating that the market integration objective has a continuing vitality.

[9] C-369/04 *Hutchison 3G v Commission* [2007] ECR I-5247, paras 36 and 38 and Laurence W. Gormley 'Competition and Free Movement: Is the Internal Market the Same as the Common Market?' (2002) 13 *European Business Law Review* 517.

[10] Case 82/77 *van Tiggele* [1978] ECR 25, 42. See also Stefaan van den Bogaert, 'Horizontality: The Court Attacks?' in Catherine Barnard and Joanne Scott (eds), *The Law of the Single European Market* (2002) 123, and Piet Jan Slot 'The Application of Articles 3(F), 5 and 85 to 94 EEC' (1987) 12 *European Law Review* 179.

[11] Luis Ortiz Blanco, *Market Power in EU Antitrust Law* (2012). For a view that market power, or at least the tests for market power, do not determine the limits of competition law intervention see M.R. Patterson 'The Market Power Requirement in Antitrust Rule of Reason Cases: A Rhetorical History' (2000) 37 *San Diego Law Review* 1.

[12] Green Paper on Vertical Restraints in EC Competition Policy COM (96) 721 final [1997] 4 CMLR 519, para 54, 65, 82, 85; Communication from the Commission on the Application of the Community Competition Rules to Vertical Restraints (Follow-up to the Green Paper on Vertical Restraints) COM(98)544 final [1998] OJ C365/3, 4, 9, 12, 21; White Paper on Modernisation of the Rules Implementing Articles 85 and 86 of the EC Treaty Commission Programme No 99/027 [1999] OJ C132/1; Commission Regulation (EC) No 2790/1999 [1999] OJ L 336/21, now Commission Regulation (EU) No 330/2010 of 20 April 2010 on the application of Article 101(3) of the Treaty on the Functioning of the European Union to categories of vertical agreements and concerted practices [2010] OJ L102/1; and Guidelines on Vertical Restraints [2000] OJ C291/1, now Commission Notice—Guidelines on Vertical Restraints [2010] C130/1; White Paper on Reform of Regulation 17: Summary of the Observations [2001] 4 CMLR 10; Council Regulation (EC) No 1/2003 [2003] OJ L1/1, and generally, http://europa.eu/documents/comm/white_papers/pdf/com99_101_en.pdf. Guidelines on the applicability of Article 101 of the Treaty on the Functioning of the European Union to horizontal co-operation agreements [2011] OJ C11/1, para 28; Horizontal Merger Guidelines [2004] OJ C 31/5, para 8; and Non-Horizontal Merger Guidelines [2008] OJ C265/6, para 23.

The modern understanding of EU competition law begins with the premise that markets work well only when market participants lack power in that market. Absent power the producer is required to offer the best quality goods or services to customers or consumers at the lowest possible price. The presence of market power is understood to be harmful in at least three ways. First, producers with market power are able to contrive a scarcity of output, refusing to supply some customers that could profitably be supplied.[13] The reduced output commands a higher price that more than compensates the producer for its diminished sales.[14] Consumers not supplied by the producer either consume nothing or instead consume an alternative good or service they desire less than that which the producer with market power has refused to produce. A second concern is that producers with market power may be less *willing* or less *able* to minimize production costs, and so consume more resources to generate a given level of output than would be consumed by a producer without market power producing the same level of output.[15] To this can be added the costs associated with obtaining or maintaining market power, expenditure that is not always socially useful.[16] A third concern is that producers with market power are less *willing* or *able* to innovate than producers lacking market power.[17] Even when a producer's market power is the result of prior innovation, that producer may seek to prevent others from developing innovations that could erode its power.[18]

EU competition law's explicit focus on market power, as distinct from other forms of power, and as distinct from other concerns, is relatively new and the extent to which market power excludes or overshadows all other concerns remains controversial.[19] An acceptance that EU competition law is to be used primarily

[13] F.M. Scherer and D. Ross, *Industrial Market Structure and Economic Performance* (3rd ed, 1990) 15–55.

[14] A.P. Lerner 'The Concept of Monopoly and the Measurement of Monopoly Power' 1 *Review of Economic Studies* (1934) 157, 157–165; Robert H. Bork *The Antitrust Paradox: A Policy at War with Itself* (1993) 90; and Richard A. Posner, *Antitrust Law: An Economic Perspective* (1976) 8–10.

[15] Massimo Motta, *Competition Policy: Theory and Practice* (2004) 46–49; Jean Tirole *The Theory of Industrial Organization* (1988) 75; Roger S. Frantz, *X-Efficiency: Theory, Evidence and Applications* (1988) 54, 64–65; and Alexander Schaub 'Competition Policy Objectices' in Claus Dieter Ehlermann and Laraine L Laudati (eds), *European Competition Law Annual 1997: The Objectives of Competition Policy* (1998) 119, 120.

[16] Roger Frantz 'X-Efficiency and Allocative Efficiency: What Have We Learned?' (1992) 82 *American Economic Review* 434, 436–437 and Richard A. Posner, 'The Social Costs of Monopoly and Regulation' (1975) 83 *Journal of Political Economy* 807, 809.

[17] Walter Adams 'Competition, Monopoly and Countervailing Power' (1953) 67 *Quarterly Journal of Economics* 469, 478–480; Dennis W. Carlton and Jeffrey M. Perloff *Modern Industrial Organization* (3rd ed, 2000) 533; and F.M. Scherer 'Schumpeter and Plausible Capitalism' (1992) 30 *Journal of Economic Literature* 1416, 1425–1430.

[18] Phillip A. Beutel, 'The Intersection of Antitrust and Intellectual Property Economics: A Schumpeterian View' (November/December 2002) *Antitrust Insights: NERA Newsletter* 1.

[19] Rein Wesseling, 'The Draft-Regulation Modernising the Competition Rules: The Commission Is Married to One Idea' 26 *European Law Review* (2001) 357; Monopolkommission, *Cartel Policy*

or exclusively to resolve problems of market power would not end all debate. EU competition law and policy has developed in the context of both continuing scepticism about the robustness of markets and a deep faith in the ability of regulators to intervene and correct problems with the functioning of those markets. This is in contrast to the 'Chicago' position, which holds a deep faith in the self-correcting nature of markets and little confidence in judicial or regulatory intervention. When markets exist, when market power exists, and when the existence or exercise of market power is problematic, and thus how the law should react to market power, remain subjects of intense debate. The judicial attitude to competition policy based (exclusively) on a concern with market power remains to be fully tested.

III. The Identification of Market Activity

Being concerned with market power, EU competition law can be applied only in relation to market activity.[20] Market activity exists, for the purpose of EU competition law, when an entity offers goods or services to meet a customer or consumer demand, but only when there is potential to make profit from that activity. Market (or economic) activity involves the interaction of supply and demand in a manner that enables the producer to profit from the interaction. This idea of market activity emerges from the Court's jurisprudence relating to the activities of undertakings.[21]

Change in the European Union? On the European Commission's White Paper of 28th April 1999; Special Report by the German Monopolies Commission Pursuant to Sec. 44, Para. 1 of the Act against Restraints of Competition (Gwb) (2000) 35–37; Mario Siragusa, 'A Critical Review of the White Paper on the Reform of the EC Competition Law Enforcement Rules' (2000) 23 *Fordham International Law Journal* 1089, 1100–1102; Robert Pitofsky, 'Antitrust Modified: Education, Defense, and Other Worthy Enterprises' (1995) 9 *Antitrust* 23; Eleanor M. Fox, 'The Elusive Promise of Modernisation: Europe and the World' (2001) 28 *Legal Issues of Economic Integration* 141; C. Townley 'Which Goals Count in Article 101 TFEU? Public Policy and its Discontents' (2011) 9 *European Competition Law Review* 441; and O. Odudu 'The Wider Concerns of Competition Law' (2010) 30 *Oxford Journal of Legal Studies* 599.

   [20] Case T-313/02 *Meca-Medina* [2004] ECR II-3291, paras 37 and 41; Case C-309/99 *Wouters* [2002] ECR I-1577, para 57; Green Paper on Services of General Interest COM (2003) 270 final, para 43 and Communication from the Commission—Services of General Interest in Europe [2001] OJ C17/4, para 28.

   [21] The activity of an undertaking is nowhere defined in the EU Treaties. Art 1 of Protocol 22 to the EEA Treaty considers the activities of an undertaking to be as 'any entity carrying out activities of a commercial or economic nature'.

Articles 101 and 102 TFEU apply only to the activities of undertakings.[22] The Court of Justice in *Höfner* defines the activity of an undertaking as 'economic activity, regardless of the legal status of the entity and the way in which it is financed'.[23]

1. The Interaction of Supply and Demand

Market activity involves the coordination of supply and demand. The demand side is normally occupied by entities providing remuneration for the goods or services provided. Ordinarily, the entity providing remuneration also receives the benefit of the good or service and is seen as the customer or consumer to whom the supply side is responsive. Markets to which competition law can be applied exist only in relation to demand sides to which a supply side is responsive. In some situations the recipient of the goods or services does not provide remuneration. Examples of third-party payment are services funded by insurance or services funded by the state.[24] In third-party payment situations the supply side may respond to the entity providing remuneration, to the entity receiving the benefit of the good or service, to both, or to neither.

Entities offering goods or services occupy the supply side.[25] The identification of supply-side actors is not normally problematic. However, the fact that an entity is entitled to collect revenue from the demand side does not mean it is offering goods or services in a market.[26] Supply and demand may not interact if the supply side collects revenue on a basis that is decoupled from the quantity or quality of goods and services supplied.[27] As noted by AG Jacobs in *Cisal*, an essential element of market activity is that 'contributions and benefits are linked'.[28] When supply is not related to the revenue collected, the basis on which those fees are collected begins to resemble taxation rather than remuneration for services rendered.[29]

---

[22] Undertaking has the same meaning under both Arts 101 and 102: Case T-68/89 *Società Italiano Vetro* [1992] ECR II-1403, para 358.

[23] Case C-41/1990 *Klaus Höfner and Fritz Elser v Macrotron Gmbh* [1991] ECR I 1979 para 21.

[24] It is recognized under Art 56 TFEU that market activity exists even then there is third-party payment: Case 352/85 *Bond van Adverteerders and others v The Netherlands* [1988] ECR 2085, para 16; Case 196/8 *Steymann v Staatssecretaris van Justitie* [1988] ECR 6159, para 12; and Gareth Davies, 'Welfare as a Service' 29 *Legal Issues of Economic Integration* (2002) 27.

[25] Case 118/85 *Commission v Italy*, para 7; Joined Cases C-180/98 to C-184/98 *Pavel Pavlov and others v Stichting Pensioenfonds Medische Specialisten* [2000] ECR I-6451, para 75; Case C-218/00 Cisal AG Opinion, para 38; and Case T-319/99 *Federación Nacional de Empresas de Instrumentación Científica, Médica, Técnica y Dental (Fenin) v Commission* [2003] ECR II-357, paras 36–37.

[26] Case 30/87 *Bodson v Pompes Funèbres des Régions Libérées SA* [1988] ECR 2479 para 18, AG Opinion, para 94.

[27] Case C-218/00 Cisal AG Opinion, para 81. Case C-67/96 *Albany International*, paras 78–79, AG Opinion, para 342, and Joined Cases C-159/91 and C-160/91 *Poucet and Pistre*, paras 10, 15.

[28] Case C-218/00 Cisal AG Opinion, para 62, also para 80.

[29] C-369/04 *Hutchison 3G*, paras 36, 38; Case C-70/95 *Sodemare SA, Anni Azzurri Holding SpA, Anni Azzurri Rezzato Srl v Regione Lombardia* [1997] ECR I-3395 AG Opinion, para 29; Leigh

2. The Potential to Make Profit

A further element of market activity is the potential for the supply side to profit from the goods or services it offers.[30] It is not necessary for the producer actually to make a profit, nor is a profit-making motive necessary.[31] Consequently, charities, professional associations, and state entities have all been found capable of participating in market activity.[32]

Circumstances in which it is not possible to profit from the offer of goods or services have been identified. A unifying feature seems to be that a service, for it is services rather than goods that are at issue, is non-excludable.[33] This means that those producing the service cannot prevent those that have not paid for the service from benefiting from the provision of that service. In *Eurocontrol* the Court of Justice accepted that it is impossible to profit from services that customers or consumers can enjoy even if they do not pay the provider for those services, air traffic control services being at issue in that case.[34] In order to function effectively, it is necessary to provide air traffic control services even to airlines that have not paid for the service. AG Tesauro noted that:

the fact we are dealing with a service, not in the economic sense and provided principally for businesses (airline companies), but aimed at the community as a whole, seems to me to be confirmed by the observation made during the hearing . . . that control is exercised in respect of any aircraft, within the air space under the authority of Eurocontrol, irrespective of whether or not the owner has paid the route charges.[35]

Hancher and Jose-Luis Buendia Sierra 'Cross-Subsidization and EC Law' (1998) 35 *Common Market Law Review* 901; and Giuseppe B. Abbamonte 'Cross-subsidisation and Community Competition Rules: Efficient Pricing versus Equity?' (1998) 23 *European Law Review* 414.

[30] This element is more clearly expressed in the Opinions of a number of AGs than it is in the decisions of the Court, in particular in Case C-343/95 *Diego Calì* AG Opinion, para 32; Joined Cases C-159/91 and C-160/91 *Poucet and Pistre* AG Opinion, paras 7–8; Case C-364/92 *Eurocontrol* AG Opinion, para 9; *FFSA* AG Opinion, para 11; Case C-218/00 *Cisal* AG Opinion, para 38; Case T-128/98 *Aéroports de Paris* [2000] ECR II-3929, para 124; Case C-67/96 *Albany International* AG Opinion, para 311; and Joined Cases C-264/01, C-306/01, C-354/01, and C-355/01 *AOK* AG Opinion, para 27.

[31] Joined Cases C-209/78 to C-215/78 and C-218/78 *van Landewyck v Commission* [1980] ECR 3125, para 88. However, compare with Case C-67/96 *Albany International*, para 74, AG Opinion, paras 214, 311, 338, and Joined Cases C-264/01, C-306/01, C-354/01 and C-355/01 *AOK*, paras 47, 51.

[32] Case C-309/99 *Wouters v Algemene Raad Van De Nederlandse Orde Van Advocaten (Raad van de Balies van de Europese Gemeenschap, Intervening)* [2002] ECR I 1577; Case C-41/1990 *Klaus Höfner and Fritz Elser v Macrotron Gmbh* [1991] ECR I 1979; and Completed Merger of Senior Link Eldercare and Aid Call Resulting from the Completed Merger between Help the Aged and Age Concern England: The OFT's Decision on Reference under Section 22(2)(a) Given on 21 July 2009, Office of Fair Trading (2009).

[33] Stiglitz *Economics of the Public Sector* at 128–129 and Buendia Sierra *Exclusive Rights and State Monopolies under EC Law*, paras 1.158–1.159, 1.188–1.190, 1.198–1.201.

[34] Case C-364/92 *Eurocontrol*, para 16.

[35] Case C-364/92 *Eurocontrol* AG Opinion, para 13.

3. The Identification of Competitive Constraints

The identification of the most immediate or powerful constraints faced by those engaged in market activity is a fundamental stage in the process of identifying and eradicating problems of market power.[36] Important constraints may exist on the demand side or the supply side.[37] Constraints are imposed by the goods or services to which a sufficient number of customers would switch, as the possibility of switching limits the behaviour in which a provider of a particular good or service may engage. Similarly, those not producing, but capable of producing the good or service, also constrain the behaviour of those currently providing the particular goods or services. It is not necessary that all customers, or even a majority of customers, are willing and able to switch in order that behaviour be constrained. If a sufficient number of customers are willing and able to switch in the event of deterioration in service or performance on the part of the supplier a deterioration in performance may be discouraged.[38]

The Court of Justice uses a qualitative method to identify the constraints faced by a provider of goods or services, asking what consumers regard as interchangeable or substitutable, by reason of the products' characteristics, their prices, and their intended use.[39] The Commission accepts that a range of quantitative techniques may be used to identify constraints on a providers' market conduct.[40]

Whether it is determined qualitatively or quantitatively, it is important to recognize the limitations of any particular method used to identify competitive constraints. Over-enforcement may occur if the method used identifies few constraints on behaviour, when the reality is that there are many. Under-enforcement may occur if the method used identifies many constraints when the reality is that there are few. One problem is that the search for competitive constraints normally examines alternatives to the good or service at the prevailing price. However, the

---

[36] C. Veljanovski 'Markets without Substitutes: Substitution versus Constraints as the Key to Market Definition' (2010) 31 *European Competition Law Review* 122. On whether this stage of analysis is necessary see Case T-62/98 *Volkswagen Ag v Commission* [2000] ECR II 2707, paras 230–231; J. Farrell and C. Shapiro, 'Antitrust Evaluation of Horizontal Mergers: An Economic Alternative to Market Definition' (2010) 10 *B.E. Journal of Theoretical Economics*, Art 9; and J. Farrell and C. Shapiro, 'Recapture, Pass-through, and Market Definition' (2010) 76 *Antitrust Law Journal* 585.

[37] Market Definition Notice, OJ 1997 C372/5, para 13 and J. Baker, 'Market Definition: An Analytical Overview' (2007) 74 *Antitrust Law Journal* 129. External constraints on behaviour may also exist—regulation being the paradigm example. These are not typically identified during the market definition stage.

[38] This insight is captured in critical loss analysis, on which, see Barry C. Harris and Cento G. Veljanovski, 'Critical Loss Analysis: Its Growing Use in Competition Law' (2003) 24 *European Competiton Law Review* 213.

[39] Case 85/76 *Hoffmann-La Roche v Commission* [1979] ECR 461, para 28; Case 322/81 *Michelin v Commission* [1983] ECR 3461, para 37; and Commission Notice on the definition of relevant market for the purposes of Community competition law [1997] OJ C 372/05, para 2.

[40] Commission Notice (n 39) and European Commission, 'Economic Evidence in Merger Control', Competition Committee, Working Party No 3, OECD, 15 February 2011.

possibility that the prevailing price is not a competitive price must be taken into account.[41] Otherwise, the constraints identified do so only when and because the undertaking is already charging a supra-competitive price, a phenomenon some-times referred to as 'the cellophane fallacy' as it was first identified in critiques of a case identifying a wide range of alternatives to cellophane or clingfilm only because the firm was charging supra-competitive prices.[42] As described in *United States v Eastman Kodak*, 'at a high enough price, even poor substitutes look good to the consumer'.[43] A second issue is that the information available to carry out the identification of competitive constraints may be incomplete or otherwise defec-tive. Finally, it should be remembered that what constrains market behaviour may change over time as conditions of competition evolve.[44] It is therefore necessary to use a variety of methods to establish the robustness of the alternative market constraints identified.[45]

IV. The Use of Article 102 to Control Market Power

Article 102 may be used to address problems of market power when those problems are caused by an undertaking occupying a dominant position within the internal market or a substantial part of it.[46] This use of Article 102 relies on an interpreta-tion of dominance that captures entities with market power. The conduct of such undertakings can then be examined to assess whether or not market power is being abused. Whilst this interpretation of Article 102 falls within the accepted under-standing of Article 102, there is debate as to whether Article 102 is broader, and so is being used, and may legitimately be used, to address problems not concerned with market power.[47]

---

[41] Commission Notice (n 39) para 19.

[42] Commission Notice (n 39) para 19 and *U.S. v EI du Pont de Nemours and Co* 351 US 377 (1956).

[43] *United States v Eastman Kodak* Co 853 F Supp 1454 (WD NY).

[44] Case T-210/01 *General Electric v Commission* [2005] ECR II-5575, para 118.

[45] Commission Notice on the definition of relevant market for the purposes of Community com-petition law [1997] OJ C372/5, para 25.

[46] See Case C-209/10 *Post Danmark*, paras 41–43; Communication from the Commission—Guidance on the Commission's enforcement priorities in applying Article 82 of the EC Treaty to abu-sive exclusionary conduct by dominant undertakings [2009] OJ C45/7, paras 28–31; and Economic Advisory Group for Competition Policy (EAGCP), Gual et al, 'An Economic Approach to Article 82' http://ec.europa.eu/dgs/competition/economist/eagcp_july_21_05.pdf, 116–120.

[47] P. Lowe 'DG Competition's Review of the Policy on Abuse of Dominance', *Annual Proceedings Fordham Corporate Law Institute* (2004) 163.

1. Market Power and Dominance

The dominance requirement under Article 102 functions as a filter, setting a threshold that must be passed before the competitive consequences of the undertaking's conduct can be assessed. The dominance requirement prevents over-enforcement and focuses administrative resources on situations most likely to be most harmful.[48] There is no universally applicable test to determine whether and when scrutiny under Article 102 TFEU ought to be triggered, the Commission and the Court instead relying on a variety of indicators to determine whether scrutiny of conduct under Article 102 is warranted.[49]

In *Hoffmann-La Roche*, the Court of Justice defined a dominant undertaking as one with the ability 'to behave to an appreciable extent independently of its competitors, its customers and ultimately of the consumers'.[50] The General Court in particular, in *AstraZeneca*, increasingly equates this idea of independence from competitors and consumers with the concept of a degree of market power sufficient to confer the ability to make profitable sales whilst lowering quality or quantity or increasing prices or without innovating.[51]

(a) Market Share

The principal practical determinant of dominance is market share.[52] As described by Landes and Posner: 'The standard method of proving market power . . . involves first defining a relevant market in which to compute the defendant's market share, next computing that share, and then deciding whether it is large enough to support an inference of the required degree of market power.'[53] The Commission's Enforcement Priorities state: 'Experience suggests that the higher the market share and the longer the period of time over which it is held, the more likely it is that it constitutes an important preliminary indication of the existence of a dominant position.'[54]

---

[48]   Jonathan Faull, Ali Nikpay, and Deirdre Taylor, *Faull & Nikpay the EU Law of Competition* (3rd ed, 2014) para 4.137 and John Vickers 'Abuse of Market Power' (2005) 115 *Economic Journal* F244.

[49]   Guidelines on Vertical Restraints [2000] OJ C291/1, paras 120–136.

[50]   Case 85/76 *Hoffmann-La Roche v Commission* [1979] ECR 461, para 38.

[51]   Case T-321/05 *AstraZeneca v Commission* [2010] ECR II-2805, para 267; Case C-457/10 P *AstraZeneca v Commission* [2012] ECR I-000, 6 December 2012, paras 177–181; Communication from the Commission—Guidance on the Commission's enforcement priorities in applying Article 82 of the EC Treaty to abusive exclusionary conduct by dominant undertakings [2009] OJ C45/7, para 8; and Giorgio Monti, *EC Competition Law* (2007) 127–130.

[52]   It has been cautioned that market share is merely 'a useful first indication' of market power: Communication from the Commission (n 51), para 13; Case T-321/05 *AstraZeneca v Commission*, para 244; Elzinga, Kenneth G., 'Unmasking Monopoly: Four Types of Economic Evidence' in Robert J. Larner and James W. Meehan Jr (eds), *Economics and Antitrust Policy* (1989) 16; and Richard A. Posner *Antitrust Law: An Economic Perspective* (1976) 55–56.

[53]   William M. Landes and Richard A. Posner, 'Market Power in Antitrust Cases' (1981) 94 *Harvard Law Review* 937, 938, also 958–960.

[54]   Communication from the Commission (n 51), para 15.

The Court of Justice has accepted the persistence of large market shares over time as a strong indication that the undertaking occupies a dominant position or possesses market power.[55] Market shares of between 70–80 per cent are a clear indication of dominance.[56] In *Akzo*, the Court established a presumption that dominance exists, and scrutiny of conduct under Article 102 TFEU is warranted, in relation to undertakings with a market share above 50 per cent.[57] Examination under Article 102 may occur even when an undertaking supplies fewer than 50 per cent of the customers in a relevant market.[58] However, it would seem that an Article 102 examination is unlikely to be triggered in relation to undertakings supplying below 30 per cent of the market.[59]

Scrutiny of conduct under Article 102 may be triggered not only when an undertaking possesses a large *absolute* market share, but also when the proportion of the market supplied by an undertaking is large *relative* to that supplied by others in the market. In *BA v Commission*, over a seven-year period, BA supplied between 530 per cent and 1286 per cent more of the market than did its nearest rival.[60] The General Court drew attention to 'the highly significant indicator [of dominance] which is . . . the *ratio between the market share held by the undertaking concerned and that of its nearest rivals*'.[61] It is important also to consider how market shares have evolved over time. It has been argued that Article 102 scrutiny is not warranted in relation to undertakings with fluctuating or declining market shares.[62] However, even the conduct of undertakings with a declining share of the market, and facing competitors that are increasing their market share, has been scrutinized under Article 102.[63] This is because an undertaking may engage in certain behaviour designed to hinder the progress of rivals, and intervention is warranted in such circumstances.

---

[55] Case 85/76 *Hoffmann-La Roche*, paras 39–41 and 48 and Case T-219/99 *BA v Commission*, para 210.

[56] Case T-321/05 *AstraZeneca v Commission*, para 243

[57] Case C-62/86 AKZO *Chemie v Commission* [1991] ECR I-3359, para 60 and R. O'Donoghue and A.J. Padilla, *The Law and Economics of Article 102* (2nd edn, 2013), 148.

[58] eg Case 27/76 *United Brands v Commission* [1978] ECR 207, paras 108–129 (40–45 per cent) and Case T-219/99 *British Airways v Commission* [2003] ECR II-5917, paras 189–225 (39.7 per cent).

[59] Communication from the Commission (n 51) para 14; Commission Notice on agreements of minor importance which do not appreciably restrict competition under Article 101(1) of the Treaty on the Functioning of the European Union (de Minimis Notice) Brussels, 25.6.2014 C (2014) 4136 final, paras 8–11; Commission Notice of 5 December 2013 on a simplified procedure for treatment of certain concentrations under Council Regulation (EC) No 139/2004 [2013] OJ C366/05, recital 32.

[60] Case T-219/99 *British Airways*, para 211; and Commission Decision 2000/74/EC Virgin/BA [2000] OJ L30/1, paras 47, 88, 90–94.

[61] Case T-219/99 *British Airways*, para 210, emphasis added.

[62] Case T-219/99 *British Airways*, paras 121, 175–176, 178, 181–183; M. Motta, *Competition Policy: Theory and Practice* (2004) 120; and D. Geradin et al, 'The Concept of Dominance' in D. Geradin (ed), *GCLC Research Papers on Article 82 EC* (2005) 6–37, 19.

[63] Virgin/BA [2000] OJ L30/1, paras 36, 41, 102, 107. Compare with the more recent Case C-209/10 *Post Danmark*, para 39 in which the Court attached significance to the competitor's ability to maintain its market share.

(b) Barriers to Entry

The easier it is for a new firm to begin to supply goods or services the less likely it is that those currently supplying such goods and services possess market power, since consumers will be able to switch to a new source of supply should prices increase or quality decline. An analysis of conduct under Article 102 may be warranted in markets in which certain factors reduce the speed and ability of other undertakings to supply the goods or services when customers which to switch.[64] These factors are known as barriers to entry or expansion. The existence of barriers is reflected by an incumbent's ability persistently to impose charges above the cost of production without attracting new competitors into the market.

There is no EU law definition of relevant barriers to entry, though it is useful to distinguish between incumbent and entrant firms, even though this may not identify all barriers.[65] Barriers can then be seen as advantages incumbents have over potential entrants.[66] The Commission's Guidance on Article 102 gives the following as examples of barriers to entry:

They may be legal barriers, such as tariffs or quotas, or they may take the form of advantages specifically enjoyed by the dominant undertaking, such as economies of scale and scope, privileged access to essential inputs or natural resources, important technologies . . . or an established distribution and sales network . . . The dominant undertaking's own conduct may also create barriers to entry, for example where it has made significant investments which entrants or competitors would have to match . . . or where it has concluded long-term contracts with its customers that have appreciable foreclosing effects.[67]

Entry barriers may be structural, such as economies of scale and cost advantages.[68] Structural barriers are distinct from strategic barriers, which involve efforts by incumbents to keep potential competitors out of the marketplace.[69] Investment in capacity, advertising, choice of location, research and development, and vertical integration can all be used to deter entry.[70] It may also be the case that an

---

[64] Communication from the Commission (n 51) para 16; Guidelines on the Assessment of Horizontal Mergers under the Council Regulation on the Control of Concentrations between Undertakings [2004] OJ C31/5, paras 68–75; M. Motta *Competition Policy: Theory and Practice* (2004) 73–75; and Richard A. Posner, *Antitrust Law: An Economic Perspective* (1976) 49–50, 57–59.

[65] Harold Demsetz, 'Barriers to Entry' (1982) 72 *American Economic Review* 47, 48–49.

[66] Joe Staten Bain, *Barriers to New Competition: Their Character and Consequences in Manufacturing Industries* (1993) 3.

[67] Communication from the Commission (n 51) para 17.

[68] Bain (n 66), 54–55, 98–109, 114–116, 144–147; Dennis W. Carlton and Jeffrey M. Perloff, *Modern Industrial Organization* (3rd ed, 2000) 79.

[69] William S. Comanor 'Vertical Mergers, Market Powers, and Antitrust Laws' (1967) 57 *American Economic Review* 254, 261; London Economics, *Barriers to Entry and Exit in UK Competition Policy*, Office of Fair Trading Report 2 (1994) 7.

[70] David Encaoua, Paul Geroski, and Alexis Jacquemin, 'Strategic Competition and the Persistence of Dominant Firms: A Survey' in Joseph E. Stiglitz, and G. Frank Mathewson (eds), *New Developments in the Analysis of Market Structure: Proceedings of a Conference Held by the International Economic Association in Ottawa, Canada* (1986) 56; Steven C. Salop, 'Strategic Entry

incumbent's possession of a portfolio or range of goods or services may deter market entry.[71] In finding dominance the General Court has taken account of 'the extent of the range' offered by an undertaking when such a range makes the undertaking an obligatory trading partner.[72]

(c) Countervailing Power

An examination of conduct under Article 102 may be unwarranted when the customers or consumers in the market possess what is known as countervailing power.[73] This exists when a purchaser of a significant quantity of goods or services has sufficient alternatives to ensure the supplier has little or no incentive to increase price or reduce quality to the market as a whole.[74] Undertakings on the supply side are then unable to exercise market power.[75] The existence of countervailing power is thus claimed to 'relieve . . . the government of its obligation—imposed by the now antiquated antitrust laws—to launch any frontal attack on concentrated economic power'.[76] In *Italian Flat Glass*, the General Court considered the threshold for examining conduct under Article 102 had not been satisfied when the Commission failed to examine whether the buyer in the market could exercise countervailing power.[77]

(d) Conduct

There exists the possibility that competition is harmed by the unilateral conduct of an undertaking that we are unable to identify as dominant.[78] In such circumstances the need to establish dominance before the prohibition can be applied will

---

Deterrence' 69 (1979) *American Economic Review* 335; and Steven C. Salop (ed), *Strategy, Predation, and Antitrust Analysis* (1981).

[71] Guidelines on the assessment of non-horizontal mergers under the Council Regulation on the control of concentrations between undertakings [2008] OJ C265/07, paras 93–118.

[72] Case T-219/99 *British Airways*, para 187, 212–217 and van den Bergh Foods [1998] OJ L246/1, paras 64–68.

[73] Communication from the Commission (n 51) para 18 and Guidelines on the assessment of horizontal mergers under the Council regulation on the control of concentrations between undertakings [2004] OJ C31/5, paras 64–67.

[74] Case T-228/97 *Irish Sugar* [1999] ECR II-2969, para 100 and Communication from the Commission (n 51) para 18.

[75] John Kenneth Galbraith, *American Capitalism: The Concept of Countervailing Power* (1957) 111–123; Alex Hunter, 'Notes on Countervailing Power' (1958) 68 *Economic Journal* 89, 103; and Paul W. Dobson and Michael Waterson, 'Countervailing Power and Consumer Prices' (1997) 107 *Economic Journal* 418, 420–426.

[76] Walter Adams 'Competition, Monopoly and Countervailing Power' (1953) 67 *Quarterly Journal of Economics* (1953) 469, 472.

[77] Joined Cases T-68/89, 77/89 and 78/89 Società Italiana Vetro, Fabbrica Pisana and PPG Vernante Pennitalia v Commission [1992] ECR II-1403, para 366.

[78] Steven C. Salop, 'The First Principles Approach to Antitrust, Kodak, and Antitrust at the Millennium' (2000) 68 *Antitrust Law Journal* 187.

lead to under-enforcement. It has been suggested that the assessment of conduct should not be separate from the determination of dominance.[79] Instead, the finding that an undertaking has harmed competition unilaterally indicates that the requirement of dominance has been satisfied. The logic may also be reversed, so that the behaviour of the undertaking may indicate that it is not dominant. For example, the fact that an undertaking has lowered its prices in response to a competitor has been recognized by the Court as 'incompatible with that independent conduct which is the hallmark of a dominant position'.[80]

2. Abuse

It has long been the mantra of students of Article 102 that the provision does not prohibit dominance, only its abuse.[81] An undertaking with market power is under a special responsibility not to allow its conduct to impair genuine undistorted competition.[82] Article 102 is used to control the conduct of undertakings with market power, rather than to prohibit the holding of market power as such. Conduct engaged in by a dominant undertaking constitutes an abuse of that dominant position (1) when the conduct leads to some prohibited consequence *and* (2) that conduct cannot be justified.[83]

The main debate is how to define the prohibited consequences and how to establish that such consequences exist—whether it is enough to show that harm from conduct is possible or whether it must be shown that such harm has occurred or is likely.[84] Some type of conduct, known as exploitative, causes *direct harm* to customers and consumers through an increase in price or reduction in quality.[85] In relation to such exploitative abuses, the issue is not so much the definition of harm as the manner in which that harm can be proven to exist. Other types of conduct, known as exclusionary abuses, cause direct harm to competitors, making it more difficult for them to participate in the market than would be the case absent that conduct.[86] It is important to distinguish, and

---

[79] Case T-219/99 *British Airways*, paras 188–189, and 218, and Economic Advisory Group for Competition Policy (EAGCP), Gual et al, 'An Economic Approach to Article 82' http://ec.europa.eu/dgs/competition/economist/eagcp_july_21_05.pdf, 116–120.

[80] Case 85/76 *Hoffmann-La Roche v Commission* [1979] ECR 461, para 71.

[81] Case 322/81 NV Nederlandsche Banden Industrie Michelin v Commission [1983] ECR 3461, para 57.

[82] Case 322/81 NV Nederlandsche Vanden-Industri Michelin v Commission [1983] ECR 3461, para 57.

[83] Case C-95/04 P *BA v Commission*, para 69, and Case C-209/10 *Post Danmark*, para 24.

[84] Case 85/76 *Hoffmann-La Roche*, para 91 provides the classic definition of abuse.

[85] P. Marsden and P. Whelan 'Consumer Detriment in EC and UK Competition Law' (2006) 27 *European Competition Law Review* 569, 577, text accompanying nn 83–89, and at 584.

[86] Case C-209/10 *Post Danmark*, para 20.

increasingly recognized as important to distinguish, between this direct harm to competitors and the harmful consequences prohibited by Article 102.[87] As stated by the Commission:

The aim of the Commission's enforcement activity in relation to exclusionary conduct is to ensure that dominant undertakings do not impair effective competition by foreclosing their competitors in an anticompetitive way, *thus having an adverse impact on consumer welfare, whether in the form of higher price levels than would have otherwise prevailed or in some other form such as limiting quality or reducing consumer choice.*[88]

It is thus clear that Article 102 will prohibit harm to competitors only when those competitors would otherwise prevent the dominant firm exercising market power to the determinant of customers and consumers.[89]

(a) Foreclosure

Foreclosure describes a situation in which the conduct of a dominant undertaking prevents competitors from entering the market or otherwise meeting consumer demand. Article 102 is applied to ensure dominant undertakings 'do not exclude their rivals by other means than competing on the merits of the products or services they provide'.[90] Foreclosure is difficult to distinguish from each customer simply receiving the best offer it can extract from the dominant undertaking.[91] There has thus been a general attempt to develop a consistent and administrable approach to identifying improper foreclosure. One approach is to ask whether profits are being sacrificed in order to exclude a rival from the market, with the expectation of high prices in a market from which rivals have been excluded. 'Profit sacrifice' cannot adequately distinguish harmful 'profit sacrifice' from beneficial 'investment' and so is of limited application. A second approach is to ask whether conduct makes no economic sense unless rivals are excluded. This approach suffers many of the same defects as the profit sacrifice approach.[92]

---

[87] Eleanor M. Fox 'We Protect Competition, You Protect Competitors' (2003) 26 *World Competition* 149.

[88] Communication from the Commission (n 51) para 19, emphasis added.

[89] Case C-95/04 P *BA v Commission* AG Opinion, para 68; *Virgin/BA* [2000] OJ L30/1, para 106; and Article 82 Discussion Paper, para 4.

[90] Communication from the Commission (n 51) para 6.

[91] Office of Fair Trading, *Selective Price Cuts and Fidelity Rebates* (2005) para 4.12; J. Temple Lang and R. O'Donoghue, 'Defining Legitimate Competition: How to Clarify Pricing Abuses under Article 82 EC' (2002) 26 *Fordham International Law Journal* 83 (2002) 108; and Robert H. Bork, *The Antitrust Paradox* (1987) 388–389.

[92] See generally, Renato Nazzini, *The Foundations of European Union Competition Law: The Objective and Principles of Article 102* (2011) 51–103.

In determining whether the inability of a competitor to enter the market is problematic, the Commission has adopted the 'efficient competitor' approach.[93] This approach allows non-dominant undertakings to compete with dominant undertakings 'on the merits'. In *Post Danmark* the Court of Justice strongly endorsed the 'efficient competitor' approach, stating:

It is settled case-law that a finding that an undertaking has . . . a dominant position is not in itself a ground of criticism of the undertaking concerned. *It is in no way the purpose of Article [102] to prevent an undertaking from acquiring, on its own merits, the dominant position on a market. Nor does that provision seek to ensure that competitors less efficient than the undertaking with the dominant position should remain on the market.*

Thus, not every exclusionary effect is necessarily detrimental to competition. Competition on the merits may, by definition, lead to the departure from the market or the marginalisation of competitors that are less efficient and so less attractive to consumers from the point of view of, among other things, price, choice, quality or innovation.[94]

(b) Objective Justification

Though Article 102 does not make express provision for exemption, the concept of abuse includes the possibility of objective justification.[95] Objective justification may be made out either on the basis of necessity or efficiency.[96] Claims based on objective justification are rarely successful. In *Syfait*, AG Jacobs suggested this was because 'the very fact that conduct is characterized as an "abuse" suggests that a negative conclusion has already been reached'.[97] There is also the question of who must satisfy the burden of proving that an objective justification exists. The General Court has ruled that 'it is for the dominant undertaking concerned, and not for the Commission . . . to raise any plea of objective justification and to support it with arguments and evidence'.[98]

---

[93] Communication from the Commission (n 51) paras 23 and 24.

[94] Case C-209/10 *Post Danmark v Konkurrencerådet*, paras 21–22, emphasis added.

[95] Case C-95/04 P *BA v Commission*, para 69; Albertina Albors-Llorens, 'The Role of Objective Justification and Efficiencies in the Application of Article 82 EC' (2007) 48 *Common Market Law Review* 1727; and Paul-John Loewenthal, 'The Defence of "Objective Justification" in the Application of Article 82 EC' (2005) 28 *World Competition* 455.

[96] Case C-209/10 *Post Danmark v Konkurrencerådet*, para 41–42 and Communication from the Commission (n 51) para 28.

[97] Case C-53/03 *SYFAIT v GlaxoSmithKline* AG Opinion, para 72.

[98] Case T-201/04 *Microsoft v Commission* [2007] ECR II-3601, para 688.

V. The Use of Article 101 to Control Market Power

Article 101 applies when an undertaking lacking the ability to obtain or exercise market power unilaterally coordinates its conduct with one or more other undertakings so as to enable market power to be obtained or exercised. The coordination of conduct may be beneficial to the undertakings but detrimental to society.[99] The coordination of certain conduct that may result in the creation, or enable the exercise, of market power may have no redeeming virtue, such conduct being labelled as hard core. Coordination may also be beneficial to both the undertakings and society.[100] The coordination of some conduct, whilst enabling the creation or exercise of market power, may nonetheless be compatible with the competition rules—either because it falls outside the scope of the Article 101(1) prohibition or because it meets the criteria for exemption set out in Article 101(3).

1. Coordination

Coordinated behaviour is a precondition for the application of Article 101.[101] Agreements and concerted practices are mechanisms by which coordination takes place. No legal consequences turn on whether competition is restricted by agreement or by concerted practice.[102] The forms of coordination have 'the same nature and are only distinguishable from each other by their intensity and the forms in which they manifest themselves'.[103] The forms of coordination are left undefined in the Treaty. However, a nuanced case law has developed that distinguishes the concept from the means by which its existence may be evidenced.

---

[99] Damien J. Neven, Penelope Papandropoulos, and Paul Seabright, *Trawling for Minnows: European Competition Policy and Agreements between Firms* (1998); F.M. Scherer and David Ross, *Industrial Market Structure and Economic Performance* (3rd ed, 1990) 235–238; Tyler Cowen and Daniel Sutter 'The Costs of Cooperation' (1999) 12 *Review of Austrian Economics* (1999) 161; Bryan Caplan and Edward Stringham 'Networks, Law, and the Paradox of Cooperation' (2003) 16 *Review of Austrian Economics* 309; and Tyler Cowen and Daniel Sutter 'Conflict, Cooperation and Competition in Anarchy' (2005) 18 *Review of Austrian Economics* 109.

[100] Stephen Martin, Industrial Organization: A European Perspective (2001) 65.

[101] Case T-41/96 *Bayer AG v Commission* [2000] ECR II-3383, para 64.

[102] Case 48/69 *Imperial Chemical Industries v Commission* [1972] ECR 619, para 64 and Case T-1/89 *Rhône-Poulenc Sa v Commission* [1991] ECR II 867 AG Opinion, 944.

[103] Case C-49/92 P *Commission v Anic Partecipazioni Spa* [1999] ECR I 4125, para 131.

(a) Agreement

The General Court judgment in *Bayer* confirms that common intention is central to the meaning of agreement under Article 101. The General Court held: '[I]n order for there to be an agreement within the meaning of Article [101(1)] of the Treaty it is *sufficient* that the undertakings in question should have expressed their *joint intention* to conduct themselves on the market in a specific way.'[104] Common intention is not only *sufficient* for an agreement to exist within the meaning of Article 101, but also *necessary*, since '[t]he proof of an agreement . . . within the meaning of Article [101(1)] of the Treaty *must be founded* upon the direct or indirect finding of the existence of the *subjective element* that characterises the very concept of an agreement, that is to say a *concurrence of wills* between economic operators'.[105]

The existence of common intention may be shown by written evidence. This may take the form of exchanges of correspondence, minutes of meetings, and other such documents.[106] The existence of an agreement may also be shown by parol evidence.[107] It is enough that words are said, so long as they can be evidenced.[108] In the event of inconsistent evidence, questions may arise as to whether there is a hierarchy of evidence between parol, written, and other types of conduct: 'Documents and testimony typically stand atop the hierarchy of proof because they tend to give the courts greater confidence that the defendants acted jointly.'[109]

There is no need for an agreement within the meaning of Article 101 to meet all the requirements of a contract or for the agreement to be legally binding, the Court having confirmed that it is unnecessary for an agreement 'to constitute a valid and binding contract under national law'.[110] It is normally irrelevant whether parties adhere to an agreement or intend to adhere to an agreement.[111] It does not matter why an agreement is entered into and duress or coercion are irrelevant for the purpose of Article 101.[112] The question of coercion is relevant at the sanctioning stage.[113]

---

[104] Case T-41/96 *Bayer AG v Commission* [2000] ECR II-3383, para 67, emphasis added.

[105] Case T-41/96 *Bayer AG v Commission* [2000] ECR II-3383, para 173, emphasis added, also 69.

[106] Case C-199/92 P *Hüls AG v Commission* [1999] ECR I 4287, paras 141–155; Case T-1/89 *Rhône-Poulenc SA v Commission* [1991] ECR II 867 AG Opinion, 955–957; and Maurice Guerrin and Georgios Kyriazis, 'Cartels: Proof and Procedural Issues' in Barry E. Hawk (ed), *Annual Proceedings of the Fordham Corporate Law Institute: International Antitrust Law & Policy 1992* (1993) 773, 790, 802–804.

[107] Case T-1/89 *Rhône-Poulenc SA v Commission*, AG Opinion 954–955.

[108] Case 28/77 *Tepea Bv v Commission* [1978] ECR 1391, para 17, 40–41; and Joined Cases 100-103/80 *Musique Diffusion Française Sa v Commission* [1983] ECR 1825 AG Opinion, 1915.

[109] Ernest Gellhorn, William E. Kovacic, and Stephen Calkins, *Antitrust Law and Economics in a Nutshell* (5th ed, 2004) 269.

[110] C-277/87 *Sandoz Prodotti Farmaceutici SpA v Commission* [1990] ECR-I 45, para 2 of the summary.

[111] Case 107/82 *AEG-Telefunken v Commission* [1983] ECR 3151 AG Opinion, 3251, 3259.

[112] Case T-9/89 *Hüls v European Commission*, para 128; Case 16/61 *Modena v High Authority* [1962] ECR 289, 303; Joined Cases 100-103/80 *Musique Diffusion Française Sa v Commission*, paras 88–90, 100; and Donald F. Turner, 'The Definition of Agreement under the Sherman Act: Conscious Parallelism and Refusals to Deal' (1962) 75 *Harvard Law Review* 655, 685–691, 694, 700–701.

[113] Turner (n 112) 655–706, 700.

In normal commercial relations, there will often be a formal written contract evidencing common intention. Undertakings do not openly acknowledge, and may actively seek to conceal, the existence of an agreement when the agreement is of a type clearly prohibited.[114] This makes it necessary to be able to infer the fact of an agreement from conduct in the marketplace.[115] The challenge is to distinguish conduct explained only by the existence of an agreement from the situation in which undertakings achieve an outcome that is similar to what would have been agreed but is not the result of agreement.[116] This second situation 'is *not* an interaction back and forth between people. It is a process in which *one* [undertaking] works out the consequences of [its] beliefs about the world—a world [it] believes to include other [undertakings that] are working out the consequences of their beliefs'.[117]

In both *Dyestuffs* and *Sugar,* the Court confirmed that 'every producer is free to change his prices, taking into account in so doing the present or foreseeable conduct of his competitors', and that the concept of collusion 'does not deprive economic operators of the right to adapt themselves intelligently to the existing and anticipated conduct of their competitors'.[118] The undertakings have simply acted rationally; it would be irrational not to take competitors' reactions into account and absurd to require undertakings to act irrationally.[119]

(b) Concerted Practice

The concept of a concerted practice captures forms of coordination that have yet to reach the stage of 'agreement properly so-called'.[120] This is required because undertakings may seek to interact in various ways and engage in various strategies that fall short of agreement. What the means of interaction have in common is that they seek to reduce uncertainty as to how competitors, trading partners, and customers will act in the future. This then enables the undertaking to 'act with greater knowledge and more or less justified expectations about other undertakings than they

---

[114] Julian Mathic Joshua and Sarah Jordan, 'Combinations, Concerted Practices and Cartels: Adopting the Concept of Conspiracy in European Community Competition Law' (2004) 24 *Northwestern Journal of International Law & Business* (2004) 647, 654–658.

[115] Case T-1/89 *Rhône-Poulenc SA v Commission*, AG Opinion, 957–960, and Julian Mathic Joshua, 'Proof in Contested EEC Competition Cases: A Comparison with the Rules of Evidence in Common Law' (1987) 12 *European Law Review* 315, 318–320.

[116] Oliver Black, 'Joint Action, Reliance and the Law' (2003) 14 *Kings College Law Journal* 65, 68.

[117] David K. Lewis, *Convention: A Philosophical Study* (1969) 32, emphasis in original.

[118] Case 48/69 *Imperial Chemical Industries v Commission*, para 118, and Joined Cases 40–48, 50, 54–56, 111, 113, and 114–173 *Coöperatieve Vereniging 'Suiker Unie' Ua v Commission* [1975] ECR 1663, para 174.

[119] Donald F. Turner, 'The Definition of Agreement under the Sherman Act: Conscious Parallelism and Refusals to Deal' (1962) 75 *Harvard Law Review* 655, 669–672, 675–681.

[120] Case 48/69 Imperial Chemical Industries v Commission, para 64.

should have had and normally would have'.[121] However, it is uncertainty as to how competitors, trading partners, and customers will act in the future environment that provides the impetus to engage in the competitive struggle.[122] A concerted practice can thus be understood as conduct reducing the uncertainty necessary for competition to exist.[123]

Communication reduces uncertainty and evidence of communication may be sufficient to establish a concerted practice.[124] Communication constitutes a concerted practice when it is of the type that 'enables each of the parties to determine its policy without having to be subject to the risks of competition'.[125] In *Suiker Unie*, the Court is clear that uncertainty about the future can be reduced if an undertaking 'disclose[s] . . . the course of conduct which they themselves have decided to adopt or contemplate adopting on the market'.[126] All that would then seem to be required to evidence a concerted practice is the disclosure of information by a single market participant. It is because communication is capable of 'influenc[ing] the conduct on the market of an actual or potential *competitor*' that the Treaties 'strictly preclude[s] any direct or indirect contact *between such operators*'.[127] Even though a commitment as to how the information will be used is absent, undertakings receiving information cannot fail to consider it when determining their future conduct; conduct is inevitably influenced. As expressed by Judge Vesterdorf, writing as AG:

undertakings will then necessarily, and normally unavoidably, act on the market in the light of the knowledge and on the basis of the discussions which have taken place . . . They will negotiate with their customers and arrange their production and so forth possessing a different body of knowledge and being in a different state of awareness than if they had only their own experience, general knowledge and perception of the market to rely on.[128]

---

[121] Case T-1/89 *Rhône-Poulenc Sa v Commission*, AG Opinion, 942.

[122] Joined Cases T-202/98, T-204/98, and T-207/98 *Tate & Lyle plc, British Sugar plc, Napier Brown & Co. Ltd v Commission* [2001] ECR II 2035, para 46.

[123] Case 48/69 *Imperial Chemical Industries v Commission*, para 64. In Case C-49/92 P *Commission v Anic Partecipazioni SpA* [1999] ECR I 4125, AG Opinion, paras 34–36, the AG questions whether 'lessening of uncertainty' as to the future' is sufficient and asks whether 'certainty' ought to be created.

[124] Joined Cases C-89/85, C-104/85, C-114/85, C-116/85, C-117/85, and C-125/85 to C-129/85 *A. Ahlström Osakeyhtiö v Commission* [1993] ECR I 1307, AG Opinion, para 172; Luis Miguel Pais Antunes, 'Agreements and Concerted Practices under EEC Competition Law: Is the Distinction Relevant?' (1991) 11 *Yearbook of European Law* 57, 61–62, 67; and Kai-Uwe Kuhn 'Fighting Collusion by Regulating Communication between Firms' Economic Policy' (2001) 167, 179–187.

[125] Luis Miguel Pais Antunes, 'Agreements and Concerted Practices under Eec Competition Law: Is the Distinction Relevant?' (1991) 11 *Yearbook of European Law* 57, 66.

[126] Joined Cases 40–48, 50, 54 to 56, 111, 113, and 114–173 *Coöperatieve Vereniging 'Suiker Unie' Ua v Commission*, para 174.

[127] Joined Cases 40–48, 50, 54 to 56, 111, 113, and 114–173 *Coöperatieve Vereniging 'Suiker Unie' Ua v Commission*, para 174, emphasis added.

[128] Case T-1/89 *Rhône-Poulenc SA v Commission*, AG Opinion, 941.

2. Restriction of Competition

Article 101 is used to examine the competitive consequences of undertakings that coordinate their conduct.[129] Coordination is prohibited under Article 101 when it enables the coordinating undertakings to exercise market power.[130] A restriction of competition is thus shown to exist when output or quality falls or prices rise as a consequence of the coordination under scrutiny.[131] In *ICI v Commission*, undertakings coordinated to enable them to increase the price of aniline dyes without the risk of losing customers to a competing undertaking.[132] In *Konica*, undertakings coordinated their conduct so as to enable them to charge 30 per cent more for goods in Germany than was charged for those same goods in the UK.[133] In *Consten and Grundig*, coordination resulted in prices 20 per cent higher in France than in Germany.[134]

The existence of a restriction of competition may be demonstrated in one of two ways. It may be shown that the *object* of coordinated conduct is to prevent, restrict, or distort competition or, alternatively, that the *effect* of coordinated conduct is to prevent, restrict, or distort competition.[135] The Court of Justice has made it clear that whilst making a distinction between the *object* of restricting competition and the *effect* of restricting competition: 'Article [101(1)] is based on an assessment of the effects of an agreement from two angles of economic evaluation.'[136] Both the object and the effect assessment share a single conception of restricted competition and both methods of assessment require that a restriction of competition be established.

The *effect* of an agreement is either measured *ex post* or may be predicted *ex ante* by use of certain economic presumptions and techniques.[137] Market share calculations are used as a first indicator of whether or not the coordination between undertakings is likely to have a prohibited effect.[138] The relevant effect is on prices,

---

[129] George A. Hay, 'The Meaning of "Agreement" under the Sherman Act: Thoughts from the "Facilitating Practices" Experience' (2000) 16 *Review of Industrial Organization* 113, 124–125.

[130] Compare with Guidelines on Vertical Restraints [2000] OJ C291/1, para 100–102.

[131] Case 56/65 *Société Technique Minière v Maschinenbau Ulm Gmbh* [1966] ECR 235, 250 and Guidelines on the Application of Article 81(3) of the Treaty [2004] OJ C 101/97, para 17. The causal element will usually be assumed in the remainder of the discussion.

[132] Case 48/69 *Imperial Chemical Industries v Commission*, para 1–6, 83–87.

[133] Konica [1988] OJ L78/34 [1988] 4 CMLR 848.

[134] Grundig/Consten [1964] JO 2545/64 [1964] CMLR 489, 493, and Cases 56 and 58-64 *Établissements Consten Sàrl and Grundig-Verkaufs-Gmbh v Commission* [1966] ECR 299, 343.

[135] Case 56/65 Société Technique Minière v Maschinenbau Ulm Gmbh [1966] ECR 235, 249; Cases 56 and 58-64 Établissements Consten Sàrl and Grundig-Verkaufs-Gmbh v Commission [1966] ECR 299, 342–343; Case T-143/89 Ferriere Nord Spa v Commission [1995] ECR II-917, para 31; and Case C-219/95 P Ferriere Nord Spa v Commission [1997] ECR I 4411, para 14–16, AG Opinion, para 15–18.

[136] Case 56/65 Société Technique Minière v Maschinenbau Ulm GmbH [1966] ECR 235, 248.

[137] See Communication from the Commission (n 51) paras 24–27.

[138] Horizontal Cooperation Guidelines OJ 2011 C11/1, paras 39ff; Vertical Restraints Guidelines OJ 2010 C130/1, paras 111–116.

output, innovation, or the variety or quality of goods and services supplied to the market. By way of contrast, the *object* approach is one in which reliance is placed on a legal presumption that coordination has or will result in the harmful exercise of market power.[139] Reliance on a legal presumption is justified on the basis that 'a full economic analysis of every case would be very costly and might not be justified by gains in identifying market situations . . . that were detrimental to competition. In those circumstances, competition policy may have to resort to relatively simple rules of thumb and do without a full economic analysis of every case'.[140]

The 'object' approach spares the expense of an 'effect' enquiry and has clear deterrent value because of the absolute nature of the prohibition.[141] However, significant analysis or investigative effort may be required to determine whether the legal presumption is properly to be applied in a particular case.[142] The effort devoted to this task may well erode the savings that justify the existence of the legal presumption.[143]

The legal presumption arises when a restriction of competition is the inevitable consequence of the agreement.[144] This is generally seen to be the case in relation to *'obvious restrictions of competition* such as price-fixing, market-sharing or the control of outlets'.[145] More controversially, a legal presumption that competition is restricted arises when it can be shown that parties intend to restrict competition.[146] Intent is relevant because undertakings coordinating their conduct with the intention of restricting competition are more likely to restrict competition than

---

[139] Case C-209/07 *The Competition Authority v Beef Industry Development Society Ltd and Barry Brothers (Carrigmore) Meats Ltd* [2008] ECR I-8637, report of the hearing, para 17; Commission staff working document—Guidance on restrictions of competition 'by object' for the purpose of defining which agreements may benefit from the de Minimis Notice Brussels, 25.6.2014 SWD (2014) 198 final; O. Odudu, *The Boundaries of EC Competition Law: The Scope of Article 81* (2006) 113–125; Communication from the Commission (n 51), para 21 and 24; Guidelines on the Applicability of Article 81 of the EC Treaty to Horizontal Cooperation Agreements [2001] OJ C3/2, paras 18 and 25.

[140] Green Paper on Vertical Restraints in Ec Competition Policy COM (96) 721 Final [1997] 4 CMLR 519, para 86. Also Communication from the Commission on the Application of the Community Competition Rules to Vertical Restraints (Follow-up to the Green Paper on Vertical Restraints) COM (98) 544 final [1998] OJ C365/3, 9, 21.

[141] ABA Antitrust Section, *Monograph No. 23: The Rule of Reason* (1999) 2–3.

[142] Guidelines on vertical restraints [2000] OJ C291/1, para 47 and ABA Antitrust Section (n 141) 128–131, 135–139, 162–163.

[143] Donald L. Beschle, 'What, Never? Well, Hardly Ever: Strict Antitrust Scrutiny as an Alternative to per se Antitrust Illegality' (1987) 38 *Hastings Law Journal* 471, 473, 486–496; and ABA Antitrust Section (n 141) 4, 9.

[144] Case C-209/07 The Competition Authority v Beef Industry Development Society Ltd and Barry Brothers (Carrigmore) Meats Ltd, para 17, AG Opinion, para 44.

[145] Joined Cases T-374/94, T-375/94, T-384/94, and T-388/94 *European Night Services v Commission* [1998] ECR II 3141, para 136, emphasis added.

[146] Case C-209/07 *The Competition Authority v Beef Industry Development Society Ltd and Barry Brothers (Carrigmore) Meats Ltd*, AG Opinion, para 46; Guidelines on the Applicability of Article 81 of the EC Treaty to Horizontal Cooperation Agreements [2001] OJ C3/2, para 22; and Case C-551/03 P *General Motors BV and Opel Nederland BV*, AG Opinion, para 64, 77–79.

if they had no such intention.[147] Thus, for example, the legal presumption arose after it was found that an agreement was '*intended to encourage the withdrawal of competitors*'.[148]

In order to determine whether the object rather than the effect approach is to be applied, it is necessary to determine whether the coordination at issue is horizontal or vertical.[149] Horizontal coordination is that between undertakings at the same level of the production or distribution chain, those producing substitutes: vertical coordination is that between undertakings at different levels of the production or distribution chain, those producing complements.[150] Vertical coordination is deemed less problematic, so that coordination, such as that concerning price or territory, can be subject to the object approach when horizontal, but subject to the effect mode of analysis when vertical. In general, vertical coordination benefits from generous presumptions of legality, a broad block exemption regime, and higher *de minimis* thresholds than is available for horizontal coordination.[151]

3. Exemption

Article 101(3) provides a framework in which to consider claims that the detrimental consequences of the coordination are outweighed by the benefits of that same coordination.[152] In *Consten and Grundig*, the Court held that the benefits of coordination should be presented as 'noticeable objective advantages such as to compensate for the inconveniences resulting therefrom on the level of competition'.[153] The Commission recognizes that coordination 'can be a means to share risk, save costs, pool know-how and launch innovation faster'.[154] It may also promote the

---

[147] L.A. Sullivan, 'Economics and More Humanistic Disciplines: What Are the Sources of Wisdom for Antitrust' (1997) 125 *University of Pennsylvania Law Review* 1214, 1229–1231; Ronald A. Cass and K.N. Hylton 'Antitrust Intent' (2001) 74 *Southern California Law Review* 657, 679–707, 712–715; and Anthony Kenny, 'Intention and Purpose' (1966) 63 *Journal Of Philosophy* 642, 649–651.

[148] Case C-209/07 *The Competition Authority v Beef Industry Development Society Ltd and Barry Brothers (Carrigmore) Meats Ltd*, para 31, emphasis added.

[149] M.A. Lemley and C.R. Leslie, 'Categorical Analysis in Antitrust Jurisprudence' (2007–2008) 93 *Iowa Law Review* 1207, 1219–1220. It can be a difficult question of fact to determine whether coordination is vertical or horizontal: see eg *Toys 'R' Us, Inc. v Federal Trade Commission*, 221 F3d 928, 930 (7th Cir 2000).

[150] Carlton and Perloff, *Modern Industrial Organization* (3rd ed, 2000), 396.

[151] M.A. Lemley and C.R. Leslie, 'Categorical Analysis in Antitrust Jurisprudence' (2007–2008) 93 *Iowa Law Review* 1207, 1224–1229.

[152] Communication from the Commission (n 51), para 33; Guidelines on the Applicability of Article 81 of the EC Treaty to Horizontal Cooperation Agreements [2001] OJ C3/2, para 4; Guidelines on Vertical Restraints [2000] OJ C291/1, para 5; and Case T-112/99 *Métropole Télévision (M6) v Commission* [2001] ECR II 2459, para 77.

[153] Cases 56 and 58-64 *Établissements Consten Sàrl and Grundig-Verkaufs-Gmbh v Commission* [1966] ECR 299, 348.

[154] Guidelines on the Applicability of Article 81 of the EC Treaty to Horizontal Cooperation Agreements [2001] OJ C3/2, para 3.

'cross fertilisation of ideas and experience, thus resulting in improved or new products and technologies being developed more rapidly than would otherwise be the
case'.[155]

As provided for in Article 101(3), Article 101(1) may be declared inapplicable if the
agreement or conduct 'contributes to improving the production or distribution of
goods or to promoting technical or economic progress'. The Commission considers
the requirement satisfied when there are 'beneficial economic effects'.[156] These 'beneficial economic effects' include productive efficiency gains.[157] It is also the case that
under Article 101(3) various non-efficiency concerns have been relied on to justify
the setting aside of Article 101(1).[158] It is contested whether Article 101(3) remains
available to be used to address non-efficiency concerns.

In some situations, there is a legal presumption that the conditions set out in
Article 101(3) have been satisfied. Instruments defining such situations are known
as block-exemption regulations.[159] The beneficial consequences that theory or experience expects to arise in a particular context are stated in the recitals of those
regulations. For example, in the fifth recital of Regulation 2790/1999 the aim of
the exemption is considered to be to identify those situations in 'which it can
be assumed with sufficient certainty that they satisfy the conditions of Article
[101(3)]'.[160] When the conditions of Article 101(3) are not satisfied, even when the
terms of the block exemption regulation have been met, the benefit of the presumption may be withdrawn.[161]

---

[155] Guidelines on the Applicability of Article 81 of the EC Treaty to Horizontal Cooperation
Agreements [2001] OJ C3/2, para 68.

[156] Guidelines on the Applicability of Article 81 of the EC Treaty to Horizontal Cooperation
Agreements [2001] OJ C3/2, para 32, and P. Roth and V. Rose (eds), *Bellamy & Child: European
Community Law of Competition* (5th ed, 2001) para 3-026.

[157] Communication from the Commission (n 51) paras 50, 59–72; Guidelines on the Applicability of
Article 81 of the EC Treaty to Horizontal Cooperation Agreements [2001] OJ C3/2, paras 102, 132, 151;
Case C-7/1997 *Oscar Bronner Gmbh & Co. Kg v Mediaprint Zeitungs- Und Zeitschriftenverlag Gmbh &
Co. Kg* [1998] ECR I 7791, AG Opinion, para 57; and Joined Cases T-374/94, T-375/94, T-384/94, and
T-388/94 *European Night Services v Commission* [1998] ECR II 3141, para 230, T-384/94, T-388/94 #20.

[158] White Paper on Modernisation of the Rules Implementing Articles 85 and 86 of the Ec Treaty
Commission Programme No 99/027 [1999] OJ C132/1, paras 56–57; Proposal for a Council Regulation
on the Implementation of the Rules on Competition Laid Down in Articles 81 and 82 of the Treaty
and Amending Regulations (EEC) No 1017/68, (EEC) No 2988/74, (EEC) No 4056/86, and (EEC) No
3975/87 [2000] OJ C365 E/284, 4; House of Lords Select Committee *Fourth Report: Reforming EC
Competition Procedures* HL 33(2000), paras 33, 60; and *Case C-2/1991 Meng*, 5770.

[159] See Richard Whish, 'Regulation 2790/99: The Commission's "New Style" Block Exemption for
Vertical Agreements' (2000) 37 *Common Market Law Review* 887.

[160] Commission Regulation (EC) No 2790/1999 of 22 December 1999 on the application of Article
81(3) of the Treaty to categories of vertical agreements and concerted practices [1999] OJ L336/21,
fifth recital.

[161] Art 29(1) of Council Regulation (EC) No 1/2003 of 16 December 2002 [2003] OJ L 1/1.

VI. Prophylactic Control of Market Power: The Control of Market Structure

1. The Need to Control Mergers

It is generally accepted by competition authorities and courts that mergers result in a number of benefits. The benefits most often claimed by merging parties are productive efficiencies, generated by achieving economies of scale (reductions in average cost across a greater volume of output) or economies of scope (costs savings from producing different products together). A second benefit often claimed is an improvement in allocative efficiency. Independent upstream suppliers and downstream distributors will both need to make a margin on their sales, known as a double margin. A merger between a supplier and a distributor may remove double marginalization as a single firm will have a greater incentive to decrease downstream prices because the benefit of increased demand will also accrue to the upstream business. A third type of benefit is dynamic efficiency. This may arise where the new firm is better able to carry out research and development and with access to a greater pool of industrial technology. Dynamic efficiencies may also result from improved management. In the 'market for corporate control', old management will be replaced. The threat of a successful takeover bid acts as an important influence upon the existing management of a firm to ensure that it functions efficiently.

Whilst mergers are often beneficial or at least benign, they may also create or strengthen the ability of one or more firms profitably to increase prices, reduce output, choice, or quality of goods and services, diminish innovation or otherwise influence the parameters of competition.[162] It may be that a merger between A and B enables AB to exercise market power, such a merger being described as having unilateral effects. It may be that a merger between A and B enables AB to coordinate its behaviour with other firms, for example with C and D, such merger being described as giving rise to coordinated effects. It may also be the case that a merger between firms operating at different, but complementary, levels of the market will foreclose third parties at one level or the merger will enable coordination between the merged entity and third parties (vertical effects), and even when undertakings are neither in horizontal competition, nor functionally related vertically, the merger may enable the merged entity to use market power to foreclose competitors (conglomerate effects).

---

[162] Guidelines on the assessment of horizontal mergers under the Council Regulation on the control of concentrations between undertakings [2004] OJ C 31/5, para 8.

The principal instrument for the control of the competitive consequences of mergers and acquisitions at the EU level is the EUMR. The current version of the Merger Regulation (Regulation 139/2004) entered into force on 1 May 2004. Prior to the adoption of the first Merger Regulation (Regulation 4064/89), which entered into force on 21 September 1990, EU law made no specific provision for the control of mergers. Any competition concerns arising were to be addressed using Articles 101 and 102.[163] However, Articles 101 and 102 are ill suited to this particular task. A merger is a one-off transaction creating a durable change in the way resources are deployed in particular markets. In a hostile takeover it is not clear that the requirement of agreement in Article 101 would be satisfied; Article 102 can be applied only if at least one of the undertakings is in a dominant position prior to the structural change; and both Article 101 and 102 are most easily applied *ex post*, but the durable nature of the changes wrought makes *ex ante* examination appropriate. If a merger were to be found problematic *ex post*, the ability to impose fines is a weak remedy, while the power to require dissolution is too strong to be of use in all but the most exceptional of circumstances. At the same time, as EU member States established their own systems of merger control, undertakings are required to comply with the requirements of multiple, not necessarily compatible, systems.

2. Principles of EU Merger Control

The EU merger control regime is guided by the same objectives as general EU competition law and in this sense complements Articles 101 and 102—controlling accretions of market power by a single undertaking.[164] What are added by a specific merger control regime are certain procedural mechanisms that enable a rapid *ex ante* assessment and give greater legal certainty than can be obtained under general competition law. This ensures the application of the competition rules does not stifle the market for corporate control.[165]

The EU merger regime achieves these objectives first by making notification of structural changes compulsory.[166] This is coupled with a standstill obligation preventing the parties proceeding with the transaction until the Commission issues

---

[163] See Case C-6/72 *Europemballage and Continental Can v Commission* [1973] ECR 215; *Mecaniver/ PPG*, OJ 1985 L35/54; and Joined Cases 142 and 156/84 *BAT and Reynolds v Commission* [1987] ECR 4487.

[164] Merger Regulation, recitals 2–6 and 24. However, on the possible role of non-competition concerns see D. Geradin and I. Girgenson, 'Industrial Policy and European Merger Control—A Reassessment' (2011) http://ssrn.com/abstract=1937586.

[165] H.G. Manne, 'Mergers and the Market for Corporate Control' (1965) 73 *Journal of Political Economy* 110.

[166] Art 4(1) of Reg 139/2004 on the control of concentrations between undertakings [2004] OJ L2004/1.

merger clearance.[167] A second feature is known as the 'one-stop shop'. Transactions within the scope of the EU merger control regime must be examined by the European Commission and may not be examined by any other authority within the EU.[168] Much work has been done to keep the burden of compliance to a minimum.[169] The Commission makes available a 'simplified procedure' for transactions that are not expected to raise significant competition concerns.[170] In addition, a 'super-simplified procedure' is available when undertakings mainly operate outside the EU.

3. Identifying Market Power Problems

The EUMR gives the Commission jurisdiction to examine certain 'concentrations'. Alongside various turnover thresholds, the concept of a concentration is used to determine the types of transaction suitable for merger review. A concentration exists when there are transactions that lead to durable structural changes in the marketplace.[171] At the same time the concept should exclude those transactions that are most appropriately addressed under Articles 101 or 102. A 'concentration' occurs when the first firm is able to exercise 'decisive influence' over the second firm.[172] At this point the second firm is no longer an independent force on the market. The enquiry then proceeds to consider the impact the loss of an independent competitor will have in the marketplace. There is debate over how to determine whether or not a transaction gives rise to the relevant degree of influence so that competitive vigour is lost. Under the EUMR this is determined by qualitative rather than quantitative criteria.[173]

---

[167] Art 7(1) of Reg 139/2004 on the control of concentrations between undertakings [2004] OJ L 2004/1.

[168] The Merger Regulation does include a mechanism enable the Commission to reallocate the assessment of a merger to national competition authorities. See Commission Notice on Case Referral in respect of concentrations [2005] OJ C56/2, paras 5 and 8.

[169] See 'Mergers: Commission Cuts Red Tape for Businesses' http://europa.eu/rapid/press-release_IP-13-1214_en.htm.

[170] http://europa.eu/rapid/press-release_MEMO-13-1098_en.htm.

[171] Commission Consolidated Jurisdictional Notice under Council Regulation (EC) No 139/2004 on the control of concentrations between undertakings [2008] OJ C95/1, paras 7–8, and 92 and OECD Definition of Transaction for the Purpose of *Merger Control Review* http://www.oecd.org/daf/competition/Merger-control-review-2013.pdf.

[172] Art 3(1) and (2) of Reg 139/2004 on the control of concentrations between undertakings [2004] OJ L2004/1.

[173] See Commission Consolidated Jurisdictional Notice under Council Regulation (EC) No 139/2004 on the control of concentrations between undertakings [2008] OJ C95/1, paras 16–23; OECD, *Antitrust Issues Involving Minority Shareholding and Interlocking Directorates* http://www.oecd.org/competition/mergers/41774055.pdf and the Commission's consultation available from http://ec.europa.eu/competition/consultations/2013_merger_control/index_en.html.

Once a concentration is deemed to have occurred its substantive impact must be assessed. The modern approach to EU merger control has it origins in three important decisions of the General Court, adopted in 2002, which challenged the Commission's approach to merger control.[174] The Commission's response has been to refocus its efforts on mergers most clearly seen as harmful, ie horizontal mergers likely to result in unilateral effects.[175] It has then sought more clearly to prescribe the circumstances in which other merger transactions might be harmful and so worthy of further investigation under the EUMR, as seen with the 2008 Guidelines on non-horizontal mergers.[176] This coupled with a revised substantive test contained in the current Merger Regulation provides that mergers are not to be viewed as problematic unless it can be shown that they are likely to lead to a significant impediment to effective competition. This is taken to mean that the merger gives 'the ability of one or more firms to profitably increase prices, reduce output, choice or quality of goods and services, diminish innovation or otherwise influence parameters of competition'.[177]

VII. Conclusion

EU competition law is best understood as a body of law capable of addressing problems of market power. The market power approach, sometimes referred to as the economic approach, provides a consistent framework in which the problems capable of being addressed by competition law can be understood. This clarity of purpose gives EU competition law a greater degree of predictability than had previously been the case and so enables those subject to the law correctly to comply with its demands—competition law now has a greater prospect of being self-executing. What remains to be tested is how the new understanding will be accommodated in the old jurisprudence and whether the interpretation of the Treaty will 'assume a significance to match the new situation which has come into being'.[178]

---

[174] Case T-342/99 *Airtours v Commission* [2002] ECR II-2585; Case T-5/02 *Tetra Laval v Commission* [2002] ECR II-4381; and Case T-310/01 *Schneider Electric v Commission* [2002] ECR II-4071.

[175] See Guidelines on the assessment of horizontal mergers under the Council Regulation on the control of concentrations between undertakings [2004] OJ C31/5.

[176] Guidelines on the assessment of non-horizontal mergers (n 175).

[177] Guidelines on the assessment of horizontal mergers under the Council Regulation on the control of concentrations between undertakings [2004] OJ C31/5, para 8.

[178] Case 73/74 Groupement des fabricants de papiers peints de Belgique v Commission [1975] ECR 1491, 1523 (AG Trabucchi).

BIBLIOGRAPHY

P. Akman, *The Concept of Abuse in EU Competition Law* (2012)

G. Amato, *Antitrust and the Bounds of Power* (1997)

C. Bellamy and G. Child, *European Community Law of Competition* (7th ed, 2012)

C. Cook and C. Kerse, *EC Merger Control* (5th ed, 2009)

J. Faull and A. Nikpay, *The EU Law of Competition* (3rd ed, 2014)

D. Gerber, *Law and Competition in Twentieth Century Europe* (1998)

A. Jones and B.E. Sufrin, *EU Competition Law* (5th ed, 2014)

G. Monti, *EC Competition Law* (2007)

R. Nazzini, *The Foundations of European Competition Law: The Objectives and Principles of Article 102* (2011)

Gunnar Niels, Helen Jenkins, and James Kavanagh, *Economics for Competition Lawyers* (2011)

R. O'Donoghue and J. Padilla, *The Law and Economics of Article 102* (2nd ed, 2013)

L. Ortiz Blanco, *Market Power in EU Antitrust Law* (2012)

R.P. Whish and D. Bailey, *Competition Law* (7th ed, 2012)

CHAPTER 25

COMPETITION LAW ENFORCEMENT

ALISON JONES

I. INTRODUCTION

WITHOUT effective enforcement, the objectives of competition laws will not be achieved. Not only do enforcement actions provide the opportunity for the meaning of the law to be developed and clarified, but they are also necessary to ensure that breaches of the rules are brought to an end, breaches are deterred and punished, and, where appropriate, that persons harmed by their violation are able to obtain compensation for loss suffered in consequence.[1] A critical issue to be determined when planning or designing a competition law system is, therefore, how effective enforcement mechanisms can be put in place that adequately respect the rights of the undertakings or persons involved. When constructing a system of public enforcement, important questions include: which institutions or persons should investigate possible breaches and initiate proceedings; which institutions should adjudicate on contested proceedings (and should it be the same institution as the investigator?); should proceedings be civil or criminal and what, if any, sanctions should be imposed on those found to have violated the rules; to what extent should competition law decisions be subject to judicial review; and what

---

[1] Wouter Wils, 'The Relationship between Public Antitrust Enforcement and Private Actions for Damages' (2009) 32 *World Competition* 3.

scope, if any, should there be for political review of, or intervention in, competition decisions?[2] A further matter is whether private enforcement of the rules should be permitted and/or encouraged and how it should be balanced with, and relate to, public enforcement.

This chapter examines and appraises the enforcement system that has developed in the EU. Although historically the rules were enforced principally by the European Commission (the 'Commission'),[3] a more decentralized system has now emerged, involving both national competition authorities (NCAs) and the courts and tribunals of the individual Member States (the national courts) in the enforcement of Articles 101 and 102 TFEU (the 'antitrust' rules).[4] These changes to the antitrust enforcement landscape have principally resulted from Regulation 1/2003's[5] removal, in 2004, of the exclusive right conferred on the Commission by Council Regulation 17 of 1962[6] to decide on the compatibility of an individual agreement with Article 101(3) following the notification of the agreement to it.[7] Prior to 2004, the set-up created by Regulation 17 meant that it was difficult for either NCAs or national courts to play a meaningful role in the enforcement process as, apart from applying block exemptions, they could not apply Article 101(3). It is seen in Chapter 24 that Regulation 1/2003 formed a critical and central plank of the EU modernization programme. In particular, it paved the way for Article 101 to become, like Article 102, directly effective in its entirety, and, consequently, for greater enforcement of the rules at the national level.

Section II of this chapter examines public enforcement of the EU Competition law rules, focusing on enforcement of Articles 101 and 102 by the Commission. One significant and contentious issue is whether the EU enforcement system, under which the Commission performs investigative, enforcement, and adjudicative functions and the role of the EU courts is confined to review of the decisions and penalties imposed, is adequate to protect the fundamental rights of the undertakings involved in investigations.

---

[2] Michael Trebilcock and Edward Iacobucci, 'Designing Competition Law Institutions' (2002) 25 *World Competition* 361.

[3] The Directorate General for Competition ('DG Comp', currently headed by Vice President Commissioner Almunia) is responsible for competition policy and enforcement.

[4] Enforcement of the EU merger rules has since the first EU Merger Regulation came into force fallen exclusively to the Commission; see now Reg 139/2004 of 20 January 2004 on the control of concentrations between undertakings [2004] OJ L24/1, Art 21(2). It is seen in Ch 24 that the purpose of the merger rules is to enable the Commission to regulate, *ex ante*, changes in market structure in the EU by deciding whether two or more commercial companies should be permitted to merge, combine, or consolidate their businesses. The rules cannot be enforced either by NCAs or by private persons before the national courts.

[5] Council Reg (EC) No 1/2003 of 16 December 2002 on the implementation of the rules on competition laid down in Articles 81 and 82 [now Arts 101 and 102] of the Treaty [2003] OJ L1/1.

[6] Reg No 17: First Regulation implementing Articles 85 and 86 of the Treaty [1959–1962] OJ Spec Ed 87.

[7] Reg No 17 (n 6) Art 9(1).

Section III examines private enforcement of the antitrust laws, occurring through civil litigation in the national courts. Although historically, private actions did not play a significant role in EU antitrust enforcement, the volume of private litigation has grown rapidly in some Member States and is now playing an increasingly important part in the enforcement process. Nonetheless, the Commission has taken the view that more has to be done, without unleashing an excessive litigation culture, to stimulate and harmonize national rules governing private enforcement. In 2013, it thus proposed a package of measures on antitrust damages actions including, in particular, a draft Directive designed to remove the main obstacles to full compensation for antitrust victims and to ensure that private and public enforcement operate harmoniously together. The Directive came into force at the end of 2014.

II. Public Enforcement

1. Introduction

A network of competition authorities, the European Competition Network (ECN) comprised of the Commission and the NCAs, is responsible for public enforcement of Articles 101 and 102. Although NCAs have, since 2004, started to perform an ever increasing and important role in EU antitrust enforcement, the Commission has sought to retain its central position 'as the guardian of the Treaty' which 'has the ultimate but not the sole responsibility for developing policy and safeguarding consistency when it comes to the application of [EU] competition law'.[8]

This chapter focuses on enforcement by the Commission, although some observations about case allocation and enforcement by NCAs are set out in Section II.7.

2. Institutional Design and Due Process

Enforcement by the Commission of both antitrust and merger rules follows the integrated administrative model.[9] In antitrust proceedings, the Commission acts, pursuant to powers conferred on it by Regulation 1/2003[10] and Regulation 774/2003

---

[8] Commission Notice on Cooperation within the Network of Competition Authorities (Cooperation Notice) [2004] OJ C101/43, para 43.

[9] See generally Alison Jones and Brenda Sufrin, *EU Competition Law: Text, Cases, and Materials* (5th ed, 2014) Chs 13 and 15.

[10] The model was first set up by Reg 17 (n 6) and is now set out in Reg 1/2003 (n 5).

(the Implementation Regulation),[11] as an integrated decision maker, deciding which cases to investigate, whether to initiate proceedings, whether an infringement has occurred and what sanctions should be imposed on undertakings in breach. It does not have to prove that the substance of an infringement has been committed before an independent tribunal or court (as it would have to under a judicial model). Rather, it adopts its own decisions and imposes penalties that are subject to review by the EU courts under Article 263 and 261 TFEU respectively (such challenges are normally made in the first instance to the General Court (GC)[12] with an appeal on points of law to the European Court of Justice (ECJ)[13]). Although the Commission's merger powers[14], reflecting the different nature of the two processes, are not identical to those governing antitrust enforcement, they do nonetheless closely follow them. This section concentrates on enforcement of Articles 101 and 102 and does not consider the merger process in detail.

It is generally accepted that the integrated agency model provides the opportunity for an expert and specialized agency to adopt and contribute to the development of a coherent competition policy and to accurate and efficient decision taking.[15] Nonetheless, the model has provoked considerable controversy over the years, which has been fuelled by a number of factors including: (1) the fact that the Commission's investigations have become less administrative/inquisitorial in nature and have taken on a more adversarial/prosecutorial appearance[16]; (2) the fact that levels of fines imposed by the Commission in its antitrust infringement decisions have increased exponentially in the last 15 years[17]; and (3) the development, and increasing importance in the EU, of European Convention on Human Rights ('ECHR') principles and case law.

Indeed as it seems now to be widely accepted that competition law fines and antitrust procedures are of a 'criminal' nature for the purposes of Article 6 ECHR,[18]

---

[11] [2004] OJ L123/18.

[12] See Art 256(1) TFEU and the Protocol on the Statute of the CJEU, Art 51, Cases C-68/95 and C-30/95, *France v Commission* [1998] ECR I-1375.

[13] Protocol on the Statute of the Court of Justice, Art 51; see further Section II 5.

[14] Set out in the EUMR itself and its implementing provisions, see Ch 24.

[15] See eg Emil Paulis (2003) 'Checks and Balances in the EU Antitrust Enforcement System' in B. Hawk (ed), *Proceedings from the Fordham Corporate International Law Institute 2002 Antitrust Law and Policy Conference* 381.

[16] See eg Heike Schweitzer, 'The European Competition Law Enforcement System and the Evolution of Judicial Review' in Claus-Dieter Ehlermann and Mel Marquis (eds), *European Competition Law Annual 2009: Evaluation of Evidence and its Judicial Review in Competition Cases* (2010).

[17] Reg 1/2003 (n 5) Art 23(5). Especially since the introduction of new fining Guidelines in 2006, 'Guidelines on the method of setting fines imposed pursuant to Article 23(2)(a) of Regulation No 1/2003' [2006] OJ C210/2, see further Section II.4.b.

[18] And in spite of their characterization in Reg 1/2003 as administrative charges, see eg *Engel v Netherlands* (1979–1980) 1 EHRR 647, *Stenuit v France*[1992] ECC 401, *Menarini Diagnostics S.R.L v Italy*, App 43509/08, judgment 27 September 2011, and most recently eg Sharpston AG in Case C-272/09 P *KME Germany AG v Commission* Opinion, 10 February 2011, para 64, and Donald Slater, Sébastien

the important question that has come to the forefront is whether the system, and/or particular aspects of it, not only upholds standards of good administration[19] and fundamental principles of EU law, especially the rights of the defence,[20] but also respects ECHR and EU Charter rights, especially the right to respect for private and family life, home and communications (see Article 8 ECHR and Article 7 of the EU Charter), and the principle of effective judicial protection,[21] as well as the right, within a reasonable time, to a fair trial before an independent and impartial tribunal[22] (see Article 6 ECHR and Article 47 of the EU Charter). Collectively, these provisions establish crucial rights for undertakings being investigated for possible violation of the antitrust laws, including the rights to a presumption of innocence;[23] to a public hearing before an independent and impartial tribunal; to give evidence in one's own defence; to have access to the evidence against one, and the supporting evidence; to be able to examine and cross-examine witnesses;[24] and to be given reasons for a decision.

Over the years, commentators and practitioners have made increasingly vociferous complaints that the EU enforcement structure does not sufficiently respect these rights, and especially does not ensure the investigated undertakings' right to a fair trial. Core concerns about the EU integrated agency model are that: it does not provide for a hearing before an independent decision maker; it creates the risk of 'confirmation' and 'hindsight' bias (so affecting the Commission's ability to take independent and balanced decisions[25]); it does not fully respect the rights of the defence; it provides for the final decision to be adopted, not by the officials

Thomas and Denis Waelbroeck, 'Competition Law Proceedings before the European Commission and the Right to a Fair Trial: No Need for Reform?' (2009) 5 *European Competition Journal* 97.

[19] EU Charter, Art 41.
[20] Case C-511/06 P *Archer Daniels Midland v Commission* [2009] ECR I-5843, para 84.
[21] Case C-389/10 P *KME Germany AG v Commission* 8 December 2011.
[22] *Jusilla v Finland* (2007) 45 EHHR 39. See, in particular eg Arianna Andreangeli, 'Towards an EU Competition Court: "Article-6-Proofing" Antitrust Proceedings before the Commission?' (2007) 4 *World Competition* 595; Ian Forrester, 'Due Process in EC Competition Cases: A Distinguished Institution with Flawed Procedures' (2009) *European Law Review* 817;Wouter Wils, 'The Increased Level of EU Antitrust Fines, Judicial Review, and the European Convention on Human Rights' (2010) 33 *World Competition* 5; Ian Forrester, 'A Bush in Need of Pruning: the Luxuriant Growth of "Light Judicial Review"', in Ehlermann and Marquis (n 16) 407; Renato Nazzini, 'Administrative Enforcement, Judicial Review and Fundamental Rights in EU Competition Law: A Comparative Contextual-Functionalist Perspective' (2012) 49 *Common Market Law Review* 971; and Wouter Wils, 'EU Antitrust Enforcement Powers and Procedural Rights and Guarantees: The Interplay between EU Law, National Law, the Charter of Fundamental Rights of the EU and the European Convention of Human Rights' (2011) 2 *World Competition* 189.
[23] See EUHR, Art 6(2) and EU Charter, Art 48(1).   [24] *Jusilla v Finland* (n 22).
[25] See Marco Bronckers and Anne Vallery, 'Fair and Effective Competition Policy in the EU: Which Role for Authorities and which Role for the Courts after *Menarini*' (2012) 8 *European Competition Journal* 283, 296–297 ('Competition law authorities have policies to defend and cases to win. It is hard to conceive of internal safeguards that could put an effective brake on these inherent biases at the time decisions are taken on the infringement and the fine').

of the Directorate-General for Competition (DGComp) who preside over the proceedings, but by the full college of Commissioners who have not heard or seen the evidence (the parties do not therefore plead their case before the actual decision maker);[26] and further that review of the Commission's decisions by the GC is insufficiently rigorous or intense. This has led some to protest that the model cannot adequately protect the rights demanded in a 'criminal' procedure or give effect to the presumption of innocence, and that profound change is warranted, for example, through separating the investigation, prosecution, and decision making functions within the Commission or the creation of a separate 'competition court' as an independent first instance adjudicator.

Despite these arguments, the Commission has remained resolute that no wholesale overhaul and restructuring of the EU enforcement system is required to meet EU and ECHR principles.[27] Rather, it takes the view that the case law of the European Court of Human Rights (ECtHR) clarifies[28] that the use of an integrated agency model in competition law cases is compatible with Article 6[29] so long as the administrative body's preliminary decision taking procedures are governed by sufficiently strong procedural guarantees and its decisions are subject to judicial control by a body with 'full jurisdiction' on questions of fact and of law, and with power to quash challenged decision in all respects.[30] In Sections II.3 and 4, it is seen that some adjustments and reforms have been made to the Commission's internal procedures to tighten process and with the aim of ensuring that essential procedural safeguards are respected, and fundamental rights protected, at the decision making stage. Further, in Section II.5, it is seen that a crucial question that remains is whether the review conducted by the GC is broad and intense enough to meet the ECtHR's full jurisdiction standard and to remedy any deficiencies occurring in the first instance.[31]

---

[26] But see n 50.

[27] See eg Joaquín Almunia, SPEECH/10/449, Due process and competition enforcement, Florence, 17 September 2010, and Alexander Italianer, 'Safeguarding Due Process in Antitrust Proceedings', Fordham Competition Law Institute, 23 September 2010.

[28] Italianer (n 27) and see eg Wouter Wils, 'The Compatibility with Fundamental Rights of the EU Antitrust Enforcement System in which the European Commission acts both as Investigator and as First-instance Decision Maker' (2014) 37 *World Competition* 5 ('it is now entirely clear that Article 6 ECHR . . . provides no grounds for abandoning the system . . . in which the European Commission both investigates suspected infringements of the antitrust prohibitions contained in Articles 101 and 102 TFEU and takes decisions finding such infringements, ordering their termination, and imposing fines.')

[29] Case law of the ECtHR establishes that proceedings which may culminate in the imposition of a criminal penalty involving civil or 'minor' (non-core) criminal offences require less stringent safeguards and protection than that required in cases of 'core' criminal offences.

[30] 'Thus, the Court must be able to quash in all respects, on questions of fact and of law, the challenged decision (see, for comparison, European Court of Human Rights *Janosevic v Sweden* . . . and *A Menarini Diagnostics S.R.L. v Italy* . . .).' Case E-15/10 *Posten Norge v EFTA Surveillance Authority*, 18 April 2012, para 99.

[31] See especially Case C-389/10 P *KME* (n 21).

3. Preliminary Investigations and Initiation of Proceedings

The Commission may commence an investigation into alleged infringements of the competition rules either on its own initiative or acting on a complaint. There are two stages to the procedure: the preliminary investigation stage—a period of fact finding intended 'to enable the Commission to gather all the relevant information confirming or not the existence of an infringement of the competition rules and to adopt an initial position on the course of the procedure and how it is to proceed';[32] and the 'inter partes' stage—covering the period from the 'initiation of proceedings', a formal notification by a Statement of Objections (the 'SO')[33] by which the Commission indicates its intention to adopt a decision under Regulation 1/2003.

In order to determine whether or not to initiate proceedings, the Commission has extensive fact finding powers, allowing it to obtain information through market inquiries, requests, interviewing persons, and/or, with the participation of NCAs, conducting investigations at business or even in certain circumstances non-business premises (the homes of staff) (and sometimes without warning, so-called 'dawn raids').[34] These broad powers, which include the right to inspect books and other records and to seal premises, were considered necessary to facilitate the uncovering of clear violations of the rules which take place in conditions of secrecy. The ECJ's 'creative jurisprudence' has, however, built in some limits to the pervasive investigative powers and has sought to balance the 'trade-off between the demands of due process and the need to allow the Commission to accomplish institutional objectives'.[35] The ECJ has, for example, confirmed that although an unannounced inspection may be appropriate and proportionate where facts justify and necessitate an inspection,[36] safeguards must be built into processes to ensure that the rights of defence are not irremediably impaired. An undertaking may therefore be compelled to provide information and have a duty to cooperate actively with the Commission (and so produce information that might be a means of establishing an infringement), but it cannot be required to provide answers that might incriminate itself by admitting to infringements.[37] Further, the Commission may not have access to 'privileged' documents provided by independent lawyers

---

[32] See Case T-99/04 *AC-Treuhand AG v Commission* [2008] ECR II-1501, para 47; see also Cases C-238 etc/99 *Limburgse Vinyl Maatschappij NV v Commission* [2002] ECR I-8375, paras 181–183; Case C-105/04 P *Nederlandse Federatieve Vereniging voor de Groothandel op Elektrotechnisch Gebied v Commission* [2006] ECR I-8725, paras 37–38.

[33] See Case 48/72 *SA Brasserie de Haecht v Wilkin-Janssen* [1973] ECR 77, para 16.

[34] Reg 1/2003 (n 5) Arts 18–20.

[35] Arianna Andreangeli and Ioannis Lianos, 'The European Union' in Eleanor M. Fox and Michael J. Trebilcock (eds), *The Design of Competition Law Institutions* (2013).

[36] Case 136/79 *National Panasonic v Commission* [1980] ECR 2033, paras 19–21.

[37] Case 374/87 *Orkem SA v Commission* [1989] ECR 3283.

(although the EU principle does not, controversially,[38] protect documents prepared by in-house counsel).[39]

With the aim of bolstering the objectiveness of the process the Commission created, in 1982, the position of an 'independent' Hearing Officer and has, over the years, expanded the role; the Hearing Officers now preside over the whole of the Commission's administrative procedure (in both antitrust and merger cases).[40] Arguably, however, further and significant amendments would need to be made before the Hearing Officers can satisfactorily fulfil their role as independent guardians of the rights of defence.[41] Commission officials are also assisted in their decision making by the Chief Competition Economist and peer-review panels. To increase understanding of its procedures, the Commission has published a Notice on 'Best Practices for the Conduct of Proceedings' and its internal manual on procedures.[42]

At the end of its investigative phase, the Commission must decide whether to close or settle a case, to take commitments, and/or whether it has sufficient evidence to proceed to a full and final decision. If it wishes to do the latter, it will open a formal procedure during the course of which it will tell the undertakings the case made against them by issuing a written SO setting out the Commission's provisional concerns. The SO forms a critical and central part of the rights of defence. It must set out the facts as understood by the Commission, a legal analysis explaining why it considers Article 101 or 102 to be infringed and any proposed remedy the Commission is contemplating adopting.[43] The Commission also holds state-of-play meetings, as well as providing the investigated persons with the opportunity to be heard (in writing and at an oral hearing presided over by the Hearing Officer) and access to the Commission's file.[44] Other interested persons may also

---

[38] See Michael Frese, 'The Development of General Principles for EU Competition Law Enforcement—the Protection of Legal Professional Privilege' (2011) ECLR 196.

[39] Case C-550/07 P *Akzo Nobel Chemicals Ltd v Commission* [2010] ECR I-8301.

[40] See Decision of the President of the European Commission of 13 October 2011 on the function and terms of reference of the hearing officer in certain competition proceedings [2011] OJ L275/29.

[41] See eg ECLF Working Group on Transparency and Process, 'Transparency and Process: Do We Need a New Mandate for the Hearing Officer?' (2010) 6 *European Competition Journal* 475.

[42] See 'Best Practices for the Conduct of Proceedings' and its internal manual on procedures (the 'Antitrust ManProc'), at http://ec.europa.eu/competition/antitrust/information_en.html. The Commission published this manual following the making of a complaint to the European Ombudsman about its previous non-disclosure, invoking the Transparency Reg 1049/2001: Complaint 297/2010/(ELB)GG, decision 26 September 2011.

[43] See Case 17/74 *Transocean Marine Paint Association v Commission (No. 2)* [1974] ECR 1063, and Cases C-68/94 and 30/95 *France & SCPA v Commission* [1998] ECR I-1375, para 174. The Commission's final decision can only deal with objection so raised and on which parties have been able to comment, Reg 773/2004 of 7 April 2004 relating to the conduct of proceedings by the Commission pursuant to Articles 81 and 82 of the EC Treaty [now Articles 101 and 102 TFEU], Art 11(2), see also Antitrust ManProc, section 11, 'Drafting of Statement of Objections' and invitation to parties to reply (Reg 773/2004, Art 11(2)).

[44] Reg 1/2003 (n 5) Art 27(1)(2) and Commission Notice on Access to the File [2005] OJ C325/7. Access to the file is an integral part of the right to be heard, Case C-51/92 P *Hercules Chemicals NV v Commission (Polypropylene)* [1999] ECR I-4235, paras 75–76.

be heard.[45] Again, it has been necessary to strike a delicate balance between competing interests in this sphere; for example, the right of access to information held on the Commission's file against the need of the Commission to protect the confidentiality of business secrets (information, the disclosure of which, would harm business interests, an undertaking or a person, for example, the identity of a whistle-blower).[46] The Commission has also frequently had to deal with requests for information held on its file (whether in relation to antitrust, merger, or state aid cases) under the Transparency Regulation.[47] Disclosure under the Transparency Regulation will not, however, ordinarily be permissible in competition cases if disclosure would undermine an inspection or investigation.[48]

On the relatively rare occasions in which the EU Courts have found that fundamental principles have not been observed, and in a way which prejudices the rights of defence,[49] they have been prepared to annul the Commission's decision, for example where the Commission has failed to disclose properly documents useful to the parties' defence—whether documents which tend to exonerate them (exculpatory documents) or which tend to incriminate them (inculpatory documents).

4. Adjudication—Decision Making

(a) Decisions by the Commission

Following a formal procedure, the Commission may take: a final decision ordering the termination of a competition law infringement; a decision making commitments binding but without making an infringement finding; or a 'positive' decision finding Article 101 or Article 102 inapplicable. Unless the taking of particular acts of management or administration has been delegated to a single Commissioner, decisions are collegiate acts of the whole Commission.[50] The Commission may also

---

[45] The procedures are set out in Reg 773/2004 (n 43).

[46] See Art 39 TFEU. The right of access to the file is thus 'subject to the legitimate interest of undertakings in the protection their business secrets' Reg 1/2003 (n 5) Art 27(2).

[47] Reg 1049/2001 [2001] OJ L145/43, adopted to implement what is now Art 15(2) TFEU (giving any natural or legal person residing or having its registered office in a Member States the right of access to documents of Union institutions and bodies, etc, pursuant to the principle in Art 15(1) that Union institutions and bodies, etc shall conduct their work as openly as possible).

[48] In Case C-404/10 P *Commission v Éditions Odile Jacob SAS*, 28 June 2012 the ECJ applied this to *closed* merger procedures as well.

[49] See Cases T-305etc/94 *Re the PVC Cartel II: Limburgse Vinyl Maatschappij NV and others v Commission* [1999] ECR II-931, paras 1011–1022, confirmed by the ECJ Cases C-238 etc/99 P *Limburgse Vinyl Maatschappij NV* (n 32) paras 315–328; Case C-51/92 P, *Hercules Chemicals NV v Commission* [1999] ECR I-4235, paras 75–101.

[50] See eg Cases T-25/95 etc *Cimenteries CBR SA v Commission* [2000] ECR II-491, para 721 where the GC rejected claims by two applicants that the principle of impartiality had been breached because the same Commission official had carried out the investigation, acted as rapporteur, drawn up the SO, and prepared the draft decision, on the grounds that the contested decision was actually taken by the College of Commissioners, not by the official.

take procedural decisions during the course of its investigation[51] or interim measures,[52] where necessary to prevent irreparable damage occurring before it can come to a final decision.

(b) Infringement Decisions and Fines

Of particular importance is the power of the Commission to adopt decisions finding an infringement[53] and, subject to the principle of proportionality, to impose remedies. In order to ensure that undertakings bring an infringement to an end and compliance with the rules is restored, not only can the Commission issue cease and desist orders but it can also impose other proportionate and necessary behavioural or structural remedies (eg an order to supply or to divest a part of the business). Regulation 1/2003 states that structural remedies may be appropriate 'where there is a substantial risk of a lasting or repeated infringement that derives from the very structure of the undertaking'. Although the Commission has never actually imposed such remedies, it has negotiated some in the context of a commitments decision.[54]

Where an infringement decision is adopted, the Commission also has power[55] to punish undertakings or associations of undertakings engaged in intentional or negligent infringements through the imposition of proportionate[56] fines up to a maximum of 10 per cent of turnover in the preceding business year. The Commission now publishes Guidelines[57] setting out how it assesses the level of fines. Since the publication of the current Guidelines in 2008, fining levels have increased dramatically (but still within the cap set out in Regulation 1/2003), as the Commission has sought to increase the deterrent effect of the competition law rules. In *Intel*,[58] for example, the Commission imposed a fine exceeding €1 billion on Intel for committing an abuse of a dominant position, and in December 2013, the Commission imposed fines totalling €1.71 billion on eight financial institutions for participating in illegal cartels in financial derivative markets (LIBOR and EURIBOR).[59] It has been seen that unease is mounting about the growing level of these fines and

---

[51] eg during the course of its investigations, it may demand information by decision (Reg 1/2003 (n 5) Art 18(3)), or order an inspection (Art 20(4)).

[52] Reg 1/2003 (n 5) Art 8.   [53] Reg 1/2003 (n 5) Art 7.

[54] See n 75 and accompanying text.

[55] Reg 1/2003 (n 5) Art 23(2). It also has the power to impose fines for procedural infringements (Arts 23(1) and 24) and for breach of Art 9 commitments (Art 23(2)(c)). (Indeed, the Commission fined Microsoft €561 million for breaching its commitments in respect of the browser choice screen; see COMP/39.530, *Microsoft*, IP/13/196).

[56] EU Charter, Art 49.

[57] Guidelines on the method of setting fines imposed pursuant to Article 23(2)(a) of Regulation No 1/2003 [2006] OJ C210/5.

[58] IP/09/745.   [59] IP/13/1208.

whether the Commission's discretion in this area is sufficiently checked by the EU Courts.[60]

Despite very high corporate fines for cartel activity, concern has nonetheless been expressed that they do not target the individuals responsible, may have spillover effects (penalizing innocent shareholders, employees, and creditors), and are not sufficiently high to ensure deterrence.[61] Indeed, some studies reinforce the view that corporate fines are not the highest concern to companies[62] and may not be deterring recidivism.[63] Consequently, it is more frequently being advocated that control which recognizes the role that individuals play in instigating, or not preventing, competition law infringements is required.[64] In the USA, for example, violation of the Sherman Act is a felony and both corporations and individuals involved in cartel activity are pursued in criminal proceedings.[65] Although the EU antitrust prohibitions are directed at undertakings, some Member States can impose administrative sanctions on individuals and/or have either criminal cartel offences or specific criminal offences against bid rigging.[66]

In cartel cases, the Commission also offers leniency to undertakings that contact the Commission.[67] Essentially, if certain conditions are fulfilled, this Notice guarantees immunity from fines to the first undertaking to submit evidence to the

[60] See Section II.5 and eg n 82 and accompanying text.

[61] See eg Wouter Wils, 'Is Criminalisation of EU Competition Law the Answer?' (2005) 28 *World Competition* 17; John Connor, 'Optimal Deterrence and Private International Cartels' Purdue Working Paper (2006); Emmanuel Combe and Constance Monnier, 'Fines against Hard Core Cartels in Europe: The Myth of Over Enforcement' (2011) *Antitrust Bulletin* 235.

[62] See eg OFT Report, Drivers of Compliance and Non-compliance with Competition Law (May 2010).

[63] John Connor, 'Recidivism Revealed: Private International Cartels 1999–2009' (2010) 6 *Competition Policy International* 3; but see Wouter Wils, 'Recidivism in EU Antitrust Enforcement: A Legal and Economic Analysis' (2012) 35 *World Competition* 5 and Gregory Werden, Scott Hammond, and Belinda Barnett, 'Recidivism Eliminated: Cartel Enforcement in the United States since 1999' Georgetown Global Antitrust Enforcement Symposium (2011) (noting that no corporation or individual convicted for cartel activity has been engaged in another cartel prosecuted in the USA).

[64] See eg Adrian Hoel, 'Crime Does Not Pay but Hard-core Cartel Conduct May: Why it Should Be Criminalised' (2008) 16 *Trade Practices Law Journal* 102, but see Alison Jones and Rebecca Williams, 'The UK's Response to the Global Effort against Cartels: Is Criminalisation Really the Solution?' (2014) 2 *Journal of Antitrust Enforcement* 100. Individual sanctions do not necessarily have to be criminal in nature, see eg Aaron Khan, 'Rethinking Sanctions for Breaching EU Competition Law: Is Director Disqualification the Answer?' (2012) 35 *World Competition* 77, 82 and see section II.7.

[65] Donald Baker 'Punishment for Cartel Participants in the US: A Special Model?' in Caron Beaton-Wells and Ariel Ezrachi (eds), *Criminalising Cartels: Critical Studies of an International Regulatory Movement* (2011) 27.

[66] See further Section II.7 and eg Gregory Shaffer and Nathaniel Nesbitt, 'Criminalizing Cartels: A Global Trend?' (2011) 12 *Sedona Conference Journal* (noting that across the world '[m]ore than thirty countries have criminalized cartel conduct in some form').

[67] Commission Notice on immunity from fines and reduction of fines in cartel cases [2006] OJ C298/11; Commission Press Release, IP/06/1705, 7 December 2006.

Commission and offers the possibility of reduction in fines to others that cooperate with it. Like many other jurisdictions around the world, therefore, the Commission has sought to deter cartel activity both through increasing sanctions for those found to have been involved in such activity whilst, at the same time, utilizing a leniency regime as an important anti-cartel enforcement tool which serves to destabilize cartels and to encourage a 'race to confess'. Since 2008, the Commission has also sought where possible to dispose of cartel cases rapidly through reliance on a formal settlement procedure.[68] This procedure allows the Commission to proceed to an infringement decision more quickly and cheaply (whilst reducing the risk of an appeal) and undertakings complying with the procedure benefit from a reduction in fine of 10 per cent.

(c) Commitments and Non-infringement Decisions

In 2004, Regulation 1/2003 conferred new powers on the Commission to adopt both commitments decisions (rendering binding undertakings given by the parties, without adopting a final decision, Article 9[69]) and 'positive' decisions finding that Articles 101 and 102 are inapplicable to particular agreements or practices (Article 10).[70] Even though, particularly in the area of Article 101, it would be extremely helpful in many situations to have clarification of when that provision is not applicable to certain practices (eg resale price maintenance),[71] the Commission has never adopted a non-infringement decision.

The Commission has, in contrast, made extensive use of the commitments procedure, adopting more than 30[72] such decisions in its first ten years;[73] not only did the Commission first use Article 9 to deal with a number of pre-Regulation 1/2003 notifications, but it has subsequently used it to close a number of proceedings,

---

[68] Commission Notice on the conduct of settlement procedures [2008] OJ C167/1.

[69] See eg Wouter Wils, 'The Use of Settlements in Public Antitrust Enforcement: Objectives and Principles' (2008) 31 *World Competition* 335; Wouter Wils, 'Discretion and Prioritisation in Public Antitrust Enforcement' (2011) 34 *World Competition* 353.

[70] The Commission was at first keen to ensure, however, that this procedure was not used by undertakings as a mechanism for gaining 'exemptions' following the abolition of the notification and exemption system.

[71] Reg 1/2003, recital 14 states that Art 10 decisions will be adopted *in exceptional cases* 'with a view to clarifying the law and ensuring its consistent application throughout the [Union], in particular with regard to new types of agreements or practices that have not been settled in the existing case-law and administrative practice'. Art 10 makes it clear, however, that these declaratory decisions will be made only when required by the Community public interest.

[72] See 'Questions and Answers' memo that accompanied the Google market test notice on 25 April 2013, MEMO/13/838.

[73] Reg 1/2003 (n 5), recital 13 states that Commitment decisions are not suitable where the Commission intends to impose a fine. Consequently, the Commission does not apply the procedure to secret cartels, 'Best Practices' (n 42) para 116. But see COMP/38.636 *Rambus* IP/09/1897; COMP/39.530 *Microsoft* (tying) IP/13/2013; COM/39.692 *IBM Maintenance Services* IP/11/1539; and Case 39.847 *e-Books* IP/12/1367.

many involving Article 102 (including a number in the energy sector[74]). Indeed, it has utilized Article 9 to quite dramatic effect, and even to secure structural solutions in some cases.[75] In *Alrosa*,[76] the ECJ confirmed that the Commission has a broad discretion to act in this area and may use Article 9 to extract concessions from undertakings, which might go beyond that which it could impose if it had to proceed to a final decision. The principle of proportionality in Article 9 cases requires only that the commitments offered address the Commission's concerns and that the interests of third parties are taken into account. The ECJ thus views the commitments not as a top-down, imposed public-law decision, but as a contract following a negotiation.[77]

The greater reliance on Article 9 since 2004 has significantly changed the face of the Commission's enforcement, creating a shift away from imposed infringement decisions towards negotiated outcomes. It is understandable that the procedure is attractive both for the Commission (enabling it to terminate cases quickly—especially important perhaps in rapidly evolving high-tech markets—whilst retaining control; it has no obligation to accept the undertakings' commitments and can proceed to a final Article 7(1) decision if it wishes) and the parties (who avoid the adverse consequences of an infringement decision and do not have to admit to an infringement). Nonetheless, there is concern that it is being used at the expense of the development and clarification of the law and the public interest, and, further, that the procedure is being operated in regulatory way, which goes beyond the conventional model of competition law and which is contributing to a blurring of the boundaries between competition law and regulation. In particular, the Commission has utilized Article 9 to settle, frequently in an interventionist manner, cases involving novel and extremely complex issues, meaning it does not have to develop legal analysis in a way that will prove its case or, importantly, help to elucidate the law. Such an approach creates risks, particularly in terms of legitimacy and error costs.[78]

---

[74] See eg Case 39.386 *EDF—Long Term Electricity Contracts in France*; COMP/B-1/337.966 *Distrigaz* [2008] OJ C9/8; COMP/39.316 *GDF, Gas market in France* OJ C57/13, IP/09/1872, 3 December 2009; COMP/39.388 *German Electricity Wholesale Markets* and COMP/39.389 *German Electricity Balancing Markets (E.ON)* [2009] OJ C36/8; Case COMP/39.402 *RWE—Gas Foreclosure* [2009] OJ C133/9; COMP 39.317 *E.ON (Gas)* [2010] OJ C278/9, 4 May 2010; COMP/39.727 *CEZ* IP/13/320, 10 April 2013.

[75] See Cases *Distrigaz* (n 74); *RWE-Gas Foreclosure* (n 74); *E.ON (Gas)* (n 74); *CEZ* (n 74).

[76] Case C-441/07 P *Commission v Alrosa* [2010] ECR I-5949.

[77] The ECJ took a very different approach to that which had been adopted by the GC in this case; see Florian Wagner-Von Papp, 'Best and even Better Practices in Commitment Procedures after Alrosa: The Dangers of Abandoning the "Struggle for Competition Law"' (2012) 49 *Common Market Law Review* 929, 933.

[78] See eg Niamh Dunne, 'Commitment Decisions in EU Competition Law' (2014) *Journal of Competition Law and Economics* 1, doi: 10.1093/joclec/nht047.

(d) Sector Inquiries

Article 17 of Regulation 1/2003 provides for the Commission to conduct general inquiries into a sector of the economy. Although Article 17(2) confers information-gathering powers, the Article does not give the Commission power to adopt remedies following an investigation. Through such an inquiry the Commission can, however, obtain a broader view of the sector and practices within it than it would when concentrating on individual agreements concluded by firms operating in those markets. Having conducted a review, it may then be in a position to take further action, either under the competition, or other Treaty, rules. Following its energy report, for example, the Commission stated that it would use the antitrust laws to remedy anti-competitive practices identified (such as long-term downstream contracts, collusion between incumbents to share markets, and lack of access to infrastructure), consider competition and regulatory remedies to deal with other identified problems, use the state aid rules where state subsidies contribute to maintenance of concentrated markets and prevent liberalization from taking root, and use the Merger Regulation to prevent increasing market concentration in this area. Indeed, a number of Article 102 proceedings have subsequently been pursued in the energy sector.[79]

5. Judicial Review

The ECJ has power to review fines and Commission Decisions under Articles 261 and 263 TFEU respectively. It has already been seen that the question of whether the review conducted by the GC is intense and quick[80] enough to satisfy the requirements of Article 6 has become a critical issue in recent years. One difficulty is that although it has unlimited jurisdiction to cancel, increase, or reduce fines under Article 261,[81] the Commission's decisions can only be challenged in judicial review proceedings under Article 263 (a review of legality).[82] It has thus been

---

[79] See n 74.

[80] The review process before the GC is often protracted. There is an expedited procedure for cases of urgency (Rules of Procedure of the General Court [1991] OJ L136/1, as amended, Art 76(a)) but this is rarely applicable to this kind of appeal.

[81] It is argued that nonetheless the GC has been too tolerant of the Commission's general approach to fining and the increased level of fines to deter infringements, and has generally confined itself to checking consistency with the fining guidelines; it is thus too deferential and has not sufficiently exercised its unlimited jurisdiction in this area, see eg Forrester (n 22) and Nils F.W. Hauger and Christoph Palzer, 'Investigator, Prosecutor, Judge . . . and now Plaintiff? The Leviathanian Role of the European Commission in the Light of Fundamental Rights' (2013) 36 *World Competition* 565.

[82] If the Commission (or GC, see n 81) has breached EU law, an action for damages may also be available against it under Art 340 TFEU. For example, a claimant may bring an action against the Commission for any damage caused to it by the defective decision: the claimant will have to establish, however, that it has committed a sufficiently serious breach of a superior rule of law intended to confer rights on individuals, and that is it has manifestly and gravely disregarded the limits on

questioned whether this review is sufficient to allow the GC to examine all, and quash in all respects on, questions of fact and law.

Article 263 provides four grounds for challenging the Commission's acts: lack of competence; infringement of an essential procedural requirement; infringement of the Treaties or of any rule of law relating to their application; or misuse of powers.[83] Competition cases are most frequently based either on pleas of procedural defects[84] or on the broad head of infringement of the Treaty or of any rule of law, including general and human right principles. This latter head enables challenges to be made on the basis that the law has been misinterpreted or misapplied, but also on the basis that the Commission committed a 'manifest error of appraisal'[85] and that the evidence relied on or the facts established by the Commission do not support the finding of law. Although the GC does not re-hear the case as it would if there was a full appeal on the merits, the GC does examine facts to determine whether the factual basis of the Commission decision was correct or sufficient, and that the Commission has produced 'sufficiently precise and coherent proof' to support its case.[86]

The most controversial aspect of the Article 263 review is that with regard to 'complex technical appraisals'[87] relating to the Commission's economic assessment, the GC states that it conducts only a limited review, and will not substitute its own assessment of matters for that of the Commission: '[E]xamination by the Community judicature of the complex economic assessments made by the Commission must necessarily be confined to verifying whether the rules on procedure and on the statement of reasons have been complied with, whether the facts have been accurately stated and whether there has been any manifest error of appraisal or misuse of powers.'[88] Some take the view that because such a 'limited review', displaying

its discretion, see eg Case C-440/07 P *Commission v Schneider Electric* [2009] ECR I-6413; Case 53/84 *Stanley Adams v Commission* [1985] ECR 3595; and Case C-352/98 P *Bergaderm and Goupil v Commission* [2000] ECR I-5291.

[83] This latter ground has never been successfully pleaded in a competition case, see eg Case 5/85 *AKZO Chemie BV v Commission* [1986] ECR 2585; Case T-5/93 *Roger Tremblay v Commission* [1995] ECR II-185.

[84] See eg Cases T-79/89 etc *BASF v Commission* [1992] ECR II-315 and Cases C-137/92 P *Commission v BASF and others* [1994] ECR I-2555.

[85] Case 42/84 *Remia & Nutricia v Commission* [1985] ECR 2545, para 34.

[86] See eg Cases 29 and 30/83 *CRAM and Rheinzink v Commission* [1984] ECR 1679, para 20; Cases C-89/85 etc *A Ahlström Oy v Commission* [1993] ECR I-1307, para 127; Case T-201/04 *Microsoft v Commission* [2007] ECR II-3601, para 564. Where it has not, it will annul the decision; see eg Case 6/72 *Europemballage Corp & Continental Can Co Inc v Commission* [1973] ECR 215; and Cases C-89/85 etc *A. Ahlström Oy* and Cases T-68/89 etc *Società Italiana Vetro Spa v Commission* [1992] ECR II-1403.

[87] Case T-201/04 *Microsoft v Commission* [2007] ECR II-3601, para 88.

[88] Cases C-204/00 P, C-205/00 P, C-211/00 P, C-213/00 P, C-217/00 P, and C-219/00 P *Aalborg Portland and others v Commission* [2004] ECR I-123, echoing Case 42/84 *Remia v Commission* [1985] ECR 2545. Reference is often made to the Commission's 'discretion' or 'margin of discretion' in this respect but arguably the term 'margin of appreciation' is most accurate, see O. Odudu, 'Article 101(3), Discretion and Direct Effect' (2002) 23 *European Competition Law Review* 17; D. Bailey, 'Scope of Judicial Review Under Article 101 EC' (2004) 41 *Common Market Law Review* 1327.

deference to the Commission when acting within its margin of appreciation, is conducted in infringement cases where fines may be imposed the EU system is flawed.[89] Others point to the fact that in some cases the GC has, despite this language, in fact conducted a very exacting, intensive, and exhaustive review of the Commission's decisions. For example, in a series of merger cases, the GC has rigorously reviewed the Commission's decisions to determine whether it had discharged its burden of establishing how the concentration might in the future alter the factors determining the state of competition on a market and whether it would give rise to a significant impediment to effective competition on the market.[90] In *KME*,[91] the ECJ rejected the argument in that case that the GC had violated the applicant's fundamental right to full and effective judicial review,[92] and had deferred too much to the Commission's discretion, holding that:

whilst, in areas giving rise to complex economic assessments, the Commission has a margin of discretion with regard to economic matters, that does not mean that the Courts of the European Union must refrain from reviewing the Commission's interpretation of information of an economic nature. Not only must those Courts establish, among other things, whether the evidence relied on is factually accurate, reliable and consistent but also whether that evidence contains all the information which must be taken into account in order to assess a complex situation and whether it is capable of substantiating the conclusions drawn from it.[93]

Given the unlimited jurisdiction to review fines, the Court concluded that the review provided for by the Treaties involves review of

both the law and the facts, and means that they have the power to assess the evidence, to annul the contested decision and to alter the amount of a fine. The review of legality provided for under Article 263 TFEU, supplemented by the unlimited jurisdiction in respect of the amount of the fine, provided for under Article 31 of Regulation No 1/2003, is not therefore contrary to the requirements of the principle of effective judicial protection in Article 47 of the Charter.[94]

The ECJ thus sent a clear message in this case: that the GC must engage with the Commission's 'complex economic assessments'. This suggests that even though there may be a disconnection between the type of review that the GC states it carries out and the type of review that it *actually* carries out, what is decisive is whether

---

[89] See Forrester (n 22).

[90] See eg Case M.2416, annulled on appeal; Case T-5/02 *Tetra Laval v Commission* [2002] ECR II-4381, *aff'd*; Case C-12/03 P *Commission v Tetra Laval* [2005] ECR I-987.

[91] Case C-272/09 P *KME* (n 21). See also Case C-501/11 P *Schindler Holding SA v Commission*.

[92] 'The principle of effective judicial protection is a general principle of European Union law to which expression is given by Article 47 of the Charter,' *Schindler Holding* (n 91) para 92.

[93] *Schindler Holding* (n 91) para 94. See also Case C-199/11 *Europese Gemeenschap v Otis*, 6 November 2012, para 63.

[94] *Europese Gemeenschap* (n 93) para 106. In relying on the EU Charter, however, the ECJ did not directly consider Art 6 ECHR or engage head on with the debate that has been raging about Art 6 and the quasi-criminal nature of antitrust proceedings. Contrast Case E-15/10 *Posten Norge* (n 30).

the judicial body in fact exercises full jurisdiction.[95] Not all agree, however, that the review conducted by the GC (either under Article 263 or Article 261) is always sufficiently intense to meet this standard. Further, even if it is correct that it does, or will in the future, then it might be better if the 'EU courts abandon the "complex appraisals" formula and devise a new description of what they actually do',[96] as there is clearly no room for deference to administrative discretion and the manifest error test where the court is reviewing infringement decisions falling within the 'criminal' sphere.[97]

6. Political Influence?

The central enforcement role in antitrust and merger cases in the EU is played by the Commission. It has been seen that a particular feature of the EU system is that decisions are, unless delegated, taken by the College of Commissioners. It is true that the College is a political body of appointees, that is not involved in the process leading up to the adoption of the decision, and that, in some controversial cases (particularly merger cases),[98] vigorous lobbying of the Commissioners has undoubtedly taken place. Nonetheless, it has also been seen that the Commission's decisions are subject to review by the EU courts and would be annulled if, for political purposes, the law were to be misinterpreted or misapplied and/or if evidence relied on or the facts established by the Commission did not support the finding of law. In practice, therefore, the College of Commissioners generally 'rubber-stamps' the decisions prepared by DGComp and the Competition Commissioner.

In some jurisdictions, competition law legislation may specifically provide for political intervention, whether generally or in identified cases. In the UK, for example, the Enterprise Act 2002 permits politicians to intervene in merger cases that raise defined public interest considerations, beyond competition and customer benefits.[99] In line with this approach, the EU Merger Regulation

---

[95] Wils (n 28).

[96] Bronckers and Vallery (n 25) 294; (it would be 'preferable for the Courts to no longer use the language of "manifest error", "margin of appreciation", "complex economic assessments" and the line when reviewing decisions imposing fines, so as to avoid any confusion', 294).

[97] Bronckers and Vallery (n 25) 295.

[98] See eg Case M.315 *Mannesmann/Vallourec/Ilva* [1994] OJ L102/1; Case M.53 *Aérospatiale-Alenia/ de Havilland* [1991] OJ L334/42; Case M.469 *MSG/ Media Services GmbH,* 9 November 1994; Case M.1672 *Volvo/Scania* [2001] OJ L143/74; and Alison Jones and John Davies, 'Merger Control and the Public Interest: Balancing EU and National Law in the Protectionist Debate' [2014] 10(3) *European Competition Journal* 453.

[99] Enterprise Act 2002, ss 42–58.

permits Member States to intervene in EU merger cases where necessary to protect certain legitimate interests not protected by the merger regulation itself.[100]

7. Enforcement by the National Competition Authorities

Although this chapter focuses on the enforcement process followed by the Commission, it has been seen that, since 2004, NCAs have begun to play a core part in the enforcement process. Indeed, Member States must designate NCAs to enforce Articles 101 and 102.[101] A few points are consequently noted here about case allocation and enforcement at the national level.

First, Regulation 1/2003 stipulates that NCAs are obliged to apply Articles 101 and 102 when applying national competition law to agreements or conduct which affects trade between Member States.[102] Although national and EU law apply concurrently,[103] where there is a conflict between a directly effective EU provision and national law, the former must prevail.[104] The principle of supremacy establishes that national law can be applied only insofar as its application does not 'prejudice the full and uniform application of [EU] law or the effects of measures taken or to be taken to implement it'.[105] This principle, which is elaborated on in Article 3 of Regulation 1/2003,[106] establishes that: (1) an NCA cannot authorize an agreement or conduct prohibited by EU law under national law or according to a national act.[107] Indeed, NCAs (like national courts) owe a duty of sincere cooperation to the EU[108] and are required *not* to apply provisions of national law that contravene EU law[109]; and (2) an NCA cannot apply national competition law more strictly than Article 101, although they are free to apply it more strictly than Article 102 to unilateral conduct.[110]

---

[100]   Reg 139/2004 (n 4) Art 21(4), Art 346 TFEU, and Ch 24.   [101]   Reg 1/2003 (n 5) Art 5.

[102]   Reg 1/2003 (n 5) Art 3(1), but see discussion of Art 11(6) in discussion in text to n 117. The obligation does not apply to (1) agreements or conduct which do not affect trade between Member States; or (2) to cases which involve the application of stricter national competition law to unilateral conduct which does not constitute an abuse of a dominant position (Art 3(2)).

[103]   Case 14/68 *Walt Wilhelm v Bundeskartellamt* [1969] ECR 1.

[104]   Case 6/64 *Costa v ENEL* [1964] ECR 585, 593–594, 456.

[105]   Case 14/68 *Walt Wilhelm* (n 103) para 9.   [106]   [2003] OJ L1/1.

[107]   Case 14/68, *Walt Wilhelm* (n 103) para 9.

[108]   See TEU, Art 4(3) which provides that the Union and Member States are to assist each other in carrying out tasks flowing from the Treaties and that Member States 'shall take any appropriate measure . . . to ensure fulfilment of the obligations' and 'shall facilitate the achievement of the Union's tasks and refrain from any measure which could jeopardise the attainment of the Union's objectives'.

[109]   See also Case C-453/99 *Courage Ltd v Crehan* [2001] ECR I-6297 and Case C-198/01 *Consorzio Industrie Fiammiferi (CIF) v Autorità Garante della Concorrenza e del Mercato* [2003] ECR I-8055 (a national authority is duty bound to disapply national legislation that violates EU law).

[110]   Reg 1/2003, Art 3(2). Arts 3(1) and (2) do not apply, however, to national merger control rules; or national legislation, which protects other legitimate interests—other than the protection of

Second, important issues are (1) when can an NCA, rather than the Commission, act under Article 101 and/or Article 102 (either on its own, possibly with the assistance of others, or in parallel with other NCAs),[111] and (2) how can it be ensured that the competition authorities act consistently? Article 11(1) of Regulation 1/2003 provides that 'the Commission and the competition authorities of the Member States shall apply the [EU] competition rules in close cooperation', and the ECN was specifically designed to ensure the success of the decentralized system; that the authorities operate according to common principles and in close collaboration and that the competition rules are applied effectively and consistently. Not only, therefore, does Regulation 1/2003 contain provisions dealing with cooperation between the Commission and the NCAs but the Joint Statement of the Council and the European Commission on the Functioning of the Network of Competition Authorities (the Joint Statement)[112] sets out the main principles governing the ECN which provides a forum to: facilitate the allocation of cases; to foster cooperation in the conduct of investigations and the sharing of information; and to ensure a continuous dialogue between the ECN authorities in relation to cases and competition policy, law, and practice. In addition, the Commission's Cooperation Notice provides fuller and more specific details of cooperation and division of work amongst ECN members.

In relation to case allocation, the general principle is that a case should be dealt with by the authority 'best placed' to deal with it and best able to restore or maintain competition in the market.[113] In order to be well placed, there must be a material link between the infringement and the territory of the authority (the conduct has substantial direct, actual, or foreseeable effects in the territory), the authority must be able to bring the entire infringement effectively to an end (either on its own or in parallel with another authority), and the authority must be able to gather the evidence required (whether or not with the assistance of another authority).[114] A single NCA is usually well placed to deal with agreements or practices that substantially affect competition mainly within its territory. Where two or more NCAs are well placed to act, then one NCA only should act where the action of one would be sufficient to bring the entire infringement to an end. If it would not, then two or more NCAs should act. The authorities should coordinate their action and where possible designate a lead authority for the case.[115]

competition on the market (the objective of Arts 101 and 102) provided that such legislation is compatible with general principles and other provisions of Community law (Art 3(3)).

[111] Commission Notice (n 8) para 5.

[112] Joint Statement of the European Council and the European Commission on the functioning of the network of competition authorities, 10 December 2002, available at http://ec.europa.eu/competition/ecn/joint_statement_en.pdf.

[113] Joint Statement (n 112) paras 11–14.   [114] Cooperation Notice (n 8) para 8.

[115] Joint Statement (n 112) para 18.

The Commission is likely to be best placed to deal with an agreement or practice where it has effects on competition in three or more Member States; the conduct is linked with other Union provisions which may be exclusively or more effectively applied by the Commission; or the Union interest requires it (to develop competition policy or to ensure effective enforcement).[116] If the Commission does initiate proceedings, Article 11(6) of Regulation 1/2003 provides that NCAs may not apply Articles 101 and 102 (this means that NCAs also lose jurisdiction to act under national competition law as they cannot apply these provisions without applying EU law[117]). The Cooperation Notice indicates that it will rarely initiate proceedings where a case has initially been allocated to another NCA, and it appears that this provision has never been relied upon by the Commission to remove jurisdiction from an NCA. Nonetheless, this provision confers significant power on the Commission and leverage over NCAs.

Regulation 1/2003 also contains provisions designed to ensure consistency in interpretation of the EU competition law rules by the Commission, the NCAs, and national courts[118] and for close cooperation between them. For example, NCAs are obliged to notify the Commission of new cases and contemplated decisions and Regulation 1/2003 provides, subject to safeguards designed to protect the rights of defence,[119] for the transfer of information between authorities, and cooperation in investigations between members of the ECN.[120] It also clarifies that an authority can suspend proceedings or reject a complaint on the grounds that it is being dealt with by another authority.

Third, the degree of 'independence'[121] of NCAs and the institutional structures vary from Member State to Member State. Questions of institutional choice and procedure have thus, as a general rule, been left to the Member States and there is considerable diversity in the national procedural enforcement frameworks. Although in some Member States NCAs have the power to fine undertakings in breach of Articles 101 or 102 (and/or national equivalents) following an administrative procedure similar to that followed by the Commission, in some Member States a judicial model is followed. In Ireland, for example, such a model is required by the Constitution, which generally requires justice to be administered, and fines imposed, by the courts, not administrative bodies. Even though processes and rights of defence diverge between Member States, NCAs when acting within the sphere of EU law must comply with fundamental principles of EU law and respect Charter rights and adhere to core principles. In some Member States, NCAs have a remit which is broader than just the enforcement of the competition law rules; for

---

[116] Joint Statement (n 112) para 19. Cooperation Notice (n 8) paras 14 and 15.
[117] See n 104.   [118] See also Cooperation Notice (n 8).   [119] See especially Arts 11–21.
[120] Reg 1/2003 (n 5) Arts 11–14 and 16.
[121] The Commission is considering whether to introduce legislation that would seek to safeguard the independence of NCAs, see statements Competition Commissioner Almunia, 'Competition Policy Enforcement as a Driver for Growth' Bruegel workshop, Brussels, 18 February 2014.

example, some have competence in regulatory fields and some (as in the UK) have both competition law and consumer protection functions.

The Commission has some concerns about the 'autonomy' the current system affords to Member States in terms of institutional design and procedural rules governing public enforcement. It is therefore considering whether further action should be taken to tackle national institutional and procedural divergences that may detract from transparency, legal certainty, and a level playing field for undertakings.[122] Although the work of the ECN may go some way to tackling these issues, the Commission is reflecting on the question of whether further harmonization measures might be required. If the Commission does pursue this route, the issue of whether and/or the extent to which, the EU has competence to harmonize in this sphere may prove to be controversial.[123]

Fourth, NCAs may adopt infringement or commitments decisions, order interim measures, and impose fines or other penalties provided for in their national law.[124] Indeed, in *Bundeswettbewerbsbehörde and Bundeskartellanwalt v Schenker & Co AG*,[125] the ECJ held that in order to ensure the effectiveness of the rules, NCAs are obliged to impose a fine on an undertaking that has infringed Article 101 intentionally or negligently, unless the undertaking's cooperation has been decisive in detecting and actually suppressing the cartel. Although Regulation 1/2003 specifically provides that NCAs can decide that there are no grounds for action on their part, in *Tele2Polska*,[126] the ECJ interpreted the Regulation in a way that imposes significant limits on the powers of the NCAs. It held that it does not permit NCAs to adopt decisions finding that Article 102 (or Article 101) has *not* been infringed.

In some Member States, NCAs may also be able to impose a broader range of sanctions than those that exist at the EU level—including sanctions for individuals as well as undertakings. For example, some NCAs may impose civil fines on individuals following its administrative procedure[127] and, in the UK, directors of companies that have breached the rules may be disqualified from acting in that capacity for up to 15 years.[128] Further, a growing number of NCAs now have the power to pursue criminal proceedings against individuals (and/or corporations) who have caused their firm to make, or to implement, horizontal cartel agreements or forms of it, such as bid rigging.[129]

---

[122] See Report on the function of Reg 1/2003 and accompanying Commission Staff Working Paper (2009).

[123] Reg 1/2003 (n 5), Art 5.

[124] K. Cseres, 'EU Competition Law and National Competition Laws' in I. Lianos and D. Geradin (eds) *Handbook on European Competition Law: Enforcement and Procedure* (2013) Art 5.

[125] Case C-681/11, 18 June 2013.

[126] Case C-375/09 *Prezes Urzędu Ochrony Konkurencji i Konsumentów v Tele2 Polska sp. z o.o. (now Netia SA)* [2011] ECR I-3055.

[127] See eg ICN Cartels Working Group, 'Defining Hard Core Cartel Conduct, Effective Institutions, Effective Penalties' (2005) 64–65.

[128] Enterprise Act 2002, section 204.   [129] See eg in the UK, Enterprise Act 2002, Part 6.

III. Private Enforcement

1. The Duties of the National Courts

Private civil actions may achieve corrective justice by allowing compensation of victims. They may also relieve enforcement pressure on public enforcement agencies and so contribute to deterring[130] violations of the rules and in helping to develop and clarify the law. Private enforcement is closely connected to public enforcement. Not only do public enforcement actions facilitate private ones,[131] but private actions can[132] reinforce public enforcement by increasing the resources available for the prosecution of competition law infringements, the likelihood of detection and the cost of non-compliance.

The TFEU contains no specific provision governing private rights of action for damages or injunctions following a violation of the EU competition law rules.[133] Private proceedings in the national courts are, however, possible by virtue of the fact that Articles 101 and 102 have direct effect; national courts[134] must protect the rights which individuals derive from directly effective provisions of EU law and respect the principle of supremacy.[135] National courts and tribunals can request the ECJ to make a preliminary ruling on the interpretation or validity of EU law[136] under Article 267 TFEU.[137]

The principle of direct effect, combined with Article 3 of Regulation 1/2003,[138] means that national courts, like NCAs, have an obligation to apply EU law in combination with national law in certain circumstances; cannot apply national law to

---

[130] See Assimakis Komninos, 'Public and Private Antitrust Enforcement in Europe: Complement? Overlap?' (2006) 3 *The Competition Law Review* 1, 9; Renato Nazzini and Ali Nikpay, 'Private Actions in EC Competition Law' (2008) 4 *Competition Policy International* 107, 109.

[131] A public finding of infringement may be relied upon to establish the existence of a competition law infringement and may provide evidence helpful in establishing causation and harm, Wils (n 1) 15–16.

[132] But private enforcement can sometimes undermine public enforcement too; see further Section III.2.

[133] Contrast the position in the USA; see Clayton Act 1914, sections 4 and 16.

[134] Reg 1/2003, Art 3(1).   [135] See Case 14/68 *Walt Wilhelm* (n 103) para 9 and Ch 7.

[136] The ECJ has accepted references relating to the interpretation of national competition law where that law mirrors the EU competition law provisions, see eg Case C-7/97 *Oscar Bronner GmbH & Co KG v Mediaprint* [1998] ECR I-7791.

[137] Although the ECJ does not accept references from NCAs (Art 267 references must be made by a 'court or tribunal', see eg Case C-103/97 *Köllensperger and Atzwanger* [1999] ECR I-551), it accepts references from tribunals or courts hearing appeals from an NCA's decision, see Case C-53/03 *Synetairismos Farmakopoion Aitolias & Akarnanias (Syfait) v GlaxoSmithKline* [2005] ECR I-4609 (reference refused); Case C-468-478/06 *Sot. Lelos kai Sia and others EE v GlaxoSmithKline AEVE Farmakeftikon Proionton* [2008] ECR I-7139.

[138] [2003] OJ L1/1.

authorize conduct prohibited by EU law; and can only apply national competition law more strictly in the circumstances specified by Regulation 1/2003. Although Article 11(6), which relieves NCAs of their competence to apply Articles 101 and 102 following initiation of proceedings by the Commission, does not apply to national courts, the ECJ has held that the duty of cooperation set out in EU law requires a national court to follow a Commission decision dealing with the same parties and the same agreement in the same Member State.[139] Further, Article 16 of Regulation 1/2003 provides that the national courts must not adopt decisions contrary to a previous Commission decision and must avoid giving decisions that would conflict with a decision contemplated by the Commission.[140]

Where an individual seeks to vindicate or protect her EU rights before a national court, the general principle is that of 'national procedural autonomy'—national law sets out the rules governing proceedings.[141] Although the protection given to EU rights and the availability of any remedy for breach of the competition rules is thus dependent on the procedural, evidential, and substantive rules applicable in each particular Member State, the national rules must of course comply with the principles of equivalence and effectiveness and ensure the availability of adequate remedies sufficient to guarantee real and *effective* judicial protection for EU rights.[142] In the context of antitrust, it is now established that national courts must ensure that:

1. Individual *clauses* in an agreement affected by the Article 101(1)—and Article 102[143]—prohibition are held to be void.[144] It is seen in chapter 24 that the agreement as a whole will also be void where those clauses are not severable from the remaining terms of the agreement (but that this is a matter for national law).[145]

2. Full compensation, must, in principle, be available to those who have suffered loss in consequence of a breach of Article 101 or 102, *Courage Ltd v Crehan*.[146]

---

[139] See eg Case C-344/98 *Masterfoods v HB Ice Cream Ltd* [2000] ECR I-11369 and Case 234/89 *Delimitis v Henninger Bräu* [1991] ECR I-935.

[140] See also Cooperation Notice (n 8) paras 11–13 and Case 314/85 *Foto-Frost v Hauptzollamt Lübeck-Ost* [1987] ECR 4199, paras 12–20. If the national court does not agree with the decision of the Commission it must either await the outcome of an appeal, if any, from its decision, or refer the question to the ECJ for a preliminary ruling.

[141] Case 33/76 *Rewe-Zentralfinanz eG and Rewe-Zentral AG v Landwirtschaftskammer für das Saarland* [1976] ECR 1989 and see further Ch 8.

[142] See Case 14/83 *Von Colson and Kamann v Land Nordrhein-Westfalen* [1984] ECR 1891, especially para 23, and Case 33/76 *Rewe-Zentralfinanz* (n 141) para 5 and Ch 8.

[143] Although Art 102 contains no declaration of nullity equivalent to that set out in Art 101, it is to be expected that Art 102 renders a contract, or severable terms of a contract, affected by its prohibition void or, at the very least, unenforceable in the same way as Art 101. See *English Welsh & Scottish Railway Ltd v E.ON UK plc* [2007] EWHC 599.

[144] Case 56/65 *Société La Technique Minière v Maschinenbau Ulm GmbH* [1966] ECR 234, 250.

[145] *Société La Technique Minière* (n 144); Case 319/82 *Société de Vente de Ciments et Bétons de l'Est SA v Kerpen & Kerpen GmbH & Co KG* [1983] ECR 4173.

[146] Case C-453/99 *Courage Ltd v Crehan* (n 109). See also Cases C-295&298/04 *Manfredi v Lloyd Adriatico Assicurazioni SpA* [2006] ECR I-6619 and Case C-557/12 *Kone AG v ÖBB-Infrastruktur AG*, 5 June, 2014.

Defences and limitations to such actions may only be applied insofar as the principles of equivalence and effectiveness are respected.

3. Interim relief must be available where necessary to protect putative EU rights;
4. National rules which conflict with EU law must be set aside.

2. Encouraging Private Litigation and its Relationship with Public Enforcement

In spite of the fact that it is clear that Articles 101 and 102 are directly effective and that national courts have a duty to protect rights derived from them, for some time there was relatively little 'antitrust litigation' brought by private individuals before national courts. Although the volume of private litigation has begun to grow dramatically in some Member States, such as the UK, Germany, and the Netherlands, the EU as a whole continues to present a stark contrast to the USA, where there is a culture of antitrust litigation and where a large proportion of competition cases are litigated privately.[147]

A key factor initially contributing to the dearth of litigation in the EU was undoubtedly the way that Articles 101 and 102 were enforced prior to modernization. In particular, the Commission's exclusive right to grant exemptions under Article 101(3), coupled with its wide interpretation of Article 101(1), gave the Commission tight control over enforcement[148] and effectively excluded the national courts from 'what the legal system of the United States understands by antitrust analysis'.[149] Further, prior to *Courage v Crehan*, there was considerable uncertainty as to whether, and if so when, there was an EU right to damages for violation of the antitrust laws. Even subsequent to modernization and *Crehan*, however, private litigation in the EU has been, and is still being, deterred by a number of other obstacles which have varied over time and from jurisdiction to jurisdiction.[150] In particular, because of the latitude that the principle of national procedural autonomy affords national courts in dealing with damages claims, the culture of litigation and the likelihood of a claim's success or failure in each state has been affected by factors such as the national institutions in place (eg the existence, or not, of specialist competition law tribunals or courts) and individual national rules on, for example, access to

---

[147] See eg William Kolasky, 'Antitrust Litigation: What's Changed in Twenty-five Years' [2012] 27 *Antitrust* 9 and Barry Rodger (ed), *Comparative Private Enforcement and Collective Redress across the EU* (2014).

[148] See eg Mario Monti, 'Effective Private Enforcement of EC Antitrust Law', Sixth EU Competition Law and Policy Workshop Florence (2001).

[149] Clifford Jones, *Private Enforcement of Antitrust Law in the EU, UK and USA* (1999) 85.

[150] See obstacles identified by the Commission in its Green Paper: Damages Actions for Breach of the EC Antitrust Rules COM/2005/0672/final.

information and evidence, follow-on actions, standing and remoteness, causation, limitation, and mechanisms for collective redress. Uncertainty has thus surrounded the question of exactly what obligations and limitations EU law imposes on national law in order to guarantee real and effective judicial protection of EU rights.

A question which has arisen therefore has been whether greater private enforcement should be encouraged and steps taken to stimulate it. Not all agree that it should or that encouragement is required (as it is already occurring in some Member States). It has been argued, for example, that private enforcement is unnecessary either as an additional mechanism for enforcement of the rules or as a mechanism for achieving corrective justice.[151] Further, that public enforcement provides a superior and less costly mechanism for ensuring that the competition rules are not violated and that corrective justice is unlikely to be served by such proceedings. Even those supporting the view that greater private enforcement would be desirable have advocated caution against unleashing too excessive a litigation culture.[152] Indeed, in the USA, there has been considerable concern that private litigation, motivated by private profit rather than public interest considerations, can be wasteful, encouraging 'anaemic' claims to be brought and settled in order to avoid protracted and expensive litigation,[153] and may sometimes deter public enforcement (in particular by deterring leniency applications). The interaction between public and private enforcement systems can therefore become strained.

In *Pfleiderer*,[154] for example, the ECJ had to give a ruling relating to the question of whether Pfleiderer, a victim of the German decor paper cartel, should be provided with access to information held on the file of the German Federal Cartel Office (*Bundeskartellamt*), including the leniency and other documents voluntarily provided by the leniency applicant. Advocate General Mazák took the view that an NCA should *not* grant injured parties access to self-incriminating statements voluntarily provided by leniency applicants as this could substantially reduce the attractiveness and, consequently, the effectiveness of the NCA's leniency programme and, in turn, the effective enforcement of Article 101.[155] An interference with the injured parties' right to an effective remedy and a fair trial was thus justified by the legitimate aim of ensuring the effective enforcement of Article 101 TFEU by NCAs, and ultimately private litigants' possibility of obtaining an effective remedy.[156] The ECJ, in contrast, supported a more balanced approach, holding that it was necessary for the national court in each case to weigh up, according to national law and taking into account all the relevant factors in the case,[157] the respective

---

[151] See Wouter Wils, 'Should Private Antitrust Enforcement Be Encouraged?' (2003) 26 *World Competition* 473 (but see now Wils (n 1) 3) and eg Francis Jacobs 'Civil Enforcement of EEC Antitrust Law' (1984) 82 *Michigan Law Review* 1364.

[152] See eg the responses to the Commission's Green Paper: Damages Actions for Breach of the EC Antitrust Rules (n 150).

[153] See eg Richard Posner, *Antitrust Law* (2nd ed, 2001); Wils (n 1) 3; and *Bell Atlantic Corp v Twombly*, 550 US 554.

[154] Case C-360/09 *Pfleiderer AG v Bundeskartellamt* [2011] ECR I-5161.

[155] *Pfleiderer AG* (n 154) paras 38–42.   [156] *Pfleiderer AG* (n 154).

[157] *Pfleiderer AG* (n 154) para 31.

interests of the leniency applicant (to have voluntarily submitted corporate statements protected) and the claimant (to have access to documents which would
facilitate the claim).[158] Further, in *Bundeswettbewerbsbehörde v Donau Chemie*,[159]
the ECJ held that an Austrian law which prohibited disclosure to third parties of
court files on public law competition proceedings, unless all parties to the proceedings agreed, was not compatible with the principle of effectiveness and so
conflicted with EU law. '[I]n competition law . . . any rule that is rigid, either by
providing for absolute refusal to grant access . . . or for granting access as a matter
of course . . . is liable to undermine the effective application of . . . Article 101.'[160] The
ECJ thus reiterated that the national court should have the opportunity to consider
the issues on a case-by-case basis, weighing up the competing interests.

Despite the concerns and tensions between public and private enforcement the
Commission has not taken the view 'that private enforcement ought to be abandoned *tout-court*'.[161] On the contrary, it has, over the years, taken a number of steps
designed to try and overcome the barriers to private litigation and to encourage
it,[162] recognizing that it (together with the NCAs) cannot bear sole responsibility
for the enforcement of the EU competition laws. 'The overall enforcement of the
EU competition rules is best guaranteed through complementary public and private enforcement.'[163] Indeed, the Commission has advocated the view that some
EU measures are required to stimulate private action, particularly by smaller businesses and final consumers ('[d]espite some recent signs of improvement in a few
Member States, to date most victims of infringements of the EU competition rules
in practice do not obtain compensation for the harm suffered'[164]). Nonetheless, it
has recognized that caution needs to be exercised to ensure that unmeritorious
claims are not encouraged and that the interaction between public and private
enforcement is properly regulated and optimized—in particular, that leniency
programmes and settlement procedures utilized by the Commission in its enforcement of the rules are not compromised by private enforcement.[165]

In 2013, the Commission published a package of measures, designed to achieve
these objectives, including: an EU Directive designed to facilitate damage claims by
the victims of antitrust violations;[166] a recommendation of non-binding principles

---

[158] *Pfleiderer AG* (n 154) para 30.   [159] Case C-536/11, 6 June 2013.

[160] Case C-536/11 (n 159) para 31.

[161] Andrea Renda, John Peysner, Alan J. Riley, and Barry J. Rodger, *Making Antitrust Damages
Actions More Effective in the EU: Welfare Impact and Potential Scenarios* (2007) http://ec.europa.eu/
competition/antitrust/actionsdamages/files_white_paper/impact_study.pdf, 57.

[162] See eg the Commission's Thirteenth Report on Competition Policy (1984) 147–149; the Fourteenth
Report on Competition Policy (1985) 59; and the Fifteenth Report on Competition Policy (1986) 52–55.

[163] Proposal for a Directive of the European Parliament and of the Council on certain rules governing actions for damages under national law for infringements of the competition law provision of
the Member States and the European Union COM (2013) 404 final, Explanatory Memorandum, 1.2.

[164] Proposal for a Directive (n 163) 1.2.   [165] Proposal for a Directive (n 163) 1.2.

[166] Proposal for a Directive (n 163) 1.2; see also IP/13/205 and MEMO/13/531.

for collective redress mechanisms for Member States;[167] and a practical guide on the quantification of harm for damages to assist national courts.[168] In the package the Commission made it clear that, although it accepts that private enforcement is important to supplement public enforcement, the two enforcement mechanisms pursue different, albeit complementary, objectives. In particular, the proposed Directive embraced the compensatory approach[169] and was designed to remove a number of practical difficulties confronted by victims of infringements of the EU antitrust rules when instigating damages claims before national courts and to establish a minimum standard throughout the EU (to deal with the problem that actions have been brought in only a few Member States). It was thus designed to ensure effective and full compensation for injured parties throughout the EU (by removing obstacles faced by victims) and optimal overall enforcement of the EU antitrust rules through regulating certain aspects of the interplay between public and private enforcement.

Although these proposals provoked some controversy and the Commission has had a difficult path to navigate, both politically and legally, to enact legislation, the Directive was finally signed into law on 26 November 2014 and must be transposed into national law by 27 December 2016.[170] Member States have to transpose the Directive into their national laws by 27 December 2016. The provisions of the proposed Directive are broad and far-reaching and will have a significant impact on the rules governing private competition actions in the individual Member States. In particular, it adheres to the principle that claimants are entitled to full compensation for actual loss suffered and loss of profits (even if they did not purchase directly from an infringer) and sets out a rebuttable presumption of harm in cartel cases (but not for other competition law infringements).[171] It also

---

[167] Commission Recommendation on common principles for injunctive and compensatory collective redress mechanisms in the Member States concerning violations of rights granted under Union law C (2013) 3539/3; see also IP/13/524 and MEMO/13/530.

[168] Commission Staff Working Document, 'Practical Guide on Quantifying Harm in Actions for Damages Based on Breaches of Article 101 or 102 of the Treaty on the Functioning of the European Union' SWD (2013) 205.

[169] Commission Staff Working Document (n 168) 4.1.

[170] See Directive 2014/104/EU of the European Parliament and of the Council of 26 November 2014 on certain rules governing actions for damages under national law for infirngements of the competition law provisions of the Member States and of the European Union [2014] OJ L349/1.

[171] A concern however is whether the Commission has done enough to achieve its objectives of increasing and harmonizing private damages action. For example, because it has not adopted a holistic approach some national obstacles and ambiguities are likely to remain. Further, significant scope for divergence in national law remains and some of the Directive's provisions will introduce considerable complexities into national proceedings.

incorporates provisions relating to: disclosure (so parties will have easier access to evidence); protection of leniency and settlement documents; joint and several liability (for any participant in an infringement except for recipients of immunity); the effect of NCA decisions;[172] establishment of clear limitation periods; the legal consequences of passing on; and consensual dispute resolution.

IV. Conclusions

Although the Commission considers that steps may need to be taken to tackle divergences in Member States' enforcement systems, public enforcement of the EU competition law rules is generally perceived to be effective. Further, a number of significant steps have been taken in recent years to increase the robustness of decision making at the EU level, to increase transparency of process, and to bolster the rights of defence. Some stakeholders continue to maintain, however, that these steps are insufficient and that further change is required to the EU architecture to ensure that the balance is correctly drawn between effectiveness and respect for the fundamental rights of those involved. One view is that further changes to both the administrative and judicial stage may suffice to achieve the correct balance. Another, however, is that a more radical change to the structure of decision making is necessary, and that a move away from the integrated agency model is required. There is no doubt that any dramatic change to the decision making structure in the EU, for example, through the creation of a specialized tribunal to adjudicate on competition law decisions, would require far-reaching change to the EU institutional structures and framework which would not be easy to achieve. A less sweeping change would be for the enforcement and adjudicative functions to be separated within the Commission itself. At the moment, however, the EU institutions consider that no such change is necessary. When the EU accedes to the ECHR, however, the ECtHR may have to determine directly whether any change is required to ensure that the EU enforcement structure complies with Article 6 ECHR.

Private enforcement is also set to change dramatically in future years, as the EU has taken radical steps to harmonize national rules governing damages claims. The

---

[172] The Commission originally proposed (see n 163) that decisions of NCAs were to constitute full proof before civil courts that an infringement had occurred provoked considerable debate and was not adopted in the compromise text agreed by the European Parliament. Instead the final text provides that NCA infringement decisions are binding only *within one and the same member state*. Final decisions of an NCA may, however, be presented before the national courts of another Member State as at least *prima facie evidence* of a competition law infringement.

volume of litigation is already increasing, and the new Directive may pave the way for a litigation culture to be built throughout the EU.

Bibliography

Arianna Andreangeli and Ioannis Lianos, 'The European Union' in Eleanor M. Fox and Michael J. Trebilcock (eds), *The Design of Competition Law Institutions* (2013)

Marco Bronckers and Anne Vallery, 'Fair and Effective Competition Policy in the EU: Which Role for Authorities and Which Role for the Courts after *Menarini*' (2012) *8 European Competition Journal* 283

Ian Forrester, 'Due Process in EC competition Cases: A Distinguished Institution with Flawed Procedures' (2009) *European Law Rev* 817

Ian Forrester, 'A Bush in Need of Pruning: The Luxuriant Growth of "Light Judicial Review"', in Claus-Dieter Ehlermann and Mel Marquis (eds), *European Competition Law Annual 2009: Evaluation of Evidence and its Judicial Review in Competition Cases* (2010)

Nils F.W. Hauger and Christoph Palzer, 'Investigator, Prosecutor, Judge . . . and Now Plaintiff? The Leviathanian Role of the European Commission in the Light of Fundamental Rights' (2013) *36 World Competition* 565

Alison Jones and Brenda Sufrin, *EU Competition Law: Text, Cases, and Materials* (5th ed, 2014)

I. Lianos and D. Geradin (eds), *Handbook on European Competition Law: Enforcement and Procedure* (2013)

Renato Nazzini, 'Administrative Enforcement, Judicial Review and Fundamental Rights in EU Competition Law: A Comparative Contextual-Functionalist Perspective' (2012) *49 Common Market Law Review* 971

Barry Rodger (ed), *Comparative Private Enforcement and Collective Redress across the EU* (2014)

Heike Schweitzer, 'The European Competition Law Enforcement System and the Evolution of Judicial Review' in Claus-Dieter Ehlermann and Mel Marquis (eds), *European Competition Law Annual 2009: Evaluation of Evidence and its Judicial Review in Competition Cases* (2010)

Michael Trebilcock and Edward Iacobucci, 'Designing Competition Law Institutions' (2002) *25 World Competition* 361

Wouter Wils, 'The Relationship between Public Antitrust Enforcement and Private Actions for Damages' (2009) *32 World Competition* 3

Wouter Wils, 'The Increased Level of EU Antitrust Fines, Judicial Review, and the European Convention on Human Rights' (2010) *33 World Competition* 5

Wouter Wils, 'EU Antitrust Enforcement Powers and Procedural Rights and Guarantees: The Interplay between EU Law, National Law, the Charter of Fundamental Rights of the EU and the European Convention of Human Rights' (2011) *34 World Competition* 189.

Wouter Wils, 'The Compatibility with Fundamental Rights of the EU Antitrust Enforcement System in which the European Commission acts both as Investigator and as First-instance Decision Maker' (2014) 37 World Competition 5

CHAPTER 26

AN EVOLUTIONARY THEORY OF STATE AID CONTROL

ANDREA BIONDI AND ELISABETTA RIGHINI

I. State Aid Policy: A Story of Resilience and Adaptation

THE Treaty articles dealing with state aid—which in the Lisbon Treaty are now numbered 107 and 108—are among the few articles that have remained largely unchanged since the Treaty of Rome came into force on 1 January 1958. The Spaak Report,[1] published the year before, identified state aid control as one of the key policies for the creation of the Common Market: the revolutionary (at least in those days) free trade zone in which goods, services, capital and labour would flow freely between the six countries then forming the European Economic Community (EEC). The abolition of tariffs and non-fiscal obstacles, the dismantling of borders and giving firms and workers the ability to operate freely in this enlarged market, would have served little purpose if Member States were allowed to interfere in the

---

[1] Intergovernmental Committee on European Integration, *The Brussels Report on the General Common Market (the Spaak Report)*, 1956, Title II, Chapter 2.

economy by lowering the costs of production through subsidies or other forms of intervention. Therefore, the founding fathers (unfortunately mothers were not involved) foresaw a generalized prohibition on state aid, together with antitrust control, as the second pillar of the internal market, next to regulatory intervention. As in the case of the fundamental freedoms of the internal market, the state aid rules were also based on the recognition that there were other objectives beyond a free market that had to be protected, objectives that could justify an exception to the absolute prohibition of state intervention in the economy. This is why, even today, the analysis of state aid takes place in two steps:

1. Whether a measure can be considered aid in the meaning of Article 107(1) TFEU and therefore, in principle, be incompatible with the establishment of an internal market; and
2. Whether it can be declared compatible, as it falls in line with one of the objectives indicated in Article 107(2) and (3) TFEU.

The classification of a state measure as 'aid', and thus the application of Article 107(1) TFEU, depends on the satisfaction of certain criteria. A national measure will be qualified as aid when: the measure entails an effective burden on the state or on a public authority (granted by the state or through state resources); when the measure would not have been adopted by a rational market operator (advantage); and if it favours certain undertakings (selectivity). Further, it must strengthen the position of the undertaking on the market (distortion of competition) and it must have an actual or potential effect on the internal market (effect on trade between Member States). The assessment as to whether a state measure is actually pursuing a legitimate objective, and can therefore be compatible with EU law, has to be carried out exclusively by the European Commission. The effectiveness of such control is ensured by Article 108 TFEU, which contains a notification mechanism under which Member States have a duty to inform the Commission of any new aid. This mechanism is reinforced by the so-called stand-still clause, under which Member States are prevented from granting the proposed aid before the Commission has made its assessment.

The system is also complemented by Article 106 TFEU, a form of *lex specialis* with respect to the above general framework. This provision has multiple purposes. On the one hand, it contains a 'reminder' that Member States should strictly comply with the rules contained in the Treaty when granting special or exclusive rights to undertakings, and that undertakings entrusted with the provision of services of general economic interest (SGEI) should also respect the Treaty rules, but only to the extent that the application of those rules does not jeopardize the performance of the tasks entrusted to them. On the other hand, it confers the main responsibility for the application of the rules above, and thus compliance with EU law, onto the European Commission.[2]

---

[2] For a general overview of how the Commission has ensured the application of Article 106 TFEU to SGEIs, see Elisabetta Righini, 'The Reform of the State Aid Rules on Financing of

Since 1958, these Treaty provisions governing state aid policy have remained formally immutable and have been deployed to monitor public interventions in the economy, to maintain a level playing field across Member States, and, ultimately, to make Europe an integrated social economy.

Notwithstanding this long period of application and the stability of its basic rules, state aid control is, however, often perceived as a rather obscure and technocratic kind of policy: a system for insiders based on few Treaty articles and affected by a constant struggle between the various actors on a battleground immersed in thick political fog. Academic debate on the nature of state aid law is also very polarized, usually entrenched in opposing views that tend not to agree even on the boundaries of such a debate. For many, it is still appropriate to speak of state aid control. As the ultimate goal is to prevent Member States using their discretion in determining economic policies as a way of directly influencing and affecting the market, state aid rules are there to enforce a strict control on any kind of state intervention through a close monitoring process operated, ideally, by an unbiased supranational institution.[3] Success is then measured in terms of a reduction of locational interventionist policies.[4] The other spectrum of opinion tends to focus on state aid policy as a form of antitrust regulation, that would come into play only, and in so far as, state aid rules can reduce anti-competitive distortive effects by preventing inefficient undertakings surviving in an artificially competitive market.[5]

In reality, the life story of state aid law can be 'humanized' as one of resilience and adaptation. Over almost six decades, state aid law has been constantly evolving and adapting to keep pace with the profound changes undergone by the European venture. Its rules have had to grow to adapt to the ever variable shift in the respective sizes and functions of the public sector and the market, as well as to the ensuing endless varieties of government intervention, through subsidies or other forms of aid. At the same time, with the progressive integration of new countries into the Union, the system has been horizontally and territorially stretched, and has also

Public Services: Paving the Way Towards a Clearer, Simpler and More Diversified Framework', (2012)2-Supplement *EStAL* 3.

[3] Vittorio Di Bucci, 'Comments on the Paper Selectivity, Economic Advantage, Distortion of Competition and Effect on Trade' in Jacques Derenne and Massimo Merola (eds), *Economic Analysis of State Aid Rules—Contributions and Limits*, proceedings of the third annual conference of the Global Competition Law Centre, College of Europe, 21–22 September 2006 (2007) 157; Luis Buendía Sierra and Ben Smulders, 'The Limited Role of the Refined Economic Approach' in *Achieving the Objectives of State Aid Control: Time for Some Realism in EC State Aid Law: Liber Amicorum Francisco Santaolalla*, (2008) 18; Andrea Biondi, 'The Rationale of State Aid Control: A Return to Orthodoxy' (2011) *Cambridge Yearbook of European Law* 35.

[4] H Friederiszick, H W Lars-Hendrik Röller and V Verouden, 'European State Aid Control: An Economic Framework' in P Buccirossi (ed), *Advances in the Economics of Competition Law* (2006) 652–654.

[5] Pietro Crocioni, 'Can State Aid Policy Become More Economically Friendly?', (2006) 29 *World Competition* 89; J Luis Da Cruz Vilaca, 'Material and Geographic Selectivity in State Aid', (2009) 4 *EStAL* 443.

become more complex, as each of the now 28 Member States has very different levels of government, and thus aid granting authorities. The rules on state aid are now supposed to cover a market of five hundred million people and a number of sectors unthinkable when the founding fathers conceived the very idea of an internal market. Similarly, the assessment of the positive contribution to the common European objectives that makes an aid measure compatible with the EU Treaty has become more and more sophisticated in order to accommodate the ever-growing needs of the complex European social economy.

Last but not least, in recent times companies and governments have had to cope with the impact of an unfortunately long and serious crisis, which has multiplied the need for public support while cutting the budgets of many Member States. Consequently, state aid policy has become an important tool to target public resources towards objectives of common interest, and thus avoid a waste of public resources, as well as to respond to the growing disparities in the fiscal capacities of different EU countries—what have been called the 'deep pocket distortions'.[6]

The results of these tumultuous events are a very changed and different landscape in terms of both national public policy objectives and market structure.[7] On the one hand, Member States are even more aware of the impossibility of pursuing purely national interests in a context where economic interdependence is now a fact and cannot be unilaterally controlled. On the other hand, a consensus seems to be emerging on the necessity of a form of renewed effort to create a *locus* where state aid rules are used to collectively identify how public spending can be beneficial to achieve aims of common interest.[8]

It is thus impossible to attempt to comprehend the 'legal' nature of state aid rules without taking into account all these transformations. This process of resilience and adaptation has shaped not only the criteria that are exclusively set by the European Commission in order to establish state intervention's compatibility with the internal market, but also the very concept of what constitutes an 'aid'. The latter, albeit defined as 'an objective notion' by the European Court of Justice,[9] is in reality dependent on constantly evolving external variables. The aim of this chapter is to present this field of European law in its dynamic evolution, looking at its principles, as enshrined in the Treaty and developed over time through case law

[6] See Joaquín Almunia, 'Doing More With Less—State Aid Reform in Times of Austerity: Supporting Growth Amid Fiscal Constraints', speech delivered at King's College London on 11 January 2013, available at http://europa.eu/rapid/press-release_SPEECH-13-14_en.html).

[7] See in general, Wolf Sauter and Harm Schepel, *State and Market in European Union Law. The Public and Private Spheres of the Internal Market before the EU Courts* (2009) Ch 1.

[8] On state aid as instrument of further integration, see the several Staff Working Documents ('SWD') accompanying the Country Specific Recommendations adopted in the context of the European Semester Package. See, for instance, European Commission SWD, 'Assessment of the 2014 national reform programme and stability programme for Germany', SWD(2014) 406 final, available at http://ec.europa.eu/europe2020/pdf/csr2014/swd2014_germany_en.pdf.

[9] Hereafter, the Court or the ECJ.

and practice, in order ultimately to provide a more general theory of the constitutional role of this area of law in the European architecture.[10]

II. Notion of Aid: An Objective Test?

According to the well-established case law of the Court, the notion of what constitutes state aid is an objective and legal concept defined directly by the Treaty.[11] 'Objectiveness' as a distinctive feature was identified very early on in the jurisprudence on the '*effect*' a certain public spending measure can produce on free movement and fair competition.[12] In line with its general economic jurisprudence,

[10] An exhaustive discussion of the procedural rules of state aid control is beyond the word limits of this contribution. We would however argue that our proposed analysis is equally 'transferable' to the procedural state aid rules. Born as a rigid centralized Commission-Member States model, the Article 108 TFEU notification system has gradually evolved into a complex and sophisticated multicentre enforcement system. This evolution has most recently been reflected in the new Procedural Regulation of 2013 ([2013] OJ L 204/15, amending Council Regulation (EC) No 659/1999). The three 'evolutionary components' of the reform of the Procedural Regulation are: (1) the improvement of the handling of complaints; (2), the codification of cooperation between national courts and the Commission; and (3) the tools that will enable the Commission to obtain complete and correct information (MIT) and conduct sector inquiries (SI). The new rules should streamline and sensibly speed up the process. They should also increase the very marginal role of national courts. Despite the fact that since the early days the ECJ declared that the violation of the stand-still clause is directly effective (C-120/73 *Lorenz* [1973] ECR 1471), in reality national courts have been considered by the Court itself as performing a merely ancillary function compared to that of the Commission. In Case C-199/06 *CELF and Ministre de la Culture v SIDE* [2008] ECR I-469, the Court held that the function of national courts is no more than to preserve, until the final decision of the Commission, the rights of individuals faced with a possible breach by state authorities of the prohibition laid down by Article 108(3) TFEU. The New Regulation instead first transforms into hard law the ability of national judges dealing with a state aid case to ask the Commission to provide information in its possession or to submit its opinion on issues regarding the application of state aid rules. This possibility was so far foreseen only in the Commission notice on the enforcement of state aid law by national courts; [2009] OJ C 85/1. Secondly, it confers on the Commission the power to intervene, on its own initiative (ie as an *amicus curiae*), in national litigation that is important for the coherent application of Articles 107(1) and 108 TFEU (mirroring the equivalent provisions of Reg. 1/2003 in the field of antitrust). This will ensure a more coherent application of state aid rules by national judges across the Union, leveling the playing field for European companies. Last but not least, through MIT and SI, the Commission will now be able to move in its investigations beyond the exclusive dialogue with Member States and finally include competitors, as well as look at state aid measures in a particular sector or based on a particular aid instrument that may materially restrict or distort competition within the internal market in several Member States at the same time. See however, for some criticism John Temple Lang, 'EU State Aid rules—The need for substantive reform', in (2014) *EStAL* (forthcoming).

[11] See eg Case C-487/06, *British Aggregates Association v Commission*, [2008] ECR I-10505 para 111.

[12] Case 30/59, *Steenkolenmijnen* v *High Authority* [1961] ECR 1; C-173/73 *Italy v Commission* [1974] ECR 409.

the approach adopted by the ECJ could be classified, to borrow a classic internal market notion, as substantive access to market.[13] The prohibition on state financial intervention would thus require not only setting aside openly protectionist measures, such as a direct subsidy, but also the elimination of any other state measures, which could have the same practical effect. Once again, in line with the *acquis* on the internal market, the substantive access to market test is not a monolithic concept but it is subject to endless modulations in an attempt to preserve the free flow of trade and national diversity in terms of both democratic process and autonomous regulatory competences.[14] The interpretation of the key factors in the notion of aid should, in our view, reflect this variable approach, which mostly depends on a continuous assessment of the economic and legal context in which the national measure was created, its object and, at the same time, the structure of the market concerned and the actual conditions in which it functions.[15]

1. The Notion of Undertaking

State aid rules only apply if the recipient is an undertaking which, according to the settled case law of the Court, means any entity engaged in an economic activity, ie in any activity consisting in offering goods and/or services in a given market.[16] The approach thus chosen has been defined as 'functional' because, to determine the applicability of state aid rules, as much as competition rules at large, it is not the characteristics of the entities concerned that are essential but rather their activities.[17] The quintessential 'evolutionary' nature of such an approach has allowed the Court and the Commission to adjust the definition of undertaking, both temporarily and spatially, so as to be able to follow the developments in the market, the changing boundaries between public activities *ius imperii* and economic endeavours, and ultimately to preserve the resilient character of state aid control by catching most of the beneficiaries of public support. The functional approach, first of all, has allowed going beyond the specific legal status of any entity under national law, to create a European homogeneous concept of what is an undertaking. A telling example of this approach can be found in the investigations the Commission opened in 2013 into alleged aid to sports clubs in the Netherlands and in Spain. In those countries, the clubs have different kinds of status under national law. In the

---

[13] Catherine Barnard and Simon Deakin, 'Market Access and Regulatory Competition' in C. Barnard and S Deakin (eds), *The Law of the European Single Market* (2005).

[14] Niamh Nic Shuibhne, *The Coherence of EU Free Movement Law: Constitutional Responsibility and the Court of Justice* (2013) Ch 7.

[15] Case C-399/93 *Oude Littikhuis and others* [1995] ECR I-4515, para 10.

[16] See Case 118/85 *Commission v Italian Republic* [1987] ECR 2599, at 2610.

[17] See Opinion of AG Jacobs in Case C-264/01 *AOK-Bundesverband and others* [2004] ECR I-02493.

Dutch cases,[18] for instance, PSV Eindhoven and FC Den Bosch are limited liability companies, while MVV Maastricht constitutes an 'association' under national law. In the Spanish cases, the alleged aid stemmed, in one instance, specifically from the preferential corporate tax treatment reserved to only four Spanish sport clubs (Real Madrid, Athletic Club Bilbao, Club Atletico Osasuna (Navarra) and FC Barcelona). The 1990 *ley del deporte* allowed these clubs to refrain from converting into sports limited companies (*sociedades anónimas deportivas*), as all others clubs had to do, and to remain sports clubs, ie non-profit entities, thus qualifying for a partial corporate tax exemption.[19] In this decision, in particular, the Commission has not contested the different status under national law as such, but rather the fiscal discrimination that the national law derives from such status.

It follows from the examples just given that another consequence of the functional approach is that being qualified as either not-for-profit or in-house is not enough to exclude the entity from the application of competition rules. If an entity offers goods and/or services in a given market in competition with others, state aid rules apply and public interventions are scrutinized as if the entity is an independent business run to make a profit. However, as the definition of an entity as an undertaking is always in relation to a specific activity, those entities that carry out both economic and non-economic activities are qualified as undertakings only with regard to the former.[20]

Another clear evolutionary facet of the functional approach lies in its ability to adapt over time to the degree of liberalization and market integration in the European economy. During their sixty-year application, state aid rules have covered more and more entities as an increasing number of economic sectors have been shifted from the control of the state to become competitive markets. Article 1(b)(v) of the Procedural Regulation[21] clearly refers to this evolutionary aspect when—in dealing with the definition of 'existing aid'—it distinguishes between liberalization that happens *de facto,* ie 'due to the evolution of the common market and without having been altered by the Member State', and *de jure,* that is to say as a result of the intervention of Union law. Two economic sectors encompassing this temporal differentiation affecting the definition of undertaking are certainly the postal sector and aviation.

In the postal sector, liberalization started in 1999 and was completed on 1 January 2011, through a gradual opening up of this public monopolistic market through

---

[18] Commission Decision of 6 March 2013 in case *The Netherlands*, SA.33584 (2013/C) (ex 2011/NN), alleged municipal aid to the professional Dutch football clubs, [2013] OJ C 116/19.

[19] Commission Decision of 18 December 2013 in case *Spain*, SA.29769 (2013/C) (ex 2013/NN), state aid to certain Spanish professional sport clubs, [2014] OJ C 69/115.

[20] Communication from the Commission on the application of the European Union State aid rules to compensation granted for the provision of services of general economic interest, [2012] OJ C 8/4, paras 9–13.

[21] Above (n 10).

EU directives.[22] In parallel, the Commission had been assessing aid granted to cover any aspects of the activities of the former incumbents once these had started operating in competitive markets.[23] This evolution is equally visible in relation to airports activities. Traditionally, the operation of airports was considered to fall within the public policy remit and hence was organized as part of the public administration rather than as a commercial entity. It followed that, until relatively recently, the financing of airports' activities and of airport infrastructure were not subject to state aid control. Over the last twenty years, however, the liberalization of airline services and the transfer of airport operations from state to regional control, coupled with privatization or a progressive opening-up of capital, have profoundly changed this sector. If, once upon a time, airports were managed as means to ensure accessibility and territorial development, recently they have also developed commercial objectives and now compete fiercely among each other to attract new airlines and traffic. Such an evolution has also brought about a different assessment of airport activities under state aid law. Already in the early 2000s, the European Courts clarified, in the *Aéroports de Paris* case, that the operation of an airport is an economic activity because it comprises 'the provision of airport facilities to airlines and the various service providers, in return for a fee at a rate freely fixed by the manager, and when the latter is public, does not fall within the exercise of its official powers as a public authority and is separable from its activities in the exercise of such powers'.[24]

A further facet of the evolutionary nature built into the functional approach has been its spatial adaptability: the behavioural concept of what constitute an undertaking in competition law has allowed state aid control to closely follow the different degrees of *de facto* liberalization and of organization of the markets between and within the Member States. In other words, it has allowed modulation of the application of the rules territorially. This is especially so when liberalization has not happened through EU law, but rather due to market forces, and the fact that the way the activity is organized, or not, by the state may differ from one Member State to another, and often also between one region and another. One of the most recurrently cited examples of this spatial adaptability are hospitals, which, at least in some countries, still form an integral part of the national health care system, are financed almost entirely from social security funds, and are based on the principles of solidarity and universal coverage,[25] while in others, hospital services are

---

[22] See, for instance, Directive 2008/6/EC of the European Parliament and of the Council of 20 February 2008 amending Directive 97/67/EC with regard to the full accomplishment of the internal market of Community postal services, [2008] OJ L 52/3.

[23] Commission Decision of 25 January 2012 in case Belgium, SA.14588 (C 20/09), *De Post-La Poste* (now bpost), [2012] OJ L 170/1, para 227.

[24] Case T-128/98 *Aéroports de Paris v Commission* [2000] ECR II-3929, para 121. See also C-288/11 P *Mitteldeutsche Flughafen, Flughafen Leipzig Halle*, judgment of 19 December 2012.

[25] See Case T-319/99 *FENIN* [2003] ECR II-357 and Case C-205/03P [2006] ECR I-6295, paras 25–28.

provided for remuneration, with a market logic, and hence with a certain degree of competition between them.[26]

2. State Resources

A second 'gatekeeper' criterion is that the measure must come from state resources and be imputable to the state in order to be classified as aid. According to the case law of the Court, the concept of 'granted by the state or through state resources' means that there must be either a direct or indirect transfer of state resources to the undertaking. In short, a specific financial burden on the state must be proven. Furthermore, for the measure to also be imputable to the state, the involvement of the state can never be assumed but must be proved on the basis of objective factors such as: the fact that the body in question could not take the contested decision without taking account of the requirements of the public authorities; or the fact that, apart from factors of an organic nature which linked the public undertakings to the state, those undertakings, through the intermediary of which aid had been granted, have to take account of *inter alia* directives issued by the state.[27]

Despite its apparent simplicity, application of the case law is difficult, because the state rarely acts in a traditional and thus easily recognizable *ex imperio* fashion, and at the same time the economic areas where the state operates are becoming extremely complex. There is no better example than the electricity market, once nearly a monopolistic state market structure and still an extremely political and sensitive policy area. The leading case on the notion of 'granted by the state or through state resources', dealt precisely with electricity. In *PreussenElektra*,[28] the ECJ found that no aid could be detected in a national measure that imposed an obligation on private electricity suppliers to purchase electricity produced from renewable energy sources at fixed minimum prices. The obligation to purchase had to be shouldered by the distributors. Even if some credit should be given to the Court because the judgment was probably supposed to bring legal certainty on the subject, its ultimate impact on the electricity market has been rather negative as it has allowed smart Member States to shield several national support mechanisms for the financing of renewable electricity from the independent and across-the-borders scrutiny of the Commission. The concomitant impressive

---

[26] Commission Decision of 28 October 2009 in case Belgium, NN 54/2009 (ex- CP 244/2005), Financing of public hospitals of IRIS network in the region Brussels-Capital, C(2009) 8120 final, para 110.

[27] Case C-482/99 *France v Commission* ('Stardust') [2002] ECR I-4397. Case C-672/11 *Doux Élevages and Coopérative Agricole*, judgment of 13 June 2013.

[28] Case C-379/98 *PreussenElektra AG v Schhleswag AG* [2001] ECR I-02099.

development of this source of electricity within the EU2020[29] climate objectives, has had a profound impact on competition in the electricity markets, both within and across Member States, and has significantly affected wholesale prices. This has not only led to significant cost increases for electricity consumers, both individuals and industry, but it has also reduced the attractiveness of the sector to investors, thus causing serious concerns about security of supply. Finally, the nature of the relationship between energy companies and state intervention has raised many concerns and criticisms.[30] Perhaps a slightly more stringent approach can therefore be detected in the more recent case law and the Commission practice. For instance, the Court has repeatedly stressed that those national regulatory measures that lead to financial redistribution from one private entity to another, without any further involvement of the state, do not, *in principle*, entail a transfer of state resources. This is so 'if the money flows directly from one private entity to another, without passing through a public or private body designated by the State to administer the transfer, and without the sums in question remaining under public control and available to the national authorities'.[31] However, it is clear that it could be argued *a contrario* that state resources are present where *a part or all* the charges paid by private persons transit through a public or private entity designated to channel them to the beneficiaries.[32] A rapid investigation into the Commission practice is equally instructive. For instance, in the Austrian Electricity decision, the Commission was confronted with a national system that conferred on a specific private entity (OeMAG) the task of administering the resources needed to support green electricity. The Commission concluded that the fact that OeMAG was a private entity was not enough to show that the measure did not involve state aid.[33] Thus, through its practice, the Commission has tried to expand the concept of state resources by accepting that the presence of the state can always be detected, even when certain forms of private contracting-out are adopted.

[29] This is the European Union's ten-year growth and jobs strategy, launched in 2010 as a response to the financial and economic crisis that has hit Europe since 2008. See Communication from the Commission, EUROPE 2020—A strategy for smart, sustainable and inclusive growth, COM(2010) 2020 final of 3 March 2010.

[30] See, in general Kim Talus, *EU Energy Law and Policy* (2013) Ch 4.

[31] Case C-206/06 *Essent* [2008] ECR I-5497 and, more recently, C-262/12 *Association Vent de Colere*, judgment of 19 December 2013.

[32] Likewise the imposition of a potential burden on state resources in the future, by a guarantee or by a contractual offer, provided that a sufficiently direct link is established between, the advantage given to the beneficiary and, on the other, a reduction of the state budget could be enough to classify the measures as coming from the state. See Joined Cases C-399 & 401/10 P *Bouygues SA and Bouygues Télécom SA v European Commission*, judgment of 19 December 2013, para 109.

[33] Commission Decision of 8 March 2011 in case *Austria*, C 24/2009 (ex N 446/2008), state aid for energy-intensive businesses under the Green Electricity Act, [2011] OJ L 235/42.

3. Selective Advantage

As far as the other conditions are concerned, some of the most difficult questions are posed by the definition of 'selective advantage'. For the measure to be classified as aid, it should constitute an undue advantage for the beneficiary. Traditionally the analysis is split into two different sub-tests.[34] First, as far as the advantage is concerned, it needs to be determined whether the state in adopting a certain measure has acted as a market investor (MIP).[35] Second, the advantage must be conferred on selected undertakings. As for the MIP, this is a concept that has clearly mutated from economic analysis and thus its application depends on the specific characteristic of the economic operation at stake. However, the Court's case law has gradually accepted that the benchmark that has to be used is not just a hypothetical 'ideal' market investor whose actions can be econometrically measured. Its effective use lies instead in the necessity of carrying out a comparison between the state's actions and those of a private actor in market circumstances as close as possible to the measure under scrutiny.[36] Thus, the EU judicature no longer refers to the expression 'investor' but tailors its analysis to more accurate comparators, for instance, the repayment of a state loan to that of a private creditor[37] or a process of privatization to a private sale.[38] Very recently, the ECJ seems to have fully embraced an 'evolutionary' approach whereby, in a case dealing with modifications of restructuring agreements for a failing bank, it spoke of whether the measure in question 'has satisfied an "economic rationality test", so that a private investor might also be in a position to accept such an amendment, in particular by increasing the prospects of obtaining the repayment of [the capital] injection'.[39]

The second part of the selectivity test is, as mentioned, that the advantage must be conferred on selected undertakings. Despite some obvious difficulties, the ECJ cannot be accused of being boring. On the contrary, it has been even more creative, experimenting with constitutional differentiation and at the same time managing to reaffirm a strict control–based application of the state aid rules. As for constitutional differentiation, the Court has now fully recognized the importance of taking into account the different internal arrangements of the member states and

[34] For a discussion, see AG Jääskinen Opinion in C-106 and 107/09 *Commission v UK ('Gibraltar')* [2011] ECR I-1111.

[35] See eg Case C-480/98 *Spain v Commission* [2000] ECR I-8717; Case T-296/97 *Alitalia v Commission* [2000] ECR II-3871; and Joined Cases C71, 73 & 76/09 P *Comitato 'Venezia vuole vivere' and others v Commission* [2011] ECR I-4727.

[36] Case C-124/10 P *Commission v EDF*, judgment of 5 June 2012.

[37] Case C-480/98 *Magefesa* [2000] ECR I-8717.

[38] Joined Cases T-268/08 and T-281/08 *Land Burgenland and Austria v Commission* [2012] ECR II-90.

[39] C-224/12 P *Commission v Netherlands and ING Groep NV*, judgment of 3 April 2014, para 213. Interestingly the Commission now uses the expression 'market operator' in Draft Commission Notice on the Notion of State Aid pursuant to Article 107(1) TFEU, available at http://ec.europa.eu/competition/consultations/2014_state_aid_notion/draft_guidance_en.pdf.

their impact on public spending decisional practice. Thus it is now well established that if a certain measure is taken by infra-state authorities that could be considered constitutionally, administratively and economically independent from the central government, the measure will be considered as general and not selective; the reference framework being the 'regional' one and not the unitary state.[40]

It is true that the Court became bogged down in a rather formalistic test on so called material selectivity. The judicial test is supposed to be composed of three parts. First, the objective of a certain measure should be identified. Then, secondly, a comparison between undertakings, which are in a legal and factual situation that is comparable in light of the objective pursued by the measure in question, needs to be undertaken. The third and final step is to ascertain whether the measure is justified by the nature or general logic of the system of which it is part. If the answer is positive, the measure does not fulfil the condition of selectivity.[41] Despite the clear lack of flair in such a convoluted test, the ECJ constantly reaffirmed that 'selectivity' will bite at any time the state behaves without taking into account—even in areas of national competence such as taxation—the impact of its action on free movement and competition and fails to act properly as the enforcer of EU law. For instance, in the *Regione Sardegna* case, the measure in question was a regional tax on aircraft stopovers and on recreational boats imposed only on undertakings which were domiciled for tax purposes outside the territory of the region of Sardinia.[42] The measure was allegedly aimed at reducing pollution and preserving the environment from excessive commercialization. Before the Court, the Regione Sardegna argued that the measure should not have been considered selective for two main reasons: first, that the tax legislation was not selective from a geographical perspective, since the Region of Sardinia has autonomous powers conferred on it by statute having the authority of constitutional law. Thus the reference, in which the 'general nature' of the measure should have been assessed, was that of the infra-state body. Secondly, the distinction between resident and non-resident is inherent in any taxation system—it is a common principle that a tax can be imposed differently on situations which are legally and factually distinct. The Court rebutted both objections. It recalled that even the autonomous power of infra-state bodies has to be exercised in a manner compatible with EU law, thus it had to be verified whether the measure in question was in reality a measure of fiscal protectionism. Then, the Court, despite accepting that environmental concerns could be a factor, concluded that undertakings having their tax domicile outside the territory of the region are,

---

[40] Case C-88/03, *Portugal v Commission*, [2006] ECR I-7115 (the 'Azores' case). See further, Francesco De Cecco, *State Aid and the European Economic Constitution* (2013) Ch 5.

[41] Case C-143/99 *Adria Wien Pipeline* [2001] ECR I-8365 and Case C-279/08 *P Commission v Netherland* [2011] ECR I-07671. The discussion of this specific point would deserve a full article. See Andrea Biondi 'State Aid is falling, falling down: an analysis of the concept of "aid" in the acquis of the EU Courts', in (2013) 50 *Common Market Law Review* 1719.

[42] Case C-169/08 *Regione Sardegna* [2009] ECR I-10821, paras 19–66.

with reference to the legal framework in question, in a factual and legal situation comparable with that of undertakings which are established in that territory. The measure had therefore to be considered as selective as it did not apply to all operators of aircraft or pleasure boats which make a stopover in Sardinia.

Only in this 'fighting protectionism' context can the very robust judgment in *Gibraltar*[43] be fully understood. In that judgment, the Court held that the Gibraltar government tax reforms had to be classified as state aid. In particular, the Court held that a tax system based on numbers of employees and on business property had to be considered as a selective measure as it discriminated in practice 'between companies which are in a comparable situation with regard to the objective of the proposed tax reform, namely to introduce a general system of taxation for all companies established in Gibraltar'.[44]

In conclusion, regardless of the national regulatory technique or legal mechanism used, a selective advantage arises anytime the national legislature has expressly or implicitly exempted some undertakings from a measure to which they would otherwise be subject, or when the national measure is asymmetrically formulated in relation to its factual elements or its scope.[45]

4. Effect on Trade and Distortion of Competition

To avoid painting an excessively rosy picture, it is abundantly clear that the last two state aid conditions 'distortion of competition and effect on trade' are instead a bit too resilient and in need of a process of transformation. These two conditions are usually called 'negative' as their fulfilment is easily satisfied. As for the distortion of competition, the ECJ case law does not require any sophisticated market analysis but it is enough that the state measure is liable to improve the competitive position of the recipient compared to other undertakings with which it competes.[46] As for the effect on free movement, all that must be shown is that the aid is such as to be liable to affect trade between Member States. The case law does not require a threshold or percentage below which it may be considered that trade between Member States is not affected. According to the Court, the relatively small amount of aid or the relatively small size of the undertaking which receives it does not as such exclude the possibility that trade between Member States might be affected.[47]

Whilst such a rigid stance was perhaps justified so as to produce some necessary deregulatory effects in very segregated markets, the undoubtedly huge success

---

[43] C-106 and 107/09 *Commission v UK ('Gibraltar')* [2011] ECR I-1111.
[44] C-106 and 107/09 *Commission v UK ('Gibraltar')* [2011] ECR I-1111, para 88.
[45] AG Kokott Opinion in *Regione Sardegna*, cited above, paras 127–128.
[46] Case 730/79 *Phillip Morris* [1980] ECR 267, para 11.
[47] Case C-280/00, *Altmark* [2003] ECR I-7747; and Case C-172/03 *Heiser* [2005] ECR I-16.

of the free movement and competition rules might require a more differentiated approach. As for distortion of competition, it is safe to claim that at least now the case law requires the Commission to provide reasons on why effects on intra-Union trade and competition can in certain cases be 'less immediate and even less discernible'.[48] Further, in relation to effect on trade, the Commission has already been toying with a form of alternative interpretation.[49] For instance, in a case dealing with financial support for cultural productions exclusively in the Basque language, the Commission spoke of a 'geographically limited attraction zone' and 'a marginal effect on the markets and on consumers in neighbouring Member States' and thus a decision of no aid was issued.[50] Arguably, the *acquis* on free movement in itself can provide some useful indications. As a breach of free movement provisions can be established only if a certain measure substantially restricts access to the market,[51] any remote, indirect and contingent effect, and, in any case, a merely hypothetical impact on trade, would not trigger the application of the Treaty. Therefore, such a 'substantial' restriction test can be transplanted into the notion of state aid. Usefully, the Court now routinely requires the European Commission to prove its case on the basis of 'conclusive evidence' in free movement cases,[52] which could include reliable estimates, figures and even patterns of trade, tools that can be easily employed in a state aid context.[53]

III. Compatibility: Work Constantly *In Fieri*

The second step in the state aid analysis consists of an assessment of whether an aid measure, which is in principle prohibited by Article 107(1) TFEU, could still be acceptable because it is 'compatible' with one of the objectives listed in Article

---

[48] Case C-494/06 *Commission v Italy and Wam* [2009] ECR I-3639, para 62.

[49] It should also be remembered that the European Commission considers that public funding to a single recipient of up to €200,000 over a three year fiscal period has a negligible impact on trade and competition, and does not require notification. Commission 'de minimis' Regulation (EC) No 1407/2013 of 18/1/2/2013, OJ L352/1.

[50] Commission's decisions in state aid cases Spain, N 257/2007, Subsidies for theatre productions in the Basque country, [2007] OJ C 173/1; Spain, N 458/2004, Editorial Andaluza Holding, [2005] OJ C 131/12; and Portugal, SA.33243, Jornal de Madeira, [2013] OJ C 16/1.

[51] Case C-518/06 *Commission v Italy* [2009] ECR I-3491 and C-565/08 *Commission v Italy* [2011] ECR I-2101.

[52] Case C-400/08 *Commission v Spain* [2011] ECR I-1915, para 62.

[53] Case C-147/03 *Commission v Austria* [2005] ECR I-5969, paras 64–66.

107(2) and (3) TFEU. This balancing of interests falls within the exclusive competence of the European Commission.[54] Over the years the Commission has thus built a very considerable practice in this delicate exercise which contains a core of common objectives that Member States are lawfully entitled to pursue; a practice that can be used as a map for a journey through the economic history of Europe.[55]

Thus, the first and sparse decisions adopted during the 60s and early 70s concerned mainly aid to the steel and coal industries, to shipbuilding, agriculture, textile, and a few cases of rescue and restructuring.[56] It is from this embryonic case practice that, in the 70s and through the mid-80s, the Commission started to draw more general criteria for assessing the compatibility of national aid measures and to codify them in frameworks, notices and letters to the Member States. Once again, the Commission's action was mirroring the state of the European economy and of a larger Community. The first 'guidelines' were not surprisingly dedicated to the textile industry,[57] to general systems of regional aid[58] and, following the first oil crisis, to environmental matters.[59] A Shipbuilding Code and rules for the steel industry followed the second energy crisis and were adopted in 1981 and 1985.[60] The Commission also used the legal basis for aid to transport, now contained in Article 93 TFEU, to propose to the Council two regulations on aid for public services in

[54] Since its early case law, the Court has recognized that Art. 107(3) TFEU confers on the Commission a broad discretion to allow aid by way of derogation from the general prohibition laid down in Article 107(1) TFEU (Case 730/79 *Philip Morris Holland BV v Commission* [1980] ECR 2671, paras 24–25). According to the Court, the question of whether a particular form of State aid is compatible with the Common Market raises problems which entail examination and appraisal of economic facts and circumstances which are complex and liable to change rapidly (Case C-301/87 *France v Commission* [1990] ECR I-307, para 15). In parallel, the Court has limited its appraisal to the illegality of a contested decision, leaving clearly to the Commission the assessment of the facts, especially in the economic sphere (Case C-225/91 *Matra v Commission* [1993] ECR I-3203, para 23).

[55] Few have attempted an historical account of state aid control. Among these, worth mentioning are Wolfgang Mederer, 'Evolution of State Aid Control' in Wolfang Mederer, Nicola Pesaresi, Mark Van Hoff (eds), *EU Competition Law—Vol. II State Aid*, (2008) Ch 2; and Juan Jorge Pierna Lopez, 'The Concept of State Aid under EU Law: From Internal Market To Competition And Beyond', *EIU*, March 2013.

[56] At that time, state aid decisions were published randomly, mostly negative ones, and in a very concise form, so that all accounts of the first attempts at controlling Member States' public interventions in the economy have to be based on an array of different sources, such as the direct reading of the *Official Journal* or the *Reports of Commission Decisions Relating to State Aid—Article 93, paragraph 2 (Negative final Decisions)*, published by the European Commission in 1996.

[57] Community framework for aids to the textile industry, Communication to Member States, SEC(71) 363 Final, July 1971.

[58] Framework on general system of regional aid: Council Resolution of 20.10.1971, [1971] OJ C 111/1; and Commission communication, [1971] OJ C 111/7

[59] Community Framework in environmental matters—Letter of the Commission to Member States S/74/38807, 07.11.1974, reproduced in *Competition Rules in the EEC and the ECSC applicable to state aids*, Commission of the European Communities, Brussels—Luxembourg, 1987, page 91.

[60] Aid to shipbuilding: Council Directive of 28.04.1981, [1981] OJ L137/39. Decision 3484/85/ECSC of 27 November 1985 establishing Community Rules for aid to the Steel industry, [1985] OJ L 340/1.

transport by rail, road and in-land waterways and for coordination of land transport that the Council adopted in 1969 and 1970.[61]

It is however, from the mid-80s, in parallel with the conception and establishment of the Single Market, that the Commission's analysis of what could constitute 'common objectives' in the meaning of Article 107(3) TFEU started to be systematic. In the White Paper, *Completing the Internal Market*,[62] the Commission stressed the importance of state aid control for the development of the internal market and for Europe's competitiveness. Even more interestingly, it sketched what almost thirty years later would be branded as 'good aid': 'an effective [state aid] Community discipline will make it possible to ensure that available resources are directed away from non-viable activities towards competitive and job creating industries of the future'.[63] From there, the Commission moved on to recognize, as common objectives, public interventions in favour of small and medium-sized enterprises (SMEs), the promotion of research and development, and the improvement of the situation of workers in the labour market and their training.[64]

Finally in 1999, the Commission proposed—and the Council approved—the so-called Enabling Regulation.[65] Under this instrument, the Council 'enables' the Commission to adopt regulations identifying certain categories of aid as compatible and exempting them from previous notification by the Member States, provided they respect a number of criteria defined in such regulations. Nowadays, therefore, compatibility is assessed on the basis of case practice, horizontal and sectoral guidelines and a block exemption regulation, that, since 2006, has captured in one single legislative text all the criteria for exempting aid from notification and harmonized, as far as possible, all horizontal aspects applying to the different aid areas concerned.[66]

---

[61] Regulation (EEC) No 1191/69 of the Council of 26 June 1969 on action by Member States concerning the obligations inherent in the concept of a public service in transport by rail, road and inland waterway, [1969] OJ L 156/1; and Regulation (EEC) No 1187/70 of the Council of 4 June 1970 on the granting of aids for transport by rail, road and inland waterway, [1970] OJ L 130/1.

[62] COM (85)310 final, 14 June 1985, paras 19 and 158.

[63] COM (85)310 final, 14 June 1985, para 158.

[64] Community guidelines on state aid for small and medium-sized enterprises (SMEs), [1996] OJ C 213/4; Community framework for state aid for Research and Development, [1996] OJ C 45/5; Guidelines on aid to employment, [1995] OJ C 334/4; Framework on training aid, [1998] OJ C 343/10.

[65] Council Regulation (EC) No 994/98 of 7 May 1998 on the application of Articles 92 and 93 (now 107 and 108 respectively) of the Treaty establishing the European Community to certain categories of horizontal state aid, [1998] OJ L 142/1.

[66] The first General Block Exemption Regulation ('GBER') consolidated five existing state aid regulations adopted by the Commission since 2001: aid to SMEs; research and development aid in favour of SMEs; aid for employment; training aid; and regional aid. In addition, the GBER block exempted another five categories of aid: environmental aid; innovation aid; research and development aid for large companies; aid in the form of risk capital; and aid for enterprises newly created by female entrepreneurs. See Commission Regulation (EC) No 800/2008 of 6 August 2008 declaring certain categories of aid compatible with the Common Market in the application of Articles 87 and 88 of the Treaty (General block exemption Regulation), [2008] OJ L 214/3.

With the recent state aid modernization programme ('SAM'), the Commission has given another turn to compatibility assessment, aligning it to the EU2020 objectives.[67] The process of revision of the state aid instruments started in 2012 and, as far as compatibility is concerned, has been based on one main objective:[68] to encourage growth through what has been defined as 'good aid', that is aid 'which is well designed, targeted at identified market failures and objectives of common interest, and least distortive'.[69] In other words, the Commission has tried to stimulate Member States to spend their often scarce public resources to facilitate and not to replace private spending, in areas which are considered the drivers of the European social economy and where the markets are indeed failing, on their own, to deliver the necessary growth. To reach this goal, the Commission has revised and consolidated almost all of the substantive rules that govern the compatibility assessment of the aid, from the guidelines on research, development and innovation, to the ones on risk capital, broadband, regional aid, aviation, and energy and environment. It has also proposed the revision of the Enabling Regulation, approved by the Council in 2013, on the basis of which the Commission has adopted an enlarged GBER,[70] whose scope now extends to block exemptions of all categories of aid that are considered 'good', have limited impact on the internal market, and for which the compatibility criteria are consolidated. New categories include aid for innovation, culture, natural disasters, sport, certain broadband infrastructure, social aid for transport to remote regions and aid for certain agriculture, forestry and fisheries issues.

Next to the revision and streamlining of all main state aid guidelines, through SAM, the Commission has also attempted to clarify the principles on which its assessment is carried out. In particular, it has identified and codified a set of seven 'common principles' applicable to the compatibility assessment of all kinds of aid,[71] a sort of common methodology that is then applied more specifically to each kind of aid. The first criterion that the Commission looks at systematically is whether the aid will contribute to an 'objective of common interest' while addressing a market failure. A telling example of how the Commission has re-oriented this requirement to target aid towards fiscal consolidation and growth is contained in the new Aviation Guidelines. Under the 2005 Aviation Guidelines, all investment aid to airports was considered compatible up to 100% of the costs,[72] with the result that many airports were developed without taking into consideration the actual demand, thus leading to

---

[67] See n 29.

[68] The other two SAM objectives are more of a procedural nature and, as highlighted above in footnote 10, have led to the revision in 2013 of the Procedural Regulation.

[69] Communication from the Commission on EU State Aid Modernisation ('SAM'), COM (2012) 209 final, 08.05.2012, para 12.

[70] Commission Regulation (EU) No 651/2014 of 17 June 2014 declaring certain categories of aid compatible with the internal market in application of Articles 107 and 108 TFEU, [2014] OJ L 187/1.

[71] Communication from the Commission on EU State Aid Modernisation ('SAM'), n 69, para 18.

[72] Community guidelines on the financing of airports and start-up aid to airlines departing from regional airports, [2005] OJ C 312/1, section 4.1, and ensuing Commission case practice.

a strong misallocation of airport capacity in Europe. The new rules will only consider investment aid that addresses a genuine transport need as fulfilling an 'objective of common interest' and will therefore result in enhanced accessibility, regional development and better traffic allocation within airports. Aid will not be allowed when other airports or other modes of transport—such as high-speed trains—already ensure the connectivity of the area.[73] Secondly, the Commission verifies the so called 'necessity of the aid'. Under this criterion, the Member States have to show that the aid is targeted at bringing about a material improvement that the market cannot deliver on its own, in other words, how the aid addresses a market failure. Thus, for instance, the new Research, Development and Innovation Guidelines ('RD&I') consider aid 'necessary' if it is for RD&I projects with positive externalities and knowledge spillovers that result in an overall societal or economic benefit but that would not be pursued by private undertakings without the aid because the mere return on the private investment would not justify them.[74] A third criterion that the Commission will from now on routinely verify is the 'appropriateness of the aid', ie whether there are alternative measures that may be cheaper for the State or less distortive. Under the new Energy and Environmental Aid Guidelines (EEAG), for instance, the Commission now foresees the possibility of granting aid to generators to ensure generation adequacy. However, in order for this so-called capacity mechanism to be considered 'appropriate' the Member States will also have to take into account the extent to which other measures, such as interconnection capacity, could be used instead of aid to remedy the problem of generation adequacy. The idea is that, while interconnections promote the internal market for energy, capacity mechanisms—by reserving a certain amount of generation over a certain period of time for given generators and compensating it through public resources—are more costly for tax payers and more distortive.[75] Under a fourth criterion, the Member States have to demonstrate the 'incentive effect' of an aid. This is a classic of the Commission's compatibility assessment, endorsed by the Court since its early jurisprudence, and it entitles the Commission to refuse the grant of aid where that aid does not induce the recipient undertakings to adopt conduct likely to assist attainment of one of the objectives referred to in Article 107(3) TFEU. Such aid must thus be necessary for the achievement of the objectives specified in that provision, with the result that, without it, market forces alone would not succeed in getting the recipient undertakings to adopt conduct likely to assist attainment of those objectives.[76]

---

[73] Guidelines on State aid to airports and airlines, [2014] OJ C 99/3, paras 84–86.

[74] Framework for State aid for research and development and innovation, [2014] OJ C 198/1, para 49.

[75] Communication from the Commission—Guidelines on state aid for environmental protection and energy 2014-2020, [2014] OJ C 200/1, para 226.

[76] Joined cases C-630/11 P to C-633/11 P, *HGA Srl and others, Regione autonoma della Sardegna, Timsas srl and Grand Hotel Abi d'Oru SpA v European Commission* judgment of 13 June 2013, quoting Case 730/79 *Philip Morris Holland v Commission*, see above footnote n. 54, paras 16 and 17.

Two further common principles are those of 'proportionality' and 'avoidance of undue negative effects'. Before declaring the aid compatible, the Commission routinely verifies that the aid granted is the minimum necessary to achieve the common objective and that the potential negative effects of the aid are sufficiently limited, so that the overall balance of the measure is positive. Since the crisis, however, these criteria have taken on a whole new significance. In both the Rescue and Restructuring Guidelines for financial and for non-financial firms, for instance, the Commission now imposes on the beneficiary's shareholders a much more pervasive 'burden sharing' as a condition for compatibility. In particular, under this reviewed mechanism, the owners of the bank or firm in difficulty will bear the losses first and public resources will only be allowed in case of remaining restructuring needs, thus greatly reducing the amount of public resources needed.[77] The Commission has presented these changes as being based on the 'good practices of the last years in dealing with bank bail-outs and restructuring' and as a key mechanism in order to level the playing field between similar undertakings located in different Member States.[78]

A last word is merited by the introduction, with SAM, of a further compatibility assessment criterion across all aid instruments: 'transparency'. From now on, for all State aid above €0.5m, Member States will have to publish on a dedicated website the identity of the beneficiary, including whether it is an SME or a large company, the location and the sector of activity; the amount of aid granted; its objective and the legal basis.[79] Although apparently just an administrative requirement, this criterion on its own has the potential to revolutionize State aid control as we know it. From now on, in fact, all levels of the Member States' administration will be accountable to their citizens for how taxpayers' money is spent and who benefits.

IV. A WORD OF CONCLUSION

The purpose of this contribution was to present an overall picture of what is undeniably a complex area of EU law, an area where 'eternal' questions about the co-existence of national and supranational elements are particularly pressing, as

---

[77] Communication from the Commission on the application, from 1 August 2013, of state aid rules to support measures in favour of banks in the context of the financial crisis ('Banking Communication'), [2013] OJ C 216/1, paras 40–46; and Communication from the Commission—Guidelines on State aid for rescuing and restructuring non-financial undertakings in difficulty, C(2014)4606 final, 9 July 2014, not yet published, paras 65–69.

[78] 'State aid: Commission Adapts Crisis Rules for Banks', Press release IP/13/672, 10.7.2013.

[79] See Communications from the Commission, C (2014) 3349 final, 21.05.2014, not yet published.

they impact on core functions of the state and on the regulatory competence of the European Union. We fully realize that in our attempt, we perhaps constructed a rather optimistic model, where these conflicting interests are considered as having been harmoniously recomposed over time to follow the process of European integration. However, we also firmly believe that a reinvigorated European project—badly needed in these times of economic crisis and ensuing *revanchisme*—can only continue to go through a sort of 'social contract' whereby the parties, the controlled and the controllers, the national and the supranational, commit to necessary public spending so as to achieve common interests, such as sustainable growth and social responsibility. As former Commissioner Sutherland wrote as long ago as 1987, state aid control is about ensuring 'that resources are channelled to industries which contribute to growth and competitiveness, that state intervention does not permit any company or sector to gain an unfair advantage over its competitors in another Member State and that state aid policy is consistent with other Community policies'.[80] This should be even truer at a time when more (better?) European regulation is considered essential, both in terms of fiscal governance, to control 'the negative externalities that unsound public finances in a Member State can generate for its neighbours' and in terms of structural policies.[81]

BIBLIOGRAPHY

Andrea Biondi, 'The Rationale of State Aid Control: A Return to Orthodoxy', in *Cambridge Yearbook of European Law* (2011) 35

Andrea Biondi, 'State Aid is Falling, Falling Down: An Analysis of the Concept of "Aid" in the Acquis of the EU Courts', in 50 *Common Market Law Review* (2013) 1719

Luis Buendía Sierra and Ben Smulders. 'The Limited Role of the Refined Economic Approach', in *Achieving the Objectives of State Aid Control: Time for Some Realism in EC State Aid Law: Liber Amicorum Francisco Santaolalla* (2008) 18

Pietro Crocioni, 'Can State Aid Policy Become More Economically Friendly?' (2006) 29 *World Competition* 89

José Luis Da Cruz Vilaca, 'Material and Geographic Selectivity in State Aid' (2009) 4 *EStAL* 443

Francesco De Cecco, *State Aid and the European Economic Constitution* (2013)

Vittorio Di Bucci, 'Comments on the Paper Selectivity, Economic Advantage, Distortion of Competition and Effect on Trade', in Jacques Derenne and Massimo Merola (eds), 'Economic Analysis of State Aid Rules—Contributions and Limits', proceedings of the

---

[80] P. Sutherland, 'Foreword', in *Competition Rules in the EEC and the ECSC applicable to state aids*, Commission of the European Communities, Brussels—Luxembourg, 1987, page 6.

[81] See Mario Draghi, 'Memorial Lecture in Honour of Tommaso Padoa-Schioppa', speech delivered in London on 9 July 2014, available at http://www.ecb.europa.eu/press/key/date/2014/html/sp140709_2.en.html.

third annual conference of the Global Competition Law Centre, College of Europe, 21–22 September 2006 (2007) 157

H. Friederiszick, H. W. Lars-Hendrik Röller, and V. Verouden, 'European State Aid Control: An Economic Framework' in P Buccirossi (ed), *Advances in the Economics of Competition Law* (2006) 652–654

Wolfgang Mederer, 'Evolution of State Aid Control' in Wolfang Mederer, Nicola Pesaresi, Mark Van Hoff (eds), *EU Competition Law—Vol. II State Aid* (2008) Ch 2

Juan Jorge Pierna Lopez, 'The Concept of State Aid Under EU Law: From Internal Market to Competition and Beyond', *EIU*, March 2013

Elisabetta Righini, 'The Reform of The State Aid Rules on Financing of Public Services: Paving The Way Towards a Clearer, Simpler and More Diversified Framework' (2-2012, Supplement) *EStAL* 3

Wolf Sauter and Harm Schepel, *State and Market in European Union Law. The Public and Private Spheres of the Internal Market before the EU Courts* (2009)

Niamh Nic Shuibhne. *The Coherence of EU Free Movement Law: Constitutional Responsibility and the Court of Justice* (2013) Ch 7

CHAPTER 27

EU INTELLECTUAL PROPERTY LAW

EXERCISES IN HARMONIZATION

CATHERINE SEVILLE

I. Introduction

INTELLECTUAL property is a powerful and increasingly global commodity. Its intangible nature allows it to move readily, but legal obstacles can hamper its passage across borders. Harmonization of IP laws is an obvious priority for the EU, given the fundamental importance of the free movement of goods and competition. Intellectual property laws can act to prevent or inhibit the free movement of goods. A balance needs to be struck between the legitimate interests of IP right holders, and the operation of fundamental principles of free movement of goods and free competition.[1] This general problem was tackled initially in the case law of the ECJ—with considerable success.[2] But legislative harmonization (if it can be achieved) offers a far better solution for these highly technical matters.

[1] IP right holders must be able to use their rights to prevent the circulation of counterfeit goods, for example. But they must be prevented from using those rights to erect barriers to trade and insulate national markets within the Community without legitimate reason (such as impairment of the goods).

[2] In both the spheres of free movement of goods and free competition, the ECJ distinguished between the *existence* of the IP right (whose protection is assured) and its *exercise* (which might

Beyond the need for harmonization, though, the EU regards an efficient system of intellectual property rights as crucial for encouraging creativity and innovation, which in turn will lead to competitive advantage, higher employment, and economic success. The contribution of IP to employment and GDP within the EU is demonstrably significant. However, there is increasing public debate about intellectual property matters, which may well be challenging to existing systems and assumptions. As a result, the EU has shown itself keen to demonstrate the worth of IP with empirical evidence. It has also made considerable efforts to review and appraise the existing systems, to engage in dialogue and consultation with stakeholders, and to raise awareness of IP among Europe's citizens. All this acknowledges that the IP system has considerable social importance, and not simply economic importance.

Yet, harmonizing EU IP law is extremely challenging. There is an external landscape. EU IP has to function within the context of important international treaties (notably the Paris, Berne, and Madrid Conventions, and the TRIPS agreement). The EU therefore has to interact with the World Intellectual Property Organization (WIPO), and with the World Trade Organization (WTO)—both of which, naturally, have different agendas and perspectives. The EU's economic success has to be seen and judged in a global context, so EU IP systems have to allow successful competition with other powerful economies. At the other end of the economic spectrum, the interests of developing countries are a matter of significant public concern. Within the EU, there may be fundamental and entrenched differences in national legal systems. Powerful national interests may prove frustratingly immovable. All these considerations and tensions are visible in the range of approaches to the harmonization of IP within the EU. There are successful unitary rights, such as the Community Trade Mark and the Community Design Right—and there may yet be a Unitary Patent. In other areas, the focus has been on removing obstacles to the single market, and on doing what is practical and possible rather than perfect. This chapter offers a succinct, high-level survey of efforts and progress so far. It aims to touch on the most important features of each area, and also the most important controversies. Given the multiple significances of IP for the EU, it is certain that there will be more to come.

in appropriate circumstances be restricted): Case 24/67 *Parke Davis & Co. v Probel* [1968] ECR 55; Joined Cases 56/64 and 58/64 *Etablissements Consten and Grundig-Verkaufs v Commission* [1966] ECR 299. This led to a considerable body of case law defining the specific subject matter of the various IP rights, addressing the nature of the consent required by a right holder if a right was to be exhausted, and setting out the boundaries of legitimate activity by parallel traders (such as repackaging of genuine goods). For further detail see Catherine Seville, *EU Intellectual Property Law and Policy*, (2009) Ch 6.

II. Trade Marks

1. Context and Introduction

The need for legally-protected trade marks was tied to the expansion of trade beyond local markets. Growth in international and global trading has only emphasized these needs. WIPO administers the Madrid System, which facilitates the acquisition of national marks, though does not offer an 'international mark' as such. The EU has been responsible for two significant developments. The first was the 1988 Trade Mark Directive (TMD), which harmonized substantive national trade mark law significantly.[3] It harmonizes the conditions for obtaining and holding a registered trade mark, but leaves Member States free to determine procedural provisions concerning registration, revocation and invalidity of trade marks. The substantive provisions regulating conflicts between confusingly similar marks and signs are also harmonized. The second important step was the establishment of a Community trade mark (CTM), by means of a regulation.[4] The CTM offers uniform protection throughout the European Union, via a single registration procedure with the Office for Harmonization in the Internal Market (Trade Marks and Designs) (OHIM). The CTM Regulation uses very similar provisions to the Trade Mark Directive to control the conditions under which a CTM may be obtained and held. OHIM opened in 1996, and has now registered approaching one million CTMs.

CTM applications can be filed either directly at OHIM or at any national trade mark office, in any of the 22 languages of the Union. The application may be refused by OHIM only on the basis of the 'absolute' grounds (which regulate the characteristics of registrable trade marks). OHIM (unlike some national systems) does not refuse applications on relative grounds—those relating to prior rights. The onus lies on third parties to raise relative grounds for refusal in opposition (or cancellation) proceedings. The initial registration period is ten years from the filing date, with the possibility of renewal for further periods of ten years (potentially indefinitely). A CTM may be revoked or declared invalid, either in proceedings in a Community trade mark court,[5] or by application to the Cancellation Division of the OHIM. Because of its unitary character, when a CTM is registered, transferred

---

[3] Dir 89/104 to approximate the laws of the Member States relating to trade marks [1989] OJ L40/1. Now replaced with Dir 2008/95/EC to approximate the laws of the Member States relating to trade marks (Codified version) [2008] OJ L299/25.

[4] Council Reg (EC) No. 40/94 on the Community Trade Mark [1993] OJ L11/1.

[5] Member States are required to designate a limited number of national courts and tribunals of first and second instance as 'Community trade mark courts', to perform the functions assigned to them by the CTMR: CTMR Art 95.

or allowed to lapse, the effect of such action is Union-wide. The CTM coexists with national trade marks, which remain useful for many undertakings.[6]

2. Registrable Mark

A trade mark may consist of 'any sign capable of being represented graphically, particularly words, including personal names, designs, letters, numerals, the shape of goods or their packaging, provided that such signs are capable of distinguishing goods or services of one undertaking from those of other undertakings'.[7] This inclusive approach is more flexible than that seen in many previous national laws. For word and figurative marks, the requirement of graphic representation is easily met. But it has defeated attempts to register smells and tastes.[8] For sounds, sonograms are now accepted in electronic CTM applications as a graphical representation, if accompanied by an MP3 sound file. Other evidentiary challenges persist. Trade mark lawyers are accustomed to weighing up the impact of word and figurative marks for purposes of registrability and infringement. In contrast, notions of how colour, shape or movement marks should be assessed (to determine their distinctiveness, for example) are much less well developed and defined.

3. Absolute Grounds for Refusal

The absolute grounds for refusal to register a trade mark are set out in Article 3 of the TMD, and Article 7 of the CTMR. These cover inherent objections to a sign's distinctiveness, and various public interest objections, including bad faith. Signs which do not comply may not be registered, or, if registered are liable to be declared invalid.

(a) Marks which are not Distinctive

A trade mark's distinctiveness is assessed by reference to the goods or services listed in the application and to the perception of the relevant public. There is also an element of public interest, aimed at ensuring that other traders offering the same type of

---

[6] In terms of fees for the relevant territory, it will be much cheaper to apply for a CTM than for many national marks. However, because the CTM is a unitary right, if it is successfully challenged (either by opposition to registration or in an invalidity action) it will be invalid for all Member States. Some businesses with very valuable marks may choose to maintain national marks to guard against this eventuality, and such a strategy will also permit forum shopping if there is an infringement. At the other end of the spectrum, a business which is firm in its intention to use a mark only in one Member State may well still find a national mark preferable.

[7] TMD Art 2; CTMR Art 4.

[8] See Robert Burrell and Michael Handler, 'Making Sense of Trade Mark Law' (2003) 4 *IPQ* 388.

goods or services will not be unduly restricted.[9] The level of distinctiveness required is not challenging: the mark must be 'devoid' of distinctive character to be unregistrable. But it must enable the relevant public to identify the origin of the goods or services protected by it, and to distinguish them from those of other undertakings. The ECJ has acknowledged that it might be more difficult to establish the distinctive character of certain categories of trade marks (shapes, common surnames, slogans, for example), but the approach is the same for all categories of marks.[10]

Descriptive trade marks may not be registered.[11] The test set out by the ECJ in the BABY-DRY case was criticized for setting a very low threshold for the registration of descriptive marks, raising concerns that ordinary language might be monopolized by a few traders.[12] It is now clear that this exclusion also has a public interest aim—to ensure that descriptive signs may be freely used by all, unless they have become distinctive through use. Geographical names fall to be considered under this provision. National trade mark laws have often been hostile to the registration of place names, to prevent a single trader from monopolizing them. However, it is now possible to register a geographic name, if it is not descriptive.[13]

Trade marks which consist exclusively of signs or indications which have become customary in the current language or in the bona fide and established practices of the trade are not registrable.[14] The ECJ has emphasized that this question cannot be considered in the abstract or separately from the goods or services applied for.[15]

There is an important qualification to these rules on distinctiveness. The three absolute grounds of refusal just discussed may be overcome if the mark has become distinctive for the relevant goods or services in consequence of the use which has been made of it.[16] Because the CTM is of a unitary character, it must possess distinctive character throughout the Union, not just a substantial part of it.[17]

(b) The Shape Exclusions

Shape marks can provide potentially indefinite protection for design elements of products. There is a risk that the registration of such marks would impede traders with a legitimate need to use similar shapes. So specific exclusions apply to signs

---

[9] Case C-329/02 P *SAT.1 SatellitenFernsehen v OHIM* [2004] ECR I-8317, para 26.

[10] Joined Cases C-53/01–C-55/01 *Linde AG, Winward Industries, Rado Uhren AG* [2003] ECR I-3161, paras 48–9.

[11] TMD Art 3(1)(c); CTMR Art 7(1)(c).

[12] Case C-383/99 P *Procter & Gamble Company v OHIM* [2001] ECR I-6251. Andrew Griffiths, 'Modernising Trade Mark Law and Promoting Economic Efficiency: An Evaluation of the Baby Dry Judgment' (2003) 1 *IPQ* 1.

[13] Case C-108/97 *Windsurfing Chiemsee Produktions- und Vertriebs v Boots- und Segelzubehor Walter Huber* [1999] ECR I-2779.

[14] TMD Art 3(1)(d); CTMR Art 7(1)(d).

[15] Case C-517/99 *Merz & Krell v Deutsches Patent- und Markenamt* [2001] ECR I-6959.

[16] TMD Art 3(3); CTMR Art 7(3).

[17] Case C-108/05 *Bovemij Verzekeringen v Benelux-Merkenbureau* [2007] ETMR 29.

which consist exclusively of: the shape which results from the nature of the goods themselves; the shape of goods which is necessary to obtain a technical result; the shape which gives substantial value to goods. These exclusions cannot be overcome by showing that the shapes have acquired a distinctive character through use.[18]

The first of these exclusions seeks to exclude basic shapes needed for use by all traders, such as the shape of a football for a football. The second exclusion requires a decision as to whether the shape of goods is necessary to obtain a technical result. The purpose of the exclusion is to preclude the registration of shapes whose essential characteristics perform a technical function, limiting competitors from supplying a product incorporating such a function. If the essential functional characteristics of the shape of a product are attributable solely to the technical result, it may not be registered, even if that technical result can be achieved by other shapes.[19] For the third exclusion, of a shape which gives substantial value to goods, the policy concern is that design protection—currently of quite limited duration in EU law[20]—should not be extended indefinitely by means of trade mark law.[21]

(c) Other Absolute Grounds

The remaining absolute grounds cover public policy and morality, deceptive marks, and certain special emblems.[22] Trade marks which are contrary to public policy or to accepted principles of morality may not be registered. The concern is with marks which are contrary to the basic norms of society, not with bad taste. Trade marks which will deceive the relevant public, for instance as to the nature, quality or geographical origin of the goods or service, may not be registered. Member States may provide that a trade mark shall not be registered if the application is made in bad faith by the applicant. However, under the CTMR this is a ground of invalidity and not a ground of refusal.

4. Relative Grounds for Refusal

Marks which conflict with earlier marks or signs may not be registered.[23] In part this is to protect the earlier trade mark owner, but it also safeguards the guarantee

---

[18] TMD Art 3(1)(e); CTMR Art 7(1)(e).

[19] Case C-299/99 *Koninklijke Philips Electronics v Remington Consumer Products* [2002] ECR I-5475. See Uma Suthersanen, 'The European Court of Justice in *Philips v Remington*: Trade Marks and Market Freedom' (2003) 3 *IPQ* 257.

[20] See below Section IV 3 (b).

[21] Case T-508/08 *Bang & Olufsen v OHIM* (6 October 2011). For discussion, see Janne Glaesel and Louise Stuhr, 'The 3D Shape Dilemma: Refusal to Register the Three-Dimensional Shape of a Loudspeaker' (2012) 7 *Journal of Intellectual Property Law & Practice* 763.

[22] TMD Art 3(1) & (2); CMTR Art 7(1) & 51(1).

[23] Both the UKIPO and the OHIM will search to determine whether the mark applied for conflicts with an earlier registered mark or CTM registration. However, the results of these official searches

of origin to the consumer. The relative grounds for refusal mirror the provisions concerned with infringement. Earlier rights present a significant risk for applicants. There are over 3 million national marks registered in EU Member States, and the identification of unregistered marks is extremely difficult.

There are three relative grounds for refusal:

(a) Identical mark on identical goods

A mark may not be registered if it is identical to an earlier trade mark and the goods or services for which registration is applied for are identical with the goods or services for which the earlier trade mark is protected.[24] In these cases of 'double identity' it is assumed that confusion will result. The concept of identity of marks is therefore construed narrowly, though from the point of view of an average consumer.[25]

(b) Identical/Similar Mark on Identical/Similar Goods

A mark will not be registered if, because of its identity with, or similarity to, the earlier trade mark and the identity or similarity of the goods or services covered by the trade marks there exists a likelihood of confusion on the part of the public in the territory in which the earlier trade mark is protected.[26]

When assessing the similarity of marks, their visual, aural or conceptual similarity is considered. What is relevant is the perception of marks in the mind of the average consumer of the goods or services in question. In assessing the similarity of the goods or services concerned, all relevant factors should be taken into account. 'Likelihood of confusion' is the risk that the public might believe that the goods or services in question come from the same undertaking, or from economically-linked undertakings.[27]

(c) Marks with a Reputation

A mark may not be registered as a CTM when an earlier trade mark has a reputation, and use without due cause of the trade mark applied for would take unfair advantage of, or be detrimental to, the distinctive character or the repute of the earlier trade mark.[28] Detriment to the distinctive character of a mark is known as

---

do not operate as an automatic bar to registration. The onus is on the owner of the earlier mark to oppose the application. This explains the commercial value of 'watching services', which alert a trade mark owner to all similar trade mark applications which have been accepted for registration.

[24] TMD Art 4(1)(a); CTMR Art 8(1)(a).
[25] Case C-291/00 *LTJ Diffusion v Sadas Vertbaudet* [2003] ECR 2799.
[26] TMD Art 4(1)(b); CTMR Art 8(1)(b).
[27] Case C-39/97 *Canon Kabushiki Kaisha v Metro-Goldwyn-Mayer* [1998] ECR I-5507.
[28] CTMR Art 8(1)(b). TMD Art 4(1)(b) permits Member States to provide for this ground of refusal in national trade mark laws, and many (including the UK) have done so.

'dilution' or 'blurring'. Detriment to the reputation of a mark is known as 'tarnishment'. This provision can be relied on whether the goods are identical, similar, or dissimilar.[29] The existence of a *link* between the marks is an essential condition—the relevant public must make a connection between them. In the absence of such a link, the use of the later mark is not likely to take unfair advantage of, or be detrimental to, the distinctive character or the repute of the earlier mark.[30] However, the earlier mark holder must do more than establish that the relevant public links the two marks—this is mere non-origin association, and insufficient to establish unfair advantage or detriment.

The ECJ stated in *L'Oréal* that unfair advantage occurs where a third party uses a similar sign, seeking 'to ride on the coat-tails of the mark with a reputation in order to benefit from the power of attraction, the reputation and the prestige of that mark and to exploit, without paying any financial compensation, the marketing effort expended by the proprietor of the mark in order to create and maintain the mark's image'.[31] Applying this ruling in the UK Court of Appeal, Jacob LJ objected that the ECJ's approach meant that all free riding was unfair, 'a conclusion high in moral content . . . rather than in economic content'.[32]

When arguing that there is detriment to the distinctive character of a mark, its proprietor is not required to demonstrate actual and present harm, though it must be proved that there is serious risk that this will occur in the future. Controversially, the ECJ has stated that such proof requires evidence of a change in the economic behaviour of the average consumer of the relevant goods or services.[33] This seems potentially a high hurdle, but the ECJ has insisted that the concept lays down an objective condition.[34]

If a trade mark proprietor shows that its earlier mark has a reputation, and the use of the later mark will take unfair advantage of, or be detrimental to, that earlier mark, then the burden is on the other party to show 'due cause' for their use.

5. Rights Conferred

The trade mark proprietor has exclusive rights in the mark, and can prevent use in the course of trade of: an identical sign on identical goods; an identical/similar sign on identical/similar goods where there is a likelihood of confusion; and, for marks

---

[29] CTMR Art 8(5). Case C-292/00 *Davidoff v Gofkid* [2003] ECR I-389.

[30] Case C-252/07 *Intel Corporation v CPM* [2008] ECR I-8823.

[31] Case C-487/07 *L'Oréal v Bellure* [2009] ECR I-5185.

[32] *L'Oréal v Bellure* [2010] EWCA Civ 535 [48]. See also Seán Mc Guinness, 'Observations on Free Riding after *L'Oréal v Bellure*', (2012) 7 *JIPL&P* 890.

[33] *Intel* (n 22) para 77.

[34] Case C-383/12 P *Environmental Manufacturing v OHIM*, judgment of 14 November 2013 and *passim*.

with a reputation, use of an identical/similar sign which takes unfair advantage of, or is detrimental to, the distinctive character or the repute of the Community trade mark.[35] It will be seen that the rights conferred mirror the relative grounds for refusal. The concepts used to determine whether a mark has been infringed are identical. The legislative requirement that use is 'in the course of trade' has caused considerable difficulty. The ECJ's case law has at times seemed inconsistent. The mainstream view is that unless the public perceives a link which would undermine one of the trade mark's functions, in particular the guarantee of origin, the use will not infringe.[36]

The sale of keywords for use as index terms by search engines led to a controversial question in the field of trade mark infringement. Could a trade mark's proprietor object to the sale and use of the trade mark—*as a search engine keyword*—to a third party, without the trade mark proprietor's consent? For example, Marks & Spencer purchased various forms of 'INTERFLORA' as keywords, so that internet consumers entering 'INTERFLORA' as a search term would receive advertisements not for Interflora's flower delivery service, but for its rival Marks & Spencer's. The ECJ has held that if the keyword is identical to the trade mark, and is being used for identical goods/services, then the advertiser will be liable for infringement if consumers cannot determine without difficulty whether the advertiser is economically linked to the trade mark owner. It may also be possible that such behaviour infringes by taking unfair advantage of a mark with a reputation. Nevertheless, the use of trade marks as keywords cannot be prevented beyond these circumstances, and in many cases may be regarded as fair competition.[37]

6. Assessment

The EU's Trade Mark system has to be counted as a success. It is popular and generally functions well. The Commission has recently adopted proposals for some revision of the legislation, but these are initiatives aimed at upgrading and streamlining the process (at both EU and national levels), rather than a major overhaul of fundamentals.[38]

---

[35] CTMR Art 9; TMD Arts 4 & 5.

[36] Case C-48/05 *Adam Opel v Autec* [2007] ECR I-1017.

[37] Case C-323/09 *Interflora v Marks & Spencer & Flowers Direct Online*, judgment of 22 September 2011. In *Google France* the ECJ held that an ISP which stores, as a keyword, a sign identical to a trade mark and organizes the display of advertisements on the basis of that keyword does not 'use' that sign within the meaning of Art 5(1) & (2) TMD (or Art 9(1) CTMR): joined cases C-236/08 C-237/08 and C-238/08 *Google France SARL and Google Inc. v Louis Vuitton Malletier SA* (C-236/08), *Google France SARL v Viaticum SA and Luteciel SARL* (C-237/08) and *Google France SARL v Centre national de recherche en relations humaines (CNRRH) SARL and others* (C-238/08), judgment of 23 March 2010, para 56.

[38] The new legislative proposals have been drafted in the light of the *Study of the Overall Functioning of the European Trade Mark System*, undertaken for the Commission by the Max Planck

III. Copyright

Copyright protects a wide range of creative works, including literary, artistic, dramatic and musical works, sound recordings, films, broadcasts and computer programs. Its subject matter has expanded very considerably since the earliest forms of legislative protection, whose roots lay in monopolies of printed books. Copyright arises without formality once a work has been recorded in a material form. Culturally and socially, copyright works have wide influence. The impact of technology in this area has been momentous. All of these features present challenges to any harmonization project. One of the most difficult issues facing legislators in the current environment is to find an appropriate balance between protecting copyright works, and facilitating access to them. For the EU, addressing these matters in the context of the Single Market is even more testing.

1. EU Harmonization—History and Summary

The Commission first considered these issues in its 1988 Green Paper, *Copyright and the Challenge of Technology*.[39] There was an urgent need for copyright protection in areas of new technology: satellite and cable television, various computer technologies, and databases. Lack of harmonization of national rights in these areas was hampering the internal market. The Commission's priorities were to address Community problems. A considerable amount of legislation followed, adopting a largely sectoral approach. Directives address the protection of computer programs, rental and lending rights, cable and satellite broadcasting, copyright term, databases, the royalty on resale of an artist's work, copyright in the 'information society', and (most recently) 'orphan works'.

Institute following a competitive tender process: http://ec.europa.eu/internal_market/indprop/docs/tm/20110308_allensbach-study_en.pdf. The careful study included analysis of extensive user surveys and consultations of user associations. It recommended that the harmonization process should continue, bringing the provisions of the TMD further into line with the CTMR, thus eliminating where possible the remaining inconsistencies between Community and national regimes. The study found a reasonable degree of satisfaction with the consistency of the decisions of trade mark offices, but noted substantial room for improvement, with the objective of converting both OHIM and the national offices into centres of excellence rather than merely centres for good or satisfactory performance. The aim is to adopt the proposals by the spring of 2014.

[39] Copyright and Challenge of Technology—Copyright Issues Requiring Immediate Action COM/88/172.

(a) Computer Programs Directive

The Computer Programs Directive was the first to be adopted, in 1991.[40] Given the current ubiquity of computer software, it is hard to believe that at this time only five of the then twelve Member States had provisions expressly protecting computer programs. The Directive requires Member States to protect computer programs, by copyright, as literary works within the meaning of the Berne Convention.[41] A computer program must be protected 'if it is original in the sense that it is the author's own intellectual creation'.[42] Ideas and principles underlying a computer program are not protected.[43] The owner of copyright in a computer program has a number of exclusive rights.[44] The exceptions to these exclusive rights were a matter of considerable controversy during negotiations, particularly that allowing decompilation where 'indispensable' to achieve interoperability.[45]

(b) The Rental and Lending Rights Directive

The Rental and Lending Right Directive was implemented on 1 July 1994.[46] These rights are now widely accepted, but some Member States did not protect them at all. The Directive gives an exclusive right to control rental and lending to authors (in respect of their works), performers (in respect of fixations of their performances), phonogram producers (in respect of their phonograms) and film producers (in respect of their films).[47] The rights may be transferred, assigned or licensed. However, there is an 'unwaivable right to equitable remuneration' when films or phonograms are rented, to protect creators' interests.[48] For the same reason, the principal director of a cinematographic or audiovisual work must be regarded as one of its authors.[49]

(c) The Satellite and Cable Directive

The Satellite and Cable Directive aims to promote cross-border transmissions of audio-visual programs, particularly satellite broadcasting and cable

---

[40] Dir 91/250 [1991] OJ L122/42 ('CP Dir'). Now codified as Dir 2009/24 [2009] OJ L111/16.

[41] CP Dir Art 1(1).

[42] CP Dir Art 1(3). At the time this required 12 Member States to lower their threshold for granting protection, and the remaining three to raise it.

[43] CP Dir Art 1(2). See Case C-406/10 *SAS Institute v World Programming*, judgment of 2 May 2012.

[44] CP Dir Art 4. Community-wide exhaustion of the distribution right (but with the clear exception of the rental right) is explicitly provided for. See Case C-128/11 *UsedSoft v Oracle* (3 July 2012).

[45] CP Dir Arts 5 & 6. There are significant competition law aspects to this issue. See eg Case T-201/04 *Microsoft v Commission* [2007] ECR II-360.

[46] The original version, Dir 92/100, has now been replaced with a codified version: Dir 2006/115 on rental right and lending right and on certain rights related to copyright in the field of intellectual property (codified version) [2006] OJ L376/28.

[47] Rental Dir Art 3(1).

[48] Rental Dir Art 5. Case C-245/00 *SENA v NOS* [2003] ECR 1251.

[49] Rental Dir Art 2(2). See Case C-277/10 *Luksan v van der Let* (9 February 2012).

retransmission.[50] Certain minimum standards are guaranteed for right holders. Authors must be given a 'broadcasting right', that is, an exclusive right for the author to authorize communication to the public by satellite of copyright works.[51] The related rights of performers, phonogram producers and broadcasting organizations are protected in accordance with the Rental Directive (at the minimum), and copyright protection remains unaffected. The Directive also sets out a system of compulsory collective management of cable retransmission rights. The Directive has not proved as effective as hoped in achieving EU-wide broadcasting. Many television channels are now encrypted and accessible by subscription only. It is common for producers to sell their programs to broadcasting organizations on condition that their transmissions are encrypted so they cannot be received beyond national borders. These contractual licensing practices have allowed broadcasters and right holders to continue segmenting markets on national lines. The dynamic nature of the audiovisual market, again in the context of rapidly emerging technology, means that this remains a live issue for EU policy.

(d) The Term Directive

The Term Directive was put in place following *EMI* v *Patricia*, a case which exemplified the problems caused by an unharmonized regime.[52] For the basic copyright term, most Member States had adopted the Berne Convention's minimum term of fifty years from the author's death; but Germany had a 70-year *post mortem* term, Spain and others 60 years. For related rights, there was a much wider degree of variation. The appropriate term for copyright has long been a matter of debate. The policy adopted was to harmonize upwards, to a basic term of the author's life plus 70 years.[53]

As enacted, the term of protection for related rights was essentially fifty years. However, the Term Directive was amended in 2011, to extend the term of protection for rights in sound recordings to 70 years. And where a musical composition with lyrics is co-written, the Directive extends copyright to life plus 70 years for both the author of the lyrics and the composer of the music, regardless of whether they are recognized as co-authors.[54] The stated aim is to protect session musicians, and is part of the Commission's wider goal of gradually aligning authors' and performers' protection. This is a controversial measure, however, which is criticized both as lacking justification in principle, and as unlikely to achieve its aims in practice.[55]

---

[50] Dir 93/83 on the coordination of certain rules concerning copyright and rights related to copyright applicable to satellite broadcasting and cable retransmission Satellite Dir) [1993] OJ L248/15.

[51] Satellite Dir Art 2.   [52] Case C-341/87 *EMI Electrola* v *Patricia* [1989] ECR 79.

[53] Dir 93/98, now replaced by Dir 2006/116 on the term of protection of copyright and certain related rights (codified version) [2006] OJ L372/12.

[54] Dir 2011/77/EU amending Dir 2006/116/EC on the term of protection of copyright and certain related rights [2011] OJ L265/1.

[55] Benjamin Farrand, 'Too Much is Never Enough? The 2011 Copyright in Sound Recording Extension Directive' [2012] *EIPR* 297.

Previously unpublished works, published for the first time after copyright protection has expired, are covered by a new right (often called the 'publication right'), which is 'equivalent to the economic rights of the author'. It lasts for 25 years.[56]

(e) Database Directive

The very issue of whether databases form suitable subject matter for copyright protection is somewhat contentious, because they may be the product simply of financial investment (so-called 'sweat-of-the-brow' databases), rather than the original authorial works which form copyright's core subject matter. However, digital technology permits ready access to an immense range and quantity of information, in a form very convenient to the user, and there is an argument for some form of protection. There is nevertheless resistance to bringing all databases within the extensive protection of copyright.

The Database Directive therefore adopts a dual strategy. Firstly, it attempts to harmonize the conditions of copyright protection for databases. This is the highest level of protection, only extended to 'databases which, by reason of the selection or arrangement of their contents, constitute the author's own intellectual creation'. For those databases which fail to reach the threshold of originality required for copyright, the Directive creates a fifteen year *sui generis* right. This is granted to the maker of a database which shows 'substantial investment' of various forms.[57] There have been several key rulings from the ECJ offering guidance on central concepts.[58] There remains dispute as to whether the *sui generis* right is satisfactorily defined, though further legislative changes are not currently a priority for the Commission.

(f) Resale Right Directive

The artist's resale royalty, also known as the *droit de suite*, gives an artist a right to a share in the proceeds of any subsequent sale of an original work of art. Its main justification is the belief that artists should be entitled to participate in the increasing value of their works as their reputation increases. However, others argue that the resale right acts simply to lower the initial sale price, and that its effect is not to support emerging artists but to reward established ones. Several Member States (including the UK) fought the proposal, fearing that major art sales would be driven out of the European auction houses into the United States and Switzerland. A Directive was eventually adopted in 2001, and was notable for its extensive transitional arrangements.[59]

---

[56] Term Dir Art 4.   [57] Dir 96/9 on the Legal Protection of Databases [1996] OJ L77/20.

[58] Case C-338/02 *Fixtures Marketing v Svenska* [2004] ECR I-10497; Case C-444/02 *Fixtures Marketing v Organismos Prognostikon Agonon Podosfairou* [2004] ECR I-10549; Case C-46/02 *Fixtures Marketing v Oy Veikkaus* ECR I-10365; C-203/02 *British Horseracing Board v William Hill Organization* [2004] ECR 10,415.

[59] Dir 2001/84 on the resale right for the benefit of the author of an original work of art [2001] OJ L272/32.

The Directive establishes an EU resale right—an inalienable right to receive a royalty based on the sale price obtained for any resale of the work. Its term is tied to the full copyright term. Payable by the seller, it applies only to resales involving 'art market professionals', not sales between private individuals. Royalty rates are set in bands, which taper off as the sale price increases, and the total royalty is capped at €12500.[60] Disagreement regarding the effects of the resale right persists.[61]

(g) Information Society Directive

The 2001 Information Society Directive aimed to provide a more harmonized framework for copyright and related rights—one which reflected recent techno-logical developments.[62] It also transposed into Union law the obligations arising from the 1996 WIPO Internet treaties.[63] The Directive harmonizes three basic exclusive rights: the reproduction right, the right of communication to the public, and the distribution right. It attempts some harmonization of the exceptions to copyright. In addition, it introduces obligations concerning anti-copying measures and rights management information.

1) Exclusive rights. The reproduction right is defined as 'the exclusive right to authorise or prohibit direct or indirect, temporary or permanent reproduction by any means and in any form, in whole or in part'.[64] There was concern that acts such as caching and browsing should not be hampered, and an exception addresses this (discussed below).

A new right of communication to the public covers the transmission and dis-tribution of copyright works in a non-physical form. This includes broadcast and cable distribution, and also on-line, on-demand distribution. For performances, phonograms and broadcasts, the right is the 'making available to the public'. There is a growing body of ECJ case law which sets out criteria for determining whether an act of communication to the public has occurred. It covers live streaming of broadcasts.[65] The right has been held to be infringed by peer-to-peer (P2P) sites, including *The Pirate Bay*. In addition, in several Member States, orders have been obtained against retail internet service providers, requiring them to block access by their customers to particular P2P sites.[66] A question which is still unresolved is

---

[60] Resale Right Dir Art 4(1).

[61] See Nobuko Kawashima, 'The *Droit de Suite* Controversy Revisited: Context, Effects and the Price of Art' (2006) 3 *IPQ* 223.

[62] Dir 2001/29 on Copyright and related rights in the Information Society (InfoSoc Dir) [2001] OJ L167/10.

[63] WIPO Copyright Treaty and WIPO Performances and Phonograms Treaty.

[64] InfoSoc Dir Art 2(1).

[65] Case C-607/11 *ITV Broadcasting v TVCatchup* (7 March 2013).

[66] In the UK, see eg *Dramatico Entertainment v British Sky Broadcasting* [2012] EWHC 1152 (Ch); *EMI v BSkyB* [2013] EWHC 379 (Ch).

whether hyperlinking as a *general* matter is covered by the right. There are concerns that a restrictive approach to hyperlinking could impact the operation of the internet severely. A reference to the ECJ is pending.[67]

The distribution right relates to distribution of the original work, or tangible copies of it. Prior to the Directive there were significant differences between Member States as to the form of the distribution right, exceptions to it, and the point of its exhaustion. Under the Directive, authors must be granted 'the exclusive right to authorise or prohibit any form of distribution to the public by sale or otherwise'. The normal rule of Union-wide exhaustion is applied.[68]

2) Exceptions. The Information Society Directive harmonizes the scheme of copyright exceptions, but there are limitations to its achievements. There is one mandatory exception from the reproduction right, to cover temporary copying such as caching and browsing.[69] There is also an exhaustive list of 20 optional exceptions.[70] Member States may enact these or not, which weakens the harmonizing effect.

3) Protection of technological measures and rights management information. The WIPO Copyright Treaty requires Contracting Parties to provide adequate legal protection against the circumvention of technological measures used by authors to prevent unauthorized acts. This is a controversial matter, as the use of technological measures brings with it a danger that it will be made difficult or impossible to enjoy lawful exceptions to copyright. The Directive does guarantee the required legal protection, but there are counterbalancing provisions to ensure that right-holders do in fact allow users to take advantage of certain permitted exceptions.[71] The Directive also offers legal protection against the alteration of rights management information.[72]

2. Current and Future Reforms

The Commission continues its efforts to harmonize aspects of copyright law and related rights. Understandably, its focus remains on the internal market. Although acknowledging that a high level of copyright protection is crucial for intellectual creation, the Commission also considers that wider dissemination of knowledge contributes to more inclusive and cohesive societies. The Commission has also

---

[67] Case C-466/12 *Svensson*.

[68] InfoSoc Dir Art 4. The rule has its origins in case law: Case 78/70 *Deutsche Grammophon Gesellschaft GmbH v Metro SB Grossmarkte GmbH & Co KG* [1971] ECR 487.

[69] InfoSoc Dir Art 5(1). Applied in C-5/08 *Infopaq International v Danske Dagblades Forening* [2009] ECR I-6569.

[70] InfoSoc Dir Art 5.2, 5.3. All exceptions are subject to the Berne three-step test.

[71] InfoSoc Dir Art 6.   [72] InfoSoc Dir Art 7.

recognized the breadth of copyright's significance within the EU—it affects not only the internal market and cultural policies but also crosses information society, competition and consumer interests. This thinking underlies many of the Commission's recent legislative plans, and its current policy. The Commission is determined to review and modernize EU copyright rules, to make them 'fit for the digital age', and is currently engaged in public consultation on various matters.

(a) EU-Wide Licensing for Online Rights

The Commission has been frustrated for some time by the fragmentation of online markets in the EU. Collecting societies, traditionally, have been nationally organized. The Commission has pressed for measures to promote EU-wide licensing of copyright. A proposal for a Directive which would allow online providers to obtain licences to stream music across national borders is currently under consideration.

(b) Orphan Works

The Commission's aspiration is a European Digital Single Market for creative content. Its 'Europeana' portal offers a multi-lingual online collection of millions of digitized items from European museums, libraries, archives and multi-media collections. One obstacle to such initiatives are so-called 'orphan works'—works still in copyright, but whose copyright holders cannot be located to negotiate permissions. The Commission, recognizing the need for common rules on digitization, has adopted a Directive on orphan works. The Directive applies to certain organizations fulfilling 'public-interest missions', allowing them to use orphan works for purposes such as preservation, and cultural or educational access.[73] Although offering a common framework requiring Member States to legislate for orphan works, there remains considerable uncertainty respecting the boundaries and definitions in the scheme.

(c) Copyright Levies

The Commission has also engaged in a consultation process regarding copyright levies, imposed by many Member States on recording hardware and/or blank recording media. Levies offer a form of indirect remuneration for right holders, justified on the basis that it is not practical to license individual acts of private copying. First introduced in the analogue environment, they are somewhat crude instruments. Copyright levies are now increasingly applied to digital equipment and media as a form of compensation for right holders whose works are subject to private copying—an approach permitted by the Information Society Directive.[74]

---

[73] Dir 2012/28/EU on certain permitted uses of orphan works [2012] OJ L299/5, Art 6(2).
[74] Art 5(2). See Case C-467/08 *Padawan v SGAE* (21 October 2010).

However, national systems vary considerably in their approaches. There are very strong views on all sides, and progress towards harmonization has been slow.[75]

(d) A European Copyright Code?

The Commission's May 2011 Communication raised the possibility of the creation of a European Copyright Code.[76] One vision of this would be a comprehensive codification of the present body of EU copyright Directives. Another would be an optional unitary copyright title. This is an ambitious plan, and the political will to achieve it ebbs and flows. Nevertheless, further harmonization of EU copyright—whether by one of these routes, via further ad hoc Directives, or by judicial activism—seems both inevitable and desirable.[77]

IV. Designs

'Design' is a term which refers to the appearance and composition of an article, and to any preliminary drawings or models used. Designs affect our lives in many ways, covering a wide range from the functional to the aesthetic. Intellectual property law has to decide how to respond. If a design can be seen as an artistic work, copyright protection may be appropriate. But even where this is not the case, design features of industrial products may be distinctive and valuable, and affect consumers' purchasing decisions. They therefore merit protection. This range within the design field has led to different forms of protection, and the picture is complex. Some national systems have used a patent-type approach, requiring registration and perhaps examination. Others have adopted a copyright-type approach, requiring neither formalities nor fees.

---

[75] Martin Kretschmer, *Private Copying and Fair Compensation: An Empirical Study of Copyright Levies in Europe* http://www.ipo.gov.uk/pro-ipresearch/ipresearch-policy/ipresearch-policy-copyright.htm; Asunción Esteve Pardo and Agnès Lucas-Schloetter, 'Compensation for private copying in Europe: recent developments in France, Germany and Spain' (2013) 35 *European Intellectual Property Review* 463.

[76] *A single market for intellectual property rights* COM(2011) 287 3.3.1.

[77] Trevor Cook and Estelle Derclaye, 'An EU Copyright Code: what and how, if ever?' (2011) 3 *IPQ* 259; Eleonora Rosati, 'Towards an EU-Wide Copyright? (Judicial) Pride and (Legislative) Prejudice'. (2013) 1 *IPQ* 47.

1. Towards EU Harmonization

The variety within national laws meant that the road to EU harmonization was a troubled one. The issue of design protection for spare parts was particularly controversial, and could not be resolved. A stand-still clause was all that could be agreed. But a Designs Directive was adopted in July 1998, harmonizing conditions for registration, the extent and term of protection, and conditions for refusal and invalidity.[78] Sanctions, remedies and enforcement remain matters for national law. Member States are free to provide for additional protection via other intellectual property regimes, such as unregistered design rights, copyright, trade marks, patents and utility models, and unfair competition. A Regulation followed in December 2001, establishing a Community-wide system of design protection, including both registered and unregistered rights.[79] Designs must be new and have an individual character.

Under the Registered Community Design (RCD) system, holders of eligible designs can register them with OHIM. There is no substantive examination procedure. Registration confers exclusive rights to use the design within the EU for up to 25 years. RCDs are protected against both deliberate copying and the independent development of a similar design. In contrast, the Unregistered Community Design (UCD) offers short-term protection for three years from the date of disclosure of designs to the public within the EU. Protection is against deliberate copying only. The two forms of protection fulfil different roles. Registration offers the certainty of a formal filing date, which will establish priority over later designs. The RCD gives rights against even designs which were independently created, and lasts significantly longer than a UCD. But if a product will have only a short life in the market (fashions, for example), the UCD may be sufficient. Nevertheless, the system of registration is cheap and straightforward, and has proved increasingly popular: 92,000 applications for registration were received in 2012.

Additionally, the EU has now acceded to the Hague Agreement concerning the international registration of industrial designs. A single application at WIPO results in protection of a design not only throughout the EU, but also in other countries which are members of the Geneva Act of the Hague Agreement.

2. Registered Community Design

(a) Application Procedure

Applications for RCDs may be filed either at OHIM, or through national offices. They must include a representation of the design, and an indication of the products

---

[78] Directive 98/71 on the legal protection of designs (Designs Dir) [1998] OJ L289/28.

[79] Regulation 6/2002 on Community designs (CDR). The substantive provisions of the Regulation and Directive are aligned.

in relation to which the design is intended to be used. The representation of the design may contain up to seven different 'views' of it. A brief description may be included.

OHIM examines whether the application complies with the formal requirements for filing, and whether the requirements concerning any claim to priority are satisfied. There is no substantive examination regarding compliance with the requirements for protection (subject matter, novelty, individual character, etc). The view taken is that these are better explored in *inter partes* proceedings, which are unlikely to arise unless there is a serious dispute. If the formal requirements are satisfied and the fees are paid, the design will be registered.

(b) The Definition of 'Design'

Although the registered and unregistered regimes differ in important ways, Community Designs must all meet the same basic requirements for protection. 'Design' is defined as 'the appearance of the whole or a part of a product resulting from the features of, in particular, the lines, contours, colours, shape, texture and/or materials of the product itself and/or its ornamentation'. The focus is thus on appearance, rather than the idea behind the design, or the design concept. The definition seeks to include the wide spectrum of design activity. 'Product' is also defined broadly as 'any industrial or handicraft item, including *inter alia* parts intended to be assembled into a complex product, packaging, get-up, graphic symbols and typographic typefaces, but excluding computer programs'. A 'complex product' is one 'which is composed of multiple components which can be replaced permitting disassembly and reassembly of the product'.[80] Designs for these are subject to special requirements, intended to address *inter alia* the controversial problem of spare parts for cars, and to limit their design protection.[81]

Three important exclusions from this inclusive definition apply to designs dictated by their technical function,[82] designs of interconnections,[83] and designs contrary to public policy or morality.[84]

(c) Grounds of Invalidity

As has been explained, Community designs must demonstrate novelty and individual character, but these matters are assessed only if the right is challenged.[85] Features

[80] Designs Dir Art 1; CDR Art 3.

[81] Designs Dir Art 3(3) & Art 14; CDR Art 4(2) & Art 110.

[82] Designs Dir Art 7(1); CDR Art 8(1): to prevent technological innovation being hampered by design protection.

[83] Designs Dir Art 7(2); CDR Art 8(2): to allow interoperability of products of different makes, and to prevent a manufacturer from monopolizing secondary markets for accessories or consumables.

[84] Designs Dir Art 8; CDR Art 9.

[85] CDR Art 24. An RCD may be declared invalid in proceedings before OHIM, or a declaration of invalidity may result from infringement proceedings before a Community design court.

dictated solely by technical function, or which allow for mechanical connection to another product, are ignored when considering both novelty and individual character (because neither is covered by design right).

A design is considered new if no identical design has been made available to the public on the relevant date. For a UCD, this is the date on which the design has first been made available to the public. For a RCD, this is the date of filing of the application for registration of the design (or the priority date, if claimed). Designs are considered identical if their features differ only in immaterial details.[86] A design is considered to have 'individual character' if 'the overall impression it produces on the informed user differs from the overall impression produced on such a user by any design which has been made available to the public'.[87] The 'informed user' is considered to be more informed than the average consumer (and so more alert to possible differences), but less informed than an expert or design specialist. The test as to individual character has not proved straightforward to apply, but a body of case law is developing. Several cases have reached the General Court,[88] and one case has reached the ECJ.[89]

The Directive provides for five further grounds for invalidity. Two—lack of entitlement and conflict with a prior design—are mandatory. The remainder are optional. Both the Directive and the Regulation state that a design must be refused registration, or, if the design has been registered, be declared invalid if the applicant for, or the holder of, the design right is not entitled to it under the law of the Member State concerned.[90] The Directive provides that a design must be refused registration (or declared invalid) if it conflicts with a relevant prior design.[91] The Regulation treats the conflicts provision as a ground only of invalidity.[92]

Member States may refuse registration of (or, treat as invalid) a design which conflicts with an earlier distinctive sign. The same provision appears in the Regulation.[93] This would commonly cover earlier trade mark rights, other regimes such as passing off, possibly Protected Designations of Origin, Protected Geographical Indications, and even some personality rights. Member States may refuse registration of (or, treat as invalid) a design which conflicts with an earlier copyright work. Again,

---

Community design courts have sole jurisdiction to determine the invalidity of UCDs. Although the intention of the Regulation was to facilitate enforcement and to avoid forum shopping, the dispute between Apple and Samsung concerning the design of their tablet computers indicates the difficulties of achieving these goals if the financial stakes are sufficiently high. See *Samsung Electronics (UK) v Apple Inc* [2012] EWCA Civ 729, and [2012] EWCA Civ 1339.

[86] Designs Dir Art 4; CDR Art 5. For rules on priority see CDR Arts 41-44.

[87] Designs Dir Art 5; CDR Art 6. The relevant dates are the same as those when assessing novelty.

[88] On the application of the test to complex products (here, internal combustion engines), see T-10/08 and T-11/08 *Kwang Yang Motor Co v OHIM* (9 September 2011).

[89] C-281/10 *PepsiCo v Grupo Promer Mon Graphic* (20 October 2011).

[90] Designs Dir Art 11(1)(c). CDR Art 25(1)(c). This ground may be invoked solely by the person in fact entitled to it.

[91] Designs Dir Art 11(1)(d).   [92] CDR Art 25(1)(d).

[93] Designs Dir Art 11(2)(a). CDR Art 25(1)(e).

the same provision appears in the Regulation.[94] Finally, Member States may refuse registration of (or, treat as invalid) a design which conflicts with protected badges or emblems. Again, there is a parallel provision in the Regulation.[95]

3. The Design Proprietor's Rights

(a) Ownership

The right to a Community design vests in principle 'in the designer or his successor in title'.[96] However, a Community design developed by an employee in the execution of his duties normally vests in the employer.[97] Since the CDR is a unitary right, it can only be transferred in its entirety, for the whole Community territory.[98]

(b) Term

The Designs Directive harmonized the term of protection for national design rights at a maximum of twenty-five years, granted in five-year periods from the date of filing.[99] The term of protection of the CDR was set at the same maximum twenty-five year term, again granted in five-year periods.[100] The Unregistered Community Design is protected for a much shorter period: three years from the date on which the design was first made available to the public within the Community.

(c) Scope of Rights

Registered Community designs and registered national designs enjoy full monopoly rights, giving the right holder the exclusive right to use the design and to prevent any third party using it without consent.[101] Unregistered Community Designs (and registered designs which have not been published) are granted only a limited monopoly. The right holder is protected only if a third party's use results from copying the protected design.[102]

Under both regimes, the scope of the protection conferred is defined to include 'any design which does not produce on the informed user a different overall impression'. The degree of freedom of the designer in developing the design is considered.[103] Where designers have a high degree of freedom, two similar designs

---

[94] Designs Dir Art. 11(2)(b). CDR Art 25(1)(f). For a recent example see Cases T-566/11 and T-567/11 *Viejo Valle* v *OHIM* (23 October 2013).

[95] Designs Dir Art 11(2)(c); CDR Art 25(1)(g).

[96] CDR Art 14(1). Joint ownership is provided for.   [97] CDR Art 14(3).

[98] CDR Art 27(1).   [99] Designs Dir Art 10.

[100] CDR Art 12.

[101] This includes all third parties, even those who have a later registered design: Case C-488/10 *Celaya Emparanza y Galdos Internacional v Proyectos Integrales de Balizamientos* (16 February 2012).

[102] CDR Art 19(2), (3).   [103] Designs Dir Art 9; CDR Art 10.

are more likely to produce the same overall impression on the informed user.[104] For registered designs, the representations in the register are used as a basis for comparison.

(d) Exceptions and Defences

There are number of exceptions to the rights conferred. These include acts done privately and for non-commercial purposes, acts done for experimental purposes, and reproductions for citations or teaching.[105] Under certain circumstances a third party who is in good faith using a design may be entitled to continue doing so.[106] Community-wide exhaustion of rights is specified in both the Directive and the Regulation.[107]

Of particular note are the provisions affecting design protection for spare parts. When the Directive was being passed, there was fierce opposition from the automotive industry to any change which would weaken the design protection they enjoyed in a number of Member States, and agreement could not be reached. There is a 'stand-still' clause in the Directive, so that Member States may only change their laws on the subject if their purpose is to liberalize the spare parts market.[108] The Regulation excludes must-match spare parts from Community design protection.[109] This was intended to be a temporary situation, pending investigation and proposals from the Commission. The Commission concluded that only by excluding design protection in the aftermarket for spare parts could an internal market be achieved. It therefore proposed that the Directive be amended to exclude design protection for 'must match' spare parts. However, disagreement remained, and there has been no change.

V. Patents

1. History and Context

A discussion of current EU patent law in a strict sense would be exceedingly brief. Decades of efforts towards a Community Patent foundered repeatedly, often over

---

[104] Case T-10/08 *Kwang Yang Motor Co v OHIM* [2011] ECR II-265*; Case T-11/08 *Kwang Yang Motor Co v OHIM* [2011] ECR II-266*.
[105] Designs Dir Art 13(1); CDR Art 20(1).   [106] CDR Art 22 (also Recital 23).
[107] Designs Dir Art 15; CDR Art 21.   [108] Designs Dir Art 14.
[109] CDR Art 110. See also CDR Recital 13. On the interpretation of this provision see *Bayerische Motoren Werke Aktiengesellschaft v Round and Metal Ltd* [2012] EWHC 2099 (Pat).

translations and jurisdictional arrangements, with national interests prevailing over the needs of the users of the patent system.[110] Given the economic significance of patents, this was very unsatisfactory. In part the failure was due to the prior success of other initiatives, notably the Patent Cooperation Treaty, and the European Patent Convention (EPC). The EPC does achieve significant harmonization of national laws, but only up to the point of grant. Issues of validity and infringement post-grant are currently matters for national law and national courts. One more EU initiative is now being attempted. If successful, it will put in place a European patent with unitary effect (a 'Unitary Patent') throughout much of the EU, and also a Unified Patent Court system. This is potentially a great achievement, not least because it would allow pan-European enforcement in a single set of proceedings. However, significant doubts remain as to the outcome of these efforts.

2. The Unitary Patent

In December 2012, the 'patent package' was approved. This has three elements. One Regulation aims to create a patent with unitary effect throughout participating EU Member States.[111] A second Regulation addresses the necessary translation arrangements.[112] The final element is an international Agreement to establish a Unified Patent Court (UPC).[113] Applications will be examined by the European Patent Office (EPO) in Munich, under the rules and procedures laid down by the EPC. If granted, the result will be a European patent with unitary effect, which will provide automatic protection in 25 of the EU's 27 Member States (not Spain and Italy) by means of a single application.[114] The scope of the protection of a unitary patent is to be uniform in all participating Member States (unlike that of European patents granted under the EPC, the extent of whose protection is defined by the national law of each Contracting State). Unitary patents can only be limited, transferred or revoked in respect of all participating Member States. To enter into effect, the UPC Agreement must be ratified by 13 Contracting States, and these must include the United Kingdom, France, and Germany.

---

[110] Justine Pila, 'The European Patent: an Old and Vexing Problem' (2013) 62 *ICLQ* 917.

[111] Regulation No 1257/2012 implementing enhanced cooperation in the area of the creation of unitary patent protection [2012] OJ L361/1.

[112] Council regulation No 1260/2012 implementing enhanced cooperation in the area of the creation of unitary patent protection with regard to the applicable translation arrangements. [2012] OJ L361/89.

[113] The agreement on a Unified Patent Court was signed on 19 February 2013, and published as the Council of the European Union Notice no. 2013/C 175/01.

[114] Spain and Italy's action challenging the Council's decision to proceed under the enhanced cooperation procedure was dismissed by the ECJ: Joined Cases C-274/11 and C-295/11 *Spain & Italy v Council* (16 April 2013).

The translation arrangements are intended to facilitate access to unitary patents. Only one translation will be required on grant. However, in the event of a dispute, the patentee will have to provide a full translation into an official language of the participating Member State where the alleged infringement took place, or the Member State in which the alleged infringer is domiciled. Additionally, the intention is to promote the dissemination of patent information and technical knowledge by making machine translations of patent applications and specifications into all official languages of the Union available as soon as possible.

The UPC Agreement provides for the establishment of a Unified Patent Court. It is made up of a Court of First Instance, and a Court of Appeal. The Court of First Instance's central division is in Paris, with specialized divisions in London and in Munich. Local and Regional Divisions of the Court of First Instance may be set up in Contracting Member States. There will normally be a panel of three judges, which must be chaired by a legally qualified judge (technically qualified judges will also be used). All appeals (which may be on matters of fact or law) will be heard in the Court of Appeal in Luxembourg. The Court will have exclusive jurisdiction over various matters, including infringement actions, declarations of non-infringement, actions for provisional and protective measures and injunctions, actions for revocation, counterclaims for revocation, and actions against decisions of the EPO.[115] It will have the power (*inter alia*) to revoke a patent, to award damages, and order the payment of costs. Decisions and orders of the Court are enforceable in any Contracting Member State. Existing European Patents, and pending European Patent applications, will fall within the jurisdiction of the new Court system—unless they are 'opted-out' under a transitional arrangement. Eventually, the UPC will have exclusive jurisdiction for all patents granted by the EPO which are brought into force in UPC Member States.[116]

The success of the Unitary Patent is far from certain. There are a number of uncertainties which will affect the outcome. One of these is costs, which have yet to be determined. The promised cost savings will not necessarily follow for all patentees. Pre-grant costs are unlikely to change much. At grant, applicants will be able to choose whether to bring their patent into force as a Unitary Patent or as separate national patents. A common strategy is to bring patents into force in only the UK, France, Germany.[117] For these patentees, translation costs will not change either. By contrast, patentees who usually validate their patents in countries where a translation of the entire granted patent is required may enjoy significant savings on these costs.

[115] UPC Agreement Art 32(1).

[116] Like any national court, the UPC will be required to cooperate with the ECJ to ensure the correct application and uniform interpretation of Union law, in particular by submitting requests for preliminary rulings in accordance with Article 267 TFEU. Decisions of the ECJ will be binding on it: Agreement on a Unified Patent Court [2013] OJ C175/1 Art 21.

[117] In deciding where to validate patents, patentees commonly consider size of market, cost of validations and cost of renewals. These three countries together represent about 50 per cent of EU GDP.

Renewal fees may be perhaps six to eight times the cost of current renewal fees. For those applicants validating only in the UK, France, and Germany, the new scheme would thus be more expensive. However, those whose practice is to validate in most European Patent states will certainly find it cheaper. The levels at which costs are set will have a major impact on patentees' practice.

Another question is how effective the UPC will be. In theory there will be a single set of rules, implementing one substantive patent law, applying standard procedures, including measures for relief. This should be cheaper and more consistent than the current position, under which patents are litigated nationally. But in practice things may not be quite so simple. The Court system will be complex, with its various divisions, and it is likely that local differences will be detectable. Since the Courts' decisions may have serious consequences (pan-EU revocations and injunctions, for example), any inconsistencies will lead to forum shopping. One focus for concern is that Local and Regional Divisions will have the discretion to deal with counterclaims for revocation themselves or to refer such claims to the Central Division. This could result in the bifurcation of the hearings on infringement and validity. A pan-EU injunction could be granted at an infringement hearing by a Local or Regional Division, effective until the patent's validity is considered by the Central Division. Some argue that this will encourage patent trolls—though others refute this.[118] Furthermore, inconsistent infringement and validity decisions would have to be resolved by the Court of Appeal, incurring further costs.

It was initially suggested that the Unified Patent system could come into force in January 2014 but this proved unrealistic; a good deal still needs to happen. The UPC Agreement has not yet been ratified. The detailed Rules of Procedure have yet to be finalized. Suitably qualified judges must be appointed. Practical matters such as the Court's IT system and the individual Courts' facilities are not yet in place. An outstanding legal challenge from Spain may yet overturn the whole system.[119] It seems unlikely that the system will come into force before 2016. Existing European patent holders may be tempted to behave defensively, opting out all their patents until the system is better established and the uncertainties have resolved. The success or failure of the Unitary Patent will eventually turn on its ability to resolve outstanding issues in a way which makes the system more attractive for patentees than the existing alternatives. Whether it can do so remains to be seen.

---

[118] A patent troll is a person or company which buys up patents with the sole intention of enforcing them to collect licensing fees rather than using them to produce goods or provide services. For discussion in this context, see Avgi Kaisi, 'Finally a Single European Right for the EU? An Analysis of the Substantive Provisions of the European Patent with Unitary Effect' (2014) 36 *European Intellectual Property Review* 170 at 179. The Commission denies that the UPC will increase the activity of patent trolls in Europe: see Commission Barnier's answer (8 January 2014) to a Parliamentary question E-012200-13 (24 October 2013).

[119] Case C-146/13, *Kingdom of Spain v European Parliament and Council of the European Union* (pending).

VI. Conclusion

As has been seen, many successes should be acknowledged in the EU legal framework for intellectual property, which reflects significant change achieved in a testing environment. Nevertheless, there is no room for complacency. Technology will continue to surprise, markets will carry on developing, economic and social goals remain challenging, and public engagement with policy matters only increases. Further harmonization of enforcement rules remains particularly contentious, as are matters of management and licensing. The Commission's repeatedly expressed aim is to strike the right balance between promoting creation and innovation, in part by ensuring reward and investment for creators and, on the other hand, promoting the widest possible access to goods and services protected by IPRs.[120] In the prevailing environment, this is easier said than done. Long transitional periods and further controversy are inevitable.

Bibliography

Robert Burrell and Michael Handler, 'Making Sense of Trade Mark Law' (2003) 4 *IPQ* 388

Trevor Cook and Estelle Derclaye, 'An EU Copyright Code: What and How, if Ever?' (2011) 3 *IPQ* 259

Benjamin Farrand, 'Too Much is Never Enough? The 2011 Copyright in Sound Recording Extension Directive' [2012] *EIPR* 297

Janne Glaesel and Louise Stuhr, 'The 3D Shape Dilemma: Refusal to Register the Three-Dimensional Shape of a Loudspeaker' (2012) 7 *Journal of Intellectual Property Law & Practice* 763

Andrew Griffiths, 'Modernising Trade Mark Law and Promoting Economic Efficiency: an Evaluation of the Baby Dry Judgment' (2003) 1 *IPQ* 1

Avgi Kaisi, 'Finally a Single European Right for the EU? An Analysis of the Substantive Provisions of the European Patent with Unitary Effect' (2014) 36 *European Intellectual Property Review* 170

Nobuko Kawashima, 'The *Droit de Suite* Controversy Revisited: Context, Effects and the Price of Art' (2006) 3 *IPQ* 223

Seán Mc Guinness, 'Observations on Free Riding after *L'Oréal* v *Bellure*', (2012) 7 *JIPL&P* 890

Justine Pila, 'The European Patent: An Old and Vexing Problem' (2013) 62 *ICLQ* 917

Eleonora Rosati, 'Towards an EU-Wide Copyright? (Judicial) Pride and (Legislative) Prejudice'. (2013) 1 *IPQ* 47

Catherine Seville, *EU Intellectual Property Law and Policy* (2009)

Uma Suthersanen, 'The European Court of Justice in *Philips* v *Remington*: Trade Marks and Market Freedom' (2003) 3 *IPQ* 257

---

[120] See eg the Commission Communication *A Single Market for Intellectual Property Rights* (2011).

PART VI

ECONOMIC, MONETARY, AND FISCAL UNION

CHAPTER 28

THE METAMORPHOSIS OF EUROPEAN ECONOMIC AND MONETARY UNION

FABIAN AMTENBRINK

I. INTRODUCTORY REMARKS

THE European financial and euro area debt crisis has revealed major weaknesses in the Union legal framework pertaining to Economic and Monetary Union (EMU) and, closely linked thereto, regulation and supervision in the internal financial market. Following the initial crisis response to the near financial collapse of several euro area Member States in the shape of unprecedented ad hoc financial assistance by Member States and the International Monetary Fund (IMF), as well as subsequently through the temporary financial assistance mechanism in the shape of the European Financial Stabilization Mechanism (EFSM) and the European Financial Stability Facility (EFSF), the European Union (EU) has set into motion a thorough conversion of the Maastricht system of EMU. The structural reform measures that have been taken so far, namely in the shape of the revision of economic policy coordination in the euro area, together with the European Central Bank's (ECB) involvement in the crisis management and resolution, arguably justify the hypothesis that the European financial and euro area debt crisis has triggered a metamorphosis of EMU.

By analogy with what is observed for the biological process, this metamorphosis is taking place at times in rather abrupt phases resulting in a substantial transformation of the overall appearance of the legal framework not only through a general growth of the body of law, but also through increased differentiation. What is more, at the time of writing, this process of transformation has not yet been completed. The fact that a study of today's Treaty on European Union (TEU) and Treaty on the Functioning of the European Union (TFEU) provides very little evidence for these major developments signals the unique character of this transformation of an important part of the Union legal framework, the effects of which are arguably not limited to European economic and monetary policy. In fact it raises more fundamental questions about the method and direction of European integration, as well as the current state and future of the complex multidimensional constitutional legal order, as the EU, including its Member States, may be characterized.

The aim of this chapter is to highlight the main characteristics of this core policy field of the EU, the stages of its metamorphosis and the main legal challenges involved, as well as the challenges of today's system that need to be addressed in the future. Considering the limited space available it is not possible to provide a complete description of all rules and procedures governing EMU or to provide an exhaustive overview of the legal debates and corresponding academic literature. Instead, the contribution is geared towards verifying the hypothesis that EMU has outgrown the tight legal framework provided by primary Union law resulting in legal constructions that challenge not only the existing supranational constitutional structure, but also that of the Member States. Finding sustainable solutions to accommodate the new economic governance framework that is emerging from the European financial and euro area debt crisis will be the main task for the years to come.

II. The Maastricht Approach to the Europeanization of Macroeconomic and Monetary Policy

In the famous 1950 Schuman Declaration reference, is made to building a united Europe 'through concrete achievements which first create a de facto solidarity', commencing with 'the setting up of common foundations for economic development as a first step in the federation of Europe'.[1] As such, the introduction of an

---

[1] Declaration of 9 May 1950.

objective to establish an economic and monetary union by the Treaty on European Union (Maastricht Treaty) may be perceived as the pinnacle of the process of economic integration between the participating European countries that had commenced roughly 40 years before with the Treaty establishing the European Coal and Steel Community. EMU has also been considered the final building block to the completion of an internal market in which all production factors could move freely and in which the interdependency between the economies of the Member States would grow. Indeed the 1969 Werner Report had already observed:

Economic and monetary union will make it possible to realize an area within which goods and services, people and capital will circulate freely and without competitive distortions, without thereby giving rise to structural, or regional disequilibrium.[2]

While the initial plan to establish an economic and monetary union by 1980 failed, the 1989 Delors Report revitalized the plan and linked it directly to the completion of the internal market, identifying the latter as the first of three consecutive stages towards the introduction of a European currency. In the report it is claimed that

The success of the internal market programme hinges to a decisive extent on a much closer coordination of national economic policies, as well as on more effective Community policies. This implies that in essence a number of the steps towards economic and monetary union will already have to be taken in the course of establishing a single market in Europe.[3]

For the authors of this influential report the greater interdependence between the national economies in the internal market reduced 'the room for independent policy manoeuvre' and amplified 'the cross-border effects of developments originating in each member country'. At the same time it was observed that with 'full freedom of capital movements and integrated financial markets incompatible national policies would quickly translate into exchange rate tensions and put an increasing and undue burden on monetary policy', thus requiring 'more intensive and effective policy coordination' both with regard to the national economies and monetary policy.[4] The Delors Report proposed the establishment of an economic and monetary union with as the two main pillars the irrevocable fixing of exchange rates between the national currencies and the adoption of a single currency, and the coordination of national economies with the aim of a higher degree of compatibility and consistency in the field of fiscal policy.[5]

---

[2] Report to the Council and the Commission on the realization by stages of economic and monetary union in the Community, Luxembourg, 8 October 1970, 9.

[3] Committee for the Study of Economic and Monetary Union, Report on economic and monetary union in the European Community, presented 17 April 1989, 11.

[4] Committee for the Study of Economic and Monetary Union, Report on economic and monetary union in the European Community, presented 17 April 1989, 10 and 11.

[5] Committee for the Study of Economic and Monetary Union, Report on economic and monetary union in the European Community, presented 17 April 1989, 13.

The drafters of the Treaty on European Union by and large followed the recommendations of the Delors Report by introducing the basic legal and institutional framework for the introduction of a single European currency and a European monetary policy authority (thereafter to become the European Central Bank) and by designing the changeover to a single currency as a three stage process commencing with the completion of the internal market and the increase of economic convergence between the Member States, followed by the establishment of the institutional framework and finally the irrevocable fixing of exchange rates for those Member States that fulfilled the pre-set economic (convergence) criteria, the coming into operation of a distinct European monetary policy for the Member States participating in the single currency, as well as the commencing of European surveillance of national budgetary positions.[6]

The drafters of the TEU also followed the recommendations of the Delors Report in another important aspect. Unlike the Werner Report, where it was argued that '[e]conomic and monetary union means that the principal decisions of economic policy will be taken at Community level and therefore that the necessary powers will be transferred from the national plane to the Community plane', the authors of the later report and thereafter also the drafters of the Treaty did not envisage a Europeanization of the economic policies of the Member States participating in the single currency.[7] In fact, in the absence of a political will to pool macroeconomic competences beyond monetary policy, EMU still stands for differentiated integration in two distinct regards. In terms of substance, this differentiation comes in the shape of a disparity in the level of integration or Europeanization of economic and monetary policy, which—as will be described in section II—has come back to haunt Europe in the context of the European financial and euro area debt crisis. What is more, despite the close link between the EMU project and the establishment/completion of the internal (financial) market, the liberalization of the free movement of capital was not accompanied by a clear vision of a European financial regulatory and supervisory system. Instead what could be witnessed until recently was a rather piecemeal approach to the introduction of European standards,[8] as well as fragmented prudential supervisory structures.

In procedural terms this differentiation resulted first of all from economic and legal criteria for determining which Member States qualified for membership in the final stage of EMU, which were separate from those applicable to accession to the EU. Put differently, accession to the EU alone did not also give the right

---

[6] See Art 109e ff EC Treaty (as amended by the Treaty on European Union) on the transitional provisions.

[7] Report to the Council and the Commission on the realization by stages of economic and monetary union in the Community, Luxembourg, 8 October 1970, p. 26.

[8] See European Commission, Implementing the Framework for Financial Markets: Action Plan, COM(1999) 232 final. Generally R.M. Lastra, 'The Governance Structure for Financial Regulation and Supervision in Europe' (2003) The Columbia Journal of European Law vol. 10 49–68.

to participation in the single currency.[9] This geographical limitation of further economic and monetary integration moreover manifested itself from the outset in the self-exclusion from the future single currency of Denmark and the United Kingdom by means of separate Protocols attached to the founding treaties.[10] Following the 2003 negative referendum on the introduction of the euro in Sweden it became apparent that such a self-exclusion could also result from an electoral rejection of EMU and, more technically speaking, from the non-observance by a Member State of the criteria for joining the single currency.[11] Thus at the time of writing of this contribution, three groups of Member States can be differentiated, including the euro area Member States (19), the Member States that have yet to fulfil the economic and legal convergence criteria formally necessary to join the single currency (6 Member States with a derogation) and Member States that *de jure* or *de facto* take a position apart (3 Member States).

If anything, the measures that have been taken in response to the European financial and euro area debt crisis have exacerbated this differentiation.[12]

1. The Original System of Economic Policy Coordination

As has been observed above, at the time of the introduction of the legal framework on EMU in primary Union law, Member States did not also choose to pool economic policy competences at the European level. Instead a rather complex coordination system was established resting on two main pillars, namely the surveillance of the economic policies of the Member States with regard to their budgetary implications (multilateral surveillance procedure), and the identification and subsequent addressing of budgetary deficits and debts based on a common procedure (excessive deficit procedure).

The basic budgetary rule is provided in Article 126(1) TFEU and the Protocol on the excessive deficit procedure according to which Member States must avoid excessive deficits, defined as government borrowing above 3 per cent for the ratio of planned or actual government deficit to GDP at market prices, or an excessive debt, defined as the total gross debt of a Member State at nominal value outstanding at

---

[9] To be sure, the accession criteria and convergence criteria are indirectly linked in the sense that the 1993 Copenhagen Criteria do refer to the requirement for candidate countries to adhere 'to the aims of political, economic and monetary union'.

[10] Protocol No. 15 on certain provisions relating to the United Kingdom of Great Britain and Northern Ireland, OJ 2012, C 326/284; Protocol No. 16 on certain provisions relating to Denmark, OJ 2012, C 326/287.

[11] In the case of Sweden, non-participation in the European Exchange Rate Mechanism (ERM II), see Art 140(1) TFEU.

[12] See Section IV.

the end of the year and consolidated above 60 per cent for the ratio of government debt to GDP at market prices. The reference values are not absolute, as becomes clear from Article 126(2) TFEU, as a deficit above 3 per cent may be acceptable if the deficit-GDP ratio has declined 'substantially and continuously' and reached a level that comes close to 3 per cent, or if the deviation is 'only exceptional and temporary' and close to the 3 per cent. Similarly, a debt level above 60 per cent can be considered acceptable, if the debt to GDP ratio is diminishing sufficiently quickly and approaching the threshold of 60 per cent 'at a satisfactory pace'.[13] German fears of a lax application of the rather broadly defined procedures in Articles 121 and 126 TFEU resulted in the adoption in 1997, and thus prior to the actual introduction of the single currency, of the Stability and Growth Pact, at the heart of which stood the adoption of two regulations laying down much more detailed—albeit far from picture perfect—procedures for the multilateral surveillance and excessive deficit procedure.[14]

As has been observed from the outset, the multilateral surveillance and excessive deficit procedures have suffered from the policy choices made at the time of the introduction of the TEU, namely the reliance on peer review to assess the budgetary situation in a Member State and the self-commitment by the latter, as well as the absence of effective enforcement mechanisms resulting from a lack of the use of legally binding measures and the exclusion of judicial review of the Member State's compliance with the basic European budgetary rules. This becomes clear, for both the multilateral surveillance and excessive deficit procedure, from a study of the legal framework and the first decade of operation of economic coordination in the euro area.

In a nutshell, the multilateral surveillance of budgetary developments in the Member States, against the background of the budgetary reference values introduced by Article 126(1) TFEU and the Protocol on the excessive deficit procedure, has been built around the Stability and Convergence Programmes that Member States submit annually to the Council and European Commission.[15] Originally

---

[13] According to the Protocol on certain provisions relating to the United Kingdom of Great Britain and Northern Ireland, Art 126(1) TFEU does not apply to the UK and the latter is only obliged to 'endeavour to avoid an excessive government deficit'. For Denmark the provisions applying to Member States with a derogation apply.

[14] Resolution of the European Council on the Stability and Growth Pact of 17 June 1997, OJ 1997, C 236. Council Regulation 1466/97 on the strengthening of the surveillance of budgetary positions and the surveillance and coordination of economic policies, OJ 1997 L 209/1; Council Regulation 1467/97 on speeding up and clarifying the implementation of the excessive deficit procedure, OJ 1997 L 209/6. See eg H. Hahn, 'The Stability Pact For European Monetary Union: Compliance with Deficit Limit as a Constant Legal Duty, 35 (1998) *CML Rev.* 77; critical on legal and economic viability, F. Amtenbrink, J. de Haan and O.C.H.M. Sleijpen, 'The Stability Pact—Placebo or Panacea?' (1997) *European Business Law Review* 8, 202–210 and 233–238.

[15] In the case of euro area Member States, they are referred to as Stability Programmes, whereas for all other Member States the phrase 'Convergence Programme' is used. Despite its special position, the UK also submits Convergence Programmes.

these programmes had to include, *inter alia,* 'the medium-term objectives for the budgetary position of close to balance or in surplus and the adjustment towards this objective for the general government surplus/deficit and the expected path of the general government debt ratio', as well as details of 'the main assumptions about expected economic developments and important economic variables' and 'a description of budgetary and other economic policy measures being taken and/ or being proposed to achieve the objectives'.[16] Thus, by means of secondary Union law, and long before the introduction of the Treaty on Stability, Coordination and Governance in the Economic and Monetary Union (TSCG), discussed hereafter, Member States were supposed to commit themselves to the achievement of a balanced or surplus budget. In formulating these programmes, Member States were supposed to take into account broad economic policy guidelines (BEPGs) adopted by the Council on a recommendation by the European Commission and conclusions of the European Council in the shape of recommendations, offering 'general orientations to Member States and the Community on macroeconomic and structural issues, ranging from budgetary policy and wage developments to labour market reform and financial market integration'.[17] Based on Article 121(4–5) TFEU and Articles 5, 6, 9, and 10 of Regulation 1466/97 in the original setup, the Council in the first instance had to assess mainly the consistency of the national programmes with the BEGP, their capacity to ensure the avoidance of excessive deficits and the achievement of the medium-term budgetary objectives, and if necessary make recommendations to adjust the programmes. Thereafter, the Council also had to monitor the actual implementation of the programmes by the Member States. In case of the detection of a significant divergence of the budgetary position of a Member State from the objectives, the Council was originally responsible for issuing a so-called early warning to a Member State in order to 'prevent the occurrence of an excessive deficit'.[18] This effectively amounted to the issuing of a recommendation to the Member State concerned to take adjustment measures.

Not least as a result of the experience with the performance of Member States under the original framework, the multilateral surveillance procedure was somewhat reinforced in 2005 to provide for country-specific medium-term objectives that now had to be specified 'within a range between -1 per cent of GDP and balance or surplus, in cyclically adjusted terms, net of one-off and temporary

---

[16] Art 3(2) Reg 1466/97.

[17] S. Deroose, D. Hodson, and J. Kuhlmann, 'The Broad Economic Policy Guidelines: Past, Present and Future' International Economics Programme Chatham House, November 2005, IEP WP 05/02, p. 2. Available at https://www.chathamhouse.org/sites/files/chathamhouse/public/Research/International%20Economics/wpeconomicpolicy.pdf.

[18] Thereafter the provision was amended to the wording of the present Art 121 TFEU, putting the European Commission in charge of issuing the early warning.

measures'.[19] Moreover, when assessing the national programmes and namely the required information on the adjustment path towards the medium-term objective, as became clear from the amended Articles 5 and 9 Regulation 1466/97, Member States were expected to improve their cyclically-adjusted balance, net of one-off and other temporary measures, by 0.5 per cent of GDP as a benchmark. Member States were expected to pursue a higher adjustment effort in economic good times. Moreover, structural economic reform measures in the pension sector were encouraged, allowing even for deviation from the adjustment path to the medium-term budgetary objective or the objective itself that corresponded with the costs of the reform measures.

The number of Member States that did not (manage to) comply with the European budgetary reference values both before and after the 2005 reform of Regulation 1466/97 highlights the limited stringency of the procedure. In fact neither today's Article 121 TFEU nor Regulation 1466/97 allowed for an enforcement of the Stability and Convergence Programmes, the BEPG or the annual improvement of the budgetary position towards a balanced or surplus budget. This can be explained by the absence of any legally binding means to sanction Member States for non-compliance, the legal nature of the measures taken, as well as the fact that the Council and thus the Member States themselves where in control of the procedure.[20]

The excessive deficit procedure, as laid down in Article 126(2)-(11) TFEU and Regulation 1467/97, suffered from similar shortcomings with the exception that on paper the application of financial sanctions in the case of non-compliance was a theoretical possibility. The main achievement of Regulation 1467/97 over what is now Article 126 TFEU was the introduction of a specific timeframe for the application of the several steps in the procedure, the definition of 'exceptional' and 'temporary' deviations from the budgetary reference values referred to in Article 126(2) TFEU and the specification of the sanctions regime foreseen in Article 126(11) TFEU.

In the original setup, the Council could decide by qualified majority vote on the existence of an excessive deficit pursuant to Article 126(6) TFEU based on a recommendation by the European Commission, which was in charge of assessing the budgetary position of the Member States on the basis of bi-annual reports by the Member States about their planned and actual government deficits and levels of government debt.[21] Astonishingly, initially the Member State concerned was not

---

[19] Art 2a Reg 1466/97, as introduced by Council Regulation 1055/2005 amending Reg 1466/97 on the strengthening of the surveillance of budgetary positions and the surveillance and coordination of economic policies, OJ 2005, L 174/1.

[20] For a detailed legal and political economy assessment, see F. Amtenbrink and J. De Haan, 'Economic Governance in the European Union—Fiscal Policy Discipline versus Flexibility' (2003) *CML Rev.* 40, 1075–1106.

[21] Council Regulation 479/2009 on the application of the Protocol on the excessive deficit procedure annexed to the Treaty establishing the European Community, OJ 2009, L 145/1. Mainly Art 3.

even excluded from voting, which was subsequently corrected through a Treaty amendment. From the outset it was foreseen that when a decision on an excessive deficit has been taken, in accordance with Article 126(7) the Council would issue a recommendation demanding that the Member State puts an end to the excessive deficit situation and identifying (in rather broad and noncommittal wording) areas on which the Member State could focus. In principle, a Member State is given a deadline of four months at the most to take effective corrective action and a deadline of no more than one year after the decision on the existence of an excessive deficit to actually rectify the situation. If the Council has decided pursuant to Article 126(8) TFEU that no effective action has been taken on its initial recommendation, in accordance with Article 126(9) TFEU, new recommendations can be decided by the Council within one month. Ultimately, if a Member State fails to comply with these recommendations the Council can decide to apply sanctions pursuant to Article 126(11). According to Article 11 of Regulation 1467/97, a non-interest bearing deposit would be required in the first instance. In case of an excessive deficit resulting from non-compliance with the government deficit criterion, the deposit would be made up of a fixed component equal to 0.2 per cent of GDP and a variable component equal to 0.1 per cent of the difference between the deficit as a percentage of GDP in the preceding year and the reference value of 3 per cent of GDP. This deposit turns into a fine if the Member State does not correct the deficit within two years of the decision on the deposit.[22] One interesting aspect is that Regulation 1467/97 did not provide details of the deposit/sanctions to be applied in case of non-compliance by a Member State with the government debt requirement. Be that as it may, the sanction regime has been the only enforcement foreseen in the context of the excessive deficit procedure as laid down in primary Union law, as Article 126(10) TFEU explicitly excludes the application of the infringement procedure pursuant to Articles 258 and 259 TFEU.

The sanction regime has never been put into effect. Moreover, the application of the excessive deficit procedure by the Council has been anything but uncontroversial, which is highlighted by the open conflict between the European Commission and the Council concerning the application of the excessive deficit procedure to France and Germany in 2004. In the face of a recommendation from the European Commission, the Council did not manage to take the required qualified majority decisions in accordance with Article 126(8) and (9) TFEU to advance the excessive deficit procedure to its next phase. Instead, the Council passed conclusions declaring that the excessive deficit procedure was to be held in abeyance and stating that it would stand ready to take a decision pursuant to Article 126(9) TFEU, if the two Member State did not comply with the self-commitments made in the context of the conclusions. The European Commission considered the failed qualified

---

[22] Art 13 Reg 1467/97.

majority vote on two occasions to effectively amount to a decision not to follow the steps foreseen in the excessive deficit procedure and the Council conclusions effectively amounting to a decision to deviate from the procedure foreseen in Article 126 TFEU. In the annulment procedure brought by the European Commission pursuant to Article 263 TFEU, the Court of Justice of the European Union (ECJ) did indeed consider that the Council's conclusions amounted to a decision to place the excessive deficit procedure in abeyance, thereby infringing ex Article 104 EC (now Art. 126 TFEU) and Article 9 Regulation 1467/97, which did not foresee in such a procedural step. However, with regard to the failure to reach qualified majorities in the context of Article 126(8) and (9) TFEU, the ECJ concluded that this could not be interpreted as a decision for the purpose of Article 126 TFEU that could be subject to review under Article 263 TFEU.[23]

Next to the basic budgetary rule and the multilateral surveillance and excessive deficit procedure, budgetary discipline is supposed to be ensured by a number of general prohibitions that were introduced in primary European law as part of the EMU legal framework. This concerns first of all Articles 123(1) and 124 TFEU, which prohibits overdraft facilities or any other type of credit facility with the ECB or a national central bank in favour of Member States governments and, moreover, forbids privileged access by national governments to financial institutions. What is more, Article 125(1) TFEU, often referred to in generic terms as the 'no bailout' clause, prohibits both the Union and other Member States from taking on or becoming liable for the financial commitments of another Member State. These provisions are essentially aimed at providing that in the currency union Member States would also remain fully responsible for the financial commitments (namely debts) they undertake and, moreover, that they have to refinance themselves at market conditions, whereby the markets would signal any negative developments in the creditworthiness of a country by means of the interest rate, forcing the country concerned to adjust its policies. As will be highlighted in Section III, the validity of the assumptions underlying these provisions has been seriously put to the test in the European financial and euro area debt crisis.

2. The Single Monetary Policy

The Union has exclusive competence to act in the field of monetary policy for the Member States that have adopted the single European currency, under Article 3(1)(c) TFEU. Within the euro area this competence has been assigned to the European Central Bank (ECB), which together with the national central banks of the euro area Member States, makes up the European System of Central Banks (ESCB).[24] The

---

[23] Case C-27/04, *Commission v Council* [2004] ECR I-6649.
[24] In accordance with Art 219 TFEU the Council is in charge of concluding formal agreements on an exchange-rate system for the euro in relation to the currencies of third countries.

overriding statutory objective of the ECB is to maintain price stability, a phrase that in the absence of a statutory definition has been quantified by the ECB itself, initially defining it as 'a year-on-year increase in the Harmonized Index of Consumer Prices (HICP) for the euro area of below 2 per cent' and, more recently, by announcing that it aims to 'maintain inflation rates below, but close to, 2 per cent over the medium term'.[25] Subject to the observance of this primary objective, according to Article 127(1) TFEU, the ECB is also supposed to support the general economic policies of the Union with a view to contributing to the achievement of the objectives of the Union.[26] Article 3 TEU in this context refers to a Europe based on balanced economic growth and a highly competitive social market economy, aiming at full employment and social progress.

At its time of establishment, the ECB was not given any specific micro-prudential supervisory tasks for credit institutions operating in the internal market, since today's Article 127(5) TFEU only provides that the ESCB contributes to the smooth conduct of policies pursued by the competent national authorities relating to the prudential supervision of credit institutions and the stability of the financial system. At the same time it, becomes clear from the opening provided for in Article 127(6) TFEU that the drafters of the Treaty legal framework on EMU did not exclude the exercise, in the future, by the ECB of 'specific tasks' in this field.[27]

Within the European institutional order, the ECB has been given a rather unique position vis-à-vis (other) European institutions as well as national government bodies.[28] The present Article 130 TFEU is aimed at shielding the ECB from any political influence at the European level or the level of the Member States. Pursuant to Article 131 TFEU, this also extents to the governors of the national central banks of the euro area that participate on the Governing Council, the main monetary policy decision-making organ of the ECB.[29] However arguably the biggest insulation of the ECB from political influence derives from the very nature of its legal basis, being primary Union law in the shape of the founding Treaties and the Protocol to the Statute of the ESCB and of the ECB that apart from a few limited exceptions can only be amended by changing the Treaties.[30] Moreover, the national central banks and the ECB are shielded from political swaying by the prohibition of monetary financing. included in Article 123(1) TFEU.[31] According to this provision, the EU and Member State governments are prohibited

---

[25] See ECB's presentation at https://www.ecb.europa.eu/mopo/strategy/pricestab/html/index. en.html accessed 15 April 2015.

[26] See also Art 2–6 Statute ESCB and ECB on the objectives and tasks of the ECB.

[27] With regard to the role of the ECB in the Single Supervisory Mechanism, see Section IV.

[28] It should be noted that it is only since the coming into force of the Treaty of Lisbon that the ECB itself has been listed as a Union institution pursuant to Art 13(1) TEU.

[29] See also Art 7 Statute ESCB and ECB. For an overview of the different aspects of central bank independence, see L. Bini Smaghi, 'Central Bank Independence in the EU: From Theory to Practice' (July 2008) *EL Rev.* 14(4), 446–460.

[30] Protocol No. 4, OJ 2012, C 326/230.

[31] J. Schwarze (ed), *Schwarze/Becker/Hatje/Schoo EU-Kommentar* (3rd ed, 2012), Art 123, para 1.

from having overdraft facilities or any other type of credit facility with the ECB or national central banks and, moreover, the ECB and national central banks are prohibited from the direct purchase of debt instruments from the Member States (prohibition on monetary financing). Overall, it can be observed that from comparative analyses of central bank statutes the ECB emerges as one of the most independent central banks existing today.[32]

With the strong focus on the establishment of the credibility of the new supranational monetary policy authority and its policy measures geared towards the stability of the new supranational currency through its legal basis, arguably less attention was initially paid to the accountability of the ECB for the exercise of what essentially amounts to public power, leading to substantive criticism of the legal setup.[33] Later practice and the voluntary appearances of the president of the ECB before the European Parliament (EP) economic and monetary affairs committee, frequently referred to as monetary dialogue, but also the clarification of the ECB's position in the Union legal order by the ECJ in *Commission v Council*, helped somewhat to correct this negative assessment of the ECB's accountability.[34] To be sure, this has certainly not removed all concerns, such as the absence of transcripts of the deliberations in the main monetary policy body of the Bank.[35]

The ECB has been set up with two main decision-making bodies, namely the Executive Board and the Governing Council. The Executive Board is charged with the day-to-day conduct of business and consists of the President, two Vice Presidents and four additional members appointed by the European Council, acting by a qualified majority, for a non-renewable period of eight years.[36] The composition of the Governing Council of the ECB, which is mainly charged with the formulation of monetary policy in the euro area and decisions relating to key interest rates and the supply of reserves in the ESCB, reveals the quasi-federal structure of the ECB. The Governing Council consists of the governors of the central banks of the Member

[32] See eg the updated Eijffinger-Schaling Indicator for central bank independence in J. de Haan, F. Amtenbrink, and S.C.W. Eijffinger, 'Accountability of Central Banks: Aspects and Quantifications' (June 1999) *Banca Nazionale del Lavoro Quarterly Review* 209 169–193, 189.

[33] See L. Gormley and J. de Haan, 'The Democratic Deficit of the European Central Bank' (April 1996) *European Law Review*, 95–112; F. Amtenbrink, *The Democratic Accountability of Central Banks—A Comparative Study of the European Central Bank* (1999).

[34] Case C-11/00, *Commission v ECB* [2003] ECR I-7147. See R.J. Goebel, 'Court of Justice Oversight over the European Central Bank: Delimitating the ECB's Constitutional Autonomy and Independence in the OLAF Case' (2005) 29 *Fordham Int'l L.J.* 610.

[35] F. Amtenbrink, 'On the legitimacy and accountability of the European Central Bank: legal arrangements and practical experiences' in A. Arnull and D. Wincott, *Accountability and Legitimacy in the European Union* (2002), 147–163. But see the speech by the ECB President, 'Monetary Policy Communication in Turbulent Times' at the conference 'De Nederlandsche Bank 200 Years: Central Banking in the next two Decades' of 24 April 2014 in Amsterdam, available at http://www.ecb.europa. eu/press/key/date/2014/html/sp140424.en.html, where he argues in favour of the non-attributed publication of a record of the ECB's policy deliberations. See also hereafter Section VI on the ECB's accountability for its new role in micro-prudential supervision.

[36] Note, by contrast, that the independent judges at the ECJ can be reappointed.

States participating in the euro area as well as the members of the ECB's Executive Board. Until the adoption of the Euro by Lithuania on 1 January 2015, decisions of the Governing Council have in principle been taken by simple majority of the members present, whereby not only all members of the Executive Board, but also of the euro area Member States have the same voting rights.[37] All national monetary policy authorities were thus treated equally, regardless of the share in the aggregated gross domestic product of the EU of the national economy they represent. Yet in the light of EU enlargement, the relevant part of the Statute of the ESCB and ECB has been amended to provide for the introduction of a rotation system for voting as soon as the total number of members of the Governing Council exceeds 21. Pursuant to Article 10.2. of the Statute of the ESCB and of the ECB, for voting purposes national central bank governors can be assigned to different groups based on the size of the economies of the Member States they represent. These groups are than assigned less votes than group members, requiring a rotation of voting rights between the participating governors. The ECB has decided to postpone the application of this system until the number of euro area Member States exceeds 18. The accession to the euro area of Lithuania has ended the voting equality of Member States. This will then increase the influence of the central banks of the Member States with the largest economies and also enhance the power of the members of the ECB's Executive Board, which notably do not participate in the rotation system.[38]

III. Testing the Outer Limits of the Maastricht Legal Framework—The European Financial and Euro Area Debt Crisis

Observing the government deficit and deficit levels on the eve of the European financial and euro area debt crisis it becomes clear that economic coordination had only partially succeeded in preventing the emergence of excessive government

---

[37] Art 10.2. Statute ESCB and ECB.

[38] See eg D. Howarth, 'Running an Enlarged Euro Zone—Reforming the European Central Bank: Efficiency, Legitimacy and National Economic Interest' (December 2007) *Review of International Political Economy* 14(5), 820–841.

deficit and debt levels and thus, that the framework had not been fully effective in ensuring the convergence of the economies of the euro area Member States. For Greece, Eurostat reported a government debt to GDP ratio of 97.8 per cent for 2006 and a deficit to GDP ratio of 3.6 per cent, which thereafter rose to 115.5 per cent and 13.6 per cent respectively by 2009.[39] In Italy, the debt level stood at 106.5 per cent in 2006, rising to 115.8 per cent by 2009. By contrast, the Netherlands for 2006 had a reported surplus of 0.5 per cent of GDP and even 0.8 per cent for 2008. By 2009, this had turned into a deficit of 5.3 per cent of GDP. The Dutch debt level stood below the European threshold at 47.4 per cent for 2006, rising only slightly above the allowed maximum in 2009 with a reported 60.9 per cent. Ireland had a deficit of 3 per cent for 2006, which even turned into a balanced budget for 2007 (surplus of 0.1 per cent), before turning into a deficit of 7.3 per cent for 2008 that further increased to 14.4 per cent for 2009. As to the debt levels, the impact of the crisis has been rather dramatic for Ireland, which in 2006 had a government debt to GDP ratio of only 24.9 per cent. By 2008 this had risen to 43.9 per cent and by 2009 to 64.0 per cent. From 2007 Member States found themselves forced to undertake major rescue operations for their financial institutions to prevent a meltdown of their own financial systems and prevent the spreading of the wildfire throughout the integrated European financial market. Soon thereafter it became clear that the budgetary position of a number of non-euro area as well as euro area Member States had become unsustainable.

The absence of an effective European financial market regulatory and supervisory regime, including a banking resolution mechanism, undoubtedly contributed to adverse budgetary developments. Yet, taking 2006 as the reference year, it also has to be noted that the budgetary situation at the time of the breakout of the crisis differed considerably between euro area Member States.[40] Indeed, some Member States were already clearly featuring deficits and debts in excess of 3 per cent and 60 per cent of GDP respectively. In these instances, the crisis that followed exacerbated an already problematic budgetary situation resulting from unsustainable fiscal policies, *inter alia*, in the shape of over-borrowing. The latter had essentially become possible because, after joining the single currency, countries such as Greece, Italy, Portugal and Spain gained access to refinancing at much more favourable market conditions, that is substantially lower borrowing costs, then before. In fact it could be argued that primary Union law allowed for this effect in the first place, since, as has been observed in Section II, the Union legal framework actually stipulates government refinancing at market conditions.

The question is of course whether the low risk premium which these Member States had to pay once they had joined the euro area reflected the actual sovereign

[39]   All data stated here: eurostat newsrelease, euroindicators, 55/2010 of 22 April 2010.
[40]   See A. van Riet, 'Early Lessons From the Crisis' in A. van Riet (ed), 'Euro Area Fiscal Policies and the Crisis', *ECB Occasional Paper* Series No. 109/April 2010 68–69.

risk of these countries, a result of a somewhat misconceived trust in the disciplining effect of the Maastricht system of economic policy coordination. In fact, despite the initially rather broad interpretation given to the prohibition of Article 125 TFEU that was echoed in its general description as 'no bail-out clause', financial market participants may have also have expected—and rightly so as it turns out—that the quasi-insolvency of a euro area Member State was no more than a theoretical possibility, since in the last resort the Union or other euro area Member States would (have to) come to the rescue of a fellow country. Be that as it may, what is clear is that in the initial ten years of the existence of the single currency 'Euro area government bonds were effectively seen as perfect substitutes by financial-market operators'.[41]

Nevertheless, as the comparison of euro area Member States also highlights, the euro area debt crisis cannot be explained by reference to the absence of budgetary discipline and an effective European financial market regulatory and supervisory system alone. Also contributing to the seriousness of the crisis were undesirable economic developments in some Member States, such as an oversized financial sector, a real estate bubble and more generally the absence of long-overdue structural reforms, that fully came to bear in the European financial and euro area debt crisis. A closer analysis of the situation in countries such as Ireland and Spain suggests that macroeconomic imbalances that could not only severely affect the functioning of the domestic economies of the Member States, but the euro area as a whole, remained largely undetected or at least unaddressed, as the focus was on budgetary surveillance. So while the application of the legal framework pertaining to economic policy coordination in EMU was already anything but trouble-free, its deficiencies were fully exposed in the context of the European financial and euro area debt crisis. In fact the system not only contributed to the emergence or at least deepening of the crisis, but at least initially, stood in the way of its effective management and resolution. What is more, the involvement of the ECB in the crisis management and solution has revealed the close link between economic and monetary policy, as well as with financial stability.

1. The Ad Hoc Financial Rescue Measures

The Union legal framework did not provide for a set of clear and uncontested legal instruments to quickly and effectively react to the euro area debt crisis. In fact, in the first instance the Union and Member States turned to intergovernmentalism and the help of the IMF when Greece was on the brink of financial collapse in

---

[41] S. Ardagna and F. Caselli, 'The Political Economy of the Greek Debt Crisis: A Tale of Two Bailouts' London School of Economics, *Centre for Economic Performance Special Paper* No. 25, March 2012, p. 1.

early 2010.[42] Doubts about the soundness of Article 122(2) TFEU as a legal basis for financial assistance in the given circumstances and, moreover, fears of a cumbersome decision-making process, made Member States and the Union for the first but certainly not for the last time during the crisis, move outside the Union legal framework by setting up a financial support programme in the shape of bilateral loans by the euro area Member States and a stand-by-agreement with the IMF, a process facilitated by the European Commission and supported by the ECB.[43] Financial support thereafter was granted in tranches and made conditional on compliance with an economic adjustment programme, a model that would thereafter also be applied to other euro area Member States.[44]

As it became clear that other euro area Member States, particularly at the time Ireland and Portugal, would also require financial assistance, it was quickly decided to make use of Article 122(2) TFEU after all to set up a temporary financial assistance mechanism under strict conditionality for euro area Member States, firstly in the shape of the European Financial Stability Mechanism (EFSM), by which the Union could grant loans or a credit line based on borrowings by the Union on the capital markets or with financial institutions.[45] Next to this, Member States could also turn for loans or a credit line to the new European Financial Stability Facility (EFSF), a private law instrument in the shape of a *société anonyme* under Luxemburg law that had been set up based on an intergovernmental agreement by the euro area Member States.[46] As shareholders of the EFSF, the Member States irrevocably and unconditionally guaranteed, towards their own contribution, the payment of all amounts payable by the EFSF following the issuance of financial instruments to generate the capital to grant financial assistance.[47]

These ad hoc measures have been criticized both in legal and economic circles for infringing the principle of monetary financing and the no bailout clause referred to in Section II, as well as, in the case of the EFSM, for falling outside the scope of Article 122(2) TFEU. With regard to the prohibition of monetary financing, it has been argued that the scope of Article 123 TFEU 'in the interest of effet utile' also

---

[42] K. Featherstone is generally critical of the crisis management of the Union: 'The Greek Sovereign Debt Crisis and EMU: A Failing State in a Skewed Regime' (2011) *JCMS—Journal of Common Market Studies* 49(2), 193–217, 201 et seq.

[43] Statement by President Van Rompuy following the Eurogroup agreement on Greece, Brussels, 2 May 2010, PCE 80/10; 'IMF Reaches Staff-level Agreement with Greece on €30 Billion Stand-By Arrangement', Press Release No. 10/176 of 2 May 2010.

[44] European Commission, Directorate-General for Economic and Financial Affairs, 'The Economic Adjustment Programme for Greece', *Occasional Papers* 61, May 2010.

[45] Council Regulation 407/2010 of 11 May 2010 establishing a European financial stabilization mechanism, OJ 2010, L 118/1, Art 2.

[46] EFSF Framework Agreement between Belgium, Germany, Ireland, Spain, France, Italy, Cyprus, Luxembourg, Malta, the Netherlands, Austria, Portugal, Slovenia, Slovakia, Finland, Greece and European Financial Stability Facility, 7 June 2010. Articles of Incorporation of 15 December 2010.

[47] For a brief overview see F. Amtenbrink, 'Legal Developments' (2011) *JCMS—Journal of Common Market Studies* 49 Annual Review, 165–186, specifically 171–172.

covers 'the budgets of the Member States and their subdivisions', since in this view the fiscal action of the Member States cannot be subject to a 'fewer restrictions' than 'the action of their central banks' to which Article 123(1) TFEU explicitly refers.[48] It was moreover argued that the crisis measures effectively amounted to a financial bailout of the Member States concerned in breach of Article 125 TFEU, *inter alia* stating that the acceptance of voluntary financial assistance of euro area Member States would effectively negate Article 125 TFEU, the purpose of which is to ensure budgetary discipline of Member States.[49] Also the choice of Article 122(2) TFEU as legal basis for the EFSM was controversial. Doubts were raised as to whether the conditions for the application of this provision were met, namely with regard to the existence of a situation beyond the control of the Member States concerned, and, moreover, whether the establishment of a general mechanism open for application to different Member States is covered by this provision.[50]

In the context of the preliminary ruling of the ECJ on the compatibility of the ESM Treaty with primary Union law in *Pringle*, the Court addressed all these legal issues by effectively defining the scope of Articles 122, 123 and 125 TFEU.[51] On Article 123 TFEU the Court states that

it must be held that Article 123 TFEU is addressed specifically to the ECB and the central banks of the Member States. The grant of financial assistance by one Member State or by a group of Member States to another Member State is therefore not covered by that prohibition.[52]

The ECJ thus applies a literal interpretation to Article 123 TFEU, arguing that that provision is not addressed to the Member States. The Court also chooses a restrictive interpretation of Article 125 TFEU, first and foremost pointing out

that that article is not intended to prohibit either the Union or the Member States from granting any form of financial assistance whatever to another Member State.[53]

Moreover, the ECJ concludes from the presence of the possibility of financial assistance to euro area Member States provided in Article 122(2) TFEU and the

---

[48] Own translation. See H. Kube and E. Reimer, 'Grenzen des Europäischen Stabilisierungsmechanismus' *Neue Juristische Wochenschrift*, 1911–1916, at 1912.

[49] T. Jeck, 'Euro-Rettungsschirm bricht EU-Recht und deutsches Verfassungsrecht', cep-Studie, 5. Juli 2010. Available at http://www.cep.eu/fileadmin/user_upload/Kurzanalysen/Euro-Rettungsschirm/CEP-Studie_Euro-Rettungsschirm.pdf. For others in favour of a strict inter-pretation of Art 125 TFEU, see D. Hattenberg on Art 125 TFEU, in J. Schwarz (Hrsg.), EU-Kommentar, 3. Auflage (Baden-Baden, Nomos, 2012), p. 1538–1539, with references to literature supporting both views. Featherstone (supra, n 42), p. 203, refers to a 'circumvention' of the no bailout rule.

[50] F. Amtenbrink, 'Legal Developments' (2011) *JCMS—Journal of Common Market Studies* 49 Annual Review, 165–186, 172–177, with further references to relevant literature.

[51] With regard to the ESM Treaty see Section IV. For a detailed critical discussion of the judgment see S. Adam and F.J.M. Parras, 'The European Stability Mechanism through the Legal Meanderings of the Union's Constitutionalism: Comment on *Pringle*, (2013) 38 *EL Rev.* 848–864.

[52] Case C-370/12, *Pringle* [2012] ECR I-756, para 125.

[53] Case C-370/12, *Pringle* [2012] ECR I-756, para 130.

stricter wording in Article 123 TFEU that the prohibition stated in Article 125 TFEU 'is not intended to prohibit any financial assistance whatever to a Member State'.[54] According to the Court

Article 125 TFEU does not prohibit the granting of financial assistance by one or more Member States to a Member State which remains responsible for its commitments to its creditors provided that the conditions attached to such assistance are such as to prompt that Member State to implement a sound budgetary policy.[55]

Referring to the Treaty establishing the European Stability Mechanism (ESM), which replaces the EFSM and EFSF as a permanent financial assistance mechanism for euro area Member States, the Court said such conditions are fulfilled if financial assistance is granted to Member States

which are experiencing or are threatened by severe financing problems only when such support is indispensable to safeguard the financial stability of the euro area as a whole and of its Member States and the grant of that support is subject to strict conditionality appropriate to the financial assistance instrument chosen.[56]

It can be argued that the predecessor of the ESM, namely the EFSM and EFSF, and even the initial bilateral loans to Greece in principle also fulfilled these conditions set by the ECJ given the economic situation at the time and the conditionality in the shape of the economic adjustment programmes attached to the granting of financial assistance.

In *Pringle* the ECJ did not interpret the scope of Article 122(2) TFEU except for stating that this provision 'does not preclude either the conclusion by the Member States whose currency is the euro of an agreement such as the ESM Treaty or their ratification of it'.[57]

2. The ECB's Non-Standard Monetary Policy Measures

The European financial and euro area debt crisis not only revealed serious shortcomings in economic policy coordination in EMU, but also the close link between economic and monetary policy in the euro area. In the face of the threat of the collapse of systemically relevant financial institutions, and more generally the breakdown of the interbank money market, as well as sovereign insolvency, the ECB found itself confronted with a major interruption of the monetary policy transition mechanism, potentially rendering the monetary policy instruments it had to achieve its statutory objective inoperable.

---

[54] Case C-370/12, *Pringle* [2012] ECR I-756, para 131–132.
[55] Case C-370/12, *Pringle* [2012] ECR I-756, para 137.
[56] Case C-370/12, *Pringle* [2012] ECR I-756, para 142.
[57] Case C-370/12, *Pringle* [2012] ECR I-756, para 122.

In order to address this, the ECB engaged in what it itself refers to as non-standard monetary policy measures from 2008, including, *inter alia,* in the first instance unlimited access to central bank liquidity at the main refinancing rate for financial institutions, extension of the maturity of liquidity provisions and of collateral eligibility in refinancing operations, as well as a purchase pro-gramme for covered bonds denominated in euro and issued in the euro area.[58] In the view of the ECB, these measures were 'aimed not at providing additional direct monetary stimulus to the economy but primarily at supporting the effect-ive transmission of its standard policy.'[59] As the threat of a sovereign default by Greece and possible domino effects on some other euro area Member States became very real, the ECB started to intervene in the euro area private and pub-lic debt securities market as part of a so-called Securities Markets Programme (SMP), namely purchasing sovereign bonds of euro area Member States on the secondary markets.[60] In the view of the ECB this became necessary, as the euro area debt crisis 'was considered to impair the transmission of policy interest rate decisions to the real economy', because of 'the crucial role of government bonds as benchmarks for private—sector lending rates and their importance for bank balance sheets and liquidity operations'.[61]

With the volatility of the sovereign debt markets persisting and speculation about the future of the European single currency mounting, the President of the ECB in a much-noted speech at the Global Investment Conference in London in July 2012 stated:

When people talk about the fragility of the euro and the increasing fragility of the euro, and perhaps the crisis of the euro, very often non-euro area member states or leaders, underestimate the amount of political capital that is being invested in the euro. And so we view this, and I do not think we are unbiased observers, we think the euro is irreversible. And it's not an empty word now, because I preceded saying exactly what actions have been made, are being made to make it irreversible. But there is another message I want to tell you. Within our mandate, the ECB is ready to do whatever it takes to preserve the euro. And believe me, it will be enough.[62]

---

[58] P. Cour-Thimann and B. Winkler, 'The ECB's Non-Standard Monetary Policy Measures the Role of Institutional Factors and Financial Structure', *ECB Working Paper,* Series No. 1528/April 2013, 11–12. The authors provide a detailed review of all non-standard measures taken by the ECB in chronological order.

[59] P. Cour-Thimann and B. Winkler, 'The ECB's Non-Standard Monetary Policy Measures the Role of Institutional Factors and Financial Structure', *ECB Working Paper,* Series No. 1528/April 2013, p. 2.

[60] Decision of the ECB establishing a securities markets programme (ECB/2010/5) (2010/281/EU).

[61] Decision of the ECB establishing a securities markets programme (ECB/2010/5) (2010/281/EU), p. 13

[62] Speech by Mr Mario Draghi, President of the European Central Bank, at the Global Investment Conference, London, 26 July 2012. Available at http://www.bis.org/review/r120727d.pdf?frames=0.

Putting words into action, in the autumn of 2012 the ECB announced what may arguably be its most controversial reaction to the crisis, namely the possibility of outright transactions in the secondary sovereign bond market without any *ex ante* quantitative limits. The ECB stated that any such outright monetary transactions (OMTs) would be subject to 'strict and effective conditionality attached to an appropriate European Financial Stability Facility/European Stability Mechanism (EFSF/ESM) programme', and that like the SMP any liquidity created through the OMT would be fully sterilized.[63]

While, according to the ECB, the OMT is aimed at 'safeguarding an appropriate monetary policy transmission and the singleness of the monetary policy',[64] even more so than in the case of the SMP, the ECB has been criticized for allegedly exceeding its statutory monetary policy mandate and violating the prohibition of monetary financing set out in Article 125 TFEU. Arguably the most powerful critique has come from the German Federal Constitutional Court (Bundesverfassungsgericht), which in January 2014, for the first time in its history, made a preliminary reference to the ECJ pursuant to Article 267 TFEU. The German Court essentially asked the Luxemburg court to rule on the question whether 'the Decision' of the ECB on the OMT is incompatible with Article 119 and Article 127(1) and (2) TFEU, and with Articles 17 to 24 of the ESCB and ECB Statute as it could exceed the ECB's mandate and trespass on the euro area Member State's competences.[65] In the view of the German Court, if this is indeed the case, in accordance with its interpretation of German constitutional law, the ECB's action would qualify 'as a manifest and structurally significant ultra vires act'.[66]

While the ECJ's response is still pending at the time of writing this contribution, it can be noted that the preliminary reference itself has already triggered a lively debate among scholars and practitioners about the actual extent of the scope of European monetary policy and the delineation between economic and monetary policy, and, more generally, the role of the judiciary in adjudicating on this policy area and even the constitutionality under German law of

---

[63] Speech by Mr Mario Draghi, President of the European Central Bank, at the Global Investment Conference, London, 26 July 2012. Available at http://www.bis.org/review/r120727d.pdf?frames=0.

[64] ECB, 'Technical Features of Outright Monetary Transactions', press release of 6 September 2012. Available at http://www.ecb.europa.eu/press/pr/date/2012/html/pr120906_1.en.html. The OMT replaces the SMP programme, whereby 'liquidity injected through the SMP will continue to be absorbed as in the past, and the existing securities in the SMP portfolio will be held to maturity'.

[65] BVerfG, 2 BvR 2728/13 of 14 January 2014, Section II.1. a). An English language version of the order is available at http://www.bverfg.de/entscheidungen/rs20140114_2bvr272813en.html.

[66] BVerfG, 2 BvR 2728/13 of 14 January 2014, Section II.1. a), recital 33.

the German Court's order.[67] Although the limited space available here does not allow for extensive analysis and engagement with the substantive arguments put forward by the German Court, it is worth pointing to the German Court's assertiveness on the issue it submitted to the ECJ, arguably not limiting itself to a neutral account of the legal background to its questions, but actually offering an extensive critique of the ECB's course of action, which becomes clear from categorical statements such as

In the view of the Federal Constitutional Court, the purchase of government bonds on the basis of the OMT Decision exceeds the support of the general economic policies in the European Union that the European System of Central Banks is allowed to pursue.[68]

In fact the order only includes two relatively brief paragraphs in which the German Court reflects on the 'possibility' of an interpretation of the OMT in conformity with Union law, whereby the German Court makes this conditional to a reading of the scope of the OMT that essentially would have to be in line with its own specific interpretation of Union law.

In the view of the Federal Constitutional Court, the OMT Decision might not be objectionable if it could, in the light of Art. 119 and Art. 127ff TFEU, and Art. 17ff of the ESCB Statute, be interpreted or limited in its validity in such a way that it would not undermine the conditionality of the assistance programmes of the European Financial Stability Facility and the European Stability Mechanism . . . and would only be of a supportive nature with regard to the economic policies in the Union. This requires, in light of Art. 123 TFEU, that the possibility of a debt cut must be excluded . . . that government bonds of selected Member States are not purchased up to unlimited amounts . . . and that interferences with price formation on the market are to be avoided where possible.[69]

Finally it is worth noting that not all judges agreed with the approach taken by the Court, as is clear from the two dissenting opinions.[70]

Overall, the crisis has highlighted the close link between economic policy, monetary policy and financial market stability and supervision. What is more, it has become apparent that the Union legal framework did not provide sufficiently robust and uncontested crisis management mechanisms, resulting in uncertainty in the financial markets and a somewhat sluggish crisis response.

---

[67] A short overview of the debate can be found in the 14 contributions to the *German Law Journal*, Special Issue, The OMT Decision of the German Federal Constitutional Court, Vol. 15, No. 02, 107–382. Available at http://www.germanlawjournal.com/pdfs/TOC/Table_of_Contents.pdf. See also Editorial Comment, 51 (2014) *CML Rev.* 375–387; W. Heun, 'Eine verfassungswidrige Verfassungsgerichtsentscheidung—der Vorlagebeschluss des BVerfG vom 14.1.2014', *Juristenzeitung (JZ)* 7/2014, 331–337. Since the first submission of this manuscript, the reasoned opinion of Advocate General Cruz Villalón on the case brought on the OMT Decision has been published on 14 January 2015.

[68] BVerfG, 2 BvR 2728/13, recital 80.   [69] BVerfG, 2 BvR 2728/13, recital 100.

[70] See the dissenting opinions of Justice Lübbe-Wolff and Justice Gerhardt.

IV. The Emerging New Economic Governance Regime

The European financial and euro area debt crisis has convinced national and European policy makers of the need to reinforce the Maastricht system of economic policy coordination mainly in respect of the euro area Member States. At the same time it has been recognized that even in a reinforced economic governance framework a situation may arise in which a euro area Member State may require financial assistance therefore requiring a permanent rescue mechanism. In the process of reinforcing macro-and micro-prudential supervision in the Union, the ECB has been given new tasks that call for a reassessment of its position.

1. European Semester, Six Pack, Two Pack, European Stability Mechanism, and TSCG

The volume and scope of these structural reform measures cannot be measured on the basis of a study of primary Union law alone.[71] In fact, with the exception of Article 136(3) TFEU, referred to hereafter, the legal framework provided by the TFEU has remained unaltered. This is first and foremost the case with regard to the distribution of competences between the Union and the Member States: Article 5(1) TFEU still only establishes a coordinating competence for the Union and Articles 119(1), 120 and 121(1) still refer to the economic policies of the Member States. Even Article 121 TFEU on the multilateral surveillance procedure and Article 126 TFEU in conjunction with the Protocol on the excessive deficit procedure have not been amended. Nevertheless it would be a mistake to conclude from this that little has changed in this regard. In fact, the opposite is true. While the foundations, in the shape of the Treaty framework, may still be standing, the building itself has been substantially altered by means of secondary Union law, namely in the shape of the

---

[71] Examples from the growing body of literature on the reform measures include M. Ruffert, 'The European debt crisis and European Union law' 48 (2011) *CML Rev.* 1777–1806; A De Gregorio Merino, 'Legal Developments in the Economic and Monetary Union During the Debt Crisis: The Mechanisms of Financial Assistance' 49 (2012) *CML Rev.* 1613–1646; P. Craig, 'The Stability, Coordination and Governance Treaty: Principle, Politics and Pragmatism' 37 (2012) *EL Rev.* 231–248; C. Herrmann, 'Legal Aspects of the European Sovereign Debt Crisis' (2013) *Hitotsubashi Journal of Law and Politics* 41, 25–40; K Armstrong, 'The New Governance of EU Fiscal Discipline' 38 (2013) *EL Rev.* 601–617.

Six Pack[72] and Two Pack[73] measures, and moreover the two intergovernmental instruments that have been adopted in the shape of the TSCG[74] and the Treaty establishing the European Stability Mechanism (ESM Treaty),[75] raising distinct legal questions identified hereafter. Overall, these amendments are directed towards the reinforcement of the European surveillance of the conduct of economic policy in the Member States on a broader scale and as such are no longer limited to budgetary discipline.

Against the background of a new, or at least reinforced, budget rule, the multilateral surveillance and excessive deficit procedures have been tightened up and streamlined to better prevent the emergence of excessive deficits and debts in the future and to address any excessive deficits and debts that may arise in spite thereof. Moreover, next to the national deficit and debt levels, the overall economic situation in the Member States is also monitored with the aim of detecting and addressing macroeconomic imbalances. All of this takes place in the context of a new annual economic policy coordination mechanism that has been baptized the European Semester.

While Article 126(1) TFEU and the excessive deficit definition provided for in the Protocol on the excessive deficit procedure have remained unchanged, the country-specific medium-term objective and the requirement of the annual reduction of the cyclically adjusted balance, introduced by the 2005 amendment of Regulation 1466/97, have been reinforced and upgraded by the TSCG. Article 3(1) TSCG obliges all contracting parties to keep the budgetary position of the general government in balance or in surplus. This is considered to be the case, if the annual structural balance of the general government is at its country-specific medium-term objective, as defined in today's Regulation 1466/97, with a lower limit of a structural deficit of 0.5 per cent of the gross domestic product at market prices. According to Article 3(1)(b) TSCG, where the ratio of the general government debt to GDP is significantly below 60 per cent and where risks in terms of long-term sustainability of public finances are low, the lower limit of the medium-term objective may reach a structural deficit of up to 1 per cent of GDP.[76] According to

---

[72] Reg 1173/2011 on the effective enforcement of budgetary surveillance in the euro area, OJ 2011 L 306/1; Reg 1174/2011 on enforcement measures to correct excessive macroeconomic imbalances in the euro area, OJ 2011 L 306/8; Reg 1175/2011 amending Council Reg 1466/97 on the strengthening of the surveillance of budgetary positions and the surveillance and coordination of economic policies, OJ 2011 L 306/12; Reg 1176/2011 on the prevention and correction of macroeconomic imbalances, OJ 2011 L 306/25; Council Regulation 1177/2011 amending Reg 1467/97 on speeding up and clarifying the implementation of the excessive deficit procedure, OJ 2011 L 306/33; Council Directive 2011/85/EU on requirements for budgetary frameworks of the Member States, OJ 2011 L 306/41.

[73] Reg 472/2013 on the strengthening of economic and budgetary surveillance of Member States in the euro area experiencing or threatened with serious difficulties with respect to their financial stability, OJ 2013, L 140/1; Reg 473/2013 on common provisions for monitoring and assessing draft budgetary plans and ensuring the correction of excessive deficit of the Member States in the euro area, OJ 2013, L 140/11.

[74] T/SCG/en 1.   [75] T/ESM 2012/en 1.

[76] Otherwise with regard to exceptional deviations see Art 3(3) TSCG.

Article 4 TSCG, Member States with an excessive debt are obliged to reduce the debt at an average rate of 1/20 annually as a benchmark. What is more, according to Article 3(2)(e) TSCG, a significant deviation from the medium-term objective, or the adjustment path towards it must automatically trigger a correction mechanism, which obliges the national government in question to implement measures to correct the deviations over a defined period of time.

While it may be argued that the balanced budget and adjustment path are not new as such,[77] the obligation to include an automatic correction mechanism that binds government to a specific course of action is. Moreover, even to the extent that Regulation 1466/97 can be interpreted as already including the substantive budgetary rules, they are given a different status by the fact that under the TSCG Member States are obliged to include corresponding rules in their own legal system. Article 3(2) TSCG states in this regard that the rules set out in Article 3(1) must take effect in the national law 'through provisions of binding force and permanent character, preferably constitutional, or otherwise guaranteed to be fully respected and adhered to throughout the national budgetary processes'. What is more, Member States are not free to decide on the nature of the automatic correction mechanisms, as according to Article 3(2) TSCG they have to be based on common principles laid down by the European Commission 'concerning in particular the nature, size and time-frame of the corrective action to be undertaken, also in the case of exceptional circumstances, and the role and independence of the institutions responsible at national level for monitoring compliance with the rules'.[78]

While Article 3(2) TSCG states that the correction mechanism shall fully respect the prerogatives of national parliaments, it seems reasonable to conclude that the obligation to introduce a balanced budget rule and automatic correction mechanism in national (constitutional) law itself already results in a limitation of the policy space of national parliaments beyond what could be observed for the old Regulation 1466/97. This is even more so since, according to Article 8 TSCG, the obligations arising from Article 3(2) are enforceable before the ECJ and may even result in lump sum and penalty payments by the Member State concerned, as the former has been given jurisdiction pursuant to Article 8(3) TSCG in conjunction with Article 273 TFEU over such cases. It is thus hardly surprising that several top national (constitutional) courts and tribunals in the context of the ratification of the TSCG have considered the consequences of these obligations for the powers of Member States in the sphere of economic policy and namely the impact on the national parliaments.[79]

---

[77] As is eg already observed by P. Craig, 'The Stability, Coordination and Governance Treaty: Principle, Politics and Pragmatism' 37 (2012) *EL Rev.* 235.

[78] Communication from the Commission, Common principles on national fiscal correction mechanisms, COM (2012) 342 final.

[79] For details see eg 'The Euro-Crisis and the Courts: Judicial Review and the Political Process in Comparative Perspective' (2014) *Berkeley Journal of International Law* (BJIL), 32(1) (forthcoming), available at http://papers.ssrn.com/sol3/papers.cfm?abstract_id=2328060##; F. Amtenbrink,

This impact on the national policy space as a result of new economic governance also becomes clear from a study of the European Semester, at the heart of which stands a six-month surveillance cycle that is primarily geared towards 'ensuring that Member States reach the agreed upon medium-term budgetary objectives in the necessary national adjustments programmes in accordance with the strategic objectives of the Union'.[80] The European Commission formulates the economic priorities of the Union in a so-called Annual Growth Survey, which is supposed to provide Member States with a general orientation for the determination of their own economic policies. Based on country reviews, as well as the Stability and Convergence Programmes and national economic reform programmes submitted by the Member States, the European Commission proposes country-specific recommendations for budgetary, economic and social policies that thereafter have to be confirmed by the European Council. Each year Member States have to submit their draft budgetary plans by 15 October to the European Commission and to the Council in the composition of the euro area Member States. These plans must be in line with the European guidelines and recommendations and moreover, comply with the annual debt reduction requirements in case of a government debt in excess of 60 per cent as laid down in Regulation 1466/97 and the TSCG.[81] The extent of the European engagement with national economic policy also becomes clear from the fact that the European Commission not only internally reviews the submitted draft budgetary plans, but actually adopts a formal opinion on them by the end on November of a given year at the latest. In this context Article 7(2) Regulation 473/2013 states:

Notwithstanding paragraph 1, where, in exceptional cases, after consulting the Member State concerned within one week of submission of the draft budgetary plan, the Commission identifies particularly serious non-compliance with the budgetary policy obligations laid down in the SGP, the Commission shall adopt its opinion within two weeks of submission of the draft budgetary plan. In its opinion, the Commission shall request that a revised draft budgetary plan be submitted as soon as possible and in any event within three weeks of the date of its opinion. The Commission's request shall be reasoned and shall be made public.

In such an instance, a Member States is expected to resubmit a revised draft budget that will be yet again subject to an assessment by the European

---

'General Report' in U. Neergaard, C. Jacqueson, and J.H. Danielsen (eds), *The Economic and Monetary Union: Constitutional and Institutional Aspects of the Economic Governance within the EU*, The XXVI FIDE Congress in Copenhagen 2014, Congress Publications Vol. 1 (2014), 73–178, particularly on Question 9; F. Amtenbrink, 'New Economic Governance in the European Union: Another Constitutional Battleground?' in K. Purnhagen and P. Roth (eds), *Varieties of European Economic Law and Regulation* (2014), forthcoming 2014.

[80] Own translation. See F. Amtenbrink and H.H.B. Vedder, *Recht van de Europese Unie* (5th ed, 2014), 21, with a more detailed description of the European Semester.

[81] For more details see Section 1-A Reg 1466/97 (as amended); Reg 473/2013 on common provisions for monitoring and assessing draft budgetary plans and ensuring the correction of excessive deficit of the Member States in the euro area, OJ 2013, L 140/11; Council Directive 2011/85/EU on requirements for budgetary frameworks of the Member States, OJ 2011, L 306/41.

Commission. Moreover, the signatory Member States of the TSCG also have to report *ex ante* on their public debt issuance plans to the Council and the European Commission.[82]

It needs little explaining that this new European economic surveillance cycle has a considerable impact on the policy space of national executive governments and parliaments. In fact this is recognized in the procedure itself, which provides for a dialogue with the national parliaments, as according to Article 7(3) 'at the request of the parliament of the Member State concerned or of the European Parliament, the Commission shall present its opinion [on the national draft budgetary plans] to the parliament making the request'.[83] Such a dialogue between the European Parliament, the (European) Council and the European Commission is also foreseen more generally in the context of the multilateral surveillance, macroeconomic imbalances and excessive deficit procedures.[84] The European Parliament can invite the President of the Council, the Commission and 'where appropriate' the President of the European Council and of the Eurogroup, consisting of the government representatives of the euro area Member States, before the Economic and Monetary Affairs Committee in a nutshell to discuss the institution's conduct in the context of the different procedures. As has been observed above, this committee has already gained considerable experience in discussing complex macroeconomic issues in the context of the regular monetary dialogue with the President of the ECB.

Turning to the multilateral surveillance procedures as laid down in Article 121, Regulation 1466/97 (as amended) and Regulation 1173/2011 it can be observed that a serious attempt has been made to increase the stringency of the procedure. This becomes clear from two key new features introduced by the Six Pack. Firstly, it is now possible to demand an interest bearing deposit from Member States that do not comply with the recommendations made by the Council in response to a significant deviation of a Member State from the adjustment path towards the medium-term objective.[85] What is more, the decision on the application of such a deposit is subject to reverse voting, meaning that unless the Council, acting by qualified majority, rejects the European Commission's recommendation within 10 days of the latter's adoption of the recommendation, the Commission's recommendation is considered to have been adopted. In the context of the excessive deficit procedure as laid down in Article 126 TFEU, Regulation 1467/97 (as amended) and Regulation 1173/2011, the decision on the existence of an excessive deficit procedure itself can already trigger a non-interest bearing deposit requirement, if the Member State in question had previously had to make an interest bearing deposit or, if the Commission decides on the existence of a 'particularly serious

---

[82] Art 6 TSCG.   [83] Brackets added.
[84] Art 2-ab Reg 1466/97; Art 2a Reg 1467/97; Art 14 Reg 1176/2011.
[85] According to Art 4 Reg 1173/2011 this amounts to 0.2 per cent.

non-compliance with the budgetary policy obligations laid down in the SGP'.[86] What is more, according to Article 5(1) TSCG, Member States subject to an excessive deficit procedure must put in place a budgetary and economic partnership programme that includes 'a detailed description of the structural reforms which must be put in place and implemented to ensure an effective and durable correction of its excessive deficit'. The programme has to be submitted to the Council and the European Commission for endorsement and is thereafter monitored as part of European budgetary surveillance. Finally, according to Article 7 TSCG, reversed voting is also supposed to apply in the excessive deficit procedure to euro area Member States.

New in its entirety is the macroeconomic imbalances procedure that also forms part of the multilateral surveillance procedure and has been established with the aim of broadening economic policy surveillance 'beyond budgetary surveillance to include a more detailed and formal framework to prevent excessive macroeconomic imbalances'.[87] For this purpose, trends 'giving rise to macroeconomic developments which are adversely affecting, or have the potential adversely to affect, the proper functioning of the economy of a Member State or of the economic and monetary Union, or of the Union as a whole' are supposed to be detected.[88] This is assumed to be achieved on the basis of a set of micro-financial indicators, including, *inter alia,* the current account balance, the international investment position, nominal labour costs, non-financial corporate, household and general government debt and rate of unemployment.[89] The European Commission draws up a so-called Alert Mechanism Report on an annual basis, which includes an economic and financial assessment of the situation in the Member States.[90] Where imbalances are expected, the European Commission can also conduct in-depth reviews. Based on a recommendation from the European Commission, the Council can address recommendations to the Member State concerned. However, if it is concluded from an in-depth review that a Member State is affected by a severe imbalance, the Council, on a recommendation from the European Commission, can adopt a recommendation establishing the existence of an excessive macroeconomic imbalance and recommend that the Member State concerned takes corrective action.[91] Such a Member State then becomes obliged to submit a corrective action plan to

---

[86] Art 5 Reg 1173/2011.   [87] Preamble No. 7 Reg 1176/2011.

[88] Preamble No. 7 Reg 1176/2011, Art 1.

[89] European Commission, Scoreboard for the Surveillance of Macroeconomic Imbalances, *Occasional Papers* 92, February 2012; Commission Staff Paper Document, 'Completing the Scoreboard for the MIP: Financial Sector Indicator', Brussels 14.11.2012, SWD(2012) 389 final.

[90] Art 3–4 Reg 1176/2011. See eg 'Report from the Commission to the European Parliament, the Council, the European Central Bank and the European Economic and Social Committee', *Alert Mechanism Report 2014*, Brussels 13.11.2013, COM(2013) 790 final.

[91] 'Report from the Commission to the European Parliament, the Council, the European Central Bank and the European Economic and Social Committee', *Alert Mechanism Report 2014*, Brussels 13.11.2013, COM(2013) 790 final, Art 7.

the Council and European Commission. The contents and implementation of this plan are monitored by the European Commission and assessed by the Council. If it is established that the Member State has not taken corrective action, the Council must impose an interest-bearing deposit. Moreover, an annual fine is imposed in cases of repeated non-compliance.[92]

The amendment of the multilateral surveillance and excessive deficit procedure, as well as the introduction of the macroeconomic imbalances procedures undoubtedly signify a new quality in the European engagement with the economic policies of the euro area Member States. In fact, considering the scope of the Six Pack, Two Pack and TSCG, the reference in primary Union law to the economic policies of the Member States and the merely coordinating competence of the Union hardly seems to reflect anymore the complex interactions that the new economic governance system introduces. At the same time, it seems premature to conclude from this that, in the new system, peer review and the need for political commitment are a thing of the past. First, much will depend on how these new procedures develop in practice. Thus, for example, the reversed voting procedure will produce little effect if the Council makes use of its power to oppose the Commission's action. Moreover, enforceability of the excessive deficit procedure continues to be hampered by the fact that Article 126(10) TFEU still rules out the application of the Treaty infringement procedure. Finally, whether the macroeconomic imbalances procedure in its current shape provides an effective toolbox to compel Member States to take necessary structural economic reforms is debatable.

The establishment of a permanent financial assistance mechanism for the euro area Member States in the shape of the ESM, which has succeeded the temporary EFSM and EFSF, shows not only that lessons have been drawn from the euro area debt crisis and the consequences of the absence of a clear and uncontested rescue mechanism, but arguably also that even with the new economic governance system in place, the possibility of a clear and present threat of a sovereign default in the euro area has not been ruled out for the future.[93] The uncertainty surrounding the admissibility of the establishment of such a mechanism within and outside the Union framework has resulted in the only substantive amendment of primary Union law in the context of the structural economic governance reform measures in the shape of the inclusion of a new paragraph 3 in Article 136 TFEU, according to which the euro area Member States can establish a stability mechanism 'to be activated if indispensable to safeguard the stability of the euro area as a whole', whereby financial assistance must be made 'subject to

---

[92] Art 3 Reg 1174/2011.
[93] While membership for a euro area Member State is obligatory, membership is open to non-euro area Member States. See Art 2 ESM Treaty.

strict conditionality'.[94] Article 3 of the ESM Treaty summarizes the purpose and working of the ESM:

The purpose of the ESM shall be to mobilise funding and provide stability support under strict conditionality, appropriate to the financial assistance instrument chosen, to the benefit of ESM Members which are experiencing, or are threatened by, severe financing problems, if indispensable to safeguard the financial stability of the euro area as a whole and of its Member States. For this purpose, the ESM shall be entitled to raise funds by issuing financial instruments or by entering into financial or other agreements or arrangements with ESM Members, financial institutions or other third parties.

Subject to a decision by the Governing Board of the ESM, on which all participating Member States that also hold the capital of the ESM are represented, Member States can be granted financial assistance, *inter alia,* in the form of a precautionary conditioned credit line, loans and financial assistance specifically for the re-capitalization of financial institutions of a Member State. This can also take the shape of a market support facility, whereby the ESM purchases the sovereign bonds of a Member State on the primary or secondary markets.[95] The first two countries to receive financial assistance were Spain and Cyprus. In the case of the former, the assistance was specifically geared towards the recapitalization of financial institutions. As part of the establishment of the Banking Union ESM has also been given the power to directly recapitalize financial institutions in the euro area that are incapable 'to attract sufficient capital from private sources and if the ESM Member concerned is unable to recapitalise it'.[96]

In principle, decisions to grant financial assistance are taken by the ESM's Board of Governors by unanimity. Yet, there is one notable exception to this rule. If the European Commission and the ECB both conclude that a failure to urgently adopt a decision to grant or implement financial assistance 'would threaten the economic and financial sustainability of the euro area' a decision to grant financial assistance requires a qualified majority of 85 per cent of the votes cast, the voting rights of Member States being equal to the number of shares allocated to them in the authorized capital stock of the ESM.[97] This effectively means that only France, Germany and Italy have a veto right. The fact that, at least theoretically, smaller Member States can be outvoted on a decision that also financially affects them is not unproblematic, as has become clear from the review of the ratification of the

[94] European Council, Decision 2011/199/EU amending Art 136 of the Treaty on the Functioning of the European Union with regard to a stability mechanism for Member States whose currency is the euro, OJ 2011, L 91/1.

[95] See Art 12ff ESM Treaty. According to the preamble to the ESM Treaty, the granting of financial assistance is subject to the ratification of the TSCG and compliance with its Art 3(2).

[96] Statement by the President of the Eurogroup, ESM direct recapitalisation instrument, 10 June 2014.

[97] See Art 4(7) and Annex II ESM Treaty.

ESM Treaty by the Estonian Supreme Court (*Riigikohus*), which found that this would interfere with the 'financial competences' of the Estonian parliament.[98]

As mentioned above, the compatibility of the ESM Treaty with Union law was reviewed by the ECJ in *Pringle*. This not only covered the question of the compatibility of the substance of the Treaty with Articles 123 and 125 TFEU, but also more generally, whether the Member States were allowed to put in place such a mechanism outside the Union legal framework in the first place. The question is addressed 'whether the stability mechanism established by the ESM Treaty falls under monetary policy and, accordingly, under the Union's exclusive competence',[99] or whether the ESM Treaty has to be otherwise considered as an international agreement for which the Union has an exclusive competence pursuant to Article 3(2) TFEU 'in so far as its conclusion may affect common rules or alter their scope'. The ECJ answered both of these questions in the negative, which triggered substantial and persuasive criticism.[100]

2. The ECB's New Role In Macro- and Micro-Prudential Supervision

As has been noted above, the European financial and euro area debt crisis has also revealed major shortcomings in financial market regulation and supervision of the internal (financial) market and the absence of effective macro- and micro-prudential supervision at the European level.[101] In a first step in 2010, the European System of Financial Supervision (ESFS) was set up, featuring three new European Supervisory Agencies (ESAs), namely, the European Banking Authority (EBA), the European Insurance and Occupational Pensions Authority (EIOPA), and the European Securities and Markets Authority (ESMA).[102] Moreover,

---

[98] Estonian Supreme Court, decision no. 3-4-10-6-12 of 12 July 2012, para 159. The Court's own English translation is available at http://www.riigikohus.ee accessed 19 December 2013, recital 159. For more details see F. Amtenbrink, 'New Economic Governance in the European Union: Another Constitutional Battleground?' in K. Purnhagen and P. Roth (eds), *Varieties of European Economic Law and Regulation*, forthcoming 2014.

[99] Case C-370/12, *Pringle* [2012] ECR I-756, recital 93.

[100] P. Eeckhout and M. Waibel, 'United Kingdom' in U. Neergaard, C. Jacqueson, J.H. Danielsen (eds), *The Economic and Monetary Union: Constitutional and Institutional Aspects of the Economic Governance within the EU*, The XXVI FIDE Congress in Copenhagen 2014, Congress Publications Vol. 1 (2014) 619–654, 624ff, with further references.

[101] See in this regard, the findings of the de Larossière Report: The High-Level Group on Financial Supervision in the EU, chaired by J. de Larossière, Brussels, 25 February 2009.

[102] Reg 1093/2010 establishing a European Supervisory Authority (European Banking Authority), amending Decision 716/2009/EC and repealing Commission Decision 2009/78/EC, OJ 2010, L 331/12; Reg 1094/2010 establishing a European Supervisory Authority (European Insurance and Occupational Pensions Authority), amending Decision 716/2009/EC and repealing Commission Decision 2009/79/EC, OJ L 331/48; Reg 1095/2010 establishing a European Supervisory Authority (European Securities and Markets Authority), amending Decision 716/2009/EC and repealing Commission Decision 2009/77/EC, OJ 2010, L 331/84.

the European Systemic Risk Board (ESRB) was established, charged with 'the macro-prudential oversight of the financial system within the Union in order to contribute to the prevention or mitigation of systemic risks to financial stability in the Union that arise from developments within the financial system and taking into account macroeconomic developments, so as to avoid periods of widespread financial distress'.[103] While formally being positioned outside the ECB, the latter is effectively in charge for the time being, since, for the first five year following the entry into force of the respective Regulation, the ESRB is chaired by the President of the ECB.[104]

The declared purpose of the ESFS is 'to ensure the supervision of the Union's financial system'.[105] Yet the EBA has not been given the task of the day-to-day supervision of credit institutions. The establishment of a more centralized micro-prudential supervisory system as part of the establishment of a Banking Union was thereafter suggested both by the European Council and the European Commission, which in two separate reports from 2012 presented their vision for the future of EMU.[106] Alongside a European Resolution Mechanism[107] and a European Deposit Guarantee Scheme, the establishment of a Single Supervisory Mechanism (SSM) has been considered as a central pillar of such a Banking Union.[108]

Rather than vesting such supervisory tasks in the EBA or establishing an additional institution or agency at the European level, the SSM has been founded by the transfer of supervisory tasks to the ECB by means of a Council Regulation based on Article 127(6) TFEU, according to which the Council may unanimously, and after consulting the European Parliament and the European Central Bank, confer specific tasks upon the ECB concerning the prudential supervision of credit institutions and other financial institutions, with the exception of insurance

[103] Reg 1092/2010 on European Union macro-prudential oversight of the financial system and establishing a European Systemic Risk Board, OJ 2010, L 331/1, Art 3(1).

[104] Reg 1092/2010 on European Union macro-prudential oversight of the financial system and establishing a European Systemic Risk Board, OJ 2010, L 331/1, Art 5(1).

[105] See eg Art 1(2) Reg 1092/2010.

[106] Communication from the European Commission, *A Blueprint for a Deep and Genuine Economic and Monetary Union. Launching a European Debate*, 28 November 2012; President of the European Council (in close cooperation with the Presidents of the Commission, the Eurogroup and the European Central Bank), *Towards a Genuine Economic and Monetary Union*, 5 December 2012.

[107] See Reg 806/2014 establishing uniform rules and a uniform procedure for the resolution of credit institutions and certain investment firms in the framework of a Single Resolution Mechanism and a Single Resolution Fund and amending Reg 1093/2010, OJ 2014, L 225/1.

[108] While a European Depository Guarantee Scheme has not been established (yet), at the time of writing of this contribution a provisional agreement had been reached between the European Parliament and the Council on the proposed Single Resolution Mechanism for the Banking Union. See 'European Parliament and Council back Commission's Proposal for a Single Resolution Mechanism: A Major Step towards Completing the Banking Union', European Commission—Statement/14/77 of 20/03/2014.

undertakings.[109] While it is not possible to analyse the SSM in any detail here, it is worth briefly highlighting the role of the ECB.[110]

Since November 2014, the ECB is exclusively competent, *inter alia,* to authorize and withdraw authorization of credit institutions, act as competent home state authority in the case of credit institutions that intend to establish a branch or provide cross-border services in non-euro area Member States, assess applications for the acquisition and disposal of qualified holdings in credit institutions and, more generally, ensure compliance with prudential requirements and conduct supervisory reviews.[111] The ECB is also in charge of the day-to-day supervision of *significant* credit institutions as defined in Article 6(4) of Regulation 1024/2013, basically taking into account the size of the credit institution, its importance to the economy of the Union or the Member State and the significance of its cross-border activities. Other credit institutions of which the ECB is in charge include credit institutions for which public assistance has been requested or received under the ESM, as well as, in all instances, the three most significant credit institutions in each Member State. National supervisory authorities remain in charge of less significant credit institutions.

The extensive role of the ECB in the SSM has triggered debate about the feasibility of Article 127(6) TFEU as a legal basis as this provision refers to the transfer of 'specific tasks'.[112] Yet, in the end, it can be argued that given the role of the national competent supervisory authorities for the day-to-day supervision of less significant credit institutions, the SSM does not stand for a full transfer of micro-prudential supervision to the ECB.[113]

Whether central banks should also be in charge of prudential supervisory tasks has been subject to debate for some time, mainly in the political economy literature. While the benefits may lie in the information advantage, expertise

---

[109]   Council Regulation 1024/2013 conferring specific tasks on the European Central Bank concerning policies relating to the prudential supervision of credit institutions, OJ 2013, L 287/63. See also Reg 1022/2013 amending Reg 1093/2010 establishing a European Supervisory Authority (European Banking Authority) as regards the conferral of specific tasks on the European Central Bank pursuant to Council Regulation 1024/2013, OJ 2013, L 287/5.

[110]   For a general overview, see eg E. Ferran and V.S.G. Babis, 'The European Single Supervisory Mechanism' *University of Cambridge Faculty of Law Research Paper* 10/2013, available at http://papers.ssrn.com/sol3/papers.cfm?abstract_id=2224538##; E. Wymeersch, 'The European Banking Union, a First Analysis', *Ghent University Financial Law Institute Working Paper* Series WP 2012–07, available at http://papers.ssrn.com/sol3/papers.cfm?abstract_id=2171785; N. Moloney, 'European Banking Union: Assessing its risk and resilience' 51 (2014) *CMLRev.* 1609–1670.

[111]   See Art 4 Reg 1024/2013.

[112]   See eg the discussion in E. Ferran and V.S.G. Babis, 'The European Single Supervisory Mechanism' *University of Cambridge Faculty of Law Research Paper* 10/2013, p. 6ff, available at http://papers.ssrn.com/sol3/papers.cfm?abstract_id=2224538##.

[113]   As eg argued by C. Herrmann, 'Germany' in U. Neergaard, C. Jacqueson, and J.H. Danielsen (eds), *The Economic and Monetary Union: Constitutional and Institutional Aspects of the Economic Governance within the EU,* The XXVI FIDE Congress in Copenhagen 2014, Congress Publications Vol. 1 (2014) 341–373, p 368.

and credibility that rest with a monetary policy authority, the disadvantage is the potential conflict of interest for the central bank in the conduct of supervisory and monetary policy tasks potentially to the detriment of the monetary policy objective. Moreover, the accumulation of tasks at a central bank may raise accountability concerns.[114] The drafters of Regulation 1024/2013 made a notable attempt to address these concerns, at least to some extent, first and foremost by placing the preparation of supervisory decisions in a new body within the Bank, the so-called Supervisory Board, consisting of one representative from each of the national supervisory authorities of the participating Member States, four representatives of the ECB, none of which may be directly charged with monetary policy tasks, as well as a chair and vice chair. While the vice chair is appointed from among the members of the ECB Executive Board, the chair of the Supervisory Board is appointed through an open selection procedure. Yet, it would be premature to conclude from this that the prudential supervisory tasks of the ECB have been completely firewalled from its monetary policy tasks. The reason for this is that the Supervisory Board in principle only prepares the supervisory decisions that are thereafter taken by the Governing Board of the ECB, that is the main monetary policy decision-making body of the Bank, even if the latter must actively oppose any draft decision within a tight deadline for it not to be considered adopted.[115] A strict separation of monetary policy and prudential supervisory tasks has thus not been achieved.

Similar to what can be observed for its tasks as monetary policy authority, both the ECB and the national supervisory authorities are supposed to be shielded from political influence when conducting supervisory tasks. To this end, Article 19 of Regulation 1024/2013 states that the members of the Supervisory Board shall neither seek nor receive instructions from Union or national bodies. At the same time, the SSM foresees a dialogue between the Supervisory Board and the European Parliament and the parliaments of the Member States participating in the SSM. Here the emphasis rests on reporting and explaining, rather than concrete instruments to sanction suboptimal performance by the new European banking supervisor. Despite this reservation, it has to be recognized in the context of the SSM that a serious effort has been made to create institutional structures that form important pre-conditions for accountability, as is also mainly highlighted by the conclusion between the EP and the ECB of an inter-institutional agreement.[116]

---

[114] F. Amtenbrink, 'Central Bank Challenges in the Global Economy' in C. Herrmann and J.P. Terhechte (eds), *European Yearbook of International Economic Law 2011* (2011) 19–42, p. 37–38, with further references.

[115] With regard to this reverse voting in the SSM see Art 14(3) Reg 1024/2013.

[116] Interinstitutional Agreement between the European Parliament and the European Central Bank on the practical modalities of the exercise of democratic accountability and oversight over the exercise of the tasks conferred on the ECB within the framework of the Single Supervisory Mechanism, OJ 2013, L 320/1.

While the SSM is primarily geared towards the euro area Member States, it is also open to participation by non-euro area Member States that can take part through the establishment of close cooperation agreements with the ECB.[117] The national supervisory authorities of such Member States also participate in the Supervisory Board. The fact that the Governing Council of the ECB can oppose draft decisions of the Supervisory Board forms a particular challenge, as non-euro area Member States do not participate in this body through their national central banks. For this reason specific safeguards are provided for in the SSM, essentially allowing non-euro area Member States to terminate the cooperation under certain conditions.[118] Yet, the non-participation in the SSM, for the time being, of some Member States and namely the United Kingdom highlights the continuing fragmentation of the internal (financial) market in the European Union.

Overall, with its involvement in macro- and micro-prudential supervision the role of the ECB in EMU has evolved from a monetary policy authority with a clear focus on price stability into a Union institution with the much more comprehensive and explicit task of safeguarding the monetary and financial stability of the euro area, thereby recognizing the interconnection between these two areas that became painfully apparent during the crisis. With this model, the Union also follows a more general trend towards assigning prudential supervisory tasks to central banks, albeit in Europe this development can also be partially linked to the loss by the euro area central banks of their monetary policy tasks.

V. Conclusions and Outlook

This brief analysis of the main legal developments triggered by the European financial and euro area debt crisis against the background of the original Maastricht system makes it clear that EMU has gone through a metamorphosis. Today's system has developed through several steps, moving from ad hoc and temporary crisis management to more permanent solutions. Rather than amend primary Union law to provide for a new legal framework, political disagreement about the need and scope of measures and, more generally, a fear about opening the Pandora's box of ordinary Treaty amendment, have lead to the seeking of solutions within the existing primary Union legal framework by means of secondary Union law and, where the viability of such an approach was considered questionable, turning to intergovernmental instruments. What has resulted from this is a complex

---

[117] Art 7 Reg 1024/2013.   [118] Art 7 Reg 1024/2013.

web of supranational, intergovernmental and—at least temporarily—private law instruments that have to be studied in combination in order to fully understand the current system of economic governance in EMU. This comes at the expense of the transparency and coherence of the legal framework, as well as resulting in the repetition of legal provisions, as has been highlighted above for the TSCG.

Viewed in combination, the scope of the Six Pack, Two Pack, TSCG and ESM arguably verify the hypothesis stated at the outset of this contribution that today's economic governance framework has in many regards outgrown the tight legal framework provided by primary Union law. This is mainly so with regard to the Treaty postulation of the economic policies of the Member States and the laconic description of the multilateral surveillance and excessive deficit procedure in Articles 121 and 126 TFEU with the exclusive focus on budgetary discipline. Moreover, considering the scope of the ad hoc and structural reform measures in response to the European financial and euro area debt crisis, as well as the ECJ's ruling in *Pringle*, a clarification of Article 123–125 TFEU seems appropriate, for which Article 125(2) TFEU could function as a legal basis. More ambitious plans, such as those identified in the European Council and European Commission reports on the future of EMU, would require a more substantial amendment of primary Union law. This is the case for ideas for a common issuance of public debt, such as proposed by the European Commission in its 2011 Green Paper on the feasibility of introducing Stability Bonds. Such a centralized debt issue would be difficult to bring into line with today's principle of government refinancing at market conditions referred to above and, thus, would require a more fundamental amendment of Title VIII TFEU. Yet, the compatibility of such proposals with today's primary Union law is not the only concern, as in some euro area Member States national (constitutional) law may stand in the way.[119]

At the time of writing the 64 000 dollar (or rather euro) question both for policy makers and students of European Union law alike is whether the reform measures that have been taken characterize a sustainable system of economic and monetary governance that will stand the test of time. While only a study of the application of the new system over a period of time will provide robust evidence, the brief analysis provided in section IV already shows that despite a notable broadening and strengthening of the multilateral surveillance, much still relies on the political will of the Member States both collectively (Council) and individually to comply with the new set of rules. The exclusion of judicial review of Member State's behaviour in the context of excessive deficit procedure arguably underlines the point that

---

[119] As has been argued eg for the introduction of Stability Bonds based on joint and several liability of Member States. See Herrmann, 356, with reference to the decision by the German Federal Constitutional Court in BVerfG, 2 BvR 987/10 from 7.9.2011 (C. Herrmann, 'Germany' in U. Neergaard, C. Jacqueson, and J.H. Danielsen (eds), *The Economic and Monetary Union: Constitutional and Institutional Aspects of the Economic Governance within the EU*, The XXVI FIDE Congress in Copenhagen 2014, Congress Publications Vol. 1 (2014) 341–373).

budgetary discipline in the euro area continues to be essentially a political pledge rather than a legally enforceable obligation, even if under the TSCG, Member States have the legally enforceable duty to introduce balanced budget rules and automatic correction mechanisms in their legal orders.

Not least, considering the wish list of the European Council and the European Commission in their respective reports on the future of EMU, it can be observed that EMU has not yet reached the final stage of its metamorphosis. At the constitutional and institutional level two main challenges that will need to be addressed are the integration method that is applied for further reform steps and ways in which the democratic legitimacy of the new economic governance system can be ensured. With regard to the former, the use of intergovernmental treaties to reform EMU may be perceived as a threat to the Community method. This is even more the case since both the TSCG and the ESM Treaty clearly aim at achieving Union objectives and, moreover, make structural use of Union institutions. What is more, the use of intergovernmental instruments in the management and solution of the European financial and euro area debt crisis has arguably widened and deepened the (political) divide between euro area and non-euro area Member States and increased the entry hurdles for Member States with a derogation. In the case of the TSCG, the route is stipulated, as Article 17 states, that within five years, at most, of the date of its entry into force 'on the basis of an assessment of the experience with its implementation, the necessary steps shall be taken, in accordance with the Treaty on European Union and the Treaty on the Functioning of the European Union, with the aim of incorporating the substance of this Treaty into the legal framework of the European Union'. Yet, this provision does not foresee an automatic or otherwise clear-cut obligation to move all substantive provisions of the TSCG into the Union legal framework.

In developing strategies to further develop economic governance, new life has to be breathed into existing possibilities of differentiation within the Union legal framework, as has, for example, been suggested for the ESM and enhanced cooperation.[120]

The restriction of the policy space of national governments and parliaments, which results from the new economic governance regime, calls for a recalibration of the existing channels providing democratic legitimacy to the system as a whole. This will be even more the case if additional steps are considered in the future, particularly with regard to the role of national parliaments. The current subsidiarity procedure, as enhanced by the Lisbon Treaty, and the envisaged cooperation of national parliaments with the European Parliament limited to the exchange of views, can hardly compensate for the increased loss of budgetary autonomy.[121]

---

[120] M. Schwarz, 'A Memorandum of Misunderstanding—The Doomed Road of the European Stability Mechanism and a Possible Way Out: Enhanced Cooperation' 51 (2014) *CMLRev.* 389.

[121] See Art 13 TSCG.

It is presently submitted that in the current state of constitutionalization in the Union, seeking this legitimacy only by means of an enhanced role for the European Parliament is not an option, not only, but also, from the national constitutional point of view. For this a more substantial role for national parliaments at the European level is required. Moreover, a conscious decision needs to be taken whether and to what extent non-euro area Member States and their MEP's should participate in decision-making pertaining to the euro area only.

BIBLIOGRAPHY

D. Adamski, 'National Power Games and Structural Failures in the European Macroeconomic Governance' (2012) *CMLRev.* 49, 1319–1364

F. Amtenbrink, 'New Economic Governance in the European Union: Another Constitutional Battleground?' in K. Purnhagen and P. Roth (eds), *Varieties of European Economic Law and Regulation* (2014)

F. Amtenbrink and J. De Haan, 'Economic Governance in the European Union—Fiscal Policy Discipline Versus Flexibility' (2003) *CMLRev.* 40, 1075–1106

F. Amtenbrink and J. De Haan, 'The European Central Bank: An Independent Specialized Organization of Community Law—A Comment' (2002) *CMLRev.* 39, 65–76

F. Amtenbrink, J. De Haan, and O.C.H.M. Sleijpen, 'The Stability Pact—Placebo or Panacea?' (1997) *European Business Law Review* 8, 202–210 and 233–238

V. Borger, 'The ESM and the European Court's Predicament in *Pringle*' (2013) 14 *German Law Journal* 1, 113–140

P. Craig, 'The Stability, Coordination and Governance Treaty: Principle, Politics and Pragmatism' (2012) 37 *ELRev*, 231–248

F. Fabbrini, 'The Euro-Crisis and the Courts: Judicial Review and the Political Process in Comparative Perspective' (2014) *Berkeley Journal of International Law* 32(1), 64–123

K. Featherstone, 'The Greek Sovereign Debt Crisis and EMU: A Failing State in a Skewed Regime' (2011) *JCMS* 49(2), 193–217

R.J. Goebel, 'Court of Justice Oversight over the European Central Bank: Delimiting the ECB's Constitutional Autonomy and Independence in the *OLAF* Judgment' (2005) *Fordham International Law Journal* 29, 610–654

C. Herrmann, 'EZB-Programm für die Kapitalmärkte verstößt nicht gegen die Verträge—Erwiderung auf Martin Seidel, EuZW 2010, 521' (2010) *Europäische Zeitschrift für Wirtschaftsrecht*, 645–646

C. Herrmann, 'Legal aspects of the European Sovereign Debt Crisis' (2013) *Hitotsubashi Journal of Law and Politics* 41(1), 23–38

D. Howarth, 'Running an Enlarged Euro-zone—Reforming the European Central Bank: Efficiency, Legitimacy and National Economic Interest' (2007) *Review of International Political Economy* 14(5), 820–841

R.M. Lastra, 'The Governance Structure for Financial Supervision and Regulation in Europe' (2003) *Columbia Journal of European Law*, 10(1), 49–68

J.-V. Louis, 'Guest Editorial: The No-Bailout Clause and Rescue Packages' (2010) *CMLRev.* 47, 971–986

H. Marjosola, 'Regulating Financial Markets under Uncertainty: The EU Approach' (2014) *ELRev.* 39, 338–361

N. Moloney, 'EU Financial Market Regulation after the Global Financial Crisis: "More Europe" or More Risks?' (2010) *CMLRev.* 47, 1317–1383

N. Moloney, 'European Banking Union: Assessing its risk and resilience' 51 (2014) *CMLRev.* 1609–1670

M. Quintyn and M.W. Taylor, 'Regulatory and Supervisory Independence and Financial Stability' (2003) *CESinfo Economics Studies*, 49(2), 259–294

M. Ruffert, 'The European Debt Crisis and European Union Law' (2011) *CMLRev.* 48, 1777–1806

W. Schelkle, 'Monetary Integration in Crisis: How Well Do Existing Theories Explain the Predicament of EMU?' (2013) *Transfer* 19(1), 37–48

M. Schwarz, 'A Memorandum of Misunderstanding—The Doomed Road of the European Stability Mechanism and a Possible Way Out: Enhanced Cooperation' (2014) *CMLRev.* 51, 389–424

R. Smits, *The European Central Bank: Institutional Aspects* (1997)

K. Tuori and K. Tuori, *The Eurozone Crisis. A Constitutional Analysis* (2014)

C. Zilioli and M. Selmayr, 'The ECB: An Independent Specialised Organisation of Community Law' (2000) *CMLRev.* 37, 591–644

CHAPTER 29

FINANCIAL MARKETS REGULATION

NIAMH MOLONEY

I. EU Financial Markets Regulation: A Primer

1. Introduction

This chapter considers the evolution and main features of EU financial markets regulation, policy, and scholarship. While often technically arcane, this field has yielded rich institutional innovation, complex constitutional conundrums as to how the requirements for optimal EU financial market governance can be fitted within Treaty constraints, powerful examples of how Member States' underlying economic models can shape their interaction with the EU, and a harmonized rule-book in support of the internal financial market the dynamic evolution of which has illustrated how the location of control over a complex and sensitive area of regulation can shift from the Member States to the EU.

The global financial crisis casts a long shadow on any discussion of EU financial markets regulation. The titanic convulsions that the crisis brought to the EU financial system in Autumn 2008, and the subsequent catastrophic damage to the EU's banking system, and consequent existential threat to the euro area as sovereigns threatened to buckle under the weight of the costs of bank rescue have led to the EU becoming the monopoly regulator of the EU financial system.[1] The upheaval has also generated radical institutional reforms that have centralized, to a precedent-setting degree, the supervision of financial institutions (and in particular euro area financial institutions) at EU level. But the crisis era is only one part of a longer and dynamic history during which the Member States have contested the location of intervention in the EU financial system and the purpose and intensity of EU intervention; the nature of EU regulatory and supervisory intervention has changed; the forces shaping EU intervention have evolved; and institutional reform has been significant and recurring.

The purpose of this chapter is to examine EU financial system regulation by considering the major features of a subset of the now behemoth EU regulatory regime—EU financial markets regulation. EU financial markets regulation addresses a core element of the modern market economy—the process of financial market intermediation[2] between suppliers of capital and firms seeking capital—and the very wide range of related market actors (such as firms seeking capital, intermediating investment firms and trading venues, 'gatekeepers' such as rating agencies and investment analysts, and capital suppliers such as investment funds), relationships, and risks that this form of financial intermediation[3] produces. The chapter does not, save by way of contrast, address other aspects of EU financial system regulation. Focusing on EU financial markets regulation serves a number of purposes. It allows for a longer historical perspective to be taken. Prior to the financial crisis, EU financial markets law was the most highly developed part of EU financial system regulation and had experienced the most advanced institutional reforms; until the crisis, banking regulation, for example, was largely concerned with capital regulation and was, for the most part, a function of the international capital standards set by the Basel Committee on Banking. This focus also sharply exposes the 'magpie' tendencies of EU financial system regulation; over its long history, EU financial markets regulation has borrowed and reshaped institutional enhancements to EU governance generally (such as 'comitology-' and agency-based governance) to meet the particular needs of financial markets governance; as they have developed, other elements of financial system regulation (mainly banking and insurance regulation) have followed this approach. It additionally reveals the longstanding and deep rifts between the Member States on the purpose, nature, and location of financial system intervention; while the euro area banking and sovereign debt crisis has thrown into sharp relief the lack of consensus across the Member States as to, for

---

[1] For reviews see David Howarth and Lucia Quaglia, 'Banking Union as Holy Grail: Rebuilding the Single Market in Financial Services, Stabilizing Europe's Banks, and "Completing" Economic and Monetary Union' (2013) 51 *Journal of Common Market Studies* 103: Eilís Ferran, 'Crisis-driven Regulatory Reform: Where in the World is the EU Going?' in Eilís Ferran, Niamh Moloney, Jennifer Hill, and John C. Coffee, *The Regulatory Aftermath of the Global Financial Crisis* (2012) 1; and the discussions in the (2009) 47 Special Edition of the *Journal of Common Market Studies*.

[2] Financial intermediation relates to the process whereby surplus funds are transferred from suppliers (savers) to those in deficit (borrowers).

[3] As noted in Section II, bank intermediation is the other major form of financial intermediation.

example, when and how banks should be supported, this newly minted location for conflict reflects longstanding differences across the Member States as to the optimum intensity of financial markets. Finally, it illustrates the extent to which EU financial system regulation is composed of multiple moving parts, many of which have been shaped by distinct influences. The recent history of banking and financial markets regulation, to take the leading example, is very different. The seismic institutional reforms to the supervision of banking in the EU, in the form of (broadly) the transfer of supervisory power over euro area banks to the European Central Bank (ECB) under the Single Supervisory Mechanism (SSM)[4] and the establishment of a Single Resolution Mechanism (SRM)[5] to manage euro area bank failure, have been driven by the euro area sovereign debt crisis; the less radical crisis-era institutional reforms to financial markets supervision have a more traditional internal-market focus, being designed to protect the internal financial market generally from supervisory failure.

Sections I.2 and I.3 below summarize the principal features of EU financial markets regulation. Sections II–IV examine the defining features of EU financial markets regulation. Section V concludes by offering brief predictions as to its future development.

2. The Evolution of EU Financial Markets Regulation

As the crisis era recedes, EU law making for financial markets is no longer an inwardly directed and somewhat technically unsophisticated business,[6] but is concerned with the construction of a sophisticated 'single rule-book' which seeks to deliver the massive regulatory repair that the financial crisis exposed as being required to almost all major regulatory systems internationally[7] and to capture emerging risks (Section II). The EU has emerged as a major force in global financial regulation[8] and EU

---

[4] Two legislative instruments support the SSM: Council Regulation (EU) No 1024/2013 [2013] OJ L287/63 (conferring supervisory tasks on the ECB) and Regulation (EU) No 1022/2013 [2013] OJ L287/5 (revising the governance of the European Banking Authority (EBA) to reflect the ECB/SSM).

[5] After very difficult negotiations, agreement was reached on the Single Resolution Mechanism in March 2014. Regulation EU (No) 806/2014 [2014] OJ L225/1. Elements of the governance of the related Single Resolution Fund are governed by an Intergovernmental Agreement.

[6] Examples of the lack of technical sophistication in the early generation of measures are legion and include eg the under-developed 1993 Investment Services Directive (Dir 93/22/EC [1993] OJ L141/27), which was replaced by the massive Markets in Financial Instruments Directive I (Dir 2004/39/EC [2004] OJ L39/1) and its dense administrative rule-book, which, until the crisis-era reforms, was the cornerstone of the regulation of investment services and trading venues in the EU.

[7] The G20-driven reform agenda was initially laid out in: Washington G20 Summit on Financial Markets and the World Economy, November 2008, Declaration of the Summit on Financial Markets and the World Economy, Action Plan to Implement Principles for Reform.

[8] Well illustrated by the many battles over the crisis era between the US and the EU over control of the new global rule-book, particularly with respect to the regulation of the global derivatives market. For a review see Atlantic Council, *The Danger of Divergence: Transatlantic Reform & the G20 Agenda* (2013).

rule making is now shaped by a technically expert agency, the European Securities and Markets Authority (ESMA),[9] a new agency established in January 2011 (Section IV). The regulatory perimeter has been significantly expanded, and harmonization is at a high level of intensity; a thick layer of administrative rules and of 'soft law' measures is being encrusted on to a detailed legislative rule-book, reflecting the enhanced capacity for administrative rule making/standard setting which ESMA has brought.[10]

While its technical sophistication and the extent to which it has displaced the Member States as regulator might distinguish EU financial markets regulation from other spheres of EU harmonization, its distinctive features are perhaps most apparent with respect to its operational quality. Market supervision, long the preserve of national competent (supervisory) authorities (NCAs) and so a safety valve for national interests and supervisory flexibility, is increasingly becoming subject to EU decision making. The supervision of the EU's financial system is now carried out through the 'European System of Financial Supervision' (ESFS), which was established in January 2011. It is composed of the NCAs which provide the foundations of the system; the three sectoral European Supervisory Authorities (ESAs), charged with a range of coordinating and supervisory functions—ESMA, the European Banking Authority (EBA), the European Insurance and Occupational Pensions Authority (EIOPA), and their coordinating ESA Joint Committee; and the European Systemic Risk Board (ESRB), which is charged with monitoring system-wide risks and macro-prudential stability. Since November 2014, the ESFS has included the ECB as the actor responsible for the supervision of the euro area's banks under the SSM. The ESFS operates on a sectoral basis. In financial markets, supervision is carried out by the NCAs for financial markets, ESMA, and the ESRB, and is, in large part, decentralized; operational supervision (and enforcement) remains at Member State level with the NCAs. But the principle of centralized supervision at EU level has been conceded with the establishment of ESMA and the conferral on it of a range of supervisory powers which extend across a spectrum from coordination of supervisory activities by NCAs to full-scale intervention by ESMA in local markets, which disables the relevant NCA.[11]

It was not always thus. EU financial markets regulation has developed incrementally reflecting, as cognate political science scholarship predicts and

---

[9] Regulation (EU) No 1095/2010 [2010] OJ L331/84.

[10] For assessments see eg Niamh Moloney, 'Resetting the Location of Regulatory and Supervisory Control over EU Financial Markets: Lessons from Five Years On' (2013) 62 *International and Comparative Law Quarterly* 955; Niamh Moloney, 'EU Financial Market Regulation after the Global Financial Crisis: "More Europe" or More Risks?' (2010) 47 *Common Market Law Review* 1317; and Peter Mülbert and Alexander Wilhelm, 'Reforms of EU Banking and Securities Regulation after the Financial Crisis' (2010) 26 *Banking and Finance Law Review* 187.

[11] For early assessments see Pierre Schammo, 'EU Day to Day Supervision or Intervention-based Supervision: Which Way Forward for the European System of Financial Supervision' (2012) 32 *Oxford Journal of Legal Studies* 771 and Niamh Moloney, 'The European Securities and Markets Authority and Institutional Design for the EU Financial Markets—a Tale of Two Competences: Part (2) Supervision' (2011) 12 *European Business Organization Law Review* 177.

documents,[12] a host of determinative factors which have, at different times and in different ways, shaped the regime, including financial market conditions, prevailing political dynamics, international financial market pressures, and institutional reforms. The EU's first attempts (in the 1970s), reflecting the then embryonic state of EU financial markets, were limited in scope and, reflecting the rudimentary nature of EU harmonization techniques generally, based on detailed, equivalence-based measures, riddled with exceptions and derogations, which failed in their objective of supporting cross-border capital raising. In the 1980s and early 1990s, the minimum harmonization/mutual recognition device pioneered by the Court of Justice and Commission, combined with policy recognition of the potential of an internal financial market to support growth, led to the first growth spurt; minimum-harmonization Directives supported regulatory 'passports' to the internal market (based on home NCA control of cross-border activity) for the actors then most strongly associated with the still nascent EU financial market (firms seeking capital, investment firms, and investment funds). A second, and more significant, growth spurt took place over the Financial Services Action Plan (FSAP) era (1999–2004), when a liberalizing agenda of great range and depth was pursued that led to an intensification of EU intervention (supported by the first serious application of administrative rule-making techniques), the conferral of regulatory passports on a much wider set of market actors, and to the first attempt at supervisory coordination. Following a subsequent 'dynamic consolidation phase' (2005–2007),[13] a further and defining growth spurt took place over the financial crisis era (2008–present).

After nearly 50 years of EU engagement,[14] the principle of EU control over financial markets regulation has largely been ceded. But unresolved tensions across the Member States as to the extent to which the internal financial market should be supported and regulated continue to open up new fault lines in EU financial market regulation.

3. Shifting Scholarly Perspectives

As the EU financial markets regime has evolved, so too has related scholarship. Legal scholarship was from the outset preoccupied with whether the EU or its Member States was the optimum rule maker for the EU financial market.[15] This

[12] eg Lucia Quaglia, *Governing Financial Services in the European Union: Banking, Securities, and Post-trading* (2010).

[13] Commission, White Paper on Financial Services Policy 2005–2010 COM (2005) 629.

[14] The starting point for EU intervention can be traced to the seminal 1966 Segre Report: Report by a Group of Experts Appointed by the EEC Commission, *The Development of a European Capital Market* (1966).

[15] As originally canvassed in the distinguished early work of Buxbaum, Hopt, and Wymeersch: Eddy Wymeersch, *Control of Securities Markets in the European Economic Community, Collection Studies,*

debate, which intensified along with EU intervention and which had significant traction until the crisis era, was largely expressed through discussion of the relative merits of harmonization and regulatory competition, drew heavily on the US federal experience with corporate law and financial market regulation, and was typically sceptical of harmonization.[16] A parallel line of scholarship focused less on the location of intervention and more on the nature of the new rules, and probed the EU's initial (and often unsophisticated) attempts to grapple with elusive concepts such as investor protection, market transparency, and market efficiency, often drawing on the US regime, given the long experience of US regulation and scholarship with financial market regulation.[17] In many Member States, the under-developed state of financial markets meant that modern financial market regulation was adopted only in response to EU requirements. As the EU's efforts intensified, and as financial markets scholarship generally became more sophisticated, legal scholarship began to grapple with the asserted transformative effect of EU financial markets law (Section II).[18] Close attention also began to focus on the EU regime as a regional example of 'international financial regulation', a burgeoning if elusive field,[19] while the solutions to regional coordination adopted by the EU came under scrutiny from US scholarship.[20] The crisis era has seen an explosion in legal scholarship that tests the logic and resilience of the new rules and the institutional reforms.[21] Increasingly, and reflecting the EU's status as monopoly rule provider, legal analysis focuses on the quality of EU rules in terms of the outcomes they seek, and with respect to their regulatory design, rather than on the EU context and the distinct process through which harmonized rules emerge.[22]

Competition, Approximation of Legislation Series No 31 (1977) and Richard Buxbaum and Klaus Hopt, *Legal Harmonisation and the Business Enterprise* (1988).

[16] Leading examples include Pierre Schammo, *EU Prospectus Law: New Perspectives on Regulatory Competition in Securities Markets* (2011); Luca Enriques and Matteo Gatti, 'Is there a Uniform EU Securities Law after the Financial Services Action Plan?' (2008) 14 *Stanford Journal of Law, Business and Finance* 43; Luca Enriques, 'EC Company Law Directives and Regulations: How Trivial Are They?' (2006) 27 *University of Pennsylvania Journal of International Economic Law* 1; and Gerard Hertig, 'Regulatory Competition for EU Financial Services' in Daniel Esty and Damien Geradin (eds), *Regulatory Competition and Economic Integration* (2001) 218.

[17] For early examples see Guido Ferrarini, 'The European Regulation of Stock Exchanges: New Perspectives' (1999) 36 *Common Market Law Review* 569 and Niamh Moloney, 'New Frontiers in EC Capital Markets Law: From Market Construction to Market Regulation' (2003) 40 *Common Market Law Review* 809.

[18] For a leading example, see Eilís Ferran, *Building an EU Capital Market* (2004).

[19] eg Eric Pan, 'Four Challenges to Financial Regulatory Reform' (2009) 55 *Villanova Law Review* 101.

[20] eg Donald Langevoort, 'Structuring Securities Regulation in the European Union: Lessons from the US Experience' in Guido Ferrarini and Eddy Wymeersch (eds), *Investor Protection in Europe: Corporate Law Making, the MiFID and Beyond* (2006) 485.

[21] eg from a massive and burgeoning literature; see the articles in the (2013) 2 edition of the *Journal of Corporate Law Studies*.

[22] For an example examining the quality of crisis-era EU rules from a behavioural finance perspective, see Emilios Avgouleas, 'The Global Financial Crisis, Behavioural Finance and Financial

EU financial markets regulation has also long been of interest to cognate fields, having strong resonances in particular with the fields of comparative political economy, given its promotion of market finance, and political science, given the rich case study that the Member States' battle for control over financial markets regulation provides (Section II). Close attention has also followed from governance scholars who have examined, inter alia, the nature and dynamics of the delegation structures deployed in this area.[23] The crisis era has prompted renewed and intense interest in the shape of and influences on EU financial markets regulation, including from governance specialists (notably with respect to the institutional reforms),[24] regulatory theorists (including with respect to the EU as a 'system manager'),[25] and, as the location of influence over EU financial markets shifted across the EU's polycentric rule making process and as the longstanding tensions between the Member State as to the nature of financial markets were laid bare, political scientists and economists.[26] Increasingly, analysis of EU financial markets regulation weaves together insights from multiple cognate disciplines, including law, political science, and political economy.[27]

II. Transformative Ambitions: Supporting an Integrated Market and Market Finance

1. Market Integration

One of the defining features of EU financial markets regulation relates to the extent to which it seeks to be transformative with respect to market integration (this section) and with respect to the embedding of market finance (Section II.2).

Regulation in Search of a New Orthodoxy' (2009) 9 *Journal of Corporate Law Studies* 23. Similarly, examining the nature of the EU's intervention in retail markets, Niamh Moloney, *How to Protect Investors: Lessons from the EC and the UK* (2010).

[23] See eg Mark Thatcher and David Coen, 'Network Governance and Multi-level Delegations: European Networks of Regulatory Agencies' (2008) 28 *Journal of Public Policy* 49.

[24] eg Michelle Everson, *A Technology of Expertise: EU Financial Services Agencies* (2012) LSE Europe in Question Discussion Paper Series No 49/2012 (2012).

[25] eg Julia Black, 'Restructuring Global and EU Financial Regulation: Capacities, Coordination and Learning' in Guido Ferrarini, Klaus Hopt, and Eddy Wymeersch (eds), *Rethinking Financial Regulation and Supervision in Times of Crisis* (2012).

[26] For a review see Daniel Mügge, *Financial Regulation in the EU: A Research Agenda* (2012).

[27] eg Daniel Mügge (ed), *Europe and the Governance of Global Finance* (2014).

EU law and policy have long assumed that a single financial market, within which, supported by a harmonized legal infrastructure, market actors can access cross-border markets, should broaden and deepen pools of capital in the EU. It has also long been assumed that integration should drive a reduction in the cost of capital for firms, promote stronger risk management, and lead to stronger growth and employment.[28] These governing assumptions can be traced back to the seminal 1966 Segré Report[29] and have been at the core of EU intervention ever since. Empirical support was some time in coming, however, and initially took the form of the 2002 London Economics report for the Commission, which provided empirical support for the FSAP reform agenda.[30]

But internal financial market construction is a complex business; integration depends on a wide range of variables, including domestic and international market conditions, taxation, infrastructure, investor demand (and the removal of the investor 'home bias' which privileges domestic investments), the availability of risk management mechanisms, and strong intermediation through investment firms and other intermediating actors. The intuition that harmonization alone is unlikely to be a 'magic bullet' received support from the 'law and finance' mode of analysis which gained significant traction internationally in the 2000s (as the EU programme intensified), and which probes the relationship between law and financial market development, and which, accordingly, can be (and has been[31]) usefully applied to EU financial markets regulation. While the nature of the causal relationship between law and strong markets remains fiercely contested,[32] there is certainly doubt as to the extent to which law can drive financial market development, domestically, regionally, or internationally.[33]

The costs of harmonization may therefore be high, particularly where harmonization does not support Member State flexibility, respond to local conditions, or allow the incubation of regulatory solutions to evolving financial market risks. The empirical evidence on EU financial market integration also bears out the need for caution, and suggests that it is not clear that there is a direct causal connection between a harmonized EU legal infrastructure and levels of market integration.[34] While strong evidence of financial market integration has been recorded in the Commission's annual assessments,[35] the financial crisis has underlined the extent to which economy-wide

---

[28] For a recent argument see ECB, *Financial Integration in Europe* (2012).   [29] See n 14.

[30] London Economics, *Quantification of the Macro-Economic Impact of Integration of EU Financial Markets: Final Report to the EU Commission* (2002).

[31] eg Ferran (n 18).

[32] See eg John Armour, Simon Deakin, Viviana Mollica, and Mathias Siems, *Law and Financial Development: What We Are Learning from Time-series Evidence*, ECGI Law Working Paper No 148/2010 (2010).

[33] The research was originally spearheaded by the work of financial economists Rafael La Porta, Florencio Lopez de Silanes, Andrei Shleifer, and Robert Vishny (LLSV) (eg 'Law and Finance' (1998) 106 *Journal of Political Economy* 1113).

[34] eg CRA International, *Evaluation of the Economic Impacts of the FSAP* (2009).

[35] The Commission reviews progress through its annual European Financial Stability and Integration Reports; the ECB reviews euro area progress in its annual Financial Integration in Europe Reports.

and market shocks can lead to a material retrenchment within domestic markets.[36] It is not unreasonable, however, to suggest that a supportive legal infrastructure is, at least, a necessary pre-condition for integration. It is also the case that the debate as to the extent to which EU financial markets law can drive integration has lost some traction, as the crisis era has led to reshaping of political and market conditions and to support for a single EU rule-book as a hedge against cross-border risk transmission.

2. Market Finance

The construction of an integrated financial market implies the adoption by the EU, to a significant extent, of the market finance model. In very broad terms, in economies based on market finance (or market-based financial intermediation), banks typically rely heavily on fee-based income sources (such as trading activities), non-bank intermediaries play a significant role in the capital intermediation process, and there is significant reliance on financial products to manage risks; firms also rely on market-based financing through the issuance of securities. In bank-based intermediation, banks take deposits and make loans and are the major form of financial intermediation, channelling funds from savers to capital seekers and relying on interest income as a main source of income. Market finance can accordingly be associated with higher levels of financial market intensity.[37]

Whatever the respective risks and benefits of different financial intermediation models, the EU's commitment to market finance is longstanding. But, as has been extensively examined in the literature, market finance has long lagged bank finance; bank finance has traditionally been associated with the major economies of France and Germany and with continental Europe generally, and market finance with the UK, and to differing degrees, the Netherlands and the Nordic Member States. The construction of an integrated financial market and the related adoption of market finance accordingly demands some very heavy policy and regulatory lifting by the EU, the dynamics of which have received close attention.

In particular, the influential Varieties of Capitalism (VoC) literature[38] relates types of financial intermediation models to states' distinct institutional structures. It has classified the dominant economy types as the Liberal Market Economy

---

[36] eg Commission, European Financial Stability and Integration Report 2011 (2012) (SWD (2012) 103) and Commission, European Financial Integration and Stability Report 2012 (2013) (SWD (2013) 156).

[37] In the EU context see eg Iain Hardie and David Howarth, *What Varieties of Financial Capitalism? The Financial Crisis and the Move to 'Market-Based Banking' in the UK, Germany, and France*, Political Studies Association Paper (2010).

[38] The foundational work is Peter Hall and David Soskice (eds), *Varieties of Capitalism: The Institutional Foundations of Comparative Advantage* (2001). For a review of the scholarship see Kathleen Thelen, 'Varieties of Capitalism: Trajectories of Liberalization and the New Politics of Social Solidarity' (2012) 15 *Annual Review of Political Science* 137.

(LME) and the Co-ordinated Market Economy (CME). This broad classification, which probes the underlying political economy of states, has important implications for the EU's financial market integration project. It describes the CME as being, inter alia, based on 'patient' (long-term) capital, typically supplied by banks through loan assets, close relationships between banks and firms, the monitoring of firms (and capital) by networks (including of banks, employees, and clients), strong stakeholder relationships, and as not dependent on publicly available information. The LME, by contrast, is based on market-based funding, a related focus on share price and current earnings, and a more short-term orientation, strong market monitoring, including through aggressive takeover activity, and publicly available information. Domestic legal frameworks for contracting and standard setting tend to reinforce these patterns of economic coordination; the LME is typically associated with more facilitative and the CME with more intrusive regulation. The VoC analysis posits that states derive a comparative advantage from these interlinked institutional infrastructures and related economy type, and can be expected to protect those institutions.

The VoC analysis accordingly exposes the scale of the EU's challenge. While it implies that law (harmonization), as an aspect of institutional structure, can shape financial intermediation models, it also suggests that Member States can be expected to protect their institutional models and their related competitive advantage in single-market-related negotiations;[39] in an over-simplification, CME states might be expected to resist moves to a more liberal, market-based system, while LME states might be expected to resist a more intrusive regulatory-intensive model for integration.[40]

The underlying institutional and related financial intermediation models of Member States represent, however, only one force among the many that shape EU financial market integration and engagement with market finance, and which are dissipated and/or concentrated across the EU's complex policy formation and rule making apparatus. A related rich scholarship examines the array of Member State/ intergovernmental, supranational, and industry/private forces that have shaped the legal infrastructure supporting financial market integration and market finance, and the extent to which and how financial markets have integrated and market finance has developed. Intergovernmental analyses, for example, have long located primary influence with the Member States and, chiming with the VoC analysis, initially characterized financial market integration as a 'battle of the systems' in which,

---

[39] In the internal market context generally see eg Jukka Snell, 'Varieties of Capitalism and the Limits of European Economic Integration' (2010–2011) 13 *Cambridge Yearbook of European Legal Studies* 415.

[40] For a VoC analysis of EU takeover regulation, see Ben Clift, 'The Second Time as Farce? The EU Takeover Directive, the Clash of Capitalisms, and the Hamstrung Harmonization of European (and French) Corporate Governance' (2009) 47 *Journal of Common Market Studies* 55.

particularly in the early stages of the integration project, Member States sought to shape financial integration to their own domestic models and to avoid conferring competitive advantage on other states.[41] More recently, intergovernmental interaction has been characterized less in terms of bank v market finance (or CME v LME), and, reflecting the array of forces that seem to shape Member States' interests, more broadly in terms of a 'market-making' coalition (led by the UK and typically including the Netherlands and the Nordic Member States, and associated with market-led, more liberal regulation), and a 'market-shaping' coalition (led by France and typically including Italy and Spain, and associated with more intrusive regulation, particularly of unregulated sectors).[42] Other accounts locate significant power with the Commission[43] and other supranational institutions, and within the networks of national and EU-level regulators/agencies and committees that have come to shape the EU rule-book for financial markets.[44] Private actors have also been identified as increasingly influential.[45] These forces change over time, as the crisis, and the ascendancy of a more intrusive EU approach to regulation and of scepticism towards financial markets, has revealed.[46] But the crisis has also exposed how coalitions can shift between Member States depending on the particular 'mix' of interests at stake, as well as the changing positions of the supranational institutions.[47]

But whatever the dynamics of the related harmonization programme and the doubts as to its impact, market finance has, reflecting wider institutional changes, taken root in the EU.[48] The extensive monitoring since the early days of the crisis of financial stability in the EU[49] paints a clear picture of the extent to which market-based intermediation had become embedded.[50] Nonetheless, the location and intensity of financial market intervention remains contested, reflecting the deep fault lines which continue to rumble beneath the relatively stable integration consensus.

[41] Classically, Jonathan Story and Ingo Walter, *Political Economy of Financial Integration in Europe* (1997).

[42] Lucia Quaglia, 'Completing the Single Market in Financial Services: The Politics of Competing Advocacy Coalitions' (2010) 17 *Journal of European Public Policy* 1007.

[43] eg Quaglia (n 11).

[44] eg Mark Thatcher and David Coen, 'Reshaping European Regulatory Space: An Evolutionary Analysis' (2009) 31 *Western European Politics* 806.

[45] Daniel Mügge, *Widen the Market, Narrow the Competition: Banker Interests in the Making of a European Capital Market* (2010).

[46] eg Lucia Quaglia, 'The "Old" and "New" Political Economy of Hedge Fund Regulation in the EU' (2011) 34 *West European Politics* 665.

[47] eg James Buckley and David Howarth, 'Internal Market Gesture Politics? Explaining the EU's Response to the Financial Crisis' (2010) *Journal of Common Market Studies* 119 and Ferran (n 1).

[48] eg Iain Hardie and David Howarth, 'Die Krise but not La Crise? The Financial Crisis and the Transformation of German and French Banking Systems' (2009) 47 *Journal of Common Market Studies* 1017.

[49] The inter-linkages between markets and the financial system generally are regularly monitored by a range of EU actors, including the ECB (through its six-monthly Financial Stability Reviews).

[50] For a recent example see ESMA, *Trends, Risks and Vulnerabilities Report No 2* (ESMA/2013/1138) (2013).

III. Shifts in the Location
and Intensity
of Financial Market Intervention

1. Ever-intensifying EU Intervention

A second defining feature of the EU regime relates to the highly dynamic and ever-intensifying nature of intervention. Intervention has, until very recently, when supervision (and enforcement[51]) came on the EU's agenda, taken the form of rule harmonization in support of the internal market. A tolerance of regulatory competition was embedded within the regime during the 'minimum standards' period (1985–late 1990s), but this period was followed by the FSAP and crisis eras which, in effect, removed regulatory competition. Over time, and reflecting the demands that market liberalization poses in the financial markets sphere, a sphere in which Member State interests in regulation are strong and cross-border risks high, harmonization has become ever more intensive,[52] thereby reordering the relationship between Member States and the EU and reshaping the scholarly debate.

Over the FSAP era (1999–2004), EU financial markets regulation went through its first major period of intensification, in support of market liberalization and reflecting vibrant market conditions and related political support for market finance (as set out in the 'Lisbon agenda'[53]). With hindsight, it is now clear that the FSAP 'rule-book' was incomplete and left large segments of the market largely unregulated. Nonetheless, under the FSAP, harmonization became a device through which centralized regulation was imposed on the EU marketplace (and on domestic and cross-border actors), albeit to support access to a rapidly evolving and increasingly sophisticated cross-border market. But the FSAP did not entirely remove Member State control. It did not formally deploy maximum harmonization in its pillar legislative measures. While a plethora of administrative rules was adopted, using the governance technology available under the then novel Lamfalussy process (Section IV.1), these rules were often based on minimum harmonization. But overall, by the end of the FSAP period and immediately prior to the crisis, a commitment had emerged to limit Member State discretion in order to curb the encrustation of national rules through 'gold-plating' and to support the cross-border market.

---

[51] The crisis-era generation of financial market measures are significantly more prescriptive with respect to the enforcement measures which must be available to NCAs and, in a significant incursion on local autonomy, specify, eg, minimum levels of pecuniary penalty.

[52] eg between 2003 and 2013, there has been (approximately) a ten-fold increase in the volume of EU law on financial services generally: HM Treasury, *Single Market: Financial Services and the Free Movement of Capital, Call for Evidence* (2013) 19.

[53] Lisbon Council Conclusions, 23–24 March 2000.

Immediately prior to the financial crisis (2005–2008) and in an indication of how closely the harmonization project had become a regulatory one that reflected global regulatory trends, there were some indications of a pulling back; the Commission sought a 'regulatory pause'[54] during which, and reflecting the global regulation-sceptical Zeitgeist, it began to rely on 'softer' mechanisms, including non-binding codes of conduct, and committed to self-regulation in some sectors (notably in relation to hedge funds). This would not last, with the financial crisis and the related preoccupation with financial stability leading to the regulatory function of EU financial markets regulation trumping the liberalization function. The perimeter of EU regulation has now been cast around a much broader set of market participants. A much wider range of asset classes and a host of trading venues have also been pulled in: for example, the combined effect of a series of measures is to impose an entirely new and intrusive rule-book on derivatives trading in the EU, which had largely been disciplined through market dynamics prior to the crisis. Actors have come within the regulatory net not because of the need to support a regulatory passport (the driver of FSAP/pre-crisis intervention), but because they pose risks to financial stability and/or have not been subject to intensive regulation. The new rule-book is characterized by detailed legislative measures which typically take the form of a Regulation, rather than a Directive, in order to avoid implementation risks, and a dense administrative rule-book, which dwarfs that constructed over the FSAP era, is under development.

The almost complete ascendancy of the EU over financial markets regulation[55] has been driven by a host of factors. The 'single rule-book' initially proposed by the EU's seminal crisis-era 'DLG' report[56] enjoyed early and widespread support from the Member States and the EU institutions. While the EU's supranational actors could always have been expected to support stronger intervention, from an intergovernmental perspective the rule-book acts as a hedge against the fiscal risks of cross-border activity and poor supervision; the rule-book consensus might also be associated with a pragmatic transfer by the Member States of the risks associated with financial market regulation at a time of intense crisis. The need to implement the extensive G20 agenda and the EU's related concern to shape the international rule-book has also led to support for more intensive intervention. In addition, the rule-book can be associated with a strong 'market-sceptical' agenda. Underlying tensions between the Member States as to the benefits of the market finance model burst out to dramatic effect as the financial crisis deepened, and became explosive as turmoil gripped the EU's sovereign debt markets over 2011 and 2012 in particular. Hostility to perceived

---

[54] Commission 2005–2010 White Paper (n 13).

[55] See further Niamh Moloney, 'The European Securities and Markets Authority and Institutional Design for the EU Financial Markets—a Tale of Two Competences: Part (1) Rule-Making' (2011) 12 *European Business Organization Law Review* 41.

[56] The High Level Group on Financial Supervision in the EU, Report (2009; the de Larosière Report or DLG Report).

excessive speculation and suspicion of market intensity and innovation have shaped, in particular, the new rating agency regime, the new regime governing alternative investment funds, and the new trading regime.

The extent to which the EU is now accepted as the rule maker for national markets is well illustrated by the Commission seizing the initiative as the crisis-era reform programme began to abate and when the global interest-rate fixing scandal broke over the summer of 2012,[57] and, in a similarly high-profile area, capturing the reform agenda with respect to the new 'crowdfunding' techniques for raising finance which are attracting regulatory attention internationally.[58] EU financial markets regulation is not yet, however, monolithic; the regulation of consumer financial markets remains, to a large extent, a creature of national law, although even here, where there are few justifications for EU intervention given the local nature of EU household engagement with markets[59] and sharp divergences across the EU in how households invest,[60] the EU is extending its reach.[61] Overall, the indications suggest an acceptance that the EU responds to emerging regulatory challenges, whether defensively with respect to risk management, or more proactively with respect to supporting strong markets.[62]

The intensification of the rule-book has been accompanied by radical changes to how cross-border supervision is organized. While NCAs retain primary responsibility for operational supervision (supervision is generally anchored to the home NCA which must coordinate with the host NCA which retains limited supervisory powers, particularly over branches of firms), a range of supervisory powers have been conferred on ESMA. First, ESMA engages in a range of cross-border home/host NCA (or home/home NCA, in the case of cross-border activity through subsidiaries) coordination activities. Second, in a significant change, it is empowered to act as a supervisor and to exercise direct, if carefully enumerated, supervisory powers. Some of these powers relate to ESMA's relations with NCAs. ESMA's NCA-orientated direct supervisory powers have given the EU a capacity to enhance NCA compliance with EU law, to take coordinated action in a crisis, and to break through NCA deadlock with binding mediation. ESMA also has direct and exclusive sector-specific supervisory powers over two actors with extensive cross-border

---

[57] eg COM (2013) 641 (proposing a general benchmark regulation regime).

[58] Commission, Consultation on Crowdfunding in the EU—Exploring the Added Value of Potential EU Action (2013) and Commission, Unleashing the Potential of Crowdfunding in the EU (2014) (COM (2014) 172).

[59] eg Decision Technology, Nick Chater, Steffen Huck, Roman Inderst, and Online Interactive Research, *Consumer Decision Making in Retail Investment Services: A Behavioural Economics Perspective* (2010).

[60] eg ECB, *The Eurosystem Household Financial and Consumption Survey, Results from the First Wave*, Statistics Paper Series No 2 (2013).

[61] eg the 2012 Commission Proposal for a horizontal disclosure regime governing 'packaged retail investment products' (COM (2012) 352/3). Agreement was reached on the new regime in April 2014.

[62] Well illustrated by Commission, Green Paper, Long Term Financing of the European Economy (2013) (COM (2013) 150/2), which, published in the final stages of the crisis-era reform programme, suggests something of an unstoppable regulatory momentum.

reach—rating agencies and 'trade repositories' (in effect, derivative market data banks). It also has more limited direct operational powers over specific areas (including with respect to short selling and product prohibition) under particular legislative measures. More generally, ESMA can exercise direct supervisory powers over financial market participants in cases of NCA breach of EU law, in emergency situations, and where ESMA is empowered to mediate between NCAs. Although all these direct supervisory powers are subject to strict conditionality of various types, they represent the first time an EU body has been conferred with binding operational authority over financial market participants and NCAs. Third, ESMA is empowered to support supervisory convergence by shaping day-to-day local supervision by NCAs through, for example, peer review and the adoption of guidance.

2. Changing the Location of Control

The changing nature of intervention has implications for the nature of contestation on EU financial market intervention.

The wider the regulatory perimeter, the greater the risk that EU intervention has asymmetric impact, given the tendency for particular financial market businesses and activities to concentrate in particular domestic markets. Prior to the financial crisis, the longstanding tensions on the nature of EU intervention were, broadly, contained; the regulatory programme was generally facilitative and regulatory costs could be offset by market access benefits. But the crisis-era programme is significantly more regulatory in orientation and reaches deep into national markets. It can more easily be associated with prejudicial regulatory costs and accordingly with the asymmetric imposition of regulatory burdens depending on the particular nature of domestic financial markets. The single market consensus therefore risks coming under pressure.

The difficult institutional and Member State negotiations on the crisis-era rule-book sharply exposed the scale of this risk.[63] But the organization of operational supervision, and in particular the related institutional reforms, has become a new source of tension. In some respects, ESMA sits on the same level as the NCAs, but with discrete responsibility for particular market actors. ESMA can also be, relatively benignly, regarded as a hub at the centre of a circle of NCA spokes, overseeing the quality, consistency, and effectiveness of supervision. But in other respects, the ESMA/NCA relationship can be regarded as hierarchical and ESMA can be regarded as limiting NCA autonomy. This ambiguity as to ESMA's characterization underlines the fact that the optimum location of financial market supervision within the EU remains unresolved (and may not be amenable to a clear resolution), and that tidy institutional solutions and allocations of competences are likely to remain elusive. It also underlines the potential for serious tension.

---

[63] See further Ferran (n 1).

In the short term these tensions are likely to be managed through the European Court of Justice. Prior to the crisis, it had not played a major role in the development of EU financial markets regulation. Its jurisprudence was mainly concerned with applying the Treaty free movement guarantees to financial markets,[64] although it has also ruled on substantive aspects of the regime.[65] As tensions have increased between the Member States, in particular with the intensification of intervention, litigation has followed. An unsuccessful challenge has been made to the validity of ESMA's powers to intervene in a national market, and displace the NCA, with respect to short selling.[66] Challenges have also been made to the validity of the major banking measure (the 2013 Capital Requirements Directive IV),[67] and (unsuccessfully) to the validity of a proposed (2013) financial transaction tax being adopted among a group of Member States under the Treaty-based 'enhanced cooperation' mechanism.[68] Together, these actions represent a significant challenge to the validity of EU intervention in financial system regulation.[69] While the substantive questions vary in each case, these challenges all require(d) the Court to rule on how the foundation Treaty settlement as to the organization of power at EU level relates to the location of control over financial system regulation and supervision.

IV. Institutional Innovation and Financial Markets Governance

1. Institutional Innovation

Finally, EU financial markets law can be strongly associated with institutional innovation and with the related constitutional conundrums which allied attempts to shoe-horn the institutional needs of EU financial markets governance into the parameters imposed by the Treaty generate.

---

[64] eg Case C-384/93 *Alpine Investments v Minister van Financiën* [1995] ECR I-1141 and Case C-101/94 *Commission v Italy* [1996] ECR I-2691.

[65] Including on the pivotal Markets in Financial Instruments Directive (MiFID I) (n 6). See eg Case C-604/11 *Genil 48 SL, Comercial Hostelera de Grandes Vinos SL v Bankinter SA, Banca Bilbao Vizcaya Argentaria SA*, 30 May 2013.

[66] Case C-270/12 *UK v Council and Parliament*, judgment of 22 January 2014.

[67] Case C-507/13 *UK v Council and Parliament*. In November 2014 the Advocate General found against the UK position and the UK subsequently withdrew the action.

[68] Case C-209/13 *UK v Council and Parliament*, judgment of 30 April 2014.

[69] In all cases, the actions have been brought by the UK, reflecting the increasingly asymmetric impact of the crisis-era rule-book on the wholesale markets in particular.

As has been well documented, financial markets governance has specific needs. Nimble and empirically informed rule making is a prerequisite for an optimal financial markets rule-book. In response, regulatory systems worldwide typically delegate technical rule making to expert regulators. Supervision, the second major element of financial markets governance had, until the crisis era, received generally less policy (and scholarly) attention than rule making. The crisis era, however, has underlined the importance of robust, judgment-based, and proactive supervision by regulators to ensuring the stability and efficiency of financial markets. But the achievement of effective financial markets governance for the EU is a challenge.

(a) Rule making

The EU's complex, inter-institutional legislative processes are ill-suited to delivering optimal financial markets rules. Incremental reforms, based on a recycling of the EU's institutional technology for administrative rule making, have, however, led to a rule making apparatus which accommodates, if somewhat uneasily, the needs of financial markets governance. In particular, the EU's agency regime and its 'comitology' process for administrative rule making have provided useful 'off-the-shelf' templates. As outlined in Section IV.2, the constraints posed by the Treaty have, however, been troublesome. Some optimism is warranted, as the forward lurches that have characterized the development of rule making governance have usually been accompanied by significant institutional learning, and review and assessment have been recurring features.[70] Nonetheless, procedural inefficiencies and institutional tensions tend to recur and are often exacerbated in each cycle of institutional reform.

The first major reform came in 2000 when the Lamfalussy Report[71] called for radical reform to financial markets rule making in order to ensure the ambitious FSAP reform agenda was realized. But this reform was dependent on wider EU reforms. The 1999 reforms to the comitology process[72] provided a framework within which a distinct model for financial market rule making could be adopted. The institutional conditions were therefore in place for the Lamfalussy Report to make its seminal recommendation that the law making process for financial markets be categorized as involving: 'level 1' high-level rules adopted by the co-legislators; 'level 2' technical (or administrative) rules adopted by the Commission under a delegation of power from the co-legislators, advised by the technically expert Committee of European Securities Regulators (CESR, which grew from the precursor Federation of European Securities Commissions), and overseen by a new committee of Member

---

[70] The Lamfalussy process was reviewed over the 2007 Lamfalussy Review, while 2013 saw the launch of the Commission's required review of the ESFS (including ESMA).

[71] Final Report of the Committee of Wise Men on the Regulation of European Securities Markets (2001).

[72] Council Decision 99/468/EC [1999] OJ L184/23.

State representatives (the European Securities Committee: ESC) which would act within the comitology framework; 'level 3' non-binding 'supervisory convergence' measures adopted by CESR; and 'level 4' enforcement activity by the Commission. Over the FSAP era, the institutions learned to play a new law making game, the ESC and CESR matured, and administrative rule making became embedded as a key element of EU financial market governance. This led to a paradigmatic shift in the intensity of EU intervention and in the balance of power between the Member States and the EU, reflected in the extensive FSAP-era administrative rule-book as well as the plethora of soft law which CESR (albeit from an insecure account-ability and legitimacy foundation) produced. The Lamfalussy model quickly came to be regarded as a success and was transplanted to the banking and insurance/occupational pension fields. A period of relative calm followed, during which, as the shadows of the crisis began to lengthen, minor changes were made. Over this period, scholarship followed the new model, with legal scholars, governance schol-ars, and political scientists examining, inter alia, the incremental development of the Lamfalussy model, the accretion of power by CESR, the accountability and legitimacy difficulties, and the shifting location of power and influence across the rule making structure.[73]

The second (current) institutional reform is unusual in that it has been crisis driven. But the institutional reforms are less radical than at first might appear. As with the Lamfalussy era, wider Treaty and institutional developments and legacy effects have been determinative. The 2009 Lisbon Treaty provided a settlement to the long-running battle between the Parliament and Council as to the nature of administrative rule making. The classification by the Treaty of EU rule making into 'legislative' rules (Article 289 TFEU, 'level 1') and 'delegated' and 'implement-ing' rules (Articles 290 and 291 TFEU, 'level 2'), and the settlement adopted in rela-tion to the oversight procedures for Article 290 and 291 rules, in combination with the EU's agency regime and the availability of CESR as an 'off-the-shelf' institu-tional template provided the foundations for the recasting, as recommended by the DLG Report, of CESR and the parallel banking and insurance/occupational pension committees into agencies (the ESAs) empowered with a range of stronger, quasi rule making powers.

With the related establishment of ESMA, administrative rule making has come a step closer to the traditional regulatory agency model. ESMA has been conferred with an array of quasi-rule making powers, chief among them the power to pro-pose a new form of administrative rule, the 'Binding Technical Standard' (BTS).

---

[73] eg Christian de Visscher, Olivier Maisocq, and Frédéric Varone, 'The Lamfalussy Reform in the EU Securities Markets: Fiduciary Relationships, Policy Effectiveness, and the Balance of Power' (2008) 28 *Journal of Public Policy* 19 and Guido Ferrarini, 'Contract Standards and the Markets in Financial Instruments Directive: An Assessment of the Lamfalussy Regulatory Architecture' (2005) 1 *European Review of Contract Law* 19.

The process for adopting BTSs is based on the Commission 'endorsing' the BTSs proposed by ESMA, and provides for a number of procedural checks to protect ESMA's position as the expert agency and the Commission's Treaty pre-eminence as the location of delegated rule making power. ESMA additionally provides technical advice to the Commission on administrative rules that do not take the form of BTSs and produces a vast array of 'soft law' measures, the most significant of which are the Guidelines in relation to which NCAs must 'comply or explain'. These powers represent a material but still incremental hardening of CESR's quasi rule making powers; like CESR, ESMA cannot adopt rules independently. But its now demonstrated technical capacity in relation to the crisis-era administrative rule-book,[74] the Commission's (general) willingness to accept its technical advice and its proposed BTSs, the close communications lines it has developed to the market, and its engagement with the international standard setting process have all placed it in a pivotal position of influence and established it as a de facto standard setter. Additionally, and like CESR before it, ESMA, from the outset, has deployed the range of soft law tools at its disposal to shape the regulatory environment more generally, and without the constraints posed by the administrative rule making process.

But ESMA has inherited many of the difficulties that troubled CESR. Legitimacy and validity opacities persist, particularly with respect to ESMA's soft law activities. While ESMA brings a demonstrated technical capacity to rule making, and inter-institutional relations have generally been strong, the effectiveness concerns which arose over the CESR era have reappeared. In particular, the control exerted by the Commission underlines the uneasy fit between ESMA's *Meroni*-dictated[75] agency governance structure and its role as an expert de facto standard setter for financial markets. Reflecting these challenges, crisis-era scholarship on EU financial market law has focused closely on ESMA's role in EU financial markets governance and on the limitations of the agency model.[76]

(b) Supervision

The multitude of challenges that effective supervision poses in domestic markets must, in the EU financial market, be met within an organizational model that in addition responds to the particular supervisory difficulties posed by cross-border activity and cross-border risk transmission. As has been extensively discussed in the pre-crisis and crisis-era literature, cross-border financial markets supervision

---

[74] By the end of 2013, ESMA had proposed a wide range of BTSs and its technical capacity was widely acknowledged during the 2013 review of the ESFS.

[75] Case 9/56 *Meroni v High Authority* [1957–1958] ECR 133. See Section IV.2.

[76] eg Madalina Busuioc, 'Rule-making by the European Financial Supervisory Authorities: Walking a Tight Rope' (2013) 19 *European Law Journal* 111 and Pierre Schammo, 'The European Securities and Markets Authority: Lifting the Veil on the Allocation of Powers' (2011) 48 *Common Market Law Review* 1911.

can draw on a number of organizational devices including the allocation of home/host (which relates to branches and cross-border services) or home/home (which relates to group/subsidiary structures) supervisory jurisdiction and of related fiscal responsibility to different supervisors; cooperation and information-sharing obligations; delegation structures; colleges of supervisors; cross-border resolution and rescue mechanisms; and, ultimately, the allocation of supervision to a central authority.[77]

There is no 'magic formula' for the optimal organizational design of EU supervision. Decentralized supervision based on NCAs allows for geographic proximity to the supervised entity, the application of local expertise, experimentation, and innovation in supervisory practices, and the location of fiscal responsibility with the supervising Member State. It sidesteps the institutional, political, and legal pyrotechnics associated with the construction of an EU supervisor. But anchoring primary supervisory responsibility for cross-border activity to a particular NCA and requiring coordination between the other NCAs engaged, as is necessary for single market efficiency, exposes the pan-EU market to any weaknesses in the quality of that supervision and in coordination. Centralization through a central EU authority provides a potentially cleaner and simpler organizational model. Prior to the financial crisis, the policy agenda (and related scholarship) periodically flirted with the 'Euro-SEC/single supervisor' model, though it never gained serious political or market traction.[78] But the legion of Treaty competence and political difficulties, in addition to the complex allocation decisions that must be made with respect to the location of fiscal responsibility, which were not fully apparent until the financial crisis, make it a highly troublesome organizational choice.

Here again, related institutional reform has been incremental. Prior to the establishment of CESR, supervision was based on loose coordination governed by the jurisdiction allocation and coordination requirements imposed on home (the main supervisor) and host NCAs (cross-border activity through subsidiaries, which requires a home/home NCA relationship, is less common in the financial markets area, although dominant in the banking area). CESR strengthened this network-based coordination model by supporting supervisory coordination and convergence through a range of 'soft' mechanisms. The crisis era led to the establishment of the ESFS, which combines centralized (ESMA/ESRB) elements and decentralized (NCA) elements. The ESFS is the product of a messy combination of political compromise and legal constraints,[79] but perhaps above all it reflects the

---

[77] eg Guido Ferrarini and Filippo Chiodini, *Regulating Multinational Banks in Europe. An Assessment of the new Supervisory Framework*, ECGI Law Working Paper No 158/2010 (2010) and, pre-crisis, Eddy Wymeersch 'The Structure of Financial Supervision in Europe: About Single Financial Supervisors, Twin Peaks and Multiple Financial Supervisors' (2007) 8 *European Business Organization Law Review* 23.

[78] For an example see Yannis Avgerinos, *Regulating and Supervising Investment Services in the European Union* (2003).

[79] See further below.

fiscal costs of supervisory failure that the crisis exposed, and the related unwill-ingness of Member States to transfer supervisory control while retaining fiscal responsibility. ESMA is, accordingly, primarily a 'supervisor of supervisors' and can exercise an array of primarily 'soft' powers to support supervisory coordination and cooperation, which together represent an incremental hardening of CESR's powers. But it has also been conferred with direct supervisory powers (Section II.2), which represent a radical change to EU financial markets governance. These are, however, limited and activate either in emergency/unusual conditions and are subject to strict conditionality, or, with respect to ESMA's more workaday direct supervision powers, apply only to pan-EU actors the centralized supervision of which has a strong logic, given their limited potential to pose fiscal risks to Member States and their strong cross-border effects. Significantly more radical solutions have since been employed in the banking area and under the SSM for euro area banks. But the drivers for institutional reform and supervisory organization are distinct in the banking field. The SSM forms part of the wider Banking Union project which is designed to provide a mutualized backstop mechanism for ail-ing banks.[80] Banking Union and the related supervision of euro area banks by the ECB under the SSM is the outcome of the fiscal and sovereign debt crisis and the destructive feedback loop which developed between bank failure, sovereign rescue of banks, sovereign fragility, and the viability of the euro, and the consequent over-whelming political imperative to break the link between sovereigns and banks. In particular, the SSM is a precondition for empowering the ESM to capitalize banks directly, thereby protecting the sovereign from the costs of bank rescue.

2. The Uneasy Relationship between Financial Markets Governance and the Treaties

Strong momentum effects and a degree of pragmatism have led to a governance model which, while somewhat rickety, provides a workable solution to the chal-lenges which financial markets governance poses in the EU. But the Treaties stand as a significant risk to, and limitation on, the development of an optimal model, given in particular the *Meroni* constraint and the limitations imposed by Article 114 TFEU, the typical legal base for institutional reform in this area.

The extent of the constraint imposed by *Meroni* only became clear with the estab-lishment of ESMA. CESR's structure was unstable; its founding Decision described it simply as 'an independent advisory group on securities in the Community'.[81] By contrast, ESMA is an EU agency. But agencies must operate within the requirements

---

[80] See eg Commission, Communication on Roadmap Towards a Banking Union (2012) (COM (2012) 510) and ECB, Financial Stability Review, June 2012.

[81] Decision C (2009) 176 (now repealed), Art 1.

of the seminal 1958 *Meroni* ruling, which provides, inter alia, that discretionary powers involving a wide margin of discretion cannot be delegated by an EU institution. Only clearly defined executive powers, subject to strict review in light of objective criteria determined by the delegating authority, may be delegated.

Reflecting *Meroni*, ESMA has not been conferred with the power to adopt binding rules. The BTS proposal power, however, brings ESMA (and the other ESAs) closer to the position of rule maker than any other EU agency. Nonetheless, the *Meroni* constraint remains a real control on ESMA's operation, particularly as there are few formal restraints on the Commission's powers to reject/revise proposed BTSs. The Commission has considerable incentives to ensure ESMA's effective operation, as one of its major architects, as a beneficiary of the intensification of EU intervention consequent on ESMA's activities, and as a consumer of ESMA's technical expertise. The likely hostility from the financial markets if the Commission were too quick to veto ESMA BTS proposals (which are subject to mandatory impact assessment and consultation) provides an additional brake. But the Commission also has the most to lose in terms of a weakening of its control over administrative rule making.

In practice, the inefficiency risks attendant on the BTS process have not, so far, crystallized. At the time of writing, all but three of the swathe of BTSs proposed since January 2011 have been adopted without revision or veto by the Commission. The three exceptions underline, nonetheless, the Commission's dominant position and its concern to protect its institutional prerogatives and the integrity of legislative/level-1 measures. The public rifts exposed between ESMA and the Commission in these cases also underline the potential for destabilizing tensions between ESMA, as the expert market regulator and location of technical expertise, and the Commission, as the guardian of the rule making process and location of competence with respect to administrative rule making.

The *Meroni* constraint also limits ESMA's powers as a nascent supervisor, as supervision can involve discretionary decisions as to how rules are applied and can have normative effects on market behaviour. In itself, operational discretion is not problematic; the difficulty lies in the extent to which discretion has been conferred and how it has been confined, such that the institutional balance under the Treaties is maintained. Delegations of operational power to ESMA have been subject to tight conditions on their operation to control discretion. ESMA's supervisory powers over rating agencies and trade repositories, for example, sit within an extensive binding rule-book, are delineated in detail, and are supported by enforcement powers that are carefully enumerated. Similarly, the 2012 Short Selling Regulation imposes a range of conditions on ESMA's powers to prohibit short sales. But these operational conditions reflect *Meroni* and the templates it has produced for agency design rather than the dictates of operational effectiveness. The conditions tend to veer between a high degree of prescription (as under the rating agency regime), which can obstruct ESMA's operational freedom, and a high degree of subjectivity (as under the short selling regime) which may, given the legal risks it may run when taking action, restrain ESMA from taking action where necessary. The conditions may inject a useful braking device as ESMA learns to exercise operational powers, but overall they sit uneasily with ESMA's status as an independent authority and with the degree of operational freedom typically enjoyed by supervisory agencies. Stability risks also follow. Given the political sensitivity associated with ESMA's operational powers, litigation risk is significant given the vagueness of some governing conditions, which often relate to competition being distorted, the orderly functioning and integrity of the market being affected, or market stability threatened. The *Meroni* constraint accordingly has the potential to become the location of significant institutional and Member State conflict on ESMA's role in supervision, and to destabilize ESMA as a nascent supervisor. Some clarity has, however, been brought by the January 2014 ruling of the Court of Justice in the *Short Selling* case.[82] Rejecting the UK challenge to ESMA's powers under the 2012 Short Selling Regulation as engaging discretionary powers which did not comply with *Meroni*, the Court found that the degree of conditionality imposed on the powers (including under the related administrative rules) meant that the *Meroni* requirements were satisfied; the Court also emphasized the importance of ESMA's technical expertise in EU financial market governance. But although some degree of certainty has been achieved, the Court did not (by contrast with the Advocate General) take the opportunity to reconsider *Meroni* in light of the 'agencification' of EU governance generally since the *Meroni* ruling and recent constitutional developments, including the clarification by the Lisbon Treaty of the nature of delegated and implementing acts and the application of judicial review to EU agencies, or in light of the particular needs of EU financial markets governance. Accordingly, the extent to which discretion has (or has not) been confined in a particular case remains the touchstone for the legality of ESMA's operational powers, the spectrum of permitted operational discretion remains fuzzy, future challenges cannot be ruled out, and the *Meroni* conditionality fetters remain clamped on ESMA as it deploys its operational powers.

Treaty competence risks also arise. As its depth and breadth increased, EU financial markets regulation became vulnerable to Member State competence challenges given, in particular, the differences across the Member States concerning the appropriate intensity of EU intervention and doubts as to the point on the harmonization spectrum at which harmonizing measures, often based on the Treaty internal market competences (typically Articles 53(1) and 114 TFEU), changed from being concerned with market construction to being, illegally, concerned, with market regulation. But only one (early) challenge was brought, and that was unsuccessful.[83] The new generation of institutional reforms are proving more troublesome. Most EU agencies have been established under Article 352 TFEU under which Member States have veto powers. In the teeth of the financial

---

[82] See n 66.   [83] Case C-233/94 *Germany v Parliament and Council* [1997] ECR I-2405.

crisis, however, Article 114 (which requires a qualified majority vote) was a significantly more attractive competence for the establishment of the ESAs, given the sharp differences across the Member States as to the extent to which supervision should be centralized which the ESA negotiations provoked. But the competence vulnerability associated with reliance on Article 114 in this area is underlined by the explicit reference in all three founding ESA Regulations to the Court's 2006 ENISA (European Network and Information Security Agency) ruling[84] as support for the reliance on the Article 114 TFEU competence. In the ruling, which relates to the establishment of ENISA, the Court supported ex Article 95 EC, now Article 114 TFEU, as the legal basis for the Agency. The Court found that Article 95 conferred discretion on the EU legislature as to the method of approximation that was appropriate, particularly in fields with complex technical features. The legislature could deem it necessary to provide for the establishment of a body that was responsible for contributing to the implementation of a 'process of harmonisation' in situations where the adoption of non-binding supporting and framework measures was appropriate. ENISA's powers fit this model, being largely concerned with data collection, advice, cooperation, best practice, and consultation activities. But ESMA's powers are significantly greater and include the power to impose binding decisions on NCAs and market participants. It now appears, however, that Article 114 is a resilient and flexible competence. In its 2014 *Short Selling* ruling, although the Court did not rule on whether Article 114 validly supported the establishment of ESMA, it found that Article 114 was a valid competence for ESMA's operational powers under the 2012 Short Selling Regulation, in a ruling which emphasized the importance of ESMA's powers to the functioning of the internal market.[85] A sympathetic approach by the Court to Article 114 as the foundational competence for the establishment of ESMA might therefore be predicted.

However troublesome the constitutional difficulties in the financial markets sphere, they are significantly greater in the banking area. Underlining the extent to which EU financial system regulation is composed of a myriad of moving parts, each with different drivers, institutional reform in the banking sector has been radical with Banking Union's SSM and SRM reforms. The constitutional difficulties have been similarly significant, reflecting the significantly greater degree to which the ECB (under the SSM) and the SRM can usurp national functions and, in particular, take decisions engaging fiscal consequences, and the related troublesome governance difficulties that can arise.[86]

---

[84] Case C-217/04 *UK v Council and Parliament* (ENISA) [2006] ECR I-3771.

[85] See n 66.

[86] See eg Eilís Ferran and Valia Babis, 'The European Single Supervisory Mechanism' (2013) 13 *Journal of Corporate Law Studies* 255.

V. Some Predictions and Conclusion

The dynamism of this area and the extent to which external shocks can reset political and market conditions caution against bold predictions. However, it can tentatively be suggested that the current trajectory is unlikely to alter significantly.

A multiplicity of factors, including the enhanced institutional capacity provided by ESMA, incentives to shape the international rule-book (including by means of deploying strict third-country equivalence techniques as a form of access control to the internal market—a striking feature of the crisis-era rule-book), the cycle of mandatory review of legislative measures (originally deployed with respect to FSAP measures and already underway for the crisis rule-book), the after-shocks from the financial crisis and the related concern to capture emerging risks, and the increasing complexity and fragility of markets are all likely to keep EU financial markets regulation in a state of close to permanent flux for the foreseeable future. It is difficult to identify countervailing factors; while industry resistance is strong, in the current political and institutional climate, it is struggling to gain significant traction, although conditions may change.

The evolution of supervisory governance is more difficult to predict. There is a strong logic to retaining primary supervisory control at Member State level, on efficiency grounds but also given acute Treaty difficulties and the absence of the compulsion to mutualize fiscal risks which drove the construction of the SSM for euro area banks. But the SSM is likely to have a destabilizing impact on the ESFS more generally. ESMA can be expected to assert its institutional position against a dominant ECB within the SSM, particularly as the ECB is expressly prohibited from engaging in financial markets supervision where its in-scope banks carry out financial market activities. It is a relatively short step from ESMA acting as the logical EU location for coordinating financial market supervision issues with the ECB/SSM to ESMA becoming a counterweight to the ECB/SSM more generally. This is all the more the case as ESMA, an internal market actor, provides a means for reinforcing the primacy of the internal market against the rifts between the euro area and the internal market that the euro area ECB/SSM has opened up, and given the potential fragility of EBA, ESMA's internal market banking counterpart, in the face of a mighty ECB/SSM. But Treaty restrictions remain a significant obstacle to ESMA acquiring extensive operational powers, and appetite for a Treaty revision is limited.

It is clear that there are significant risks to this new settlement. Rule making for financial markets is difficult given, not least, the scale of the information asymmetries between regulators/legislators and the markets, the speed of innovation, and the complexity which regulation must capture. The EU's current status as the monopoly supplier of financial markets regulation makes the production of effective regulation all the more difficult, particularly as EU law-making is often obstructed by intractable political disputes reflecting longstanding institutional differences, as experience with the 2011 Alternative Investment Fund Managers Directive,[87] which became the 'poster-child' for politically driven (and often sub-optimal) rule making over the crisis, attests.[88] In addition, the ability of Member States to innovate, experiment, respond to distinct local market features, and correct regulatory errors has been almost entirely removed, But experimentation in the highly dynamic financial markets sphere is important—the EU's crisis-era rules were, in places, able to draw on solutions previously incubated at national level. The production by the EU of optimum regulation is all the more a challenge given the novelty of the regulatory challenges now being faced by the EU as monopoly regulator (as opposed to internal market facilitator) and the related dearth of empirical data. With respect to supervision, EU-level supervision is almost entirely untested and, as it has the potential to close the safety valve which national operational supervision provides, represents a potential source of risk.

But if there is one lesson from the previous 50 years or so of engagement, it is that the EU has proved resilient, pragmatic, and often imaginative in responding to threats, whether to the quality of rule making and supervision, or to the internal financial system more generally.

BIBLIOGRAPHY

Emilios Avougleas, 'The Global Financial Crisis, Behavioural Finance and Financial Regulation in Search of a New Orthodoxy' (2009) 9 *Journal of Corporate Law Studies* 23

Julia Black, 'Restructuring Global and EU Financial Regulation: Capacities, Coordination and Learning' in Guido Ferrarini, Klaus Hopt, and Eddy Wymeersch (eds), *Rethinking Financial Regulation and Supervision in Times of Crisis* (2012)

James Buckley and David Howarth, 'Internal Market Gesture Politics? Explaining the EU's Response to the Financial Crisis' (2010) 48 *Journal of Common Market Studies* 119

Madalina Busuioc, 'Rule-making by the European Financial Supervisory Authorities: Walking a Tight Rope' (2013) 19 *European Law Journal* 111

Luca Enriques and Matteo Gatti, 'Is there a Uniform EU Securities Law after the Financial Services Action Plan?' (2008) 14 *Stanford Journal of Law, Business and Finance* 43

Michelle Everson, *A Technology of Expertise: EU Financial Services Agencies* (2012) LSE Europe in Question Discussion Paper Series No 49/2012 (2012)

Eilís Ferran, *Building an EU Capital Market* (2004)

---

[87] Dir 2011/61/EU [2011] OJ L174/1.

[88] The intense politicization of this measure (commonly termed the hedge fund Directive) has led to an extensive literature querying the capacity of the EU to regulate financial markets effectively. eg, Eilís Ferran, 'After the Crisis: The Regulation of Hedge Funds and Private Equity in the EU' (2011) 12 *European Business Organization Law Review* 379 and Cornelia Woll, 'Lobbying under Pressure: the Effect of Salience on EU Hedge Fund Regulation' (2012) 51 *Journal of Common Market Studies* 555.

Eilís Ferran, 'After the Crisis: The Regulation of Hedge Funds and Private Equity in the EU' (2011) *12 European Business Organization Law Review* 379

Eilís Ferran, 'Crisis-driven Regulatory Reform: Where in the World is the EU Going?' in Eilís Ferran, Niamh Moloney, Jennifer Hill, and John C. Coffee, *The Regulatory Aftermath of the Global Financial Crisis* (2012) 1

Eilís Ferran and Valia Babis, 'The European Single Supervisory Mechanism' (2013) *13 Journal of Corporate Law Studies* 255

Guido Ferrarini, 'The European Regulation of Stock Exchanges: New Perspectives' (1999) *36 Common Market Law Review* 569

Guido Ferrarini, 'Contract Standards and the Markets in Financial Instruments Directive: An Assessment of the Lamfalussy Regulatory Architecture' (2005) *1 European Review of Contract Law* 19

Peter Hall and David Soskice (eds), *Varieties of Capitalism: The Institutional Foundations of Comparative Advantage* (2001)

Iain Hardie and David Howarth, 'Die Krise but not La Crise? The Financial Crisis and the Transformation of German and French Banking Systems' (2009) *47 Journal of Common Market Studies* 1017

David Howarth and Lucia Quaglia, 'Banking Union as Holy Grail: Rebuilding the Single Market in Financial Services, Stabilizing Europe's Banks, and "Completing" Economic and Monetary Union' (2013) *51 Journal of Common Market Studies* 103

Niamh Moloney, 'EU Financial Market Regulation after the Global Financial Crisis: "More Europe" or More Risks?' (2010) *47 Common Market Law Review* 1317

Niamh Moloney, *How to Protect Investors: Lessons from the EC and the UK* (2010)

Niamh Moloney, *EU Securities and Financial Markets Regulation* (2014)

Daniel Mügge, *Financial Regulation in the EU: A Research Agenda* (2012)

Daniel Mügge (ed), *Europe and the Governance of Global Finance* (2014)

Peter Mülbert and Alexander Wilhelm, 'Reforms of EU Banking and Securities Regulation after the Financial Crisis' (2010) *26 Banking and Finance Law Review* 187

Lucia Quaglia, *Governing Financial Services in the European Union: Banking, Securities, and Post-trading* (2010)

Pierre Schammo, *EU Prospectus Law: New Perspectives on Regulatory Competition in Securities Markets* (2011)

Christian de Visscher, Olivier Maisocq, and Fréedéeric Varone, 'The Lamfalussy Reform in the EU Securities Markets: Fiduciary Relationships, Policy Effectiveness, and the Balance of Power' (2008) *28 Journal of Public Policy* 19

Eddy Wymeersch, 'The Structure of Financial Supervision in Europe: About Single Financial Supervisors, Twin Peaks and Multiple Financial Supervisors' (2007) *8 European Business Organization Law Review* 23

CHAPTER 30

DEATH, TAXES, AND (TARGETED) JUDICIAL DYNAMISM

THE FREE MOVEMENT OF CAPITAL IN EU LAW

THOMAS HORSLEY

I. Introduction

THE free movement of capital is an integral component of European integration. As the fourth economic freedom, the Treaty provisions on capital movements contribute directly to the objective of establishing a functioning internal market. Uniquely amongst the provisions on free movement, the Treaty rules on capital also apply externally to regulate capital movements between Member States and third countries. The extended reach of the capital provisions is not merely geographical. The free movement of capital is closely intertwined with the realization of broader economic and political objectives of European integration—principally, economic and monetary integration[1] and, in the area of freedom, security and justice, counter-terrorism.[2]

---

[1] See eg Art 116(2)(a) EC.   [2] Art 75 TFEU.

This chapter reviews the Treaty rules regulating the free movement of capital set out in Title IV of the TFEU (Articles 63–65 TFEU). It begins in Section II by providing a brief overview of the unique evolutionary trajectory that has shaped their development. Attention then turns to consider the key features governing the internal dimension of the free movement of capital. Reflecting current divisions in the case law, Sections III and IV explore the impact of capital liberalization on two distinct categories of market participant. Section III examines the impact of the Treaty rules on the activities of corporate actors. Section IV then reflects on the liberalization of capital movements from the perspective of the (Union) citizen. Section V focuses on the free movement of capital's unique distinguishing feature. It surveys the legal framework regulating capital movements between Member States and third countries.

Looking internally, the regulation of intra-EU capital movements is now very much in line with established trends across the Treaty freedoms. Intra-EU liberalization is driven by the Court of Justice (CJ) and is shaped by an increasingly shared language of 'restrictions' on intra-EU movement and proportionate 'overriding public interest objectives'. Transposing established principles to the capital sphere, the Court has extended the reach of the internal market into new areas. This has benefited not only the interests of corporate actors, but also added considerably to the body of rights enjoyed by Union citizens and others. Tension over the outer limits of the Court's jurisprudence on Article 63(1) TFEU—a reoccurring theme across the Treaty freedoms—is largely contained within a particular regulatory strand of EU corporate governance: the 'golden shares' case law. In the external context, an emerging growth area, the Court is also at the centre of the liberalization process. However, its interpretative choices in that sphere are determined in the shadow of a system of residual political control managed, ultimately, by the Member States.

II. The Evolution of the Free Movement of Capital

1. From Forgotten to Fourth Freedom

The free movement of capital has followed a unique and 'non-linear' evolutionary trajectory.[3] In contrast to the Treaty provisions on goods, persons, and services,

---

[3] For earlier surveys, see J. Snell, 'Free Movement of Capital: Evolution as a Non-Linear Process' in P. Craig and G. de Búrca (eds), *The Evolution of EU Law* (2nd ed, 2010); S. Hindelang, *The Free Movement of Capital and Foreign Direct Investment* (2009); J. Usher, 'The Evolution of the Free

THOMAS HORSLEY

where liberalization was driven by the Court, a step ahead of the Union's political branches and often against the natural instincts of national governments, the development of the Treaty rules on capital movements was for many years essentially left to the Member States as a matter of policy.[4]

The Court's decision to secede control over the pace and depth of capital market liberalization to the Member States was taken in *Casati*.[5] In that decision, the CJ famously concluded that Article 67(1) EEC—the central provision on intra-EU capital movements in the founding EEC Treaty—was not directly effective. According to the Court, the wording of that provision was non-absolute, requiring Member States to liberalize intra-EU capital movements only 'to the extent necessary to ensure the proper functioning of the common market'.[6] The Court's ruling in *Casati* effectively left the Member States to manage the opening up of the EU capital market using their legislative competence in Article 69 EEC. Acting through the Council, the Member States took a series of steps in the 1980s to liberalize progressively intra-EU capital movements through secondary legislation.[7] This process culminated in the adoption of Directive 88/361 EEC, which required, in Article 1(1), the full liberalization of capital movements within the EU.[8] The Court, for its part, confirmed that Article 1(1) of the Directive had direct effect.[9] The Maastricht Treaty subsequently revised the original Treaty provisions to reflect the substance of Article 1(1) of Directive 88/361 EEC. Crucially, that Treaty also extended the scope of the principal prohibition to capture restrictions on capital movements between Member States and third countries—a key distinguishing feature amongst the Treaty freedoms. Article 63(1) TFEU now prohibits 'all restrictions on the movement of capital between Member States and between Member States and third countries'.

The Court's historic display of interpretative restraint in the field of capital is atypical across the Treaty freedoms. In the case law on goods, persons, and services, the CJ did not hesitate to assume a leadership role in the integration process.[10] By conferring direct effect on individual Treaty provisions, the Court created for itself an important space to reshape fundamentally the boundaries of Member State competence in pursuit of one of the Treaty's primary economic objectives: the

Movement of Capital' (2008) 31 *Fordham International Law Journal* 1533; L. Flynn, 'Coming of Age: The Free Movement of Capital Case Law 1993–2002' (2002) 39 *Common Market Law Rev* 773; S. Peers, 'Free Movement of Capital: Learning Lessons or Slipping on Spilt Milk?' in C. Barnard and J. Scott, *The Law of the Single European market: Unpacking the Premises* (2002).

    ⁴ See here also Snell (n 3) 554.   ⁵ Case 203/80 *Casati* [1981] ECR 2595.
    ⁶ *Casati* (n 5) para 8.
    ⁷ The First Directive for the implementation of Art 67 of the Treaty [1959–1962] OJ Spec Ed 49, the Second Council 63/21/EEC Dir [1963–1964] OJ Spec Ed 5, Council Dir 85/583/EEC [1985] OJ L372 39–41, and Council Dir 86/566/EEC [1986] OJ L332 p. 22. For discussion, see Usher (n 3) 1535–1539.
    ⁸ Council Dir 88/361/EEC [1988] OJ L178/5.
    ⁹ Joined Cases C-163/94, C-165/94, and C-250/94 *Sanz de Lera* [1995] ECR I-4821, para 48.
    ¹⁰ See eg Case 2/74 *Reyners* [1974] ECR 631, Case 8/74 *Dassonville* [1974] ECR 837, and Case 33/74 *Van Binsbergen* [1974] ECR 1299.

establishment of a functioning internal market. The differentiated judicial approach to liberalization in the field of capital movements cannot adequately be explained with reference to distinctions in the wording of Article 67(1) EEC. As Snell argues, the drafting of the original Treaty freedoms was such that the Court could legitimately have opted to make the applicability of the rules on goods, services, and persons equally conditional on prior legislative intervention.[11] The difference in approach is better understood with reference to judicial awareness of the distinguishing features of the free movement of capital. Perhaps first and foremost, the Court in *Casati* was undoubtedly sensitive to the fact that an abrupt and unstructured liberalization of capital movements had the potential to disrupt the as yet largely uncoordinated economic and monetary policies of the Member States.[12]

2. Residual Political Control in the Field of Capital

The introduction of revised, directly effective capital provisions into the Treaty framework at Maastricht has not entirely displaced political influence over the development of the free movement of capital.[13] The liberalization of capital movement stills displays unique features in this respect. First and foremost, the scope of the term 'capital movements' continues to be defined with express reference to the discrete categories of economic transactions outlined in Annex I of the now defunct Directive 88/361 EEC. These categories include, *inter alia*, the acquisition and transfer of shares[14]; the purchase of property (real estate)[15]; the transfer of moveable and immoveable property by inheritance or gift[16]; and the provision of loans.[17] According to the Court, Annex I of Directive 88/361 EEC retains 'indicative value' for the purposes of defining the term 'capital movements' in Article 63(1) TFEU.[18]

The Court's approach to the definition of capital movements certainly differs from that adopted for the other freedoms. By continuing to adhere to the terms of lapsed Directive 88/361 EEC, the Court has indeed passed on an opportunity to construct a broad, functional definition of 'capital movements'—an opportunity exploited as regards the provisions on goods and workers.[19] Nevertheless, this

---

[11] Snell (n 3) 549.   [12] *Casati* (n 5) para 9.

[13] For an inter-institutional perspective on the evolution of the free movement of capital, see R. Murphy, 'The Dynamic Relationship of the Legislature and the Judiciary in the Pursuit of Capital Liberalisation' in P. Syrpis (ed), *The Judiciary, the Legislature and the EU Internal Market* (2012).

[14] Case C-367/98 *Commission v Portugal (Golden Shares)* [2002] ECR I-4731, para 38.

[15] Case C-302/97 *Klaus Konle* [1999] ECR I-3099, para 22.

[16] Case C-364/01 *The heirs of H. Barbier* [2003] ECR I-15013, para 58.

[17] Case C-452/04 *Fidum Finanz AG* [2006] ECR I-9521, para 42.

[18] Case C-222/97 *Trummer and Mayer* [1999] ECR I-1661, para 21 and, thereafter, eg Case C-510/08 *Mattner* [2010] ECR I-3553, para 19.

[19] eg Case 7/68 *Commission v Italy (Article Treasures)* [1968] ECR 423 p 428 (goods) and Case 66/85 *Laurie-Blum* [1986] ECR 2121 para 16 (workers). For services, see Art 57 TFEU.

difference in approach ought not to be read as an expression of residual Member State control over the scope of Article 63 TFEU. The Court's continued adherence to the definition of 'capital movements' in that Directive rests on a deliberate judicial choice, which it may yet opt to change. Supporting this view, the CJ recently stated that Directive 88/361 EEC now has 'no normative value in the legal order of the European Union' insofar as the scope of the primary Treaty provisions on capital movements is concerned.[20]

Effective political control over the development of the free movement of capital is now largely restricted to the external dimension of the freedom. Article 64(3) TFEU, for example, empowers the Council, using the special legislative procedure, to adopt measures that constitute a step backwards as regards the liberalization of capital movement between Member States and third countries.[21] The differentiated regime applicable to external capital movements was bolstered further following the entry into force of the Lisbon Treaty. That Treaty inserted an important new provision—Article 65(4) TFEU—enabling the Council, at the request of a Member State, to reintroduce national tax measures declared by the Court to constitute restrictions on the movement of capital between Member States and third countries. That provision is comparable to Article 108(2) TFEU, which permits the Council, acting unanimously and on application by a Member State, to decide that aid granted by a Member State is considered compatible with the internal market.

III. Intra-EU Capital Movements and Corporate Actors

Recent years have witnessed rapid growth in the number of cases on the free movement of capital. Much like services in the 1990s, the jurisprudence on intra-EU capital movements has, over the last 15 years, shifted from the shadows to the foreground of market integration. The growth in capital case law has shaped the economic activities of two distinct categories of market participant: corporate actors and individual citizens. This section explores developments affecting the activities of the first category of participants within the internal market. It begins by examining the impact of Article 63(1) TFEU on Member State competence in the field of taxation. Thereafter, it considers the jurisprudence on 'golden shares', an area of

---

[20] Case C-476/10 *Projektart*, Order of the Court [2011] ECR I-5615, paras 44 and 45.

[21] See also Art 64(1) TFEU, which 'grandfathers' restrictions on capital movements between Member States and third countries in force prior to the entry into force of the Maastricht Treaty.

particularly contentious judicial law making that presently marks the outer limits of the case law on intra-EU capital movements.

1. Article 63(1) TFEU and Corporate Taxation

Tax disputes now make up a considerable part of the Court's jurisprudence on intra-EU capital movements—46 out of 57 decisions between 2008 and 2013.[22] The rise in number of tax cases can be explained in part with reference to the definition of capital movements under Article 63(1) TFEU. Following Annex 1 of Directive 88/361 EEC, the Court reads that concept to include 'direct' and 'portfolio' investments.[23] The inclusion of both direct and portfolio shareholdings within the scope of Article 63(1) TFEU has opened up for corporate investors in particular fresh opportunities to scrutinize unfavourable provisions of Member State tax legislation against benchmark principles of EU market integration. Both categories of investments fall out with the scope of Article 49 TFEU on establishment by reason of the fact that they do not confer lasting controlling stakes in undertakings.[24] The financial stakes in this new sphere of internal market law are considerable. Member States are concerned not only to protect their fiscal autonomy from scrutiny at Union level, but also their national budgets.[25]

In the field of corporate taxation, the Court's interpretation of Article 63(1) TFEU has developed into a prohibition of discrimination.[26] This approach recognizes, as a matter of principle, the fundamental right of Member States to structure their own tax systems, whilst requiring them, at the same time, to accommodate the demands of cross-border movement.[27] It is the least intrusive of the current approaches employed to manage the division of competence between the Member States and the Union in EU free movement law—an area of shared responsibility.[28] It also broadly follows the Court's approach to taxation measures across the related provisions on establishment.[29] At odds with the substance of its own case law on

---

[22] Data from *InfoCuria* http://curia.europa.eu/juris/recherche.jsf?language=en.

[23] Case C-182/08 *Glaxo Wellcome* [2009] ECR I-8591, para 40.

[24] On the boundary between capital and establishment, see eg Joined Cases C-436/08 and C-437/08 *Haribo* [2011] ECR I-305, para 35. For a detailed critique, see Hindelang (n 3) Ch 3.

[25] eg R. Murphy, 'Why Does Tax Have to Be so Taxing? The Court Revisits the Franked Investment Income Litigation' (2013) 38(5) *European Law Review* 695.

[26] eg Case C-35/11 *Test Claimants in the FII Group Litigation*, judgment of the Court (Grand Chamber) of 13 November 2012, para 40. See also Snell (n 3) 557–563, Usher (n 3) 1560, and S. Kingston, 'A Light in the Darkness: Recent Developments in the ECJ's Direct Tax Jurisprudence' (2007) 44 *Common Market Law Review* 1321, 1359.

[27] eg Case C-35/98 *Verkooijen* [2000] ECR I-4071, para 32.   [28] Art 4(2)(a) TFEU.

[29] eg Case C-374/04 *Test Claimants in Class IV of the ACT Group Litigation* [2006] ECR I-11673 and Case C-446/04 *Test Claimants in the FII Group Litigation* [2006] ECR I-11753. For discussion, see Kingston (n 26) 1335–1347 and C. Barnard, *The Substantive Law of the EU: The Four Freedoms* (4th ed, 2013) 343–353.

taxation, the Court rarely uses the language of discrimination in its tax case law.[30] Following its approach across the freedoms, the Court instead interprets the scope of Article 63(1) TFEU more broadly in terms of a prohibition of national measures that exhibit potential 'deterrent' and/or 'dissuasive' effects on intra-EU movement.[31] In practice, however, this expansive, effects-based language masks the true scope of that provision in connection with the review of national tax measures.[32]

The basic requirement imposed by Article 63(1) TFEU in the field of taxation is one of equal treatment.[33] That provision is focused on the scrutiny of national measures that introduce differences in treatment based on the nationality or place of residency of investors and/or the source of their taxable income. The prohibition of differences in treatment based on Member State nationality and/or residency is the hallmark of the non-discrimination principle in EU law.[34]

Not every difference in treatment qualifies as a restriction on intra-EU movement. The Court's discrimination-based approach in the area of direct taxation employs a key distinction between the situations of resident and non-resident taxpayers. That distinction borrows from international tax law, and is applied to manage the relationship between national tax systems and the demands of a functioning internal market across the Treaty freedoms.[35] On the one hand, the CJ asserts that the situations of resident taxpayers are considered objectively comparable.[36] Article 63(1) TFEU therefore prohibits any national measure that introduces or maintains a difference in treatment between resident taxpayers (subject, of course, to possible justification).[37] By contrast, the CJ acknowledges that, with respect to direct taxation, the situations of resident and non-resident taxpayers are generally not comparable.[38] As a matter of international tax law, states enjoy primary jurisdiction over the worldwide income of resident taxpayers, whereas they may tax non-residents only on income generated within that state.[39] Member States may, in principle, therefore treat resident and non-resident taxpayers differently without infringing Article 63(1) TFEU.[40]

---

[30] For an exception, see eg Case C-250/08 *Commission v Belgium*, judgment of the Court (First Chamber) of 1 December 2011, para 65.

[31] eg Case C-35/98 *Verkooijen* (n 27), paras 34–35.

[32] The Court has concluded only most exceptionally that such rules infringe that provision. See eg Case C-439/97 *Sandoz GmbH* [1999] ECR I-7041.

[33] Case C-35/11 *Test Claimants* (n 26) para 40.   [34] Art 18 TFEU.

[35] eg Hindelang (n 3) 146 and Kingston (n 26) 1330. See also eg the OECD Model Convention with respect to taxes on income and capital (2010) http://dx.doi.org/10.1787/9789264175181-en and Case C-279/93 *Schumacker* [1995] ECR I-225, paras 32–33.

[36] eg Case C-35/98 *Verkooijen* (n 27).

[37] eg Case C-379/05 *Amurta* SGPS [2007] ECR I-9596, Case C-377/07 *STEKO Industriemontage* [2009] ECR I-299. and Joined Cases C-338/11 to C-347/11 *Santander*, judgment of the Court (Third Chamber) of 10 May 2012.

[38] eg Case C-169/03 *Wallentin* [2004] ECR I-6443, para 15.

[39] See eg Kingston (n 26) 1330.

[40] eg Case C-513/04 *Kerckhaert and Morres* [2006] ECR I-10967 and Case C-157/10 *Banco Bilbao*, judgment of the Court (First Chamber) of 8 December 2011 (nyr).

Although firmly orientated on the narrower discrimination model, Article 63(1) TFEU has emerged as a powerful legal tool for corporate actors. In particular, the CJ has proved willing to scrutinize national measures closely for evidence of differences in treatment that exist in law or fact at every stages of the taxation cycle: imposition, calculation, and/or collection of tax revenue.[41] The scope of Article 63(1) TFEU is further enhanced by the Court's approach to the comparability of taxpayers. In specific circumstances, and following principles of international tax law, the Court has collapsed the distinction between resident and non-resident taxpayers. Most significantly, it has ruled that the situation of non-resident taxpayers becomes comparable to that of resident taxpayers *as soon as* a Member State elects to tax the income of non-residents generated within that state.[42] The comparability of both groups of taxpayer in such circumstances gives rise to an obligation on the part of the taxing Member State to extend the benefits of any arrangements for the prevention or mitigation of double taxation to non-resident taxpayers.[43]

On the other hand, Article 63(1) TFEU does not prohibit double taxation that arises simply as a consequence of the parallel existence of two sets of non-discriminatory Member State tax systems.[44] Member States are not obliged to offset taxes paid by resident taxpayers in another Member State on income received abroad.[45] As the Court (Grand Chamber) held in *Test Claimants*:

An obligation on the Member State where [an] undertaking resides to exempt foreign-sourced dividends from corporation tax would affect the competence of the Member State concerned to tax, in compliance with the principle of non-discrimination, the profits thereby distributed at the rate prescribed by its own legislation.[46]

According to the CJ, it falls to the Member States to respond to the challenges of double taxation, for example by means of international conventions.[47] Prior to the entry into force of the Lisbon Treaty, Article 293 EC positively required Member States, so far as possible, to enter into negotiations with each other with a view to abolishing double taxation within the (then) Community. There is no longer any comparable provision in the amended Treaties.

The Treaty contains two express derogations as regards restrictions on intra-EU capital movements. The first of these, Article 65(1)(a) TFEU, has proved to be of no value to Member States.[48] That provision, inserted at Maastricht, provides that Member States may apply tax rules that distinguish between taxpayers 'who are

---

[41] See esp Case C-35/11 *Test Claimants* (n 26) para 52.
[42] eg Case C-374/04 *Test Claimants ACT* (n 29) para 68 and Case C-284/09 *Commission v Germany* [2011] ECR I-9879, para 56.
[43] eg Case C-284/09 *Commission v Germany* (n 42) para 57.
[44] eg Case C-157/10 *Banco Bilbao* (n 40) para 38. See also Hindelang (n 3) 152.
[45] eg Case C-513/04 *Kerckhaert and Morres* (n 40) paras 19 and 20.
[46] Case C-35/11 *Test Claimants* (n 26) para 40.
[47] eg Case C-540/07 *Commission v Italy* [2009] ECR I-10983, para 31.
[48] See also Snell (n 3) 552, Hindelang (n 3) 154–157, and Barnard (n 29) 608.

not in the same situation with regard to their place of residence or with regard to the place where their capital is invested'. On one view, supported by Peers, the insertion of that sub-paragraph was expressly intended to provide an additional sphere of protection for Member States in the field of intra-EU capital movements.[49] Several Member States have indeed invoked Article 65(1)(a) TFEU in this vein in an attempt to enhance their autonomy in the field of taxation policy.[50] In *Manninen*, for example, the Finnish, French, and United Kingdom governments argued that, on the basis of that provision, Finland was entitled to restrict the award of a particular tax credit to dividends paid by companies established within that state.[51]

The Court has squarely rejected efforts to use Article 65(1)(a) TFEU as a tool to carve out an additional sphere of protection. According to the CJ, that provision 'cannot be interpreted as meaning that all tax legislation which draws a distinction between taxpayers on the basis of their place of residence or the State in which they invest their capital is automatically compatible with the Treaty'.[52] Instead, the Court takes the view that Article 65(1)(a) TFEU does nothing more than simply codify its pre-existing body of case law on discriminatory national tax measures developed under the related Treaty freedoms.[53] If, as Peers has argued, Article 65(1)(a) TFEU was indeed conceived by the Member States to introduce a specific point of differentiation between the free movement of capital and the related Treaty freedoms in the field of taxation, it clearly failed in its objective.

Despite its mere 'declaratory' status, Article 65(1)(a) TFEU does affect the structure of the Court's analysis under Article 63(1) TFEU.[54] Under the free movement of capital, the CJ conducts its assessment of the comparability of taxpayers at the justification stage. In other words, it examines whether specific national tax measures should be *removed* from the scope of Article 63(1) TFEU on the basis that they do not give rise to prohibited differences in treatment between taxpayers in comparable situations. This approach differs markedly from that employed across the provisions on persons and services. Under these related provisions, the Court conducts the same assessment at the first stage of its enquiry—the scope of Article 63(1) TFEU. In practical terms, this difference in approach between the Treaty freedoms has no material impact on the scope of Union competence in the area of direct taxation. It simply reflects the unique existence of Article 65(1)(a) TFEU in the Treaty framework as a derogating provision.

To justify discriminatory tax measures—in the Court's vocabulary, 'restrictions' on intra-EU movement—Member States may turn to a second express derogation, Article 65(1)(b) TFEU. That provision empowers Member States:

to take all requisite measure to prevent infringements of national law and regulations, in particular in the field of taxation and the prudent supervision of financial institutions, or to

---

[49] Peers (n 3) 348–349.   [50] eg Case C-35/98 *Verkooijen* (n 27) para 38.
[51] Case C-319/02 *Manninen* [2004] ECR I-7477, para 27.
[52] eg Case C-11/07 *Eckelkamp and others* [2008] ECR I-6845, para 57.
[53] Case C-35/98 *Verkooijen* (n 27) para 43.   [54] See here also Hindelang (n 3) 155–157.

lay down procedures for the declaration of capital movements for the purposes of administrative or statistical information, or to take measures which are justified on grounds of public policy or public security.[55]

Member States may also seek to justify discriminatory tax measures (and restrictions on capital movements generally) on the basis of non-discriminatory proportionate overriding public interest objectives.[56] The recognition of that additional category of case-law-based justifications is in line with earlier developments across EU free movement law.[57] In the area of taxation, accepted justifications include, most significantly, 'securing the cohesion of the tax system'[58] and 'effective fiscal supervision'.[59]

The Court interprets both the express derogation in Article 65(1)(b) TFEU and the complementary overriding public interest justifications restrictively. This follows its general approach to justifications across EU free movement law.[60] Member States may not, amongst other things, maintain restrictions on intra-EU capital movements based on 'a general presumption of tax evasion or tax fraud'.[61] Equally, and following established principles of EU free movement law, obstacles to the free movement of capital may not be justified on purely economic grounds (eg a reduction in tax revenue).[62] The objective of 'securing the cohesion of the tax system' is particularly narrowly construed. It applies only to justify national tax restrictions where Member States are able to show a 'direct link' between a particular tax advantage and an offsetting tax payment.[63] The direct link test is a straightforward transposition of the case law on Articles 45 and 49 TFEU.[64]

Directive 77/799 EC on administrative cooperation in the field of taxation plays a particularly important role in connection with the justification of restrictions on intra-EU capital movements.[65] That instrument, now superseded by Directive

---

[55] See earlier, Art 4 of Dir 88/361 (n 8).

[56] eg Case C-319/02 *Manninen* (n 51) para 29 and, most clearly, Case C-367/98 *Commission v Portugal (Golden Shares)* (n 14) para 38. For discussion, see eg Kingston (n 26) 1347–1355.

[57] eg Case 120/78 *Cassis* [1979] ECR 649, para 8 and Case C-55/94 *Gebhard* [1995] ECR I-4165, para 37.

[58] Case C-319/02 *Manninen* (n 51) para 29 and Case C-493/09 *Commission v Portugal* [2011] ECR I-9247, para 35.

[59] eg Case C-478/98 *Commission v Belgium (Eurobonds)* [2000] ECR I-7587, para 39.

[60] For a review, see eg C. Barnard, 'Derogations, Justifications and the Four Freedoms: Is State Interest Really Protected?' in C. Barnard and O. Odudu, *The Outer Limits of European Union Law* (2009) 273–305.

[61] eg Case C-478/98 *Commission v Belgium (Eurobonds)* (n 59) para 45.

[62] eg Case C-35/98 *Verkooijen* (n 27) para 48. However, note Case C-182/08 *Glaxo Wellcome* (n 23) paras 82–88 on the allocation of tax jurisdiction between Member States.

[63] eg Case C-35/98 *Verkooijen* (n 27) para 57 and Case C-250/08 *Commission v Belgium* (n 30) paras 70–77.

[64] eg Case C-204/90 *Bachmann* [1992] ECR I-249.   [65] [1977] OJ L336/15.

2011/16 EU, is frequently cited by the Court to support its decision to reject Member State attempts to invoke Article 65(1)(b) TFEU in order to justify discriminatory tax measures.[66] Directive 77/799 EC established an EU-wide system of mutual cooperation between Member State tax authorities with a view to ensuring the efficient functioning of national tax regimes and combating tax evasion and fraud. The existence of that Directive has significantly curtailed the scope for Member States to appeal, in particular, to the justification grounds listed in Article 65(1)(b) TFEU.[67] Its express aim is to manage legitimate Member State concerns regarding, *inter alia*, potential tax evasion through the establishment of a detailed EU system of mandatory administrative cooperation in the field of taxation.

2. Judicial Dynamism Unleashed: Golden Shares

Whereas the Court has opted to tread rather carefully in the fiscal context, it has taken a far more intrusive approach in the regulatory sphere.[68] In its assessment of the regulatory preferences of the Member States, the CJ has pushed the scope of its case law on Article 63(1) TFEU beyond the discrimination model to capture genuinely non-discriminatory 'restrictions' on intra-EU movement. This expansion in scope has considerable implications for Member State autonomy. Moving beyond the discrimination model enables litigants (including the Commission using Article 258 TFEU) to scrutinize the existence of Member State regulation *per se*. Under this 'restrictions' approach, Member States may be called to justify national measures that merely 'dissuade', 'deter', or 'render less attractive' intra-EU capital movements.

The impact on Member State autonomy in the regulatory context is most apparent in the area of corporate governance.[69] In particular, the Court has repeatedly concluded that so-called 'golden shares' constitute restrictions on intra-EU capital movements. Golden shares are special categories of shareholding created by Member States—typically in previously nationalized undertakings—in deviation from ordinary rules of national company law.[70] The creation of such shares is designed to enable the Member State concerned to retain a degree of control over the ownership and management of privatized undertakings (disproportionate to

---

[66] See now Dir 2011/16 EU [2011] OJ L64/1.

[67] eg Case C-540/07 *Commission v Italy* [2009] ECR I-10983, para 60 and Case C-493/09 *Commission v Portugal* (n 58) para 49.

[68] For a critical view of the distinction between fiscal and regulatory measures, see Snell (n 3).

[69] With respect to other regulatory measures, see eg Case C-302/97 *Konle* (n 15), Case C-300/01 *Doris Salzmann (No. 2)* [2003] ECR I-4899, and C-213/04 *Burscher* [2005] ECR I-10309.

[70] For discussion see eg E. Szyszczak 'Golden Shares and Market Governance' (2003) 40(2) *Common Market Law Review* 493; W.-G. Ringe, 'Company Law and Free Movement of Capital' (2010) 69 *Cambridge Law Journal* 378; and C. Gerner-Beuerle 'Shareholders between the Market and the State' (2012) 49 *Common Market Law Review* 97.

the value of the 'golden share'). The Court has established a clear principle that *any* deviation from the ordinary framework of company law linked to the exercise of Member State authority constitutes a restriction on the free movement of capital. This approach leaves Member States only limited scope to use golden shares as regulatory tools to achieve specific policy objectives or to develop models of corporate governance that depart from the basic principle of one share, one vote.

Starting with its decision in *Commission v Portugal (Golden Shares)*, the Court has consistently taken the view that golden share provisions fall within the scope of Article 63(1) TFEU.[71] According to the CJ, even if genuinely non-discriminatory, such provisions are 'liable to impede the acquisition of shares in the undertakings concerned and to dissuade investors in other Member States from investing in the capital of those undertakings'.[72] That case concerned Portuguese provisions that (1) prohibited the acquisition by investors from other Member States of more than a given number of shares in certain Portuguese undertakings and (2) required *all* private investors to obtain prior authorization before acquiring shares in certain Portuguese undertakings in excess of a specified level. Subsequent cases have addressed a range of other golden share instruments across different economic sectors. These include, *inter alia*, measures granting Member States specific powers with respect to the management of the relevant undertakings; for example, the right to approve or veto certain corporate resolutions or to appoint members of the board.[73]

The Court's 'catch all' approach to the review of genuinely non-discriminatory golden shares against Article 63(1) TFEU has attracted particular criticism.[74] For instance, Advocate General Ruiz-Jarabo Colomer sought repeatedly to convince the Court to reconsider its analysis in light of the demands of Article 345 TFEU.[75] That provision provides that 'the Treaties shall in no way prejudice the rules in Member States governing the system of property ownership'. On his analysis, Article 345 TFEU protected the right of Member States to use non-discriminatory golden shares to achieve strategic economic policy objectives, ie objectives *other* than profit maximization.[76] In *Commission v Spain*, the United Kingdom Government appealed to a

---

[71] Case C-367/98 *Commission v Portugal* (n 14).

[72] Case C-367/98 *Commission v Portugal* (n 14) para 45.

[73] eg Case C-98/01 *Commission v United Kingdom (BAA)* [2003] ECR I-4641, C-112/05 *Commission v Germany (Volkswagen)* [2007] ECR I-8995, and Case C-171/08 *Commission v Portugal (Telecom)* [2010] ECR I-6817.

[74] See T. Horsley, 'The Concept of an Obstacle to Intra-EU Capital Movement in EU Law' in N. Nic Shuibhne and L. Gormley, *From Single Market to Economic Union: Essays in Memory of John A. Usher* (2012). See also Gerner-Beuerle (n 70) and Ringe (n 70).

[75] See the Opinion of the Advocate General in Case C-367/98 *Commission v Portugal* (n 14) para 54, Case C-112/05 *Commission v Germany* (n 73) para 48, and Case C-326/07 *Commission v Italy* [2009] ECR I-2291, para 36.

[76] See the AG's Opinion in Case C-367/98 *Commission v Portugal* (n 14) at paras 49–56. To reach this point, the Advocate General adopted a historical and teleological approach to the interpretation of Art 345 TFEU.

second line of internal critique in an attempt to persuade the Court to reach a similar end result.[77] In that case, it was argued that certain categories of non-discriminatory golden shares should fall out with the scope of Article 63(1) TFEU on the basis of the Court's decision in *Keck*.[78] In its view, non-discriminatory golden shares that grant Member States a degree of control in the continued *management* of undertakings have effects on intra-EU movement comparable to measures excluded from the scope of Article 34 TFEU in that decision as 'certain selling arrangements'.

Attempts to argue that certain or all genuinely non-discriminatory golden share provisions should escape scrutiny at Union level have fallen on deaf ears. With respect to the first argument, the Court recognizes that Article 345 TFEU is a statement on the neutrality of the Treaty as regards Member State rules on property ownership.[79] That provision does not compel Member States to privatize (or re-nationalize) sectors of their economies.[80] At the same time, however, the CJ is clear that Article 345 TFEU does not shield Member State rules governing public or private property ownership from the fundamental rules of the Treaty, including Article 63(1) TFEU on the free movement of capital.[81] On the second argument—the transposition of *Keck*—the CJ asserts that golden shares do not have 'comparable effects' to the measures at issue in *Keck*.[82] In its view, golden shares, even if genuinely non-discriminatory and restricted to management rights, 'affect the position of a person acquiring a shareholding as such and are thus liable to deter investors from other Member States from making such investments and, consequently, affect access to the market'.[83]

Member States may, of course, attempt to justify golden shares. It is open to them to demonstrate that the restrictive effect of their special shareholdings is necessary in order to secure a non-discriminatory proportionate overriding public interest objective.[84] The Court has acknowledged a range of such objectives—including, *inter alia*, the need to guarantee services of general interest[85] or the protection of workers and minority shareholders.[86] However, Member States rarely succeed in their efforts to persuade the Court that the relevant proportionate public interest objective justifies the creation and maintenance of golden shares. In the final analysis, the CJ often rejects Member State justifications on proportionality grounds.

---

[77] Case C-463/00 *Commission v Spain* [2003] ECR I-4581 at paras 49–50. See also thereafter eg the arguments of the Portuguese Government in Case C-171/08 *Commission v Portugal (Telecom)* (n 73) at para 43.

[78] Joined Cases C-267/91 and C-268/91 *Keck and Mithouard* [1993] ECR I-6097.

[79] eg Joined Cases C-105/12 to C-107/12 *Staat der Nederlanden v Essent NV*, judgment of the Court (Grand Chamber) of 22 October 2013, para 29.

[80] Joined Cases C-105/12 to C-107/12 *Staat der Nederlanden v Essent NV* (n 79) para 30.

[81] Joined Cases C-105/12 to C-107/12 *Staat der Nederlanden v Essent NV* (n 79) para 36.

[82] Case C-463/00 *Commission v Spain* at (n 77) para 59.

[83] Case C-463/00 *Commission v Spain* at (n 77) para 61. See also Case C-171/08 *Commission v Portugal (Telecom)* (n 73) para 67.

[84] Case C-367/98 *Commission v Portugal* (n 14) para 49.

[85] eg Joined Cases C-282/04 and C-283/04 *Commission v Netherlands* [2006] ECR I-9141, para 19.

[86] eg Case C-112/05 *Commission v Germany (Volkswagen)* (n 73).

However, on occasion, Member States have managed to square particular national policy objectives with the Treaty framework. The Court has accepted, for instance, that 'certain concerns may justify the retention by Member States of a degree of influence within undertakings that were initially public and subsequently privatized, where those undertakings are active in fields involving the provision of services in the public interest or strategic services'.[87] However, to invoke that justification successfully, Member States must comply with a good governance test.[88] To escape Article 63(1) TFEU, golden share provisions may only empower Member States to oppose corporate resolutions *ex post* and on very specific non-economic grounds.[89] These grounds must be clearly defined in advance. Further, the exercise of golden shares must be subject to strict procedural safeguards and, ultimately, judicial review.

The Court's most recent case law suggests that it may be loosening its grip on the Member States slightly—at least with respect to certain types of non-discriminatory provisions. For instance, in *Essent NV*, the Grand Chamber upheld as compatible with Article 63(1) TFEU Dutch legislation that effectively prohibited private investors and/or upstream market participants from acquiring shares in undertakings engaged in the distribution of gas and electricity within that state.[90] The Court placed particular weight on the absolute nature of the Dutch ban on private investment. This was interpreted as a direct expression of that state's preferred approach to structuring its system of property ownership within the meaning of Article 345 TFEU.[91] Of course, this did not have the effect of shielding the contested provisions from review against Article 63(1) TFEU. Nevertheless, the Grand Chamber held that the *reasons* underpinning the Dutch legislature's preferred choice of ownership model for the energy sector *could* constitute overriding objectives in the public interest capable of justifying restrictions on intra-EU capital movements.[92] The final assessment was left to the referring court.

Justifications aside, the extension in scope of Article 63(1) TFEU to capture all non-discriminatory golden share provisions expresses an important statement of principle. It indicates that the Treaty rules on intra-EU capital movements are firmly anchored to a particular view of corporate governance. That view privileges shareholder value maximization ahead of all other economic and non-economic values.[93] It is also Commission policy.[94] Any deviation from the basic principle of one shareholder, one vote is taken, by default, to constitute a restriction

---

[87] eg Joined Cases C-463/04 and C-464/04 *Federconsumatori and others* [2007] ECR I-10419, para 41.

[88] Case C-503/99 *Commission v Belgium (Golden Shares)* [2002] ECR I-4809, paras 48–52.

[89] Case C-503/99 *Commission v Belgium (Golden Shares)* (n 88) paras 48–52.

[90] Joined Cases C-105/12 to C-107/12 *Staat der Nederlanden v Essent NV* (n 79).

[91] Joined Cases C-105/12 to C-107/12 *Staat der Nederlanden v Essent NV* (n 79) para 54.

[92] Joined Cases C-105/12 to C-107/12 *Staat der Nederlanden v Essent NV* (n 79) 55.

[93] See also eg Szyszczak (n70) at p. 283 and Gerner-Beuerle (n 70) 125.

[94] See the Commission Communication 'on Certain Aspects Concerning Intra-EU Investment' [1997] OJ C222/15.

on intra-EU movement. This approach to Article 63(1) TFEU has fundamentally reconfigured—and effectively unified—key aspects of corporate governance across the Member States.[95] As a consequence of this, particular Member States, most notably Germany, have been forced repeatedly to defend against the Treaty economic models that were expressly designed to balance shareholder value with *other* fundamental policy objectives, such as the protection of workers.[96]

On one view, the preceding approach is unproblematic. The application of the Treaty freedoms is such that obstacles to intra-EU movement—including genuinely non-discriminatory ones—may be justified. Moreover, the Court's preferred approach actually has the added benefit of increasing market transparency: Member States are required to outline in advance and in clear terms the conditions under which they seek to depart from the objective of maximizing shareholder value. At the same time, however, the nature of EU free movement law is such that policy objectives *other* than shareholder maximization are automatically placed on an unequal footing.[97] To survive, complementary and/or opposing objectives must be subsumed within a legal framework that interprets justifications narrowly and subjects accepted grounds of derogation to a strict proportionality test. Of course, this is not a phenomenon that is unique to the free movement of capital. The same tension reverberates across the Treaty freedoms.[98]

With specific respect to Article 63(1) TFEU, it is appropriate to question whether the Court has opted for a reading of that provision that is best able to give effect to a full range of Member State preferences without sacrificing the Treaty's objective of establishing a functioning internal market. By way of illustration, an approach inspired by the Court's decision in *Keck*, would arguably achieve the same end result with considerably less impact on the regulatory autonomy of the Member States.[99] Under that test, investors would only be able to trigger the review of genuinely non-discriminatory special rights retained by Member States as regards the management of undertakings where states exercised these in a *discriminatory* manner. Critics of this view may object that this places too great a burden on private investors. Yet it is a unique feature of capital markets that any such disadvantage would be automatically *priced into* the market value of the affected shares.[100] In light of that fact, it is certainly questionable

---

[95] See also Ringe (n 70).379.

[96] eg Case C-112/05 *Commission v Germany (Volkswagen)* (n 73) paras 22 and 70, and Case C-95/12 *Commission v Germany (Volkswagen)*, judgment of the Court (Grand Chamber) of 22 October 2013.

[97] See also eg N. Nic Shuibhne, *The Coherence of EU Free Movement Law: Constitutional Responsibility and the Court of Justice* (2013) 46 and C. Barnard 'Social Dumping or Dumping Socialism' (2008) 67 *Cambridge Law Journal* 262, 264 on the hierarchy between the Treaty freedoms and other policy objectives in EU free movement law.

[98] See eg Case C-112/00 *Schmidberger* [2003] ECR I-5659, Case C-36/02 *Omega* [2004] ECR I-9609 and Case C-341/05 *Laval un Partneri* [2007] ECR I-11767. See eg Barnard (n 97) 264.

[99] Horsley (n 74) 168–170.

[100] A reality overlooked by the CJ. See eg Case C-171/08 *Commission v Portugal (Telecom)* (n 73) para 61.

whether judicial intervention is warranted where this serves only to increase share prices further.

An open issue at present is whether Article 63(1) TFEU may be used to review special shareholdings created for the benefit of, or acquired by, private investors.[101] If confirmed, this would indeed mark a significant expansion in the scope of the Treaty rules on capital movement with considerable potential implications for Member State autonomy. A whole new range of discriminatory and non-discriminatory provisions of Member State company law would be opened up for potential scrutiny at Union level against Article 63(1) TFEU.

The case law to date indicates that such a development is unlikely. The golden shares jurisprudence thus far is squarely focused on scrutinizing the creation and maintenance of special shareholdings directly linked to the exercise of Member State authority. The *Volkswagen* judgments, in particular, illustrate this point clearly. In that series of cases, it was argued that golden shares held by German *Länder* in Volkswagen AG should fall out with the scope of Article 63(1) TFEU by virtue of the fact that they were contained within that company's articles of association—a private law contract.[102] The CJ rejected this argument outright. In its view, even if the contested provisions were contained within a private instrument, 'the fact that [that] agreement has become the subject of a Law suffices for it to be considered as a national measure for the purposes of the free movement of capital'.[103] The CJ's response clearly accentuates the requirement for a direct link between the special rights included with the company's articles of association and the exercise of state authority.[104] It does not fire the starting gun in a race to confer horizontal direct effect on Article 63(1) TFEU.

IV. Intra-EU Capital Movements and the Citizen

The free movement of capital does not only serve the financial interests of undertakings and corporate shareholders. It also enables Member State nationals to manage some of the consequences arising from the exercise of their rights (or those of their relations) to move and reside freely within the Union as economic

---

[101] For reflections on this issue, see Ringe (n 70) 390–402.

[102] Case C-112/05 *Commission v Germany (Volkswagen)* (n 73) paras 22–24.

[103] Case C-112/05 *Commission v Germany (Volkswagen)* (n 73) para 26.

[104] Case C-112/05 *Commission v Germany (Volkswagen)* (n 73) para 26. See also Case C-171/08 *Commission v Portugal (Telecom)* (n 73) at para 55, in which the CJ noted that the creation of the contested shares was 'not the result of the normal application of company law'.

and/or non-economic actors. The existing body of scholarship on capital movements currently underplays this important, growing aspect of cross-border movement within the internal market.[105]

The reach of Article 63(1) TFEU into the economic lives of Union citizens follows directly from the definition of 'capital movements' adopted by the Member States in Directive 88/361 EEC and presently affirmed by the Court. The Treaty provisions on intra-EU capital movements do not simply ensure, for the benefit of corporate investors and undertakings alike, that financial resources are free to be directed towards the most favourable investment environment within the internal market. 'Capital movements' also cover, *inter alia*, property purchases,[106] mortgages,[107] inheritances,[108] and personal loans[109]—routine economic transactions for millions of mobile Union citizens. On the other hand, key financial transfers affecting the lives of Union citizens do not fall within the scope of Article 63(1) TFEU. The payment of social assistance is the prime example. The Court's adherence to the discrete categories of 'capital movements' defined in Directive 88/361 EEC ensures that the free movement of capital regulates only acts of private redistribution, such as inheritance transfers or charitable donations.

A growing body of case law addresses challenges to Member State regulations instigated by Union citizens. Several such cases have concerned inheritance tax disputes arising as a result of the exercise of the Treaty rights on intra-EU movement. In *Fernandez*, for instance, the Court held that Article 63(1) TFEU prohibited German tax rules that granted residents tax deductions on income or losses from property only with regard to property owned within that state, but not elsewhere in the Union.[110] The applicants, Spanish nationals resident in Germany since birth, had inherited, let, and then sold a family property situated in Spain. In other instances, the Court has protected Union citizens' right to acquire property in host Member States and access mortgages on equal terms with nationals.[111] In its approach to the review of tax measures, the CJ adopts the same discrimination-based model developed for corporate investments (see Section III above).

In *Commission v Belgium*, the Commission sought to develop a closer relationship between Article 63(1) TFEU and the emerging status of Union citizenship.[112] In that decision, concerning Belgian rules on the 'portability' of property registration duties, it argued that: 'The right of a citizen of the European Union to "reside" in a Member State other than that person's Member State of origin includes the right to

---

[105] For an exception, see Kingston (n 26).   [106] Case C-302/97 *Konle* (n 15) para 22.
[107] Case C-222/97 *Trummer and Mayer* (n 18) para 21.
[108] Case C-364/01 *The heirs of H. Barbier* (n 16) para 58.
[109] Case C-452/04 *Fidum Finanz* (n 17) para 42.
[110] Case C-35/08 *Fernandez* [2009] ECR I-9807. See also eg Case C-540/10 *Mattner* (n 18).
[111] eg Case C-222/97 *Trummer and Mayer* (n18), Case C-302/97 *Konle* (n 34).
[112] Case C-250/08 *Commission v Belgium* (n 30).

establish a principal residence in that Member State, *which implies the right to buy or build that residence*.[113]

The Court chose not to take up the Commission's invitation to borrow from its jurisprudence on intra-EU capital movements in order to expand further the scope its Article 21 TFEU citizenship case law. It concluded instead that Article 63(1) TFEU alone governed the purchase of new-build properties in the Flemish region of Belgium by Member State nationals who sought to transfer, 'without economic reason', their principal residence from another Member State.[114] This follows established principles. The application of the economic freedoms *lex specialis* to situations involving the exercise of rights by Union citizens is a familiar feature of EU free movement law.[115]

Article 63(1) TFEU does not only enable Member State nationals to manage the economic consequences associated with the exercise of their rights under the Treaty. Third-country nationals may also invoke the protection afforded by that provision. There is as yet no express judicial pronouncement on this point. Nevertheless, it follows logically from the wording of Article 63(1) TFEU, which refers only to the abolition of restrictions on internal and external capital movements.[116] Moreover, it is also implicit in several key judgments of the Court, including *Sanz de Lera*—the first decision interpreting the revised Maastricht provisions on capital.[117] In that decision, the CJ applied Article 63(1) TFEU to review a decision by the Spanish authorities to arrest a Turkish national resident in Spain, who had boarded a flight for Istanbul with a large quantity of banknotes without having first obtained an export authorization.

The inclusion of third-country nationals distinguishes the free movement of capital from the related provisions on establishment and services. The latter sets of provisions confer rights exclusively on Member State nationals. As the CJ concluded in *FKP Scorpio* with specific respect to services, '[the] Treaty does not extend the benefit of those provisions to providers of services who are nationals of non-member countries, even if they are established within the Community and an intra-Community provision of services is concerned'.[118] Conceptually, the Treaty provisions on capital should therefore be considered alongside Articles 34 and 35 TFEU on goods—at least in terms of their personal scope. The latter provisions on goods also apply without regard to the nationality of the transacting parties.[119]

---

[113] Case C-250/08 *Commission v Belgium* (n 30) para 11.

[114] Case C-250/08 *Commission v Belgium* (n 30) para 32. Contrast Case C-197/11 *Libert*, judgment of the Court (First Chamber) of 8 May 2013 in which the Court considered restrictions against all freedoms.

[115] eg Case C-104/06 *Commission v Sweden* [2007] ECR I-671, para 15.

[116] On this point, see also Nic Shuibhne (n 97) 67 and Hindelang (n 3) 204.

[117] Joined Cases C-163/94, C-165/94, and C-250/94 *Sanz de Lera* (n 9). See also eg the Opinion of AG Geelhoed in Case C-452/01 *Ospelt* [2003] ECR I-9743, paras 45–47.

[118] Case C-290/04 *FKP Scorpio Konzertproduktionen GmbH* [2006] ECR I-9461, para 68.

[119] Nic Shuibhne (n 97) 67.

V. Global Markets: The External Dimension of Capital Movements

The external application of Article 63(1) TFEU is the key distinguishing feature of the free movement of capital. It is the point where discussion of that provision's scope moves beyond comparative analysis with the related Treaty freedoms to break new ground. Snell articulates three possible explanations for the extension in scope of Art 63(1) TFEU to regulate capital movements between the Member States and third countries.[120] First, the liberalization of intra-EU capital movements inevitably affects global capital flows by enabling investors to enter and exit the Union through national markets with the least restrictive controls on capital. A uniform approach to external capital movements is therefore desirable. Second, the global dimension of capital serves to bolster the credibility of the Euro by safeguarding for international investors the right to invest and repatriate their capital freely. Third, Snell suggests that the extension application of Article 63(1) TFEU may be linked to the objective of establishing 'an open market economy with free competition' expressed in Article 119 TFEU.

The nature of Article 63(1) TFEU as a provision of 'unlimited scope' presents new challenges and opportunities for both the Court and the Member States.[121] For its part, the Court has been required to determine the extent to which differences between internal and external capital movements preclude the direct transposition of its case law on intra-EU movement. Further, given that only Article 63(1) TFEU applies beyond the frontiers of the internal market, it has also had to adjudicate on the precise boundaries between that provision and the Treaty rules on persons and services. The judicial response so far points clearly to the emergence of a distinctive, second-tier regime as regards extra-EU capital movements. The absence of the internal market as a unifying legal framework, together with provision in the Treaty for residual Member State control in this sphere, function as important limits on the Court's interpretative choices.

The case law on the external dimension of capital is presently centred on the review of tax measures. In this field, the Court of Justice has, to a greater extent, directly transposed its case law on internal market restrictions to the global context. Its approach to the scrutiny of Member State tax measures in connection with capital movements between Member States and third countries is informed by the same *de facto* discrimination test.[122] In its first full substantive ruling on extra-EU capital movements, *Skatteverket v A*, the CJ was requested to consider Swedish

---

[120] Snell (n 3) 564–565. See also Hindelang (n 3) 24–30.
[121] Case C-384/09 *Prunus and Polonium SA* [2011] ECR I-3319, para 20.
[122] See also Usher (n 3) 1569 and Snell (n 3) 567.

legislation that granted resident taxpayers a tax emption with respect to the receipt of specific dividend payments.[123] That exemption applied only to dividends distributed by undertakings establish in Sweden or within an EEA State. According to the Court, the exclusion of distributions made by undertakings established in third countries outside the EEA constituted a restriction to Article 63(1) TFEU. The difference in treatment introduced by the Swedish rules had the effect of 'discouraging' taxpayers residing in Sweden from investing their capital in companies established outside the EEA.[124]

The Court's uniform approach to restrictions on intra-EU capital movement and those between Member States and third countries no doubt alarmed Member State governments. However, the regulation of external capital movements at Union level has, in practice, had less impact on Member State autonomy. This is due principally to the Court's more generous approach to the justification of national measures that are caught by the prohibition in Article 63(1) TFEU. The Court is alert to the very different legal and political dynamics governing capital movements between Member States and third countries.[125] In particular, it has repeatedly acknowledged the limitations of the current framework for mutual cooperation between national tax administrations in Directive 77/799 EC.[126] As an instrument of EU law, that Directive imposes legal obligations only on Member States and not third countries.[127] In light of this, the Court has indicated that Member States may seek to justify restrictive tax measures affecting external capital movements on grounds that would not constitute valid justifications in the internal market context.[128]

The Treaty framework provides additional safeguards for the benefit of Member States in connection with the external application of Article 63(1) TFEU. First, the Treaty permits Member States to maintain certain restrictive measures regulating, *inter alia*, direct investment or the provisions of financial services with third countries that existed on or before 31 December 1993.[129] Second, the Treaty permits Member States to introduce new restrictions on capital movements between Member States and third countries. Article 64(3) TFEU empowers the Council to 'adopt measures which constitute a step backwards in Union law as regards the liberalization of the movement of capital to or from third countries'. Finally, Article 66 TFEU provides a legal base to address specific concerns linked to the free movement of capital with third countries and affecting the operation of economic and monetary union.

---

[123] Case C-101/05 *Skatteverket v A* [2007] ECR I-11531. See, thereafter, eg Case C-72/09 *Rimbaud SA* [2010] ECR I-10659 and Joined Cases C-436/08 and C-437/08 *Haribo* (n 24).

[124] Case C-101/05 *Skatteverket v A* (n 123) para 42.

[125] Case C-101/05 *Skatteverket v A* (n 123) para 60.

[126] See now Dir 2011/77 EU (n 67).

[127] eg Case C-101/05 *Skatteverket v A* (n 123) paras 37 and 61 and Case C-72/09 *Rimbaud SA* (n 123) paras 40–41.

[128] eg Joined Cases C-436/08 and C-437/08 *Haribo* (n 24) para 120.

[129] Case C-541/08 *Fokus Invest* [2010] ECR I-1025.

Most significantly, however, Article 65(4) TFEU grants Member States direct political control over the external dimension of capital movements. That provision, introduced at Lisbon, empowers the Council to adopt a decision that a restrictive national tax measure adopted by a Member State concerning one or more third countries is considered compatible with Union law. Article 65(4) TFEU is expressly conceived to 'claw back' from the Court the final say over the legality under EU law of national tax rules in the global capital movement context. That provision is yet to be tested and, indeed, may never be invoked. Its introduction into the Treaty framework is arguably sufficient in itself to ensure that the Court does not exercise a degree of judicial leadership that is not sustained by the (unanimous) political will of the Member States. At the same time, the Court is likely to be aware of the practical difficulty in activating Article 65(4) TFEU. The requirement to secure unanimity in Council effectively casts that provision as a mechanism to affect a minor Treaty amendment.

The Court has also been required to adjudicate on the relationship between Article 63(1) TFEU and the related Treaty freedoms. Given that only the Treaty provisions on capital apply externally, delineating Article 63(1) TFEU from the related provisions on persons and services is a critical issue.[130] Internally, it is far less important to maintain clear distinctions between the scope of the individual Treaty freedoms. To a greater extent, the CJ now adopts a uniform approach to restrictions on intra-EU movement across EU free movement law. Any blurring of the distinction between, for instance, Article 49 TFEU on establishment and Article 63(1) TFEU on capital has little practical impact on the outcome of the Court's review. Indeed, on occasion, the CJ simply transposes its review of national measures as restrictions on intra-EU movement from one freedom directly to another.[131]

The Court falls back on established principles to delineate the scope of Article 63(1) TFEU from that of the related Treaty provisions. To distinguish between establishment and capital, the Court looks specifically to the purpose of the relevant national provision. Article 45 TFEU on establishment is deemed to apply to Member State rules that exclusively affect investments granting shareholders 'definite influence' in an undertaking's decisions and activities.[132] Article 63(1) TFEU, on the other hand, governs situations falling short of that threshold.[133] With respect to Article 56 TFEU on services, the CJ's approach focuses on the identification of the 'centre of gravity' in particular cases.[134] Where a national measure relates to both the freedom to provide services and the free movement of capital, it examines whether the application of one of the two freedoms is entirely secondary to the other. In such

---

[130] eg Case C-31/11 *Scheunemann*, judgment of the Court (Second Chamber) of 19 July 2012, paras 33–34.

[131] eg Case 310/09 *Accor SA* [2011] ECR I-8115, para 64.

[132] Joined Cases C-436/08 and C-437/08 *Haribo* (n 24) para 35.

[133] Joined Cases C-436/08 and C-437/08 *Haribo* (n 24) para 35.

[134] Case C-452/04 *Fidum Finanz* (n 17) at para 43.

cases, the Court will scrutinize the relevant national measure exclusively against the dominant Treaty freedom.[135]

The application of both the 'definite influence' and 'centre of gravity' tests leaves the Court a considerable degree of flexibility to manage the external reach of the Treaty rules on capital. With respect to the boundary between capital and establishment, the Court's scope for manoeuvre is further enhanced by the broad interpretation given to 'direct investments' under Article 63(1) TFEU. In line with Directive 88/361 EEC, that concept includes investments intended to 'establish or maintain lasting and direct links' in the relevant undertaking. Moreover, the 'direct investments' concept has been held to presuppose that shareholders enjoy 'the possibility of participating effectively in the management or control of an undertaking'.[136] That broad definition brings the scope of the free movement of capital very close to that underpinning Article 45 TFEU on establishment.

In *Test Claimants*, the Court (Grand Chamber) arguably took advantage of the blurred boundary between capital and establishment in order to extend the extra-EU dimension of the former freedom.[137] In that decision, the CJ held that Article 63(1) TFEU may be invoked to scrutinize national tax measures that applied without distinction to investments that confer definite influence and those that do not. On its analysis:

A company that is resident in a Member State and has a shareholding in a company resident in a third country *giving it definite influence over the decisions of the latter company and enabling it to determine its activities* may rely upon Article 63 TFEU in order to call into question the consistency with that provision of legislation of that Member State which relates to the tax treatment of dividends originating in the third country and *does not apply exclusively to situations in which the parent company exercises decisive influence over the company paying the dividends.*[138]

That decision greatly enhances the potential scope of Article 63(1) TFEU in connection with capital movements between Member States and third countries. This has clear benefits for investors.

On the other hand, there is also evidence to support the Court's use of its preferred delineating tests to contain the external reach of Article 63(1) TFEU. *Fidum Finanz*—another Grand Chamber decision—stands out in this respect.[139] That case addressed German legislation that effectively prohibited credit institutions established in third countries from providing loans to individuals resident in that state. In that judgment, the CJ concluded that the free movement of services prevailed over Article 63(1) TFEU on capital.[140] As a result, the contested provisions fell out

---

[135] Case C-452/04 *Fidum Finanz* (n 17) at para 43.
[136] eg Case C-112/05 *Commission v Germany (Volkswagen)* (n 73) at para 43.
[137] Case C-53/11 *Test Claimants* (n 26).
[138] Case C-53/11 *Test Claimants* (n 26) para 104 (emphasis added).
[139] Case C-542/04 *Fidum Finanz* (n 17).   [140] Case C-542/04 *Fidum Finanz* (n 17) para 50.

with the scope of the Treaty. In its view, the German legislation primarily affected access to the national market for credit operators established in third countries. Its impact on extra-EU capital movements was considered to be 'merely an inevitable consequence of the restriction imposed on the provision of services'.[141] That finding arguably underplays the independent character of loan provision as a 'capital movement' under Article 63(1) TFEU. In *Eurobonds*, for instance, the CJ had previously held that Belgian legislation prohibiting residents from investing in loans issued in other Member States constituted a restriction on the free movement of capital.[142]

VI. Concluding Remarks

A review of the Treaty framework on capital movement exposes an unusual marriage of the exceptional and the familiar. On the one hand, the Treaty rules on capital may be defined with reference to distinctive features: a unique evolutionary trajectory; an external scope of application; and an uncharacteristic degree of direct Member State control. At the same time, discussion of the free movement of capital raises key issues familiar to internal market lawyers. What constitutes an obstacle to movement under Article 63(1) TFEU? On what grounds may Member States seek to justify restrictions caught by that provision? Do the Treaty rules on capital have horizontal direct effect?

Looking internally, Article 63(1) TFEU is now very much part of the established framework of EU free movement law. The CJ has modelled its approach to that provision to match its interpretation of the related rules on persons and services. That approach is underpinned by a broad distinction between fiscal and regulatory measures. In the fiscal sphere, the Court has opted for a less intrusive, discrimination-based assessment of Member States preferences. This leaves Member States the maximum degree of manoeuvre permitted by the Treaty. By contrast, in the regulatory sphere, the Court has been much bolder. Following established patterns across the economic freedoms, it has decoupled the scope of Article 63(1) TFEU from the discrimination concept in *substance* as well as language. That move grants the Court a much more direct stake in market making. Nowhere is this clearer to see than in its golden shares jurisprudence. In that sphere, the Court has given its full backing to a contestable vision of EU corporate

---

[141]   Case C-542/04 *Fidum Finanz* (n 17) para 49.
[142]   Compare eg Case C-478/98 *Commission v Belgium (Eurobonds)* (n 59).

governance advanced by the Commission. That vision privileges shareholder value over all other economic and non-economic policy objectives.

In key respects, the external dimension of Article 63(1) TFEU follows the same approach developed for the internal market. Most notably, the CJ has directly transposed its case law on restrictions from one context to the other. Yet, the liberalization of extra-EU capital movements remains a fundamentally distinctive aspect of EU law. The CJ is acutely aware of the different political and legal framework within which capital transactions between Member States and third countries take place. Indeed, the parallel jurisprudence on external capital transactions reminds legal scholars—in the negative—of the extraordinary character of EU integration. Recalling *Costa*:

By creating a [Union] of unlimited duration, having its own institutions, its own legal personality, its own legal capacity and . . . real powers stemming from a limitation of sovereignty or a transfer of powers from the States to the [Union], the Member States have limited their sovereign rights, albeit in limited fields, and have thus created a body of law which binds their nationals and themselves.[143]

The absence of a unifying legal and political legal framework to govern capital movements between Member States and third countries is not the only brake on the CJ's dynamism. In the key area of taxation, the Court's decisions in the external sphere are also subject to political revision by the Member States. Time will tell just how far Article 65(4) TFEU serves to shape its interpretative choices.

BIBLIOGRAPHY

C. Barnard, 'Social Dumping or Dumping Socialism?' (2008) *67 Cambridge Law Journal* 262

C. Barnard, 'Derogations, Justifications and the Four Freedoms: Is State Interest Really Protected?' in C. Barnard and O. Odudu (eds), *The Outer Limits of European Union Law* (2009)

C. Barnard, *The Substantive Law of the EU: The Four Freedoms* (4th ed, 2013)

L. Flynn, 'Coming of Age: The Free Movement of Capital Case Law 1993–2002' (2002) *39 Common Market Law Review* 773

C. Gerner-Beuerle, 'Shareholders between the Market and the State' (2012) *49 Common Market Law Review* 97

S. Hindelang, *The Free Movement of Capital and Foreign Direct Investment* (2009)

T. Horsley, 'The Concept of an Obstacle to intra-EU Capital Movement in EU Law' in N. Nic Shuibhne and L. Gormley (eds), *From Single Market to Economic Union: Essays in Memory of John A. Usher* (2012)

S. Kingston, 'A Light in the Darkness: Recent Developments in the ECJ's Direct Tax Jurisprudence' (2007) *44 Common Market Law Review* 1321

---

[143] Case 6/64 *Costa v ENEL* [1964] ECR 585.

R. Murphy, 'The Dynamic Relationship of the Legislature and the Judiciary in the Pursuit of Capital Liberalisation' in P. Syrpis (ed), *The Judiciary, the Legislature and the EU Internal Market* (2012)

R. Murphy, 'Why Does Tax Have to Be so Taxing? The Court Revisits the Franked Investment Income Litigation' (2013) *38 European Law Review* 695

N. Nic Shuibhne, *The Coherence of EU Free Movement Law: Constitutional Responsibility and the Court of Justice* (2013)

S. Peers, 'Free Movement of Capital: Learning Lessons or Slipping on Spilt Milk?' in C. Barnard and J. Scott (eds), *The Law of the Single European Market: Unpacking the Premises* (2002)

W.-G. Ringe, 'Company Law and Free Movement of Capital' (2010) *69 Cambridge Law Journal* 378

J. Snell, 'Free Movement of Capital: Evolution as a Non-Linear Process' in P. Craig and G. de Búrca (eds), *The Evolution of EU Law* (2nd ed, 2010)

E. Szyszcazak, 'Golden Shares and Market Governance' (2003) *40 Common Market Law Review* 493

J. Usher, 'The Evolution of the Free Movement of Capital' (2008) *31 Fordham International Law Journal* 1533

CHAPTER 31

DIRECT TAXATION AND THE FUNDAMENTAL FREEDOMS

PAUL FARMER

I. INTRODUCTION

TAXATION, particularly indirect taxation, has been an important area for the EU since its foundation. The focus in the early case law on the prohibition of discrimination against foreign products under what is now Article 110 TFEU gave way, with progressive harmonization of value added tax (VAT) and other indirect taxes, to a succession of cases on the interpretation of the Community legislation. The key area of VAT was substantially harmonized in 1977 and has since been the subject of continual refinement, the most substantial changes coming in the early 1990s to bring about the removal of fiscal frontiers as part of the single market programme.[1]

The present chapter is devoted to another area that has become increasingly important over the last few decades, namely the impact of the fundamental freedoms on direct tax rules. Surprisingly, perhaps, it was not until 1986 that the Court first encountered direct tax obstacles to the freedoms. The *Avoir Fiscal* case[2]

---

[1] For an up-to-date guide to the VAT legislation and case law see B. Terra and J. Kajus, *A Guide to the European VAT Directives* (2014).
[2] Case C-270/83 *Commission v France* [1986] ECR 273.

concerned the refusal to grant branches of insurance companies whose registered office was situated in another Member State a tax credit (the *Avoir Fiscal*) granted to resident companies receiving dividends from other French companies. The Court held the different treatment to be discriminatory on the ground that the branches and resident companies were subject to corporate profits tax on the same basis and that therefore there was no objective difference in their situations. The Court thus applied the by then familiar covert[3] discrimination analysis used in cases such as *Sotgiu*[4] some 12 years earlier.

By the time of the *Avoir Fiscal* case, however, the general case law on the fundamental freedoms had moved on. The *Cassis de Dijon* case,[5] extending the case law to restrictions arising from disparities between national product regulations, had been decided in 1979. *Gebhard*,[6] using a form of words that extended the Cassis-style analysis to all the freedoms, was decided nine years later in 1995; and in the same year came *Bosman*,[7] concerning genuinely non-discriminatory obstacles imposed by private associations. The case law on direct taxation was therefore born during a period of rapid evolution of the general case law. That evolution is reflected in the language used by the Court in the tax case law, although in substance its decisions remain rooted firmly in discrimination.

II. Particular Features
of Tax Restrictions

Unlike legislation on indirect taxes, such as VAT and excise duties, direct tax rules remain largely unharmonized. The reason for that is the continuing unanimity requirement under Article 115 TFEU (fiscal provisions being explicitly excluded from Article 114(1) TFEU by Article 114(2)) and the reluctance of Member States to cede sovereignty in matters of direct taxation.

Legislative activity in the direct tax field has so far been confined to three directives dealing with specific aspects of cross-border company taxation (cross-border

---

[3] Technically, the different treatment was directly on grounds of the company's seat but the Court treated this as equivalent to different treatment on grounds of the residence of a natural person.

[4] Case C-152/73 *Sotgiu v Deutsche Bundespost* [1974] ECR 153.

[5] Case C-120/78 *Rewe-Zentral v Bundesmonopolverwaltung für Branntwein* [1979] ECR 649.

[6] Case C-55/94 *Gebhard v Consiglio dell'ordine degli Avvocati e Procuratori di Milano* [1995] ECR I-4165.

[7] Case C-415/93 *Union Royale Belge v Bosman* [1995] ECR I-4921.

restructuring of groups,[8] intra-group dividends,[9] and interest and royalty[10] payments) and three directives facilitating cross-border fiscal supervision and enforcement (a specific Directive providing for automatic information exchange on savings interest[11] and two Directives providing more generally for administrative cooperation[12] and mutual assistance in recovery of tax claims[13]). Remaining initiatives of note comprise a multilateral convention between Member States in the field of transfer pricing[14] and the Council Code of Conduct group on business taxation, a political or soft law initiative, operating somewhat uneasily in parallel to the state aid rules, designed to curb the shifting of tax base through 'harmful' tax competition between Member States.

While it has shown little appetite for proposing harmonization of income taxes, the Commission has consistently sought to make the case for more general harmonization of company taxation,[15] pointing to the fiscal obstacles for multinational groups operating in multiple jurisdictions. However, its more ambitious proposals, most recently a proposal for a common consolidated tax base for multinational groups,[16] have made little progress. The main focus for Member State governments in recent years, reflecting a wider international agenda,[17] has been less the removal of fiscal barriers for multinational taxpayers than preventing perceived tax avoidance and tax-base shifting. Such support as there is for harmonizing initiatives stems

[8] Council Dir 2009/133/EC of 19 October 2009 on the common system of taxation applicable to mergers, divisions, partial divisions, transfers of assets and exchanges of shares concerning companies of different Member States and to the transfer of the registered office of an SE or SCE between Member States [2009] OJ L310/34.

[9] Council Dir 2011/96/EU of 30 November 2011 on the common system of taxation applicable in the case of parent companies and subsidiaries of different Member States [2011] OJ L345/8.

[10] Council Dir 2003/49/EC of 3 June 2003 on a common system of taxation applicable to interest and royalty payments made between associated companies of different Member States [2003] OJ L 157/49.

[11] Council Dir 2003/48/EC of 3 June 2003 on taxation of savings income in the form of interest payments OJ L157/38.

[12] Council Dir 2011/16/EU of 15 February 2011 on administrative cooperation in the field of taxation and repealing Dir 77/799/EEC [2011] OJ L64/1.

[13] Council Dir 2010/24/EU of 16 March 2010 concerning mutual assistance for the recovery of claims relating to taxes, duties and other measures [2010] OJ L84/1.

[14] 90/436/EEC Convention on the elimination of double taxation in connection with the adjustment of profits of associated enterprises [1990] OJ L225/10.

[15] See eg the Report of the Committee of Independent Experts on company taxation (Ruding Committee), European Commission 1992; and more recently Commission Staff Working Paper SEC (2001) 1681: Company Taxation in the Internal Market SEC (2001) 1681 and Communication from the Commission to the Council, the European Parliament and the Economic and Social Committee, 23 October 2001, COM (2001) 582: *Towards an Internal Market without tax Obstacles: A Strategy for Providing Companies with a Consolidated Corporate Tax Base for their EU-wide Activities.*

[16] Proposal for a Council Directive on a Common Consolidated Corporate Tax Base 2011/0058(CNS).

[17] Organisation for Economic Co-Operation and Development, *Harmful Tax Competition: An Emerging Global Issue* (1998).

more from that agenda than the desire for liberalization of cross-border movement and investment. Consequently, were the Council to adopt a common corporate tax base—which probably could at most occur by way of enhanced cooperation—it seems unlikely that it would be the elective regime, ie a regime which groups could choose whether to opt into, currently proposed by the Commission and supported by industry. This would not serve the tax competition agenda.

Consequently, in the EU, as elsewhere, countries continue to operate individual tax systems and are free to determine the scope of their taxing rights. In accordance with international practice, they generally assert jurisdiction on the basis of two criteria: the residence of taxpayers and the source of their income. Those criteria are reflected in systematic differences of treatment under national rules between resident and non-resident taxpayers and taxpayers with domestic- and foreign-source income. For example countries commonly grant resident individuals whom they tax on their worldwide income deductions to take account of their personal circumstances, whereas traditionally non-resident individuals are taxed on an objective basis without such deductions.

The existence of individual tax systems and treasuries implies the need for rules ensuring that countries are able to tax an amount of income or profit commensurate with the taxing rights asserted by them. Common examples are rules to ensure proper pricing of transactions within multinational groups of companies ('transfer pricing' and 'thin capitalization' rules), rules determining how much profit should be allocated to company branches, provisions imposing charges on uncrystallized gains on the migration of taxpayers or assets and 'controlled foreign corporation' (CFC) rules which tax the profits of non-resident subsidiaries resident in low tax jurisdictions in the hands of their resident parent companies. Such rules are generally limited to cross-border situations because they would be redundant in a domestic one.[18] The thinking behind the Commission's proposal for a consolidated corporate tax base was in large part to eliminate the need for such rules, with their associated tax and compliance costs, by replacing Member States' individual company tax systems with a single system.[19]

The use by countries of the dual criteria of residence and source for asserting taxing rights is liable to result in 'international juridical double taxation' of persons subject to more than one jurisdiction, ie taxation of the same income in the hands of the same taxpayer by more than one country. For example, taxpayers receiving dividend payments from another Member State may suffer a withholding tax at source on the dividend and then be subject to taxation on the same income in their

---

[18] See however the discussion of the cases on thin capitalization rules below.

[19] The Commission's proposal envisages a system under which, at the election of the taxpayer, corporate profits would be consolidated on an EU-wide basis and then apportioned between Member States on an agreed formulary basis (as they are eg between US and Canadian states). This would create a single EU-wide tax system, eliminating the need to ensure proper pricing of individual intra-group transactions and allowing cross-border consolidation of losses and profits.

state of residence. Countries have partly addressed this problem by entering into a network of bilateral double taxation conventions, often based on a model published by the OECD.[20] However, the treaty network within the EU is not complete and instances of double taxation remain.

In the absence of harmonization countries are free to design their own tax systems, for example systems for the taxation of corporate groups and distributed profits. Such systems often provide for arrangements to prevent economic double taxation of distributed profits, ie multiple taxation of profits as they pass up the group and onwards to shareholders, and to prevent losses and profits from being stranded in different companies belonging to what is in substance a single economic entity. Countries commonly place territorial restrictions on such systems to protect their tax base.

It is obvious from the above survey that the potential for conflict with the Treaty freedoms is considerable. Unsurprisingly, the trickle of cases that followed *Avoir Fiscal* in the late 1980s became a steady flow by the mid to late 1990s to the point where direct tax cases are now a major component of the case law with several hundred decisions. The challenge for the Court, as in other areas of freedoms case law, has been to strike a proper balance between the Treaty freedoms and the need for Member States to safeguard their taxing rights to protect their tax base. The tax area has posed particular challenges due to the inherent complexity of tax rules and the interaction between national systems.

III. The ECJ's Approach in the Tax Area

The basic principle established by the Court is that, in the absence of harmonized rules, Member States remain competent to define their taxing rights and tax systems. Ultimately, Member States' sole obligation is not to discriminate, in the exercise of those taxing rights, on grounds of nationality or, more broadly, against persons exercising the fundamental freedoms (whether inbound or outbound).[21] The Court's inquiry focuses on whether source state rules place non-resident taxpayers at a disadvantage by comparison with resident taxpayers or whether residence state rules place resident taxpayers investing or establishing themselves in another Member State or third country at a disadvantage by comparison with

---

[20] OECD *Model Tax Convention on Income and on Capital 2010 (Full Version)* (10 August 2012).

[21] See the discussion on this point in the opinion of Advocate General Poiares Maduro in Case C-446/03 *Marks & Spencer* [2005] ECR I-10837, in particular at para 28.

taxpayers operating purely domestically[22] or, occasionally, with taxpayers operating in a third Member State.[23] The Court has been reluctant to extend to the direct tax area its case law on non discriminatory restrictions (even though it often uses the language of such cases).

Thus the Court has held that there is no obligation on Member States to eliminate disadvantages arising from disparities between Member States' tax rules. A state of residence is not, for example, obliged to indemnify a taxpayer for the fact that part of his income is subject to higher taxation in another Member State because of a higher tax rate or wider tax base.[24]

Nor are Member States obliged to eliminate the double taxation which may arise from the parallel exercise of fiscal sovereignty by two Member States.[25] A Member State may even enact legislation overriding an existing provision of a bilateral convention so as to remove the double tax relief previously granted; this does not involve a breach of the Treaty freedoms or the duty of cooperation.[26]

Double taxation does not arise from a disparity between Member States' rules: it arises from double exercise of taxing rights over the same income or capital, and occurs even where the rules are identical in both states. Unlike disparities in tax rates and base, double taxation acts as a very real barrier to free movement and investment. Whereas in the absence of harmonization, taxpayers subject to the jurisdiction of more than one state must accept that they will be subject to different sets of rules and rates on different parts of their income or capital, they may be surprised to learn that the Treaty has nothing to say about their being charged tax twice on the same income or capital. As it stands, EU law permits, for example, an individual resident in one Member State who owns a property in another to be subject to income, capital gains, or inheritance tax on the property in both states without any recognition of the tax borne in the other. The Court's explanation for this limitation on the scope of the Treaty is that EU law does not, as it currently stands, lay down any general criteria for the attribution of competence between Member States in relation to the elimination of double taxation.[27] In the case law

---

[22] Case C-293/06 *Deutsche Shell* [2008] ECR I-01129 raised the intriguing question of whether Germany should be required to take account of an exchange rate loss in relation to an Italian branch in a case where there was no convincing domestic comparator. The Court held there to be an unlawful restriction, noting that the loss only showed up in the German accounts and could only be taken into account by Germany.

[23] Case C-196/04 *Cadbury Schweppes plc v Commissioners of Inland Revenue* [2006] ECR I-7995, para 45, and Case C-194/06 *Staatssecretaris van Financiën v Orange European Smallcap Fund* [2008] ECR I-3747, para 56.

[24] Case C-336/96 *Mr and Mrs Robert Gilly v Directeur des services fiscaux du Bas-Rhin* [1998] ECR I-2793.

[25] Case C-513/04 *Kerckhaert and Morres v Belgium State* [2006] ECR I-10967; Cases C-436 and 437/08 *Haribo and Salinen v Finanzant Linz* [2011] ECR I-305 at paras 168–170; Case C-540/11 *Levy and Sebbag v Belgium State*, Order of 19 September 2012.

[26] *Levy and Sebbag* (n 25).   [27] See eg *Kerckhaert and Morres*, para 22.

on goods and services, the Court resolved the problem of dual regulation by giving priority to home state regulation, requiring the importing state to recognize the home state's regulations unless there are overriding general interest requirements. While in the case of dual fiscal regulation there is no principled reason why one state should surrender revenue in favour of the other,[28] it would arguably have been open to the Court to impose a shared obligation on the states concerned, rendering either of them liable to give double taxation relief pending the conclusion of an agreement. Any risk that a taxpayer might avoid taxation in either state could be resolved by requiring evidence from the taxpayer, reinforced where necessary by recourse to the EU administrative cooperation machinery.[29] The Court's failure to give the same stimulus to the removal of barriers arising from dual regulation that it gave in other areas means that instances of international juridical double taxation continue to be widespread within the enlarged EU. The Court's unduly cautious approach has effectively disarmed the Commission, which can do no more than encourage the Member States to complete their network of bilateral agreements and render them more comprehensive (something which is not high on their agenda but would be readily attainable).

In practice the distinction between discrimination and disadvantages arising from disparities or parallel exercise of taxing rights is not always an easy one. This is discussed below in the context of frontier workers and dividend taxation.

1. Differences of Treatment Incorporated in Bilateral Tax Treaties

In a series of decisions,[30] the Court has held that it is open to Member States to conclude bilateral treaties with other Member States which limit the reciprocal advantages conferred by the Treaty to their respective residents. It has justified this on the basis that such a limitation is inherent in the nature of bilateral treaties and that residents of other states are not in a comparable position to residents of the two contracting states. Thus, for example, in *ACT Class IV*, the Court held that the UK was free to hand back to Netherlands shareholders part of the corporation tax paid by UK resident companies in the form of a tax credit while refusing to make an equivalent refund to German-resident shareholders.

---

[28] See however the discussion of the cases on dividend taxation below.

[29] Council Dir 2011/16/EU of 15 February 2011 on administrative cooperation in the field of taxation [2011] OJ L64/1.

[30] Case C-376/03 *D v Inspecteur van de Belastingdienst* [2005] ECR I-5821; Case C-374/04 *Test Claimants in Class IV of the ACT Group Litigation v Commissioners of Inland Revenue* [2006] ECR I-11673 ('ACT Class IV'); Case C-194/06 *Orange European Smallcap Fund* [2008] ECR I-3747.

ACT Class IV and similar cases may be contrasted with the ruling in *Saint Gobain*,[31] where the Court held that Article 49 TFEU required Germany to extend to the branch of a French-resident company the benefits granted to German residents under a bilateral treaty with a third country. While in *ACT Class IV* and similar cases the Court concluded that requiring the contracting states to extend the benefits of the agreement to residents of other Member States would disrupt the overall balance of the agreement, it thought this would not be the case in *Saint Gobain*.

The apparently unqualified acceptance that different treatment of taxpayers subject to different tax treaties may be justified by the inherent nature of bilateral agreements and the overall deal between the Contracting Parties is surprising. For example, if the UK were to provide in its tax laws that a German resident earning UK income was subject to tax at 10 per cent whereas an equivalent French resident was taxed at the normal statutory rate of 30 per cent, this would surely be discriminatory. So why should the inclusion of such different treatment in a bilateral agreement—perhaps as part of a deal imposing on Germany a reciprocal obligation to give a similar tax break to UK residents—make it immune from challenge? Certainly, many differences in treatment under tax treaties may be explained by countervailing advantages or disadvantages under the agreements. The central purpose of most agreements is simply to allocate taxing rights between the two states: in simple terms, taxation in one state is simply the corollary of exemption in the other. But a justification of this type is quite different from that in *ACT Class IV* and similar cases because it relates to the overall tax treatment of the same taxpayer in the two countries. The Court's willingness to accept different treatment favouring residents of certain countries over others simply as part of an overall horse trade between the two states in relation to their taxpayers in general is more difficult to understand. The result is that Member States are free to introduce discriminatory rules provided they collaborate with other Member States to do so in their tax treaties.

IV. Member State Defences

1. Overriding Interests

Since the *Avoir Fiscal* case the Court, in line with the general trend in the case law, has gone beyond *Sotgiu*-style covert discrimination and introduced into its analysis a series of overriding interest justifications. Indeed, ensuring proper fiscal

---

[31] Case C-307/97 *Saint Gobain v Finanzant Aachen-Innenstadt* [1999] ECR I-6161.

supervision was among the interests originally referred to in *Cassis de Dijon*. Since then the Court has added the interest in ensuring fiscal coherence or cohesion,[32] the interest in preventing tax avoidance,[33] and, more recently, the interest in preserving the balanced allocation of taxing powers.[34]

The Court's analysis in this area varies and may sometimes be considered somewhat unorthodox.[35] The existence of overriding interests may be examined in cases where discrimination has or could have been found,[36] and the language of discrimination is used equally in cases concerning outward investment by a Member States' own residents. For example in the line of cases concerning tax restrictions on foreign-source dividends, the Court considers whether the rules are discriminatory, ie involve different treatment of objectively comparable situations, and then goes on to consider whether the Member State concerned can rely on any relevant overriding interest.[37] However, while the Court uses different language, its inquiry is ultimately directed at the single basic question of whether the different treatment of non-residents or of residents according to the source of their income is sufficiently explained by a Member State's allocated taxing rights or by the purpose of the tax regime in question. Selected examples from the case law are discussed below. The narrow tax focus of the inquiry in the freedoms case law, involving considerable overlap between the various justifications, may be contrasted with the analysis in state aid cases where there are two levels of justification: determining whether a fiscal benefit constitutes state aid involves an inquiry into whether the benefit is in accordance with the logic of the tax system, whereas the examination of compatibility entails a broader enquiry into public interest grounds. It may also be contrasted with the diverse range of general policy interests that may be in issue in the general freedoms case law, such as consumer protection, health, environment, and so forth.

The fiscal cohesion defence is concerned predominantly with symmetry between deductions and taxing rights. The enquiry is into whether there is a link between a particular tax advantage and a tax charge. Thus in *Bachmann*,[38] where the defence first appeared, the Court held there to be a direct link between the deduction allowed for life assurance and pension contributions and the taxation of the benefits, a link which would be broken if Belgium were required to allow deductions for contributions paid to providers established in other Member States.[39]

---

[32]   Case C-204/90 *Bachmann v Belgium State* [1992] ECR I-249.

[33]   Case C-264/96 *ICI v Colmer (Her Majesty's Inspector of Taxes)* [1998] ECR I-4695.

[34]   *Marks & Spencer plc* (n 21). The need to ensure effective collection of taxes is also separately referred to in recent case law: see Case C-498/10 *X v Staatssecretaris van Financiën*, 18 October 2012.

[35]   See eg the criticisms made by Advocate General Jacobs in Case C-136/00 *Danner* [2002] ECR I-8147.

[36]   See eg Case C-204/90 *Bachmann v Belgian State* [1992] ECR I-249, where a rule which discriminated overtly against insurers established in other Member States and was 'contrary to . . . the Treaty' was nevertheless held to be justified on the overriding ground of preserving fiscal coherence.

[37]   eg Case C-310/09 *Accor* ECR I-8115, para 44.

[38]   See n 36.

[39]   It is clear that Bachmann would now on its particular facts be decided differently (see Case C-80/94 *Wielockx* [1995] ECR I-2493 and Case C-296/12 *Commission v Belgium*, 23 January 2014).

The interest in preventing tax avoidance focuses on whether a restriction is justified by the need to combat artificial arrangements designed to gain the benefit of—or circumvent—Member State tax rules. The enquiry is therefore into the commerciality of the taxpayer's arrangements. In order to be proportionate, a restriction must be specifically targeted at wholly artificial arrangements.[40]

Since the fiscal coherence defence is not limited to combating non-commercial arrangements, it is therefore potentially of broader application. In the 1990s and early 2000s, however, the Court, retreating from the *Bachmann* decision, severely restricted Member States ability to rely on this defence, imposing the condition that there must be 'a direct link . . ., in the case of one and the same tax payer, between the grant of a tax advantage and the offsetting of that advantage by a fiscal levy, both of which related to the same tax'.[41]

What was missing from the case law during this period was the recognition that there was a need for Member States not merely to apply rules specifically targeted at instances of tax avoidance but more general rules designed to protect the integrity of their tax base. The Court saw no distinction between that objective and (merely) preventing loss of revenue. While it can be no defence for a Member State to complain that eliminating discrimination will mean losing tax revenue (as otherwise the freedoms would be a dead letter), proportionate rules protecting the integrity of a Member State's tax base are the necessary corollary of separate unharmonized tax systems. This was finally recognized with the introduction of the defence based on balanced allocation of taxing powers in *Marks & Spencer*, discussed below.

2. Differences in Tax Rates and Tax Competition

In the absence of harmonization Member States' general tax rates and bases vary widely. In addition many states have traditionally operated special regimes designed to attract certain types of activity into their territory, such as regimes for coordination centres and finance and holding companies. Disparities in tax rates and base may, if sufficiently large, influence patterns of movement and investment, depending on the degree of mobility of the taxpayer and the investment.

Ultimately though, tax is a cost like any other cost, and a degree of competition between Member States is generally thought to be healthy. Distortions caused by

---

[40]   eg Case C-264/96 *ICI* [1998] ECR 1-4695, para 26; Case C-524/04 *Test Claimants in the Thin Cap Group Litigation v Commissioners of Inland Revenue* [2007] ECR I 2107 ('Thin cap'), para 72.

[41]   Case C-168/01 *Bosal Holdings v Staatssecretarias van Financiën* [2003] ECR I 9409, para 29. The requirements have since been relaxed somewhat, allowing Member States more success with the defence: see eg case C-35/11 *Test Claimants in the FII Group Litigation* v *Commissioners of Inland Revenue*, judgment of 13 November 2012 ('FII II'), paras 57 and 58, and case law cited. However, the defence has in the meantime been overtaken somewhat by the broader defence based on balanced allocation of taxing powers: see the discussion of *Marks & Spencer* (n 21).

selective tax measures can be addressed by the state aid rules or at the political level by the Code of Conduct group. Recent developments in the law of state aid have potentially expanded the range of fiscal measures that fall within the scope of the rules. The Court has emphasized that the legislative technique employed is not determinative. It is the effect or impact of the rules on competition that must be considered.[42] The assessment of selectivity does not necessarily involve identifying a reference framework, ie normal taxation from which a derogation is provided. Thus, a tax system, achieves the same result as granting a specific derogation by adjusting and combining tax rules in such a way that their very application results in a distortion of competition, may involve state aid.[43]

Despite this there are inherent limits on the scope of the state aid rules. Some smaller Member States have sidestepped the state aid rules and Code of Conduct process by introducing low general rates of corporate tax, calculating that the lower rate would be outweighed by the tax and other benefits of increased inward investment. The best-known example is probably Ireland, which replaced the reduced rate for finance companies under the Dublin Docks regime with a generally applicable low corporation tax rate.

There is an incentive for higher-tax Member States to seek to neutralize lower rates applied by other States. The Court has held, however, that a Member State is not permitted to impose taxes to offset lower taxation imposed on service providers or lenders in other Member States. Such compensatory measures are regarded as being contrary to the very foundations of the single market. Thus in *Eurowings*,[44] the Court refused to permit Germany to apply a rule imposing a disallowance or add-back of rental payments on the lease of an aircraft from an Irish lessor on the ground that the lessor was subject to an abnormally low rate of tax. Moreover, CFC rules discouraging parent companies from setting up subsidiaries in lower-tax Member States by taxing them on their subsidiaries' profits are not permitted unless they are directed at wholly artificial situations, ie cases of abuse where there is no genuine establishment.[45]

Member States are, however, permitted to counteract lower rates of foreign tax applied to their residents' foreign-source dividend income by topping up the foreign tax to the domestic rate.[46] Thus, in the taxation of residents' foreign-source income the Court has opted for an approach promoting capital export neutrality, aimed at placing foreign-source income on an equal footing with domestic-source income.

---

[42] Case C-487/06 P *British Aggregates v Commission* [2008] ECR I-10515, Opinion of Advocate General Mengozzi, para 100.

[43] Cases C-106/09P and C-107/09P *Commission and Spain v Gibraltar and UK* [2011] ECR I-11113. See also the English Court of Appeal in *Lunn Poly* [1999] STC 350.

[44] Case C-294/97 *Eurowings Luftverkehrs AG v Finanzamt Dortmund-Unna* [1999] ECR I-7447.

[45] Case C-196/04 *Cadbury Schweppes plc v Commissioners of Inland Revenue* [2006] ECR I-7995.

[46] Case 446/06 *Test Claimants in the FII Litigation v Commissioners of Inland Revenue* [2006] ECR I-11753 ('*FII I*').

V. Interaction of Tax Systems

Repeating the principles established under general case law, the Court held early on[47] that the absence of harmonization of tax rules did not justify different treatment contrary to the Treaty freedoms. This is plainly a defence that the Court could not accept as the freedoms would have been a dead letter. The direct tax area does, however, have the complicating factor that whether taxpayers are truly disadvantaged may depend on their overall treatment in the jurisdictions to which they are subject. In some cases, this is virtually impossible to determine, for example where income passes through investment vehicles and on to shareholders who may be resident in other EU or third countries.[48] In other simpler cases it may be more obvious that the different treatment simply transfers revenue from one state to another and that the taxpayer is not disadvantaged because there is a countervailing advantage in another state.

The Court has accepted in principle that it is open to a source Member State to impose an otherwise unlawful withholding tax on dividends paid to shareholders resident in other Member States where relief for the withholding tax is given against the liability of the shareholder in the residence state. However, it rightly imposes strict conditions. The relief must actually be given and given under a binding agreement with the other state.[49] A Member State cannot rely on another Member State giving the countervailing relief unilaterally.[50]

Conversely, the Court has held that Member States may in some cases require taxpayers to show that eliminating the different treatment will not give the taxpayer an unwarranted advantage. Thus, in the cases on cross-border loss relief,[51] the Court has permitted Member States to refuse relief for losses incurred in other Member States unless the taxpayer can demonstrate that they were unable to obtain relief for the losses locally. Similarly, under the Court's case law on dividend taxation,[52] a Member State of residence that applies a system giving relief for economic double taxation is in principle obliged to extend the same treatment cross-border only if the taxpayer shows that they have actually incurred corporation tax in another Member State (and therefore suffered economic double taxation).

---

[47] Case C-270/83 *Commission v France* [1986] ECR 273 (*Avoir Fiscal*), para 24.

[48] See eg Joined Cases C-338/11 to C-347/11 *Santander Asset Management v Directeur des Résidents à L'étranger et des Services généraux*, 10 May 2012.

[49] Case C-540/07 *Commission v Italian Republic* [2009] ECR I-10983.

[50] Compare the cases on frontier workers (discussed below), where the Court has recognized that resident and non-resident taxpayers are in principle in different positions so that a host state can rely on the residence state to provide tax reliefs taking account of the taxpayers' personal circumstances.

[51] eg *Marks & Spencer* (n 21), discussed below.   [52] See eg *FII I* (n 46).

VI. Selected Areas

1. Frontier Workers

The tax situation of workers and self-employed individuals has been a recurring theme in the case law. Many cases have proved relatively straightforward. The Court has had little difficulty, for example, in finding the following to be discriminatory: a higher rate of tax imposed on a non-resident,[53] refusing to deduct professional expenses incurred by a non-resident self-employed person,[54] or refusing a refund of overpaid tax to non-residents.[55] The particular situation of frontier workers has led to the more difficult question of how the personal reliefs and allowances that are commonly granted to individual taxpayers should be treated. The convention under international tax law is that it is the state of residence, as the state which taxes an individual's worldwide income, that is best placed to take account of an individual's personal circumstances, whereas the source state taxes on an 'objective basis'. The problem that arose in the early case of *Schumacker*[56] was that the taxpayer, a frontier worker, earned all his income in the host state and was not taxed in his state of residence. The only state that could take account of his personal circumstances was the host state. The Court held that in those circumstances Mr Schumacker was in a comparable position to a taxpayer resident in the host state and should be granted the same reliefs. Mr Schumacker's case, however, was a rather special one. In other cases the income of two spouses may be split across two or more countries, and in those circumstances it becomes much harder to distinguish discriminatory disadvantages and those arising from the parallel exercise of taxing powers.[57]

2. Cross-border Losses and the Defence Based on Balanced Allocation of Taxing Powers

The recognition of the defence of preserving the balanced allocation of taxing powers came in *Marks & Spencer*, where the Court was asked to rule on

---

[53] Case C-107/94 *Asscher v Staatssecretaris van Financiën* [1996] ECR I-3089; Case C-234/01 *Gerritse v Finanzamt Neukölln-Nord* [2003] ECR I-5933.

[54] *Gerritse* (n 53).

[55] Case C-175/88 *Biehl v Administration des contributions* [1990] ECR I-1779.

[56] [1995] ECR I-225.

[57] See eg Case C-391/97 *Gschwind* [1999] ECR I-5453; Case C385/00 *De Groot v Staatssecretaris van Financiën* [2002] ECR I-11819; Case C-303/12 *Imfeld v Belgian State*, 12 December 2013; and Case C-168/11 *Beker v Finanzamt Heilbronn*, 28 February 2013. For further discussion of the difficulties encountered by the Court in this area see Richard Lyal, 'Elimination of Tax Disadvantages for Frontier Workers: Non-Discrimination and Exceptions' (2006) 7 *ERA Forum* 336.

whether UK provisions restricting group relief (ie surrender of losses between group members to UK resident companies or companies carrying on trade in the UK) was justified. The restriction was a general territorial limitation on the relief rather than one directed specifically at non-commercial arrangements. The UK sought to defend the restriction on the ground that resident and non-resident group members were not in a comparable situation or on grounds of fiscal cohesion. Either way the argument was basically the same: the UK did not tax the profits of the taxpayer's non-resident subsidiaries and should not therefore be required to give relief for their losses. In essence, therefore, the UK's argument was based on symmetry between deductions and taxing rights.

In its judgment the Court reformulated the UK's argument and expressed it as three separate justifications: the need for symmetry in order to preserve the balanced allocation of taxing powers, the need to prevent double use of losses, and the interest in preventing tax avoidance in the form of jurisdiction shopping for the highest tax rate.[58] The Court held that those three points, taken together, justified the UK rules. The Court rightly realized that if it refused Member States the right to impose territorial restrictions on their systems of group relief, this would allow taxpayers freely to choose where to obtain relief for their losses (which would inevitably be in the country with the highest tax rate). The tax base of group members could be shifted at will from one Member State to another.

The Court went on to consider the proportionality of the restriction and concluded that it was disproportionate to those aims for the UK to apply the restriction where there was no possibility for the taxpayer to use the losses locally.[59] The Court considered that where there was no possibility of local use 'the essential part of the objectives pursued' would be achieved.

It may be noted that even relief for losses that are incapable of local use entails a breach of symmetry between deductions and taxation and hence an erosion of tax base.[60] What concerned the Court, however, was the lack of symmetry when combined with the ability of taxpayers to choose where to set off their losses. It was that additional element of free choice that threatened the integrity of the UK's tax system. The Court therefore required Member States to give cross-border relief only in limited circumstances where this concern did not arise, namely where there was no possibility of local use. The Court has followed this approach in a number of

---

[58] *Marks & Spencer* (n 21) paras 43–51.   [59] *Marks & Spencer* (n 21) para 55.
[60] The taxpayer's argument that the profits of the subsidiary were taxed when they were distributed to the UK as dividends was rejected.

later cases[61] (although the decision remains controversial because of the breach of symmetry[62]).

In the nine years since the *Marks & Spencer* decision, the interest in preserving the balanced allocation of taxing powers has become increasingly prominent in the case law. It can perhaps best be viewed as an overarching justification that responds to the basic inquiry into whether a restriction follows logically from a Member State's allocated taxing rights and its particular tax regime. While it encompasses the concept of symmetry underlying the fiscal coherence defence,[63] it may subsume the interest in preventing tax avoidance.[64] Where the purpose of the particular national rules is to combat non-commercial arrangements, then the result should be the same, whichever justification is used. This is reflected in the cases on thin capitalization and transfer pricing discussed below.

3. Exit Taxes

The balanced allocation defence has also recently featured in cases concerning exit charges, that is to say charges imposed on the migration of taxpayers or assets outside the jurisdiction of a Member State.[65] Most countries have rules which tax any uncrystallized gains and recapture reliefs given in relation to assets which leave a Member State's territory or over which it loses taxing rights. Like the rules on group relief, these are not specific rules targeted at instances of avoidance or abuse, but are general rules designed to preserve the integrity of the Member State's tax base. In essence they are based on the same concept of symmetry that underlay the restriction on group relief in *Marks & Spencer*. The Court has recognized the

---

[61] Contrast Case C-123/11 *A Oy,* judgment of 21 February 2013, which concerned a situation not dissimilar to that in *Marks & Spencer,* with Case C-231/05 *Oy AA* [2007] ECR I-6373 and Case C-337/08 *X Holding BV v Staatssecretaris van Financiën* [2010] ECR I-01215. See also Case 414/06 *Lidl Belgium v Finanzamt Heilbronn* [2008] ECR I-3601 concerning the temporary losses of a branch. The Court has found it easier to deal with restrictions imposed on domestic loss relief merely because a link company in the group was non-resident: *Papillon v Ministère du Budget* [2008] ECR I-8947; Case C-18/11 *Commissioners for Her Majesty's Revenue & Customs v Philips Electronics UK,* 6 September 2012; Case C-80/12 *Felixstowe Dock and Railway Company Ltd v The Commissioners for Her Majesty's Revenue & Customs,* 1 April 2014.

[62] Opinion of Advocate General Geelhoed in *ACT Class IV,* para 65; see also Advocate General Kokott in *Oy AA* and *A Oy*; and, very recently, Case C-172/13 *Commission v United Kingdom.*

[63] *Marks & Spencer* (n 21) para 43.

[64] As Advocate General Kokott noted in Case C-311/08 *SGI v Belgian State* [2010] ECR I-487, para 59, 'Such abuse of arrangements therefore constitute simply a particular form of interference in the allocation of the part of tax between Member States.'

[65] Case C-371/10 *National Grid Indus BV v Inspecteur van de Belastingdienst Rijnmond* [2011] ECR I-22273 and Case C-164/12 *DMC Beteiligungsgesellschaft v Finanzamt Hamburg-Mitte,* judgment of 23 January 2014.

legitimacy of such rules but has sought to balance the national fiscal interest with the interest in free movement using the proportionality principle. The need for Member States to tax accrued gains in order to preserve their taxing powers has to be balanced against the fact that in a domestic situation the tax charge would arise only on the ultimate disposal of the asset by the taxpayer. The Court has reconciled the two by allowing Member States to impose a charge on exit but requiring postponement of the charge.

4. Thin Capitalization and Transfer Pricing Rules

At the risk of excessive generalization, the *Marks & Spencer* decision can be seen as something of a watershed in the Court's case law. Before then Member States' attempts to justify their rules were nearly always rejected, often rather summarily. Since then the Court's case law has generally been more nuanced, often turning on an inquiry into proportionality left in varying degrees to the national court. This can be illustrated by comparing the Court's approach to national rules on thin capitalization in *Lankhorst-Hohost*[66] and the later cases of *Thin Cap* and *SGI*.[67]

Lankhorst-Hohorst concerned German rules on thin capitalization under which intra-group interest payments made under non-arm's-length arrangements to lenders whose seat was outside Germany were treated as disguised distributions of profits. The effect of this was to convert the payments from interest payments that were deductible against profits into non-deductible dividends. The rules were of a kind operated by a number of countries and were designed to prevent the shifting of taxable profits from the country of the borrower to the country of the lender by means of excessively high interest deductions.

The application of the thin capitalization rules in the particular case was rather perverse. The loss-making German subsidiary of a Netherlands parent company sought to *reduce* its interest payments in Germany by replacing third-party bank borrowing with a loan from its parent. The German tax authorities nevertheless treated the interest as a disguised distribution on the basis that the arrangements were not arm's length because the subsidiary could not have obtained a loan on similar terms from a third party. The national court found that the arrangements were entirely commercial and non-abusive. On the facts, the thin capitalization adjustment was plainly disproportionate to any legitimate interest served by such rules, and it would have been open to the ECJ to dispose of the case on that ground.

However, the Court's reasoning was more sweeping. It held first that the legislation was not justified by the need to prevent tax avoidance because it did not have the specific purpose of preventing wholly artificial arrangements designed

---

[66] Case 324/00 *Lankhorst-Hohorst v Finanzamt Steinfurt* [2002] ECR I-11779.
[67] Case C-311/08 *SGI*.

to circumvent German tax legislation, but applied wherever the parent company had its seat abroad. It also rejected the German and UK governments' arguments based on fiscal cohesion and the internationally recognized arm's length principle, holding that there was no *Bachmann*-style direct link between the less favourable treatment and the countervailing advantage.

The Court's dismissive attitude to the arm's-length principle alarmed a number of Member States and led them to extend their thin capitalization and intra-group transfer pricing rules to domestic situations so as to avoid different treatment (even though in a domestic context such rules are entirely redundant).

The *Lankhorst-Hohorst* decision led to further challenges to thin capitalization and transfer pricing rules, but it was not until 2007 that the Court had occasion to consider such rules again, this time in the UK case of *Thin Cap*.[68] The case concerned a challenge by a number of UK-resident subsidiaries of non-resident parent companies to the UK thin capitalization and transfer pricing rules. The underlying transactions for which the finance was granted varied but all were entirely commercial. The dispute focused on the financing arrangements, the tax authorities refusing to allow the deduction of interest because the amount of the loans was deemed excessive and non-arm's length.

In *Thin Cap* the ECJ's approach was more nuanced than in *Lankhorst-Hohorst*. Although it rejected arguments based on the cohesion of the UK tax system, it held that such rules could in principle be justified by the objective of preventing abusive practices insofar as their specific object was to prevent wholly artificial arrangements transferring tax liability to a state with a lower tax liability. Referring to *Marks & Spencer*, it added that such practices could undermine the right of the Member States to exercise their tax jurisdiction in relation to the activities carried out in their territory and thus jeopardize the balanced allocation of taxing powers.[69]

Turning to proportionality the Court held that it was permissible for a Member State to apply the arm's-length principle as an objective means of determining whether the transaction was wholly or in part a purely artificial arrangement whose essential purpose was to circumvent the legislation of the Member State. However, it then added the proviso that, 'on each occasion on which the existence of such an arrangement cannot be ruled out, the tax payer [must be] given an opportunity, without being subject to undue administrative constraints, to provide evidence of any commercial justification that there may have been for that arrangement'. It was also necessary that any adjustment should be limited to the non-arm's-length proportion of the interest.

---

[68] Case C-524/04 *Test Claimants in the Thin Cap Group Litigation v Commissioners of Inland Revenue* [2007] ECR I-2107.

[69] *Test Claimants* (n 68) paras 74 and 75.

The recognition of objective and subjective tests follows the pattern in other cases on abuse. The inquiry required by the subjective limb of the test does not involve, as such, an inquiry into the taxpayer's intentions or state of mind. The inquiry is into whether there is (objective) evidence of genuine commercial reasons for the financing arrangements.[70] In other words, the distinction between the objective and subjective limbs of the proportionality test is that the former focuses solely on whether the arm's-length standard is met and ignores whether in the particular circumstances there were commercial reasons explaining the taxpayer's departure from that standard. If no commercial explanation can be shown for non-arm's-length financing arrangements then a Member State is justified in refusing a tax deduction because it would lead to unwarranted erosion of its tax base; and that is so regardless of whether the taxpayer gains a tax advantage through the arrangements because the lender is subject to a lower tax rate.

The findings in *Thin Cap* have been repeated in similar terms in cases such as *SGI and Itelcar*,[71] although with greater emphasis on the balanced allocation defence recognized in the *Marks & Spencer* line of cases. There is, however, an important distinction between the rules in the two types lines of cases. Whereas the specific purpose of the regimes in *Thin Cap* and similar cases was to combat non-commercial transactions, group relief and similar regimes permit groups to transfer results between different group members at will in order to prevent profits and losses from being stranded in different companies. Territorial restrictions on group relief and similar systems serve the broader aim of preserving the integrity of Member States' tax bases by imposing limits on that freedom to transfer profits or losses at will from one company to another. They respond to the more general threat that such regimes would pose to the integrity of Member States' tax systems if they were applied cross-border. Intra-group lending threatens that integrity only to the extent that interest deductions are uncommercial and artificially high.

5. Dividend Taxation

Another area that has featured prominently in the case law is the taxation of distributed company profits. The cases in this area, particularly *FII I and II*[72] and *ACT Class IV*, provide further illustrations of the difficulty in drawing the line between discriminatory disadvantages and those arising from disparities in or parallel exercise of taxing rights.

---

[70] See similarly the comments of Advocate General Poiares Maduro in Case C-255/02 *Halifax v Commissioners of Customs & Excise* [2006] ECR I-1609, paras 70–71; see also Advocate General Leger in *Cadbury Schweppes*, para 117.

[71] Case C-282/12 *Itelcar v Fazenda Publica*, 3 October 2013.

[72] See also the earlier cases of C- 35/98 *Staatssecretaris van Financiën v B.G.M. Verkooijen* [2000] ECR I-4071 and Case C-319/02 *Manninen* [2004] ECR I-7477.

Countries have various systems for taxing distributed corporate profits but a distinction is commonly drawn between classical systems under which companies and shareholders are taxed independently of each other and systems that integrate the two. For example, from 1973 onwards, the UK operated an integration system, known as the imputation system, under which shareholders received a credit against their tax liability for part of the tax paid by the company. Where a company paid a dividend it was required to make an advance payment of corporation tax (ACT) in an amount equal to the credit received by the shareholder. Systems like the UK system are directed at relieving economic double taxation, ie taxation of the same income in the hands of the company and the shareholder.

In addition, most countries, even those applying classical systems, have rules preventing economic double taxation from arising at the corporate level where one company distributes taxed profits to its parent company or corporate shareholder. Domestic dividends are often exempt. Most countries also provide relief for foreign-source profits either by exempting them or by allowing a credit for tax paid (the tax credit or imputation method).

Traditionally many countries have imposed withholding taxes on dividends paid to non-resident shareholders. Such taxes, although collected by the paying company, are technically taxes on the shareholder rather than the company.

In a succession of cases the Court has laid down a number of principles under which it makes a sharp distinction between the obligations of the country of residence and the source country, and between economic double taxation and international juridical double taxation.

As noted above, disadvantages arising from international juridical double taxation fall outside the scope of the Treaty insofar as they are the consequence of the parallel exercise of taxing powers by two states. However, the Court has held that, where a state of residence applies a domestic system for relieving economic double taxation of distributed profits, it cannot lawfully restrict that system to domestic-source income.

FII I and *II* concerned the UK corporation tax system which provided relief for the UK corporation tax paid by dividend-paying subsidiaries by exempting the dividends in the hands of their parent companies. For foreign-source dividends it taxed the income at the normal statutory rate but gave a credit for foreign corporation tax paid up to the UK rate.

In addition the UK operated a system which ensured that the ACT payable on distribution of dividends under its imputation system was paid only once within the domestic corporate group through a system of tax credits given to higher-tier companies (the *FII* system). Where a company received a dividend on which ACT had been paid it received a tax credit that it could set against its own liability to ACT on its own dividends. This was not replicated in the case of foreign-source dividends, which were subject to ACT without regard to the foreign corporation tax already paid on the underlying profits.

The question in *FII I* was whether the different arrangements for foreign-source dividend income were contrary to Articles 49 and 63 TFEU. In relation to the corporation tax charge on foreign-source dividends, the Court held that the domestic exemption system and the tax credit or imputation arrangements applied to foreign-source dividends were equivalent and could be applied in tandem provided that the same rate of tax was applied to the profits of resident dividend-paying companies and foreign-source profits, and that relief was given for the underlying corporation tax paid on foreign-source profits up to the UK rate. As noted above, this finding was based on the principle that the UK was entitled to top up the foreign tax rate to the UK rate so as to put foreign-source income on an equal footing with domestic-source income.

The issue was however referred back to the Court in *FII II*. The difficulty that had arisen following *FII I* was that the national court found that the tax rates on domestic- and foreign-source profits were not the same. Resident dividend-paying companies often benefited from reliefs and allowances in computing their taxable profits which reduced their actual or effective rate to a rate substantially lower than the UK statutory rate applied to foreign-source dividends. Yet dividends paid by resident companies were still exempt in the hands of their parent companies, allowing the benefit of such allowances and reliefs to flow through. The tax burden on foreign-source profits was therefore often higher.

Learning of this the Court held that there was a difference of treatment, but one which was justified by the aim of ensuring fiscal cohesion. However, the UK rules were disproportionate to that aim because a less restrictive approach could have been adopted. The Court reasoned that the domestic exemption had the same effect as taxing the dividend while giving a credit not merely for tax actually paid but, where it was higher, at the statutory or nominal rate of tax. This allowed the benefit of any reliefs and allowances lowering the actual tax burden to pass up to the recipient of the dividend. The UK could have transposed this approach to foreign-source dividends by giving relief at the foreign nominal rate. The Court noted that this solution might not resolve all the disadvantages for companies with foreign-source dividends but held that any remaining disadvantages arose from the parallel exercise of taxing powers rather than from discrimination.

In truth, the Court had taken a wrong turn in *FII I*.[73] By the time of *FII II* the principle of equivalence of the exemption and the tax credit or imputation methods was well established.[74] However, as a matter of simple arithmetic the two methods rarely lead to the same tax burden being imposed on domestic- and foreign-source income. The only way the exemption and tax credit methods could be rendered truly equivalent

---

[73] See the Opinion of Advocate General Jääskinen in *FII II*, who agreed with the views of Advocate General Geelhoed *in FII I* (whose opinion the Court had not followed on this point).

[74] Case C-436/08 *Haribo* [2011] ECR I-00305; Case C-310/09 *Ministre du Budget v Accor* [2011] ECR I-8115; Case C-310/09; and Case C-201/05 *Test Claimants in the CFC and Dividend GLO* v *Commissioners of Inland Revenue* [2008] ECR I-2875.

would be by converting the foreign profits to domestic tax principles (which would be very cumbersome). The idea of granting a credit at the foreign nominal rate credit was a clever solution, although not a complete or conceptually pure one.[75] Moreover, as a matter of analysis, the remaining disadvantages did not, as the Court thought, arise from parallel exercise of taxing rights but from the simple application of a discriminatory UK tax base to foreign-source profits.[76]

In relation to ACT, the Court held in *FII I* that the UK was required in charging ACT to allow a deduction for underlying foreign corporation tax. A UK-resident company receiving foreign-source dividend income was in a comparable position to a UK-resident company receiving domestic-source income judged by reference to the purpose of the UK regime of relieving economic double taxation. Double taxation arose whether the corporation tax paid by the distributing company was UK ACT or foreign corporation tax.

In its judgment, the Court subtly alters the true aim of the UK system, which, as far as ACT was concerned, was limited to relieving multiple charges to *UK ACT* within the domestic group. The Court evidently considered the aim of the system to be legitimate only if it relieved both UK and foreign corporation tax. The fundamental question of why this should be the case is not discussed. The judgment is perhaps to be understood as establishing the principle that, where a Member State of residence makes the policy choice of relieving economic double taxation of distributed profits domestically, it is obliged to carry through that aim to comparable foreign taxes.[77]

There is by contrast no equivalent obligation on a source state which operates a system of relieving economic double taxation. *ACT Class IV* concerned the grant by the UK of tax credits to resident company shareholders to take account of tax borne at the company level. The Court held that the restriction of the payment of tax credits to resident shareholders was not discriminatory because non-resident shareholders were not in a comparable position. The UK granted the credits to resident shareholders in its capacity as their state of residence, whereas it did not exercise taxing rights over the dividends paid to non-resident shareholders.

Thus, whether there is discrimination depends on whether the Member State concerned exercises taxing powers over the dividend and whether the comparators are to be seen as being in a comparable position in the light of the aim of the regime. In *FII I* and *II*, the UK as country of residence exercised taxing rights over

---

[75] Granting a credit at the foreign nominal rate would not correct the difference between the effective tax rates applied to UK- and foreign-source profits, but would allow the UK taxpayer to benefit from whatever allowances and reliefs were granted in the source country by allowing them to pass up to the UK without further taxation.

[76] The disadvantage would arise whenever the UK nominal rate exceeded the foreign nominal rate even where the tax bases were identical in both states.

[77] See K. Lenaerts, 'The Court of Justice and EU Law' in G Maisto (ed), *Taxation of Intercompany Dividends under Tax Treaties and EU Law* (2012).

the foreign-source income whereas in *ACT Class IV*, the UK as source country did not.

ACT Class IV may be contrasted with *Denkavit*,[78] another source state case decided in the same year. *Denkavit* concerned a withholding tax imposed by the state of the dividend-paying company on dividends paid to a shareholder in another Member State. The Court distinguished *ACT Class IV* on the ground that, as soon as a Member State taxes the dividend income of the non-resident shareholders, their situation becomes comparable with that of resident shareholders. A withholding tax applied solely to the income of non-resident shareholders was therefore discriminatory.

The distinction drawn by the Court is rather fragile and formalistic. It is comparatively easy to convert taxation of the shareholder into taxation of the company and vice versa. Companies ultimately do not bear tax themselves—they are merely a vehicle for collection of taxes. Corporation tax imposed on distributed profits is in essence a tax on the company's shareholders, albeit one collected by the company. That is particularly true of a system such as the UK imputation system under which ACT was specifically designed to be prepayment of the shareholder's tax liability.[79] The built-in bias against inward investment inherent in the UK system in *ACT Class IV* was equivalent in effect to a discriminatory withholding tax. This can be demonstrated by a simple example.

Suppose that a Member State has a corporation tax rate of 30 per cent and imposes a withholding tax of 15 per cent on a dividend paid to another Member State. It learns from *Denkavit* that it cannot impose the withholding tax because it is discriminatory. It therefore changes its legislation, raising its corporation tax rate to 45 per cent and giving a tax credit of 15 per cent to resident shareholders alone. The net result is the exactly same as the corporation tax rate of 30 per cent and withholding tax of 15 per cent previously applied.

What the Court overlooked in *ACT Class IV* was that under its imputation system the UK did effectively assert taxing rights at source over non-resident shareholders, and imposed a discriminatory tax on them. If the deeper rationale for *FII I* is that the obligation to remedy the different treatment arose from the policy choice made by the residence state, then the same would logically apply to a source state that, by its choice of system, effectively discriminates against non-resident shareholders. An obligation on the source state to correct the problem would be

---

[78] Case C-170/05 *Denkavit Internationaal v Ministre de l'Économie* [2006] ECR I-11949. See also Case C-379/05 *Amurta v Inspecteur van de Belastingdienst* [2007] ECR I-9569; Case C-284/06 *Finanzamt Hamburg-Am Tierpark v Burda* [2008] ECR I-4571.

[79] See eg 1971 Budget Statement of the Chancellor of Exchequer announcing the imputation system, HC Deb, 30 March 1971, vol 814 col 1384: '[T]here is an alternative system under which all company profits, whether distributed or not, are taxed at the same rate, but part of the corporation tax on the distributed profit is treated as a payment on account of the shareholder's eventual income tax liability on his dividends. The system [is] normally known as the imputation system.'

consistent with international tax treaty practice under which countries giving a tax credit to resident shareholders often agree to extend the credit to residents of the other contracting state. Indeed, as noted above, the UK followed that practice itself in its treaties, albeit selectively. The Court appeared to accept that this was not a problem that could necessarily be cured by the residence state. The conclusion that the disadvantage was, as Advocate General Geelhoed put it, a 'quasi-restriction' that could only be resolved by harmonization[80] was by no means a necessary one. This was a problem caused by the UK's choice of system.

6. Third Countries

Thin Cap and *FII I* and *II* also raised novel points concerning the scope of Article 63 TFEU in relation to investment from and into third countries. Article 63, unlike the other freedoms, applies to third-country situations, subject to the standstill clause in Article 64(1) TFEU for restrictions relating inter alia to direct investment and establishment existing on 31 December 1993. The clear inference to be drawn from Article 64(1) is that Article 63 applies to establishment situations. At the same time, it was surely not the intention of the authors of the Treaty to confer the right of establishment on third-country taxpayers via the back door of Article 63.

The Court resolved this conundrum by reference to the purpose of the legislation in question. Legislation that was directed exclusively at situations which in an intra-EU context would fall within the scope of the freedom of establishment was excluded from the scope of Article 63.

Thus, in *Thin Cap*, the Court held that groups whose parent companies had their seat in third countries could not rely on Article 63 to challenge the UK thin capitalization rules, which were solely concerned with interest payments between group members. That principle even extended to transactions between the parent company's EU-resident subsidiaries. The Court reasoned that a loan transaction between two sister companies resident in the EU was covered not by the free movement of services but by the freedom of establishment. This meant that, where their parent company was resident in a third country, the loan was excluded from the scope of the Treaty. This aspect of the Court's decision is a little curious as, followed to its logical conclusion, it would remove a significant proportion of intra-EU services from the scope of the Treaty.

By contrast, rules that are not directed exclusively at establishment situations fall within the scope of Article 63 and, subject to the standstill clause in Article 64(1), can be challenged in third-country situations. Thus, in *FII I*, the Court held that taxpayers could rely on Article 63 to challenge the UK dividend taxation rules,

---

[80] Advocate General Geelhoed, paras 38–39.

which applied generally to dividends from holdings of any size, in respect of dividends from third countries. In *FII 2*, the Court confirmed that this was so even where on the facts there was a parent-subsidiary relationship which in an intra-EU context would be dealt with under Article 49 TFEU.

7. The Scope of Restitutionary Claims

The *Thin Cap* and *FII* cases also raised a number of remedies issues of general interest. In *FII I*, the claimants, in addition to claiming repayment of overpaid tax, had a number of more sophisticated claims. These included claims for the value of statutory reliefs and allowances used to set off the unlawful tax, claims for additional corporation tax paid where the claimants had waived certain reliefs in order to allow set off of unlawful ACT, and claims for the value of enhancement of dividend payments made to shareholders to compensate them for the unlawful refusal of shareholder tax credits. The Court held that the right to restitution extended to the unduly levied tax and to amounts which related directly to that tax. It did not extend to other matters that were not the inevitable consequence of the discrimination.[81]

As a matter of EU law, the distinction between restitutionary and damages claims appears to be essentially one of causation and remoteness. Restitution is limited to claims that flow directly from and are an inevitable consequence of the breach without any independent act by the claimants. In *FII I*, the Court made it clear that the claims for waiver of reliefs and enhanced dividend payments fell on the damages side of the line. It was less clear from the judgment whether the Court thought statutory reliefs used to meet the unlawful tax liability were too remote to qualify as restitutionary claims. This question is currently an outstanding appeal issue in the *FII* litigation before the Supreme Court.[82]

It seems clear from the case law that as a matter of EU law the amount of restitution is to be measured, as with a damages claim, from the perspective of the claimant, the difference between the two types of claim being the categories of loss that can be recovered. The English law of restitution looks at restitution from the perspective of the recipient of the unlawful tax. This issue is of particular significance in measuring the time value of money. It would seem to follow that, as a matter of principle, the relevant interest rate in determining whether a claimant receives an adequate indemnity for the unlawful levying of tax is the borrowing cost of the claimant rather than that of the defendant. This could be particularly important

---

[81] *FII I* (n 46) paras 205–208.

[82] *Test Claimants in the FII Group Litigation v Revenue and Customs Commissioners* [2010] ECWA Civ 103, paras 175–184 (time for applying for permission is currently suspended by the Supreme Court order of 8 November 2010).

where a smaller company is deprived of funds as its borrowing rate is likely to be much higher than that of the government. In the recent High Court decision in *Littlewoods*,[83] given following the reference to the Court, the Judge commented on this but noted that the claimants were content to settle for the government's borrowing rates.

VII. Conclusion

The Court's case law on direct taxation has now reached a level of maturity with a number of well-established principles. While over the last 20 years or so there have at times been significant adjustments to the course taken, in the short to medium term we are more likely to see a process of refinement and development of the existing principles.

Developments at the political level are harder to predict. The single currency has assisted capital mobility and made disparities in levels of taxation more transparent, exacerbating the concerns about tax competition. Perceived abuse by multinationals in shifting profits to low tax jurisdictions is high on the political agenda. The financial crisis has also highlighted the need for greater budgetary control and cooperation. Whether this will translate itself into legislative action in the direct tax field remains to be seen; but if there is further harmonization, the impetus is more likely to come from those factors, with the efficiencies offered by the removal of tax barriers to cross-border activity a by-product. Notwithstanding the Court's significant contribution to this area of the law, many obstacles, particularly in the field of company taxation, ultimately require action by the legislator.

Bibliography

V. Edwards and P. Farmer, 'The Concept of Abuse in the Freedom of Establishment of Companies: A Case of Double Standards?' in A. Arnull, P. Eeckhout, and T. Tridimas (eds), *Continuity and Change in EU Law: Essays in Honour of Sir Francis Jacobs* (2008)

R. de le Feria and S. Vogenauer (eds), *Prohibition of Abuse of Law—A New General Principle of EU Law?* (2011)

J. Ghosh, *Principles of the Internal Market and Direct Taxation* (2007)

T. Kaye, 'Tax Discrimination: A Comparative Analysis of US and EU Approaches' in Avi-Yonah, Hines and Lang (eds), *Comparative Fiscal Federalism: Comparing the European Court of Justice and the US Supreme Court's Tax Jurisprudence* (2006)

---

[83] *Littlewoods Retail v HMRC* [2014] EWHC 868 (Ch).

G. Kofler, 'Tax Treaty "Neutralization" of Source State Discrimination under the EU Fundamental Freedoms?' (2011) 65 *Bulletin for International Taxation* 684

M. Lang, *CFC Legislation and Community Law* (2002) 42 *European Taxation* 374

M. Lang, 'ECJ Case Law on Cross-border Dividend Taxation—Recent Developments' (2008) 17 *EC Tax Review* 67

M. Lehner, 'The Influence of EU Law on Tax Treaties from a German Perspective' (2000) 54 *Bulletin for International Taxation* 461

G. Maisto (ed), *Taxation of Intercompany Dividends under Tax treaties and EU Law* (2012)

T. O'Shea, 'Dividend Taxation Post-*Manninen*: Shifting Sands or Solid Foundations?' (2007) 45 *Tax Notes International* 887

T. O'Shea, *EU Tax Law and Double Tax Conventions* (2008)

P. Pistone, 'Ups and Downs in the Case Law of the European Court of Justice and the Swinging Pendulum of Direct Taxation' (2008) 36 *Intertax* 146

P. Pistone, 'The Impact of European Law on the Relations with Third Countries in the Field of Direct Taxation' (2006) 34 *Intertax* 234

B. Terra and P. Wattel, *European Tax Law* (6th ed, 2012)

S. Van Thiel, *Free Movement of Persons and Income Tax Law: The European Court in Search of Principles* (2002)

F. Vanistendael, 'The ECJ at the Crossroads: Balancing Tax Sovereignty against the Imperatives of the Single Market' (2006) 46 European Taxation 413

F. Vanistendael, 'In Defence of the European Court of Justice' (2008) 62 *Bulletin for International Taxation* 90

D. Weber, *Tax Avoidance and the EC Treaty Freedoms* (2005)

D. Weber (ed), *The Influence of European Law on Direct Taxation* (2007)

PART VII

AREA OF FREEDOM, SECURITY, AND JUSTICE

CHAPTER 32

EU CRIMINAL LAW UNDER THE AREA OF FREEDOM, SECURITY, AND JUSTICE

CHRISTOPHER HARDING

As a description and as a concept 'EU criminal law' is novel, contestable, and potentially misleading, yet it has now become established as a convenient label which is being used to indicate a significant body of emergent policy and law within the EU system, providing the title now for some recently published books on this subject area.[1] So far the term has yet to make an appearance in any formal Treaty provision, and indeed its Treaty location—although now more focused and evident compared to the pre-Lisbon state of affairs—remains somewhat obscure, sited in the section of the TFEU dealing with the Area of Freedom, Security and Justice (AFSJ). To say this at the beginning of the discussion in fact serves to make an important point about EU criminal law as a subject. Expectations should not be raised that this is criminal law in the conventional sense, as understood at the national level, and this is a feature of the topic that makes its understanding and study challenging, at least on first acquaintance. It would be helpful, therefore, to preface the account given in this chapter with some probing questions about the nature and role of this body of EU policy and rules, and how the concept of criminal law should be understood at

[1] For instance: Valsamis Mitsilegas, *EU Criminal Law* (2009); Samuli Miettinen, *Criminal Law and Policy in the European Union* (2012).

the supranational European level. The opening questions should be: in what sense is this criminal law, in what sense is it European, and how does this area of policy and law relate to criminal law and crime policy at both the Member State level and the international or inter-governmental levels? Care should also be taken in choosing vocabulary—is there a difference between 'EU criminal law' and 'European criminal law'? It would be preferable to reserve the former term for those rules and instruments arising directly under the EU legal order (*sensu stricte*), and employ the term 'European criminal law' to refer to the range of inter-governmental criminal law activities, particularly under the umbrella of the Council of Europe, at the European level (*sensu largo*).

Also, one of the first things to say about the idea of EU criminal law is that for many people it is a matter of surprise or even objection that it should have emerged at all. It was widely felt that the former European Community had and should have no interest in criminal law, as an area which was outside the agreed competence of the Community and one that should remain so as a politically and legally reserved domain of national sovereignty.[2] Although definitely expressed, the argument that criminal law should be regarded as a matter of national sovereignty par excellence was rarely reasoned in an explicit way and required some reading between the lines. On closer inspection, the strong national interest in the matter would seem to reside in two important qualities of criminal law: its employment of actual force, and its expressive role.

In its modern incarnation, criminal law involves a forcible authority, an exercise of compulsory and repressive power in relation to the processes of investigation and trial and the imposition of sanctions.[3] The extremity and special intrusiveness of criminal law result in a constitutional significance, and have given rise to two major principles: first, the state's claim to a monopoly of the legitimate use of violence or force against the individual; and second, the use of criminal law as a measure of last resort, the *ultima ratio* principle. Following on from its extreme character, criminal law then possesses a strong expressive power, in relation to the core values, interests, and identity of a society or polity. As the German *Bundesverfassungsgericht* argued in 2009: 'By criminal law, a legal community gives itself a code of conduct that is anchored in its values, and whose violation, according to the shared convictions on law, is regarded as so grievous and unacceptable for social co-existence in the community that it requires punishment.[4]

On such reasoning, if a state or society loses command of its criminal law, it loses something of its identity and the self-determination of its core values, and thus any

---

[2] 'Criminal law was firmly considered the exclusive province of the member states': Jenia Iontcheva Turner, 'The Expressive Dimension of EU Criminal Law' (2012) 60 *American Journal of Comparative Law* 555, 555.

[3] Turner (n 2) 556.

[4] BVerfG, 2BvE 2/08 vom 30/6/2009, para 355 (the so-called 'Lisbon Judgment', reviewing the compatibility of the Treaty of Lisbon with the German Basic Law).

formal commitment to transferring or sharing sovereignty in that area is a sensitive and even controversial issue in political and legal terms. Nonetheless, there is now a phenomenon that is widely described as EU criminal law, which, no doubt partly for the above reasons, appears to have emerged by stealth. A brief account of how this has happened will also serve to indicate, in broad lines, what kind of legal species is contained within the description of EU criminal law.

I. The Pre-history of EU Criminal Law

1. Multi-level Origins

Historically, it is possible to summarize the pre-history of the present *corpus* of EU criminal law[5] as the accumulation of much that comprised the former Third Pillar *acquis*—that developing inter-governmental arm of the EU dealing broadly with 'Justice and Home Affairs' (JHA) and 'Police and Judicial Cooperation in Criminal Matters' during the period between the Treaties of Maastricht in 1993 and Lisbon in 2009. But the Third Pillar had its antecedents, in particular the Trevi process originating in the 1970s. Trevi (Terrorism, Radicalism, Extremism, Political Violence) was an inter-governmental network of national officials set up in 1975, whose remit gradually extended from terrorism to a wider range of crime control and public order matters.[6] Trevi became a kind of organizational platform for the Third Pillar in 1993 within the broader JHA competence. Another antecedent was the Schengen regime, based on the 1985 Schengen Agreement and 1990 Implementing Convention and providing for the removal of border controls at EC internal borders and 'compensatory' security at the external perimeter of the Community, giving rise to significant measures of police cooperation and exchange of information.[7] The Schengen crime and control measures were in due

---

[5] See generally: Mitsilegas (n 1) Ch 1; Estella Baker and Christopher Harding, 'From Past Imperfect to Future Perfect: A Longitudinal Study of the Third Pillar' (2009) 34 *European Law Review* 25, 27–43.

[6] Juliet Lodge, 'Internal Security and Judicial Cooperation', in Juliet Lodge (ed), *The European Community and the Challenge of the Future* (2nd ed, 1993).

[7] For background on the earlier, more separate phases of the Schengen regime, see: H. Meijers et al., *Schengen: Interntionalisation of Central Chapters of the Law on Aliens, Refugees, Security and the Police* (1991); C. Fijnaut, 'The Schengen Treaties and European Police Cooperation' (1993) 1 *European Journal of Crime, Criminal Law and Criminal Justice* 37. On the integration of the Schengen regime into the EU structure, see: Cyrille Fijnaut, 'Police Co-operation and the Area of Freedom, Security and Justice', in Neil Walker (ed), *Europe's Area of Freedom, Security and Justice* (2004) Ch 6; European Council (ed), *The Schengen Acquis Integrated into the European Union* (1999).

course absorbed into the Third Pillar structure under the Treaty of Amsterdam, albeit importing a certain degree of optionality,[8] as the latter also slimmed down[9] the JHA remit to police and judicial cooperation in criminal matters. The Amsterdam Treaty supplied a new framework for much of this activity, the Area of Freedom, Security and Justice (AFSJ), seen in its most ambitious light as something that could stand alongside the other grand projects of the single market and the Eurozone. The AFSJ has itself been driven forward by a series of multi-annual programmes agreed at meetings of the European Council, starting with that at Tampere in 1999,[10] followed successively by the second and third programmes, the Hague programme in 2004,[11] and the Stockholm programme in 2009.[12] Even with a sense of steady progress based on these programmes and accompanying 'road maps', the latter days of the Third Pillar were complex, with further discussion within the framework of the Convention on the Future of Europe,[13] the subsequent failure of the Constitutional Treaty, the appearance of fresh inter-governmental initiatives (the Prum Convention and the formation of the G6 Group),[14] before the final mainstreaming of the Third Pillar *acquis* under the Lisbon Treaty and the present provisions of the TFEU.

These main developments are summarized in Figure 32.1.

2. Legislative Competence

It is also worth recalling, if only briefly for present purposes, the earlier disputes during the Third Pillar phase regarding the respective First and Third Pillar

[8] Protocol No 2, on the right of the UK and Ireland not to be bound by the Schengen *aquis.*

[9] That part of the Third Pillar relating to population movement was transferred to the First Pillar, becoming a new Title IV of the EC Treaty, on 'Visas, Asylum, Immigration and Other Policies Relating to the Free Movement of Persons'.

[10] Council of the European Union, 15–16 October 1999, *Presidency Conclusions: The Tampere Milestones.*

[11] Council of the European Union, *The Hague Programme: Strengthening Freedom, Security and Justice in the European Union,* 16054/04, Brussels, 13 December 2004 [2005] OJ C53/1.

[12] Council of the European Union, *The Stockholm Programme: An Open and Secure Europe Serving the Citizen,* 17024/09, Brussels, 21 December 2009 [2010] OJ C115.

[13] See the Final Report of the Working Group X, 'Freedom, Security and Justice', Brussels, 2 December 2002, CONV 426/02. See now Part Three, Title V of the TFEU.

[14] Prum Convention, 27 May 2005 (originally Austria, Germany, Belgium, Luxembourg, and the Netherlands). The treaty was based on a German initiative and concerned further cross-border cooperation (hence the colloquial title of 'Schengen III'); core provisions were subsequently incorporated into Council Decision 2008/15/JHA of 23 June 2008. The G6 Group (an unofficial grouping of interior ministers) comprises France, Germany, Italy, Poland, Spain, and the UK. See: House of Lords European Union Committee, *Behind Closed Doors, 40th Report of Session 2005-06,* 2006, HL Paper 221.

Trevi (1975)	Intergovernmental network of officials: terrorism, radicalism, extremism, violence—and beyond.
Schengen Agreement (1985) and Implementing Convention (1990)	Crime and control measures following from removal of internal border control and compensatory measures on external EC borders.
Maastricht Treaty (TEU) (in force 1993)	Third Pillar (first incarnation) established: Justice and Home Affairs (intergovernmental). Trevi absorbed.
Treaty of Amsterdam (in force 1999)	Third Pillar (second incarnation): AFSJ and Judicial and Police Cooperation in Criminal Matters. Schengen regime incorporated.
Tampere European Council and Programme ('Milestones') (1999)	First EU policy and legislative programme laid down.
Working Group X on Freedom, Security and Justice (Convention on the Future of Europe (2002) Hague Programme (2004)	Second policy and legislative programme.
Constitutional Treaty fails (2005) Prum Convention and G6 (2006)	Further partial intergovernmental initiatives.
Stockholm Programme (2009)	Third policy and legislative programme.
Lisbon Treaty and TFEU (2009)	Pillar system removed and Third Pillar *acquis* mainstreamed in supranational Part III Title V of the TFEU A.

Figure 32.1 Historical Route Map of EU Criminal Law: Key Developments

legislative competence about criminal law matters, since to some extent these have informed the present competence as established in the TFEU. A historical feature of the longer term evolution of EC/EU competence in the broad field of criminal matters was its haphazard location across the First and Third Pillars of the EU, and to some extent (as noted immediately above) also in the wider European inter-governmental sphere of action. Alongside Trevi, Schengen, and the growing Third Pillar *acquis*, it had also been increasingly asserted that there was a 'parasitic' EC (First Pillar) competence in relation to criminal law, in that single market objectives could either prevent or require Member State action in the criminal law field. Put simply, it was argued, and in due course affirmed by the Court of Justice, that national criminal law should not obstruct the application of single market rules,[15] or could be called in aid if necessary to ensure an effective application of the latter.[16] The development of this EC Treaty based competence can also be viewed in terms of 'neo-functionalist' argument[17] and 'spill-over' theory, insofar as integration in one sector of activity (eg the economic) may spill over into other and related areas, when achievement of goals in the first field become dependent on further action in a second related field (in this case, enforcement process and criminal law). By the early years of this century, the Commission and the Parliament had seized upon this 'subdued but stable . . . selective and opportunistic method of construction'[18] to argue in favour of a First Pillar rather than Third Pillar basis for EU legislation directing the use of national criminal law. The matter came to a head in the so-called 'Environmental Crime' and 'Ship-Source Pollution' cases[19] as a matter of some constitutional significance, with the Commission confronting the Council and a clutch of Member States[20] in challenging the legality of Council Framework Decisions and arguing for action by means of EC Directives. The real prizes in this dispute were command of the legislative process, legal effect, transparency, and judicial scrutiny—that is, being able to use the supranational, Community method.[21] The Court of Justice, taking a notably adventurous approach reminiscent of some of its earlier 'activism',[22] supported the Commission's argument, confirming that the Council's clear legislative competence under the Third Pillar could not trump the need for 'effective, proportionate and dissuasive penalties', as may be deemed necessary for purposes of the EC Treaty.[23]

Following the Lisbon changes, this debate has become historical and all bases for an EU competence in criminal law matters have become mainstreamed under Part III, Title V of the TFEU. But the earlier and largely judicial assertion of an 'effective implementation' competence is now codified in Article 83(1) of

---

[15] Case 203/80 *Casati* (1981) ECR 2595.

[16] Case 50/76 *Amsterdam Bulb BV v Produktschap voor Siergewassen* (1977) ECR 137. See generally for a fuller account, Mitsilegas (n 1) 60ff, and in particular, Estella Baker, 'Criminal Jurisdiction, the Public Dimension to "Effective Protection" and the Construction of Community–Citizen Relations' (2002) 4 *Cambridge Yearbook of European Legal Studies* 25.

[17] Associated in particular with the work of Ernst Haas (see Ernst B. Haas, *The Uniting of Europe* (1958). For a more recent discussion of this approach, see Alec Stone Sweet, *The Judicial Construction of Europe* (2004).

[18] Baker and Harding (n 5) 28.

[19] Case C-176/03 *Commission v Council* (2005) ECR 1-7879 ('Environmental Crime Case'); Case C-440/05 *Commission v Council* (2007) ECR 1-9097 ('Ship-Source Pollution Case').

[20] In the Environmental Crime case the Commission was supported by the European Parliament, while the Council was supported by 11 Member States (Denmark, Germany, Greece, Spain, France, Ireland, the Netherlands, Portugal, Finland, Sweden, and the UK). In the Ship-Source Pollution Case (n 19), 20 Member States intervened in support of the Council.

[21] For a fuller account and overview of the legal argument in these cases, see Mitsilegas (n 1) 70–84.

[22] Mitsilegas (n 1) 72.

[23] See eg the Court's 'Ship-Source Pollution' judgment (n 19) para 66.

the TFEU, as one of the principal bases for EU legislative action in this field, as discussed below.

3. Tracing Development through the Programmes

Another way in which to gain some sense and direction in this field of EU competence, especially during the last 15 years, is to track main policy developments as articulated in the successive European Council Programmes, Action Plans, and Roadmaps. These instruments and documents, drafted and adopted within the framework of the AFSJ from the occasion of the Tampere European Council in October 1999 onwards, have served to drive forward policy and law in this field within an inter-governmental energizing process. At the broadest level, the successive five-year programmes, adopted by the European Council at Tampere (1999), The Hague (2004), and Stockholm (2009),[24] have set targets for legislative action. The Programmes have been supplemented by more detailed Action Plans, most importantly those dealing with organized crime (1997 and 2000, together with a Joint Action in 1998[25]) and terrorism (2001)[26] as additional spurs to legislative action, in the form principally of a tranche of Third Pillar Framework Decisions and implementation 'Roadmaps'. This process of policy mapping and legislative implementation has possessed a characteristically inter-governmental character and, pre-Lisbon, largely reflected the European Council and Member State governments' preoccupation with securitization within the AFSJ umbrella. A reading of these instruments and documents, and their successive legislative outcomes, provides an idea of the substantive content of EU criminal law and criminal justice in the first years of this century, while also reflecting the somewhat reactive and top-down direction of this field of action. A general view of such action taken under the Third Pillar would lead to an impression of 'crime control' rather than 'criminal law'. In a stock-taking exercise in relation to the Third Pillar, published in 2009, Baker and Harding commented that a main focus of criticism of Third Pillar activity was:

the striking imbalance between the Union's enthusiasm for investing in crime control and its reticence about ensuring appropriate protections for defence rights. For example, all but one of the framework decisions that have been adopted under the Third Pillar concern crime control in some guise or other, the exception being an instrument to protect victims' rights.[27]

---

[24] See notes 10–12 above.   [25] 98/733/JHA, 29 December 1998 [1998] OJ L351.
[26] Action Plan on combating terrorism, 21 September 2001, SN 140/01, subsequently updated.
[27] Baker and Harding (n 5) 34.

To some extent, this drift and flavour of Third Pillar EU criminal law may be explicable by its location within the AFSJ. This dimension of the subject, and its present post-Lisbon supranational aspects, will be explored further in Section II.

II. The Area of Freedom, Security, and Justice as a Legitimation of EU Criminal Law

1. Human Mobility

It has already been noted that the neo-functionalist 'spill-over' argument serves to explain some of the EU direction of national criminal law in favour of single market interests. Such an interpretation of the integration process and its consequences can also be used to explain the appearance of the AFSJ and the development of EU crime policy and criminal law under that umbrella. In a nutshell, the underlying issue here is *human mobility*. Increased opportunity and freedom of movement of persons, especially in the European context, have been major features of life in the second part of the twentieth century and into the present time. The European Community project in itself, of course, fostered human mobility—the free movement of persons within the Community was one of the key freedoms of the single market. But also, more widely, globalizing tendencies and the greater permeability of borders in the post-Cold War period, have also contributed to greater human mobility.[28] Consequently, such mobility, although in one sense economically positive within the EU, has increasingly become a matter of concern as the less desirable outcomes have made themselves evident, in the form of crime flows and the undermining of security. By the time of the Treaty of Amsterdam, the longstanding but narrowly interpreted security derogation in relation to the free movement of EC nationals[29] had become elevated to a strong EU concern, emerging in the Amsterdam revisions as the incorporation of the Schengen regime and the advent of the AFSJ. To quote the Council's website on Justice and Home Affairs: 'Lifting the frontiers between the Member States to permit people to pass freely cannot

---

[28] For an overview, see Khalid Kosser, *International Migration: A Very Short Introduction* (2007) Ch 3.

[29] Originally Art 48(3) of the EC Treaty, see now Art 45(3) TFEU ('limitations justified on grounds of public policy, public security or public health').

take place to the detriment of the security of the population, of public order and of civil liberties. To obviate this, flanking compensatory measures were adopted.'[30]

On this reasoning, some of EU criminal law may be viewed as 'flanking compensatory measures', taking its place under the AFSJ alongside policy and rules on external border regulation, immigration, asylum, and—it should be added—citizenship and the protection of basic rights (the JHA remit). This line of argument also served during the 1990s to underscore EU claims to legitimacy, summed up in the Tampere European Council's 'AFSJ milestones', which included a reference to the AFSJ as a 'project which responds to the frequently expressed concerns of citizens and has a direct bearing on their daily lives'.[31] The formulation of the AFSJ served to combine an internal focus—the security and protection of those within the EU—with an external context—the relation to the world outside the EU, whether that comprises the needs of immigrants and asylum seekers or the security and crime threats emanating from beyond the European borders. In short, managing human mobility, in both its positive and negative aspects, supplied further legitimation for a new phase of European integration.

2. Security v Rights Protection

However, as the concept of the AFSJ became fleshed out, concerns began to emerge regarding a bias towards security,[32] and the overall coherence of the AFSJ package of policy and activity.[33] The question remains concerning the interrelation between and the precise interpretation and role of the elements of freedom, security, and justice. It may be plausibly argued that, insofar as the AFSJ is a matter of crime control, then the balancing of *individual freedom* and *collective or public security* reflects a natural tension within the field of criminal law, as articulated in Packer's classic analysis[34] and then mediated through a legal balancing exercise within the framework of human rights protection. The discussion excited by the flurry of anti-terrorist activity, which resulted in a number of EU measures in the early years of this century, provides a characteristic example of such freedom v security critical debate. The 'justice' element of the AFSJ may then be seen as that mediating process which seeks to reconcile and accommodate these competing objectives, and in the European context signals the significant relevance of both the European

---

[30] www.consilium.europa.eu.

[31] Tampere European Council, 15–16 October 1999, milestone 2.

[32] See eg Cathryn Costello, 'Administrative Governance and the Europeanisation of Asylum and Immigration Policy', in Herwig C.H. Hofmann and Alexander H. Türk (eds), *EU Administrative Governance* (2006) 287.

[33] See for instance, Neil Walker, 'In Search of the Area of Freedom, Security and Justice: A Constitutional Odyssey', in N Walker (ed), *Europe's Area of Freedom, Security and Justice* (2004).

[34] See generally Herbert L. Packer, *The Limits of the Criminal Sanction* (1968).

Human Rights Convention (ECHR) and the EU Charter of Fundamental Rights for developing EU criminal law. It is significant also in this connection to note the emphasis placed on human rights arguments in the 2009 Stockholm Programme. In its opening statement for the Programme, the European Council refers first to the need to focus on the interests and needs of citizens and to ensure respect for fundamental freedoms and integrity while guaranteeing security, and that the AFSJ must 'above all be a single area in which fundamental rights are protected'.[35] The stronger commitment to the 'rights agenda' that has emerged post-Lisbon, evident for instance in the revitalized legislative programme in relation to defence rights, may be seen as a move towards rebalancing the freedom/security tension within the AFSJ.

The evolution of the AFSJ as a legal concept is now best encapsulated in Article 67 of the TFEU, located at the beginning of Title V of the Treaty. Article 67 represents some reconfiguration and different emphasizing of the previous Treaty provisions relating to the AFSJ (Articles 29 EU and 67 EC). In particular, the present Article 67 emphasizes in its first paragraph the respect for fundamental rights and the diversity of national legal systems and traditions, so giving rights protection and legal diversity a sure place and guiding role in the whole AFSJ project. This tenor is maintained in the following paragraphs, with references to fairness towards third-country nationals in paragraph 2 and the role of the Union in facilitating access to justice in paragraph 4. Moreover, the role of mutual recognition as the 'cornerstone' of legal development in this field of action is recognized in both the third and fourth paragraphs of Article 67. Meanwhile, the substance of the AFSJ is summarized in two main objectives: internal freedom of movement, secured through a common position on external borders, immigration and asylum; and internal security secured through a common position and effective cooperation on crime, racism, and xenophobia. It is also significant that the latter are grouped together as threats to security, justifying common EU action.

3. Reacting to Outsiders

Another significant component of the AFSJ, which also has a bearing on crime policy and criminal justice, arises more directly from the policy and rules on immigration and asylum (relocated in the First Pillar between Amsterdam and Lisbon, and now sited in Title V of the TFEU). Immigration and asylum are both important legal routes into the EU for nationals of third states, and the presence of migrant workers, refugees, and asylum seekers within EU countries has emerged as an increasingly sensitive political issue in recent years. One question that may

---

[35] *Stockholm Programme* (n 12).

be posed is whether such significant outsider groups import distinctive criminality or crime-related issues in their wake, so adding to the crime control agenda in the Member States. Limited research findings to date suggest that such third-country nationals resident in the EU do not add so much to the range of offending conduct, but simply in terms of additional numbers replicate established patterns of criminality as found in the existing population of host countries.[36] But what is an emerging certainty in a number of EU states is a degree of suspicion and apprehension regarding the presence of migrant workers, refugees, and perceived invasive organized crime groups on the part of host country populations. This has clearly appeared as an issue within political debates, criminological rehearsals in contemporary fiction and drama, and as a tension which, for instance, informs understanding of the Breivik massacre in Norway in 2011.[37] The relevant point to note here is how such an outsider presence may become a trigger for xenophobia, racism, and hate crime, and these categories of criminality have appeared in recent years on the EU crime control agenda, culminating in a Framework Decision in 2008 on combating certain forms of expression of racism and xenophobia by means of criminal law.[38]

The measures to deal with racism and xenophobia provide an instructive case study within the field of EU criminal law. The expression of racism and xenophobia, as specific types of 'hate-speech' crime, are not listed in the category of 'Euro crimes' in the TEU and TFEU provisions, since it does not fit into the model of transnational criminality. The Framework Decision and its forerunner, the Action Plan of 1997, were based broadly on Articles 29, 31, and 34(2)(b) of the TEU—Article 29 (see now Article 67(3) TFEU) put forward combating racism and xenophobia as a main route to achieving the AFSJ, and the first recital of the Decision explained that 'racism and xenophobia are direct violations of the principles of liberty, democracy, respect for human rights and fundamental freedoms and the rule of law, principles upon which the European Union is founded and which are common to the Member States'. In one sense, this provides an example of a value-led initiative within the EU criminal law field, basing the need for common action on the need to protect certain core values and interests, rather than performing a more instrumental role in dealing with the transnational challenge in enforcing criminal law or in supporting single market policies. But having embarked on legal action in this sector and in its quest for a common position, the project also made evident

---

[36] See eg the findings of some recent British research: Grahame Maxwell and Peter Fahey, *Comment on Migration and Policing*, ACPO Report (2008); Brian Bell and Stephen Machin, *The Impact of Migration on Crime and Victimisation* (2011); Peter Aspinall and Charles Watters, *Refugees and Asylum Seekers: A Review from an Equality and Human Rights Perspective*, Equality and Human Rights Commission, Research Report 52 (2010), Ch 6.

[37] The so-called Utoya Massacre, perpetrated by Anders Breivik in July 2011. Breivik's subsequent defence manifesto was based on a xenophobic world view.

[38] Framework Decision 2008/913, 28 November 2008 [2008] OJ L328.

some divergence of views and interests as between Member States. In particular, the exercise revealed a strong 'rainbow' of views regarding the criminalization of certain forms of expression, and the compatibility between the use of criminal law and the entitlement to basic rights in relation expression,[39] so testing the limits on harmonization in the criminal law field.

III. EU Criminal Law as a System of Pan-European Coordination: Legislative Competence

The discussion so far has traced the evolution and emergence of the body of policies and rules now described as EU criminal law and its present Treaty location in the provision of an AFSJ. It is necessary now to explain further what is comprised in more substantive terms in this corpus of EU rules, by reference to the now more explicit provision for mainstream legislative action in Chapter 4 of Title V of the TFEU.

The formal heading of Chapter 4 is 'Judicial Cooperation in Criminal Matters' (and that of the following Chapter 5 is 'Police Cooperation'), and this immediately suggests something different from a conventional criminal code or catalogue of criminal offences. The map of Chapter 4 is something of a patchwork. Article 82 describes the *method* of cooperation, along with some legislative competence in relation to broad procedural matters. Articles 83 and 84 provide for a legislative competence with reference to substantive criminal law matters. Article 85 describes the establishment and role of Eurojust. Article 86 deals with the protection of the financial interests of the Union and the setting up of a European Public Prosecutor's Office. The provisions of Chapter 5 (Articles 87–89) cover police cooperation, the operation of Europol, and agency operation across the Member States. The overall package of Chapters 4 and 5 therefore supplies a legal basis for the EU direction of national criminal law for certain purposes, by means of steering European-level legislation and other instruments. Any search for coherence in this corpus of Treaty provisions is likely to result in the idea that this is all about the coordination of criminal justice.

Within this package perhaps the core and most innovative provision in relation to the *scope* of legislative competence is Article 83, which codifies and develops

---

[39] See the discussion in Mitsilegas (n 1) 98–101.

two main bases for EU action in the criminal law field: dealing with serious trans-national crime (Article 83(1)—ex-Article 29 TEU); and supporting the effective implementation of EU policy (Article 83(2)—from the case law of the Court of Justice). Article 83(1) and (2) may be quoted in full:

1. The European Parliament and Council may, by means of directives adopted in accordance with the ordinary legislative procedure, establish minimum rules concerning the definition of criminal offences and sanctions in the areas of particularly serious crime with a cross-border dimension resulting from the nature or impact of such offences or from a special need to combat them on a common basis. These areas of crime are the following: terrorism, trafficking in human beings and sexual exploitation of women and children, illicit drug trafficking, illicit arms trafficking, money laundering, corruption, counterfeiting of means of payment, computer crime and organised crime.

   On the basis of developments in crime, the Council may adopt a decision identifying other areas of crime that meet the criteria specified in this paragraph. It shall act unanimously after obtaining the consent of the European Parliament.

2. If the approximation of criminal laws and regulations of the Member States proves essential to ensure the implementation of a Union policy in an area which has been subject to harmonisation measures, directives may establish minimum rules with regard to the definition of criminal offences and sanctions in the area concerned. Such directives shall be adopted by the same ordinary or special legislative procedure as was followed for the adoption of the harmonisation measures in question.

As already noted, these two grounds for legislative competence have developed along different routes, the first very much within the Third Pillar and the AFSJ, the second largely with its origins in strategies of First Pillar effectiveness. Article 83 now casts them as areas of sibling competence, sharing common objectives and methods—the adoption of Directives to establish minimum rules concerning the definition of criminal offences and sanctions. In this way, the EU legislature may require the amendment or new provision of Member State criminal and penal law, as necessary, to secure the two objectives of Article 83(1) and (2). The impact on the Member States is likely to be variable, ranging from no necessary action to the enactment of new criminal offences and, as an exercise in legal development, it has brought (in the case of some Third Pillar framework decisions) and will bring (in the case of Directives) into sharper relief the diversity of criminal law and penal philosophies and practices across the Member States (a 'European penal rainbow').

The essential thrust of Article 83 competence is to ensure that there is a necessary common provision regarding criminal law enforcement in certain areas ('Euro crimes' and to support implementation of EU policy). In both branches of Article 83 it is really a matter of effectiveness, a European-level monitoring of national enforcement and coordination of the latter across the EU. This is therefore best described as managerial rather than substantive criminal law, a reading of the situation that is underpinned by the constitutional confirmation that Union intervention in this field is predicated upon principles of subsidiarity, complementarity, and proportionality, and summed up in the idea that it has to add value to what is already done at the national level. In a significant step towards steering developments on the basis of Article 83 (and arguably more generally in the field of EU criminal law), the Commission issued a Communication on EU criminal policy in September 2011,[40] and in this document emphasized the 'added value' role of EU crime policy and criminal law, the need for the Union legislature to base itself on the above basic principles, and the objectives of coherence and consistency in the field. This led the Commission to sound a cautionary note on the use of criminal law, as embodied in the *ultima ratio* principle:

Criminal investigations and sanctions may have a significant impact on citizens' rights and include a stigmatising effect. Therefore criminal law must always remain a measure of last resort. This is reflected in the general principle of proportionality (as embodied in [Article 5(4) of] the Treaty on European Union and, specifically for criminal penalties, in [Article 49(3) of] the EU Charter of Fundamental Rights). For criminal law measures supporting the enforcement of EU policies [as laid down in Article 83(2) TFEU], the Treaty explicitly requires a test of whether criminal law measures are 'essential' to achieve the goal of an effective policy implementation.

Therefore, the legislator needs to analyse whether measures other than criminal law measures, eg sanction regimes of administrative or civil nature, could not efficiently ensure the policy implementation and whether criminal law could address the problems more effectively. This will require a thorough analysis in the Impact Assessments preceding any legislative proposal, including for instance and depending on the specificities of the policy area concerned, an assessment of whether Member States' sanction regimes achieve the desired result and difficulties faced by national authorities implementing EU law on the ground.[41]

Of particular note within this document is the stress placed on the use of criminal law impact assessments, signalling a more systematic steering by the EU of the use of criminal law in these areas.

The Treaty provisions flanking Article 83 lay down further areas of EU competence. Article 84 enables measures to be adopted to promote and support Member State activity in the field of crime prevention, outside the scope of harmonization. Article 82, on the other hand, allows for the enactment of infrastructural rules (in paragraph 1) and procedural rules (in paragraph 2) to support the processes of mutual recognition of judgments and approximation

---

[40] European Commission, 'Towards an EU Criminal Policy: Ensuring the Effective Implementation of EU Policies through Criminal Law' COM (2011) 573 final.

[41] European Commission (n 40) section 2.2.1.

of rules, and this can perhaps be broadly described as a criminal justice and procedure competence. The listed subject matter in those provisions includes matters such as conflicts of jurisdiction, judicial training, and the rights of defending parties and of victims.

At present, the legislative programme based on these TFEU provisions is of course largely prospective, but some idea of the present and future corpus of coordination and common minimum rules may be gained from a glance at the list of Third Pillar Framework Decisions and First Pillar Directives adopted during the pre-Lisbon period of legislative activity. At first glance, this list might appear haphazard and broad in scope, but it gains some coherence from a retrospective mapping of the TFEU provisions referred to above. A retrospective reading also reveals a character of wayward vitality in this legislative process. In terms of substantive criminal law and associated penal measures, there may be identified a determined jostling of First and Third Pillar activity, dealing with three main kinds of issue: protection of the Union's own interests (especially the Union budget), transnational criminal activities, and the achievement of Community policies.[42] In relation to procedural questions and criminal justice, despite an uncertain Treaty basis for legislation in that field, a number of Framework Decisions were adopted, for instance to support mutual recognition or deal with the standing of victims, further encouraged by an expansive interpretation of such measures by the Court of Justice, confirming their indirect effect[43] and application to corporate persons.[44] The TFEU provisions will now introduce a clearer sense of order into this enterprise, already supplying, for example, a surer legal basis in Article 82 for the emerging tranche of Directives on defence rights.

The programme of defence rights legislation, comprising common minimum standards in support of the principle of mutual recognition, had been urged successively in the Tampere, Hague, and Stockholm Programmes. In a Council Resolution attached to the Stockholm Programme at the end of 2009, recalling the issue of an increasing number of persons involved in criminal proceedings in Member States other than their own and the fact that discussion on procedural rights had not so far been productive, the comment was made that it was 'now time to take action to improve the balance between' measures of judicial and police cooperation to facilitate prosecution and the protection of procedural rights of the individual.[45] The Council endorsed a Roadmap, annexed to the Resolution, setting out a step-by-step programme of measures: the right to translation and interpretation; the right to information on legal entitlement and

---

[42] Mitsilegas (n 1) 86–87.

[43] Case C-105/03 *Maria Pupino, Criminal Proceedings* (2005) ECR 1-5285.

[44] Case C-467/05 *Giovanni Dell' Orto* (2007) ECR 1-5585.

[45] Resolution of the Council of 30 November 2009 on a Roadmap for strengthening procedural rights of suspected or accused persons in criminal proceedings ([2009] OJ C295/1).

about charges; the right to legal advice and legal aid; the right to communicate with relatives, employers, and consular authorities; safeguards for vulnerable persons; and rights in relation to pre-trial detention.[46] Now having a clear Treaty basis in Article 82(2)(b) of the TFEU, some Directives have appeared as part of this programme: Directive 2010/64 on the right to interpretation and translation;[47] Directive 2012/13 on the right to information in criminal proceedings;[48] and Directive 2013/48 on the right of access to a lawyer and to communicate upon arrest.[49] This emergent codification of defence rights thus serves to redress the imbalance in relation to enforcement powers, which, as noted already, had become a matter of increasing critical concern.

Another field of policy development and legislative action which has gained a significant momentum more recently is that of victim protection, following on from an earlier commitment and exhortation in the 1999 Tampere Conclusions and the Stockholm Programme in 2009, regarding the broader need to protect citizens and especially those who are especially vulnerable and in 'particularly exposed situations'.[50] A Commission Communication on strengthening victims' rights in the EU[51] outlined a programme of protective legislation, which has now materialized in a number of measures: Directive 2011/99 providing for the European Protection Order[52]; Directive 2012/29, establishing minimum standards on the rights, support, and protection of crime victims[53]; and Regulation 606/2013 on the mutual recognition of civil protection measures,[54] all adding to the earlier Directive 2004/80 on compensation for crime victims.[55] As such, this body of rules represents another emergent code, of victim protection and victims' rights. But, reporting on this line of development, alongside that relating to defence rights referred to just above, raises some wider questions regarding the overall direction and coherence of policy and the underlying relation between victim protection and defence rights. There is a natural tension in the subject, and at least an opportunity for this to be addressed in itself as an underlying constitutional issue at the EU level.

---

[46] Annex to Resolution; see also, 'Analysis of the Future of Mutual Recognition in Criminal Matters in the European Union', report of 20 November 2008 by the Université Libre de Bruxelles, locating such procedural protection as a necessary element of trust and confidence in underpinning mutual recognition.

[47] [2010] OJ L280/1.   [48] [2012] OJ L142/1.

[49] [2013] OJ L294/1. For a recent study of present national positions regarding the areas covered by these first three Directives, see Jodie Blackstock, Edward Lloyd-Cape, Jacqueline Hodgson, and Taru Spronken, *Inside Police Custody: An Emprical Account of Suspects' Rights in Four Jurisdictions* (2013), covering interpretation and translation, information and legal assistance in France, Scotland, the Netherlands, and England and Wales.

[50] See the listing of victims in this sense in point 2.3.4 of the *Stockholm Programme* (n 12).

[51] COM (2011) 274 final, 18 May 2011.   [52] [2011] OJ L338.   [53] [2012] OJ L315.

[54] [2013] OJ L181/4.   [55] [2004] OJ L261/15.

IV. The Method of EU Criminal Law: The Rise of Mutual Recognition

1. Origins

One of the most interesting and significant developments so far in the history of EU criminal law is that of the rise to prominence of the strategy of mutual recognition to serve as a governing operational principle and also as a trigger for a fast developing case law on matters of real legal and penological substance. The device has its origins in the context of the EC single market rules (for instance, freedom of establishment via the mutual recognition of qualifications) as a means of expediting market integration through bypassing the need for a complete uniformity or harmonization of measures across the Member States. In analytical terms, it is a matter of locating regulatory control, whether in the host or receiving state (subject to non-discrimination, that country determines the standard to be applied); or at the supranational EU level ('vertically' agreed harmonization of the standard as the same for all); or in the home or sending state (whose standard is accepted or 'mutually recognized' on the basis of trust by all other receiving countries). Thus the third option appears the speediest and the easiest since all originating standards are accepted elsewhere, so as to remove 'standard barriers' and facilitate the movement of goods, services, professional activities, or—the case of EU criminal law—national enforcement tools. So, in the last context, an official decision to start criminal proceedings (by charging an offence) or to initiate a penal measure (eg commit to prison) can be enforced in another state by a complementary measure (arrest and rendition) to send an individual to the first state, even if the procedure leading to the first state's decision or its legal basis differs from that applicable in the second. The second state will agree to the transfer on a basis of trust and confidence in the different process or standard. The most important actual example of this approach is that contained in the Framework Decision on the European Arrest Warrant (EAW),[56] which facilitated precisely that process of arrest and rendition for purposes of prosecution or serving a sentence in another Member State as a means of effecting criminal law cooperation across the EU.

In the Third Pillar context of criminal law cooperation, mutual recognition was seized upon in the late 1990s (largely on the initiative of the UK Presidency of the EU in l998) when EU harmonization of standards was proving slow and difficult to achieve.[57] The strategy was rapidly taken on board—endorsed by the European

---

[56] Council Framework Decision 2002/584/JHA, 13 June 2002, on the European Arrest Warrant and the surrender procedures between Member States [2002] OJ L190/1.

[57] See the summary in Mitsilegas (n 1) 116.

Council in its Tampere Conclusions as the 'cornerstone' of judicial cooperation in criminal matters, explored as such in a Commission Communication of 2000,[58] and adopted as the preferred method in relation to a proposed programme of 24 measures in the field in 2001. The superficial appeal of mutual recognition is that it facilitates transnational cooperation (and to that extent integration) while respecting diversity and removing the agonies of harmonization. But in the context of criminal law, the matter is less straightforward than in the context of single market mutual acceptance of economic policy.

A problem resides in the sensitivity and special constitutional values inherent in criminal and penal law in a transnational and European context, where the different standards of other states may be less readily accepted and trusted. The fact, for instance, that the same conduct is criminalized in one state but not another may reflect strongly embedded national philosophies, traditions, and values that may not be readily compromised (and indeed may already have appeared as obstacles to harmonization). Politically, it was quickly apparent that there should be some tolerance of host or receiving state reluctance to accept unreservedly the standards elsewhere, and so some qualification of the automaticity of mutual recognition. Legally, this could be done through a number of devices, notably the agreement at EU level on agreed 'minimum' standards (as a limited harmonization measure, an approach now embodied in Article 82 TFEU, as the main provision on criminal law mutual recognition); or through derogation from the obligation to recognize, based on either a test of functional equivalence or comparability, or the recognition in turn of 'mandatory requirements' as a trump card to be played by the host state. Thus, realistically, mutual recognition in this field has not proven automatic, but subject to a balancing of diverse criminal law and penal interests, mediated through a legislative working out of minimum standards or a judicial assessment of claims to derogate. As such it has emerged as a revealing field of legal discourse on crime policy and constitutional standards across the European 'penal rainbow'.

There is a further connected argument relating to the role of mutual recognition in this field compared to the single market context. In the latter area, the role of mutual recognition is rights enhancing for individuals in promoting freedom of movement and economic opportunity. In the context of JHA, however, it operates differently, promoting the movement (or more exactly, extra-territorial effect) of official decisions *against* individuals,[59] thus rights restricting in outcome.[60] This fact has contributed to the concern regarding an enforcement priority within the EU criminal law field,

---

[58] 'Mutual Recognition of Final Decisions in Criminal Matters' COM (2000) 495 final.

[59] What Mitsilegas, for instance, has termed the 'enforced movement' (as compared to 'free movement') of individuals: Valsamis Mitsilegas, 'The Limits of Mutual Trust in Europe's Area of Freedom, Security and Justice: From Automatic Inter-State Cooperation to the Slow Emergence of the Individual' (2012) 32 *Yearbook of European Law* 319, 319.

[60] See, for instance, S. Lavenex, 'Mutual Recognition and the Monopoly of Force: Limits of the Single Market Analogy' (2007) 14 *Journal of European Public Policy* 762.

leading to argument in favour of the more explicit integration of human rights protection (eg the promotion of defence rights, as discussed in Section II(2)), and the coupling of legislative provision of minimum standards with mutual recognition obligations.

2. The Field of Legislative and Judicial Action

Mutual recognition has been used significantly during the first decade of the century as a basis for EU criminal law cooperation in some crucial areas of enforcement: arrest and transfer for trial or custodial sentences,[61] collection and exchange of evidence,[62] and the enforcement of financial penalties.[63] Two measures in particular, the Framework Decisions on the EAW and the European Evidence Warrant (EEW), have led to both extensive comment and some important litigation, at both national and European levels. Such mutual legal assistance legislation has in a relatively short space of time codified a set of obligations to cooperate in criminal law enforcement across Member State boundaries and to do so promptly, without formality, and without too many questions. The thrust of this policy was most evident in the terms of the EAW Framework Decision, which itself came into being speedily, almost as a species of emergency legislation, later in 2001. The obligation on the part of the requested state to surrender individuals was not automatic but was strongly presumptive, especially regarding the removal of any double criminality requirement in relation to more serious offences,[64] the scope of the mandatory and optional grounds for refusal,[65] and the Court of Justice's subsequent confirmation that the measure complied with general principles of legality.[66]

Unsurprisingly, resort to the EAW procedure became a fertile site of legal appeal and challenge, and questions regarding the compatibility of Member State implementing legislation with national constitutions in a number of countries.[67] One notable outcome of such resistance and concern has been (somewhat ironically) to fall

---

[61] Council Framework Decision on the European Arrest Warrant (n 56).

[62] Council Framework Decision on the European Evidence Warrant, 18 December 2008, 2008/978/JHA [2008] OJ L250/72.

[63] See in particular Council Framework Decision on the application of mutual recognition to financial penalties, 22 March 2005, 2005/214/JHA [2005] OJ L76.

[64] See eg the discussion in S. Alegre and M. Leaf, 'Mutual Recognition in European Judicial Co-operation: A Step Too Far Too Soon? Case Study—the European Arrest Warrant' (2004) 10 *European Law Journal* 200.

[65] eg incompatibility with human rights protection was not listed as a ground for refusal to surrender. National Parliaments, defence lawyers, and media have expressed reservations: see Valsamis Mitsilegas, 'The Constitutional Implications of Mutual Recognition in Criminal Matters in the European Union' (2006) 43 *Common Market Law Review* 1277.

[66] Case C-303/05 *Advocaten voor de Wereld VZW v Leden van de Ministerraad* (2007) ECR 1-3633.

[67] Germany, Cyprus, Poland, and the Czech Republic—eg in relation to the extradition of nationals.

back on harmonization, in the form of an EU framing of minimum standards of legal protection for suspects and defendants, as laid down in the 2009 Roadmap and present programme of Directives described in Section III, and in the 2009 Framework Decision on double jeopardy (or *ne bis in idem*).[68] The level of concern regarding the enforcement imperative contained in the EAW provisions has also been reflected in the greater element of compromise evident in the later Framework Decision on the EEW, which was subject to a much longer process of legislative negotiation and not enacted until 2008. This measure is more explicit about human rights and other constitutional safeguards—there are clear references to necessity and proportionality in the collection of evidence, and greater concession is made to the principle of double criminality.[69] The longer-term prospects for the EEW have been rendered more uncertain by the appearance of a new proposal, to be embodied in a Directive, for a European Investigation Order, which, among other things, would enable investigations to be undertaken in other states, but this proposal has already been subject to critical scrutiny.[70] To be sure, the technique of mutual recognition has released a vigorous and full rehearsal and debate regarding the need to balance competing interests in the criminal justice process across the European spectrum.

V. Institutional Developments: System or Happenstance?

EU criminal law also comprises the activity of a growing number of European bodies and agencies with specific criminal law roles, in particular Europol, Eurojust, the proposed office of a European Public Prosecutor, and OLAF.[71] Again, it is characteristic that this institutional infrastructure has evolved gradually and unevenly and not in any carefully planned way—more a matter of happenstance than system, with the TFEU being used in an attempt to superimpose some more coherent ordering.

---

[68] Framework Decision 2009/948, 30 November 2009, on prevention and settlement of conflicts of exercise of criminal jurisdiction in criminal proceedings ([2009] OJ L328/42).

[69] See Art 7(a) of the Framework Decision on necessity and proportionality, and Art 14 on double criminality.

[70] See eg Steve Peers, *EU Justice and Home Affairs Law* (3rd ed, 2011) 715. See the compromise text for a Directive on the European Investigation Order, Council Document no. 18918/11.

[71] For a fuller discussion and overview of the role and development of Europol, Eurojust and OLAF up until the changes brought about by the Treaty of Lisbon, see Mitsilegas (n 1) Ch 4.

1. OLAF

From a historical perspective, the earliest example of a European-level criminal justice agency was the body established by the Commission in 1987 to deal with fraud against the financial interests of the EC—an anti-fraud unit within the Commission, UCLAF (*Unité de coordination de la lutte anti-fraude*). UCLAF was replaced in 1999 by OLAF (*l'Office européen de lutte anti-fraude*) following the fall of the Santer Commission.[72] OLAF's role has been the investigation and collection of evidence relating to internal and external[73] cases of suspected fraud affecting the EC/EU budget, cases then handed over for prosecution at the national level. The haphazard development of UCLAF and OLAF has led to the latter's status being described as 'hybrid and ambiguous' by the French National Assembly,[74] reflecting concerns and uncertainty regarding the use of its evidence and the implications for the exercise of defence rights in national criminal proceedings. OLAF's status and activities are governed mainly by a Commission decision and regulation (both of 1999) but its accountability is opaque—a certain degree of scrutiny is exercised by a Supervisory Committee and the Court of Auditors, but the latter body in particular has questioned the effectiveness of these scrutinizing procedures.[75] There is, in addition, uncertain opportunity for judicial review of OLAF action, especially in the context of the division of responsibility between OLAF and national authorities. However, there are signs of an increasing willingness on the part of European Courts to probe the legality of OLAF's conduct of its cases—in contrast to the Court of First Instance's earlier hands-off approach in *Tillack v Commission* in 2006,[76] the European Court of Human Rights in *Tillack v Belgium*[77] and then the Court of First Instance in *Franchet and Byk v Commission*[78] adopted a more vigorous approach to protecting individual rights in relation to OLAF's procedure.[79] Some of these issues are characteristic consequences of establishing in an ad hoc manner, within an institution whose main role is not in the field of criminal law, a body with criminal law functions, and this rehearses again some of the

---

[72] The Commission under the presidency of Jacques Santer resigned as a body on 15 March 1999 following the publication of Report by a Committee of Independent Experts: *Report on allegations regarding fraud, mismanagement and nepotism in the Commission.*

[73] That is, internally within the institutions and bodies of the EU, and external in the sense of the activities of others (for instance traders) within the framework of EU policies.

[74] Assemblée Nationale, *Rapport d'information depose par la Délégation de l'Assemblée Nationale pour l'Union européenne sur l'Office européen de lutte anti-fraude (OLAF)*, No 1533, 8 April 2004, 10.

[75] See the Special Report No 1/2005 of the Court of Auditors, *Concerning the Management of the European Anti-Fraud Office (OLAF)* [2005] OJ C202.

[76] Case T-193/04 *Tillack v Commission* (2006) ECR II-3999.

[77] Application no 20477 *Tillack v Belgium*, judgment of the European Court of Human Rights, 27 November 2007.

[78] Case T-48/05 *Franchet and Byk v Commission* (2008) ECR II-2841.

[79] See generally the summary provided by Mitsilegas (n 1) 215–218.

longer-standing arguments concerning the Commission's role in investigating and sanctioning serious competition infringements.

OLAF has emerged as a significant initiative and model of European-level crime control. Its own information depicts a substantial body of activity: since 1999, some 3500 investigations completed, over 1.1 billion Euros recovered, and during 2011 a cumulative 511 years of prison sentences handed down in EU Member States following OLAF investigations.[80] In the longer term, its future role will be bound up with the projected setting up of the European Public Prosecutor's Office (now provided for in Article 86 of the TFEU), which in some respects would involve a widening of OLAF's present remit on the basis of a more secure legal platform in the Treaty. At the present time, however, Member State support for the Prosecutor's Office remains limited.[81]

2. Europol

While OLAF evolved within the mainstream of EC and EU activity, as a body within the Commission, Europol (European Police Office) has inter-governmental origins but has now been mainstreamed under Article 88 of the TFEU. Its legal basis was originally located in the Third Pillar Europol Convention of 1995, supplemented by three Protocols and then a Council Decision,[82] and its role has developed incrementally, both in terms of scope and powers. Police cooperation is now firmly embedded as a Union objective and area of competence in Article 87 of the TFEU, while Article 88 confirms Europol's mission in support of Member State criminal law enforcement in relation to 'serious crime affecting two or more Member States, terrorism and forms of crime which affect a common interest covered by a Union policy'.[83] As laid down in Article 88(2), Europol has two main fields of action: an intelligence role (collection, storage, processing, analysis, and exchange of information); and investigative and operational action, carried out jointly with Member States' authorities. Both these fields of action are highly significant in legal terms, and the operational role represents a more recent leap forward in relation to Europol's original competence.

While Europol's investigative and operational role remains largely prospective, its intelligence role is well established, and the collection, analysis, and exchange of personal data give rise to a number of questions relating to the protection of individual rights. In this respect, the mainstreaming of Europol's activities and

---

[80] http://ec.europa.eu/anti_fraud/index_en.htm.

[81] Principally, France, Germany, Spain, and Italy.

[82] Europol Convention [1995] OJ C316/1; Council Decision on Europol (2009/371/JHA) [2009] OJ L121/37.

[83] As provided also in the 2009 Decision; originally its remit was limited to dealing with organized crime.

their future legal basis in the form of EU regulations will enhance the possibility of judicial and other forms of scrutiny within the framework of the TFEU.[84] What remains less certain is the relationship between Europol and the other principal EU actors in this field, OLAF and Eurojust, especially pending the setting up of the European Public Prosecutor's Office.

3. Eurojust

Once again, the story of Eurojust is one of incremental development, and drift from the inter-governmental to the supranational sphere of operation, but broadly speaking concerned with the facilitation of judicial cooperation, just as Europol has been concerned with police cooperation. The pre-historical background to Eurojust is therefore the international field of mutual legal assistance, and its nearer history resides in the setting up of the European Judicial Network in 1998,[85] the emergence of the concept of Eurojust in the 1999 Tampere Conclusions, and its formal birth in the Council's Eurojust Decision in 2002.[86] Eurojust now has its formal legal basis in Article 85 of the TFEU, as a European-level body with a role in supporting and strengthening coordination and cooperation between national investigating and prosecuting authorities. An idea of the scale and substance of the work of Eurojust may be gained from its annual reports. The Report for 2011,[87] for example, records over 1400 requests for assistance from Member State authorities during that year, and the setting up of 33 joint investigation teams at national level with Eurojust's assistance. Eighty per cent of Eurojust's coordination meetings that year were concerned with 'EU priority crimes': drug trafficking, fraud, money laundering, trafficking in human beings, terrorist activity, corruption, and cybercrime. In sum, this indicates a significant facilitating role in the national investigation and prosecution of cross-border criminality.

Article 86 TFEU envisages the establishment of a European Public Prosecutor's Office (EPPO) 'from Eurojust'. In fact, the idea of a European Prosecutor dates back some time, to a Commission initiative in the 1990s, which funded an academic study resulting in the *Corpus Iuris* proposals. The latter comprised a kind of criminal code relating to the protection of EC financial interests, laying down offence definitions and procedures for prosecution, trial, and sanctions across the territory of the Member States as a single legal area.[88] Unsurprisingly, these ambitious ideas

---

[84] There is also a more explicit provision for judicial review (although in Third Pillar terms) in the 2009 Decision. For a recent review of Europol's activities, see: Report by RAND Europe, 'Evaluation of the Implementation of the Europol Council Decision and of Europol's Activities, prepared for the Europol Management Board' (2012) http://www.rand.org/pubs/technical_reports/TR1264.html.

[85] Joint Action of 7 July 1998 [1998] OJ L191.   [86] [2002] OJ L63.

[87] www.eurojust.europa.eu.

[88] For a detailed overview of the project and its proposals, see M. Delmas-Marty and J.A.E. Vervaele (eds), *The Implementation of the Corpus Iuris in the Member States* (2000); House of Lords

encountered some strong resistance on the part of a number of Member States, anxious regarding such an encroachment on criminal law sovereignty,[89] and the later outcome of further debate is contained broadly in the Article 86 version of the EPPO. The latter would be in many respects the successor body to OLAF, being responsible for the investigation and prosecution of offences against the Union's financial interests, acting in liaison with Europol as appropriate, and undertaking the role of prosecutor in national criminal trials. The establishment and functioning of the Prosecutor's Office would be through Council regulations—not the ordinary legislative procedure. But the whole project remains highly prospective at present. In October 2013, the Commission's latest proposal resulted in a 'yellow card' from the national Parliaments of 14 Member States, under the early warning system laid down in Article 7 of Protocol No 2 to the Lisbon Treaty, leaving the Commission to revise the proposal so as to take into account these national parliamentary concerns.[90]

There is a real sense in which all these institutional developments remain half-formed with still uncertain prospects, poised now on the cusp between an inter-governmental role of cooperation and a supranational role of direction. As Mitsilegas noted, writing on the eve of the Lisbon changes, real doubts endure regarding the emergence of genuine EU criminal law institutions and agencies: 'as with mutual recognition, transposing the features of Community agencies to criminal law may not reflect the reality of action in criminal matters. Market considerations cannot be equated with criminal justice considerations.'[91]

VI. The Judicial Development of EU Criminal Law: A European Common Law of Criminal Law

In the historically haphazard legislative shift from inter-governmental to hybrid Third Pillar, then to supranational First Pillar and post-Lisbon mainstream, it is important to note and reflect upon the role of the Court of Justice in drawing

European Union Committee, *Prosecuting Fraud on the Communities' Finances—the Corpus Iuris*, 9th Report, 1998–99, HL, paper 62.

[89] For a broad account of the fate and transformation of the *Corpus Iuris* proposals, see Mitislegas (n 1) 229–232.

[90] Council of the EU, Interinstitutional File 2013/0225 (App), 28 November 2013.

[91] Mitislegas (n 1) 232.

(or perhaps inserting) an EU logic from these complex developments and legal moves. It has been mentioned already that, just as the Court of Justice performed a dynamic role in developing the concept and practice of a *sui generis* legal order within the framework of the single market, something similar may be happening in the field of JHA, the AFSJ, and what is now being termed EU criminal law. Just as the practical demands of economic integration were translated into a logical transfer of sovereign power, so too the imperatives of criminal law cooperation may now translate into a similar logic of legal integration, which for political reasons may be difficult to spell out in Treaty terms but may be articulated through judicial intervention.

The role of the Union Courts, and in particular that of the Court of Justice, in this respect is potentially very significant but also very challenging. It has already been seen that some of the case law so far arising in this field of activity has involved constitutional as much as criminal law and criminal justice issues, addressing questions of legislative competence and the relation between the European and national orders, inviting the Court of Justice to explore and even determine the emerging configuration of legal authority and legal action. While the Court of Justice is clearly well versed in the constitutional dimension of the subject, it has also had to enter a largely new domain in appreciating the sensibilities and methodology of criminal law. Nonetheless, an increasing number of questions have been brought to the Court, even within the context of its more limited Third Pillar jurisdiction.[92] Following the Treaty of Lisbon, its jurisdiction is that much fuller and the scope for judicial development correspondingly large. Henceforth, the Court can rely upon a broadly based jurisdiction,[93] and invoke both the full panoply of 'effectiveness' principles and an integrated Charter of Fundamental Rights.

The judicial record to date suggests for the most part an 'activist' approach on the part of the Court, generally enabling the development of a corpus of EC and EU rules on criminal law matters. At an earlier date, its resort to principles of assimilation and effectiveness[94] confirmed the European reach into the national domain of criminal law, while at the same time respecting the need for individual protection

---

[92] Most importantly, jurisdiction to give preliminary rulings depended on a Member State declaration accepting such jurisdiction, the Commission could not bring enforcement actions, and no actions for damages were available.

[93] Subject, however, to complex transitional provisions during a five-year period from the entry into force of the Lisbon Treaty: see the Protocol on Transitional Provisions to the Treaty of Lisbon. Art 10(4) of the Protocol provides for a UK opt-out from the transitional provisions regarding Third Pillar acts preceding the Lisbon changes, exercisable until six months before the end of the transitional period.

[94] That is, Member State enforcement of EC/EU rules via criminal law should be no less 'diligent' than that accorded to comparable national rules (assimilation), and the principle of 'effective, dissuasive and proportionate' application; see in particular Case C-68/88 *Commission v Greece* (1989) ECR 2965.

by limiting the retrospective and aggravating impact on criminal liability through reference to human rights norms.[95] In the disputes regarding legislative competence, the Court favoured the award of First Pillar competence in the interests of effectiveness.[96] Moreover, and very significantly, the Court in its *Pupino* ruling transposed the First Pillar method as far as possible into the Third Pillar, by ruling that Framework Decisions were subject to the obligation to interpret national law in conformity with EU law—so-called indirect effect—even though their direct effect had been explicitly excluded in Article 34(2)(b) of the former EU Treaty.[97] The main thrust of this case law may be termed 'integrationist' in that it seemed designed to ensure the implementation and application of EC and EU policy and measures within the national criminal law domain.

On the one hand, this may be seen as the Court of Justice performing its natural role as a European Court. But, on the other hand, the substance of this case law and its expressive outcome are more complex and uncertain in their reading. In particular, it may be asked whether the Court's guiding spirit has been *instrumental*, in the sense of being mainly concerned to ensure the effectiveness of European rules, or also *expressive* of certain core values in this field. It is difficult at present to provide a certain answer to such a question. The *Pupino* ruling, so striking in its broad assertion of the indirect effect of Framework Decisions, is also an example of mixed signals—suggesting on the one hand that defence rights may be trumped by victim rights,[98] while also drawing a distinction between substantive and procedural criminal law,[99] both of which arguments might be seen as contestable in terms of criminal justice.

Post-Lisbon, the legal landscape is different: effectiveness is firmly embedded in the TFEU provisions, and the general method is that of the old First Pillar. As a result, the Court of Justice may now have the psychological and legal space within which to consider more fully issues of criminal law substance and move on from a preoccupation with constitutional questions. Indeed, the Court's role in the more immediate future may be the interpretation of what is now emerging as a more balanced legislative programme of EU Directives on criminal law matters, and the mediation of conflicting national positions on crime matters as they emerge from the growing litigation on the extent of mutual recognition. In short, the focus of attention may shift to traditional criminal justice balancing (enforcement interests weighed against justice and rights argument) and navigating the European criminal and penal rainbow. In carrying out these kinds of task, the judicial role may in effect amount to some elaboration of a 'general part' for EU criminal law. One

---

[95] Joint Cases C-387/02, C-391/02, C-403/02 *Berlusconi, Adelchi, Dell'Utri and others* (2005) ECR I-3585; *Maria Pupino* (n 43) 58, 59.

[96] See the discussion above: 'Environmental Crimes' and 'Ship-Source Pollution' Cases (n 19).

[97] *Maria Pupino* (n 43).   [98] *Maria Pupino* (n 43) para 56.

[99] *Maria Pupino* (n 43) para 46.

view of the development of EU criminal law (and certainly that presented here) is that of a reactive response to crime problems as they have arisen historically, with limited opportunity to consider fundamental questions regarding the scope and approach of criminal law. The haphazard and event or problem-driven nature of EU crime policy and legislation has resulted in fundamental questions concerning the role and objectives of criminal law, agency in criminal law, and an appropriate idea of *mens rea*, being decided in particular contexts and from time to time, rather than as a matter of general principle. Moreover, even though the Commission's 2011 Communication on Crime Policy does essay some discussion of the process and method of criminalization,[100] it does not stray very far into the substantive realm, which is the more logical starting point. It may be argued then that a valuable steering role for EU criminal law would now be to pose some basic and critical, though difficult, questions. In particular:

- What should be the scope for using criminal law in a material sense, especially in a European context, and should that be determined via the transnational significance and impact justification embedded now in Article 83(1) of the TFEU?
- What kind of actor should be dealt with by criminal law, at both the national and EU level, and in particular to what extent should corporate and organizational actors be viewed as agents of criminal conduct, and how should the relationship between human and corporate or collective entities be understood for purposes of criminal responsibility?
- To what extent can a European solution tolerate cultural, legal, and penal diversity, without losing coherence and efficiency—what are the limits of uniformity, harmonization, and mutual recognition?
- What values should inform the fundamental component of *mens rea* in the determination of criminal liability, in drawing the more exact boundaries of criminal mindset, participation, and justifiable defensive action, and do such values have a distinctively European character?
- What is the constitutional and legitimating basis for a European direction of these fundamental aspects of crime policy and criminal jurisprudence, and what are the appropriate respective roles of legislator and judiciary in this field of legal activity?

Such an agenda, although undoubtedly ambitious, could in the first instance be taken up by the Commission in its role of policy formation and initiation of legislation, but would be given most substance through the work of the European Courts, as the opportunity to exercise jurisdiction in the criminal law field grows apace.

---

[100] See the discussion in Christopher Harding and Joanna Beata Banach-Gutierrez, 'The Emergent EU Criminal Policy: Identifying the Species' (2012) 37 *European Law Review* 758.

VII. EU Criminal Law at the Crossroads

Following the changes finally brought about by the Treaty of Lisbon, EU criminal law is a field of legal activity awaiting more substantial and hopefully more systematic development. Much is there already, although the routes leading to the present position have been diverse and to some extent accidental. Some degree of uncertainty remains regarding the more precise contours of future development and on some topics political willingness is likely to govern the speed and detail of the emerging law. Moreover, a certain amount of variable geometry (at present well illustrated by the UK's 'purchase' of this area of EU action[101]) is likely to remain a feature of the overall picture. In terms of scope and content, perhaps the main question to be posed at this juncture concerns the extent to which EU policy and law in this field will move beyond a predominantly instrumental, coordinating, and managerial role to something more distinctive regarding the expression of core values and main concepts. A possible agenda in this respect has been sketched out immediately above. There are one or two glimmers of a more distinctively European approach in matters of substance. For instance, the listing of xenophobia and racism as 'priority' areas of concern in terms of EU criminal policy signals a particular and perhaps distinctively European interest in combating such conduct and attitudes. Similarly, the recent emphasis on the *ultima ratio* principle and a more considered choice of sanctions and methods of legal control suggest the emergence of a supranational position on criminalization as a legal strategy. An important speculation concerns the extent to which EU criminal law is or will be about basic rights protection or about the effective legal control of transnational criminality.[102] It may also be asked, in broader terms, how the emergent regimes of EU criminal law and the AFSJ fit into evolving European—or European

---

[101] The extent to which the UK is bound by the overall body of EU criminal law is a matter of some complexity, depending on that country's opt-out of certain bodies of EU policy and law—very broadly speaking the UK is bound by pre-Lisbon First Pillar law, post-Lisbon law, those parts of the Schengen *aquis* where the UK has opted in, but not by pre-Lisbon Third Pillar law. Regarding the present Government's proposal for a block opt-out of pre-Lisbon criminal law and policing measures (129 measures with a proposal to rejoin 35 of these), see the report of the UK Parliament's European Scrutiny Committee (21st Report, 7 November 2013), which is critical of an incoherence in government policy.

[102] On this issue, it is interesting to note the two 'manifestos' that have been issued as a result of the European Criminal Policy Initiative, which is a project established by an autonomous group of criminal law scholars from a number of Member States: *The Manifesto on European Criminal Policy*, December 2009 (for the text, see (2011) 86 *European Criminal Law Review*); and *A Manifesto on European Criminal Procedure Law*, November 2013. Each Manifesto identifies and urges the application of a number of principles and standards relating to the rule of law and rights protection, and applies such principles in an illustrative way to existing and proposed EU criminal law measures.

alongside national—governance. Taking up Jonathan Simon's argument[103] about 'governing through crime' in the American context, Estella Baker has posed similar questions regarding the EU and its increasing incursion into the criminal law domain.[104] Baker's analysis and conclusions suggest a somewhat equivocal set of developments in the European context regarding the extent to which the EU may fashion its evolving pattern of governance 'around the imaginary ideal subject of the citizen-victim'. But this kind of reflection serves as a valuable reminder of the significant relation which may exist between crime policy and criminal law on the one hand, and contemporary methods of governance on the other hand.

For the present, therefore, there is a great deal that remains prospective, and one important immediate task is to ensure an awareness and appreciation of the scope and nature of this new body of law and how it relates to the wider legal and policy landscape of the Union.

BIBLIOGRAPHY

S. Alegre and M. Leaf, 'Mutual Recognition in European Judicial Co-operation: A Step Too Far Too Soon? Case Study—the European Arrest Warrant' (2004) 10 *European Law Journal* 200

Peter Aspinall and Charles Watters, *Refugees and Asylum Seekers: A Review from an Equality and Human Rights Perspective* (2010) Ch 6 Legal and criminal justice system

Estella Baker, 'Criminal Jurisdiction, the Public Dimension to "Effective Protection" and the Construction of Community–Citizen Relations' (2001) 4 *Cambridge Yearbook of European Legal Studies* 25

Estella Baker and Christopher Harding, 'From Past Imperfect to Future Perfect: A Longitudinal Study of the Third Pillar' (2009) 34 *European Law Review* 25

Estella Baker, 'Governing through Crime—the Case of the European Union' (2010) 7 *European Journal of Criminology* 187

Brian Bell and Stephen Machin, *The Impact of Migration on Crime and Victimisation* (2011)

Jodie Blackstock, Edward Lloyd-Cape, Jacqueline Hodgson, and Taru Spronken, *Inside Police Custody: An Empirical Account of Suspects' Rights in Four Jurisdictions* (2013)

European Commission, 'Towards an EU Criminal Policy: Ensuring the Effective Implementation of EU Policies through Criminal Law' COM (2011) 573 final

M. Delmas-Marty and J.A.E. Vervaele (eds), *The Implementation of the Corpus Iuris in the Member States* (2000)

Christopher Harding and Joanna Beata Banach-Gutierrez, 'The Emergent EU Criminal Policy: Identifying the Species' (2012) 37 *European Law Review* 758

[103] Jonathan Simon, *Governing through Crime: How the War on Crime Transformed American Democracy and Created a Culture of Fear* (2007).

[104] Estella Baker, 'Governing through Crime—the Case of the European Union' (2010) 7 *European Journal of Criminology* 187.

S. Lavenex, 'Mutual Recognition and the Monopoly of Force: Limits of the Single Market Analogy' (2007) 14 *Journal of European Public Policy* 762

Grahame Maxwell and Peter Fahey, *Comment on Migration and Policing*, ACPO Report (2008)

Samuli Miettinen, *Criminal Law and Policy in the European Union* (2012)

Valsamis Mitsilegas, *EU Criminal Law* (2009)

Valsamis Mitsilegas, 'The Limits of Mutual Trust in Europe's Area of Freedom, Security and Justice: From Automatic Inter-state Cooperation to the Slow Emergence of the Individual' (2012) 32 *Yearbook of European Law* 319

Steve Peers, *EU Justice and Home Affairs Law* (3rd ed, 2011)

RAND Europe, 'Evaluation of the Implementation of the Europol Council Decision and of Europol's Activities, prepared for the Europol Management Board' (2012) http://www.rand.org/pubs/technical_reports/TR1264.html

Jonathan Simon, *Governing through Crime: How the War on Crime Transformed American Democracy and Created a Culture of Fear* (2007)

Jenia Iontcheva Turner, 'The Expressive Dimension of EU Criminal Law' (2012) 60 *American Journal of Comparative Law* 555

Neil Walker, 'In Search of the Area of Freedom, Security and Justice: A Constitutional Odyssey' in N. Walker (ed), *Europe's Area of Freedom, Security and Justice* (2004)

CHAPTER 33

EU ASYLUM AND IMMIGRATION LAW UNDER THE AREA OF FREEDOM, SECURITY, AND JUSTICE

NADINE EL-ENANY

I. Introduction

THIS chapter examines EU asylum and immigration law under the Area of Freedom, Security and Justice (AFSJ). It begins with a historical account of European cooperation on these matters. The chapter then maps developments in EU asylum law, providing an analysis of the nature and effectiveness of the Common European Asylum System (CEAS). It is argued that the quality and effectiveness of the asylum Directives is questionable because they suffer from incomplete or mal-implementation, resulting in vast differences in practice between the Member States in the level of protection afforded to asylum seekers, and diverse rates of recognition of refugees across the Union. The CJEU has indicated in a number of judgments that it is prepared to interpret EU asylum provisions in a manner that ensures the protection of refugees. Some of the key judgments are discussed. The protracted negotiations on the recently adopted recast asylum Directives suggest that there is an acute divergence between the views of the Member States and the Commission on what is to be considered a sufficient level of harmonization of asylum norms.

The second part of the chapter examines the current state of EU immigration law. While Member States have in general been eager to adopt legislative and operational measures in the interests of curbing irregular migration, they have shown markedly less enthusiasm for harmonization of rules on regular migration into the Union. Where such legislation does exist, the Court of Justice has played an important role in placing a brake on Member States' narrow and seemingly contrived interpretations of the rights granted to third-country nationals. Some of the key case law and legislative instruments are discussed, including the Long Term Residents Directive and the Family Reunification Directive.[1]

The final part of the chapter examines the relationship between the fields of EU asylum law and immigration and border control, arguing that the EU's highly restrictive wider migration and border control policy subverts protective elements that might be observed in its asylum legislation. Access to EU territory is severely limited for all migrants, irrespective of their motives for moving. Migrants' departure points are being pushed further afield and their journeys to the EU are becoming more dangerous. With this in mind, reform of substantive internal protection standards is insufficient in the absence of comprehensively addressing the relationship between migration policy and asylum.

II. History of European Cooperation on Asylum and Immigration

The economic crisis of the 1970s and the closing of legal immigration routes along with the demise of refugee resettlement regimes in the 1980s meant that asylum became one of the only routes of entry to Western European countries and the only avenue to refuge. Pressure on national asylum regimes was building with the outcome of 'an almost total paralysis of European asylum systems by the beginning

---

[1] Despite the existence of an important body of country-specific immigration law based on bilateral agreements, in particular the very rich legislation and court jurisprudence on the rights of Turkish workers and their families, discussion of this is beyond the scope of this chapter.

of the 90s'.[2] European states began to consider the adoption of an international approach in place of 'purely national asylum strategies'.[3]

The process of European cooperation in the field of asylum and immigration began within the framework of ad hoc groups, the first being Trevi, established in 1976 by the then 12 EC Member States. At this time, the EC did not have competence in this field and so cooperation between interior ministers took place intergovernmentally, and so to the exclusion of the European Commission, the European Parliament, and the CJEU. Operating outside the treaty framework and the auspices of the supranational institutions, it was nigh impossible to exercise political or judicial scrutiny over the work of Trevi at either national or European level.

The intergovernmental cooperation that eventually led to the introduction of asylum and immigration as 'matters of common interest' in the 1992 Maastricht Treaty on the European Union and their later move to the First Pillar in the 1997 Amsterdam Treaty began in 'two partly overlapping, and partly differing intergovernmental fora'.[4] These fora consisted of the Ad Hoc Group on Immigration, which brought together representatives of the then 12 Member States, and the Schengen group, which comprised five Member States at its inception: France, Germany, and the Benelux countries.[5]

The evolution of European cooperation on immigration and asylum took place in the context of Member States' attempts to remove restrictions on the movement of EU citizens within the Union. The Schengen project was originally the product of a Franco-German scheme whereby the two governments agreed to move towards the steady removal of checks at their shared borders.[6] The Benelux countries chose to participate shortly afterwards and the First Schengen Agreement on the Gradual Abolition of Checks at the Common Borders was agreed on 14 July 1985. This core group of Member States believed that the principle of free movement of persons was reliant upon the abolition of internal border checks coupled with compensatory controls at the external border. The objective of cooperation was said to be the realization of the single market.[7] Lavenex writes of the 'dynamic process of cooperation, particularly among the interior ministries of the Schengen countries' that led to the adoption in 1990 of the Second Schengen Agreement applying the Schengen Agreement of 14 June 1985.[8] Only three provisions made reference to 'illegal immigration' in the 1985 Agreement, while the 1990 Agreement was predominantly on the subject of third-country nationals.[9] The 1990 Schengen Agreement created an area within the EU in which residents and visitors (with a valid visa) are free to travel without systematic passport checks at national borders.

[2] I. Boccardi, *Europe and Refugees: Towards an EU Asylum Policy* (2002) 27.

[3] Boccardi (n 2) 28.

[4] S. Lavenex, *The Europeanisation of Refugee Policies: Between Human Rights and Internal Security* (2001) 83.

[5] Lavenex (n 4).   [6] The Schengen Agreement 1985. See Lavenex (n 4) 87–88.

[7] Lavenex (n 4) 88.   [8] Lavenex (n 4) 88.   [9] Lavenex (n 4) 88.

However, it was argued by policy makers that the area of free movement demanded heightened external border controls and close cooperation between the Member States on issues such as cross-border crime, police, and judicial matters, as well as visa and asylum policy.

In 1990, the Dublin Convention was signed,[10] limiting the number of claims for protection an individual could make in the Union to one and establishing a system for the allocation of responsibility for asylum applicants between Member States. The Convention came into force in 1997. The Dublin Regulation[11] is now the central binding EU instrument for the implementation of the 'safe third-country' concept, which assumes that all EU countries are safe for the purposes of returning asylum seekers, and incorporates the Dublin Convention into EU legislation. The rules for the determination of the Member State responsible for hearing the claims of asylum seekers are premised on the notion that responsibility lies with the first Member State with which an asylum applicant establishes contact, whether by the issue of a transit visa, legal presence of a close family member, or, in the absence of these, the first physical contact with the territory.[12] States are required to readmit individuals transferred on the basis of the Dublin regime. Lavenex has observed that European cooperation is founded on 'the assumption of common standards of refugee protection that would justify the loosening of the exclusive responsibility of sovereign States under international law'.[13] Article 17 of the recast Dublin Regulation provides for the possibility of Member States derogating from the responsibility criteria on humanitarian grounds.[14] However, this clause has been interpreted restrictively. In the UK, for instance, the Court of Appeal has held that Article 15 does not create a right for asylum seekers and was instead intended 'to regulate the relationship between two or more member states'.[15]

To ensure the functioning of the Dublin Regulation, the Eurodac system was set up as a means of establishing the transit route of asylum applicants.[16] This (along

---

[10] Convention determining the state responsible for examining applications for asylum lodged in one of the Member States of the European Communities, 15 June 1990 [1997] OJ C254/1.

[11] Reg No 604/2013 of the European Parliament and of the Council of 26 June 2013 establishing the criteria and mechanisms for determining the Member State responsible for examining an application for international protection lodged in one of the Member States by a third-country national or a stateless person (recast) OJ L180/31 29.6.2013.

[12] Arts 7-15 of Regulation No 604/2013 (n 11).

[13] S. Lavenex, '"Passing the Buck": European Union Refugee Policies towards Central and Eastern Europe' (1998) 11 *Journal of Refugee Studies* 130.

[14] Reg No 604/2013 (n 14).

[15] *R (on the application of G v Secretary of State for the Home Department* [2005] EWCA Civ 546, para 25.

[16] Council Regulation (EC) No. 2725/2000 of 11 December 2000 concerning the establishment of 'Eurodac' for the comparison of fingerprints for the effective application of the Dublin Convention [2000] OJ L316/1; Council Regulation (EC) No. 407/2002 of 28 February 2002 laying down certain rules to implement Regulation (EC) No 2725/2000 of 11 December 2000 concerning the establishment of 'Eurodac' for the comparison of fingerprints for the effective application of the Dublin Convention [2000] OJ L316/1.

with the Temporary Protection Directive)[17] was the earliest post-Tampere, CEAS measure to be adopted. Eurodac requires Member States to take fingerprints of asylum seekers as well as those crossing EU external borders irregularly, and grants a power to fingerprint those present unlawfully on Member State territory. The Commission manages Eurodac's Central Unit, which consists of the Automated Fingerprint Identification System, receiving and transmitting the recorded information to the National Access Points of the Member States. An informal comitology structure described as an 'informal expert group' was created by the Commission to aid in the running of the Central Unit.[18]

In a Protocol to the 1999 Treaty of Amsterdam, the UK, Ireland, and Denmark secured opt-outs from EU treaty provisions on immigration, asylum, and civil law. Unlike Denmark, which cannot opt in, the British and Irish opt-outs allow for the countries to choose whether to participate in legislation in this area. While the UK has cooperated closely on asylum and refugee policy with other EU Member States for many years, more recent developments in British policy suggest that a new period characterizing the UK's attitude towards the CEAS is dawning. Maria Fletcher has argued that since the introduction of opt-outs 'into the EU governance armoury . . . the United Kingdom . . . has exploited the . . . mechanism as a tool of diversity management to the greatest extent'.[19] In practice, until recently the UK has opted out of nearly all proposals concerning visas, borders, and legal migration, but has opted into all proposals on asylum and civil law, and nearly all proposals concerning irregular migration.[20] Recently, the approach of the UK and Ireland has changed and their participation in common policies on irregular migration and asylum has become more selective. At present, the Dublin and Eurodac regulations apply to all Member States and associated countries (Norway, Iceland, Switzerland, and Liechtenstein). The Refugee Fund and European Asylum Support Office arrangements apply to all Member States except Denmark.[21] The second-phase qualification, procedures, and reception Directives apply to all Member States except the UK, Ireland, and Denmark. The UK and Ireland continue to be bound by the first-phase qualification and procedures Directives, and the UK by the reception Directive.[22]

---

[17] Council Directive 2001/55/EC on minimum standards for giving temporary protection in the event of a mass influx of displaced persons and on measures promoting a balance of efforts between Member States in receiving such persons and bearing the consequences thereof. OJ L212 7.8.2001, 12.

[18] *First Annual Report on the Activities of the EURODAC central unit* SEC (2005).

[19] M. Fletcher, 'Schengen, the European Court of Justice and Flexibility Under the Lisbon Treaty: Balancing the United Kingdom's "Ins" and "Outs" ' (2009) 5 *European Constitutional Law Review* 74.

[20] The Irish practice has been almost identical to that of the UK.

[21] Negotiations are currently ongoing with associated countries.

[22] S. Peers, 'The Second Phase of the Common European Asylum System: A Brave New World—or Lipstick on a Pig?' (2013) http://www.statewatch.org/analyses/no-220-ceas-second-phase.pdf 3.

Before turning to the EU asylum legislation itself, we begin with a brief introduction to the development of the CEAS. The formulation of common policies on asylum at the European level is driven by the assumption that the movement of asylum applicants is determined by 'pull factors', policies deemed attractive to asylum seekers, who are perceived as rational actors deciding on their destination countries according to these factors. European policy makers claim that controlling these pull factors will reduce the numbers of asylum seekers in any particular Member State, despite the empirical evidence contradicting this thesis.[23] However, the appeal of a thesis that promises to reduce the number of asylum seekers cannot be underestimated. Not only do such policies have populist appeal, but they also promise to reduce the administrative costs of Member States' asylum regimes.

Just as its Member States have long promised to protect refugees, the European Union made a similar commitment when initially expressing its intention to build the CEAS. At Tampere in 1999, the European Council agreed 'to work towards establishing a Common European Asylum System, based on the full and inclusive application of the Geneva Convention, thus ensuring that nobody is sent back to persecution, ie maintaining the principle of non-refoulement'.[24]

The Hague Programme of 2004[25] called for the establishment by 2010 of a CEAS with unified procedures and status within the second stage of implementation provided for in the Amsterdam Treaty.[26] It was decided that decisions on asylum would be taken on the basis of qualified majority voting as opposed to unanimity and in co-decision with the European Parliament rather than by consultation, and the Commission was to have an exclusive right of initiative.[27] An action programme for reinforcing practical cooperation on asylum between Member States was proposed by the Commission, which foresaw the establishment of a single procedure for the determination of asylum claims, the agreement of a common procedure for assessing the situation in countries of origin and investigating the potential for practical funding for states under particular pressure due to their geographical location.[28]

The single asylum procedure envisaged by the Commission has yet to come to fruition. In the Hague Programme, the European Council requested the Commission to 'present a study on the appropriateness as well as the legal and

---

[23] See E. Neumayer, 'Asylum Destination Choice: What Makes Some West European Countries More Attractive Than Others?' (2004) 5 *European Union Politics* 155.

[24] Tampere European Council Presidency Conclusions 1999, para 13.

[25] European Council, *The Hague Programme: Strengthening Freedom, Security and Justice in the EU* (2004).

[26] See Communication from the Commission to the Council and the European Parliament *A More Efficient Common European Asylum System: The Single Procedure as the Next Step* COM (2004) 503 final.

[27] Council Decision OJ 2004, L396/45.

[28] Commission Communication on strengthened practical cooperation: New structures, new approaches: Improving the quality of decision making in the common European asylum system COM (2006) 67 final of 17 February 2006.

political implications of joint processing of asylum applications within the Union',[29] which is to consist of the sharing of country-of-origin information and the monitoring of the pressure levels on Member States' asylum administrations. It was anticipated that once the common asylum procedure had been achieved, this system of cooperation would be converted into 'a European support office for all forms of cooperation between Member States'.[30] In 2010, the EU Asylum Support Office was established.[31] This is a new development over and above the limited cooperation between Member States' asylum services through EURASIL, a European network of asylum specialists which replaced the Centre for Information, Discussion and Exchange on Asylum.

Asylum is one of the Union's competences that form the AFSJ, itself comprising a number of policies found in Article 67 of the TFEU (ex Article 61 TEC and ex Article 29 TEU). In relation to asylum, it provides that the Union 'shall ensure the absence of internal border controls for persons and shall frame a common policy on asylum, immigration and external border control, based on solidarity between Member States, which is fair towards third-country nationals. For the purpose of this Title, stateless persons shall be treated as third-country nationals'.

Towards the realization of the first stage of the CEAS, in 2000 and 2001, the Commission drafted a number of proposals for Directives. Initially four Directives were adopted: on asylum procedures,[32] reception conditions,[33] and recognition and content of refugee and subsidiary protection.[34] Since the emergence of the EU asylum regime, there have been increasing pressures for reform, originating both from within the EU governance framework and outside. The failings of the first round of asylum Directives are seen to have various effects, ranging from in-built inefficiency to curtailing the rights of those seeking asylum in the EU. Mal-implementation is the problem that plagued the initial asylum Directives. We know from other more established areas of EU law that the CJEU can play a crucial role in narrowing implementation gaps. Initially, it was hoped that proper implementation of uniform standards of protection across the Union only awaited court rulings on the interpretation of EU asylum legal provisions. The 2009 Lisbon Treaty extended the jurisdiction of the CJEU, bringing the whole of the AFSJ within its general jurisdiction. No longer is the preliminary reference

---

[29] European Council (n 25) 9.   [30] European Council (n 25) 9.

[31] EU Reg 439/2010 of the European Parliament and of the Council of 19 May 2010.

[32] Council Directive 2005/85/EC on minimum standards on procedures in member states for granting and withdrawing refugee status OJ L326 13.12.2005.

[33] Council Directive 2003/9/EC laying down minimum standards on the reception of applicants for asylum in Member States OJ L31 6.2.2003.

[34] Council Directive 2004/83/EC on minimum standards for the qualification and status of third country nationals and stateless persons as refugees or as persons who otherwise need international protection OJ L304 30.09.04.

procedure limited to national courts or tribunals against whose decisions there is no judicial remedy; it is now available to all national courts.[35] Arguably, the CJEU's activity in this area has led to some limited legal protection for the rights of individuals.[36] The Court has been willing to interpret provisions of EU asylum law in a manner that protects the rights of asylum seekers at the implementation stage, for instance in the *Elgafaji* case.[37] Mr Elgafaji and his wife, both Iraqi nationals, brought a case against the Netherlands after being refused temporary stay permits on the grounds that they had failed to demonstrate that they faced a real risk of serious and individual harm in Iraq. Under the Qualifications Directive, an individual may not be returned to a country in which she faces risk of suffering 'serious harm', which, pursuant to Article 15(c) of the Directive, includes a 'serious and individual threat to a civilian's life or person by reason of indiscriminate violence in situations of international or internal armed conflict'. The CJEU interpreted 'individual threat' broadly, stating that it

must be understood as covering harm to civilians irrespective of their identity, where the degree of indiscriminate violence characterizing the armed conflict taking place . . . reaches such a high level that substantial grounds are shown for believing that a civilian, returned to the relevant country or, as the case may be, to the relevant region, would, solely on account of his presence on the territory of that country or region, face a real risk of being subject to the serious threat referred in Article 15(c) of the Directive.[38]

In spite of some positive judgments, uniformity and complete application of the asylum Directives have not been achieved through the extension of the Court's jurisdiction. Higher EU asylum standards matter only to the extent to which they are properly implemented by the Member States.[39] According to Steve Peers, the problem of mal-implementation 'should have been ameliorated somewhat by the increased jurisdiction for the Court of Justice on asylum matters following the Treaty of Lisbon, but the increase in its case load has only been modest and reportedly a number of Member States' authorities and courts are finding ways to refuse to implement the Court's judgments properly'.[40]

---

[35] See House of Lords European Union Committee, *The Treaty of Lisbon: An Impact Assessment: Vol. I Report* (10th Report, Session 2007–2008) 125–126.

[36] See eg Joined Cases X (C-199/12), Y (C-200/12) and Z (C-201/12) *v Minister voor Immigratie en Asiel* (Judgment of the Court (Fourth Chamber) of 7 November 2013); Joined Cases C-411/10 and C-493/10 *NS and others v Secretary of State for the Home Department* and *M.E. and others v Refugee Applications Commissioner and Minister for Justice, Equality and Law Reform* (Judgment of the Court (Grand Chamber) of 21 December 2011).

[37] Case C-465/07 *Elgafaji and another v Staatssecretaris van Justitie* (Judgment of the Court (Grand Chamber) of 17 February 2009).

[38] *Elgafaji and another* (n 37) para 35.

[39] See eg European Parliament, *Setting Up a Common European Asylum System: Report on the Application of Existing Instruments and Proposals for the New System* (2010).

[40] Peers (n 22) 8.

In 2008, the Commission released a Policy Plan,[41] which was the product of a public consultation in the form of a Green Paper presented in 2007.[42] The objective of the Green Paper was to identify 'the possible options for shaping the second phase of the CEAS', which was set out in the 2004 Hague Programme as being the creation of a common asylum procedure and a uniform status for those granted refugee status or subsidiary protection.[43] The 2010 Stockholm Programme, which followed the Tampere Programme (1999–2003) and the Hague Programme (2004–2009), expressed a commitment to achieving the CEAS by 2012.[44] In its Policy Plan, the Commission identified three trends that are to inform future developments in asylum policy. The first trend identified by the Commission was that the Member States, bar 'some border States', are 'under less pressure than in the recent past', making the improvement of the quality of protection standards in the EU a timely enterprise.[45] Second, the Commission reported that despite the achievement of some level of legislative harmonization at the EU level, 'a lack of common practice, different traditions and diverse country of origin information sources are . . . producing divergent results'. According to the Commission, the differing implementation records of the Member States work against the principle of providing equal access to protection and create secondary movements.[46] Finally, the Commission found that where individuals are granted protection, an increasing number receive a subsidiary protection status and other forms of protection based on national law rather than refugee status according to the 1951 Refugee Convention. As a result, the Commission highlights the importance of paying particular attention to subsidiary and other forms of protection during the second phase of the CEAS.[47] The Commission expressed its intention to put forward proposed amendments to the existing Directives as well as to consider the possibility of new instruments.[48]

With regard to the Qualifications Directive, the Commission reported on the significant variation in the recognition of protection needs of applicants from the same countries of origin,[49] in part due to 'the wording of certain provisions' of the Qualifications Directive.[50] According to the Commission, a level

[41] Communication from the Commission to the European Parliament, the Council, the European Economic and Social Committee and the Committee of Regions on the 'Policy Plan on Asylum: An Integrated Approach to Protection Across the EU' of 17 June 2008 COM (2008) 360.

[42] European Commission, 'Green Paper on the Future Common European Asylum System', Brussels, 6.6.2007 COM (2007) 301 final.

[43] European Council (n 25).

[44] The Stockholm Programme, An Open and Secure Europe—Serving and Protecting Citizens OJ C 115/1 4.5.2011.

[45] Communication from the Commission to the European Parliament, the Council, the European Economic and Social Committee and the Committee of Regions on the 'Policy Plan on Asylum: An Integrated Approach to Protection Across the EU' of 17 June 2008 COM (2008) 360, section 1.2.

[46] COM (2008) 360 (n 45) section 1.2.   [47] COM (2008) 360 (n 45) section 1.2.

[48] COM (2008) 360 (n 45) section 3.   [49] COM (2008) 360 (n 45) section 3.3.

[50] COM (2008) 360 (n 45) section 3.3.

playing field 'has not been fully achieved during the first phase of harmonization'.[51] ECRE reported that '[i]n application, the Qualifications Directive largely reflects pre-existing Member State practice'.[52] The Commission put forward a proposal for a recast version of the Qualifications Directive in 2009,[53] which was eventually adopted in 2011.[54] The purpose of the Directive is to establish 'standards for the qualification of third-country nationals or stateless persons as beneficiaries of international protection, and for the content of the protection granted'.[55]

In June 2007, the Commission reported that the Reception Directive left too much discretion to Member States and had resulted 'in negating the desired harmonization effect'.[56] Through its proposal to recast the EU Reception Directive,[57] the Commission aimed to establish higher common reception standards for asylum seekers. The changes proposed in the recast proposal were significant. ECRE concluded that '[m]any of the amendments proposed would contribute to the further approximation of national reception conditions on the basis of higher standards, in particular by closing outstanding legal gaps which have allowed Member States to interpret the Directive in a restrictive manner'.[58] However, ECRE's hope that the Member States would 'maintain the positive elements of the Commission proposal, while at the same time introducing further safeguards where necessary'[59] during negotiations was not realized. While the European Parliament adopted its position on the Commission's proposal in May 2009, agreeing with the most part of the document,[60] no decision could be reached in the Council, the Member States expressing concerns about the complexity of the reforms, the potential for abuse of their reception systems, and the financial and administrative implications of some provisions.[61] In particular, many Member States resisted the adoption of provisions requiring substantial legislative

---

[51] COM (2008) 360 (n 45) section 3.3.

[52] ECRE, *The Impact of the EU Qualification Directive on International Protection* (2008) 7.

[53] European Commission, *Proposal for a Directive of the European Parliament and of the Council on minimum standards for the qualification and status of third country nationals or stateless persons as beneficiaries of international protection and the content of the protection granted* (Recast COM (2009) 551 final/2).

[54] Directive 2011/95/EU of the European Parliament and of the Council of 13 December 2011 on standards for the qualification of third-country nationals or stateless persons as beneficiaries of international protection, for a uniform status for refugees or for persons eligible for subsidiary protection, and for the content of the protection granted (recast) OJ L 337/9 20.12.2011

[55] Qualifications Directive, Art 1.

[56] European Commission, Report from the Commission to the Council and to the European Parliament on the application of the Directive 2003/9/EC of 27 January 2003 laying down minimum standards for the reception of asylum seekers COM (2007) 745 final.

[57] Proposal for a Directive of the European Parliament and of the Council laying down minimum standards for the reception of asylum seekers (Recast) COM (2008) 815 final (Brussels, 3.12.2008).

[58] COM (2008) 815 final (n 57) 14.   [59] COM (2008) 815 final (n 57) 14.

[60] OJ C212 E, 5.8.2010, 348.

[61] European Commission, Explanatory Memorandum on the Amended proposal for a directive of the European Parliament and of the Council laying down standards for the reception of asylum seekers (Recast) COM (2011) 320 final, 3.

changes because of the costs they would incur.[62] In June 2011, the Commission withdrew its proposal and adopted a modified version due to the 'slow and difficult' legislative progress.[63] According to the Commission, its new proposal was designed to 'give an impulse to the stalled negotiations'[64] and included 'clearer concepts and more simplified rules and grants Member States more flexibility in integrating them in their national legal systems',[65] suggesting a retreat to a discretionary framework. The Directive,[66] the purpose of which is to establish standards for the reception of asylum seekers in Member States, was finally adopted in June 2013.[67]

If any of the original measures can be said to have been in need of recasting, it is the Procedures Directive. From the outset it was criticized from a humanitarian point of view by lawyers, NGOs, and academics.[68] In 2010, the Commission concluded that the Directive's 'optional provisions and derogation clauses had contributed to the proliferation of divergent arrangements across the EU, and that procedural guarantees vary considerably between Member States'.[69] The Commission proposed a recast Procedures Directive in 2009,[70] but following stalemate in negotiations, it put forward an amended proposal.[71] Despite the

---

[62] COM (2011) 320 final (n 61) 3.

[63] Communication from the Commission to the European Parliament and the Council, *Annual Report on Immigration and Asylum (2010)* COM (2011) 291 final, 5; the legal base is Art 78(2)(f) of the Treaty on the Functioning of the European Union (TFEU).

[64] COM (2011) 291 final (n 63) 5.

[65] European Commission, Explanatory Memorandum on the Amended proposal for a directive of the European Parliament and of the Council laying down standards for the reception of asylum seekers (Recast) COM (2011) 320 final, 3.

[66] Dir 2013/33/EU of the European Parliament and of the Council of 26 June 2013 laying down standards for the reception of applicants for international protection (recast) OJ L 180/96, 29 June 2013.

[67] Reception Directive, Art 1.

[68] See eg ECRE, ILGA Europe, Amnesty International, Pac Christi International, Quaker Council for European Affairs, Human Rights Watch, CARITAS-Europe, Médecins Sans Frontières, Churches' Commission for Migrants, Save the Children in Europe, Call for withdrawal of the Asylum Procedures Directive (22 March 2004); UNHCR Press Release, 'Lubbers Calls for EU Asylum Laws Not to Contravene International Law' (29 March 2004); European Parliament legislative resolution on the amended proposal for a Council directive on minimum standards on procedures in Member States for granting and withdrawing refugee status (14203/2004—C6-0200/2004—2000/0238(CNS)); C. Costello, 'The Asylum Procedures Directive and the Proliferation of Safe Country Practices: Deterrence, Deflection and the Dismantling of International Protection?' (2005) 7 *European Journal of Migration and Law* 35.

[69] Report from the European Commission to the European Parliament and the Council on the application of Directive 2005/85/EC of 1 December 2005 on minimum standards on procedures in member states for granting and withdrawing refugee status COM (2010) 465 final, 15.

[70] European Commission, Proposal for a Directive of the European Parliament and of the Council on minimum standards on procedures for granting and withdrawing international protection (Recast) COM (2009) 554 final.

[71] Amended proposal for a Directive of the European Parliament and of the Council on common procedures for granting and withdrawing international protection status (Recast) COM (2011) 319 final.

Commission's acknowledgment that 'the proliferation of disparate procedural arrangements at national level and deficiencies regarding the level of procedural guarantees for asylum applicants which mainly result from the fact that the Directive currently allows Member States a wide margin of discretion',[72] the main aim of the proposal was described as being 'to simplify and clarify rules, in order to make them more compatible with the variety of national legal systems and to help Member States to apply them in a way that is more cost-effective'.[73] The concessionary approach of the Commission is discernible throughout the Directive, which was eventually adopted in June 2013.[74] For instance, the tone of suspicion around the credibility of asylum claims is identifiable in its provision for the possibility for the acceleration of procedures 'where the applicant has made clearly false or obviously improbable representations which contradict sufficiently verified country-of-origin information, thus making his/her claim clearly unconvincing'.[75] This is despite the existence of evidence that accelerated procedures lead to poor quality decision making at first instance and thus result in secondary claims.[76]

The protracted nature of the negotiation process entailed in the adoption of the second round of asylum Directives reflects the forces existing in tension in the harmonization project. Although there is a desire to set adequately high minimum standards, Member States are simultaneously desirous to reduce the administrative costs of implementing new legislation by retaining existing national standards. The unhappy compromise has been the introduction of a high level of discretion in the asylum Directives, which has allowed not only for diverse practices across the Member States, but also contradictory or nullifying effects of provisions in the same Directive, as well as uncertainty as to whether breaches of the law are taking place.

At the heart of a harmonization project is the necessity for the limitation of Member States' discretion to legislate differently. This is particularly important with regard to asylum because of the persistence of the Dublin system's 'one chance of asylum' rule. Different levels of protection across the Member States 'produce an "asylum lottery" in the EU'.[77] ECRE reports that 2005 recognition rates for Chechens varied from approximately 0 per cent in Slovakia to 90 per

---

[72] European Commission Explanatory Memorandum to the Proposal for a Directive of the European Parliament and of the Council on minimum standards on procedures for granting and withdrawing international protection (Recast) COM (2009) 554 final, 2, para 1.1.

[73] COM (2009) 554 final, 2 (n 72) para 2.

[74] Dir 2013/32/EU of the European Parliament and of the Council of 26 June 2013 on common procedures for granting and withdrawing international protection (Recast) OJ L180/60 29.6.2013.

[75] Procedures Directive, Art 38(1)(8)(e).

[76] UNHCR, *Improving Asylum Procedures: Comparative Analysis and Recommendations For Law and Practice* (2010), Section 9, 2–3.

[77] UNHCR (n 76), Section 9, 2–3.

cent in Austria. The problem is also significant in the case of Iraqis with 2007 recognition rates showing an 87.5 per cent success rate in Cyprus, 85 per cent in Germany, 82 per cent in Sweden, 30 per cent in Denmark, 13 per cent in the UK, and 0 per cent in Slovenia and Greece.[78] With these figures in mind, it is inappropriate to deprive asylum seekers of the choice of a destination host country on the premise that they receive the same treatment across the Member States. ECRE has warned that '[l]ack of equal protection can create a real risk of *refoulement*, and thus of failing to conform to international legal obligations'.[79] The contribution of the Dublin system to the pressure on border states creates the risk that these states will work to limit access to territory or asylum procedures.[80] There is also the danger that asylum seekers will try to avoid being transferred or elude the asylum system altogether.[81] Jonathan Aus has noted the 'immediate reaction' to Eurodac's fingerprinting system of asylum seekers in Nordic countries has been to 'deliberately *cut or burn their fingertips* . . . A member of the *Swedish Migration Board* reported "scars from knives and razors, or entire [fingerprint] patterns that are entirely destroyed because they've used acid or some other kind of product to destroy their hands".'[82] The deleterious effects of the interaction between the Dublin system and a context of differing levels of reception conditions became apparent in the case of *MSS v Belgium and Greece*, a landmark case in being the first in which the European Court of Human Rights (ECtHR) has held that the transfer of an asylum seeker between two EU countries under the Dublin rules was in violation of a series of Convention rights by both the sending and receiving states. Despite 'leading to significant human rights abuses',[83] acknowledged by the ECtHR[84] and the CJEU,[85] radical reform of the Dublin system was not considered an option in the latest round of reforms. Instead, the Dublin system has been tinkered with, primarily for purposes of efficiency, and partly in the interests of protection, in the course of the adoption of the new Dublin regulation.[86]

[78] ECRE, *Five Years on Europe is Still Ignoring Its Responsibilities towards Iraqi Refugees* (2008), cited in UNHCR (n 76) 15.

[79] ECRE, *Sharing Responsibility for Refugee Protection in Europe: Dublin Reconsidered* (2008) 16.

[80] ECRE, *The Way Forward Towards Fair and Efficient Asylum Systems in Europe* (2005) 13.

[81] ECRE (n 80) 16.

[82] J.P. Aus, 'Eurodac: A Solution Looking for a Problem? (2006) 10 *European Integration Online Papers* 12 (emphasis in original).

[83] Aus (2006) 8.

[84] *MSS v Belgium and Greece*, [2011] Application No 30696/09, 21 January 2011.

[85] Joined Cases C-411/10 and C-493/10 *NS and others v Secretary of State for the Home Department* and *M.E. and others v Refugee Applications Commissioner and Minister for Justice, Equality and Law Reform* (Judgment of the Court (Grand Chamber) of 21 December 2011); See also *R (on the application of EM (Eritrea) v Secretary of State for the Home Department* [2014] UKSC 12.

[86] S. Peers, 'Court of Justice: The NS and ME Opinions—The Death of "Mutual Trust"? (2011) 6.

III. EU Immigration Law

The process of development of EU immigration law has been a protracted and differentiated one. Despite the EU having had extensive competences to adopt measures in the field of immigration and to create a common immigration policy since the entry into force of the Amsterdam Treaty in 1999, the EU has not yet established an intelligible and comprehensive common immigration policy. Article 79(1) of the TFEU reiterates the objective of achieving a common immigration policy:

The Union shall develop a common immigration policy aimed at ensuring, at all stages, the efficient management of migration flows, fair treatment of third-country nationals residing legally in Member States, and the prevention of, and enhanced measures to combat, illegal immigration and trafficking in human beings.

While Member States have in general shown willingness, even enthusiasm, for the adoption of legislative and operational measures in the field of irregular migration, including border control and the negotiation of readmission agreements with third countries,[87] they have shown markedly less enthusiasm for harmonization of rules on regular migration into the Union. As noted by Pascouau, this reticence on the part of Member States was evinced in their refusal to consider the European Commission's 2001 proposal to establish common rules on the entry and residence of third-country nationals for the purposes of work and self-employment.[88] The result is the absence of a coherent and comprehensive EU immigration law. Instead, the EU's method has been to adopt common rules on the entry and residence of specific categories of individuals. This is in accordance with the first part of Article 79(1) of the TFEU, which entrusts the Union with the task of developing a 'common immigration policy aimed at ensuring, at all stages, the efficient management of migration flows, fair treatment of third-country nationals residing legally in Member States'. Categories that have been the subject of legislation include students,[89] researchers,[90] and highly skilled migrants.[91] A Directive on intra-corporate

---

[87] See further, S. Peers, E. Guild, D. Acosta Arcarazo, K. Groenendijk, and V. Moreno-Lax, *EU Immigration and Asylum Law*, Vol 2 (2nd ed, 2012).

[88] Proposal for a Council Directive on the conditions of entry and residence for the purpose of paid employment and self-employment activities COM (2001) 386 final, 11.07.2001. See Y. Pascouau, 'Intra-EU Mobility: "The Second Building Block" of EU Labour Migration Policy' (2013) 74 European Migration and Diversity Programme 1.

[89] Council Dir 2004/114/EC of 13 December 2004 on the conditions of admission of third-country nationals for the purposes of studies, pupil exchange, unremunerated training or voluntary service OJ L375 23.12.2004.

[90] Council Dir 2005/71/EC of 12 October 2005 on a specific procedure for admitting third-country nationals for the purposes of scientific research OJ L289 03.11.2005.

[91] Council Dir 2009/50/EC of 25 May 2009 on the conditions of entry and residence of third-country nationals for the purposes of highly qualified employment OJ L155 18.06.2009.

transferees is presently being negotiated,[92] and a Directive on seasonal workers looks shortly to be adopted.[93] The Commission has recently expressed its intention to consolidate the rules on entry for a number of specific purposes with its proposal for a Directive on the conditions of entry and residence of third-country nationals for the purpose of research, studies, school exchanges, training, voluntary work, and au pairing.[94]

Pursuant to the Lisbon Treaty of 2009, the migration field has been uniformly legislated through the co-decision procedure. Following the 2010 Stockholm Programme, the Commission expressed its intention to work towards developing 'a genuine common migration policy consisting of new and flexible frameworks for the admission of legal immigrants'.[95] However, in spite of the Commission's ambitious goals, Member States' reluctance to take action on harmonization of legal migration rules in a concerted manner has stymied progress towards a comprehensive common immigration policy.

Despite Member States' reluctance to adopt common rules on first entry and access to the Union, harmonized rules have been adopted in relation to migrants who have secured access to the Union in the form of the Long-term Residence Directive,[96] which applies to all third-country nationals who meet the five-year residency threshold, except excluded categories such as refugees, and the Family Reunification Directive.[97] These Directives comprise the most significant legal developments in the field of regular migration and have prompted important jurisprudence from the CJEU on the interpretation of the rights contained within them.[98]

---

[92] Proposal for a Directive of the European Parliament and of the Council on conditions of entry and residence of third-country nationals in the framework of an intra-corporate transfer COM (2010) 378 final 13.07.2010.

[93] See European Commission Press Release, 'Commissioner Malmström Welcomes European Parliament Vote on Migrant Seasonal Workers' (4 February 2014) Available at http://europa.eu/ rapid/press-release_MEMO-14-82_en.htm; Proposal for a Directive of the European Parliament and of the Council on conditions of entry and residence of third-country nationals for the purpose of seasonal employment COM (2010) 379 final 13.07.2010. See Y. Pascouau (n 88) 1–2.

[94] Proposal for a Directive of the European Parliament and of the Council on the conditions of entry and residence of third-country nationals for the purposes of research, studies, pupil exchange, remunerated and unremunerated training, voluntary service and au pairing COM (2013) 151 final 25.03.2013.

[95] Communication from the Commission to the European Parliament, the Council, the European Economic and Social Committee and the Committee of the Regions, 'Delivering an Area of Freedom, Security and Justice for Europe's Citizens. Action Plan Implementing the Stockholm Programme' COM (2010) 171 final 20.04.2010.

[96] For a comprehensive analysis of Dir 2003/109, see D.A. Arcarazo, *The Long-Term Residence Status as a Subsidiary Form of EU Citizenship: An Analysis of Directive 2003/109* (2011).

[97] Council Dir 2003/86/EC of 22 September 2003 on the right to family reunification OJ L 251/12. The United Kingdom and Ireland opted not to participate in the adoption of this Directive.

[98] See Arcarazo (n 96).

The Long-term Residents Directive[99] and the Family Reunification Directive emerged following the Tampere Conclusions of 1999, in which the Member States agreed to work towards granting third-country nationals 'residing lawfully on the territory of the Member States'[100] rights approximating those of Union citizens. It took three years for a decision to be reached on the text of the Long-term Residents Directive, which has two main goals. First, to approximate national norms and practices in relation to the granting of long-term resident status to third-country nationals legally residing in a Member State, and second, to determine the conditions according to which long-term residents can exercise freedom of movement.[101] The Directive has been criticized for assuming 'fundamental inequality between TCNs [third-country nationals] who have acquired long-term residents status and EU nationals' due to its method of specifying areas to which equality of treatment should apply, rather than 'introducing an overarching principle of equality'.[102] The Directive contains, through the use of 'may' clauses in Article 11(2)(3) and (4), a broad scope for the discretion of Member States to qualify and restrict the areas in which third-country nationals are to be granted equal treatment with Union citizens delimited in Article 11. The rights include equal treatment in relation to access to employment,[103] education, and[104] social security.[105] In view of the lack of certainty in the Directive, its application is 'dependent on how the Member States choose to implement these optional derogation clauses and on how restrictively the ECJ can/ will approach the Directive' in its interpretation of its provisions.[106]

In relation to the Commission's initial proposal for the Family Reunification Directive, negotiations followed the usual pattern of Member States expressing their reluctance to depart from existing national norms, making the negotiation process a protracted one.[107] Despite the heavily watered down nature of the adopted version, it succeeded in creating for the first time a right to family reunification for third-country nationals in some Member States.[108] The purpose of the Directive is to determine the conditions for the exercise of the right to family reunification by third-country nationals residing lawfully in Member States.[109]

---

[99] Council Dir 2003/109/EC of 25 November 2003 concerning the status of third-country nationals who are long-term residents OJ L016. The UK and Ireland opted not to participate in the adoption of this Directive.

[100] Recital 3, Preamble to Council Dir 2003/86/EC of 22 September 2003 on the right to family reunification OJ L251/12.

[101] Art 1.

[102] L. Halleskov, 'The Long-term Residents Directive: A Fulfilment of the Tampere Objective of Near-equality' (2005) 7 *European Journal of Migration and Law* 183.

[103] Art 11(1)(a).   [104] Art 11(1)(b).   [105] Art 11(1)(d).   [106] Halleskoy (n 102) 200.

[107] J. Hardy, 'The Objective of Directive 2003/86 Is to Promote the Family Reunification of Third Country Nationals' (2012) 14 *European Journal of Migration and Law* 441.

[108] K. Groenendijk, 'Legal Concepts of Integration in EU Migration Law' (2004) 6 *European Journal of Migration and Law* 118, cited in Hardy (n 107) 442.

[109] Art 1.

According to the Preamble to the Directive, family reunification 'helps to create sociocultural stability . . . and social cohesion'.[110] Diego Acosta Arcarazo has pointed out the contradiction here in that 'the discourse on social cohesion is usually employed by Member States in the opposite direction . . . [ie] to further restrict immigration'.[111]

In the *Family Reunification Directive* case, the European Parliament challenged the legality of the Directive on the basis that certain of its provisions compel Member States to breach their obligations under the ECHR, despite the Community's clearly expressed intention to be bound by the Convention in Article 6(2) TEU and in Recital 2 of the Preamble to the Directive, which claims to 'respect' and 'observe' the ECHR and the European Charter of Fundamental Rights (the Charter).[112] The CJEU concluded that the Directive left scope for the Member States to act in accordance with their ECHR obligations and thus could not be said to be in breach of the Convention. Nevertheless, the case well illustrates the problems that can result from legislation couched in uncertain terms. Not only is this case the first in which the CJEU made direct reference to the Charter, but it also has great significance for the increasing legislation on asylum and immigration matters. The case emphasizes the importance of clarity and coherence in the drafting of legislation which has the potential to impinge on fundamental rights. From paragraph 23 of the judgment it is possible to derive an argument that any such legislation will be in breach of fundamental rights protected in international legal instruments if they merely *permit* rather than *oblige* Member States to breach their obligations to respect these rights. The Court stated that, 'a provision of a Community act could, in itself, not respect fundamental rights if it *required, or* expressly or impliedly *authorised*, the Member States to adopt or retain national legislation not respecting those rights' (emphasis added).

Advocate General Kokott, in her Opinion, seemed to realize precisely this problem of legal uncertainty rendering breaches of fundamental rights more likely. Unlike the Court, Kokott argued that Article 8 of the Directive was contrary to Article 6(2) TEU. Article 8 of the Directive permits Member States to establish waiting periods:

Member States *may* require the sponsor to have stayed lawfully in their territory for a period not exceeding two years, before having his/her family members join him/her.

By way of derogation, where the legislation of a Member State relating to family reunification in force on the date of adoption of this Directive takes into account its reception capacity, the Member State *may* provide for a waiting period of no more than three years between submission of the application for family reunification and the issue of a residence permit to the family members [emphasis added].

---

[110] Recital 4.   [111] Arcarazo (n 96) 167.
[112] *Parliament v Council* [2006] ECR, I-5769 C-540/03, 27 June 2006.

Kokott articulated the problems liable to arise due to the uncertainty created by the use of the word 'may'. By Article 8, the EU appeared to empower Member States 'to provide for waiting periods of up to two or even three years. If a Member State were to transpose that provision, as it were, one-dimensionally, with disregard for its human-rights obligations, national rules on waiting periods would also be enacted which failed to allow for the possibility, required by the case-law of the [ECtHR], of having regard to hardship situations.'[113] She added that Recital 2 of the Preamble to the Directive, which states that it both 'respects' and 'observes' fundamental rights, contributed further to the likelihood of a failure to protect fundamental rights occurring by fostering 'misconceived and one-dimensional transposition'. She states that '[i]nstead of reminding Member States of their responsibilities in regard to fundamental and human rights, the recital asserts that the Directive, as drafted, is compatible with them'. Her conclusion is that should any breach occur on account of such provisions liable to being 'misunderstood . . . responsibility would lie not only with the national legislature . . . but also with the Community legislature'.[114]

Although the Court did not adopt this line of argument, it nevertheless recognized in paragraph 23 of its judgment that an EU law provision might be held not to respect fundamental rights if 'it required, or expressly or impliedly authorized, the Member States to adopt or retain national legislation not respecting those rights'. It is possible to argue that where a Directive contains numerous highly uncertain provisions that could be interpreted as both compliant or non-compliant with binding international obligations, and contains no safeguard clause making clear that any application of the Directive provisions *must* respect these obligations, it amounts to an 'impliedly authorised' breach.

The Commission has produced a report on the implementation of the Family Reunification Directive in which it highlights Member States' mal-implementation of some of its provisions, for instance those relating to the imposition of integration requirements. This is an area which is likely to become a point of contention for Member States and the EU Institutions, with the European Council having called on the Commission to put forward proposals for an evaluation or review of the Directive, 'taking into account the importance of integration measures'.[115] The 2010 Stockholm Programme reiterated the 1999 Tampere Conclusions in calling for an approximation of the rights of EU citizens and third-country nationals 'legally residing' in Member States: 'The European Union must ensure fair treatment of third country nationals who reside legally on the territory of its Member States. A more vigorous integration policy should aim at granting them rights and obligations comparable to those of EU citizens'.[116]

---

[113] *Parliament v Council* (n 112) Opinion of Advocate General Kokott, para 103.
[114] *Parliament v Council* (n 112) Opinion of Advocate General Kokott, para 103.
[115] Stockholm Programme, Brussels, 2 December 2009, 17024/09, 6.1.4 http://eur-lex.europa.eu/legal-content/EN/ALL/?uri=CELEX:52010XG0504(01).
[116] Stockholm Programme (n 115) 64.

Diego Acosta Arcarazo notes that this is an 'acknowledgement that the Tampere objective has not been achieved in the previous ten years'.[117]

In exercising its jurisdiction over EU immigration law, arguably the CJEU has in general subjected the provisions of relevant Directives to a rights-expansive interpretation. However, through an analysis of a selection of recent cases, it is argued below that rather than interpreting the provisions of the Directives broadly, the Court has merely put a brake on Member States' excessively narrow, restrictive, and contrived interpretations of the rights granted to Union citizens and their family members.

In its judgment in *Chakroun*, the Court, in interpreting the Family Reunification Directive, adopted a narrow interpretation of the scope for Member States to impose resource conditions on family reunification. The Dutch authorities refused to grant Mrs Chakroun, a Moroccan national, a provisional residence permit on the grounds that her husband, a Moroccan national with a permanent Dutch resident permit in receipt of an unemployment benefit did not have sufficient income pursuant to Dutch legislation.[118] The Court stated that '[s]ince authorisation of family reunification is the general rule', Article 7(1)(c) of the Family Reunification Directive, which allows Member States to require evidence that the sponsor has stable and regular resources sufficient to maintain herself and members of her family without recourse to the social welfare system of the Member State, 'must be interpreted strictly'. The Court added that 'the margin for manoeuvre which the Member States are recognized as having must not be used by them in a manner which would undermine the objective of the Directive, which is to promote family reunification, and the effectiveness thereof'.[119] Rather than this being a case in which the Court has interpreted the Directive in a particularly broad light, this statement from the Court seems to confirm that the role it is playing is one of reining in Member States seeking to exploit the potential for restriction in the Directive, perhaps aided by the lack of clarity in drafting.

In its recent judgment in the *Reyes* case,[120] the CJEU was called upon to interpret Article 2(2)(c) of Directive 2004/38 on the free movement rights of family members of EU citizens.[121] Article 2(2)(c) includes in the definition of a 'family member' of a Union citizen 'the direct descendants who are under the age of 21 or are dependents'. In interpreting the term 'dependant', the Court rejected Sweden's restrictive application of the requirement for 'dependence' between an adult child and her EU citizen

---

[117] Arcarazo (n 96) 71.

[118] *Rhimou Chakroun v Minister van Buitenlandse Zaken* Case C-578/08 (Judgment of the Court (Second Chamber) of 4 March 2010), para 21.

[119] *Rhimou Chakroun* (n 118) para 43.

[120] *Flora May Reyes v Migrationsverket* Case C-423/12 (Judgment of the Court (Fourth Chamber) of 16 January 2014).

[121] Dir 2004/38/EC of the European Parliament and of the Council of 29 April 2004 on the right of citizens of the Union and their family members to move and reside freely within the territory of the Member States.

parent. Ms Reyes, a Philippines citizen over the age of 21, whose mother, having moved to Germany and obtained German citizenship, had been supporting her all her life through the sending of remittances, had been denied a Swedish residence permit on the grounds that Ms Reyes could have sought work and supported herself. In rejecting this rationale, the CJEU stated that there was no need to determine the reasons for dependence once factual material dependence has been established. Despite the factual existence of a material relationship of dependence, the Swedish authorities had argued that Ms Reyes had failed to show she was economically dependent on her mother because she was young, had studied and lived in Manila, and had a higher education diploma.[122] The Swedish authorities' reasoning seems particularly contrived in their denial of a relationship of dependence despite acknowledging that Ms Reyes was being economically supported by her mother, as she had no income of her own. In order to justify this *contra legem* reasoning, the Swedish authorities were selective with the particular facts relating to Ms Reyes's situation that they chose to regard as relevant and opted not to consider as relevant other facts, such as her having spent her time helping her now deceased sister to take care of her children and that unemployment is endemic in the Philippines. The Court of Justice, in rejecting the premise that a descendent ought to show she has tried to find work, considered that such additional evidence 'is not easy to prove in practice' (with all due respect, it would be near impossible to prove in practice), and would 'make it excessively difficult for that descendent to obtain the right of residence in the host Member State'.[123] The Court stated that its chosen interpretation 'is dictated in particular by the principle according to which the provisions, such as Directive 2004/38, establishing the free movement of Union citizens, which constitute one of the foundations of the European Union, must be construed broadly'.[124] While this may be the case, it is submitted that rather than the Court's interpretation of the Directive being particularly broad, it is merely *intra legem* and it is the Swedish authority's interpretation of Article 2(2)(c) that was excessively narrow, and arguably *contra legem*.

IV. The Impact of EU Immigration and Border Control on Asylum

This section examines the relationship between the fields of EU immigration and asylum law, in particular examining the implications of the EU's immigration and border control regime on refugee protection. In what follows, it is argued that under

---

[122] *Flora May Reyes* (n 120) para 14.   [123] *Flora May Reyes* (n 120) para 26.
[124] *Flora May Reyes* (n 120) para 23.

the AFSJ, the fields of immigration and border control and asylum have not been developed in a coherent and complementary manner. In the case of the Union's asylum regime, it is crucial that it be considered in the context of wider immigration policy, both in its formulation at the policy level and in any evaluation of its functioning and the quality of its protection. It is argued that the EU's asylum law is being subjected to and subverted by its border control regime. One of the implications of this process is that a number of characteristics, which are not stated in refugee legislation, are implicitly required of the European refugee and result in the exclusion of the most vulnerable individuals from this category. Refugees are effectively being required to demonstrate characteristics over and above those found in the legal definition, including possession of financial resources, economic mobility, and a willingness to take risks.[125]

Measures deployed to limit access for migrants to EU territory have proliferated over the years and include the imposition of visa requirements on refugee-producing countries and host countries in regions of origin, carrier sanctions, the use of 'safe country' concepts, juxtaposed border controls, and the activities of Frontex, the EU Borders Agency. Frontex was created as a specialized agency to coordinate the cooperative border security operations of the Member States. Concerns have been raised in relation to the *refoulement* of asylum seekers by Frontex. Thomas Gammeltoft-Hansen has noted that Italy, Spain, France, and Greece have engaged in migration control activity on the high seas. It is well known that Italy has returned thousands of individuals to Libya under a 2005 agreement with the Libyan authorities without ensuring that there were no asylum seekers amongst these, despite the fact that Libya has no asylum procedure and is not party to the 1951 Refugee Convention.[126] Frontex was involved in coordinating a number of the returns from Italy, a practice which has been criticized by Human Rights Watch as a breach of *non-refoulement*.[127] In the recent European Court of Human Rights Grand Chamber ruling in the case of *Hirsi v Italy*,[128] it was held that Italy's interception of migrants in international waters and their action in returning them to Libya exposed them to inhuman and degrading treatment in breach of Article 3 ECHR and amounted to *refoulement*.

In impacting indiscriminately on all migrants, whatever their motive for seeking to enter the Union, immigration control practices are inhibiting the effectiveness of existing limited protection mechanisms available in the EU. The EU and the Member States have imposed visa requirements on refugee-producing countries as well as host countries in regions of origin. Common EU visa rules are applicable to nationals of 128 countries, including the majority of African

---

[125] See N. El-Enany, 'Who Is the New European Refugee?' (2008) 33 *European Law Review* 313.

[126] Human Rights Watch, *Pushed Back, Pushed Around: Italy's Forced Return of Boat Migrants & Asylum Seekers, Libya's Mistreatment of Migrants and Asylum Seekers* (2009).

[127] Human Rights Watch (n 126).

[128] ECtHR 23 February 2012, Appl No 277765/09 *Hirsi v Italy*.

countries, Asia, and significant parts of Central America.[129] Further, a special air-port transit visa is required for nationals originating from countries producing high numbers of asylum seekers. Consular officials are instructed to be 'particu-larly vigilant when dealing with . . . unemployed persons or those with irregular income' and to demand that such high-risk cases provide supporting documenta-tion.[130] Gammeltoft-Hansen has queried the fairness of these rules, considering 'that asylum-seekers are likely to fall into this category and are often unable to produce such documentation'.[131]

The restrictive migration control measures in place serve to prevent individuals in need of protection from penetrating European borders and accessing asylum procedures.[132] There has been an obvious decrease in the number of applications for asylum lodged in the EU, and a parallel admission from the Commission that this does not necessarily mean that the number of those individuals in need of protection has decreased.[133] This does not of course allow us to conclude that there is a definitive causal relationship between EU migration control and the number of asylum seekers entering the EU. There are geopolitical factors, such as patterns of conflict, that affect the numbers of asylum seekers that might seek protection in the EU. That said, there is no doubt that there is a concerted effort on the part of Member States and the EU to reduce the number of those entering the EU irregu-larly, including those seeking asylum, and this continues to raise concerns in the literature and amongst human rights organizations that are not unfounded.[134] This concern can be said to be at least partially plausible if we consider that government initiatives have been shown to have some, if limited, practical effects.[135] However, while it may be that policy makers are relatively unsuccessful in reducing over-all numbers of entrants, their efforts to control borders are not altogether with-out implication. In studying migration at the EU border, Spijkerboer concludes that the impact of intensified border control on migrants seeking to enter Europe irregularly by sea is increasing migrant deaths.[136] Spijkerboer found that increased patrol at the external border has not reduced the number of irregular migrants entering the Union, but instead has led them to use more hazardous routes into the EU.[137] Following a crackdown by the Moroccan government as a result of European

---

[129] T. Gammeltoft-Hansen, *Access to Asylum: International Refugee Law and the Globalisation of Migration Control* (2011) 133.

[130] Gammeltoft-Hansen (n 129) 133.   [131] Gammeltoft-Hansen (n 129) 133.

[132] See N. El-Enany, 'The EU Asylum, Immigration and Border Control Regime: Including and Excluding the "Deserving Migrant"' (2013) 15 *European Journal of Social Security* 171.

[133] Commission Communication on Regional Protection Programmes COM (2005) 388 final.

[134] See T. Gammeltoft-Hansen (n 129).

[135] E. Thielemann, 'Does Policy Matter? On Governments' Attempts to Control Unwanted Migration', Institute for International Integration Studies Discussion Paper 9.2003, 1.

[136] T. Spijkerboer, 'The Human Cost of Border Control' (2007) 9 *European Journal of Migration and Law* 127.

[137] Spijkerboer (n 136) 127.

migration policy,[138] which works to persuade the authorities at departure points to prevent migrants from travelling to Europe, migrants have shifted their departure points further south, to Libya, Tunisia, Guineau Bissau, Ivory Coast,[139] as well as Mauritania and then to Senegal.[140] Thus, while the number of migrants entering at particular points of the Union can be reduced, this merely has a 'displacement' effect whereby migrants move their departure points further away, making more dangerous journeys to the EU. Between 1993 and 2006, 7182 deaths at the European border were documented by the NGO, United, which gathers detailed data on the basis of press reports.[141] Since then, the number has leapt to 17 306.[142]

V. Conclusion

This chapter has argued that the quality and effectiveness of the CEAS legislation is questionable in that the asylum Directives contain broad scope for discretion in application and suffer from incomplete or mal-implementation, resulting in vast differences in practice across the EU in the level of protection afforded to asylum seekers, as well as diverse rates of recognition of refugees. Despite the CJEUs willingness to interpret EU asylum provisions in a manner that protects refugees, uniformity and complete application of the asylum Directives have not been achieved through the Court's exercise of its jurisdiction. The protracted negotiations on the recently adopted recast asylum Directives suggests that there is an acute divergence between the views of the Member States and the Commission on what is to be considered a sufficient level of harmonization of asylum norms.

With respect to EU immigration law, Member States' muted enthusiasm for harmonization of rules on regular migration into the Union has meant that a coherent and comprehensive EU immigration law remains elusive. Instead, common rules on the entry and residence of specific categories of individuals have been adopted. Where such legislation does exist, the Court of Justice has played an important role in placing a brake on Member States' narrow and seemingly contrived interpretations of the rights granted to third-country nationals.

---

[138] Amnesty International, 'Spain: The Southern Border' (June 2005), cited in Spijkerboer (n 136) 130.

[139] M. Lahlou, *Les Migrations Irregulieres Entre Le Maghreb et L'Union Europeenne: Evolutions Recentes* (2005) cited in Spijkerboer (n 136) 130.

[140] Spijkerboer (n 136) 130.

[141] United, Amsterdam 2006, cited in Spijkerboer (n 136) 136.

[142] United, see http://www.unitedagainstracism.org/campaigns/the-fatal-realities-of-fortress-europe/.

Despite Member States' reluctance to adopt measures on regular migration into the EU, they have in general been eager to adopt legislative and operational measures in the interests of curbing irregular migration. This chapter has argued that the EU's highly restrictive wider migration and border control policy subverts protective elements that might be observed in its asylum legislation. Access to EU territory is severely limited for all migrants, irrespective of their motives for moving. Migrants' departure points are being pushed further afield and their journeys to the EU are becoming more dangerous. With these effects in mind, it has been argued that reform of substantive internal protection standards is insufficient in the absence of comprehensively addressing the relationship between migration policy and asylum, in particular the effects of border control measures in restricting access to protection.

Acknowledgments

The author would like to thank Bruno de Witte for comments on earlier drafts of this chapter. Any omissions are the author's own.

Bibliography

D.A. Arcarazo, *The Long-Term Residence Status as a Subsidiary Form of EU Citizenship: An Analysis of Directive 2003/109* (2011)

J.P. Aus, 'Eurodac: A Solution Looking for a Problem?' (2006) *European Integration Online Papers* 10

I. Boccardi, *Europe and Refugees: Towards an EU Asylum Policy* (2002)

C. Costello, 'The Asylum Procedures Directive and the Proliferation of Safe Country Practices: Deterrence, Deflection and the Dismantling of International Protection?' (2005) 7 *European Journal of Migration and Law* 35

ECRE, *The Way Forward Towards Fair and Efficient Asylum Systems in Europe* (2005)

ECRE, *The Impact of the EU Qualification Directive on International Protection* (2008)

ECRE, *Sharing Responsibility for Refugee Protection in Europe: Dublin Reconsidered* (2008)

N. El-Enany, 'Who is the New European Refugee?' (2008) 33 *European Law Review* 313

N. El-Enany, 'The EU Asylum, Immigration and Border Control Regime: Including and Excluding the "Deserving Migrant"' (2013) 15 *European Journal of Social Security* 171

M. Fletcher, 'Schengen, the European Court of Justice and Flexibility under the Lisbon Treaty: Balancing the United Kingdom's "Ins" and "Outs"' (2009) 5 *European Constitutional Law Review* 71–98

T. Gammeltoft-Hansen, *Access to Asylum: International Refugee Law and the Globalisation of Migration Control* (2011)

B. Ghosh (ed), *Managing Migration: Time for a New International Regime?* (2000)

L. Halleskov, 'The Long-term Residents Directive: A Fulfilment of the Tampere Objective of Near-Equality' (2005) 7 *European Journal of Migration and Law* 181

J. Hardy, 'The Objective of Directive 2003/86 Is to Promote the Family Reunification of Third Country Nationals' (2012) 14 *European Journal of Migration and Law* 439

Human Rights Watch, *Pushed Back, Pushed Around: Italy's Forced Return of Boat Migrants & Asylum Seekers, Libya's Mistreatment of Migrants and Asylum Seekers* (2009)

S. Lavenex, '"Passing the Buck": European Union Refugee Policies towards Central and Eastern Europe' (1998) 11 *Journal of Refugee Studies* 2

S. Lavenex, *The Europeanisation of Refugee Policies: Between Human Rights and Internal Security* (2001)

E. Neumayer, 'Asylum Destination Choice, What Makes Some West European Countries More Attractive than Others?' (2004) 5 *European Union Politics* 155

Y. Pascouau, 'Intra-EU Mobility: The "Second Building Block" of EU Labour Migration Policy' (2013) 74 *European Migration and Diversity Programme*

S. Peers, 'Court of Justice: The NS and ME Opinions—The Death of "Mutual Trust"'? (2011)

S. Peers, E. Guild, D. Acosta Arcarazo, K. Groenendijk, and V. Moreno-Lax *EU Immigration and Asylum Law*, Vol. 2 (2nd ed, 2012)

S. Peers, 'The Second Phase of the Common European Asylum System: A Brave New World—or Lipstick on a Pig?' (2013) http://www.statewatch.org/analyses/no-220-ceas-second-phase.pdf

T. Spijkerboer, 'The Human Cost of Border Control' (2007) 9 *European Journal of Migration and Law* 127

E. Thielemann, 'Does Policy Matter? On Governments' Attempts to Control Unwanted Migration', Institute for International Integration Studies Discussion Paper 9 (2003)

UNHCR, *Improving Asylum Procedures: Comparative Analysis and Recommendations for Law and Practice* (2010)

CHAPTER 34

THE HARMONIZATION OF CIVIL JURISDICTION

RICHARD FENTIMAN

I. INTRODUCTION

THREE instruments form the core of the European Union's private international law regime in civil and commercial matters. The 'Brussels Regulation' (newly amended)[1] governs jurisdiction, and the effect of foreign judgments. Regulation 593/2008 (the 'Rome 1' Regulation)[2] regulates the identity and effect of the law governing a contract. Regulation 864/2007 (the 'Rome 2' regulation)[3] regulates the law applicable to non-contractual liability. Together these instruments ensure that most significant issues arising in civil proceedings before the courts of EU states are governed by a common European regime. The general effectiveness of this regime is undisputed, and states such as the UK, for which adoption of these instruments is optional,[4] have accepted that harmonization in the area of jurisdiction is in principle desirable.[5] But

---

[1] Council Reg (EC) No 1215/2012 of 12 December 2012 on jurisdiction and the recognition and enforcement of judgments in civil and commercial matters [2012] OJ L351/1.

[2] Reg (EC) No 593/2008 of 17 June 2008 on the law applicable to contractual obligations (Rome I) [2008] OJ L 177/6.

[3] Reg (EC) No 864/2007 of 11 July 2007 on the law applicable to non-contractual obligations (Rome II) [2007] OJ L199/40.

[4] An optional matter concerning civil judicial cooperation, within Art 3 of the Protocol on the position of the United Kingdom and Ireland, annexed to the TEU.

[5] See eg the response by the UK Ministry of Justice to proposals to amend the Brussels 1 Reg: *Revision of the Brussels 1 Regulation—How Should the UK Approach Negotiations?* (December

serious doubts remain as to whether each of the components of the EU regime offers the optimal solution to the private international law issues they address, doubts which concern not merely matters of detail, policy, and drafting, but reflect more fundamental problems surrounding the harmonization of European private international law.

The following remarks are concerned only with the Brussels 1 jurisdiction regime, in its original and recast form, and with identifying and assessing the tensions underlying its operation.[6] This focus is justified for two reasons. First, the Regulation in its present form, and in its earlier guise as the 1968 Brussels Convention,[7] has long been in force, and has generated a considerable body of case law. Second, the issues of jurisdiction that it addresses are at the heart of cross-border litigation.[8] Jurisdictional disputes are numerous. Much cross-border litigation involves a challenge to the court's competence, and many involve parallel proceedings in different courts, requiring each court to assess which action should proceed. Again, it is a truism that disputes concerning jurisdiction are hard fought, but that cases normally settle once the forum for adjudicating the merits has been determined.[9] A defendant unable to extricate itself from a court's jurisdiction is likely to compromise, while a claimant unable to sue in its preferred court is likely to desist. As this implies, forum shopping is the principal operation in multi-state litigation, and rules of jurisdiction the major battleground. As this suggests, the proper regulation of jurisdictional disputes is the central challenge facing the harmonization of EU private international law. The Brussels jurisdiction regime is the engine of European private international law, and it is not inappropriate to test the EU harmonization project by reference to its successes and failures.

There is, of course, a contiguous debate to be had about how best to harmonize the rules for choice of law in the EU,[10] and a tension between the harmonization of those rules, and the harmonization of substantive private law.[11] Moreover, much attention has been focused on the substantive harmonization, in particular on such initiates as the Common European Sales Law[12] and the Common Frame of

---

2011). Of those who submitted evidence 88 per cent agreed that it was in the UK's national interest to opt in to the revised Reg.

  [6] For treatment of related themes in the context of the Rome 1 and Rome 2 Regs, see R. Fentiman, 'Choice of Law in Europe: Uniformity and Integration' (2008) 82 *Tulane Law Review* 2021.

  [7] Convention of 27 September 1968 on jurisdiction and the enforcement of judgments in civil and commercial matters, OJ 1972 L32.

  [8] R. Fentiman, 'Theory and Practice in International Commercial Litigation' (2012) 2 *International Journal of Procedural Law* 235, 238–240.

  [9] *Spiliada Maritime Corporation v Cansulex Ltd* [1987] AC 460, 468.

  [10] Fentiman (n 6).

  [11] R. Brand, 'The Evolving Private International Law/Substantive Law Overlap in the European Union' in P. Mankowski and W. Wurmnest (eds), *Festschrift für Ulrich Magnus* (2014).

  [12] Proposal for a Regulation on a Common European Sales Law, Brussels 11 October 2011 COM (2011) 635 final; European Parliament legislative resolution of 26 February 2014 on the proposal for a regulation of the European Parliament and of the Council on a Common European Sales Law COM (2011) 0635—C7-0329/2011—2011/0284(COD).

Reference.[13] In practice, however, which law applies in a given case may be less significant to litigants than where it will be heard. Certainly, although such harmonization ensures that in principle the same law will apply wherever in the EU a case proceeds, this may not substantially reduce the significance attached to the question of venue. Disputes about venue often concern cases, for example, where a party has initiated tactical proceedings in a given court with the object of benefiting from the mandatory rules, or public policy considerations, applicable in that court irrespective of the law governing the contract—matters that substantive harmonization is unlikely to address.[14] In any event, given that the substantive laws of EU states are in many areas functionally similar, if conceptually diverse, matters such as the convenience, cost, and speed of proceedings are likely to be more pressing considerations for litigants, reinforcing the role of rules of jurisdiction. However the uniform application of substantive law is approached, through a private international law strategy or by substantive harmonization, jurisdiction remains the core of private international law.

The following discussion is particularly concerned with an examination of some controversial cases on Regulation 44/2001, and with attempts to reform the Regulation in an effort to solve the problems they have caused. Those problems are technical, and specific, but exemplify more generally the difficulties presented by the harmonization of private international law within the EU. As will become apparent, those difficulties are severe, and the capacity of the Regulation to regulate civil jurisdiction effectively must be doubted.

But two preliminary issues must first be addressed. First, it is necessary to identify the conflicting assumptions that explain the frequent controversies surrounding the Brussels 1 regime, its operation, and objectives. Second, it is necessary to sketch the requirements of any regime intended to regulate international civil procedure, and in particular issues relating to jurisdiction—the measure against with the EU regime must be judged.

II. Conflicting Assumptions

Any discussion of the EU jurisdiction regime is impeded by fundamental differences of opinion about its objectives, about its practical context, about the nature of jurisdictional rules, and about the judicial role in determining matters of jurisdiction. Six principal tensions underlie the debate.

---

[13] C. von Bar, E. Clive, and H. Schulte-Nölke (eds), *Principles, Definitions and Model Rules of European Private Law Draft Common Frame of Reference (DCFR)* (2009).

[14] eg *JP Morgan Europe Ltd v Primacom AG* [2005] 2 Lloyd's Rep 665.

First, assumptions differ as to the context in which the regime operates. For many practitioners throughout the EU, and for English lawyers in particular,[15] cross-border litigation is commercial litigation. It involves high-value, multi-state litigation between well-funded commercial parties. This says much about the perennial disquiet amongst commercial practitioners—especially English practitioners—about the perceived inadequacies of the Regulation. Most such disputes are likely to involve the possibility of parallel proceedings elsewhere, and in consequence proceedings concerning jurisdiction and the staying of actions are the norm. Moreover, many cases involve parallel proceedings in non-Member States, a matter with which the regime has struggled. In this environment, tactical forum shopping is commonplace, and the parties are able and willing to invest in expensive litigation. Above all, perhaps, the fact that commercial litigation is a commercial matter, with the decision to claim or defend being an investment decision, means that the object is not a legal but a commercial victory. This has several consequences. It fosters the belief that settlement not judgment is the object of proceedings. It emphasizes the paramount importance of ensuring that disputes are heard in the forum where they can most cost effectively be determined. Above all, it creates an expectation that the law, and especially judicial decisions, will reflect commercial considerations. It is apparent, however, that the central case assumed by the EU regime is very different, as the decisions analysed below attest.

Second, issues of jurisdiction, and the allocation of proceedings between competing courts, are the core issues in cross-border litigation. It is a truism that the issue of jurisdiction is paramount in substantial, cross-border litigation. Only once the location of proceedings is known can each party assess the risk of pursuing or defending a claim. Only then does a dispute's legal framework crystallize, governed by where it occurs, and according to which law. Only then can litigants measure their chance of success, and weigh that chance against the cost of litigating. Only then can they gauge the possibility of securing capitulation or a favourable compromise, and assess the risk of investing in litigation. Most importantly, only then are the parties equipped to achieve the settlement that is almost certainly their objective.

Third, the important consequence is that cross-border disputes invariably end in capitulation or compromise once the location of proceedings is established. They seldom proceed to trial on the merits, still less to judgment. This reality is, however, strikingly at odds with the overriding objective of the EU jurisdiction regime, the avoidance of irreconcilable judgments in two Member States.[16]

---

[15] For this perspective, see: C. McLachlan, 'International Litigation and the Reworking of the Conflict of Laws' (2004) 120 *Law Quarterly Review* 580; T. Hartley, 'The European Union and the Systematic Dismantling of the Common Law of Conflict of Laws' (2005) 54 *International & Comparative Law Quarterly* 813; R Fentiman, *International Commercial Litigation* 2nd edn., (2015) Ch 1.

[16] Evident in decisions such as Case C-116/02 *Erich Gasser GmbH v MISAT Srl* [2003] ECR I-14693, considered below.

Fourth, as this suggests, jurisdictional disputes are not mere preliminaries to the determination of liability. They are often the means by which the dispute is finally determined.[17] For that reason, the assumption apparently underlying the EU regime that jurisdictional disputes should be resolved swiftly, and not be the subject of extended litigation, may seem particularly inapt.[18]

Fifth, the decisive importance of jurisdictional disputes, combined with the scale and cost of much cross-border litigation, suggest that any sophisticated jurisdictional regime must ensure that any given dispute is allocated to the most appropriate forum. The most appropriate forum in this sense is that where the dispute can most efficiently be heard, but also that in which justice for both parties can best be achieved. For that reason, many legal systems have adopted in some form the doctrine of *forum non conveniens*. In English law, for example, a court has discretion whether or not to exercise jurisdiction, on the basis that the *forum conveniens* is the court 'having competent jurisdiction, in which the case may be tried more suitably for the interests of all the parties and for the ends of justice'.[19] Strikingly, however, the doctrine has no overt role in the EU jurisdiction regime,[20] and has been held to be incompatible with the regime's objectives of certainty and predictability.[21] Conspicuously, and somewhat inconsistently, elements of the doctrine are evident in the regime's rules regulating parallel proceedings in related actions,[22] and in the rules in Brussels 1bis concerning parallel proceedings in non-Member States. But, although this consideration must now be regarded as somewhat qualified, the regime's starting point is that the allocation of jurisdiction should be a matter of rule, not discretion.[23] As Professor Schlosser has stated,[24] 'A plaintiff must be sure which court has jurisdiction. He should not have to waste his time and money risking that the court concerned may consider itself less competent than another.'

Sixth, a fundamental divide separates those for whom the objective of the EU regime is to achieve optimal rules of international civil procedure, and those for whom the regime is but one element in the broader project of European integration.[25] The first, pragmatic constituency give prominence to the practical solution of real problems. But for them the regime deals only inadequately with the true

---

[17] *Spiliada* (n 9) para 468.

[18] An assumption not confined to the EU regime: see *Deripaska v Cherney* [2009] EWCA Civ 849, at para 7, per Waller LJ, 'It surely would have been better for both parties and better use of court time if they had expended their money and their energy on fighting the merits of the claim'.

[19] *Sim v Robinow* (1892) 19 R665, 668 a passage cited as stating English law in *The Abidin Daver* [1984] AC 398, 411 (HL); *Spiliada* (n 9) para 474–475 (HL); see further, Fentiman (n 15) Ch 13.

[20] *Re Harrods (Buenos Aires) Ltd* [1992] Ch 72 (CA).

[21] Case C-281/02 *Owusu v Jackson* [2005] ECR I-1383, considered below.

[22] Art 22 of Reg 44/2001; Art 30 of Reg No 1215/2012 of 12 December 2012 on jurisdiction and the recognition and enforcement of judgments in civil and commercial matters (recast) [2012] OJ L 351/1 (Brussels 1bis); Case C-129/92 *Owens Bank Ltd v Fulvio Bracco* [1994] ECR I-00117 (Opinion).

[23] P. Schlosser, *Report on the 1968 Brussels Convention* [1979] OJ C59/71, 97, paras 76–82.

[24] Schlosser (n 23) para 78.   [25] See further Fentiman (n 6).

problems of multi-state litigation, particularly in cases where a court is required to allocate venue between competing courts. At least in the past, it has said nothing about cases involving parallel proceedings in a non-Member State,[26] and its rules allocating jurisdiction between Member States are simplistic and easily manipulated.[27] Such pragmatists are tolerant of disparities between national approaches, where national laws (or some at least) offer a better solution than the harmonized rules of the regime. And they tend to favour a discretionary approach to such questions as being the only approach sufficiently flexible to respond to the complexities of cross-border litigation.[28]

Others, however, may consider the harmonization of European civil procedure as an end in itself, a position controversially expressed in the view of the European Court of Justice in *Owusu v Jackson*[29] that 'the consolidation as such of the rules on conflict of jurisdiction and on the recognition and enforcement of judgments' serves the objectives of the internal market.[30] Such a view favours whatever solution best achieves harmonization, not the optimal solution of practical problems. Importantly, it discountenances any discretionary approach to jurisdiction, and favours harmonization over resort to national law. As this suggests, a stark difference of perception exists between those whose concern is to achieve optimal rules of jurisdiction, and those for whom uniformity is an end in itself. Those favouring an instrumental approach, whereby uniformity is an end in itself, are frustrated with those whose approach is pragmatic, whose constant complaint is that the proposed rules will not work, or are not optimal.

Seventh, this opposition between competing goals is paralleled by conflicting views concerning the EU's competence in matters of jurisdiction. Differently expressed, it concerns the EU regime's legitimate territorial reach. The matter remains controversial, although as a matter of law it is now clear which the CJEU has preferred.[31] It is easy to suppose that such an EU instrument is properly concerned only with persons established in a Member State, or with matters uniquely tied to a Member State, or with parallel proceedings in different Member States. Certainly, the jurisdictional rules of the recast Regulation generally apply only to defendants domiciled in a Member State, who may be taken to have submitted to those rules by their presence. Exceptionally, and reflecting established principles of private international law, the regime also applies if either a Member State has a unique interest in the subject matter of the dispute[32] or the defendant has agreed to submit to the courts of a Member State.[33]

---

[26] See further Fentiman (n 15) Ch 13.   [27] Fentiman (n 15) para 11.75–11.76.

[28] See further, Financial Markets Law Committee, *Legal Assessment of Problems Associated with the Brussels 1 Regulation and Suggested Solutions* (2008); *Green Paper on the Brussels I Regulation, Report with Evidence*, House of Lords European Union Committee, HL Paper 148 (2009).

[29] Case C-281/02 [2005] ECR I-1383.   [30] Case C-281/02 (n 29) para 34.

[31] *Owusu* (n 21) considered below.

[32] As in cases involving immovable property: Art 24.   [33] Art 25.

It does not follow, however, that the scope of the Regulation (still less its successor) is territorially confined. It is evident from the Court's decision in *Owusu v Jackson*[34] that the 1968 Brussels Convention (the Regulation's precursor) applies notwithstanding that the claimant is established in a non-Member State, notwithstanding that the subject matter of the dispute is connected with such a state, and notwithstanding that the issue is whether the courts of a Member State or non-Member State should exercise jurisdiction. As *Owusu* makes clear, the scope of the Regulation is not defined by reference to territorial connection with the Member States, but by the objective of harmonizing their private international law. More precisely, the goal of facilitating the functioning of the internal market does not imply that the Regulation applies only in cases involving a territorial connection with the Member States. That objective is satisfied merely by the harmonization of European private international law.[35]

Finally, an important difference of opinion concerns the role of judicial discretion in the exercise of jurisdiction. This divide reflects in turn different assumptions about the judicial role, which fundamentally distinguishes common law and civil law approaches to jurisdiction. In English national law, for example, the exercise of jurisdiction is invariably discretionary.[36] An English court has discretion whether to stay proceedings in which the claimant has established jurisdiction as of right, and discretion whether to exercise jurisdiction over a defendant domiciled in a non-Member State. In its present form, the discretion draws upon and conflates the court's traditional power to stay vexatious or oppressive proceedings, and their discretion to ensure that a foreign defendant was only brought to an English court if it was the proper forum. The exercise of adjudicatory discretion is the core of the English approach to jurisdiction. It is highly prized by English lawyers as a means of ensuring procedural justice and efficiency, and responding to the complexities of cross-border litigation in which the balance of interests and policies differs markedly between cases.

Not only is this approach almost entirely absent in civil law systems,[37] it has been disapproved in the context of the Brussels 1 Regulation. Consider (once more) *Owusu v Jackson*,[38] in which the Court of Justice denied English courts the power to stay proceedings in favour of the courts of a third state on *forum conveniens* grounds. In doing so, the Court made clear that adjudicatory discretion is incompatible with the certainty and uniformity required by the Regulation.[39]

---

[34] Case C-281/02 [2005] ECR I-1383.   [35] Case C-281/02 (n 34) para 34.
[36] As famously revealed in *Spiliada* (n 9).
[37] W. Kennett, '*Forum non conveniens* in Europe' (1995) 54 *Cambridge Law Journal* 552.
[38] Case C-281/02 [2005] ECR I-1383.   [39] Case C-281/02 (n 38) para 37–46.

III. Regulating Multi-state Litigation

It might be expected that any regime governing jurisdiction in civil and commercial matters will seek to address the central issues affecting civil litigation.[40] Four matters above all others preoccupy the parties in commercial disputes. The first is the issue of venue—where will proceedings occur? The second is the issue of enforcement—will any judgment be effective? The third is the issue of party management—to what extent may these issues be regulated contractually by the parties themselves? The fourth is the issue of fairness—will one party have an unfair advantage in proceedings, perhaps achieved by its abusive conduct?

These concerns are common to domestic and multi-state proceedings. But they acquire special significance in international disputes. In such cases the legal process may be distorted, leading to inefficiency, and obstructing a fair settlement, where a dispute is heard in a non-optimal forum. Enforcement may be prevented because a defendant's assets are abroad. And fairness may be jeopardized in multi-state cases, partly because proceedings may not be heard in the optimal forum, and partly because of the possibility of abusive proceedings in a foreign court.

This suggests that the objective of legal regulation in this area should be to prevent distortions in the process of resolving the dispute, in particular those which impede litigation in the natural forum. Litigation in a non-optimal forum should be controlled, as being inefficient, and potentially unfair to the weaker party, as should abusive forum shopping. Where proceedings occur in a non-optimal forum, or when a party is threatened with abusive parallel proceedings, the process of resolving the dispute, not least by settlement, is distorted. Equality of arms and the proper assessment of advantage and risk are prevented.

As this suggests, legal techniques that promote litigation in the optimal forum should be promoted, together with mechanisms for avoiding tactical foreign proceedings, and enforcing contractual dispute-resolution provisions. A legal landscape in which these objectives were prized would presumably devolve substantial control to the court to ensure that disputes are resolved in the natural forum, permit the restraint of abusive foreign proceedings by means of anti-suit injunctions, and give strong protection to exclusive jurisdiction or arbitration agreements. It is apparent, however, as the jurisprudence of the CJEU confirms, that these are not the objectives of the EU jurisdiction regime.

---

[40] See further Fentiman (n 8).

IV. Brussels 1 through the Cases

1. Four Cases

Perhaps surprisingly, the general objectives of legal regulation in matters of jurisdiction may not be the primary concerns of Regulation 44/2001 ('Brussels 1'),[41] and its successor, Regulation 1215/2012 ('Brussels 1bis'),[42] or of the CJEU in applying them. It would be an exaggeration to claim that the CJEU, in applying Brussels 1 and Brussels 1bis is unconcerned with the resolution of particular disputes, or with crafting the best solutions to particular problems. But it has proved to be difficult for the Court to fashion a regime that is responsive to the problems of procedural justice and efficiency inherent in cross-border litigation, and that supplies appropriately commercial solutions to essentially commercial problems. The approach of the CJEU to the Brussels 1 Regulation has proved to be both *instrumental* (serving wider objectives of EU integration) and *institutional* (preserving the logic of and integrity the regime itself).

The approach of the Court of Justice is *instrumental* insofar as it has not sought the optimal outcome in particular cases, but has sought above all to serve the goals which animate the harmonization of private international law in Europe, and in particular the goal of serving the internal market.[43] This instrumental approach was articulated by the Court of Justice in *Opinion 1/03*, the Lugano Opinion, in a statement referring to the Brussels Regulation:[44] 'The purpose of that regulation, and more particularly Chapter II thereof, is to unify the rules on jurisdiction in civil and commercial matters, with the objective of eliminating obstacles to the functioning of the internal market which may derive from disparities between national legislations on the subject.'

Similarly, the approach of the Court is markedly *institutional*, intended to serve the integrity and coherence of the common scheme imposed by the Regulation. This is most apparent in the Court's unswerving adherence to the principle that irreconcilable judgments must be avoided.[45] It reflects the Regulation's origins in the 1968 Brussels Convention, intended to ensure the 'free movement of judgments' between Member States, and the objective underlying the Regulation's rules

---

[41] See further Hartley (n 15); J. Harris, 'The Brussels I Regulation and the Re-Emergence of the English Common Law', *European Legal Forum* (E) 4-2008, 181.

[42] See n 22.

[43] R. Fentiman 'The Significance of Close Connection' in J. Ahern and W. Binchy (eds), *The Rome II Regulation on the Law Applicable to Non-Contractual Obligations* (2008) 85.

[44] Opinion 1/03, Opinion pursuant to Art 300(6) EC (Competence of the Community to conclude the new Lugano Convention on jurisdiction and the recognition and enforcement of judgments in civil and commercial matters) [2006] ECR I-1145, para 143.

[45] Exemplified by *Erich Gasser* (n 16).

preventing parallel proceedings. As might be expected, the twin requirements of uniformity[46] and certainty[47] are also of considerable importance when applying the regime. Again, being a reciprocal regime, mutual trust between Member States is required when handling the Regulation. No court may review another court's assertion of jurisdiction or its competence to determine that jurisdiction.[48]

These two orientations serve to explain four prominent decisions concerning the relationship between the EU regime and national law. *Owusu v Jackson*[49] illustrates the instrumentalism of the Court's approach. *Turner v Grovit*,[50] *Allianz v West Tankers*,[51] and *Erich Gasser v MISAT*[52] demonstrate the power of the argument that the institutional integrity of the regime must be defended regardless of the consequences.

(a) Owusu

In *Owusu v Jackson*,[53] the Court ruled that an English court, having jurisdiction under the Brussels jurisdiction Regulation, cannot decline to exercise that jurisdiction on discretionary *forum conveniens* grounds, even where the alternative forum is that of a non-Member State. In doing so, the European Court of Justice reveals its broader position on the harmonization of European private international law.

In *Owusu*, the claimant, Mr Owusu, sued in England in respect of injuries sustained swimming in Jamaica. Being English-domiciled, Mr Jackson was subject to the English court's jurisdiction pursuant to Article 2 of the 1968 Brussels Convention.[54] But he argued that the court should decline to exercise jurisdiction, on the basis that Jamaica was the *forum conveniens*. The courts of Jamaica represented a forum, having competent jurisdiction, in which the case might be tried more suitably for the interests of all the parties and the ends of justice.[55] This begged the question as to whether an English court may legitimately stay proceedings, in which it has jurisdiction under the European regime, on the ground that a court in a third state is the *forum conveniens*. The trial judge held that no such power exists, because Article 2 is unqualified, save as the Convention itself provides. The Court of Appeal in *Owusu* referred the issue to the European Court of Justice, which

---

[46] *Owusu* (n 21).

[47] A. Dickinson 'Legal Certainty and the Brussels Convention – Too Much of a Good Thing?' in P. de Vareilles-Sommières (ed), *Forum Shopping in the European Judicial Area* (2007), Ch 6.

[48] Case C-351/89 *Overseas Union Insurance Ltd v New Hampshire Insurance Co* [1991] ECR I-3317.

[49] See n 21.　　　[50] Case C-159/02 [2004] ECR I-3565.

[51] Case C-185/07 [2009] 1 Lloyd's Rep 413.

[52] See *Erich Gasser* (n 16); R. Fentiman, '*Erich Gasser GmbH v MISAT*' (2005) 42 *Common Market Law Review* 241; R. Fentiman, 'Jurisdiction Agreements and Forum Shopping in Europe' (2006) 21 *Journal of International Banking and Financial Law* 304; Rt Hon Lord Mance 'Exclusive Jurisdiction Agreements and European Ideals' (2004) 120 *Law Quarterly Review* 357.

[53] Case C-281/02 [2005] ECR I-1383.

[54] Proceedings were started before Reg 44/2001 came into force.　　　[55] *Spiliada* (n 9).

answered emphatically. National courts have no discretion to decline to exercise jurisdiction under Article 2 of the Brussels regime, on the ground that a court in a third state would be a more appropriate forum. This is so even if no other Member State is implicated, either because its courts have jurisdiction, or are otherwise connected with the dispute.

Powerful arguments of principle suggested, however, that such a stay was permissible. The regime is silent as to whether and on what basis national courts may decline to exercise jurisdiction opposite third states. It might have been supposed that the allocation of jurisdiction between a Member State and a third state should not be, and was not intended to be, regulated by the Community rules. Moreover, the animating purpose of the regime's rules governing jurisdiction is the avoidance of irreconcilable judgments in two Member States, which leaves it no role in cases involving a third state. Yet the European Court of Justice held that national law could not apply in such a case.[56] Significantly, the argument that the Convention's defining objective would not be served by that conclusion was defeated by a higher-order, instrumental argument. The Brussels regime serves the objectives of the internal market, which require uniformity in all matters of jurisdiction, leaving no room for the subsidiary application of national law.[57] That objective was not served only in cases involving Member States. It was served by the uniform application of the Convention's rules of jurisdiction in any case to which those rules applied. As the Court expressed it, in a passage of considerable importance:

Suffice it to observe in that regard that the consolidation as such of the rules on conflict of jurisdiction and on the recognition and enforcement of judgments, effected by the Brussels Convention in respect of cases with an international element, is without doubt intended to eliminate obstacles to the functioning of the internal market which may derive from disparities between national legislations on the subject.[58]

Having determined that the EU regime applied to allocate jurisdiction between the courts of Member States and non-Member States, the Court further held that it was incompatible with the regime for a court to cede its jurisdiction under the Convention to the courts of a third state on *forum conveniens* grounds.[59] In particular, the objectives of the Convention would be undermined by allowing courts discretion to qualify their jurisdiction. To do so would impair legal certainty. It would also prejudice those established in the Community, by removing the benefits of legal certainty for both parties, and by putting obstacles in the way of Community claimants wishing to establish jurisdiction under the Convention. Finally, it would undermine the uniform application of the Convention, because the doctrine of *forum non conveniens* was known in some Member States, but not others.

---

[56] Case C-281/02 (n 53) paras 29–35.   [57] Fentiman (n 43).
[58] Case C-281/02 (n 53) para 34.   [59] Case C-281/02 (n 53) paras 37–46.

The decision in *Owusu* has been widely criticized, in terms of the quality of the reasoning as much as its substance.[60] It is important in the present context, however, because it suggests two broad principles of considerable significance. First, the interpretation of Union instruments depends ultimately not upon the particular objectives of the instrument in question, but the needs of European integration and the internal market. This is both legitimate and necessary where such higher-order considerations inform the interpretation of any instrument, but is striking, and introduces considerable uncertainty, when used to amend an instrument's scope *ex post facto*. Second, effective integration in private international requires uniformity in the relevant Union rules, which means that the exercise of discretion by national courts cannot be tolerated.

The effect of *Owusu* was to ensure uniformity in the application of the EU jurisdiction regime in a way that denied a role for both judicial discretion in national courts, and any role for national law at all. The immediate consequence was to deprive courts of the power to allocate proceedings to the *forum conveniens*. A court must accept jurisdiction over a party domiciled within its territory, notwithstanding that the dispute is more closely connected with another court, and although justice and efficiency would not be served. More generally, the decision generated damaging uncertainty by exposing (and leaving unanswered) a series of important questions concerning the power of national courts to decline jurisdiction in favour of proceedings in third states.[61] To leave unanswered questions that are moot in the context of a given case is itself both proper, and usual for the CJEU. But it is hard to understand how the Court could have addressed the issue in *Owusu* without placing it in a wider context of principle. The practical effect was to leave open a matter of considerable commercial importance concerning the extent to which jurisdiction should be declined on the basis that the parties had contractually agreed to the exclusive jurisdiction of a third state's courts.[62]

(b) Gasser

A different example of the drive towards institutional integrity is a prominent case in which the internal logic of the regime was enforced at the expense of commercial and practical considerations, and fairness to the parties. In *Erich Gasser GmbH v MISAT Srl*,[63] a case under the Brussels Convention, MISAT had sued Gasser in

---

[60] See eg A. Briggs, 'The Death of Harrods: *Forum Non Conveniens* and the European Court', (2005) 121 *Law Quarterly Review* 535; A. Briggs, '*Forum Non Conveniens* and Ideal Europeans' (2005) *Lloyd's Maritime and Commercial Law Quarterly* 378; E. Peel, '*Forum Non Conveniens* and European Ideals' (2005) *Lloyd's Maritime and Commerical Law Quarterly* 363; R. Fentiman, 'Civil Jurisdiction and Third States: *Owusu* and After' (2006) 43 *Common Market Law Review* 705.

[61] See further Fentiman (n 15) Ch 13.

[62] Answered (by an English court) in favour of permitting a stay in *Konkola Copper Mines plc v Coromin* [2005] EWHC 898 (Comm).

[63] *Erich Gasser* (n 16); Fentiman (n 52) (2005) 42 *Common Market Law Review* 241; Fentiman (n 52) (2006) *Journal of International Banking and Financial Law* 304; Mance (n 52).

Italy for a declaration that its contract with Gasser had terminated. Before the Italian court addressed its jurisdiction, Gasser sued MISAT in Austria under the contract, relying upon a contractual agreement to the Austrian court's jurisdiction, and thus upon Article 17 of the Convention (now Article 25 of the recast Regulation). Uncertain whether it had jurisdiction, the Austrian court referred to the European Court of Justice the question as to whether it could assert jurisdiction under Article 17, notwithstanding that another court was seised under Article 21 of the Convention (now Article 29 of the recast Regulation).

The Court concluded that Article 21 prevailed, preventing the Austrian court from asserting jurisdiction under Article 17. Chronological priority must be strictly enforced in such cases. A court may not assert jurisdiction under Article 17 if another court is seised. The court first seised has the task of determining whether the court second seised has jurisdiction under Article 17. The overriding need to avoid parallel proceedings meant that Article 21 was to be interpreted broadly.[64] Nor could it be said that the second court was ever in a better position than the first court to determine its jurisdiction, since the common rules of the Convention were applicable in both courts.[65] However, insofar as differences might arise in the application of those rules, it was desirable that one court should have responsibility for doing so. This should be the court first seised because Article 21 clearly stated that the court first seised was responsible for determining its own jurisdiction. This was reinforced by Article 19, which made it clear that a court must of its own motion decline jurisdiction where another court has jurisdiction under Article 16, but does not mention Article 17. Moreover, the motives of a claimant in bringing proceedings other than in the agreed court were irrelevant. The Convention contains no reference to motives. Nor could it be said that Gasser's human rights would be infringed if delay in the Italian courts postponed resolution of the issue of jurisdiction. The operation of Article 21 did not depend on such considerations. It would also be contrary to the principle of trust between Member States, implicit in the European regime, to allow a court to criticize (even if implicitly) the procedures adopted in another Member State.[66]

Moreover, the Court explicitly rejected any suggestion that the practical difficulties associated with such a decision, notably the encouragement of tactical proceedings, could undermine its wording and logic. As the judgment states, in an arresting passage:[67]

the difficulties of the kind referred to by the United Kingdom Government, stemming from delaying tactics by parties who, with the intention of delaying settlement of the substantive dispute, commence proceedings before a court which they know to lack jurisdiction by reason of the existence of a jurisdiction clause are not such as to call in question the

---

[64] *Erich Gasser* (n 16) para 47.   [65] *Erich Gasser* (n 16) para 48.
[66] *Erich Gasser* (n 16) para 48.   [67] *Erich Gasser* (n 16) para 53.

interpretation of any provision of the Brussels Convention, as deduced from its wording and its purpose.

The alarming, and strikingly uncommercial, implications of the decision in *Gasser* are highlighted by the English decision in *JP Morgan Ltd v Primacom AG*.[68] Several banks, acting through JP Morgan as agent, had lent substantial sums to Primacom, a German company. The loan agreement was subject to English law, and provided unambiguously that any disputes between the parties were to be submitted to the exclusive jurisdiction of the English courts. Having failed to make two successive interest payments, Primacom initiated proceedings in Germany for a declaration that it owed no interest. JP Morgan responded by initiating proceedings on the banks' behalf in the English courts, pursuant to the jurisdiction agreement, in part for a declaration that interest was payable. It was clear that both actions turned on Primacom's obligation to pay interest, and that those in Germany were initiated first. Article 27 of Regulation 44/2001 was thus engaged, apparently requiring the English court, as the court second seised, to stay its proceedings, pending the outcome of the inevitable jurisdictional dispute in Germany. The only question was whether the English court was competent nonetheless under Article 23, given the jurisdiction agreement. But since the decision of the European Court of Justice in *Gasser*, the answer was clear. Given that Article 27 applied, the express submission to English jurisdiction was irrelevant. The court second seised must stay its proceedings, even if it considers that it has jurisdiction under Article 23. Indeed, Article 27 forbids it from considering that issue at all. Only if the first court declines jurisdiction, because it recognizes that the contractual forum has jurisdiction under Article 23, may the claim in the contractual forum proceed.

Superficially, the defendant in the first court in such cases is in no worse a position than it would be in a case outside the Regulation in which one party invokes the jurisdiction of a court other than that nominated in a jurisdiction agreement. However, the Regulation penalizes the defendant in a unique fashion, by preventing the defendant from launching counter-proceedings in the named court. Again, *Gasser* does not weaken jurisdiction agreements subject to Article 23. The first court is bound to cede jurisdiction if it considers that Article 23 confers exclusive jurisdiction upon the nominated court. But it may prejudice the defendant in the first court in several ways: by forcing the defendant to defend proceedings in a non-contractual forum; by exposing the defendant to the risk of possibly irrecoverable costs in the first court; by exposing the defendant to the risk that the first court will treat the jurisdiction as ineffective, or non-exclusive; by exposing the defendant to the risk that the first court, if it accepts jurisdiction, will reach a conclusion on the merits different from that which the contractual forum would reach; or by forcing the

---

[68] [2005] 2 Lloyd's Rep 665.

defendant to settle or withdraw any claim it may have against the claimant in the first court, in the light of such risks.

Moreover, it is unrealistic to suggest that the integrity of Article 23 is left intact by *Gasser*. The problem directly raised by *Gasser* and *Primacom* concerns *Kompetenz-Kompetenz*—jurisdiction to determine jurisdiction. But *Gasser* may also affect a court's substantive jurisdiction. Suppose that the first court eventually decides that the named court has exclusive competence, and accordingly declines jurisdiction pursuant to Article 23. In principle, the named court has jurisdiction. The party wrongfooted by proceedings in the first court may at last bring proceedings in the agreed court, and indeed has the right to do so under Article 23. It is far from clear, however, that the vindicated party will in fact do so, or will be able to do so. This may be unrealistic, given the cost and delay occasioned by proceedings in the first court. The wrongfooted party, even if successful in ousting the jurisdiction of the court first seised, may be more inclined to settle or withdraw. The effect of giving priority to Article 27 in cases such as *Gasser* and *Primacom* is thus to render ineffective the rights of each party under Article 23. In theory, *Gasser* merely confirms which court is entitled to determine the parties' rights under Article 23. But, in practice, it may render Article 23 valueless.

The risks to the defendant in such a case are illustrated by the predicament of the bank in *Primacom*. First, it is hard to see how the jurisdiction agreement could have been clearer. Unambiguously exclusive in effect, it clearly contemplated that all disputes between the parties were to be determined in England. It was perhaps unsurprising that the German courts eventually said as much, and declined jurisdiction—but only after the bank's right to sue in England was suspended for several months. Second, Primacom had sought a negative declaration in Germany, thereby exploiting the tactical possibilities of such relief in the European context. As the European Court of Justice has established, a defaulting party, lacking a positive claim, may always shelter behind Article 27, merely by claiming in its preferred forum that it is not liable for any wrong of which it might be accused.[69] In the scheme of Article 27, a desire not to be sued is effectively a cause of action. Third, although they had sued in Germany, it is not apparent that Primacom had any grounds for objecting to the English court's exclusive jurisdiction. It is telling that Primacom's counsel in the Commercial Court seemed unable to identify any reason why the jurisdiction agreement was ineffective,[70] and that the German court eventually upheld it. As this suggests, a party may obstruct proceedings in a contractually agreed court without having any substantial reason for doubting the effectiveness of that agreement. Article 27 engages immediately the first court seised, whether or not there are grounds for disputing the agreement. The ruse may eventually be exposed, when the first court declines jurisdiction and upholds the

---

[69] Case C-406/92 *The Tatry* [1994] ECR I-1517 (ECJ); R. Fentiman, 'Tactical Declarations and the Brussels Convention' (1995) 54 *Cambridge Law Journal* 261.

[70] [2005] 2 Lloyd's Rep 665, para 34.

agreement, but the defaulting party will still have succeeded in delaying (and per-haps preventing), proceedings in the agreed court. Fourth, German procedural law (in common with that of many civilian systems) allowed the banks no opportunity to mount a preliminary challenge to the German court's jurisdiction, in advance of a hearing on the merits. This postponed examination of Primacom's invocation of German jurisdiction. But it also exposed the banks to the costs of preparing a defence to Primacom's substantive claim that interest was not payable. Yet such costs were inevitably wasted (and were always likely to be wasted) given the existence of the English jurisdiction agreement. Legal systems may legitimately manage disputes in the manner they consider appropriate. But the effect of such a process is inevitably to underwrite Article 27's role as an instrument of obstruction and delay. Fifth, what-ever the strength of their case, the banks were placed in a position in which com-promise must have seemed the best-worst option. Certainly, it is revealing that the parties appear to have settled once the German court had declined jurisdiction, and confirmed the exclusive jurisdiction of the English court. Only the parties can know why and on what terms such settlements are achieved. But it is all too likely that a party in the position of the banks in *Primacom* will compromise even if the court first seised declines jurisdiction. Presented with an inevitable delay in pursuing its claim, and exposed to the costs of unwelcome litigation in the first court, any unwillingness to commence proceedings afresh in the agreed court is understandable.

The effect of the decision in *Gasser* is therefore to challenge the most basic assumptions underlying the conduct of cross-border litigation. By preventing the court designated in a jurisdiction agreement from entertaining proceedings, party autonomy and the power of the parties to manage the risk of litigation by express agreement are ignored. And by permitting a counter-party to pre-empt proceed-ings in the agreed court tactical forum shopping is both rewarded and encouraged.

(c) Turner *and* West Tankers

In a controversial pair of cases, the Court of Justice comprehensively prevented the use of ant-suit injunctions to allow the courts of one Member State to restrain proceedings in another such State. In *Turner v Grovit*,[71] Mr Turner, formerly employed in Spain by a company owned and controlled by Mr Grovit, had success-fully obtained a judgment for unfair constructive dismissal in the UK employment tribunal. When Mr Grovit then brought proceedings in damages in Spain against Mr Turner, Mr Turner obtained an injunction from the English courts restrain-ing Mr Grovit from pursuing the Spanish proceedings, on the basis that they were an abuse of the process of the English court because they intended only to harass Mr Turner. The House of Lords referred to the European Court of Justice the

---

[71] Case C-159/02 [2004] ECR I-3565; T. Hartley 'How to Abuse the Law and (Maybe) Come Out on Top' in J. Nafziger and S. Symeonides (eds), *Law and Justice in a Multistate World* (2002) 73.

question whether such relief was incompatible with the 1968 Brussels Convention, precursor to Regulation 44/2001. The European Court held that such relief was incompatible with the Convention. It was inconsistent with the mutual trust required between the courts of Member States, and the principle that the jurisdiction of one national court could not be determined by another such court, because the effect of the injunction was to prevent the Spanish court from ruling on its jurisdiction.[72] It was irrelevant that such interference was only indirect, insofar as such relief is not concerned with a court's jurisdiction, but with controlling the abusive conduct of a party to English proceedings.[73]

In *Allianz SpA v West Tankers Inc*,[74] the question was whether an English court could restrain, by injunction, civil proceedings in Italy in breach of an English arbitration agreement. The Court had already prohibited such relief in principle,[75] but *West Tankers* was arguably different because Article 1(2)(d) of the Regulation provides that 'arbitration' is outside the Regulation's scope. The Court held that relief enforcing arbitration agreements was in principle outside the Regulation's scope, but that this was not decisive. The question before the Italian court, whether it should decline jurisdiction in favour of the arbitration agreement, was an issue within the scope of the Regulation insofar as it was ancillary to substantive proceedings in which jurisdiction depended on the Regulation.[76] In consequence, the principle in *Turner* applied. To restrain a party from bringing that issue before the Italian court would be to interfere indirectly with the Italian court's power to determine its jurisdiction under the Regulation.[77]

The principle to be derived from both cases is that the *effet utile* of the Regulation demands that it cannot be overridden by national law. Such an injunction represented an indirect interference in the exercise of jurisdiction pursuant to the Regulation. The argument from *effet utile* represents the purest argument for the institutional integrity of the regime. It neutralizes any suggestion that an issue is beyond the regime's scope, because the scope of the regime is irrelevant. In doing so it potentially jeopardizes any feature of national law that might be said to affect the operation of the regime, however indirectly. It also suggests how closely the Court defends the regime's integrity. As the English courts have repeatedly emphasized, restraining orders operate *in personam* to control the conduct of a claimant in foreign proceedings, and have no effect on the foreign court's jurisdiction.[78] Yet in *Turner* and *West Tankers*, even an indirect threat to the regime was unacceptable.[79] Moreover, what might be regarded as a real threat to the regime did not arise

---

[72] Case C-159/02, paras 25 and 27.   [73] Case C-159/02, para 29.
[74] Case C-185/07 [2009] 1 Lloyd's Rep 413; R. Fentiman, 'Arbitration and Antisuit Injunctions in Europe' (2009) 68 *Cambridge Law Journal* 278.
[75] *Turner v Grovit* (n 71).   [76] *Turner v Grovit* (n 71) para 26.
[77] *Turner v Grovit* (n 71) para 27.
[78] *Turner v Grovit* [2001] UKHL 65 [2002] 1 WLR 107, para 29.
[79] As also in *Turner v Grovit* (n 71).

in *West Tankers*. Given that arbitral proceedings, and civil proceedings for ancillary relief, are outside the scope of the Regulation, Articles 27 and 28 did not apply to allocate priority between the English and Italian proceedings. There was no sense in which those important rules were overridden by the grant of a restraining order. In that sense, the *effet utile* of the Regulation was jeopardized, not because of any threat to its operation, but because the rules of national law were different.

The role of anti-suit injunctions begs important questions concerning comity and the territorial effect of injunctions.[80] But the task of the Court of Justice was merely to assess the compatibility of such relief with the objectives of the EU jurisdiction regime. The decision that it was not rests on defensible grounds. But the decision in neither case was inevitable. The Court could easily, and defensibly, have concluded that the purpose of anti-suit injunctions is to control the abusive conduct of claimants in foreign proceedings, not to control the jurisdictional competence of other courts. They could have decided that such relief (at least in cases such as *Turner*) is an aspect of a court's power to control its own process, a matter arguably beyond the scope of the EU regime. More obviously still, they could have concluded that the policing of arbitration agreements is a matter outside the scope of the EU regime, and thus decided *West Tankers* differently. As it is, the Court chose to defend the institutional integrity of the regime, despite powerful arguments that the issues before it belonged properly to national law, and despite the practical consequences. For the consequences of both decisions are dramatic. National courts are deprived of a means to control abusive forum shopping, and (as *West Tankers* illustrates) to grant injunctive relief to prevent a breach of contract. The effect is to expose litigants to abusive proceedings, and to undermine the value of jurisdiction and arbitration agreements, the key tools in the effective management of litigation risk.

V. Brussels 1bis

From 10 January 2015, Regulation 44/2001 is replaced by a recast Regulation, Regulation 1215/2012 ('Brussels 1bis').[81] Nothing in the recast Regulation deviates from the rule in *Turner* to the effect that the courts of one Member State may not

---

[80] See eg R. Fentiman, 'The Scope of Transnational Injunctions' (2013) 11 *New Zealand Journal of Public and International Law* 323.

[81] See n 22. For assessment of Reg 44/2001, establishing the parameters of the recast, see, Burkhard Hess, Thomas Pfeiffer, and Peter Schlosser, *The Brussels 1 Regulation 44/2001: Application and Enforcement in the EU* (2008); Financial Markets Law Committee (n 28).

restrain abusive litigation in the courts of another such state. Importantly, however, the difficulties exposed by *Owusu* and *Gasser* are addressed in the new instrument. But the lessons to be drawn from both cases remain, and point to tensions at the heart of the EU regime which are likely to manifest themselves in other ways in future. It is especially significant, however, that attempts to solve the problems exposed in those cases reveal precisely the tensions that caused them.

Importantly, the practical effect of *Gasser* is lessened in the recast Regulation. But it is not removed. The recast Regulation now ensures that the designated court has priority in determining the effect of a jurisdiction agreement.[82] Any other court must stay its proceedings unless the named court declines jurisdiction.[83] Strikingly, this protection to jurisdiction agreements is offered only if the designated court is seised of the dispute between the parties. The awkward practical consequence is that a party relying on such an agreement must initiate proceedings in that court to preserve its position. But the underlying message is significant. The protection of jurisdiction agreements is not perceived primarily as a matter of upholding party autonomy or vindicating legitimate expectations, as practitioners and their clients would naturally assume. Instead, it is regarded as an aspect of preventing parallel proceedings. The implication is that any qualification of the court-first-seised rule is only justified if it serves the objective which that rule is intended to promote—the avoidance of irreconcilable judgments. Just as in *Gasser* itself, the protection of party autonomy, the promotion of commercial certainty, and fairness between the parties are relegated to a secondary role, behind considerations of case management, and the efficient administration of justice.

Again, Articles 33 and 34 of Brussels 1bis seek to regulate the allocation of proceedings between the courts of a Member State and a non-Member State, the issue addressed in *Owusu*. They now confer discretion on courts seised under the Regulation to stay their proceedings in favour of pending proceedings in a third state. Superficially, a notable methodological departure, this more flexible approach reflects the distinct issues which arise when parallel proceedings occur in a state which does not share the internal uniform rules of the EU, and is more a concession to a different situation, than a conceptual retreat. Certainly, the scope and nature of the discretion remains unclear. Not least, it is uncertain to what extent scope remains for the operation of national law. The present discussion is concerned, however, only with the assumptions underlying the new regime.

Article 33 applies in cases equivalent to those intra-EU proceedings which are subject to Article 29 of the recast Regulation,[84] insofar as both proceedings must involve the same cause of action and the same parties. Article 33 is not primarily concerned with identifying the most appropriate forum for the dispute, but with avoiding irreconcilable judgments. For that reason, a stay is possible only in cases

---

[82] Recital 22.   [83] Art 31(2).   [84] Art 27 of Reg 44/2001.

in which 'it is expected that the court of the third State will give a judgment capable of recognition and, where applicable, of enforcement' in the Member State seised.[85] Article 34 permits a stay of proceedings where a related action is pending in a third state. Such a stay is permitted only if (1) the courts of a third state are already seised; (2) it is expedient to hear both the local and foreign actions together to avoid the risk of irreconcilable judgments resulting from separate proceedings; (3) it is expected that the foreign court will give a judgment effective in the Member State concerned; and (4) a stay is necessary for the proper administration of justice. The stay may be lifted, and proceedings in a Member State reinstated, if (1) there is no longer a risk of irreconcilable judgments; (2) the foreign proceedings have been stayed or discontinued; (3) it appears that the foreign proceedings are unlikely to be concluded within a reasonable time; or (4) continuation of the proceedings in the relevant Member State is required for the proper administration of justice.

The discretion to stay proceedings in favour of the courts of a third state is, however, significantly circumscribed. Importantly, no power to stay exists in the event of subsequent proceedings in a third state. This is the case even if the foreign court is seised second, and its proceedings are substantially advanced before the application to stay is heard. The practical effect is to encourage pre-emptive proceedings in the courts of a Member State, and (conversely) to encourage such proceedings in the courts of third states by parties wishing to avoid the torpedo effect of proceedings in a Member State.

Surprisingly, moreover, Articles 33 and 34 provide no rules for handling cases where the courts of a non-Member State have exclusive jurisdiction, notably by virtue of an express agreement to the jurisdiction of those courts. The second case will in future be addressed when the Hague Convention on choice of court agreements is ratified by the EU.[86] But even in this event, numerous jurisdiction agreements will fall outside the Convention's scope, notably those in favour of non-contracting states. The absence of any express treatment of third-state jurisdiction agreements in the recast Regulation may therefore generate significant problems in practice.

The recast Regulation does, however, address obliquely cases where a court in a third state has exclusive jurisdiction. Recital 24 permits a court, when exercising its discretion to stay, to consider whether the court of the third state would have had exclusive jurisdiction. A court in a Member State may therefore consider the fact that a court in a third state would have exclusive jurisdiction under Article 25 pursuant to a jurisdiction agreement had it been a Member State. The Regulation therefore recognizes the significance that should be attached to the fact that a court in a third state is regarded as having exclusive jurisdiction. But the weight to be given to that fact is weaker than might be supposed. This is for three reasons. First,

---

[85] Art 33(1)(a).
[86] *Proposal for a Council Decision on the approval, on behalf of the European Union, of the Hague Convention of 30 June2005 on Choice of Court Agreements*, 30 January 2014.

in sharp contrast with cases under Articles 24 and 25 themselves, the fact that a court in a third state has exclusive jurisdiction is relevant only if proceedings are pending in that court. Importantly, therefore, a stay could not be sought merely because, for example, the parties have agreed to the exclusive jurisdiction of a third state's courts. A party seeking such a stay is required to commence proceedings in the agreed court before doing so.

Second, even if a third state's courts would have had exclusive jurisdiction under the Regulation, the effect is not to require the courts of a Member State to decline jurisdiction. A court must apply those articles reflexively to the extent that it must ascertain whether the foreign court would have had exclusive jurisdiction *mutatis mutandis* according to those provisions. It must decide, for example, whether a jurisdiction agreement in favour of such a court would have conferred exclusive jurisdiction under Article 25. But at that point the reflexive effect of Article 25 is exhausted. A court is not required to decline jurisdiction as it would under Article 25. Instead, it must exercise its discretion under Articles 33 and 34, having regard to the fact that the foreign court would have had exclusive jurisdiction.

Third, the Regulation does not attach special weight to the foreign court's perceived exclusive jurisdiction. Far from creating any presumption of a stay, Recital 24 provides only that the factors relevant in the exercise of discretion 'may also include consideration of the question whether the court of the third State has exclusive jurisdiction'. It is unclear, therefore, what weight should be attached to a foreign court's exclusive jurisdiction. Indeed, the language of the Recital, and the absence of any presumption, suggests that a court will find it difficult to attach any such weight. This has serious implications in cases involving jurisdiction agreements in favour of the courts of third states. At present, the English courts have applied the Regulation so as to permit them to stay their proceedings in such cases exactly as they would had their jurisdiction derived from national law.[87] The effect is that a stay will be granted in all but the most unusual circumstances, and effect given to the jurisdiction agreement. As this suggests, it is at least possible, even likely, that the protection afforded to third-state jurisdiction is significantly weaker than presently under English law.

The effect of Articles 33 and 34 is therefore to reduce significantly a court's power to prevent the inefficiency and potential abuse of process caused by parallel proceedings, and to encourage tactical litigation. Articles 33 and 34 permit a stay only if the foreign court is first seised. Their effect is also potentially to diminish the protection given to exclusive jurisdiction agreements in favour of third-state courts. This is for two reasons. First, a court in a Member State has no power to give effect to such agreements in their own right, but can do so only if the agreed court is seised. Second, the fact that a third state has agreed exclusive jurisdiction is not

---

[87] *Konkola Copper Mines plc v Coromin* [2005] 2 Lloyd's Rep 555.

decisive, and may not be particularly significant, but is apparently merely a factor in exercising the discretion to stay. The effect will be to encourage torpedo claims in the courts of Member States. If the agreed court is not seised, a court in a Member State will be unable to stay its proceedings. Even if the foreign court is seised, the protection afforded to such a jurisdiction agreement may be relatively weak.

As this suggests, the new regime is likely to hinder, not promote, the proper administration of justice. The requirement that proceedings must be pending in a third state at the time when the relevant court in a Member State is seised makes it impossible for such a court to respond comprehensively to the inefficiency and potential abuse of process caused by parallel proceedings. A stay is impossible where the foreign court is seised second, but proceedings in that court are substantially advanced before proceedings go to trial in a Member State, even where the foreign court is likely to give judgment first. The familiar consequences of such parallel proceedings are increased costs, wasted legal resources, and potentially a rush to judgment in both courts.

Significantly, therefore, the recast Regulation purports to address the difficulties addressed in *Owusu* and *Gasser*. But it does so in a way that reflects the same assumptions which created those difficulties. In particular, it reveals once again a preoccupation with the avoidance of irreconcilable judgments, a diminished regard for the value of party autonomy, and an insensitivity to the problems of tactical litigation.

VI. CONCLUSIONS

As the decisions in *Owusu, Turner, West Tankers*, and *Gasser* confirm, the interpretation of Regulation 44/2001, and the design of the recast Regulation, is constrained by considerations secondary to achieving the best outcome, and secondary to creating a successful regime for the regulation of international commercial disputes. This has prompted unease amongst practitioners, and those who bear the risk of litigation. It prompts three reflections about the utility of the EU jurisdiction regime.

First, practitioners increasingly seek respite from the difficulties caused by the EU jurisdiction regime by opting for arbitration, not litigation. By doing so, they exploit the fact that arbitration is excluded from the Regulation's scope.[88] It is increasingly common either to favour arbitration instead, or to provide for arbitration as an alternative to litigation.[89] This reflects the perception that the

---

[88] Art 1(2)(d).

[89] Fentiman (n 52) (2005) 42 *Common Market Law Review* 241; R. Fentiman, 'Parallel Proceedings and Jurisdiction Agreements in Europe' in Pascal de Vareilles-Sommières (ed), *Forum Shopping in the European Judicial Area* (2007) Ch 1.

Brussels Regulation is too unsophisticated, too uncommercial in its ideology, to regulate substantial commercial disputes. The effect is to allow a party to arbitrate in circumstances where the Regulation would hinder the effective resolution of the dispute.[90] This promises a future in which commercial disputes in Europe are resolved almost invariably by arbitration, leaving only other matters for the Brussels Regulation. It suggests a mixed economy, in which high-value, high-cost commercial litigation occurs beyond the Regulation, and in which the Regulation governs consumer complaints, debt collection, and personal injury claims. The ironic consequence is that a regime intended to harmonize the law on civil jurisdiction within the EU, by subjecting it to uniform rules, may have the effect of encouraging litigants to arbitrate, a matter beyond the regime's scope, and subject to national law.

Second, consider again the principle at the root of the EU jurisdiction regime, that parallel proceedings must at all costs be avoided, so as to guard against the spectre of irreconcilable judgments. No tenet is more central to the Brussels regime, none more often repeated. But for those with experience of commercial litigation this preoccupation is puzzling, indeed misguided. It is very possible that two courts will be seised concurrently in a substantial dispute, given the likely importance to each party of manoeuvering proceedings into their preferred forum. But the likelihood that proceedings will advance significantly in both places is remote. This is not because both courts are likely to agree that only one has competence. Even if the parties intend to pursue the dispute to judgment, the cost of fighting on two fronts is likely to deter them. But litigants in costly cross-border disputes seldom have any intention of taking the dispute to judgment, or even to trial—certainly not to a trial on the merits. The jostling for position so common in transnational disputes, each party seeking to seise its preferred forum, is invariably intended to promote settlement, or surrender by the other party. The notion that either is seeking a judgment on the merits is unrealistic. Indeed, it is an axiom of cross-border litigation that to win the battle of forums is to win outright. As claimants know to their advantage, defendants sued in an inconvenient forum are apt to capitulate, and, as any defendant knows, claimants unable to sue where they wish are likely to withdraw. It is striking that the risk of irreconcilable judgments, the principal leitmotif of the Regulation, is a danger that is at best exaggerated, at worst an illusion.

Third, it is inevitable that not all procedural models will satisfactorily implement the objectives of efficiency and justice in cross-border litigation. These centre on the need to prevent the distortions in the legal process that arise when litigation occurs in a non-optimal forum, and when a party is threatened with abusive

---

[90] As in cases following the decision in *Erich Gasser* (n 16).

parallel proceedings. Legal techniques are therefore required that promote litigation in the optimal forum, and control tactical foreign litigation.

There may be legitimate juridical or constitutional reasons why some legal systems are better equipped than others to address the problems of cross-border litigation. Experience teaches that the devices necessary to achieve these goals fully—such as discretion to allocate proceedings to the natural forum, and the power to restrain abusive foreign proceedings—involve a distinctive, activist conception of the judicial role rejected in many systems. Again, not every legal system is required to regulate the complex, high-value, multi-jurisdictional commercial disputes that call for such treatment. But particular questions arise concerning the capacity of Regulation 44/2001 (and its successor, Brussels 1bis) to regulate international commercial disputes effectively. Properly, the Regulation is animated by important and legitimate objectives of its own, such as the furtherance of European integration, and achieving simplicity in litigation. It is apparent, however, that these objectives are often incompatible with the resolution of substantial cross-border disputes. As we have seen, it is striking that the threat that underpins the logic of the Regulation—the existence of irreconcilable judgments—is one that practitioners will seldom if ever encounter. Nor have the decisions of the Court of Justice generally reflected the realities of commercial dispute resolution, or promoted the policies identified above. It is certainly unclear how such disputes can be regulated effectively by a regime that encourages abusive forum shopping,[91] undermines contractual jurisdiction agreements,[92] prevents recourse to mechanisms for discouraging such abuse,[93] and prevents the allocation of disputes to the most appropriate forum.[94]

In the end, however, the lesson to be drawn from these difficulties is not perhaps that the EU jurisdiction regime is flawed, but that it seeks to achieve objectives different from those normally associated with the regulation of cross-border disputes. The imperative of preserving a certain and uniform regime may be inherently at odds with any aspiration to serve 'the interests of the parties and of justice'.[95] And the complexity of multi-state litigation may demand a degree of flexibility, and a central role for judicial discretion, which is incompatible with any attempt to achieve true harmonization.

[91] Case C-406/92 *The Tatry* [1994] ECR I-5439; for critique see R. Fentiman, 'Tactical Declarations and the Brussels Convention' (1995) 54 *Cambridge Law Journal* 261.

[92] *Erich Gasser* (n 16).

[93] *Turner v Grovit* (n 71); see R. Fentiman, *International Commercial Litigation* 2nd ed, (2015) 532–535.

[94] *Owusu* (n 21).

[95] *Sim v Robinow* (n 19) 668, per Lord Kinnear; cited in *Spiliada* (n 9) 474, per Lord Goff.

Bibliography

Christian von Bar, Eric Clive, and Hans Schulte-Nölke (eds), *Principles, Definitions and Model Rules of European Private Law Draft Common Frame of Reference (DCFR)* (2009)

Ronald Brand, 'The Evolving Private International Law/Substantive Law Overlap in the European Union' in P. Mankowski and W. Wurmnest (eds), *Festschrift fur Ulrich Magnus* (Sellier, Munich, 2014)

Adrian Briggs, '*Forum Non Conveniens* and Ideal Europeans' (2005) *Lloyd's Maritime and Commerical Law Quarterly* 378

Richard Fentiman, 'Choice of Law in Europe: Uniformity and Integration' (2008) 82 *Tulane Law Review* 2021

Richard Fentiman, *International Commercial Litigation* 2nd ed, (OUP, Oxford, 2015) Chs 1 (Introduction), 13 (Declining Jurisdiction: English National Law)

Richard Fentiman, 'Brussels I and Third States: Future Imperfect' (2011–2012) 13 *Cambridge Yearbook of European Law Studies* 65

Richard Fentiman, 'Theory and Practice in International Commercial Litigation' (2012) 2 *International Journal of Procedural Law* 235

Financial Markets Law Committee, *Legal Assessment of Problems Associated with the Brussels 1 Regulation and Suggested Solutions* (2008)

Green Paper on the Brussels I Regulation, Report with Evidence, House of Lords European Union Committee, HL Paper 148 (2009)

Jonathan Harris, 'The Brussels I Regulation and the Re-emergence of the English Common Law' (2008) 4 *European Legal Forum* (E) 181

Trevor Hartley, 'The European Union and the Systematic Dismantling of the Common Law of Conflict of Laws' (2005) 54 *International & Comparative Law Quarterly* 813

Burkhard Hess, Thomas Pfeiffer, and Peter Schlosser, *The Brussels 1 Regulation 44/2001: Application and Enforcement in the EU,* (2008)

Wendy Kennett, '*Forum non conveniens* in Europe' (1995) 54 *Cambridge Law Journal* 552

Campbell McLachlan, 'International Litigation and the Reworking of the Conflict of Laws' (2004) 120 *Law Quarterly Review* 580

Rt Hon Lord Mance, 'Exclusive Jurisdiction Agreements and European Ideals' (2004) *120 Law Quarterly Review* 357

Edwin Peel, '*Forum Non Conveniens* and European Ideals' (2005) *Lloyd's Maritime and Commerical Law Quarterly* 363

PART VIII

BEYOND THE REGULATORY STATE?

CHAPTER 35

....

PURSUING EQUALITY IN THE EU

....

ELISE MUIR

I. From the Principle of Equal Treatment to EU Equality Law

....

THE principle of equality or non-discrimination[1] constitutes one of the cornerstones of the process of European integration. Pursuing equality among the people and states of Europe are primary objectives,[2] it has long been perceived as a precondition to progressing towards 'an ever closer union among the peoples of Europe'[3]—to the extent that the Union is actually 'founded' on the value of equality.[4]

It flows from the importance of the principle that EU law entails multiple references to non-discrimination.[5] Certain references are fairly specific, such as the duty to ensure equal treatment between agricultural producers and consumers,[6] or the prohibition of discriminatory internal taxation on products from other Member States.[7] Others are more open-ended as is the case of the prohibition of nationality

---

[1] These notions are used interchangeably; see Takis Tridimas, *General Principles of EU Law* (2nd ed, 2006) 64

[2] eg Arts 3(3), 4(2) TEU, Art 8 TFEU.   [3] Art 1 TEU.   [4] Art 2 TEU.

[5] See further Koen Lenaerts, *L'égalité de traitement en droit communautaire* (1991) 27 *Cahiers de droit européen* 3, 3.

[6] Art 40(2) TFEU.   [7] Art 110 TFEU.

discrimination within the scope of application of the Treaties[8] or the prohibition of discrimination based on any ground such as sex, race, colour, ethnic or social origin, genetic features, language, religion or belief, political or any other opinion, membership of a national minority, property, birth, disability, age, or sexual orientation.[9]

References to equality are therefore very diverse. Yet they all find a common origin in a 'meta-principle of equality' defined by reference to the Aristotelian formula adjusted in the context of EU law to the effect that compliance with the principle of non-discrimination requires that comparable situations must not be treated differently and that different situations must not be treated in the same way unless such treatment is objectively justified.[10] This principle has been granted constitutional status and is frequently referred to as a general principle of EU law.[11]

As such, the general principle of equality and its expressions in primary and secondary law serve as benchmarks[12] to assess the soundness of decision making by EU actors[13] as well as by the Member States acting within the scope of EU law.[14] It demands that decision makers be capable of explaining the legitimacy, appropriateness, and necessity of specific distinguishing criteria and the negative impact of a decision on a certain category of actors or products. It is thus a tool for good governance.

Among the diversity of references to non-discrimination there also exist a number of specific expressions of the principle that substantiate the meta-principle in the context of a specific policy. Many of these references have in common that they are primarily driven by the goal of market-making for goods, services, legal and natural persons, as well as capitals. In this context, the principle of equality is framed in terms of non-discrimination on grounds of nationality and is designed progressively to erase boundaries among the Member States for such economic entities.

Other references to equality are the expression of a more ambitious societal goal: they operationalize the 'transformative'[15] function that the principle plays in

---

[8] Art 18 TFEU.   [9] Art 21 CFEU.

[10] Joined Cases 117/76 and 16/77 *Ruckdeschel* [1977] ECR 1753, para 7. The first limb of this formula is the most classic expression of the principle but the second limb is also of practical relevance, eg Case C-149/10 *Chatzi*, judgment of 16 September 2010, paras 68–75.

[11] *Ruckdeschel* (n 10) para 7. See also Case C-115/08 *Čez* [2009] ECR I-10265, para 91.

[12] On the functions of the principle, eg Gillian More, 'The Principle of Equal Treatment: From Market Unifier to Fundamental Right?' in Paul Craig and Gráinne de Búrca (eds), *The Evolution of EU Law* (2011) 517; Gráinne de Búrca, 'The Role of Equality in European Community Law' in Alan Dashwood and Siofra O'Leary (eds), *The Principle of Equal Treatment in EC Law* (1997) 13.

[13] Including the legislator, eg Case C-236/09 *Test-Achats* [2011] ECR I-773.

[14] By analogy Case C-617/10 *Akerberg Fransson*, judgment of 26 February 2013, paras 16–31.

[15] The expression is borrowed from Alec Stone Sweet and Kathleen Stranz, 'Rights Adjudication and Constitutional Pluralism in Germany and Europe' (2012) 19 *Journal of European Public Policy* 92, 96.

EU law. These latter provisions, which may be found in primary as well as secondary law, belong to policies driven by the intent to further equality among the people of Europe.[16] Here non-discrimination is more than a principle regulating the mechanics of institutional law or a tool to regulate the relationship among national markets; it is one of the central constituents of a project for greater harmony between, as well as within, the societies of Member States. The identification of the social function of equality is commonly illustrated by reference to the landmark statement of the Court in *Defrenne II* according to which the principle of equal pay between men and women 'forms part of the social objectives of the [Union], which is not merely an economic union, but is at the same time intended [. . .] to ensure social progress and seek the constant improvement of the living and working conditions'.[17] Today, the Union is, for example, expected actively to seek to combat discrimination on a variety of grounds,[18] as well as to combat it while defining and implementing its policies and activities,[19] with the emphasis on equal treatment between men and women.[20]

The pursuit of equality with this social connotation is both an ancient competence and a particularly modern and dynamic EU policy. The Rome Treaty contained provisions that have set the floor for a wealth of legislation and case law on equal treatment in employment with the prohibition of nationality discrimination against workers from another Member State[21] as well as sex discrimination as regards pay.[22] This legal framework quickly developed through political initiatives as well as judicial law making.[23] It was considerably broadened following the entry into force of the Amsterdam Treaty. What is today Article 19 TFEU indeed empowers EU institutions to take appropriate action also to combat discrimination based on racial or ethnic origin, religion or belief, disability, age, or sexual orientation, thus paving the way for a spectacular broadening and modernization of EU equality law. Legislation giving flesh to the principle of equality has also blossomed in the context of employment and migration law, as will be detailed in Section II.2.[24]

The set of references to equality that seeks to give effect to the transformative function of the principle in EU law is what will be the focus of this chapter insofar as it is constitutive of EU equality policy. In seeking to pursue this transformative function, EU actors have considerably broadened the scope of EU law, yet it is not unlimited. We will therefore pinpoint the perimeters of EU equality law and explore the rationale behind the external boundaries of this policy

---

[16] Fritz W. Scharpf, 'Perpetual Momentum: Directed and Unconstrained?' (2012) 19 *Journal of European Public Policy* 127, 132–133.

[17] Case 43/75 *Defrenne II* [1976] ECR 455, para 10.   [18] eg Arts 18, 19, 157 TFEU.

[19] Art 10 TFEU.   [20] Art 8 TFEU.   [21] Art 45(2) TEEC.   [22] Art 119 TEEC.

[23] Alec Stone Sweet, *The Judicial Construction of Europe* (2004) 147

[24] Also introducing these aspects of the principle together: Mark Bell, 'The Principle of Equal Treatment: Widening and Deepening' in Paul Craig and Gráinne de Búrca (eds), *The Evolution of EU Law* (2nd ed, 2011).

field (Section II). Taken together, these specific expressions of the principle of equality have two main characteristics that shape the implementation of the principle. First, they are strongly embedded in a fundamental rights rationale. Non-discrimination is indeed considered to be a precondition to the respect for human dignity and personal autonomy.[25] Therefore, limitations to the principle should be narrow and the relevant rights, irrespective of whether they are expressed in EU primary or secondary law tinted with a high moral value. Second, these references to the principle of equality are destined to impact on societal habits. The technicalities of this field of EU law are thus marked by an advanced procedural framework. This results in a sophisticated web of concepts that can be assessed in terms of their contributions to different normative models of equality (Section III).

II. An Ambitious yet Circumscribed Project

1. The General Architecture

The fact that the constituent powers regularly seek to broaden the ambit of this policy field points at a truism: EU equality law is finite. Unlike the meta-principle of equality, policies designed to further equality among people are shaped by a tight legal framework. Each prong of equality law identifies specific grounds of differential treatment as well as specific fields in which differences of treatment are suspect. Differences of treatment on grounds other than those identified or in other fields fall outside the scope of EU equality law. For instance, until a decade ago, EU law addressed sex discrimination but not discrimination on grounds of sexual orientation, which was deemed to be a distinct concept.[26]

EU equality law is also fragmented. The applicable legal tools may—and often do—differ from one ground to the other and from one field to the other. The rules on sex equality in employment are, for instance, distinct from those relating to statutory social security schemes. EU equality law thus specifies for (1) each ground (2) the fields in which the prohibition of discrimination applies and the corresponding (3) legal regime without it being possible to dissociate the three elements.

---

[25] AG Maduro Case C-303/06 *Coleman* [2008] ECR I-5603, paras 8ff.
[26] eg Case C-249/96 *Grant* [1998] ECR I-621, para 47.

The definition of grounds and fields is therefore a precondition to the identification of the relevant legal framework. Nevertheless, EU legislation rarely provides a clear definition of these *grounds*, thus leaving it for the domestic arena and ultimately the European judiciary to clarify. For instance, there has been much controversy on the definition of 'disability'. While the Court had first adopted a rather narrow definition of the concept,[27] it modified its approach in the *HK Danmark* case[28] so that an illness may be covered by the concept of 'disability'.[29]

Nor does legislation systematically define the *fields* it covers. When possible, the Court favors an autonomous as well as a uniform definition of the terms used to define the substantive scope of this policy. An illustration is the notion of 'pay' that has been subject to vivid debate in the context of sex equality law.[30] The CJEU ruled that it should include any consideration (including contributions to contracted-out occupational pensions schemes) provided that the worker receives it, albeit indirectly, in respect of his employment from his employer; this broad definition has been further transposed to other prongs of equality law.[31]

The complexity created by the fragmentation of EU equality law has a dual origin. A first set of reasons relate to the nature of the EU legal order. EU competences to develop an equality policy have only progressed in stages. Although today's version of the TFEU includes a Part entitled 'Non-discrimination and citizenship of the Union' with a prohibition of nationality discrimination (Article 18 TFEU) and an enabling provision to combat discrimination on grounds of sex, racial or ethnic origin, religion or belief, disability, age or sexual orientation (Article 19 TFEU), multiple expressions of the prohibition of discrimination are spread throughout the Treaty. As a consequence, the identification of specific grounds, fields, and legal regimes depends on different legal bases, institutions, and procedures. For example, while qualified majority voting at the Council is required to regulate nationality or sex equality in employment,[32] Article 19 TFEU requires unanimity; hence the difficulty of finding agreement on the proposal to expand the scope of the prohibition on grounds of religion or belief, disability, age, or sexual orientation beyond the field of employment.[33] There are also external constraints affecting the shape of equality law. EU law is influenced by several international instruments on fundamental rights.[34] This is particularly strong insofar as disability law is concerned since the EU has been

---

[27] C-13/05 *Chacón Navas* [2006] ECR I-6467, paras 46–47.

[28] Joined Cases C-335/11 and C-337/11 *HK Danmark*, judgment of 11 April 2013, para 38.

[29] *HK Danmark* (n 28) para 41.

[30] Deirdre Curtin, 'Scalping the Community Legislator: Occupational Pensions and "Barber"' (1990) 27 *Common Market Law Review* 475.

[31] eg Case C-546/11 *Toftgaard*, judgment of 26 September 2013, paras 26–30.

[32] Arts 46 and 157(3) TFEU.

[33] Proposal for a Directive on implementing the principle of equal treatment between persons irrespective of religion or belief, disability, age or sexual orientation COM (2008) 426.

[34] eg Art 14 ECHR, Protocol 12 ECHR.

bound by the United Nations Convention on the Rights of Persons with Disabilities since December 2010.[35]

A second set of reasons is more specific to equality policy as such. For certain Member States, the very choice of equality law as a tool to address social injustices has demanded a significant shift of regulatory paradigm that contributes to explaining the gradual approach adopted at European level. In France, for instance, illegitimate differential treatment was primarily a problem tackled through criminal law but not through employment and civil law; the EU approach thus demanded profound legal changes.[36] Besides, the specific need to structure this discipline by reference to different grounds is in fact dictated by the distinct characteristics of each of these grounds and the perception thereof by the legislator. For instance, while anti-discrimination law is usually symmetrical insofar as the two groups (such as men and women) should in principle be treated in the same way, disability discrimination is often said to be asymmetrical. The specific situation of disabled people generally justifies that they be protected while the reverse is not true.[37] Similarly, the prohibition of age discrimination is atypical insofar as, as a matter of fact, everyone will experience being part of a different age group;[38] as a consequence, policy makers may have a certain leeway in structuring age related policies.

More generally, the limits of equality policy ought also to be understood in light of other forms of intervention in favour of disadvantaged groups[39] as well as in the context of the relationship between the right to equal treatment and other fundamental rights. The legislature may, for instance, be reluctant to expand the scope of equality law where the duty of non-discrimination leads to a head-on conflict with the freedom to conduct a business or fundamental right to private autonomy. Furthermore, in the more specific context of EU law, the level of political support for equality legislation is affected by the perception that the EU should focus on economic integration, leading policy makers to be more reluctant to support intervention in non-economic domains such as access to housing or education. It is unsurprising therefore to observe that while EU equality law prohibits non-discrimination in employment on grounds of sex, religion or belief, disability, age, sexual orientation and race or ethnic origin, it only prohibits discrimination in education and social advantages on the latter ground, as we shall now see.

---

[35] As a consequence, the CJEU adjusted its interpretation of the notion of 'disability': *HK Danmark* (n 29) paras 36–38.

[36] Sophie Latraverse (ed), 'Le droit français en matière de discriminations', in Organisation Internationale pour les Migrations, *Pour une société plus juste: Le droit international, communautaire et français en matière de discriminations* (2004) 126.

[37] Lisa Waddington, 'Implementing the Framework Employment Directive' in Anna Lawson and Caroline Gooding, *Disability Rights in Europe: From Theory to Practice* (2005) 107, 113–117.

[38] See further Peter H. Schuck, 'The Graying of Civil Rights Law' (1979) 89 *Yale Law Journal* 27, 82.

[39] See further Sandra Fredman, *Human Rights Transformed: Positive Rights and Positive Duties* (2008).

2. The Actual Perimeter

The definition of the specific *grounds* and *fields* to which EU equality law is applicable has significantly evolved over time. We can today distinguish between four broad sets of rights characterized by the relative breadth of their substantive scope as well as distinctive underlying dynamics and institutional frameworks.

(a) Equal Treatment on Grounds of Nationality among EU Citizens

We start with the oldest broad non-discrimination clause: today's Article 18 TFEU. This provision already existed in the Treaty of Rome and makes it clear that nationality discrimination is prohibited within the scope of application of the Treaties. Article 18 TFEU is complemented by numerous specific provisions.[40] Some may be found in EU primary law such as those forming the backbone of the rules on the free movement of workers (Article 45(2) TFEU), establishment (Article 49(2) TFEU), and services (Article 56 TFEU),[41] while others appear in legislation.[42]

The prohibition of nationality discrimination has been primarily designed to serve the process of economic integration through the elimination of unjustified differential treatment among the factors of production of the internal market. However, the CJEU as well as the legislature have stressed the importance of ensuring that natural persons pursuing a cross-border economic activity be ensured equal access to a set of advantages going well beyond the needs of their economic function. In particular, besides equal treatment in access to, performance, and termination of employment or self-employment activities, as well as in matters of vocational training and unionism, economic actors shall have equal access to a whole range of tax and social advantages,[43] such as to remain with an unmarried partner in a host state which permits the unmarried companion of its own nationals to reside in its territory.[44]

The notion of EU citizenship has been progressively fleshed out with the effect of prohibiting nationality discrimination against non-economically active EU citizens.[45] Ever since the *Martínez Sala* case, the CJEU has developed the equal treatment rights of mobile EU citizens irrespective of the absence of a genuine

---

[40] The CJEU repeatedly stresses that more specific expressions of the principle should be used whenever available, yet Art 18 TFEU has been a useful gap filler in a number of symbolic cases, eg Case 293/83 *Gravier* [1985] ECR 593, para 26.

[41] On the distinction between discrimination on grounds of nationality, on grounds of cross-border movement and the prohibition of obstacles to free movement, see further in Part IV of this edited collection.

[42] eg Art 7(2) Reg 492/2011 on the freedom of movement for workers within the European Union [2011] OJ L141/1 and Art 24 Dir 2004/38 on the right of citizens of the Union and their family members to move and reside freely within the territory of the Member States [2004] OJ L158/77.

[43] Art 7(2) Reg 492/2011.   [44] Case 59/85 *Reed* [1986] ECR 1283, para 30.

[45] See further Síofra O'Leary, *The Evolving Concept of Community Citizenship* (1996).

economic activity.[46] Today, Article 24 of the Directive on the right of citizens of the Union and their family members to move and reside freely within the territory of the Member States spells out (and specifies derogations from) this prohibition of nationality discrimination.[47]

This prong of EU equality law has therefore unquestionably gained a social dimension besides its economic purpose. Non-discrimination on grounds of nationality is also now a fundamental right as confirmed by Article 21(2) CFEU. Yet the prohibition of nationality discrimination is atypical when compared to other dimensions of EU equality law.[48] It remains closely intertwined with its function as a device for further integration among the Member States through the elimination of borders so that significant limitations persist on its ability to operate as a genuine tool for the transformation of European societies.

First, the right to be protected against discrimination on grounds of nationality may not be invoked in purely internal situations. The Court has repeatedly said that the prohibition of nationality discrimination is only applicable to situations in which EU citizens and their families have a cross-border dimension.[49]

Second, the applicability of the rules on the prohibition of nationality discrimination has been subject to important temporal limitations resulting in certain categories of EU citizen being significantly restrained in their ability to invoke these rules. In the past decade, the large scale of enlargements of the Union have indeed been made conditional upon the acceptance of transitory regimes for the free movement of workers that could last up to seven years and which entitled the old Member States in particular to maintain restrictions to access to their labour market.[50] It was feared that divergences in the economic performance of new and old Member States could constitute push and pull factors capable of unsettling the employment market of the old Member States.

Third, the prohibition of nationality discrimination does not in principle apply to third-country nationals.[51] The Court has indeed ruled that Article 18 TFEU is 'not intended to apply to cases of a possible difference in treatment between nationals of Member States and nationals of non-member countries'.[52] There is uncertainty as to whether this provision would be applicable to differences of treatment on grounds of nationality between third-country nationals covered by EU law. In fact, as things currently stand, EU law only addresses the equal treatment rights of non-EU citizens whose status is regulated by EU law on an ad hoc basis, as will be discussed below.

---

[46] Case C-85/96 *Martínez Sala* [1998] ECR I-2691, paras 60–62.   [47] Dir 2004/38.
[48] Cf Art 21(1) and (2) CFEU. See also Bell (n 24) 613.
[49] Joined cases 35-36/82 *Morson and Jhanjan* [1982] ECR 3723, para 15.
[50] See Samantha Currie, *Migration, Work and Citizenship in the Enlarged European Union* (2008).
[51] See Martin Hedemann-Robinson, 'Third-Country Nationals, European Union Citizenship, and Free Movement of Persons' (1996) 16 *Yearbook of European Law* 354. On third-country nationals family members of an EU citizen or lawfully employed by an undertaking established in the EU and having a cross-border economic see further in Part IV of this edited collection.
[52] Joined Cases C-22/08 and C-23/08 *Vatsouras and Koupatantze* [2009] ECR I-4585, para 52.

(b) Equal Treatment on Grounds of Sex, Racial or Ethnic Origin, Religion or Belief, Disability, Age, or Sexual Orientation

These limitations on the material, temporal, and personal scope of the prohibition of nationality discrimination are in sharp contrast with the next set of provisions on equal treatment on grounds of sex, racial or ethnic origin, religion or belief, disability, age, or sexual orientation. The latter may be considered as forming the bulk of EU equality law insofar as these rules have been adopted in order to perform a genuinely transformative function; that is to implement or '[put] into effect in the Member States' the principle of equal treatment.[53] This prong of EU equality law is detached from the objective of eliminating physical borders among states and seeks to pursue 'inter-personal equality per se'.[54] They thus apply to cross-border as well as—if not in particular—to internal situations, as of accession to the EU and, although subject to certain limitations,[55] to EU and non-EU citizens alike.

Although jointly referred to by Article 19 TFEU and driven by a similar rationale, the history and substantive scope of the law applicable to these six grounds of discrimination differ. The starting point is the prohibition of sex discrimination enshrined in the Rome Treaty and today's Article 157(1) TFEU. At the time, the prohibition only applied to equal pay for equal work and was mostly perceived as a way to prevent unfair competition on the cost of the female workforce across the newly created internal market. This soon developed into a sophisticated web of rules on equal treatment in employment, social security schemes, and self-employment, and was perceived, starting from the *Defrenne II* case, to be the spearhead of EU social policy.[56] The legal framework evolved significantly over time so that it may have appeared fragmented by the late 1990s. However, the entry into force of the Amsterdam Treaty and the adoption of Directives creating a new legal framework to give effect to the principle of equal treatment in relation to racial or ethnic origin, religion or belief, disability, age and sexual orientation ('the other Article 19 TFEU grounds') resulted in the consolidation, modernization, and alignment of sex equality law. Today, the latter is therefore governed by four main instruments (beside Article 157(1) TFEU) that cover employment,[57] self-employment,[58] statutory social security,[59] and access to and supply of goods and services.[60]

---

[53] Art 1 of Dir 2000/78 establishing a general framework for equal treatment in employment and occupation [2000] OJ L303/16.

[54] Scharpf (n 16)   [55] Below subsection (d).   [56] *Defrenne II* (n 17) paras 10–16.

[57] Dir 2006/54 on the implementation of the principle of equal opportunities and equal treatment of men and women in matters of employment and occupation (recast) [2006] OJ L204/23.

[58] Dir 2010/41 on the application of the principle of equal treatment between men and women engaged in an activity in a self-employed capacity [2010] OJ L180/1.

[59] Dir 79/7 on the progressive implementation of the principle of equal treatment for men and women in matters of social security [1979] OJ L6/24 is still applicable.

[60] Dir 2004/113 implementing the principle of equal treatment between men and women in the access to and supply of goods and services [2004] OJ L373/37, the adoption of which was only made possible owing to the new Art 19 TFEU.

In contrast, it is only with the entry into force of the Amsterdam Treaty that it became possible to develop legislative instruments covering the other Article 19 TFEU criteria. The adoption of legislation has been remarkably quick in reaction to a worrying xenophobic context in certain Member States as well as the result of mobilization of civil society organizations.[61] The Race Equality Directive[62] prohibits discrimination on grounds of racial or ethnic origin in the fields of employment and vocational training but also social protection, social advantage, education, and access to goods and services that are available to the public. The second instrument adopted in the immediate aftermath is the so-called Framework Directive.[63] It is both broader and narrower than its twin. It covers four grounds of discrimination, namely religion or belief, disability, age, and sexual orientation, but it only applies in the field of employment and vocational training. The legal framework provided by this second instrument is also more fragmented since each of the four grounds attract legal arrangements to accommodate the specificities of the grounds as well as the particular sensitivity of certain forms of differential treatment.[64]

(c) Equal Treatment Rights for Those Involved in Flexible Forms of Employment

The third set of equal treatment clauses that deserves attention relates to non-discrimination against flexible forms of employment. Its institutional framework is unique insofar as it emanates from European-level bargaining among social partners. The Social Protocol attached to the Maastricht Treaty (and today's Articles 154 and 155 TFEU) empowered social partners to request that a collective agreement be implemented through a Council decision. These actors soon indicated their wish to establish legal frameworks for the elimination of discriminations against flexible forms of employment and the improvement of the quality of such work. These have been given binding effect by means of Directives with the same legal value and effects as ordinary Directives.[65]

The first agreement relates to part-time workers. The latter 'shall not be treated in a less favourable manner than comparable full-time workers solely because they work part time unless different treatment is justified on objective grounds' in respect of employment conditions.[66] A similar provision was also agreed upon to prohibit discrimination between fixed-term workers and comparable permanent workers.[67] In this context, much attention ought to be placed on the comparability

---

[61] Virginie Guiraudon, 'Construire une politique européenne de lutte contre les discriminations'(2004) 53 *Sociétés Contemporaines* 11.

[62] Dir 2000/43.   [63] Dir 2000/78.

[64] See Lisa Waddington and Mark Bell, 'More Equal than Others: Distinguishing European Union Equality Directives' (2001) 38 *Common Market Law Review* 587.

[65] Case C-268/06 *Impact* [2008] ECR I-2483, para 58.

[66] Dir 97/81 on part-time work [1998] OJ L14, 9–14, Cl.4(1).

[67] Dir 1999/70 on fixed-term work [1999] OJ L175, 43–48, Cl.4(1).

of the situations at hand, without which the prohibition of discrimination does not apply.[68] Social partners also attempted to reach an agreement on temporary agency workers. Although the negotiations failed, the Commission relied on this preliminary work on the Directive according to which 'the basic working and employment conditions of temporary agency workers shall be...at least those that would apply if they had been recruited directly by that undertaking to occupy the same job'.[69] This is an atypical expression of the principle of equal treatment; it is used as a minimum threshold more than as an objective as such.

As these equal treatment rights have been adopted as a social policy, they are also detached from the internal market rationale. They apply in cross-border and purely internal situations alike and benefit EU citizens as well as third-country nationals. The case law available to date concerns the first two framework agreements and it is striking that the Court seeks a uniform interpretation of these instruments[70] as well as, insofar as possible, with other EU equality law provisions.[71] It also stresses the relationship between these provisions and the general principle of non-discrimination[72] and insists that the principle of non-discrimination between fixed-term and permanent workers is a principle of EU social law of 'particular importance'.[73] Nevertheless, the legal framework accompanying the equal treatment clauses on flexible forms of employment is remarkably poor. The actual content of the prohibition of discrimination in this context is closer to the meta-principle of equality than to the advanced legal tools applicable to the latter forms of discrimination, described in Section III. As a consequence, the level of protection thereby afforded is significantly lower.

(d) Equal Treatment for Third-country Nationals Legally Residing in the EU

The final category of equal treatment provisions relates to third-country nationals legally residing in the EU.[74] This set of equal treatment rights is clearly distinct from the previous three for two reasons that are closely interwoven: it primarily serves a gap-filling function and is highly fragmented.

The reluctance of the Member States to see the EU interfering with their migration policies has deep implications for the protection of third-country nationals against discrimination. The main provisions of EU equality law are biased against third-country nationals. Although today a large majority of those lawfully residing

---

[68] eg Case C-313/02 *Wippel* [2004] ECR I-9483, paras 57–65.

[69] Dir 2008/104 on temporary agency work [2008] OJ L327, 9–14, Art 5(1).

[70] Case C-361/12 *Carratù*, judgment of 12 December 2013, paras 34–35.

[71] eg *Impact* (n 65) paras 131–132.

[72] eg Case C-307/05 *Del Cerro Alonso* [2006] ECR I-7109, paras 26–27.

[73] *Del Cerro Alonso* (n 72) para 27.

[74] See Bell (n 24).

in the EU have a legal status covered by EU law (in their quality of long-term residents or family members of another third-country national),[75] the CJEU maintains that the prohibition of nationality discrimination contained in Article 18 TFEU does not apply to them.[76] Furthermore, the Race Equality Directive (although it largely benefits third-country nationals) explicitly excludes from its scope discrimination on grounds of nationality. Nor does it cover provisions governing the entry and residence of third-country nationals or stateless persons and treatment that arises from the legal status.[77]

Nevertheless, the entry into force of the Amsterdam Treaty[78] and a political context characterized by the will to approximate the rights of third-country nationals to those of EU citizens have made it possible to consolidate the rights of the former.[79] As a result, EU law is now dotted with a series of equal treatment rights for selected categories of third-country nationals.[80] These rights are tailored to prevent the equal treatment provision from entitling the third-country national to claim advantages (such as access to the labour market or entitlement to social benefits) beyond those for which her specific legal status in the host Member State allows.

The starting point is the equal treatment provision relating to third-country workers who have been admitted for the purpose of work or are allowed to work.[81] The Single Permit Directive provides for a common set of rights including a right to equal treatment with nationals of the host state with regard to a fairly broad range of advantages such as working conditions, recognition of diplomas, or advice services afforded by employment offices.[82] However, the Member States have reserved the rights significantly to restrict equal treatment as regards several of these advantages in particular education and vocational training, social security, tax benefits, and access to and supply of goods and services.[83]

A more protective equal treatment provision concerns third-country nationals who have legally and continuously resided for five years in a given Member State.

---

[75] Kees Groenendijk, 'Access of Third-country Nationals to Employment under the New EC Migration Laws' in François Julien-Laferrière, H. Labayle, and O. Edstrom (eds), *The European Immigration and Asylum Policy: Critical Assessment Five Years after Amsterdam* (2005) 149, 172.

[76] *Vatsouras* (n 52).   [77] Dir 2000/43, Recital 13 and Art 3(2).

[78] In particular today's Art 79(2)(a)-(b) TFEU.

[79] eg Arts 67(2) and 79(1) TFEU; European Council, Presidency Conclusions (Tampere, 15-16.12.1999).

[80] See Elspeth Guild and Steve Peers, 'Out of the Ghetto? The Personal Scope of EU Law' in Nicholas Rogers and Steve Peers (eds), *EU Immigration and Asylum Law* (2006) 96.

[81] Both are assessed in accordance with national or Union law.

[82] Dir 2011/98 on a single application procedure for a single permit for third-country nationals to reside and work in the territory of a Member State and on a common set of rights for third-country workers legally residing in a Member State [2011] OJ L343, 1–9, Art 12(1).

[83] Dir 2011/98 (n 82) Art 12(2-4), see Tamara Jonjić and Georgia Mavrodi, 'Immigration in the EU: Policies and Politics in Times of Crisis 2007–2012' (EUdo Report, 2012/5), 17–20.

These so-called 'long-term residents' enjoy equal treatment with nationals of the host state not only in working conditions but also in access to an economic activity as well as a range of other advantages such as access to education and tax benefits.[84] Although significant, the possibilities for Member States to restrict these equal treatment rights are more limited than regarding third-country workers in general.[85] Moreover, the first case on the matter—*Kamberaj*—suggests that the Court will interpret the equal treatment rights of long-term residents in light of their social purposes insofar as possible.[86]

These key equal treatment provisions as well as several others enshrined in EU migration Directives[87] contribute to counterbalancing the limits on the scope of the prohibition of nationality discrimination and on racial and ethnic origin discrimination. The equal treatment rights of third-country nationals tend to be more protective as the length of stay, the degree of integration, as well as the economic input of the third-country national increase.[88] Nevertheless, they lack coherence and are primarily defined in the context of the host state.[89] As for flexible forms of employment, the content of these equal treatment rights is closer to the meta-principle of equality than to the sophisticated tools giving shape to the prohibition of discrimination on grounds of nationality for EU citizens, sex, and the other Article 19 TFEU criteria (Section III).

3. Policing the Boundaries

Equality law therefore has a variable geometry suggesting that certain forms of equal treatment may attract more attention than others, that certain grounds may necessitate more attention or that the protection of certain equal treatment rights is more central to the project of European integration.[90] Interestingly, the

---

[84] Dir 2003/109 concerning the status of third-country nationals who are long-term residents [2004] OJ L16, 44–53, Art 11(1).

[85] Dir 2003/109 (n 84) Art 11(2–4).

[86] Case C-571/10 *Kamberaj*, judgment of 24 April 2012, paras 76–93. See further Steve Peers, 'Case Note on Kamberaj'(2013) 50 *Common Market Law Review* 529.

[87] See also Dir 2003/86 on the right to family reunification [2003] OJ L251, 12–18, Art 14(1).

[88] Contrast for instance Dir 2009/50 on the conditions of entry and residence of third-country nationals for the purposes of highly qualified employment [2009] OJ L155, 17–29, Art 14 with Directive on the conditions of entry and stay of third-country nationals for the purpose of employment as seasonal workers (Document PE 113 2013 REV 1), Art 23.

[89] See also Dir 2003/109, Arts 11 and 21(1); Bell (n 24) 621–622.

[90] Waddington and Bell (n 64). Erika Howard, 'The Case for a Considered Hierarchy of Discrimination Grounds in EU Law' (2006) 13 *Maastricht Journal of European and Comparative Law* 445.

definition of the actual perimeter of EU equality policy has triggered tensions with the meta-principle of equality.

The assessment of whether the legislature does comply with the general principle in defining the reach of EU equality law may result in a dialogue between political and judicial institutions. An illustration may be found in the *Test-Achats* case on the validity of EU equality legislation in light of the principle of equal treatment for men and women enshrined in Articles 21 and 23 of the CFEU.[91] The legislature having asserted that EU sex equality law would in principle apply to the insurance service sector, the Court could review the mechanisms designed for the protection of sex equality in this field in light of the higher principle of equality. It concluded that the legislation was in breach of the higher principle: the Directive could not enable Member States to maintain derogations from the rule of unisex premiums and benefits without temporal limitations.[92]

The political negotiations at the Council had resulted in a rather broad substantive scope for the legislation on sex equality in access to goods and services so as to cover the insurance sector; this was counterbalanced by a rather flexible set of legal tools allowing the Member States to derogate from the prohibition of discrimination as regards premiums and benefits. As for the Court, it acknowledged the broad scope of the legislation but prevented the Member State from using the flexibility they had desired. The case thus points at the close interconnection between the definition of the perimeter of EU equality law and the design of the inner technicalities which we will now examine.

III. Operationalizing the Principle of Equal Treatment

In searching how best to serve the transformative function of EU equality law, the legislature and the judiciary have sought to develop concepts and rules empowering victims of overt as well as covert forms of discrimination to take legal action. Although the legal rules vary for each grounds and field, the present section outlines the common features of the legal regime of the most ambitious and advanced prongs of EU equality law.

---

[91] *Test-Achats* (n 13).   [92] *Test-Achats* (n 13) paras 30–32.

1. The Technical Implications of the Prohibition of Discrimination

(a) Equal Treatment of Comparable Situations

As is clear from the first limb of the Aristotelian expression of equality, the prohibition to treat two situations differently requires that these situations be comparable.[93] This very first stage in the legal analysis may pose conceptual challenges, since making a decision on the comparability of two situations amounts to either acknowledging or denying the applicability of equality law.

An illustration of the dilemma may be found in the *Hay* case, where the CJEU had to assess the comparability of claims for equal treatment in access to benefits normally granted to married couples in the context of their employment but denied to same-sex registered partners, a particularly sensitive question in the French context. In earlier cases, the Court had deferred, at least in the abstract, the assessment of the comparability of situations to domestic courts, thus leaving them the final word on whether the EU law would be applicable.[94] The Court was more assertive in *Hay*: persons of the same sex who are not allowed to marry and may only register their partnership by means of a PACS (*pacte civil de solidarité*) are in a comparable situation when claiming benefits normally granted to married couples, such as days of leave and bonuses at the time of the marriage.[95] This is so, explained the Court, because the comparability is to be assessed in a 'specific and concrete manner in the light of the benefit concerned' and does 'not consist in examining whether national law generally and comprehensively treats registered life partnership as legally equivalent to marriage'.[96] The situation could thus be further analysed in light of EU rules.

Assessing the comparability of situations may also pose practical challenges. That is so in cases where there is no identifiable complainant or victim of a discriminatory behaviour, as may be the case in proceedings brought by public interest bodies. The Court has addressed this challenge by making it possible to claim discriminatory treatment if a specific behaviour 'is clearly likely to strongly dissuade certain [persons] and, accordingly to hinder their access' to an advantage covered by the Race Equality Directive.[97] Even when there is a clear complainant it may be difficult to establish a clear person or group of persons with whom this complainant could be compared. Most equality Directives thus

---

[93] This is of lesser importance in the context on EU free movement law where the Court often adopts a flexible test to identify not only discriminations but also more generally restrictions to free movement rules.

[94] eg Case C-267/06 *Maruko* [2008] ECR I-1757, paras 69, 72–73.

[95] Case C-267/12 *Hay*, judgment of 12 December 2013, paras 33–37.

[96] *Hay* (n 95) paras 33–34.   [97] Case C-54/07 *Feryn* [2008] ECRI-5187, paras 23–25.

make it possible to provide evidence that comparable situations *would* be treated differently; that is, to rely on the existence of a hypothetical comparator subject to certain conditions.[98]

(b) The Prohibition of Overt as well as Covert Discrimination

The principle of non-discrimination has often been further interpreted as addressing overt as well as all covert forms of discrimination insofar as they in fact lead to the same result.[99] The prohibition of nationality,[100] sex, and the other Article 19 TFEU criteria discrimination includes legal tools to combat both direct and indirect discrimination.[101] In the case of sex equality in employment, for example, direct discrimination is deemed to exist where one person is treated less favourably on grounds of sex; and indirect discrimination exists where an apparently neutral provision, criterion or practice would put persons of one sex at a particular disadvantage compared with persons of the other sex.[102] This broad definition of the notion of discrimination looks at the potential discriminatory effect and is designed to tackle insidious forms of discrimination, including differences of treatment that may appear harmless (or well-intended) but actually perpetuate a bias against a protected group. As a consequence, national law implementing EU equality law may not require evidence of an intention to discriminate.[103]

Besides drawing attention to a broad range of practices with a discriminatory effect, the distinction between direct and indirect discrimination has an impact on the nature of legal regime. Although the rules differ for different grounds and fields of equality law, exceptions to the prohibition of direct discrimination are in principle rare, while possibilities of being exempted from the prohibition of indirect discrimination are broader. There may indeed be a range of valid reasons explaining the need for different treatment of comparable situations irrespective of the incidental discriminatory effects that may arise thereof, as will be illustrated below. The classification of a specific set of facts as being constitutive of direct or indirect discrimination, therefore, often has a decisive impact on the control of lawfulness. It is in that sense remarkable that the CJEU has framed certain settings such as pregnancy-related differential treatment as being inherently constitutive of direct discrimination.[104]

---

[98] eg Dir 2006/54, Art 2(1)(a), see also n 134.

[99] Case 152/73 *Sotgiu* [1974] ECR 153, para 11.

[100] See further Part IV in this edited collection.

[101] In the instruments providing a definition of direct and indirect discrimination (the sex and other Art 19 TFEU Directives with the exception of Dir 79/7) the prohibition of discrimination includes a prohibition of harassment and instruction to discriminate.

[102] Dir 2006/54, Art 2(1)(a) and (b).   [103] Case C-170/84 *Bilka* [1986] ECR 1607.

[104] See also *Hay* (n 96) para 44 and see further Catherine Barnard, *EU Employment Law* (2012) 406.

(c) Limitations to the Duty of Equal Treatment

There exist several ways to make differential treatment tolerable in the light of the law despite the suspicion raised by the discriminatory effects of a measure or practice. The first and main avenue is built in the meta-principle of equal treatment; that is, objectively to justify the design of the instrument under scrutiny. Objective justifications constitute an open-ended category of reasons that decision makers may invoke to explain the rationale for their action and legitimize their approach. Nevertheless, equality law imposes a twofold straitjacket.

On the one hand, EU equality law may exclude the possibility to resort to justifications. This is so when the law is worded more narrowly than the meta-principle, and prohibits unequal treatment without allowing for justifications. It is largely established that the prohibition of direct discrimination on grounds of nationality, sex, and the Article 19 TFEU criteria does not make space for an open-ended list of justifications.[105] In particular, it is hardly possible to escape from the prohibition of direct discrimination on grounds of racial or ethnic origin[106] as well as on grounds of sex.[107] However, the prohibition of direct discrimination is seldom that absolute. Instead, the arguments that may be raised to legitimize differential treatment are usually exhaustively listed in EU law.[108]

On the other hand, when it is possible for decision makers to invoke objective justifications (as is usually the case for indirect discrimination or for less advanced prongs of EU equality law), these are under scrutiny. Justifications ought to be legitimate insofar as they must be acceptable in a democratic society. They are only acceptable if they are not of an economic nature and are genuinely 'objective'. In other words, EU equality law presupposes that the society must bear the cost of equal treatment if there is such a cost and a justification may not perpetuate a bias against the group that the law seeks to protect.[109]

The second way to legitimize differential treatment is for the Member States to provide that a difference of treatment based on a characteristic related to criteria covered by EU equality law does not constitute discrimination where 'by reason of the nature of the particular occupational activities concerned or of the context in which they are carried out, such a characteristic constitutes a genuine and determining occupational requirement'.[110] This 'genuine occupational requirement' exception exists across several prongs of EU equality law (including nationality discrimination although under a different form)[111] but is only destined to cover

---

[105] With the exception of the prohibition of age discrimination: Dir 2000/78, Art 6; see further Christa Tobler, 'Putting Mangold in Perspective: In Response to Editorial Comments, Horizontal Direct Effect—A Law of Diminishing Coherence?' (2007) 44 *Common Market Law Review* 1177, 1181–1182.

[106] Dir 2006/54, Art 14(2).   [107] eg Case C-356/09 *Kleist* [2010] ECR I-11939, para 42–43.

[108] eg Arts 45(3) TFEU, 2(5) Dir 2000/78; eg Case C-341/08 *Petersen* [2010] ECR I-47, paras 51–64.

[109] eg Joined Cases C-444/09 and C-456/09 *Gavieiro and Torres* [2010] ECR I-14031, para 57.

[110] eg Dir 2000/43, Art 4.   [111] Art 45(4) TFEU.

exceptional cases in which there is a unique match between certain characteristics, a suspect ground, and the nature of a position.[112]

(d) Proportionality of Limitations to Duty of Equal Treatment

Invoking one of these limitations does not amount to successfully legitimizing differential treatment in the light of EU law. It must be established that the negative effects of a measure or practice on a disadvantaged group is minimal. The discriminatory impact must therefore be proportionate to achieving the legitimate aim pursued by decision makers. This test, which is often a crucial part of the implementation of equality rules, has two components;[113] it must be ascertained that the measure under scrutiny provides an appropriate avenue to pursue the legitimate objective invoked, and that the discriminatory effects of this act do not go beyond what is necessary to achieve the legitimate objective identified.

Uncertainty on the proportionality of attacks on equal treatment rights most often arises in the context of domestic disputes and is brought to the attention of the CJEU by way of preliminary rulings. As a consequence, the Court is torn between the constraints of this procedure that limits its jurisdiction to the analysis of EU law and the will to provide practical guidance to the national court. The degree of scrutiny may also vary depending on the sensitivity of the policy area involved. For instance, much attention has been devoted to the analysis of justifications for measures that have a discriminatory effect on different age groups.[114] The Court has repeatedly asserted that the Member States as well as social partners have broad discretion in choosing to pursue a particular objective in the field of social and employment policy—frequently invoked as legitimate objectives—as well as in defining the measures to implement it. The Court has subsequently often made final statements on whether the measure was or was not in breach of the principle of proportionality, instead of deferring to the national court.[115]

2. Beyond Equal Treatment? Different Models of Equality

If the pursuit of equality is to be an ambitious policy goal, it must be asked whether this goal could actually make space for unequal treatment in favour

---

[112] For an example where it was successfully invoked: Case C-229/08 *Wolf* [2010] ECR I-1.
[113] As indicated in a multitude of cases, eg Case C-141/11 *Hörnfeldt*, judgment of 5 July 2012, para 31.
[114] See n 105 and Colm O'Cinneide, 'Age Discrimination and European Law' (2005) Report for the European Commission.
[115] eg *Toftgaard* (n 32) para 72. Contrast with Case C-141/11 *Hörnfeldt* (n 113) para 47.

of the disadvantaged group so as actively to strengthen the position of its members in society. This question illustrates a tension between two models of equality. One may favour formal equality and thus the idea that parties should be treated strictly equally, irrespective of the broader context. On the other hand, the concern to ensure equality of outcomes, or substantive equality, may call for specific intervention to help redress discriminations deeply anchored in the society.

EU law does not clearly take sides in the dispute between the partisans of each model. One thing that it does not (yet) do is impose positive action measures. If such measures ought to be developed, this is primarily at domestic level.[116] In contrast, what EU law does is to provide a legal framework against which positive action measures may be checked for compliance with the principle of equal treatment. This legal framework has been hotly debated in the context of sex equality law and the CJEU has relaxed its reluctance towards a substantive model of equality.[117] Today, the wording of the TFEU, as well as of the sex and Article 19 TFEU Directives, indicates that the Member States will be allowed to pursue 'full equality in practice',[118] and thus suggests a more substantive understanding of the concept of equality than in the past. However, positive action measures will be checked against the safeguards established by the CJEU that requires that measures not be too burdensome for those to the detriment of which positive action operates and allow for a case-by-case analysis of their individual situations.[119]

One way in which EU law has sought to support the vulnerable position of women on the labour market has been through the adoption of legislation establishing minimum rights on pregnancy and maternity rights.[120] Another interesting set of rules relates to the duty of reasonable accommodation for disabled persons.[121] In these contexts, the law seeks to match the special needs of a group better to ensure integration in society. These instruments support equality policy but do not amount to positive action as such; they are designed to address circumstances that do not vary with societal context.[122]

---

[116] See Commission Proposal for a Directive on improving the gender balance among non-executive directors of companies listed on stock exchanges and related measures (COM (2012) 614).

[117] See further Sandra Fredman, 'Changing the Norm: Positive Duties in Equal Treatment Legislation' (2005) 12 *Maastricht Journal of European and Comparative Law* 369.

[118] eg Art 157(4) TFEU and Art 3 Dir 2006/54. Gareth Davies, 'Discrimination and Beyond in European Economic and Social Law' (2011) 18 *Maastricht Journal of European and Comparative Law* 17.

[119] eg Case C-407/98 *Abrahamsson* [2000]ECR I-5539.

[120] Dir 92/85 on the introduction of measures to encourage improvements in the safety and health at work of pregnant workers and workers who have recently given birth or are breastfeeding [1992] OJ L348, 1–7 and, although less directly, Dir 2010/18 on parental leave [2010] OJ L68.

[121] Dir 2000/78, Art 5.

[122] Lisa Waddington and Mark Bell, 'Exploring the Boundaries of Positive Action under EU Law' (2011) 48 *Common Market Law Review* 1503.

3. The Quest for Greater Effectiveness of EU Equality Rules

The legislation fleshing out the principle of equal treatment on grounds of sex[123] and the other Article 19 TFEU criteria goes one step further in seeking to fulfil a transformative mandate. It provides a remarkable framework for the judicial and non-judicial enforcement of EU equality law. Combating discrimination involves addressing mindsets that may only result from a combination of techniques and with recourse to a variety of players.[124] This has been complemented by a distinct yet similar set of rules to enhance the effectiveness of the prohibition of discrimination against migrant EU workers.[125]

(a) A Remarkable Framework for the Invokability of EU Equality Provisions

As the CJEU acknowledged that the most advanced prongs of EU equality law were destined to perform a transformative function, it also asserted that the key provisions were capable of both vertical and horizontal direct effect. In other words, the European judiciary revealed the possibility for those affected by discriminatory treatment to invoke their rights before domestic courts irrespective of the public or private nature of the defendant. It is now established not only that the prohibitions of discrimination on grounds of nationality and sex enshrined in the Treaty are capable of the two forms of direct effect,[126] but also that the general principle of non-discrimination on grounds of age, enshrined in Article 21 of the CFEU, and given specific expression by Directive 2000/78, may be relied upon in horizontal disputes to set aside contravening domestic rules.[127]

Although the Court has so far declined invitations to expand this approach to the invokability of general principles given specific expression in Directives outside the scope of equality law,[128] there is no reason why it should not prevail when individuals seek to invoke the other Article 19 TFEU criteria given expression in equality Directives. In contrast, it is unclear whether the equal treatment provisions contained in the Directives for the protection of those involved in flexible forms of employment[129] or in the migration law Directives could be granted horizontal

---

[123] With the exception of Dir 79/7.

[124] Oliver de Schutter, 'Fundamental Rights and the Transformation of Governance in the European Union' (2006–2007) 9 *Cambridge Yearbook of European Legal Studies* 133.

[125] Directive on measures facilitating the exercise of the rights conferred on workers in the context of freedom of movement of workers (PE-CONS 4/1/14).

[126] eg Case C-415/93 *Bosman* [1995] ECR I-4921; *Defrenne II* (n 17).

[127] Case C-476/11 *Kristensen*, judgment of 26 September 2013, para 31.

[128] eg Case C-176/12 *Association de médiation sociale*, judgment of 15 January 2014, paras 41–49.

[129] On their vertical direct effect *Impact* (n 66) and Case C-486/08 *Zentralbetriebsrat der Landeskrankenhäuser Tirols* [2010] ECR I-3527, para 25.

effects that are traditionally unavailable for provisions enshrined in Directives. Indeed, unlike the prohibition of discrimination on grounds of nationality against EU citizens, on grounds of sex or on the other grounds listed in Article 19 TFEU, the prohibition of discrimination on grounds of employment status or nationality against non-EU nationals remains primarily anchored in EU secondary law.

(b) The 'Proceduralization' of EU Equality Legislation

In parallel to, and in conjunction with this judicial process, the legislature has been increasingly concerned to set procedural safeguards[130] for those willing to enforce equal treatment rights. The Directives that today flesh out the prohibition of discrimination on grounds of nationality against mobile EU workers, sex, and the Article 19 TFEU criteria provide for a set of rules that are remarkably detailed.

Naturally, all those who consider themselves wronged by a failure to comply with the prohibition of discrimination shall be granted access to judicial (or administrative) procedures (possibly after conciliation procedures).[131] EU legislation then notably codifies case law on a partial shift in the burden of proof. As soon as facts are established from which it may be presumed that there has been discrimination, it is for the respondent to prove that there is no breach of the principle of equal treatment.[132] The CJEU tends to be flexible in accepting evidence allowing a shifting of the burden of proof. For instance, in *ACCEPT*, homophobic declarations made by someone who presents himself and is perceived as playing a leading role in the recruitment policy were enough to shift the burden of proof on the recruiter.[133] The Court as well as the legislator also allow for the use of statistical data to establish facts triggering a shift in the burden of proof.[134]

Furthermore, the equality Directives require that it should be possible for associations, organizations, or other legal entities that have a legitimate interest to engage, on behalf or in support of the applicant and with his approval, in judicial or administrative procedures.[135] This has been criticized for supporting an individual model of access to justice, risking leaving aside the most vulnerable victims. This may now be read in conjunction with the 2013 Commission Recommendation that encourages Member States to develop legal tools for collective redress.[136]

Finally, EU legislation may be unusually precise on matters of remedies, requiring not only that the Member States introduce effective, proportionate, and dissuasive sanctions, but also, for instance, that they provide for compensation or reparation,

---

[130] I am grateful to Mariolina Eliantonio for suggesting the expression 'proceduralization'.
[131] eg compare Art 7(1) Dir 2000/43 and Art 17(1) Dir 2006/54.
[132] eg Art 19 Dir 2006/54.   [133] Case C-81/12 *ACCEPT*, judgment of 25 April 2013, para 53.
[134] See Evelyn Ellis and Philippa Watson, *EU Anti-discrimination Law* (2012) 155.
[135] Art 17(2) Dir 2006/54.
[136] Commission Recommendation on common principles for injunctive and compensatory collective redress mechanisms in the Member States concerning violations of rights granted under Union Law [2013] OJ L 201, 60–65.

clarifying that this may not be restricted by the fixing of upper limits.[137] In addition, the equality Directives require that the Member States put in place a system for the protection of complainants against victimization.[138]

(c) Pursuing Equality beyond Litigation

Although not in a uniform manner, the Directives adopted since the entry into force of the Amsterdam Treaty have also modernized equality policy by stressing the importance of non-judicial approaches. Much emphasis has been placed on the need to disseminate information on equality policy as well as to promote social dialogue and dialogue with NGOs with a view to fostering equal treatment.

The key innovations are 'Equality bodies'. Member States are expected to create or designate bodies whose task will be to promote, analyse, monitor, and support equal treatment. These bodies shall be competent to provide independent assistance to victims, conduct surveys, and publish reports and recommendations (and exchange information with their peers in other Member States).[139] Although such organs are not warranted to implement the prohibition of discrimination on grounds of religion or belief, disability, age, or sexual orientation or on grounds of sex in social security matters, they are under the other Directives on sex, racial, or ethnic origin equality as well as under the new Directive on mobile EU workers.[140] It may be inferred from the *Belov* Case that the Court is concerned to protect the non-judicial function of equality bodies where their genuine added value lies.[141] Nevertheless, the multiplicity of the relevant entities at domestic level as well as their lack of independence and competences still constitute bars to their effectiveness in certain Member States.[142]

The Commission has also deployed a large set of initiatives destined to further equality policy.[143] These range from funding programmes,[144] information portals as well as networks of experts to spread knowledge and Europeanize relevant areas of domestic policies,[145] and strategies to monitor and benchmark progress at domestic level in designated areas such as the integration of Roma[146] to recommendations to the Member States on how to enhance equal treatment.[147]

---

[137] Art 18 Dir 2006/54.   [138] eg Art 24 Dir 2006/54.   [139] eg Art 20 Dir 2006/54.

[140] The new one(s) will have a particularly broad scope, see n 125 Art 4(1).

[141] Case C-394/11 *Belov*, judgment of 31 January 2013, paras 42, 47, 51, 53.

[142] Bruno de Witte, 'National Equality Institutions and the Domestication of EU Non-discrimination Law' (2011) 18 *Maastricht Journal of European and Comparative Law* 157.

[143] Gráinne de Búrca 'EU Race Discrimination Law: A Hybrid Model?' in Gráinne de Búrca and Joanne Scott (eds), *Law and New Governance in the EU and the US* (2006) 97.

[144] eg see the European Social Fund at http://ec.europa.eu/esf/main.jsp?catId=50&langId=en.

[145] eg European Network of Legal Experts in the field of Gender Equality http://ec.europa.eu/justice/gender-equality/tools/legal-experts/index_en.htm.

[146] eg http://ec.europa.eu/justice/discrimination/roma/index_en.htm.

[147] eg Recommendation on strengthening the principle of equal pay between men and women through transparency [2014] OJ L69/112.

IV. EU EQUALITY LAW IN PERSPECTIVE

EU equality law is destined to regulate as well as to transform societal habits. It is unquestionably an example of EU intervention beyond the regulatory state. This ambitious policy objective is matched by the growing personal and substantive scope of equality provisions, the broad definition of the key legal concepts as well as a set of precise rules to ensure the efficiency of the policy. Yet, this is not to say that EU equality law is always at the forefront of social change. One could find several examples in which the legislator is reluctant to expand the scope of equality law[148] or the Court to take progressist steps.[149] Equality law is thus both a most advanced fundamental rights policy and a policy that remains constrained by the heavy institutional mechanics of the EU legal order, as well as the lack of consensus on the role of equality law to address social imbalances.

It is with this tension between ambition and constraints in mind that we ought to look at the future. Beside the broadening of equality law, which remains highly sensitive, enhancing the coherence of the existing set of rules would be desirable. The role of special bodies should be clearly asserted for the prohibition of discrimination on grounds of religion or belief, disability, age, and sexual orientation as it has been recognized for the prohibition of nationality discrimination against workers, while other forms of nationality discrimination against EU citizens may also need to be accompanied with greater procedural rules. The efficiency of mainstreaming provisions could also be enhanced to ensure the promotion of equality across EU policies,[150] and the implementation of existing legislation should be carefully monitored. The novel areas of EU equality law concerned with third-country national rights could also be fleshed out more clearly.

Some of these improvements may result from legislation. Other may flow from more coherent institutional practices; it is in that sense regrettable that the competences on equality matters are so spread out within the Commission.[151] Certain changes may also be induced by the CJEU. Much attention has been devoted to the general principle of equality that has been used in conjunction with written equal treatment clauses to enhance their invokability. It will be particularly interesting to observe how the Court addresses questions on the interaction between the fundamental right to equal treatment and the various equal treatment provisions that are not yet fully fleshed out, such as those on third-country nationals.

---

[148] See n 33.   [149] See n 26 and 27.

[150] Israel de Jesús Butler, 'Ensuring Compliance with the Charter of Fundamental Rights in Legislative Drafting: The Practice of the European Commission' (2012) 4 *European Law Review* 379.

[151] Four different Directorate Generals are competent for these matters.

BIBLIOGRAPHY

Mark Bell, 'The Principle of Equal Treatment: Widening and Deepening' in Paul Craig and Gráinne de Búrca (eds), *The Evolution of EU Law* (2nd ed, 2011)

Gráinne de Búrca, 'The Role of Equality in European Community Law' in Alan Dashwood and Siofra O'Leary (eds), *The Principle of Equal Treatment in EC Law* (1997)

Gráinne de Búrca, 'EU Race Discrimination Law: A Hybrid Model?' in Gráinne de Búrca and Joanne Scott (eds), *Law and New Governance in the EU and the US* (2006)

Evelyn Ellis and Philippa Watson, *EU Anti-Discrimination Law* (2012)

Sandra Fredman, *Human Rights Transformed: Positive Rights and Positive Duties* (2008)

Elspeth Guild and Steve Peers, 'Out of the Ghetto? The Personal Scope of EU Law' in Nicholas Rogers and Steve Peers (eds), *EU Immigration and Asylum Law* (2006)

Virginie Guiraudon, 'Construire une politique européenne de lutte contre les discriminations' (2004) 53 *Sociétés Contemporaines* 11

Martin Hedemann-Robinson, 'Third-Country Nationals, European Union Citizenship, and Free Movement of Persons' (1996) 16 *Yearbook of European Law* 354

Erika Howard, 'The Case for a Considered Hierarchy of Discrimination Grounds in EU Law' (2006) 13 *Maastricht Journal of European and Comparative Law* 445

Koen Lenaerts, *L'égalité de traitement en droit communautaire* (1991) 27 *Cahiers de droit européen* 3

Gillian More, 'The Principle of Equal Treatment: From Market Unifier to Fundamental Right?' in Paul Craig and Gráinne de Búrca (eds), *The Evolution of EU Law* (1st ed, 2011)

Oliver de Schutter, 'Fundamental Rights and the Transformation of Governance in the European Union' (2006–2007) 9 *Cambridge Yearbook of European Legal Studies* 133

Alec Stone Sweet, *The Judicial Construction of Europe* (2004)

Lisa Waddington and Mark Bell, 'More Equal than Others: Distinguishing European Union Equality Directives' (2001) 38 *Common Market Law Review* 587

Bruno de Witte, 'National Equality Institutions and the Domestication of EU Non-discrimination Law' (2011) 18 *Maastricht Journal of European and Comparative Law* 157

CHAPTER 36

THE EU AND NATIONAL SYSTEMS OF LABOUR LAW

PHIL SYRPIS

I. INTRODUCTION

THIS chapter considers the variety of ways in which the EU has an impact on the development of national labour law systems. It thus considers not only 'EU labour law' but also other aspects of EU law and policy (in particular EU internal market law, and the EU responses to the unemployment and debt crises) that have an impact on the world of work.

The relationship between EU internal market law and Eurozone governance, on the one hand, and labour law, on the other, raises profound questions as to the nature of EU integration and the (changing) structure of the Treaties. These questions can be conceptualized in a variety of different ways—for example, in terms of the relationships between 'positive' and 'negative' integration, between 'old' and the 'new' Member States, and between uniformity and diversity within Europe. The relationship between the European integration process and labour law has been, and will continue to be, a difficult one. It is therefore unsurprising that the vast majority of labour lawyers are pessimistic about the future for labour law in Europe.[1] This is for three main reasons. First, there has, in recent years, been little

---

[1] It is hoped that this chapter follows the example of Freedland and Countouris, who manage to combine the 'pessimism of the intellect' with the 'optimism of the will'; see M. Freedland and N. Countouris (eds), *Resocialising Europe in a Time of Crisis* (2013) x.

social legislation adopted at the European level. Moreover, the legislation that has been adopted is flexible, and is interpreted in creative ways—often against the interests of workers—by the Court of Justice. Second, EU internal market law imposes restrictions on states' (and trade unions') capacity to apply labour law standards to mobile factors of production. And third, the demands of Eurozone (and crisis) management are resulting in sharp downward pressures on social standards in all Member States, in particular in those relying on the EU and IMF for financial support. While it is of course possible that the future will bring more positive news on each of these three fronts, the current constellation appears bleak.

It seems to me that the two most difficult questions, which will be addressed in the remainder of this chapter, are the following. First, what is the relationship between European integration and labour law, and how has that relationship evolved since the compromise reached in the Treaty of Rome? And second, at the level of both constitutional principle and practical reality, how does one ensure that a fair balance is struck between 'the economic' and 'the social'?

II. European Integration and Labour Law

Many people assume that when intervention in the labour law field occurs at European level, it must be based on what may be termed a 'social' rationale—ie it must be motivated by the desire to improve the lot of the worker, and to ensure that wealth is redistributed within society. There are a variety of conceptual lenses through which the social rationale is analysed.[2] At its most basic, it is about the protection of workers. Workers, it is said, need protection because of the imbalance of power inherent in the employment relationship.[3] Their interests may be protected either through the development of substantive standards, or alternatively through the development of procedures through which workers can bargain or negotiate with employers on equal, or at least more equal, terms. But the social rationale may also be conceptualized in other ways. It may, for example, be about the preservation of the values associated with the 'European social model'.[4] In this

---

[2] See eg B. Hepple, 'Social Values and European Law' (1995) 48 *Current Legal Problems* 39.

[3] See P. Davies and M. Freedland, *Kahn-Freund's Labour and the Law* (3rd ed, 1983) 18.

[4] See C. Crouch, *Industrial Relations and European State Traditions* (1993) and F. Scharpf, 'The European Social Model: Coping with the Challenges of Diversity' (2002) 40 *Journal of Common Market Studies* 645.

context, ideas such as solidarity,[5] cohesion, and distributive justice come to the fore. Alternatively, it may be linked with democracy.[6] But most significant in the EU context have been the various attempts to harness the powerful languages of 'rights' and of 'citizenship' to the social rationale.[7]

It is perhaps a shock to discover that it is not (always) so. In fact, the social rationale co-exists with an 'integrationist' and an 'economic' rationale.[8] It is (perhaps) helpful to use a pie analogy here. The economic and social rationales are easy to grasp. The economic rationale is concerned with the size of the pie, while the social rationale is concerned with the distribution of the slices; specifically with ensuring that workers get their fair share. The integrationist rationale is rather more complex. It is concerned with the integrity of the pie, with ensuring that the ingredients are bound together properly.

The relationship between European integration and labour law is not a straightforward one. It has been contested since the early years of the (then) European Economic Community. Many of the uncertainties arise as a result of the fact that it is difficult to pin down what European integration must, may, or should entail. There are considerable disagreements at both theoretical and practical levels, and neither the Treaties nor the key institutional actors have a clear or consistent position. Neoclassical economists see an opposition between the market and the state, and view regulation as exogenous interference with the market mechanism. Others challenge the idea that markets are a separate realm, arguing that they are social constructs, embedded in social relations, constituted by law and social norms.[9] As for the creation of markets, there are those who argue that it is possible, and desirable, for market order to emerge spontaneously, but others who suggest that it is prudent, even necessary, for political institutions to intervene so as to ensure that markets are constituted and organized in particular ways.[10] Next, those who agree on the need for intervention often disagree in fundamental ways over the intervention that might be required. It is not at all obvious, for example, whether the establishment of the

---

[5] See eg T. Hervey, 'Social Solidarity: A Buttress against Internal Market Law', in J Shaw (ed), *Social Law and Policy in an Evolving European Union* (2000) 31, and M. Dougan and E. Spaventa (eds), *Social Welfare and EU Law* (2005).

[6] See R. Dahl, *A Preface to Economic Democracy* (1985). See further S. Smismans, *Law, Legitimacy, and European Governance: Functional Participation in Social Regulation* (2004), and A Mitchell, 'Industrial Democracy: Reconciling Theories of the Firm and State' (1998) 14 *International Journal of Comparative Labour Law and Industrial Relations* 3.

[7] See G. de Búrca, 'The Language of Rights and European Integration' in J. Shaw and G. More (eds), *New Legal Dynamics of European Union* (1995), and P. Alston (ed), *The EU and Human Rights* (1999).

[8] See P. Syrpis, *EU Intervention in Domestic Labour Law* (2007).

[9] See M. Granovetter, 'Economic Action and Social Structure: The Problem of Embeddedness' (1985) 91 *American Journal of Sociology* 481.

[10] See M. Egan, *Constructing a European Market* (2001). See also A. Supiot, 'The Dogmatic Foundations of the Market' (2000) 29 *Industrial Law Journal* 321, and C. Joerges, 'The Market without the State? The Economic Constitution of the European Community and the Rebirth of Regulatory Politics' (1997) 1 *European Integration Online Papers*.

market calls for harmonization of legal regimes, or whether there should be scope for regulatory competition between different regimes, and if so, whether that competition should be bounded by rules, and if so, what those rules should be. These debates have been present since the inception of the then European Economic Community, and continue to influence the development of European integration.

First of all, it is important to be clear about the nature of the compromise reached in the Treaty of Rome. While the initial position reached in the Treaty is much criticized, in particular for the way in which it seems to create an asymmetric constitutional structure that appears to prioritize economic freedoms over social rights,[11] it should not be mistaken for a neoliberal charter. The Treaty was based on the analysis in the Ohlin and Spaak Reports, which relied on theories claiming that free international trade would bring about a removal of economic and social disparities between different regions. For the framers of the Treaty it was seen as axiomatic that, through the establishment of a common market, social and economic benefits would result.

Giubboni identifies 'embedded liberalism' as the idea at the heart of the Treaty. He states that

the apparent flimsiness of the social provisions of the Treaty of Rome was in reality consistent with the intention, imbued within the embedded liberalism compromise, not only to preserve intact but hopefully to expand and strengthen the Member States' powers of economic intervention and social governance.

In the scheme of things as viewed by the founding fathers, the construction of a strong transnational market in Europe would open up and integrate the member countries' economies *without* creating any threat to their respective national sovereignty in social matters, which would in fact be able to count on the beneficial effects of the spontaneous and progressive harmonisation of their social systems or, at least, on the greater fiscal *dividend* deriving from the creation of the common market.[12]

In this way, the 'out-and-out constitutionalization of free-market principles at transnational level would be based on the guarantee, no less secure for being implicit, of the preservation of strong and deeply rooted *national* welfare-state systems'.[13]

Thus, the initial assumption was that market-building would lead to spontaneous and progressive harmonization of social systems in the Member States, and that, in any event, those states would not lose any of their ability to exercise powers in the social field.

Given the nature of the 'embedded liberalism' compromise, it is understandable that the competence afforded to the European institutions to act in the social

---

[11] See F. Scharpf, 'The European Social Model' (2002) 40 *Journal of Common Market Studies* 645.
[12] S. Giubboni, *Social Rights and Market Freedom in the European Constitution: A Labour Law Perspective* (2006) 16. The emphasis is in the original.
[13] Giubboni (n 12) 17.

field was restricted. The Ohlin and Spaak Reports are explicit on this.[14] Ohlin states that as 'differences in the general level of wages and social charges between different countries broadly reflect differences in productivity',[15] 'the notion that a *general* harmonization of social policy is justified by reference to "distortions of competition" brought about by differences between the labour law regimes of Member States is a delusion'.[16] Adjustments in, for example, the rate of exchange, can accurately reflect changes in relative productivity among countries,[17] and this renders harmonization unnecessary. Only where there are 'specific distortions which favour or handicap certain branches of economic activity'[18] is there a need for harmonization of laws to assist in the establishment and functioning of the market. This was the basis for the inclusion (at the behest of the French) of one of the few social competences in the Treaty of Rome, the then Article 119 EEC on equal pay.[19]

In what follows, consideration will be given to the extent to which the compromise reflected in the Treaty of Rome—which Giubboni aptly describes as an 'unstable chemical compound'[20]—has unravelled. This will be done via an enquiry into the continuing ability of states to act in the ways suggested in the Ohlin and Spaak Reports, and via an examination of the extension of the social competence of the EU. It would appear that states do not, and as a result of developments in European law and policy may no longer be able to, act in the ways assumed by the authors of the Treaty of Rome. And although there has been a gradual increase in the social competence of the EU, it is striking that this competence has, for a variety of reasons, not been utilized in order to provide meaningful European level protection for workers.

1. On the Ability of States to Act in the Labour Law Field

The above analysis makes it clear that the authors of the Treaty of Rome relied on two assumptions. First, they envisaged that the market-building process, and

---

[14] The Ohlin Report is at (1956) 74 *International Labour Review* 99; the Spaak Report is summarized in 'Political and Economic Planning' (1956) 405 *Planning*.

[15] (1956) 74 *International Labour Review* 99, 102.

[16] S. Deakin, 'Labour Law as Market Regulation: The Economic Foundations of European Social Policy' in A. Davies, P.L. Davies, and S. Simitis (eds), *European Community Labour Law: Principles and Perspectives: Liber Amicorum Lord Wedderburn* (1996) 92.

[17] P. Davies, 'The Emergence of European Labour Law' in Lord McCarthy (ed), *Legal Intervention in Industrial Relations: Gains and Losses* (1992) 321.

[18] Spaak Report (n 14) 233–234.

[19] The latest incarnation of the provision on equal pay is Art 157 TFEU. See also the reasoning in Case 43/75 *Defrenne II* [1976] ECR 455 at 9.

[20] Giubboni (n 12) 18.

the constitutionalization of free-market principles, would be based on active social policies at the national level, and the preservation of strong and deeply rooted national welfare state systems. Second, they relied on the ability of states to revise their rates of exchange to reflect differences in productivity. Both assumptions have come under increasing threat in recent years, first as a result of the way in which the EU's internal market law has developed, and second as a result of the creation of the euro, and the policies subsequently adopted in order to ensure the success, or survival, of the single currency, and to avert crises. The effect has been to destabilize the compromise reached in the Treaty of Rome, with predictable, and worrying, results for national systems of labour law.

The first assumption relates to the preservation of social competences, and strong welfare state systems, at the national level. It should first be noted that this assumption depends on the willingness of states to preserve and develop national social systems, and has always been, at least to some extent, vulnerable. This is because the process of regulatory competition may operate so as to create incentives for states to reduce social standards in an attempt to attract inward investment from mobile factors of production. It is indeed possible to point towards examples of competitive deregulation in the labour law field, but commentators are divided on whether the phenomenon they are witnessing is best described as a 'race to the bottom' or a 'race to the top'. The debate relating to regulatory competition will not be pursued further here; though it is necessary to be aware of the way in which the process of regulatory competition may lead to the pursuit of suboptimal policy choices on the part of the Member States eager to appeal to mobile investors.[21]

Of far greater concern is that the capacity of states to develop and maintain strong social systems, to my mind paradoxically, may be undermined by developments in law and policy at the European level. First, the Court's internal market case law itself threatens the maintenance of high social standards. Second, the policy prescriptions called for as part of the response to the Eurozone debt crisis, leave states with little option but to reduce social standards and social spending.

Let me begin with the internal market case law. Under the legal framework established by the Court, the need to provide justifications for national labour laws (and indeed for the actions of trade unions) only arises once it becomes apparent that these laws (and actions) create obstacles to the establishment of the market, within the meaning of the relevant Treaty provisions. These obstacles may amount to either 'barriers to free movement' or 'distortions of competition'. For many years, the Court managed to avoid conflicts between internal market norms and national labour laws; allowing states to preserve their national social systems.[22] For

---

[21] See further S. Deakin, 'Regulatory Competition after *Laval*' (2008) 20 *Cambridge Yearbook of European Legal Studies* 581.

[22] See further S. Deakin, 'The Lisbon Treaty, the *Viking* and *Laval* Judgments and the Financial Crisis: In Search of New Foundations for Europe's "Social Market Economy"' in N. Bruun, K.

example, in *Seco* and *Rush Portuguesa*, in the context of the transnational provision of services, the Court felt able to hold that 'Community law does not preclude Member States from extending their legislation, or collective labour agreements entered into by both sides of industry, to any person who is employed, even temporarily, within their territory, no matter in which country the employer is established.'[23] In *Albany International*, in similar vein, it held that collective negotiations between management and labour must 'by virtue of their nature and purpose' be regarded as falling outside the scope of the competition law provisions of the Treaty.[24]

However, while the statement in *Albany* that collective agreements will not be analysed with reference to the competition law provisions of the Treaties remains good law,[25] *Viking* and *Laval* make it clear that, notwithstanding the earlier indications in *Seco* and *Rush*, national labour laws and the actions of trade unions may constitute barriers to free movement to the extent that they are applied to mobile factors of production.[26] The *Viking* and *Laval* line of case law destroys any cosy assumptions to the effect that labour law may be insulated from the internal market case law of the Court. First, the Court held that the actions of trade unions fall within the scope of the free movement provisions, despite significant doubts over the extent to which those provisions should be able to catch the conduct of non-state actors.[27] Second, and more important, the Court chose to define the 'barrier to free movement' very broadly, holding that a barrier exists whenever an out-of-state service provider faces a situation that has the effect of making the exercise of rights to freedom of establishment 'less attractive'.[28] The fact that undertakings may be 'forced' into 'negotiations with the trade unions of unspecified duration', and would not be able to ascertain in advance the minimum wage rates to be paid to workers, was said to confirm for the Court that a restriction on the freedom to provide services had occurred;[29] thereby triggering the need to provide a justification.

Lörcher, and I. Schömann (eds), *The Lisbon Treaty and Social Europe* (2012). He states (at 24) that prior to *Viking* and *Laval*, the Court 'more or less held the deregulatory tendencies of free movement law at bay'.

[23] See Joined Cases 62 and 63/81 *Seco v EVI* [1982] ECR 223 at 14, and Case C-113/89 *Rush Portuguesa* [1990] ECR I-1417 at 18.

[24] Case C-67/96 *Albany International* [1999] ECR I-5751 at 60.

[25] See further S. McCrystal and P. Syrpis, 'Competition Law and Worker Voice: Competition Law Impediments to Collective Bargaining in Australia and the European Union' in A. Bogg and T. Novitz (eds), *Voices at Work: Continuity and Change in the Common Law World* (2014).

[26] See Case C-438/05 *International Transport Workers' Federation (ITF) and Finnish Seamen's Union (FSU) v Viking Line* [2008] ECR I-10779 (hereinafter '*Viking*'); and Case C-341/05 *Laval un Partneri v Svenska Byggnadsarbetareförbundet* [2008] ECR I-11767 (hereinafter '*Laval*'). For comment, see P. Syrpis and T. Novitz, 'Economic and Social Rights in Conflict: Political and Judicial Approaches to their Reconciliation' (2008) 33 *European Law Review* 411.

[27] See *Viking* (n 26) 33–37.   [28] See eg *Viking* (n 26) 72; *Laval* (n 26) 99.

[29] *Laval* (n 26) 100.

Of course, it is still possible for the autonomy of States to set high labour standards to re-emerge at the justification stage. Indeed, for all bar internal market scholars, there is not a big distinction between a judgment holding that national labour law rules do not amount to barriers to free movement, and a judgment holding that they do constitute barriers, but ones that are nevertheless lawful, as courts are able to satisfy themselves that the rules are both justified and proportionate. I would nevertheless seek to argue that latter approach helps to create an institutional tension between market integration and the autonomy of states to set high labour standards and apply those standards to mobile factors of production, which need not, and should not, exist.

Be that as it may, the Court sees the justification stage as the stage at which the economic and social objectives of the EU can be balanced and reconciled. In *Viking* and *Laval*, it made reference to the aims and objectives of the then Community in acknowledging that 'since the Community has thus not only an economic but also a social purpose, the rights under the provisions of the Treaty on the free movement of goods, persons, services and capital must be balanced against the objectives pursued by social policy'.[30] It also held that 'the right to take collection action' must 'be recognised as a fundamental right which forms an integral part of the general principles of law the observance of which the Court ensures'.[31] Nevertheless, in *Viking*, the Court concluded that the collective action of trade unions was liable to restrict the exercise of enterprises' free movement rights, and that while the protection of workers is, in general, able to serve as a justification for restrictions on free movement rights, the legality of industrial action turns on the ability of unions to convince courts that the action 'does not impose disproportionate limitations on the employer's cross border activities'.[32] In *Laval*, where posted workers were involved, the Court conceded that 'in principle' trade union action aimed at the prevention of social dumping could be permissible,[33] but considered that action connected to negotiations on rates of pay for such workers could not be justified on public interest grounds, since this would make it 'impossible or excessively difficult' for service providers to determine their obligations.[34] At the justification stage, the Court was prepared to countenance arguments to the effect that restrictions could in principle be justified on the ground of the protection of workers, but it applied the proportionality test strictly—insisting that the state (and the trade unions) be able to demonstrate, first, that any restrictive action was suitable for ensuring the attainment of the legitimate objective pursued and, second, that it did not go beyond what was necessary to achieve that objective.

---

[30]   *Viking* (n 26) 79; *Laval* (n 26) 105.   [31]   *Viking* (n 26) 44; *Laval* (n 26) 91.

[32]   A. Davies, 'One Step Forward, Two Steps Back? The *Viking* and *Laval* Cases in the ECJ' (2008) 37 *Industrial Law Journal* 126, 145.

[33]   *Laval* (n 26) 107.   [34]   *Laval* (n 26) 110–111.

The key message is that states which choose to have high social standards that may deter inward investment are likely to be placed in a position in which they will have to demonstrate that those high standards are justifiable and proportionate. A similar burden has been placed on trade unions choosing to take action to seek to defend these high social standards. The case law to date indicates that it is not easy for states and unions to satisfy courts that their policies and actions are justifiable and proportionate, thus undermining one of the assumptions built into the Treaty of Rome.

Next, we consider economic and monetary union and the governance of the Eurozone. The first point is simple. The Ohlin and Spaak Reports assumed that Member States have the freedom to set their own exchange and interest rates. Clearly then, at least for those states which have adopted the euro as their currency, economic and monetary union threatens 'the very freedom of action at the level of the nation State which the Ohlin Report considered essential if economic integration was to lead to improved living and working conditions'.[35]

This much has been obvious from as long ago as the 1990s, when the Treaty provisions on economic and monetary union were first introduced, and the Court held that the Treaty provisions relating to the free movement of capital were directly effective.[36] The Treaties make provision for the coordination of economic policy,[37] and for the responsibility for monetary policy to shift from the Member States to the European System of Central Banks, whose 'primary objective' is stated in the Treaties to be 'to maintain price stability'.[38] The mechanisms put in place for the operation of the single currency not only affect the ability of states to revise their rates of exchange to reflect differences in productivity, but are also 'intended to limit the discretion of Member States to run their own economic policies, and in particular to curb the use of fiscal deficits as a response to recessions'.[39] The economic model adopted stresses 'price stability and fiscal conservatism above all else', and treats the welfare state 'as a fetter on the operation of the self-equilibrating market'.[40] The contrasts with the approaches adopted in the Ohlin and Spaak Reports are stark.

---

[35] Deakin (n 16) 82–83. There are fears that 'monetary union would strip national governments of significant macro-economic policy levers, and a Community-wide macro-economic stance will create significant regional unemployment problems. Somewhat flexible exchange rates allow local adaptations to local economic conditions. Once these instruments are dismantled, combatting pockets of regional unemployment at the national level will be more difficult'; S. Leibfried and P. Pierson, 'Social Policy' in H. Wallace and W. Wallace (eds), *Policy-Making in the European Union* (1996) 202.

[36] See Joined Cases C-163/94, C-165/94, and C-250/94 *Sanz de Lera* [1995] ECR I-4821.

[37] See Art 121 TFEU, which also provides that all Member States are to 'regard their economic policies as a matter of common concern'.

[38] See Art 127 TFEU. Stronger systems of coordination and surveillance exist for those (now 18) Member States who have adopted the euro as their currency; see Arts 136–138 TFEU.

[39] See Deakin (n 22) 30.

[40] Deakin (n 22) 32. See further Arts 119 to 144 TFEU on economic and monetary policy.

Over time, and in particular as the financial and sovereign debt crises have developed since 2008, the level of fiscal discipline has increased. This is not the appropriate forum in which to explore in detail the many changes that have taken place, or to comment in detail on the impact which EU crisis management is having on the labour law systems of the Member States.[41] Instead, I merely draw attention to the wide range of strategies employed by the EU institutions in order to enforce fiscal discipline and to dictate the way in which Member States should act in order to emerge from the crisis[42] in order to illustrate just how far-reaching, and entrenched, the politics of austerity have become.

The states whose labour laws are most directly affected by the crisis are the bail-out countries (Greece, Portugal, and Ireland). In return for financial assistance from the EU and the IMF, these countries have agreed to Memoranda of Understanding, which call for huge cuts to public spending and structural reforms to systems of labour law. However, the message that fiscal discipline and deregulation provide 'the blueprint for escaping the crisis[43] is far more widespread. It can be seen, for example, in the strengthening of the Stability and Growth Pact (via the so-called 'six-pack' of measures adopted in late 2011, and the 'two-pack', applicable only to Eurozone countries, adopted in 2013), and in the provisions of the Treaty on Stability, Coordination and Governance, agreed by all states, except the UK and the Czech Republic, in 2012, in response to the perceived inability to enact the necessary budgetary rules under the existing EU Treaties. It can moreover be seen in the Europe 2020 strategy (the European Union's ten-year growth strategy, which has replaced the Lisbon Strategy),[44] now operationalized via the European Semester.[45] The EU Treaties, EU legislation, and the general tenor of EU coordination of economic policy all point in the same direction, a direction which seems to exasperate a growing number of academic writers in the field. To quote Simon Deakin: 'the EU institutions have yet to move beyond the view, which has become

---

[41] See eg C. Barnard, 'The Financial Crisis and the Euro Plus Pact: A (Labour) Lawyer's Perspective' (2012) 41 *Industrial Law Journal* 98; P. Craig, 'The Stability, Coordination and Governance Treaty: Principle, Politics and Pragmatism' (2012) 37 *European Law Review* 231; the Special Issue, 'The Sovereign Debt Crisis and European Labour Law' (2012) 41 *Industrial Law Journal*; the Special Issue, 'Economic and Monetary Union and the Crisis of the Eurozone' (2012) 50 *Journal of Common Market Studies*; M.-C. Escande Varniol, S. Laulom, E. Mazuyer, and P. Vielle (eds), *Quel droit social dans une Europe en crise?* (2012); C. Degryse, M. Jepsen, and P. Pochet, 'The Euro Crisis and its Impact on National and European Social Policies' ETUI Working Paper 2013.05.

[42] See also K. Armstrong, 'The New Governance of Fiscal Discipline' (2013) 38 *European Law Review* 601.

[43] See Barnard (n 41).

[44] See COM (2010) 2020, Communication from the Commission, 'Europe 2020: A Strategy for Smart, Sustainable and Inclusive Growth'; and COM (2012) 173, Communication from the Commission, 'Towards a Job-rich Recovery'.

[45] See P. Copeland and D. Papadimitriou (eds), *The EU's Lisbon Strategy: Evaluating Success, Understanding Failure* (2012).

commonplace during the crisis, that labour law acts as a distorting factor in the operation of the single market and currency union. It is surely a matter of urgency for alternatives to that position to be articulated and advanced.[46]

To sum up, the Eurozone crisis has affected not only national economic policies, but also national systems of labour law. EU law and policy in relation to the governance of the Eurozone, as in relation to the internal market, are adversely affecting the ability of states to pursue a progressive social policy of the sort called for in the Ohlin and Spaak Reports. However, there is an important difference between developments in the internal market arena, and the Eurozone, which is of particular relevance to the future of European labour law. In relation to the internal market, it is the case law of the Court of Justice, and in particular, the Court's controversial interpretation of the free movement provisions, which is responsible for many of the difficulties facing national systems of labour law and trade unions. In relation to the Eurozone, the downward pressure on national labour law systems is attributable to a combination of the Treaties, the European Central Bank, and the various systems of economic and monetary policy coordination in which actors at both European and national level are implicated. In this case, the judiciary (at the European, national, and indeed international level) may well come to operate as a constraint on the political institutions.

Next, I consider the second way in which the assumptions in the Treaty of Rome were undermined. Not only has the social policy making power of the Member States been compromised, but, perhaps to some extent in recognition of that tendency, the social policy-making power of the EU institutions has also, gradually, been increased. However, while the competence of the EU has developed with each revision of the Treaties, the main conclusion of Section II.2 is that, for a variety of reasons, this competence has been little used. Thus, while the social competence of the Member States has been eroded, there has been no significant regulatory shift to the EU level. The charges of imbalance and asymmetry that have, in my view wrongly, been directed towards the Treaty of Rome, are much more aptly levelled at today's emerging system.[47]

2. On the Extent of Social Competence at the EU Level

Another sign of the unravelling of the embedded liberalism compromise is the gradual increase in the competence of the EU to intervene in the social field. The need for European-level action in the social field was first acknowledged in the 1970s, with

---

[46] S. Deakin, 'Editorial: The Sovereign Debt Crisis and European Labour Law' (2012) 41 *Industrial Law Journal* 251, 253.

[47] See also Deakin (n 22), who charts the shift from 'ordoliberal' to 'neoclassical' conceptions of the market in EU law.

the acceptance that European integration needed to have a 'human face'.[48] However, by the end of that decade, market orthodoxy had returned. The mid to late 1980s witnessed a more significant shift, though, as will be discussed in Section III, the suspicion nevertheless remains that the EU is paying no more than lip-service to the social rationale. In 1989, the European Parliament stated that 'market forces should not be allowed to determine the social framework conditions of the internal market'.[49] Also in 1989, the European Community's Charter of the Fundamental Social Rights of Workers was adopted.[50] It represents the assertion 'that the completion of the internal market could not be achieved without fully recognising that the aspirations, the interests and thus the rights of Europe's citizens—especially the workers—needed to be guaranteed'.[51] From the early 1990s, the competence of the EU in the social field has indeed developed—not only in relation to social policy (see Articles 151 to 161 TFEU), but also in anti-discrimination law (see Article 19 TFEU),[52] employment policy (see Articles 145 to 150 TFEU), and in terms of the development of fundamental rights at EU level (most visibly via the Charter of Fundamental Rights, solemnly proclaimed in 2000, and afforded 'the same legal value as the Treaties' at Lisbon in 2009, via Article 6 TEU).

While it is not possible to trace the scope of the EU's social competence in detail in this chapter,[53] it is worth pausing to reflect on Article 151 TFEU, the first provision in the 'Social Policy' title of the Treaties. It outlines the objectives of the Union and the Member States in the social field, and exposes some of the tensions that have influenced the development of the EU's competence in this field. It provides that the Union and the Member States:

having in mind fundamental social rights such as those set out in the European Social Charter signed at Turin on 18 October 1961 and in the 1989 Community Charter of the Fundamental Rights of Workers, shall have as their objectives the promotion of employment, improved living and working conditions, *so as to make possible their harmonisation while the improvement is being maintained*, proper social protection, dialogue between

---

[48] See B. Hepple, 'The Crisis in EEC Labour Law' (1987) 16 *Industrial Law Journal* 77, and M. Shanks, 'The Social Policy of the European Communities' (1977) 14 *Common Market Law Review* 375. In the mid 1970s, much of the most significant EU-level social legislation was adopted (notwithstanding the lack of a specific social competence), ie the Equal Pay and Equal Treatment Directives (now consolidated as Dir 2006/54 ([2006] OJ L204/23)), the Collective Redundancies Directive (now Dir 98/59 ([1998] OJ L225/16)), the Acquired Rights Directive (now Dir 2001/23 ([2001] OJ L82/16)), and the Insolvency Directive (now Dir 2008/94 ([2008] OJ L283/36)). In the mid 1990s, the Posted Workers Directive (Dir 96/71 ([1997] OJ L18/1)), which was at issue in *Laval*, was also adopted under an internal market legal base.

[49] [1989] OJ C96/64.   [50] See COM (89) 568 final.

[51] Vasso Papandreou, the then Commissioner for Employment, Industrial Relations and Social Affairs, in (1990) 1 *Social Europe* 8. Note, however, that the Preamble of the Community Charter states that 'the completion of the internal market is the most effective means of creating employment and ensuring maximum well-being in the Community' (46).

[52] See chapter on 'Equality' by Elise Muir.

[53] For more detail, see C Barnard, *EU Employment Law* (2012).

management and labour, the development of human resources with a view to lasting high employment and the combating of exclusion.

To this end, the Union and the Member States shall implement measures which take account of the diverse forms of national practices, in particular in the field of contractual relations, and the need to maintain the competitiveness of the Union economy.

They believe that such a development will ensue not only from the functioning of the common market, which will favour the harmonisation of social systems, but also from the procedures provided for in the Treaties and from the approximation of provisions laid down by law, regulation or administrative action.[54]

Article 153 TFEU sets out the detailed competence of the EU, which is authorized to adopt both 'measures designed to encourage cooperation between Member States . . . excluding any harmonisation of the laws and regulations of the Member States', and 'by means of Directives, minimum requirements for gradual implementation, having regard to the conditions and technical rules obtaining in each of the Member States'. In some areas the ordinary legislative procedure applies while in others EU intervention is only possible if the Council is unanimous.[55] Article 153(4) provides that provisions adopted pursuant to Article 153 'shall not prevent any Member State from maintaining or introducing more stringent protective measures compatible with the Treaties', while Article 153(5) makes it clear that the competence of the EU under Article 153 does not extend to 'pay, the right of association, the right to strike or the right to impose lock-outs'.

Articles 154 and 155 TFEU create the opportunity for the social partners (ie management and labour at the Union level) to conclude agreements at Union level, which, at the joint request of the signatories, may be implemented by Council decision, and thereby acquire the force of Union law.[56]

Thus, a clear, if restricted, competence to legislate in the social area exists in the current Treaties, and has existed since the early 1990s. The first paragraph of Article 151 TFEU sets out the objectives of the 'Social Policy' Title of the Treaties. These are broadly social, though with an emphasis on the promotion of employment. There is a noticeable tension between harmonization, which is said to be likely to ensue not only from the operation of the market but also, to quote directly from Article 151(3) TFEU, 'from the procedures provided for in the Treaties and from the approximation of provisions laid down by law, regulation or

---

[54] The section in bold was introduced at Amsterdam in 1997. The sections in italics are from the old Art 117 EEC (ie they date from the Treaty of Rome). The remaining sections are from the Agreement on Social Policy, which dates from the Maastricht Treaty in 1992.

[55] See Art 153(2) TFEU. The ordinary legislative procedure is outlined in Art 294 TFEU.

[56] For a full treatment of the social dialogue, see A. Lo Faro, *Regulating Social Europe: Reality and Myth of Collective Bargaining in the EC Legal Order* (2000).

administrative action', and national diversity, acknowledged in Article 151(2) TFEU, and protected via Articles 153(2) and (4) TFEU. As explained above, the internal market case law of the Court complicates matters here, increasing the pressure towards harmonization and rendering the preservation of national diversity more difficult. Where there are differences between national laws that are liable to create barriers to free movement (*Viking* and *Laval* state that national rules require justification where they are liable to make the exercise of rights to freedom of establishment 'less attractive'), states are put on the defensive, and have to demonstrate that their rules are justified and proportionate. The freedom of Member States to maintain or introduce more stringent protective measures, which appears to be preserved by Article 153(4), is in reality tightly controlled by the internal market case law of the Court.

These social provisions have existed in the Treaties (or the Agreement on Social Policy) since the early 1990s. While one could discuss the innovations they contain, or the way in which they set out the social priorities of the EU, or the unresolved tension between harmonization and diversity, the most striking is how little they have been utilized.[57] In addition, the few items of legislation that have emerged have been flexible, allowing states and/or social partners (and in the case of the Working Time Directive, even individual workers) to derogate from European standards of protection.

The reasons for this are rather difficult to fathom. One might imagine that the application of the principles of subsidiarity and proportionality would provide an obstacle to EU-level action;[58] but, despite some salience at the political level, and the greater role afforded to national Parliaments in the Nice and Lisbon Treaties,[59] these principles have not operated as a significant block to the development of social policy at EU level.[60] Instead, there seems to have been a lack of political will to utilize the social competences that the states chose to afford to the EU institutions (though the UK only agreed to the provisions once

---

[57] There has been a considerable amount of legislation adopted in the occupational health and safety field, including, most controversially, the Working Time Directive (now Dir 2003/88 ([2003] OJ L299/9)), which was the subject of an (unsuccessful) legal challenge by the UK in Case C-84/94 *UK v Council* [1996] ECR I-5755. Beyond that, there have been Directives providing limited information and consultation rights for workers, first on transnational matters via the European Works Councils Directive (see now Dir 2009/38 ([2009] OJ L122/28)), and then in all undertakings with more than 50 employees (Dir 2002/14 ([2002] OJ L80/29)); and Directives on parental leave (see now Dir 2010/18 ([2010] OJ L68/13)), and various sorts of 'atypical' work (see Dir 97/81 ([1998] OJ L14/9), Dir 99/70 ([1999] OJ L175/43) and Dir 2008/104 ([2008] OJ L327/9)) all based on agreements reached between European-level social partner organizations.

[58] See Syrpis (n 8) Ch 3.

[59] See Art 12 TEU, and the Protocols on the role of national Parliaments in the EU, and on the application of the principles of subsidiarity and proportionality.

[60] See F. Fabbrini and K. Granat, ' "Yellow Card but no Foul": The Role of the National Parliaments under the Subsidiarity Protocol and the Commission Proposal for an EU Regulation on the Right to Strike' (2013) 50 *Common Market Law Review* 115.

a Labour government came into office in 1997, resulting in the extension of measures agreed since 1992 to the UK, and the absorption of the Agreement on Social Policy into the EU Treaty at Amsterdam). In part, as Scharpf has explained, this is the result of problems inherent in the process of joint decision making in federal systems.[61] More fundamental, I would argue, is the shift towards 'new forms of governance' in the EU, and in particular towards the open method of coordination.[62] This development in EU governance can be observed across a number of policy fields. The employment guidelines, first developed in 1997, have now been subsumed under broader systems of policy coordination, first within the Lisbon Strategy, and now within Europe 2020. The aim is to steer the economic policy of the Member States in particular directions, ensuring that attention is paid to the big issues—most notably, unemployment, and today, deficit and debt reduction. Many have commented on the unhappy fate of social priorities within such broad, holistic, policy processes in which economic and social goals are combined.[63]

The conclusion of this section is, therefore, rather pessimistic. The compromise arrived at by the authors of the Treaty of Rome has, to a large extent, unravelled. The faith of the authors of the Treaty, in the spontaneous harmonization of social systems and in the ability of the Member States to preserve and build national social systems, appears to have been misplaced. As shown above, developments in the EU internal market law and Eurozone governance have played a large part in destabilizing national social systems, and in contributing towards the dismantling of protective labour laws (which are said either to amount to unjustifiable barriers to free movement, or to be unsustainable in times of financial crisis). While the social competence of the EU has developed with each revision of the Treaties, the relevant actors have not succeeded in adopting legislation at European level to replace that which has been lost at national level.

However, there are grounds for (some) optimism. Section III will consider the question of the how the balance between the economic and the social may best be achieved, paying particular attention to the constitutional dimension, and to the responsibilities of all actors in the policy making process.

[61] See F. Scharpf, 'The Joint-decision Trap: Lessons from German Federalism and European Integration' (1988) 66 *Public Administration* 239.

[62] See G. de Búrca, 'The Constitutional Challenge of New Governance in the European Union' (2003) 28 *European Law Review* 814; D. Trubek and L. Trubek, 'Hard and Soft Law in the Construction of Social Europe' (2005) 11 *European Law Journal* 343; and C. Sabel and J. Zeitlin, 'Learning from Difference: The New Architecture of Experimentalist Governance in the EU' (2008) 14 *European Law Journal* 3.

[63] See eg M. Dawson, 'The Ambiguity of Social Europe in the Open Method of Coordination' (2009) 34 *European Law Review* 55; R. Hyman, 'Trade Unions, Lisbon and Europe 2020: From Dream to Nightmare' (2012) 28 *International Journal of Comparative Labour Law and Industrial Relations* 5.

III. The Balance between the Economic and the Social

The above sections show that the relationship between 'the economic' and 'the social' rationales is crucial as regards the impact of the EU on national systems of labour law. It is important in relation to both internal market case law and the development of economic and social policy in the (crisis-ridden) Eurozone. The debate is, of course, of high political salience. As Maduro has argued, 'debates on efficiency versus distributive justice never have been peaceful and are not likely to be in the context of a "contested" European political community whose degree of cohesion and solidarity can only be said to be weak'.[64] The current situation, in which 'the economic' appears to be systematically privileged over 'the social', has been the focus of much criticism, in particular from labour lawyers.

This section reflects on the constitutional settings in which the balance between 'the economic' and 'the social' is sought, and points towards some ways in which the debate may be reconceptualized—in the hope that greater space may be afforded to the development of the social dimension of European integration.

The Treaty of Lisbon, which came into force in 2009, made substantial changes to the common provisions of the Treaties. The changes are such as to invite some reflection on whether Europe may have made a stronger commitment to the social rationale.[65]

The new Article 2 TEU states that:

The Union is founded on the values of respect for human dignity, freedom, democracy, equality, the rule of law and respect for human rights, including the rights of persons belonging to minorities. These values are common to the Member States in a society in which pluralism, non-discrimination, tolerance, justice, solidarity and equality between women and men prevail.

The new Article 6 TEU affirms the Union's commitment to human rights. It states for the first time that the rights, freedoms, and principles set out in the Charter of Fundamental Rights of the European Union 'shall have the same legal value as the Treaties'. It also makes provision for the EU to accede to the European Convention for the Protection of Human Rights and Fundamental Freedoms, and states, in

---

[64] M. Maduro, 'Europe's Social Self: "The Sickness Unto Death"' in J Shaw (ed), *Social Law and Policy in an Evolving European Union* (2000) 341.

[65] See N. Bruun, K. Lörcher, and I. Schömann (eds), *The Lisbon Treaty and Social Europe* (2012); C. Semmelmann, 'The European Union's Economic Constitution under the Lisbon Treaty: Soul-searching among Lawyers Shifts the Focus to Procedure' (2010) 35 *European Law Review* 516; and P Syrpis, 'The Lisbon Treaty: Much Ado ... But About What?' (2008) 37 *Industrial Law Journal* 219.

much the same way as in previous Treaties, that fundamental rights 'shall constitute general principles of the Union's law'.

Further, the under-explored Articles 7 to 17 TFEU introduce a proliferation of integration principles, requiring the integration of a wide range of EU policy objectives. Article 7 TFEU states that the Union shall 'ensure consistency between its policies and activities, taking all of its objectives into account', and Article 9 TFEU on social policy integration reads as follows:

In defining and implementing its policies and activities, the Union shall take into account requirements linked to the promotion of a high level of employment, the guarantee of adequate social protection, the fight against social exclusion, and a high level of education, training and protection of human health.

However, while there have been changes made to the common provisions, the detailed provisions dealing with the internal market, and with economic and monetary policy, remain substantially unchanged.

In my view, there is room for optimism in relation to the internal market. The Court itself acknowledges that a balance has to be struck between fundamental freedoms and fundamental rights. Advocate General Trstenjak's Opinion in *Commission v Germany* invokes the equivalence between fundamental freedoms and fundamental rights in order to argue that the balancing process in *Viking* and *Laval* was fundamentally flawed.[66] She seems to have correctly identified the rather one-sided attempt by the Court to balance fundamental freedoms and fundamental rights—or economic freedoms and social rights—in *Viking* and *Laval*. Instead, she advocates an approach which examines not only whether, and to what extent, social rights may have to yield to economic freedoms (social rights yield once found to conflict with economic freedoms, with the Court imposing a considerable burden to show that restrictions on economic freedoms are justified and proportionate), but also whether, and to what extent, economic freedoms may have to yield to social rights. There is no doubt that such an approach would be complex. Part of the focus of attention would be on EU free movement law, specifically on Directives such as the Public Procurement Directives (which were at issue in *Commission v Germany*) and the Posted Workers Directive (at issue in cases such as *Laval* and *Rüffert*), with the Court examining whether the Directives were appropriate and necessary for the achievement of the EU's free movement goals, and whether the restrictions on fundamental social rights were justifiable and proportionate.

The position as regards the governance of the Eurozone is more problematic. That is largely because of the way the relevant provisions of the Treaties are written.[67] Article 127 TFEU states that the 'primary objective of the European System of Central Banks shall

---

[66] Case C-271/08 *Commission v Germany* [2010] ECR I-7091. See P. Syrpis, 'Reconciling Economic Freedoms and Social Rights: The Potential of *Commission v Germany* (Case C-271/08, judgment of 15 July 2010)', (2011) 40 *Industrial Law Journal* 222.

[67] See M. Herdegen, 'Price Stability and Budgetary Restraints in the Economic and Monetary Union: The Law as Guardian of Economic Wisdom' (1998) 35 *Common Market Law Review* 9.

be to maintain price stability'. Article 127 TFEU goes on to provide that the European System of Central Banks 'shall support the general economic policies in the Union with a view to contributing to the achievement of the objectives of the Union as laid down in Article 3 TEU', but 'without prejudice to the objective of price stability'. Article 126 TFEU provides that 'States shall avoid excessive government deficits'; this now should be read in conjunction with the Treaty on Stability, Coordination and Governance, whose Article 3 reinforces the commitment to balanced budgets. These commitments to price stability and balanced budgets are hardwired into the EU Treaties, and as a matter of EU law, it is difficult to mount arguments to the effect that these commitments should be softened, or even abandoned, when they come into conflict with (for example) fundamental rights. It is, however, possible for such arguments to be made within national legal orders (witness recent developments in Germany, Portugal, Spain, and Greece), and with reference to international labour standards (in particular the International Labour Organization and the Council of Europe).[68]

However, while the constitutional setting is, of course, important, and operates as the framework within which political contestation occurs, it is perhaps liable to be over-emphasized by lawyers. The reality is that actors responsible for the development of the law have considerable freedom of manoeuvre. For example, the Court's understanding of the meaning of 'the barrier to free movement' has changed markedly over the years, as has the way it approaches the proportionality test. In addition, the Commission and the European Central Bank's understanding of the 'convergence criteria', now set out in Article 140 TFEU, has been inconsistent, as has the enforcement of rules against excessive deficits.[69]

Thus, attention should be devoted not only to the constitutional dimension, but also to the actions of all those involved in the formulation of law and policy. While I welcome the increasing prominence given to fundamental rights in the Treaty of Lisbon,[70] and look forward to seeing the creative ways in which rights may come to be used in order to promote a fairer balance between the economic and the social, it is also important that attention is paid to the way in which 'the economic' and 'the social' are reconciled at all levels of the decision making process; for example, in the various iterations of the European Semester, where social goals are currently marginalized as a result of the priority accorded to employment creation and fiscal conservatism.

---

[68] See eg the 269th session of the Council of Europe's European Committee of Social Rights, 27 to 29 January 2014, held in Brussels, which considered austerity measures and fundamental rights.

[69] See eg Case C-27/04 *Commission v Council* [2004] ECR I-6649. See also D. Hodson and I. Maher, 'Soft Law and Sanctions' (2004) 11 *Journal of European Public Policy* 798.

[70] For an indication of the continuing need for caution, see J. Prassl, 'Freedom of Contract as a General Principle of EU law? Transfers of Undertakings and the Protection of Employer Rights in EU Law' (2013) 42 *Industrial Law Journal* 434, discussing Case C-426/11 *Alemo-Herron v Parkwood Leisure*, judgment of 18 July 2013. See also T. Novitz and P. Syrpis, 'The EU Internal Market and Domestic Labour Law: Looking Beyond Autonomy' in A. Bogg, C. Costello, A. Davies, and J. Prassl (eds), *The Autonomy of Labour Law* (2015).

IV. Conclusion

Academic efforts should be, and are, in fact, directed not only towards the constitutional dimension, but also towards the more day-to-day attempts of actors in policy making processes to balance 'the economic' and 'the social'. In particular, efforts have been made to find synergies and complementarities between the economic and the social. New institutional perspectives on regulation have been used to make what are essentially economic arguments for legal regulation of the labour market.[71] Under these approaches, attention is directed towards the fact that private ordering may lead to suboptimal outcomes,[72] that there may be a tendency towards damaging short termism in the unregulated decisions of enterprises,[73] and that labour market institutions may therefore be viewed as governance mechanisms designed to enhance efficiency.[74] What may be termed Third Way ideology had a big influence on the development of EU policy around the turn of the millennium, aiming at 'a synthesis between economic and social policy, market and state'.[75] More recently, the hybrid term 'flexicurity' has been seen as a way of combining the economic and the social,[76] though there is already ample evidence to suggest that in practice, it offers rather more by way of flexibility than security, and that it has been used to dismantle various national employment protection systems.[77]

While it is possible that this linkage between the economic and the social will occur in the context of an activist social policy, it is perhaps more likely to mask the sacrifice of social objectives on the altar of economic efficiency. Barnard argues that 'the development of the Community's 'social' policy is constrained—perhaps fatally—by the need to operate within both an economic and a social framework'.[78] Fredman's view is that 'the power of the market will always subordinate social rights where there is a conflict with efficiency, unless there is a bedrock of fundamental

---

[71] See R. Coase, 'The Problem of Social Cost' (1960) 3 *Journal of Law and Economics* 1, and A. Ogus, *Regulation: Legal Form and Economic Theory* (1994) Chs 2–4.

[72] See eg G. Majone, 'The European Community Between Social Policy and Social Regulation' (1993) 31 *Journal of Common Market Studies* 153, and B Langille, 'Eight Ways to Think about International Labour Standards' (1997) 31 *Journal of World Trade* 27.

[73] See W. Hutton, *The State We're In* (1995) Ch 6.

[74] See D. Ashiagbor, *The European Employment Strategy: Labour Market Regulation and New Governance* (2006) 22–28.

[75] S. Fredman, 'Transformation or Dilution: Fundamental Rights in the EU Social Space' (2006) 12 *European Law Journal* 41, 44.

[76] See COM (2007) 359, Commission Communication, 'Towards Common Principles of Flexicurity: More and Better Jobs through Flexibility and Security'.

[77] See eg M. Bell, 'Between Flexicurity and Fundamental Social Rights: The EU Directives on Atypical Work' (2012) 37 *European Law Review* 31.

[78] C. Barnard, 'EC "Social" Policy', in P Craig and G de Búrca (eds), *The Evolution of EU Law* (1999) 501.

rights that owe their genesis to fairness and justice for its own sake, rather than as a means to efficiency ends'.[79] Lord Wedderburn puts it characteristically well: 'the social can of course contribute to competitiveness, but when it conflicts with the economic, whatever the rhetoric, it has few friends.'[80]

Perhaps in recognition of these difficulties, other writers have begun to focus not so much on co-opting economic arguments in order to make the case for labour regulation and labour law, but on ways of reconceptualizing the relationship between the economic and the social. Of particular interest are Mark Freedland and Nicola Countouris' suggestion that 'the idea of the mutualisation and demutualisation of risks to workers' can shape future thinking about resocializing Europe,[81] as well as the human development perspective which builds on the work of Amartya Sen,[82] and is used in the labour law context by, for example, Simon Deakin, in which 'the role of social and economic policy is to provide a framework within which individual "capabilities", understood as substantive economic freedoms, are advanced within the constraints set by given resources'.[83] Both these approaches rely on a reconceptualization of the role of the state. The first focuses on the movement of risks and risk costs, to and from individual workers to other entities and communities (be they employers, groups of workers, or society at large). The second moves away from an essentially protective view of the role of the state, and instead focuses on the establishment of frameworks that develop the capacity of individuals within society to thrive.

These developments are profoundly interesting, and offer the prospect of a redefinition of 'social Europe' and of the relationship between European labour law and other European policies including EU internal market law and Eurozone governance. They will become especially significant if they enable actors—be they judges, policy makers or social partners, be they at the national or the European level—to overcome their legacy of 'ambivalence of the social',[84] to rethink the nature of the balance between 'the economic' and 'the social', and to appreciate more fully the social consequences of their policies. In order for that to be possible, the ideas have to be fully developed and tested. They also, to adopt the language of many research councils, have to have impact: they have to be communicated to key actors, who then have to be convinced to change course. The task is a huge one. But it is a crucially important one. The preservation of the European social model is at stake, and with it, perhaps, the legitimacy and ultimately the very survival of the European Union.

---

[79] Fredman (n 75) 46.

[80] Lord Wedderburn, *Labour Law and Freedom: Further Essays in Labour Law* (1995) 391.

[81] Freedland and Countouris (n 1) 7.   [82] See A. Sen, *Development as Freedom* (1999).

[83] Deakin (n 24) 36. See also J. Fudge, 'The New Discourse of Labour Rights: From Social to Fundamental Rights?' (2007) 29 *Comparative Labor Law and Policy Journal* 29.

[84] See C. Joerges, 'On Disregard for History in the Convention Process' (2006) 12 *European Law Journal* 2, 3.

Bibliography

D. Ashiagbor, *The European Employment Strategy: Labour Market Regulation and New Governance* (2006)

C. Barnard, *EU Employment Law* (4th ed, 2012)

A. Bogg, C. Costello, A. Davies, and J. Prassl (eds), *The Autonomy of Labour Law* (2015)

N. Bruun, K. Lörcher, and I Schömann (eds), *The Lisbon Treaty and Social Europe* (2012)

M.-C. Escande Varniol, S. Laulom, E. Mazuyer, and P. Vielle (eds), *Quel droit social dans une Europe en crise?* (2012)

M. Freedland and N. Countouris (eds), *Resocialising Europe in a Time of Crisis* (2013)

S. Giubboni, *Social Rights and Market Freedom in the European Constitution: A Labour Law Perspective* (2006)

J. Shaw (ed), *Social Law and Policy in an Evolving European Union* (2000)

P. Syrpis, *EU Intervention in Domestic Labour Law* (2007)

CHAPTER 37

....

WELFARE POLICY AND SOCIAL INCLUSION

....

MARK DAWSON AND BRUNO DE WITTE

I. INTRODUCTION: THE CONSTITUTIONAL FRAMEWORK OF WELFARE AND SOCIAL PROTECTION IN THE EUROPEAN UNION

THE Lisbon Treaty inserted into primary EU law new language in relation to social protection and social inclusion.[1] This language denotes the ambition of the authors of the Treaty to give the European Union a more social face, but it did not radically modify the existing legal framework nor did it herald a new role for European law in shaping national welfare policies. The Lisbon Treaty has, generally speaking, considerably expanded the formulation of the basic values and objectives of the EU. The relevant Treaty articles (Articles 2 and 3 TEU) now include wording that rebalances the weight of market and non-market values in the foundational provisions of the EU. Solidarity is included among the values, listed in Article 2, on which the Union is based. Article 3, which lists the Union's main objectives, starts

[1] For a more detailed discussion (on which some of the ideas discussed in this chapter draw), see Mark Dawson and Bruno de Witte, 'The EU Legal Framework of Social Inclusion and Social Protection: Between the Lisbon Strategy and the Lisbon Treaty', in Bea Cantillon, Herwig Verschueren, and Paula Ploscar (eds), *Social Inclusion and Social Protection in the EU: Interactions between Law and Policy* (2012) 41.

with the ringing sentence that 'The Union's aim is to promote peace, its values and the well-being of its people', and then mentions, among the other main objectives, 'a highly competitive social market economy' and 'social progress'. The Union is, furthermore, directed to 'combat social exclusion' and 'promote social justice and protection'. In this way, the central values and principles that underlie national welfare systems are recognized and incorporated at the European level.

At first sight, these amendments to the EU Treaty may seem purely rhetorical because they are not fleshed out, elsewhere in the Treaties, by new law making competences and decision making procedures. In this respect, welfare differs from most of the other policy domains mentioned in Article 3 TEU, which can be effectively pursued by means of binding EU acts or binding international treaties of the Union. For welfare and social protection policies, the division of competences between the EU and its Member States remains what it was prior to the Lisbon Treaty. Article 153 TFEU, in the chapter on Social Policy, maintains a strict distinction between the available means of EU action:[2] whereas the social protection of workers may form the object of minimum harmonization by the EU, the 'combating of social exclusion' and the 'modernization of social protection' may form the object only of measures 'designed to encourage cooperation between Member States', which is an oblique reference to the OMC process described in Section III of this chapter. A clear law making competence only exists in respect of the free movement of persons, allowing for the coordination of social security regimes for mobile EU citizens (as discussed in Section II.1 of this chapter) (Article 48 TFEU).

This disjunction between Treaty proclamations and lack of law making instruments was not an oversight of the drafters of the Lisbon Treaty, but rather the result of a power struggle. A consensus was eventually reached on including the lofty but rather innocuous statements of principles, while excluding—due to the opposition of a number of country delegations—any extension of the Union's law making competences.[3] The effect of the disjunction can be illustrated by a (post-Lisbon) own-initiative Resolution of the European Parliament, in which it pleaded for the introduction of guaranteed minimum income schemes in all EU Member States, and gave detailed guidelines on how those schemes should be shaped.[4] The Resolution made some intriguing references to a possible 'Commission initiative' or to 'a legislative proposal it [ie the Commission] may submit',[5] but it did not specify what kind of legal basis the Commission could use for a legislative initiative in

---

[2] See, for this distinction, points (a) and (b) of Art 153(2) TFEU.

[3] Oliver Treib, *Der EU-Verfassungsvertrag und die Zukunft des Wohlfahrtsstaates in Europa*, IHS Working Paper, Political Science Series 99 (2004) 26–27. Treib lists, among the most reluctant national governments, those of Ireland, the UK, Spain, Estonia, and the Czech Republic.

[4] European Parliament Resolution of 20 October 2010 on the role of minimum income in combating poverty and promoting an inclusive society in Europe, 2010/2039(INI).

[5] See, respectively, points 36 and 21 of the Resolution.

this field (understandably so, since no Treaty basis for EU legislation seems to be available).[6]

This does not render the new language contained in Articles 2 and 3 TEU entirely useless or misleading. That language may come to play another, more indirect, role by prompting the EU institutions, including the Court of Justice, to give more consideration to social welfare implications when applying and interpreting *other rules* of EU law. Article 9 TFEU contains a new mainstreaming clause that aims precisely at achieving this. It states that, in defining and implementing all its policies and activities, 'the Union shall take into account requirements linked to the promotion of a high level of employment, the guarantee of adequate social protection, the fight against social exclusion, and a high level of education, training and protection of human health'.

This horizontal clause, again, does not transfer any new competences to the EU. It cannot be used as a legal base for the establishment of a proactive and comprehensive EU social policy, covering the domains mentioned in the text of the article. What then could its practical legal significance be?[7] By mainstreaming social policy into all EU policy fields, Article 9 TFEU affirms that social objectives are equivalent to economic objectives within EU primary law. Thereby it requires all EU actors to find a proper balance between economic, social, and other aims in all fields of public policy making and implementation in which the EU is engaged.

The fields that are particularly relevant in this context are internal market law, competition law, and European citizenship law. In those areas, EU law has created important conditions and constraints for the organization of national welfare and social protection systems, as we shall see in Section II of this chapter. 'To find a proper balance' concretely means—one might argue—that social considerations should play a greater role than they have done so far in EU policies outside the strict domain of social policy. Only such an understanding of the clause could make a difference compared to the pre-Lisbon situation and could thereby adequately mirror the increased recognition given to the idea of a social Europe by the text of the Treaties in their post-Lisbon version.

Finally, as discussed in Section III of this chapter, the question of balancing social welfare with the EU's economic goals has also guided the EU's governance and policy making structure for welfare and social inclusion. While the EU has developed mechanisms for coordinating national welfare policies, these mechanisms have been used to tie social policy closely to a competitiveness agenda.

---

[6] For a discussion of this competence issue, see Herwig Verschueren, 'Union Law and the Fight against Poverty: Which Legal Instruments?' in Bea Cantillon, Herwig Verschueren, and Paula Ploscar (eds), *Social Inclusion and Social Protection in the EU: Interactions between Law and Policy* (2012) 205, 210–214.

[7] See also the reflections on this point by Pascale Vielle, 'How the Horizontal Social Clause Can Be Made to Work: The Lessons of Gender Mainstreaming' in Niklas Bruun, Klaus Lörcher, and Isabelle Schömann (eds), *The Lisbon Treaty and Social Europe* (2012) 105.

The euro crisis has only furthered this trend, rendering EU coordination both more prescriptive and more aligned to the Union's larger economic goals. In this sense, the existence of social welfare and inclusion as a relatively autonomous field of EU policy faces an uncertain future.

II. THE IMPACT OF FREE MOVEMENT, INTERNAL MARKET LAW AND COMPETITION LAW ON NATIONAL WELFARE POLICY

1. Access to Welfare Rights for Mobile European Citizens

As was mentioned above, the only explicit legislative competence of the EU in relation to welfare and social protection is to be found in Article 48 TFEU.[8] This is a long-standing competence, since the original EEC Treaty already provided, in the chapter on free movement of workers, that the Council, acting unanimously, could enact measures to ensure that the Member States' social security schemes do not inhibit labour mobility (Article 51 EEC). Indeed, for many years, the main way in which European law impacted on national welfare systems was through the regime of inter-state coordination of social security, which was enacted as part of the legislative framework on the free movement of workers. The EEC Treaty provision was quickly implemented by Regulation 3/58, which was one of the very first legislative instruments adopted by the EEC, although its practical relevance for the lives of migrant workers became more tangible in the adapted version contained in Regulation 1408/71.[9] The latter followed shortly after the adoption of Regulation 1612/68,[10] which fleshed out the Treaty principle that migrant EEC workers should

---

[8] This section of the chapter draws, in part, on Dragana Damjanovic and Bruno de Witte, 'Welfare Integration though EU Law: The Overall Picture in the Light of the Lisbon Treaty' in Ulla Neergaard, Ruth Nielsen, and Lynn Roseberry (eds), *Integrating Welfare Functions into EU Law: From Rome to Lisbon* (2009) 53.

[9] Reg 1408/71 of the Council of 14 June 1971 on the application of social security schemes to employed persons, to self-employed persons, and to members of their families moving within the Community, [1971] OJ L149/2. This text was amended several times and then repealed and replaced by Reg 883/2004 of 29 April 2004 on the coordination of social security systems, [2004] OJ L166/1, which was itself lightly amended by Reg 988/2009 ([2009] OJ L284/43) and implemented by Reg 987/2009 ([2009] OJ L284/1).

[10] Reg 1612/68 of 15 October 1968 on freedom of movement for workers within the Community [1968] OJ L257/2. This foundational piece of legislation was also amended several times in the course

not be discriminated in the sphere of employment by adding some ancillary guarantees of equal treatment for EU migrants in the social sphere. Thus, as of the late 1960s, national welfare systems had to be adapted to those two fundamental pieces of European legislation. Regulation 1408/71 basically prescribed equal treatment of the migrant worker as regards social security, as well as a right to aggregate social security entitlements acquired in various Member States, and a right to export social security benefits across the territory of the EC. It also indicated which national social security regime was to apply to persons in a cross-border situation (frontier workers, seasonal workers, etc). Regulation 1612/68, for its part, guaranteed equal treatment of Community workers as regards all conditions of employment, but in addition granted them the same 'social and tax advantages' as the nationals of the host state (Article 7.2), as well as the same conditions of access to vocational training, to social housing, and to education for their children.

In enacting those rules, the European legislator intended to confer specific rights of cross-border access to welfare, and in particular only to a limited group of EU citizens, namely 'workers' and their families. However, in the following years and decades, the European Court of Justice adopted a consistently broad interpretation of those provisions. It first established the fundamental rule that this legislation only facilitated the exercise of the rights conferred directly by the Treaty rather than actually creating these rights. This approach has preserved an important and independent legal role—until today—for the general principle of non-discrimination on grounds of nationality (now in Article 18 TFEU) also in respect of welfare rights. The Court, furthermore, continuously extended both the personal and the substantive scope of the legislative provisions. It construed the term 'worker' as broadly as possible, to include basically any economically active person, and applied the principles of cross-border access to virtually all welfare benefits, whereas they were originally intended only to cover the benefits closely linked to the employment context.[11] In particular, the notion of 'social advantages' to which migrant EU workers and their families have equal access, was interpreted by the Court as including social assistance benefits and minimum income schemes.[12]

The European legislator followed the extensive interpretation adopted by the Court and gradually codified the extended welfare rights of economically active migrant citizens when amending the relevant EU legislation. That process culminated in

---

of the EU's existence. It was replaced by a new consolidated version in 2011: Reg 492/2011 of 5 April 2011 on freedom of movement for workers within the Union [2011] OJ L141/1.

[11] On the extensive interpretation of these provisions by the ECJ, see Eleanor Spaventa, *Free Movement of Persons in the European Union: Barriers to Movement in their Constitutional Context* (2007) 1; Anne Pieter van der Mei, *Free Movement of Persons within the European Community: Cross-border Access to Public Benefits* (2003).

[12] Case 249/83 *Vera Hoeckx v Openbaar Centrum voor Maatschappelijk Welzijn Kalmthout*, judgment of 27 March 1985, para 22.

the adoption of Regulation 883/2004 on the coordination of social security systems and Regulation 492/2011 on freedom of movement for workers within the
Union,[13] which consolidated and updated the existing secondary legislation on the
free movement of persons. The European Commission played a major role in this
process, by trying quite often, when drafting these legislative instruments, to take
welfare integration a step further even than the ECJ did, thereby imposing pressure
on the Council and the Parliament to widen the scope of the non-discrimination
rule. The most obvious example of this closer-integration trend is the expansion
of the personal scope of the social security coordination regime. Whereas it was
originally limited to 'workers', it applies, in its current version, to all nationals of
an EU state, as well as to stateless persons and refugees, on the sole condition that
they were previously affiliated to the social security system of another Member
State (that is, a cross-border social security element is required).[14] Recently, the EU
legislator took a further step by adopting a Directive which requires the Member
States to create specific remedies and monitoring mechanisms that are modelled
on those tried out earlier in other areas of EU non-discrimination law. This piece of
legislation does not confer new rights but its transposition in national law should,
ideally, facilitate the effective access of EU migrant workers and their families to
their welfare rights.[15]

In addition to the granting of equal welfare rights to economically active EU
citizens, a more general set of rights has been granted also to the non-economically
active ones, and their third-country family members, based on the legal concept
of Union citizenship introduced in 1992 by the Maastricht Treaty. The European
Court's inventive line of argument, and now its well-established doctrine, is that
any EU citizen who has exercised rights of movement and/or residence finds herself
for that reason alone within the 'scope' of the Treaty and can therefore challenge,
on the basis of Article 18 TFEU, any discrimination on grounds of her nationality.[16]
This applies also, in principle, to welfare rights and social protection schemes.

In the area of welfare integration, the Court has, however, been cautious and
has tended to accept national provisions that link welfare benefits to durational
residence requirements: only if they have resided for a certain length of time in

---

[13] See the references in n 9 and 10.

[14] For a complete analysis of the social security coordination regime, see Frans Pennings,
European Social Security Law, (5th ed, 2010).

[15] Dir 2014/54 of 16 April 2014 on measures facilitating the exercise of rights conferred on workers in the context of freedom of movement for workers [2014] OJ L128/8. Note, however, the limited
scope of this Directive: it applies only to EU migrant *workers* and their families, and not to EU citizens generally nor to third-country nationals who are not a member of the worker's family.

[16] See, for a synthesis of the relevant case law, Paul Craig, *EU Administrative Law* (2nd ed,
2012) 508. For a critical reading of the Court of Justice's approach, see Michael Dougan, 'Judicial
Activism or Constitutional Interaction? Policymaking by the ECJ in the Field of Union Citizenship'
in H.-W. Micklitz and B. de Witte (eds), *The European Court of Justice and the Autonomy of the
Member States* (2012) 113.

the host Member State are EU migrants able to demonstrate the required degree of integration into the host society which entitles them to benefit from its social solidarity in the form of welfare benefits. This position is now reflected in the EU's regulatory framework, namely Directive 38/2004 on free movement of citizens. The Directive provides that all (non-economically active) Union citizens and their (third-country) family members are entitled to complete equal access to welfare benefits once they have resided lawfully for a continuous period of five years in the host state (that is, when they obtain the status of a permanent resident citizen). Within the first five years, by contrast, those EU citizens must be able to provide for themselves and the members of their family, ie they have to be covered by health insurance and must have sufficient resources to avoid becoming a burden on the social assistance system during that early period of residence. But what happens if, during that initial five-year period, their financial means become insufficient and they wish to apply for social assistance? Can this be refused or, worse, can this be taken by the host state as a reason for withdrawing the right of residence (since the right of residence was conditional on the existence of sufficient resources)?

The Court's case law on this question remains hesitant. The Court recognizes that 'transnational solidarity as regards Community citizens who are economically inactive cannot but remain conditional and, in particular, can only be affirmed to the extent that it does not jeopardize the vitality of national welfare systems'.[17] But that general position does not exclude that individual EU citizens may have a right to receive welfare benefits. In *Grzelczyk*, decided prior to the Directive of 2004, the Court had decided that a (non-economically active) EU citizen could apply for social assistance, but that such a request could have as a consequence the non-renewal of that person's residence right.[18] In *Brey*, decided after the adoption of the Directive, the Court found that if an EU citizen applied for social assistance, the host state could not automatically invoke the 'burden on public finances' argument to reject a demand for a welfare benefit. The unreasonable nature of the burden could not be based on that individual claim alone, but only on the overall burden that all similarly situated Union citizens could lay on the system[19]—which is hard to prove for the host Member State. After *Brey*, the question of the access of non-economically active EU citizens, and their families, to the welfare system of their country of residence, remains therefore uncertain in legal terms.[20] That

---

[17] Stefano Giubboni, 'Free Movement of Persons and European Solidarity' (2007) 13 *European Law Journal* 360, 375.

[18] Case C-184/99 *Rudy Grzelczyk v Centre public d'aide sociale d'Ottignies-Louvain-la-Neuve*, judgment of 20 September 2001.

[19] Case C-140/12 *Pensionsversicherungsanstalt v Peter Brey*, judgment of 19 September 2013, paras 75–78.

[20] See the critical comment on the *Brey* judgment by Herwig Verschueren, 'Free Movement or Benefit Tourism: The Unreasonable Burden of *Brey*' (2014) 16 *European Journal of Migration and Law* 147.

question is, at the same time, very controversial in political terms, with a number of Member State governments openly complaining about 'benefit tourism' by large groups of non-economically active EU citizens.[21] Demands to tighten the welfare rights entitlements of EU citizens by means of an amendment of the Directive 38/2004 were rejected by the Commission but, in order to assuage those national governments, the Commission did publish a communication in November 2013 in which it confirmed that Member States could take measures to tackle fraud and abuse of the system, and promised to offer some guidance and help, for example, in fighting marriages of convenience, and in applying the habitual residence test for access to social security benefits.[22]

2. Internal Market Law and Welfare Services

It is not obvious, at first sight, why social security schemes and welfare policies would come within the scope of EU internal market and competition law. In *Duphar*, a judgment from 1984, the ECJ for the first time used a formula which it repeated several times in later years, namely that: 'Community law does not detract from the powers of Member States to organize their social security systems.'[23] Even at that time, the formula sounded rather unconvincing, since the system of coordination of social security regimes put in place in the 1960s (see Section II.1) seemed like an obvious 'detraction' from that power of the Member States, and in fact, the statement in *Duphar* was made fleetingly and without much sustained argument. Stronger judicial statements, exempting the social security regimes from internal market and competition law, were made in later cases. In *Poucet and Pistre*, decided in 1993, the ECJ stated emphatically that bodies belonging to a country's social security system were not undertakings, so that EC competition law did not apply to them.[24] In *Sodemare*, decided in 1997, the Court held that the Region of Lombardy could organize its social welfare system (in the particular case, the provision of

---

[21] For a short reflection on this political discussion, see the 'Editorial Comments: The Free Movement of Persons in the European Union: Salvaging the Dream while Explaining the Nightmare' (2014) 51 *Common Market Law Review* 729. For a comprehensive panorama of the legal and political issues, see Elspeth Guild, Sergio Carrera, and Katharina Eisele (eds), *Social Benefits and Migration: A Contested Relationship and Policy Challenge in the EU* (2013).

[22] Commission Communication, *Free Movement of EU Citizens and their Families: Five Actions to Make a Difference* COM (2013) 837 of 25 November 2013.

[23] Case 238/82 *Duphar v The Netherlands*, judgment of 7 February 1984, para 16. Later repetitions of the formula include: Case C-70/95 *Sodemare and others v Regione Lombardia*, judgment of 17 June 1997, para 27; Case C-158/96 *Raymond Kohll v Union des caisses de maladie*, judgment of 28 April 1998, para 17.

[24] Joined Cases C-159/91 and C-160/91 *Poucet and Pistre*, judgment of 17 February 1993, paras 7–19. Confirmed by the Court of Justice in Case C-218/00 *Cisal*, judgment of 22 January 2002; and by the Court of First Instance in Case T-319/99 *FENIN v Commission*, judgment of 4 March 2003, paras 38–39.

homes for non-autonomous elderly persons) in such a way that only non-profit private organizations could be reimbursed for their contribution to the system; the fact that commercial firms from other EU countries could not obtain public funding was found not to be a restriction of their market freedoms, since, basically, there was no market to begin with.[25]

A similar exclusionary approach was adopted in secondary legislation. The General Services Directive of 2006 does not apply to healthcare services, to 'social services relating to social housing, childcare and support of families and persons permanently or temporarily in need', or to 'non-economic services of general interest'.[26] In this way, most of the welfare sector is excluded from its scope of application.[27]

However, there is another line in the Court's case law which does effectively bring parts of the welfare sector within the scope of application of internal market and competition law. This has been the case, most prominently, with health services. Although the Court acknowledged that the regulation of access to medical services was part of the social security system, this fact alone was not enough to keep this sector of activity outside the scope of internal market law. In fact, the Court repeated in Kohll, one of its early health service cases, the formula mentioned above that 'Community law does not detract from the powers of the Member States to organise their social security systems'. However, it immediately added that the 'Member States must nevertheless comply with Community law when exercising those powers' and that 'the special nature of certain services does not remove them from the ambit of the fundamental principle of freedom of movement'.[28] This composite and ambiguous formula, whereby the States retain their powers in the social protection domain but must exercise them in conformity with EU law, has been repeated many times since.[29] It makes sense only if one accepts that EU law does actually detract from the welfare policy powers of the Member States, but not to the extent of affecting their general policy making responsibility in this domain.

In fact, the extent of this EU-law based 'detraction' differs between the health sector and other welfare policy sectors. In the former domain, the Court has pursued a consistent line of treating patients going abroad to seek medical help as

[25] Case C-70/95 (n 23) paras 28–34.

[26] Dir 2006/123 of 12 December 2006 on services in the internal market [2006] OJ L376/36, Art 2(2).

[27] But see the more detailed analysis of this question in Ulla Neergaard, Ruth Nielsen, and Lynn Roseberry (eds), *The Services Directive: Consequences for the Welfare State and the European Social Model* (2008).

[28] ECJ, Case C-158/96 *Raymond Kohll v Union des caisses de maladie*, judgment of 28 April 1998, respectively paras 17, 19, and 20.

[29] Se eg Case C-228/07, *Jörn Petersen v Arbeitsmarktservice Niederösterreich*, judgment of 11 September 2008, para 42; Case C-211/08 *Commission v Spain*, judgment of 15 June 2010, para 53. The use and meaning of this judicial formula is discussed by Lena Boucon, 'EU Law and Retained Powers of Member States' in Loïc Azoulai (ed), *The Question of Competence in the European Union* (2014) 168.

'receivers of services', who can invoke the Treaty provisions on the free movement of services, even when the service provided to them is part of the social security system and even when it is provided without any direct payment by the receiver. It is enough that 'someone' remunerates the service, even if that someone is a public healthcare fund. If all cross-border provision of medical care is now covered by the freedom to provide services, so that any obstacles placed in the way of such services become suspect restrictions of that freedom, the ECJ has been rather lenient at the justification stage, by accepting that those restrictions may be justified if they are required to preserve the financial balance of a country's social security system.[30] The Court thus accepted an economic interest as a good reason to restrict a fundamental freedom, which is rather unusual in its internal market case law.[31] In this respect, the healthcare case law developed in a similar direction as EU citizenship law, where social budget arguments were also accepted by the Court and the European legislator as grounds for restricting the welfare rights of EU citizens (see Section II.1).

Welfare services other than healthcare are not so 'fully' covered by internal market law.[32] The Court tends to find a restriction of the freedom to provide services only where the national welfare system is organized in such a way that it provides services which could equally be offered by a commercial provider based in another EU state. In such cases, a national policy choice to exclude the operation of the market may be challenged on internal market grounds. Take the example of the *Kattner* judgment.[33] In that case, German law provided for the compulsory affiliation of employers in a particular economic sector to a social insurance scheme for accidents at work, based on the principle of solidarity. On the basis of the *Poucet and Pistre* and *Sodemare* approach, one could have expected the Court to find the Treaty inapplicable to the case. Nevertheless, the Court considered that this scheme restricted the possibility for foreign insurance companies to offer contracts covering some of the risks covered by the scheme, and that it therefore created a restriction to the freedom to provide services. In the next step of the

---

[30] See eg Case C-368/98 *Abdon Vanbraekel and others v Alliance nationale des mutualités chrétiennes (ANMC)*, judgment of 12 July 2001, para 47. For a comprehensive view of the abundant case law, see Vassilis Hatzopoulos, 'Health Law and Policy: The Impact of the EU', in Gráinne de Búrca (ed), *EU Law and the Welfare State: In Search of Solidarity* (2005) 111; and Damian Chalmers, Gareth Davies, and Giorgio Monti, *European Union Law: Text and Materials* (3rd ed, 2014) 835.

[31] Niamh Nic Shuibhne and Marsela Maci, 'Proving Public Interest: The Growing Impact of Evidence in Free Movement Law' (2013) 50 *Common Market Law Review* 965, 997ff.

[32] In fact, the line of case law on patient mobility has been criticized for its contribution to the 'blurring of the economic and welfare spheres at the EU legal level and hence to the legal uncertainties ... on the application of the EU market rules to the Member States' welfare regimes' (Dragana Damjanovic, 'The EU Market Rules as Social Market Rules: Why the EU Can Be a Social Market Economy' (2013) 50 *Common Market Law Review* 1685,1701).

[33] Case C-350/07 *Kattner Stahlbau GmbH v Maschinenbau- und Metall-Berufsgenossenschaft*, judgment of 5 March 2009, paras 74–83.

reasoning, when examining possible justifications for restrictions to free movement, the Court invariably accepts welfare policy objectives as overriding reasons in the public interest that may offer a justification[34] but then the final outcome of the assessment depends, as usual in internal market cases, on the proportionality of the concrete national measure.

Public procurement law is, of course, a special case. Since it is concerned with the award of public service contracts, the public system of social welfare is naturally covered by it, but only to the extent that the private sector is called upon to contribute to social protection. As the Court observed, the public procurement legislation does not make 'a distinction between public contracts awarded by a contracting authority for the purposes of fulfilling its task of meeting needs in the general interest and those which are unrelated to that task'.[35]

A consequence of the fact that certain welfare services fall within the scope of internal market law is that they also fall within the competence of the EU to adopt harmonization measures to ensure the smooth functioning of the internal market. This consequence has been drawn most clearly, again, in the health sector. Following on the Court's complex case law on cross-border access to medical services, in 2011 the EU adopted a Directive on cross-border patient rights which aimed at codifying the principles developed by the ECJ in its case law as well as providing procedural guidance on how to apply those principles.[36] This is, in legal terms, a piece of internal market legislation but it does impact on the organization of national healthcare systems in a manner that could seem at odds with the Treaty article on public health which states that 'Union action shall respect the responsibilities of the Member States for the definition of their health policy and for the organization and delivery of health services and medical care'.[37]

3. State Aid Law and 'Social Services of General Interest'

To the extent that welfare services are not provided directly by public authorities but by public or private bodies funded by them, this funding could be considered

---

[34] *Kattner* judgment (n 33) para 85; similarly, in the case of a social housing scheme, Case C-567/07 *Minister voor Wonen, Wijken en Integratie v Woningstichting Sint Servatius*, judgment of 1 October 2009, para 31, and Joined Cases C-197/11 and C-203/11 *Eric Libert and others v Gouvernement flamand*, judgment of 8 May 2013, paras 52 and 67.

[35] Case C-271/08 *Commission v Germany*, judgment of 15 July 2010, para 73.

[36] Dir 2011/24 on the application of patients' rights in cross-border healthcare [2011] OJ L88/45. See for an analysis of this instrument Stéphane de la Rosa, 'The Directive on Cross-border Healthcare or the Art of Codifying Complex Case Law' (2012) 49 *Common Market Law Review* 15; Wolf Sauter, 'Harmonization in Health Care: The EU Patients' Rights Directive' in Bea Cantillon, Herwig Verschueren, and Paula Ploscar (eds), *Social Inclusion and Social Protection in the EU: Interactions between Law and Policy* (2012) 105–129.

[37] Art 168(7) TFEU.

as 'state aid' in the sense of the Article 107 TFEU, and therefore in need of noti-fication to, and authorization by, the Commission. The state aid rules apply only where certain economic criteria are fulfilled, namely that the public funding must benefit undertakings, affect trade in the common market and distort competition by favouring the country's own firms over those based in other Member States. One might, at first sight, think that the funding of welfare services does not ful-fil those criteria and is therefore outside the scope of state aid law, and indeed this was the implicit understanding for many years. When, however, in 2006 the Commission adopted its first general policy document on what it called 'social ser-vices of general interest' (SSGI),[38] it stated that those SSGI could be subject to the application of state aid rules, depending on the particular characteristics of the funding and of its beneficiaries.[39] An example of a welfare scheme coming within the scope of EU state aid policy would be where private operators provide publicly defined long-term care services (eg house cleaning, laundry, and personal care) to the elderly in return for remuneration by public authorities at fixed rates.[40]

The Commission's approach caused some uncertainty on whether specific wel-fare funding schemes, especially the ones operating at the regional and local levels, should henceforth be notified to the Commission and on whether they would be held permissible under EU law. The Commission's expansive approach, and the initial uncertainty about its practical implications, caused widespread misgivings in the welfare sector against the Commission's seemingly aggressive attitude, as well as critical comments in the scholarly literature.[41] In his report on the state of the internal market of May 2010, Mario Monti called this controversy a 'persistent irritant in the European public debate' and he recommended 'to further increase the flexibility of the State aid rules applicable to financial compensation'.[42] In view of the controversy, and also perhaps in view of the introduction of 'social' lan-guage by the Lisbon Treaty,[43] the Commission gradually backed down and has, in its most recent policy documents (in particular in the 'Almunia package' of

[38] This concept was coined by the Commission but does not appear in the text of the EU Treaties.

[39] Commission Communication, *Implementing the Community Lisbon programme: Social services of general interest in the European Union* COM (2006) 177 of 26 April 2006.

[40] We draw this example from Leigh Hancher and Wolf Sauter, 'Public Services and EU Law' in Catherine Barnard and Steve Peers (eds), *European Union Law* (2014) 539, 541.

[41] See, in particular, the contributions in Ulla Neergaard, Erika Szyszczak, Johan van den Gronden, and Markus Krajewski (eds), *Social Services of General Interest in the EU* (2013).

[42] *A New Strategy for the Single Market*, Report by Mario Monti to the President of the European Commission, 9 May 2010, respectively at 73 and 75.

[43] See the provisions of the Lisbon Treaty discussed in Section I of this chapter. See also, and in particular, *Treaty Protocol no. 26 on Services of General Interest* whose Art 2 states that 'the pro-visions of the Treaties do not affect in any way the competence of the Member States to provide, commission and organize non-economic services of general interest'. This Article could be seen as an attempt to 'grant to these services a sort of constitutional immunity from the opening logic of the integration process' (Maurizio Ferrera, 'National Welfare States and European Integration: In Search of a Virtuous Nesting' (2009) *Journal of Common Market Studies* 219, 227).

December 2011[44]), adopted a much more lenient view which basically exempts social services from the application of state aid rules.

First, the Commission confirmed that parts of the welfare sector are entirely outside the scope of application of state aid rules. Rehearsing the complex case law of the Court of Justice on the definition of 'economic activity', the Commission held that state aid rules only apply where a certain activity is provided in a market environment; therefore, the Commission declares, state aid rules do not apply at all to certain parts of the welfare sector, namely social security schemes that are solidarity based and public hospitals offering their services free of charge.[45] However, the Commission could hardly have provided a full list of non-economic social services, since, according to the Court's case law, the economic or non-economic character of an activity does not depend on its intrinsic characteristics (eg its welfare policy nature) but on the way it is regulated in each national or regional legal system.[46] There is thus still much uncertainty as to where the dividing line must be traced. Second, the Commission fixed a special *de minimis* threshold for state aid to services of general economic interest which is higher than the general threshold for state aid schemes: such aid is exempt from the notification requirement if the total amount granted to one 'undertaking' does not exceed €500,000 over a period of three years.[47] Many welfare schemes, especially those at the regional or local levels, may thereby be exempted without further ado. Third, financial support exceeding that threshold does not have to be notified to the Commission and is held *ipso facto* compatible with the common market if it is awarded to hospitals and to services 'meeting social needs as regards health and longterm care, childcare, access to and reintegration into the labour market, social housing and the care and social inclusion of vulnerable groups'.[48] This list of services seems to cover the entire welfare

---

[44] The 'Almunia package' (named after the Commissioner in charge of competition policy) sought to clarify the rules on state aid as regards the funding of services of general economic interest (and thus applies more broadly, well beyond welfare services). For general discussions of the Almunia package see special issue of (2012) 2 *European State Aid Law Quarterly*; Wolf Sauter, 'The *Altmark* Package Mark II: New Rules for State Aid and the Compensation of Services of General Economic Interest' (2012) *European Competition Law Review* 307; Marianne Dony, 'Les règles régissant le financement public des services d'intérêt économique général après la réforme de 2011' (2014) *Cahiers de droit européen* 97.

[45] Communication from the Commission on the application of the European Union state aid rules to compensation granted for the provision of services of general economic interest [2012] OJ C8/4, points 2.1.3 and 2.1.4.

[46] Julio Baquero Cruz, 'Social Services of General Interest and the State Aid Rules' in Ulla Neergaard, Erika Szyszczak, Johan van den Gronden, and Markus Krajewski (eds), *Social Services of General Interest in the EU* (2013) 287, 295.

[47] Commission Reg 360/2012 of 25 April 2012 on the application of Arts 107 and 108 of the Treaty on the Functioning of the European Union to *de minimis* aid granted to undertakings providing services of general economic interest [2012] OJ L114/8.

[48] Commission Decision of 20 December 2011 on the application of Art 106(2) of the Treaty on the Functioning of the European Union to State aid in the form of public service compensation granted

sector. This exemption is, however, subject to procedural and substantive conditions: procedurally, there must be an 'act of entrustment' in which the public authorities spell out the content of the public service tasks and the funding parameters; and substantively, the amount of compensation 'shall not exceed what is necessary to cover the net cost incurred in discharging the public service obligations, including a reasonable profit'.[49] The Commission thus preserves the power to intervene when it considers, on the basis of either a complaint by a potential competitor or its own information, that a social service has been over-funded by state, regional, or local authorities, but in practice that power is seldom or never used.[50] One should note, however, that this legal regime is rather fragile, since it is based on a package of hard law and soft law instruments adopted autonomously by the Commission, without the involvement of the other EU institutions, and is therefore also subject to later unilateral change by the Commission. It is also subject to review by the European Courts who may refuse to approve this flexible approach to the interpretation of the Treaty's state aid rules. On this point, it may be too early to tell—the new regime was put in place only recently and has, so far, not been challenged before the Courts.

III. Governing Social Welfare and Inclusion in Europe

1. Social Inclusion and the Lisbon Strategy

As Section II has highlighted, the legal framework for EU social welfare and inclusion policy has oscillated between different approaches. Early ideas about the 'separateness' of national welfare from EU economic law have given way (often after considerable national resistance) to attempts to balance and mediate between economic law and welfare services. At a political level, the EU's own social welfare policy architecture has also carried an ambiguous character. While the Union has made considerable steps to give some weight to its social objectives, these objectives have often been closely tied and, in the view of some, even subordinated, to market and competitiveness goals.

---

to certain undertakings entrusted with the operation of services of general economic interest [2012] OJ L7/3, Art 2(1) (b) and (c).

[49] Commission Decision of 20 December 2011, Arts 4 and 5(1).

[50] For a convenient summary of the Commission's current policy line on social services, see the Commission Staff Working Document, *3rd Biennial Report on Social Services of General Interest* SWD (2013) 40 of 20 February 2013.

This phenomenon can be seen in one of the first significant twenty-first century moves to provide an overall blueprint for EU social policy—the Lisbon Strategy, established in March 2000.[51] The strategy had three central goals: to construct a knowledge-based economy in Europe; to close the Union's growth gap towards its main economic competitors; and finally to 'modernize the European Social Model, investing in people and combating social exclusion'.[52] Ambitiously (overly so as it turned out) all of this was to be achieved by 2010. While Lisbon therefore placed the social dimension on the EU's agenda, its three-pillar structure, and ambitious inter-locking of different policy goals, meant that it did so in an ambiguous '3rd way'.[53]

First, as a matter of institutional design, EU policy makers differed on the mechanisms through which Lisbon's social goals could be delivered. Should EU social policy be highly prescriptive and thus based on enumerated EU legal competences in the social domain, or should the welfare state be seen instead as a domain of 'thick' obligations that must be intentionally insulated from the transnational sphere, including from the direct effect of EU economic law?[54] The policy structure created to deliver Lisbon's goals was effectively a compromise between these competing visions.[55] Lacking the political will to create strong EU obligations in the welfare domain, the guiding framework for delivering the strategy's goals—the Open Method of Coordination (OMC)—was designed as a multilateral coordination process, intentionally developed outside of 'hard' EU law.

The OMC process was developed to monitor Lisbon's social inclusion goals; therefore, it mixed hierarchical institutions with a heavily decentralized implementation structure. The OMC involved the central EU institutions, with the Council setting out overarching guidelines and the Commission monitoring national implementation. At the same time, policy delivery was largely inter-governmental, with national governments asked flexibly to implement EU targets and guidelines according to domestic processes and preferences (with civil society and regional actors playing an active role). The OMC's central procedural obligation was to ask Member States to report to the EU level on the process of domestic reform. In contrast with traditional EU law, the OMC was thus designed as a 'two-way street': EU

---

[51] See Dawson and de Witte (n 1) 43–45.

[52] European Council, 'Presidency Conclusions', 23–24 March 2000, [5].

[53] Damian Chalmers and Martin Lodge, 'The Open Method of Coordination and the European Welfare State' (2003) *ESCR Centre for Risk and Regulation Studies Discussion Papers* 11; Mark Dawson, 'The Ambiguity of Social Europe in the Open Method of Coordination' (2009) 34 *European Law Review* 55–79.

[54] See Claus Offe, 'The European Model of "Social" Capitalism: Can It Survive European Integration?' (2003) 11 *European Journal of Political Philosophy* 437.

[55] Jonathan Zeitlin, 'Social Europe and Experimentalist Governance: Towards a New Constitutional Compromise?' (2005) 5 *European Governance Papers*.

policy making was not just to inform but *to be informed by* national experience, learning from and adapting to the best practices of successful Member States.[56]

Second, the Lisbon strategy carried a substantive ambiguity: what should be the relationship between social policy coordination and the strategy's other objectives? Should social policy coordination under the OMC be conducted separately or in combination with other coordination processes, for example in the employment and fiscal domains? While originally operating as a series of separate coordination processes in social inclusion, employment, and fiscal policy, Lisbon was heavily criticized during its 2004 mid-term review for being about 'everything and thus nothing'.[57] The solution, the review argued, was to 're-focus' the strategy along a central guiding arc. This would be delivered through joining the EU's fiscal and employment strategies into a singular 'strategy for jobs and growth'. Alongside this central strategy, separate coordination processes in health, pensions, and social inclusion were also consolidated into an overarching OMC for social protection and social inclusion (OMC SPSI).

The downsizing of social inclusion—from a separate multilateral process, to a smaller part of an ancillary strategy—was seen by many as a betrayal of Lisbon's original design.[58] Was social inclusion part of three mutually supporting pillars or potentially subordinated to a new master narrative, focused on 'growth and jobs alone'? In a final substantive sense, what was EU social inclusion under Lisbon really about: the 'modernization' of European welfare states, or instead the creation of a national social state more amenable to the 'meat' of EU policy making—a competitive and open trans-national market?

2. Evaluating the OMC SPSI

While these two founding ambiguities continue to represent fault-lines in the academic and institutional debate over the Lisbon strategy's utility, the debate over EU social inclusion policy has also been dominated by the question of how effective Lisbon has been at delivering on its original social commitments. On the positive side of the coin, the experience of the OMC SPSI seems to suggest

---

[56] See Milena Büchs, 'The Open Method of Coordination as a Two-level Game' (2009) 36 *Policy & Politics* 21.

[57] *Facing the Challenge: The Lisbon Strategy for Growth and Employment*, Report from the High Level Group Chaired by Wim Kok, November 2004, 16.

[58] See eg the EMCO/SPC Joint Opinion on the Kok Report http://ec.europa.eu/social/keyDocuments. jsp?pager.offset=10&langId=en&mode=advancedSubmit&policyArea=0&subCategory=0&year=0 &country=0&type=46; EAPN, 'The Kok Report Ignores the Commitment to Eradicate Poverty and Exclusion' http://www.eapn.eu/index.php?option=com_content&view=article&id=521%3Apress-re lease-lisbon-strategy-the-kok-report-ignores-the-commitment-to-eradicate-poverty-and-exclusion &catid=7%3Apress-releases&Itemid=100002&lang=en.

some concrete benefits for EU social inclusion policy from the Lisbon experiment. In many countries, for example, social inclusion issues have been placed on the national agenda for the first time.[59] In others, states have shifted towards a common 'multi-dimensional' view of the *causes and nature* of social exclusion, with poverty seen not only in monetary terms, but as requiring a broad societal response, incorporating proactive health, housing, employment, and social assistance policies.[60] Finally, the OMC SPSI has given many social actors, such as NGOs, a right of 'structural entry' into national discussions previously closed off to them, or allowed them—through EU programmes such as the PROGRESS fund (discussed in Section III.5)—to form into pan-European networks able to lobby for policy changes at EU and national levels.[61]

For all these benefits, however, the OMC's operation in the social inclusion domain thus far also points to important deficits. First, while the ability of EU targets and objectives to influence national policy depends on governments willing to take EU guidelines seriously, there is evidence to suggest that national reports under the OMC have often served merely a 'dissemination' function, listing national reforms, but rarely serving as an engine of change for the domestic policy agenda.[62] The problem may be exacerbated by the OMC's participative shortcomings. While anti-poverty policy is primarily a regional or local competence in many Member States, national reporting has most often been conducted at a federal level, with regional authorities shut out.[63] The exclusion of the very authorities with the power and authority to *implement* the Lisbon strategy's most important social objectives has brought into question the ability of EU coordination to provide a 'common frame of reference' for national social policies.

---

[59] See Mark Dawson, *New Governance and the Transformation of European Law,* (2011) 184–185; Milena Büchs and David Friedrich, 'Surface Integration: The National Action Plans for Employment and Social Inclusion in Germany' in Jonathan Zeitlin and Phillippe Pochet (eds), *The Open Method of Coordination in Action: The European Employment and Social Inclusion Strategies* (2005) 249, 267.

[60] See Dawson (n 59) 181–184; Stefan Bernhard, 'The European Paradigm of Social Exclusion' (2006) 2 *Journal of Contemporary European Research* 41.

[61] See Dawson (n 59) 197–201; Jonathan Zeitlin, 'The Open Method of Coordination in Action: Theoretical Promise, Empirical Realities, Reform Strategy' in Jonathan Zeitlin and Phillippe Pochet (eds), *The Open Method of Coordination in Action: The European Employment and Social Inclusion Strategies* (2005) 468; Kenneth A. Armstrong, 'The Europeanization of Social Exclusion: British Adaptation to EU Co-ordination' (2006) 8 *British Journal of Politics and International Relations* 79, 90–91.

[62] See eg the assessment of the Lisbon 2020 evaluation document: 'While the OMC can be used as a source of peer pressure and a forum for sharing good practice, evidence suggests that in fact most Member States have used OMCs as a reporting device rather than one of policy development.' Lisbon Evaluation (n 57) at 21. See also Dawson (n 59) 230.

[63] Sandra Kröger, 'When Learning Hits Politics or: Social Policy Coordination Left to the Administrations and the NGOs?' (2006) 10 *European Integration Online Papers* 6; Mark Dawson, 'EU Law Transformed? Evaluating Accountability and Subsidiarity in a "streamlined" OMC for Social Inclusion and Social Protection' (2009) 13 *European Integration Online Papers.*

Finally, there is evidence to suggest that the OMC SPSI has been placed in a secondary position when compared to other objectives, such as the economic goals pursued under the 'integrated guidelines' for jobs and growth. While these guidelines, for example, are supposed to 'feed into' and reflect upon social inclusion objectives there is scant evidence of them doing so.[64] As noted by one key EU-level anti-poverty organization, EAPN: 'While it is clear that the economic and employment processes, whether "wrapped" in the national reform programme or not, dominate and constrain the social processes (feeding in) . . . there is little evidence of poverty proofing of strategies or measures in other dimensions of the Lisbon process (feeding out).[65]

This final deficit has led to a common perception among social actors that Lisbon is primarily about growth, with social protection systems considered relevant only insofar as they can be recalibrated to support further growth in the future.[66] These empirical findings suggest that while concrete benefits have been derived from the OMC's emergence in the social inclusion and protection domains, its impact has been far below Lisbon's original social ambitions.

3. Social Inclusion under 'Lisbon 2020'

The failures of the original Lisbon strategy framed much of the debate from 2010 onwards about creating a new strategy for the current decade. The relaunched 'Lisbon 2020' strategy attempted to tackle both of the principal 'ambiguities' about social inclusion mentioned above. At a substantive level, the 2020 strategy included for the first time an explicit EU-wide poverty target—to lift 20 million individuals across the EU out of poverty by 2020.[67] The new strategy also addressed the concern that Lisbon had become too growth-centric by re-establishing the strategy's original three-pillar structure. The new strategy would have three guiding arcs—of inclusive, sustainable, and smart growth—supplanting the old strategy's focus on 'growth and jobs', with an emphasis on making economic growth sustainable in economic and environmental terms. This included—within the 'inclusive growth' pillar—a specific 'flagship programme on poverty', designed to allocate

---

[64] See the Report of the Social Protection Committee, 'The Mutual Interaction between the Common Social Objectives and the Integrated Guidelines for Jobs and Growth' (2007) http://www.google.de/url?sa=t&rct=j&q=&esrc=s&source=web&cd=1&ved=0CCMQFjAA&url=httt p%3A%2F%2Fec.europa.eu%2Fsocial%2FBlobServlet%3FdocId%3D4034%26langId%3Den&ei=PQGUVMKyIcvcaLulgZgH&usg=AFQjCNGZ2FfWRVI_xCoTqoqfs8lLQ7Mo8g&sig2=zthrmjBpR-dX_sdSKC-e4w&bvm=bv.82001339,d.d2s.

[65] EAPN, 'The 2006–2008 National Reports on Strategies for Social Protection and Social Inclusion: What Do They Deliver for People in Poverty?' (2006) 23.

[66] See eg EAPN, 'Making Lisbon Deliver for People Experiencing Poverty: EAPN Response to 2006 Implementation Reports on the National Reform Programs' (2007) 3; Offe (n 54).

[67] European Council, 'Presidency Conclusions', 17 June 2010, EUCO 13/10 [12].

EU structural and cohesion funding to better target the least advantaged, as well as assessments of the adequacy of pension and social security systems for the socially excluded.[68]

Procedurally—facing severe criticism of the previous strategy's 'implementation gap'—the 2020 proposals saw a shift in the actors responsible for delivering Lisbon's goals. Faced with criticisms under the first strategy that the Commission had made itself responsible for the achievement of targets that could only be delivered at the national level, the Commission used the 2020 revision to loosen the chain of responsibility hanging from its own neck. The European Council, the Commission insisted, 'will have full ownership, and be the focal point, of the new strategy'.[69] As part of this, the new strategy supplements EU-wide targets with specific national targets, ensuring that each Member State takes its own share of responsibility for the performance of the whole.[70]

While this move may seem sensible given the strategy's deep penetration into areas of national competence, this reform has the potential to re-enforce the frequent criticisms of Lisbon's 'implementation deficit'. The problem with national targets—as evidenced by the first round of target setting—is that Member States have tended to set disparate and unambitious goals. Analysing target setting in 2012, Daly and Copeland highlighted severe disparities between national poverty targets, with three Member States failing to set any quantitative target for poverty reduction at all. Taken as a whole, they calculate that the accumulation of national targets—even if achieved by 2020—would fall short of the EU target by some five to eight million persons.[71] To this extent doubts as to whether the strategy can overcome the implementation gap of its predecessor remain.

Finally, Lisbon 2020 also involved reforms to the relationship between the OMC SPSI and economic and employment coordination. Reflecting fears that the OMC SPSI was being sidelined and subordinated through its inclusion within the larger guidelines for fiscal and employment policy, the EU's Social Protection Committee (SPC) recommended the re-establishment of a standalone OMC SPSI from 2012, with Member States submitting separate 'National Social Reports' on social inclusion and welfare reform.[72] While this approach has the merit of reintroducing some level of autonomy to social policy coordination, it also carries the danger of placing social

[68] See on this, the specific measures proposed in the Commission Communication, 'The European Platform against Poverty and Social Exclusion: A European Framework for Social and Territorial Cohesion' SEC (2010) 1564 final.

[69] Commission Communication, 'Europe 2020: A Strategy for Smart, Sustainable and Inclusive Growth' COM (2010) 2020, 4.

[70] European Council 'Presidency Conclusions', 25 March 2010, EUCO 7/10 [5].

[71] Mary Daly and Paul Copeland, 'Poverty and Social Policy in Europe 2020: Ungovernable and Ungoverned' (2014) 42 *Policy and Politics* 351 at 361.

[72] See European Council Opinion, 'The Future of the Social Open Method of Coordination—Endorsement of the Opinion of the Social Protection Committee' SOC (2011) 418 final.

inclusion at the side-lines of the larger Lisbon framework. A worrying sign emerges from national compliance—by the deadline for submission of the 2012 Social reports, only 14 out of 27 Member States had done so.[73] As will be highlighted in Section III.4, the onset of the economic crisis in the euro area has created a policy environment in which welfare and inclusion policy has struggled to enter the EU policy agenda.

4. Social Inclusion and the Euro Crisis

The Lisbon 2020 reforms seem to tinker with but not fundamentally alter the centrality of policy coordination rather than hard law to the EU framework for social inclusion. Even if, however, the policy framework has not changed significantly from 2000 to the present day, the surrounding social context has been altered irreparably by the consecutive financial and euro crises that rocked the world economy from 2008 on. One cannot underestimate the substantive impact the crisis has had on poverty and social deprivation. To give a brief snapshot, the 2012 report of the SPC indicated an increase of 4 million in the number of Europeans living in poverty from 2010 (to 24 per cent of the total EU population).[74] An increase in child poverty was registered in ten Member States with the percentage of children at risk of poverty higher than the percentage of adults. Unsurprisingly, the report illustrates that Europe's widening North–South divide is not just economic but social: lower economic growth and weaker systems of social protection have ensured that the biggest increases in poverty and decreases in household income have taken place in southern economies.[75]

Given this, how is EU policy influencing the ability of national welfare states to cope with the social effects of the euro crisis? We can talk here about both negative effects, ie constraints on welfare states and the range of social policy choices available to governments emerging from EU policy in the economic field, or of positive effects, ie efforts by the Union to improve national social capacity.

In the first case, the constraints emerging on national social policy have significantly increased as a consequence of efforts by the EU to place the euro on a more secure footing. It may be helpful further to divide these constraints into two different categories: first, constraints emerging from economic coordination processes designed for the Union as a whole (which themselves may include different instruments for Eurozone and non-Eurozone states),[76] and second, constraints specifically applicable to obligations arising from EU and IMF bail-outs of struggling peripheral economies.

---

[73] Daly and Copeland (n 71) 11.

[74] 'Social Europe: Current Challenges and the Way Forward', Annual Report of the Social Protection Committee (2012) 9.

[75] 'Social Europe' (n 74) 25–27.

[76] To use the example of the MIP discussed below, this procedure is applicable to all EU states, yet its sanctions cannot be applied to non-Eurozone states.

In the former case, while a classical criticism of OMC methods has often been their low level of prescription and enforceability, several reforms to EU governance have significantly 'hardened' the range of instruments available to EU policy makers to discipline governments in the fiscal and social fields.[77] One of these is the adoption by the Council and Parliament of a 'six-pack' of measures on strengthening EU economic governance in 2011.[78] Among other reforms, the package includes an EU Regulation establishing a Macro-Economic Imbalances procedure (MIP), designed to monitor those elements of national policy (beyond debt and deficits) likely to have a significant bearing on the stability of the Eurozone. The broad remit of the MIP—covering any element of national policy, from unsustainable pension and social security systems to levels of private debt, likely to create macro-economic risk—brings levels of social spending and investment clearly within its ambit. By contrast to the relatively weak OMC SPSI, the MIP carries the possibility of binding Council recommendations, 'corrective plans' to be drawn up bilaterally between offending states and the Commission, and an interest-bearing deposit of 0.1 per cent of GDP (convertible into fines), where Member States deviate from agreed upon deadlines or reforms.

The broad scope of this procedure speaks to a long-standing critique of EU social inclusion and welfare policy already discussed. While EU policies designed to encourage Member States to improve social provision carry few carrots and no sticks, policies for macro-economic coordination are highly prescriptive. This may have the consequence that national social policy is increasingly monitored and steered, but largely through the lenses and priorities of fiscal consolidation. This perceived bias has already been the subject of significant political contestation. Responding in June 2013 to the Commission's planned scoreboard for measuring such imbalances, the Green Group of the European Parliament lambasted the Commission's omission of measurements relating to income inequality or poverty as 'incomplete' and likely to 'lead to socially and environmentally regressive policies'.[79] We have here the fear that measuring macro-economic imbalances is

---

[77] See Sonja Bekker, 'The EU's Stricter Economic Governance: A Step Towards a More Binding Coordination of Social Policies?' (2013) *WZB Discussion Paper* 501; M. Dawson, 'Modes of Flexibility: Framework Legislation v Soft Law', forthcoming in Andrea Ott, Ellen Vos, and Bruno de Witte, *Between Flexibility and Disintegration: The State of EU Law Today* (2015).

[78] Reg (EU) No 1173/2011 of 16 November 2011 on the effective enforcement of budgetary surveillance in the euro area; Reg (EU) No 1174/2011 of 16 November 2011 on enforcement measures to correct excessive macroeconomic imbalances in the euro area; Reg (EU) No 1175/2011 of 16 November 2011 amending Council Reg (EC) No 1466/97 on the strengthening of the surveillance of budgetary positions and the coordination of economic policies; Reg (EU) No 1176/2011 of 16 November 2011 on the prevention and correction of macroeconomic imbalances; Council Reg (EU) No 1177/2011 of 8 November 2011 amending Reg (EC) No 1467/97 on speeding up and clarifying the implementation of the excessive deficit procedure; Council Dir 2011/85/EU of 8 November 2011 on requirements for budgetary frameworks of the Member States

[79] http://www.greens-efa.eu/fileadmin/dam/Documents/Letters/Letter_on_the_Social_Dimension_of_the_EMU_11_06_13.pdf.

no mere economic coordination measure but one likely to reach deeply into the national social state.

This fear may be exacerbated by certain procedural reforms undertaken in response to the crisis. The creation of the 'six-pack' has coincided with greater efforts to streamline EU policy coordination under a single roof. Under the 'European Semester', national reporting under the Lisbon Strategy is to be assessed by the European Council in conjunction with parallel reports on national 'Stability and Convergence Programmes' designed to assess the soundness of public finances. While it is too early to gauge the effect of this change, a number of social NGOs have expressed concerns that social policy is likely to be marginalized through the semester cycle—to take one example, the Commission's 2013 Communication on recommendations for the next semester cycle does not use the language of social inclusion at all.[80]

The possibility of fundamental reorganization of social policy under the umbrella of fiscal reform is even more tangible for states facing the need for financial assistance.[81] As highlighted by the Court of Justice in its *Pringle* decision, high levels of conditionality are seen by the EU institutions as underpinning both the legality and the efficacy of EU lending arrangements to struggling economies.[82] Even if one were to leave out specific policy prescriptions, governments facing the need to balance their books under conditions of economic and monetary union (EMU) face a dwindling number of policy options. With currency devaluation and 'counter-cyclical' spending forced off the table, the only route towards the balanced budget obligations demanded by EMU has often been deep cuts in social spending.[83]

On top of this general pressure on the social state, the Memorandums of Understanding agreed between bail-out states and the EU/IMF troika as a precondition for financial rescue have often included specific commitments relating to social rights and social spending. The Irish government, in its 2011 Memorandum of Understanding with the EU, promised to cut by one euro per hour its minimum wage and to repeal a number of collective agreements inhibiting 'wage adjustment' in the labour market.[84] In Portugal's Memorandum of the same year, it committed to reducing severance and bonus salary payments in the public sector, to limiting the entitlement period for unemployment benefits, to reducing state subsidies of pharmaceuticals, and to reforming its labour code to ease the grounds under which

---

[80] Commission Communication, '2013 European Semester: Country Specific Recommendations', COM (2013) 350 final.

[81] See Catherine Barnard, 'The Charter, the Court and the Crisis' (2013) *Cambridge Legal Studies Research Paper Series* 18, 8.

[82] See Case C-370/12 *Thomas Pringle v Government of Ireland*, judgment of 27 November 2012.

[83] Fritz W. Scharpf, 'Monetary Union, Fiscal Crisis and the Preemption of Democracy' (2011) *MPIfG Discussion Papers* 11, 27.

[84] Council Implementing Decision on granting Union financial assistance to Ireland, 2010/0351 (NLE) of December 10 2011 http://register.consilium.europa.eu/pdf/en/10/st17/st17211.en10.pdf.

workers could be dismissed.[85] Both states committed to raising indirect forms of taxation, such as VAT (taxes which, unlinked to income, tend to have socially regressive effects). For states requiring financial assistance, centralized EU intervention in areas far beyond the normal reaches of EU competence is not only a reality but backed up by a sanction above and beyond even the most hierarchical form of EU law: withdrawal of bail-out funding and potential economic catastrophe.

These 'negative' impacts have to be seen alongside more positive measures, ie EU efforts to mitigate the social welfare impacts of the economic crisis.[86] While the EU's response to the social effects of the crisis is still in its infancy, the package of social policy proposals adopted to date are highly limited in scope, tinkering with, rather than breaking from, the Lisbon 2020 framework. While asked, by the European Parliament among others, to present a Communication on strengthening the social dimension of EMU, the Commission's October 2013 proposals offer few concrete options for improving the EU's capacity to address its social shortcomings.[87]

The main proposals presented are statistical: they include, for example, including indicators on employment and poverty in the MIP, and developing a scoreboard of social indicators (essentially similar to the scoreboards already developed in the context of the OMC SPSI).[88] The Communication does envisage one much more radical option—of creating a large social investment fund, which states could draw upon in times of economic downturn. As the Commission puts it:

A common instrument for macroeconomic stabilisation could provide an insurance system to pool the risks of economic shocks across Member States, thereby reducing the fluctuations in national incomes. In its simplest formulation, a stabilisation scheme to absorb asymmetric shocks could require monetary net payments that are negative in good times and positive in bad times. For example, a simple scheme could determine net contributions/payments by countries as a function of their output gap (relative to the average). Such a system would need to be financially neutral in the medium term for each country, and it would also depend on country size.[89]

While such a reform—a kind of EU stimulus fund—could address the serious disparities in the social safety net between different EU members, this type of

---

[85] Portugal Memorandum of Understanding on Specific Economic Policy Conditionality http://ec.europa.eu/economy_finance/eu_borrower/mou/2011-05-18-mou-portugal_en.pdf.

[86] For a more positive appraisal, see Bart Vanhercke, 'Under the Radar? EU Social Policy in Times of Austerity' in David Natali and Bart Vanhercke (eds), *Social Developments in the European Union 2012* (2013) 91.

[87] See eg the disappointed reaction of the President of the European Parliament https://twitter.com/MartinSchulz/status/385349244086784000.

[88] An interesting question is whether the inclusion of social indicators in the MIP is consistent with its legal basis under Art 121(6). See on this, Kenneth A. Armstrong, 'The Social Dimension of EMU: Socialising Economic Governance' http://eutopialaw.com/2013/10/04/the-social-dimension-of-emu-socialising-economic-governance/.

[89] Commission Communication, 'Strengthening the Social Dimension of the Economic and Monetary Union' COM (2013) 690, at 11

scheme is acknowledged in the Communication as a long-term project requiring Treaty change,[90] providing little immediate impetus for reform. The admission, for example, that such a fund would have to be financially neutral between
states seems to undercut the utility of the proposal as a mechanism of healing
the significant North–South gap emerging in European social welfare provision.

5. Social Inclusion and the EU's Social Funds

A more realistic set of future changes may relate to the reform of existing EU funding schemes. A decisive push from the EU level to address problems of poverty and
social deprivation—as well as the severe deficiencies of capacity in some Member
States—would require the deployment of significant financial resources. While EU
leaders have floated and developed several funding schemes with a social element,[91] the
resources available from traditional sources, such as the EU budget, remain limited.

The two funding schemes most relevant for social welfare and inclusion are the
European Social Fund (ESF) and the EU Programme for Employment and Social
Innovation ('EaSI') scheme, designed to support financially the social pillar of the
Lisbon 2020 strategy. Of the two, the ESF is by far the most expansive. Its current
funding line of €10 billion per year under the 2014–2020 budget supports Operational
Programmes co-agreed between the Member States and the Commission under particular priority areas. Improving 'the social inclusion of less favoured persons' is a
priority area to which roughly 20 per cent of the ESF budget is allocated from 2014
to 2020.[92] The 'EaSI' scheme carries resources of €919 million over the same funding
period.[93] Under both schemes, NGOs and regional and local authorities can apply for
EU co-financing for any projects that falls within the broad objectives of each programme (for the latter fund, Progress, this includes a focus on building transnational
networks able to effectively implement and monitor EU policy in the social field).

Both programmes face significant challenges. One is the overall scope of funding.
Reflecting the relative size of the EU budget, one has to keep in mind the limited capacity of EU funds to do the 'heavy lifting' of poverty reduction, which has historically required significant investment and social transfers. Whereas the budget of the
entire ESF is €10 billion per year, even tiny Ireland (hardly the most expansive welfare state) spent over €37 billion on social security and protection in 2011.[94] A second

[90] Commission Communication (n 89) at 12,

[91] See eg the Commission Communication on an EU Youth Employment Initiative COM (2013)
0144 final.

[92] See Reg 1304/2013 of 17 December 2013 On the European Social Fund and Repealing Council
Reg (EC) No 1081/2006 OJ L347/470.

[93] Reg 1296/2013 of 11 December 2013 on a European Union Programme for Employment and
Social Innovation [2013] OJ L347/238, Art 5.

[94] See OECD social expenditure database 2011 http://www.oecd-ilibrary.org/social-issues-
migration-health/government-social-spending_20743904-table1.

limit is pressure on budgets emerging from general national and EU budgetary constraints. After agreement in November 2013 between the EU institutions for a cut of some 6 per cent in the EU budget from 2014, €71 billion were allocated to the ESF in the 2014 budget, a lower amount than the prior 2007–2013 allocation. Social spending—in an EU budget required to support ever more functions and institutions—is in significant competition with other EU tasks and funding lines.

One concrete innovation of some import for EU social welfare policy in the new funding period is the Commission's proposed EU Fund for Most Deprived Persons.[95] This programme would involve broadening the mandate of the prior 'Food to the Most Deprived' programme (designed to utilize surplus crops produced under the Common Agricultural Policy) to include clothing, housing assistance, and other essential goods. This proposal has been the subject of political contestation. When first mooting the Fund in October 2012, the Commission proposed a €2.5 billion funding line, €1 billion below the total allocated to the fund's predecessor. The Social Affairs Committee of the European Parliament, however, rejected this in April 2013, successfully demanding the restoration of the €3.5 billion allocation.[96] The Fund (like other EU schemes, such as the planned guarantee scheme for youth unemployment) is in any case not 'new money'—the funding would come in its entirety from the EU's general cohesion budget (thus potentially subtracting from other projects of social value). The role of the Parliament in these negotiations, however, also provides an interesting lesson: the side-lining of the Parliament in the multilateral coordination processes already discussed could itself be to the significant detriment of developing a more robust social response to the crisis.

IV. Conclusion: Welfare in Europe from 'Autonomy' to 'Balancing'

Given these legal and political developments, where is welfare and social inclusion policy in Europe headed in the future? Certainly one model of welfare—that of a national social state that is seen as autonomous from the reaches of EU law and

---

[95] See Reg 223/2014 of 11 March 2014 on the Fund for European Aid to the Most Deprived [2014] OJ L72/1

[96] See European Parliament Press Release, 'Social Affairs Committee Rejects Cut to Fund for the EU's Most Deprived' (21.05.13) http://www.europarl.europa.eu/news/en/news-room/content/20130520IPR08568/html/Social-affairs-committee-rejects-cut-to-fund-for-the-EU%27s-most-deprived.

EU intervention—seems to be increasingly difficult to achieve. While we have seen many efforts by the EU institutions, such as in the example of social services of general interest mentioned above, to insulate national welfare policy from internal market law, we also see many of the legal and political boundaries between national welfare and the larger structure of EU policy making being broken down.

The impact of the euro crisis seems likely to accelerate this trend. In so far as the crisis provides the EU with an enhanced capacity to steer national budgets, this capacity is likely to have knock-on effects on all areas of significant national spending. Social inclusion and welfare, if not already coordinated under the rubric of 'soft' processes like the OMC SPSI, will increasingly be affected by more binding mechanisms of EU economic governance, particularly for the euro area.

This trend poses its own dangers, as well as opportunities. The opportunity may be that the insertion of new social language into the constitutional framework of the Union, and new EU capacities, will also gradually lead to a more autonomous EU social policy being developed. In the 2014 parliamentary elections, social policy was no longer seen merely through a national prism. Rather, the demand and limits of an austerity agenda on growth, jobs, and equality across Europe became a significant campaigning issue.

The danger may be that enhancements of EU capacity in the social field—like many of the developments observed in existing mechanisms such as the Lisbon Strategy—will not 'balance' economic and social objectives, but rather subordinate the latter to the former. So long as social inclusion remains largely a rhetorical commitment, rather than one backed up by significant resources and steering capacity, social goals are likely to play second fiddle to goals such as financial stability, where an EU mandate to act is clearest. With significant problems of unemployment, inequality, and social deprivation persisting both during and after the euro crisis, social inclusion is likely to remain an area of significant fluctuation and change in the coming decade.

BIBLIOGRAPHY

Sonja Bekker, 'The EU's Stricter Economic Governance: A Step Towards a More Binding Coordination of Social Policies?' (2013) *WZB Discussion Paper* 501

Stefan Bernhard, 'The European Paradigm of Social Exclusion' (2006) 2 *Journal of Contemporary European Research* 41

Gráinne de Búrca (ed), *EU Law and the Welfare State: In Search of Solidarity* (2005)

Bea Cantillon, Herwig Verschueren, and Paula Ploscar (eds), *Social Inclusion and Social Protection in the EU: Interactions between Law and Policy* (2012)

Mary Daly and Paul Copeland, 'Poverty and Social Policy in Europe 2020: Ungovernable and Ungoverned' (2014) 42 *Policy and Politics* 351

Dragana Damjanovic, 'The EU Market Rules as Social Market Rules: Why the EU Can Be a Social Market Economy' (2013) 50 *Common Market Law Review* 1685

Mark Dawson, *New Governance and the Transformation of European Law* (2011)

Elspeth Guild, Sergio Carrera, and Katharina Eisele (eds), *Social Benefits and Migration: A Contested Relationship and Policy Challenge in the EU* (2013)

Ulla Neergaard, Ruth Nielsen, and Lynn Roseberry (eds), *Integrating Welfare Functions into EU Law: From Rome to Lisbon* (2009)

Ulla Neergaard, Erika Szyszczak, Johan van den Gronden, and Markus Krajewski (eds), *Social Services of General Interest in the EU* (2013)

Frans Pennings, *European Social Security Law* (5th ed, 2010)

Fritz W. Scharpf, 'Monetary Union, Fiscal Crisis and the Preemption of Democracy' (2011) *MPIfG Discussion Papers* 11

Eleanor Spaventa and Michael Dougan (eds), *Social Welfare and EU Law* (2005)

Jonathan Zeitlin and Phillippe Pochet (eds), *The Open Method of Coordination in Action: The European Employment and Social Inclusion Strategies* (2005)

CHAPTER 38

EXPERTS AND PUBLICS IN EU ENVIRONMENTAL LAW

MARIA LEE[*]

I. INTRODUCTION

SINCE a brief overview of EU environmental law is probably impossible, this paper focuses on two striking and pervasive themes of EU environmental law: the preoccupation with gathering information on the state of the environment, impacts upon it, and risks to it; and the emphasis on participatory, collaborative, and (possibly) open modes of decision making. The self-conscious effort to institutionalize information generation in EU environmental law is not a new development. Damian Chalmers noted the 'increasing importance of informational capital' some years ago,[1] and the EU's relatively small bureaucracy has meant that the search for informational resources has always been a preoccupation.[2] 'Public participation', in turn, was perhaps the dominant theme of EU environmental law in the final years of the twentieth century and the early years of the twenty-first, promising a response to all sorts of concerns about environmental decision-making.

  [*] I am grateful to Damian Chalmers for his very helpful comments on an earlier draft of this paper.
  [1] Damian Chalmers, 'Inhabitants in the Field of EC Environmental Law' in Paul Craig and Grainne de Búrca (eds), *The Evolution of EU Law* (1st ed, 1999), 68.
  [2] eg Sonia Mazey and Jeremy Richardson, 'Environmental Groups and the EC: Challenges and Opportunities' (1992) 1 *Environmental Politics* 109.

This paper begins with a discussion of the relationship between these two themes. The two themes of expertise and participation are by no means inher-ently incompatible, and few would advocate one without the other; indeed, in certain respects they are mutually reinforcing. But the tension between them can sometimes be challenging.[3] I then explore the attention paid to the generation of information, knowledge and expertise in EU environmental law. A number of areas are highlighted, specifically: the regulation of industrial activities under the Industrial Emissions Directive (IED);[4] EU level authorization of products, such as genetically modified organisms (GMOs)[5] and certain chemical substances; the more general regulation of chemicals under REACH (the Regulation on the Registration, Evaluation, Authorisation and Restriction of Chemicals);[6] and the national environmental impact assessment (EIA) of projects under the EIA Directive.[7] The limitations of using expertise as a sole decision-making resource are well known. Environmental protection depends not only on detailed, specialized information about the physical state of the world, but also on political judgments about values and priorities, distributing goods and bads between rich and poor, current and future generations, prioritizing between different environmental goods, and between the environment and other social goods. Concerns about the legitimacy of expert processes are further exacerbated by the regulated industry's central role in the provision of expertise in the legislation examined here. After a discussion of some of these challenges, I explore the place of broader public participation in EU environmental law. Lay public participation does not resonate easily at EU level,[8] and the legislation takes a notably parsimonious and instrumental approach to guarantees of participation in some cases.

A routine institutional response to the need for politically legitimate environmental decisions is to insist that final (political) decisions are taken by politically legitimate principals, rather than delegated to 'experts'. In practice, at EU level, this means that final decisions are taken by the Commission with comitology, the limitations of which are discussed in the final section of this paper.

---

[3] See the detailed empirical review in Mariano-Florentino Cuéllar, 'Rethinking Regulatory Democracy' (2005) 57 *Administrative Law Review* 411.

[4] Dir 2010/75/EU on industrial emissions (integrated pollution prevention and control) [2010] OJ L 334/17.

[5] Dir 2001/18/EC on the deliberate release into the environment of genetically modified organisms [2001] OJ L106/1; Reg 1829/2003/EC on genetically modified food and feed [2003] OJ L268/1. See Maria Lee, *EU Regulation of GMOs: Law and Decision-making for a New Technology*, (2008).

[6] Reg 1907/2006/EC concerning the Registration, Evaluation, Authorization and Restriction of Chemicals (REACH), establishing a European Chemicals Agency [2006] OJ L396/1.

[7] Dir 2011/92/EU on the assessment of the effects of certain public and private projects on the environment (codification) [2012] OJ L26/2.

[8] Maria Lee, *EU Environmental Law, Governance and Decision-Making*, (2014), Ch 8.

II. The Relationship Between Expertise and Participation

The reasons for a focus on information in EU environmental law are diverse, but are at least to some degree inherent in the complex nature of ecological challenges. Neither the causes of, nor the solutions to, environmental problems are intuitively observable. The limited 'in-house' resources available to the EU administration may also, as suggested in the introduction, have contributed to a concern to elaborate processes and fora for the generation of detailed information and knowledge. The emphasis on public participation both feeds into and mediates the resulting focus on expertise. The recognition of the informational challenges faced by environmental governance has in many cases been inherently participative, in the sense of extending participation beyond public sector regulators. This includes, in particular, efforts to harness the superior informational resources of the regulated industry. Broader public participation, including lay publics and environmental interest groups, extends the potentially available information, to include, for example, local knowledge and environmental perspectives.

To understand, even very precisely, the impact of (for example) a particular industrial activity on the environment, and the costs of either environmental harm or environmental regulation, does not, however, in itself tell us what to do.[9] How safe is safe enough, how much risk is acceptable, what sort of world we want to live in, are always value judgments. Environmental regulation is distributive of risk, benefits, harm and costs, and we might be concerned about who gains and who loses, as well as the overall environmental costs and benefits. The essentially political nature of environmental decision making is widely appreciated. By 'political decisions', I mean decisions based on values as well as facts, which might properly be subjected to debate in a political forum. 'Public participation' can provide information on the values that are crucial to political decision making. Participation is also often part of the mosaic of responses to weak political legitimacy at EU level. Like robust fact-finding, inclusive processes may contribute more generally to the legitimacy of decision making. Even in the absence of perfect solutions, ensuring transparency, inclusion, and opportunities for political and legal contestation are important efforts to enhance the 'building blocks' of legitimacy.[10]

Uncertainty enhances the importance of legitimate political intervention in environmental decision making, since it further undermines any assurance that

---

[9] This is recognized by cases such as Case T-13/99 *Pfizer Animal Health SA v Council* [2002] ECR II-3305, which insist on decisions being taken by political institutions rather than experts.

[10] In a different context, see Grainne de Búrca, 'Developing Democracy Beyond the State' (2008) 46 *Columbia Journal of Transnational Law* on 'democratic striving'.

'the facts' will legitimize a decision. No matter how developed and rigorous the processes for generating information, uncertainty remains an inevitable and necessary part of environmental decision making. Science at best provides 'a robust consensus based on a process of inquiry that allows for continued scrutiny, re-examination and revision'.[11] Limits to intellectual capacities and resources of information, time, and money mean that the gathering and assessment of all information on facts and values for all possible alternatives, is generally simply impossible.[12] And the behaviour of complex and dynamic ecological and social systems, can be literally unpredictable.

Some of the great hope for 'public participation' as a route to political legitimacy seems to have waned since the turn of the century. The challenges of enabling genuinely participatory processes have been more painfully recognized. Further, broad participation is messy and unpredictable, and the questions raised may not be easily incorporated in or held alongside technical expertise. It is probably fair to say that an instrumental view of public participation dominates in EU environmental law, in which participation is valued for the contribution it makes to the expert resolution of environmental issues, in terms of information-gathering and scrutiny. This instrumental understanding of the role of public participation is likely to reduce the space for open involvement, as indeed we see below under both the IED and REACH. Expertise, and contributions framed in dominant technical terms, are prioritized,[13] and it is assumed that we already know precisely what is at stake.[14]

This means that the decisive effort to address the political nature of decisions must be found elsewhere. EU environmental law insists that final decisions are not delegated to experts, but are taken by political bodies. The arrangements at *national* level, where the final authorization decision is often taken in EU environmental law, including under the EIA Directive and the IED, will vary.[15] At EU level, influential cases like *Pfizer* confirm that 'scientific legitimacy is not a sufficient basis for the exercise of public authority'.[16] The usual approach is to leave the final decision, for the benefit of which so much effort has gone into enriching knowledge, to the Commission and comitology, in which the Member States (in 'committee') participate in Commission implementation of EU environmental law. This (Commission plus comitology) approach applies to a number of key EU-level decisions taken in

---

[11] Naomi Oreskes, 'Science and Public Policy: What's Proof Got to do With it?' (2004) 7 *Env Sci and Policy* 369, 369–370. Also Lee (n 8), Ch 2.

[12] Charles E. Lindblom, 'The Science of "Muddling Through"' (1959) 19 *Public Administrative Review* 79.

[13] Cuéllar (n 3).   [14] eg Lee (n 8), Ch 9, on narrow participation under REACH.

[15] In the UK, many of the final decisions subject to EIA are taken by democratically elected local authorities, whilst IED permits are decided by the Environment Agency.

[16] *Pfizer* (n 9), [201]. Whilst alternative scientific evidence is necessary for any disagreement with scientific advice, the political nature of the decision is clear.

product authorization, and under REACH and the IED. Reconciling expertise and politics is difficult for any decision maker. The challenges are intensified by comitology's own somewhat delicate legitimacy. I return below to the limits of comitology in this context.

III. Information and Expertise in EU Environmental Law

Environmental legislation sets up more or less elaborate processes for the generation of environmental 'facts' about the physical and social world. My focus in this paper is on the gathering of information for the benefit of public 'regulators'. Access to information can also serve a range of other regulatory purposes,[17] allowing third parties to place pressure on polluters and regulators,[18] possibly incentivizing behaviour change, or even supporting cultural change, through the evolution of a self-critical, more environmentally self-aware, organization.[19] Scholars of 'new' or 'experimental' environmental governance, with their concern for learning and adaptation in response to new information, also often pay careful attention to the creation of governance frameworks 'which encourage the generation of rich, up-to-date, information about environmental quality'.[20]

The EU's formal gathering of information and expertise has conventionally taken place through a plethora of committees, and increasingly through agencies such as the European Food Safety Authority (EFSA) and the European Chemicals Agency (ECHA), as well as the European Environment Agency. In the first part of this section, I briefly outline the arrangements that can be found in the IED,

---

[17] eg Karen Yeung, 'Government by Publicity Management: Sunshine or Spin?' [2005] *Public Law* 360.

[18] eg Neil Gunningham, 'Corporate Environmental Responsibility: Law and the Limits of Voluntarism' in Doreen McBarnet, Aurora Voiculescu and Tom Campbell (eds), *The New Corporate Accountability: Corporate Social Responsibility and the Law* (2007).

[19] Explored, eg in Jane Holder, *Environmental Assessment: The Regulation of Decision-Making*, (2004).

[20] Joanne Scott, 'Preface' in Joanne Scott (ed), *Environmental Protection: European Law and Governance* (2009), v; also eg Joanne Scott and David Trubek, 'Mind the Gap: Law and New Approaches to Governance in the European Union' (2002) 8 *European Law Journal* 1, 5–6. More generally, see eg Julia Black, 'Enrolling Actors in Regulatory Systems: Examples from UK Financial Services Regulation' [2003] *Public Law* 63; in environmental law scholarship, Elen Stokes and Steven Vaughan, 'Great Expectations: Reviewing 50 Years of Chemicals Legislation in the EU' (2013) 25 *Journal of Environmental Law* 411.

REACH, product authorization and environmental assessment for generating information, before turning to some more general observations. Other areas could be singled out for attention, but this demonstrates a range of approaches across a range of areas of environmental protection.

The IED is the main piece of EU legislation on the environmental impact of industrial operations, requiring the Member States to put in place an authorization system that imposes various controls on industry. It aims to take a holistic approach to different aspects of the operation, and to the environmental media of air, water and soil. Industries regulated under the IED must be required under their permit to comply with the standards achievable by use of the 'best available techniques' (BAT). According to the definition in the Directive:

'best available techniques' means the most effective and advanced stage in the development of activities and their methods of operation which indicates the practical suitability of particular techniques for providing the basis for emission limit values and other permit conditions designed to prevent and, where that is not practicable, to reduce emissions and the impact on the environment as a whole.[21]

'Best', 'techniques' and 'available techniques' are all further defined, bringing 'the way in which the installation is designed, built, maintained, operated and decommissioned' into consideration as well as technology, economic and technical viability, costs, and advantages.

Identifying BAT for the purposes of including appropriate requirements in a permit demands an enormous amount of information and expertise, on issues including the activities and costs of the industry, the industry's impacts on the environment throughout its activities, and the range of potential techniques at each stage of the process. Under the predecessor to the IED, the Integrated Pollution Prevention and Control (IPPC) Directive,[22] determining BAT was ultimately in principle a question for national or local regulators. But an elaborate process, led by the Seville-based European IPPC Bureau, emerged to provide detail on BAT for particular industries and processes. Information was produced in the form of lengthy BAT Reference Documents (BREFs), which were one consideration for regulators called on to apply BAT in any particular case. BREFs, more particularly the BAT Conclusions within them, play a more significant role in the regulation of industrial operations under the IED. They are '*the* reference' for setting permit conditions, and once adopted by the Commission (plus comitology), set prima facie minimum standards for 'emission limit values' (ELVs).[23]

---

[21] IED (n 4), Art 3(10).

[22] Dir 2008/1/EC concerning integrated pollution prevention and control [2008] OJ L24/8.

[23] IED (n 4), Arts 14(3), 15(3). On the complexity of this apparent shift from 'soft' to 'hard' law, see Maria Lee 'The Ambiguity of Multi-Level Governance and (De)-harmonisation in EU Environmental Law' (2014) *Cambridge Yearbook of European Legal Studies* 357.

The 'Seville process' is now set out in the Directive, and further detailed in a Commission Implementing Decision.[24] The initial 'exchange of information' on BAT for any particular sector takes place in a Technical Working Group (TWG), composed of 'Member States, the industries concerned, non-governmental organisations promoting environmental protection and the Commission'.[25] Members of a 'forum', composed of 'Member States, the industries concerned, non-governmental organisations promoting environmental protection', but not the Commission[26] nominate members ('their representatives') to the TWGs.[27] Of 44 participant organizations in the TWG for the BREF for iron and steel production, two were classified by the European IPPC Bureau as environmental interest groups (the European Environment Bureau and ÖKOPOL[28]), 14 were from industry,[29] and the rest represented the Member States.[30] The European IPPC Bureau seeks information from members of the TWG, and presents formal and informal drafts to the TWG for comment.[31] 'Consensus . . . is sought' in the TWG, but 'it is not a prerequisite' for a decision.[32] We might note that by contrast with the areas of law discussed below, in which either market access for a product or the grant of a permit for a process is conditional on information provision, the IED does not compel industry participation in TWGs.[33] The opportunity to influence regulation provides an important incentive to contribute resources to the TWG.[34] In the absence of regulatory intervention, industry has no incentive to carry out costly safety research, let alone to share the results of that research.[35] Gathering and disclosing information on its

[24] Commission Implementing Decision 2012/119/EU laying down rules concerning guidance on the collection of data and on the drawing up of BAT reference documents and on their quality assurance [2012] OJ L63/1.

[25] IED (n 4), Art 13(1). http//:eippcb.jrc.ec.europa.eu/about/who_is_who.html. Bettina Lange *Implementing EU Pollution Control: Law and Integration* (2008).

[26] IED (n 4), Art 13(3).   [27] Decision 2012/119/EU (n 24), [4.3].

[28] ÖKOPOL does not describe *itself* as an environmental advocacy organization; it emphasizes its scientific credentials, and works closely with public authorities and industry, http//:www.oekopol.de/en/.

[29] Including individual iron and steel producers, such as Corus Group and ArcelorMittal; industry associations at the national and EU level; and suppliers to the industry.

[30] Email communication from European IPPC Bureau, 25 July 2012. For further discussion of participation in TWGs, see Carolyn Abbot and Maria Lee, 'Economic Actors in EU Environmental Law' (2015) Yearbook of European Law, forthcoming.

[31] Decision 2012/119/EU (n 24), Table 1, [1.2.4].

[32] Decision 2012/119/EU (n 24), Table 1, [4.4.2].

[33] Although at a later stage in the process, applicants for a permit do have to provide information on their activity.

[34] We might contrast the involvement in TWGs with eg the low levels of participation in Defra and US EPA voluntary reporting scheme for nanomaterials, discussed by Carolyn Abbot, 'Bridging the Gap—Non-state Actors and the Challenges of Regulating New Technology' (2012) 39 *Journal of Law and Society* 329, 342–343.

[35] Wendy Wagner, 'Commons Ignorance: The Failure of Environmental Law to Produce Needed Information on Health and the Environment' (2004) 53 *Duke Law Journal* 1619; Linsey McGoey, 'The Logic of Strategic Ignorance' (2012) 63 *The British Journal of Sociology* 553.

own costs and environmental and health impacts, may be preferable for industry to less well-informed regulation.[36]

The IED provides perhaps the most elaborate arrangements for information generation and sharing in EU environmental law.[37] REACH is the perhaps the piece of regulation that turns most emphatically around new demands on industry to supply information. The 'no data no market' principle requires importers and manufacturers, and some others in the supply chain, to register with the ECHA a range of information about any chemical imported or manufactured in quantities of one tonne or more. Additional information is required as the ten, 100 and 1000 tonne threshold is passed.[38] At the ten tonne threshold a chemical safety report, which assesses the risks of the substance's specified uses (essentially a risk assessment), must be included.[39] The registrant also has to 'identify and apply the appropriate measures to adequately control the risks'.[40] For substances imported or manufactured in annual quantities over 100 tonnes, if the regulated party does not already have adequate information on safety, it has to be produced, if necessary after submitting testing proposals to the ECHA.

Product authorization in the EU tends to turn around risk assessment, the details of which are in some cases set out at length in the legislation and/or subsequent guidance.[41] The industry applying for permission to market its product is usually responsible for providing this information in the first instance. Under the Directive on GMOs, for example, an applicant seeking authorization of its GM plant has to provide a 'notification' including a range of information on the plant, the genetic modification and the applicant, and an 'environmental risk assessment'.[42] Chemicals that have been identified as 'substances of very high concern' (SVHC) under REACH are subject to an authorization requirement.[43] An applicant for authorization has to provide a range of information, including a chemical safety report, 'covering the risks to human health and/or the environment from the use of the substance(s)'.[44]

The obligation on applicants to provide information is not limited to product authorization. Most process authorization regimes, including the IED permitting process, also require applicants to provide detailed information.[45] The same applies in EIA. EIA is a systematic attempt to gather information on the environmental

---

[36] Bradley C Karkainnen, 'Information-Forcing Environmental Regulation' (2006) 33 *Florida State University Law Review* 861. Lange (n 25) notes that participants (Member States as well as industry) withhold information, 113.

[37] See also the 'Common Implementation Strategy' under Dir 2000/60/EC establishing a framework for the Community action in the field of water policy [2000] OJ L327/1.

[38] REACH (n 6), Art 12. Set out in detail in Annexes VI to X

[39] REACH (n 6), Art 14, Annex I.   [40] REACH (n 6), Art 14.

[41] eg Deliberate Release Directive (n 5), Annexes II and II.

[42] Deliberate Release Directive (n 5), Art 6.

[43] REACH (n 6), Art 56; Art 57, Annex XIV.   [44] REACH (n 6), Art 62.

[45] IED (n 4), Art 12.

impacts of a project, before its authorization. The proposing developer must gather a range of information on the potential impact of its proposal, including at least a description of the project and proposed mitigation measures; the data required to identify and assess the main effects; an outline of 'the main alternatives studied by the developer; and an indication of the main reasons for his choice'.[46]

Additional information generation mechanisms can be found in the routine obligations on operators of permitted facilities or activities to monitor and report (often publicly) their emissions or activities. IED permits must include 'suitable emission monitoring requirements', as well as obligations to monitor ground water and soil.[47] The Commission has proposed introducing a monitoring obligation into the EIA Directive,[48] filling a palpable gap in the regulatory scheme. In the EU's multi-level governance context, obligations imposed on the Member States to report to the Commission, each other, and the public, are equally important. Such obligations are a routine feature of EU environmental legislation, including the IED and EIA Directives.[49] The Commission is often under a corresponding obligation to respond, and in some cases expressly to consider whether to put forward a legislative proposal.[50]

Reporting obligations are primarily concerned with enhancing implementation, but if the information is well-organized and searchable, it could become a valuable resource for enriching the information available to environmental governance. Farber has criticized US environmental assessment for the failure to organize information in an easily accessible and useable form;[51] Stokes and Vaughan raise similar questions about the real 'availability' of information provided under REACH.[52] There is little in the way of specific obligations to maintain information or to ensure that it is accessible and searchable in the legislation discussed here. The difficulty is to some extent recognized, and there are efforts to create information systems for the EU,[53] but given the high priority placed on generating expertise, surprisingly little.

---

[46] EIA Directive (n 7), Art 5.   [47] IED (n 4), Art 14, 16.

[48] European Commission, Proposal for a Directive amending Directive 2011/92/EU on the assessment of the effects of certain public and private projects on the environment COM (2012) 628 final, proposed new Art 8(2).

[49] Joanne Scott and Jane Holder, 'Law and New Environmental Governance in the European Union' in Grainne de Búrca and Joanne Scott (eds), *Law and New Governance in the EU and the US* (2006), on environmental assessment.

[50] eg IED, (n 4), Art 73.

[51] Dan Farber, 'Bringing Environmental Assessment into the Digital Age' in Jane Holder and Donald McGillivray (eds) *Taking Stock of Environmental Impact Assessment: Law, Policy and Practice* (2007).

[52] N 20. European Commission, *Staff Working Document accompanying General Report on REACH* SWD (2013) 25 highlights the importance of avoiding registration becoming a 'data cemetery', 107, although without inspiring much confidence (also Stokes and Vaughan, n 20, 428).

[53] http://www.eea.europa.eu/about-us/what/shared-environmental-information-system-1.   Also European Commission (n 52).

Acquiring adequate information for a good understanding of the environment, and of the impact of human activities upon it, is dauntingly difficult.[54] The deliberate construction of a space in which information and knowledge will be gathered, shared and reflected upon, is a significant development in EU environmental law. As well as the customized approaches discussed so far, some more general observations can be made.

The type of information being sought in EU environmental law seems primarily to be information on the physical impacts of activities and the risks posed to the environment and human health by different economic activities. The Court of Justice of the EU generally demands 'scientific risk assessment' before the EU's administrative bodies can take a protective measure in an area of high complexity,[55] and environmental legislation, especially but not exclusively product regulation, is also often built explicitly around risk assessment.[56] We may be witnessing the slow development of a 'common' European approach to risk assessment. Although the European Environment Agency plays a relatively marginal role in the implementation of legislation, EFSA and the ECHA both make important contributions to the regulation of areas with strong environmental implications, including pesticides and herbicides, chemicals, and GMOs. The risk assessments produced by EFSA exercise an enormous influence over the Commission,[57] and are used both in authorization decisions, and in decisions disciplining autonomous national action (under a safeguard provision, or Article 114 TFEU). It is too soon to comment on the influence of the ECHA's risk assessments, which like EFSA may face competing risk assessments (from the Member States, from industry, or from environmental and consumer groups), as well as concerns not related to risk to the environment or human health.

Reliance on 'common' EU risk assessments is not inherently problematic, and in terms of environmental protection will sometimes be highly (pre)cautious, sometimes less so.[58] In any event, it would be wrong to suggest that EU level agencies provide any simple centralization of power or authority, given the significant guarantees of national involvement in the agencies themselves, and in subsequent decision making.[59] But risk assessment is not a neutral, objective tool that provides

---

[54] Karkainnen (n 36), 864.   [55] eg *Pfizer* (n 9).

[56] eg Deliberate Release Directive (n 5). Environmental legislation does not always require risk assessment before administrative action, eg Case C-343/09 *Afton Chemical Limited v Secretary of State for Transport* [2010] ECR-I-7027, especially Kokott AG.

[57] Ellen Vos, 'Responding to Catastrophe: Towards a New Architecture for EU Food Safety Regulation?' in Charles F. Sabel and Jonathan Zeitlin (eds), *Experimentalist Governance in the European Union: Towards a New Architecture* (2010).

[58] eg GMOs and neonicitinoids in Lee (n 8), Ch 2.

[59] Of EFSA, see Vos (n 57); of ECHA, see Joanne Scott, 'REACH: Combining Harmonization and Dynamism in the Regulation of Chemicals' in Scott (n 20).

universally applicable answers, answers that anyone in possession of the relevant facts could agree on. So who decides can matter.

We may also be witnessing the beginnings of a common EU approach to other forms of knowledge. Economic information on the costs and benefits of regulation plays an increasingly significant role in environmental governance. Cost-benefit analysis (CBA) is an important aspect of regulatory impact assessment,[60] and is sometimes required or encouraged as part of decision-making processes, as for example in the authorization and restriction of chemicals under REACH, and in the IED.[61] We might note that the EU institutions resist the language of CBA, preferring for example 'multi-criteria analysis'[62] or 'socio-economic analysis'.[63] This perhaps reflects the fact that EU law and policy does not *demand* quantification of all costs and benefits.[64] More likely, the intention is to side-step the controversy generated by CBA in other jurisdictions,[65] since quantification is certainly encouraged in the EU,[66] and all but the most extreme approaches to CBA would acknowledge the significance in principle of impacts that are difficult or impossible to quantify.

Whilst it is fair to conclude that various approaches to risk assessment and CBA dominate EU knowledge generation, other sources of expertise may also be important. 'Ethical' expertise has an increasing (and controversial) role in public life, although so far to a limited extent in EU environmental law. The 'task' of the European Group on Ethics in Science and New Technologies (EGE) is to 'advise the Commission on ethical questions relating to sciences and new technologies, either at the request of the Commission or on its own initiative'.[67] The clearest legal space for the EGE in environmental law is in the law applying to GMOs, which explicitly refers to the possibility of calling on its advice. Even here, the consultation of ethics committees is explicitly not to affect the legislation's 'administrative procedures', and references to *European* ethics are matched by references to the continued authority of the Member States on ethical matters.[68]

A turn to economic or ethical expertise, whilst they look very different, may share a concern with side-stepping messy participatory processes. For

---

[60] European Commission, Impact Assessment Guidelines SEC (2009) 92, 4.

[61] REACH (n 6), Art 60(4); European Commission, BREF on Economics and Cross-Media Effects (2006).

[62] Commission (n 60).   [63] Under REACH (n 6).

[64] eg Commission (n 60), 38; European Chemicals Agency, Guidance on the Preparation of Socio-Economic Analysis as Part of an Application for Authorisation (2011).

[65] Frank Ackerman and Lisa Heinzerling, *Priceless: On Knowing the Price of Everything and the Value of Nothing* (2004).

[66] See eg the Annual Impact Assessment Board Reports, European Commission, *Impact Assessment Board Report for 2012*, 26.

[67] Commission Decision 2010/1 on the Renewal of the Mandate of the European Group on ethics in Science and New technologies [2010] OJ L1/8.

[68] Deliberate Release Directive (n 5), Art 29(3), Recitals 9, 57, 58.

example, one of the routes for the authorization of a chemical deemed to be a SVHC under REACH is if 'socio-economic benefits outweigh the risk to human health or the environment arising from the use of the substance and if there are no suitable alternative substances or technologies'.[69] This is examined through a socio-economic analysis, which addresses a potentially wide range of issues, including distributive questions about the impact of (non-)authorization or restriction on consumers, employment, trade, competition, and economic development, and a catch all 'any other issue that is considered to be relevant'.[70] These are the sorts of issues that we may expect to identify through political processes, including public participation, even if some detail on the scale of some effects, for example on employment, may be sought through economics.[71] But instead, under REACH, information on how we value the broad impacts of (non-)authorization, is sought from experts in economics. And the first draft of the analysis will generally be provided by the applicant for authorization.

The danger that we turn political debates about the organization of society into technical 'expert' discussions is real. This may reflect a process of learning about the difficulty of managing public participation, combined with a genuine recognition that more is at stake than we can learn from the natural sciences. It may also be about a preference for articulating reasons for decisions in terms amenable to technical expert assessment. One reason for emphasizing in this paper the *political* nature of environmental decision making, when the questions raised might just as easily be conceptualized as 'ethical' questions, is that politics is less readily appropriated by expert processes than ethics. Although ethical expertise may have a valuable contribution to make to environmental decisions (for example, highlighting and articulating taken-for-granted assumptions), an expert process cannot substitute for politically legitimate decision making.

The emphasis on information and knowledge in EU environmental law at least implicitly recognizes the weakness of regulatory knowledge, and the tendency for commercial research to move ahead of safety research. Ignorance may have considerable strategic importance, possibly allowing the command of resources, the denial of responsibility in the aftermath of trouble, and the continued assertion of expertise when outcomes are unpredictable.[72] Regulation that incentivizes the generation and sharing of information is in part at least an effort to respond to these challenges.

---

[69] REACH (n 6), Art 60(4).   [70] REACH (n 6), Annex XVI.

[71] REACH (n 6), Art 62. 'Socio-economics' may allow the use of a substance identified as being 'of very high concern', but there is not provision for it to tip the balance against the use of a substance.

[72] McGoey (n 36) for discussion of the literature, noting that strategic ignorance may be valuable to regulators as well as industry.

IV. ECONOMIC ACTORS AS PARTICIPANTS AND EXPERTS

Technical expertise, based on excellent information and knowledge, is clearly crucial to tackling our environmental problems, and the mechanisms discussed in the previous section may contribute to countering disincentives to expand knowledge. The limits of expertise as a decision-making resource have, however, been well rehearsed in different areas of EU law, especially in the context of comitology and agencies, and increasingly in the context of new or experimental governance.[73] One issue has already been raised: the inherently political nature of environmental decision making means that expertise alone does not equip a group or individual to reach a final decision. Most would now agree that the resources of expertise alone cannot determine responses to environmental questions, and that political resources are also required. But further, and in a phenomenon so common that it almost goes unnoticed, economic actors,[74] (that is the industry, even the particular firm being regulated) are very heavily involved in information generation and expert processes. There are many good reasons to enrol economic actors in environmental governance, not least their superior resources of information and knowledge. Their role, however, does raise questions about the legitimacy of processes and decisions.[75]

It is clear from even the brief outline in the previous section that it is routine for economic actors to play a central role in providing information when their product or activity has been identified for regulatory attention.[76] The close engagement of economic actors in environmental regulation is in part a response to the familiar question of information asymmetry between regulator and regulated: the regulated industry knows more about its activities than regulators and can acquire further information most easily and cheaply.[77] Far-reaching collaboration is necessary since 'no single actor has all the knowledge required to solve complex, diverse and dynamic problems'.[78] The enrolment of regulated parties in regulatory processes

---

[73] Virtually any of the citations in this article touch on this; see also eg Carol Harlow and Richard Rawlings, 'Promoting Accountability in Multilevel Governance: A Network Approach' (2007) 13 *European Law Journal* 542; Mark Dawson, 'Transforming into What? New Governance in the EU and the "Managerial Sensibility" in Modern Law' [2010] *Wisconsin Law Review* 389.

[74] Bridget Hutter, 'The Role of Non-State Actors in Regulation (2006)' *CARR Discussion Paper* No. 37)

[75] Abbot and Lee (n 30).   [76] For more discussion, see Abbot and Lee (n 30).

[77] The 'enrolment' or 'surrogacy' of private parties in regulation is a more general phenomenon; Abbot (n 30); Black (n 20).

[78] Julia Black, 'Decentring Regulation: Understanding the Role of Regulation and Self-Regulation in a Post-Regulatory World' (2001) 54 *Current Legal Problems* 103, 107.

may also enhance the legitimacy of the process (at least to the regulated parties),[79] and may help with the dissemination, implementation, and enforcement of norms.

Demanding technical information from the regulated industry is a central governance technique in EU environmental law and beyond, for good reason. But the confidence in the 'neutrality' of the technical information produced, the reluctance to countenance the possibility that providers of information may be selective or self-interested about the information they share, is a little puzzling. History is littered with chilling examples of 'slow and sometimes obstructive behaviour by businesses whose products endangered workers, the public and the environment'.[80] To say that provision of information may be selective or self-interested does not even need to imply deliberate efforts to mislead: a slow response to information provided by outsiders can be attributable to complex epistemological and psychological phenomena, as well as to 'cupidity and arrogance'.[81] And there are choices, sometimes implicit rather than conscious, to be made in the gathering and interpretation of information,[82] and those choices are likely to be affected by the values and interests of the participants. Too much trust can be placed in regulated parties' ability and willingness to control their own risks.[83] This means that very strong mechanisms for the scrutiny of industry's contributions to expertise, and for the contribution of alternative perspectives, must be in place, adding perhaps a further dimension to the demands for 'public participation' discussed above.

Especially when set against the weaknesses, discussed below, of lay publics and environmental interest groups relative to industry (in many, not all, cases), the centrality of economic actors also emphasizes the continued need for expert, experienced (and costly) public-regarding, publicly accountable scrutiny of information. The ECHA plays this role under REACH. It is responsible for the 'evaluation' of registration dossiers, checking at least 5 per cent of dossiers submitted for compliance with the requirements of the Regulation.[84] In products authorization at EU level, a public authority generally scrutinizes the risk assessment provided by the industry, and provides an opinion to the final decision maker. In respect of GMOs, this role is carried out by EFSA.[85] Applications for authorization of SVHCs are submitted to the ECHA, and scrutinized by its Committee for Risk Assessment and Committee for Socio-Economic Analysis, whose opinions are provided to the Commission and Member States.[86] National public authorities should provide

---

[79] Legitimacy in this context is complicated, see n 78.

[80] European Environment Agency, *Late Lessons from Early Warnings: Science, Precaution, Innovation* (2013), 10.

[81] European Environment Agency (n 80), Ch 25 and panel discussion, 177.

[82] See text below at n 130.

[83] See Julia Black, 'Paradoxes and Failures: "New Governance" Techniques and the Financial Crisis' (2013) 75 *Modern Law Review* 1037; Christie Ford, 'New Governance in the Teeth of Human Frailty: Lessons from Financial Regulation' (2010) *Wisconsin Law Review* 441.

[84] REACH (n 6), Art 41.   [85] Deliberate Release Directive (n 5).

[86] REACH (n 6), Art 64.

scrutiny of the information provided by developers in EIA: 'authorities likely to be concerned by the project by reason of their specific environmental responsibilities' (such as nature conservation or environmental agencies) are invited to provide comments;[87] and the body that makes the final decision on whether permission should be granted should provide additional expert scrutiny. Under the IED, the European IPPC Bureau exercises a potentially important role in mediating information and expertise. It produces drafts on the basis of information received, collates comments, checks, and verifies the information,[88] and is able to carry out its own research into sources of information.[89] At least some Bureau employees see themselves as 'a necessary counterbalance in particular to the influence of EU trade associations'.[90] The role of the Member States in the TWGs is equally important. Numerically, the majority of participants in the TWGS are Member State representatives, usually from the government ministry or environmental regulator, although sometimes clearly from an industry body.[91] The ECHA scientific committees are also composed largely of national regulators, nominated by (although not representing) the Member States. This provides the opportunity for a broadly 'regulatory' perspective, potentially 'an active, public-regarding counterweight in [the] interpretive community'.[92]

A skilful, expert regulator within a public authority has the potential to exercise significant control over knowledge generation activities, and should provide expert, public-regarding scrutiny of information. However, economic actors were called on in the first place precisely because of the difficulty of generating adequate information and expertise in public institutions. It is not uncommon to come across concerns about the ability of regulators to provide adequate scrutiny of industry's claims. The role of the ECHA in dossier evaluations, and the general quality of the information provided, has, for example, been criticized.[93] And in recognition of a recurring concern about capacity in EIA, and in order to 'guarantee the completeness and sufficient quality of the environmental reports', the Commission has proposed that the environmental information provided by developers is either prepared by 'accredited and technically competent experts' or verified by 'accredited and technically competent experts and/or committees of national experts'.[94] This means turning first to other private parties, effectively accredited auditors. Environmental consultants are already frequently contracted

---

[87] EIA Directive (n 7), Art 6(1).   [88] Decision 2012/119/EU (n 24), [4.5].

[89] Decision 2012/119/EU (n 24), Table 1.   [90] Lange (n 25), 123.

[91] Email (n 30): the Hungarian Steel Association was Hungary's representative in the Iron and Steel Bref; BPEX, an organization representing pig levy payers in England and Wales (www.bpex. org.uk), was a UK representative (along with the Environment Agency) in the TWG on the intensive rearing of poultry and pigs; and three industry members represented the UK, alongside the Environment Agency, in the Large Combustion Plants TWG.

[92] Ford (n 83), 471, in the context of financial regulation.

[93] Stokes and Vaughan (n 20).   [94] Commission (n 48), proposed new Art 5(3).

by developers to prepare reports, and the requirement that they be subjected to some national accreditation scheme may enhance their competence and probity. The additional possibility, that specialist public 'committees' will verify the reports, looking for the development of more specialist expertise in the public sector, is potentially interesting.

V. Public Participation
in EU Environmental Law

A broad consensus emerged towards the end of the twentieth century that 'public participation' is a necessary part of good environmental decision making. Two key events, one internal and one external, both strengthened this consensus and contributed to the institutionalization of public participation in EU environmental law. These events were symbolic of the (perhaps now lapsing) faith that public participation can respond to all manner of ills. First, a strong rhetoric of participation was central to the Commission's *White Paper on European Governance*, which was the response to a period of intense concern about the Commission's legitimacy.[95] The Aarhus Convention, built on three pillars of access to environmental information, public participation in decision making on environmental matters, and access to justice in environmental matters, is well-known to environmental lawyers.[96] Although public participation was an important part of EU environmental law before the Aarhus Convention, the Convention remains a rallying point, and led to some changes of detail and perspective. Obligations on Member States to provide opportunities for public participation became routine in EU environmental law, and an expectation of open and transparent decision-making was increasingly part of the rhetoric of 'good' decision-making at EU level.

A call for participation can respond to a variety of concerns about environmental decision making,[97] contributing both to the legitimacy and fairness of the process by which decisions are taken, and to the quality of decisions and environmental outcomes. There is no clean line between these rationales: for example, because environmental decision making is political as well as technical, substantively good

---

[95] European Commission, White Paper on European Governance COM (2001) 428 final.
[96] Aarhus Convention on Access to Environmental Information, Public Participation in Decision-Making, and Access to Justice on Environmental Matters United Nations Economic Commission for Europe (1998) 38 ILM 517 (1999).
[97] Lee (n 8), Chs 7 and 8.

decisions (and deciding what is 'good'), require broad contributions. For current purposes, 'publics' (whoever they might be) potentially play a number of important roles. They provide information, both technical information and information on values, and deliberative participatory processes may even contribute to the constitution and evolution of these values. They are given the opportunity to scrutinize information developed in fora dominated by privileged economic actors, and provide alternative perspectives that could broaden the range of solutions available.[98] And more ambitiously, their presence, and ability to challenge and dissent, can enhance the legitimacy of political decision making.

Precisely what 'public participation' is for, and precisely what it should consist of (Who is our public? How do they participate?) in any particular case is rarely clear. Participatory processes can range from simple consultation, through to more ambitious shared problem solving, and from the inclusion of a relatively narrow group of elite participants, to a more open and 'public' process. The TWG in Seville might be described as a participatory forum, given that it includes a range of public and private actors: 'Member States, the industries concerned, non-governmental organisations promoting environmental protection and the Commission'.[99] The collaboration of the participants in the TWG implies something more than consultation, in the rich potential for deliberation and interaction; and less than 'public' participation, given that only invited organizations can participate. But it is an effort to institutionalize a space for information to be provided from different perspectives, particularly for current purposes industry and environmental groups. The ECHA does not embrace industry within its committees (as the European IPPC Bureau does), but economic actors do have a major role in providing the information for regulation. There is no compensating formal role for environmental interest groups. The Commission is, however, allowed up to six (non-voting) representatives on the ECHA Management Board, including three individuals from 'interested parties' (currently two individuals working in the chemicals industry, one environmental legal academic[100]). The Parliament can also appoint two 'independent persons'.[101] In addition, the Management Board shall 'in agreement with the Commission', 'develop appropriate contacts' with 'relevant stakeholder organisations'.[102] 'Accredited stakeholder organisations', including environmental interest groups, are able to send observers to the ECHA's two scientific committees, for risk assessment and for socio-economic analysis.[103]

---

[98] Jenny Steele, 'Participation and Deliberation in Environmental Law: Exploring a Problem-solving Approach' (2001) 21 *Oxford Journal of Legal Studies* 415.

[99] IED (n 4), Art 13(1).

[100] REACH (n 6), Art 79(1). http://echa.europa.eu/web/guest/about-us/who-we-are/management-board/management-board-members.

[101] REACH (n 6), Art 79(1). They have appointed a professor of applied environmental science, and a consultant engineer who is also a former MEP.

[102] REACH (n 6), Art 108.

[103] EFSA also arranges for 'stakeholder' participation, Vos (n 57).

This sort of collaboration between diverse public and private actors is replete with possibilities for deliberation and sharing knowledge, for the identification of problems, and of a broader range of possible solutions.[104] But actually ensuring adequate representation by public interest groups is not straightforward. Whilst inclusion of accredited stakeholders seems to be slightly more balanced in the ECHA[105] (although industry has the initial advantage of providing the information on which regulation is based), industry certainly dominates the TWGs in quantitative terms. And whilst embedding diverse voices within the institution is important, such close collaboration exacerbates the likelihood that a shared *technical* or professional framework between participants can mean that political or ethical questions are unthinkingly re-conceptualized as purely technical. Close collaboration may reduce the distance that is necessary if participants are really to challenge the approach being taken, at worst degenerating into an 'old boys network'.[106] Important as it is, ensuring a balancing voice within the institution is not a simple matter.

Beyond these opportunities for participation within the organization, we turn to more general guarantees of transparency and consultation. The arrangements are patchy. There is no legal obligation to do so, but draft documents are made public (in English only) during the Seville process, although there is no clear process for feeding external comments into the decision. The opinion of the Forum on the BREF proposed by the TWG,[107] which must be taken into account by the Commission, is also published, again without any settled process for making comments. The ECHA maintains a database of information provided under REACH, although subject to some potentially problematic exceptions, especially in respect of information that would undermine commercial interests.[108] There are some opportunities for general public contributions to REACH processes, on very tightly defined issues.[109] Other product authorization decisions also create the space for some public consultation. For example, when a food or feed GMO is authorized, the application is made available to EFSA, the Commission and all Member States, and the summary is made available to the public. EFSA's opinion

---

[104] Steele (n 98). Note that data sharing between industry actors seems to have worked poorly in the pre-registration stages of REACH, see Commission (n 52), 24–26.

[105] http://echa.europa.eu/documents/10162/13579/rac_loa_sto_en.pdf; Abbot and Lee (n 30).

[106] Harlow and Rawlings (n 73).   [107] IED (n 4), Art 13(4).

[108] REACH (n 6), Arts 118, 119. Reg 1049/2001/EC regarding public access to European Parliament, Council and Commission documents [2001] OJ L 145/43; Reg 1367/2006/EC on the application of the provisions of the Aarhus Convention on access to information, public participation in decision-making and access to justice in environmental matters to Community institutions and bodies [2006] OJ L 264/13; ECHA, Decision on the Implementation of Reg 1049/2001/EC regarding public access to documents (2009).

[109] Veerle Heyvaert, 'The EU Chemicals Policy: Towards Inclusive Governance?' *LSE Law, Society and Economy Working Paper 7/2008*; Lee (n 8) Ch 9.

on the application is published, and there is an opportunity for the public to 'make comments'.[110]

Stronger processes are required of the Member States. Environmental assessment is perhaps the high point of the participatory ethos in EU environmental law, requiring the Member States to ensure that the 'public' is informed of the request for development consent, and given details about the decision-making procedure.[111] The 'public concerned'[112] is given 'early and effective opportunities to participate', and is 'entitled to express comments and opinions when all options are open' and before the decision is taken.[113] The role of 'non-governmental organizations promoting environmental protection' is formally recognized in EIA, since the Directive explicitly includes them in the rights granted to the 'public' and the 'public concerned'. Member States have considerable discretion in respect of the 'detailed arrangements' for public participation, which could be very ambitious, or a simple opportunity to provide written comments. All of the information gathered during the EIA, including the results of the consultations, 'shall be taken into consideration' in the decision.[114] Both public participation and environmental protection feature explicitly in the reason-giving obligation: the decision and 'the main reasons and considerations on which the decision is based, including information about the public participation process' and 'a description, where necessary, of the main measures to avoid, reduce and, if possible, offset the major adverse effects' are to be made available to the public.[115] A similar opportunity for third parties to feed into the regulatory process is provided during the national or local process for permitting particular facilities under the IED, although this does not provide an opportunity to scrutinize or challenge the BREF, agreed at EU level.[116]

These general public participation provisions allow for contributions to be made by environmental and consumer interest groups, and economic competitors, as well as lay publics. It is important not to underestimate the contribution of 'lay' participants in providing different information and perspectives, and contributing to the shaping of the questions to be asked. But whilst lay publics may have a great deal to contribute to environmental decision making, it can be difficult to contribute to a process framed in highly technical terms. Highly technical information is really 'available' only to a very few experts; information requires some

[110] Food and Feed Regulation (n 5), Arts 5 and 6.

[111] EIA Directive (n 7), Art 6(2).

[112] Defined broadly: those 'affected or likely to be affected' or having 'an interest in' the procedures; environmental interest groups are 'deemed to have an interest', EIA Directive (n 7), Art 1(2)(e).

[113] EIA Directive (n 7), Art 6.   [114] EIA Directive (n 7), Art 8.

[115] EIA Directive (n 7), Art 9(1)(c). The Member States enjoy considerable discretion over the detailed arrangements for public participation, eg C-216/05 *Commission v Ireland* [2006] ECR I-10787.

[116] The impact of earlier decisions (whether subject to consultation or not) on participation is always difficult, see Maria Lee et al. 'Public Participation and Climate Change Infrastructure' (2013) 25 *Journal of Environmental Law* 33.

sort of 'translation' if it is to be used by general publics.[117] This is often another job for environmental or other public interest groups,[118] although the EIA and the IED require the applicant to provide a 'non-technical summary' of information provided.[119] We should also note that the volume and density of information provided can mean that even expert capacity is challenged.[120] The demands made of participants should not be underestimated, and the more technical the activity, the greater the demands on the party doing the holding to account.[121]

The role of the expert accountor, including environmental interest groups, in scrutinizing information, and in providing an alternative perspective on a problem, is crucial. As well as being potentially expert enough to engage, environmental interest groups are most likely to have sufficient detachment to 'want to query the objectives and methods' of industry.[122] We should note though that even in Seville, no particular environmental interest group has a legally protected role, so it cannot be taken for granted that the most expert (or challenging) groups will find themselves around the table. More generally, the ability of environmental interest groups to compete with industry for influence is problematic.[123] It is hard to draw generalizable conclusions, but quantitatively, environmental interest groups are often less well-represented in EU level decision-making processes, as indeed they are in the TWGs.[124] Influence is even more difficult to measure, but environmental interest groups are generally less well resourced (in time, money, information, people) than industry groups, and have less ready access to the information valued in these regulatory processes. So whilst the inclusion of environmental interest groups in decision-making is crucial, we cannot be confident that it adequately counters the perspective of economic actors. We should also note that environmental interest groups are not inherently more accountable or representative than industry. Environmental values are multifaceted and there is no guarantee that the values of pan-European environmental interest groups reflect citizens' or even their members' environmental values;[125] nor are environmental values the only important issues at stake. Whilst inclusion of the 'general' public and of environmental interest groups is extremely important, the inherent difficulties they face emphasize the continued centrality of regulators and other public institutions, as suggested above.

---

[117] Sheila Jasanoff 'Transparency in Public Science: Purposes, Reasons, Limits' (2006) 69 *Law and Contemporary Problems* 21.

[118] As under REACH (n 6), see the discussion in Scott (n 59).

[119] IED (n 4), Art 12; EIA Directive (n 7), Art 5.

[120] See eg Commission (n 53) on 'safety data sheets' under REACH.

[121] Julia Black, 'Calling Regulators to Account: Challenges, Capacities and Prospects' *LSE: Law, Society and Economy Working Papers* 15/2012.

[122] Jasanoff (n 117), 37 and 34.   [123] Abbot and Lee (n 30).   [124] Abbot and Lee (n 30).

[125] Alex Warleigh '"Europeanising" Civil Society: NGOs as Agents of Political Socialisation' (2001) 39 *Journal of Common Market Studies* 619.

VI. Political Decision Making

The space for public participation in environmental decision making at EU level (especially) is narrow, and it is difficult to envisage 'publics' providing adequate legitimacy for administrative decisions. As noted at the beginning of this paper, ultimately, the politics of environmental decision making are embraced by the requirement that final decisions be taken by political rather than expert institutions. In most cases, at EU level, that involves the Commission acting through comitology. Strictly, the member states *supervise* the Commission implementing powers through comitology, but the process has evolved to allow for cooperation between the different actors. Essentially, whilst the comitology process can be complicated and elaborate, in the environmental field it generally proceeds from an initial draft decision presented by the Commission to an 'examination committee', composed of national representatives.[126] Committee members can suggest amendments, and the Commission can present amended drafts, providing opportunities for negotiation, collaboration and consensus seeking. The committee votes on the Commission's draft by qualified majority. In the vast majority of cases, comitology committees simply agree with the Commission, and the measure is adopted.[127] In more controversial cases, if the examination committee either rejects the draft, or does not reach an opinion in either direction, the draft must (in most environmental cases) be put before an Appeal Committee, again made up of national representatives, but at a higher political level. Again, after opportunities for discussion, the Appeal Committee votes by qualified majority. If there is a positive opinion, the Commission 'shall' adopt its draft; if there is a negative opinion, it 'shall not adopt' it. If there is no opinion, the Commission 'may adopt' its draft.

There are limits to the reliance on comitology to mediate expertise and politics. First, it takes for granted the ability to maintain a clear separation between facts and values, to ensure that experts simply assess the facts, prior to, and independently of, political value judgments, when facts and values are inextricably linked. Value judgments and assumptions are made at every stage of fact gathering:

What are the relevant forms of risk (human health, environmental burdens, ecological integrity, monetary values, social disruption, ethical offence)? How should we measure these (for instance, health can be measured alternatively as frequency or mode of death or injury, disease morbidity, or quality of life)? . . . What weight is placed on wellbeing of humans compared with non-humans, or future generations compared to the present? . . . When as often happens, technical parameters like the mechanical reliability of a

---

[126] Reg 182/2011/EU laying down the rules and general principles concerning mechanisms for control by Member States of the Commission's exercise of implementing powers [2011] OJ L 55/13.

[127] See eg Ellen Vos, '50 Years of European Integration, 45 Years of Comitology' *Maastricht Faculty of Law Working Papers* 2009–3.

human-fabricated, maintained, and operated technology embody social-behavioural factors which are contingent, how does risk assessment represent these?[128]

The assumptions applied during technical assessments are often not consciously adopted as such, and so are rarely externally questioned.[129] Professional judgments are legitimate, and necessary. But there is no such thing as a single neutral assessment, which stands above politics and values.[130]

The reliance on comitology to take final decisions may pay too little attention to the challenges of explaining a decision on grounds other than expert advice. Politics is not independent of expertise, but is properly dependent on it. The inscrutability of complex technical processes may result in an apparently inevitable response that reduces the space for political value judgments. The limitations of 'hard' technical assessments, in terms of quality and certainty, as well as value judgment, may not be taken into account.[131] There may well be political pressure to justify decisions by reference to the 'facts', rather than by more contentious political values. Or we may simply not yet be sufficiently skilled at articulating the political, rather than technical, reasons for a decision.

There is something of a paradox in worrying that the need for political judgment is sidelined, and expertise granted too much authority. It is notorious that organizations request information that they never use, and are not aware of what others know or used to know.[132] The European Environment Agency has provided a number of dispiriting, detailed case studies of our failure to take action in respect of harms on which evidence exists in the public domain.[133] It is perfectly plausible that *political* decisions, in the pursuit of short-term economic advantage, are failing to heed the warnings of science. But ignoring warnings, complexity, and relevant scientific information is not inconsistent with an institution that is overly-deferential to technical expert judgments. Perhaps a decision is expressed as if it rested on the 'facts' as established by EU expertise, when in fact it rests on a political calculation about for example, the employment generated by a risky industry. This creates very

---

[128] Expert Group on Science and Governance, *Taking European Knowledge Society Seriously* (2007), 34, from a longer passage with many more examples.

[129] Expert Group (n 128), Ch 6; Michael Polanyi, *The Tacit Dimension* (1966). See also Amartya Sen's foreword to the 2009 edition.

[130] eg Andrew Stirling et al., 'Empowering Designs: Towards More Progressive Appraisal of Sustainability' (2007) *STEPs Working Paper* 3.

[131] eg Theodore M. Porter, *Trust in Numbers: The Pursuit of Objectivity in Science and Public Life* (1995).

[132] eg Martha S. Feldman and James G. March, 'Information in Organizations as Signal and Symbol' (1981) 26 *Administrative Science Quarterly* 171. Brian Wynne, 'Uncertainty and Environmental Learning: Reconceiving Science and Policy in the Preventive Paradigm' (1992) 2 *Global Environmental Change* 111 discusses advice on the consumption of sheep meat from the English Lake District after the Chernobyl nuclear accident, which was based on the behaviour of radiocaesium in alkaline chalky soils (rather than acid peaty soil). In fact, scientists had carried out the relevant studies some decades before, but that knowledge had been lost to decision makers.

[133] EEA (n 80).

serious problems of accountability, since the 'real' reasons for a decision are hidden from challenge, which is more important than ever in conditions of controversy and uncertainty.[134] It should not be thought that 'politics', including politics accessed through 'public participation', is necessarily more environmentally protective than 'expertise'. Other important human values compete politically with environmental protection, especially in the short term. The advantages of the regulated industry in shaping expertise, however, add to concerns about the legitimacy of a decision that does not take the politics of environmental protection sufficiently seriously.

Perhaps the more profound difficulty with relying on comitology is the fragile legitimacy of administrative decision makers (including, even especially, Commission plus comitology). This is likely to increase the appeal of objective 'facts', since it makes any call on shared political values potentially problematic. The Court in *Pfizer* (and subsequent cases) takes for granted 'the political responsibilities and democratic legitimacy' of the Commission, referring also to political control by the European Parliament.[135] Comitology in principle allows national interests, priorities and values (and national politics) into the EU-level decision. There is of course an enormous literature on the legitimacy of comitology, concerned largely with the relative distance of comitology committees from the public, including the media and those affected by the decision.[136] This is not the moment to explore this literature. However, given that formal approaches to delegation and agency (ie the retention of final decision-making authority by political institutions) do not provide a simple solution to the challenges posed by the role and identity of experts in EU environmental law, the legitimacy and accountability of all parts of the decision-making process move centre-stage. The questions of transparency and inclusion, raised in the first place by the authority of expertise, are raised afresh.

VII. Conclusions

Environmental decision making demands resources of both expertise and politics. A strong emphasis on the generation of knowledge and information in EU environmental law is coupled with an expectation of openness to scrutiny and participation in decision making. The preoccupation of EU environmental law with information

---

[134] See the discussion in Maria Lee, 'Beyond Safety? The Broadening Scope of Risk Regulation' (2010) *Current Legal Problems* 242.

[135] *Pfizer* (n 9), [201].

[136] Post-Lisbon see eg Paul Craig, 'Delegated Acts, Implementing Acts and the New Comitology Regulation' (2011) 36 *European Law Review* 671.

and knowledge is in itself a positive development, an improvement on any assumption that information will emerge 'serendipitously' or that industry will volunteer 'incriminating information without fuss or fanfare'.[137] The EU institutions have devoted far less effort to the ways in which the need for expertise can be reconciled with an emphasis on public participation that used to be equally strong, and remains equally important. Nor is much explicit attention paid to the challenges created by our reliance on economic actors for knowledge generation. Constant attention needs to be paid to who plays the role of expert in environmental governance, and to ensuring diverse input into decisions. The challenge faced by EU environmental law is essentially the same as in national processes: ensuring that political decisions are taken by politically legitimate processes. The simplicity of the question is in direct contrast with the difficulty of the response. The EU institutions make some effort to respond, but the recourse to comitology is problematic. What remains is a need for inclusion and scrutiny (including by well-resourced, well-trained, skilled and experienced regulators), with guarantees of participation and transparency. These prescriptions might sound banal, and certainly familiar. They are however extremely challenging, and the discussion above suggests that they are only partially acknowledged in EU environmental law. Equally importantly, the final political decision-makers need to be more comfortable, and more skilled, at articulating political reasons for a decision, if that decision is indeed based on politics rather than expert technical input.

BIBLIOGRAPHY

Julia Black, 'Enrolling Actors in Regulatory Systems: Examples from UK Financial Services Regulation' [2003] *Public Law* 63

Grainne de Búrca, 'Developing Democracy Beyond the State' (2008) 46 *Columbia Journal of Transnational Law*

Jane Holder, *Environmental Assessment: The Regulation of Decision-Making* (2004)

Bridget Hutter, 'The Role of Non-State Actors in Regulation (2006)' *CARR Discussion Paper* No. 37

Bettina Lange *Implementing EU Pollution Control: Law and Integration* (2008)

Maria Lee, *EU Environmental Law, Governance and Decision-Making* (2014)

Naomi Oreskes, 'Science and Public Policy: What's Proof Got to do with it?' (2004) 7 *Environmental Science and Policy* 369

Joanne Scott, 'REACH: Combining Harmonization and Dynamism in the Regulation of Chemicals' in Joanne Scott (ed), *Environmental Protection: European Law and Governance* (2009)

Brian Wynne, 'Uncertainty and Environmental Learning: Reconceiving Science and Policy in the Preventive Paradigm' (1992) 2 *Global Environmental Change* 111

---

[137] Wagner (n 35) (of US environmental law), 1622–1623.

Index